THE PARTY'S INTERESTS COME FIRST

STANFORD-HOOVER SERIES ON **AUTHORITARIANISM**

Edited by Paul R. Gregory and Norman Naimark

THE PARTY'S INTERESTS COME FIRST

The Life of Xi Zhongxun,
Father of Xi Jinping

JOSEPH TORIGIAN

Stanford University Press | Hoover Institution, Stanford University

Stanford, California

Stanford University Press
Stanford, California

© 2025 by Joseph Torigian. All rights reserved.

No part of this book may be reproduced or transmitted in any form or by any means, electronic or mechanical, including photocopying and recording, or in any information storage or retrieval system, without the prior written permission of Stanford University Press.

Library of Congress Cataloging-in-Publication Data
Names: Torigian, Joseph (Political scientist), author.
Title: The party's interests come first : the life of Xi Zhongxun, father of Xi Jinping / Joseph Torigian.
Other titles: Stanford-Hoover series on authoritarianism.
Description: Stanford, California : Stanford University Press : Hoover Institution, Stanford University 2025. | Series: Stanford-Hoover series on authoritarianism | Includes bibliographical references and index.
Identifiers: LCCN 2024047832 (print) | LCCN 2024047833 (ebook) | ISBN 9781503634756 (cloth) | ISBN 9781503640986 (epub)
Subjects: LCSH: Xi, Zhongxun, 1913-2002. | Xi, Jinping—Family. | Zhongguo gong chan dang—Biography. | Revolutionaries—China—Biography. | Communist parties—China—History. | China—Politics and government—1912-1949. | China—Politics and government—1949-
Classification: LCC DS778.X519 T67 2025 (print) | LCC DS778.X519 (ebook) | DDC 951.04092 [B]—dc23/eng/20250113

LC record available at https://lccn.loc.gov/2024047832
LC ebook record available at https://lccn.loc.gov/2024047833

Cover design: Martyn Schmoll
Photographs: Xi Zhongxun, 1946, Wikimedia US Public Domain; Xi Zhongxun and his family members in 1959.

The authorized representative in the EU for product safety and compliance is: Mare Nostrum Group B.V. | Mauritskade 21D | 1091 GC Amsterdam | The Netherlands | Email address: gpsr@mare-nostrum.co.uk | KVK chamber of commerce number: 96249943

Contents

Map	x
1 The Party's Interests Come First	1

PART I
THE PARTY'S "FOOTHOLD"
The Shaanxi Years

2 *The Young Wanderer*	13
3 Who Saved Whom?	28
4 The Yan'an Era	45
5 Love and Revolution	69
6 War on the Nationalists and the Peasants	82

PART II
BUILDING THE NEW REGIME

7 King of the Northwest	99
8 "Political Means, with Military Force as a Supplement"	107

9	Ideology and Power Politics in the Beijing of the Early People's Republic	123
10	The Perils of Intimacy at Home and Abroad	136
11	"Military Suppression Combined with Political Struggle"	153
12	Home Life in the Capital	174

PART III
CATASTROPHE

13	The Great Leap Forward	185
14	*Liu Zhidan*	208
15	The Cultural Revolution	219
16	The Xi Family Slowly Rebuilds	241

PART IV
THE PARTY'S "LAUNCHPAD"
The Guangdong Years

17	Facing the Consequences of the Cultural Revolution	255
18	Blazing a Bloody Trail	271
19	Opening to the West	287

PART V
TRYING TO SAVE THE REVOLUTION

20	A New Order at the Secretariat and the National People's Congress	303
21	Princeling Politics	323
22	The United Front Restored and Restrained	350
23	A New Era in Ethnic and Religious Affairs	367
24	"Things Were Going So Well!"	396
25	Xi and the Fate of Global Communism	411

PART VI
CATASTROPHE AGAIN

26	"It Is Necessary to Also Have a Spiritual Civilization"	433
27	The Deep Waters of Zhongnanhai	468
28	Tiananmen Square	488
29	The Final Years	515
30	Fathers and Sons	532
	Acknowledgments	547
	Abbreviations	549
	Notes	551
	Bibliography	635
	Index	681

THE PARTY'S INTERESTS COME FIRST

FIGURE 1. The geography of Xi Zhongxun's life.

Shaanxi: The Foothold

- Yulin
- Hengshan
- Yangjiagou
- Suide
- Wayaobu
- Liangjiahe
- Huan County
- Yan'an
- Nanliang
- Guanzhong
- Zhaojin
- Fuping
- Sanyuan County
- Xi Family Village
- Xi'an
- Liangdang County

- Yekejuu League
- Hohhot
- Beijing
- N. KOREA
- Pyongyang
- SHANXI
- Gaoyang
- Zhengding
- S. KOREA
- NINGXIA
- Taiyuan
- Changzhi SHANDONG
- Yuncheng
- Zhengzhou
- Luoyang Changge
- SHAANXI HENAN JIANGSU
- Dengzhou
- JAPAN
- HUBEI
- ANHUI
- Shanghai
- CHONGQING
- Lushan
- ZHEJIANG
- JIANGXI
- GUIZHOU HUNAN
- Ningde
- FUJIAN
- Fuzhou
- Taipei
- Xiamen
- GUANGXI GUANGDONG
- Shantou
- TAIWAN
- VIETNAM
- Haikou
- HAINAN

PHILIPPINES

0   250   500 km

1
THE PARTY'S INTERESTS COME FIRST

Fourteen months after the crackdown on protesters in June 1989, Chen Jianzhong, one of the late Chiang Kai-shek's top spymasters, departed from Taiwan to meet Xi Jinping's father, Xi Zhongxun, in Beijing. Nearing the end of his political career, Xi Zhongxun had hoped to establish a secret back channel that would facilitate unification between Taiwan and mainland China. Sixty-two years before Chen's trip, when they were fourteen-year-old best friends growing up in Shaanxi Province, Chen and Xi had committed their first revolutionary act together. They tried to poison an academic administrator but failed and instead sickened many of their teachers. The two young boys were swiftly arrested and spent months in prison. Five years later, Chen betrayed the top Shaanxi Chinese Communist Party leadership, joined the Nationalists, and spent the remainder of his life working against his former comrades—including Xi.

The meeting of the two old friends and comrades in arms was bittersweet. Chen later vividly described the experience:

> Xi Zhongxun had suffered from brutal factional struggles inside the party, causing psychological damage; in his later years, he would have a hallucination that a figure was following him from behind; later, the pressure became so great that he developed a mental illness. Xi Zhongxun spoke with me on two occasions; it was probably because when he saw me that his emotional state became calmer, his illness took a turn for the better.... One time when we were chatting at his home, he took me outdoors to the courtyard where

no one could hear what we were saying. He looked left and right and then said to me, "Regarding our situation on the inside, you, elder brother, know everything. I have to be careful. Nobody will hear us talking in this place today." His wife even patrolled from a distance so that no one would approach us. Xi Zhongxun and Deng Xiaoping both had been Zhou Enlai's subordinates, and they both had been sent to the countryside for labor reform. In such a situation, Xi was extremely careful. He dared not utter one careless word; at the time, I thought the Chinese Communist Party system was truly terrifying.[1]

Chen Jianzhong had arrived in Beijing at a troubled time in Xi's life. Over four months in 1988 and 1989, three of Xi's closest friends had died: the prominent Mongol cadre Ulanhu; the tenth Panchen Lama, Choekyi Gyaltsen; and the former party general secretary Hu Yaobang. Two months before Chen's appearance in the Chinese capital, Liu Jingfan, the younger brother of Xi's first great mentor, Liu Zhidan, had passed away as well.

Yet Xi was not only witnessing the loss of his companions—the party was rapidly moving away from the new policies he had helped implement during the 1980s to overcome the tragic legacy of the Cultural Revolution. The special economic zones, first established while Xi was party boss in the southern province Guangdong and in which he took great pride, were under threat as the party debated whether the liberal economic policies might have led to the mass protests in 1989. As the politburo member whose bailiwick had included ethnic and religious policies for much of the decade, Xi championed a model of ethnic relations in Xinjiang and Tibet that prioritized addressing grievances, allying with local minority leaders, and promoting economic growth. But after a series of protests in those regions, by 1989, the party leadership had decided priority should instead be placed on cracking down on "splittists." Xi had helped rebuild relations with foreign Communist parties after such ties were destroyed under Mao Zedong, but now global Communism was at a moment of crisis. Even though Xi hoped the party could overcome the strongman rule of the Mao era, the autocratic Deng Xiaoping had brazenly removed Xi's direct superior, Hu Yaobang, from power in 1987 and forced a violent solution to the student protests in 1989.

From the outside, no one could have guessed Xi's frustrations. Publicly and within the party, Xi always faithfully toed the official line and defended even those decisions with which he most vociferously disagreed. Yet people who truly understood Xi—for instance, Mao Zedong—would not have been surprised by this behavior. During the revolution, Mao often gave short, pithy formulations to characterize his favorite cadres. For Xi, Mao wrote the words "The party's interests come first" on a white cloth and gave it to him as a gift. It became one of Xi's most treasured possessions.

Although the party's interests came first, Xi was still human. He struggled to balance the multiple centers of emotional gravity that shaped his life. In August 1990, Xi momentarily lost his ability to contain his frustrations. According to the diaries of Li Rui, one of Mao's former secretaries, at a meeting of the National People's Congress Standing Committee, Xi screamed at Premier Li Peng, leading Li Rui to write, "This demonstrates that his mental situation has, at the very least, completely lost control." Li Rui concludes that "this was the result of several years of pent-up resentment." Xi refused to see a doctor and spent the night after his outburst on the couch in his office.[2] It was soon after that incident that Xi met with Chen Jianzhong. Xi then departed for Guangdong, only to return to Beijing in 1999.

XI ZHONGXUN, THE LEGEND

During his career, Xi Zhongxun had his setbacks, but he did succeed in one regard: he established a reputation as the very best kind of individual that the party could produce. According to that narrative, shared widely among Chinese elites, Xi was a righteous individual who was almost uniquely practical, open-minded, and merciful. The legends are numerous. He tried to protect his corner of the Yan'an base area during the notorious Rescue the Fallen Campaign—a party rectification that went off the rails in 1943. He helped end the excesses of the party's land-reform campaign in 1947 and 1948. After the People's Republic of China was founded in 1949, Xi tempered the Suppression of Counterrevolutionaries Campaign in his Northwest Region. He was a quintessential reformer in Guangdong during the early years after the Cultural Revolution. And, perhaps most famously, he allegedly exploded emotionally at the meeting when Hu Yaobang was removed from power.

Xi, according to one of his closest associates, once claimed, "With regard to me at least, in my whole life, I never persecuted anyone; in my whole life, I never made a leftist [radical] mistake."[3] One of Xi's daughters claimed that after his retirement, he told her, "Your father, in his whole life, did not leave you all with anything. I only left you all with a sense of uprightness."[4]

In a letter to his father, Xi Jinping once wrote, "You instructed me that in your entire life, you never persecuted people and you always maintained the truth."[5] Some analysts even conclude that one of the reasons for Xi Jinping's ascendancy to top leader is the reputation of his father as a reformist titan who had not used brutality to rise to power.[6]

Xi Jinping's aggressive attacks on potential challengers and reluctance to introduce political and economic reforms disappointed people who thought he would be more like their understanding of his father.[7] Even after Xi Jinping started demonstrating these tendencies, Wu Jiaxiang, who previously had worked in the secretariat, argued that Xi would never betray his father's legacy as a reformer: "He is his father's son; he was born into the family of the most proreform faction, and according to the legacy of the party and Chinese history, he will not betray the faction that includes his father. . . . He is an egg laid by his father, an egg of reform. . . . [Xi Zhongxun] was not a typical reformer—he was the greatest reformer."[8] After Xi Jinping's political direction became clear, Xi Zhongxun's life turned into a weapon against him. Hu Ping, a prominent Chinese liberal intellectual living in the United States, called Xi Jinping an "unfilial son."[9]

Xi Jinping's supporters, on the other hand, emphasized another one of Xi Zhongxun's legacies—his absolute devotion to the revolution and the party. Despite the misfortunes Xi Zhongxun encountered throughout his life, including the suffering he experienced at the hands of the party itself, he never lost faith. In that same letter to his father, Xi Jinping wrote, "No matter whether it was the era of the White Terror [i.e., the Nationalists] or the period of extreme leftism; no matter whether you were libeled against or you were in a difficult situation, in your heart, there was a bright lantern that always kept you on the correct path forward. When people yelled at us for being bastards, I always stubbornly believed that my father was a great hero, that he was a father most worthy of feeling proud."[10]

XI ZHONGXUN, THE FATHER

As Xi Jinping's words suggest, Xi Zhongxun was not only a legend within the party. He was also a legend within his family. As a child, during the Lunar New Year, Xi Jinping would kowtow in front of his father (an incorrect kowtow would earn him a spanking).[11] Jinping later described how his father inspired his children: "'You will certainly make revolution in the future.' ... He would then explain what a revolution is. We heard so much about this that our ears got calluses."[12] In early 1989, when Xi Zhongxun could no longer chew on garlic ribs because they were too tough, he gave a piece that had already been in his mouth to Jinping to finish—which he promptly did.[13] Even during Zhongxun's last years, when his son had already achieved prominence as a politician, Jinping would politely stand to one side, only sitting down after his father gave the word.[14] As an adult, on the Lunar New Year, Jinping would still kowtow before his father, who would smile and say, "That's right, that's right, that's enough, thank you."[15]

Xi Jinping repeatedly refers to his father when he meets with foreigners. In August 2011, when Xi met with then vice president Joe Biden, he spoke of Zhongxun and his family's traumatic experiences.[16] Unprompted, Xi also brought up his father during a cozy fireside chat at the Lodge, the official residence of Australian prime minister—at the time, Kevin Rudd.[17] In March 2013, Xi told a group of Russian sinologists that his father was the "supreme life example" and was "humane to the highest measure of wisdom." "We took the historic baton and will carry it with honor," Xi said.[18]

XI ZHONGXUN AS PARTY HISTORY

An inescapable irony sits at the heart of *The Party's Interests Come First*. It is a book about party history, and the life of its subject, Xi Zhongxun, is itself a story about the politically explosive nature of competing versions of the past. The men and women who gave their lives to the party were enormously sensitive to how this all-encompassing political organization would characterize their contributions. Such a sentiment was powerful not only because revolutionary legacies were reflected through hierarchy and authority within the party but also because their lives as chronicled in party lore had a fundamental significance for their own sense of self-worth.

For Xi Zhongxun, party history was a landmine that, throughout his career, threatened to explode and sometimes did. Even before he began working in the Communist-controlled rural base areas in 1932, the party in Shaanxi Province was riven by mutual antagonisms and violence, which resulted in hatreds that would last for decades. The year of 1935 was a watershed—Xi and more prominent leaders, such as Liu Zhidan and Gao Gang, were incarcerated by fellow Communists. For the rest of his life, Xi would claim that the party's plan had been to bury him alive. Mao and the rest of the central leadership, nearing total exhaustion after months of fleeing Nationalist forces on the Long March, stumbled upon the Shaanxi Communists. Soon after, Xi and the others were released and the Central Committee under Mao proceeded to settle in the region. That moment would tie Mao and Xi together but in a dangerous way. As one of the last corners of Communist-controlled territory, its discovery was a great boon for Mao at a critical moment, but its existence also suggested that Mao was not the only one who had devised a way to make revolution work.

In 1942, Mao used his own interpretation of party history to "adopt" the men who had survived the 1935 purge. According to this narrative, Xi and others from the Northwest had suffered leftist dogmatic persecution in ways that mirrored Mao's own experiences in Jiangxi before the Long March. Yet Mao would abandon Xi twenty years later. When the sister-in-law of Xi's comrade Liu Zhidan began drafting a book about Liu, Xi initially discouraged her, but others persuaded him to relent. After segments were published, the book was characterized as an attempt by Xi to rewrite party history for his own nefarious goals. Under intense emotional pressure, he spent the next sixteen years of his life rewriting self-criticisms about his history in the party. Even after Mao's death, the issue of the party's past in the Northwest was a sensitive topic—*Liu Zhidan* would be banned twice more, once in the 1980s and again in 2009.

The weaponization of Xi Zhongxun's life by both his son's detractors and his son's boosters, as well as by the inherently political nature of party history described above, raises serious challenges for any potential biographers. Jia Juchuan, the author of Zhongxun's official biography, admits, "So many officials and people want to make up and change things. Lots of political factors have been introduced. Everyone, no matter whether they have jobs or are retired, wants to leave something behind for their own status.... People who don't know about history are writing history, and people who don't know how to write biography are writing biography."[19] Xi Jinping himself has characterized the negative portrayals of the past as "historical nihilism" and therefore an existential threat to regime stability. Thus, any book on party history, especially on Xi Jinping's own father, is necessarily only the latest draft.

XI ZHONGXUN, THE MAN

But what does the evidence we do have tell us about Xi Zhongxun, the man who allegedly epitomized the party's most humane and open tendencies and who also happens to be the father of China's current president and general secretary, Xi Jinping, one of the world's most powerful and mysterious people? The purpose of this book is not to contrast a "good" father with a "bad" son or to claim that the father was not as "good" as the legends go. Although this book has both caves and a pipe, it is not intended to be a Freudian analysis of Xi Jinping. Instead, it uses the life of one rather unique individual to tell the story of the Chinese Communist Party in the twentieth century. He was witness, often in special ways, to many crucial events in the party's history, and he helped to shape several controversial policies that are still essential for how we view Chinese history and China today.

Xi Zhongxun was a man whose life was marked by personal tragedy. Shortly after he was released from jail at the age of fourteen, his father, whose health had collapsed out of worry over his son, died. His mother and two sisters, weakened by famine, passed shortly thereafter. In the following years, he was almost killed on numerous occasions by enemy forces, causing him to experience nightmares for the rest of his life. During the Cultural Revolution, he was kidnapped by Red Guards and forcibly brought to another province, held in solitary confinement, sent to struggle sessions, and sometimes beaten. Many of his former colleagues, as well as his own family, suffered terribly because of their connections with him—some were even persecuted to death, including a daughter.

While Xi felt undeniable anguish and sadness throughout his life, it would be a mistake to assume that these difficulties diminished his devotion to the party and the revolution. Understanding why requires a sensitivity to the political culture in which Xi lived. In the party, suffering meant "forging," or strengthening one's willpower and dedication. Undergoing such trials would signify true faith in the cause, and caring too much about oneself was a symptom of a bourgeois, individualistic privilege. Xi's favorite novel, *The Young Wanderer*, tells the story of a series of personal disasters that befall a young man on his course to joining the revolution.[20] When Xi was incarcerated during the Cultural Revolution, as he paced back and forth every day to maintain his health, he memorized Mao's writings. When people complained about party policies, Xi often bragged about his hardships to delegitimize their grumblings. In the early 1990s, Xi even boasted to a Western historian that although Deng Xiaoping had suffered at the hands of the party on three occasions, he had been persecuted five times.[21]

Yet Xi still had an impressive career that saw him carry heavy responsibilities at tender ages. When he was sixteen, he infiltrated a warlord army as an undercover agent, and only two years later, he led a failed mutiny of a battalion. At twenty, he was chairman of a local soviet base area. On arriving in that region, Mao saw posters about a "Chairman Xi," and when he finally met him, Mao was shocked by his youth. After the revolution, Xi was by far the youngest leader of a major regional bureau. In 1959, he was the youngest vice-premier. Over and over again, Xi served as the trusted right-hand person to others who were much older, including such legendary figures as Peng Dehuai, He Long, and Zhou Enlai. In the 1980s, he served as the trusted assistant to the slightly younger Hu Yaobang on the secretariat.

Under Zhou and then Hu, Xi twice served as the "chief implementer for the chief implementer." He also executed the party's policies as the head of regional powerhouses in the Northwest and the South. On first glance, such a figure might not seem worthy of a biography. Why would someone whose job was to follow orders be interesting? The answer is that party life is much more complicated than simply doing what one is told. As Xi's life shows in dramatic fashion, the "implementers" often faced an impossible situation. They were told to pursue multiple goals at the same time without clear guidance on what mattered more or how to achieve them. Commands would often include two parts separated by a "but": make sure the campaign is thorough, they were told, but avoid going too far too fast. If they went too far in one direction, either to the "left" (too radical)" or "right" (too capitulationist), they could face charges of ideological heresy. Setbacks might mean losing authority to someone else. As paramount leaders, Mao and then Deng were often distant, vague, mercurial, and suspicious. If a deputy reported too much, they might feel overwhelmed and distracted from big issues. But not enough communication could lead to suspicions that underlings were trying to run the country themselves. Private frank meetings between a leader and his lieutenants were extremely rare, and even then there was no guarantee that an understanding had been achieved or would prove resilient. Working for both Zhou and Hu, Xi saw how all these challenges were further exacerbated by the explosive politics of course correction—a common problem given the constant swinging from left to right—and worries about succession.

For people outside the party, Xi was most famously a high-ranking figure in the so-called United Front: an influence campaign to co-opt other parties, prominent unaffiliated individuals, powerful ethnic-minority leaders, and the Chinese diaspora. His deep faith in the revolution made him an especially capable person to make the party's case to these outsiders. Displaying the party in a positive light was much easier when Xi actually held office. Before 1949, the party was an attractive alternative to the corrupt Nationalists. In the 1950s, many had hopes that the party would finally build a strong China. Then, in the 1980s, as the party moved away from the disastrous policies of the Mao era, people once again had reason to believe that it was moving in the right direction.

Xi was an earthy, humorous individual who often impressed people with his sincerity. He was memorably courteous and friendly toward much younger people. His friendships with former Nationalist leaders and ethnic-minority figures had genuine elements. Yet although he could be a charmer, he was no pushover. He often reminded these individuals that friendship with the party could only be based on "principles." Toward other party members, he could display an explosive rage, although never toward top leaders, such as Mao or Deng. At times, he overreacted to perceived slights or jumped to conclusions, often apologizing after wrathful encounters. His tenure on the secretariat was memorable for its open atmosphere, but he could also be longwinded and monopolize conversations. When necessary, he served effectively as the party's enforcer. Xi respected toughness—Jinping was his favorite son precisely because of a belief that Jinping had the most "mettle."[22] In part because of his fixation on hardship as a character-building enterprise, at home, Xi Zhongxun was a brutal disciplinarian.

Although Western scholars often use "left" or "right," or even "good" or "bad," to characterize Chinese leaders, a closer look at the supposed inveterate "reformer" Xi Zhongxun reveals the problems with such terminology. Although he helped establish the special economic zones, at first, he strongly opposed the household-responsibility system in the countryside that allowed peasants to farm their own plots—perhaps the most important policy change that led to China's economic takeoff. He thought the Cultural Revolution was a disaster, and he believed Mao's style of strongman rule should never be repeated, but throughout his life, he remained deeply devoted to the chairman's memory. Xi was comfortable with policy flexibility, but he was sensitive to the importance of justifying such innovations with ideological explanations, and he found consumerism and materialism deeply distasteful. He thought dialogue and listening to grievances could help resolve contradictions within society, but he had a phobia of chaos. He used co-optation and a lighter touch to win the loyalty of ethnic minorities, but such policies were still forms of control for Beijing to maintain its power along its borders. He cared deeply about the principle of protecting differing opinions, but he also fetishized party unity. Although he often shared policy views with his protégés, he simultaneously felt a responsibility to regularly rein them in and to push them to pursue unity with competitors.

As Russian historian Roi Medvedev writes, no one in a Leninist system could occupy a top post and not "from time to time betray one's own friends, associates, or completely innocent people. Everyone made their own choice, and everyone sought justifications for their transgressions."[23] In this book, the traditional "heroes" of Chinese history come out a bit worse, and the "villains" a bit better. Personalities matter, but no one's behavior can be understood out of the context of a particular system: the Chinese Communist Party.

A tough man with chauvinistic tendencies, Xi Zhongxun was still someone who struggled to find meaning in the face of desperation. As a young person, he went through a period of doubt and depression, but ultimately, he found motivation in the self-sacrifice and dedication of the professional revolutionary. Life as a member of the party presented new challenges: how to balance his own "humanity" (*renxing*)—in the form of ambition, friendship, family, mercy, and personal political views—with the values of "partyness" (*dangxing*)—organizational discipline, unity, societal transformation, and protecting the "core" leader.

Sometimes these elements aligned, but at other times, they did not. And although the party betrayed Xi Zhongxun, Xi Zhongxun never betrayed the party. Xi's choice was always inevitable, but it was never easy. Terror, guilt, regret, sadness, and fury mixed with dedication and a coolly rational conclusion that opposing the party would make any situation worse. For many observers, such a life might seem tragic, but Xi Zhongxun made his choice, and it was deeply meaningful for him. It was a life lived according to party morality, a life that afforded him the excitement of participating in the grand adventure of revolution in an organization that he believed was a manifestation of the iron laws of history. And now his son, who intimately watched his father balance these competing tendencies for decades, is the leader of the People's Republic of China.

PART I **THE PARTY'S "FOOTHOLD"**

The Shaanxi Years

2
THE YOUNG WANDERER

Xi Zhongxun's ancestors arrived in Fuping County in the Guanzhong area of central Shaanxi Province in the 1880s when Xi's grandparents, Xi Yongsheng and a woman with the surname Zhang, fled from economic hardship in Dengzhou in Henan Province. Throughout his life, Xi Zhongxun would demonstrate a strong interest in his family's past. In 1976, when a young man told him that Henan people were bad (a stereotype sometimes seen in other provinces), he responded furiously, "I'm a Henanese! My ancestral home is Deng County in Henan."[1] In 1962, when he was purged from the leadership, Liu Shaoqi, then president, gave a speech claiming that Xi was interested in anyone with the Xi surname and liked hearing about how his ancestors had served as dynastic officials.[2]

It would have been hard for someone growing up in Shaanxi not to have such a preoccupation with the past. Shaanxi was where Emperor Qin Shi Huang had forged the first unified Chinese state, and the imperial dynasties had ruled for millennia from the capital of Xi'an. Yet, by the time the Xi family had arrived, the region had suffered a prolonged period of political and economic calamities.[3] It was a place of contradiction that led one of Zhongxun's close childhood friends to later say that the region made "people develop a sort of extreme way of thinking—on the one hand, it has a rich cultural legacy, but on the other hand, the people face a difficult situation and the chaos of war never ends."[4] The Xis' village of Dancun was on a tract of elevated land that allowed many ancient tombs to be visible.[5] When Zhongxun's future wife, Qi Xin, told an author that Xi repeatedly complained about how the imperial tombs had ruined Dancun's feng shui, the man reflected that Xi had indeed grown up surrounded by the physical geography of feudal abuse.[6]

Yongsheng, Zhongxun's grandfather, worked as an itinerant peddler but soon died by the side of a road near a Buddhist temple close to Fuping City. He had gone on a trip there, about thirteen kilometers away, to find food for his hungry family. He was placed in a nearby gorge by local people while his relatives were waiting for him to return. He was not buried at home until 1958.[7] Yongsheng's oldest son, Tiger, joined the army, while his second son, Zongde, remained at home to take care of the family. A daughter, Danu, and his third son, Zongren, helped with the farming. In 1900, Tiger was a member of the escort force that protected Empress Dowager Cixi and Emperor Guangxu as they fled to Xi'an from Beijing when a multinational force invaded the capital after the Boxer Rebellion. Tiger visited home very briefly, leaving behind sixty taels of silver that allowed the Xi family to escape abject poverty, purchase several acres of land, and build a house with nine rooms.[8]

Less than two years after the last Qing emperor abdicated, Zhongxun was born on October 15, 1913, to Yongsheng's second son, Zongde. According to tradition, the first character of the names of all the boys in Xi Zhongxun's generation included the character for *zhong*, meaning "awarded." For the second character, Xi's father selected *xun*, meaning "meritorious service," "merits," "achievements," or "decoration." Xi's birth name could therefore roughly be translated as "winner of achievements." Yet those same characters could also mean "Chinese founding father." In middle school, Xi's teacher Yan Musan, a Marxist, convinced Xi to change the original *zhong* character to another one that means "impartiality" or "integrity."[9]

Xi also had a childhood name (a common Chinese practice): Xiangjin. In October 2009, at the China Cultural Center in Berlin, Xi Jinping claimed his father's childhood name was related to an excerpt from the Confucian *Analects*:

> The second line of the *Three Character Classic* is "By nature [*xing*], men are close to and inseparable from one another [*xiangjin*]; through practice [*xi*, the same character as the Xi surname], they become different [*xiangyuan*]." Let me tell you a secret. My father, Xi Zhongxun, is also known as Xi Xiangjin. Why is that? At the time, there was a teacher from a private school who said, "The *Three Character Classic* talks about how people through practice become far apart from one another [*xi xiangyuan*], but why should practice

[xi] lead to people growing far apart? We should use practice to grow closer; it is definitely necessary to become closer." So he was called Xi Xiangjin [literally, "to become closer through practice"].[10]

Xi Zhongxun had positive memories of his parents. Later in life, he recalled,

> My father was an extremely kind-hearted peasant. He often said to us: "When you grow up, do not be an official and do not go into business. Officials tyrannize regular people; businesspeople have difficulties avoiding the habit of seeking nothing but profit, and they care a lot about money. If you have an education, be a teacher, and use your own talents to teach others and gain respect. Otherwise, be a farmer or a peasant who knows his place."
>
> My mother was diligent and virtuous. She was extremely pious toward my grandmother. When grandmother was sick, she brought carefully prepared lotus-seed soup to the foot of her bed. She herself ate and used little. Until the day she died, she did not enjoy a single day of leisured life.[11]

Discipline was severe in the Xi household, however. Zongde "treated the children strictly; we were all afraid of him," according to Zhongxun, and Zongde would scold his children even for speaking loudly.[12] Zongde's "amiable face" would often shoot looks of fierceness. Zhongxun's sister described a powerful family patriarch: "Often when the children would kick up a serious row, father, with one cough, would silence everyone immediately."[13]

In 1940, in an autobiography the party asked him to write, Xi described growing up in an unwealthy, although not desperately so, peasant family with a gradually improving economic standing: "My background was poor, and when I was young, my family situation was still not very good. I remember we farmed the land of others as well as a few dozen *mu* we farmed for ourselves. It was not until 1919 or 1920 that we finally became middle peasants."[14] Despite the escape from total poverty, Zhongxun began to work in the fields at the age of five, digging out weeds and hoeing and later learning to plow the fields as well. A cousin-in-law later remembered the young Xi as an intelligent, uninhibited, decisive, and courageous boy who dressed simply. On break from school, Xi behaved like the son of a peasant who "ate anything and would do any kind of work." He liked to spend time with his aunt, whose family had moved into Zongde's household because they were so poor. While she sat spinning cloth, Zhongxun would read to her, occasionally reciting with enough animation to make her laugh.[15]

When Xi helped with the farming, old men from the village would tell him stories from *Romance of the Three Kingdoms* and *The Water Margin*, two classic Chinese novels. The novels had a profound impact on the young Xi, and as a boy, he enjoyed acting out with friends the sections from those novels in which heroic men swore brotherhood to one another. When children played "war," Xi was the commander, and he would use bamboo to make a helmet for himself. When he participated in games like cudgel dancing, rock throwing, or hide-and-go-seek, he often bested an older, stronger cousin.[16] But he had a kind side as well. When a close friend developed malaria, Xi carried the young boy on his back to the doctor.[17]

STUDENT DAYS

In 1922, when Xi was nine years old, he enrolled as a student at the local primary school, where he studied traditional Confucian texts, arithmetic, society, and the natural world.[18] In February 1926, Xi began his studies at Licheng Middle School, which had been established in 1920 by Hu Jingyi, a "progressive" warlord from Fuping County. In March 1926, Xi joined the Licheng Youth Society, an organization founded by the Communists. In the spring, a traveling party member came to Licheng to teach about Marxism, marking the beginning of Xi's understanding of Communism. By May, Xi had joined the Communist Youth League. In June, Xi's teacher Yan Musan led sixty students, including Xi, to the sprawling complex of a local militia leader named Zhang to shout slogans such as "Grab the local despot and get even with him!" The marchers stormed his home, and local peasants who had joined the fray started smashing Zhang's possessions. Yan was swiftly fired from his position.[19]

Xi's attraction to Communism at this time was more emotional than ideological. When he was older, Xi would say of his time as a young teenager, "At the time, the revolutionary situation allowed all kinds of revolutionary books and newspapers for reading, but regrettably, because my individual study was too poor, even if I read more, it would only mean that there was more I did not understand. Because I was too young, my memory only allowed for half-baked knowledge, and my understanding of Communism was still not deep. Ultimately, my understanding at the time was that the party was good and that, in any case, I wanted to work with the party until the end."[20]

Xi's experience in this regard was rather common. A very close friend at the time later recalled a similar abundance of emotion but lack of clear understanding: "At the time, the thinking of young people was all very leftist. . . . They had an inexplicable awe for leftist personages. Because only leftism gave you a kick. Even when dating, everyone would pick a partner who was leftist in thinking. At the time, everyone wanted to 'make revolution.' They thought joining the Nationalists was not progressive enough . . . but young people simply could not distinguish the difference between the Nationalists and the Communists, so it could not be said that they opposed the Nationalists."[21]

Yan Musan became dean of Fuping First Primary School, and after the Lunar New Year of 1927, he brought Xi and other radical students to study there. At some point in the second half of that year, the party branch in Fuping debated whether to let Xi join the party. Because Xi was so young and had only just transferred, his application was rejected. In January 1928, Xi, again at Yan's command, began studies at No. 3 Normal University in Sanyuan County. Under the leadership of his friend and classmate Song Wenmei, who was also Xi's sponsor into the Communist Youth League, Xi participated in student movements at the school as well as in activities off campus.[22]

At this time, the party was operating in Shaanxi in a relatively benign environment, especially in places of learning where Communist teachers radicalized an entire generation of individuals who would go on to become Shaanxi party leaders. The Communists were united with the Nationalists, and Communists often joined the Nationalist Party. According to historian Joseph Esherick, "the Nationalist Party apparatus in Shaanxi was largely built by communists." In 1926, the year that Xi entered Licheng Middle School and began his political awakening, the Nationalists and Communists were even fighting together as allies in a desperate battle to defend nearby Xi'an from a warlord.[23]

However, after using the Communists as allies in his battles with the warlords, in April 1927, Chiang Kai-shek, the leader of the Nationalists, betrayed the party and launched a series of purges against them. In early July, Feng Yuxiang, in an alliance with Chiang, formed a new government in Shaanxi and launched the White Terror against the Communists. The impact was devastating—by September of that year, 496, both students and others, had been either arrested or killed.[24]

The central party authorities demanded that the Shaanxi party branch launch a series of peasant revolts in response. Communists Xie Zichang and Yan Hongyan had been building up a party organization within an enemy battalion in Qingjian, and in September, they led the unit to mutiny. But they started to argue about the proper course of action, and by early January 1928, the first violent Communist insurrection in the region had already failed.[25] The Nationalists then began to focus on the party presence in schools. On February 28, students and teachers were assaulted at Xuanhua Higher Primary School. The next day, the party and Communist Youth League led hundreds of peasants and students to occupy the school. Four people who worked at the school were killed: three were beaten to death with staffs and bricks and another was thrown headfirst into a well. In March, the Shaanxi party leadership called for a violent response—an incident that became known as the Weihua Uprising, the second major violent Communist insurrection in the region. A man named Liu Zhidan, who would go on to be Xi's great mentor, was head of the military committee. However, as in the case of the Qingjian Uprising, the plans were too ambitious. It triggered a Nationalist crackdown that led to mass arrests of party members, including many students.[26] In one county alone, sixty-two members of the Communist Youth League were executed.[27] It would have been a deeply frightening moment for the young Xi.

To support the Weihua Uprising, the Communists in Sanyuan County, where Xi was studying, began to mobilize. On March 13, the Shaanxi leadership explicitly called for "striving to mobilize students to fight for their own interests and struggle to resist counterrevolutionary teachers, and to extend and expand the great wave of killing every last counterrevolutionary teacher and student."[28] In the winter of 1926, he and other students had already used force to drive out the dean of their school, and one year later, Xi and his classmates violently evicted the head of education in Fuping County.[29] Yet he had never tried to kill anyone. That was about to change.

In late March 1928, the party member in charge of student movements in Sanyuan County, Wu Tingjun, summoned Xi and two other students, Song Wenmei and Cheng Jianwen, all close friends, and they decided to assassinate Wei Hai, the head of instruction at Xi's No. 3 Normal University. At first, they considered blowing him up or setting the school on fire, but they decided those plans were too dangerous. They settled on poison instead.

Cheng mistakenly put poison in a porridge bowl intended for teachers to share, not for Wei, and several teachers became sick. Xi Zhongzhi, an uncle, offered to let Zhongxun hide in his guild for people from Henan. The boy refused, reasoning that it would implicate others. Fourteen people, members of the party and Communist Youth League as well as regular students, were arrested and sent to prison—including Zhongxun.[30]

Xi demonstrated a tough side in jail. According to an individual who was present, when one student began to waver, Xi threatened him. "At this point, no one is allowed to talk nonsense," Xi said. "We won't allow anyone who sells out other people to leave here alive."[31] Xi himself later asserted that incarceration had a profound impact on his revolutionary path: "At the time, I was just dissatisfied with the old society; I did not understand what Communism was. I merely relied on my own enthusiasm to make revolution, and it was totally based on my own bravery. I only truly came to understand some revolutionary principles in prison from Wu Tingjun."[32] Xi had proved himself enough to win party membership, and Wu was the man who sponsored his candidacy.[33] Instances of individuals joining the party while in prison were exceptionally rare during the revolution, so Wu had made an exception for the young boy.[34] Xi's career would outshine this early mentor. Shortly after release from prison, Wu committed suicide in Shanghai.[35]

Xi spent more than two months in the Sanyuan County detention center. As a member of a secret party cell, he participated in a hunger strike to win better food for inmates and did political work on Nationalist deserters. In early June, Xi was sent by oxcart to a special jail for party members and other revolutionaries. When Xi was interrogated, he only answered by saying "I don't know" or "I did not participate."[36]

Years later, during the Cultural Revolution, Xi was accused of being allowed to leave prison because he shamefully begged for mercy from Song Zheyuan, the newly installed Nationalist leader in Shaanxi.[37] Xi's official biographer confirms that in August, Xi and students from another school were indeed summoned to a meeting with Song. Song told them that Shaanxi's previous leader, Feng Yuxiang, had taken the wrong path, which had caused the students to make poor decisions. He also said that given their youth, they should study well at school and not cause trouble with student movements. Their parents had waited for them to return home for several months, and they would now be allowed to go home and comfort their families, Song promised.[38]

Song was a progressive general who took pity on the tender age of the students and agreed to let them go if two people would serve as guarantors. Xi's uncle Zongren convinced a man from the same village who sold silk in Xi'an to serve as one guarantor. When they could not find a second individual, they fabricated one, using a fake official seal as his stamp. When Zongren picked up his nephew from jail, he burst into tears at the sight of Zhongxun. Zhongxun, though, remained calm. "Don't cry, uncle," he said. "Let's go."[39]

DESPERATION AND RESOLUTION

Xi disappeared from the revolution from August 1928 to May 1929. It was one of the hardest periods of a difficult life. While incarcerated, he had developed eczema and boils on his body, which were so serious that he was unable to walk. And in December, Xi faced yet another emotional experience—the death of his father Zongde. Zongde had been ashamed of his son's arrest, and he was so anguished by Zhongxun's imprisonment that he suffered depression during the four months his son was incarcerated, finally suffering a mental breakdown. Zhongxun later recalled, "My father was an honest peasant; when I was freed from jail, I was afraid he would scold me, but he not only did not blame me, he said to me that I was too young. I could work as a party representative when I grew up, but for the time being, it would be best that I help the poor. For a peasant at the time to say something like that was already not easy." Zhongxun's brother said that their father "became ill because of pent-up sorrow, and he died with sadness." Less than a year later, in June 1929, Xi's mother suddenly died of an illness as well. Xi could not afford a burial. Instead, she was put in a cheap coffin for two years until he had enough money for a funeral. In his 1940 autobiography, Xi wrote, "Because I was arrested and put in jail, both my parents died of illness." He soon also lost two sisters to famine.[40]

Xi felt trapped and was not sure what to do next. He could not continue his studies. In 1967, he wrote, "I wanted to pick a school and study for a few more years to increase my knowledge." However, "because I was suspected of being a member of the party and had been in prison, it was as if I was already marked: no school that knew about this situation would dare to accept a student like me; this left me bitterly disappointed." He was particularly hurt because not only former classmates and teachers but also members of the youth organization with whom he had participated in revolutionary activities refused to interact with him.[41] In spring of 1929, Song Wenmei, one of the students who had taken part in the failed assassination attempt, went to Xi's village and suggested they enroll students at Whampoa Military Academy in southern Guangdong Province. Xi told Song such a step was impossible. With Wu dead, it was impossible to prove Xi's party membership, and Xi was so ill that he still had trouble moving.[42]

While Xi remained at home, the Communists in the region continued to suffer severe setbacks. In February 1929, the head of the Communist Youth League was apprehended in Xi'an and betrayed the party, leading to the arrest of most of the leadership of the Shaanxi Party Committee. During the subsequent crackdown, the number of party members dropped from three thousand to thirteen hundred. In Guanzhong, Xi's home region, barely two hundred party members remained.[43] Those pessimistic about the future were expelled; many others defected. Released prisoners like Xi often did not resume their party work because of lingering doubts about the loyalty of individuals who were jailed.[44]

With his father dead and an uncle sick, Xi was forced to help take care of his family, which included more than ten people. Moreover, Xi's home region of Weibei was suffering an extremely severe drought. One party report in September 1930 describes the situation there as the most serious in the province. More than half the population was unemployed. One entire village was dismantled to be sold as firewood. Almost all of Weibei was under the control of bandits or militias led by landlords. To support his family, Xi joined other refugees and panned salt in flats east of Fuping, trading it for basic food at a location more than a hundred kilometers from Dancun.[45]

In May, Xi continued to live near home, but he returned to his revolutionary activities. He fought with peasants against a local militia led by a man named Zhang Changqing. They tied Zhang to a gate tower and held a rally, but Zhang escaped and led a counterattack on the village. One member of the peasant group and an uncle-in-law of Xi's were arrested and held in a gate tower. Xi tried to free his relative with a piece of rope but failed, and the man was executed. Many years later, Xi told his brother that the experience had been traumatic.[46] His revolutionary activities caused great suffering to those close to him. Around this time, Xi also convinced four individuals to join the party—two of them would die in 1933, one executed by the Nationalists and the other in battle.[47] Xi often hid with the family of a childhood friend, and when the local Nationalist commander learned that Xi might be hiding there, he raided the household. But because Xi had been tipped off, the enraged commander broke the legs of the mother of Xi's friend.[48]

More than sixty years later, at another low point of his life after his career had cratered for the last time, Xi wrote wistfully in his personal diary about this formative year:

> It is impossible to overstate the influence of my family on my ability to become a revolutionary. Out of my grandmother, father, mother, uncles, aunts, and cousins, not a single one of them wanted me to become an official or a moneybags. My father and mother dearly loved me. They dearly loved that I dared to make revolution. They were extraordinarily good-hearted and righteous. They did not oppose my sitting in jail and did not oppose my beating of local tyrants or killing of evil people. They only said one thing: be careful and don't make any big mistakes. My father and mother died at a very young age. In 1928, I came out of prison and my father died in November. My mother died in between the spring and summer of 1929. She was only thirty-five years old. It was so terribly tragic; it was an enormous blow to a fifteen-year-old boy like me.
>
> In 1928, there was a great drought in Henan and Shaanxi, and the turmoil of war raged everywhere. Nineteen twenty-nine was the historic famine of the eighteenth year of the Republic of China. In the eight hundred kilometers of the Qin Plain in Guanzhong, where the spread of cholera made the situation even worse, nine out of ten habitations were empty. It was truly a horrific scene of human barbarity. My family could not escape either. After my father died, his brother became sick, and then my uncle's wife died. I became head of the family. A crowd of brothers and sisters all relied on me. It was so difficult. I not only led them into the fields to labor, I also picked things to bring home for them to eat that should not be used for human consumption. We ate what even the pigs would not eat. I wanted my younger brothers and sisters to live—I wanted them to live like human beings. The influence of this year on me was truly great, and it established the basis for a life of revolution.[49]

These traumatic experiences help explain Xi's obsession with the novel *The Young Wanderer*, by Jiang Guangci.[50] According to Xi Jinping, Xi Zhongxun repeatedly told his children that "at the time, the reason I understood that society was so black and that the old exploitation system needed to be overthrown was primarily because of the deep influence of *The Young Wanderer*."[51] Jiang Guangci was not interested in the intricacies of Marxist theories. "All revolutionaries are romantics. Without being romantic, who would come to start a revolution?" he asked. Within the Communist literary world, Jiang erred on the side of "lawlessness and hollowness"—a very different approach from that of other writers such as Guo Moruo, who chose to flatter the party (Jiang would ultimately be expelled from the party for his "romantic" inclinations). The great scholar of Chinese literature Tsi-an Hsia criticizes not only Jiang but also his readership, which would have included Xi: "He no doubt had his fans among the barely literate youths who did not care so much about the quality of the writing as the emotions he so 'frankly' expressed. . . . Did not his popularity in his lifetime constitute rather an unfavorable comment on the intellect of his readers of those days, who seemed merely excitable in temper and indiscriminate in taste?"[52]

The book begins with a forward by the author in which Jiang describes his *Young Wanderer* as a "crude scream." It is an epistolary novel, in which Wang Zhong, the main character, recounts a series of unfortunate events that befall him. Wang's parents, like Xi's, die at an early age. Wang watches helplessly as patriotic student protestors are massacred. While in prison, Wang writes, "Time in jail truly passes quickly. . . . It doesn't matter whether you are in jail or not, our lives are always prison-style lives." Wang concludes that only violence can save China. The book ends with him enrolling in Whampoa Academy, only to die in battle shortly thereafter.[53]

Xi, like Wang, would constantly face situations he deemed fundamentally unfair. Still, sadness and fortitude had a complicated relationship: "From birth I loved to resist, I loved to champion the cause of those who suffered." And his own suffering contributed to that sentiment: "The more pain that evil society brought me, the more powerfully did my resistance develop." These contradictions in Jiang's hero—resignation coexisting with intense motivation, a desire for change that persists despite constant failure, and a sense of justice that regularly conflicts with matters beyond one's own control—would be reflected in Xi's life for decades to come.[54]

THE LIANGDANG MUTINY

Under party investigation during the Cultural Revolution, Xi was depicted as a dissolute young man: no work and only gambling.[55] Xi, however, later claimed that he fabricated gambling debts as a cover story for leaving Fuping to continue fighting in the revolution.[56] In February 1930, after the health of his uncle began to improve, he told two of his younger sisters, "Our parents are dead. You must take care of one another, and you must take care of our little brothers and sisters. Do not make things difficult for uncle." When Xi left, he did not tell his uncle, fearing that the stress of the news would cause the man's old illness to reoccur. Xi, only sixteen years old at the time, allegedly nevertheless felt guilty about leaving and had tears in his eyes as he departed.[57] Xi Zhongzhi complained to Xi's cousins about him: "Xi Yongsheng died tragically on the road; your aunt and uncle became sick from famine and cold and died, but your big brother Zhongxun did not take the path of individual determination to change the fate of his own family."[58]

For two years, from 1930 to 1932, Xi served in a Nationalist military unit. His goal was to infiltrate the unit and persuade its soldiers to defect—an extremely optimistic, if not foolhardy, objective.[59] This choice to engage in "mutiny work" was particularly dangerous for Xi as he already had a prison record. He later wrote that he would never have dared to participate in such a mission "without the greatest determination for sacrifice." According to Xi, his conviction sprang from what he had seen: "More than a year in the countryside after leaving prison forced me to personally experience the tragic mistreatment of the laboring people and the extreme darkness of the old society."[60]

Xi cleverly used his hometown and school connections to develop a network of friends in the military—a goal facilitated by his position as the man in charge of logistics and food within his company. Xi also adopted the traditional Chinese practice of "swearing brotherhood" to establish relationships with locals, and he regularly relied on these "sworn brothers" to help him with underground party work.[61]

Xi slowly convinced other members of a battalion to secretly join the Communists, and he became head of the unit's party committee in the winter of 1931. When the First Battalion was ordered to switch locations with the Second Battalion, thus leaving the Liangdang area of Gansu Province, the mood deteriorated. The move meant they would now be in cold, mountainous areas. At around this time, in March 1932, Liu Linpu—secretary and special delegate of the Shaanxi Provincial Military Committee—arrived, and he agreed the time was ripe for an insurrection. On April 1, in a mule-and-horse store, Xi held a battalion committee meeting that decided that Liu would lead the mutiny and Xi would serve as commander of the battalion. The Communists immediately killed three company commanders, but the battalion commander escaped. On April 3, the mutineers, numbering about two hundred individuals, declared their loyalty to the party. Liu served as commissar, Xi as secretary of the party committee, and a man named Xu Tianjie was commander. But the next step was not obvious. When the forces departed Liangdang, they had only a general sense that they wanted to go to Northern Shaanxi, and they had not yet come up with a precise route. All Liu had was a small map ripped from a textbook, and no one had any clue about the location of either the Nationalist forces or the bandits.[62]

They crossed the Wei River into Shaanxi but were soon blocked by Nationalist troops. Some of the leadership had already lost hope and wanted to join another Nationalist military leader. Another group, which included Xi, believed that such a move would be foolish—after all, they had just led a mutiny. Then, a questionable decision was made. Both Liu Linpu and Xi Zhongxun left the troops, apparently to find a way to get across the Jing River. Xi, disguised as a teacher, narrowly passed an inspection by an undercover Nationalist agent, who asked whether he had participated in the mutiny. Three days after Xi departed, the battalion was defeated: the soldiers were still wearing Nationalist uniforms and flying a Nationalist flag, which led a local bandit to believe they were coming to attack him. The entire battalion was captured. Xi, who had still not returned to the unit, hid successfully in a cave, but Liu was soon captured while on a trip to Xi'an.[63] The Nationalists tortured Liu, but he refused to give up his true identity, so he was declared to be a "Shandong bandit." As he was paraded through the streets to his execution with someone else's name hanging from his neck, he finally shouted the truth. "I am a member of the Chinese Communist Party! Down with Chiang Kai-shek!" he yelled. He died at the age of twenty-three.[64]

Du Heng, the leader of the party in Shaanxi at the time, described the Liangdang mutiny in a report as an especially poor display of planning and execution. The soldiers only knew that they would mutiny, not for what reason or what they would do afterward. The night of the insurrection was planned so poorly that the mutineers accidentally attacked one another. Old officers were left in charge, and some of them ran away with the troops. After

FIGURE 2. Xi Zhongxun shortly before the Liangdang mutiny, 1932. Source: *Xi Zhongxun huace* (Shenzhen: Haitian, 2006), 2.

the mutiny, political work was done poorly, and officers were so terrified of enemy forces that they fought incompetently.[65]

Many years later, Xi provided his own reasons for why the mutiny failed. First, they did not sufficiently link up with local Communist forces. Second, at the time, they did not understand the importance of quickly establishing a cooperative relationship with the local peasants to form a base area—instead, they kept moving. Third, they failed to work closely with potentially friendly military forces: "When we arrived at a new place, even the chickens and dogs ran away." Fourth, "wavering elements" were not swiftly expelled from the group. If such people are not managed severely, Xi said, "their damaging influence can be more powerful than the party's political influence at critical moments." Finally, goals should be clear; because they did not raise the Red flag or provide slogans, "the masses did not understand." Xi's mutiny was a disaster, but it was not the only one. Liangdang was the first of about nine such mutinies that occurred in the region between April 1932 and early 1933. All but one, aided by local guerrilla forces, were unsuccessful.[66]

In June, Xi briefly again returned home, still a hunted man. In early July, he tried to link up again with the party for the first time since the Liangdang mutiny through a teacher named Shi Zhongwei in the Fuping County seat. When he arrived in the city, Xi was quickly arrested and brought to the military garrison for interrogation. Xi claimed that his surname was Jiao, and he wrote a note to Shi claiming he wanted to become a teacher. A Nationalist soldier brought the note to Shi to determine whether Xi was telling the truth. Shi falsely claimed that Xi was indeed a student, and thus Xi was released—yet another close brush with death. By September, Xi was at a Communist base area in Zhaojin, over a hundred kilometers north of Xi'an. He was only nineteen years old, and he had already experienced one failed assassination, one failed mutiny, and two incarcerations.[67]

3

WHO SAVED WHOM?

The Rise of the Base Areas and the Arrival of Mao

In Shaanxi during the revolution, the infighting within the party left a legacy that is sensitive in China even today. "The scars left behind by the brutal killings within the revolutionary units made a deep mark on their hearts forever, hurting them for their whole lives," Wang Xiaozhong, who participated in managing these grudges decades later, writes in his memoirs. According to Wang, "In party-history propaganda, such a major historical event as the Northwest issue is played down, skirted around, and treated casually. As for the internal turmoil and butchery that are unbearable to look back upon, they are simply not brought up."[1]

The most crucial issue shaping the history of revolutionary activities in the Northwest is the relationship among three key leaders: Liu Zhidan, Xie Zichang, and Yan Hongyan. In September 1931, Liu successfully combined three militia groups and formed the Nanliang Guerrilla Unit.[2] In October, Liu was joined by a group led by Yan. The top Communist leadership in Shaanxi sent Xie to find them. In January 1932, the Northwest Anti-imperialist United Army of seven hundred men was officially formed, with Xie as commander and Liu as vice-commander. The army was divided into a First and Second Unit, with the former made up of Yan's men and the latter based on Liu's forces. They swore a secret society–style oath of loyalty to each other.[3]

However, this declaration of brotherhood could not prevent the outbreak of violence that would have reverberations throughout party history—the

Sanjiayuan incident. The origins of the incident lay in two vexing issues. First, Xie Zichang wanted their forces to "raise the Red flag" of the party and to declare themselves Communists. Liu Zhidan believed it was too early for such a decision, calling instead to act as a part of a nearby warlord's army. Second, the units came from very different backgrounds. The Shaanxi Party Committee believed that Liu's unit was a "conglomeration of former bandits" with a penchant for rape who followed the Communists only when given opium.[4] Liu thought that education was enough to reform these men, while hard-liners wanted to disband the questionable units and take their weapons.[5]

In early February, Xie secretly met with Yan Hongyan. They decided to execute Zhao Erwa, one of Liu's close compatriots, take all the Second Unit's weapons, and raise the Communist banner. The showdown occurred a day later at a rally in Sanjiayuan. When Xie declared that Zhao Erwa was a criminal and that the Second Unit's weapons would be confiscated, Zhao was killed as he started to realize what was happening.[6]

An official report in 1986 notes that "in regular circumstances, the method of one group of people taking the weapons of another group of people" was already wrong, but this case was especially egregious because the main leaders, Liu and Xie, had not yet reached a consensus, and the process led to a loss of life. The report praises Liu Zhidan for seeing the bigger picture and still maintaining unity after his poor treatment.[7]

XI ARRIVES IN THE BASE AREAS

It was shortly after this incident that Xi joined the Communists north of Xi'an. This was dangerous work. Xi told a friend about this period years later, "We were people who lived carrying our heads on our belts," meaning they could have died at any time.[8] But by 1932, Xi did not have much of a home to which he could return anyway. A cousin from Henan who had moved to Shaanxi looking to start a new livelihood learned that the Xi family in Dancun had been "broken up and destroyed"—five or six of them had starved to death and a warrant was out for Xi's arrest.[9] To avoid harming his remaining family, when he wanted to meet them, he had them brought to him secretly. Xi's sister, who was only twelve at the time, later recalled their meeting in a cave: "I said to older brother that we should return together because our family lacked hands. He interrupted me and said never to tell him to return again." He told her to instead stay with their uncle, as Xi, in his words, still had "very, very far to go." She asked him why he had burned down a local man's home and divided his grain. Xi responded, "Because he's a landlord, of course!"[10]

He found a new father figure in Liu Zhidan. When they first met in the summer of 1932, Xi was only nineteen and, by his own description, depressed about the failure of the Liangdang mutiny. Xi felt he lacked experience in "the struggle." "I did not know what to say," he recalled many years later. "Comrade Zhidan understood me very well, and he encouraged me by saying, 'How can those who engage in revolution be afraid of failure? If you fail, just keep going. Failure is the mother of triumph. I failed many more times than you.'"[11]

Liu sent Xi to work in the Weibei Soviet, an extremely dangerous area given its close proximity to the Nationalist stronghold of Xi'an. There was one advantage, however. Xi could draw upon his old family connections to supply the base areas. Zhongzhi, the same relative who thought Zhongxun should have stayed at home to help the family's fortunes, nevertheless used his Henanese guild to help Zhongxun. The guild smuggled weaponry, as well as members of the Xi family, to the party. Later, Zhongzhi would say, "At the time, I never thought about revolution. . . . [Zhongxun's father] gave me a bite to eat and a good boss, and his child [Zhongxun] was on the north shore [at the base area]. We should help our own family do a bit." Yet he would also bitterly joke that "Zhongxun, on behalf of the revolution, would have his own family members do things that were punishable by death."[12]

Weibei was the first soviet base area in Shaanxi, but it soon failed. Joseph Esherick concludes that "the rural party . . . was built upon existing structures of local power, which allowed it to sink roots and grow, but limited its ability to transform society."[13] Moreover, the area was much too close to cities dominated by the Nationalist government, and the local cadres were forced to act too ambitiously. Provincial party leaders, for example, criticized Huang Ziwen, a local soviet official, for not aggressively dividing up the land for the peasants. Later, Xi would admit that Huang had been right—after a big open celebration of the Soviet Union's October Revolution, the Nationalists attacked, and dozens of party members were killed.[14] "It was impossible to create base areas in core areas controlled by the enemy," Xi said. He blamed the "leftist" opportunists for stubbornly holding on to the idea that "the cities are key" in the effort to overthrow the government.

"They wanted to take Xi'an and Sanyuan, and they opposed the so-called go-to-the-mountains surrenderism; they did not take into account the actual situation in the base areas; they forced a redivision of the land, and they continuously opposed the 'rich-peasant line' and 'rightist opportunism' of the soviet comrades. This kind of leftist opportunist line proved to be a failed line."[15]

In February 1933, Jin Like, a special representative of the Shaanxi Party Committee, called for a group of "political and military" talents to be sent to join the guerrilla forces in Zhaojin, which would become the second major soviet after the collapse of Weibei. One month later, Xi, one such talent, arrived there.[16] Despite his youth, he was rapidly promoted. In March 1933, the Shaanxi-Gansu Border Region Special Committee, a party organization, was created, with Jin as its secretary. Xi was secretary of the Military Affairs Committee and the youth organization. The next month, the Shaanxi-Gansu Border Region Revolutionary Committee (a "government" body) was established, with Zhou Dongzhi, a peasant, as chairman, and Xi as vice-chairman and party secretary. Although nominally Zhou was the leader, he was picked primarily because of his peasant status, and Xi made most decisions. He spent his time on forming and mobilizing militia units. He also enforced party rules against gambling and the tradition of binding women's feet.[17] This was a weighty assignment for twenty-year-old Xi. In 1993, Xi wrote that Liu Zhidan explained why he had been promoted so quickly: "Currently, most of the leading cadres in our party finished middle school or university, but they do not understand reality. However, grassroots cadres are illiterate. You both finished middle school, and you farmed, and you understand the peasants—that is your strength."[18]

Although now more distant from Nationalist areas, work remained treacherous. In late May 1933, Xi was ambushed. He told the main group to flee, and he stayed behind to provide cover. In the fighting, Xi was hit with a bullet. He told the others not to bother with him. Four or five others were injured as well. When they were surrounded, he used his eyes to hint that they all should run off into the forest, but no one understood what he meant, so they were captured. In 1986, Xi recalled,

> Under those circumstances, they could not be blamed for what happened. They all came from the villages and became guerrillas because they had been child cowherds. They had never been trained and had never participated in

fighting. Moreover, they were on their way to a meeting to collect grain, and we had pack animals. It was a surprise ambush by the militia. But during the Cultural Revolution, leftist rebels made a big deal of this; they said that the guerrilla unit gave up its weapons and surrendered. Because of this, I wrote materials for people to explain the true situation.[19]

Xi and some of the wounded Communists were taken prisoner. Xi later described the harrowing experience:

After I was injured, I could not stop bleeding, and my whole body had no energy. A little boss in the militia named Zhou Zhixiang took me away. He curiously said to me, you look like a big official to me. I said, I'm a regular person. The [limited] grain sent by the government gave me no option but to join the Red Army. He said no, you are a big official. What's your surname? Where are you from? I said my surname was Jiao and I was from Fuping. As I was saying that, I took out six pieces of silver from my pocket. He took three of the pieces and said that he knew I was a big official and he would let me run away. When I heard this, I did not know if it was true or false, but I summoned up the energy to run out of the ravine. When I passed the village of Chenjiapo, several dozen people appeared behind me, fired their guns rapidly, and shouted, 'Capture him alive! Capture him alive!' I ran toward the great ravine in front of me and rolled down the incline. The result was that I got caught on a tree, and it was only then that my injury began to hurt. The bandits fired a bunch of wild shots, then they made a signal to assemble. Finally, I slowly climbed down tree by tree.

Later Xi came to realize why he had been allowed to escape: "Although, at the time, Zhou Zhixiang was in the Nationalist militia, he had written us a letter saying he wanted to join the party. Because we could not clearly verify his letter, we did not respond. So he remained in the militia, but he continued to sympathize with the Red Army and wanted to make revolution." Only that remarkable coincidence saved Xi's life. But still it was a close call. As Xi fled, he used his hands to try to stop his wound from bleeding. He drank some bad water in a river and could not defecate for almost ten days. In 1986, Xi recalled, "At the time, it was good that I was young; otherwise, I would have died."[20]

The month after Xi's brush with death, the base-area party committee met near Zhaojin to discuss plans. Xi did not attend, as he was still recuperating. Du Heng, head of the party in Shaanxi, demanded that their forces march south to attack Weihua, reasoning that the city had more resources and that controlling the region would allow them to threaten Xi'an. However, the Nationalists understood the importance of Weihua, which made it unlikely that the small Red Army forces could hold it. Although Xi had not attended the meeting, he communicated that he thought Du's plan was problematic.[21]

The assault was a disaster, and again Xi drew some important lessons. Years later, he remembered,

> Du Heng himself acted willfully; he was completely foolhardy. First, he attacked the Miaowan Xia Yushan militia, which upset the nearby militias and led them to unite and to counter the Red Army. Then he burned Xiangshan Temple, so more than one thousand monks became enemies as well. The more the enemies were attacked, the more numerous they became; the more territories we attacked, the less territory we controlled. All that was left was Xuejiazhai, and we were surrounded by enemies. It was so bad that the injured had nowhere to go, no one supplied them with food, and it was impossible to remain in Zhaojin.[22]

In July 1933, Du was captured by the Nationalists because of the treachery of Xi's former close friend Cheng Jianwen. Du and Cheng then turned against the Communists. Cheng's act essentially destroyed the Shaanxi Communist leadership.[23]

The situation was dire. Liu Zhidan was missing. Connections with higher party authorities had been severed. The few remaining Communists were under attack and could not agree on what to do next. In August, the remnants of Communist forces, along with Wang Taiji, a Nationalist military leader who had recently defected, met in Chenjiapo. Huang Zixiang, commander of the most important military unit, argued that the provincial party committee had been destroyed, and therefore, the only option was for the individual units to split up, flee, and make their own decisions. He also believed it was inappropriate for Wang Taiji, who was not a party member, to be a leader of a united army. Huang Zixiang also opposed a proposal that Gao Gang, who had just narrowly avoided capture in Xi'an, become commissar of the unit. Huang's proposals were rejected but only after intense debate. If two more votes had gone the other way, they would have dissipated into multiple groups, given up on the base areas, and engaged only in guerrilla warfare.[24]

Huang had every reason to expect Xi would support him. Huang was eighteen years older than Xi and had vast influence within the region, and the two had interacted repeatedly over the years. On the day before the meeting, Huang demanded that Xi support his position, but Xi demurred. "I don't understand the situation," he said. "Let's discuss exactly how I will decide after the meeting starts." Yet Xi rejected Huang's positions, and because Xi chaired the meeting, his opposition to Huang had a very important influence on the outcome.[25] Opposing Huang, Xi supported Gao Gang instead.[26]

Yet another catastrophic defeat soon followed. By October 1933, Nationalist forces had finally surrounded Zhaojin. To escape, the remaining Red Army forces used a rope to lower soldiers one by one down a precipice, and then they ran down a ravine into a dense forest. Xi was the last to leave. When he tied the rope to a tree and started to crawl down, a local militiaman recognized him and shot him, wounding him in the leg. But he was found by some peasants, who hid him in a cave. When Xi finally left, he took the son of the woman who had cared for him to join the Red Army, but the son soon perished.[27]

After the base area in Zhaojin was destroyed, the Communists retreated to Nanliang—already the third base area in the region. In early November 1934, the Shaan-Gan (Shaanxi-Gansu) Border Region Congress of Workers, Peasants, and Soldiers was held in Nanliang to elect a soviet government—deliberately on the anniversary of the October Revolution in Petrograd. Workers, peasants, soldiers, and women were each given a set number of seats in the congress, but the elections were held in a generally democratic fashion, including anonymous voting. Liu Zhidan and Xi Zhongxun gave key speeches about using the countryside to envelop the cities and to lead "the great suffering and laboring masses to rule all under heaven." Liu told one of the representatives that "when it comes to constructing political power and engaging in civilian work, I am not as good as Comrade Xi Zhongxun." Xi, only twenty-one years old, was elected chairman of the soviet.[28]

Liu, Xi, and the others in the base area developed a close relationship with the peasants and lived an egalitarian lifestyle. Xi often visited country markets, where crowds would surround him to ask friendly questions. To raise funds for party activities, they often kidnapped local landlords. Some of the victims would be released after payment, whereas the more infamous ones were executed or subjected to manual labor. The base-area leadership also supported local merchants who engaged in trade with the Nationalist-held areas. Xi was commissar of the First Lenin Primary School, where political education for local children included simple songs with lyrics like "Marx and Engels are mentors of world revolution" and "Kill the despotic gentry with knives and shoot the White Army with rifles."[29]

One sticking point was opium. The peasants told the Communists that if the production of opium were banned, they would all leave and live in the areas controlled by the Nationalists, where they could plant and smoke in peace. So the Communists tacitly decided to allow it. Zhang Xiushan, one leader in the soviet, later rationalized, "If they had really left after [we] came, there would not even be a pot to cook food in and [be] no rice to eat. Therefore, we yielded to the common people; we said we would not ban it that year or the next year, but it would be banned within two years."[30]

Infighting among the local Communists persisted. In January 1934, Gao Gang was removed from his position as commissar after Huang Ziwen told Liu Zhidan that Gao had raped a woman. However, Gao's replacement, Zhang Xiushan, fought poorly. When people asked Xi Zhongxun to become commissar instead, Xi refused, saying that Gao had more experience and that Gao should again become commissar. In May, just a few months after being punished, Gao again assumed the position.[31]

In the spring of 1935, an attack by Ma Hongbin, a Muslim leader allied with Chiang Kai-shek, forced the Communists to give up on Nanliang as well. As the leadership fled, Ma sent his cavalry in pursuit. On April 16, Xi and some of his soldiers were surrounded. The survivors lost Xi in the mayhem, and they had to search for a long time before they discovered him hiding in a ravine. Xi rallied forty men, but Ma's forces caught up with them again a few days later. Only after escaping did Xi realize that he had ridden his white horse with such force that the stirrups had caused two bloody injuries on his feet and his face was covered with the horse's blood. He had beaten the horse so severely that, in his own words, "the white horse became a red horse." The experience deeply affected Xi. According to Qi Xin, Xi's future wife, nightmares about horses and gunfire would wake him "countless times."[32]

LIU ZHIDAN

Liu Zhidan had a profound impact on the young Xi. Liu had a "big-tent" philosophy when it came to revolution. In 1929, he described his vision in stark terms: "All we have to do is transform the existing popular armed groups, along with the enemy's armed forces, into a revolutionary armed force! Achieving this will require us to actively employ various practical methods, but the key must always be to unite with the masses and with people from all walks of life, including Nationalist officials, gentry figures, and even old gentlemen." Liu constantly clashed with radicals, whom he described as "old widows, dreaming of a perfect world but oblivious to the problems of the real world."[33]

According to the Ten Great Policies, signed by Liu and Xi and disseminated in November 1934, only some of the land of the landlords and rich peasants was to be redistributed, and those landlords who participated in labor could be given land. Conscription was not imposed: people only joined the armed forces voluntarily. Friendly local militias were not to be attacked, and neutral militias were to be won over. Bandits who could be educated were not to be destroyed. Although unambiguous counterrevolutionaries were to be executed, those individuals supported by the masses were to be protected.[34]

In 1979, Xi wrote that Liu had taught him that "revolution demands a united line." Liu's policies, in Xi's mind, showed that "the fewer the enemies the better. The more friends the better. If we add one piece of strength, the enemy loses one piece of strength." Xi described how Liu had demonstrated an impressive ability to bring to his banner members of secret organizations, such as the Gelaohui, warlords, Nationalist officers, and militias. Liu never purged those with different opinions. Instead, he used logic to convince his opponents.[35] In 1993, Xi again reflected on Liu's lessons: "During my entire life, I took care to listen to different opinions, to listen to the opinions of people outside the party, and to do a good job with United Front work. This came from respecting the guidance of Comrade Zhidan and the practical experiences of the time."[36]

Two scholars on the party in Shaanxi, Xu Youwei and Philip Billingsley, theorize that Liu's need to cooperate with these politically problematic forces made Northern Shaanxi different from Mao's Jinggangshan base area, where the Communists were more powerful.[37] Despite Liu's general approach, he was still violent. Liu once disarmed and killed a militia commander after coaxing him to relax and share an opium pipe. On another occasion, he slit the throat of a traitor and let him bleed to death.[38]

Xi demonstrated special care for his new mentor. After Nationalist troops attacked Liu's home and dug up the graves of his ancestors, Liu's family fled and faced a large bounty on their heads. Xi sent a group to bring them to the base area. Liu's wife, Tong Guirong, had not yet met Xi, but she knew that the peasants called him the "Baby Chairman" because of his tender age. When Xi introduced himself to her, she thought to herself, "He really is a baby." But Xi gave off an air of approachability—he quickly called Liu Zhidan's father "uncle" and played with Liu's daughter. Tong described Xi as a man who "never puts on airs; as soon as he meets someone, with just two or three words, they become close. His memory is also good. He would remember people's names after meeting them just once."[39]

THE PURGE

As Liu was building up what would become known as the Shaan-Gan Border Region, farther north, a second base area was also developing: the Shaan-bei (Northern Shaanxi) base area. Du Heng had expelled Xie Zichang from the region, but in January 1934, Xie returned to Shaanxi to lead this base area.[40] Around the same time, Guo Hongtao joined them as head of its Organization Department. Xie and Guo shared a more dogmatic approach to revolution.[41]

In July 1934, they traveled to Xi's Shaan-Gan Border Region base area. Xie read two letters from higher party authorities that accused Liu's army of "rightist opportunism," "surrenderism," and "mountainism," meaning hiding in the mountains. Liu's men allegedly focused too much on military issues and not enough on politics. The listeners were shocked, wondering how it was possible that Shaan-bei cadres were telling Shaan-Gan Border cadres what they were doing was wrong. They were flabbergasted to hear Xie accuse Liu of "rightist" mistakes given that Xie himself had been expelled from the region after suffering from such labels.[42]

Xi Zhongxun was deeply upset, remarking, "We were waiting in expectation, but we were given a cold shower."[43] In 1942, he described his reaction to this affront: "When Comrade Hongtao arrived, he acted like an imperial envoy. At the time, I was indeed careless. I did not know whether he was a representative of the Central Committee of the Northern Bureau. I did not look at his recommendation letter, and at that meeting, I was very restrained. In the past, I did not like to talk, and as soon as I talked, my face would turn red. I couldn't really talk, and at this meeting, I said little. At the time, I was a member of the meeting's presidium, but I didn't really understand what the debate was all about."[44] Despite the insults from Xie and Guo, Liu worked to keep the meeting from spinning out of control. He allowed Xie Zichang to become commissar of his Shaan-Gan Border Region forces, replacing Gao Gang. Liu even sent some of his forces and supplies to go to Shaan-bei to help the other base area.[45] Despite Liu's generous gestures after the meeting, both Guo Hongtao and Xie Zichang wrote letters to the Northern Representative Party authorities criticizing Liu.[46] In 1942, at a meeting held to discuss this history, Xi mocked Guo (but not Xie) for writing the letter, making the audience laugh: "Everyone think for a moment, who, at the time, did not want to build a base area on a plain, so we wouldn't have had to climb up and down all the time!?"[47]

About a month after Xie Zichang criticized his fellow Shaanxi Communists, he was seriously injured in battle. In early 1935, Liu Zhidan went to Shaan-bei to visit Xie, who lay on his death bed. They decided to combine the Shaan-Gan Border Region and Shaan-bei party and military organizations. Xie and Liu each tried to convince the other to assume the role of head of the military commission. For decades, the northwesterners would fight about who would finally assume the role of head of the military commission, but, in any case, Xie was dead by the end of the month. The two base areas combined into the Northwest Work Committee.[48]

Liu brought most of the Communist forces into the northeast of Shaanxi, where they reached a new peak of power and influence. The party heavily recruited among peasants, bandits, and the disaffected. Killing gentry was a ticket into the party, as it showed commitment. Liu shifted from ransoming local rich individuals to publicly executing them. In Esherick's words, "The region descended into a brutal cycle of revenge killings." In one case, when twelve of their soldiers were executed, the Communists killed thirty-two village functionaries in retaliation. Even Communist reports from the time spoke of "indiscriminate arson and executions" as well as "frequent violations" of discipline, including rape and looting. When a former colleague begged Liu to spare his life, Liu was merciless. "Kill the bastard," he ordered.[49]

Even as the party's power grew, Liu faced a new challenge. In May 1935, Kong Yuan, who was in charge of Communist operations in the north of China, sent Zhu Lizhi to Shaanxi to enforce a more ambitious strategy. Kong even gave Zhu a handbook called *Sufan* (Purge) as a guide.[50] When Zhu arrived in the Northwest, Guo Hongtao told him that Liu Zhidan came from a family of landlords and had always engaged in rightist deviation.[51]

In July 1935, the Northwest Work Committee held an enlarged session, where letters from the Northern Representative and Hebei Party Committees were transmitted and the base area was ordered to struggle against rightist opportunism. Xi was deeply distressed, but he did not fight back. "Some people became rightist opportunists, though I did not dare say this aloud. It was necessary to demonstrate a supportive attitude, but in my heart, I was depressed," he later said.[52]

In Northern Shaanxi, which had a smaller population concentration, the peasants were primarily concerned about debt and income inequality, not about the division of land. Liu Zhidan's group therefore had not prioritized land reform. However, the "leftists" without experience in the region interpreted this behavior as insufficiently revolutionary.[53] In August, three men described by Xi as "imperial envoys" arrived to "help" the local soviet overcome its "rightist" mistakes. Xi was furious. One of the "envoys," Hui Bihai, wanted to confiscate land from the rich and middle peasants and, in Xi's words, "force them into the mountains to eat grass." Li Jinglin, another new arrival, disagreed with Xi's plans to punish Hui, but Xi emerged victorious. Xi believed that "Li Jinglin was all about extremism, adventurism, and acting unscrupulously. If someone were to say that guy is a rich peasant, he would immediately say 'go struggle' against him!"[54]

Still cut off from other Communists, the situation fundamentally changed with the arrival of Xu Haidong's Twenty-Fifth Army, on the run from Nationalist forces. Xu immediately supported Zhu Lizhi and Guo Hongtao. A new Shaanxi-Gansu-Shanxi party committee was established, with Zhu as secretary and Guo as vice-secretary. All military forces in the region were combined into a new army commanded by Xu. Liu Zhidan was relegated to vice–chief of staff, whereas Gao Gang was made head of the Political Department. Liu, Gao, and Xi, who had done the most over the previous years to expand Red power in the Northwest, were relieved of any real political or military power. Zhu, now more comfortable with Xu's military support, ordered an investigation into local traitors—and that moment signified the official beginning of an inner-party purge.[55]

Although this incident is usually seen as an attack by outsiders on the leaders of the Shaan-Gan Border Region base area, at first, Liu Zhidan, Gao Gang, and Xi Zhongxun all supported the action. Officially, the purge was about finding and eliminating people who supported Zhang Mutao, a man who had been stripped of his party membership and had tried to start a new party. The first arrests included Cai Ziwei, Huang Ziwen, and others—figures who had some connection with Zhang Mutao or had a "mysterious background.""[56] Xi himself helped to facilitate these arrests by writing letters in his own name to summon people back for investigation.[57] He would invite men to speak with him, ask to see their gun, and then place the weapon under his leg, providing an opportunity for them to be hogtied. Xi said, "Listen to the orders of the organization, and the matter will ultimately be clarified." Because Xi was chair of the soviet government and was seen as a kind person, they did not resist.[58]

But torture led the detained cadres to lie, and the investigation soon spread even to Liu and Xi.[59] After Liu accidentally discovered a letter calling for his own arrest, he surrendered himself. In an article published in *People's Daily* in 2000, Xi Zhongxun notes that because Liu had control over some military forces, he could have refused to surrender. Some comrades wanted to fight back, but Liu had told them to be patient—after all, if they caused trouble, they would be labeled "antiparty," and the enemy could take advantage of the split. Moreover, by staying in the system, Liu reasoned, they could continue to raise their own opinions and resist leftist mistakes.[60]

Xi, too, did not resist arrest. When Xi was summoned to a suspicious meeting, his bodyguard said, "You can't go! They arrested Old Liu and Old Gao!" But Xi said, "That doesn't matter. Things always get figured out." He told his associates, "After I go to this meeting, I may come back. But I might not come back. No matter who is leader, you must all work hard." He even told his bodyguard, "No matter what happens, you must not speak or act irresponsibly!"[61] When Liu Jingfan, Liu Zhidan's brother, suggested that Xi hide for a while, Xi responded, "Even if I am killed, I cannot go; these comrades were all summoned back under my name. How can I leave?" At the last opportunity to flee, he instead gave his gun and some money to a friend. Alone, he traveled on a thin horse to meet his accusers. While incarcerated, someone suggested to Xi the possibility of helping him escape. But Xi made a brave face of it with a promise to "be faithful until death for the party."[62] "I believe that the Central Committee will definitely clarify this matter. I absolutely am not a counterrevolutionary," Xi said to a friend who had snuck, with a blanket, into the freezing pawnshop where Xi was confined. "If I die, that is also dying for the revolution. And if I survive, I will redouble my efforts for the party."[63]

Despite these strong words, Xi suffered terribly. Still in summer clothes, he slept in the cold Shaanxi weather tied up with ropes and crawling with lice.[64] When he greeted two colleagues with a smile and a nod as they were also brought into jail, a guard struck him twice in the head with a whip.[65] About two hundred of his fellow cadres were executed by their own party.[66] In 1943, Xi left a deep impression on a young cadre who had been assigned to write on the early history of the base area when he took off his shirt to show that the scars had yet to heal.[67]

THE LONG MARCHERS APPEAR

Mao Zedong and the central leadership staggered into the Northwest in the middle of this purge. In 1934, the main party leadership had been forced to leave the central base area in southern Jiangxi to start the Long March, in large part because of "leftist" mistakes committed by individuals more radical and dogmatist than Mao as well as because of improved Nationalist military tactics.[68] Mao learned of the existence of the Shaanxi base area in a newspaper while at a remote village in Gansu Province. At the time, the situation was so dire that the Red Army was considering a retreat to distant Inner Mongolia to win support from the Soviet Union. Meanwhile, there was trouble in the ranks—complaints led the security services to start executions.[69]

Xi would claim that Mao's arrival saved his life. "If things had continued, heads would have had to move homes; many heads would have been finished [meaning executed]," Xi later claimed.[70] In 1950, he told a journalist that if the party center and Mao had arrived only four days later, he and his comrades would have been buried alive.[71] This story of how Mao "saved" Xi's life is one of the most famous narratives in party history. Yet the historical record about what exactly happened is a little more complicated: Xi's death was not imminent, Mao's own role is overstated, and it took years for Xi to achieve complete rehabilitation.

The leaders of the purge later asserted to have already started to realize the seriousness of the situation before Mao appeared. Guo Hongtao said that he never believed allegations that Gao and Liu were rightists, even saying to have remarked, "Even if you kill me, I will not believe that Liu and Gao are counterrevolutionaries." Sometime around September 24 or 25, likely before he knew of the approach of the Long Marchers, Guo went to the front to tell Xu Haidong that arresting Liu and Gao had been a mistake and that a decision had been made to cease the arrests. No one was released and the investigations continued; however, the evidence suggests that executions were indeed probably not imminent.[72]

According to the conventional narrative, Mao declared a halt immediately after arriving in the region. For example, Wang Shoudao, who was sent by Mao to investigate the purge, wrote that Mao said that "cutting off heads is not like harvesting garlic." "After harvesting garlic, it can grow back," but, he said, "heads cannot grow back."[73] Mao's role, however, was not as decisive as Wang suggests. Sometime between October 19 and 22, Wang first heard about the arrests and executions from two low-ranking cadres in the region. Mao promised to solve the matter, but he did not end the purge that early. Historian Li Donglang writes that declaring an end to the purge merely after listening to a report from two commanders was "something that a cautious Mao Zedong would clearly never do." Liu, Gao, Xi, and the others were not freed until after a close examination, probably sometime between November 10 and 25.[74]

The decision to release them was a collective one, and Mao would have been at least somewhat involved. Yet Mao was distracted by the continued fighting with the Nationalists, and it was the general secretary of the party, Zhang Wentian, who personally managed the investigation.[75] Although official party histories tend to mark Mao's ascent to head of the party at the Zunyi Conference in January 1935, Mao was only head of the military and Zhang continued to take the lead in managing party affairs. Zhang's wife, Liu Ying, later recalled, "At the time, whenever anybody had a problem, they looked for Wentian, not Chairman Mao. . . . Things that Wentian did right, many good things that he did, it seems it was said they were not done by him; it was said they were done by Chairman Mao."[76]

In subsequent years, Zhu Lizhi and Guo Hongtao would forcefully reject Xi's version of the purge. In 1945, Zhu said Xi himself could substantiate the claim that by the time of the arrival of the party center, there was no intention to bury anyone alive.[77] In a commemorative article about Zhu, one of his official biographers writes that during the purge, Zhu had told Xi, "For the moment, we can't clarify the situation, so we must temporarily inconvenience you a bit. But I guarantee that the party will seek truth from facts and will not wrongfully convict a good person."[78] In 1999, Guo Hongtao privately said that the idea of plans to bury anyone alive or that Mao had ordered to "spare their lives" was "bullshit." "The first person to claim that Mao said to 'spare their lives' was Xi Zhongxun, and then the story spread widely," Guo complained.[79]

Although the investigation by the party center called for the prisoners to be released, it did not reverse the purge's verdicts against Xi and the others. On November 18, Mao, Zhou Enlai, and Peng Dehuai confirmed that "a group of people had been wrongly incarcerated—that is a fact," but they did not say the purge as a whole had been incorrect. On November 26, an official Central Committee document acknowledged the purge had made "a severe mistake," yet it still affirmed that the struggle against "rightist surrenderism" and the "purge of counterrevolutionary rightists" were "generally necessary and accurate."[80] Those individuals who were arrested at the beginning of the purge were not released.[81]

Because they continued to carry the label of "rightists," Liu Zhidan's associates, such as Gao Gang, Zhang Xiushan, and Xi, served only in low-ranking positions for years. Zhang Xiushan and Gao Gang both cried over their treatment.[82] Gao even considered suicide.[83] In 1986, Xi claimed that Li Weihan, who managed personnel for the party, later apologized to Xi for how he had been treated. Li repeatedly said, "I did not understand the situation at the time, and I listened to their opinions too much. I was especially unfair to Comrade Xi Zhongxun, sending him to be a county secretary."[84]

As those who suffered during the 1935 purge continued to work in low-level positions but with the accusations against them still not cleared, they suffered another emotional blow—the violent death of Liu Zhidan. Rumors persist among elites in China to this day that Mao ordered Liu's execution. However, most party historians discount this possibly—Mao's authority was too much higher than Liu's for the Shaanxi man to be a threat, and Mao probably understood Liu's fanatic party discipline. The more likely reasons for Liu's demise were his need to move to the front to better manage his Red Army unit and, most importantly, to put himself in harm's way to provide evidence of his dedication. Zhang Xiushan recalled Liu saying, "Let them see on the battlefield" whether he and the other men were "rightists." Zhou Enlai similarly ascribed to this viewpoint, arguing that Liu "was trying to clean himself, to prove that he was not an agent. He preferred to charge ahead into battle to sacrifice himself."[85]

Despite Liu's valiant efforts, however, his record when he died still included the verdict that he had "previously committed the serious mistake of rightism." And not all of his comrades in arms believed that Liu's death was glorious. During the Yan'an era, some of Liu Zhidan's comrades who had also been purged told Liu's daughter, "Your father is good in every way except that he gives in to other people too easily. He even put his life on the line. That much should not be emulated."[86]

The disgraced status of Liu's comrades only started to change in the spring of 1937 during elections for the Shaan-Gan-Ning (Shaanxi-Gansu-Ningxia) Base Area Assembly, when many people started to express dissatisfaction with Guo Hongtao.[87] The party center failed to convince everyone to support Guo's election as regional party secretary. Xi did, however, agree to support Guo, and many people who survived the purges saw Xi's act as a betrayal. In 1942, Xi tried to justify his behavior, reasoning that "we understood the Central Committee's goal at the time was to achieve unity in the party, so in order to achieve this, they had me go explain matters." But when trying to make the case to many comrades, he noted, "I was not successful; some lower-ranking cadres said I sold them out."[88]

When the assembly elected seventeen members of the Shaan-Gan-Ning Border Region party leadership, Xi won the tenth most votes. Gao Gang came in first with eighty-three votes, and even Guo Hongtao did better than Xi with sixty-four votes.[89] Participants at the assembly called for an investigation into Zhu Lizhi and Guo Hongtao's responsibility for the purge. Xi and others finally convinced the party leadership that the Central Committee's earlier conclusion about the nature of the purge was wrong. Finally, in January 1938, the Politburo Standing Committee met to discuss the issue, and, for the first time, Zhu and Guo were held accountable.[90]

Crucially, some of the initial targets of the purge who had been arrested with the approval of Gao and Liu were never rehabilitated. In 1939, Cai Ziwei was expelled from the party—an act that would not have happened without the explicit approval of Gao, who was secretary of the Shaan-Gan-Ning Border Region by that time. In 1942, Gao accused Huang Ziwen, the man who had complained about Gao's rape of a woman, as well as other individuals, such as Cai Ziwei, of engaging in "rightist" activities in the early 1930s. In other words, Gao did not subscribe to the belief that the purge was wrong; he simply thought it went too far when he too was dragged into it.[91]

4
THE YAN'AN ERA

In January 1936, only a few weeks after his release from a Communist prison and at just twenty-two years old, Xi was sent on another dangerous mission. He was ordered to work in the Guanzhong Special Region, located along the precarious southern border of Communist-controlled territory. Some weaknesses there had been self-inflicted. Xi later recalled that at the time, "because of a misguided purge, many cadres had been executed in Guanzhong, and the masses were in a state of terror. This had affected work so deeply that it almost came to a standstill." In April, a Nationalist assault captured five counties, and the local Communists were forced to dissolve the Special Region and engage in guerrilla warfare. Xi would later describe this period as an "arduous and terrifying moment." In early May, he was told to return to the party center to await a new assignment.[1]

In June, the Red Army seized Qu and Huan Counties in neighboring Gansu Province, and Xi went to lead the area. The area was still so volatile that he regularly slept with an armed pistol under his pillow.[2] The local contest for power was brutal. On one occasion, two individuals who worked for the party were kidnapped by Zhao Sizhong, a local Nationalist security official. One of the detained men escaped, but Zhao burned the other man to death. After Xi captured two men who worked for Zhao, he immediately held a mass rally to sentence them to death, and he had them executed on the spot. "With regard to our enemies," Xi said, "if you show them mercy, they will ride on your neck. This is a bloody lesson!" To retaliate, Zhao grabbed another one of Xi's men, strung him up over a pit, and tortured him for several days. This time, instead of launching an assault, Xi engaged in careful negotiations to win the man's freedom. But Zhao continued to cause trouble—on one occasion, an assault by Zhao's forces on the Huan Party Committee led Xi to flee to a cave behind a waterfall for an entire day and night.[3]

In August 1936, Xi was sent back to the Guanzhong subregion. It was still a challenging time for the area. Guanzhong was situated immediately north of Xi'an, and Chiang Kai-shek was planning to launch an assault on the Communist base areas. But in December, warlord Zhang Xueliang captured Chiang in Xi'an and demanded that the Nationalists establish a new, second United Front with the Communists to address the growing threat from imperial Japan. Chiang and Zhou Enlai struck an agreement, and for the next ten years, the Nationalists and the Communists existed in what Chinese historian Yang Kuisong describes as a situation with "both love and hate, both cooperation and enmity, symbolizing both equality and inequality, and implying both peace and war."[4] Xi even named his first child Heping, the Chinese word for "peace," because she was born around the time of the birth of this second United Front.[5]

The agreement between the Nationalists and Communists created an extraordinarily complex environment, and Guanzhong was the frontline. Without the United Front, the party would have simply not been able to survive there. Xi would later describe the situation: "On the one hand, we re-established all sorts of secret organizations, and on the other, we developed all sorts of United Front connections." "Each individual, each faction, each social group, and each armed group" had its own situation. Xi faced the challenging task of "contacting them, consulting with them, negotiating with them, establishing with them all sorts of agreements, complete or partial, temporary or long-term, and written or oral, to establish different levels of United Front relations with some people and some groups."[6]

Loyalties were mixed and shifting. Tian Pingxuan, Nationalist leader of Guanzhong's southernmost county of Xunyi, had grown up close to Xi, and the two had attended school together. From 1936 to 1938, despite their status as the local Nationalist and Communist leaders respectively, Xi would often visit Tian at his home and sometimes even spend the night. They would sleep on the same *kang*, a heated stone platform bed common in northern China, in the Nationalist county headquarters. Tian gave the Communists twenty-five pistols and rifles and even a machine gun. On multiple occasions, Tian would request to become a member of the party, but Xi always refused, reasoning that Tian could do more for the cause if he remained with the Nationalists. Tian was able to live in peace the first few years of the new regime after the Communist victory in 1949. However, in 1964, Tian, like so many others, was targeted for his long-term relationship with Xi. In August of that year, Tian wrote in a letter to his wife, "Please warmly support the party, obey the party, and follow the party." He committed suicide by jumping into a river.[7]

For years, Guanzhong remained relatively calm, but as Xi later admitted, it was really "a rising wind foreboding a coming storm."[8] At first, Chiang hoped that the Nationalists and the Communists would unite into one party. Chiang admired the morale among Communist forces, and he hoped that the infusion of Communists would help the Nationalist cause.[9] Yet Chiang was increasingly disappointed by the lack of Communist help in the war against Japan, and he worried about the party's growing strength. In January 1939, Nationalist leaders made an official decision to limit the growth of Communist power.[10]

In that same month, the new Nationalist chief of Xunyi laid siege to a hospital for Red Army soldiers. When Xi learned of the situation, he carefully removed the patients from the hospital. Then, the Communists went too far. A Nationalist report from this period suggests that Xi's forces were using "sly tricks," staging incidents, improving fortifications, and enlarging their numbers. In May, a Red Army hospital worker who had been trying to buy supplies was killed. The Nationalists denied responsibility, but the Communists demanded "justice" and launched demonstrations in an apparent attempt to evict the Nationalists from the county seat. The Nationalists resorted to force. At the time, Xi was at a meeting in Yan'an, but he rushed back to send reinforcements. It was already too late. The party had suffered serious losses and been pushed out of a strategic, highly productive region.[11]

The members of the Red Army unit that had fled were furious and wanted to counterattack. Xi acknowledged that it was their right to do so, but he argued against it, noting that the enemy was more powerful than they were. Moreover, the Nationalist hard-liners wanted to use the fighting as an excuse for even more provocative acts. Xi and the Guanzhong leaders decided to proceed prudently, so instead, they wrote a letter to the high-ranking Nationalist military leader in the region to reason with him. After reviewing the incident, internal Communist documents blamed themselves for adopting a tough line that sparked Nationalist violence when their own forces were still too weak to resist.[12]

The Communists were not well prepared to deal with the increasingly precarious situation. In December 1939, the Shaanxi provincial leadership, which focused on underground work and whose hidden headquarters were located within Nationalist-controlled areas, fled to Guanzhong. This created serious organizational issues, as Xi's Guanzhong was technically under the control of the headquarters of the entire Shaan-Gan-Ning Border Region, not the Shaanxi provincial party.[13]

Xi struggled to get the United Front to work right. On January 13, 1940, the United Front Department of the Border Region Party Committee criticized Xi and his comrades for not being able to explain how they would manage "allies" who caused trouble, strengthen cooperation with prominent local individuals, or engage with ordinary people. The central leadership in Yan'an warned Xi to be careful with regard to the most stubborn Nationalist supporters, informing him that it was necessary to deal with the Nationalists using a variety of methods. The goal was to convince them to resist Japan and not to engage in open enmity. Xi had failed to establish any serious party-front organizations.[14]

On January 21, Xi penned a warning to the leaders of the Shaan-Gan-Ning Border Region. Having successfully integrated political warfare into their program, the Nationalist forces were preparing for another attack. Communist defections were facilitating Nationalist espionage, and spies were overwhelming the party. The Communists would focus on "political attacks," not military offensives. He promised to strengthen antispy activity by sending special cadres to investigate, but he would also mobilize the entire party to find agents. "The most important thing is to focus on the outside and destroy their foundation for spying while also strengthening our own ranks," Xi wrote.[15]

The next month, Xi was commended for writing a "very good" report on United Front work. But the leadership still had concerns. Xi should not casually use the word "traitor" against people who had only committed acts that had *helped* the traitors. Accentuating the secretive nature of United Front work, Xi was ordered to only submit oral reports and not to again submit reports in writing. He was tasked with winning over the local militias while also infiltrating them with party members to gradually gain control of them, as well as with better educating cadres on "commonsense secret work."[16]

Yet the situation did not improve. On March 30, Nationalists attacked the headquarters of the Guanzhong Communist leadership in Malanbao even as the Communists were holding a rally in support of Chiang Kai-shek. In April, Xi warned that Nationalist forces were building fortifications around Guanzhong in an attempt to seal off the area. In mid-May, the Shaanxi Standing Committee informed the central leadership that Communist control over certain parts of Guanzhong had become so weak that the Communists had been forced to shift to guerrilla warfare. By the end of the month, the Communists had fled Malanbao.[17]

Xi faced criticism again at the end of the month when a company of soldiers defected to the party, and yet Xi still decided to confiscate their guns. In a telegram, Xi's superiors wrote that "doing this has an extremely bad political influence." They demanded that Xi hold a meeting and openly acknowledge that he had made a mistake and that he had been criticized for it by his superiors. The telegram continued, "Guanzhong must avoid all kinds of activities that violate the principles of the United Front, especially guerrilla units that go out, which need strong leadership. We expect a detailed discussion to research experiences and lessons from Guanzhong United Front work."[18]

On June 5, Xi was censured for planning a retreat from the city of Chunhua, yet another setback for Guanzhong, without requesting permission from his superiors.[19] Four days later, Xi's superiors warned him in a document that because Guanzhong was weaker than other party-controlled areas, it was likely that Nationalist general Hu Zongnan would first concentrate on seizing that region. Guanzhong, according to the document, was not ready for such a challenge, and the slaughter of party cadres was causing terror in the ranks. The local party leadership under Xi was committing an "intolerable mistake" by engaging in conventional, as opposed to guerrilla, warfare. Political messaging was too abstract, and the local Communist forces were not taking advantage of internal contradictions among the enemy. The reasons for these mistakes were summed up as "an inability to concretely use or understand United Front tactics."[20]

Xi resorted to more dangerous measures. The Communists captured Yao Chungui, a Nationalist militia commander, even though Xi and Yao had developed a cooperative relationship. At first, Xi wanted Yao to go to Yan'an to study, but then Xi changed his mind and decided it would be more in the party's interests for Yao to continue to work for the Nationalists. Just as in the case of Tian Pingxuan, this decision had a devastating impact on the course of Yao's life. If Yao had gone to Yan'an, he likely would have officially joined the party. However, because he remained with the Nationalists, he came under suspicion by the party for the rest of his life. "I once had some interactions with Xi Zhongxun," Yao said in an interview years later. "Because of this I suffered a life of torment! What the hell did I accomplish in life? I wasn't a Communist; I wasn't a Nationalist. My life was a mess!" In 1988, when asked about a similar case of an individual who had secretly worked for the party and was later mistreated, Xi said that "there were lots of this kind of problem in Shaanxi."[21]

Changing political winds could hurt longstanding members of the party as well. In September 1940, Xi summoned a party cadre named Yang Zongyao and told him he had been selected to work as a secret agent. Yang was shocked that his name had already been given to the Nationalist political police as someone interested in working for them as part of a cover story. Yang was very unhappy, and he asked what would happen if, many years later, someone discovered his name in the Nationalist archives but forgot that his name was there only because of a party trick. Xi tried to convince Yang to accept the assignment, but Yang continued to refuse. Finally, Xi grew upset. "Are you a member of the party or not?" Xi asked. "Do you obey the decisions of the party? If you don't accept the party's work, the local party committee will punish you!" Xi then tried to reason with Yang in a lighter tone but to no effect. A week later, Zhang Zhongliang, who was in charge of security in the region at the time, told Yang that Guanzhong had been criticized by the top leadership numerous times for its poor intelligence about the enemy, so Yang finally accepted the job. Between October 1940 and 1943, Yang delivered fifty secret documents to Xi. But after Xi was purged in 1962, Yang was labeled a Nationalist agent, just as he had feared four decades earlier. He died in 1973 in prison after seven years of incarceration.[22]

Despite these attempts to improve the situation in Guanzhong, in September, Xi was again criticized by the leadership of the Shaan-Gan-Ning Border Region. The recent reports from Guanzhong lacked practical solutions and applicability to real problems. Although the Guanzhong leaders had submitted self-criticisms, they still "lacked a concrete plan for work in the future," which meant that lower-ranking cadres did not know what they were to do. Xi's work in establishing local governance structures that did not include party members was praised, although he was reminded to make sure that these institutions really did win over the people and they were not mere window dressing.[23]

In December, the Shaan-Gan-Ning Border Region leaders decided that the immediate danger in Guanzhong had passed. No massive attack on the base areas was imminent. Therefore, they counseled Xi to hold off on any changes to military policy and instead to focus on "using contradictions within the enemy, winning over the majority, isolating the minority, and attacking a small minority" to weaken the ability of the Nationalist forces. Moreover, Xi was told to "do everything possible" to increase underground work in Nationalist-controlled territory. The complete annihilation of the secret Communist operations in Xunyi had been "a huge loss," so Xi and the others were to draw lessons about that defeat and engage in special discussions on how to improve underground work. They were to plan on developing long-term assets that could be activated when the time was right.[24]

But this brief lull ended in February 1941 when the Shaanxi and Guanzhong leaderships concluded that the enemy was planning to destroy the Communist hold on Guanzhong once and for all.[25] On April 11, Xi and other Guanzhong leaders sent a panicked telegram that began with the words "Extreme urgency!" Organization in Guanzhong was still so poor, they claimed, that it was deeply necessary to centralize control over the Communist forces to manage the deteriorating war situation.[26] As a result, the Guanzhong Subregion Party Committee was transferred from the Shaan-Gan-Ning Border Region to the Shaanxi Party Committee, centralizing leadership and providing the leaders of Shaanxi Province with a border region that could be used as a base of operations for underground work in the Nationalist areas. Xi joined the Shaanxi Party Committee as a standing committee member, although he continued as leader of Guanzhong as well.[27]

In a speech at the first session of the new Shaanxi Party Committee in May, Zhang Desheng, who the next month would officially become Shaanxi party secretary, emphasized Guanzhong's "major significance" given the possibility of a Japanese attack on Yan'an. Defending Guanzhong was the same as "defending the front door of the Shaan-Gan-Ning Border Region." Yet Zhang had critical remarks about Xi's area. He stated that many ordinary people and even cadres were "pessimistic" about future Nationalist attacks, and, therefore, they lacked initiative. Leaders in Guanzhong held too many meetings but failed to carry out serious investigations, Zhang warned. As for United Front work, Zhang praised Xi, but he criticized past policies. Guanzhong was supposed to be a "resist Japan model democratic region," and it had already established legislative assemblies and granted "all kinds of democratic freedoms." However, there were "still many undemocratic elements." Zhang mentioned that the assemblies had no power and the government's work environment lacked "a democratic style." Zhang suggested it was necessary to "improve elections and improve government bodies at every level."[28]

These organizational improvements did not immediately help the situation. Xi continued to struggle with intelligence and the United Front. In August 1941, Yan'an sent a special group to Guanzhong to improve intelligence work there. They discovered that the Shaanxi Party Committee had overestimated Chiang Kai-shek's operational capabilities. The cadres from Yan'an told the Shaanxi leadership that not every single Nationalist party and government organization was actually a spy organization.[29] Xi was impressed by Bu Lu, the man who led the delegation and was once described by Mao as "the Red Sherlock Holmes." Bu helped Xi with an intransigent local Nationalist military commander. Killing the man would be too escalatory, but United Front policies were not winning him over either, so Bu openly treated the Nationalist to expensive meals on several occasions. They never talked about politics, but the commander's superiors lost faith in him and gave him a transfer. Xi was delighted. "You won without firing a shot!" he said to Bu.[30]

Xi's ability to at least hold the situation together in a place like Guanzhong was generally considered impressive among his colleagues. In a January 1937 report, Li Weihan, a key figure who managed the party's United Front work policies, praised the region, writing that Guanzhong was "one of the best soviets" he had visited. "The Guanzhong party is a Bolshevik party forged in struggle," Li wrote. "It has many leaders who are truly beloved by the masses," Li noted, specifically mentioning Xi.[31] In May 1941, Shaanxi party secretary Ouyang Qin applauded Xi in strong terms:

> Although work in the Guanzhong subregion still has many unsatisfactory elements and deficiencies, from a historical point of view, when looking at it practically from many perspectives, [the Guanzhong leaders] basically completed the mission given by the party center, and they indeed achieved successes. That is because during the era of Nationalist rule, Guanzhong was politically and culturally backward, and bandits were brazen. After it became part of the border region, to reach its current situation, despite the countless sieges by the Nationalists and to still be able to stand proudly up-

right was, of course, the result of hard struggle. Now, compared to other border regions, it is not backward, and it is even relatively stronger—its military forces are numerous and strong, the conditions of the masses are good, and all these naturally count as victories.[32]

Xi was noticed by the Nationalists as well. The military intelligence file on Xi in Taiwan expresses grudging praise. "This bandit is clever and has many stratagems," it notes.[33]

The Nationalists were not the only problem about which Xi had to worry, however. Feuding within the party continued as well. Shortly after he joined the leadership of the Shaanxi party, it began feuding with Gao Gang, who, in May, had become head of the new Northwest Bureau. Gao told a member of the Shaanxi party leadership that he did not want to lead them because he thought its underground work was a "horrible mess." In response, on June 13, the Shaanxi Party Committee, including Xi, wrote a telegram requesting that they remain directly under the Central Committee, arguing that Gao did not have experience with undercover work. But the Shaanxi party was still given to the Northwest Bureau, thus infuriating Gao.[34]

PARTY RECTIFICATION AND THE RESCUE CAMPAIGN

With Xi on the frontlines trying to stabilize Communist positions, Mao, back in Yan'an, slowly moved to transform the very nature of the party. In spring 1942, he launched a rectification campaign against "dogmatism," the impractical application of foreign ideas, and "bourgeois individualism," the putting one's own feelings and desires ahead of those of the party. The campaign was not only about achieving ideological cohesion. By demonstrating the right to tell party members how they should think about the world, Mao was turning the party into an institution in which his authority was paramount.[35]

This drive to achieve transformation through education began with a focus on the study of a set of documents approved by Mao.[36] On April 6, Xi and the Guanzhong party leaders ordered cadres to spend two hours every day participating in this campaign. They were instructed to record in their personal notebooks their reactions to the classes, reports, discussions, and readings. Despite the continuing challenges for the party in the region, these regulations strictly prohibited "regular" work from interfering.[37]

The campaign's strong anti-intellectual elements had special meaning for Xi, who, in July 1942, moved from Guanzhong to Yan'an to become dean of the Northwest Bureau Party School. With "bookish" knowledge without practical application a special target of rectification, the Northwest Bureau Party School under Xi's tenure instead focused on something else entirely: the forging of teachers and students at the school into a completely new kind of human being. Concerned about private conversations that criticized the leadership, the party explicitly attacked "sentimental relationships and friendships" that separated the people from the organization. Throughout Yan'an, party members wrote in their journals introspective self-criticisms, and they shared them not only with colleagues but also with the study committees, which then "helped" party members to confess their crimes publicly at meetings. Participants in these activities often felt extreme levels of guilt and shame about their previous behavior and thoughts. Cadres "even embellish[ed] their personal secrets in a masochistic fashion," according to the late Chinese historian Gao Hua.[38]

In June, on the eve of Xi's arrival at the Northwest Bureau Party School, the school's leading party committee had launched an investigation into the progress of the campaign among its teachers and discovered that it was reaching a crescendo. The teachers, afraid of falling behind, competed with one another, some continuing to write in their notebooks late into the night and even refusing to admit when they were sick so they could continue to participate in discussion meetings. In August, with Xi now officially the dean, the school started to inspect whether the rectification had succeeded. Students were asked questions like what kind of deficiencies they had found at the school and in themselves and how they were overcome. Students were evaluated based on whether their self-reflections were sincere, honest, deep, and systematic.[39]

The campaign had both coercive and voluntary elements. At its heart, rectification was about solving a fundamental problem: how a group of young, individualistic, and self-important people motivated by romantic and heroic dreams to save the nation could be transformed into a force so disciplined that it could solve the problems that motivated them in the first place. As Chinese scholar Huang Daoxuan argues, the answer was a total attack on every party member's sense of self, and it was a goal understood by the targets themselves. He writes, "Pressure from without is indispensable for inducing an individual's awakening. But more crucial in rectification was self-transformation. External pressure had to be internalized as self-aware voluntarism." When the transformation was achieved, Huang writes, "it often brought about feelings of complete rebirth" and joy. One young woman described how, on "sleepless nights," she would remember that "I myself have become a useful screw (even if only a very, very small one), a genuine smile, so rare in the daytime, dawns on my face."[40]

Rectification would soon evolve into something even more intense—a spy hunt—and Xi had to run the campaign in a particularly troubled area. In February 1943, Xi became top party leader in the Suide subregion, with a population of 544,000. Located on the northeast border of the Shaan-Gan-Ning Border Region, Suide was the commercial center of Northern Shaanxi, connecting this border region with the Jin-Sui base camp.[41] American military officers and journalists were struck by the apparently symbiotic relationship between the party and the local powerbrokers in Suide. In the border region, Suide was "known as the home of big landlords and wealthy gentry," according to journalist Harrison Forman. In Suide's Mizhi County, Forman witnessed a cooperative relationship between the government and the local business owners. He wrote in his notebook, "The whole experience left me with the thought that this was not Communism; that a man could start and own his own business, which could be developed into a profitable venture—as in any other capitalistic state. This, then, was capitalism, not communism in the Soviet sense."[42] Israel Epstein, another American journalist, described Suide in the *New York Times* as different from Yan'an "in every way as any two towns could be." While landlords in Yan'an had fled after land distribution, in Suide the "retired military and civil officials, scholars and gentry, who gave luster to the city's ancient reputation as the greatest cultural center of North Shensi [Shaanxi], are still here and still in power, though reduced, in the administration."[43]

Only two months after Xi arrived in Suide, the political atmosphere in this complicated and strategic region suddenly grew more tense. On April 5, the secretariat in Yan'an launched a confession movement to convince alleged spies to come clean—a program that eventually became known as the Rescue the Fallen Campaign.[44] On April 19, the Suide Subregion Party Committee held a study-mobilization rally, at which Xi announced that the campaign would be the top priority from April to October. Although Guanzhong cadres had been told to study two hours a day, Xi was now ordering a three-hour regimen.[45]

Just as Yan'an was launching the confession movement, anonymous letters complaining about party policy began to appear on a wall at Suide Normal College. While the letters were under investigation, several more suspicious notes were found in a class taught by Yang Dian, dean of Academic Affairs. Two or three weeks later, Yang was hurt with a rock, and martial law was declared at the school. Students who did not live on campus were forced to move there. They were forbidden from speaking with one another privately, and those students under investigation could not even go to the bathroom without someone accompanying them. Due to the pressure, a second-grade student admitted to trying to kill Yang, and he named other students who allegedly had helped him. It was not until the following year that an investigation determined that Yang had injured himself and had written the anonymous notes, as he apparently wanted either to direct the campaign away from himself or to win entrance into the party by appearing to be a victim of enemy actions.[46]

For months, the Rescue Campaign in Suide under Xi descended into a persecutorial mania that combined elements both farcical and terrifying. When one young student was pressured to confess, he "admitted" to eating black beans so he could disrupt class with flatulence—a ridiculous claim that, under that particular political atmosphere, was nevertheless believed.[47] When another student falsely confessed to hiding a gun at a rally, the audience, excited by the news, demanded that he show them where it was hidden. The student suddenly became nervous since he had made up the entire story. He led them to multiple locations where they dug holes but never found anything. Then the student claimed he had given the gun to someone else. When the two students then drew pictures of the made-up weapon, the sketches appeared to be very different, so suddenly it seemed as if there were multiple guns. Then the second student said he had given his gun to a third student. The process kept repeating itself until finally the first student was charged with leading a group of ten armed boys. Local military forces were mobilized. One day, all the students at the school were brought outside to be searched for weapons. "Turn around! Stand apart! No moving!" someone yelled. Soldiers with loaded weapons surrounded the terrified students. Teachers then frisked them, one by one.[48]

As the campaign heated up at Suide Normal, one fifteen-year-old student, Ma Fengchen, suddenly felt as if he were being followed. Soon thereafter, he was detained at the Suide party headquarters and subjected to repeated interrogations. He learned that another student whom he did not even know had claimed that he was a Nationalist agent. Qi Xin, who was Ma's classmate and was already involved in a budding romantic relationship with Xi, often visited Ma. She told him that no one under suspicion would be released until they "confessed." Ma felt that Qi was looking out for his best interests and had given him this information so he could avoid torture.[49]

Ma knew about at least two forms of physical punishment that were being used on fellow prisoners. One was "pressing the anvil": an anvil with four legs was placed on someone's posterior while the torturer sat on it, pressing the legs of the anvil into the flesh of the tortured person and almost immediately causing bleeding. Another method was "rolling dough": if anyone under interrogation bent their head and waist, then, as punishment, they would be pushed against a hard surface with their hands tied behind their back. The interrogator would then grind wooden sticks into the back of the prisoner's head and feet, just like rolling dough.[50]

For Ma, the fear was worse than the physical punishment. During an interrogation, as Xi himself watched, Ma finally admitted that he was a spy for the Nationalists. As he spoke, Ma saw a small grin appear on Xi's face. It seemed to Ma that Xi was skeptical. After the interrogator left, Ma immediately told Xi that his "confession" had been false. But Xi asked him, "Why did you confess then?" Ma responded, "If I did not confess, my health would simply not be able to withstand your torture." Xi dismissively gave Ma a faint smile and said nothing.[51] Tempers, including Xi's, ran high. On one occasion, Xi personally interviewed one young person suspected of being an agent. When the young man realized what was happening, he picked up a brick and threw it at Xi. "I'm a Guanzhong *lengwa*," he screamed, using a word in the local dialect that referred to people from Guanzhong. "Don't you know that?" Xi then picked up a chair to defend himself and shouted back, "You're a Guanzhong *lengwa*. Does that mean I'm not a Guanzhong *lengwa*?"[52]

The campaign soon spread from the school to the party and beyond. Suspects recited their histories in front of big groups, and the audiences would interrupt to raise a series of "issues," making the case that they were in fact secret agents.[53] Some of those under suspicion confessed on stage. "Admitting meant 'making progress,' so they could eat a bowl of noodles," one individual wrote later. "At the time, the living conditions in Northern Shaanxi were poor, so eating noodles was a form of special treatment. But when many people were eating noodles, they had a long face, and some of them even suddenly burst into tears."⁵⁴ At one rally, an old woman demanded she take the stage. The participants discouraged her, asking what she could possibly confess. But she kept saying, "It is good to confess; it is good to confess." One student who watched as the campaign started to touch the higher party ranks later wrote, "I understood a certain principle: all those who start a fire to burn others will ultimately be burned as well."⁵⁵

Even though famous authors, such as Yang Shu, were targeted. Like many others who had been at least briefly arrested by the Nationalists, Yang Shu quickly came under suspicion. "At the time," Yang's wife, Wei Junyi, later recalled, Xi "banged on the table every day and was extremely angry." Wei soon started spending her days holding her young child in her cave dwelling and weeping. Finally, she told Yang to submit. "The situation demands that you must confess, so go confess." Yang then broke down crying and made a false confession. The situation was farcical—Yang could not name a single crime. He simply claimed to have tried to somehow sabotage party policy.⁵⁶

Even though Yang had admitted to being an agent, he soon wrote a letter to Mao, stating, "Chairman Mao, Xi Zhongxun decided I was an agent. I am not an agent," whereupon Mao wrote a letter to Xi: "Comrade Zhongxun, it is necessary to be careful about this kind of person." But no one was sure how to interpret Mao's vague language. Finally, the group in charge of Yang's case reached out to Bo Gu, then head of the New China News Agency, who previously had been head of the Organization Department. Bo explained that the guards who had freed Yang were underground party members.⁵⁷ Yang was cleared, but not before Wei's health had collapsed under the stress and her young daughter had died, at least in part because of their difficult conditions. "Xi Zhongxun persecuted both my husband and me," Wei wrote in her memoirs.⁵⁸

The situation in Suide deteriorated so badly that Li Dingming, who was vice-chairman of the Shaan-Gan-Ning Border Region government but not a party member, complained to the central leadership. Xi had locked up one hundred people at the regional government headquarters, yet repeated interrogations had achieved nothing, so even Xi asked Yan'an for help. In response to these entreaties, Shi Zhe and Bu Lu, two security officials, arrived in Suide in late May, where the campaign had already "expanded to a point where it lost control." In Shi's words, in Suide, "the more lies someone made up, and the more ridiculous they were, the more that person would be appreciated and glorified." He later claimed that in the month after his arrival, the situation was basically resolved, including the case of one young man who said that Xi had locked him up merely for kissing a woman. Yet after Shi's arrival, the abuses not only persisted but even got worse. One of Xi's close associates later privately claimed that Shi was actually sent to Suide to be a "hatchet man."[59]

In July, Kang Sheng, the man in charge of the Rescue the Fallen Campaign and who was also in charge of the Social Department, the party's security and intelligence agency, gave a long speech about the threat of spies. He used the opportunity to invite a female student from Suide to describe how she had been persuaded to "confess" to her (fabricated) crimes, which included the seduction of local party cadres.[60] That same month, Yuan Renyuan, the man in charge of the party's governing apparatus in Suide, visited Yan'an, where he met with Mao. According to Yuan, Mao said he had heard that many "evil people" had been found at Suide Normal College, but he was unfamiliar with the details. The chairman then warned that previous purges had demonstrated that forced confessions should not be used as people would lie under pressure. However, Yuan later claimed, "We did not sufficiently understand the spirit of Chairman Mao's order," and, when Yuan conveyed Mao's message to Xi, "The regional party leaders did not end the campaign. They continued to engage in 'Rescue the Fallen,' but their methods were somewhat milder."[61]

In fact, the situation in Suide continued to deteriorate. At a mass rally on July 19, Xi warned that "anti-Communist elements are conducting sabotage throughout the border region. Everyone must heighten their vigilance."[62] On August 15, Kang Sheng reported to Mao in positive terms on Xi's use of mass rallies to expose spies.[63] At the end of the month, Gao Gang, head of the Northwest Bureau, wrote to Xi, saying, "Your method in Suide of inviting the family members of students to participate in the big confession meetings is very good."[64]

By mid-September, the spy hunt in Suide reached a climax. *Liberation Daily* published a lengthy article delineating, in lurid detail, the alleged behavior of a secret Nationalist spy group known as the Renaissance Society. These agents, the article claimed, wanted to wreak havoc in preparation for a Nationalist invasion. The most explosive claim was about Xi. The plotters, worried about his success, felt a need to murder him. They allegedly said that Xi "arrived less than two months ago. . . . Local gentry and regular people, as well as his cadres, all feel very positive about him. Obviously, he is a big cadre with great talent. At the same time, he is a great enemy hindering our work." Therefore, they concluded, Xi had to die. They considered ambushing him at night with a stone, stick, or axe.[65]

The most dramatic moment of the campaign was an extraordinary "Mass Rally of All Types of People Denouncing the Nationalist Spies." At 8:00 a.m. on September 13, the rally began with 2,500 participants facing Xi on a dais. On the left side, there was a picture of a group of people in a morass who had dropped their knives so that the party members could grab them. On the right side, another picture displayed Nationalist agents throwing young people into an abyss. Xi castigated the so-called agents who, in order to achieve their goal of sabotage, had "colluded with enemy traitors." "We are now extending both of our hands," Xi said. "We hope that the young people who have fallen, all traitors and agents, quickly crawl out of the pit to become good sons and daughters of the Chinese people." When Xi finished, the crowd yelled, "The Communist Party is our mother! Let us extend our hands and correct our ways to make a fresh start!"[66]

During the following ten days, about 190 supposed agents were exposed. The focus of the rally was Suide Normal College—particularly the young women, even the girls, at the school. At the rally, one supposed agent claimed that Nationalist spymasters had commanded him to "libel" female students by claiming that they charged different rates for sex based on their looks and that these women were then used to seduce people. One female student "admitted" to seducing a math teacher to steal Communist secrets, and another claimed her Nationalist handler had told her, "The frontline for you female spies is the bed." One girl, only fourteen years old and only slightly taller than the table on the dais, admitted to such "crimes." On September 22, the last day of the rally, *Liberation Daily* depicted the college as a model in the struggle against spies and quoted one parent who credited Xi for "saving" the children.[67]

Kang Sheng was impressed again. On October 8, he personally approved of Xi's methods and recommended that Suide's use of mass rallies to expose spies be adopted as a model more broadly. Two days later, writing this time in the name of the Social Department, Kang again praised the Suide mass-rally approach, stating not only that Xi's actions were completely correct but also that they should be adopted by the entire party.[68]

At the end of the year, Suide sent the Advanced Model Cadre Campaign Reporting Group of students and teachers to a Yan'an rally. Ma Hongchen, the same young student whom Qi Xin had urged to confess, brought a giant rock to the rally, claiming (falsely) that he planned to kill Xi with it. Liu Shaoqi, who had previously been convinced that the spy threat was real, saw the group and found the claims unbelievable, leading him to doubt the entire campaign. Mao, under pressure from the Soviet Union, also agreed that it was time to bring the campaign to an end. On December 22, the secretariat finally decided to begin the process of reviewing potential wrongful verdicts.[69]

Although the campaign was never declared to have been a complete mistake, the party did begin to look at what went wrong. In February 1944, Mao and Kang issued a joint directive that acknowledged that the Renaissance Society in Suide, which had allegedly plotted to kill Xi because he was a threat to its plans, did not actually exist.[70] In March, Kang recognized the campaign's mistakes in a key speech to the Northwest Bureau. "In some places," Kang said, "because there was not enough experience, they did not pay attention to the guideline of not arresting big numbers of people."[71] The Northwest Bureau cadres determined that although the campaign had achieved "major accomplishments," there were also serious mistakes, like hounding people to death and false verdicts. Although not named directly, Xi's methods were criticized: "At some schools, entire classes, even twelve- or thirteen-year-old middle school students, were labeled agents." Two months later, the secretariat accepted that including the "masses" in the hunt for spies, a technique Xi had widely used, inevitably had led to the "disease" of "leftism." "Mass-confession rallies must be used carefully," the secretariat warned.[72] By May or June of 1944, all the verdicts against students in Suide had been reversed.[73]

In many ways, the Rescue Campaign was a disaster, and Mao expressed regret on several occasions.[74] Tragedy also extended to Xi's own family. When Xi Yongsheng, Zhongxun's grandfather, had left Henan many decades earlier, his oldest daughter remained at home, later giving birth to a boy named Zhao Tianxian. In the early 1940s, Zhao's middle school was forced to close because of Japanese military operations in Henan, so he fled to Yan'an, in large part because his cousin Xi Zhongxun was there. Zhao, who arrived in the midst of the Rescue Campaign, was arrested and died in jail. Decades later, Zhongxun would still sob when speaking about this incident.[75]

Although Xi did not know it at the time, he too was under investigation. His history made him vulnerable. Many figures from the Shaanxi party who, like him, had led underground work were suspected of working for the Nationalists. As Xi noted in the forward to a book on such work in Shaanxi during this period, "Many were treated unfairly, they were investigated as 'agents,' and many were forced to make false confessions."[76] In November 1943, Shi Zhe was summoned to meet with Ren Bishi, a member of the secretariat, as well as with Gao Gang and Kang Sheng. Ren revealed to Shi that the reason for Xi's transfer away from Guanzhong the previous year was that the party had intercepted multiple Nationalist intelligence documents that included Xi's name on them. Ren told Shi that technically Xi was not under suspicion, but it was necessary to understand why his name appeared so frequently on these materials. Shi went to Guanzhong to investigate. Shi finally determined that because Nationalist intelligence agencies paid for information based on the rank of the original source, a double agent working for the party had tried to make extra money by claiming the false information had come from Xi himself.[77]

The campaign also provided a lesson on the negative effects of radicalism within the party on its broader strategic goals, such as the United Front. Since such work, by its nature, necessitated contacts with nonparty individuals, every single Suide cadre involved in the United Front was brutally persecuted as an "agent" or "traitor."[78] Rebuilding the United Front proved difficult. One Northwest Bureau report disseminated in September 1944 noted that since the start of the antispy campaigns the previous year, many party cadres were displaying wrongful thinking about United Front policies. In Xi's own Suide, the United Front Work Department was referred to as the "ignored department" because cadres believed it was unimportant and irrelevant. Even people who led United Front work refused to interact with anyone who was not a party member because of fear that they themselves might come under suspicion again. When the cadre in charge of United Front work in Suide's Mizhi County acted too cautiously, Xi confronted his subordinate. "I have many contacts, but I simply do not dare approach them," the man told Xi.[79] The purge also affected military readiness. Xi was commissar of the Suide Garrison, where 425 individuals came under suspicion in August and September. Five of them were tortured by the Suide authorities.[80]

Some evidence suggests that Xi, at least occasionally, tried to rein in the abuses. Two former colleagues, for example, wrote that Xi saved the lives of people whom Gao Gang had sought to execute, including former Shaanxi stalwarts, like Huang Ziwen.[81] Xi himself later wrote that Gao Gang wanted to kill Huang "on multiple occasions" because Huang had exposed a sexual assault by Gao Gang when the two had worked together. "But I saved him each time," Xi claimed. Decades later, in a private conversation, Xi told an associate that during the Yan'an era, relations with Gao Gang had "been strained for a time" because of his support for Huang.[82] One subordinate later wrote that during a morning walk after the campaign was over, Xi meaningfully raised the earlier purge, in which he himself had suffered. "We absolutely must be careful," Xi told him. "Regardless of who, if there was a mistake, they should be rehabilitated and given a position."[83] As leader of a Suide Subregion High-Ranking Cadre Study Group created in July 1944 to review the mistakes of the Rescue the Fallen Campaign, Xi again discussed the painful story of his own persecution.[84]

Yet it is precisely that history that raises a difficult question: How could someone who had suffered from the torment of a purge just eight years earlier allow his own region to see such high levels of persecution? In 1935, Zhang Xiushan had "confessed" when he was strung up for torture, and the information he provided was used to arrest Xi and the others. Zhang would retract what he had said as soon as the punishment ended. Xi, knowing about Zhang's role, should have understood that confessions under duress were not credible testimony.[85] In fact, the slaughter and persecution that had raged in base areas throughout the country before 1936 were clearly on the minds of the party leadership, and at first, they thought the Rescue Campaign could be structured to avoid repeating the same abuses. The mass deaths marked by previous campaigns were absent, and the security services played a much less prominent role. This time, rectification was intended to transform people, not destroy them, and the masses were included.[86] Yet the party had still not figured out a way to cleanse its own ranks without hurting innocent people and causing extraordinary emotional suffering.

While impossible to definitively account for Xi's actions, one possible answer, perhaps the most obvious one, is that Xi was a party member, so when he was told to find spies, he did. The charged environment was not conducive to expressing any doubts. Ambitious party members would have also understood that catching many "spies" might help their careers. Furthermore, cadres, such as Xi, could have genuinely believed that spies were a real threat. In Guanzhong, such agents had been a challenge for him. The Nationalists had been able to recruit some students to work in the base areas, although they were all discovered by May 1942, and Nationalist records reveal that in August of that year, they had no agents working for them in Communist-controlled areas.[87] The Communists were themselves conducting espionage against the Nationalists, so it was no great leap to think that Nationalist agents were infiltrating their ranks as well. There were also fears of an imminent Nationalist invasion. In the summer of 1943, after Joseph Stalin dissolved the Comintern, Chiang Kai-shek seriously considered a major assault on the base areas in Shaanxi, a plot later dropped in part because the Communist spies had gotten wind of the war preparations (although by August 2, the party leadership knew that the threat was over).[88]

Xi's aggressive hunt for spies did not make him unique. Although Kang Sheng is usually described as the villain in the story, even Kang does not stand out for his radicalism. Liu Shaoqi, Peng Zhen, and Gao Gang all aggressively supported the campaign because that was what Mao wanted.[89] And when Mao wanted the campaign to end, none of them resisted. It was Kang who gave the report at the December 22 secretariat meeting that signified an end to the campaign, and in March 1944, at the meeting of Northwest Bureau cadres, Kang blamed "extremely serious problems," such as forced confessions and overly high estimates of the number of spies, on some regions that failed to understand central directives correctly.[90] Figures such as Hu Yaobang, who unlike Kang still enjoys a sterling reputation, actively persecuted members of their own party during this era.[91]

Yet cadres like Xi did have some leeway to interpret the directives from Yan'an. According to the "leading-cadre-responsibility" guideline for the campaign, Xi was fully in charge and had room for creativity. Giving regional leaders like him more power had in fact been one of the steps the party took in an attempt to avoid abuses that had marked previous campaigns.[92] Xi used that space to impress Kang Sheng with a zealous approach that stood out for its effective inclusion of the "masses" and the targeting of young women at a school—a school, moreover, where Xi's future bride was a student leader.[93] As late as April 1944, when the leadership was already reigning in the abuses, Xi still said that in his region "the schools are primarily what the enemy agents use as a foothold to screw us."[94]

MAO AND THE NORTHWESTERNERS

Xi had one other plausible reason to do everything possible to demonstrate his loyalty to Mao—gratitude. The rectification campaign was intended to unify everyone around one way of thinking, and that included a single version of the past. Cadres were taught that the history of the party was one of constant battle between dogmatic leftists trained in Moscow (Mao's opponents) and pragmatists (Mao) who effectively combined theory and the real world. This careful cultivation of history was Mao's way of establishing a powerful legitimation narrative for himself.[95] It fatefully tied Mao to Xi and some of the other northwesterners.

For Mao, Liu Zhidan's experiences in 1935 resembled what had happened in the Jiangxi Soviet, where Mao was stripped of authority by cadres sent from Moscow and whose overly aggressive policies had contributed to the Communist failures in the region. Mao made this comparison explicit during the eighty-eight-day Northwest Bureau High-Ranking Cadres meeting in 1942–1943.[96] Over the previous years, Mao had gradually developed his own views of party history, but it was during these sessions that he used what had happened in the Northwest to affirm more broadly the legitimacy of his views.[97] For the first time, party history was officially understood as a contest between a correct and an incorrect "line," and Mao and Xi were on the right side.[98] The northwesterners, who felt ignored and disrespected by the Communists who had come to Shaanxi from other regions, must have felt thrilled to earn Mao's respect. Yang Shangkun had joked with Xi Zhongxun about local flyers calling Wayaobu a "central city." "What kind of central city can Wayaobu be considered!" Yang asked.[99] But now Mao was mocking cadres who had come with him for thinking they were better simply because they had walked more kilometers.[100]

Xi's own speech at the Northwest Bureau High-Ranking Cadres meeting was fiery. He accused his nemeses of making dishonest speeches: "Comrade Guo Hongtao's incorrect individualist thinking made up the bulk of his entire history, but he did not do a good job deeply reflecting." Xi mocked the self-criticisms of his enemies, joking that they "all said they wanted people to help them take off their trousers, to make the matter clear. When you take off your trousers, it is necessary to show a naked leg, but for them, taking off trousers meant taking off a hat [a political accusation]. They showed a naked head instead!" The audience laughed. "They vaguely acknowledged a mistake, but concrete content and concrete facts were lightly passed by.... You are like crazy people fighting, you can't find a reason for what you did. Why is that?" Again the crowd laughed. "They said they want to take off their trousers, but in reality, they were taking off the belts of other people!" Xi concluded by warning that "if past history is not clarified, it means that in the future, the party in the border region will suffer a major failure!"[101]

During the meeting, the party completed a new set of judgments for Xi's official organizational evaluation. This assessment stressed Xi's ability to get along with regular people. "All of the people in Guanzhong, no matter whether they are adults or children, know him and like him," the document concluded. He was someone who "never put on airs" and understood the "moods, habits, and needs" of the "masses." The writers of the appraisal also noted Xi's near-miraculous ability to escape close brushes with death: "In the past, when he led the masses in struggle, he often faced extraordinary dangers, but each time, he survived. That was because the masses protected him, stood guard over him, and hid him. People from dozens of kilometers away even took special trips to express their regard."[102]

Mao was struck by Xi's organizational discipline. He was impressed by Xi's relatively more measured style at the Northwest Bureau High-Ranking Cadres meeting compared to that of Gao Gang, who had tried to assault Guo Hongtao at one point. "Xi Zhongxun was a good model at this meeting," Mao said. "His words and behavior in every way demonstrate that he thinks about the party's interests. He always puts the party's interests first." Mao then wrote the formulation "The party's interests come first" on a white cloth and gave it to Xi. Qi Xin later said Mao chose those words because of the impression that Xi, despite his own sufferings, worked hard to carry out Liu Zhidan's request shortly before his death to convince those who suffered in the 1935 purge to put the nation first and not to hold grudges.[103]

To consolidate his alliance with the northwesterners, Mao had to select someone to represent them and to demonstrate unity between the local cadres and the central Red Army. Yet Mao lacked a clear candidate. Both Liu Zhidan and Xie Zichang, even though they sometimes had a difficult relationship, had claim to the loyalty of the group of northwesterners as a whole. Their deaths, to a significant extent, orphaned the Northwest cadres.[104] After investigation, Mao determined that among those who were left, Gao Gang's historical legacy was the most impressive.[105] In February 1942, Mao even stated, "I have been in Shaan-bei for five or six years, but in terms of understanding Shaan-bei and relations with the people of Shaan-bei, I am nowhere near as good as Comrade Gao Gang and those people."[106]

Mao's version of party history and his selection of Gao was not accepted by all the Northwest cadres. By 1945, these tensions over history came to a head. In the lead-up to the Seventh Party Congress that year, Yan Hongyan,

Guo Hongtao, and Zhu Lizhi forged a new alliance to oppose Gao's ascension. Another "Northwest history discussion meeting" was held to address the complaints. But it did not go in the direction that the dissenters had hoped. Yan Hongyan's historical contributions were mocked.[107] Gao's own speech reveals that some in the party were unhappy about Xi's rise too. Gao claimed that some people had said, "Promoting Zhang Xiushan, Wang Shitai, and Xi Zhongxun but not promoting Yan Hongyan is unfair; it is factionalism." According to Gao, Xi's opponents denigrated him. They said Xi was a baby, that he was stupid and confused, and even that he smoked opium.[108]

In a remarkably prescient speech at the meeting, He Jinnian, a close Xie Zichang associate, warned his fellow northwesterners that not solving their squabbles about historical legacies was extremely dangerous: "I once said to Zhang Bangying [who was close to Liu Zhidan] that because there are some careerist comrades in the party, there are some misunderstandings and opinions that they want to use to create convenient conditions for their black market activities, often because of our regional relations." He Jinnian hoped that Gao Gang would give people such as Xie Zichang and Yan Hongyan more credit and that the northwesterners could achieve unity. But Gao chose not to walk that path.[109]

In Xi's speech at the meeting, he emphasized that while it was "no big deal" if people did not know history, "the most damaging is the distortion and falsification of history." He criticized those who opposed the "correct line" represented by Liu Zhidan, Xie Zichang, and Gao Gang: "Those who sit in Western-style buildings can only order students to struggle and to shout slogans, and they achieve nothing—all they get from their struggles is a prison sentence. They isolate themselves, and they damage the influence and power of the party among the masses." Confident in his own contributions, Xi made a statement that can be interpreted as a sort of comparison between Mao and Liu Zhidan: "In the south, there was Ruijin, and in the north, there was Zhaojin."[110]

At the subsequent Seventh Party Congress, Xi was promoted to the highly coveted position of candidate member of the Central Committee—its youngest member and the only leader of a subregion. Also in that year, Xi replaced Gao as head of the Northwest Bureau. These were stunning promotions for a person only thirty-two years old. One cadre who lived in Yan'an during this period and who later became one of its best historians concludes that Xi's dramatic promotion was a reward for demonstrating so much zeal during the Rescue the Fallen Campaign.[111] A former journalist for *Liberation Daily*, however, wrote that Xi won the position because of his especially strong performance correcting the wrongful verdicts during the subsequent review stage.[112] Whatever the reason for his promotion, Nationalist military intelligence believed that Xi's entrance to that weighty body was controversial. Described as Mao's "faithful henchman," Xi allegedly encountered "much envy and dissatisfaction" from among the local Shaanxi cadres.[113]

Unhappiness about the rapid rise of Gao Gang, and of Xi as well, did not only exist among party members in the Northwest. Two of Mao's comrades from Jiangxi were removed from the potential list of members and candidate members to the Central Committee, and one of those spots went to Xi. One of the men who lost his spot complained, "Chairman Mao, have we somehow wronged you?"[114] Another old comrade from the Jiangxi base area said that they felt like "old rain" passed over by "the new favorites." Mao's trusted secretary Hu Qiaomu thought that Mao treated them like "his own children." "He really loved and protected them."[115]

5
LOVE AND REVOLUTION

In June 1916, Hao Mingzhu, Xi Zhongxun's first wife, was born into a poor family in Anding County (now Zichang County) of Shaanxi Province. When her father told her that the family could not afford for her to go to school, she stopped doing household chores and began a hunger strike. Her father, worried that she might commit suicide, finally relented. At school, many of Hao Mingzhu's classmates were underground party members, including one young woman named Ren Zhizhen, who would sometimes dress like a man to do propaganda work among peasants. Ren and Hao became close, but Ren was soon arrested after someone betrayed her. Hao went to visit her friend, who was held in manacles. "It looks like I will not be able to leave here alive," Ren told her. "I hope you can continue the revolution. Do not be scared away by the reactionaries' temporary arrogance; they will ultimately be annihilated." Soon thereafter, Ren was executed at the age of seventeen or eighteen. Hao's first husband also died a young death. When Hao was seventeen years old, she married a Communist named Yan Zhongling. After their marriage, she spent little time with him, who was off fighting guerrilla battles. Soon Yan, too, was betrayed to the Nationalists, who tortured and executed him—at the age of eighteen. With the help of friends, Hao found her dead husband's body and decapitated head, which she buried.[1]

In 1935, Guo Liben, a Communist official, told Hao that he had someone in mind for her as a new husband. That same day, Hao's mother, who had dreamed the night before of a bright moon coming to shine over her cave, hosted Guo and a group of men that included Xi Zhongxun. Hao was struck by Xi's poor clothing. She learned later that it was the result of his just recently having been released from incarceration. The next morning, the wife of a local cadre asked Hao to cut her hair. As soon as Hao arrived at the cadre's home, Guo and the group of men from the previous day suddenly appeared, pointed at Xi, and yelled, "This is the one, do you like him or not?" Hao ran to hide. The group of men chased her as they continued to shout, "Are you willing or not?" Hao said nothing, but she did get a quick peek at Xi, whom she thought was the most handsome of the lot. That night, when she returned home, Hao's mother suggested that she marry him. Hao said she could not understand Xi's dialect, but her mother argued that she would get used to it after they lived together. Hao never explicitly expressed an opinion, but her lack of opposition was taken to mean she accepted the proposal.[2]

That version rings true based on common practice at the time, and Xi himself acted as a matchmaker for others in similar ways on several occasions. When Li Liqun, a young woman from southern Jiangsu, graduated from the party school in Yan'an, Chen Yun, as leader of the Organization Department, introduced her to Gao Gang as an appropriate match. Li was not interested, as Gao was fifteen years older than she and she wanted to focus on party work. But one day, Gao brought her to meet Mao, and Mao told Li that Gao was a great revolutionary who was widely revered in the Northwest. Li returned home distressed. Then, one night several days later, Xi showed up with several other leading figures and tried to bring her to a party. She refused. Xi said to her, "You, little girl, you're so feudal." Finally, she gave in to their pressure and went to the party, where she was suddenly forced to marry Gao.[3]

In Guanzhong, Xi asked a colleague named Liu Maogong what he thought of two young women whom they had just passed on the street. Liu said that he had not noticed them. Xi informed Liu that the two women were single and had just graduated from Yan'an Women's College. One of them, Yu Qun, worked for Hao Mingzhu. Xi and Hao formally introduced Yu to Liu, and the two of them met repeatedly at Xi's home. One night, Liu and Yu stayed up late chatting at another friend's home, when they suddenly found themselves locked inside. Liu later recalled, "We knew we were tricked, so I could only say to Comrade Yu Qun, 'How about getting married!' She had no choice; she could only agree. Our 'event of lifelong significance' was settled in that way. Some comrades had a negative opinion of such a simple method, but

Comrade Xi Zhongxun took the initiative to come out and explain that he approved of it."[4]

Xi kept up his habit of matchmaking. Around 1947, he summoned a twenty-year-old woman to his office and told her he had a match in mind—a man she did not know and who was almost twenty years older than her. Since Xi's position was so weighty, she was terrified. Yet, in a quiet voice, she said, "No!" Xi grinned, but he continued to press her. Softly, she refused again. He lost his patience. "If you don't agree, I won't let you go home!" Pretending to accede so she could leave and hide, she just said, "Mmm." Xi laughed and said, "Good! Good! Good! That's right! 'Mmm' means yes!" She jogged home and told her grandmother what happened. But before she could conceal herself, Xi and other officials arrived at her home banging on drums. It was a wedding party. Neighbors started shouting along with the commotion. She was married by the end of the day.[5]

After Xi and Hao's own wedding, Hao started washing clothes and killing lice for Xi's colleagues.[6] As the only woman on Xi's early travels, she faced intense personal difficulties: on her first trip, her feet swelled up so much she had trouble walking, and she was too embarrassed to say when she was menstruating.[7] In September 1936, when Xi moved again, Hao carried her infant on her back in a basket.[8] Despite the challenges of motherhood in the base areas, she held significant positions in the party. When Xi was in Guanzhong, she was a fellow member of the party committee, and she also served as both vice-head and later full head of the Women's Affairs Department.[9]

The work was not easy. In areas that often moved between Nationalist and Communist control, many local women did not want to become involved in politics. Frightened by Hao's short hair and military uniform, they kept their doors closed and sometimes even sent their dogs to chase her away. She often cried in frustration. But she eventually won over the peasants—in one case, saving a woman's life by bringing her to see a doctor and, after moving to another location, again winning a woman's trust by saving her child who had fallen into a well.[10]

Sometimes the goal of empowering women conflicted with the party's competition with the Nationalists. A local woman named Zhang Fengying refused to participate in an arranged marriage. Zhang had been influenced by Hao, who often talked about a woman's right to choose her own husband. On the day of her wedding, Zhang hid among firewood to escape the marriage. Xi and Hao regarded her as a model progressive youth and supported her education. However, one day, Yao Chungui, the nearby Nationalist militia commander who was the target of United Front work and a friend of Xi, came to visit the Xi home and happened to meet Zhang. Xi pressured her to marry him to strengthen Yao's positive attitude toward the Communists, but Yao was ten years older than Zhang, and at first, she was reticent. After she finally agreed, the marriage became one of the reasons that Yao would later engage in secret underground work for the party.[11]

Like many other young women in the party during this time, Hao faced a contradiction between the demands of married life and the desire to devote her life to the revolution.[12] Going through five pregnancies and having to give up three children to foster families were emotionally difficult. Giving birth in the countryside came with serious challenges—on one occasion, a peasant midwife pulled on a baby coming out feet first, killing the child and nearly Hao as well. Another child died a few days after birth. According to Hao's daughter, Xi Qianping, these experiences devastated her mother emotionally, but Xi Zhongxun was never present for any of them. When Xi did visit her, he often came with a group, and Hao, weak from childbirth, still had to cook for them. Xi and his friends would play with the new child briefly and then quickly depart, leaving Hao feeling desperately lonely.[13] Meanwhile, Xi was receiving a lot of attention from other women. On one occasion, after Xi addressed a group of students at a rally, so many of the women asked to have their picture taken with him that Li Weihan, who was leading the rally, said, "Will the students please listen to the lecture; Secretary Xi is already married."[14]

Hao decided that the only way to protect herself from another pregnancy was to stop having sex. As a result, she refused to travel with Xi, and when they were together, she avoided him. At the same time, she did not tell him the real reason for her behavior. Xi was confused by her actions, and he began to think that she disliked him or that she loved someone else. So he started to distance himself or to deliberately upset her, thinking that such behavior could get her to pay more attention to him. Hao, who still cared for Xi, did not consider the possibility that he would lose his feelings for her. When Xi was in Suide, Hao stayed in Yan'an.[15] He did not seem to understand that Hao did not want to make children; she wanted to make revolution. And she was not the only one. As one male intellectual wrote in his diaries about the Yan'an era, "The women are always sick and tired of sex. Every Saturday, they do it perfunctorily out of obligation, but there are even fights, which leads to the men masturbating in front of the women."[16]

"A WHITE PIECE OF PAPER": QI XIN

The gap that emerged between Xi and Hao created room for someone else: Qi Xin. Qi Xin had a very different background from Hao. Her father, Qi Houzhi, had graduated from Peking University's Law Department. In 1926, he participated in the famous Northern Expedition, when Chiang Kai-shek marched north from Guangdong and seized control of much of China from the warlords. In 1929, he became head of a county and then, a year later, secretary of Zhili (later, renamed Hebei) Province. Qi Xin's mother, Deng Yaozhen, born in 1893 in Hebei's Gaoyang County, was the daughter of a Qing dynasty military official. The Deng family was a rich clan that included dozens of people living together in an enormous complex. The Dengs owned a pigment company, from which, over the years, Deng Yaozhen would draw funds to support her children's political activities.[17]

Qi Yun, Qi Xin's elder sister, was born in 1919, and Qi Xin was born in 1923. A younger brother, Bu, who later changed his name to Ruixin, was born in 1927. In 1931, Qi Houzhi went to work for the warlord Yan Xishan. Five years later, after he became the head of a county in Shanxi, he separated from Deng Yaozhen to marry an actress, ceasing to provide material support to his former wife and children. In 1937, Deng, Qi Xin, and Ruixin moved to Gaoyang County in Hebei, where they were supported financially by Qi Houzhi's brother and Deng's siblings.[18]

On July 7, 1937, just as Qi Xin was delighted to hear that the elite Beiping City First Women's Middle School had accepted her as a student, the Marco Polo Bridge Incident occurred, which signified the beginning of unrestricted warfare between Imperial Japan and China. Because she was already in the capital, Qi Xin could hear the fighting on the bridge, and she personally witnessed citizens preparing for urban warfare against the Japanese. As she watched the Japanese tanks enter the city on July 28, she promised to resist the invasion to the very end. She later told a friend, "I furiously gave those Japanese devils an angry look! Big sister Qi Yun praised me, but she was worried about me, and she said I was too brave!" When she and other students entering the Beiping Train Station had to pass through two rows of Japanese soldiers holding bayonets, the young Chinese started singing patriotic songs to rally their spirits. The two Qi sisters escaped by pretending to be the family members of a Tianjin businessperson; all the other students from their group were captured.[19]

The two sisters left Beiping for Taiyuan, the capital of Shanxi Province.

The sisters then met their father in the southeast Shanxi county of Changzhi, where he was then the county head. In an autobiography written in 1956, Qi Yun writes that she had fled to her father because she "did not have a clear understanding of how to carry out a revolution." In the fall, after losing his position as county head, Qi Houzhi brought his two daughters to Yangcheng to rest and to avoid the fighting. There, Qi Yun met local party's members and started working for them by the beginning of December. In her words, she had become ashamed of her father's pessimism in the face of the Japanese aggression, and this cowardly attitude was what convinced her to join the revolution: "I not only thought that fleeing to be with him had no future but also felt it was extremely disgraceful."[20]

While her sister Qi Yun participated in revolutionary activities, Qi Xin met with party cadres and read books about the Long March and Mao, including Edgar Snow's *Red Star Over China*. When she was trying to make up her mind about whether to do work with a children's corps or to join the Eighth Route Army, she became very ill with a fever and had trouble walking. Qi Yun arrived at the family home in a military uniform, saluted her father, and then said she was going to join a guerrilla unit. She told her sister Qi Xin that she was too sick to accompany her. Qi Xin later wrote, "As a result, I lost the opportunity to join the revolution in the spring of 1938." Qi Houzhi then brought Qi Xin to a small village, where she spent her time terribly missing her mother, brother, and sister. One day, when a messenger brought a letter from Qi Yun, Qi Xin tried to follow the man without telling her father, but her father chased her into the mountains and brought her back. After they moved to yet another village, Qi Yun hid some eggs and grain as she prepared to flee, but she was caught again. When Qi Houzhi took her to Xi'an, she became depressed. In early fall of 1938, she finally received permission from her father to go to Shanxi and join the revolution.[21]

After spending the Lunar New Year together in 1939, Qi Yun brought Qi Xin to a local satellite campus of a party school. Qi Yun told the people at the school that her sister was "a white piece of paper. She will be whatever color she is dyed." Qi Xin, then only fifteen years old, dates March 18 as the date she officially "stepped onto the revolutionary path," but she did not become a candidate for party membership until August. The commissar of the women's unit warned her, "Comrade Qi Xin's family background is relatively advantaged; after she enters the party, she should strengthen her ideological forging." The forging started quickly, as she was assigned to a "battlefield workgroup" during a Japanese offensive later that year. In the winter, she was nearly killed when enemy cavalry and artillery forces surrounded the local party county-level government leadership. Under a hail of gunfire, Qi Xin and others narrowly escaped.[22]

During the fighting, Qi Xin saw some homes had been covered with white paper, which meant that bodies of the murdered family members were still inside. On one occasion, she witnessed a group fleeing during a raid. The group included women carrying their children and the wounded who were crying out, "I want to die! I want to die!" Life was tough—Qi slept on a *kang* that was too hot to sleep on during the first half of the night and then too cold to sleep on during the second half, and she developed a long-term pain in her waist. Yet her performance was impressive enough for her to be granted official membership in the party in 1940—at the age of sixteen years old.[23] By then, the party was her primary family. That same year, a party cadre told her that her father's attitude toward the Communists was "relatively good," but Qi immediately said, "I have terminated any father-daughter relations with him."[24]

Between January 1941 and the summer of 1942, Qi was a student at the party school in Yan'an. That placed her at the very epicenter of the rectification campaign, as the party school was where Mao launched the campaign in February 1942 and honed its techniques. In the summer of 1942, she transferred to the middle school attached to Yan'an University, where she became class president.[25] Although her own family background was problematic, most of her classmates were the sons and daughters of Communist martyrs or high-ranking officials.[26] One classmate, Li Peng, the son of a man executed by the Nationalists in 1931, would later rise to the position of premier. Still, conditions were tough. Every year, they were given only one pair of shoes, which would wear out by summer, and they all had to participate in physical labor.[27]

The middle school students at Yan'an University, like Qi Xin, were too young to participate directly in the rectification campaign. They were certainly proximate to it, however. Their teachers disappeared every afternoon to join study sessions, so the students had to learn on their own during that time. Once a month, the vice-dean of the university reported to them on the campaign, and the middle schoolers went to some of the big rallies. Qi would have known that the head of middle school, Lin Disheng, suffered terribly, even though he had serious party bona fides. Years previously, he had been dean of a school in Guanzhong, where Xi had helped him when Lin had a falling out with the school's commissar. During rectification, Lin was persecuted for an entire year. Along with many others, he was detained in a ravine and forced to study and do physical labor while waiting for a verdict.[28]

COURTSHIP IN A CAMPAIGN

Every evening after dinner, Xi would stand outside the door of a journalist who lived in the Suide leadership compound. "Tian Fang, let's go play basketball at Suide Teachers' College!" he would yell. During their twenty-minute walk, Xi asked Tian many questions about the local situation. When they arrived at the basketball court, Xi took off his jacket, rolled up his sleeves, and started playing with the students. But Tian would soon notice that Xi had disappeared. At first, Tian figured that Xi had gone to speak with the university leadership. Later, Tian learned that Xi, the thirty-year-old party boss of the strategic Suide subregion, was courting the seventeen-year-old student Qi Xin.[29]

In the spring of 1943, the Northwest Bureau had sent a group of Yan'an University students, led by Qi, to Suide Teachers' College. She arrived around the same time that Xi became leader of the region and the Rescue the Fallen Campaign was enveloping the area. Because the parents of the students were so furious, Xi made a trip to the university to investigate the situation. Xi's mobilization report at a large meeting was the first time Qi ever saw him. Soon after, Xi met Qi and another student in a cave that was serving as his bedroom and office, where she saw for the first time the characters Mao had written for him: "The party's interests come first." Xi told them to resist mistakes in the Rescue the Fallen Campaign. Otherwise, she and her classmate would come under suspicion as well. As a student representative on the university's presidium, she later met Xi on numerous occasions. During the next few months, Xi regularly wrote Qi letters about her work and study plans. Despite the electrified political environment of fear and accusation at the school, they developed a close relationship with one another.[30]

In October 1943, Xi traveled by mule to visit Hao. According to his daughter Qianping, he hoped she would reunite with him. When he knocked on the door of her cave, she opened the door a crack, saw it was Xi, and then quickly slammed it. Xi shouted at the door for more than an hour. Hao, furious that Xi thought she was having an affair, refused to speak with him. Xi, who by then was tired, thirsty, and hungry, finally squatted in the rain in front of her door and cried. It was too late to return home, so he spent the night in a stable. The next morning, he left before dawn. The divorce was finalized in the early winter of 1944. Although she was only twenty-six, Hao never remarried. Later, Xi would tell one of his daughters, "There was no real reason why your mother and I divorced. At the time, we were young and quick-tempered. Neither of us would surrender to the other. We acted willfully. Ultimately, we took the path we did."[31] It was a common path too. In the base areas, many rough-and-tumble men divorced their peasant wives to marry the much younger intellectual women who ran to Yan'an to join the revolution.[32]

According to Qi Xin, Xi raised the issue of marriage in the "winter of 1943," a vague date—one that was apparently after Xi's last trip to see Hao but before his official divorce. Xi asked her to write an autobiography of herself for him. Qi Xin found the task somewhat difficult, believing she had little to say. The vice-dean of her school wrote in a letter to Xi, "She did not grow up until after she arrived in Yan'an," which helped Xi decide that Qi would be a good match. She impressed Xi with her story about fleeing from home twice to join the revolution, only to be brought back by her father. Xi laughed and said that when he was young, he was just like her.[33]

After her divorce, Hao continued a career working on women's issues. In 1946, during elections for the local Communist-run government in Zichang County, she was one of the two highest vote getters. She was even elected to serve on the Shaan-Gan-Ning Border Region Assembly—one of only seven women on the 135-person body.[34] In 1949, she helped create the Northwest Women's Federation, and between 1951 and 1953, she served as head of its Organization Department.[35] In subsequent years, Hao had an impressive career as one of the only women in the top Shaanxi party hierarchy.[36]

During the Cultural Revolution, Hao's ties with Xi Zhongxun, who was then facing intense persecution, were investigated. According to a subsequent report intended only for internal circulation, Hao and Xi remained close after their divorce, and Xi even gave her gifts of a radio and watch. Hao, "who, on the one hand, in terms of personal emotions, hated Xi but, on the other, was also envious of him," requested that Xi help their children with their work and income. Xi, to "hide his ugly face," used "economic means to win Hao over." Hao was treated leniently by the investigators, who decided

78   CHAPTER 5

that although she was proximate to a "black-line person," she herself was not one, and she was released.[37]

Xi and Qi officially married in a cave on April 28, 1944. The individual who took their wedding picture was Bu Lu, one of the most notorious spymasters in Chinese history. In 1952, after Bu was labeled a British spy (Bu had served in the Malayan Communist Party in Singapore), Bu's wife went to beg for Xi's help. Before she could open her mouth, Xi knew why she had come and said, "British spy—that's bullshit!" After hearing Xi's words, Bu tried to visit his old boss, but he was turned away at the door because he looked like a beggar. Arrested soon thereafter and never rehabilitated while he was alive, Bu died in 1972 after decades of prison and "reform through labor."[38]

After their wedding, Xi said to Qi, "From now on, we are bound together. But I am not willing to become a small faction," meaning they should not put their interests above those of the party. That summer, Qi graduated from Suide Teachers' College and went to do grassroots work with peasants. They lived separately until October 1945, when Xi became head of the Northwest Bureau and they moved together into a cave in Yan'an, where Qi again stud-

FIGURE 3. Xi Zhongxun and Qi Xin at the Northwest Bureau headquarters in Yan'an, spring 1947. Source: *Xi Zhongxun huace*, 166.

ied at the party school. But the reunion was brief as, in the fall of 1946, Qi became vice-secretary of Yihe Township in Suide. When the party brought Qi to see Xi in May 1947, right in the midst of intense battles following the loss of Yan'an, Xi yelled at her publicly, "It's so arduous. What the hell are you doing here?" She returned to Yan'an in 1949 to work as a researcher for the Northwest Bureau on agricultural issues until 1952, but she still spent a great deal of time outside of Yan'an.[39] During the period of their separation, Xi regularly wrote her letters encouraging her to do her best for the party. He told her that the countryside was like a "big university" where she could gain great knowledge. A friend who saw one of the letters laughed and said, "How is this a regular family letter?"[40]

By 1949, Qi Houzhi, Qi Xin's father, was an adviser to the top Nationalist general in Beiping, Fu Zuoyi. Along with Fu, Qi defected to the Communists, which allowed the party to take the city peacefully. Xi participated in the ceremony marking the People's Liberation Army's entrance into Beiping in March, where he met both Qi Houzhi and Qi Yun. Much to Qi Xin's delight, Xi brought a letter back to Yan'an from her sister.[41] In September, Qi Houzhi went to Xi'an and began work at the Northwest Branch of the Highest People's Court. When the Communists began investigations after their total victory, Qi Houzhi took the initiative to explain his historical problems and was treated leniently.[42]

RAISING THE NEXT GENERATION

Xi's eldest daughter with Hao Mingzhu, Heping, was born in October 1936. One month after her birth, she was carried in a basket on the back of a secret messenger through several layers of a Nationalist blockade to see her father.[43] A second daughter, Qianping, was born in 1938 and quickly given to a wet nurse. But the area was beset by violence between the Communists and the Nationalists, and the woman soon returned to her home in a Nationalist-controlled area—along with tiny Qianping. For about a decade, Xi had no idea where his daughter was, and Qianping did not know who her parents were. After Xi'an was taken by the party, Xi sent out some people to find her, and they finally reunited after many years apart. At first, Qianping was frightened of Xi and refused to call him father. One day, Xi took her by the hand during a stroll and said, "Tomorrow, a sister and mother are going to come. The mother did not give birth to you; your birth mother and I divorced." Qianping later told one of Xi's secretaries, "The first mother I saw was Qi Xin; she was very kind and warm." Qi Xin taught Qianping to read, and both she and Xi often told Qianping they were all one's flesh and blood.[44]

Xi's first son, Zhengning, was born in 1941 (his birth name was Fuping, after Zhongxun's home county, but the name was later changed to commemorate the name of the town where he was born). Like Qianping, he was given over to a peasant family. During that time, a strange man showed up and claimed to be Hao Mingzhu's cousin. The peasants were suspicious, and the foster father hid Zhengning in a cave. That evening, their home was burned to the ground.[45] Unlike Qianping, Zhengning was soon returned to his family as the peasants were unable to feed him and he became malnourished.[46]

On one occasion, after Zhengning reunited with his father, the little boy was playing in his father's office when it began to hail outside. Xi told his son to go and collect it. When Zhengning went outside, he immediately felt the pain of the hail striking him, so he ran back inside. Xi pushed him back outside, saying, "Don't be so afraid. You not only want to forge bravery; at the same time, you need to use your brains to think of a way to bring back the hail without letting it hit you!" Zhengning froze, and then his father placed two washing basins on their heads, and they went out together. Zhengning finally started to have fun, and his father praised his bravery. Zhengning later also recalled his father asking him one day why he did not go outside to play with the other children. Zhengning explained that he had had a fight with them, and so he did not want to see them again. Xi said nothing and told Zhengning to go to sleep. The next morning, Xi put peanuts, melons, and other tasty treats on a table in his cave and asked a bodyguard to bring the other children inside to eat. When everyone started to have fun, Xi said to his son, "The way you do things is no good! How can it be that after only one fight, things become awkward and you stop talking and you no longer interact with each other or play together? What's there to be afraid about fighting; if you don't fight, you don't get to know each other. It is only after fighting that you can become better friends."[47]

Xi's first child with Qi Xin was born in March 1949—six years after they were married. The baby was born in a Catholic church in Yan'an that had been converted into a Communist hospital. Since the church was in the Qiao'ergou neighborhood, Qi Xin's mother named the baby Qiaoqiao. Xi'an was taken by the Communists in May 1949, and a month later, Qi Xin, by then one of the last Northwest Bureau workers still living in Yan'an, brought the baby to the city. She traveled alone, sitting in the back of a truck, and because they had no shade or water, Qiaoqiao developed heat stroke, suffered a fever, and nearly went into shock.[48]

Although Xi was head of the Northwest Bureau after 1949, he did not arrange for Qi Xin to permanently live with him in Xi'an. When Xi traveled to Chang'an County during an anticorruption investigation (sometime between 1951 and 1952), he brought Qiaoqiao to see her mother, who was then working in the county. When Qiaoqiao saw Qi Xin, she jumped into her mother's arms and cried, demanding that she return to Xi'an with them. Qi did not have any activities planned for that night, and she could have taken a bus back the next morning without affecting her work, but Xi did not agree—the optics would be bad. Xi carried his daughter away as she cried for her mother.[49]

Xi's cleverness, quick temper, and preoccupation with party affairs all manifested in his personal life. He enjoyed mahjong, but according to one of his former subordinates, he was a shifty player: "When playing, Xi was quick of eye and deft of hand, and after putting his tiles down, he would often steal another tile and yell, 'Mahjong!' Because the others had poor eyesight, they did not know that he was deceiving them." He could also be an angry player. At the beginning of a game of Chinese chess, he told his secretary he would give up one piece at the beginning, and the secretary picked a cannon. Xi started to lose, and he said, "This game does not count," and they started over. The next time, when Xi started to win, the secretary became nervous, made a mistake, and asked to reverse the move. Xi agreed, but then the match turned around. When Xi saw he was losing, he pushed away the board and said, "I'm done! We'll play again some other day." He was an accomplished dancer, and he danced every Saturday night, yet he apparently liked to combine work and pleasure. One former cadre in the Northwest Bureau gradually understood why Xi liked to dance so much: "After going to the parties a few times, I realized that Old Xi danced with both men and women, young and old; he did not refuse anyone, and he danced and talked at the same time. It was only then that I understood that although it appeared he was dancing, in actuality, he was trying to understand the situation and he was carrying out an undercover inspection."[50]

6
WAR ON THE NATIONALISTS AND THE PEASANTS

As Japan's defeat loomed, the Nationalists already started putting more pressure on Communist positions. In July 1945, General Hu Zongnan seized the southern tip of the Communist-controlled area north of Xi'an. The party center named Zhang Zongxun and Xi Zhongxun as commander and commissar, respectively, of the forces assigned to launch a counterattack, which became known as the Yetaishan Campaign. Their three brigades came from different areas, and the commanders had so little trust for one another that their first planning meeting ended in acrimony without a clear plan, but Xi did a good job bringing them together.[1] Xi also successfully ran the political campaign to condemn the Nationalist assault. Because he was deeply familiar with the area after having spent so many years running the Guanzhong subregion, Xi effectively mobilized the population to support the Communist forces and to discover any spies. The Communists succeeded in retaking all the territory that they had lost, and in the public-opinion war, the Nationalists suffered for having attacked the Communists so soon after the defeat of the Japanese.[2]

In subsequent years, with the top party leadership in the same city as the Northwest Bureau, Xi worked very closely with Mao, especially during a rescue mission to save Wang Zhen's retreating forces in 1946. Two years earlier, the Communists had sent the 359th Brigade under the leadership of Wang to establish a presence in Hunan Province. However, after the Japanese surrender in 1945, Chiang Kai-shek launched a ferocious attack on the

Communist forces in the region. In June 1946, Mao placed Xi in charge of supporting the retreat. Between July 26 and September 2, Mao wrote nine letters to Xi, in which he provided specific directions. Years later, Xi said the experience of working with Mao to save Wang demonstrated the chairman's ability to both "give cadres free space to work but also give specific guidance."[3]

Beginning in October 1946, the party repeatedly received warnings about an impending attack on Yan'an by Hu Zongnan. When Hu finally did launch a major attack in spring of the next year, many civilians simply did not believe the news and reacted slowly. The Communists lacked bullets and grenades and sometimes had to fight the enemy forces with bayonets, even as the Nationalist air force and artillery pummeled their positions. The situation became more critical after the battle of Xihuachi in eastern Gansu between March 2 and 5. Zhang Zongxun, commander of the Communist forces in the battle, and Xi, the commissar, fought poorly. Lack of familiarity with the terrain, poor reconnaissance, inappropriate deployments, and lack of coordination meant severe losses at precisely the moment the Communists needed to conserve their forces. On March 5, Zhang and Xi wrote a self-criticism claiming that their desire to defend Yan'an had made them too aggressive. The situation became so critical that, on March 16, when the Nationalist forces were on the outskirts of the city, the Central Military Commission released a notification declaring that Peng Dehuai would become commander and commissar of all Northwest forces and Xi, his vice-commissar. Peng, who had previously been vice-chairman of the Central Military Commission, had accepted a major demotion to a regional command to manage a full-blown crisis.[4]

On the afternoon of March 18, Peng Dehuai, Xi Zhongxun, and Wang Zhen urged Mao to flee Yan'an. Only late that evening did Mao agree. Peng and Xi escorted Mao as he left the city that had served as the Communist capital for ten years. A bomb destroyed his cave just after Mao departed. According to a story Xi told many years later, Mao said, "OK, this is a firework set by Hu Zongnan to see me off." Peng and Xi did not leave until after Mao was safely outside Yan'an. Morale was poor, and as the rearguard finally withdrew, some individuals continuously stopped to look back. On March 19, Peng and Xi reported to the Central Military Commission that Yan'an had fallen.[5]

Communist forces were in full retreat. Hu Zongnan's troops thought they would soon be able to leave the bitter Northwest. On March 25, Hu triumphantly visited the cave in Yan'an where Mao used to live. Hu found a piece of paper in the drawer. It read, "Hu Zongnan has arrived in Yan'an. His situation is like riding a tiger. He can't move forward, but he can't retreat either. Helpless! Helpless!" Hu burst out laughing. It would be his last laugh. On that very same day, Peng and Xi ambushed Nationalist soldiers at nearby Qinghuabian.[6] Some of their commanders had feared that this strategy was too risky, as the plan would only work if Nationalist intelligence had not figured out their location. Yet the battle was a success, and Peng credited local civilians for the outcome as they did not provide the enemy with any information. Intelligence provided by Communist spies in Xi'an was also vital. Shortly thereafter, Peng and Xi destroyed an entire Nationalist brigade at Yangmahe. The two battles helped improve morale and turn around the battle for the Northwest.[7]

Fresh with those two successes, Peng and Xi planned a more ambitious attack on Panlong, a logistical station for Hu Zongnan's troops. As the Communists planned their attack, their command center was so close to the front lines that Xi paced worriedly back and forth in his cave. Peng told Xi not to worry as the Nationalists would never enter a ravine because of fear of an ambush. Peng was right, and the Communist forces were able to seize Panlong—and all its crucial supplies.[8]

Over the course of a month and a half, the triumphs at Qinghuabian, Yangmahe, and Panlong stabilized the situation in the Northwest. In early May, the Communists considered moving more forces into Shaanxi to help Peng and Xi retake Yan'an.[9] At a rally marking their recent victories, Xi spoke powerfully to stir up his audience: "The people in the border region have experienced an unprecedented disaster—homes were destroyed, grain was stolen, animals were slaughtered, men were taken away, women were raped, and the happy life that the people in the border region had spent ten years of hard work to establish has been destroyed. But the people of the border region will never surrender. We must take revenge!"[10]

Plans to make the Northwest a primary battlefield soon shifted, however. On June 30, Liu Bocheng and Deng Xiaoping's Second Field Army seized territory on the south side of the Yellow River in Shandong, devastating Nationalist plans to use that river as a defense line. Mao summoned Peng and Xi to Xiaohe to discuss whether to continue to focus on the Northwest or on the new possibilities in central China. At their meeting, which began on July 16, Mao said that the Northwest simply could not support a major campaign.

While the situation in Shandong might shift in the Communists' favor, that was not the case in Shaanxi.[11] At Xiaohe, the party also decided to combine the Shanxi-Suide Military Region with the Shaanxi-Gansu-Ningxia-Shanxi Suide Joint Defense Army, with He Long as commander and Xi as commissar. Xi Zhongxun was now commissar of a massive region, working with Peng on the front lines and with He Long in the rear.[12]

Working with Peng meant learning to manage the older man's famously explosive temper. In April 1948, the Communists seized the strategic city of Baoji between Xi'an and Shaanxi's border with Gansu. Xi had expressed skepticism about such a daring campaign, and, at the end of the month, the Communists were forced to give up the city after Hu Zongnan reacted more quickly than expected. Peng chaired a meeting to debrief on the catastrophe. The atmosphere at the meeting was extremely tense. Peng was particularly furious at one commander, Wang Shitai, who Peng believed had committed the mistake of "severe individualism," which included not executing orders and missing opportunities. Peng slammed his hands angrily on the table, pointed his finger at Wang and told him, "Given the losses that the revolutionary war has suffered, your head should roll!" Xi was also furious: "What's wrong with getting rid of a few people who are dishonest, have a bad character, and suffer from individual heroism? They should be fired. We must resolve to cut out these pieces of rotten meat."[13]

After the meeting, Xi acted as peacemaker. Xi told Wang that Peng's criticisms "do not spare any sensibilities, but they are for the common good. Commander Peng only told you that he wanted to execute you. That is already very polite." Wang was impressed that Xi could protect Peng's authority while also convincing Peng's subordinates not to fear him—a crucial skill that allowed for freer discussion.[14] Not everyone was impressed with Xi, however. At a meeting on the history of the Northwest battlefield many decades later, one general criticized Xi for "saying nice things" about the commanders who had made severe mistakes.[15]

Peng and Xi did not always agree, but they established a functional working relationship. Peng was struck by how closely Xi interacted with regular people. Peng repeatedly lambasted administrators for not providing Xi with living conditions that were as comfortable as his own. Peng's vice–chief of staff wrote in his memoirs that Peng would always exchange views with Xi Zhongxun before expressing a position on military affairs at a meeting.[16] Xi would later jokingly tell the story of how, at night, while sleeping in the same bed, Xi's snoring would often prevent Peng from sleeping soundly, so Peng would get up and put shoes on Xi's face to wake him up.[17]

The Northwest battlefield was a unique one during the war. It was seen as a backwater, and many people believed that putting Peng Dehuai in charge was deeply unfair to the legendary hero. Mao played a closer, direct role managing decisions there than he did in other areas. When the First Field Army was created on November 11, 1948, some people believed that those forces, made up of Northwest units, were not big enough to deserve the appellation of a "field army." The battles fought in the region were smaller than those in other areas, but the conditions were especially difficult: twenty thousand soldiers faced 220,000 Nationalist soldiers. Most of the best supplies went to the other field armies.[18]

Spy craft also played a prominent role on the Northwest battlefield. Between 1948 and 1949, Communist agents working for the Northwest Bureau penetrated Hu Zongnan's headquarters. Xi later said that the intelligence provided by this group proved to be "100 percent correct."[19] In the summer of 1949, Xi even gave special permission for these spies to join the party, although the decision remained secret as they continued to work for the Nationalists. Every single one of these individuals, however, would later be persecuted during the Cultural Revolution.[20]

Although the campaign in the Northwest lacked the glory of the other fronts, Xi cared deeply about how his legacy would be remembered. In 1990, the Central Military Commission created an Editing and Compilation Committee on the Fighting History of the First Field Army, with Xi as chairman. During the deliberations, a dispute arose about how much the official history should emphasize Xi. One general, Wang Enmao, stated emphatically that although Peng deserved the lion's share of the credit for the triumphs in the Northwest, He Long, followed by Xi Zhongxun, should also be considered two other key figures. Another main leading commander, however, said Peng Dehuai and He Long should be equals, and he did not name Xi. In 1994, Qi Xin told representatives of the First Field Army History Office that "Old Xi pays very close attention to the history of the First Field Army; he has asked about it many times." "When writing war history, it is necessary to respect history. Old Xi's position and contributions to the Northwest Field Army should be written clearly," she said.[21] The final edition of the history lists Xi after Peng and He as the "main leaders and direct commanders" on the Northwest battlefield.[22]

THE HENGSHAN UPRISING AND THE "YULIN MODEL"

Xi had some claim to the legacy of the military victories in the Northwest. However, his primary contributions to the victory were not brilliance on the battlefield. Given his role in the Northwest Bureau, Xi spent a great deal of time and effort ensuring that the army had the resources it needed. He did well in that regard, although deficiencies persisted. In November 1947, he made a self-criticism for the Northwest Bureau about failings in the war effort, and the People's Liberation Army had to call off a campaign that month because of lack of supplies.[23] In February 1948, Gao Gang complained that the Northwest Bureau suffered from bureaucratism and was doing poorly with war preparations.[24] Xi's most obvious talent lay elsewhere—in political warfare against waffling Nationalist leaders.

One of his greatest triumphs between the defeat of the Japanese in 1945 and the establishment of the People's Republic in 1949 was his role in convincing two powerful generals, Hu Jingduo and his nephew Hu Xizhong, to defect to the Communists at a crucial moment. Xi had attended Licheng School in Fuping County with both Hus. In subsequent decades, Xi and Hu Xizhong regularly kept in touch. Because Xi knew that Hu was a sympathizer, he regularly wrote him letters in which he reminded Hu that although the current priority was to defeat the Japanese, it was also necessary to remember that afterward, the Nationalists would have to be defeated militarily. In the winter of 1943, a messenger sent to deliver one such letter was captured. Hu was arrested, and only the intervention of several Nationalist elders saved him (seven years later, Xi had the messenger executed). Xi convinced Hu to prioritize gaining control over troops and then defecting instead of trying to change the Nationalists from the inside. In Xi's mind, only violence could defeat the Nationalists.[25]

In October 1945, Hu Jingduo sent a secret letter to Xi informing him that he and his nephew Xizhong were ready to defect. At the time, their forces were located in Hengshan, a part of Yulin City, which was in a strategically important area located north of the base areas. In September 1946, Xi told the Hus that the party was ready to welcome the revolting troops, and on October 16, about two thousand soldiers joined the Communists. Xi said that this was his proudest moment as a revolutionary.[26]

Hengshan was not the only dramatic case of United Front work leading to positive results—Xi also played a significant role in the defection of General Deng Baoshan and the subsequent fall of the Nationalist stronghold in Yulin. In June 1947, when the party was in an especially vulnerable position in Shaanxi, at a meeting of the Northwest Bureau, Xi decided to intensify political pressure against Yulin. The meeting decided to draw upon the party's already established connections in Deng's forces and also utilize the "many familial and societal connections" that the military shared with people living in the Communist-controlled territories.[27]

In the summer of 1947, Deng still refused to defect, so Peng Dehuai and Xi decided to try to take Yulin by force. During the battle, Peng and Xi were not able to seize the city, but Deng suffered 5,200 casualties. In October, Peng and Xi attacked the city, but, once again, they were unsuccessful.[28] Xi determined a policy of "winning over politically and sieging militarily to strive for an uprising." He wrote to Deng two letters in which he said that a Nationalist defeat was a historical inevitability. By August 1948, Yulin was the last key remaining Nationalist position in the Northwest, and Deng left for Beiping. As the Communist forces were surrounding Yulin and cutting it off from the outside world, the Northwest Bureau was directing underground party members to organize front organizations, put up posters, hand out flyers, and launch protests. After Beiping surrendered peacefully in January 1949, Deng wrote a letter to Zuo Shiyun, the commander in Yulin, urging him to give up as well. In February, Zuo finally entered into secret negotiations with the Communists, and Xi dictated the terms. In April, Zuo finally decided to surrender. Xi suggested to the party leadership that they accept Zuo's offer; as the People's Liberation Army did not have sufficient forces in the area to easily seize Yulin, the region would suffer less damage, and Deng's soldiers "had ten plus years of relations with us, so if matters are settled appropriately, the political influence will be a little better."[29]

Xi proudly characterized Yulin as a model for using force and inducements to convince the enemy forces to surrender. "In the future, when enemies are defeated in the Northwest, not only military methods should be used; in some cases, the specific situations will demand peaceful methods," he said. For Xi, the "Yulin model" was marked by a long period of preparation with both patience and activity; the use of both political and military methods together; the sublimation of external pressures into internal contradictions to combine the former and the latter; not giving up on principles but providing as much to the opponent as possible; and the effective use of contradictions.[30]

LAND REFORM

While the Communists were fighting with Hu Zongnan's forces on the front lines, in the rear, from 1946 to 1948, the party was fighting a war of sorts with the peasants in the form of land reform. Xi's behavior during this campaign, one of the most infamous disasters in party history, is often described as one of the best examples of Xi's steady, gradualist approach and his willingness to take risks to criticize radical policies. The available evidence does provide some support for such a view, but Xi's bravery should not be overstated, and land reform still reached levels of extreme violence.

Given his peasant roots and extensive time working at the grass roots, Xi intimately understood the countryside. The question for him and the party was how to balance transformational politics with practicality. Without a clear answer, the party often shifted between extremes, a problem Xi described vividly in a 1943 self-criticism about his time in Guanzhong. Before Mao arrived in the Northwest, Xi said, party policies had "violated the interests of the middle peasants during land reform, and economic policy was to confiscate some things from businesspeople, and there were the 'purge' policies of the 'leftist' opportunists as well, so there was significant terror among the masses in the Guanzhong Soviet." But after Mao arrived, the land-reform policies then made a mistake in the other direction. "The land of the landlords that had been confiscated was returned to the landlords, and the hired laborers and poor peasants who had been given land felt their land rights were unstable, and they began to have doubts about the revolution." Thereafter, there was a *third* reorganization of land according to a joint principle based on population and labor power. But that, according to Xi, "dissatisfied the poor peasants who were small in number and who had previously been given more land, as well as the middle peasants because they used to have land, but they were not given land, so they also doubted the revolution."[31]

In the Shaan-Gan-Ning base area, half the land had undergone reform decades earlier, while the other half had experienced reforms during the war against the Japanese. None of the region had ever been occupied by Japan, so there were few "traitors" to eliminate and no need to physically exterminate the landlords. The base area's rich peasants were of the "new-rich-peasant" variety, meaning they had become wealthy through their own hard work after acquiring land from the Communists during the war. Leaders in the

Shaan-Gan-Ning base area therefore believed that purchasing land was the best policy to further land reform.[32]

At first, the top party leadership supported the peaceful land purchases in Shaan-Gan-Ning. However, on December 10, 1946, Mao sent a group that included Kang Sheng to eastern Gansu to investigate. Kang discovered that, despite the previous reforms, landlords and rich peasants still held 53 percent of the land. In February 1947, at a meeting of Xi's Northwest Bureau, Kang suggested combining purchases with "exposing and condemning" landlords.[33] Liu Shaoqi, the second most powerful figure in the party, was concerned that the party had become less zealous than the peasants. At a nationwide land meeting in Xibaipo that lasted from July until September 1947, Liu proposed a policy that targeted a wider number of people for attack and empowered the peasants at the expense of party cadres.[34]

On October 10, the party disseminated its Outline on Chinese Land Law, which signified the beginning of the more radical policies.[35] On October 18, at a rally, Xi said the new land-reform plans were as "worth celebrating" as any wins on the battlefield.[36] On November 1, the Northwest Bureau arranged a meeting in Yihe, Suide Province, to discuss the outcome of the Xibaipo meeting. The atmosphere was electric. The director of propaganda of the Northwest Bureau used slogans such as "Set fires to every village" and "Every household should be smoking."[37]

After the Yihe meeting, land reform in the Northwest Bureau became extraordinarily violent. In one area, the local Poor Peasants Association set a rule that anyone who was not active in struggles against landlords was to be put to death by stoning.[38] In another area, 357 cadres were killed as a result of either perceived laxity in implementing land reform or after they were branded as "landlords" or "rich peasants" by impassioned party or peasant activists. The chaos led to starvation. Crowds appeared at party, government, and military buildings and chanted, "You want to eat; we also want to eat." Food was so scarce that one work group devised a rule that only those individuals whose legs had gone black from hunger would be given some grain.[39]

Xi made a self-criticism at a high-ranking cadre meeting held by the Northwest Bureau that lasted from November 1 to 23—not because of the violence but because previously he had not acted with enough ardor. "In the past, the Northwest Bureau, when solving land issues, did not resolutely rely on the poor peasants, did not give free rein to the masses, did not investigate and criticize the thinking and positions of cadres at every level, and did not influence the thinking of the landlords in a timely fashion." Xi admitted that he had "committed the mistake of individualism and bureaucratism." On December 18, Lin Boqu (head of the Shaan-Gan-Ning government), He Long, and Xi Zhongxun publicly affirmed the need to divide up all land, annihilate the landlords and feudal forces, and work under the leadership of the Poor Peasants Associations and mass meetings. The Northwest Bureau was clearly still pursuing land reform in its most radical form.[40]

The situation began to change only a few days later at the December Meeting at Yangjiagou. The Xi family takes pride in Zhongxun's role at these sessions. According to accounts of the December Meeting by Xi and his son Yuanping, Zhongxun went to Mao's residence to report on "leftist" mistakes on the very night of his arrival. At the official sessions, Xi did not plan to speak at first, but Mao said, "Zhongxun, are you going to say something? Are you going to give a speech?" As Xi spoke for three hours, Mao sat closer and closer until he was right in front of him. When Xi finished, Mao said, "I haven't heard such a truthful report in a long time!"[41]

Yet Xi does not deserve sole credit for the correctives that the Yangjiagou meeting approved. He certainly had not raised any concerns before Yangjiagou, and a year later, in December 1948, he would say in a self-criticism that he should have said something sooner.[42] Xi was clearly not the only person worried about the direction of the campaign. On December 19, Kang Sheng and Yang Shangkun warned of famine in a region they inspected.[43] During a preparatory session for the meeting between December 7 and 24, Ren Bishi, a man who ranked fifth in the leadership and was already worried about leftist excesses, chaired a small group on land reform and listened to concerned reports from Xi Zhongxun but also from several others. On December 27, Ren gave a speech at the formal proceedings that castigated radical mistakes. The next day, Mao said, "When the 'leftist' tendency becomes a wave, the party must oppose this wave!"[44]

Many years later, in December 1978, Xi wrote that seeing Mao at Yangjiagou was the most "unforgettable" of his encounters with the Chinese leader. Xi recounted Mao's remarks to him in detail. Mao emphasized the importance of reading more and developing a stronger command of theory: "For a long time, you have been involved in practical work with no time to study. That's no big deal. If you have no time, you can make time. Now we are in mountain ravines, but in the future, we will run the cities. If, in one year, you read one small book, in two years, that will be two books! In three years, that's three books! In that way, in ten-plus years you can read ten-plus books. Doesn't that mean you can gradually become proficient in Marxism-Leninism?!" "One person's experience is narrow; it is restricted by time, location, and conditions," Mao said. "In order to turn experience into theory, it is necessary to study." Xi wrote that Mao's instructions were like a "flame" that made him "feel warm" inside and made his "heart light up."[45]

With a sense that the party, especially Mao, was beginning to recognize that land reform had gone wrong, Xi finally began to make the case for a new direction. On January 4, in a message to Mao, Xi warned that wherever the masses were mobilized for struggle in areas that had already undergone land reform many years before, "generally it was too leftist." Because the middle peasants, previously the foundation of the party's social coalition, were not included, many decisions on land reform were made by poor or landless peasants, leading to mass confiscations of property from people who had earned the land through their own considerable efforts. If these matters were allowed to continue, "it would necessarily lead to disastrous results divorced from the masses." A few days later, Xi wrote a report to the Northwest Bureau on land reform in Suide that continued these themes. Some individuals were attacked simply because they had food to eat. Landlords and rich peasants, despite their differences, were tortured in the same way—in some cases, knives, heated until they were red, were placed on their tongues. Many people came to believe that land reform simply meant more killing and more torturing.[46]

On January 19, Xi wrote another report that Mao then distributed for study. In that document, Xi complained about the "extreme leftist deviation" in the areas undergoing land reform. Xi drew attention to the very serious situation in Xue County in particular: "Very few relatives of party cadres were spared struggle. . . . Some relatives of martyrs were expelled from their homes. Some people were drowned in earthen jars filled with salty water. People were burned to death by pouring boiling oil on their heads. Xue County was in chaos for more than five days, and everything was in a terrible state. I believe that as soon as there is a leftist deviation, in less than half a month, everything is wrecked." No one dared to bury the dead or treat the sick. Allowing the Poor Peasants Associations to lead land reform "meant giving the power of leadership to evil people." People were hesitant to produce, lest they acquire any modicum of wealth and be branded a rich peasant or a landlord. Some party members were fleeing or committing suicide. Mao wrote on the document, "I completely agree with these opinions of Comrade Xi Zhongxun."[47]

As a native cadre with concrete knowledge of the situation, Xi's reports helped Mao convince Liu Shaoqi that something had gone wrong. Liu did not accept the attacks on land reform at first, but Xi's findings forced him to react. In Liu's mind, without first scaring the middle peasants a bit, it would have been impossible to create an atmosphere conducive to land reform. Liu sent a telegram to Mao in which he said that extreme leftist mistakes had only taken place in Jin-Sui and in Northern Shaanxi. Moreover, cases of incorrect beatings and murders were because of poor leadership, not a wrong policy. But, on February 3, at least in part because of Xi's opinion, Mao sent a telegram to Liu arguing that the party had made a mistake treating regions long controlled by the Communists the same way as new territories.[48]

On February 6, Mao met again with Xi. Then, on February 8, Xi wrote another frank report: "We deeply feel that land reform during the last two months, as well as the work of the Poor Peasants Associations, not only accomplished little but in fact created many difficulties." In the Shaan-Gan-Ning Border Region, Xi explained, most of the land had already been divided before the land-reform campaign. In those areas, the middle peasants had the most land, not the landlords or the rich peasants. Therefore, Xi wrote, "dividing again, generally speaking, means touching most or all of the land of the middle peasants, or even touching 10 percent of the land of the poor peasants." That would "create a lack of confidence among peasants toward the ownership of land." Peasants would refuse to work, wondering "whether in a few years another division will take place again." Peasants who were poor because they drank, visited prostitutes, and gambled made up a full quarter of the number of poor peasants, so as soon as they were given power in a Poor Peasants Association, they aggressively attacked the middle peasants. Liu finally accepted the views of Mao and Xi.[49]

Over the next few months, as vast swathes of the nation fell to rapidly advancing Communist forces, Xi worried the party was not ready. In July, he expressed his concern to Mao. The Communists poorly understood the situation in these new regions, and the cadres the party was sending were arrogant, dogmatic, and emotional. Xi admitted that regular peasants "were not as poor as we had imagined." Moreover, the people who lived in those new areas, including some from the middle and upper classes, hoped to see the party succeed. Xi asserted that the "correctness" of the party's policies was the main explanation for why it was winning new adherents. The greatest worry for these party supporters, Xi claimed, was that the party would change its own promises.[50]

Therefore, Xi wrote, the Communists should first stabilize the regime and only then pursue societal transformation. He even recommended that the party not raise the issue of land reform too quickly. Otherwise, "in actual fact, it would be the hoodlums who will take advantage." Landlords were not afraid of losing their land, he continued. They were afraid of being killed. Xi made a remarkable proposal: that the government peacefully accept land that the landlords gave up on their own. "Is this a case of 'bestowing favors'?" he asked. "I don't think so. If the landlords are willing, then what's the harm?" The lessons of the previous year appeared to weigh on him: "In the past, we treated formulaic revolution as the best kind of revolution. But in reality, we were acting in a way that really lacked strategy."[51]

He gave a somewhat fuller account of the party's mistakes over the last year during a speech to Northwest cadres the following month. "The deficiencies of the Yihe meeting" that launched land reform in the Northwest were the result of an inability to "analyze the specific situation in the border region and set a concrete guideline," he said. In particular, there were no rules about determining class labels, and torture was not explicitly banned. Yet the main thrust of his speech was an attempt to deny that the Yihe meeting had been a complete disaster and to protect his own record. "Looking at this now, the nature of these deficiencies was all in terms of tactics and pace. Therefore, it cannot be said that the deficiencies were the primary nature of the Yihe meeting," Xi said.[52]

Now facing accusations of "leftism" himself, Xi spoke of his old nemeses who had persecuted him in 1935. Whereas the party had correctly criticized Guo Hongtao and Zhu Lizhi in 1942 for their "leftist-opportunist line," the Yihe meeting had, also correctly, "criticized rightist phenomena." That was a necessary course correction, Xi claimed. During the ten years before the Yihe meeting, "in terms of thinking and style, serious phenomena like a muddled class view, a weak sense of struggle against the enemy, bureaucratism, individualism, and even corruption had appeared." Land reform was a disaster, but whipping up revolutionary fervor was still necessary: "Currently we still do not dare give free rein to the masses, our work lacks efficiency, and cadres are not willing to join the military or to go to new areas. That means a class mindset and a will to struggle against the enemy have not received the attention they deserve. Lack of vigilance is still a big problem."[53]

Xi tried to make the case for a middle line between dogmatic radicalism and lack of sufficient zeal: "Our party grew up in a struggle between two different lines. At all times, it is necessary to struggle against the two incorrect deviations of left and right. When a right deviation blocks the revolution from moving forward, it is necessary to concentrate forces to oppose it. When a left deviation becomes the main danger, it is also necessary to stubbornly defeat it. Of course, opposing rightism, that does not mean leftist things are entirely absent. Similarly, when opposing leftism, it is intolerable to ignore the existence of rightist things." Channeling Mao's words to him at Yangjiagou, Xi then proceeded to criticize "empiricism"—the view that experience and practicality, not ideological guidance, were the only skills necessary: "Empirical thinking does not analyze problems, does not research problems, and does not try to connect problems to find their true nature and determine patterns." For Xi, it was this kind of empiricism that was the main challenge facing the party. "Studying theory is not the mistake of dogmatism" but instead a combination of "the universal truth of Marxism-Leninism and the practice of the Chinese revolution," he said.[54]

Xi's behavior during land reform and especially his self-criticisms are enormously revealing both in terms of what they tell us about him as an individual and also about the Communist Party as a system. The land-reform debacle was shaped by perennial challenges: the tensions between political expediency and social transformation, the need to rally enthusiasm while not going too far, the fraught politics of course corrections, and the relationship between "Marxism" and "empiricism." In that context, it would be inappropriate to portray Xi Zhongxun as either a quintessentially practical individual or as a radical ideologue—he was a politician facing a fluid situation that demanded caution. His reports to Mao helped the chairman understand the seriousness of the situation, and the evidence Xi submitted helped persuade figures such as Liu Shaoqi. Yet he failed to stop the violence, and he did not speak out on the problems until he had a sense that he was pushing on an open door. Everyone wanted the same outcome. The question was how to achieve it in the least costly way.

On the eve of the party's great victory over the Nationalists, Xi warned Mao, "I believe that, in the new areas, there are still leftist mistakes in all kinds of policies. We should overcome these leftist attitudes and mistakes in the party. As long as our policies are not wrong, we can unite the broad masses and defeat the enemy."[55] Yet, in his self-criticism a month later, Xi very clearly did not characterize himself as a "gradualist." He made a case for a sort of middle path—one that avoided the atheoretical cowardliness of the "rightist" and the tactless dogmatism of the "leftist." While Xi had eloquently identified the two dangers, he failed to provide a clear answer for how to maneuver between the two. It was precisely this ambiguity that would make Xi, and many others, vulnerable to charges of "line errors" in the soon-to-be-established People's Republic.

PART II **BUILDING THE NEW REGIME**

7
KING OF THE NORTHWEST

As Mao declared the founding of the People's Republic of China in Beijing on October 1, 1949, Xi listened to the ceremonies on the radio in Xi'an. The following day, he braved a rainstorm to address two hundred thousand people in celebration of the Communist triumph. "We declare to the world: We Chinese people have also stood up," he told the huge crowd. "We Chinese people have suffered all kinds of misery and all kinds of torment, and finally we have stood up. We Chinese people will never be humiliated again." Xi warned "American imperialists and reactionaries in every nation" that if they attempt to sabotage China's newfound independence and freedom, they will "definitely suffer a severe blow." The remaining Nationalist forces that refused to surrender will be "wiped out." Mao was now "the flag of the victory of the Chinese people."[1] The moment was certainly a heady one. Xi had nearly died on multiple occasions fighting for the revolution, and he had personally witnessed numerous disasters, many of which had been self-inflicted by leftist policies or party infighting on the final course to victory. Now, as the man in charge of the Northwest Bureau, Xi faced a new challenge: how to incorporate vast swathes of territory into the newly established People's Republic.

The thrill of victory soon faded among debates about how to properly build Communism and avoid degeneration among the party's own ranks. When the Communists seized Xi'an in May 1949, chaos ensued. "Bureaucratism" and "closed doorism"—Communist code words for inefficient, unresponsive government—were endemic. A summary report of the situation complained that the plan for moving into the city had been woefully insufficient.[2] In December 1950, an internal report warned that cadres, many of them new and untrained, were using beatings to achieve production quotas. Some were even tying up people and then suspending them in the air—holding the view that "when working, there must be three methods: the first is to beat, the second is to detain, and the third is to threaten."[3]

Xi tried desperately to prevent the party from "divorcing" itself from the masses. In May 1950, he argued that the biggest problem facing the party in the previous year had been "bureaucratism" and "commandism." Because the party did not yet have a chance to educate and reform itself, "many people still use the old style of the Nationalists." Cadres did not listen to criticism and did not explain to people their commands. Xi did not mince words: this poor work style was "the greatest threat."[4] The following January, he was still hammering away at the same theme. In a speech laying out the work ahead for the new year, Xi warned that meetings, decisions, notifications, and laws meant nothing if cadres did not spend time interacting with regular people and understanding their thinking. "Currently, we must create a foundation, and such a foundation is working with the masses." The problem was that new cadres simply did not know how to interact with civilians, while old cadres had been promoted to levels from which they did not meet with people on a regular basis.[5] "It is necessary to take care to correct the styles of issuing and monopolizing decision-making," Xi said that same month at a meeting on agricultural production in Shaanxi. "To avoid impetuosity, especially in terms of leading the masses in production, too much rashness is damaging." In Xi's mind, all cases in which people were forced, rather than persuaded, "experienced brutal failures."[6]

LAND REFORM AND THE SUPPRESSION OF COUNTERREVOLUTIONARIES CAMPAIGN

Yet brutality quickly manifested during more land reform and the Suppression of Counterrevolutionaries Campaign. In one village, forty households were not even left with mugs for tea because their homes had been ransacked so thoroughly. In another region, landlords and rich peasants regularly "suffered beatings, were forced to kneel, had their beards plucked out, and were stripped of their clothes." In Weinan County, twenty-two individuals died because of extreme punishment. Scores more in several counties committed suicide by hanging, jumping into wells, or cutting their own throats in the face of persecution.[7]

When Mao demanded more violence against supposed counterrevolutionaries, Xi did not resist. In February 1950, the Northwest Bureau reported that more than five hundred people had been executed during the previous two months. "When executing the plan of suppression," the report added, "it is necessary to be careful and decisions to execute should always be made at the provincial level." Mao disagreed and wrote a notification that decisions to execute should be made at the prefectural level to facilitate more killing.[8] In October, the internal party newspaper *Neibu cankao* reported that the Suppression of Counterrevolutionaries Campaign in Shaanxi was insufficiently radical.[9] The next month, Xi raised the temperature. "In the past, there were mistakes in how our lenient policy was applied." Since the beginning of the Korean War, "the whole country has seen hundreds of cases of active bandits and agents, so it is necessary to overcome the peaceful view among cadres."[10]

On March 3, 1951, at a meeting with the top party leadership in Gansu Province, Xi said it was necessary for them to "make the atmosphere a bit more tense." He suggested that the top leadership send people to the lower levels to "turn around their thinking" and make them understand the seriousness of the campaign. The war in Korea had created a newly charged atmosphere, and, according to Xi, everyone supported more killings. "We should use this external force to be brutal for a bit before May in the Han regions—to kill enough to create awe and terror," Xi said. "We should remember the past: every time a base area was created, didn't we kill a few bastards whom the peasants opposed? Otherwise, the dictatorship of workers and peasants and the creation of soviet power would have been simply impossible."[11]

Two days later, at another meeting in Gansu, Xi said, "It is necessary to remember that the more bad people whom we kill, the more they will be afraid." His words suggested that the party could somehow achieve a "right" number of executions:

> Revolution demands killing, but in the process of killing, it is still necessary to maintain a principle of caution: resolutely kill those who should be killed; don't kill those who could either be killed or not killed; and don't kill those who should not be killed. We need to expand propaganda to make people

understand that every killing should have an educational effect. Definitely do not kill in secret, but in terms of methods, it is necessary to remember not to create an atmosphere of mass killing. The walls of Xi'an are covered with notifications on killings. When people see them, it is offensive to the eyes.[12]

After returning to Xi'an, Xi used violent, even Stalinist language: "As long as reactionary forces exist inside and outside the country, the struggle will remain. Moreover, as the counterrevolutionary forces come closer to annihilation, the struggle will intensify and become more brutal. In every place where counterrevolutionary activities have been attacked, such activities will definitely become more secretive and frenzied." He warned that the Suppression Campaign had achieved some, but not enough, triumphs. "We have not done a good job yet," he said. "We have not suppressed enough yet."[13] In a report to Mao the next month, Xi said that there was "mass enthusiasm" for the crackdown on counterrevolutionaries, and, in fact, the masses wanted even more. The people, Xi wrote, felt that the killings that did take place were not brutal enough.[14]

Neibu cankao began publishing reports on the number of deaths. The party executed 119 people in Lanzhou—a number some cadres and civilians believed was too high, leading them to say, "Secretary Xi Zhongxun came to Lanzhou to order more executions."[15] Over the course of one year in the entire Northwest Region, more than five thousand individuals were arrested as enemy agents or bandits; twelve thousand agents and counterrevolutionaries were subjected to *guanxun*, a form of education during incarceration.[16]

In Gansu again, in August, Xi finally tried to rein in the campaign. He warned against "incorrectly giving a free hand, with indiscriminate beatings, indiscriminate struggle, and indiscriminate confiscation." He noted that the beatings had not been invented by the peasants—they were a reaction to their own sufferings that they themselves have experienced. Still, the peasants should understand that indiscriminate beatings were not beneficial. Even landlords should be treated differently based on the scale of their crimes. "In the land-reform struggle," he said, "it is necessary to fight under guidance and in an organized fashion." But he also engaged in a self-criticism about not using more violence earlier, explaining that in May 1950, the provincial leadership had adopted a cautious attitude because of resistance to the party in the non-Han areas. By the end of 1950, though, the situation had stabilized enough to adopt more aggressive policies. Xi apologized for not taking advantage of the new situation sooner and not accelerating the killings at the time: "Being a bit late does not mean being rightist, but when the leadership is late, the influence on the lower levels is very big; this is a mistake of the leadership."[17]

Soon after Xi's purge in 1962, land reform and the Suppression of Counterrevolutionaries Campaign during his tenure as leader in the Northwest were severely criticized as "incomplete," especially in his home Guanzhong region. That verdict led to the Democratic Revolution Remedial Class Campaign that labeled, in Guanzhong alone, 58,865 households as rich peasants, including the families of old party members.[18] When Hu Yaobang became first acting secretary of the Shaanxi Party Committee in November 1964, he attempted to end the mass arrests and the expulsions of party members, even saying, "Some things that occurred in the past are unclear. My opinion is to stop and cease debate." For these policies, Hu was persecuted so severely that he was forced to leave Shaanxi, and, during the Cultural Revolution, he was accused of having "formed a team" with the "nails hammered in Xi'an by the Xi Zhongxun antiparty clique."[19] In 1980, the Central Committee reversed the verdict that land reform and the Suppression of Counterrevolutionaries Campaign in the Northwest had been incomplete, noting that the execution of 0.48 per thousand was close to the number of 0.5 per thousand set in May 1951 by Beijing.[20]

THE THREE ANTIS

Land reform and the Suppression of Counterrevolutionaries Campaign were about transforming society. But how should party members act toward one another as members of a new ruling elite? In June 1951, Xi spoke about the issue of how to handle the party's internal contradictions. "Do not fear disputes during meetings," he said in Gansu, adding that the "truth becomes clearer the more it is debated." He warned not to "indiscriminately attach labels and draw conclusions too quickly." Party members should criticize each other's positions, not make personal attacks. "Leading and grasping the ideological struggle within the party," he went on, "is a form of art." Xi recognized that party members were afraid of being corrected because criticism had been taken too far in the past. "In the future, problems must be corrected, but it is necessary to pay attention to the method. It is necessary to be gentle and mild, to engage in concrete analysis and to use reasoning to persuade." In Xi's mind, 90 percent of all the party's tasks could be solved through effective political work among cadres.[21]

Yet Xi's "mild" approach soon faced a new challenge. In late 1951, Mao became increasingly concerned about degeneration among the party's ranks, which led to the so-called Three Antis Campaign against corruption, waste, and bureaucracy. In December, Xi reported that 30 percent of the cadres in the tax apparatus in the Tianshui region were corrupt. In Shaanxi, seven of the twenty-seven county-level heads of public security had engaged in illicit activities. "These facts show that indulgent, depraved thinking has indeed grown inside the party," he wrote. "Corrupt degeneration has already become the main threat. That is because in the victorious peaceful environment, bourgeois thinking and the old traditional bad habits have viciously attacked us." He blamed this turn of events on the rapid expansion of the party and the small number of old cadres, some of whom could not withstand the "new tests." In Xi's views, they had "themselves given up on the weapon of Marxist-Leninism and had been conquered by the sweet bullet of the enemy."[22]

Mao was elated. He forwarded Xi's report to the heads of the other regional bureaus and included a note of praise for Xi: "I believe your analysis, planning, and other opinions are all correct. The discussion meeting you held on December 8 was terrific. You held a meeting for one day and you already understand the situation. You grasped the heart of the issue. Now, when mobilizing the masses and expanding struggle, the bamboo is already cut, so it will be easy to split it all the way down."[23]

In January 1952, while in his office, Xi listened on the radio to the proceedings of a large public meeting declaring sentences for some individuals who had been accused of corruption. When Xi realized that seven convicts had been given sentences that were too heavy, he immediately summoned the leaders of the meeting and told them that it was inappropriate to think that just because of the ongoing campaign against corruption that heavy sentences were no big deal.[24] Yet that same month, on January 6, Xi complained that the Three Antis Campaign was still not aggressive enough: "We've just brushed the dust off ourselves a bit, but the dirt on our bodies has not been cleaned." The extent of corruption discovered by the campaign was "shocking." Xi called corrupt cadres "people without souls" who had been "infected by the poison of the exploiting class." He concluded his speech by describing corruption as "a germ in our blood" that needed to be expelled to stabilize the regime and to stay in touch with the masses.[25]

Some cadres found the campaign entirely unnecessary. *Neibu cankao* complained about incorrect thinking about the movement among cadres at all levels in the Northwest—party members believed that the Northwest had few, if any, cases of waste and corruption, partly because the Northwest had "special conditions." They were tired of repeated campaigns, and they believed they did not have to take this one seriously. Some of the complaints indicated that the lack of enthusiasm for fighting waste and corruption was based on a feeling that party members were still living less luxuriously than the Nationalists had and that, having played such a great role in the revolution, they deserved some enjoyment.[26] To combat these sensibilities, on the last day of January, Xi declared a ten-day campaign against "tigers," warning that if that was not enough, there would be a second and third campaign, or even a month-long campaign—whatever it took to achieve a complete victory.[27]

Although Mao was initially happy with Xi's performance that month, the mood of the chairman, whose mercurial nature could be hard to predict, shifted. On February 1, he sent a telegram to Xi and Zhang Zongxun, then vice-commander of the Northwest Military Region, complaining that they were not planning to spend all of February on the Three Antis Campaign and noting that the number of purged corrupt figures was still very low. Not a single "tiger" who had stolen more than 100 million yuan had been caught, and the chairman demanded a "budget for attacking tigers"—in other words, a concrete number of individuals to be targeted.[28]

On February 10, Mao wrote again, complaining that a plan to study staffing issues would only distract from the Three Antis: "The Northwest Military Region system is the least enthusiastic and has the fewest victories in the Three Antis struggle." "Why is it that you all are not enthusiastic about the Three Antis and instead before the Three Antis even reaches a climax, you become so enthusiastic about rectification?" Mao asked.[29] On February 17, Mao finally approved Xi's "budget" for "hitting tigers." But Mao told Xi to use the South Central Bureau's goal of eight thousand tigers—the highest goal in the country—as a reference for later increasing the Northwest Bureau's own target.[30] By May, the Northwest Region had discovered two hundred thousand corrupt individuals, including 120,000 in the military. The lower the level, the worse the abuse: in the provincial leadership, numbers reached 26 percent, while at the county level, 62 percent of all officials were implicated.[31]

Although the campaign helped arrest growing corruption within the party, it had devastating economic implications. Markets emptied and trade between cities and the countryside rapidly deteriorated. The Northwest Bureau introduced a series of policies in an attempt to continue the "struggle to strike tigers" while also bringing order back to the economy.[32] Nevertheless, waste continued to be a problem: in Shaanxi, a full year of medicine was wasted within six months because of a focus on the optics of the health campaign as opposed to really helping the people.[33] As in the other campaigns, the Three Antis often targeted innocent people. In Xinjiang, when forty-three cases were later reinvestigated, it was discovered that none of them held up to scrutiny. The numbers in the Shaanxi Military Region were even more shocking. Originally, 1,231 "tigers" were caught, but after several rounds of investigation, ultimately only 227 of those convictions remained.[34]

8

"POLITICAL MEANS, WITH MILITARY FORCE AS A SUPPLEMENT"

Ethnic Minorities in the Northwest

During the Yan'an era, Xi had already started to brush up against an issue on which he would spend much of the rest of his career: just exactly how the party should define its relationship with ethnic and religious minorities. A significant Muslim population lived in Guanzhong, and in his memoirs, Li Weihan praised Xi for arming a unit of Muslim Hui with sixteen rifles to fight against the Nationalists in the region.[1] In 1941, he established the Guanzhong Hui People's Japan Resistance and Save the Nation Branch Organization, which elected a local imam as its leader.[2]

Yet Xi was still a novice, and he was not always popular with the Hui. He endured criticism from the border-region leadership when Hui representatives from Guanzhong, who were attending a meeting in Yan'an, were "in a bad mood" because they felt their presence was forced. The border-region leadership also disapproved when Xi allowed a government employee to marry the Hui wife of a man who was away fighting against Japan. "Please immediately transfer this employee and convince the couple to end their love affair and marriage," the leadership ordered Xi.[3]

Xi also began a special relationship with the Mongolian community. He developed a close friendship with Ulanhu, a high-ranking party figure with Mongolian ancestry who had been trained in Moscow and traveled to Yan'an in 1938. Qi Xin studied together with Ulanhu's daughter Yun Shubi. In 1943, Yun went to her father to talk about a potential romantic partner. During the conversation, Xi walked into the room and jokingly said, "Father and daughter look so happy. Whom are they going to meet? Could it be me?" As Yun poured a glass of water for Xi, Ulanhu said his daughter had found a match. Xi asked if it was a man who had previously worked for him and then mysteriously said he had a "spy" keeping an eye on them. When Yun asked who the spy was, Xi laughed and said the "spy" had been Qi Xin. The relationship between Xi and Ulanhu was so cordial that Xi felt comfortable making fun of Ulanhu for paying too much attention to his wife, as Ulanhu allegedly would not "dare" go out to eat or to dance without his wife's permission.[4]

After Xi became head of the Northwest Bureau in 1945, he was in charge of party work in the Mongolian Yekejuu League north of Shaanxi, although the majority of Mongolian areas fell outside his purview. The Communists tried to partner with Zhang Wenxuan (Jamyang Sherob), a Mongolian military commander in Yekejuu's Otog Banner. Although the party wanted to support Zhang and rally Mongolians around his leadership, Xi instructed party cadres to also secretly seek control of the league. The need for subterfuge, Xi explained, was "to prevent Zhang from becoming suspicious and then distancing himself from us." This plan to use Zhang failed in January 1946, when Zhang lost a power struggle to his subordinates and committed suicide. Members of the Northwest Bureau leadership, including Xi, subsequently met to discuss the debacle. Given that the Communists had connections with the conspirators, "we had been prepared to stop this incident from occurring," but some cadres not only failed to enact party policy but even supported the coup. Zhang might have been dictatorial, but at least he was a Mongol and anti-Nationalist, so he should have been saved. The problem was that the Communists tried to control and reform the Mongols too quickly and too brazenly. "We cannot avoid responsibility for Zhang Wenxuan's suicide, and the implications are very bad," they concluded. The banner soon split into dueling factions.[5] Nevertheless, the Communists ultimately turned the situation around. In June 1948, Xi determined that the Han and Mongols would govern the Yekejuu League jointly and they would establish a wide United Front with many elements from Mongolian society. Red Guards from the Cultural Revolution era would later provide numerous quotes by cadres in Yekejuu who praised Xi's contribution to the region.[6]

As Communist forces marched from victory to victory throughout the region in the last years of the decade, the party understood that the vastness of the territory and the large population of non-Han residents in the Northwest required special attention. In August 1949, Mao instructed Peng Dehuai,

He Long, and Xi to combine military force with "political means." "We believe," Mao wrote, "that the Northwest Region is huge, the ethnic situation is extremely complicated, and our party has very few Hui cadres with authority." Therefore, Mao warned, "it is necessary to use political means, with military force as a supplement." Since they had military superiority, such a policy would be less costly, he explained.[7] Xi echoed those themes at a speech to Hui cadres graduating from a December 1949 training program: "Because the Northwest area has many ethnicities, minorities make up one-half of the population. If comrades are not willing to engage in ethnic work, that means they are not willing to work in the Northwest. If it can be said that the Northwest has a defining characteristic, that defining characteristic is ethnic work."[8]

Yet ethnic work was challenging. It was not popular among party cadres because many simply did not take ethnic issues seriously and saw United Front work as "eating and drinking, welcoming visitors and seeing them off."[9] As Xi noted in March 1951, cadres feared involvement in United Front work because it meant listening to forces outside the party, and such work was dangerous. "Our comrades in the party are always afraid of the 'rightist' hat, and as soon as the 'rightist' hat goes on, they become afraid," Xi said. But even Xi warned that United Front policies could go too far, noting that in some areas, "there is only unity and no struggle—that is 'rightist,'" while in other areas "there is only struggle and no unity—that is 'leftist.'"[10]

Still, the United Front component of Communist policy during those years was significant, and Xi demonstrated an ability to learn from these early experiences with the Hui, Uyghurs, Kazakhs, and Tibetans under his jurisdiction. Although he clearly believed that force and the threat of violence were necessary tools, he also revealed a sensitivity to the usefulness of other methods of control: gradual co-optation of local leaders and effective propaganda. Although the party did not give up on the goal of socialist transformation, cadres were at least occasionally aware of how rushed policies could be unnecessarily costly. In the early years of the People's Republic of China, securing the help of powerbrokers, not class struggle, was the priority.[11]

XI ZHONGXUN AND ISLAM

Even after the Nationalist presence was destroyed, the People's Liberation Army fought against numerous uprisings in the constituent provinces of the Northwest Bureau for years.[12] Throughout 1949, as Benno Weiner writes, "repeated lapses in Party and military discipline" were having "negative effects on the [party's] efforts to court Muslim communities" in Qinghai. In December, more than 1,700 fighters launched multiple assaults across Datong County. That same month, insurgents in Xunhua attacked a regiment, killing 104, including the party secretary.[13]

Two major incidents in neighboring Gansu Province especially caught the attention of the authorities. In Linxia, Han vigilantes were regularly robbing Muslim communities, and Hui were not given meaningful positions in local power structures. In October 1949, when the bodies of Muslims who had died in prison were left in the wilderness, up to five thousand Muslims resisted party rule with force. Then, in May 1950, two thousand Hui began resisting Communist encroachments in Pingliang. Hui fighters were able to resist for six months, allegedly killing more than one hundred cadres. The party leadership understood that its own actions had played a role in the uprising. On May 13, the Northwest Bureau criticized local cadres and warned that "one mouse can ruin a whole soup."[14] On June 17, Zhang Desheng, head of the Gansu Party Committee, blamed the Pingliang incident in part on a lack of vigilance against enemies, yet he also acknowledged that party cadres were not attentive enough to Hui customs. Cadres ate pork in Hui homes, threw pork in Hui wells, planted crops in Hui cemeteries, raised pigs in Hui schools, and even sent public-security officials to watch Hui reading the Koran.[15] Decades later, in 1982, Xi referred to these events: "In Gansu, two Hui rebellions erupted on a massive scale. On one occasion, Pingliang was occupied, and on another occasion, the number of casualties reached almost two thousand. How was this ultimately solved? Force was no good; it was necessary that patriotic high-ranking religious figures organize a group of representatives to peacefully resolve the situation."[16]

However, the following year, 1951, was even more violent. Some eight thousand people surrounded the Gansu city of Ningding, which led to a crackdown that caused more than one thousand deaths.[17] In neighboring Qinghai Province, three uprisings led to the deaths of almost ten thousand Hui.[18] Although the party, at one point, tried to offer Kazakh leader Osman Batur a post in either Urumqi or Altai, it later (incorrectly) decided that he was working for the Americans. He was marched through the streets of Urumqi and then shot in April.[19] Ironically, despite the brutal treatment of Batur, Xi was later accused of excessive mercy. Cultural Revolution materials claimed that Xi believed Batur was an "ethnic problem" and that he was not supported by either American or Nationalist agents. Xi supposedly made the case it was cheaper to buy off the rebels than to use resources to suppress them—a clear case of supposed "right opportunism."[20]

Large-scale fighting did not end until May 1953, when the forces of Muslim generals Ma Yuanxiang and Ma Liang were finally defeated. Given the sensitivity of the topic, reliable numbers of casualties are difficult to find. According to the memoirs of one general, between January 1950 and March 1951, the People's Liberation Army "eliminated" seventy-two thousand "bandits" through surrender, defeat, or death. Another source reports that by July 1953, the number of casualties was ninety thousand.[21]

But this does not mean that the party relied exclusively upon military force to achieve control over the Hui areas. In early April 1952, in Gansu's Xiji region, five to six thousand Hui, led by Ma Guo'ai, leader of the Sufi Jahriyya, rallied under the Nationalist flag and attacked the county capital. The party responded to the threat with intense military pressure, but after achieving a number of victories on the battlefield, it tried to win over the remaining insurgents by political means. Xi personally spoke to Ma Guo'ai's uncle Ma Zhenwu, a prominent nonparty leader, and promised that if Ma Guo'ai were to surrender, he would not be executed. The plan worked.[22] Xi would later regret that Ma Liang, who was defeated on the battlefield, "was not given a position, and the result was that the bandits were able to win him over."[23]

These alliances did not, however, represent a rejection of socialist transformation—they only meant doing it in a better way. In a report to Mao and the rest of the central leadership in April 1951, Xi wrote that some comrades in Gansu's Linxia area wanted to delay land reform because of contradictions between Han and Hui, "feudal strength," and lack of party cadres. However, Xi said, these skeptics "ignore another truth of Marxism-Leninism," which is that to truly solve ethnic problems, it is necessary to deepen the struggle against imperialism and feudalism. Instead of being happy with the status quo, Xi proposed to separate the ethnic minority's "laboring masses" from "feudal power." To achieve the goal of land reform in Linxia, Xi recommended working with prominent Hui and with "progressive forces," "making the area of attack as small as possible."[24] However, several months later, in November, Xi admitted that this pursuit of land reform in the Hui regions had created "lots of new problems." "It is necessary to be more careful," Xi said. "Any carelessness is intolerable." In minority areas, "everything must go through the local ethnic cadres, everything must rely on the self-mobilization of local ethnic peoples, and everything must be done on the basis of ethnic unity."[25]

PURGE OF THE XINJIANG LEADERSHIP

Although everyone in the leadership agreed that the party should not abandon its long-term goals, they did, at least occasionally, differ on how quickly it should move forward. In 1952, those differences manifested dramatically in a showdown on policy in Xinjiang's nomadic regions between the Northwest Bureau and the Xinjiang Subbureau. Xi won the contest, and the party boss of Xinjiang, Wang Zhen and his deputy, Deng Liqun, were fired from their positions. This affair has long been shrouded in mystery, and in an internal speech on party history, Deng Liqun told the authors of Wang Zhen's official biography not to write the entire truth.[26]

Xi certainly wanted to transform Xinjiang, and he was very worried about political trends in the region. In May 1951, he wrote to Mao, "I believe that it would be better to carry out land reform in Xinjiang sooner rather than later." Moreover, he felt that Xinjiang was more dangerous than Gansu, Ningxia, or Qinghai because of "conspiratorial sabotage by pan-Turkists with international backgrounds." Some party cadres in Xinjiang with "nationalist inclinations" wanted to establish an "independent nation." Their manner of speaking and behaving, according to Xi, was exactly to the imperialists' liking. Support for a Uyghur republic, similar to what the Central Asian republics enjoyed in the Soviet Union, was a violation of party policy, Xi believed.[27]

Nevertheless, Xi wanted to move cautiously. On May 4, 1952, he addressed a full session of the Northwest Bureau and argued that with regard to land reform in minority areas, it was necessary that local people act according to their own will, that minority cadres participate in the land reform, that struggles against minority landlords be led by minority people, and that local religious customs be protected. For Xi, the first priority was to form an alliance with important local personages and bring them on board with United Front work, and mobilizing the masses was only to be addressed later. "These two steps should not be turned around," he said.[28]

Xi used the expression "unite with feudalism to oppose feudalism" to describe this policy. Speaking in a conversational tone to make his case, he said that local minority intermediaries could "exchange" their support for land reform, or at least not oppose it, for "reform in a way that is a bit more peaceful." Thus, the party could "preserve a bit of feudalism to smash a lot of feudalism." Many Northwest cadres thought that such talk was too lenient, and some comrades in Beijing were even surprised by it. When one Beijing cadre asked a northwesterner involved in United Front work about the idea, the man responded, "Without an individual like Comrade Zhongxun, other people would probably not have dared to suggest it. Even some of us who work on drafting documents were surprised."[29]

In the nomadic regions, land reform was not to proceed, and religious institutions were to remain untouched. Xi again referenced the Pingliang incident, warning that "it was precisely propaganda in this area that had been problematic since it gave the reactionary landlords an opportunity to incite believers to engage in insurrection." After two years of campaigning against counterrevolutionaries and against corruption, some cadres concluded that United Front work was no longer necessary. But Xi reminded that "United Front work in the Northwest represents competition with the enemy over ethnic and religious affairs." He continued, "During the last two years, we came up with some valuable lessons regarding work in minority areas. These include the importance of both maintaining caution and progressing slowly. Any carelessness or recklessness will definitely create chaos. There have been many lessons about this."[30]

Drawing upon the themes of his May 4 speech, Xi wrote a special directive to the Xinjiang Subbureau on May 7. Although land reform was to proceed in Xinjiang, the nomadic areas were not to be included. Moreover, territory owned by mosques and Buddhist temples was not to be seized, as that would turn the "masses" against the party. The priority was to establish an "antifeudal United Front" as wide as possible. The nomadic leaders were to be forgiven for past "uprisings." The number of investigations into "cases" of "Greater Turkestan" and "Islamism" was to decline and all cases to be carefully inspected. Anyone already under arrest was to be swiftly released if no incriminating evidence was found.[31] Beijing approved of Xi's decisions. On May 8, Liu Shaoqi, in the name of the Central Committee, penned a notification on Xi's report on the May 4 Northwest Bureau meeting, saying it was "very good." Mao added, "You should all pay more attention to the issues raised." The notification was then forwarded to all central and regional bureaus.[32] On May 17, the party center affirmed Xi's May 7 special directive to Xinjiang.[33]

Yet Wang Zhen and Deng Liqun resisted the May 7 directive. They believed that they had a better understanding of local on-the-ground conditions.[34] Wang, as a military figure, might have disregarded Xi as only a civilian cadre. Wang had joined the party a year before Xi, and they were both candidate members of the Central Committee. Moreover, at this period in the party's history, the precise relationship between the subbureaus and regional bureaus was somewhat unclear. On the one hand, the subregions were supposed to pay attention to local conditions, but on the other hand, they could easily stumble into conflict with their direct superiors. In the South China Subbureau, Ye Jianying had pursued a more gradual form of land reform, reasoning that connections with the Chinese diaspora and the presence of patriotic businesspeople necessitated such an approach. On a trip to the capital in the early summer of 1952, Xi would learn that Beijing and the South Central Bureau had both accused Ye of "localism" and a "rightist" inclination.[35]

While Ye made a "rightist" mistake, Wang Zhen and Deng Liqun committed a "leftist" one. Deng showed Xi's May 4 speech to Wang and pointed out the differences with their own policies. The problem was that if the speech were to be published in Xinjiang, the differences would immediately become clear, but not publishing the speech would also be a bad decision as Xi was secretary of the Northwest Bureau. Wang, who was, in Deng's words, "a little too naïve," told Deng that he and Xi were "old brothers" who had fought together under Peng Dehuai, so it would be fine if they disagreed. "After arguing, we are still brothers and everything is OK," Wang said. Wang and Deng decided to cut Xi's words in the speech that were in obvious conflict with their policies. On May 26, Wang Zhen, ignoring signals from Xi'an and Beijing, ordered suppression of the party's enemies in the nomadic areas. The next day, *Xinjiang Daily* published Xi's May 4 speech—but without the original content about how no classes were to be identified and no one was to be struggled against in the nomadic areas.[36]

When Mao learned what had happened, he was livid. In early June, he met with Xi. Wang Zhen "had not asked for guidance and had not obeyed," Mao told him. He called Wang's behavior a serious breach of discipline. "If this were war, he would have been executed." In Mao's mind, Wang had "buried the results of all our hard work, so the punishment should be even worse than execution." On June 18, according to Mao's instructions, the Central Committee sent a telegram to the Xinjiang Subbureau and the Northwest

Bureau declaring that the May 26 suppression decision had been a mistake. More than one thousand people who had been arrested were to be freed. Deng Liqun was given the task of temporarily managing the daily affairs of the subbureau.[37]

In late June, a meeting was held in Beijing to address Wang's behavior. Xi's words were tough. He accused Wang of forcing his hand: "The mistake of the Xinjiang Subbureau led by Comrade Wang Zhen, especially the mistake of Comrade Wang Zhen, violated the guideline to move forward carefully. The subbureau and Wang Zhen used the method of struggle against the Northwest Bureau to force the Northwest Bureau to conform. They crudely and unreasonably attempted to split the Central Committee and the Northwest Bureau, arguing that the Central Committee was correct and the Northwest Bureau was 'rightist.'" Wang's failures, Xi continued, were "the summary result of a whole series of mistakes. Xinjiang has serious ethnic issues, but there has been no ethnic work. It has serious religious problems, but there has been no religious work."[38] Liu Shaoqi supported Xi, and he, too, accused Wang Zhen of trying to force the Northwest Bureau to submit to the subbureau and to force a split between the Northwest Bureau and the Central Committee.[39]

To enforce this line from Beijing, the Second Xinjiang Party Congress was held in Dihua (later renamed Urumqi) from July 15 to August 5, 1952. Xi delivered an opening speech in which he explained that the nomadic economy depended on herd owners. The regime's policy was not to destroy them but rather to unite with them. Local notables were to participate in government organs, and they were not to be arrested or killed. Armed force was to be used against uprisings only when it had been made clear that every political attempt to solve the problem had been exhausted. "As long as there is a shred of opportunity," Xi said, "it is necessary to continue our work of political persuasion." Drawing on Friedrich Engels, he argued that religion should not be considered a part of feudalism. Feudal forces used religion, but they did not create it. Therefore, he explained, religion would not disappear together with feudal exploitation (Mao would edit this part of Xi's speech before it was distributed, changing it to argue instead that religion would disappear after classes had been destroyed and the ability to control nature and society had been dramatically improved).[40]

The congress also signified a major policy shift in one of Wang Zhen's most treasured contributions: the creation of massive military-style agricultural and industrial enterprises that in later years would become known as *bingtuan*. By the summer of 1952, Xi had concluded that sending thousands of soldiers to engage in huge industrial projects was a mistake—big factories should be left to regional civilian authorities. The congress decided to turn over nineteen factories to the government and that, henceforth, the People's Liberation Army would confine itself to more limited agricultural endeavors. In a discussion of this history in 2007 by a group of former high-ranking *bingtuan* leaders, they angrily described the congress as a mistake and a setback.[41]

On July 17, Deng Liqun was forced to openly publish a self-criticism in *Xinjiang Daily*. He admitted to opposing the guidelines set by the Central Committee and the Northwest Bureau by editing Xi's May 4 speech. "This was a serious mistake of violating organizational discipline," he wrote. "It was a mistake of individualism against the party and against my superiors." Deng even accepted the charge that his "partyness" was "unclean." In the same issue of the newspaper, the full version of Xi's speech was published with an editorial note castigating Deng for his "severe mistake of lacking organizational discipline."[42] The critiques were humiliating, but Deng Liqun had demonstrated some character by taking the public-facing blame from Wang Zhen.

In a report sent to Mao in August, Xi stated that Wang Zhen had a correct understanding of his mistakes and had conducted a sincere criticism. In the future, "opposing Greater Turkestan" would no longer be used as a slogan, and Greater Turkestan organizations would no longer be targets for suppression. Those who supported a Greater Turkestan would be treated to long-term and patient education so as to persuade the vast majority. Han chauvinism was roundly condemned.[43]

Xi's intervention was not well received by the Xinjiang politburo. One cadre later wrote that everyone was thinking the following about Xi: "What the hell is going on? Who does this person think he is? How could he represent the party center? He's talking so big; how dare he fire our commander?" To signal their dissatisfaction with Xi, they all tried to share responsibility for Wang's alleged crimes.[44] Deng and Wang never forgot the humiliation. During the meetings, Deng lost ten kilograms.[45] At a small reception during the congress, an inebriated Wang Zhen raised his cup to Xi and said, "Zhongxun! We . . ." and then he burst into tears.[46]

Yet some evidence suggests that Xi also helped to protect Wang and

Deng from Mao's wrath. On the way back to Xi'an from Xinjiang, Xi said that it would be necessary to help find new work for Wang: "This guy is also an old comrade with significant military exploits; we can't beat him to death in one blow, right?" In early September, Xi went to Mao and told him that Wang understood his mistake and should be given a new opportunity. Because the incident was the result of friction between Xinjiang and the Northwest Bureau, Xi's intervention carried special weight, as it would have been awkward to transfer Wang elsewhere without Xi's permission.[47] Mao also twice demanded that Deng Liqun be expelled from the party for his actions in Xinjiang, but Xi merely transferred Deng to a lower-level position.[48]

XI AND PROMINENT TIBETAN FIGURES

The Northwest Bureau also included huge regions populated by Tibetans, and Xi developed an apparently genuine friendship with Apa Alo (Huang Zhengqing), the powerful Tibetan leader in control of the area surrounding the famous Labrang Temple in Gansu. In September 1949, Apa Alo defected from the Nationalists, and shortly thereafter, he went to Lanzhou, where Xi told him, "Even though this is the first time we are meeting, I have known of your situation for a long time. Although we were unable to connect, all is fine now, and we warmly welcome you." Xi, Apa Alo writes in his memoirs, "not only guided me and encouraged me in my work, but he also demonstrated great care with regard to my thinking and my life." Apa Alo describes heart-to-heart conversations as well as invitations to attend dance parties or to bathe at the Huaqing Hot Springs used by high-ranking leaders of the Chinese imperial dynasties. "We were on very intimate terms with each other," he asserts.[49]

Personal intimacy had political benefits. In January 1953, Apa Alo participated in the elimination of the anti-Communist forces led by Ma Liang in Gansu. Prior to leaving Xi'an, Xi met with Apa Alo. Apa Alo recalls that Xi praised him for his previous work for the party in Gansu. "On this trip, you should work even more bravely. The party believes in you. We have worked together for years, and you are very well understood," Xi said. He then warned Apa Alo, "Currently, Taiwan is looking for you everywhere. They are even dropping letters of appointment from the air. There are official seals, and there also is a radio station. After going to Gansu, if anyone tries to give them to you, do not be afraid. Accept them and report to the top." Indeed, after Apa Alo arrived in Gansu, he received documents from Chiang Kai-shek that bestowed on him "official" positions. But Xi continued to rely upon him.[50]

Xi's ability to manage party relations with another Tibetan figure, Wangchen Dondrup, head of the Nangra Tibetans in Qinghai, elicited the highest praise from Mao, who compared Xi to the famous ancient strategist Zhuge Liang.[51] For a brief period after the Communists entered the region, Wangchen Dondrup cooperated with the party. Yet, shortly after, he launched a rebellion. On seventeen separate occasions over a period of eighteen months, the party sent delegations to try to convince him and his small group of armed men to come into the fold. Repeatedly, the Northwest Bureau told the Qinghai authorities not to use force unless it was absolutely necessary. Some high-ranking members of the Qinghai Party Committee were upset about the Northwest Bureau's directives, and they believed Xi was demonstrating a "rightist" inclination. After the party's seventeenth attempt, in May 1952, the People's Liberation Army finally invaded Wangchen Dondrup's region, whereupon his forces collapsed, and in July, he surrendered. Despite his behavior, he was given the opportunity to write a self-criticism. Xi, meeting Wangchen Dondrup at a banquet, told the Tibetan that "only by following the party will the path be bright."[52]

Xi wrote a summary report on the experience that revealed his logic: "The Qinghai Nangra tribe had some relations with us after Liberation, but later things went wrong. Now, after a self-criticism, there is also the issue of us not having good policies, which caused the head of this tribe to rob people everywhere." Xi acknowledged that the use of co-optation instead of just violence was counterintuitive, but he also recognized the role of violence in the process of co-optation: "Doesn't this make you angry? How can it not be appropriate to attack? But we did not attack, and we slowly won him over. Because this is not an issue of annihilating him as one person. It would have been easy to kill him. More than ten thousand soldiers could have been sent there, then where would he run? But we did not do that because he, as one person, influenced many others. After our seventeen attempts did not work, we did attack. But this attack was in order to win him over."[53]

Out of all Xi's friendships with Muslim and Tibetan figures that began at this time, by far the most significant was his relationship with the tenth Panchen Lama. During the following several decades, this relationship would prove fateful not only for the two men themselves but also for the entire trajectory and tragedy of Tibetan history. Historically, the Panchen Lamas had lived at Tashilhunpo in Shigatse, located about 270 kilometers west of Lhasa. However, in 1923, after a dispute with the Dalai Lama, the ninth Panchen Lama fled Tibet. In June 1949, the tenth Panchen Lama, Choekyi Gyaltsen, was enthroned at Kumbum Monastery, near Xining, capital of Qinghai Province. Chiang Kai-shek's government tried to convince the tenth Panchen Lama to move to Taiwan, but the party was able to persuade the young Tibetan to remain, and the Northwest Bureau played a prominent role in those negotiations.[54]

The Northwest Bureau almost took the lead in seizing Lhasa. At first, Mao believed that Peng and Xi's First Field Army should be the main force entering Tibet, as military activities in the First Field Army's area of operation had ended. But Peng Dehuai asked Fan Ming, then head of the Northwest Bureau Liaison Office, to research the difficulties of such a mission. When Fan revealed how difficult it would be to move troops from Qinghai to Tibet, Peng suggested to Mao that the Southwest Military Region assume primary responsibility. In January 1950, Mao accepted Peng's advice and decided to task the Second Field Army under Liu Bocheng and Deng Xiaoping.[55] Just like what had happened in 1947 at the Xiaohe meeting, the glory of leading one of the party's most historic military campaigns once again slipped from Peng and Xi to Liu and Deng.

Yet the Northwest Bureau still hoped for a prominent role in the Communist presence in Tibet. In November 1950, the party center decided that the Northwest Bureau would manage Back Tibet (the area surrounding Shigatse), the Ali region, and the Panchen Lama, while the Southwest Bureau would primarily focus on Front Tibet, the Dalai Lama, and the area around Lhasa. In other words, Tibet was to be split into two parts, with figures from the Northwest Bureau controlling a giant swathe of the region and working closely with the Panchen Lama. Xi Zhongxun was put in charge of making the relevant preparations.[56] That same month, Xi suggested to Beijing that they should reject the Panchen Lama's request to return to Shigatse until matters were settled with the Dalai Lama.[57]

In December, Xi Zhongxun sent Fan Ming to Beijing to report on the Northwest Bureau's preparations to establish Back Tibet. However, the need to persuade the Dalai Lama not to flee the country forced Beijing to recalibrate its policies in favor of Liu and Deng's Southwest Bureau. In March or April, the party decided not to support two separate regions of equal status in Tibet after all. The Southwest Bureau would assume the primary role of managing all of Tibet, although the Northwest Bureau would still send some supplies and cadres to participate in the new government in Lhasa.[58] This change of plans deeply upset cadres in the Northwest Bureau.[59]

In April 1951, the Panchen Lama met with Xi on the way to Beijing. This was the first time the Panchen Lama, then only twelve-years old, ever met a high-ranking party official. According to Jambey Gyatso, who was close personally to the Panchen Lama, from that point on, "the Panchen Lama and Xi Zhongxun worked together for a long time and established a very good friendship. The Panchen Lama deeply respected Xi Zhongxun, and he treated him as his own good teacher and helpful friend. Whenever there were any problems, he would always speak with Xi and seek his advice."[60]

After the Panchen Lama returned home from the capital, Xi visited him at Kumbum Monastery on December 14. The Panchen Lama had prepared an extraordinary welcome. When Xi's delegation arrived, lines of monks and local laity reaching as long as two kilometers stood outside the ancient monastery to greet him. As Xi approached the monastery, drums started beating and the sound of a horn shook the valley. When Xi walked up the stone steps

FIGURE 4. Xi Zhongxun and the tenth Panchen Lama in Xi'an, April 1951. Source: *Xi Zhongxun huace*, 33.

covered in red carpet, a lama held an umbrella over his head as a sign of respect. After Xi took his seat, he told the Panchen Lama he had come as a representative of the party and of Mao to prepare an escort for him back to Shigatse. The Panchen Lama responded, "Without the party, without Chairman Mao, I could never return to Tibet." After a short break, Xi was given a tour. He visited the nearby tomb of Genghis Khan, which had been sent there from Japan-occupied Mongolia. Xi bowed three times, shocking the other Communists who were with him. But Xi brushed them off, saying that the Mongol was a "national hero, extraordinary, and great."[61]

The following day, the Panchen Lama traveled to the nearby provincial capital of Xining for a meeting at party headquarters. His coterie asked for more weapons and silver taels as provisions for the trip as well as for a sleeper car for the Panchen Lama. Xi, promising to do his best, referred to the Panchen Lama as *foye*, or "buddha." Again, Xi's generosity and patience surprised those party cadres who were present. Afterward, one journalist even told Xi that he had felt uncomfortable when Xi had used the word *foye*, but Xi said, "That's nothing; it is just part of our ethnic policy."[62]

On December 16, the Communists held a rally to commemorate the Panchen Lama's impending departure to Shigatse. The Panchen Lama again said his return would have been impossible without the party and Chairman Mao, and he referred to them as "the great emancipators of the Tibetans."[63] At the ceremony, the Panchen Lama bowed to Xi and gave him a *khata*, a traditional white Tibetan scarf. Xi held the Panchen Lama's hand and said, "I wish the *foye* a smooth trip and a victorious arrival."[64]

Two days later, Xi met with two officials who would be traveling with the Panchen Lama to Tibet. Xi said that it was too early to begin talking about opposing feudalism and that they should meet local notables as often as possible. He described the Panchen Lama as "a progressive force." "They were repressed in Tibet," he went on. "They cannot get by without relying on us. They will cooperate with us to the utmost." He continued, "Today they stand with us in terms of the general direction, which is right." This meant "Do not make too many demands with regard to their backwardness. As long as 'big similarities' are achieved, 'small differences' are OK. Of course there will be 'small differences.' Having 'small differences' is what the United Front is about. You should really pay attention to this. This exemplifies the boldness of our party's vision." Xi concluded with a plea to the Northwest cadres to get along with the Southwest cadres.[65]

Despite Xi's attentiveness to the Panchen Lama, serious problems undermined the expedition. Most of the cadres were Han Chinese who could not speak Tibetan and who did not understand Tibetan customs, and planning was poorly coordinated across different agencies. Dozens died, especially those among the Han who were not used to the cold weather. Xi's congratulatory telegram on their "victorious" passing through the Tanggula Mountains on the Qinghai-Tibet Plateau was not remembered fondly in one memoir: "That was not accurate; how could it be called a victory if so many people and livestock died?"[66] Xi also included a number of nonparty individuals in the team that escorted the Panchen Lama, including those who were members of other parties or who were former Nationalist officers and functionaries. More than a decade later, when he was purged from the leadership, this legacy was sullied. No longer praised for helping incorporate Tibet into the People's Republic, Xi was instead accused of leading more than one hundred counterrevolutionaries into Tibet.[67]

9
IDEOLOGY AND POWER POLITICS IN THE BEIJING OF THE EARLY PEOPLE'S REPUBLIC

In the early 1950s, Minister of Finance Bo Yibo went to see Mao Zedong. He found the chairman reading a report written by Xi on the situation in the Northwest. When Mao asked Bo what he thought of Xi, Bo answered that he was "a promising youth." Mao shook his head and said Xi was instead "a pure blue flame in the stove"—an expression that refers to Daoist priests making pills of immortality, meaning someone with extremely high talent. But his words also implied that Xi's prowess had been forged in the fires of the revolution—perhaps denoting the suffering he had experienced in 1935. Mao's words became famously associated with Xi.[1]

Soon thereafter, Mao brought Xi to Beijing to assume work as part of one of the most famous personnel reassignments in Chinese history, known as "the five horses entering the capital." Gao Gang, Rao Shushi, Deng Zihui, Deng Xiaoping, and Xi Zhongxun all left their positions as powerhouse figures in the regional bureaus to take up new positions in the capital. Mao's thinking was almost certainly related to worries that these figures were too dominant in their respective regions and might present a threat to centralized control. But they also could serve as useful new allies in Zhongnanhai.[2] Once again, Xi stood out due to his youth. Born in 1913, he was eight years younger than Gao Gang and nine years younger than Deng Xiaoping. Xi became vice-minister of the Culture and Education Committee, a member of the new State Planning Commission (which was chaired by his former leader Gao), and minister of propaganda.[3]

At a meeting in Xi'an prior to his departure, the leaders of the four provinces in the Northwest Bureau told Xi they did not want him to leave. Xi replied that he, too, did not want to depart, and he had said to Mao that he was not qualified to lead culture, education, and propaganda at a national level. But Mao, according to Xi, had told him that people in India could still tame snakes even though they appeared to be frightening. All that was necessary, according to Mao, was the humble study of the snake's nature. In his parting words, Xi still expressed doubts: "I am an uncouth person. I cannot speak in a roundabout way. Whether inside the party or outside the party, I seek truth from facts. I am frank and honest. I seek a situation in which everyone speaks their true thoughts. If I make a mistake, you criticize me; if you make a mistake, I criticize you. This is the principle by which I interact with everyone. Perhaps this means I lack the skill of leadership. I have many defects."[4]

MINISTER OF PROPAGANDA

As Xi had admitted to his colleagues in Xi'an, managing the party's role in ideology and culture was a curious assignment for someone who had ended his formal schooling at the age of fourteen. Decades later, during a private conversation, a close associate of Xi expressed bafflement that someone with so little education would manage the Ministry of Propaganda.[5] Xi requested a transfer on multiple occasions, believing he was not a good fit.[6] During the Cultural Revolution, he would claim he had actually spent little time managing the ministry. Instead, Vice-Minister of Propaganda Hu Qiaomu "took complete responsibility."[7] But it was an extraordinarily prestigious position. In 1953, An Ziwen, vice-minister of the Organization Department, proposed to Gao Gang that Liu Shaoqi should replace Xi, reasoning that the Ministry of Propaganda in the Soviet Union was the most important ministry and it was run directly by the first secretary.[8] Xi had been tasked with the weighty job of making the Chinese people learn to support Communism. As someone whose own life's path was sparked more by a novel than Marxist theory, Xi understood the power of literature and movies on the imagination.

Reaching the masses, however, was also a practical challenge. When he first arrived in the capital, there was a sense, in the ministry, that work was suffering from severe deficiencies. After consulting with Mao, Xi decided that these problems could be solved by "combatting bureaucratism." The main problem, according to Xi, was that cadres were trying to achieve too much too quickly. An earlier plan to end illiteracy within just a few years was scrapped, as the intensity of the drive, according to Xi's assistant at the time, was leading to mental illnesses and even suicides. The shift to a Soviet five-year university program was similarly abandoned because it was too ambitious, as neither students nor professors could work that hard and it had severely damaged their health.[9] When Mao read Xi's report on fighting bureaucratism, he forwarded it to the Central Committee and the Central Military Commission, praising it as a "very good report" that should be used as reference.[10]

Xi also impressed people working beneath him. After he complained about too many meetings and suggested a more efficient approach to cultural and education work, one senior cultural official, Ye Shengtao, commented in his diary, "It is obvious that he has a spirit of seeking truth from facts, and his behavior is laudable." At another meeting, Xi criticized the habit of forcing peasants to buy books. Xi's remarks made Ye think of the focus on the countryside "that had marked the beginning of each preceding dynasty."[11] Even Hu Qiaomu was impressed with Xi, telling one of Mao's secretaries that Xi's skills were "a cut above those of other people."[12]

Intellectuals also favored Xi's tenure as head of the Ministry of Propaganda, as it came at a time of relatively liberal policies. In October 1952, Zhou Enlai told Xi that governance of movies should be "political and ideological" rather than asserting direct leadership. Otherwise, movies would suffer from "monopolized thought."[13] In May 1953, Xi echoed these themes in a speech at the conclusion of the first meeting on movies in the People's Republic. He began by admitting that he was a "nonprofessional." In fact, "since coming to the party center, I have grasped very little, and I have seen few of our movies." But that did not prevent him from making sweeping statements.[14]

Xi's solution for China's serious lack of good cultural products was not centralized control or more exacting standards but rather the opposite. Unsurprisingly, Xi did speak of the need for the party leadership to "regularly inspire, guide, and help" authors, and he strongly criticized those individuals who said "I am an author and I experience life myself. I'll write on my own. Why do I need you to lead me?" But Xi clarified that leadership over cultural work should primarily be ideological and not by "administrative decree." He complained that when cultural products were problematic, no one took care to explain what exactly was wrong or to carefully measure the seriousness: "We just take an easy position: you are wrong, go back and experience real life." When faced with such a situation, authors lost hope in their ability to improve.

Xi warned that if standards were too high, no one would dare to write: "In terms of literature and art, we study the Soviet Union. We will absolutely never stop studying the method of socialist realism, and we must not waver. But that does not mean it is necessary for every author's product to reach the level of the Soviet Union, to completely reach the standards of socialist realism."[15]

Party leadership of cultural work should not be like "placing orders" in a factory, he continued. Cultural products were "ideological and political," meaning they were more "meticulous" than physical goods. "Our engineers are a higher level. They are ideological engineers, political engineers." Except in cases of "opposing the ideology of class enemies," "patient persuasion" should be used. The party should be like a "gardener who cultivates." Thus, authors could raise their pens like "living dragons and tigers."[16] Intellectuals were delighted. One author wrote in his diary that he and a friend had read Xi's speech on movies aloud to each other, and "we felt that even if we had half a day, we could not give a speech as lively and deep as Xi's."[17]

At a nationwide United Front work meeting in July 1953, Xi again used relatively measured language: "Our mission is to unite all of the old intellectuals, old cultural figures, and old doctors who can be used," he said, adding, "in order to transform, it is necessary first to unify." But cultural and education work was not following that principle, he complained. "Before unity is achieved, transformation starts; it pushes the target, especially high-ranking intellectuals. Before unity is achieved, they are scolded; that is no good." If the direction of the nation were positive and the nation's achievements significant, why would intellectuals not follow? he asked. In Xi's mind, if they did not come around on their own, it would be impossible for them to do so through force: "These people grew up for many years in a liberal environment; suddenly using rectification to solve their problems of thought is, in my mind, impossible."[18]

Yet like in so many other cases, Xi's "liberal" sensibilities were only relative, and they could swiftly change, as the case of the famous author Hu Feng demonstrates. In March 1954, Hu started the 280,000-word *Report on the Real Situation in Literature and Art since Liberation*, and, several months later, he submitted it directly to Xi. In the report, Hu Feng complained about the restrictions authors faced in terms of creativity and then, on a personal level, the fact that the party had not allowed him to work. He criticized Zhou Yang, vice-minister of propaganda and one of the party's leading cultural theorists and writers, for his "factional" behavior. Xi welcomed Hu Feng's approach, and the two engaged in a friendly discussion about the cultural world. When

Hu complained that his works were not getting reviewed, let alone published, Xi said, "That is not right, you should be commended for however much you do correctly understand." As their conversation was ending, Xi escorted Hu to the door of his office. When Hu returned home, he excitedly described how Xi had told him that "you should trust the party center. Submitting your opinion to the Central Committee was correct."[19]

Hu's report triggered decades of persecution. He had specifically asked that Xi not share the report with Zhou Yang, but Xi so did anyway. "At the time, we all thought that was laughable," high-ranking cultural figure Li Zhi recalled. "How could an opinion given to the Ministry of Propaganda not be shown to Zhou Yang!" Li believed that "Xi Zhongxun did not really understand the situation in the cultural world; he only knew that there were many opinions, so he thought having them discussed was very normal."[20] Zhou Yang used Hu's letter as a weapon against him. A nationwide campaign to criticize Hu was launched in early 1955, and later that year, Hu was arrested. He spent more than two decades in prison.[21]

By the end of Xi's tenure as minister of propaganda, he was already expressing a much more radical tone. Two months after Hu Feng submitted his report, Xi warned that because the party sought a "fundamental change" in society, it would be necessary to engage in a long struggle to replace capitalist thought with socialist thought "in people's brains." Meanwhile, capitalists would try to stop the progress of socialism at every step. Any difficulties on the road to socialism would be used by "the disgruntled" to libel and slander the party and to "mobilize the backward classes." The idea that a majority of businesspeople and industrial capitalists supported socialism was "outrageous talk." Even within the party, most cadres did not understand socialism, and they lacked a "sufficient recognition" that "class struggle" was still "extremely sharp and complicated," Xi said. Imperialists and capitalist reactionaries were still seeking to find sympathizers and agents within the party.[22] And one of those alleged traitors was Xi's old comrade Gao Gang, whose purge was the reason for this sudden shift in language.

THE FALL OF GAO GANG

Xi began to learn more about the dangers of politics at the party center immediately after arriving in Beijing. The first lesson was Mao's rough treatment of Zhou Enlai, something that Xi would see over and over in subsequent years. In August 1952, Xi joined the board of the party-committee secretaries of the Central People's Government, which was led by Zhou. The board reported to the party center while managing the various government organs, but it soon came under Mao's suspicions for acting too independently. In early 1953, *People's Daily* published a guideline on taxation that treated public and private enterprises equally. Mao, who was not informed about this ahead of time, was furious. In February, Zhou announced that government ministries would report directly to the party center, not to the board, which was thereafter dissolved. It was to facilitate this concentration of power at a higher level that Xi was placed in charge of cultural and education work. Xi was already witnessing firsthand the danger of any kind of initiative that had not been explicitly approved by the chairman.[23]

Xi had a front-row seat to the first great purge of the People's Republic: the so-called Gao Gang incident.[24] At the time of his defeat, Gao's power was awesome—he had been brought to Beijing from the Northeast, where he had fought against the Nationalists and helped support Peng Dehuai and the People's Liberation Army in Korea, to assume a number of influential positions, including chairman of the State Planning Commission. Gao's stature was so great that Xi believed that he was likely to be Mao's successor.[25]

Gao's improving position was related to Mao's increasing dissatisfaction with Liu Shaoqi, the second most powerful man in the party. In previous years, Liu had swung wildly between "leftist" (as in the 1948 land-reform debacle) and "rightist" positions, often not matching with Mao's own shifting inclinations. Mao also believed that Liu was not keeping him in the loop on important decisions. Gao, in contrast, impressed Mao by consistently holding similar views, so Mao decided to use Gao to put pressure on Liu.[26]

Gao had his own reasons to dislike Liu. In 1935, Gao, in the "Red area" of Northern Shaanxi, had suffered, along with Xi, at the hands of young, inexperienced Communist leaders who had been sent from the "White areas"—the cities controlled by the Nationalists. As early as 1941, Mao was seen as the embodiment of the correct line in the Red areas, while Liu was seen as a representative of the correct line in the White areas—an assessment that implied a certain amount of equality.[27] In 1953, Gao complained that White-area figures like Liu Shaoqi and Bo Yibo "love to make mistakes; they are a faction."[28] Gao believed that it was inappropriate to equate the historical contributions of the White-area cadres with those of the Red-area cadres. He also hoped that the northwesterners in particular would see their legacy affirmed: "When discussing revolution, it seems there is only the South; in the North, there are only riffraff and bandits."[29]

Significantly, despite their long relationship, Xi did not actively assist Gao in his machinations against Liu. Xi said that his caution stemmed from a belief that the new regime needed to "put unity first," or "our enemies will see us as a joke." Moreover, he cautioned, "We Northern Shaanxi comrades should not, at every turn, have this idea that Northern Shaanxi saved the party center," as that was an out-of-date view. "Right now, it's best that no one discuss this." He clearly appreciated the greater political capital of those individuals who knew Mao from the days of the Jiangxi Soviet: "Those comrades who came down from Jinggangshan can say a bit more; they have such capital. We, on the other hand, should not say too much, and even more so, we should not speak out."[30]

Xi stood out during this time for his wariness, especially at the Second Nationwide Organization Work Conference held in September and October 1953. Zhang Xiushan, a fellow northwesterner who had gone with Gao to the Northeast in 1945 and who was in charge of personnel in the region, made remarks critical of national-level cadre policy. Liu Shaoqi had encouraged Zhang Xiushan to speak out, and beforehand, Zhang had even reported to Mao. In his memoirs, Zhang would state that his behavior was fully legitimate according to party rules.[31]

Although the conference, and Zhang's speech, appeared to be a normal discussion of policy, Xi was savvy enough to understand things were not that simple. After Zhang spoke, Xi's former subordinate Fan Ming went to Xi's home. Xi referred to Zhang as "an old bandit." "I told him not to say anything, but he did so anyways," Xi said. "Now he has caused an upheaval." Worse, Zhang refused to take responsibility. "He slapped his ass and walked away," Xi said of Zhang, using an idiom that means he showed little concern for what he had done. Mao sent Xi and Zhu De to restore unity. Under pressure during the Cultural Revolution, Xi claimed (falsely) that Gao Gang had wanted to use the conference to remove An Ziwen as vice-head of the Organization Department and put his own people in charge. Yet Xi still refused to accept that he had "executed Gao Gang's black orders," claiming that Mao had met with him, Liu Shaoqi, and Deng Xiaoping on two occasions to give them direct guidance for the meeting.[32]

Although Gao did not try to use the Organization Work Conference to remove An Ziwen (one of many false charges Gao would face after he came under attack), Gao was acting incautiously during this period. While Mao had probably only wanted to warn Liu, Gao, believing Mao sought to remove the man, went too far. Gao even started to tell people about his private conversations with the chairman.[33] Gao's biggest mistake was reaching out to Deng Xiaoping, even though, according to Xi, "Gao looked down on Xiaoping."[34] Deng immediately betrayed Gao's confidence. We can only guess why Deng behaved in this way. Perhaps because of real concern about political unity? Skepticism about Gao Gang as an individual? Xi had his own views of the matter, believing that Deng was not pleased with Mao's promotion of Gao. "Xiaoping participated in the Long March, was boss of the Southwest Bureau," Gao's widow Li Liqun recalls Xi saying. "Do you really think he would submit to Gao Gang or could respect Gao Gang? Isn't it very clear?"[35]

Xi warned Gao about Chen Yun as well. Gao had worked with Chen in the Northeast, and they had met repeatedly to talk about elite politics after they both were transferred to Beijing. But when Deng Xiaoping went to complain to Mao, Chen betrayed Gao and supported Deng. Xi complained to Li Liqun that Gao had "treated Chen Yun like a saint." When Xi entered Gao's home after Gao came under attack, Xi began the conversation by saying, "Now you know what kind of person Chen Yun is!" Xi had warned Gao about individuals like Deng and Chen on numerous occasions, but Gao, in Xi's words, "didn't listen." "He simply lost his head" and "thought he was so great."[36]

Yet even Deng and Chen needed help to "expose" Gao's mistakes. Deng decided to go to Zhou Enlai, and Zhou went to report to the chairman, who, put on the spot, decided to give up on Gao. As Taiwanese historian Chung Yen-lin suggests, such an act reveals that Deng and Zhou not only shared a similarly dismal view of Gao but also were willing to jointly assume political risk by opposing an individual whom Mao, by all appearances, continued to favor. Together, Deng and Zhou successfully defeated a potentially dangerous opponent.[37] Xi had learned something about the premier. Zhou had moved against Gao even though, before his death, Gao would tell his secretary, Zhao Jialiang, that he had never opposed Zhou and had even refused an offer from Mao to replace the premier. When Zhao told Zhou about this conversation, Zhou was stunned into silence. Zhou then said, "Chairman Mao told me this. Chairman Mao says Gao Gang opposed Zhou." Nevertheless, before Gao killed himself, it was to Zhou that Gao wrote an emotional letter begging that the party care for his children.[38]

After a discussion meeting on Gao's "problems," Xi went to the home of

Li Liqun and wept. He had just seen a terrifying side to Zhou Enlai that he had not witnessed before. "I do not understand. The attitude at this discussion meeting toward Gao Gang was fierce. I never saw the premier like this." Zhou would not even give Gao an opportunity to explain. Xi reflected on how the treatment was "similar to that in 1935 when Zhu Lizhi and Guo Hongtao arrested us and wanted to kill us." "Who knows who else is going to be persecuted?" he wondered. "If it is to be death, we'll die together." He worried that Gao's personality was "too strong" to survive such humiliation.[39] Most of the charges ultimately brought against Gao were entirely fallacious, and the characterization and treatment of Gao's "crimes" as a manifestation of class struggle within the party was a prologue to the brutality of Chinese politics during the entire Mao era.[40]

Scattered evidence suggests Xi did take limited steps to help Gao once he was in trouble. According to a Cultural Revolution–era document, after realizing Mao was upset with him, Gao sent Xi to speak with Shi Zhe, who then was working as Mao's Russian translator. Other accusations against Xi for supporting Gao include helping to draft a letter from Gao to Mao, showing Peng Dehuai Gao's self-criticism, and pressuring fellow northwesterners, such as Zhang Xiushan and Wang Shitai, not to air too much of Gao's potentially dirty laundry. Xi was allegedly upset that Zhang had told Liu Shaoqi about Gao's sexual crimes from when Gao was in the Northeast. "Zhang Xiushan has no bones," Xi is said to have remarked. "During the purge [in 1935], as soon as he faced pressure, Zhang Xiushan would say anything. But now he is not even under pressure, and he speaks out."[41] During a Cultural Revolution struggle session, Xi admitted to helping write a letter to Mao, but he claimed to have rejected Gao's request to ask Shi Zhe for information.[42]

Most evidence, however, suggests that Xi did not take risks to defend Gao; on the contrary, he treated Gao roughly and tried to distance himself. According to a document written by Li Liqun during the Cultural Revolution, Xi advised Gao not to try to defend himself by implicating people like Peng Dehuai and Lin Biao who had supported Gao's criticisms of Liu Shaoqi. "They all hold power in the military," Xi reasoned. "If they are dragged in, things will be even worse."[43] This charge is partially corroborated by Xi's later acknowledgment that he destroyed material written by Li Liqun that touched upon Peng Dehuai. (Xi defended himself by saying he did not think the party intended to "expose" Peng at the time.)[44] At the Cultural Revolution struggle session, Xi claimed that he refused Gao's requests to talk with

Chen Yun and Peng Dehuai, knowing that Chen had been the one to expose Gao and that Peng was denying any relationship with Gao.[45]

Xi was right to be concerned about Gao's inability to survive the pressure. On February 17, Gao tried to shoot himself in the head. At the last moment, right before he was to pull the trigger, his secretary, Zhao Jialiang, lunged forward and knocked the nozzle of the gun away so that the bullet hit a wall. Gao's suicide attempt was reported to Zhou Enlai, who sent a delegation of northwesterners, including Xi, to meet with Gao. Gao tried to smile and said, "Welcome, welcome! Please sit, please sit!" Gao sat on his bed and the visitors sat on his couch. Then Xi suddenly said, "We are here representing the Central Committee to negotiate with you. Your mistakes are extremely serious, and today you added another mistake to the earlier ones! We are here to save you, but you must rein in at the brink of the precipice, stop all incorrect thinking and actions, and not make your mistakes worse. You must undergo a radical transformation and become a new person. Now the main task is to calm down and relax. With regard to a self-criticism, wait until you are calm, and then do a good job." Gao, while listening, bowed his head, cried, and nodded. Xi said, "Zhao Jialiang and the others saved you; they did the right thing, and you should thank them. You absolutely must not hate them and hold a grudge." Xi told Gao that henceforth he would be under "surveillance and reeducation through labor" and that he was forbidden from "suicide, murder, or fleeing." Xi criticized Gao for trying to kill himself: "How could you be so petty; it was only a discussion meeting, and people were just talking; if you had had a little forbearance, wouldn't it have passed?" The meeting ended with Gao promising to obey the party and thanking Zhao Jialiang for saving him. Xi and the others left without shaking hands with Gao. Gao sent Xi the latest draft of his self-criticism, but that very evening, Xi returned the document, complaining that Gao "did not say one word" about usurping the party and stealing power. Gao's face went red, and he struck himself in the temples. "Take it away, take it away!" After a night of thinking on it, Gao finally added this admission, though he qualified it by using terms that indicated it was not his intention to seize power. Gao complained to his wife that Xi had forced him to write the more damaging self-criticism against his will, but he also regretted not having listened to his friend in the first place. "Only now do I understand," Gao said.[46]

At a discussion meeting on Gao after this suicide attempt, Zhou Enlai described the action as representative of "self-alienation from the party and the people." The first charge Zhou leveled against Gao was "fabrication of party history." By saying that "the party appeared on the barrel of a gun" and that "the party was created by the military," Gao, according to Zhou, had tried to separate Mao's Red areas from Liu Shaoqi's White areas to win over several high-ranking military figures.[47] Xi found such charges ridiculous. Two months later, when Fan Ming, Xi's protégé, went to see Xi, Xi jumped up, picked up a copy of the *Selected Works of Mao Zedong*, and said, "Look, 'political power comes out of the barrel of a gun.' Those are the words of Chairman Mao: how can this be described as Gao Gang's problem?" Xi recognized that the suicide attempt had exacerbated Gao's situation. "The deal with this person, Gao Gang, is that he screwed everything up by firing that gun. Otherwise, after doing a few self-criticisms, he could have put his dick back in his pants," Xi said to Fan.[48]

Gao's second suicide attempt in August of that year, that time with sleeping pills, was successful. Li Liqun blamed Gao's death in part on Xi. According to Li, Zhou Enlai informed her that Mao had asked Xi to tell Gao that he could remain a member of the Central Committee and return to work in Shaanxi. Zhou asked if Xi had ever delivered the message. When Li said no, Zhou called Xi a coward. If Xi had delivered the message, Zhou suggested, Gao might not have died. When Li later asked Xi about why he had not conveyed Mao's message, Xi said that visiting Gao's home would have required asking for permission from Liu Shaoqi, Zhou Enlai, and Deng Xiaoping—"Could I dare to go? You should understand my situation and difficulties."[49] Although Xi's act seems cowardly, he had reason to fear that without written confirmation the chairman might change his mind.[50] Whatever the reason, Xi's decision hurt his prestige. "I think it was because Xi Zhongxun wanted to protect himself," one former Gao subordinate later told Li Liqun.[51]

Rumors spread that Xi even played a role in Gao's death. In 1962, Yang Jingren, Xi's former close associate, accused Xi of hiring someone to kill Gao.[52] In the mid-1960s, Mao made a callous statement that blamed Gao's suicide partly on hounding by Xi.[53] In 1984, Bo Yibo said he suspected that Gao's death had been "facilitated" by Xi (possibly referring to Xi's decision to break ties with Gao, thus causing Gao to lose hope).[54] Li Liqun believed that Mao came to suspect that Gao had not committed suicide but rather had been assassinated as part of a coverup.[55] Xi, however, blamed Li Liqun for Gao's death. Xi was furious with her for not heeding his warnings to take special care to prevent Gao from killing himself with sleeping pills.[56]

For unclear reasons, Mao decided to only purge Gao's associates from his period in Northeast China after 1945. Zhou singled out Xi for protection, saying at one meeting at Zhongnanhai, "Their activities caused certain extremely important comrades, for no apparent reason, to join them for a moment. It's good that they now understand. We welcome them back. Isn't Comrade Zhongxun sitting here?"[57] And Xi declared loyalty to Zhou. During a self-criticism in 1955, Xi included (false) claims that Gao had opposed the premier.[58] But Xi still had to write a successful self-criticism. That was a significant challenge—he had to appear to be sincere while not admitting too much, and he also had to deal with his own strong feelings. He was not sure what other people would say either. During a discussion meeting on the history of the Northwest in 1955, Xi summoned Fan Ming to his home to get their stories straight: "You see that I already did a self-criticism at the national party conference, and at the Northwest discussion meeting, no one had any problems with me. In your speech, don't get carried away," Xi said.[59]

Deng Xiaoping directly managed Xi's case, and Xi had to write three self-criticisms about his relationship with Gao before a full exoneration in 1955.[60] And Deng was tough. After the Cultural Revolution, Xi said to Li Liqun, "Deng Xiaoping kept saying to me, 'Gao Gang is like milking a cow, he doesn't talk. What did you say when you saw Gao?'"[61] Yet after Mao's death, Deng said he had tried to protect Xi: "A group of cadres from the Northwest was deliberately protected. Comrade Xi Zhongxun was deliberately brought from the Department of Propaganda to become secretary general of the State Council, and later he became vice-premier."[62]

As Deng said, Xi not only survived but also won increasingly prominent roles. In October 1954, he was made directly responsible for the twelve institutions run directly by the State Council. In May 1955, he was put in charge of all major issues that had not specifically been assigned to Zhou or Vice-Premiers Chen Yun and Chen Yi.[63] Xi's position included managing tiny details, such as planning meetings and approving the membership of delegations sent overseas, but he was also involved in major issues, such as the structure of State Council ministries and the national economic plans.[64] In 1955, the party gave Xi the extraordinary distinction of reciting the orders by Mao and Zhou bestowing honors and the rank of general on more than a thousand revolutionaries at a ceremony (Peng Zhen read the orders for marshals earlier that day).[65]

Yet Xi understood that Gao's fall was a setback for him. According to

Fan Ming's memoirs, Xi complained that, although he had achieved great triumphs in the Northwest, after Gao's fall, even Wang Zhen began to attack him for what had happened in Xinjiang in 1952.[66] Documents from the Cultural Revolution assert that Xi lost votes at the 1956 Eighth Party Congress when delegates from the Northeast argued that no one with ties to Gao should be allowed into the Central Committee, thus embittering Xi. "It was just these opinions—how badly did they decrease my votes?!" he asked. He certainly had reason to feel upset. At the 1945 Seventh Party Congress, Xi had been the youngest Central Committee candidate. In 1956, he finally entered the Central Committee, but he came in eighty-fourth place—a very weak performance for secretary general of the State Council. Even Hu Yaobang, who in 1949 was merely the director of a corps-level political department, was three spots ahead. In 1957, Xi said to Fan Ming, "Now, I am no longer the sun at twelve in the afternoon but rather the sun at two or three in the afternoon."[67]

FIGURE 5. Xi Zhongxun at the time of the Eighth Party Congress, 1956. Source: Zhonggong zhongyang dangshi yanjiushi, ed., *Xi Zhongxun huace* (Beijing: Zhonggong dangshi, 2013), 155.

10
THE PERILS OF INTIMACY AT HOME AND ABROAD

The Gao Gang affair was an emotionally devastating experience for Xi and also a chastening one. Yet, for a time, Xi's career was far from over. His most significant new tasks were outward-facing ones. On the international stage, he helped Beijing manage its relations with the Soviet Union. At home, he was one of the party's leading figures in United Front policy. These were weighty assignments. Not only was the Soviet Union China's most valuable strategic ally, but also Moscow was helping China rebuild after decades of war. And in the early years of the People's Republic, the Chinese Communist Party valued certain parties and unaffiliated intellectuals who remained after 1949. In 1957, Mao even briefly believed that they could help supervise the party and prevent it from deteriorating into a new bureaucratic caste separated from the masses.

Yet serving as the gateway to forces outside the party was dangerous work. While such relationships created the possibility for enlisting powerful allies, the Communists feared those same connections would be used in the other direction: to infiltrate and change the party itself. Winning people over required charming them, but such behavior could also be seen as "accommodationist." During periods of intense political radicalism, any connections with outsiders were suspect. Although Xi was purged from the leadership in 1962 for reasons mostly related to ambitious rivals, historical antagonisms, ideological radicalism, and Mao's suspicious nature, Xi's past with the Soviets and nonparty figures in China was included in the serious charges against him. He was labeled a Soviet spy and chief of an "antiparty clique" that sought to secretly control the United Front Work Department. Xi would have found such labels ridiculous: no evidence suggests he was particularly "pro-Soviet," let alone a spy, and, during the notorious Antirightist Campaign in 1957, he had helped to prepare an infamous party crackdown against prominent United Front targets.

XI AND THE OUTSIDE WORLD

Xi's interactions with foreigners during his younger years were limited. But that changed in 1944 when several Americans passed through his Suide subregion. Some of these individuals were members of the Dixie Mission, the American military's observer group sent to Communist-controlled areas, and others were journalists writing about the region for audiences back home. At the time, the Communists, hoping to woo Washington's support away from the Nationalists, went to great lengths to court them. It was an early lesson for Xi on how seriously the party took its relationship with outsiders. Before the journalists arrived, the entire subregion was ordered to disappear opium dens, prostitution, gambling, punks, and beggars. Roads were repaired, new slogans written, and garbage cleaned up. This preparation work was inspected several times, even including a trial visit by Suide cadres, and people were told to practice answering political questions.[1]

Dixie Mission officers such as David D. Barrett and Wilbur Peterkin later recalled how they were repeatedly feted in Suide City. In a letter home, Peterkin reports that he had met "all the big shots civil and military" during a feast in his honor. He was delighted by the gift of a heavy blanket, which is now at Stanford's Hoover Institution. When he attended a play, he noticed signs up in Chinese "welcoming the American friends."[2] The Americans were also shown propaganda plays, whose emotional power deeply impressed them. Journalist Harrison Forman wrote in his diary, "I came away with a sense of exhilaration. These boys are really fighters and not afraid of Japs. If only they had proper weapons."[3]

Yet Xi's most meaningful early relationships with foreigners would have been with Soviet representatives. The Soviets helped the First Field Army and the Northwest Bureau exert power over Xinjiang. Without Moscow's help, that process would have been much more difficult and drawn out. Xi met Soviets who were advising on railroad construction in the region.[4] In

December 1949, Xi and Peng Dehuai proposed to the Central Committee that Xinjiang and the Soviet Union should cooperate to develop resources in the province. A year later, Xi became head of the Northwest Chinese-Soviet Friendship Association.[5]

After moving to Beijing, Xi became involved in foreign policy at the national level. Zhou Enlai even recommended that Xi become minister of foreign affairs, but Xi was not interested. "I wouldn't work as minister of foreign affairs even if you expelled me from the party," Xi said, although he later bragged that Zhou almost always took him along when meeting foreign delegations.[6] Xi and Vice-Premier Chen Yi would decide which Foreign Ministry documents were to be forwarded to Zhou, and urgent documents sent directly to Zhou were also given to Xi and Chen for later review.[7] Xi was regularly copied on documents relating to Chinese foreign policy.[8]

The fall of Gao Gang was an early lesson about the dangers of close contacts with foreign powers. Gao was so close to the Soviet advisers in Manchuria in 1949 that he felt comfortable complaining to them about his colleagues in the party, something Mao learned about from Stalin.[9] Mao came to suspect Gao's ties with Moscow. In November 1956, Mao referred to some individuals who had "illicit relations with a foreign power" and who had provided intelligence to the Soviet Union—a clear reference to Gao.[10] The Soviets did not help allay suspicions. During a Moscow banquet attended by Deng Xiaoping in 1960, Nikita Khrushchev said, "Gao Gang is our friend, but you purged him. That was an unfriendly act toward us, but he is still our friend!"[11]

Tensions gradually grew over just how much China should learn from the Soviet Union. In the early years of the People's Republic, Beijing planned to copy the Soviet Union wholesale. Subsequently, Chinese leaders decided that they could not simply copy Soviet economic and political organization. The Soviet Twentieth Party Congress in February 1956, when Khrushchev gave his famous speech denouncing Stalin, deepened the feeling that China should not mechanistically study Moscow's experiences. In April 1956, Mao delivered the speech "On the Ten Major Relationships," which criticized certain Soviet approaches to economics and politics, especially the overconcentration of authority at the center. In response, on May 11, at a State Council Standing Committee meeting, Zhou established seven research groups, with Xi in charge of the comprehensive group. Xi managed the deliberations, which proceeded slowly as the participants did not feel prepared and differences persisted between central and local leaders.[12]

At a State Council Standing Committee meeting on July 17, 1956, Xi presented the results of the research on institutional reform to Zhou Enlai. The meeting decided that the heads of the small groups would go to Beidaihe—the summer resort for Beijing's elite—and they would send revised drafts of their research to Xi, who would then combine them into a first full draft. When Zhou finally presented the finished report to the full Eighth Party Congress in August, he explained that the purpose of the reform was to give greater freedom to local authorities, who were more responsive to the masses and better understood local conditions.[13]

As discussions on moving away from the Soviet model proceeded, Xi also warned that the era of blindly following Soviet experts was over. In June, Xi complained that although only 70 percent of Soviet advice should be adopted, the Soviets expected complete obedience. Xi identified a new guideline: "Do not hire when unneeded, when needed hire as few as possible, fully use the ones that are hired." He stated, "For our country to approach an advanced global scientific level within twelve years, it is necessary to primarily rely on a big group of experts whom we have trained ourselves; foreign experts can help us, but relying on the thinking of foreign experts is dangerous."[14]

However, that did not mean the Chinese no longer had anything to learn from the Soviets, and Xi identified those problems requiring correction. Some of the experts had "died, been poisoned, been injured, become ill, or been robbed." One jumped off a building in Harbin; another killed himself in Luoyang; still another died of disease in Lanzhou. Xi declared that those Soviet experts who were seriously ill should be immediately sent home, as "the political influence will be different if they die in China or elsewhere." He proposed establishing a system to identify Soviet experts who might be considering suicide "because people always show that they are going to attempt suicide ahead of time." Xi also warned that when Soviet experts behaved poorly, their Chinese counterparts were not to be too strict.[15]

In February 1959, Xi, who was born in October 1913, left China for the first time in his life. He led China's delegation to the Leipzig Trade Fair in East Germany.[16] In the early 1950s, Beijing had used the fair to break the Western embargo by importing goods through East Germany. By the middle of the decade, China had established enough direct ties with West Germany that the Leipzig Trade Fair lost favor, and Beijing even considered ending its participation. China's presence in 1958 was mainly to demonstrate political support for East Germany. Xi's presence in 1959 signified a renewed interest. The Chinese more than doubled their exhibition area to better showcase the Great Leap Forward, and they signed a massive trade deal with East Germany to import equipment. In the words of historian Tao Chen, "In short, the Chinese trade officials had rediscovered the Leipzig Trade Fair." Xi concluded that "the support of [East Germany] could not be changed."[17]

On March 19, Xi joined a delegation led by Zhu De, the head of the National People's Congress, to a country where recent developments had rocked the entire Communist world: Hungary. Less than three years earlier, a violent uprising triggered a Soviet invasion, a series of events that frightened leaders throughout the socialist bloc. Xi would have been intensely interested in what had gone wrong and how the Hungarians had fared in subsequent years. A memorandum on the trip in the Hungarian archives noted that the trip was a "great success," as evidenced by private and public comments by the Chinese on the quality of life in Hungary and repudiation of the 1956 events.[18]

On March 21, Zhou Enlai urged Zhu and Xi by telegram to hurry back for a Central Committee meeting in Shanghai. They could relax in Moscow for one day on the way home, but they should refuse a Soviet negotiation for an official visit.[19] On March 25, Zhu and Xi flew to Kyiv, where they were met at the airport by the first secretary of the Communist Party of Ukraine, Nikolai Podgornyi, and visited the Ukrainian Supreme Soviet. The Chinese toured monuments to the Red Army officers Nikolai Vatutin and Mykola Shchors (both statues would be removed after Russia's full-scale invasion of Ukraine in 2022). Xi also saw Stalin Square, later named European Square, and the Sophia Museum, a cathedral where religious services were illegal under Soviet rule. As souvenirs, Xi was given a figurine of a Cossack, a Ukrainian shirt, and a photo album of Kyiv.[20] The next day, the delegation briefly stopped in Moscow. The Chinese delegation was met at Vnukovo Airport by top Soviet leaders, including Aleksei Kosygin, chairman of Gosplan, and Iurii Andropov, who was in charge of the Department for Liaison with Communist and Workers' Parties and who had been Soviet ambassador to Hungary in 1956.[21] Andropov's experience in Budapest had been so harrowing that it would shape his conservative, repressive policies for decades as head of the KGB and then Soviet leader (his wife was so horrified by scenes of butchered Communists that she developed a lifelong mental illness).[22]

Three months later, Zhou Enlai placed the Foreign Experts Bureau directly under the leadership of Xi.[23] Xi was scheduled to again visit the Soviet Union in July, and Moscow had decided that Dmitrii Ustinov, the powerful deputy premier in charge of military-industrial issues, would host Xi and his delegation.[24] However, Xi had to delay that trip because of the second great purge in the history of the People's Republic after Gao Gang. This time the purge included Xi's former commander, Defense Minister Peng Dehuai.[25] Mao was incensed after Peng had written a letter criticizing certain aspects of the Great Leap Forward, and he suspected that Peng's criticisms had something to do with Soviet leader Nikita Khrushchev. In December, Mao even linked Moscow's alleged support for Gao Gang in 1953 to Peng's "subversive activities" at Lushan six years later.[26] Mao, in other words, had come to suspect that two of Xi's closest associates had committed treason.

These developments meant that Xi's rescheduled trip, which began at the end of August 1959, came at a deeply sensitive moment for him politically. It also occurred at a watershed moment in the Sino-Soviet alliance. On June 20, the Soviets had informed China that they would renege on a promise to support China's nuclear-weapons program.[27] And then an event unforeseen in both capitals threatened to push the alliance to its very limits. On August 25, People's Liberation Army forces killed one Indian soldier and wounded another at Longju, north of the McMahon Line (the 1914 border claimed by Delhi). It was on precisely the same day that Councilor Nikolai Sudarikov, a Soviet diplomat in Beijing, invited Xi to lead a government delegation to Moscow, and Anastas Mikoian proposed to the leadership that Vice-Chairman of the Soviet Council of Ministers Aleksandr Zasiad'ko would meet with Xi (by then, Ustinov was on vacation).[28]

On August 28, Xi met with Zasiad'ko in Moscow. Xi began the conversation by explaining that the delegation had not visited in July as planned because of the Lushan plenum. He informed his interlocutor that the Chinese would closely study Soviet achievements in industry so, in particular, that the imperialists could not claim China was uninterested in Soviet experiences. On his own initiative, Xi then (falsely) claimed that the recent Lushan plenum had solved the Great Leap Forward's overambitious goals. He explained that the party in China had long understood that the economic figures were inflated but an earlier reconsideration had been impossible because "this could have exerted an unfavorable influence on the activities of the masses." Xi then proceeded to sing the praises of the communes, which would ultimately lead to mass starvation. He "repeated the idea several times that the right opportunists, who had made use of the difficulties, opposed the high rates of socialist construction and the people's communes." Xi did admit the presence of "undue haste" in the construction of the communes and the principle of distribution, but he quickly claimed that Mao had noted such mistakes only a month after they occurred. Xi smiled and said, "Now, our Soviet comrades need not worry about us." "Naturally," said Xi, "we always studied the positive experience of the Soviet Union and the mistakes that the Soviet comrades had to fix. We knew of the possible consequences of such mistakes, but we were not able to avoid them."[29]

On August 28 and 29, the delegation visited the Exhibition of Achievements of National Economy, where it showed a special interest in the construction of apartments, energy, metallurgy, and agriculture.[30] On August 30, they went to the mausoleum of Vladimir Lenin and Joseph Stalin in Red Square (Khrushchev had yet to remove Stalin's body), and they placed wreaths with inscriptions dedicated to "the great leader and teacher of the proletarian revolution V. I. Lenin" and "the great Marxist-Leninist I. V. Stalin."[31] The next day, the delegation moved on to Kyiv, Xi's second trip to the city, and then to Czechoslovakia.[32]

Xi had told Zasiad'ko on August 28 that the delegation would return home on September 18. But on September 4, Zhou wrote to Xi with an order to end the overseas trip early. As soon as business in Czechoslovakia concluded, Zhou wanted Xi to immediately return to Moscow for just two more days. Xi was told to be back in China before September 12.[33] Two days after Zhou's telegram, the Chinese provided Soviet diplomats in Beijing with Beijing's version of what happened on the border with India.[34] On September 9, back in the Soviet Union, Xi's delegation again saw the Exhibition of Achievements of National Economy, where, this time, they spent three hours at the pavilion run by the Academy of Sciences and at a pavilion on the peaceful uses of nuclear energy. The Chinese viewed satellites, meteorological rocket models, electronic computing machines, miniatures of atomic power plants and the *Lenin* atomic icebreaker, and a uranium-fueled reactor.[35]

Despite this outward sign of business as usual, on that same day, Soviet chargé d'affaires Sergei Antonov provided the Chinese with a draft Soviet statement on the recent border clash between China and India that infuriated Beijing. Although China and the Soviet Union were treaty allies, the statement took a neutral position, declaring the incident "certainly deplorable" and affirming that the Soviet Union "maintains friendly relations both with the People's Republic of China and the Republic of India." Foreign Minister Chen Yi tried to convince the Soviets to change or delay the document. Although the Soviets had indicated that the statement was planned for release the following day, it was released by TASS (Telegrafnoe agentstvo Sovetskogo Soiuza) at seven o'clock Moscow time that same night instead.[36]

The following day, Xi's delegation traveled to the Kremlin, where Xi met again with Zasiad'ko. Xi's delegation also spent time sightseeing at Lenin's old office and apartment in the Grand Kremlin Palace.[37] That evening, at a reception at the embassy, Xi hosted Zasiad'ko and described the trip as "meaningful and difficult to forget." "The Chinese people thank the assistance from our Soviet big brother from the bottom of our hearts," he said.[38] But behind the scenes, the Chinese and Russians were trying to manage a full-blown crisis in their relationship. As Xi was meeting Zasiad'ko in the Kremlin and touring Moscow, the Chinese embassy finished a report (with a copy to Xi) that furiously condemned the TASS statement for "lacking a clear, principled stance." Moscow, the Chinese concluded, was afraid of "offending India" and wanted to avoid trouble during the upcoming meeting between Khrushchev and President Dwight Eisenhower. Late that night, on September 10, Xi and a vice-minister of the First Ministry of Machine Building left for home.[39] One savvy East German journalist publicly raised the likelihood that Xi's departure was related to the TASS statement.[40] When Khrushchev met Mao in Beijing in early October later that year, Mao rebuked him: "The TASS announcement made all the imperialists happy."[41]

Still, for a time, Beijing and Moscow tried to stop the relationship from completely collapsing. On the same trip to Beijing, Khrushchev brought gifts, and Xi received a Temp-3 television, a selection of perfumes, and a picture album of Moscow.[42] In January 1960, he hosted some of the Soviet experts for a Lunar New Year celebration and thanked them: "Socialist construction in our country is flying ahead, and this is inseparable from the selfless support the Soviet Union has given our country."[43] In April, the Foreign Experts Bureau reported that work with experts had "achieved big progress."[44] In May, during a private conversation with the Soviet chargé d'affaires, Xi praised the recent Fifth Session of the Supreme Soviet in extraordinarily friendly terms. "The decisions taken at the session have colossal political significance not only for the Soviet Union, China, and the countries of the socialist camp, but for all people of the world as well," Xi said. "The Soviet Union is a shining example of tireless concern for the welfare of the people. Khrushchev's report and the decisions of the session are wise."[45]

Yet the Soviets were worried they were not getting good press in China. One Soviet embassy document complained that, in early May, Xi had gone to Shenyang with the ambassador from Czechoslovakia to give a speech at a ceremony marking the naming of a factory—christened Chinese-Czechoslovak Friendship. In his speech, Xi praised the significance of Czechoslovak technological assistance many times, which the Soviet embassy saw as an example of the Chinese emphasizing the Eastern European countries at the expense of Moscow.[46]

Despite the deteriorating relationship, in April 1960, more than 1,500 Soviets still remained in China. A report submitted that month to Chen Yi and to Xi noted that the Soviets working in China were in a better mood and they better understood Chinese policies. The situation was far from perfect, however. Many experts felt ignored during the relentless political campaigns,

FIGURE 6. Xi Zhongxun hosts a banquet for Soviet specialists, January 1960. Source: Zhonggong zhongyang dangshi yanjiushi, *Xi Zhongxun huace*, 200.

and they were afraid the Chinese would accuse them of being too "conservative"—the Soviets were especially concerned they would be targeted by big-character posters. Moreover, the Soviet experts—even those helping China's nuclear program—felt they were not treated as well as they deserved. The leadership approved proposals to improve matters.[47]

The report suggested that the Chinese still saw great usefulness in Soviet assistance. Yet in the summer of 1960, Khrushchev, furious at China's criticisms of the Soviet Union, decided to remove them all, thus ending Xi's role in managing their presence there. In a letter of explanation provided to the Chinese on July 16, Moscow accused the Chinese of treating the Soviet experts disrespectfully, trying to convince them to oppose Moscow, and even spying on them—all claims that Chinese historian Shen Zhihua shows were either false or exaggerated. The specialists were told to leave immediately. The Chinese were both stunned and outraged by this sudden decision and hoped that Moscow would change its mind. Around July 24, Xi delivered a series of directives: do not discuss politics with the experts so the Soviets will not be able to "exploit the situation," take Soviet criticisms seriously, and, if there were any significant new developments, immediately and secretly inform the State Council. On July 31, the Chinese Foreign Ministry officially urged Moscow to reconsider. But at the same time, Xi was put in charge of a committee to guide their departure, and, on August 1, the State Council decided that the experts would be given a warm farewell in hopes that after they returned to the Soviet Union, they would have positive views of China.[48]

The next month, September, Xi briefly passed through Moscow on the way to the funeral of Wilhelm Pieck, the president of the German Democratic Republic. Kosygin treated Xi to a meal, during which he asked Xi about the situation in China's countryside and told him, "According to decades of experience in the Soviet Union, material incentives are very important." That night, Xi arrived in Berlin, where he was treated coldly by the East Germans. One member of Xi's delegation later blamed the Soviet Union. The East Germans "were not friendly enough," he wrote in his memoirs. "Their reception of us was at a low standard. It was clear to everyone that they were doing this for the Soviets." Yet the East Germans had their own reason to be upset with Beijing. China was failing to meet contractual obligations because of the Great Leap Forward, and Beijing had used the spring 1960 Leipzig Trade Fair solely to flaunt the supposed superiority of the Chinese system, which both infuriated and frightened their hosts. In any case, Beijing was so upset that they demanded no future delegations to Berlin be treated the same way.[49]

The East Germans had humiliated Xi, but, over the following months, their economic situation deteriorated, and more refugees fled west. In January 1961, they sent Hermann Matern, a politburo member, to China to ask for butter, as Beijing had finally limited food exports to fight the famine caused by the Great Leap Forward. The Chinese, unhappy at the sudden imposition, had Xi meet him at the airport and host him for dinner. Matern acknowledged that the standard of living in his country was the highest among socialist nations, but, he told Xi, the point of comparison for its citizens was West Germany, not China or the Soviet Union, so many East Germans were running away. Xi, who knew that millions of his compatriots were dying from hunger, listened as Matern told him that if East Germany could achieve a better life for its people than West Germany, that would have a "huge influence" on Western Europe. Matern got nowhere with Xi. Matern said he had a letter he wanted to give to Mao, but Xi said he would take it—a sign that Mao would not meet the German. When Zhou met Matern two days later, the premier said, "If you insist on demanding the undelivered goods, there will be mass starvation in China." "You're talking and thinking in a certain way, that is: Germans above all others. I can't accept it," Zhou warned. Matern did not get more butter, but he did get something else. Khrushchev, worried about losing the Germans to China after Matern's visit, gave up on his reticence and agreed to supply the East Germans with more goods.[50]

Publicly, Xi continued to describe the Sino-Soviet alliance in warm terms. On July 26, 1962, at a reception held by the Cuban ambassador, he expressed support for the recent Soviet nuclear tests.[51] The next month, at a cocktail party celebrating the safe return of a Soviet spacecraft, Xi said that the Soviet victories in conquering space once again demonstrated the superiority of the socialist system over the capitalist system and Soviet triumphs were leading to "great horror and depression" in the United States.[52] But soon after the reception, Xi would be removed from the leadership. When he returned to power sixteen years later, it would be to lead Guangdong Province—where the failures of socialism and the virtues of capitalism could not be more visible.

Just like his close colleagues Gao Gang and Peng Dehuai, Xi was accused of illicit relations with Moscow. The idea was fanciful: as one former high-ranking official in the Chinese Foreign Ministry wrote in his memoirs, when it came to foreign policy, everyone just did what Mao wanted: "There were never two voices."[53] Nevertheless, Xi was charged with serving Moscow's interests. One secretary who betrayed Xi claimed that his boss had asked him to copy by hand a secret document so it could be given to the Soviet ambassador.[54] Xi had been treated roughly on his trip to Berlin, yet Xi came under suspicion for his relations with East Germany as well. According to one Cultural Revolution document, Xi asked to visit the border with West Berlin, but he was not given permission. He went anyway, which caused a commotion among his minders, who asked him to leave. After returning home, the Germans reportedly gave him equipment to make a photography darkroom, and he had his secretary study the process. "What was the purpose?" the document asked. "It deserves deep thinking."[55] The main reason for Xi's purge, however, would not be any supposedly suspicious relations with foreign powers. Instead, it was Mao's growing fear of "revisionism" at home—a worry initially sparked by his conclusion that Moscow's insufficiently aggressive position toward the West was the result of political degradation within the Communist Party of the Soviet Union.

XI AND THE UNITED FRONT

Extended exposure to foreigners was dangerous but so was United Front work, which included regularly consulting with former Nationalist leaders, the "democratic" parties under Communist control, and intellectuals. Although they were fellow Chinese, the party still considered them outsiders. When Xi told Zhou he did not want to lead the Foreign Ministry, he offered instead to become Zhou's "minister of Internal Foreign Affairs"—meaning the United Front.[56]

To work well, such "diplomacy" required a personal touch. Xi was particularly close to Zhang Zhizhong, who had once been a confidante of Chiang Kai-shek and later played a key role convincing the Nationalist leadership in Xinjiang to surrender to the Communists. Zhang felt comfortable discussing whatever was on his mind with Xi, and he would regularly visit Xi's home without invitation.[57] When Zhou was busy, he would send Xi to meet with Puyi, the last emperor of the Qing dynasty—the father of China's future leader courting its last emperor.[58] Xi's mahjong buddies included many prominent nonparty figures. He continued his habit of cheating—and when his opponents caught him, they would complain to his wife. But Xi apparently never gave up the habit, and he would hum Shaanxi opera when he played well.[59]

Despite Xi's deserved fame for his close relationship with United Front targets, that history is tarnished by his role during the Antirightist Campaign. The origins of the campaign, one of the most notorious in China's history, lay in Mao's momentary hope in the spring of 1957 that intellectuals and non-Communist officials would criticize the party to prevent it from deteriorating into a bureaucratic body that was out of touch with the needs of society. Mao had concluded that this "soft" approach would help the party avoid the kind of insurrection recently witnessed in Hungary.[60] Although some scholars have argued that Mao was planning a trap from the start, the evidence suggests that initially Mao had sincerely hoped that these individuals would indeed help supervise the party during the so-called Hundred Flowers Campaign.[61]

But the intellectuals were more critical than Mao had expected, and he soon turned against them. On May 14 and 16, 1957, two secret notifications called on newspapers to publish the views of the intellectuals "so the masses will see their true face"—a clear sign that Mao had begun to plot. The two documents were distributed broadly, and Xi almost certainly saw them. Xi encouraged nonparty officials and intellectuals to speak out when he already knew a crackdown was coming.[62]

In late May, as secretary of the State Council, he began a series of meetings with nonparty leaders. At the first session, he invited more than thirty individuals who worked in the State Council's Legal System Bureau, Office of Consultants, and Secretaries Office. He began by requiring the participants to dispel any doubts and raise whatever opinions they had. The participants immediately started arguing with one another. One nonparty State Council councilor complained that the leaders at the State Council, including Xi, rarely met with their subordinates. Other participants criticized the United Front for only working with high-ranking officials.[63]

Over the next few days, Xi held several more such meetings in which State Council councilors who were not Communists issued serious criticisms.[64] At meetings not hosted by Xi, his work at the State Council was criticized as well—on June 3, a specialist in the Ministry of Electric Power complained that Xi had given a speech on managing petitions, but "the State Council itself is bad at managing petitions. Theory is divorced from reality."[65] At a meeting in Tianjin, Zhang Bojun, one of the most prominent nonparty figures, complained that "Xi Zhongxun says the democratic parties should only be involved in technical work and they should not engage in political thought work."[66]

For a very brief period, partly with Xi's encouragement, nonparty officials and intellectuals were enjoying a moment of unprecedented freedoms. But on June 6, at a meeting chaired by Xi, the atmosphere suddenly changed for the entire country. The session began with State Council Assistant Secretary Lu Yuwen, a man who worked directly under Xi, describing an anonymous threatening letter he had received. The letter warned Lu, who was always strongly proparty, to "turn back as soon as possible," or "you will not be spared." The party "will ultimately be annihilated" if it continues to "only acknowledge people like you."[67]

At the time, some believed that the letter was fake, but later it was determined by security officials that it had been written by a student in the History Department of Peking University. In any case, Mao used this incident at a meeting run by Xi as an excuse to launch a counterattack. Mao told Wu Lengxi, editor of *People's Daily*, that he had been looking for an excuse to begin for days; the anonymous letter that was brought to Xi's attention was perfect for his purposes. On June 8, *People's Daily* published an article headlined "Why Is This?," marking the start of the Antirightist Campaign.[68] The new atmosphere was palpable two days later when Xi held another meeting with nonparty officials. Li Zhonggong added that he, too, had received a threatening anonymous letter. Xi interrupted to say he had received anonymous letters as well. "Keep your eyes open at all times and in all places," Xi told them ominously. "Your whole family too."[69]

On June 19, at his last meeting with nonparty officials, Xi delivered the concluding speech. Xi thanked the participants for raising opinions on a wide variety of issues, including the work of the State Council. "This is very good; we sincerely welcome this," adding that "there is nothing strange" about noting the numerous mistakes and deficiencies. He continued,

> At the discussion meetings, there were also some incorrect opinions, even some opinions that left the position of socialism and went in the direction of opposing socialism. But even this is beneficial for us. It is also beneficial for those who revealed their incorrect thinking. Both correct and incorrect opinions have the function of enlightenment and education to help the party

undergo rectification. What the party does not welcome is antisocialist opinions. Other than that, as long as the opinions are good for our work and good for socialist construction, even if things are put a little too strongly, we welcome them. Of course, we also understand that not everyone can put things in exactly the right way. It is impossible for things to be put just right with regard to every issue. It is normal if words are said too strongly or are exaggerated.[70]

The encouraging tone of Xi's remarks was deeply misleading. The massive crackdown during the Antirightist Campaign would not distinguish between "antisocialist opinions" and "things that are put a little too strongly."

A prominent target of the campaign and one of the founders of the All-China Federation of Industry and Commerce, Zhang Naiqi, saw Xi as a potential savior. On July 22, Zhang wrote directly to Xi, claiming that he had never planned to oppose the party or socialism and requesting that the State Council investigate. However, his letter achieved nothing. In January of the next year, Zhang met with Zhou Enlai and Xi together. Xi watched as Zhou told a stunned Zhang that the party had decided to remove him from all of his positions. Zhou was blunt, almost mocking. When Zhang said there was no point for him to attend the State Council meeting held to discuss his punishment since the party had already made up its mind, Zhou responded, "That's also fine. If there is to be a debate, we are in the majority, and you cannot convince us." When Zhang promised to "forge" himself better so that he could return to work in the future, Zhou laughed and said, "You sure are optimistic."[71]

When the party finally decided to move against nonparty leaders and intellectuals, Xi clearly played a role in helping them dig a hole for themselves. But in a private conversation in the 1980s, Xi claimed to have protected several nonparty figures like Zhang Zhizhong. He also tried to take credit for making the Antirightist Campaign less serious than it might have been. The "rightists" were divided into multiple categories of seriousness, like "extreme rightist" and "middle rightist." According to Xi, he had suggested that the middle rightists not be "labeled" so they would not suffer even more serious consequences. His proposal was accepted.[72]

Xi also tried to help Yu Xinqing, who had graduated from Columbia University and later worked as a pastor for the troops of warlord Feng Yuxiang, the so-called Christian General. After 1949, Yu served in several significant government positions, including under Xi's leadership as head of the Department of Government Offices Administration. Although Yu was in danger of being labeled a rightist in 1957, Xi protected him, arguing that his contribution to the Communist victory and his work as head of a department made up for his mistakes. Yu committed suicide during the Cultural Revolution. Xi later spoke of Yu's death: "At that time, when people were persecuted, shit was simply dumped on their heads! When it comes to democratic personages, if you don't respect them, how can they respect you?"[73]

The Antirightist Campaign was primarily targeted against figures without party membership—except for at the party school, which employed Xi's wife, Qi Xin, as an assistant researcher and lecturer.[74] The party school was a place where, for a time, people felt comfortable expressing somewhat critical ideas, but when Mao heard a report on the school in mid-June, he concluded that "rightist" thinking had infected the party itself. Deng Xiaoping led the charge, and Qi Xin would have witnessed what one employee at the school at the time called "a battlefield of class struggle." Of the people studying there, 4.12 percent were ultimately declared rightists as well as 6.4 percent of the teachers. Three of them committed suicide.[75]

The Antirightist Campaign was doubly embarrassing for Xi. He had helped set the trap, and then he participated in the persecution of nonparty colleagues with whom he had developed close relations. But the reason why Xi had been tasked with cultivating such people was to win them over to the party's cause; when their criticisms went beyond what the party expected, it almost certainly raised questions about Xi's own effectiveness. At the Ninth National United Front Work Meeting in December 1957, participants argued that nonparty officials had been given too much power and respect in the new People's Republic. Some individuals even wanted to end United Front work altogether, believing that it was to blame for the appearance of so many "rightists."[76]

United Front work suffered during the years of the Great Leap Forward, but the party briefly tried to overcome its "leftist" excesses in the spring and early summer of 1962.[77] This brief period of rectification decisively ended with the Tenth Plenum of the Eighth Party Congress later that year when Mao returned to his fixation on class struggle. That plenum saw Xi come under attack for several reasons, including his role in United Front work.[78] In 1964, Mao declared that the United Front Work Department had been "in contact with the bourgeois class," and yet "some people there do not speak of class struggle." By the beginning of the Cultural Revolution, the department was denounced as a "revisionist headquarters."[79]

One of Xi's former secretaries, Tian Fang, filled two hundred notebooks with accusations against his boss, which included details about Xi's alleged treason on behalf of the Soviet Union but also about his relationship with nonparty officials. Tian denounced Xi for making United Front targets "feel very comfortable."[80] During the Cultural Revolution, Xi was pressured into admitting that he had been part of an antiparty clique that ran United Front efforts. When his health started to deteriorate because his accusers refused to allow him to rest, Xi finally accepted the charges and claimed that Li Weihan, head of the United Front Work Department, was "chief" of the clique and he had been second-in-command. However, when the investigators told Xi to describe the group's activities, Xi, temporizing, said he needed time to list everything. Luckily for Xi, the interrogators never followed up, probably because the charges were inherently ridiculous: the party had tasked Xi and Li Weihan with running United Front work.[81]

11
"MILITARY SUPPRESSION COMBINED WITH POLITICAL STRUGGLE"
The Radicalization of Ethnic and Religious Policy

During the last years of the civil war against the Nationalists and the first years after the founding of the People's Republic, the party faced the task of incorporating a massive expanse of territory inhabited by ethnic and religious minorities—especially in the Northwest, where Xi was in charge of such efforts. After Xi moved to Beijing—by then, an expert on ethnic affairs—he helped the party devise its national-level ethnic policies. Although he was a powerful individual, he faced a nightmarish policy environment, because of both the dilemmas inherent to the party's model for managing the nation's Muslim, Buddhist, and Christian population and the sizable danger of managing such a delicate and volatile issue within the cutthroat political context of party politics.

In 1952, when Xi was still in the Northwest, his showdown with Wang Zhen over Xinjiang policy had revealed that members of the party could reach very different conclusions about fundamental questions, such as, How quickly should the party pursue socialist transformation? How much should the party try to achieve more peaceful, and less costly, change? Yet perhaps the most fraught question was whether to continue to rely upon intermediaries to achieve its goals. Winning over figures like the Dalai Lama and the Panchen Lama or prominent Catholic cardinals and bishops had clear benefits. But such individuals were imperfect vectors for control. They had their own interests and sources of power, as well as their own deeply held personal beliefs. They had to win respect in their own communities while at the same time assuaging Communist fears of betrayal. They could convey to the party important information, but complaints could also be interpreted as threats. The party struggled to effectively combine intimidation and inducements without either frightening potential allies into becoming enemies or giving too much freedom for United Front targets to cause "trouble."

The party was not blind to the full extent of the challenge. It knew that the religious faithful in China included the "masses," and it was aware that Soviet attempts to destroy religion had failed. Moreover, a policy of immediate and forced atheism would damage China's reputation abroad. Christians posed a special problem. In 1950, Zhou Enlai had described Islam and Buddhism as "ethnic" religions, but he said Protestantism and Catholicism were "political" religions that were connected to imperialism.[1] Of the two Christian faiths, Catholics were considered the more dangerous. At a meeting on religious affairs held by Xi Zhongxun and Li Weihan in late 1953, Li warned that Catholics were "very good at struggle, and they are extraordinarily cunning." They "secretly send agents, engage in underground work, steal documents, infiltrate patriotic organizations, and they may even sneak into the party itself."[2]

Looking back at Xi's own words on ethnic and religious affairs during this period, a clear tension immediately becomes apparent. On the one hand, Xi deeply feared anti-Communist sentiment, wanted to achieve socialist transformation as quickly as possible, and did not shrink from devious and brutal methods. On the other hand, often even in the same speech, Xi would reveal a strikingly sensitive, practical, and flexible side. He appreciated the difficult circumstances in which United Front targets found themselves. At the same time, however, determining just what Xi really thought over these years is especially challenging. Xi had to be careful. Not only was it difficult to achieve real progress, but failures could lead to dangerous political accusations of "leftism" or "rightism."

Factionalism, as well as Mao's own shifting views, meant such labels were prominent weapons in the incessant political warfare within the party. The situation in the Tibet Autonomous Region presented an almost impossible situation for Xi. Most of the leaders in Tibet, such as Zhang Guohua, were cadres from the Southwest Bureau. With Deng Xiaoping as their backer, they supported the Dalai Lama over the Panchen Lama and pursued a more gradualist approach. In contrast, the northwesterners, led by Fan Ming, had arrived in Tibet with the Panchen Lama, and they were supported by Peng Dehuai and Xi Zhongxun. From Beijing, Deng and Xi danced carefully around each other, both supporting and reining in their protégés as the situation demanded.

Xi had reasons to fear Deng, but the most challenging figure was Mao. The purge of Gao Gang, the Antirightist Campaign, the Great Leap Forward, and the return to class struggle at the 1962 Tenth Plenum all shaped how the party approached ethnic and religious affairs. Despite occasional attempts to stop abuses, during the 1950s and the early 1960s, Mao was responsible for the increasingly leftist policies that signified a decisive break from the model Xi had previously triumphed in the Northwest. By the end of 1962, Xi, too, faced the devastating accusation that he had committed the mistake of "rightism" in party ethnic affairs.

THE "PANMUNJOM" MEETING ON TIBET

The party repeatedly tried and failed to get a handle on the feuding within the party in Tibet. In March 1952, Beijing named Zhang Jingwu as first party secretary of the Tibet Work Committee. Zhang had worked closely with both Xi in the Northwest and with Deng in the Southwest. Zhang Guohua, from the Southwest Bureau, became Zhang Jingwu's first deputy secretary. Fan Ming was the third deputy secretary, but he was also director of the United Front Work Department—the body in charge of relations with Tibetans.

This new appointment failed to arrest the political infighting. In October, Xu Danlu, head of the Liaison Department of the Tibet Military Region, met with Li Weihan, director of the central United Front Work Department, in Beijing to tell him about the continuing tensions. When Li asked Xu to name two individuals who he thought should be informed about the situation, Xu suggested Deng Xiaoping and Xi Zhongxun. Li grinned and immediately praised Xu's choice—Xu had correctly identified the two primary patrons of the different groups. The next day, Xu Danlu met with Deng, Xi, and Li Weihan at Deng's office. Deng asked Xu about his personal views of Zhang Guohua, Zhang Jingwu, and Fan Ming. Xu said that both Zhang Guohua and Fan Ming suffered from "heroism" but that Zhang was a bit worse. Deng stood up and asked several times, "Is that really the case?!" Deng then quieted down and said, "Of course, people change." When Xu said Zhang Jingwu, who had served with both Deng and Xi, was seen as someone who tried to paper over differences at the expense of principle, Deng laughed and said if the party had not sent such an individual, "who knows how much trouble you people there would have caused!"[3]

When Fan Ming himself traveled to Beijing in March 1953, Xi Zhongxun and Li Weihan asked him to write a report on the situation in Tibet. Li liked what Fan wrote, but when Xi read the document, he said, "When this person, Fan Ming, looks at a problem, he is always too careless. So arrogant." However, Xi did not offer any specific criticisms of the document.[4] In April, Fan, in a meeting with Peng Dehuai, expressed opposition to paying the Tibetan aristocrats, who owned the wholesale grain shops, to stabilize prices. Peng told Fan to speak to Mao, but Fan refused, characterizing his view as a tactical difference and not serious enough to bother the chairman. After Peng brought up the issue at a politburo meeting, Xi warned Fan that, in the future, he was not to casually talk to Peng about political issues, as Peng "often fired cannons."[5]

In October, the leadership in Tibet was summoned to a Tibet Work Conference held in Beijing. The participants argued about the Panchen Lama and the Dalai Lama, whether a Front and Back Tibet should be established, and how quickly the party should pursue change. Fan constantly pushed a more radical agenda. He reported to Xi privately, and, after Fan finished, Xi's only response was that he disagreed with Fan's proposal to use force to reform the Tibetan military. In Fan's words, "In actuality, he was giving silent assent." Fan claimed that another meeting participant, on the other hand, went to give regular reports to Deng, implying that Deng and Xi were having a subtle contest through their former subordinates from the Southwest and Northwest.[6]

The debates were so rancorous that Deng compared them to the site of the peace talks underway to end the Korean War. "You are making this meeting into the Panmunjom of Beijing," he said. To settle the disputes, Deng notified the delegates to the Tibet Work Conference about the resolution on Gao Gang. According to the historian Xiaoyuan Liu, if not for the Gao Gang incident, Fan Ming might have been removed from his position in Tibet, but Gao's fall made party unity the top priority. Liu concludes, "Given that Fan Ming was a subordinate of Xi Zhongxun's and maintained contact with Xi during the Tibet Work Conference, Deng's gesture was probably more meaningful to Xi than to anybody else."[7]

Finally, a draft of the *Tibet Work Conference Summary Report* was completed—a compromise document that affirmed the unity of Tibet but declared that the Dalai Lama was a "centrist" and the Panchen Lama was a "leftist." Zhao Fan, who managed Tibet on behalf of the central Ethnic Affairs Commission, did not support these conclusions, believing they were too ambiguous and that they failed to clarify which Tibetan leader had seniority. Zhao immediately went to Liu Shaoqi. At a politburo meeting, Liu asked Li Weihan to read Zhao Fan's complaint, although Liu hedged a bit by adding, "I think his opinion is not necessarily correct." After Li read the first part of Zhao Fan's complaint, Xi immediately said, "I believe that the conclusion of the *Tibet Work Conference Summary Report* is correct; Zhao Fan's opinion is wrong." After a discussion, Deng Xiaoping said, "The conclusion is indeed not complete, but for the purpose of unity, it should still be distributed in the name of the Central Committee!"[8]

Both Xi and Deng had tried to serve as peacemakers. Before Fan Ming returned to Tibet, Xi told him to treasure unity and to pay closer attention to the opinions of Zhang Guohua.[9] Back in Lhasa, however, it was Zhang Guohua, Deng's protégé, who offered a self-criticism and accepted primary responsibility for the tensions with Fan. The compromise proved to be short-lived. In August 1954, Mao would tell Li Weihan that the Dalai Lama came first, saying, "When walking out the door, two people cannot do it at the same time!"[10]

THE BIRTH OF THE XINJIANG UYGHUR AUTONOMOUS REGION

After they moved to Beijing in 1952, Deng and Xi also worked together to determine the party's formative policies toward Xinjiang. Again, they faced tough questions about how aggressively they should seek transformative goals and whether they should accommodate leading non-Han figures. Xinjiang presented a challenge that was different from that in Tibet. Even though Xinjiang was not riven by factional divides, policymaking there was still complicated, as Deng outranked Xi but was less familiar with the region. Furthermore, Xinjiang leaders, such as Burhan Shahidi and Saifuddin Azizi, did not command the formidable authority of the Dalai Lama or the Panchen Lama. Although dominated by a large Uyghur population, Xinjiang was more ethnically diverse than Tibet.

In fact, the party was not even sure what to call the region, as none of the options could please everyone. On February 20, 1953, Deng and Xi, as well as Li Weihan and Liu Geping, a Hui cadre, met and decided to support a draft document that would establish an autonomous region. The group concluded that if residents of the area did not like the term Xinjiang, then Tianshan Uyghur Autonomous Region was an acceptable option. They also raised the problem of "chauvinism" among some Uyghurs toward other ethnic groups in the region and the need for "education" to resolve the problem. On March 17, Deng, Xi, and other central leaders met with Burhan Shahidi and Saifuddin Azizi to discuss these issues. Azizi explained that some non-Han cadres opposed the name Xinjiang (its Qing-dynasty name meaning "new territory") and instead preferred Tianshan (the name of a mountain range in the region). With no consensus, a decision on the name was delayed.[11]

The situation was complicated by Mao's opposition to using the word Uyghur anywhere in the official name of the region. On March 27, Deng, Xi, and Li Weihan reported to Mao that Xi had discussed Mao's position with Shahidi and Azizi. Shahidi did not express support or opposition. Although Azizi finally agreed to accept Mao's proposal, he emphasized that he held a different view, arguing that the law on autonomous regions included a stipulation that regions would be named after the relevant ethnic group. Temporizing, Xi told Shahidi and Azizi that establishing an autonomous region in Xinjiang would not take place until the following year and that, in the meantime, research on the issue of what it would be named could continue.[12]

In early 1955, Mao sent Xi to speak with Shahidi and Azizi once again. Azizi explained that it did not make sense to refer to mountains or rivers as "autonomous"—only an ethnicity could be called "autonomous." Xi promised to report this to Mao, and then, two days later, Xi returned to tell Azizi that Mao had accepted his logic—the word "Uyghur" would indeed be included in Xinjiang's official name.[13] The moment was a remarkable one—the persistence of non-Han leaders, with Xi as interlocutor, had led to Mao changing his mind.

FROM THE FIRST NATIONAL PEOPLE'S CONGRESS TO THE FALL OF FAN MING

In subsequent years, Xi's role in managing ethnic politics continued to grow. In September 1954, the first session of the First National People's Congress established the State Council and placed the Ethnic Affairs Commission directly under its leadership. To facilitate its work, the State Council established a number of small groups, with Xi in charge of the Internal Affairs Group, which included the Ethnic Affairs Commission. Xi was also given responsibility for party relations with the Panchen Lama.[14]

Xi was clearly disappointed by the better treatment the Dalai Lama received at the first National People's Congress, the Chinese legislature. According to Bapa Phuntsok Wangchuk, who had founded the Tibetan Communist Party in 1943, Xi "shook his head when he saw the different level of arrangements for the Panchen Lama but did not say anything." Deng, however, "praised us and said everything had been arranged perfectly."[15] The Panchen Lama's living quarters were originally going to be at Fuyou Temple on Beichang Street. However, Xi conducted a personal investigation and concluded that Fuyou Temple was "too small, and it was far inferior to where the Dalai Lama was staying." Hence, Xi moved the Panchen Lama's residence to the Changguan Tower to the west of the zoo in Xizhimenwai.[16]

After the two Tibetan leaders arrived in Beijing, the party leadership struggled to manage their relationship. When the Panchen Lama learned that he would be selected as a vice-chairman of the Chinese People's Political Consultative Conference, whereas the Dalai Lama would be assigned a position as a vice-chairman of the National People's Congress, he flew into a rage. Li Weihan and Xi Zhongxun tried to calm him down, but he said to them, "You sent me back to Tibet to suffer repression everywhere [by the Dalai Lama]. Now, I am here at the center, and you are still not acting justly."[17]

During an interview conducted for this book, the Dalai Lama described Xi as "relatively open-minded" compared to other high-ranking party officials, like one who had made fun of him for wearing his traditional clothing to an official ceremony. "I remember very clearly that, at different venues, whether it was at an individual meeting or at a big event, I found him to be easygoing," the Dalai Lama said. In fact, he had liked Xi enough to give him an expensive watch as a gift, although he could not recall many years later whether he gave such watches to other leaders as well. He sensed Xi was someone whom Mao trusted. When asked whether Xi's relationship with Fan Ming and the Panchen Lama affected his feelings toward Xi, the Dalai Lama responded that it was "difficult to say.... Fan Ming was indeed more distant from me." Yet he also said, "I felt that Xi Zhongxun probably also was relatively supportive of my side."[18]

Given the favoritism that Xi Zhongxun had shown for the Panchen Lama, what are we to make of the Dalai Lama's stated fondness for Xi? Both the distance of memory and the Dalai Lama's personality are important for interpreting his remarks. He was only twenty years old when he met Xi, and he was eighty-eight years old when the interview was conducted. During the interview, the Dalai Lama admitted he could remember few specific details about Xi. The Dalai Lama typically refrains from disparaging others, and denigrating the father of Xi Jinping would likely not suit his political approach to Beijing. However, it is also very possible that Xi Zhongxun, a charismatic individual, did indeed charm the young man. Whatever Xi's personal feelings for the Dalai Lama, Xi was working for the party, and he knew what it wanted: to win the Dalai Lama's affection for the regime in Beijing.

Yet, behind the scenes and whenever possible, Xi continued to promote his own agenda. In 1955, he exacted vengeance on Zhao Fan. After the "Panmunjom" meeting, Zhao, who had supported the Dalai Lama over the Panchen Lama, continued to feud with United Front Work Department officials, such as the northwesterner Wang Feng. Deciding that he could not defeat them, Zhao Fan finally sent a report to Xi Zhongxun asking for a transfer. In Zhao's own words, he did not suspect that he "had fallen into their trap." Xi told Wang Feng about Zhao's report and then sent it to the Central Committee. Suddenly, a meeting was called to discuss Zhao's request for a transfer, but no information was given to him ahead of time. Zhao concluded that Xi had severely mistreated him, later writing, "This can be described as striking when the enemy is unprepared, 'a sneak attack.' This trick by Xi Zhongxun 'knocked me off my horse with a gust of wind.'"[19]

THE FALL OF FAN MING

In the winter of 1955 and the spring of 1956, officials in Sichuan started to enact wrenching social reforms in the Tibetan regions, which led to a mass outbreak of rebellions. In the summer, reforms began within the Tibet Autonomous Region itself. The party became worried that the Dalai Lama, who was on a trip to India, would not return to China if the problems were not addressed. In March 1957, the secretariat met to discuss the situation. The participants all agreed that a "great retraction" was necessary. However, two practical questions remained: Would the removal of the government bodies that Beijing wanted to impose in the region imply a political retreat? And if the reforms in Tibet proper were to be reversed, what about the changes in the Tibetan areas of Sichuan? Some participants were skeptical about a "political retraction." Deng Xiaoping expressed the worry that "if we do that, it can be hypothesized that they will think they were victorious and they will want to kick us out." Xi also worried about backing off from the hardline policies too quickly. "Even though our general purpose is to extricate ourselves from the current predicament, should we give up what has already been gained politically?" he asked.[20]

Fan Ming arrived three days after the beginning of the secretariat meeting. That very evening, Xi, who had been partying at the Beijing Hotel, went to Fan's room and told him that Zhou Enlai, while still dancing, had said, "The situation in Tibet is all screwed up, and it looks as if Fan Ming might have some responsibility?" Xi said he agreed with Zhou, so he wanted to warn Fan to be careful. Fan concluded that Deng Xiaoping was planning to punish him.[21] When participating in the last session of the secretariat meeting on March 9, Fan criticized a proposal to completely cease the reform plans. Fan recalled later, "Weihan and Zhongxun gestured for me to stop, but I did not. Not responding to what I said, Deng Xiaoping pushed over some documents on the table and said that everything had already been decided. Then he left."[22]

Fan, furious at Deng, decided to write a letter directly to Mao. Mao opted to support him, and "the Central Committee accepted my opinions and asked Xi Zhongxun and Li Weihan to talk with me," Fan later wrote.[23] Xi and Li then drafted a report that distinguished between the tasks that were "doable" and those that were "undoable" and allowed for "preparation for indirect reforms." Fan believed that this new decision allowed the party to retreat without entirely abandoning the reforms.[24]

Fan had emerged triumphant, but he was making powerful enemies. Before returning to Lhasa, he met with An Ziwen, head of the Organization Department. An told him that when it came to inner-party struggles, it was necessary not to "grow horns that were too long," meaning that Fan should not be too obstreperous when arguing and he should accept defeat. When Fan went to bid farewell to Xi and described his conversation with An, Xi asked, "Did An really say that?" When Fan responded positively, Xi merely said oh and nothing else. Xi left Fan with the impression that he believed An's behavior had been unprincipled.[25]

But this was only a brief victory for Fan. Several months later, in September 1957, the party center suddenly ordered that both direct and indirect reform preparations were to cease.[26] In early 1958, Fan Ming launched a rectification campaign in Tibet to punish dissenters, but in February and March, he himself became a target. The trigger was the posting of a big-character poster regarding Fan Ming's book *New Journey to the West*, a novelized version of the party's history in Tibet. Fan would later claim it was Peng Dehuai who had entrusted him to write the book, but a Cultural Revolution–era Red Guard publication blames Xi.[27]

When Xi was presented with evidence of Fan's supposed crimes, he agreed that Fan should be punished. Fan "even dared to oppose Mao," Xi said. To win Xi's support, Fan's supposed "opposition" to Xi was included as a crime, although the evidence was flimsy. It was enough—according to Fan, Deng Xiaoping did not decide to launch his attack against Fan until Xi and other Northwest cadres had agreed.[28]

In April 1958, at a meeting of cadres from the county or regiment level and above throughout Tibet, Fan was savagely criticized. A document listing fifteen of Fan's crimes, put together by the leadership in Tibet, included one crime related to Xi: "Not only that, he [Fan] even attributed factionalism to leading comrades at the party center; said Comrade Xiaoping is the Southwest and supports Guohua; that Guohua engaged in a personality cult with Comrade Xiaoping; that Comrade Xiaoping personally trusted Guohua; and that Comrades Dehuai and Zhongxun were the Northwest and supported him, Fan Ming."[29]

The Dalai Lama was apparently delighted by Fan's downfall. According to Zhang Jingwu, the Dalai Lama jumped up in excitement when he heard the news. Zhang told the Dalai Lama, "The Central Committee's Xi Zhongxun and Li Weihan carried out self-criticisms, with each saying that their eyes had been blinded and that they had misjudged Fan Ming."[30] When Xi traveled through Xi'an in June 1959, Fan, then at a reform-through-labor camp, asked to meet with him, hoping to win Xi's sympathy and support. But, in Fan's words, Xi adopted a "slippery attitude"—Xi met with Fan for only half an hour, and during the entire time, probably at Xi's instigation, a security guard repeatedly urged Xi to leave for another meeting. Xi's only promise was to share some material with the party center.[31]

Fan's defeat was a major setback for all the northwesterners who had traveled with him to Tibet. Henceforth, none of them would be entrusted with sensitive positions, and many of them would be purged.[32] Li Weihan and Xi Zhongxun did, however, nominate Fan's replacement, Zhou Renshan. In 1947 and 1948, when Zhou had managed party work in the Mongolian Yekejuu League, Xi had been Zhou's superior.[33] According to a Red Guard publication, Xi selected Zhou Renshan from the "Northwest faction" to replace Fan as representative of his interests in Tibet—a charge Xi was forced to acknowledge in a struggle session during the Cultural Revolution.[34]

CATHOLICS AND PROTESTANTS

Xi was one of several important individuals involved in Tibetan affairs during this period, but he was the party's primary point man for its policies toward Christians. Xi was sensitive to Catholic resistance to the party. On June 17, 1953, at an enlarged session of the secretariat in Beijing chaired by Mao, Xi proposed that the party not apply the "Three-Selfs" (self-evangelization, self-governance, and financial self-support) to Catholics in Shanghai but instead use the less offensive terminology of "patriotism" to win over more supporters. But this was clearly a case of the party using both "tough" and "soft" measures simultaneously. Two days before the secretariat meeting, Fernand Lacretelle, the top Catholic leader in Shanghai, and six other foreign missionaries had been arrested. Some were held for months, others for years, and they all suffered extensive psychological and physical torment. Lacretelle was interrogated for 550 hours and forced to write 769 pages of "confessions," which were later used as a powerful weapon against the Chinese Catholics.[35]

Yet, remarkably, just one month after this crackdown, the party demonstrated a more flexible side. On July 10, the party center—recognizing that fear of excommunication was a "major obstacle" preventing making any inroads with Chinese Catholics—decided that as long as Catholics avoided "political or economic" relations with the Vatican, their "religious" connections were tolerable (although, if such "religious" connections were used for "counterrevolutionary activities," the culprits were to be "punished by law").[36]

This jarring mix of brutality and practicality was on full display in Xi's speech to the Third Nationwide Work Meeting on Religion in 1955. He began by bragging about the mass expulsion of foreign missionaries and the destruction of the Catholic organization Legion of Mary. That did not mean the threat had diminished—far from it. Precisely because socialism was triumphing, enemies both inside and outside China were accelerating their efforts to "use religion to engage in all kinds of conspiratorial activities." Yet, immediately after this Stalinist language, Xi bluntly brought up the party's own mistakes. The party was not good at mobilizing the religious masses—especially the pious believers. With regard to Catholic priests, the party's "demands are too high. There is a lack of concern for their situation and difficulties. In many places, their economic interests are often infringed upon, and their normal religious activities are interfered with by the party. In some places, they are even arbitrarily detained or beaten." Xi acknowledged a different problem with the nation's leading Protestants, some of whom were so proparty that they were losing believers. "Their activities have too much of a political air, and their religious hues are too weak," Xi said. In other words, he was telling Protestants to be more devout so they could serve as better intermediaries for the party.[37]

Xi then tried to put the challenge in a less threatening way than he did at the beginning of his speech. Yes, Catholics and Protestants were used by the imperialists as a "tool of invasion," but only a small number of Christians were really enemies. If the danger were to be overstated, then the imperialists and counterrevolutionaries would benefit. "If religious matters are addressed by a simple administrative approach, that will not only fail to eliminate religion but actually make their religious prejudices deeper and stronger," he said. Later in the same speech, the radical nature of Xi's long-term goals, and the devious nature of his methods, once again reappeared. With regard to China's most powerful Catholic, Bishop Ignatius Kung Pinmei of Shanghai, Xi said it was "necessary to struggle against him but also slacken his vigilance." For now, "a face-to-face struggle" against Kung would be a mistake, but a "daily struggle" should be waged against members of his circle. In the meantime, the party should collect compromising material to later "expose his counterrevolutionary political goals." Once a sufficient amount of "enemy intelligence" was acquired, the conditions would be ripe to "seize this reactionary fortress."[38]

Then, jarringly, he returned to a softer touch. He recognized that the fear of excommunication among Catholic priests was the "central issue" in making it difficult to win them over. Therefore, Xi said, "it is necessary to have an appropriate response." For the time being, "anti-imperialist patriotic thinking" and "maintaining close relations with us" will be sufficient for most priests. But for priests who wanted to move further in their support for the party, Xi was strikingly practical: "It is necessary to make it clear that they must express devotion in their religious life so they do not lose their 'spiritual power.'"[39]

Xi had expressed both ambition and patience in his speech, but, several months later, his tougher side manifested forcefully when Kung Pinmei's "reactionary fortress" was assaulted (probably as part of the nationwide Eradicate Hidden Counterrevolutionaries Campaign, which the Hu Feng case had triggered). On September 8, 1955, on the Feast of the Nativity of the Blessed Virgin Mary, the party launched a coordinated assault on Shanghai's Catholic community. In one night alone, more than three hundred Catholics, including Kung himself and a number of high school students, were arrested in multiple locations throughout the city. But that was only the beginning. A total of twelve hundred would be taken by the end of September.[40]

With Kung gone, the party moved more quickly to exert direct control over Chinese Catholics. In February 1956, Xi held a discussion meeting with Catholic leaders visiting Beijing for a session of the Chinese People's Political Consultative Conference. Louis Zhang Jiashu, a proparty priest who would become Shanghai's bishop in 1960, made two requests: first, that the government help "raise patriotic consciousness" through education and, second, that the party help Chinese Catholics establish their own organization. Xi told the group that the 1955 campaign of repression and the arrest of Bishop Kung had signified that the "representatives" of the "foreign powers" had been annihilated. The Catholic Church was "basically" no longer under external control. Now, Xi told them, conditions were ripe to establish a nationwide patriotic association.[41]

During a series of preparatory meetings before the first official meeting of the Catholic Patriotic Association in the summer of 1957, Catholic leaders were somewhat outspoken in their concerns about party policy. At the time, Mao was still allowing criticism of the party in the lead-up to the Antirightist Campaign. According to internal documents, the "rightists" allegedly expressed opposition to socialism, the anti-imperialist patriotic campaign, and the purge in the Catholic Church. The most important "struggle," however, was over the Vatican, with the "rightists" supposedly arguing for "absolute" obedience to the pope. In particular, Catholics worried about the recent excommunication of a priest in Nanjing. But the winds shifted dramatically with the beginning of the Antirightist Campaign. Party documents claim that after more than twenty days of "vicious arguments and sharp struggles," a "majority" of the participants at these preparatory meetings agreed to criticize the Vatican.[42]

On July 15, with the preparatory meetings over, Catholic leaders opened a full congress in Beijing. In his keynote speech, given on July 16, Xi referred to the differences that allegedly existed among the participants. He criticized those Catholics who believed that "loving religion automatically means loving the nation" or "first love religion, then love the nation." He queried whether it was better to love "churches run by the Chinese people" or "churches under the control of imperialism." He complained about some individuals who were still unhappy that the imperialists had been expelled between 1951 and 1953: "If they had stayed until now, they would have been poisoned even more and the government would have used even tougher measures. Many foreign missionaries did evil things. Their crimes are numerous. If the number of their crimes were counted, one could write several books full of their evils." Catholics could not be apolitical, he asserted: "Drawing lines between friends and enemies is an extremely important issue; not drawing lines will not only mean chaos in terms of thinking, but it will also lead to serious mistakes in action." Xi claimed that "there are many religions in China, but only Catholics now listen entirely to directions from foreigners and are controlled by the Vatican." Because the Vatican had opposed the party both before and after 1949, viewing the Vatican entirely in religious terms was incorrect, according to Xi. In fact, "the Vatican is a tool of invasion by the American imperialists," Xi said.[43]

According to an internal State Council report on the congress, the participants concluded that the Vatican would no longer be allowed to approve of the choices made by Chinese Catholics about new bishops and priests. Therefore, the names of newly promoted Catholic leaders subsequently would no longer be reported to the Vatican for approval—"just quickly informing the Vatican is enough." After sufficient time had passed, not even a notification would be necessary, as Chinese Catholicism would "gradually separate from control by the Vatican and achieve independence."[44]

CIVIL WAR IN THE NORTHWEST AND TIBET

While the Catholic Church kept Xi busy during the summer of 1957, United Front work cadres meeting in the coastal city of Qingdao were reacting to the new "antirightist" turn in Beijing in a way that would soon bring devastation to the ethnic minorities in the Northwest whom Xi had helped to incorporate into the People's Republic earlier in that decade. Those at the meeting in Qingdao were afraid that Uyghur cadres in Xinjiang wanted to establish a Soviet-style federal system and to end the influx of Han Chinese into the region. In October, the party launched the Rectification and Socialist Education Campaign against ethnic minorities. Although the party would always oppose Han chauvinism, it now declared that the focus was on primarily combatting "local nationalism." In January 1958, the Xinjiang Party Committee opened a four-month enlarged session to criticize nationalist sentiment. Unable to withstand the emotional pressure of the looming purges, shortly after the meeting began, a deputy chairman of the Ili-Kazakh Autonomous Prefecture cut his own throat. On previous occasions, Xi and Deng Xiaoping had managed Xinjiang affairs together, but this time Deng, from Beijing, was directing the entire meeting on his own.[45]

As Benno Weiner writes, by early 1958, the party was moving decisively away from "gradualism and volunteerism" in the direction of "revolutionary impatience."[46] In March, Mao lost his temper with what he viewed as excessive caution in the party's ethnic policies. Whether someone had a particular ethnic heritage, Mao said, was less important than asking whether they were Communist. In subsequent discussion meetings, the Ethnic Affairs Commission, which fell under Xi's bailiwick, was savaged for lacking zeal. Liu Chun, who was second in command at the Commission at the time, wrote that "it was like the Ethnic Affairs Commission achieved nothing since its establishment."[47]

Swept up by the radicalism of the Great Leap Forward, provincial leaders in Qinghai and Gansu decided to pursue collectivization in the nomadic regions. By March, mass uprisings by Tibetans and Muslims began to erupt. Li Weihan quickly led a group to Gansu to investigate. On April 3, they submitted a report that concluded that the earlier policy of "giving precedence to political struggle" was outdated. "Military suppression combined with political struggle, flexibly utilized," should be the new policy of the day. Although the party had refrained from executions in the past, now "several principal instigators should be killed with great fanfare." On June 24, Mao expressed delight. "An armed rebellion by Qinghai reactionaries is excellent," he wrote on a report from Qinghai. "The greater the disturbance, the better," as that would give the party reason to use force to more rapidly achieve socialist transformation. In July, Zhu De reported that "more than twenty-six thousand" enemies had been "knocked off" in Gansu, Qinghai, and Sichuan, but fifteen thousand still remained at large. The party was at war against its own people.[48] Since the violence was occurring in Xi's old territory, these developments might have raised questions about whether Xi had failed to fully eradicate opposition to party rule when he was master of the Northwest Bureau.

In this new situation, many ethnic-minority leaders whom Xi personally had convinced to support the party in the early years of the People's Republic were now targeted for persecution. Mao had praised Xi in superlative terms for convincing Wangchen Dondrup to surrender, but, in 1958, Wangchen Dondrup was criticized and stripped of his positions. After a brief period of arrest, he died a depressed man in 1959 at the age of fifty-five.[49] Decades later, Xi would express regret over such outcomes. In the 1980s, during a conversation with a Hui cadre, Xi recalled how Ma Zhenwu had helped the Communists end an uprising peacefully. Yet, in 1958, Ma had been removed from the Ningxia government leadership. Xi angrily referred to this treatment as "absolutely ridiculous" and "a painful historical lesson that absolutely must be carefully remembered."[50]

Whatever Xi thought about the new approach at the time, he still made efforts to assuage the concerns of party allies. In the summer of 1958, Sherab Gyatso, a Tibetan scholar Xi had befriended years earlier, visited Qinghai, where he was stunned by the violence he saw. After returning to Beijing, he warned Xi that the party had gone too far: local Communists were killing innocents, closing temples, and terrifying people into believing the party wanted to destroy religion once and for all. Xi tried to calm him. He praised Sherab Gyatso for presenting his concerns: "If you do not speak on behalf of Buddhism, no one else will do so." Xi explained the Suppression Campaign was targeted against counterrevolutionaries, not against religion itself, and although mistakes had been made in implementation, the party was correcting them. He asked Sherab Gyatso to speak to local Tibetans on behalf of the party.[51]

Shortly after this conversation, Xi, too, visited his old territory of the Northwest to investigate the party's ethnic policies (as well as the economic policies of the Great Leap Forward).[52] On September 28, on a trip to the nomadic region of Aksay Kazakh Autonomous County in Gansu, he expressed concern about the party's growing extremism: "Currently, in some places in Lanzhou, Ningxia, and Xining, they are engaged in some kind of struggle against feudal privilege, forcing Muslim people to raise pigs and women to remove their veils and wear Han clothing. Imams are also struggled against. They are forced to shave their beards, and some religious figures are even expelled from the mosques." When Xi was told about the recent arrest of nineteen individuals during a crackdown, as well as of five Han who had been charged during the Antirightist Campaign, he was furious:

> Nineteen "rebels" plus five rightists are already more than 1 percent of the entire county. No other county in the whole country is like that. If little babies are not included, then the percentage would be even higher. That means out of every few dozen, one individual was arrested; how could there have been so many bad people? Among those so-called rebels who were arrested, was there really a problem? Are there any facts or evidence? After the end of the nationwide Eradicate Hidden Counterrevolutionaries Campaign in 1955, the Central Committee had already enacted a policy of fewer arrests, fewer executions, and fewer incarcerations. . . .
>
> I also want to stress that the current Central Committee work guideline on minority areas still emphasizes "cautious progress" and "unity with the upper levels." When engaging in this work, it is necessary to stay in touch and consult with local personages to win their support and assistance to push progress forward. . . .
>
> With regard to ethnic customs, you absolutely must not see them as backward, feudal things. The dozens of ethnic groups in the country each have their own customs; how could the Han not have its own customs as well? What is the logic behind treating minority women wearing the veil and wearing a dress or men growing a beard as feudal. . . . Some of these customs are even connected to their environment and their conditions. . . . That is a kind of life demand; is it possible for you to want to eliminate it?[53]

Although Xi seemed to be worried about "leftism" in late September 1958, the Communists moved even more ambitiously against religion soon after he returned to Beijing. In November, the Ethnic Affairs Commission, which fell under Xi's purview, submitted a report on Islam and "Lamaism" (a term denoting Tibetan Buddhism) to the Central Committee, calling for the complete elimination of religious counterrevolutionaries and the "total abolishment of religious feudal privileges and exploitation." This report blamed "upper-class elements" for the "insurrections" in Gansu and Qinghai during the previous year as well as for the uprisings in the Tibetan areas of Sichuan in 1956. The party remained aware of the "mass" nature of these religions, and it worried about reputational costs in Africa and Asia, where many Muslims and Buddhists lived. Beijing called on cadres to only oppose religious customs that damaged productivity. But the report was an official, central directive calling for total transformation of Islam and Buddhism.[54]

This document excluded the Tibet Autonomous Region, but the party leadership in Beijing was increasingly convinced that there, too, the gradualist approach to change was failing. Khamba fighters, with American support, were acting brazenly, and the Dalai Lama was unwilling to stop the uprising. Tensions between the Tibetans and the Chinese finally boiled over in March 1959. Tibetan officials, without the Dalai Lama's knowledge, secretly summoned the people of Lhasa to stop him from attending a gala at the Chinese military headquarters, a situation that rapidly spiraled out of control and ended with the Dalai Lama fleeing to India.[55]

The northwesterners in Tibet felt vindicated. In his memoirs, one of them wrote that, less than a year after their persecution by southwestern cadres, "the Dalai clique had already openly launched an armed insurrection. Tibet seized the opportunity to engage in comprehensive democratic reforms. This demonstrates completely that Fan Ming's estimation of the situation at the time had been correct. Truth was on Fan Ming's side."[56] By extension, by party logic, Xi was right and Deng Xiaoping was wrong.

In June, just three months after the Dalai Lama's dramatic flight to India, Zhou Enlai declared that when Ulanhu was not in Beijing, Xi would *directly* manage the Ethnic Affairs Commission. He would henceforth also include the Religious Affairs Bureau as part of his direct purview.[57] Xi, and by extension Zhou Renshan, his supposed protégé in Tibet, thus must have played a key role in the mass violence that ensued in Tibet over the subsequent months. In May 1960, at a meeting with local security officials, Zhou Renshan said that even though many "bandits" had been destroyed and the "feudal slave system" had ended, that did not mean that "enemy class resistance and sabotage had concluded." In fact, "the struggle between dictatorship [of the proletariat] and antidictatorship is extremely serious, and some of our comrades do not take seriously the enemy's opposition to dictatorship." Finally, in October, the regional leadership concluded that the violence had gone too far. Despite a guideline noting that 2 percent of the population would have to be punished, that quota was often surpassed. In January 1961, Deng Xiaoping stated that it would subsequently be necessary to emphasize opposing "leftism" in order to stabilize the situation.[58]

THE PANCHEN LAMA'S "SEVENTY-THOUSAND-CHARACTER PETITION"

The Panchen Lama was disgusted by this treatment of his fellow Tibetans. He started to draft a petition, seventy thousand characters in length, hoping to alert the party to its mistakes. While writing the document, the Panchen Lama refused to receive any Chinese guests other than Chen Yi, He Long, and Xi Zhongxun.[59] In it, he criticized the arbitrary killings that took place after the Dalai Lama had fled, complaining that "religious activities were as scarce as stars in the daytime, and there were hardly any complete sets of religious activities." The destruction of Buddhism is "something that I and more than 90 percent of the Tibetans cannot endure."[60]

As the Panchen Lama was working on his petition, Xi was already trying to arrest party abuses in the ethnic-minority regions. Between April 21 and May 28, 1962, Xi, along with Ulanhu and Li Weihan, chaired a nationwide ethnic work conference, which called for a move away from radicalism and a correction of the party's previous mistakes. An interim report prepared by Xi and other high-ranking figures, issued on May 15, concluded that the top priority should now be unity, gradual restoration of the economy, and improvements in the people's livelihoods. For the next five years, everything else would be secondary. The writers of the report suggested that "minority people and cadres should be strongly encouraged to manage internal affairs on their own in the autonomous regions, especially their special economic characteristics, cultural forms, language and writing systems, and customs and habits." The construction of people's communes and collectives could be delayed, and teaching was the appropriate method for avoiding great Han chauvinism and local nationalism: "In the future, generally speaking, do not engage in struggle." The interim report even stated, "Apparently, the tendency of great Han chauvinism has grown in some places." The report said its writers were prepared to make a self-criticism at future meetings. Deng Xiaoping approved of the report, and, on June 20, it was disseminated by the Central Committee.[61]

But those proceedings were not meaningful enough or fast enough to assuage the Panchen Lama's concerns. Hoping to stop him from finishing the petition, in mid-May, Zhou Enlai, Xi, United Front leaders, and officials from Tibet met with him to hear his views. In strong language, the Panchen Lama argued with those who were present.[62] Zhou said that the party's triumphs in Tibet were greater than its deficiencies, and he warned that the party did not have to listen to "everything that is incorrect" according to the Panchen Lama's views.[63]

Afterward, Zhou summoned Xi Zhongxun, Li Weihan, Zhang Jingwu, Zhang Guohua, and Liu Chun, head of the Ethnic Affairs Commission. Zhou hoped that they could convince the Panchen Lama not to deliver his petition officially. But the Panchen Lama could not be consoled, and he submitted it on June 7.[64] Li Weihan and Xi then met with him on three occasions to discuss the report. Xi began the first session on June 21 by saying, "The purpose is to engage in free discussion; if once is not enough, then we can talk again." Li presented the main remarks; when he complained that the leadership in Qinghai had been hiding its mistakes in its treatment of the Tibetans, Xi interrupted to concur: "The first secretary took the lead in concealing such mistakes." Xi compared the situation to what had occurred during the "peaceful reform" of Xinjiang in 1952 and noted, "Mistakes are difficult to avoid completely."[65]

The next day, when the Panchen Lama demanded to know how Tibetans could have been persecuted so severely without an explicit order from Beijing, Xi said that the Panchen Lama "should not think about things in that way. When things are screwed up, it is possible that is because of an order from the top, but for some things, there is no order. For example, in the Han areas, women also cut their braids. I once went to the local levels where the top had not issued any orders, but in some counties, the women's braids had nevertheless been cut off. There was just that kind of wind. As soon as it starts blowing, it spreads everywhere."[66] But Xi was conciliatory, admitting it had been wrong to damage religious texts, images or statues of the Buddha, and temples as they were part of "historical culture." He said, "Vent your anger. Doing it here is very good. I welcome you to vent your anger here. If today you are not done venting your anger, we can hold another meeting to allow you to vent your anger. You vent your anger, and we accept your anger.... Every time there is a fight, then unity becomes much better; it does not make unity worse."[67]

On the third day of the meeting, June 25, Xi spoke the most. He said, "In my personal opinion, this is a good report. When I studied it, it was like taking a class. It was very beneficial." But he criticized the petition for treating individual problems as universal. The problems were in implementation. He tried to blend conciliatory attitudes with criticism: "Your petition is not comprehensive, but it can be understood." Xi explicitly asked the Panchen Lama to confirm that his petition was not meant to contradict "the main guidelines and policies" for work in Tibet—in other words, he was asking that the

Panchen Lama be more deferential. Xi told his old associate, "As I have told you, you are required to be honest with us. We must also be direct and honest. There should be no gaps between us." Xi also warned that the Dalai Lama was watching from India and "dreaming" that the party in Tibet would fail and the Panchen Lama would "collapse." According to Xi, Jawaharlal Nehru and the Dalai Lama were sending agents to "overthrow the current leadership in Tibet." The Panchen Lama thereafter thanked Li and Xi for meeting with him even though their "health was not very good" and they were so busy.[68]

Liu Chun, who attended these meetings, was dumbstruck by Xi. "At the time, I simply could not stand the way that they spoke to the Panchen Lama," he wrote in his memoirs. "But what could I do? They had already said it! Even now, I think that they were speaking inappropriately."[69] Disappointed that Xi and Li could not solve the problem on their own, Zhou Enlai, together with Xi and several other high-ranking officials, met the Panchen Lama on July 24. Zhang Jingwu promised Zhou Enlai that the previous mistakes would be corrected and that errors would not be hidden. Zhou Enlai praised the Panchen Lama for being fundamentally different from the Dalai Lama, who, according to Zhou, refused to be honest with the central leadership. Zhou said the Dalai Lama, as "ethnic, people's, national, and religious scum," should not be allowed to reincarnate. He asserted that reform in Tibet would necessarily result in losses, just like how during surgery "some good blood must be spilt too."[70]

The situation seemed to be stabilizing—until the work meeting before the Tenth Plenum when Mao demanded that the party return to a greater emphasis on "class struggle." Both the Panchen Lama and Xi Zhongxun came under attack. Mao said, "You want to cultivate the Panchen Lama into a people's hero. I believe he cannot become a hero."[71] Deng Xiaoping, using a Chinese expression, remarked that the Panchen Lama was so haughty that his "tail is even higher than a U-2 jet; he is wagging it up to outer space."[72] Peng Zhen, who worked for Deng at the secretariat, accused Xi of being the Panchen Lama's "backstage supporter."[73] Xi, who had spent so much time helping the party manage Tibetan affairs, watched helplessly as his legacy was savaged over the following years as the leadership concluded that the Panchen Lama's behavior was the result of Xi's inability to control him.[74] During the Cultural Revolution, Xi's former boss, Zhou Enlai, would himself ominously tell Tibetan students that Li Weihan and Xi Zhongxun were rightists who had catered to the Panchen Lama "without principle."[75]

12
HOME LIFE IN THE CAPITAL

At work, Xi faced a dizzying array of policy challenges and the vicissitudes of his own shifting fortunes. But in party culture, home life was no escape from the political. Everything from schooling and leisure to even the clothes and food in the Xi household were shaped by broader preoccupations within the elite. Aaron Solts, the Soviet Union's most famous theorist of Bolshevik ethics, had asserted that "the family of a Communist must be a prototype of a small Communist cell" and "the members of the family must, in all their work and life, represent a unit of assistance to the Party." Domesticity presented an existential challenge to the Communist war on bourgeois weakness and materialism.[1] Having fought decades of war to establish a transformational regime, party leaders in China were proud of what they had achieved yet concerned about their families losing the revolutionary elan that had proven so instrumental to earlier victories. The party leadership, including Xi, worried that the next generation would grow up spoiled and separated from the so-called masses.

Before he arrived in Beijing, Xi was already a father to three surviving children with his first wife (a son, Zhengning, and two daughters, Heping and Qianping), as well as two daughters with Qi Xin (Qiaoqiao and An'an). Two more sons, Jinping and Yuanping, were born in the capital in 1953 and 1955, respectively. While the sons were allowed to carry Xi's surname, his daughters were not because Zhongxun did not want their teachers and classmates to know the identity of their father. Since the parents were so busy, all the children lived at school during the week. That was a traumatic experience for Qiaoqiao, who cried so hard that she passed out on the first day.[2]

They all attended special institutions for the children of high-ranking elites. Zhengning went to the Beijing 101 Middle School, where his classmates included Mao Zedong's nephew as well as the children of Gao Gang, Yang Shangkun, Wang Zhen, and Guo Hongtao (Guo's son was the class prankster). Zhengning must have been popular as he was elected class president by his peers.[3] Qianping similarly demonstrated leadership skills at a young age. Before leaving the Northwest, all her classmates in Xi'an had short hair, which was common at schools for the children of top cadres where military discipline was the norm. One day, having decided that she did not like the way her forehead looked, Qianping put on a hairclip. That night, at roll call, an older boy saw her and said she had manifested "bourgeois ideology," and other students soon joined him. She felt dejected, but she proved resilient to bullying. One night after dinner, she hugged another classmate from behind, believing it was one of her female friends. It was in fact a male student, who, embarrassed, then yelled at her. Fed up with the lack of distinction between genders, she decided to grow braids over the winter break.[4]

By the time her hair was long, the family had already moved to Beijing, where Qianping went to study at Yuying Middle School. She worried about the "uncouth" qualities she had picked up in Xi'an. The girls in the capital spoke the standard Mandarin Chinese, while Qianping had a strong Shaanxi accent. She also wore poorly fitting clothes. Yet the other girls, who all had bob cuts, loved her braids. When the students heard that a teacher was planning to cut them off, they surrounded the teacher and shouted, "Don't cut off Qianping's braids!" Before class, they even wrote on a blackboard "Defend the braids! Long live the braids! We also want to grow braids!" The teacher relented and even let the other students grow their hair long as well. "Girl students, by nature, like to look pretty," Qianping later wrote in a reminiscence about the school.[5]

Qiaoqiao, An'an, Jinping, and Yuanping all went to middle school at the August 1 School, where the students were primarily the children of high-ranking military, not political, figures. One graduate described the school as a place where "softness and delicateness were especially despised." The students often fought nastily, and they were less interested in academics than their peers at other schools, as the August 1 School student body proudly expected to become "cannon fodder" in a war—"good students" were simply "pursuing their own futures."[6] Physical sports were strongly emphasized. They were assigned physical labor and underwent military training. Male and female students were completely separated, which led one student to regret that his cohort, which included Jinping, developed a "feudal" view that the girls were inferior.[7]

Although it was tough, the August 1 School was also an exciting place. The students "were full of resolution to give their lives to the desire to struggle, the will to serve, the collective spirit, and sincere beliefs and traditional pursuits, and at the same time, they were full to the brim with the special confidence and pride of victors," according to one former student.[8] The education system emphasized class struggle, teaching that enemies could be lurking behind any problem, that anyone could be an enemy, and that such enemies were to be treated viciously.[9] During political-education class, they read books such as *Be a Successor to the Revolution*, which in Jinping's own words "influenced the idealistic beliefs and life choices of our generation."[10] Graduates of the August 1 School credit the education they received there with giving them the spiritual power not to lose hope during the dark times that were to come during the Cultural Revolution.[11]

As the son of a civilian, not a military leader, however, Jinping felt somewhat out of place. In 2014, he recalled,

> The August 1 Middle School is a school for military children, so most of the parents of my classmates were in the military. Every weekend, when the parents came to pick up my classmates, they wore epaulettes and badges. It was very impressive. I thought to myself, Why does father not have an epaulette? When I returned home on the weekend, I asked my family, Why is it that my father does not have a military uniform, does not have a military rank? My family told me that father was not in the military system, father was vice-premier [*fu zongli*]! The next day, I returned to the dormitory, and I proudly told my buddies what my father did! He is vice-director [*fu jingli*]! But my classmates chipped in and asked, vice-director? Your father runs a market?[12]

In 2003, an interviewer bluntly asked whether Xi Jinping had enjoyed a privileged lifestyle as a child. Xi responded, "It can be put this way: there were no worries about clothes or food, but my father's demands upon us made us live very frugally." As an example, Xi said that he was forced to wear the clothes of his older sisters as hand-me-downs. He tried to depict his own family as especially thrifty, but in doing so, he also revealed the "privileges" he enjoyed when participating in activities with the party elite: "At the Lunar New Year, we participated in several evening parties; when we went to the

Great Hall of the People or to Tiananmen Square, the staffers would ask whose children were wearing such run-down clothing? Those who understood would reply that we were the children of the Xi family."[13]

Although Xi Zhongxun's children spent most of their time at school, he did have time to spend with them on weekends. Xi even cleaned their clothes and bathed them, although bath time was not fun. In 1993, Jinping told his sister,

> When I was young, I was most afraid of father coming home late at night and waking me up from a dream to take a bath. He thought the water he had used for his own bath after coming home was clean, and he did not want to waste it, so he felt a need to wake up Yuanping and me and force us into his used bath water for a dip and a bit of cleaning. After a terrible time in the bath, father still did not dispose of the water; he would force us to put our clothes in it to be washed the next morning.[14]

By several accounts, Xi Zhongxun was a ferocious disciplinarian. Even Qi Xin wrote, "Sometimes, I really believed that your demands on the children were too strict."[15] Xi's children often spoke of their father's thriftiness. Qianping wrote, "I remember, when we were little, none of us were willing to eat at the same table as father. We were terrified of his strict rules on frugality. For his entire life, father was extremely economical, and he cared about thriftiness. For example, when eating, he never allowed us to drop a single piece of rice or bits of food; if we were not careful and dropped any food, he would immediately pick it up and eat it."[16] In 2001, Jinping told two interviewers at the end of a conversation that he would not ask them to stay and eat. "Actually, eating with me is a form of suffering," he said. "I am the son of a peasant. I have never been picky about eating, and, moreover, I never allow people to leave any leftovers."[17] Despite his frugality, Xi Zhongxun put on weight as he settled into his office in Beijing; Liu Shaoqi would often pat him on the belly and joke, "Look—doesn't this seem like the stomach of a capitalist?"[18]

Xi's harshness also included physical punishment. In his diaries, Li Rui described a conversation with Ren Zhongyi—who would later succeed Xi Zhongxun as party boss of Guangdong—in March 1998: "[We] discussed how Xi raised his three sons; he was extremely brutal based on feudal rules of etiquette that included beatings."[19] Journalist John Garnaut, who has conducted extensive interviews with elite political families in China, writes,

FIGURE 7. Xi Zhongxun with his sons Jinping (*left*) and Yuanping (*center*), 1958. Source: *Xi Zhongxun huace*, 167.

"Xi Zhongxun, despite his noble exterior, drank too much and would occasionally explode with anger. His children were sometimes on the receiving end of his anger, according to a close family friend who witnessed such occasions."[20] According to another journalist with deep ties in Beijing, on one occasion, Xi was so angry that he lined up his children, as well as the child of another high-ranking leader who often visited their home, and struck them one by one.[21]

Xi was tougher than most, but his behavior was still reflective of the context of the times. Many "cadre offspring" deeply worried their parents because they played too much and did not study hard.[22] The Xi household was not the only "Red aristocratic" family in which children would kowtow; many elite families had such strict protocols.[23] When a friend asked Xi why he was so cruel, he responded, "I do not do this to make them fear me. It is to make them feel a sense of awe and veneration for heaven and earth so that, from a young age, they have understood that one cannot act in an anarchic fashion." In Xi's words, children who did not respect their parents were a disaster when they entered society.[24]

The behavior of the children of party leaders was a serious, and extremely sensitive, political issue. In June 1952, Mao called for an end, as soon as possible, to "aristocracy schools" that exclusively admitted children of top-ranking officials. Even after Mao's order, however, those schools still primarily catered to the children of the new elite. In May 1953, shortly before Xi Jinping's birth, Zhou Enlai warned the offspring of high-ranking cadres that if they became separated from the people, "the people will not forgive you, and Chairman Mao will not agree." Zhou argued that the Qing dynasty had collapsed because the Manchus spoiled their children, who then became "corrupt opium addicts."[25]

Yet Zhou's words were not heeded. In September 1960, the Political Department of the Beijing Military Region summoned the leadership of the elite Beijing schools to a meeting that determined that one of the main challenges facing the schools was "the sense of superiority" and "privilege" among students. To combat this tendency, teachers were to emphasize revolutionary idealism, and students were required to behave politely toward their teachers, mix with the masses, wash their own underwear, and take public transportation. Parents were told not to give their children nice clothes, allow them to bring hunting rifles or cameras to school, bring them to dances or banquets, or allow them to look at classified documents.[26]

Yet still the situation did not improve. In 1962, a student at Harbin Military Engineering Institute, the son of a commander of an important military district, contacted an enemy agent. An investigation concluded that the treachery was the result of a "Red-by-birth" sense of superiority. When Mao saw the report, he demanded that the department write another, more detailed one. The results were sobering; of all cadre offspring at the school, 54.3 percent were "mediocre," and 18.5 percent were "ideologically backward, had poor academic records, displayed a privileged lifestyle, and learned very slowly."[27] In 1965, Mao told his daughter Li Min that "the offspring of cadres are a huge disaster."[28]

Xi understood this political environment, but he had a softer side too. On one occasion, he picked up Jinping and carried him around on his head. When Jinping started urinating on him, Zhongxun waited patiently until Jinping had finished. Xi believed that when children were urinating, they should not be frightened, otherwise they will "have an illness for the rest of their life."[29] Xi and Qi Xin would help their children play jump rope, and the siblings played "horse," riding on their father's back. Although the children feared their father, they cherished the time they spent together with him. In Qiaoqiao's words, "I was happiest at those times, but the time we had together with father and mother was truly too little."[30]

On the weekends, when Xi's children were home from school, he would include them in his United Front work, bringing them to the homes of individuals such as Fu Zuoyi, Qu Wu, Burhan Shahidi, Saifuddin Azizi, Ulanhu, Deng Baoshan, and the Panchen Lama.[31] Drinking was a significant part of United Front work, and the children knew it. On one occasion, when Xi hosted a banquet at Beijing Friendship Hotel, the Panchen Lama poured a large cup of Moutai for Xi's assistant. When the man waved his hand and said he could drink no more, the Panchen Lama grew upset. Xi convinced his assistant to drink the Maotai to protect the Panchen Lama's sensibilities, causing a severe hangover.[32] In 2015, at the beginning of a dinner conversation following their historic first meeting in Singapore, Ma Ying-jeou, the president of Taiwan, asked Xi Jinping how well he could handle his liquor. Xi Jinping laughed and said, "My tolerance for liquor is low!" He then started to reminisce about his father. When Zhou Enlai drank, the late premier would put away a whole *jin* (0.5 liters) of Maotai. As Zhou's right-hand man, according to Jinping, "my father would usually have to join the battle." Jinping emotionally said, "When I was a child, I often saw him stumbling home in the middle of the night. I once asked him, Why are you always like this? It was not until I was a little older that I finally understood that this was part of my father's work." Ma recalls feeling touched by the "love of his father that was clearly visible" on Jinping's face when he told this story.[33]

Xi regaled his children with tales of the revolution. Qiaoqiao recalled, "Father told us about how, when creating the Shaan-Gan Border Region base area, he was always in a state of high readiness; he not only never parted from his gun, even when he was sleeping, he never undid his puttees. He kept his head facing the wall and his feet facing the door while sleeping on the *kang* to be ready at all times for any emergency situation." That habit saved Xi's life on one occasion: two enemy soldiers with swords rushed into his cave, and Xi ran toward the door screaming. His voice stunned the enemy soldiers long enough that he could rush past them. He later told his daughter that if he had kept the habit of old peasants and had slept with his head facing the door, he probably would have died. Xi also described two occasions when he was almost eaten by a leopard. The second occasion was the most dangerous: Xi had just fled from enemies and entered a forest when he encountered the animal. He could not fire his gun because his pursuers would then find him, so he simply faced the leopard for a prolonged period from about ten steps away. He was so frightened that his hair stood on end and sweat soaked his clothes. When Xi's children commended him for his bravery, he said, "The two leopards I encountered had probably just finished eating, or perhaps it was because I made my eyes bigger than theirs."[34]

Qi Xin saw the children less than their father did. Later, as top leader, Xi Jinping would recall how his mother taught him a "beautiful moral viewpoint" by sharing with him children's books such as *Biography of Yue Fei*, about a famous general from the Southern Song dynasty. Jinping described one memorable volume that included the story about how the famous patriot's own mother tattooed the words "Serve the country with the utmost loyalty" on his back.[35] But Qi Xin lived at the party school during the week since it was so far away from the Xi household. Despite their lengthy separation, Qi later wrote, "I never considered staying at home with the children for even a moment longer or even changing my job to be closer to home. At the time, all I could think about was to serve the decisions of the organization; work could not be delayed. Even when the children suffered from serious illnesses, I did not ask for leave." Because she had so little time, Qi Xin did not even participate in fun weekend activities with her husband and the children. Zhou Enlai found the situation a little strange when he regularly observed that Xi would bring along his children on his own.[36] When Zhou finally did see Qi, he was surprised by how young she looked and decided that she should participate in activities with foreigners. Xi refused. Some people who encountered her asked, "Why is it that Vice-Premier Xi's wife dresses so much like a bumpkin?" Her feelings were hurt, but Xi consoled her by saying, "It's better to look like a bumpkin than to look like a foreigner!"[37]

PART III CATASTROPHE

13
THE GREAT LEAP FORWARD

Xi performed poorly in the vote count for membership on the Central Committee in 1956, probably because of the Gao Gang incident, but he remained near the apex of power. Although not a member of the politburo, he still attended its meetings during this period.[1] As secretary general of the State Council, he was the most important assistant to Zhou Enlai, who largely ran the country for much of the 1950s. Their working relationship was especially close. Before 1958, the secretaries in the Office of the Premier served not only Zhou but also Xi as well as Vice-Premiers Chen Yi and Chen Yun.[2]

The relationship between Zhou and Xi had casual elements. Zhou made fun of Xi's Shaanxi accent, especially his pronunciation of "Soviet Union." But Zhou was an extremely difficult boss. He frustrated subordinates by often ignoring basic organizational tasks. Busy work could distract him from longer term strategic planning. Zhou was extremely attentive to certain details, especially interactions with foreigners and United Front targets, and he did not trust his lieutenants to take an initiative on their own. When people were late for meetings, he would demand an explanation and criticize them for wasting time. Additionally, Zhou was a workaholic. Xi later acknowledged that he lacked the extraordinary energy of Premier Zhou, who could recharge by simply closing his eyes for a moment. When two of Xi's direct subordinates became sick from exhaustion in 1959, Zhou joked about the brutal working conditions. "The climate inside the 'Red walls' [Zhongnanhai] is tough," Zhou said. "Everyone should be careful. Working with no breaks is not good."[3]

On at least two occasions, Xi privately described an example of Zhou's fury that had left a deep impression on him. After a visiting dignitary's plane took off, the group that wished him farewell at the airport immediately began to disperse. Zhou was furious. He yelled, "Come back! Come back!" and he sent his assistants to summon them. After everyone returned, Zhou lined them up in a row and demanded, "Who was the first to leave?" When no one answered, Zhou named Xi and Chief of the General Staff Huang Kecheng. "Step forward!" Zhou shouted, using martial language. Xi and Huang obeyed while everyone else stood at attention. "At ease!" Zhou ordered. Then he spoke in a serious tone: "When the plane of a guest takes off, it will fly around in a circle three times to bid farewell. How could you leave as soon as it took off! That's outrageous! In the future, you must strictly adhere to discipline." No one left until Zhou finally, again speaking in military language, said, "Dismissed." When Xi told the story, he blamed Huang Kecheng for leaving early and left himself out.[4]

On the State Council, Xi was positioned not only to observe Zhou Enlai; he was also in a special, almost unique, position to understand China at the grass roots as well. When Xi joined the State Council, he assigned one of his secretaries the task of regularly visiting the Petition Receipt Office to help manage petitions and visits by civilians. That secretary reported to Xi about local situations throughout the country. In late 1954, Xi received word that people in the Northwest were upset that cooking oil was so difficult to procure. One individual wrote a clever poem, indicating that the situation was better before the party came to power. Another individual urinated on the noisy wheels of his cart and said, "I don't have [cooking] oil to eat, but here you want to eat [lubricating] oil!" Xi's secretary removed those colorful anecdotes from the report, but Xi wanted them to remain. When he learned that some peasants were begging on their knees for mercy, or even committing suicide, because they could not pay back their debts to the state, he said, "If we party cadres oppose the masses, then we should worry that the masses will beat us with poles. This is the lesson of the collapse of the Nationalist regime."[5]

He knew that tensions in society were increasing yet not getting the attention they deserved. In May 1957, Xi and Yang Shangkun, who was director of the General Office, held the People's Republic's first nationwide meeting on the petition system. In his speech to the participants, Xi criticized those cadres who ignored or punished petitioners. What was the reason for this careless behavior? Xi answered, "After victory in the entire nation and after the leading organs entered the cities, the living and work environments changed. This kind of change had a definite influence on the thinking of our cadres. A real change occurred. What was the nature of this change? It was a move far away from the masses, a weakening in the consciousness of the masses, and a cooling in the care for the difficult living conditions of the masses." Xi told his audience that petitions were a crucial way for the party to understand when mistakes occurred during campaigns. If problems were not exposed, they could not be solved. "What is the current trend with regard to petitions?" he asked. "In my opinion, the situation is increasingly tense, but just how long these tensions will last is currently difficult to say. That is because the current trend consists of contradictions manifesting as a group, and the nature of the petitions has changed. Especially with regard to petitions delivered in person, now it is not just one or two people petitioning. Often it is several or several dozen all at once," he said. Xi concluded by addressing the challenge in apocalyptic terms. "It is necessary to be emotionally prepared, to strengthen ideological thinking, to stand up, and to take responsibility for solving the problems. There is no other way. Otherwise, our days will be numbered," he said.[6]

As the top central leader managing petitions in Beijing, Xi learned that starvation appeared even before the Great Leap Forward. In the winter of 1957, he received a letter from Gansu about cadres using force against peasants and "damaging production," which led to deaths from lack of food.[7] As early as April 1958, Xi forwarded a report to Vice-Premier Chen Yun about starvation, even death, across thirteen provinces—a problem which was attributed, at the time, to weather problems, false reporting at the grass roots, and the greed of party cadres.[8]

One of Xi's answers to these problems of "bureaucratism" that petitions were revealing was to subject government employees in his purview to physical labor. He clearly saw such work as redemptive. In his speech on the petition system in May 1957, he said, "A few days ago in the State Council, more than a hundred people went to the countryside to participate in the building of a fence for tomatoes. That should have been easy labor, but after four hours, my legs were sore for many days. If you do not labor, you cannot know the taste of labor."[9]

The party's methods would soon go far beyond building tomato fences. In a new rectification campaign, which Xi led within the government apparatus, he affirmed elements of "mass democracy," such as the "airing of views" (*mingfang*), which encouraged subordinates to criticize leading cadres, and "big-character posters" (large political messages mounted on walls). In November, Xi said proudly that the number of big-character posters had reached 220,000, and he described them as "very good weapons. They not only expose problems very quickly and sharply. They are also deep and broad." Mass meetings for the airing of views could no longer be restrained: "If anyone has an opinion, they should speak up; if they do not speak up now, they can blame only themselves for falling behind." Any attempts to oppose criticism, he warned, were a "suppression of democracy."[10]

Xi's warnings seemed prescient when, on November 30, *People's Daily* published an explosive article about the situation in Guanzhuang, an area officially governed by Hebei Province but also the home of ten central government organs that all fell under the purview of the city of Beijing. Hebei, Beijing, and the Ministry of Building Materials Industry, Guanzhuang's biggest employer, all neglected to take a severe deterioration in public security there seriously. Hoodlums, thieves, and rapists scared the local population so badly that women refused to go anywhere alone.[11] Xi sent a five-person work group to investigate, and he was furious when Minister Lai Jifa still failed to take the issue seriously enough. Xi did not believe the problem was simply organizational. On December 25, he said to Lai, "The situation in Guanzhuang is so chaotic. Could the presence of so many abnormal phenomena simply be a problem of weak ideological leadership, or is there a bigger problem? Could there be counterrevolutionaries and evil people there? Could they be in control of some of our institutions? Otherwise, how could antisocialist power there be so strong?"[12] It was a radical reaction, and Xi used radical methods. He turned Guanzhuang into a model for "airing of views," and Lai was subjected to the extraordinary humiliation of publishing a self-criticism in the *People's Daily*.[13]

FROM OPPOSING RASH ADVANCE TO THE GREAT LEAP FORWARD

Xi was Zhou's right-hand man running the government and the individual in charge of the State Council's internal "intelligence" apparatus, and the story of Xi and the Great Leap Forward, one of the most tragic famines in human history, is revealing in special ways about how such a terrible calamity could have occurred. Xi saw Mao humiliate Zhou Enlai, his boss at the time, and purge Peng Dehuai, his former superior during the war against the Nationalists for the Northwest years earlier—in both cases, for expressing, at different times, doubts about a fanciful economic agenda. He had seen how a wish to please Mao, as well as a real desire to catch up with the West, had led to unrealistic agricultural and industrial policies. He had also witnessed how fear and ambition created silence when those policies failed. And he beheld, both on his own inspection trips and in reports from throughout the country, the waste, hunger, and death that ensued.

In 1955, the party successfully established collectives in the countryside. Fresh off from this triumph, in January 1956, with Mao's encouragement, the State Council accelerated China's plans for economic modernization. But the new agenda proved too ambitious for both industry and agriculture, and, in February, Zhou began to sound the alarm. At the end of March, Xi was tasked with implementing a somewhat cautious State Council directive on spring plowing. The collectives had not yet fully organized their resources and labor, the document warned, and some were losing work time to bad planning and spending their budgets on wasteful projects.[14]

Crucially, Zhou did not believe that such acts were a challenge to Mao—all that would be required was a correction in implementation. But Mao was not convinced that anything was seriously wrong with the economy. In April, at a politburo meeting, Mao pushed for a higher-capital construction budget. The other participants disagreed, believing that would lead to shortages. But Mao stuck to his position and ended the meeting. A few days later, Zhou told Mao privately that he could not "in good conscience" agree to Mao's proposal. Mao was unhappy and their meeting was tense, but finally Mao acceded to Zhou's view. When Mao was sent a draft of the *People's Daily* editorial that was to introduce the so-called Oppose Rash Advance, Mao wrote on it, "Will not read this," but nevertheless the editorial was soon published. At the time, even individuals who understood Mao very well did not believe the chairman disagreed in principle with Oppose Rash Advance.[15]

It only later became clear that the incident deeply rankled Mao. Oppose Rash Advance would prove to be a serious and rare lapse in Zhou's political ability to manage Mao. In the last months of 1957, he started to express disappointment that Zhou had poured cold water on rapid development the previous year. In January 1958, at the Nanning Conference, Mao took his criticisms of Zhou to a new level. He accused Zhou of wanting to develop the

State Council into another "core" within the leadership. The State Council, Mao believed, had prevented him from participating in economic policy, only allowing him to give the plans a thumbs up or a thumbs down. Vice-Premier Bo Yibo felt Mao's words were unfair—the State Council had consulted carefully with the politburo, but in practice, it would have been impossible to pester Mao for approval on every single issue. Even more worrisome, Mao said that Oppose Rash Advance was only "fifty meters" away from the rightists. Zhou delivered a self-criticism, lasting from 8:00 p.m. until 1:00 a.m., in which he admitted to "rightist, conservative thinking." Mao's attack on Zhou was a watershed moment in the degradation of party norms for open discussion on key issues at the elite level.[16]

Although Xi did not attend the Nanning Conference, back in Beijing, Zhou and Xi discussed the debacle. "I made yet another mistake," Zhou told Xi—a subtle criticism of Mao, as the premier's words meant that the chairman kept criticizing him no matter what he did. Xi responded, "We will all take responsibility."[17] Xi's words revealed more loyalty and character than Chen Yun had displayed. Mao believed Chen was even more to blame than Zhou for Oppose Rash Advance, but Chen conveniently fell sick in late 1957 just as Mao began to criticize the policy. With Chen absent from Nanning, Zhou took full responsibility.[18]

Yet Zhou's torment was not over. West Flower Hall, Zhou's residence and office, which used to be full of energy and people, suddenly became very quiet. The premier took to drinking late at night to console himself. He even started to catalog his books in case he were to lose his position.[19] In February, Mao ordered that economic decision-making be transferred from Zhou's State Council to Deng Xiaoping's secretariat, which had been established in 1956 to manage party affairs. It was an ironic decision, as Deng, too, had supported Oppose Rash Advance, but Deng had won Mao's affection by supporting the chairman's new ambitious economic agenda and demonstrating toughness in the Antirightist Campaign. In May, Zhou tried to resign, and a secretary saw tears in Zhou's eyes and more gray hairs as the premier prepared yet another self-criticism. Zhou was allowed to retain his position, but Mao established five small groups to supervise the government and to report directly to Deng. Mao declared that, in the future, "primary political principles will be decided by the Politburo, and specific deployment will be decided by the secretariat."[20]

Deng and Zhou had a high level of personal trust, and Deng tried to protect Zhou and consult with him. Yet the situation put the State Council in a difficult position. Over the course of the Leap, Deng as well as his deputy Peng Zhen, who had a fraught relationship with Zhou, would prove to be enthusiastic true believers, constantly pushing for targets that even surpassed what Mao wanted in both steel production and the socialist transformation of agriculture. But the State Council would be expected to implement those policies. Chen Yun complained that "some people went to the secretariat to find enthusiasm and went to the premier to complain about difficulties." Zhou knew the goals were fanciful. While the secretariat sometimes neglected to conduct regular investigations, the State Council had a clearer sense of the problems. Now chastened, however, Zhou's priority was not good policy. Rather, Xi saw his superior at the State Council put political survival and Mao's authority first.[21]

Although the secretariat was now in charge of the economy, within the State Council, Xi still had the power to harangue government cadres. By March 1958, ten months into the rectification campaign, he was no longer only emphasizing ideological transformation. The campaign was taking on a heavier policy component that emphasized politics over practical know-how. Xi was delighted that even cooks and drivers were discussing politics. Henceforth, Xi said, the priority would be to better integrate ideology with production. Everyone had to take a Great Leap: "Anyone who wants to crawl will not survive." Leaders had to trust and rely upon the masses, he said, and he praised the role of "mass airings of views" in the development of more ambitious planning.[22]

In June, Xi, Zhou, and hundreds of central government employees went to the giant Ming Tombs Reservoir project to engage in manual labor. The purpose of the trip was to provide a model for cadres throughout the country to engage in such work. Together with Xi, Wen Jize, who worked in China's broadcasting apparatus, formed a small group to transport stones in a cart. Xi pushed and Wen pulled. But Wen, not used to the work, gashed his leg. They worked until 6:00 p.m., when they ate some steamed buns and salted vegetables and soup from a common bucket. They continued until 11:00 p.m. and then spent the night in a workers' dormitory.[23]

A few days after his own participation in tough physical labor, Xi gave remarks that stand out not only for their strong anti-intellectualism but also for his praise of the new politically charged approach within the Second Ministry of Machine Building—China's fledgling nuclear industry. He sav-

FIGURE 8. Members of the party leadership on their way to engage in physical labor at the Ming Tombs Reservoir, including Deng Xiaoping (*sixth from right*), Liu Shaoqi (*fourth from right*), Xi Zhongxun (*third from right*), and Zhou Enlai (*second from right*), June 1958. Source: Zhonggong zhongyang dangshi yanjiushi, *Xi Zhongxun huace*, 162.

aged the cadres there for previously suffering from "empiricism," meaning a nonideological worldview. When their "old empirics" had failed them, they started to believe superstitiously in "experts" and "foreigners," Xi said. But the Second Ministry of Machine Building had turned the situation around. Now, everyone, including nonexperts, could make suggestions. Many people stayed up all night working. Some plans formerly thought to have needed ten to fifteen years to complete could be finished in three or five years or even in just a few months in the newly charged atmosphere. Some goals that were previously unimaginable because of the low technological foundation were now on track to reach the level of the capitalist countries by the July 1 or October 1 holidays. Everyone was included—cooks were mobilized to have food ready all night long and to send food straight to offices.[24]

Xi did not attend the August Beidaihe meeting, when the party dramatically raised steel targets and ordered the establishment of people's communes in the countryside—fateful decisions that officially signified the beginning of the Great Leap Forward. His absence seemed significant to Xi—he mentioned it to Mao's former secretary Li Rui in 1985, and a Cultural Revolution–era document claims that Xi was not allowed to attend the meeting, which "left a grudge in Xi's heart."[25]

Yet, curiously, it was around this time that the chairman reached out to Xi directly. One evening in the summer of 1958, after nine o'clock in the evening, Xi went to the Zhongnanhai swimming pool. Mao was still swimming when Xi entered. Mao said, "Zhongxun, you come in too; let's swim together for a bit." But Xi said, "Chairman, go ahead and swim, I won't go in for a swim today." Mao got out of the pool, took a towel, sat down, and gifted Xi with a book. He asked the younger man if he still felt burdened by the political fallout after the Gao Gang affair. When Xi replied no, Mao encouraged him to continue working hard. "I said to Enlai, you are still young, your health is good, you're a tough person, you're a promising youth, and it is necessary to give you a bit of a heavier burden," Mao said.[26]

Mao's encouraging words must have excited Xi—perhaps the stigma he had carried for several years was passing. But at the same time, Xi roundly condemned anyone who cared more about themselves than about the party. During a conversation with writers from *China Youth*, Xi described a "battlefield of class warfare" between "the advanced and those who were behind, the correct and incorrect, proletariat thinking and bourgeois thinking" in the minds of all young intellectuals. He claimed that, rather than knowledge, the most important skill was a "Communist consciousness." He went so far as to say that "the lowly are the most intelligent; the elite are the most ignorant." Xi warned about people who were too smart for their own good and those who refused to acknowledge criticism about their own problematic thinking. Individualism was a "germ." Even if small, this germ "does not fear the heavens, does not fear the earth, and it is extraordinarily daring." He continued, "Even if you weigh eighty kilograms, even if today you have only a tiny, tiny bit of individualism in your body, once it develops, it will devour you whole." This germ, moreover, was contagious, and healthy people who did not continuously examine themselves would also "become sick."[27]

On August 14, Xi finally had some good news for the cadres working in national government bodies—the rectification campaign that had begun fifteen months earlier was finally over. But that only meant that a "new revolutionary campaign" was beginning. Now, the party would focus on a "technological revolution" and, ominously, a "cultural revolution." The purpose of these campaigns was to serve the Great Leap Forward by mobilizing the revolutionary fervor of party members. This would require continuous, personal ideological transformation. Such a process was "long-term" and "arduous," Xi said. No one was safe. "Some old cadres relaxed their ideological self-transformation, and the result was that they committed a major mistake and were removed from the party. This is a serious lesson." Moreover, as the Great Leap Forward achieved its extraordinary promises, Xi said, it would be even easier to fall into complacency.[28]

THE LUSHAN PLENUM

Although the secretariat was now firmly in command of the economy, Zhou tried to better understand how the Great Leap Forward was proceeding. For that purpose, between August and October 1958, he sent Xi on a trip to Shaanxi, Gansu, Qinghai, Inner Mongolia, and Ningxia. Xi's former secretary Tian Fang later asserted that, during the trip, Xi could tell something had gone wrong. When Xi visited the Fenghuo People's Commune, a national model, in Shaanxi's Liquan County, he was baffled to see small mounds covering the fields. "What are these for?" he asked. He was told that a scientist in Beijing had discovered that if more soil was exposed to sunlight, then the crops would grow faster. Doubtful, Xi crouched down and examined the roots in the dirt. Xi, who had grown up in the countryside, knew better. "The surface of the mound seems to have increased exposure, but the roots underneath are still only concentrated in a small area. Even if there is sunlight but soil and fertilizer are limited, how can production be increased?!" he asked. A welcome banquet served thirty-plus dishes of chicken, duck, and fish for only a few more than ten people. His hosts told the guests that Communism was no longer distant. Xi furrowed his brow and quietly said, "How can it be that fast if it is still the same people and the same land?"[29]

While in Shaanxi, Xi visited more than five hundred employees of the State Council and the Shaanxi government who, six months earlier, had been sent down to engage in manual labor. He praised them for their transformation: "Many among you, when working in the government apparatus, were in poor shape, too weak to withstand a gust of wind. Many knew little about the countryside and could not get along with peasants. But now? Everyone has ruddy faces, everyone is in top shape, and you are full of spirit. You understand the value of labor and the glory of peasant collective power. You have developed a deep friendship with the laboring people." Xi named ambitious goals: "to annihilate the difference between mental and physical labor and to transform oneself into a Communist new person." Xi described why that was necessary: "Compared to the peasants, all you have done is only read a few more books. In that regard, the peasants cannot compete with you. But we must understand that the peasants, through practice, have collected a rich understanding of class struggle and productive struggle. The intellectuals cannot compete with that." Xi would have known that his audience would be skeptical of these remarks. He noted reports that stated that 80 percent of the sent-down workers were upset. "But I think that even the other 20 percent cannot say that they do not have any ideological problems either," he said. Yet Xi doubled down, warning them that even physical labor might not save them if they did not "continuously engage," through their own initiative, in an "ideological revolution."[30]

Xi's secretary claims that when Xi then arrived in Lanzhou, the capital of Gansu, he was concerned about construction of the Yintao Dam in a region that lacked electricity and industrial machinery. Workers from Sichuan and Henan were coming to labor, but there was not enough infrastructure to support them. Xi told Zhang Zhongliang, the provincial party leader and an old comrade from his revolutionary days, "You can't do this! In the future, the common people will suffer." But Zhang replied, "Let me try, and then we will see!" In public, however, Xi was supportive. When he visited the site, he said, "This project has . . . international significance. . . . It demonstrates that we are not only the masters of society but also the masters of nature. The crucial factor here is daring. . . . This is the spirit of Communism. . . . Gansu has let us see the future of Communism." The project was a disaster. Workers labored for months at a time on segments that were later abandoned. By late spring of the next year, Gansu was facing mass starvation, a situation exacerbated by the Yintao Dam. Zhou tasked Xi to hold a meeting to determine a plan for the neighboring provinces to send emergency aid. But they were too late, and a shocking number of people had already starved to death. In December 1960, the Yintao project was abandoned.[31] A year later, local officials complained that Xi knew about the endeavor, and even visited it, but did not discover any problems at the time.[32]

On the 1958 trip, Xi visited other sites in Gansu as well. On September 28, he went to Aksai Chin, which was heavily populated by nomadic Kazakhs. He warned the local leadership to act cautiously with regard to the establishment of communes and free mess halls, which could lead to waste and lazy behavior.[33] A few days later, in Gansu's northwestern Dunhuang County, Xi said that he had noticed people were not paying sufficient attention to production in many places. He warned that the county lacked enough resources to achieve Communism; Communism meant machines, electricity, and a high level of Communist sensibility. Ending the differences between city and countryside to establish communes did not constitute Communism. Xi continued, "Now, the consciousness of the masses has indeed grown, and the authority of the party and Chairman Mao are very high. The problem is that the leadership and the party only have to say one word and the masses will follow. This requires us to be more careful, to strive for care and accuracy. Things must be managed appropriately."[34]

In his official November 6 report to Zhou and the politburo, Xi did not explicitly raise questions about false numbers. He wrote that, other than Shaanxi, all the provinces he visited had, in the past, been poor agricultural regions. Now, however, they were bountiful. "Average grain per capita in several provinces is more than five hundred kilograms, Ningxia averages 850 kilograms per person, Gansu averages 750 kilograms per person, and some counties in Shaanxi reach two thousand kilograms," he wrote.[35] Yet he raised some concerns as well. Although collectivization in the countryside was the right policy, he wrote, it was necessary to pay attention to local conditions and tempo. The party was promising too many social benefits, and waste was also a problem. Material incentives had weakened. Peasants were spending their time making steel instead of producing food in the new communes, which were not receiving enough attention.[36]

This report may have been one contribution to greater caution on Mao's part. Although the party had decided at Beidaihe to move from "socialist collective ownership" to "socialist ownership by the whole people" in the countryside within three to six years, in November, Mao decided to back off from that brazen goal.[37] At the end of the year, Xi spoke out again. He provided a measured voice when he attended the enlarged politburo sessions and the Central Committee's Sixth Plenum in November and December in Wuhan. He warned about the communes going too far—they should not encompass an entire county or provide for everything, like what he had seen in Dunhuang. It was impossible to leap directly from socialism to Communism, he said. China could not yet give up on "distribution for work" for "distribution according to need." If productive relations went beyond productive forces, Xi argued, production would be negatively affected.[38] Despite Xi's remarks, in Wuhan, the Central Committee decided to increase the grain target from four hundred to five hundred million tons to 525 million tons. The next month, Deng's secretariat further raised the target to 650 million tons.[39]

In March 1959, Xi traveled to Shanghai for a politburo meeting. On the night of his arrival at the Jinjiang Hotel, a representative of the party's General Office came to see Xi with two expensive Panda brand cigarettes—and a new draft proposal naming Xi a vice-premier. The purpose of the visit was not only celebratory but to gauge Xi's reaction. Xi immediately said thank you but declined the position. He then drafted a letter and, after multiple revisions, sent it to Mao and Deng: "I considered the matter repeatedly, but my mood was extremely anxious. Thinking back on the past few years working as secretary general of the State Council, I did not do good work and that was primarily because of my own faults. . . . Therefore, my conscience is extremely guilty. I will still gladly remain in the same position for the next State Council to do some more work and to do it a bit better. This way, work will not be hindered, and perhaps this will be more beneficial for me." According to Xi's secretary, the letter honestly reflected Xi's feelings at the time. Despite his protests, on April 28 Xi became a vice-premier.[40]

The reasons for Xi's surprise—and reticence—have never been made explicit. But certainly the promotion came at a strange time for him. The previous summer, Mao had praised him during a poolside chat. Yet, after

Gao Gang's downfall, Xi might have feared any expression of ambition was dangerous. Additionally, for more than a year, Mao had been regularly humiliating Zhou Enlai and attacking the State Council, and Xi had become increasingly aware of the problems of the Leap. Although Xi's secretary believed the promotion was Mao's idea, Xi would later claim that Chen Yi, his comrade on the State Council, had suggested the promotion.[41] In any case, the position signified that he had entered the very top echelon of the government structure—a welcome change for someone who had spent the last several years suffering from the aftermath of the Gao Gang incident. He was the youngest of the sixteen vice-premiers by four years (after Li Xiannian).[42]

In subsequent months, Xi helped the top leadership understand the growing crisis. April 1959 was a key moment. On April 6, the office of the secretary general of the State Council wrote a report directly to Xi, with copies to Zhou Enlai and the vice-premiers, on starvation in five provinces. On April 11, Xi wrote to Zhou asking the premier to read the document. Cautiously, Xi asserted that "this situation might have improved recently, but certain places will not have done a good job, so it appears that they should be contacted separately to remind them to keep an eye out." On April 12, Zhou forwarded the document, as well as another one submitted by a central commission on disaster relief, to Mao and other leaders. Four days later, Xi forwarded to Zhou yet another document from the office of the secretary general of the State Council—this one based on reports from cadres who had been sent to the countryside. This time, Xi included a warning that "the problem is still very serious, and I believe that the measures taken to address the issue are still not resolute enough." Delays would "make repercussions even worse." "The demands of the masses are not high," Xi wrote. "They say that as long as they eat their fill, they will climb a mountain of swords. I think that every location that lacks food should be sent grain. Otherwise, the impact on production will be too great."[43]

On April 17, Mao ordered that the two documents he received on April 12 be distributed by plane to fifteen provincial leaders. Those two documents were apparently the first official information that Mao saw about the famine. Mao now warned that twenty-five million people faced starvation, although he saw it as a "temporary" problem.[44] Zhou tasked Xi with meeting the heads of the five provinces that were described in the April 6 State Council document. Eleven provincial leaders ended up attending an important meeting in Beijing that began on April 18. Xi chaired the first day's session as the regional leaders delivered their reports, and they confirmed that edema and death by starvation were already occurring. Xi told them to write summaries of their findings by the end of the day.[45]

Problems grew so serious that, in May, Xi frankly admitted to a delegation from East Germany who were visiting China's precision mechanics and optics factories that, during the Great Leap Forward, quality had been neglected in favor of quantity.[46] In the middle of the month, Zhou proposed that eight vice-premiers make individual inspection trips to investigate steel production, and Xi was sent to Henan.[47]

In late June, while still outside Beijing, Xi was ordered to travel through the capital to Jiangxi Province's Lushan Mountain for an enlarged session of the politburo. By then, Mao, who had just visited Hunan and had heard warnings from his own family, had decided that it was time to "cool things down a bit and study some political economy." Back in Beijing, Xi read a report from the petition office that, since the beginning of June, the capital had received nineteen letters from Gansu about the lack of food. In one commune, the cafeterias had been disbanded, and each person was only allowed one hundred to 150 grams of food per day, so the people were forced to eat wild herbs. In another commune, more than 620 people in April and May became bloated from lack of nutrition. When a commune had no choice but to feed people flaxseed residue, which normally was only given to livestock, the peasants vomited or suffered diarrhea. One petition even included a sample of the "food" that starving people were eating to survive. When Xi tasted it, he said, "How the hell are people eating this!" A report summarizing these petitions warned that local authorities were doing nothing, and they were even trying to stop people from telling the truth. Anyone who complained was labeled a rightist, so the masses "dared to be angry but dared not speak." The views in these petitions matched exactly the conclusions Xi had reached in Henan. He asked the office of the secretary general of the State Council to write up a report based on these materials for him to take to Lushan, and he also sent an investigation team to Gansu.[48]

On June 30, as Xi's vehicle was halfway up Lushan Mountain, the car in front of him stopped at a turn that faced out on Hanjiang's plateau far below. Defense Minister Peng Dehuai exited, so Xi got out to chat with him. Both had gone on inspection tours of the Northwest in 1958, and they had similar views of the dangerous situation in the country. Peng, and probably Xi as well, had seen peasants fleeing famine from the train window on the way to the Lushan meeting. As they looked out into the distance while conversing, Xi's secretary, Tian Fang, watched and could not help but feel that he was witnessing a repeat of their partnership of years past.[49]

When the Lushan meeting officially started on July 2, Peng and Xi were both in the Northwest Small Group. Peng's remarks were critical but measured and not nearly as sharp as what people were saying privately. Xi had sent the materials he had collected from the office of the secretary general of the State Council to Zhou Enlai, who forwarded them to Mao. Soon thereafter, it was distributed via a newsletter to all the meeting participants. The party leadership seemed to be effectively discussing the Leap's problems. But, seven or eight days later, Zhou Enlai's secretary told Tian Fang about ominous words spoken by Zhou the previous night: "Right now, a rising wind forebodes a coming storm at Lushan. So many members of the Central Committee are present in Lushan, but they do not understand the true face of Lushan. They are still having fun like tourists!" Tian recounted this news to Xi, who "also began to notice some irregularities in the atmosphere, so he started to act cautiously," Tian recalled.[50]

It was not long thereafter that the storm arrived. On July 12, Peng Dehuai, worried that Mao was still too optimistic, went to have a private conversation with him, but he was told Mao was already asleep. The following day, Peng wrote a note to Mao. Although Peng tried to couch his concerns in positive language, he also used sharp terms like "bourgeois enthusiasm," and Mao took the letter as a personal affront. A few days later, Mao launched an attack and ultimately purged Peng from the leadership—another turning point in the new country's history.[51] This was an extraordinarily dangerous moment for Xi. He was linked by career ties to Peng, he had spent time with Peng both before and during the Lushan meetings, and he had even submitted his own evidence critical of the Leap. Additionally, during the Korean War, Peng had grown close to Gao Gang, and Peng's letter was labeled "the continuation and development" of Gao Gang's behavior in 1953.[52]

Xi was probably vulnerable because of his contacts with other individuals as well. He had called Gansu party boss Zhang Zhongliang and told him, "If there is trouble in terms of grain, you should reflect upon this problem accurately."[53] But Zhang was fully on board with the Leap and did not listen to Xi. Xi had better luck with Huo Weide, the party's second secretary of Gansu. Over the phone, in order to convince Huo to act, Xi mocked him, asking Huo if he was afraid of criticism or afraid of a "hat" (meaning a dangerous political label). While Zhang was in Lushan, Huo submitted a report warning that 2,200 people had already starved to death and tens of thousands of people were fleeing. As a result, together with ten thousand party members, Huo was labeled a rightist. Many of them starved to death in "reform-through-labor" camps. In 1962, when it was understood that the Leap had failed, Gansu cadres demanded to know whether Xi had reevaluated Huo's case. Huo was rehabilitated in July of that year, but he was persecuted again just several months later.[54]

Xi was expected to join in the criticism of Peng, but while working on his speech, he could not think of what to write. He finally said, "Forget it; I won't write it. When the time comes, I will just say a few words according to the situation."[55] Xi criticized Peng primarily for comments made during the war in the Northwest—Peng allegedly had blamed Xi for not adequately mobilizing the masses and not achieving the goal of "enough food and clothes," a party slogan at the time.[56]

Yet, at Lushan, Mao affirmed the necessity of working with the Northwest cadres. Mao singled out Xi, among others: "Now Xi Zhongxun's performance is very good."[57] It was enough for Xi to survive, although several men fell along with Peng, including Zhang Wentian, the former party general secretary who had investigated the case of Xi's imprisonment in 1935, as well as Mao's secretary, Li Rui. Li Rui would later claim that Xi had tried to protect him but to no avail. "Xi," Li claimed, "said I could still be considered to be in the middle but leaning to the left"—a somewhat milder criticism.[58]

Lushan was not only a tragedy for Peng Dehuai and the other men who suffered Mao's wrath. Peng had mismanaged the difficult politics of course correction. Before Lushan, even Mao was open to the idea that the Leap had gone too far, too fast. But the style of Peng's letter had infuriated Mao. Instead, the party would double down on the failing policies that so much of the leadership had already begun to doubt. After Lushan, Peng Zhen not only forced the State Council vice-premiers, such as Li Xiannian and Bo Yibo, to self-criticize but also launched an investigation into rightists in central government ministries—a task that implied Xi's calls for "self-transformation" did not satisfy Mao. Ultimately, 7 percent of the party members working in the central apparatus were targeted during the campaign, which did not conclude until January 1960. Under those circumstances, criticizing the Leap would have been difficult for Xi, if not unthinkable.[59]

THE SLOW PATH TO COURSE CORRECTION (AGAIN)

But even sounding the alarm did not always get attention. Finally, in February 1960, a director from the Ministry of Internal Affairs arrived in Henan's Xinyang County to investigate claims of starvation, and the county's vice-secretary of the party told him that two hundred thousand to three hundred thousand had already perished. The director returned to Beijing after only two days, whereupon the ministry's leadership told him to immediately report his findings to Xi. Xi, who had also learned about the seriousness of the situation in Henan from the Ministry of Public Health, reported to Dong Biwu, head of the Central Control Commission, and Dong sent an investigation team to Xinyang for three months. The group saw corpses along the road and learned that four hundred thousand people had died. They considered going directly to Mao, who was also in the province at the time, but they thought better of it. Back in Beijing, they did submit a report, but Tan Zhenlin, the vice-premier in charge of agriculture, refused to forward it.[60] In March, Xi forwarded a letter to Zhou about people starving to death in two Anhui counties, which led Zhou to demand that the provincial party secretary immediately investigate.[61] But, for months, Mao still believed that starvation was not a dangerous nationwide problem, and the party took no serious actions.

Finally, in September, Mao's own relatives went to Beijing to tell the chairman that his deputies were lying. His family members begged him to act swiftly to stop the threat of mass starvation. On November 3, the party adopted emergency measures to address the growing crisis. Tragically, those measures were almost exactly what the leadership had planned to introduce before the Lushan plenum.[62] Xi fought hard to get the party leadership to realize the seriousness of the situation during those weeks. On October 21, the Ministry of Internal Affairs reported on a meeting of civil-affairs cadres that concluded a hundred million people lived in areas that faced hunger. Xi reacted swiftly. On October 22, he attached a notice to the document: "If there are no big mistakes, I recommend that this is approved and disseminated to lower levels for reference." Vice-Premiers Li Fuchun and Tan Zhenlin disagreed. But on November 8, Zhou backed Xi and ordered that the Ministry of Internal Affairs send the document to all provincial civil-affairs offices.[63]

On November 11, Xi assumed a significantly enhanced role in these delayed attempts to combat the famine. The Ministry of Internal Affairs, which, at the time, was one of the government's chief tools for helping the starving people and reporting on their situation, was placed under the direct supervision of the State Council. That ministry, the Ethnic Affairs Commission, and all bureaus led by the State Council were placed under Xi's command as part of the new Internal Affairs Group, which reported directly to the secretariat.[64]

One of the reasons the party center had struggled to appreciate the extent of the starvation was the petition system had suffered from catastrophic failures. The beginning of the Antirightist Campaign in September 1957 signified the start of a yearslong decline in the number of petitions as leftist political campaigns swept the country. Under such conditions, complaints, or reporting on such criticisms, could easily be interpreted as an attack on the party. The number of petitions received by central agencies in 1960, a year of terrible famine, was 32.2 percent of those received in 1957. The percentage of anonymous letters increased too. Career incentives played a role as well: fearful of punishment, regional cadres either ignored or persecuted those who tried to submit petitions. Finally, in February 1961, acting under instructions from Liu Shaoqi, Xi held a major meeting on petitions.[65]

He was blunt. It was normal to receive petitions, he said, as they showed that the peasants trusted the party leadership to solve problems. Withholding petitions broke the connection between the party and the masses and "blockaded" the party center. In several provinces, cadres had ordered public-security officials and postal workers to illegally suppress petitions en masse. Some counties had openly set a guideline that every letter to the party center or Mao should be stopped. In certain cases, Xi said, people had been arrested or persecuted to death for warning about starvation. According to the spirit of Xi's remarks, the meeting presented new policies to protect petitioners, including a ban on public-security officials from intercepting letters or telegrams, except in very special circumstances with explicit permission from Beijing.[66]

Despite these attempts by Xi to fix the petition system, Beijing was still not clear about what exactly was going on in the countryside. In the early months of 1961, the top leaders started to visit the provinces themselves to find out. They were shocked and ashamed by what they saw. This time, they talked to peasants instead of local officials, and they witnessed for themselves the poverty and destruction. On the late side of these trips, Xi left the capital in April.[67]

He went to Changge County, Henan Province, where what he found was appalling. One local commune party secretary told him that women were suffering from uterine prolapse because of lack of food, even providing specific details about the number of women and the severity of their symptoms. Xi responded, "Are there measuring instruments in the countryside? How do you know just how prolapsed? It is enough just to say how many women have uterine diseases." People were hungry and angry, but they were still afraid to criticize the disastrous commune canteens. Xi allowed the peasants to dissolve them. He also ended the policies that made the brigades the accounting units, that permitted eating together as big groups, and that supported paying people according to need, not performance—all approaches that eroded peasant initiative.[68]

On May 2, Xi gave a fiery speech at an enlarged meeting of the Changge County party leadership. He complained that since the establishment of the communes, the "most fundamental principle of socialism"—distribution according to work—had been abandoned. Therefore, the masses had lost their initiative. He castigated leaders for launching giant, costly projects, such as big public roads and huge office buildings for the local government. "Their brains aren't full of the interests of the masses; they are only full of individual interests. This kind of person is not qualified to be a party member," he said. He warned that "the mood of the masses is not stable," both because of a lack of food and because of the poor performance by the party. Xi complained that local leaders were not returning land and other property that had been confiscated earlier in the Great Leap Forward: "The question is whether the nation should have a bit more. Or should the masses have a bit more? My opinion is that, especially now, it is better for the masses to have a bit more."[69]

Xi wrote two reports to the Central Committee on what he found, couched in positive language. "Now, everywhere in the countryside, there is a new atmosphere of prosperity." But having affirmed the big picture, a necessary step for "partyspeak," he then shifted to what he really wanted to emphasize: "In the countryside, currently, there are still extremely large production and livelihood difficulties." Peasants were afraid policies would change again. He pointed out the problems in the mass cafeterias, suggesting they should be disbanded. Peasants were in such poor health that two or three people were needed to do the work of what one peasant could do in the past. For Xi, the biggest problem with the communes was that they negatively impacted the initiative of the masses.[70]

During Xi's trip, local officials had privately warned Xi's secretary that his boss should not go too far with his criticisms. Politburo members, ministers, and even Mao himself had visited, they said. When Xi's secretary told Xi about the warnings, he was incensed: "Do they seriously expect me to praise them if they did something wrong?!"[71] But many years later, Xi would complain that local officials did indeed successfully "settle scores" with him later:

> The Great Leap Forward was all about targets that were too high! Especially in Henan. I went to Henan in 1958 when the mass creation of steel began. In 1961, I went back to Henan three times with a work group. At the time, the relevant leading comrades on the Central Committee said, "You're in charge; bring whatever people you want." ... I brought with me a viewpoint of opposing "leftism." After the investigation, I filled an entire notebook with information and gave it to the Henan Party Committee. Because of this, I was persecuted terribly. People bided their time to settle their scores with me! Especially those in Changge County. That's a county Chairman Mao had visited, they said. Had it been determined in Beijing that your visit to Changge County was for the sole purpose of opposing Chairman Mao? After I arrived in Henan, the party committee held a meeting and said that Changge was neither a good nor a bad county. What in the world did they mean by not good and not bad? It was "leftist" as hell! As soon as you took a look, it was clear they were exaggerating. They were growing wheat in the corners of the fields, but there were only weeds in the center. At the time, the line was to have everyone exaggerate![72]

That "settling of scores" would come later. At the time, Xi's report was one of the many such evaluations that led Beijing to finally understand the massive scale of the disaster. At a politburo meeting held in Beijing between May 21 and June 12, top party officials finally conducted a series of self-criticisms that revealed that they knew the Leap had failed in a fundamental way.[73]

In October 1961, a retired Ministry of Public Security cadre in Shandong named Cao Shuli wrote a letter to Mao that began with "A shocking number of people are dying here! You simply should not sit securely in Beijing and only rely on official communications and notifications, Marxism, and political work." Cao wrote that both of his parents had died, leaving him "absolutely inconsolable" but such losses were no longer "anything special" given that so many people had lost loved ones. Cao knew Mao would only see the letter if it was forwarded to him, so, at the end of the letter, he wrote to whomever might read it first: "Responsible comrade: if you are a loyal minister who loves the motherland and the chairman and has a conscience, you will definitely send this honest letter to the chairman to read. If you do not do this and you throw it in the trash, then you must examine your conscience!" It landed on Xi's desk. Bravely, he forwarded the letter but not to Mao. He sent it to Zhou Enlai and Vice-Premiers Li Xiannian and Tan Zhenlin. Zhou then wrote a letter to the party boss of Shandong demanding an investigation and warning him not to punish Cao.[74] Later that month, Xi learned from the Ministry of Internal Affairs that 162.36 million people had been affected by the disaster sweeping the country.[75]

Although the party was now trying to remedy its mistakes, at the end of 1961, Xi received letters reporting that in his home county of Fuping, people were committing suicide by jumping into wells or hanging themselves and selling their children. Seventy percent of the peasants did not have enough food, so some were starving to death. Xi immediately forwarded the letters to the Shaanxi party leaders and asked them to conduct an investigation.[76] When Xi fell from power, Zhang Desheng, party boss of Shaanxi, was forced to delineate some of Xi's "crimes." Under duress, he claimed that Xi had not helped Shaanxi in 1961 but rather had asked that it send high-quality flour for the exclusive use of the leadership. Xi also had allegedly demanded that the Shaanxi party leadership send aid to his home county of Fuping.[77]

Not even Xi's own family in Beijing could avoid hunger. In 1961, Apa Alo's wife became sick because of the serious hardships, and Xi brought her to Beijing to treat her. Apa Alo later wrote that Xi's health suffered, as did that of Qi Xin: "During the time of hardship, the health of both [Xi] and Big Sister Qi Xin was not very good, and even they could not eat their fill. But they still specially found a way to take care of our ethnic eating habits. They often brought food and drink to the hospital and had time to chat."[78] At Xi Jinping's August 1 Middle School, which catered to the children of the party elite, students ate stale rice contaminated with rat feces.[79]

In February 1962, the party finally held the Seven Thousand Cadres Conference to come up with a verdict on what had happened. At least for the moment, the party, including Mao, was fully on board with rectification. Decades later, Xi would praise the conference as a rare moment in party history during which people felt comfortable expressing what they genuinely thought.[80] But the party had not yet fully overcome the crisis. That same month, Xi was still receiving reports from the party committee of the Ministry of Internal Affairs about relief efforts.[81] And as late as March 28, Zhou and Xi pulled an all-nighter to find ways to deliver grain, coal, and relief funds to Henan.[82]

At a struggle session during the Cultural Revolution, Xi would defend his alleged attempts to correct the Leap, saying that peasants did not have enough freedom. Xi had been afraid, he said, that if matters had continued to deteriorate, peasants would "use carrying poles to beat us."[83] In a 1985 private conversation, Xi claimed that he had done his best, given the circumstances. He believed his concerns helped to bring an end, for example, to the wasteful and damaging campaign to kill sparrows. He hinted that what he could do was limited, asserting that after the Leap began, he had been "sidelined" and that Kang Sheng was plotting to label him a rightist.[84]

The Leap was a national tragedy, but it had special significance for Xi. He knew better than most about the severity of the situation in the countryside, while, at the party center, he witnessed firsthand the degradation of inner-party norms as Mao persecuted two of Xi's closest associates: Zhou Enlai and Peng Dehuai. Yet the party rectification that Xi himself led in the government ministries descended into a persecutorial mania that presaged the Cultural Revolution.[85] The attacks on technical expertise, according to historian Lin Yunhui, "not only failed to spark the enthusiasm of intellectuals and members of the non-Communist parties but instead caused severe injury in the deepest areas of their hearts, created chaos in academia, and blocked developments not only in the social and physical sciences but also in the economy and society." Whatever Xi tried to do, whatever small change he managed to achieve, the Great Leap Forward proved to be one of the greatest disasters in Chinese history—a catastrophic failure of party rule that killed up to thirty million people.[86]

14
LIU ZHIDAN

Already on two occasions since the founding of the People's Republic, Xi had narrowly escaped falling along with two close compatriots—Gao Gang and Peng Dehuai. In the wake of the Great Leap Forward, the third great purge in the history of the People's Republic was targeted against Xi himself. The organization that had given his life meaning for decades had turned against him. "Thirty-six years of affection were ruined all at once," he wrote shortly after the humiliation began.[1] Xi was stunned. It came like "a thunderbolt out of nowhere," he said. Worse, he could not comprehend why it was happening: "I failed to understand it after thinking about it one hundred times."[2] He would tell a friend that he felt like "a person who fell off an eighteen-floor building."[3]

In time, Xi would blame his fall on a single individual: Kang Sheng. Xi may have genuinely believed that the problem was Kang, or he may simply have wanted to protect Mao. In reality, the attack on Xi was a collective effort. As Taiwan's leading historian of party history, Chung Yen-lin, writes with regard to Xi's purge, if Kang Sheng "had not achieved agreement from the Politburo Standing Committee led by Chairman Mao Zedong as well as assistance at every step from Deng Xiaoping and Peng Zhen, head and vice-head of the secretariat, Kang Sheng alone simply would have been unable to achieve his goal."[4]

Gao Gang and Peng Dehuai were uncouth individuals whose ambition and frankness got them into trouble. Xi was a much more cautious man, and his mistake was more prosaic. Against his better judgment and after years of pressure, he reluctantly gave his approval to a novel. In 1956, Workers' Publishing House asked Li Jiantong, the wife of Liu Zhidan's younger brother Liu Jingfan, to write a book about Liu Zhidan. Xi gave his approval for a project on Liu Zhidan, but he believed it would be most appropriate to only publish vignettes of his life. Ignoring him, Li Jiantong, who interviewed more than three hundred old revolutionaries and visited the archives in Shaanxi, produced a draft manuscript for a full book. Xi warned Li Jiantong, "Writing such a large novel is not a game. It touches upon too many issues, especially some issues about the party history of the Northwest. If it is not managed well, it will cause differences of opinion. Wouldn't it be better just to write a few short revolutionary memoirs?" He encouraged Liu Jingfan to put pressure on his wife, telling him that she would probably not be able to do a good job because she had not fought with them during the early period and there was too much she did not know. Even if she were to do a good job, he told Liu, it would probably still cause problems—especially with regard to Gao Gang, who was very difficult to deal with in a novel.[5]

But Li was undeterred. In 1959, Xi received another draft of the book. At the time, Xi was so busy that he only skimmed it, but it was enough for him to again express opposition to the project, in part because of the new political sensitivities surrounding Peng Dehuai's fall at Lushan. Li refused to accept Xi's verdict, in part because many other old northwesterners supported her. Liu Jingfan appealed to Xi by saying that all the other leading Northern Shaanxi cadres "either had died or had gone bad." Liu said to Xi, "If you don't support this book, *Liu Zhidan*, who will?" Finally, under pressure from his old friends, Xi consented.[6]

After Xi was given a fourth draft of the book in the late spring or early summer of 1961, he met with the editors at Workers' Publishing House on two occasions to discuss it. Xi emphasized the importance of depicting Liu Zhidan as a "microcosm" of Mao Zedong thought: "Chairman Mao's correct thinking on leading the revolution was brought into concrete reality through Zhidan," he said. But some of his remarks were rather incautious. He said leftist adventurism had destroyed every base area except for the one in the Northwest, which then became both a "landing point" and "springboard" for the party. Still, Xi stated that if Mao had not arrived at the last minute, "things would have been all over!" When the fifth draft was completed, Xi repeatedly told Li to send it to those Northwest cadres who held different opinions so they would have an opportunity to express their own views before publication.[7]

Xi had good reason to worry. Gao Gang's fall had created an opening for those dissatisfied with the decisions on party history made during the Yan'an era. Gao played an integral role in the 1942 and 1945 decisions that criticized figures such as Guo Hongtao, Zhu Lizhi, and Yan Hongyan. With Gao himself now tarnished, his former nemeses attempted to force a reconsideration of the verdicts against them. Deng Xiaoping himself encouraged Guo and Zhu to officially challenge the 1942 decision, and, in 1959, the Central Committee Control Commission finished a report that absolved them of the most serious crimes.[8]

With everything moving in their favor, Gao's enemies, especially Yan Hongyan, would have seen the novel *Liu Zhidan* as a threat. When the editor, He Jiadong, who was helping Li Jiantong write *Liu Zhidan*, interviewed Yan, Yan was dismissive of the novel's subject. "Liu Zhidan's forces were all bandits. They stole from everyone, raped everyone's women, smoked opium, and rode into battle on donkeys with women on their backs." Yan even said that capturing Liu Zhidan and not killing him was already going easy on him.[9] When Yan finally received a draft of the novel that had been sent to him by Li Jiantong, he wrote her a furious letter: "In actuality, this is using the form of a novel to summarize the history of the revolutionary struggle in the Northwest, and this unavoidably touches upon numerous issues of principle, some of which must be decided by the Central Committee." Yan warned that it would be inappropriate to publish the book, but Li ignored Yan's warnings.[10]

On July 28, excerpts of *Liu Zhidan* appeared in *Workers' Daily*. Yan, who was at the beach resort of Beidaihe for a meeting of the party leadership, was incensed. He called Xi and demanded to know whether he had known about the novel. Xi responded, "Before 1960, I did not support the writing of this book. I later agreed, but I also wanted the author to send drafts to the relevant comrades for review and to seek their opinions before publication." Xi suggested that Yan again meet with the author.[11]

Instead, Yan reached out to the All-China Federation of Trade Unions, demanding that it stop publication. On August 17, Yan wrote a letter to Yang Shangkun, head of the General Office of the party, in which he claimed that the book was an attempt to propagate Gao Gang. Yan warned that, although a decision had been made to end publication, "it has already been disseminated, and discussions have already begun." If the matter were not managed carefully, *Liu Zhidan* would become a banned book and spread secretly, he worried. Yan proposed that a copy of the book be shared with the Northwest cadres who were already at Beidaihe and that the Department of Propaganda hold a special meeting to clarify the "issues of principle" upon which the book touched. Yan also provided materials suggesting that certain characters in the book were actually Xi Zhongxun and Gao Gang.[12]

When the issue of *Liu Zhidan* first started coming up in discussions during the party deliberations at Beidaihe, leading ministerial figures who had worked with Xi in the State Council were not concerned. After all, it was only a novel, and Yan himself was from the Northwest. They thought it was merely a historical dispute.[13] But around this time, Yan also contacted Kang Sheng, although it is unclear why and when he did so.[14] On August 24, Kang wrote a letter demanding an investigation—a key moment in the saga that suddenly exacerbated matters. "This is not simply an issue of a cultural written product," Kang warned ominously. "It seems that this has a political direction." Kang accused Xi of trying to use the novel to reverse the verdict on Gao Gang.[15]

But why did Kang attack Xi so vociferously? Kang, known for his work in counterintelligence, was sensitive to vulnerabilities and weaknesses.[16] Xi told one friend that Kang was using the novel as an excuse to purge the northwesterners as a whole.[17] Yet Kang's own career goals are possibly the most powerful explanation for his behavior. When Yan raised the issue of *Liu Zhidan* at the meetings in Beidaihe, Mao was already returning to the theme of class struggle. In February 1962, the party had decided to implement a less radical line to overcome the devastation of the Great Leap Forward. However, during the next few months, Mao decided that Liu Shaoqi, Chen Yun, Zhou Enlai, and Deng Xiaoping had gone too far. Mao interpreted their policies as a political problem, not merely a policy dispute. By early August, Mao started to signal his displeasure at the Beidaihe meetings, and then, throughout the month, he gave several speeches criticizing other leaders and emphasizing class struggle in powerful terms.[18]

Just as the economic policies were beginning to worry Mao, in June, Peng Dehuai wrote a long letter to the leadership explaining why he should be rehabilitated. Initially, Peng's letter did not receive a great deal of attention during the Beidaihe sessions. But on August 22, two days before the meetings ended and two days before Kang wrote his letter about *Liu Zhidan*, Peng submitted a second letter to the leadership requesting rehabilitation.[19] Because Peng and Xi were so connected, both to each other and to Gao as well, Peng's second letter so close in time to the publication of *Liu Zhidan* was extraordinarily unfortunate timing for Xi.[20]

In that kind of environment, Kang almost certainly understood that attacking Xi would improve his own status. Kang worked in Shandong Province for three years after 1949, and, even after finally returning to Beijing, he still did not hold a prominent position. For years, he suffered from a debilitating illness, but his health finally began to improve in 1956. Slowly, with the support of Deng Xiaoping and by impressing Mao with the toughness he demonstrated in the negotiations with the Soviets, Kang was able to restore some of his power.[21] The *Liu Zhidan* incident was an opportunity to further that process.

But Kang's role should not be overstated. Deng, as head of the secretariat, almost certainly deserves more blame than even Kang for what happened to Xi. Deng and Yan Hongyan were close—after Yan's falling out with Gao Gang in Yan'an, Yan had served for years directly under Deng in the Second Field Army. Yan would probably have sought Deng's permission before acting.[22] According to one of Yan's close assistants, Deng was very supportive of Yan's attack on Xi. "Old Yan!" the assistant claimed Deng had said. "You did a really great thing. Keep it up!" Deng's biographer Chung Yen-lin surmises that Deng's behavior might have been his own attempt to return to Mao's good graces after displeasing the chairman by supporting greater rights for individual peasants, expressing too much pessimism about the economy, and rehabilitating cadres who had been persecuted in earlier campaigns.[23] After the Dalai Lama's flight to India in 1959, Deng may have also worried about his legacy in Tibet—punishing Xi and the Panchen Lama would shore up the position of Deng's own protégés in the region.

On September 6, Li Jiantong submitted an explanation to the leadership about why she had written the novel in the way she did. With regard to the character that Yan Hongyan believed was based on Xi, Li said her intention had been to portray a typical soviet chairman involved in governance work. However, she admitted that most of the material she used for that character had been drawn from Xi's life.[24] Li also wrote two letters to the Department of Propaganda that belittled Yan's historical legacy, claiming that Yan was so disliked that his own men had wanted to execute him. The letter only made the situation worse. In a fit of pique, Yan blamed Xi Zhongxun for writing the letters, believing that Li was incapable of producing them.[25] Such sexism was widespread. The party's cultural tsar Zhou Yang did not even think Li Jiantong wrote *Liu Zhidan*. "Who was the person who really wrote the book?" he asked Li. She replied, "Me, of course." Then Zhou said, "But some people say it was written by Xi Zhongxun. How could someone your age and status know so many things from the time of the land revolution?"[26]

On September 6 and 7, the participants in the Central Committee preparatory meeting began to directly link Peng Dehuai's pleas for rehabilitation with Xi's support for *Liu Zhidan*.[27] On September 8, Yan said, "Xi Zhongxun presided over the writing of the novel *Liu Zhidan*. He is the first author. He uses the propagation of Liu Zhidan to propagate Gao Gang and to reverse the verdict on the traitor Gao Gang. It propagates Xi Zhongxun himself." Kang Sheng asked, "Now the core question is why Gao Gang is being propagandized at this time?" These comments appeared in the meeting newsletter and led to an explosion of criticism of Xi. On the night of September 8, a nervous Xi returned home. He told his secretary that Li Jiantong had not listened to his concerns and had created big trouble.[28]

Two days later, Xi wrote a letter to Liu Lantao, another man who hated Gao Gang and who was then head of the Northwest Bureau. "I am not responsible for this book, *Liu Zhidan*," Xi wrote. "I never even participated in the planning for the book." He told Liu that he never wanted Li Jiantong to write the book in the first place because she had never written anything before and lacked life experiences. Moreover, the book would not be able to avoid sensitive historical issues. When Li pressed the issue, Xi explained to Liu he told her to first send it to other comrades for their approval. Xi had not even read the latest draft, which she had sent earlier that summer. On July 23, Xi had conveyed to Li a message from Yan Hongyan that the book should not be released. He had no idea that excerpts were going to appear in party newspapers shortly after that conversation. Xi's letter was immediately published in the preparatory meeting's newsletter.[29]

Xi then decided to write directly to the Central Committee. On September 13, he consulted with Liu Jingfan and Li Jiantong about the matter. Xi was not happy with the current draft and asked his secretary to rewrite it. After he submitted the letter, Xi felt as if a great weight had been lifted. He went dancing at a Mid-Autumn Festival celebration in the National Political Consultative Hall. When he ran into Kang Sheng, he denied the accusations against him. Xi raised both of his hands and said, "Look, this affair has fallen onto my own head." Kang just smiled and walked away.[30] At the same event,

Zhang Zhiyi, vice-minister of the United Front Work Department, asked Xi what was going on. As Xi tried to explain, Kang Sheng walked by, saw them, and yelled loudly, "Ah, here's the one who escaped the net! Are you two plotting something?" Xi said to Zhang, "Ignore him! He's a crazy person! He wants to take a few bites out of anyone he sees. I should keep away from you so they don't target you as well."[31]

Shortly after the party, the situation became even more dangerous. On September 18, Xi met with Zhou Enlai, Chen Yi, and Liu Lantao.[32] We do not know what they discussed, but the following day, on September 19, an explosively compromising document written by Gao Gang's widow, Li Liqun, in 1959 about Peng Dehuai and Xi was released to the party elite. Xi subsequently requested permission from Zhou Enlai to leave the meeting so as to prepare a self-criticism.[33] On September 23, Deng Xiaoping proposed that Kang Sheng be promoted to the secretariat. Mao immediately granted approval.[34]

When Mao opened the full Tenth Plenum on September 24, Xi's fate was already sealed. "Isn't writing novels very popular now?" Mao began sardonically. He said that "using a novel to engage in antiparty activities" was "a great invention." "Whenever there is a desire to overthrow a regime, it is necessary to first shape public opinion, to conduct ideological work, to engage in the superstructure—both revolution and counterrevolution are like this," he said. Mao then asked Deng Xiaoping to declare who would not be allowed to attend the plenum. Deng listed Xi along with four others who were under investigation, including Peng Dehuai. Mao then said, "The crimes of these individuals are truly too great" and that they would no longer be allowed to participate in other important meetings or to stand on Tiananmen Square. Mao declared that the party had successfully crushed "an attack by the Peng antiparty clique," exposing "the Peng antiparty activity and the Gao-Rao antiparty-person Xi Zhongxun."[35] Did Mao actually believe that Xi had betrayed him in such an extraordinary way? Or was it simply that Mao found it politically expedient to use Xi's misstep to make a bigger point to the elite about class struggle? The answer is lost to history.

In any case, Xi's fate was sealed. On September 27, the last day of the plenum, the Central Committee established two full investigation committees to look into the cases of Peng Dehuai and Xi Zhongxun. The group to investigate Xi was huge, including seventy-three members.[36] Kang Sheng demanded that investigators look for evidence that *Liu Zhidan* propagated the ideas that "the Northwest had saved the party center," that "Gao Gang was the king of the Northwest," and that Xi was Gao's heir.[37] They compared the ideas of Liu Zhidan in the novel with the *Selected Works of Mao Zedong*, claiming that any instance in which Liu's words predated Mao's was plagiarism.[38] According to the preliminary decision on Xi's crimes made by the Tenth Plenum, *Liu Zhidan* sought to portray Shaan-Gan Border Region as the "center" of the Chinese revolution.[39] In a later self-criticism, Xi would be forced to say, "My primary motivation with regard to writing the book *Liu Zhidan* was to use this book to make the Shaan-Gan-Ning Border Region the orthodoxy of the revolution. I plotted to propagate myself as the first heir of the Shaan-Gan-Ning revolutionary base and I plotted to become the leader of the Northwest after Liu Zhidan and Gao Gang, all in order to collect further capital to be able to demand more from the entire country." Xi further "acknowledged" that, while he and Gao Gang were both "careerists," Xi, by using a novel, had found a better method, which was "more hidden, more clever, and more difficult for people to see."[40] Xi accepted the charge that he had tried to "use the propagandizing of a dead person to propagandize the living me."[41] As time passed, Xi would also face charges of smoking opium, inappropriate relations with women, and spying for the Soviets.[42]

The attack on Xi Zhongxun and *Liu Zhidan* over the next several years gradually turned into a full-scale assault on cadres from the Northwest. In November, Liu Shaoqi said, "The Northwest had a few bad leaders, such as Gao Gang and Xi Zhongxun. They wanted to do mountaintopism [participate in factionalism]. For them, right and wrong are determined by mountaintops."[43] The same month, Deng, too, spoke of factions: "There is no need to fear open opposition factions. Peng Dehuai and Xi Zhongxun were not members of an open opposition faction. They schemed in secret."[44]

It was not only top leaders who were targeted after publication of the novel. The head of Workers' Publishing House was arrested and persecuted to death. A regular worker at the press was beaten brutally; another was tortured with electric currents. Two people who had served as Li Jiantong's guides when she was conducting interviews died while under investigation. A manager at a restaurant where Xi ate was declared an "underground agent," and he was linked to fifty-nine other restaurants, leading to the arrest of nineteen other people and the deaths of five.[45] Ultimately, twenty thousand people were persecuted as part of the "Xi Zhongxun antiparty clique." At least two hundred were beaten to death, driven mad, or seriously injured.

According to Xi's secretary, the fact that so many people suffered because of him produced "great pain in his heart." For years, even the word "implicate" would upset him.[46]

Xi was betrayed by his own secretary, who claimed that after a visit by an actress one morning, blood was found on Xi's bed—implying that Xi took her virginity. When presented with this information, Zhao Shouyi, secretary for daily affairs of the Shaanxi Party Committee, was skeptical. Why would a woman who did acrobatic work for an opera group still have an unbroken hymen? he wondered. The secretary removed that charge, along with a charge that Xi had copied a document for the Soviets. However, during the Cultural Revolution, those issues were raised again, and Zhao Shouyi was accused of protecting Xi.[47]

The investigation upended Xi's life at home. When Xi's wife Qi Xin heard the news, "it was like a bolt from the blue; I was immediately scared stupid, and I wanted to cry but dared not."[48] An individual close to the family claimed that the stress led Xi to lash out against his wife.[49] When Xi's daughter An'an saw her father sitting silently alone in the dark, she questioned, "Father, what's wrong?" His son Yuanping asked his father why he no longer went to work. His children were all frightened by Xi's countenance.[50] Meanwhile, Zhou Enlai worried that Xi might commit suicide. Xi assured Zhou, "I am prepared to return to the countryside to become a peasant. To make revolution, it is not necessary to be an official. Farmers can also make revolution." Still, Zhou had Qi Xin return home to keep an eye on Xi and make sure he did not kill himself.[51]

The investigation into Xi was kept secret, and the outside world picked up on the fact that he was in trouble only in April 1964. Even then, information was scarce. An American diplomat in Hong Kong cabled home that Xi had operated a "love nest" in which he was "alleged to have had illicit relationships with at least thirty women, 'though not at the same time.'" Two of the women were wives of other leaders, including Qu Wu, the nonparty deputy director of the Commission for Cultural Relations with Foreign Countries. Qu, the diplomat reported, had a "nervous breakdown" but soon returned to work (Xi would later write the forward to Qu's *Selected Works*). That same month, the *New York Times* referred to a "university professor from Peking" who said Xi was attacked for antiparty thinking and also was accused of "imposing his favors on young girls." A local bulletin for China watchers in Hong Kong similarly claimed that "a professor of a mainland university" and "the sixth son of a well-known 'democratic element'" had seen a circular that "laid stress" on Xi's "profligate living": "At the rally against him over 20 young girls gave testimony, charging [Xi] with rape." Although Xi had a reputation for groping stewardesses in Zhongnanhai, no available Chinese-language written sources have spoken of these accusations, and they all should be treated skeptically, especially since it appears these rumors might have come from the same problematic source. No one on the outside came close to guessing the deeper reasons for Xi's fall.[52]

THE FIRST STEP TOWARD A NATIONAL TRAGEDY

The fall of Xi Zhongxun was a turning point in Chinese history. Despite Mao's more practical inclinations earlier in the year, at the Tenth Plenum, he again turned decisively toward a preoccupation with revolutionary class struggle. The cultural space was a special target. In the summer of 1962, the writer Ke Zhongping had finally finished the first volume of a second draft of an epic poem about Liu Zhidan (the first draft was destroyed when Gao Gang fell). Swept up in the same fervor that targeted Xi, Ke's health collapsed after sitting through a month of criticism, and he died two years later. The work was never published.[53]

Other than *Liu Zhidan*, however, the most prominent target during this turn in cultural policy was an article written by Wang Chaobei, the party's top agent in Nationalist-controlled Xi'an from 1939 to 1949. During Wang's years in Xi'an, he provided more than 31,460 pieces of intelligence.[54] Xi encouraged Wang on multiple occasions to write an article about this history. Wang Chaobei sent drafts of the article "Fighting against Hu's Cavalry in an Ancient City," regarding Hu Zongnan, to Xi. Wang believed that the Central Investigation Department, China's spy ministry, had also given approval, but a former editor of *Hongqi piaopiao*, a party magazine, claimed the piece went forward on Xi's recommendation alone. After *People's Daily* published an advertisement for the forthcoming article, the Central Investigation Department called Xi to complain, but Xi said, "You have your opinion, but other people have the right to publish! You interfere too much!" and he hung up the phone. A few days after publication, all copies of the magazine were recalled, and three hundred thousand copies were destroyed. In September, the Ministry of Public Security was given permission to arrest Wang.[55] Years later, Kang Sheng declared that "the traitor Wang Chaobei snuck into our party, and, through Xi Zhongxun, he treated all the enemies' spies as our own people, and he put them into the public-security system."[56] Kang was referring to an intelligence organization created by Xi that employed numerous former Nationalist agents to track down any remaining operatives.[57] During his persecution, Wang's teeth were beaten out of his mouth.[58]

Wang Chaobei's "Fighting against Hu's Cavalry in an Ancient City," Ke Zhongping's epic poem on Liu Zhidan, Fan Ming's *New Journey to the West*, Li Jiantong's *Liu Zhidan*—all these cases show that history was dangerous, and that was especially the case for Xi and those around him. Lack of caution could destroy careers and, in some cases, even lives. The party was, at this point, in a vastly different place compared to less than a decade earlier when Xi, as director of propaganda, had called upon cadres to allow writers to make mistakes.

The purge of Xi and his colleagues from the Northwest presaged something far worse. Four years after the *Liu Zhidan* incident, the opening salvo of the Cultural Revolution was an attack on the play *Hai Rui Dismissed from Office*—a work that was seen as a defense of Peng Dehuai. In the words of Chinese historian Han Gang, the criticisms of *Hai Rui Dismissed from Office* were an "extension" of the *Liu Zhidan* case: "It can be said that the case of the novel *Liu Zhidan* was a signal of the direction of Chinese politics after 1962. In that sense, the case of the novel *Liu Zhidan* was not an individual case. It was not only a personal tragedy but also a societal tragedy."[59] In 1967, Kang Sheng himself would say the Cultural Revolution was imperative precisely because of people like Xi. "Why is it said that the Cultural Revolution is a great revolution that will touch upon individual souls?" he asked. Because, he said, the bourgeoisie understand that to destroy a regime, it is necessary to first "prepare public opinion"—and that was, according to Kang, the purpose of *Liu Zhidan*.[60]

15
THE CULTURAL REVOLUTION

In the first months after the Tenth Plenum, Xi was under house arrest. Finally, in the fall of 1963, once it was obvious that the investigation into his case would not end any time soon, he was sent to live in a facility near the party school known as Xigongsuo, a small, quiet, and isolated courtyard that formerly had been inhabited by Qing dynasty officials who managed the nearby Summer Palace, a beautiful and expansive imperial garden. He began a yearslong process of writing constant self-criticisms about his past.[1] In the morning, Xi read Karl Marx, Vladimir Lenin, and Mao Zedong, and in the afternoon, he gardened in the yard.[2] During the Cultural Revolution, Xi later described this period of self-study as "a long and painful process."[3]

It was difficult for his family to witness his torment, but he tried to put on a brave face. At the first May Day celebration after his fall, the children asked him why he would not be going to Tiananmen. "We want to go to Tiananmen!" they said. But Xi responded, "Today we will have a real May 1 Labor Day!" Then Xi took them to help with weeding and fertilizing.[4] Qi Xin recalled, "In those years, the children were still young and could not understand what had happened." But Xi was resolute. When his sister visited him, she started crying when she saw him. But he said, "You are still so weak despite having been educated by the party for so many years. How can you break down and burst into tears so easily?"[5]

In a self-criticism, he admitted to feeling unhappy when he was first attacked: "I continued to be fussy about which materials about me were true and which were false. I had a strong sense of being wronged regarding just how much I should be held responsible. I always felt that some self-criticisms were forced, that my level of unwillingness was high. This lack of consciousness lasted a long time." But he also finally acknowledged the charges against him: "After victory, I was one of the individuals who had been struck down by the bourgeois sugarcoated bullets. I abandoned the gun of class struggle."[6]

The investigation into Xi's crimes dragged on without a conclusion. In 1963, Deng Xiaoping read an initial report from the Department of Propaganda's investigative small group. It asserted that *Liu Zhidan* had "exaggerated and misconstrued" the party's history in the Northwest and had replaced Mao Zedong thought with Liu Zhidan thought to "puff up Xi Zhongxun." The book was said to be "a program for the Xi Zhongxun antiparty clique." But no official verdict was made, and the investigative small group essentially stopped working. Deng said that a verdict should not be reached for at least two years.[7]

In February 1965, the United States dramatically increased its involvement in the war in Vietnam, and Mao decided that the intensifying international situation meant that Peng Dehuai and Xi Zhongxun should leave the capital.[8] That summer, Xi wrote a pleading letter to Mao: "Send me to join a production brigade in the countryside, to join a furnace of collective labor, to transform myself into a new ordinary laborer in the style of Mao Zedong. For a long time, I have been confined in a room and divorced from real life, which makes transformation difficult." But instead, the head of the Organization Department, An Ziwen, told Xi that he was to become vice-manager of a mining-tool factory in Luoyang, Henan Province. Xi made three promises: to steadfastly believe in Marxism and Mao Zedong thought, to do nothing that would harm the party or the people, and to not kill himself.[9]

In September 1965, the Peng-Xi Special Case Committee met. Kang Sheng revealed that one reason for their transfer was to trick them into letting their guard down to better facilitate the ongoing investigation. Someone interrupted to say, "As soon as they leave, they will start shouting." Kang continued, "On the other hand, we will express hope that they will turn around. Whether or not they do that completely depends on them."[10] The factory Xi was sent to had been completed in 1958 with the extensive help of the Soviet experts whom he previously helped manage; a local newspaper had described it as a "crystallization" of the "glorious Sino-Soviet friendship."[11]

Xi would later describe his time at the factory as "a year of schooling at a university for industry." After he requested that he be moved to the frontline of production, he was assigned to work with a group of electricians at the No. 2 Metalworking Workshop. Although he had been disgraced, the people at the factory welcomed him. They tried to give him lighter work, but Xi refused to accept it. They called him Old Revolutionary Xi, not Vice-Premier Xi. And he was generous back to them. Workers interviewed many years later recalled how Xi would remember their names after meeting them one time. He gave one young man a cigarette case that had been a gift from Zhou Enlai. On one occasion, Xi told his friends that several of them would have to share one cigarette, as the pack they were smoking that day had been a gift from the prime minister of India to Zhou and then had been given to Xi by the premier.[12]

INITIAL EXCITEMENT GIVES WAY TO HORROR

When the Cultural Revolution first began, Xi was enthralled. In a letter to his children, he asked, "When will the fires of the Cultural Revolution finally burn my body?" to express his hope that the campaign would improve his ideological worldview. Xi told the editor of the factory newspaper, "The Cultural Revolution is also a campaign of the masses. Mobilizing the masses is a good thing. It is necessary to support it. It should be treated correctly. Do not pour cold water on it. It is even more important not to treat the campaign like an enemy." Xi said, "The Cultural Revolution personally initiated and led by Chairman Mao makes me very excited; even more, it makes me determined to reform myself in the world-shaking Cultural Revolution."[13]

But as the campaign swept the country during the following months, Xi began to have doubts. According to a barber, Xi was outraged when he saw the radicals who had been unleashed by Mao ransack a state-owned shop, burning cigarettes and alcohol. The barber warned him not to become involved, but Xi replied that he was not afraid of them and that he had never seen anyone dare to burn state property. Xi told his secretary to write a report to Premier Zhou.[14]

Xi asked the head of the factory's newspaper why the man had been targeted for brutal criticism. After listening to the explanation, Xi produced a set of comments that suggested he was trying to embrace the Cultural Revolution but to avoid its worst excesses:

No one has ever before experienced the Cultural Revolution, and since it is a revolution, it means conducting revolution against old things and constructing new things. So do not be afraid. You should be prepared. Actively jump into this great revolution. You should have an accurate attitude toward the opinions expressed by the masses on the big-character posters. This is the same as the Yan'an Rectification. It is like Chairman Mao said: Correct your mistakes if you have committed any and avoid mistakes if you have not. The Cultural Revolution is a mass campaign. The masses have risen. Some people maybe went too far, but even so, they should be treated correctly. Do not refuse to understand. Do not adopt inappropriate methods. That would be bad for the campaign.

Yet the editor could see that Xi was "under extremely intense emotional pressure."[15]

In late 1966 and early 1967, students throughout the nation descended into vicious factional infighting.[16] Bands at universities started to secretly kidnap high-ranking central and provincial leaders—the rank and number of such figures were seen as important indications of the "successes" of the Cultural Revolution. One faction in Xi'an decided to kidnap Xi. On the night of January 4, 1967, Xi was reading in his Luoyang dormitory when, at 11:00 p.m., a group of more than ten Red Guards entered the room. They forced him to change his clothes and put on a mask. The students then put him on a train, pretending he was a sick patient, and they ordered him not to speak.[17]

Unfortunately for the students, however, at the moment of the kidnapping, Kang Sheng, then an advisor to the Central Cultural Revolution Small Group, disbanded the group that had nabbed Xi. When, on their way home, Xi's kidnappers heard what had happened, they were unsure about how to proceed. They hid Xi outside Xi'an and subjected him to struggle sessions by workers as they negotiated a deal to turn him over as a "gift" to facilitate their entry into a rival group. On January 10, students from the other group arrived in the middle of the night to pick up Xi and to transfer him to Northwest University, arriving at the school at 11:00 a.m.[18]

One young Red Guard, Meng Deqiang, was assigned to watch over Xi and to ensure that he did not run away, commit suicide, or end up captured by another rival Red Guard faction. Meng and Xi shared the same small room, sleeping right next to one another. On days when the dormitory did not have electricity, the two would have long chats in the dark after dinner to pass the time. Meng was surprised that Xi would dare express such a positive attitude toward people like Liu Shaoqi and Deng Xiaoping who had already come under attack. Meng and Xi were so close that when they bathed, they would use the same shower nozzle, taking turns one after another to rinse and even rubbing each other's backs. Xi often told Meng that the biggest gain from his time in Xi'an was to have met a young friend like Meng. Xi apparently maintained his sense of humor—on one occasion, when Meng went out to make some purchases, Xi went into hiding to trick the young man into believing he had been stolen away by another faction. Xi then stepped out and made a face at him.[19] But the camaraderie with Xi would come at a cost for Meng. As the Cultural Revolution consumed its own fighters, Meng was later labeled a reactionary and exiled to an isolated part of Shaanxi.[20]

On a chilly January 24, Xi's captors dragged him to a struggle session at the Xi'an People's Stadium. He was forced to bend over and bow his head while the crowds screamed slogans through megaphones. "Down with Peng, Gao, and Xi," they yelled. "Enemies who do not surrender will be annihilated!" Xi was then put on a truck and paraded through the town. He felt dizzy, heard a buzzing sound in his ears, and then lost hearing in his right ear. The university clinic told him that he should go to the hospital, but he refused, afraid that someone would recognize him, kidnap him, and maybe subject him to beatings or even worse.[21]

At a struggle session in a university auditorium, students forced Xi into the "jet-plane" position with his arms twisted behind his back. They placed a sign weighing more than ten kilograms around his neck with the words "Three-anti element Xi Zhongxun." Two burly students pushed his head so low that it hovered less than two feet from the ground. After two hours, the struggle session ended in screams of "Topple! Set on fire! Deep-fry!" as more than ten students rushed on stage to punch and kick Xi and the other men suffering along with him. One of Xi's old comrades, implicated as a member of the "Peng-Gao-Xi" clique, fell off the two-meter-high stage during the turmoil. Blood sputtered out of the man's mouth as he lost consciousness.[22]

As the Cultural Revolution raged around him, Xi's thoughts returned to the 1935 purge in Shaanxi, as they did during so many other moments in his life. On one occasion, when Meng Deqiang escorted Xi on a walk by the northern entrance to Northwest University, Red Guards from another school in Xi'an, Jiaotong University, were arriving in a truck. The students used thick wire attached to their vehicle to tear the gate out of the ground. Meng told

Xi that the Northwest and Jiaotong Red Guards used to be allies, but in early 1967, they had split when the Jiaotong students were labeled "rightist opportunists." That night, Meng and Xi did not go to sleep until late, as Xi was deeply disturbed by what he had seen that day. Xi told Meng about the 1935 purge and "spoke of many principles to strengthen unity and resolve contradictions."[23]

Distressed by what he had seen, on February 2, Xi wrote directly to Mao, addressing him as "chairman":

> On January 11, I was taken to Xi'an by Red Guards. Now I am living at Northwest University. Please inform the premier so that he does not worry.
>
> After arriving in Xi'an, the Red Guards beat me twice, and one of my ears was beaten so badly that I became deaf. In the early years of the People's Republic of China, I worked in Xi'an. Now, the Red Guards are bringing me to the streets of Xi'an to be struggled against. This can only delight the families of counterrevolutionaries.
>
> Recently, a slogan has spread throughout society calling to "attack with words and defend with force." It is very easy for this slogan to result in the masses struggling against the masses. "Struggle with words, don't struggle with violence" is better.[24]

On February 17, Xi sent a long letter to the head of the Central Cultural Revolution Small Group, Chen Boda. In the letter, which he asked to be sent to Mao and the Politburo Standing Committee, Xi denied that he was a "capitalist roader" or a "revisionist," and he asked to be allowed to return to Luoyang to "forge through labor and continue to reform myself." He also criticized the Cultural Revolution: "Now we are struggling against old cadres in a worse way than when we struggled against landlords and old money. If matters continue in this way, the situation will spiral out of control."[25]

On March 2, he again wrote to Mao: "Chairman: Recently, Xi'an has become like the rest of the country. Red Guards are seizing power everywhere. Now it is already March; the spring plowing is about to begin. The Red Guards are all kids. They do not understand farming. If they are allowed to seize the production teams and the power of the production brigades, it is possible that this year's agricultural production will be affected. I recommend that the Central Committee release a document that clarifies that no one shall seize control over the production teams and the production brigades during the spring plowing." Mao never answered either of these entreaties.[26]

Around this time, Xi also sent a letter to his brother Zhongkai, a man Xi had not seen for more than a decade, begging that he visit: "We have not seen each other for ten years. After you receive this letter, if it is convenient, I hope you will come to the university so we can see each other." He wrote that he hoped to see Zhongkai's children as well. Meng Deqiang delivered the letter. Afterward, Meng told Xi that Zhongkai had taken the note and put it into his pocket without saying anything. Xi suggested that perhaps his brother was unable to visit but that maybe his nephews could visit instead. Over the next few days, Xi waited excitedly, but when no one arrived, his face revealed his disappointment.[27]

In February 1967, Zhou Enlai met in Beijing with the leaders of two Red Guard factions in Xi'an. When Zhou saw a picture of Xi at a struggle session, he said, "None of us knew about this. Why did you arbitrarily take Xi Zhongxun to Xi'an?" "You grabbed Xi Zhongxun," Zhou told them. "You thought you were getting a treasure, but in fact you got a porcupine." He ordered that the Shaanxi Military Region detain Xi. On March 14, the military established a site to "observe" Xi and five other former high-ranking leaders. On March 23, Xi wrote a letter to his secretary in Luoyang requesting that the factory send word to Zhou that Xi wanted to return to Henan to treat his deaf ear. The letter was never sent—that night around midnight, three soldiers of the People's Liberation Army came to take Xi away.[28]

Xi and the other officials ended up at 73 Jianguo Road—a location that became known simply, notoriously, as "Number 73." Although officially labeled a "guardianship management facility," it was in fact a prison. All those sent to Number 73, eventually totaling fifty-five individuals, were treated as enemies of the people. The prisoners were confined separately, referred to by number, and only allowed outside briefly twice a day. At night, they could not turn off the lights. They were forced to defecate and urinate in their cells, and not even family members could visit. Beatings were common. In the morning, they were given one ladle of vegetables and one cornmeal bun; for lunch, they received one more scoop of vegetables and two more buns. One prisoner became so hungry that he fought with the pigs to steal their slop.[29] Another inmate who was able to survive spoke of the intense loneliness he experienced: "Depression and pain became the main content of my life. On more than one occasion, I thought about the nature of will, belief, and ideals. . . . But none of these could end the anxiety and uneasiness when loneliness attacked. At times, I wondered, Is this guardianship really better than a prison? In prison, many criminals are together. They can speak a bit to one another. But here, unless someone is angry with you, no one speaks to you. . . . In the guardianship rooms that held only one person, the people were overcome with loneliness, suffocation, and darkness."[30]

The transfer to Number 73 did not spare Xi from abuse. Leftist rebels now needed permission from the Shaanxi Military Region to subject Xi to struggle sessions, but soldiers complied, escorting him to the sites.[31] When the Cultural Revolution reached another crescendo in the summer of 1967, Xi was subjected to more than ten big struggle sessions and to ten smaller ones.[32] At one session in September, under interrogation, Xi admitted that he thought Gao Gang had been treated too severely and that Gao's treatment would be difficult to explain to the people in the Northwest. When his interrogators asked him why he had said such a thing, Xi broke: "The goal was to oppose the Central Committee, to oppose Chairman Mao." The participants then yelled, "Down with whoever opposes Chairman Mao!" When Xi's persecutors asked how his opposition to Mao Zedong thought had manifested itself, Xi replied that he had opposed the party as well as Mao and that he had "plotted" the publication of *Liu Zhidan*. When Xi was accused of not reading books and for saying that if practical experience is used, then the management of any problem naturally fits Marxist principles, he accepted the charges.[33]

Xi became resigned to his fate. On April 5, he wrote a desperate letter to Zhou Enlai: "My value as a negative example is over. Now I just accompany other people as they suffer criticism and struggle. . . . It has already been fifteen years since I left Xi'an. Even with regard to the prior evil influence, there can no longer be much left anymore." Xi suggested to Zhou that because his "problems" had already been addressed after 1962, he should be treated differently from other people and allowed to continue to "forge through labor, to continue to completely transform myself."[34]

But Zhou did not save his old deputy. On August 27, 1967, student radicals from Jiaotong University brought Xi to yet another mass rally. An article in the student newspaper about the event described how "the mass struggle rally began in an atmosphere full of hatred and rage toward the class enemy." The student who led the rally began by describing Xi as a "local emperor" who had opposed Mao and the party and who was the "sworn enemy" of the people in the Northwest. "We dragged this dog out of the water to show him to the masses," the student went on. "We will not retreat until total victory is achieved and he is knocked down and struggled against to the point that he stinks." As Xi entered, the students shouted slogans like "Down with the counterrevolutionary revisionist Xi Zhongxun!" Xi listened as the students accused him of sabotaging land reform in the Northwest, of failing to sufficiently purge the enemies of the party during the Suppression of Counterrevolutionaries Campaign, and of distorting the party's United Front policies. Xi was called a "big feudal foreman," who allegedly used practices from secret societies, like the Green and Red Gangs and the Gelaohui, such as swearing blood brothers and adopting goddaughters.[35] One Red Guard tabloid described Xi's behavior at a struggle session when he was pressured to confess to his "crimes" on Tibet policy: "This old fox is very cunning; with regard to some key issues, he always speaks evasively, he hums and haws, and only in the face of ironclad evidence does he admit his crimes."[36]

But not all of these stunts convinced ordinary people. On October 2, 1967, Red Guards took Xi to Yishan Middle School in Xi's home county of Fuping. The locals told the Red Guards to stop shouting as they credited Xi with saving them from starvation in 1962. Many years later, Xi recalled, "I was criticized and struggled against at Yishan Middle School. For fear that I would faint under the intense heat, someone held an umbrella for me. After the meeting, I told the local people, 'I'm back,' and I said jokingly that they should treat me to a meal in my hometown. They then prepared for me some local snacks, such as minced green bean paste and red bean noodles."[37]

In January 1968, Zhou had Xi brought to Beijing to be placed under the authority of the Beijing Garrison.[38] While confined in the capital, Xi occupied a small room at Beixinqiao Communications School. When his son Yuanping later asked him how he had managed, Zhongxun explained, "When there was no one to talk to, I talked to myself!"[39] Xi had no idea who else was incarcerated there—the shower nozzles had been separated by wooden boards, so the inmates could only see each other's feet while bathing.[40] But the situation was better than what he had experienced in Xi'an, even though, on at least one occasion, he was beaten with belts by two guards from Shandong. As a result, Xi long held a grudge toward anyone from the province. "Even after I die, I won't forget," he said. "Those two soldiers had no human nature!"[41]

Zhou gave no sign that the situation would improve. In April 1968, he praised a delegation from Shaanxi for their "investigations" into the cases of Xi and other disgraced leaders. He called upon the leaders of the mass organizations in the province to "join together and continue to investigate" Xi, even as he was encouraging them to "liberate" other fallen comrades.[42] On a trip to Yan'an in March 1970, Zhou declared that Xi "was a traitor and an enemy agent who had snuck into the party." Liu Zhidan was admirable for his "extreme" party discipline, Zhou said. Gao Gang and Xi, on the other hand, were "domineering and extremely arrogant."[43]

THE XI FAMILY STRUGGLES

Even before the Cultural Revolution, the situation for Qi Xin was far from easy. In 1964, the party school was subjected to another round of investigations and persecutions. One hundred and fifty-four cadres at the school were punished, and the former deputy director of the Philosophy Department committed suicide after someone spit in his face. The individuals under investigation were not allowed to go anywhere without being watched, and anyone who dared to speak to them would also come under suspicion. One former party school official described the situation there as a "true White terror" in which "revolutionary comrades" were treated as "enemies."[44]

Qi's relationship with Xi exacerbated her situation. She later wrote that, at the time, she felt deeply conflicted. She wanted to stand with the party, but she still felt emotions toward Xi. She claimed that she decided to join the new Socialist Education Campaign away from the party school to escape this conundrum. However, she was only one of many party-school cadres who participated in this campaign in a rural area of Haidian District of Beijing, where many high-ranking figures from the party school held leading positions.[45]

Regardless of whether she was forced to join the Socialist Education Campaign as an employee of the party school or had joined voluntarily to escape an already difficult situation, she would have found herself in the middle of one of the most notorious cases of mass persecution in the party's history. The Tenth Plenum in 1962 marked the beginning of not only her husband's purge but a renewed emphasis on class struggle. In the ensuing years, the central leadership took an increasingly dim view of class enemies infiltrating the party, especially in the countryside. Liu Shaoqi, who fully accepted Mao's warnings about the dangers of "revisionism" and "peaceful evolution," meaning departure from Communist values or regime change, came up with a solution—to send work teams from the cities to struggle against rural cadres who had departed from the revolutionary agenda. The Socialist Education Campaign soon led to beatings, physical punishments, and suicides. The work teams, who spent prolonged periods living with peasants, were shocked by the poverty and backwardness they witnessed, even in the environs of Beijing. In Haidian District, where Qi Xin was working, one local cadre even believed that the peasants "were only capable of criticizing or struggling; it is so disillusioning!"[46] In early December 1965, she was allowed one day of leave from the campaign to visit Xi before he was to leave for Henan. She cleaned his bedding as a way of saying goodbye. They would not see each other again for eight years.[47]

When the Socialist Education Campaign ended and the Cultural Revolution began, it was Qi Xin's turn to face persecution. Party-school cadres who had led the Socialist Education Campaign in Haidian District were swiftly targeted in the ensuing turmoil for allegedly suppressing the masses.[48] Kang Sheng, who oversaw the party school, actively supported the rebels persecuting the school's leadership and many of its employees. On August 20, 1966, Kang warned against physical punishment at the party school, but he clarified that "putting on big hats and hanging signs on people" were still acceptable. "In my opinion," Kang said at a mass rally at the school in April 1967, "the party school is a stubborn castle that for a long period of time opposed Mao Zedong thought."[49]

Qi Xin was particularly vulnerable not only because of Xi but because of her own blood relations as well. Her brother Ruixin was criticized, accused of having a "Nationalist boss" for a father.[50] Qi Xin was put on a "black name list" of five hundred people at the school and later labeled an "antiparty element." The entire school was covered with big-character posters criticizing her. "Down with Qi Xin," radicals wrote on the ground in front of the entrance to the school cafeteria. To humiliate her, the characters for her name were written upside down, with a one-meter-wide X written across them. When Yuanping, who was only eleven years old at the time, passed by, he was terrified.[51]

Such a situation was extraordinarily difficult for young children. Swept up in the moment, the Xi siblings treated their mother in ways they would later regret. When Qi returned home after a struggle session, her children started crying: "Mother, did you talk nonsense?" Qiaoqiao blurted out. "You cannot be a traitor!" When describing this experience, Qiaoqiao later reflected, "Looking back now, speaking that way to my mother was a bit too much."[52] When Qi Xin walked Yuanping to school, he would deliberately keep his distance from her. "I both could not stand to look at the black-and-blue scars on her face and was also worried my classmates would surround her and look down on her, and I would feel ashamed," Yuanping wrote later. "I often cried silently out of humiliation for my mother and family. But looking back now, I often feel overwhelmed by guilt about my childishness at the time."[53]

Qi Xin often stayed up all night trying to understand how she could write a self-criticism that would pass muster without betraying her husband. She was so stressed that she would smoke two packs of cigarettes every day, leading her to develop emphysema later in life. One night, Yuanping and one of his sisters woke up to discover that their mother was missing. Yuanping's sister grabbed his hand. "Quickly, let's go find mother," she urged him, fearing any number of dreadful possibilities, even suicide. "Don't let something bad happen." They found her alone, at the memorial arch of the party school, pacing back and forth and looking at the sky. When Qi Xin saw her children, she embraced them while in tears. She later told Yuanping that she had feared that she had already reached a breaking point. "I could hardly hold on any longer," she told him, "but I thought about father, and I thought about our young children."[54]

Qi Xin and Yuanping were exiled to the party school's so-called May 7 Cadre School, one of many such institutions throughout the country established to subject party cadres, especially intellectuals, to reform through labor. The school was in Henan Province's Huangfan District, an area of extreme poverty because of regular flooding due to the nearby Yellow River (Qi's own dormitory was destroyed by a flood). She was forced to engage in work that exceeded her physical capabilities because she was a key target of "reform." She had a form of arthritis that became worse in the damp conditions, so she wore boots into the fields where she grew her own carrots, and she also used a skincare product to treat Yuanping's mosquito bites. These acts were used by people as evidence of her acting like a "stinking bourgeois missy." In Zhongxun's absence, the family was so poor that, in order to send care packages to the other siblings, Qi Xin would allow Yuanping only half a meal of food. Qi Xin rarely had breaks from her reeducation at the May 7 Cadre School, but when she did, she spent all of her salary on tickets to Shanxi, Shaanxi, and Inner Mongolia to visit her children. Because she could only buy the cheapest tickets, she often would stand for days at a time on the train.[55]

Xi's children suffered as well. Xi Qianping graduated from China Foreign Affairs University with a major in French in 1965. After graduation, she went to work at *Peking Review*, the party's foreign-language magazine intended primarily for foreign leftist parties. In April 1966, along with other cadres at the Foreign Languages Publishing House, she was sent to participate in the Socialist Education Campaign in an isolated area of Ningxia Autonomous Region. No one except the two leaders of her work team actually knew that she was Xi Zhongxun's daughter. During one meeting, someone criticized Xi, and, unable to restrain herself, Qianping defended him. After the team returned to Beijing, the Foreign Languages Publishing House suffered from intense factional infighting for years, and at least one employee of *Peking Review* died an "irregular" death. Ma Baoshan, a fellow employee at *Peking Review* who would later marry Qianping, was imprisoned for nine years.[56]

Qiaoqiao was incarcerated in a Mao Zedong–Thought Study Group along with criminals. In the spring of 1969, she joined a construction corps in Inner Mongolia. Her experience there was tough—she was tormented by tuberculosis, rheumatic fever, heart problems, and dysentery. "At that time, people really did not fear hardship or death," she said later. But she believed that by engaging in more arduous experiences, it would be easier for her to show her value and to escape her status as a "black child" of a disgraced official.[57]

An'an attended the Beijing Foreign Studies University School, which was heavily populated by the offspring of high-ranking cadres because they were seen as more trustworthy for future positions in the foreign policy establishment. Even before the Cultural Revolution, one group of students, known as the Four Young Ladies, refused to let An'an join their group because her father had become a local official in Henan. Perhaps suffering from financial difficulties at home, An'an's reputation at the school suffered further after she borrowed ten *kuai*, a hefty sum at the time, and never repaid it. She avoided her fellow classmates and instead associated with hooligans and pickpockets who hung out at Ganjiakou, the park near her school. After the Cultural Revolution began, she was sent to work on a production team in Shanxi.[58]

Jinping faced a difficult situation at the August 1 School. At least one student there was not permitted to enter the Communist Youth League simply because his father was connected with Xi Zhongxun.[59] According to journalist John Garnaut, "That's why Xi Jinping sometimes jokes that he could never actually be called a 'princeling'—the ubiquitous and disparaging term for children of senior Chinese leaders—because his father was in political purgatory for most of the years he had known him, says a close family friend, whose father worked directly under Xi."[60]

The situation became worse with the onset of the Cultural Revolution. In 1996, Jinping's former teacher Chen Qiuying recalled, "Because of the irregular political life of his mother and father during the Cultural Revolution, he suffered extremely unfair treatment, and Xi Jinping was seen by some as 'one of the five black elements, a bastard' and 'a reactionary student.'"[61] Chen remembers Jinping as someone "calmer than other people his age," someone who always let the teacher walk in front and who loved to read, especially poetry by Tang dynasty poet Du Fu.[62] Jinping, who was beaten and forced to march, asked Chen why something like that could occur; she later admitted that she did not have a good answer for such a young boy at the time. Chen knew that Jinping was in pain but also claimed that he did not participate in "doing bad things."[63]

While no available evidence ties Jinping to any particularly brutal violence, he did become the "little king" of a group of young boys near the party school whose parents had been swept away by the Cultural Revolution. These children organized themselves according to where they lived and fought with neighboring groups. Military belts were their preferred weapon.[64] At one point, Jinping went with a friend to find a physical education teacher who had previously bullied him because of his father's status to give the man a "lesson."[65]

Only thirteen years old, Jinping probably would have felt disappointed that he was too young to join any official Red Guard organizations. These early Red Guards were often the children of high-ranking leaders, and they chanted that "if the father is a hero, then the son is a brave man; if the father is a reactionary, then the son is a bastard."[66] At first, members of the Central Cultural Revolution Small Group praised the bloodline theory. However, when the Red Guards realized that their parents were the targets of the campaign, they swiftly fell out with the others. They formed their own faction called the United Action Committee. Subsequently, the Small Group attacked the bloodline theory, and the United Action Committee was smashed by the central authorities.[67] On January 25, 1967, Jinping's own August 1 School was assaulted by more than twenty thousand people looking for the leaders of the United Action Committee. More than thirty-three students and two employees at the school were detained and placed in a Ministry of

Public Security facility in Beijing.⁶⁸ Shortly thereafter, the August 1 School was closed down and turned into a public exhibition hall showcasing the alleged special privileges of the students.⁶⁹

After his school was closed down, Jinping transferred to the Beijing No. 25 Middle School. Jinping and two friends were looked down upon and considered the "blackest" students in their class because of their parents. Although Jinping was almost certainly not allowed to join the early Red Guards or the United Action Committee, he had connections to those groups, and, on one occasion, he and his two friends from No. 25 were invited by the old Red Guards to debate students at another school. Hundreds of students arrived at the event. Suddenly, a gate opened, and a smaller number of organized students armed with clubs ran onto the campus and started attacking everyone they saw. Jinping was fast and escaped, but one friend, who was too slow, was beaten severely.⁷⁰

Jinping was persecuted at the place of his mother's employment, the party school. He later claimed that it was there that he was "dragged out" for persecution by Kang Sheng's wife, Cao Yi'ou, as a "family member of a 'black gang.'" On one occasion, likely in the spring of 1967, the party school held a mass rally to criticize six "capitalist roaders," including some other adults as well as one child—Jinping. Because of his young age, Jinping had trouble with the humiliating heavy steel cap they were all forced to put on their heads as part of the spectacle. He had to hold it onto his head with his hands. Qi Xin attended this rally, and when the slogan "Down with Xi Jinping" was shouted, she too raised her hands and yelled along with everyone else. Although mother and son were only a few feet away from each other, they were not allowed to speak.⁷¹

One night during a rainstorm, when the guard was distracted, Jinping crept out of his confinement at the party school and returned home. He told his mother he was hungry, but she refused to give him any food. Worse, despite the rain, she went to report him to the authorities. According to a family friend, Jinping understood his mother's behavior—if she were to be caught, she would have been arrested. Jinping cried in front of An'an and Yuanping and then departed, still hungry, back into the night. He found a place to stay with an old worker near the Summer Palace. The next day, however, he was arrested and put into a juvenile detention facility for "reform through labor."⁷²

In 1984, Xi described his experiences during the Cultural Revolution to two journalists:

> During the ten years of chaos [the Cultural Revolution], my entire family was attacked. At the time, I was fifteen. Because of my "dissatisfaction with the Cultural Revolution," the Special Case Committee placed me in isolation for investigation, and, from morning until night, I was questioned and forced to persevere while standing up in the "jet-plane position" as punishment. One time, during the Lunar New Year, my younger brother sent me a plate of dumplings. I really wanted to eat them, but the people on the Special Case Committee stole them away and said, "Do you know what kind of people ate dumplings in the past? You do not want to eat those dumplings. You want to relive the heavenly lifestyle from the past that you lost. That's just a dream!" Soon thereafter, in August, I was imprisoned. I had only one, unlined, item of clothing, and by December, it was already very cold. At night, I slept on the icy floor. I used an icy brick as a pillow. My entire body was covered in lice. I collapsed from sickness, and I even thought of death.[73]

In 1997, Jinping said frankly to an interviewer, "Actually, I suffered more than most people."[74]

In January 1969, carrying a bag knit by his mother bearing the words "Mother's heart" on it, Jinping went to Shaanxi as a "sent-down student," one of the millions of young people exiled by Mao to the countryside to learn from the peasants.[75] If Jinping had stayed in Beijing, he faced the strong possibility of continued incarceration. After the hardship at the detention center, Jinping felt elated. He later recalled, "On the special train to Yan'an, I remember very clearly—that was January 1969—everyone was crying; on the entire special train there was no one who was not crying, except for me, who was laughing. At the time, my family members, standing outside the train, asked, How can you be laughing? I replied that if I had had to stay in the prison, I would have been crying. If I had not gone to the countryside, I don't know if I would have lived or died."[76] On January 23, Jinping and more than 1,300 others arrived in Yanchuan County in the region of Yan'an, where most of them lived in caves.[77]

One sent-down youth in Yanchuan described the county in 1969 as a place of chaos. Local markets were full of gangs of youth who fought and stole from each other. Only in 1970 did the situation improve, primarily because "sent-down youth stealing from each other could not solve the problem of finding food to eat." He wrote, "From the Cultural Revolution to becoming a sent-down youth, many people came to the realization that to evolve into a benevolent person was an exceptionally lengthy process, but to turn a person into an animal, on the other hand, was very easy. Just extinguish a bit of affection and light a bit of fire, then smash a plate of food, and that is enough."[78]

Shaanxi was such a desolate and poor region that the treatment of the sent-down youth there attracted the attention of the national leadership. One youth, while on a trip back to Beijing, met with Zhou Enlai and warned him about the situation. Beggars were common. Family members were forced to share only one blanket. Daughters were sold into marriage, and the dowry was based on how much the girl weighed. Locals complained that conditions had been better during the early years of the revolution. When the sent-down youth fought among each other, no one intervened. Zhou met with the participants at a special meeting held by the State Council to address the problems that the sent-down youth faced in Yan'an. He expressed shame that, despite the contributions of the people in Northern Shaanxi to the Communist victory, Yan'an remained so shockingly poor.[79]

The situation clearly wore on Jinping—when he finally got his hands on some local sorghum *baijiu* liquor (Xifengjiu), a rare achievement in that desperately poor region, he got so drunk that he fell asleep in the snow. "Good thing I was young—only sixteen—so I was in good physical condition," Jinping later told Taiwanese president Ma Ying-jeou, "otherwise I would have frozen to death."[80] He admitted that when he first arrived in Yan'an, he had refused to work and did not get along well with the peasants. When the peasants sat on his hot *kang*, he would become angry, fearing that they were carrying lice. News that Jinping had fed a dog a piece of stale bread, at the time regarded as an unbelievable waste of food, spread throughout the entire county. He asked the other students whether they also felt like "cavemen."[81]

Jinping fled all the way back to Beijing, where he was again incarcerated for four or five months and forced to work in the Haidian area sewers.[82] While pondering his future, he went to visit his aunt Qi Yun and uncle Wei Zhenwu. Qi Yun and her husband had been transferred to Beijing in 1955. Wei was assigned to work in the Ministry of Forestry, where he became a vice-minister in 1960. In 1964, Wei also faced political persecution. Although the ostensible reasons were related to his behavior in the ministry, the real reason was his relationship to Xi Zhongxun. After an investigation concluded, Wei was lucky to escape the worst punishment, but he was reassigned to become a vice-county head—a drop of eight grades.[83]

Before the Cultural Revolution, the Xi and Wei families rarely met, as everyone was busy, and they lived in different parts of Beijing. After the Cultural Revolution began, however, Wei Zhenwu and Qi Yun went to great lengths to help the Xi family. For a time, all four of the Xi children, lacking money and food, lived with Wei and Qi, which placed significant stress on their family. The Xi children would have seen how even their grandmother Deng Yaozhen, who also found refuge with Wei and Qi, was harassed because of her class origins despite her fame as a revolutionary mother who "rode a donkey up [the Communist base area of] Taihang." At one point, the authorities threatened to exile the old lady from the city—a prospect that devastated the entire family. Qi Yun resisted the decision until she herself was sent to the countryside. For the final years of her life, Deng lived alone and continued to suffer harassment by young radicals.[84] Yet the family remained devoted to the revolution. When Jinping spoke to his aunt and uncle, they told him stories about their own decision to leave the cities decades earlier. Qi Yun said, "At the time, we all were running to the countryside; now, all you young people are afraid to go there. That is wrong!"[85]

After Jinping returned to the Northwest, it seemed to him that he might never be allowed to leave. In September 1970, representatives of the sent-down youth in the province were told at a meeting held by the Shaanxi Revolutionary Committee that they should prepare to spend their entire lives in the countryside. Morale was poor, especially because some high-ranking leaders were using connections so that their children could return to the cities. There were also cases of mistreatment or abuse. Between 1970 and August 1973 alone, Shaanxi recorded 621 cases of youth abuse, most of which involved the rape of young women.[86]

But Jinping suffered special mistreatment due to his father's situation. There was no hope that he could leave by either joining the People's Liberation Army or finding work in a city.[87] On one occasion, he went to visit a friend he knew from the August 1 School, who was living nearby. While away, their commune suddenly decided to hold a meeting, but Jinping did not have time to return to his village of Liangjiahe, so he went instead with his friend's work brigade, which was being led by the local party secretary holding a Red flag. Shortly before they reached the commune, Jinping returned to his own brigade. This act led to the absurd accusation that "the son of Xi Zhongxun does not march with a Red flag"—implying that he was a counterrevolutionary. The charge was so devastating to Jinping that he lost the energy to work.[88] Jinping was even forced to denounce his father and read aloud from articles that criticized him. Jinping later bitterly recalled that experience: "Even if you do not understand, you are forced to understand. It forces you to mature earlier."[89]

Jinping had to apply eight times to join the Communist Youth League, and he became furious when he heard that a local party leader had been criticized for even attempting to support the application despite Zhongxun's status. "Who am I?" Jinping reflected. "What did I do? Did I write reactionary slogans, or did I yell a few reactionary slogans? I am a young person; I want to advance—what is wrong with that?"[90] Early attempts to join the party also failed. In 1973, the village party branch approved Jinping's application, but the commune leader did not. The commune leader criticized the man who supported Jinping's application: "You even dare to introduce the 'son of a black gang' into the party!" Jinping was not accepted into the party until 1974.[91] But even as his father made it harder for him to climb the ranks, Zhongxun's fall from grace was one motivation for that striving in the first place. One of Jinping's friends at the time later said that Jinping overcame several years of emotional distress and confusion after a local leader spoke about his father's revolutionary exploits and the respect he enjoyed in the region.[92]

The sufferings of his mother seemed to motivate Jinping as well. In 1971, he visited her and joined her to work in the fields. After working six hours, she was told that she would still have to work another shift. According to Yuanping, Jinping took her by the hand and led her away. A family friend tells another version: When Jinping asked for someone to cover for his mother, the brigade leader called him a bastard. Jinping became furious and struck the man.[93] Shortly thereafter, Jinping, wearing his father's old uniform, went for a walk with Yuanping. After remaining silent for a moment, Jinping said, "Little brother, your brother will not be sticking around any longer; I simply can't! I cannot bear to watch what our mother must endure! I am leaving tomorrow, and I will return to Liangjiahe in Northern Shaanxi! Your big brother will make a good showing for dad and mom to make a good showing for our whole family! Take good care of mom." Even though Jinping had not seen his family for three years, he departed the very next day, only five days after his arrival, without even having used up all his vacation time.[94]

Jinping's desire to "make a good showing" marked a transformation during his time in Shaanxi. Despite everything, he still could imagine a brighter future. One peasant recalled preparing porridge for Jinping as he lay on the *kang* with a high fever. "I don't want to die like this," he told the peasant as he continued reading a book. "I still want to do some great things." The peasant, with the benefit of hindsight, recalled, "At that point, I became sure that this person would one day become a big person."[95]

Jinping has often spoken about how the Cultural Revolution challenged his worldview. He was stunned by the poverty he witnessed. Xi later said his "heart trembled" thinking about how the Northern Shaanxi peasants, who had supported the revolution with their lives and blood, lived in the "disaster" caused by the "false socialism" brought about by the Gang of Four.[96] As an adult, he would reflect that his generation had been "stirred up" by radicalism, but "by the time of the Cultural Revolution, our ideals had been destroyed."[97] He would claim that he had decided to leave Beijing for a job at the grass roots because "only if millions of people willingly devote their lives to the party can the tragedy of the Cultural Revolution be prevented."[98] Precisely because he underwent a period of trial and serious reflection, Jinping would later say, his decision that only socialism could save China was felt all the more powerfully.[99]

If true, it would demonstrate that both Zhongxun and Jinping were shaped by a Bolshevik political culture that fetishized "forging"—the idea that desperation actually *increases* dedication to the cause. While Zhongxun was inspired by Jiang Guangci's novel, Jinping told a group of Russian scholars in 2013 that his model was a puritanical and revolutionary character in Nikolai Chernyshevskii's novel *What Is to Be Done?* The character, Rakhmetov, slept on a bed of nails to forge his will. Xi imagined a parallel as he wandered through rainstorms and blizzards.[100]

In 1997, Xi Zhongxun, nearing the end of his life, would tell an old associate, "The Cultural Revolution honed my children."[101] However, one member of the Xi family did not survive the "forge"—Zhongxun's daughter Heping. Much remains mysterious about her personal torment. In Hebei Province's Zhangjiakou, she worked at a foreign-language military academy that trained young people to conduct signals-intelligence surveillance against China's enemies. The school suffered from repeated political campaigns throughout the 1960s, but when the Cultural Revolution began, sheer chaos ensued: students went to Beijing to besiege the Ministry of Defense, one of the founders of the school was persecuted to death, and many young and middle-aged teachers were forced to leave. In July 1969, the school moved to Luoyang in Henan Province.[102]

FIGURE 9. Heping (*right*) and Qianping (*left*), sometime before the Cultural Revolution. Source: *Xi Zhongxun huace*, 168.

At some point during this turmoil, Heping, by then a mother of two, went to Beijing to stay with her sister Qianping in the Foreign Languages Publishing House dormitories in the Weigongcun neighborhood. One day, when Qianping left for work, Heping hanged herself from a pipe in the toilet.[103] Jinping learned about his sister's death while he was in Liangjiahe. When he received the letter, he was digging an air-raid shelter in preparation for a possible Soviet attack. He stepped away so that no one would see him cry.[104] Zhongxun was not told about Heping's death until 1978, which would have been several years later than Jinping received the news. Zhongxun "could not stop crying for an entire day. He cried so much that his eyes swelled up," Qianping recalled. She believed that the loss was a "major blow" to her father.[105]

Heping's death created a sense of empathy for Xi with others who suffered during the tragedy of the Cultural Revolution. In January 1989, Wang Yuqi, who for many decades had worked in the Northwest, visited Xi in Beijing to ask for help resolving difficulties related to his rehabilitation. Xi invited Wang to his bedroom to discuss the problem. Xi said, "The Cultural Revolution brought many unhappy things." Xi's voice then became softer, and a look of melancholy spread across his face. He told Wang about Heping's suicide. Wang later wrote of the moment, "My father was persecuted to death as a 'Nationalist agent' during the Cultural Revolution. Old Xi connected my father's unjust case with that of his own daughter. The Cultural Revolution brought disasters to so many families!"[106]

16
THE XI FAMILY SLOWLY REBUILDS

During eight years of exile, persecution, and incarceration, Xi Zhongxun did not see his wife or children, though the family continued to hear rumors about him: that he was dead, had gone mad, committed suicide, or simply disappeared. His son Yuanping, who was nine at the time his father departed for Luoyang before the Cultural Revolution, later described his feelings: "In my heart, for a long time, my father was already a distant dream that could be thought about but not seen."[1]

In 1972, Qi Xin's status as a party member was restored.[2] That winter, her sister Yun wrote to warn her that their mother was dying. Qi Xin asked for leave and returned to Beijing. Her children were also allowed to temporarily visit the capital. Homeless and with no money, they met at Yun's home. Qi Xin used the occasion to write Zhou Enlai a letter asking if she and the children could meet Xi. Zhou granted the request. The reunion was emotional. She recalled, "What I did not expect was that when Zhongxun saw the children and me, this man who had been indomitable his entire life, started crying and repeatedly said, 'This is happy; this is happy.'"[3] Xi could no longer distinguish between Qiaoqiao and An'an, and he could not recognize his sons. Zhongxun later described the experience: "One day, someone from the Special Case Committee abruptly brought me to a place in the city; I suddenly saw Qi Xin and the children sitting there. One child warmly called me father, but I was temporarily dumbfounded. Only after Qi Xin told me did I recognize my youngest son."[4]

Jinping offered his father a cigarette and also lit up one for himself.

When Zhongxun asked him why he was smoking, Jinping answered, "I am depressed. These last few years we also suffered many difficulties and hardships." Zhongxun was silent for a moment. "I give you permission to smoke," he said. The next time the family was reunited, Zhongxun, knowing that his son did not have rolling papers, gave Jinping a pipe. "I have taken care of it ever since," he said later. But Zhongxun mixed kindness with characteristic toughness. On one trip to visit his incarcerated father, Jinping complained about the difficulties of life in rural Shaanxi. He expected his father to commiserate, but Zhongxun responded, "Being a sent-down youth is a good thing. Don't look at the fact that I'm locked up here; even after they let me out, I will still tell you to hurry back to the countryside; you must be one with the masses at the grass roots!"[5]

BACK IN LUOYANG

The investigation into Xi's alleged crimes had never officially concluded. On December 21, 1974, Liu Zhidan's widow wrote a letter to Mao begging for Liu Jingfan to be released from prison to treat an illness. Mao penned a notification. "This case has already been under investigation for a long time," the chairman wrote. "It is inappropriate to delay further. I suggest they be released and no longer investigated." In February the following year, Xi wrote to Mao from confinement: "I have now passed sixty years of age. That's not old. My health is pretty good. I am very optimistic. As long as I don't develop a weird illness, it's totally possible that I could work for the party another twenty years." He asked to participate in "arduous labor" so that he could "further forge in real struggle and once again become an enlightened soldier that continues to make revolution." In March, Mao approved Zhou Enlai's proposal to release most of the nearly seven hundred individuals under investigation by the central special case committees.[6] In May, Xi was told that his problem was a case of "contradictions among the people," although he was still accused of having committed an "antiparty" mistake. The Special Case Committee declared that Xi should "change his environment, rest, and recuperate."[7] Not everyone who was released received such treatment. For example, Peng Zhen, a man loathed by Zhou, was let out of Qincheng Prison only to see a new resolution labeling him a "traitor" and suggesting he be expelled from the party.[8] Had Zhou tried to help his old deputy Xi by applying the more positive language of "contradiction among the people" to his case?

And what was Xi's reaction to his new freedom? The answer is unknown, but Liu Jingfan told his family that Mao had "saved him again"—a clear reference to the party center's appearance in Shaanxi in 1935.[9]

Xi, accompanied by his wife, returned to Luoyang but to a different factory. Change was already in the air. In the summer of 1975, Deng Xiaoping, who after his purge at the beginning of the Cultural Revolution had spent years in internal exile, had been entrusted by Mao to get the economy back on its feet. However, Mao remained mercurial. Just a few months after Xi's arrival in Luoyang, Mao decided to purge Deng once again. During the subsequent Criticize Deng, Strike against the Right Deviationist Wind of Reversing Verdicts Campaign, Xi's factory produced 28,400 fewer tons of material and suffered a financial loss of 328.79 million yuan. On top of that, it became a very dangerous place to work. Between April 1975 and December 1976, four work incidents had led to fatalities. Yet hints of China's more open stance to the outside world were starting to appear. In July 1975, a 1,250-ton hydraulic brick press arrived at the factory from West Germany, and, a year later, a West German technician came to help adjust it.[10]

At first, Xi was extremely cautious because the verdict against him had still not been fully reversed, so he avoided speaking with people, fearing that he might implicate them in his troubles with the party. When he and Qi Xin visited a friend from Shaanxi, he asked them to close the blinds, refusing to sit down until they had absolute privacy. When Xi was asked how long he would stay in Henan, he responded, "It's hard to say," sighed, and continued, "I guess we'll just have to see what the party is planning?" Qi Xin then cut in to say that the circumstances of this stay in Luoyang were worse than the last time as Xi's special treatment had been canceled. But Zhou Enlai had arranged for Qi Xin to take care of him this time. Emotionally, Xi said, "I was able to survive the suffering during the war era. The conditions today are much better."[11] At the time, they were living in a forty-meter apartment that was so small that the bathroom and the kitchen were in one room. Qi Xin slept together with their daughter An'an in an eight-meter bedroom, while Xi stayed in the common room (An'an, then twenty-four, had recently graduated from a medical school in Taiyuan and become a doctor in the factory).[12] Furthermore, Xi was still not receiving an official salary. To survive, he had to borrow money from the factory every month, and the workers, who were also very poor, often helped.[13]

The long ordeal had taken a toll on Xi's physical and mental well-being.

When Zhou Enlai died in January 1976, Xi was so sad that when he cried, he also hit his legs—his blows were so strong that his legs began to well up. His weeping was so loud that he frightened the neighbors, and for three days, Xi refused to eat. On one afternoon, he wept so hard while facing an image of Zhou at his home that he passed out, and his neighbors had to take him to the hospital. Xi's weeping became a regular occurrence. According to a Chinese journalist, "Xi Zhongxun's neighbors all said that each day, after he cried, Xi would go out for a jog at Luoyang's Nancun Reservoir."[14] When someone saw Xi reading the novel *Defend Yan'an*, he asked, "Isn't that book about Peng Dehuai?" a highly familiar yet rude way for a young person to refer to a man who had been one of the People's Republic's great military legends. Xi scolded him for more than an hour and then started crying again.[15]

Nevertheless, Xi's frailty was mixed with resolution. On one occasion, Xi overheard two old women saying that normal people would have committed suicide if they had to experience what had happened to him. Xi turned around and said, "I, Xi Zhongxun, would absolutely never do such a stupid thing as kill myself! In Luoyang, I made many worker and peasant friends,

FIGURE 10. Xi Zhongxun in Luoyang, 1975. Source: *Xi Zhongxun huace*, 55.

why wouldn't I continue to struggle, to fight for an opportunity to serve them better? Why would I leave them because of personal setbacks?"[16] Xi, according to accounts about this time, would talk about those who had sacrificed their lives for the revolution, claiming that "the fact that I have lived until today is something that I simply could not have imagined at the time."[17] To a visiting relative, he revealed a fascination with the Tang dynasty figure Lou Shide, an individual famous for having an uncouth background but a drive for self-study and an ability to accept repeated career-related setbacks. Xi explained to his visitor how Lou, a chancellor at the time, told his younger brother that if someone spit in his face, it was necessary to let the saliva dry, instead of wiping it off, to show deference.[18]

He tried to use his time in Luoyang to improve his health. In October 1982, during a meeting with North Korean leader Kim Il-sung, Xi said, "Every morning, I woke up at 5:00. Then I would jog until 7:30. Each time, I jogged nine kilometers, rain or shine. The reason my health is still so good is because, at that time, I stubbornly forged myself."[19] He seems to have sincerely enjoyed interacting with ordinary people, and he was able to win their affection. Members of the Xi family recalled a "favorite hobby": waking up to bathe in the public baths at 9:00 a.m. with a group of workers who had just gotten off the night shift. Yuanping believed that it was during those moments, while joking with the workers, that his father was happiest. Zhongxun would pick up the workers' children by putting his hands on their bellies and then float them on top of the water, and he often would ask a neighbor's son to give him a back massage.[20]

Zhongxun clearly saw value in the tribulations Jinping was experiencing—when Yuanping visited Luoyang in 1975, Zhongxun suggested that he accompany Jinping to Liangjiahe: "You are a worker, and even though your salary is relatively low, compared with where your brother is, you are in a much better situation. The Northern Shaanxi countryside is really the cruelest!"[21] But Jinping did not want to remain in Shaanxi. He tried to use his family's connections to escape, although Jinping was not unique in that regard. In the early 1970s, a "wind" of "taking the back door"—a Chinese expression that means engaging in nepotism—led to more than one million young urban people departing the countryside by 1973.[22] Qi Xin admits that Yuanping, who was not allowed to continue as a student because of his father's status, was able to find a job working in a factory in Beijing in 1972 only because of one of his father's "old comrades in arms."[23]

Jinping and Qi Xin placed their hopes on the director of research at the People's Hospital in Beijing, Wang Shuqi. Wang's family was from Shaanxi, knew the Xi family well, and was friends with Qi Xin. Qi asked Wang to provide a certificate that would allow Jinping to leave the countryside for medical reasons. But Wang, a righteous woman who believed in Mao's rationale for the sent-down-youth program, angrily refused. She herself had three daughters in the countryside, and none of them had tried to leave for medical reasons. By 1975, when Jinping finally left the countryside, only 3.7 percent of the original sent-down youth remained in the vicinity of Yan'an in Shaanxi Province, where Jinping was living, and those who had remained mostly did so because they had married peasants.[24]

But when Jinping finally did leave the countryside, it was to study at China's prestigious Tsinghua University in Beijing. He had applied as early as 1973 but had been rejected because of his father's status. In 1975, Tsinghua University gave the entire Yan'an region only two slots, and when Jinping applied, he put Tsinghua University as his first, second, and third choices. He would later remark that it turned out to be good timing because, in the summer of 1975, the leftist radical leaders at the university were distracted and not managing the university's practical affairs. A vice-dean, Liu Bing, used the opportunity to approve Jinping's application.[25]

It was also Liu Bing who inadvertently triggered Deng Xiaoping's downfall. In August and October 1975, Liu had written two letters to Mao complaining about Chi Qun, a colleague at the university, alleging that Chi was a careerist despot who lived a "bourgeois" lifestyle. Mao interpreted the letters as a direct challenge and believed that Deng was somehow involved. Jinping would have arrived on campus for a welcome rally for students on October 20; less than one month later, on November 18, about ten thousand Tsinghua students, faculty, and staff held a rally marking the beginning of a campaign to criticize Liu Bing. In the subsequent weeks, big-character posters, accompanied by struggle sessions, appeared on campus. Jinping had left the countryside and walked directly into the epicenter of a new political explosion.[26]

As the attacks on Deng swept the nation and dashed hopes that the worst of the Cultural Revolution was over, Zhongxun worried about how his son Jinping was faring. In June 1976, at about eight o'clock one night, Yang Ping, a young man whom Xi Zhongxun had befriended at the factory, visited Xi's tiny apartment. Yang was surprised to find Xi drinking strong cheap liquor

THE XI FAMILY SLOWLY REBUILDS 247

and crying alone in the dark. Xi explained that it was his son Jinping's birthday. Xi said, "Your father is better than I am; he took such good care of you. I am also a father, but because of me . . . Jinping only narrowly escaped death!" Xi then proceeded to tell Yang about Jinping's experiences during the Cultural Revolution. Yang later wrote, "That night, Old Xi spoke to me, and at the same time, he cried. He kept saying he had let down everyone in his family. He said that in terms of taking care of his entire family, his behavior had been criminal and so on. One could say that his emotional state was approaching a total lack of control. It made me feel extremely sad. Normally, his words would be very concise. He wasn't verbose, and he didn't repeat himself. He definitely was never incoherent." On July 18, Xi told Yang Ping that Jinping and Yuanping would be arriving two days later. After they arrived, Xi asked Yang to take Yuanping out to play because "I want to talk to Jinping." Zhongxun had hoped they would stay out for a whole day, but, after watching a movie, Yuanping rushed home around noon. When they got back to the sweltering apartment, Yang was surprised to find Jinping and Zhongxun sitting in their underwear smoking as Jinping recited Mao's speeches from memory while Qi Xin watched. Jinping stood up to put on some clothes, but Zhongxun stopped him. Jinping laughed to apologize for the situation.[27]

Jinping and Yuanping were only home for two days. When they departed, Yang asked whether Zhongxun had a special place in his heart for Jinping. Xi did not deny such feelings, and he said that his two sons would take different paths. Yang asked Xi about the content of their conversation. Xi said it went pretty well as Jinping had successfully memorized "On Contradiction" and "On Practice," two famous speeches by Mao. Yang was shocked: Why would Xi invite his son to visit only to have him recite speeches by Mao Zedong while sitting in their underwear? Later Yang would learn that Xi had also wanted his son to memorize the entirety of volume four of Mao's *Selected Works*. Xi said that if an old man like him could memorize it, then his young son should be able to as well.[28]

XI AND MAO

When Mao died in September 1976, Xi and his wife went to pick wildflowers to place in front of the late leader's picture.[29] The next month, the Gang of Four—a group associated with the worst abuses of the Cultural Revolution and which included Mao's own wife—was arrested. Xi, who almost never cooked, started to prepare a meal to celebrate, and he sang joyfully while chopping up vegetables.[30] During his years in the political wilderness, Xi had reflected on the role of Mao in Chinese history. He told a friend from Shaanxi that Mao's achievements were mighty "especially before 1957." After 1957, however, Xi believed that Mao "indeed did become arrogant, and every day the cult of personality and personal dictatorship became more severe," according to the friend. That ultimately led to the "long-term, comprehensive" mistakes of the Cultural Revolution. Yet like so many of his colleagues, Xi was careful to say that Mao's achievements were "number one," that Mao Zedong thought was the eternal "guiding thought" of the party, and that Mao's mistakes were ultimately the mistakes of a "glorious Marxist."[31]

In November 1977, a younger relative of Zhongxun named Zhonggun came to visit, and the two had another intimate conversation about Mao. In Zhongxun's mind, Mao Zedong thought was the "first great leap forward" in the Sinicization of Marxism. Before 1949 and in the early years after the founding of the People's Republic, the party never strayed from the path of "seeking truth from facts." The Great Leap Forward and the Cultural Revolution, however, had departed from that tradition. Xi praised Mao's ability to convey complicated ideas in a simple way to uncouth men. "Striving to unite all possible forces is the source of wisdom that allows party members to always achieve an invincible status," Xi told Zhonggun. Mao, according to Xi, always, no matter what, opposed evil people within the party. Xi praised Mao for "liberating" Liu Zhidan and others. Significantly, however, Zhongxun also said that "up until 1953, [Mao] was always extremely wise; he basically made no mistakes." The year of 1953, of course, marked the fall of Gao Gang.[32]

Yang Ping recalled Xi already expressing concerns about dictatorship at this time:

> The behavior of any person must be limited to a certain extent. There must be a monitoring system that cannot be broken. Otherwise, law and the heavens will end up being ignored, and there will be a problem. . . . As long as there is a personal monopoly of power, from the perspective of human nature, one will find it difficult to avoid the following four stages. The first stage is sharing weal and woe; he [i.e., the dictator] will go through fire and water with his sworn brothers in order to survive and in order to conquer

some land. During the second stage, he will dominate. Hong Xiuquan occupied Nanjing, and those great kings of the sky had to kneel when they saw him, they had to listen to him, and only him. The third stage is when he will focus on women over friends; that I won't explain to you now. You'll understand this when you grow up and marry. In a word, he will believe that only with women by his side will there be security and happiness. In the fourth stage, he will become isolated. It is during this stage that problems are most likely to appear. He will believe no one, and he will believe that even his own women will hurt him. He is suspicious of everything, and he will arbitrarily slay the innocent.[33]

Yet Xi never abandoned his emotional attachment to Mao. In February 1983, on a visit to Mao's hometown of Shaoshan, Xi wrote that Mao Zedong thought is "the crystallization of the revolutionary desires and practices of hundreds of millions of people. In the past, present, and future, it is the guiding thought of all our work."[34] Xi helped arrange for Mao's son-in-law Kong Linghua to work in Shenzhen despite dissatisfaction by powerful figures about Kong's actions during the Cultural Revolution. "Mao Zedong's son-in-law must also be given an opportunity to make a living!" Xi once said.[35] During the 1990s, whenever anyone met with Xi in Shenzhen and criticized the late chairman, Xi would bang on the table, stand up, and tell them to leave.[36] A documentary about this period in Xi's lifetime includes a video of Xi making a jolly rendition of the song "The East Is Red," including the following lyrics:

> The East is red; the sun is rising.
> From China comes Mao Zedong.
> He strives for the people's happiness.
> Hurrah, he is the people's great savior!

When Xi finished, Qi Xin commented, "That is his favorite song."[37]

SLOW REHABILITATION

After the defeat of the Gang of Four, on November 15, 1976, Xi wrote to the central leadership. He promised "to be a better heir to the work bequeathed by Chairman Mao" and "to contribute the entirety of the rest of my life to the party." He signed the letter, "A party member of Chairman

Mao who has not yet returned to organizational life, Xi Zhongxun."[38] Xi's family and friends told him to go to Beijing to plead his case, but, according to Jinping, Zhongxun replied that he believed the Central Committee would understand his situation. He remained proud. "If one wants to go to Beijing, one has to buy a train ticket and then beg for survival," he told his son. "Is that appropriate? I'll do nothing of the sort!"[39]

Yet Xi Zhongxun faced an uphill battle for rehabilitation even after Mao's death. After the cases of Gao Gang and Peng Dehuai, Xi's case was the third-biggest verdict of the pre–Cultural Revolution era. Many other old revolutionaries who had been persecuted had already returned to work prior to Mao's death, and other major cases, like those of Bo Yibo and Peng Zhen, were already much closer to reversal by that point.[40] As late as May 1977, a Special Case Committee report still accused Liu Jingfan of having worked together with Xi to use the *Liu Zhidan* novel to reverse the verdict on Gao Gang.[41]

When Jinping visited Luoyang in July 1977, he asked two men to help his father write a document to submit to the Central Committee. Zhongxun told the two men that he had not yet written to the top leadership about his case because they were so busy, but he no longer wished to wait. He wanted to request that the party revisit his situation as it was not only about him—many others were implicated as well. The biggest issue was still the novel itself. Xi complained that Li Jiantong "did not listen." "There was nothing I could do," he said. Xi refused to acknowledge that *Liu Zhidan* was antiparty or that he was its true author.[42]

Two other issues irked Xi as well. First, the Special Case Committee was trying to claim that Zhongxun had joined the revolution in 1928, not 1926, when he became a member of the Communist Youth League. In the political culture of the party, the difference between those dates was enormously important—if Xi had started working for the party in 1928, then it would have been *after* the Nationalist crackdown and the subsequent revolution. In a system that fetishized seniority and status, the committee's claim would severely undermine Xi's prestige as a party elder. "This must not be ambiguous," Xi insisted. "I joined when I joined—the truth must be sought from the facts!" Xi also cared deeply about how the party understood his family background. He complained that although in the past he had always written on party documents that his family was of "rich-middle-peasant" background, the Special Case Committee wanted to change this to "rich peasant" (the reason for this accusation was Xi's uncle had been given this label during land reform). Xi grew increasingly angry as he discussed these issues.[43]

Shortly after the Thirteenth Party Congress in August 1977, Xi began sending letters to the top leadership asking to return to work. At the congress, Deng Xiaoping had finally returned to his former positions, but the top party leader was still Hua Guofeng, Mao's named successor at the time of the chairman's death. Wang Dongxing, whose control over the palace guards had proven decisive in the move against the Gang of Four, was in charge of ideology and the Special Case Committees. Wang Zhen became the first person to speak in favor of Xi's rehabilitation.[44] On September 19, 1977, Wang sent a notification and one of Xi's letters to Wang Dongxing. "I met with some old Northwest cadres to discuss the issue of Xi's work," Wang Zhen wrote. The charges that Xi was a spy had been resolved during rectification in Yan'an, Wang Zhen asserted. On October 6, Wang Dongxing wrote his own notification: "I think Comrade Xi Zhongxun should be given work. I request Chairman Hua to give guidance."[45]

Xi paid a price for Wang Zhen's support. Ye Xuanning, one of the sons of the powerful marshal Ye Jianying, had told Qi Xin that if Wang Zhen supported Xi's rehabilitation, the process would be easy—implying that Wang was a key stumbling block. Qi Xin and Xi Jinping went to Wang's home with a letter from Zhongxun that expressed remorse over his treatment of Wang Zhen in Xinjiang in 1952.[46] Similarly, Zhongxun's daughter Qiaoqiao went to Wang's home to deliver a letter as well. Waiting outside his front door for his car to arrive, she introduced herself as the daughter of Zhongxun and told him that her father had asked her to seek him out "at this most difficult moment."[47] A March 1979 Central Committee decision stated explicitly that the criticisms of Wang Zhen in 1952 "did not correspond with reality," meaning that, technically, Xi Zhongxun was blamed for at least one Mao-era verdict that was reversed during the reform era.[48]

After Hu Yaobang became head of the Organization Department in December 1977, his son Deping arranged a secret meeting between Qi Xin and Hu Yaobang at the request of Xi Jinping.[49] Hu Yaobang asked Qi Xin how her husband was faring in Luoyang. Although he was friendly, Hu noted that it would be "very easy" for the party to make mistakes at the current moment, so it was necessary to be careful and to act according to policy. This was probably Hu's way of telling Xi not to lose hope but that full rehabilitation would not be immediate.[50] On December 24, Xi was finally given a new draft of his case. He was still unhappy. It was better than the draft he had seen in 1975, a development he welcomed, and the new document restored his relationship with the party (and his salary). Yet Xi expressed opposition to the charges that he was an "important member" of Gao Gang's faction and that he had a rich-peasant background. He also could not accept some of the characterizations of his work in the Northwest, and he wanted more clarity on when he joined the party.[51]

Despite his recalcitrance, the first small but significant breakthrough finally came shortly after. At an Organization Department preparatory meeting for the Fifth Chinese People's Political Consultative Conference, after listening to a report citing the list of attendees, Hu Yaobang added Xi's name to it. Xi was invited to attend the meeting in Beijing, which began on February 24, 1978.[52] "I now feel as if I have returned to the party's embrace," Xi told the man sent to escort him from Luoyang to Beijing. He claimed to have never lost hope. He described how, while in prison, he would walk back and forth, counting up to ten thousand and then back again. "In order to do more work for the party and the people, it was necessary to walk back and forth, to forge willpower, and to also forge my body. I was full of confidence in the party. I believed the party center would ultimately correct its verdict regarding my case." Xi explained that he had kept this habit a secret so no one could stop him from "forging."[53]

The return to Beijing was deeply emotional. One old associate later described the scene: "[Xi] went to see old comrades, and they had heartfelt conversations with one another. With his white hair, he continuously asked the old comrades how they were doing and whether their families and children were settled. He asked so much that his throat became hoarse and he could no longer speak, but Secretary Xi was very happy. His entire face was red. This was the first time I saw him like this."[54] Yet he was still not officially rehabilitated, and the future remained unclear. He was still so "frightened" that he sent an intermediary to meet with Ji Dengkui, who had managed the investigation cases of the top leaders during the Cultural Revolution, because Xi dared not go himself.[55]

PART IV ***THE PARTY'S "LAUNCHPAD"***
The Guangdong Years

17
FACING THE CONSEQUENCES OF THE CULTURAL REVOLUTION

At first, the top party leaders could not decide where Xi should work. Possibilities included the Seventh Ministry of Machine Building, which ran China's missile and satellite programs, the Ministry of Agriculture, or Shaanxi Province—all significant yet not leading positions. Marshal Ye Jianying, one of the three most powerful men in the leadership at the time, selected Xi to run affairs in Ye's home province of Guangdong. Xi was not the only party heavyweight who was sent to Guangdong. Yang Shangkun, who would become Xi's deputy there, had been in charge of the party's General Office before the Cultural Revolution. Having two such former high-level figures in one province was unique, but Guangdong was a special case given Ye's special interest and the scale of the challenges.[1]

In April 1978, Xi flew to Guangzhou, the southern province's capital, to become the second secretary of the party committee. Jinping, still a student at Tsinghua, was present to see him off at the Beijing airport.[2] Because the first secretary, Wei Guoqing, was still in Beijing as head of the military's General Political Department, Xi effectively ran affairs in the province. He would later tell a friend that he had been shocked to receive such an important position—he thought serving as a vice-minister in a place like the Ministry of Agriculture would have already been a great victory.[3] By the end of the year, Xi would officially become first secretary.[4] Qi Xin was finally given a position outside of the party school. In May 1978, she began working for the

Guangdong Party Discipline Inspection Committee, before later serving as vice-director of the Guangzhou Party Organization Department.[5]

When Xi was first freed from a Communist prison in 1935, he was not fully rehabilitated, nor was he given a position that matched his seniority or contributions. In 1978, Xi was sent to work in a distant province, and the accusations against him were still not officially reversed. Xi told an old friend that Hua Guofeng's plan was to have him "first start working and then, at the same time, solve the [historical] problems."[6] Xi, however, did not mind. He told another associate that too much time had passed without working and that he wanted to make good on his promise to "struggle his entire life for the party." Xi's friend thought that this was not a good decision. He encouraged Xi to instead fight for his complete rehabilitation before going to Guangdong. But Xi ignored him.[7] The Organization Department would not determine that the *Liu Zhidan* novel was not part of a conspiracy until July 1979. The decision that Gao Gang and Peng Dehuai were not members of an antiparty faction came even later—in January 1980. Xi's own "antiparty clique" was declared nonexistent the next month.[8]

LEADERSHIP STYLE

Xi's "forging" while in the political wilderness seems to have been effective. He would often work until 3:00 a.m. and even read documents while eating, bathing, or sitting on the toilet. He wanted to "make up for lost time and do a few things for the people," he said.[9] One colleague from Shenzhen recalled how Xi used to say that he never expected he would be able to return to work before dying, but he later came to believe that all his patience and perseverance had been worthwhile.[10]

But how much had Xi learned about the party's previous mistakes? On certain occasions, Xi seemed to hope that China would move away from its radical past. In September 1978, a local cadre named Mai Zican wrote a letter to Xi that criticized him for being a cadre who "loved to listen to reports, loved hearing pretty words, and loved braggards." Mai was upset that Xi had repeatedly made positive comments about an irrigation project that the people hated. Mai was concerned that the leaders were talking about starting yet another, even larger-scale project despite the fact that the peasants were exhausted after the Cultural Revolution. "I think what you say about taking into account letters from the masses is just pretty, empty words!"

Mai wrote, daring Xi to respond. "Don't you always say you like to hear unpleasant words and say that 'medicine that tastes bad is good for diseases'?" Instead of punishing Mai, Xi gave the impression that he was listening to the man's complaints. In October, Xi expressed "sincere acceptance" of Mai's criticisms. On November 8, both *People's Daily* and *Nanfang Daily* published Mai's letter, Xi's response, and Xi's comments on the exchange.[11]

Xi's act deeply impressed his patron, Ye Jianying. At the work conference prior to the Third Plenum later that year, Ye referred to Hua Guofeng, still the country's leader, and to Xi Zhongxun as the two people within the party who most clearly exemplified having the ability to accept constructive criticism: "A cadre in the leadership, in order to develop democracy, must modestly listen to the opinions of the masses and bravely have a spirit of self-criticism." He went on, "Comrade Hua Guofeng is a model for everyone, and I also must make reference to Comrade Xi Zhongxun. You comrades have probably all seen the letter from a grassroots cadre in Guangdong's Huiyang District to Comrade Xi Zhongxun and Comrade Xi Zhongxun's response. Comrade Xi Zhongxun's spirit of not fearing to listen to unpleasant opinions, encouraging people to speak, and bravely engaging in self-criticism deserves study by all of us comrades."[12]

According to Ye's daughter, this section on Xi was added only at the last minute to the final draft of the speech. Her father's purpose was to stress the importance of developing real democracy within the party. "Comrade Xi Zhongxun was precisely the model for self-criticism and for stubbornly taking the mass line," she said. Ye's speech was one of the most important documents calling for true inner-party democracy in party history.[13] Yet Ye's praise of Xi for this behavior was cut from both the public version of his speech and from later collections of Ye's speeches.[14] In 1982, Ye's speech was absent entirely from a collection of important documents after the Third Plenum.[15] The reason was almost certainly Deng's falling out with Ye over Hua Guofeng as well as Ye's distaste for Deng's autocratic style.

Xi returned to the theme of leadership style in a speech to discipline investigators in June 1980. For Xi, "feudal thinking" in the party had produced problems, such as "lifelong tenure, a personality cult, cronyism, a stress on seniority for promotion, factionalism, treating friends well and others coldly, a refusal to tolerate different views, bootlicking, and using one's position to pursue personal perquisites and prestige." "When the picture of the leader is posted everywhere, isn't this idolization?" he asked. "China was a small-scale production society for thousands of years. That means it needed a boss or an emperor, so it was easy to continue that kind of thing," he explained. The "feudal thinking of the landlord class has not been criticized systematically, so its pernicious influence still exists everywhere."[16]

Despite Xi's constant talk about inner-party democracy, he often displayed a poor temper. A colleague in the Guangdong leadership, Wu Nansheng, got along well with him but was forthcoming about Xi's less-attractive qualities. In an interview, he described Xi in scathing terms: "His thinking was a little abnormal. He was very excitable. Whenever he spoke, he would not shut up. Also, he would make irresponsible remarks. There were many things he did not know. He had been isolated for too long. Some old Guangdong cadres had poor relations with Xi because he was always saying the wrong thing. . . . Zhongxun's brain was no good; he would lose his temper for no reason and say the wrong thing."[17]

Another individual who worked with Xi later recalled a meticulous man, influenced by the late Zhou Enlai, who could display both anger and calm: "When Xi Zhongxun gave orders, he was very specific; that was because he had worked as a secretary [on the State Council] and he came from working with Premier Zhou. He had a temper. Sometimes, when he got excited, he would shout out 'That's bullshit' several times. But other times, he was very patient."[18] Cheng Kai, who worked as a journalist at Guangdong's top newspaper *Yangcheng wanbao* similarly gave mixed reviews. He described Xi as a "relatively honest old man." However, Xi was very long-winded, and because people were afraid of him, no one dared to interrupt him when he spoke during meetings.[19]

Xi was warned about his temper. Vice-Governor Wang Quanguo chided him at a party-life meeting. "Comrade Zhongxun," he said, "your personality is too hot-tempered, and your demands are too strict. In the future, this must be fixed." Xi did not refute Wang. Afterward, while taking a stroll, he said to a colleague in the Guangdong party office, "Quanguo says I am hot-tempered and make harsh demands. Am I really impatient? How can this behavior compare to Premier Zhou's impatience? Whatever Premier Zhou assigned at the beginning of the day, he would ask whether it had been finished at the end of the day. I am not as impatient as Premier Zhou!"[20]

Age and years of confinement began to take a toll. He was now sixty-five years old and had just undergone sixteen years of physical and emotional suffering. On one occasion, Xi struck the new minister of finance,

Wang Bingqian, while Wang was giving a report.[21] In the late summer of 1980, during a trip to Zhanjiang, he was so tired that he tripped and fell.[22] Xi spent a prolonged period in the hospital in early 1981—two separate individuals remember visiting Xi in a hospital in Beijing in January and February, respectively.[23]

Qi Xin has proudly referred to the fact that she not once left the Chinese mainland, even to go to Hong Kong when her husband was party boss in Guangdong.[24] But some incipient signs of special privileges were present. When Xi visited the Chonghua Hot Springs to meet county leaders, he brought his family along to play while he worked, although, at the time, this behavior was not considered particularly egregious.[25] A more serious act occurred when Xi and Yang Shangkun finally left Guangdong, taking with them an entire vehicle full of local delicacies that had been given to them as gifts, which left a very bad impression.[26]

ADDRESSING THE LEGACIES OF THE CULTURAL REVOLUTION

In Guangdong, Xi faced several severe challenges. One of the most explosive was continued investigations into suspicious figures and wrongful Cultural Revolution–era verdicts. The situation in Guangdong was particularly serious. When Defense Minister Lin Biao died while fleeing China in 1971, he left behind a top lieutenant, Huang Yongsheng, who had served as party boss of Guangdong for years. Jiang Qing, Mao's wife and a member of the Gang of Four, had allegedly made inroads with some of the provincial leadership. Fifteen percent of all Guangdong cadres had been investigated by Special Case Committees during the Cultural Revolution, including 74.5 percent of cadres at the level of vice–office head and above. By some early estimates, thirty-nine thousand people had died due to "unnatural" causes, suggesting the upheaval's human toll.[27] Xi was besieged with grumbling about the legacies of these earlier campaigns. During the first eight months of his tenure in Guangdong, the party received 8,611 complaints about cadres acting like dictators, taking vengeance, violating discipline, and engaging in corruption. In 1979, the situation became even worse—the provincial leadership received 1,700 complaints every month, totaling 20,066 for the year.[28]

Before Xi even arrived in Guangdong, he already had a negative impression of both Liang Xiang and Jiao Linyi, the top party boss in Guangzhou and the secretary for daily affairs of the Guangdong Party Standing Committee, respectively. Wu Nansheng recounted that Xi enlisted his help to attack them in a rather underhanded fashion. "You go! Dig up some problems about these two people for me," Xi told him, offering him Jiao Linyi's job once they were ousted. Wu balked. "As soon as I heard his words, I thought he had gone too far," Wu later wrote. He continued, "If I were to knock down Jiao Linyi and then became secretary for daily affairs, what would I be doing? I'm not that kind of person. To be honest, I look down on such a method."[29]

In August and September 1978, the Guangdong Party Committee held an enlarged standing committee session to fault the province for failing to attack the legacy of the Gang of Four. The meeting, led by Xi, was clearly targeted against Jiao and Liang, who faced the serious charge of factionalism. The harshest critics were those cadres who had returned to work during the later stages of the Cultural Revolution. They had a special mistrust for people who had survived the tumult mostly unscathed, such as Jiao. Participants at the standing committee session raised dangerous questions: Why was Jiao Linyi allowed to return to work so early? Why did Lin Biao first consider fleeing to Guangdong? Why did Jiang Qing come to Guangdong so many times?[30]

Xi shared these suspicions. He wanted Liang gone immediately, but Wu Nansheng implored Xi to wait until Yang Shangkun arrived to work as party boss of Guangzhou. Finally, a decision was made to send Liang to study at the party school in Beijing for a year. Later, when Liang was about to finish his term in Beijing, Xi was in a hospital, and Liang went to wish him well. But by the end of the visit, the two of them started yelling at each other. Finally, Liang was expelled from Guangzhou and sent to Shenzhen.[31]

Cleaning up after the Cultural Revolution was not just about punishment; it was also about rehabilitation, and again Guangdong presented special difficulties. One of the most difficult cases from the Mao era that Xi had to address was the so-called 1957 Oppose Localism Campaign. Gu Dacun and Feng Baiju, two Guangdong natives who had led the province in the early years of the People's Republic, were removed from the leadership that year for allegedly blocking central directives by relying on close-knit local networks. They were punished along with huge swathes of the local party apparatus. In 1978, many individuals in the Guangdong party leadership still believed that the purge had been justified. Mao himself had approved of the campaign, and it had predated the Cultural Revolution. Moreover, powerful figures like former Guangdong leaders Zhao Ziyang and the late Tao Zhu had led the campaign and had benefited from it, so Xi had reason to worry about how Zhao and Tao's influential widow might react. Multiple meetings of the provincial leadership were held to discuss the case, but a decision could not be reached. Although Xi was the top provincial leader and he supported a full rehabilitation, he remained in the minority. The discussions reached a stalemate. Xi asked a military commander to help him engage in "guerrilla warfare" by arranging for the publication of short but positive articles about Feng Baiju in the provincial newspapers.[32] Xi told Gu Dacun's widow, "There are two possibilities. One possibility is that I am cast out of Guangdong. The other possibility is that I am able to reverse the verdict on Oppose Localism."[33]

In early 1979, the Guangdong leadership finally launched an official reinvestigation into the matter. In the summer, Xi asked the same military commander whom he had asked to engage in guerrilla warfare to now arrange a "nuclear bomb"—meaning a single newspaper article that would be powerful enough to really shake up the case. But for months, no newspaper agreed to publish such a piece. In August, Xi finally submitted a draft decision on Feng and Gu to the Central Committee. The draft, written by Xi himself, affirmed that it was indeed appropriate for Gu and Feng to have been criticized, thus giving face to Zhao and Tao. Yet it also asserted that the campaign suffered from both "simplicity and expansion." Moreover, it also claimed that Gu and Feng had not actually forged an "antiparty alliance." Xi's decision to first seek approval from Beijing was not the only sign of his political caution and cleverness—the draft document also displayed a sensitivity to the need for compromise. In October, the Central Committee approved the document, which, given the restrictions of the time, was a significant achievement, though it disappointed those who had hoped for a full exoneration.[34]

In 1982, the party leadership in Guangdong finally submitted a report to Beijing requesting a total rehabilitation for both Gu and Feng. But the central party authorities did not approve, probably because of opposition by Zhao Ziyang, who was premier at the time. Gu's family members went directly to Xi—who was then working in the secretariat—to ask for help, but they were told that there were still some people who opposed rehabilitation. The next year, Xi and Qi Xin invited Gu's widow and his son to their home. Xi told them that he had supported full rehabilitation, and he expressed confusion as to why the 1982 Guangdong proposal still had not been approved. Shortly thereafter, the persecution of Feng and Gu was finally declared to have been a complete mistake.[35]

Xi also struggled to rehabilitate Peng Pai, the first revolutionary leader to create a Communist base area and whose forces were a prototype of the Red Army but who posthumously had been declared a "leftist adventurist."[36] Xi was furious that Peng Pai's mother had been persecuted, a son was driven to death, and two nephews were killed, with one of their heads put up on public display. More than sixty people had died as a result of Peng's case.[37] In July and August 1978, Xi went to Peng's home county, where he referred to some local leaders as murderers. "There is blood on their hands," he said.[38] According to Xi's secretary, Xi acted so aggressively that there was a worry that the cadres whom he attacked might commit suicide. Xi, however, was furious about the killings in that area. "If they kill themselves, that's their business!" he said. The individuals who had participated in the persecution of Peng's family were treated as criminals.[39] They threatened to complain, but Xi called their bluff: "If you do not make a report, you're bastards!"[40]

To overcome resistance to the reversal of these verdicts, Xi relied on support from Ye Jianying. In August 1978, Ye visited the home of Hu Yaobang and told Hu to write a supportive letter to the Guangdong party leadership. "We completely support the work of Comrade Zhongxun," Hu wrote. "If any comrades feel there is a problem, they should speak directly with Comrade Zhongxun."[41] In June 1979, during a trip to Guangdong, Ye praised Xi and other cadres from outside the province, even though they could not speak the local Cantonese dialect. "Comrades from outside the province have come to Guangdong and do a lot of work for the province," he said. "This is a very big contribution."[42]

Despite Xi's aggressive moves against Guangdong's Cultural Revolution–era leaders, such as Jiao Linyi, he was cautious when it came to correcting injustices at lower levels. While on an inspection trip in the city of Zhaoqing, shortly before he went to bed, Xi noticed two letters on his table from local people who were seeking justice for their family members who had died during the Cultural Revolution. Xi decided to delay his departure so that he could meet with the two people who had sent the letters. The next day, twenty people showed up, most of whom were peasant women. They screamed and wept, imploring that Xi return their dead husbands and sons and have the culprits executed. Because of Xi's age and because he was surrounded, the party leaders traveling with him began to feel nervous. Xi tried to calm down the crowd. "In the past, he killed your family; today, we kill his family," he said. "In this way, you start a feud between your two families. You start a grudge, and then it will never end—it will last forever. When does such a circle of vengeance end?" The women responded, "When a murder takes place, a life must be given in exchange! The government should execute those murderers!" Xi went on emotionally, "How many people joined in the struggles during the Cultural Revolution? How many people have to be executed before it will be enough? During the Cultural Revolution, so many people were beaten to death; our government can no longer kill people in that way! Things cannot be done like that anymore, otherwise what would be the difference between then and now?" Inevitably, perhaps, Xi turned to his personal experience. He understood their feelings, he said, but he called upon them to move on, just as he himself was trying to do:

> Actually, I understand you! Your family members died during the chaos, and you feel this misfortune. I am also very sad! Today, I came to help you solve this problem as a representative of the province, but do you know what? It was only a little while ago that I too was sent down. I was sent down for sixteen years, and I also experienced a great injustice. But what is to be done? The Cultural Revolution already caused such great losses. But we still have to live, we have to live happily, and we have to look to the future. Only if you can all get along will the future go well.[43]

Under Xi, the provincial leadership developed a reputation for a lack of courage to punish individuals who had committed abuses during the Cultural Revolution. The scope of the injustices is one explanation for such a delay, but Xi and Yang also believed that if they were to move too quickly, the cases would have to be investigated again in the future. In their minds, a swift campaign would be no different from the persecutions of the Cultural Revolution era.[44] Despite the final count of 42,237 "irregular" deaths in the province during the Cultural Revolution, only 586 cadres were punished by legal means, while 908 were subjected to party discipline.[45]

Moreover, Xi continued to demonstrate caution in areas in which he was potentially vulnerable. At the work conference before the Third Plenum in 1978—a historic meeting that signified a major breakthrough for the old guard—at first, Xi did not dare to speak about the verdict against Peng Dehuai or other historic cases. Chen Yun—who Mao Zedong had once privately complained was "the type of person who is afraid that a falling leaf will hurt his head"—raised the issue even before Xi did.[46] When Xi finally did express his position, he did not argue for a complete rehabilitation of his old friend Peng Dehuai; instead, he said that Peng's contributions were greater than his mistakes and suggested that when describing Peng's mistakes, the party center should use terms that were a bit milder.[47]

When Gao Gang's widow, Li Liqun, asked for support in reversing the verdict on Gao, Xi disappointed her. She recalled, "Xi said, while in tears, what can I say now? Everything is linked to me. In 1935, Liu Zhidan, Gao Gang, and I were arrested. They prepared to bury us alive. You also know I was investigated once again because of the *Liu Zhidan* novel. To be honest, I sympathized with Gao Gang; I felt very sad about his death"—not sad enough to intervene, however. He did not think it was possible for Gao to be given an honest verdict at the time.[48] He was right. Hu Yaobang, who was in charge of rehabilitating the fallen cadres, similarly did not believe Gao was "antiparty."[49] But Deng Xiaoping said to Hu, "Do you dare to reverse even verdicts like this? You are crazy!"[50]

Li Jiantong, the author of *Liu Zhidan*, started campaigning for her own rehabilitation. "Do not worry," she told Qi Xin. "I will appeal for justice. As soon as the case is reversed, the problem for Zhongxun and the others will be completely solved." Qi was terrified, however, and urged Li Jiantong not to push for rehabilitation. "My old man was just released," she said of Xi. "As soon as you appeal, he will be thrown into prison again!" According to Li, Qi was "scared into stupidity." When Qi Xin saw Li Jiantong and He Jiadong—the man who had supported publication of *Liu Zhidan* from Workers' Publishing House—at a restaurant, she was too frightened to even say hello. Li alleged that, after the Organization Department decided to rehabilitate her, Xi blocked the decision. "Comrade Zhongxun does not agree that you should be rehabilitated," a vice-minister had told her. "He believes if you were to be rehabilitated, it would be bad for Chairman Mao."[51]

The old antagonisms had never gone away. Guo Hongtao also sought to protect his legacy. In 1978, at his request, the party disseminated the 1960 Central Committee decision that revised the Yan'an-era verdict against him. Mao Zedong's official *Selected Works* were also stripped of a footnote that criticized Guo for his role in the 1935 purge. In 1981, Guo published two articles on the history of the Northwest.[52] The leaders of the Shaan-Gan Border base area immediately complained.[53]

Attempts to find a compromise failed, and, in February 1983, former Shaan-Gan-Bian cadres demanded a meeting to discuss Northwest history. In April, the Central Advisory Commission—an institution created for old cadres before complete retirement—was tasked with dealing with this problem, and a five-person small group led by Li Weihan was formed. In June, Li's small group submitted to the secretariat a report in which Guo Hongtao was charged with executing a leftist line and with drafting an inaccurate report that led directly to the 1935 purge. However, at the same time, the document accepted Guo's claim that, after the purge began, he had said, "Even if you kill me, I do not believe they were counterrevolutionaries." The personal responsibility of those who had led the persecution would no longer be emphasized. Therefore, the document both partially confirmed and partially annulled the Yan'an-era verdict. Even Guo, very reluctantly, accepted these conclusions. In July, the report of the Central Advisory Commission was sent by the Central Committee to the entire party as *Document No. 28*.[54]

Yet still the disputes among the Northwest cadres did not subside. When a new version of *Liu Zhidan* was published in 1985, Xie Zichang's relatives and Xie's close associate He Jinnian wrote letters to the secretariat that accused the novel of violating *Document No. 28*. In January 1986, according to directives from Hu Yaobang and Xi Zhongxun, a meeting was held to discuss the issue. This gathering, attended also by Xi, decided to forbid publication of the book. For it to be reissued, it would have to meet the spirit of *Document No. 28*.[55]

Li Jiantong wrote a letter to the leadership in protest. She refused to edit *Liu Zhidan*, arguing that she was not writing party history and that those who criticized her book were the same "killers" who had close relations with the leftists who had led the purge.[56] She then wrote an open letter to Xi. The language was extraordinarily caustic. She accused him of becoming a different person: "I already do not understand you. You have changed now. You cannot resist the 'leftist' opportunism and the repeated attacks by the factionalists. You are beaten with fear. Soon you will be a fool. . . . As soon as you fall into disarray, the 'leftist' factionalists will drink in celebration. . . . This book should not be banned. The more it is banned, the more people will want to read it!" At the conclusion of the open letter, Li wrote she would use the constitution to protect her right to publish.[57]

Li held to her position despite repeated visits from the Organization Department. Her intransigence dragged on in the secretariat, the Central

Advisory Commission, the General Office, Organization Department, and Propaganda Department. He Jinnian wrote two letters to Bo Yibo—who managed daily affairs in the Central Advisory Commission—demanding that debate over the novel be resolved and criticizing articles that Xi Zhongxun had written about Liu Zhidan in 1978 and 1979. Bo agreed that *Liu Zhidan* should meet the spirit of *Document No. 28*, but he defended Xi's articles, pointing out that they had been published before *Document No. 28* was issued. The leadership put even more pressure on Li Jiantong, but she refused to buckle. Bo was furious. He complained that the relevant comrades had already been criticized many times, "but they just don't listen!" Xi concurred, writing, "I agree with Comrade Yibo's position." Li finally gave up after Hu Yaobang was removed from power in 1987.[58]

Li Jiantong made a clear and strong moral judgment about Xi's behavior, and she was not the only northwesterner dismayed by Xi's lack of support. After the Cultural Revolution, Fan Ming, Xi's former protégé in Tibet, was partially rehabilitated, and, in 1980, Xi met with Fan and his grandchildren at the Xi family home in Beijing. But Fan's verdict was not fully reversed, and Xi was the reason. In September 1985, Fan met with the party leadership of the Tibet Autonomous Region, and they finally decided to submit a report in favor of Fan's complete rehabilitation. Xi quashed the proposal. Fan wrote in his memoirs that Xi, "in order to avoid suspicion and not attract attention," said "in a very irresponsible fashion" that the Central Committee had "already reached a conclusion and managed the matter, and that is enough for [Fan]. Why is [Fan] still causing trouble?" Around the time of the Lunar New Year in 1986, during a meal at Beijing Hotel hosted by the head of the Tibet Autonomous Region, one of the attendees asked Xi how Fan's requests for full rehabilitation should be treated. "He should stop causing trouble," Xi replied. "His treatment is already good enough."[59] Similarly, when Wang Chaobei—the former spy who had been thrown into prison in 1962 for writing an article on the Xi'an spy ring—asked for Xi's help, Xi told him to look at the big picture and sign a decision that only provided for a partial rehabilitation. It took many more years before the verdict against Wang was completely reversed.[60]

Are such examples emblematic of moral cowardice and self-protection? The disappointment of those individuals whom Xi failed to support suggests that they thought so. Yet Xi probably faced multiple considerations. Through compromise, Xi could unite the northwesterners and claim to represent them as a whole. Given his weighty position within the party, the top leadership would have expected him to rise above petty "factional" allegiances. In a way, opposing the novel *Liu Zhidan* was an act of dedication to the historic figure Liu Zhidan, who, shortly before his death on the battlefield, had implored Xi to forget past hatreds and put the party's interests first.

MANAGING THE INCIPIENT PRODEMOCRACY MOVEMENT

The question of rehabilitations touched upon a broader issue: Just how far should the party go recognizing its past mistakes? The path forward faced serious questions without obvious answers. Could voices in favor of change be harnessed to promote the needed reforms? What kind of criticisms were a healthy sign of debate, and what accusations were "antiparty"? When overly negative views were expressed, were they to be addressed through dialogue or quashed with force?

In certain ways, Xi shared critical views of the past—he certainly loathed the Cultural Revolution. He was so optimistic about the post-Mao future that he believed the party's message was powerful and persuasive. At the same time, however, one of the most unambiguous lessons of the Cultural Revolution for Xi was the need for stability and unity. A clear fear of chaos thus shaped Xi's reactions. When dialogue did not work, he did not shrink from more repressive methods.

In Guangdong, the most prominent test of how much China had changed after Mao involved a group of three former Red Guards—Li Zhengtian, Chen Yiyang, and Wang Xizhe—as well as one cadre, Guo Hongzhi, who had all confronted Guangdong officials and written incisive posters against the violence of the late Cultural Revolution. They became known as the Li Yizhe Writing Group—a mashup of their names. Their most famous poster criticized the personality cult of Mao, the radical slogans, the lack of material incentives at factories, and the illegal detentions. Although the group occasionally cooperated with the Guangdong leadership, particularly with Zhao Ziyang, Jiao Linyi decided that their attacks on a "new class" within the party and calls for mass democracy were too dangerous. In March 1977, they were thrown in prison.[61]

Later released, they requested that Xi fully rehabilitate them, and he took managing the issue extremely seriously—one of his former assistants recalls that for four days Xi did not return home even for a shower.[62] At his first meeting with the group, on January 24, 1979, Xi adopted a conciliatory tone, telling them, "No matter how you lose your temper or speak, it will be OK because we made a mistake." However, he also downplayed their suffering. Compared to him, they had suffered very little in their lives, he claimed. He said, "My legs were in manacles, but probably yours were not." In Xi's mind, time in prison could be a "big forging experience" for young people. He warned them about putting too much faith in the West: "It is necessary to make a clear line of distinction between socialist democracy, proletarian democracy, and Western democracy or bourgeois democracy."[63]

During their conversation, Wang Xizhe referred to an article Xi had written about Mao for *People's Daily* that described the chairman as someone who could accept criticism. Xi happily responded, "That's right; that's right. How could someone carelessly say someone is a counterrevolutionary? In the past, the Nationalists' policy was that it was preferable to incorrectly kill one thousand in order to not let anyone go. We in the Chinese Communist Party should be the opposite; it is preferable that we let one thousand go and not make a single unjust verdict!" Xi went on to mention how someone who wanted to overthrow the party had recently posted counterrevolutionary slogans. "I said it will be good enough just to tear it down. It is not necessary to investigate. Could posting such a slogan be enough to instigate the masses to oppose the Chinese Communist Party? Does the Chinese Communist Party have that little self-confidence?"[64]

But Xi could mix a conciliatory attitude with fury, especially when he felt cornered or tricked. The group requested a better venue for the ceremony at which their rehabilitation would finally be announced. They also wanted Xi's personal attendance and a meeting between the Guangdong leadership and all the individuals who had been implicated in their case, going far beyond only the four writers. They were afraid that if the scale and visibility of their rehabilitation were insufficient, they would remain vulnerable.[65]

When Xi tried to emphasize the prestige of the already-established venue, Wang Xizhe disagreed, and he also emphasized the importance of Xi's presence. Xi grabbed his briefcase, stood up, took a few steps to leave, and said, "Wang Xizhe, with an attitude like that, I will not speak with you anymore. I am leaving! OK?" Wang was shocked, but when he noticed that Xi's colleagues had not reacted, Wang concluded that Xi was playacting in the style of a high-ranking cadre.[66]

The next day, when Xi met with other individuals who had also been implicated in the case, one of them demanded that the rehabilitation ceremony be held at the Sun Yat-sen Memorial Hall. Xi jumped up, turned around to face Wang Xizhe and said, "Wang Xizhe, did you kidnap me? Did you kidnap me to bring me here to threaten me?" Wang Xizhe explained that these participants did not know about the outcome of the conversation the day before. The man who had made the demand then admitted he was acting on his own, and Xi calmed down.[67]

Xi was incensed when people seemed to be taking the political loosening too far. Without party permission, a proreform rally was scheduled for April 5. *Future* magazine held a discussion meeting at which Wang Xizhe gave a speech stating that Tito, not Mao, was the greatest Marxist and that Mao had not made any innovative contributions to Marxism. Wang pointed to a 1959 speech by Mao, "Talks on Reading Socialist Political Economy," as evidence that the late chairman had not understood anything about economics.[68]

Xi's view was that it was most important that "a rally does not occur but that forceful, simple, command-style methods cannot be used to force its cancellation." He acknowledged that it would be difficult to use "persuasion and education" to stop the rally from occurring within just a few days' time, but he said that the rally must definitely not take place.[69] Xi met with Li Zhengtian to learn more about Wang's speech and the upcoming rally. An agitated Xi said, "Their behavior, if that is not anarchism, what is it? They don't even have a concept of the nation. If they act in this way, why can't the nation interfere? . . . Some evil elements are taking advantage, and they intend to create chaos. . . . What kind of democracy is that? It is extreme democracy—anarchism."[70]

On April 2, Xi tried to convince the planners to cancel the rally. As soon as Xi walked into the planning room, before shaking hands with anyone, he shouted at Wang. "Wang Xizhe, how can you reject Chairman Mao? How can you not raise high the banner of Chairman Mao?"[71] Xi betrayed a fear that the actions in Guangdong would link up with those in Beijing, Shanghai, and even Ningxia—a poor region far from the country's main urban centers. He pleaded that the country itself was at stake: "Our stable situation was achieved with a difficult struggle. . . . How much did Lin Biao and the Gang of Four wreck the country? It can survive no more tossing and turning. If the nation cannot be protected, how can the individual be protected? . . . Of course, you can also say this is democracy, that you support the party center, and that you support the provincial party leadership, but your activities do not. We must treasure today's great situation." Xi's words ultimately swayed them, and they canceled the planned meeting.[72] According to Wang, gratitude to Xi for his rehabilitation helped shape the decision.[73]

Although Wang had backed down, Xi's remarks were broadly disseminated. Wang felt betrayed. He wrote a protest letter to the city and provincial party leaders. Xi responded by saying that his criticisms of Wang were his own personal opinions, not a political verdict.[74] Wang doubled down. In a 1979 interview with *People's Voice*, an independent newspaper, Wang bitingly suggested that Xi needed to refresh his memory about Mao's "Talks on Reading Socialist Political Economy," and he acerbically compared Kang Sheng's treatment of Xi in 1962 to what Xi himself had done to Wang in Guangdong. "In sum, I feel that Comrade Xi Zhongxun has not been careful in the handling of this matter," Wang wrote.[75]

Xi had faced a different situation in Guangzhou than his colleagues in other cities—local democracy activists there presented relatively mild criticisms and lacked wide public support. Guangdong still stood out for its *relatively* softer touch, at least in the early months.[76] Yet Xi's style did not spread as a model in part because of the changing political winds at the party center. During a theory conference held in the capital in 1979, Yu Haocheng—who worked for Masses Publishing House, which was connected with the Ministry of Public Security—saw material on how Xi had reversed the verdict on the Li Yizhe case. Yu asked the vice-minister of Public Security to publish a booklet about the episode, reasoning that the theme of the conference was socialist democracy and law and that the participants at the theory conference could use the material for reference. Yu received initial approval, but the next day the decision was reversed. Deng, concluding that the early stages of the meeting had given too much space for liberal viewpoints, had introduced the very conservative formulation of the Four Cardinal Principles. The participants never learned of Xi's approach.[77]

Xi did not oppose the new conservative direction set in Beijing. The grassroots movement in Guangdong, like those in other provinces, would not survive. In April 1980, Xi accused the activists of "carrying out secret liaison work" and "establishing secret contacts abroad." Their behavior constituted "an antagonistic stand against the Party and people."[78] In August, Guangzhou police arrested a group involved in the National Association of People's Publications. In November, Xi left Guangdong to assume a position in Beijing. A few months later, in April 1981, Wang Xizhe was arrested.[79]

18

BLAZING A BLOODY TRAIL

In 1978, the People's Republic was approaching a troubled thirtieth anniversary, and the extent of the party's failings was especially evident in the place where, after sixteen years, Xi had first resumed work. Thousands of migrants were choosing capitalism over socialism with their feet, fleeing from Guangdong to Hong Kong. In China, a laborer could only make a few jiao in a day, but a laborer in Hong Kong could make 2,000 yuan in one month.[1]

In July, two months after arriving in Guangdong, Xi traveled to the border county of Bao'an to investigate the problem. What he saw was shocking. Although July and August should have been peak harvest time, Xi found only a few old women and children. A particularly dramatic moment occurred during a trip to Sha Tau Kok, where Chung Ying Street was controlled on one side by the mainland and the other side by Hong Kong. On the capitalist side, business was brisk, but in the mainland, the scene was desolate; buildings were run-down, and weeds were growing in abandoned areas. "Liberation happened so long ago, almost thirty years," Xi said. "That side is prosperous, but on our side, everything is shabby."[2]

Fang Bao, a local leader, later remembered what it was like for Xi during the inspection trip: "Comrade Xi Zhongxun was an old revolutionary proletariat. He firmly believed in the superiority of the socialist system. But ten years after he had been incorrectly punished and he had been dismissed from work, what he saw and heard was not the superiority of the socialist system but rather prosperity of the capitalist Hong Kong New Territories and the bleak conditions in the border areas that had been socialist for nearly thirty years." The starkness of the divide seemed to strike Xi deeply. "The life of peasants in the mainland was not nearly as good as that of peasants in the New Territories; we could clearly imagine the size and depth of his feelings about the differences between reality and his ideals," Fang recalled. "The comrades who were there could sense, both in his words and his facial expressions, his feelings of anxiety, sadness, and worry."[3]

In September, the Guangdong Public Security Office reported that, in the previous month alone, 6,709 individuals had fled. This was the highest number since the Great Leap Forward. In one case, it was the leadership of a production brigade that organized a group that hijacked a boat to flee. The relatives of soldiers were saying openly at meetings that illegal migration was "more glorious" than joining the military. Wu Nansheng forwarded the report to Xi. "Comrade Zhongxun," he wrote, "it is worth nothing the situation this report describes."[4] In late November, Xi organized a mass operation of more than ten thousand cadres, militia, and People's Liberation Army troops to forcefully stop those trying to flee. Xi's operation helped address the symptoms but not the underlying causes of the problem.[5] A hundred thousand migrants were incarcerated in Shenzhen between January and June 1979.[6]

In May, Vice-Minister of Civil Affairs Liu Jingfan, the younger brother of Liu Zhidan, visited an overcrowded detention facility in Shenzhen. Dozens of migrants were locked up in the same room, with no access to toilets. Liu immediately demanded that Fang Bao—the local official who had seen Xi react so strongly to the economic disparities on the border several months earlier—let them go. But Fang refused, arguing that they would simply try to flee again. When Liu told Xi what had happened, Xi was furious, believing that Fang was treating contradictions among the people as a fight against enemies. He ordered their immediate release. The Shenzhen leadership warned that even if they were to be let go, that very day, a new wave of illegal migration would begin. The Shenzhen leadership was right—word got out that the city leadership had been criticized, and that night, seventy thousand people tried to flee to Hong Kong. Two border crossings were totally overwhelmed. Xi summoned Fang to his room and admitted that Fang had been correct.[7]

Meanwhile, the party leadership in Beijing became increasingly dissatisfied with Xi's inability to resolve the situation. On June 13, the State Council listened to a report by Kou Qingyan, a member of the Guangdong leadership. When Kou reported on the tough Hong Kong response and the local media reaction, Vice-Premier Li Xiannian complained about the "extremely bad influence" the news was having on the outside world. He demanded that the Guangdong Party Committee place the issue on its agenda and that Xi go directly to the grass roots to address the problem. When Kou described how even local cadres were trying to develop relations with people in Hong Kong and Macau, Li Xiannian exploded in anger: "It is necessary to severely punish some people. Shameful! The situation is extremely serious. It is necessary to discuss this with Comrade Zhongxun to really grasp this issue. . . . The party committee should discuss the issue of production seriously! How could it have become so bad? Just listening to this makes one disillusioned!" Another vice-premier, Gu Mu, responded that the answer was not to provide Xi with more resources, including funds and vehicles; instead, the Guangdong Party Committee itself needed to improve. "I think this is a work issue, and some concrete issues will not be difficult to resolve," Gu Mu said. The State Council ordered that Xi end the crisis by July 5, the same day that Hua Guofeng would depart for the United Kingdom.[8]

Xi was under intense pressure. On June 17 and 18, he held two standing committee meetings on migration and created a ten-person leadership small group, with himself as the head. The struggle was to be treated as a "great battle" for three months. After the meeting was over, Xi and Kou headed south. On their way, they saw numerous groups of people—ranging from a handful to twenty or thirty—heading south. After arriving in Huiyang District, not far from the border with Hong Kong, Xi learned that all those whom they had seen had already been arrested, but then the migrants had escaped from the buses at the detention facility. On June 20, Xi acknowledged the leadership failures. "We in the provincial party committee did not grasp this issue well," he said. "Now it is an issue the Central Committee worries about. As the individual responsible for the provincial party committee, I feel guilty."[9]

On a trip to a detention facility, Xi complained that the security forces were resorting to methods that violated the law and the constitution. "Public-security people are using methods on the detainees that are for use against enemies." He sounded exasperated: "What kind of policy is this?"[10] When their vehicle passed a police operation, Xi exclaimed, "Are you really arresting people again?" As he exited the vehicle, he saw three peasants, with their hands tied behind their backs, squatting on the ground. One of the guards saluted Xi and then proceeded to curse the prisoners and to kick one in the butt.

Xi yelled, "Hey, how can you kick these people?! You must set up a system with no hitting." He demanded that the peasant be released. Xi then proceeded to politely call the prisoner "young fellow" and ask him about his life.[11]

When he returned to his vehicle, Xi criticized Fang Bao, arguing that "ideological education" was not being conducted properly and that the differences between the old society and the new regime had to be better emphasized. Xi pointed at his head and said, "The key is to grasp this." However, one of the other officials in the vehicle contradicted Xi, pointing out that such arguments had little weight given how obvious it was that Hong Kong had developed so well. At first, Xi was stunned. He still had not absorbed the truth about how far behind the People's Republic had fallen: "That is wrong! What is that? That is a corrupt, bourgeois lifestyle! The landlord class exploits the peasants; everyday, they eat fish and meat. Can we eat that? Can this be a correct comparison?" "Back then, engaging in revolution was so much more arduous," he told them, but it was the Nationalists who ran to join the Communists.[12]

When Xi met with a group of brigade leaders, he was surprised that no one applauded, and some did not even turn around. Xi told the bodyguards with guns to exit, and he asked the cadres to speak. Even though Xi promised that no one would be punished for giving their opinions, there was still silence. Xi reminded them that he too had suffered, and he asked whether there was a method to ultimately stop people from fleeing to Hong Kong. One brigade leader, a man named Wen Fuxiang, said it was best *not* to stop the phenomenon. He tried to explain why people were leaving. When a baffled Xi asked how it would be possible for people to freely enter Hong Kong and noted that the party had already decided this was illegal, the brigade leader pointed out that the constitution guaranteed freedom of residence. "It is we, the Chinese Communist Party, whose words cannot be counted on," he said.[13]

Xi lost his patience and asked what was so great about Hong Kong, and he even questioned whether Wen was a party member. Still, Wen was not cowed—he informed Xi he had been a member of the party for twenty years. Xi responded by asking about his class background—Wen was a third-generation poor peasant. Xi then asked if he had been fulfilling his work quotas—in fact, Wen had been exceeding them. When Fang interceded to remark that Wen's work brigade was in fact "advanced" in terms of production, Xi burst out saying, "What is 'advanced'? How can this kind of work brigade leader be advanced?" Xi demanded to know his name, and Wen, with no fear at all, gave his full name and the name of his work brigade. Though perturbed, Xi was impressed by the man's bravery and his achievements. As they conversed, Xi began to relent. Wen said, "Secretary Xi, you also suffered—and only because of that did I tell you the truth.... If the policies of our Chinese Communist Party continue in this way, with no change, so many will run away that there will be no one left!" Finally, Xi fell silent.[14]

When the meeting ended, Xi gave remarks that suggested he was struggling with what China should do next. On the one hand, he made conservative comments: "Only socialism can save China; only if our thinking is straightened out can socialism be done well. Now, there are some problems. We can reform them ourselves. It is definitely possible to develop well. We still have to continue the revolution—to take the socialist path. This cannot be doubted. As soon as it is doubted, we will be headed in the wrong direction, and in the future, there will be big problems." At the same time, however, Xi believed new approaches were possible: "It is necessary to allow a process of practice and a process of understanding. Expressing different ideas must be allowed. Making mistakes and saying the wrong things must be allowed."[15]

Xi tried to work with the capitalist colonial authorities in Hong Kong. He spent December 6 to 12 in the city—the first such official visit by a Chinese provincial leader to Hong Kong since the founding of the People's Republic. According to the British record of Xi's meeting with Chief Secretary Jack Cater, Xi was "obviously pleased with the attention shown to him" and was "animated and friendly." Cater complained that the number of refugees crossing into the territory had begun to rise again after slowing down over the summer. Xi described the illegal border crossings as a problem for both sides and that China did not wish to create difficulties for Hong Kong. But Xi also accused people in Hong Kong of soliciting migrants from inside the mainland. Xi told Cater that there were no easy solutions and that 260,000 people had been stopped by Chinese security forces that year alone. Xi acknowledged that corruption at local levels in China was part of the problem. He promised that the challenges were temporary and would ultimately end as China's economy improved. The British were worried, however, that the Chinese crackdown would be "unduly harsh" because Xi had told local officials to attack the border problem "in the same spirit as China's first lesson in Vietnam," referring to the Chinese invasion of that country earlier that year.[16]

Still, Xi failed to completely solve the crisis by the end of his tenure. In

June 1980, Deng Xiaoping received a letter from overseas Chinese in Hong Kong and Macau that complained about social disorder in Guangdong and the continuing problem of out-migration. Deng forwarded the letter to Xi and wrote on it, "Without determination, without a concrete approach, and if violators of the law (especially public officials and the children and relatives of cadres) are not treated severely, there cannot be significant improvement."[17] That same month, in a meeting with discipline inspectors, Xi referred to Deng's notification. Yet he was cautious. Although it was necessary to discipline the worst offenders according to the law, "of course, the problem for most people is education," Xi said. "Encouragement and punishment" were both necessary, but the former was to be the priority. "Self-criticism" was better than criticism. "If you made a mistake but admit it, then it's OK!" Do not be afraid to punish, he warned, as that was in the party's interest. But it was also absolutely imperative that the party not produce more wrongful verdicts, Xi said.[18]

THE SPECIAL ECONOMIC ZONES

Xi decided that opening Guangdong to the outside world economically was one possible way to solve the structural reasons for the migration crisis. "The only method is to improve people's livelihoods," he said in 1990 on the tenth anniversary of the establishment of the Shenzhen Special Economic Zone. "Otherwise, they will vote with their feet."[19] While, during the 1950s, China had looked to the Soviet Union for answers on how to build socialism after decades of war, now Beijing looked in other directions.

In 1978, Duan Yun, vice-chairman of the State Planning Commission, conducted a twenty-eight-day inspection tour of Hong Kong and Macau. When the trip concluded on May 6, Duan reported to the Guangdong leadership that the economies of Hong Kong and Macau had developed very quickly over the last ten years. He was cautious—he noted that Hong Kong and Macau relied on capitalism and were therefore susceptible to international economic crises and a large income gap: "The parasitism and rot inherent in capitalism never stops growing, and there is a great deal of societal waste." But Duan also noted that Shenzhen and Zhuhai were close to Hong Kong and Macau, which allowed them certain possibilities: "The conditions are very advantageous for the development of the production of exports and commodities, and in terms of perishable commodities in particular, no country or region can compare [with us]." "Why is it that even though there are so many beneficial conditions, we don't use them?" Duan asked.[20]

Xi held a series of meetings with the provincial standing committee to determine what they should request from the central leadership. On November 9, shortly after arriving in Beijing, Xi urgently asked for a meeting with Hua Guofeng. The two agreed that the exodus of people from Guangdong was not merely a political problem but also an economic one. To solve these difficulties, the center would have to allow Guangdong some policy flexibility. Hua supported the creation of "foreign trade bases" in Shenzhen and Zhuhai.[21]

On February 21 of the following year, Wu Nansheng, secretary of the Guangdong Party Committee, drafted a report to the provincial leadership that proposed an idea even more ambitious than "export bases." Wu told the provincial party leaders that Shantou—which he was visiting as he wrote his report—should use foreign capital to expand trade.[22] After Wu returned to Guangzhou, Xi visited Wu's home and thanked him. Xi urged Wu to bring up the issue at a provincial party meeting the next day. At the meeting, Wu pointed out that Taiwan, Hong Kong, and Singapore had all developed quickly and that Guangdong had the most propitious conditions in the country to do the same. "Both Xi and Yang are here," Wu said, referring also to Yang Shangkun. "If it is still impossible to improve things, then what can be done?" Xi agreed: "That's right, Guangdong has such good conditions. If matters still do not improve, as a member of the party, I will feel guilty." Xi argued that the key was how Guangdong's demands would be framed. Wu suggested that Shantou be used as a testing ground for a different approach because the city already enjoyed a high level of outside trade, and many Shantou people were living overseas. Xi lost his temper and said, "If this is to be done, the whole province should do it!" Wu later told a journalist that Xi "did not know that the whole province could not do it; if the whole province were to do it, it would be disastrous!"[23]

Shortly after that meeting, Xi traveled to Beijing for a work conference on economic affairs. Li Xiannian gave a major speech on the economy, but he did not go far enough for Xi. On April 8, Xi told the South China discussion group that "Comrade Xiannian's speech did not clearly indicate that power is too concentrated, and it did not mention this 'serious defect'; it only generally said it was necessary to develop the initiative of the party center and the regions." Xi continued, "Now power is overly concentrated.

This problem has not been solved. . . . The right to flexibility in the localities is too small. The country and the central ministries manage everything to death. This is not beneficial to the development of the national economy." Xi even said that if "Guangdong were an independent country," it would be able to develop more quickly. On April 17, at a politburo meeting, Hua Guofeng, Deng Xiaoping, and Li Xiannian listened to the reports of the leaders of the discussion groups. On this occasion, Xi extended his comments: "Guangdong is planning to copy the form of foreign-processing zones to observe, study, test, and use foreign practices, to set aside a place in areas bordering Hong Kong and Macau, such as Shenzhen and Zhuhai, and Shantou—a city with important connections to overseas Chinese—to engage in independent management, to serve as a venue for investment by foreign businessmen in the Chinese diaspora and compatriots from Hong Kong and Macau, to organize production according to the demands of the international market, and initially to call these areas 'trade-cooperation zones.'"[24] Xi won the support he needed from Hua Guofeng, who replied, "Comrade Zhongxun says that if Guangdong were its own country, it would have developed a long time ago. Too much control affects speed. After two years of study, this fact is even more obvious. . . . It is necessary to carry out a big reform. Guangdong must have a new system."[25]

Deng's own support for the creation of the special economic zones at the work conference is often heavily emphasized in historical accounts. Deng is said to have told Xi to "blaze a bloody trail," to forge ahead without money from the center, and to call the new experiments "special zones" based on the Shaan-Gan-Ning special zone that surrounded the party leadership in Yan'an during the revolution.[26] Deng's imprimatur was indeed significant. Xi was still working out the rehabilitation of a previous campaign against "localism," and even Xi's deputy, Yang Shangkun, was initially skeptical about the special economic zones. One high-ranking Guangdong official asserted that provincial leaders would never have dared to build the zones if Deng did not approve.[27]

Still, Deng's role should not be overstated. He did not attend most of the work conference that discussed the new policies for Guangdong, and the famous conversation between Xi and Deng might not have happened. According to the director of a documentary about Xi, "When we were interviewing, we still heard some different voices, and some people even did not believe that this conversation occurred."[28] Credible accounts differ on the exact nature of the interactions between Xi and Deng in April 1979. According to Wu Nansheng, Deng's famous words were not spoken to Xi at all; instead, Deng suggested a "special zone" in a conversation with Gu Mu, who had reported to Deng that no one was sure what exactly to call the new areas. That was when Deng said, "Why not just call them special zones? Shaan-Gan-Ning was a special zone."[29]

More importantly, whatever the exact details of the interactions between Deng and Xi at the conference, Xi's behavior in Guangdong afterward demonstrates that he gave more credit to Hua than to Deng. On May 3, Xi did tell the Guangdong Party Standing Committee that Deng Xiaoping had said that "it is necessary to blaze a bloody trail," but, crucially, most of Xi's comments were about Hua. He credited Hua for the guiding thought of the work meeting, and with regard to giving more powers to Guangdong, Xi asserted that "Chairman Hua and the comrades on the politburo all got the message."[30] As Wu Nansheng explained to one historian, "When Xi Zhongxun returned, he only talked about Chairman Hua; he did not talk about Deng Xiaoping. When he talked about Deng Xiaoping, it was only in reference to one thing, he said: 'Xiaoping says to blaze a bloody trail; I think he is also very active in terms of Reform and Opening.'"[31]

Still, the April 1979 work conference was not a total win for Xi. Guangdong had planned to make expansive investments in giant construction projects, but the meeting put a stop to these hopes and introduced a program of rectification in the economy.[32] And Xi's detractors were still not impressed. In his memoirs, Deng Liqun claimed that Xi's speech during a session held by Hua to discuss this rectification policy was "rambling" and "irrelevant."[33] Moreover, the Guangdong leadership was still unclear about just how they should proceed to establish the zones. On May 26, Xi expressed both excitement and doubt to the Guangdong party leaders. "No matter what, we must have resolute determination and confidence," he told them. He knew big steps were needed, but he was afraid about going too far too quickly:

> My mood is both joyful and terrified. I am happy that under the unified leadership and great support of the Central Committee, we can use the advantageous conditions in our province to implement the Four Modernizations by taking the first step and accumulating some experience for the whole country. This is a glorious mission. But I am terrified that the burden is great, the mission is arduous, and we also lack experience. The difficulties are numer-

ous, so I am a little nervous about how to do things well and whether or not things can be done well. . . . Of course, it is impossible to avoid even a little chaos; do not be afraid if some problems arise, but it is absolutely necessary to avoid big chaos.[34]

On July 20, the party approved *Document No. 50*, which awarded Guangdong, as well as Fujian, with three key policies. First, according to a "contract" system, Beijing would require that Guangdong give a set amount of yuan every year to Beijing, but whatever income the province generated beyond that amount could be used locally. Second, the two provinces were promised more autonomy to make decisions. Third, the Central Committee officially gave the provinces permission to start the special zones.[35] In September, when Vice-Premier Gu Mu visited Guangdong to discuss how to implement these plans, Xi raised the issue of whether to pick a small, medium, or large plan. Gu was clearly disappointed with Xi's lack of confidence. "I believe we cannot have a plan B," he said. "We can only set out with determination to go big and fast."[36]

In April 1979, Xi Zhongxun had criticized Li Xiannian for concentrating too much economic decision-making authority in the capital. In the early spring of 1980, Xi was an even more assertive advocate for devolving rights to the provincial leaderships. In February of that year, the Ministry of Finance warned that China's budget deficit was too high and that the country should pursue slower growth. At a meeting of regional and central leaders between March 3 and 6, some participants simply did not believe the report, and they thought that the Ministry of Finance was not supportive enough of development.[37]

Xi was one such individual, and his speech on March 5 was forceful. He could not understand how finances could be in such a difficult position when the broader political and economic conditions were so strong. Xi thought it was smarter to improve finances through rapid growth, not cutting off the spigot of funds. The special privileges supposedly given to Guangdong and Fujian had simply not materialized, he complained, and the Ministry of Finance had broken its promises—something Xi labeled a "bad style." Yet on the same day of Xi's speech, Chen Yun called Yao Yilin, a vice premier, to express support for the Ministry of Finance. At the end of the conference, Li Xiannian and Hua Guofeng sided with the center. Hua tried to console Xi: "You have had some difficulties this year, Comrade Xi Zhongxun, but in the future, things will gradually get better, and some people are even envious of you." "I suppose that some semiautonomous rights were given," Xi allowed. Hua promised he would send Gu Mu to help, but he warned Guangdong not to move too quickly. Once the economy had stabilized and China had more money, then the country could grow faster, Hua said. Hua spoke of the future, but this was the last time he ever gave a meaningful policy directive. Control over the economy was moving into the hands of Zhao Ziyang, who, unlike Xi Zhongxun and Hu Yaobang, shared Chen Yun's conservative approach.[38]

At the end of March, Gu returned to Guangdong to hold a meeting with the leaders of both Guangdong and Fujian. The resultant *Document No. 41* approved by the Central Committee in May had tough words for the two provinces. With regard to the economic problems, "leadership work is not keeping up," the report stated: "The two provinces must take another step forward in terms of redirecting emphasis and leadership energy to economic construction, to completely implement *Document No. 50*, and to undertake new structural experiments. The main leaders must personally manage and the provincial-level cadres must lead the special economic zones."[39] That very same month, in a speech to the Guangzhou Military Region leadership, Xi emphatically stated that the purpose of the zones was only to obtain foreign currency, solve employment problems, and learn advanced technology and management practices. He called for ideological vigilance: "When using Hong Kong and Macau, there inevitably will be struggle. The special economic zones mean directly interacting with the capitalists too, and that means even more struggle."[40]

Members of the Guangdong leadership saw real challenges. On June 19, Vice-Governor Liu Tianfu warned that "we have not used well the privileges given to us by the party center in terms of the structural reforms and the changing policies, and, therefore, we have not truly mobilized as much as possible in every area."[41] Also in June, Wu Nansheng described Shenzhen as a basket case: "Everyone feels that order in Shenzhen is very chaotic and that it must be rectified. We are at the entrance to the southern gate of the motherland, and as soon as people come in, their impression is very bad. At first, they want to invest, but when they see the situation, they start to have doubts, and they run away."[42]

On September 24 and 25, the secretariat in Beijing held two meetings on Guangdong. The sessions began with Xi complaining about the threat of cold spells on agriculture. Premier Zhao Ziyang responded by acknowledging that agriculture in Guangdong had been less and less stable since 1972. Hu Yaobang criticized Xi's idea of decreasing grain production and increasing cash crops. The next day, Gu Mu again lambasted the leadership in Guangdong for not taking advantage of the new policies. According to Gu, the provincial leaders needed to be brave, comparing them unfavorably to others in provinces that did not have Guangdong's special privileges. "Jiangsu does not have these preferential policies," he said, "but it has made things livelier than you." Yao Yilin told the Guangdong leaders that they needed to think about their province on its own terms: "For example, if Guangdong were an independent country and Comrade Xi Zhongxun were president, how would your country develop?" Zhao raised the most ideological concerns. He warned about the "Hong Kong wind" that might affect the province. "Aren't there people in Hong Kong who want to Hong Kong–ify and Macau-ify Guangdong?" Zhao asked. "This is a major struggle." Hu Yaobang concluded the meeting by reminding the participants that the special economic zones were only to study the management practices of the bourgeoisie, not their "lifestyle" or ideology.[43] The party center released a *Summary of the Secretariat Meeting*, giving Guangdong and Fujian greater authority to act. Liu Tianfu would describe the summary as an "imperial sword" that Xi had won for Guangdong. Still, Liu believed that even this document did not yet allow for true flexibility and autonomy.[44]

XI AND ECONOMIC REFORM

Xi's contribution to the special economic zones was very significant, although they had not taken off by the time he departed Guangdong. His record in other areas was more mixed. Shortly before his arrival in Guangdong, Liang Xiang, second party secretary of Guangzhou, relaxed price controls on some vegetables. Liang's act—which was an attempt to motivate peasants to work harder—led to more supplies, but, just as Xi was assuming his new position, some citizens started complaining about higher prices. Xi concluded that, from the outset, the Guangzhou City leadership had wanted to discredit him. On his second day on the job, he yelled at Liang. Liang, furious at the accusations, fought back. Wu Nansheng interceded. "Comrade Liang Xiang, it is not good to be like that. Comrade Zhongxun has just arrived," he told Liang. "There are many things he does not understand. Explain matters clearly to Comrade Zhongxun. Don't fight." But the price controls were quickly reversed. Xi's first act in Guangdong thus was to interpret early economic reforms as a political challenge against him that had to be stopped immediately.[45]

Xi was deeply aware of problems in the countryside, and he was comfortable using forthright language to criticize past failures. At the work conference in 1978, he frankly stated that the document on agriculture under discussion was written poorly, had no key message, and if it were to be disseminated, it would not solve any problems. Even more bravely, Xi criticized the commune system, which, until then, had been described as one of Mao's greatest victories. In Xi's mind, some of the communes were not as productive as the collectives. He demanded a thorough investigation into the past twenty years of agricultural policies.[46]

Crucially, however, Xi Zhongxun did not support the household-contracting system, which gave more individual rights to peasants.[47] It was the single most important breakthrough in the early years of the reforms, but, at least initially, Xi was convinced that it was "a low-level form of management." According to one individual deeply involved in agricultural issues in Guangdong during this time, Xi was afraid that giving more rights to individual households would lead to an explosion of societal contradictions, weaken party leadership, and hurt the collective welfare system.[48]

On a trip to Zhanjiang in August and September of 1980, Xi listened to a report on the benefits of household contracting. Xi allowed for its temporary use to solve emergency needs, but he remained opposed to a permanent change. "If it continues for the long term, it will not be in accordance with the directives and guidelines. People will be held accountable!" Xi threatened to fire any commune or county leader who shifted completely to the policy. He repeatedly demanded that a brigade leader named Wu Tangsheng, who had adopted the approach, admit to at least one problem the policy had created, but Wu was unable to come up with any. Xi asked Wu how long he planned to use household contracting. When Wu said he would use it as long as policy allowed, Xi said, "We on the socialist path must take the collective road, the road of common prosperity." Everyone went silent. Then Wu lost his temper and replied in his local dialect. "In the past, we had to make it so no one would have anything to eat to fit the policy," he said. "Now we make it so we have food to eat, but this does not fit the policy. How do local cadres know what to do in such a situation?" After listening to the translation, everyone once again fell silent. Then Xi said, "How should your words be understood? There must be a bridge between socialism and Communism. Therefore, this kind of household contracting can only be a form of a transitional bridge—temporary work." Again, silence. After a bit more discussion, the meeting ended unhappily.[49]

THE LEGACY OF REFORM IN GUANGDONG

When Xi left for Beijing in 1980, he could take some pride in what he had accomplished, but Guangdong's greatest successes were yet to come. According to journalist Cheng Kai, who worked in Guangdong at the time, Xi did not enjoy a high level of prestige because, other than the special economic zones, he had not introduced many innovative policies. The Chinese expression "Sticking to old habits" (*xi yi wei chang*), which includes the Chinese word *xi*, was used to satirize Xi's old-fashioned approach. The word on the street was that Xi's previous suffering had made him cautious.[50] Ezra F. Vogel, in his classic book on reform in Guangdong, shares this assessment about Xi and Yang Shangkun, who, "perhaps because of their experience in guiding regional economies, did not live up to the hopes of many in getting the economy moving."[51]

Still, Xi was protective of his legacy. He complained to the top leadership that his successor, Ren Zhongyi, did not praise him enough for his role establishing the special economic zones. Ren felt this was an unfair accusation, and he later determined that a misunderstanding had occurred because the record of one of Ren's speeches did not include the segment on Xi for some reason.[52] In September 1987, Xi was also unhappy that Yang Shangkun was taking credit for the changes in Guangdong when, in Xi's mind, it was he who had bucked the pressure.[53]

Yet contributing to the special economic zones was not universally seen as useful political capital. After a trip to Shenzhen, Mao's former secretary Hu Qiaomu said that the city had turned completely White, meaning reactionary and capitalist. The only Red left, Hu thought, was the flag.[54] Others in the top leadership believed that the area was undergoing "Hong Kong-ification." They compared the special economic zones to the "concession areas" forced on China by the colonial powers in the nineteenth century. One senior revolutionary cried when he visited Shenzhen, believing that the country he had helped conquer for socialism was turning capitalist. Nonideological problems persisted as well—the reforms led to increased smuggling and the open markets drained commodities from other provinces.⁵⁵

The man who led the charge against the special economic zones was Chen Yun. In December 1981, he said that the primary mission for the special economic zones was to "summarize experiences"—a political euphemism indicating that he opposed any expansion of the zones.⁵⁶ Guangdong bore the brunt of this conservative political offensive, and the Politburo Standing Committee released a special document on smuggling in the province. For reasons that can only be guessed, Xi seemed to support the crackdown. On a trip to Yunnan in January 1982, Xi affirmed that although the opening to the outside world was correct, "the resulting struggles between infiltration and counterinfiltration and corruption and anticorruption are inevitable and long-term." Whether or not the party could achieve victory in this battle was a matter of "survival." In a report to Hu Yaobang about his trip, he also complained that party cadres in the countryside were paying too much attention to individuals who were making a lot of money, not the "path of common prosperity."⁵⁷

The next month, at the Two Provinces Meeting (referring to Guangdong and Fujian) in Beijing, Hu Qiaomu interrupted a speech by Hu Yaobang to demand distribution of a report titled *The Origins of Old China's Concessions*.⁵⁸ Xi was relatively quiet at the meeting and limited himself to one interjection. When Peng Chong, a member of the secretariat, stated that current corruption was much worse than it had been during the Three Antis and Five Antis Campaigns in the 1950s, Xi responded, "In the past, they were small tigers; now, they are big tigers."⁵⁹

At this critical moment, Deng did almost nothing.⁶⁰ Xi later told Ren Zhongyi that when the Politburo Standing Committee listened to a report on the debate about Guangdong and Fujian, Deng was silent.⁶¹ Deng's first real major contribution to the special economic zones came in January and February of 1984 when the success of the policy was finally clear. On a trip to Shenzhen, Zhuhai, and Xiamen, Deng declared, "It's not the time for retraction but rather for expansion"—words that were clearly directed against Chen Yun's earlier call for "summarizing experiences." By then, Deng was taking credit for everything. "I proposed setting up special economic zones," he said. "It appears that the correct path was taken."⁶²

Like the special economic zones, the household-contracting system proved its worth in practice, and, in the following years, Xi's views of the countryside developed. In 1983, Xi told the French ambassador, "The household-responsibility system brought unprecedented prosperity to the countryside." "In spite of some local resistance," the government intended to expand the practice, as results had proven it correct, Xi said. Xi even showed some bravado, claiming that, in some places, they "might lack silos to store grain."[63] In a meeting with a cadre from Shanghai, Xi would even deny that the practice of peasants hiring employees constituted capitalist exploitation of labor. "It is possible that even if it is exploitation, it is still a good thing," Xi said.[64]

19
OPENING TO THE WEST

In 1962, when Xi was purged from the leadership, the Sino-Soviet split was worsening, but the relationship had yet to completely collapse. When Xi returned to work, the world looked very different. Now, the Soviet Union was China's main enemy. Worried about Moscow's expanding ties with Hanoi, China attacked Vietnam in February 1979, seven months after Xi became second commissar of the Guangzhou Military Region, which bordered Vietnam. It was a disaster. After Xu Shiyou's poor display as a commander, Xu told his staff not to tell anyone in Guangzhou that he would be returning because he did not want a welcome ceremony. Xi learned of Xu's plans and went to the airport to greet him anyway. When Xi warmly approached with a smile on his face and his hand extended, Xu grabbed his hand so tightly that Xi said "*Aiya!*" (a Mandarin interjection of surprise, frustration, or exasperation) and nearly collapsed to the ground in pain. "Fuck," Xu said. "Who told you to come welcome me?" He then got into a vehicle and sped away.[1]

China's security posture facilitated a new economic opening to the West. In 1979, Deng Xiaoping told Li Shenzhi, then a member of the International Issues Writing Group, that it was those countries and regions that were with the United States, not the Soviet Union, that had become rich and powerful. Li came to believe that whether Sino-American relations were good or bad would "determine the fate of China's Reform and Opening."[2] During Xi's years in Guangdong, he participated in this shift that would so fundamentally shape global power in subsequent decades.

AUSTRALIA

Australia, a capitalist democracy without the historical baggage that other Western countries had in China, represented a special opportunity to learn about the outside world on a more relaxed footing. In June 1979, the New South Wales treasurer J. B. Renshaw brought a delegation of government and industry officials to China, where Renshaw discussed a sister-province relationship with the Guangdong leadership and invited Xi Zhongxun to visit Australia. Neville Wran, the governor of New South Wales, later repeated the invitation, adding that Xi would be a guest of his government. In October, Xi finally cabled confirmation of a sister-province relationship and accepted the invitation.[3] Before Xi arrived the next month, Australian diplomats penned a rather dismissive description of him. They wrote that Zhang Guotao, who split from Mao during the Long March, described Xi "as a man who gave no indication of significant individuality either in thought or expression, but one who was politically reliable and obedient." Another source, the cable continued, referred to Xi "as able and conscientious but by no means brilliant."[4]

At a banquet on November 26, Wran told Xi that the visit was "a landmark in the further development of the close and increasingly fruitful relations between the People's Republic of China and Australia."[5] Geopolitics pushed Australia and China in similar directions. Xi said, "Australia's friendship with China made a positive contribution to the maintenance of regional stability," and he "stressed the importance which China attached to Australia as a source of modern technology, particularly in the field of agriculture."[6] On his way back to China, the Australian commissioner for Hong Kong, Ian Nicholson, met Xi at the airport and again later at a reception. Nicholson informed Canberra, "Chairman Xi waxed enthusiastic about the delegation's visit to N. S. W. He told me they had seen 'everything from Dubbo to Leeton and Newcastle.' He said that N. S. W. was three times the size of Guangdong Province and had only one-third of the population—as Chairman, he suggested that he therefore had six times the problems of Mr. Wran.... He said that the prosperity of N. S. W. and its advanced technology would make cooperation for Guangdong valuable. He also praised the warm hospitality the delegation received wherever they went."[7] Back in China, he wrote a report on his trip to the Central Committee with two proposals. First, Chinese diplomats abroad should intensify their efforts to learn about economic development and advanced scientific technologies in the developed world. And second, Beijing should think more about how to utilize the Chinese diaspora. Xi was impressed by the friendliness of the overseas Chinese he met in Australia, including individuals who were from Taiwan that were "friendly, polite, and willing to approach us."[8]

In April 1980, Wran himself visited China. Expectations for the trip were low, but he was treated with such pomp that the *Sydney Morning Herald* concluded that "wily" Chinese officials had given the politically ambitious Wran "publicity" instead of oil in exchange for the coal he promised to send to Guangdong.[9] Wran met Hua Guofeng in Beijing, where Xi and Guangdong's relationship with Australia were a top priority in their discussions. Hua told Wran that Australia exported much more to China than vice versa and that Guangdong could help solve that problem. For Hua, "the establishment of a sister relationship between Guangdong and New South Wales would further promote the already existing relationship between the two countries."[10] The Hua-Wran meeting was highly irregular because Wran was only a state premier. Australian diplomats assumed that Xi, whom they believed was "very influential," might have successfully lobbied for Wran's meeting with the top leader.[11]

Xi also wined and dined Wran in Guangdong. The *Sydney Morning Herald* reported that Wran was "over-awed" by the reception he received in Guangzhou: "They've put him up at heavily guarded guesthouses that are normally reserved for Presidents and Prime Ministers, he's had fleets of black limousines, airport receptions, banquets, and a bodyguard trained in martial arts. Governor Xi even gave Mr. Wran his own limousine, and while Mr. Wran has been in Canton, the Governor has been traveling in a mini bus!"[12]

MACAU

Xi was head of Guangdong during a crucial moment in the history of the neighboring Portuguese colony of Macau. In 1979, Portugal and China finally established diplomatic relations. The agreement included a secret clause that avoided Portugal admitting Chinese sovereignty but allowed China to claim sovereignty without exercising it.[13] In March of 1980, Governor Nuno Viriato Tavares de Melo Egidio of Macau visited China. While in Guangzhou, Egidio invited Xi to visit Macau, which Xi did between June 4 and 7, 1980—the first ever such visit by a top leader of Guangdong.[14]

Xi's visit happened at a moment of intense political crisis. Delegates to the legislative assembly could not agree to a revision of Macau's Organic Law.[15] Delegates proposed selection of the governor through direct elections instead of the Portuguese president making the appointment. Beijing, however, believed that direct management of Macau by the Portuguese president fit the terms of the secret agreement with China. Moreover, Chinese nationals had to be residents of Macau for five years in order to vote, but Portuguese and Macanese were exempt from the policy, so direct elections would put the Chinese at a disadvantage. The party was clearly concerned about the long-term implications that direct elections, however limited, might mean for control and stability.[16] To oppose the new law, China relied on local tycoons, known as the Red Fat Cats, such as Ho Yin, Henry Fok, and Ma Man-kei. Another key figure was the general manager of the Nam Kwong Trading Company, Ke Zhengping, who served as secretary of the Macau Subbureau of the Chinese Communist Party's Hong Kong–Macau Work Committee. In Macau, Ke was known as the "Underground Governor." To fight the electoral reforms, Chinese members of the municipal council, led by Ho Yin, refused to attend sessions of the legislative assembly so that a quorum could never be reached. All these men worked closely with Xi during his trip, and Ke even escorted Xi from Zhuhai into the colony.[17]

A Hong Kong reporter working for Television Broadcasts Ltd. asked Xi whether he was there because of the debates on reforming the local constitution. Xi asked for a response from his vice-governor, Liang Weilin, who, speaking in Cantonese, strongly implied that the answer was yes. Macau did not pass the reforms in time for the Portuguese legislature to approve them prior to it taking a break before a major election. Xi's intervention, with the help of local Chinese and Governor Egidio, thus prevented a major, albeit limited, political reform in the direction of universal elections.[18]

Xi had something else to worry about as well during his trip. An editorial in Hong Kong's *Sing Tao Daily* had claimed that the use of the term "visit" instead of "inspection" to characterize Xi's trip meant that "Beijing was not prepared to retake Hong Kong and Macau." Possibly in response to that editorial, Xi departed from his written remarks in a speech to the municipal council on June 5 to say that Hong Kong and Macau were Chinese territory that would certainly be returned to the mainland. "Hong Kong and Macau are actually special zones and their historical status quo should be maintained to promote stability and prosperity," he said. "Since China has such a vast territory, why can we not allow the existence of some special zones?

Are we not now designating special economic zones?" His vision extended to Taiwan, which could also be a "special zone" when it "returns to the embrace of the motherland in the future." One reporter for *Hong Kong Daily News* picked up on the importance of the statement, and both his newspaper and Macau's *Tai Chung Daily* reported on it. The claims were explosive and caused a big stir, as they were the first case of a Chinese leader publicly saying that Beijing would ultimately take back the two cities while allowing them to maintain their respective systems.[19]

THE UNITED STATES

In January 1979, the United States and China finally established official diplomatic relations after seven years of negotiations and false starts following President Richard Nixon's 1972 trip. Just as with the Australians, Guangdong was at the forefront of China's new opening up to the outside world. On August 30, 1979, Vice President Walter Mondale arrived in Guangzhou to establish the first American consulate outside of Beijing since the establishment of the People's Republic. Xi attended the welcoming at the airport with his wife, Qi Xin, and other top leaders in Guangdong.[20]

At a luncheon held by the Asian Pacific Chamber of Commerce, Mondale asked for help turning "normal relations between the United States and China into concrete reality." After providing a long list of breakthroughs in relations, he continued, "What it all adds up to is this: Our new relations with China are mutual and they are reciprocal. Both of us benefit."[21] At a speech commemorating the opening of the consulate, Xi listened to Mondale speak of Guangdong's historic role in US-China relations: "It is appropriate that the first American consulate be opened here. By far the largest portion of Chinese-Americans trace their ancestry to this area. Guangzhou was the first point of contact between the United States and China."[22]

In October and November 1980, Xi led the first delegation of Chinese governors to ever visit the United States, a trip hosted by the National Committee on US-China Relations, a nonprofit established in 1966 to pursue closer relations between the two countries.[23] Lian Zhengbao—who, at the time, was second-in-command at the Department of North American and Oceanian Affairs in the Chinese Foreign Ministry and who was also a member of the delegation—said that originally Xi was not on the list of participants, but when secretariat member Wan Li saw the proposed list, he suggested an important change. "The number of overseas Chinese from Guangdong in America is relatively high," Wan wrote. "Drop Yunnan or Guangxi for Guangdong." When the newly added Xi met the other delegation members on October 10, he told them that its task was to learn about America's economy, cities, and cultural and education policies to serve China's modernization. "We should look more, listen more, and think more," he said.[24]

Xi arrived in New York on October 20 and moved into the Biltmore Hotel with the other governors on the delegation. The next day's activities included a meeting with Chinese community associations, visits to the World Trade Center and the New York Commodities Exchange, a helicopter ride, lunch at Chase Manhattan Bank, a meeting with Mayor Edward Koch, and finally a welcome dinner with the National Committee on US-China Relations. On October 22, the delegation visited Bloomingdales, followed by the committee's annual luncheon, at which Xi spoke. He explained that the Chinese people, who had experienced ten years of chaos during the Cultural Revolution, had decided to turn China into a "modernized, highly democratic and civilized socialist country." Strengthening friendship and cooperation between China and the United States had "an extremely important strategic meaning" for world peace, he said. He warned about the Soviet Union's "southward drive strategy," meaning the Soviet invasion of Afghanistan. He argued that the present international situation "urgently calls for the unity of all countries in the world to check and frustrate Soviet expansion and aggression, and not wait until they are forced by the Soviet completion of its global strategic deployments to make a choice between surrender and war."[25]

The delegation then moved on to Washington, where American diplomats had been preparing carefully for their arrival. One memorandum requesting National Security Advisor Zbigniew Brzezinski meet with the group suggested that he "underline the importance we attach to the development of our long-term strategic relationship with China."[26] Another memo noted, "Many of them are likely to become senior officials in the central government of China over the next five years."[27] Executive Secretary Peter Tarnoff informed Brzezinski that this was "the highest level provincial delegation ever to visit from China." According to Tarnoff, the Chinese would probably be most interested in strategic issues, "particularly Soviet behavior and intentions, Asian regional questions and US-China relations." Tarnoff also warned that they may also raise the subject of Taiwan.[28]

Brzezinski did agree to meet with the delegation in the Roosevelt Room, and they also toured the White House. That afternoon, they went to the State Department to meet Deputy Secretary of State Warren Christopher and to the Department of Commerce to speak with Robert E. Herzstein, undersecretary for international trade. One National Committee translator at these meetings provided a description of a very pro-American Xi:

> He is a strong advocate of Sino-American friendship and unity against the Soviets. Time and again he sought to impress his hosts that the delegation represented not just seven provinces and a few hundred million people but all of China's 29 provinces and one billion people. Time and again he played up the theme that the world will have peace if China and America stand together, but that the world will be plunged into turmoil if the two countries are not united. His concern about the impregnability of the North America Air Defense seems real. His request to Under Secretary of State Christopher for the U.S. to help China reunite with Taiwan, though somewhat un-diplomatic, seemed sincere. If there are differences of views within the Chinese leadership as to how close China should align itself with the U.S., Xi's utterances during the tour would seem to side him with the faction that wants a closer tie with the U.S.

The next day, a Saturday, was more casual. The delegation visited the National Air and Space Museum, the National Gallery of Art, Capitol Hill, and the Lincoln and Jefferson monuments. Although one of the governors was quite interested in the translation of the quotes at the Jefferson Memorial and even asked for them to be repeated back to him the next morning, Jefferson's words seemed to bore Xi.[29]

On October 26, the delegation arrived in Iowa to meet Governor Robert Ray and Kenneth Quinn, a State Department Foreign Service officer on detail to the governor of Iowa. In the back of the limousine on the way from the airport, Xi was struck by the countryside. "Iowa is very clean," he told Ray.[30] The next morning, the governors went to the Pioneer Hi-Bred International Research Center, a seed research facility, and to a John Deere manufacturing plant, where many of the delegation donned bright green Pioneer seed-corn caps. Xi told journalists, "We wish for a greater bumper harvest next year so we can buy more grain from you."[31] Xi, who was completely comfortable with the farmers even though they smelled like pigs, asked them very specific questions.[32]

At 5:30 p.m., they had a formal meeting with the governor. Xi stuck to his talking points and was not particularly gregarious. Quinn believed they were being careful because they were entering new territory.[33] The meeting was nevertheless important. Governor Ray's discussions of state-federal relations in the United States made a powerful impression on the delegation. Some of the governors expressed a belief that the party center should give more rights to the provinces and not fear chaos. Some even wondered whether it might be possible for some provinces to test out something like the US federal system. Others pointed to China's longstanding "evil tradition" of warlordism and worried that China's unity, which they had worked so hard to achieve, would come under threat.[34]

Another memorable moment was a meal at the Amana Colonies, which were formed in 1854 based on strict communal and religious principles but were dissolved by vote in 1932. "Xi Zhongxun was enthralled, and he and the other delegates were more animated and asked more questions than at any other stop," according to Quinn. "At the time, I thought the Chinese visitors were so interested in this topic because it seemed a historical oddity—Communism in a capitalist America." He recalled that Xi "went on and on and on" in such a way that it left an impression for many years. Xi suddenly "became a different guy" when discussing Amana—"more animated, more aggressive in his questioning. He was almost climbing across the table."[35]

Quinn thought that Xi was reacting so strongly because he was surprised to hear that "household contracting" had proven so efficient. But does that fully explain the strength of Xi's response? The story of the Amana Colonies was not just about how to best organize agricultural production. Xi was visiting a Communist society that had become a destination for tourists. Only eighty-eight years after its founding, the younger generation, inspired by the outside world, wanted a more materialist, consumerist lifestyle. When Wang Huning—who would later become one of Xi Jinping's closest advisors on ideology—went to the Amana Colonies, he was struck by how generational turnover represented an existential threat to collectivist projects. Wang accepted that economic inefficiencies played a role in the failure of the Amana Colonies, but, for him, the primary reason for collapse was young people losing faith in the mission of their forebears.[36]

After Iowa, the delegation spent a few hours in Dallas—a stop that had been added because Dresser Industries had lent a private jet for the delegation. The group visited the Security Division of Dresser Industries, had lunch with the president of Dresser, and toured the Dresser Leadership Center (years later, Dresser would merge with Halliburton).[37] After the brief excursion in Texas, the group continued on to Colorado, where the trip experienced a small hiccup. At a reception with the governor, the group suddenly said they did not want to visit a molybdenum mine. Jan Berris, who worked for the National Committee, theorized that they were afraid about six top leaders "deep in the bowels of the earth." The Colorado stop did include highlights such as a Halloween dinner at the homes of the state commissioner of education and state commissioner of higher education, and visits to the Air Force Academy, the Garden of the Gods, and the North American Aerospace Defense Command, where they were hosted by the commander in chief, Lieutenant General James V. Harpinger.[38] One translator recalls that Xi demonstrated there a "huge interest, more than anywhere else" and asked numerous questions.[39]

Los Angeles was not originally on the itinerary, but the National Committee added this trip when it learned that Xi would be the leader of the delegation. At the time, Los Angeles was negotiating a sister-city relationship

FIGURE 11. Xi Zhongxun shakes hands with American military power: with Major General Warren C. Moore at the North American Aerospace Defense Command in Colorado, fall of 1980. Source: National Committee on United States–China Relations.

with Guangzhou, part of the national effort to open up ties. However, right before the delegation departed China, the Los Angeles city government had declared October 10 to be the Day of the Republic of China, the official name of Taiwan, and raised the Taiwan flag at a ceremony. In response, the party boss of Guangzhou, Yang Shangkun, informed the mayor of Los Angeles that official plans to make Guangzhou and Los Angeles "friendly cities" had been canceled.[40] Once again, just like Xi's experiences in the Soviet Union in 1959 and East Germany in 1960, bad timing threatened to turn an overseas trip into a humiliation.

Given that history, Xi's handling of the situation was remarkably confident. On the day of his arrival in the United States, during a discussion of the trip, Xi had asked, "in a rather puckish manner," whether there would be any trouble in Los Angeles. The Americans tried to explain to Xi that the people in Los Angeles were very much looking forward to the visit. Xi responded that "some people" in China had suggested bypassing the city, and he seemed to be afraid that weak security might allow someone to stage an incident. They tried to assure him that the Chinese would be welcomed even if some people found it difficult to drop old friends (meaning Taiwan). When Xi then "launched into the two-China lecture," he was told to save it for Los Angeles. Finally, Xi and the others were convinced that there would be security precautions and the likelihood of an incident was low. As the date of arrival approached, the Americans were surprised that "the Chinese seemed to be upgrading it."[41] Lian Zhengbao recalled that the delegation had varying opinions about how to respond to the Los Angeles situation, but Xi supported the visit, saying that he believed friendship between China and America was the general trend.[42]

When the delegation finally arrived in Los Angeles, Xi received a key to the city at a dinner attended by hundreds of people. Xi told them, "Those who wish to damage the growing relationship will not succeed. Chinese-American relations are irreversible and of great importance to the two countries. If that relationship is damaged it will be bad for the whole world." He went on to tell the guests that "an unfortunate incident" had occurred prior to the delegation's arrival. Brushing it aside, he said,

> This is a minor thing, if we let it pass, it will pass. When Mayor Yang Shangkun raised his protest regarding that event, I was in Beijing, not Guangzhou. As I understand, he protested because this event involved a principle embodied

in the communiqué establishing the friendship city relationship, so this was not an issue between L.A. and China.

In short, I wish to say that we cherish only one aim and purpose—the friendship and unity between the two countries. For those who have worked hard for the growing relations, we regard them as old friends. For those who tried differently, we also regard them as friends. China has an old saying that unless you quarrel with someone, you can't really be friends.

Xi concluded his speech by unexpectedly promising to send a delegation to celebrate Los Angeles's bicentennial the next year, which caused the audience to jump up in applause. The Chinese translator told his American counterpart that this announcement had not been discussed previously by the delegation.[43]

The trip to the West Coast included a trip to Disneyland, where the delegation was allowed to cut the lines. Xi rode the Space Mountain roller coaster and, grinning, shook hands with Mickey Mouse.[44] On November 3, after a visit to University of California, Los Angeles (UCLA), and the Fluor Corpo-

FIGURE 12. Xi Zhongxun shakes hands with American cultural power: with Mickey Mouse at Disneyland, fall of 1980. Source: National Committee on United States–China Relations.

ration, the delegation departed for Hawaii on a Fluor Corporation plane.[45] Although Governor Ryoichi Ariyoshi was a Japanese American, on a trip to Pearl Harbor, Xi did not refrain from talking about Japan in remarkably strong terms: "Japanese people cannot be trusted easily. They consistently use sneak attacks and tricks. . . . Now, it is still necessary to be extremely on guard about Japanese right-wingers reconstructing militarism. The two countries of China and the United States that formally stood together in the same bunker to resist the Japanese invasion forces must together still oppose the revival of Japanese militarism; historical tragedies must absolutely not be allowed to repeat."[46] Xi twice addressed Governor Ariyoshi as "mayor," only to be caught and corrected by the translator. Xi referred to Tokyo as "your motherland"—another lapse caught and omitted during translation. A memo by the National Committee after the trip was unflattering. "Perhaps because of his age and the fact that he was under a political limbo for so long," the memo said, Xi "sometimes seems unable to form coherent speech and a little ignorant of foreign countries."[47]

Despite these mishaps, this last leg of the tour seems to have gone well in the eyes of the Chinese. An American translator believed that Hawaii was "the climax" of the trip for Xi. "He will probably never forget his visit to the Polynesian Cultural Center and his participation in the Tahitian dance." At the Tahitian dance, Xi, according to Jan Berris, even allowed himself to "shake his bottom a bit." Shortly before leaving, Xi repeatedly said his group had been "immersed in the friendship of the American people ever since we arrived" and told Ariyoshi that "soon we will leave America, but our hearts will stay behind." Xi's American translator believed that by the end of the tour, Xi was visibly relaxed and enjoying himself. "Whether the glisten in Gov. Xi's eyes at the airport was that of a tear or not, he had evidently been touched by the warm friendship shown by Americans wherever he went."[48] After returning to China, at a meeting intended to summarize the experiences, Xi described the trip as a diplomatic success. "We deeply felt that the American people have friendly attitudes toward the Chinese people," he said. He concluded by saying "America has many methods and experiences that we can use for reference."[49]

In a report written shortly after the trip, Berris wrote that Xi had been less active than Song Ping, the deputy leader, "but this could be due to his advanced age." Still, she believed that Xi "can be a real charmer."[50] Late in the trip, Xi even let his hair down enough to enjoy an impromptu rock 'n' roll dance party with his delegation and American interpreters in a hotel room. Susan Levine, one of the translators, remembered Xi as a warm man with a "really lovely smile" but also someone who sometimes could be disengaged and "look like he had a lot on his mind." "It was clear he was going into different modes, but it was not clear why," she said.[51] A note written by another one of the translators depicted a complicated individual:

> Gov. Xi of course is not a simple man. He is a seasoned veteran in the political arena, shrewd, conservative, patriarchal, intensely jealous of his newly regained power. He is careful not to say or do anything that is not in line with official policy, and is concerned most of all that no incident of any kind happens to the delegation. Occasionally, he is critical of some of the things he saw, as for example he once remarked that the high standard of living in America "consists mainly of eating, drinking, and having fun." And he thinks the pace of life in America is too fast, even the life of the students at UCLA seems to be "rushed." . . . [H]e likes to admonish his subordinates in the typical fashion of a Party bigshot, even corrects his deputy leader at dinner tables in front of his hosts.[52]

For a few months after the trip, Xi continued to interact with Americans. On December 1, a delegation from the National Committee met Xi in Guangdong. David Lampton, who participated in the meeting, recalled that Xi "was a bit rotund, a commanding presence." Lampton also remembered being "disappointed that a person with such a battle-hardened history" resorted to trying to inebriate his guests while Xi's own shot glass had been filled with water after the first toast.[53] When Xi was promoted to a high-level new position in Beijing, the Americans were delighted. In July 1981, Arthur Rosen, president of the National Committee, penned an effusive congratulatory letter to Xi.[54]

Just a few days after Rosen's enthusiastic letter, at a meeting on political work in China's universities, Xi mocked the United States: "Are capitalist countries really that great? America's economy is going downhill; their economic problems are worse than ours. I once told an American, you have difficulties, we also have difficulties. But I believe our system is good, we will solve our problems faster than you. Don't just look at external manifestations. In our country, a billion people have food to eat. That's a big deal."[55] Xi's last meeting with the National Committee came in November of that year.[56] Subsequently, his foreign policy focus would be directed to a very different corner of the world: foreign leftist, revolutionary, and Communist parties.

PART V *TRYING TO SAVE THE REVOLUTION*

20
A NEW ORDER AT THE SECRETARIAT AND THE NATIONAL PEOPLE'S CONGRESS

In late 1978, party elders achieved significant promotions at the Third Plenum of the Central Committee. It was Deng Xiaoping who proposed that Chen Yun, Deng Yingchao (Zhou Enlai's widow), Wang Zhen, and Hu Yaobang all join the politburo. Xi and eight others became members of the Central Committee. Technically, a plenum was not allowed to select members of the Central Committee. Only a party congress could do that. But Deng did not care. "It will be enough to recognize it retroactively," he said.[1] In any case, the victory was deeply meaningful to these individuals who had been pushed aside during the Cultural Revolution and replaced by younger cadres. But now, the party faced new problems. Many of the old guard were too old to work long hours, and their return to power created serious questions about looming succession challenges.

On December 11, the day after the promotions were publicly announced, Xi expressed support for reestablishing the secretariat, which had been replaced by the Central Cultural Revolution Small Group. Xi thought that while the politburo and Politburo Standing Committee should focus on big questions, the secretariat could manage running the country. If it was not possible for the secretariat to reappear immediately, Xi said, then perhaps, in the meantime, a work group for daily affairs could serve as a temporary measure. He proposed that Hu Yaobang lead such a body. In part based on Xi's recommendation, Hu became a new "secretary" of the Central Committee.[2]

In February 1980, the secretariat was finally reinstalled, and Hu Yaobang was named party general secretary. The secretariat was an extraordinarily powerful institution. Ye Jianying declared that politburo and Politburo Standing Committee members, whom he referred to as the "second line," should research "major international and domestic issues." The secretariat, the "first line," was to assume the task of executing those policies—and serve as a crucial step for achieving a stable succession. "Those comrades who later are to enter the politburo and Politburo Standing Committee should first work for a bit in the secretariat," Ye said.[3]

Xi did not immediately join the secretariat, but he soon received a series of promotions. During the National People's Congress session in August and September 1980, he was promoted to that body's list of vice-chairmen. In November, the top leadership decided to bring him from Guangdong to work in Beijing, and then, in March 1981, it was decided he would join the secretariat. In June of that year, Xi formally started working there.[4]

Xi's seniority in the party was much greater than Hu's, and Hu knew it. Before Xi went to work in Guangdong, Hu had told Qi Xin that Xi was "a good comrade." "He did more work than me," Hu said and then added, "He is more skilled than me, and his contributions are greater than mine."[5] Xi recognized Hu's abilities as well. In 1978, Xi went to see Bo Yibo to praise Hu's performance.[6] Yet, years later, Xi would privately complain that he, not Hu, originally had been considered for the position of general secretary.[7] And, curiously, rumors often floated that Xi would replace Hu. In September 1981, the Swedish ambassador to China reported that there was "unconfirmed and unofficial information that Xi can become the successor to the newly appointed Party chairman Hu Yaobang as general secretary of the party."[8] In November, the Central Intelligence Agency concluded that, in the preceding June, Xi had "appeared to be the candidate of Deng and Hu for the general secretary position."[9] Media accounts fared no better with their predictions. In July 1981, the *South China Morning Post* reported on "keen speculation" that Xi would become general secretary. Soon thereafter, the Toronto *Globe and Mail* reported that Xi, "Deng's choice for Party general secretary," had been denied the post.[10]

In May 1982, the top leadership formed two small groups to determine the new makeup of the Central Committee, the Central Commission for Discipline Inspection, and the Central Advisory Commission at the upcoming Twelfth Party Congress, and Xi led one of those groups.[11] Yet Xi's own future was unclear—he himself had requested retirement from the secretariat, noting he was already sixty-nine years old. But, on September 1, the first day of the congress, Hu Qili, who was about to join the secretariat, wrote to Hu Qiaomu to express worries about the size of his workload and his lack of familiarity. Hu Qili, who was much younger and more inexperienced than Xi, expressed the hope that Xi would remain on the secretariat. In a subsequent letter to Deng Xiaoping and Hu Yaobang, Hu Qiaomu wrote that he agreed with Hu Qili. Deng's response was that "it can be considered. If Zhongxun remains, Comrade Hu Qili should remain as secretary in charge of daily affairs."[12]

At the Twelfth Party Congress, Xi was elected to both the politburo and the secretariat. At a secretariat meeting convened shortly after the plenum, in addition to assisting Hu Qili, Xi was assigned a number of special responsibilities. He was placed in charge of personnel, the United Front, ethnic policy, and religion, as well as given responsibility for specific bodies like the General Office, the Organization Department, and the United Front Work Department. He was also assigned to be in charge of liaison work with the National People's Congress, Chinese People's Political Consultative Conference, the Central Commission for Discipline Inspection, the trade unions, Youth League, and the Women's Federation. He was even entrusted with arranging for the meetings of the secretariat and the politburo. Xi now held "a position of great responsibility," as one of his secretaries put it. "He worked night and day." Raidi, a Tibetan cadre, recalled how Hu Yaobang explained why Xi had been given such sensitive assignments. "Because Comrade Zhongxun is impartial and honest; he dares to hold on to principles," Hu had said.[13]

The secretariat ran the country, and Xi ran the secretariat. Yet he was still distant from the true center of power. As a Long March veteran with major military victories against the Nationalists and an individual who had spent years as general secretary of the party directly under Mao, Deng was paramount. Although the secretariat, not Deng, was managing the day-to-day execution of policy, Deng was the undisputed top authority. At the closing session of the Sixth Plenum in June 1981, Hu Yaobang declared that "even foreigners know that Comrade Deng Xiaoping is the main decision-maker in China's Party today.... The members of the old revolutionary generation are still the core figures who play the main role in the Party."[14] The exact nature of Xi's personal relationship with Deng at this point remains murky, but the two men would have remembered their previous differences over Gao Gang and Tibet. Given that history, putting Xi on the secretariat under Hu might have been Deng's way of using Xi even though he did not fully trust him.

Chen Yun and Peng Zhen had first joined the politburo even earlier than Deng—at the Seventh Party Congress in 1945. At that same congress, Li Xiannian and Bo Yibo became full Central Committee members. Xi was only a candidate member. Li and Bo had become vice-premiers in 1954 and 1956, respectively, and Xi did not become a vice-premier until 1959. Yet Xi enjoyed certain advantages that even these heavyweights did not have. Chen Yun was in very poor health during the reform era. Deng Liqun later recalled that Chen was "no longer of the age that he could meet all facets of work."[15] Peng Zhen, although still a workaholic, was deeply unpopular among the elite (especially with Chen) because of historical antagonisms.[16] Xi too complained that Peng "never apologized" for persecuting so many people.[17]

Li Xiannian and Bo Yibo may have become vice-premiers earlier than Xi, but, as former head of the Northwest Bureau, Xi's contributions to the revolution outweighed theirs. And although Li had survived the Cultural Revolution better than almost anyone else in the old guard, which contributed to his position in the party, questions persisted about how he had survived that era so well. Moreover, Li was associated with Zhang Guotao, an early defector from the party, so Li knew he had to be careful.[18] Bo suffered from weaknesses as well. He often worked as Deng's hatchet man, which meant that while Deng was able to maintain a positive reputation among the leadership, Bo was widely disliked—the lonely image of Bo walking with only a bodyguard or secretary at dusk was a common sight.[19]

Xi's long period away from the center of power hurt him, but it also meant that he was able to avoid more "leftist" mistakes than others. His age placed him in between the old guard like Deng and the rising stars like Hu Yaobang and Premier Zhao Ziyang, and his health was (relatively) good. Moreover, Xi had another advantage as well—he was likeable, even charming. Bao Tong, Zhao Ziyang's secretary, remembers Xi as an individual who got along well with everyone: "Old Zhongxun was an extremely amiable person. Whenever he saw someone, no matter who it was, even if it was a young person like me.... At the time, I was very young, but he still nodded at me when he saw me and shook my hand. He was extremely easygoing. Whenever he saw anyone, he would cup one hand in the other before his chest and say hello."[20] Qin Chuan, former editor of *People's Daily*, described Xi as someone with a consensual style: "Among all the leaders I have seen, Comrade

Zhongxun was someone who really did have a democratic style. When working, he would absolutely never simply issue orders or take everything into his own hands, even when dealing with issues regarding the missions of the Central Committee that had been assigned to him. He would first have the relevant ministry express its opinion, and then he would determine a course of action."[21] Gao Kai, who worked with Xi at the National People's Congress, was struck by how Xi would walk around with a cup of tea during breaks, chatting and politely introducing himself to people who did not know him. "My name is Xi Zhongxun, we are in the same small group," he would say. Although high-ranking officials normally took the elevator alone, Xi would refuse. "Come, come, come, altogether," he would say, and then he would joke around with everyone.[22]

Xi did continue to demonstrate a habit for wordiness. Li Rui described Xi at one particular meeting in 1984: "As usual, he was the only one who talked."[23] Du Daozheng, who was long involved in media affairs, similarly recalled that "Xi had an ailment common to all high-ranking party cadres, especially after they got old": "Every time Hu Yaobang made an important speech, Xi would always say 'I have three things to add,' but after those three things, he would say, 'I still have something else to add,' then he would say again, 'I still have something else to add!' Everyone would become very irritated, and they really did not want to listen to his 'additions.' But Xi Zhongxun still earnestly 'added things' and he was always courteous and had a smile on his face." Despite this annoying habit, Du wrote that Xi made significant political contributions during the Hu era, so "everyone would say good things about him and wish him a long life."[24]

Xi was slowing down. In 1982, he told a colleague that he would soon retire. "My brain is not so good," he said.[25] In 1986, Xi and Wan Li held a discussion about grain. Xi suddenly went off on a long tangent about how much he liked red bean porridge. Wan clearly was concerned by Xi's sudden digression. Later that day, Xi exited the bathroom with his fly open and shirt in disarray. A witness recalled being surprised by how such a legendary man could show such curious behavior, worrying that something was wrong with Xi's mind.[26]

PARTY ENFORCER

Xi's return to the party center near the end of 1980 coincided with the final push not only to remove Hua Guofeng, Mao's initial successor, but also to falsely tarnish Hua's record as relentlessly dogmatic, leftist, and authoritarian. Xi knew better—Hua, not Deng, was the individual in the party center who deserved the most credit for supporting the special economic zones. Hua was also accused of opposing the rehabilitation of old cadres—another untrue claim, especially with respect to Xi's case. When Xi went to Beijing in 1978 after sixteen years of persecution, Hua was the first person to treat him to a meal and to suggest that he go to Guangdong. "Why is it that some old cadres cannot be liberated?" Hua asked a colleague around this time. "Why can't there be reciprocal forgiveness? Isn't it good that Xi Zhongxun and Song Renqiong have come back?" Hua told Xi that Guangdong would be a first step to a key post back in the capital; at one point, Hua even considered assigning Xi the position of vice-chairman of the Central Military Commission as a balance against Deng.[27]

Curiously, the decision to bring Xi back to work in Beijing, but not yet with any specifics on what he would do there, was made on November 9, 1980—one day before the beginning of the enlarged politburo session that detailed Hua's alleged mistakes and signaled his complete political defeat.[28] Xi quickly demonstrated an ability to adapt to the new situation in the capital. According to the notes of Li Erzhong, a senior official in Hebei Province, on July 15, 1981, shortly after the Sixth Plenum when Hua finally formally stepped down as the party's top leader, Xi castigated Hua in extraordinarily sharp terms: "He took his cult of personality further than Chairman Mao did. Everywhere he went, he wrote inscriptions. In some cases, Chairman Mao's inscriptions were taken down and Hua's were put up. When some people try to carry a sedan chair for you, the issue is whether or not you sit down on it. If you see it, you should resist it." Xi then went on to praise Hua's replacement, Hu Yaobang: "I believe that after the fall of the Gang of Four, we can see Comrade Yaobang thinks further and stands taller in every area. . . . Comrade Yaobang dares to struggle against evil winds and perverse trends, and he studies hard. This is something we should study. Hua Guofeng plays poker as soon as he goes home. Not even Chairman Mao did that." Xi also used strong language to declare his allegiance to Deng: "In Lankao County, peasants are shouting, 'Long live Deng Xiaoping.' But some people speak foolishly about Comrade Xiaoping. He is a seasoned leader of the party. Since the Third Plenum, he has raised a whole series of correct guidelines. He is the spirit of the party. Why overthrow him?"[29]

Marshal Ye Jianying, who, after Mao's death, along with Hua and Deng, had briefly formed part of a leading triumvirate, was also gradually stripped of any real authority. Ye was impressed with Hua's dedication to a more collective form of leadership, and he believed that Deng was a bully and a tyrant.[30] Ye and Xi were close—Ye sent Xi to Guangdong, defended Xi after his arrival in the province, and often visited Xi there. Ye spent most of his final years unhappily in Guangdong. Despite Ye's delicate political situation, Xi continued to visit him, including twice in 1984 (once along with Hu Yaobang).[31]

Xi helped manage disgraced high-ranking officials who were unhappy about being punished for their supposed mistakes during the Cultural Revolution. One such individual was Qiao Guanhua, the former foreign minister who had been fired and cast under suspicion for his supposed ties to the Gang of Four. Qiao was deeply upset about this treatment. In December 1982, Xi met with him at Zhongnanhai. "You are an old comrade in the party. When you suffer a little, you should get over it," Xi told Qiao. Xi said China's foreign policy needed Qiao and that he would receive a new assignment within half a month. However, even after repeated delays, Qiao was only given a sinecure. The following September, Xi again went to see Qiao, who was then on his deathbed. "Comrade Zhongxun has come to see you," Qiao's wife said to her husband, and then remarked, "If you have any words for the Central Committee, maybe you could say them to Comrade Zhongxun?" Qiao laughed and simply said, "Thank you for coming to see me!" He then turned his head away and whispered to his wife, "I won't speak. Anything I will say is useless." He died the next day.[32]

In the 1980s, Xi regularly visited Ji Dengkui, a man who had been unfairly labeled as part of Hua Guofeng's "faction" and who had been removed from the leadership as Deng began to assert power. When Xi and Ji were both in a hospital in early 1981, Xi visited him. Ji, the former party boss of Henan, tearfully said to Xi, "You were exiled to Luoyang for so many years, but when I was working in Henan, I never visited you. Now, you are coming to see me." During one of their friendly chats, Xi tried to comfort Ji: "Sometimes you are in power, sometimes you are not. You should take a broader view: if you are allowed to be in power, you should work more. If you are removed from power, then you should be happy to be idle and just read some more books."

When Ji died in 1988, Xi, along with Zhao Ziyang, fought hard during the funeral arrangements to give him full vice-premier honors.[33]

As Hu Yaobang's trusted assistant and with a special assignment for party organization, Xi was tasked with the job of reorganizing the provincial party leaderships. The Cultural Revolution had left a legacy of strong personal animosities and distrust within the provincial party committees, and those personal squabbles usually were connected in complicated ways with the question of whether individual leaders had been doing enough to demonstrate their loyalty to reform. Some of them abused their positions for personal gain or did not take organizational discipline seriously enough.[34] In April 1982, the secretariat assigned Xi and Wan Li, to work with the Organization Department and the State Council in holding discussion meetings on the reorganization of party leaderships in the provinces, cities, and autonomous regions.[35]

The work was difficult, often emotionally grueling, as in the case of Gansu. In early 1983, Xi sent an inspection group to the province. Then, in March, he summoned the provincial leaders to Beijing, where he met with them individually. On the morning of March 11, Xi summoned Gansu party secretary Feng Jixin to Qinzheng Hall in Zhongnanhai. Feng did not want to retire, and he felt deeply wronged by the accusations made against him by his colleagues. As he broke down crying, he told Xi that detractors had overexaggerated his mistakes for political reasons. But Feng accepted the decision that he retire. In the afternoon, acting as peacemaker, Xi met with the entire Gansu provincial party committee. He acknowledged that people were unhappy with Feng, and he affirmed that it was permissible to criticize him. But with Feng on his way out, Xi defended his record, noting that Feng had supported the line of the Third Plenum, even though Feng might have not listened enough to the opinions of others in some cases. Xi was self-deprecating: "I joined the work on managing personnel issues. If there are any areas of thoughtlessness that caused you to have misunderstandings, that is primarily my fault. Do not blame Comrade Jixin." Xi told the group that the era of factionalism and infighting was over: "Maintaining old positions is bad. It all ends here. It is easy to create a grudge but difficult to remove it. Stop allowing past matters to vex you and influence your work." Remarkably, the meeting ended in a spirit of unity.[36]

Gansu had been a difficult case, but Hunan, Hua Guofeng's home province, presented a special problem. The party boss of Hunan, Mao Zhiyong, was young, had been promoted quickly during the Cultural Revolution, and had served for a long time in the leadership, thus making him vulnerable to the old revolutionaries who were skeptical of such individuals. At a meeting during the Second Plenum on October 9, 1983, Xi complained that Hunan was still under the control of Hua Guofeng's "original group." The next day, Xi spoke for close to two hours in extremely sharp terms, accusing the Hunan leaders of being Hua Guofeng's "old group."[37] Hu Yaobang, however, believed that trying to eliminate Hua Guofeng's influence in Hunan would be a mistake, as everyone who had had contact with Hua would then have to do a self-criticism. In essence, Hu was arguing against the Cultural Revolution method of "line struggle"—finding the head of a particular group, then moving down and destroying every person associated with that person.[38]

Cleaning up the party while avoiding a line struggle was not an easy task, however, especially in October 1983 when the party launched a new, historic rectification. The leadership politics of the campaign were complicated. Technically, Xi was merely an advisor to the Central Party Rectification Leadership Committee, but in fact he was the direct supervisor. Therefore, Bo Yibo, who was the committee's vice-chairman in charge of day-to-day affairs, believed he had no authority, thus making his relationship with Xi strained. Xi, on the other hand, believed Bo was simply a "bully" who arrogated too much power, even complaining that although Bo's job was to "rectify" other people, it was Bo's own committee that should have been rectified. Xi thought it was a mistake even to have created such a committee; he thought that an office would have been enough.[39]

With rectification, the party wanted to push out any last cadres who might be harboring sympathy for the Cultural Revolution or who had manifested disciplinary problems, such as factionalism. But it was not immediately obvious how rectification could be carried out successfully without repeating the same Cultural Revolution–style purge tactics that had become so unpopular. Although Xi had been aggressive toward Mao Zhiyong, he did believe that rectification should avoid the mistakes of the past. In August 1984, when party leaders met to discuss how the campaign was proceeding, Xi stated emphatically that rectification was not like previous political campaigns. The purpose of rectification, according to Xi, was to benefit unity, the economy, and reform, not persecution.[40]

Rectification also had to deal with the profoundly challenging issue of how to manage younger individuals who had come of age during the Cultural Revolution. The top leadership had different views about this. Chen Yun, along with many other elders, hated the so-called leftist rebels who had been promoted rapidly during that period; the label of "three types of people" was created as a weapon to be used against them.[41] Deng saw the danger in apocalyptic terms, believing that they represented a hidden time bomb within the party that might explode when the old revolutionaries passed from the scene.[42]

But the question of the three types of people was far from simple. It was very difficult to determine who had been promoted quickly because of the mass purges and who had actively persecuted their previous superiors. Almost everyone had engaged in violence, so digging up the past threatened hard-won stability. Moreover, in most cases, the "leftist rebels" had simply been executing what they believed to be Mao's commands. To a significant extent, the desire for revenge on the part of the old guard stemmed from their inability to fully break with Mao: attacking these young individuals allowed them to blow off steam without undergoing a real process of coming to terms with the past.[43]

Hu Yaobang was more supportive of the so-called three types of people than either Chen Yun or Deng Xiaoping.[44] Xi, too, despite his own humiliations, was remarkably forgiving of these individuals, including those among his own staff who had acted aggressively during the Cultural Revolution.[45] "People can change," he said during a conversation with a writer in 1983. "It is not true that the 'three types of people' can never change."[46]

In June 1984, Xi published an article on the topic in *People's Daily*, in which he wrote that "given such drastic turmoil as the 'Cultural Revolution,' if these young people in their teens or early twenties did something wrong, the main blame should not be placed on them." Xi noted that "even some of our old comrades . . . could not clearly realize the evil nature and harmfulness of the 'Cultural Revolution' and also said and did something wrong at the initial stage of the movement." Xi even asserted that the Cultural Revolution had some unintentional positive benefits: "Although many young people were influenced by the erroneous 'leftist' ideology and behaved in a sort of frenzy, the reality of life has gradually made them skeptical about what they were told and has enabled them to gradually realize the mistakes of the 'Cultural Revolution.'" Once again, he drew upon Bolshevik political culture to use the imagery of a "forge": "Having been poisoned and having had a traumatic experience, the younger generation which has gone through years of turmoil has been tempered in the special circumstances that young people in other periods cannot experience."[47] In November 1985, in a private meeting with members of the Shanghai leadership, Xi called for forgiveness: "Many of those below who wrote big-character posters and great criticism articles should not be investigated. Investigation should be limited to those ministries and units in which the Gang of Four directly interfered."[48]

Xi even hired Jia Yanyan as his secretary—a man who, twelve years earlier, had been a leading student of the Red Guards at the No. 2 High School attached to Beijing Normal University. On the same day in August 1966, Jia had been involved in the deaths of two people. After participating in the beating to death of a female teacher at No. 36 Middle School, he returned to his own school, where Fan Ximan—the vice-secretary of the party school at the Ministry of Railways and the mother of a classmate—had been forced to kneel on a brick ping-pong table. Students took turns beating her with a massive wooden stick while the crowd shouted "Good!" after each strike. Jia hit her with a cord, causing her clothes to tear. One individual who was present recalled that Fan never uttered a sound or resisted in the slightest way. After she lost consciousness, someone yelled, "She's faking death! The counterrevolutionary is still stubbornly resisting!" They dumped cold water on her, covering her in mud, but still she did not move. They then put salt on her wounds to stir her, but she never woke up.[49]

As was the case for other early Red Guards, Jia's own parents soon became targets as well (his mother tried to flee, but she was found in Wuhan, brought back to Beijing, and later confined to a mental institution).[50] Yet Jia seems to have learned little from these experiences. In 1970, as a sent-down youth in Inner Mongolia, he and other young Han persecuted their commune's party secretary, a member of the Evenk ethnic minority. The man had been kind to Jia, but the students from Beijing not only beat the commune leader during a struggle session but also set his hair on fire. Decades later, Jia would express remorse that he had participated in the humiliation of this Evenk cadre even as his own parents were suffering in Beijing.[51]

Why would Xi hire such an individual as his secretary? It was common for cadres who, like Xi, had been betrayed by their secretaries to choose the offspring of high-ranking cadres for such positions after the Cultural Revolution, and Jia had impeccable credentials in that regard: He was born in Yan'an in 1945. Furthermore, his father, Jia Yiping, was a useful man to know. As a vice-director of the Beijing City Capital Construction Committee from

1973 to 1980, Jia Yiping often helped rehabilitated cadres find places to live and their children find jobs in the capital.[52] Although Jia Yanyan was recommended to Xi by unidentified "old cadres" and their families, Xi was still cautious before making the hire. Xi spent two days interviewing him, and Xi's family met Jia as well.[53]

Xi's focus on stability and mutual forgiveness extended even to Guangxi Province, where astonishingly high levels of violence had occurred during the Cultural Revolution.[54] On May 27, 1983, he demanded that rehabilitations there go through careful procedure. "Don't be reckless," he wrote in a notification. As for punishing offenders, he opposed an approach that was similar to "demanding the repayment of debts." "It will only heighten contradictions and make disputes worse," he argued.[55] On July 1, Xi and other party leaders met with Party Secretary Qiao Xiaoguang and Vice–Party Secretary Wei Chunshu of Guangxi. Xi, admitting that managing the problems in Guangxi had been put aside for a long time, remarked, "It can be said that this is a special case with special circumstances." Despite the horrific nature of the crimes in Guangxi, Xi made stability paramount. "With regard to dealing with people, it is necessary to be extremely cautious," he said. "The Guangxi problem is a historical problem. Policy must be controlled and grasped in a very meticulous way. Do not go too far. Do not see anything as too serious. The more serious the matter, the more it should be carefully distinguished."[56]

On August 31 and September 2, Xi hosted two meetings to make line-by-line edits to two documents the Guangxi leadership had prepared. When Wei Chunshu discussed a case of murder and rape in Shanglin County, Xi said, "These people should be punished. . . . This kind of person is the social basis for Lin Biao and the Gang of Four. Lin Biao and Jiang Qing wanted to bring these people into the party. Jiang Qing had said, 'Those who come out of prison are the most revolutionary; they can all enter the party.' Those people must not be treated mercifully." However, Xi still clearly believed that stability was most important: "When addressing historical problems, it is still best not to kill a lot of people." He criticized an earlier version of a document in which it was written that those who murdered people would be required to write a "Guilt Admission Statement." "That is not a good method," Xi said. "That's the method that was used to screw us during the Cultural Revolution, and it should not be used again." Xi was also attentive to Guangxi's position on China's periphery, and he warned that "counterrevolutionaries will use this issue to cause trouble." "This is precisely the reason for an emphasis on caution," he explained.[57]

In January 1984, Hu Yaobang, Xi Zhongxun, and Li Rui met with a Guangxi Central Work Group and the Guangxi provincial leadership. Hu began by saying, "More than eighty thousand people died in your Guangxi; this was a historical tragedy." Xi chimed in: "The Cultural Revolution was special. Guangxi was a special case at a special time. Deaths were relatively numerous. Addressing that legacy now is relatively late, so special policies are needed." Hu warned the Guangxi leadership to be careful when it came to removing old cadres from the party even if they had made "mistakes." As for managing the younger cadres who had committed "leftist" mistakes, Hu advised caution, and Xi agreed: "Treat each case separately."[58] Only 1,120 people in Guangxi ended up facing criminal punishment in the 1980s.[59]

Xi's own personal experiences might have affected his views on these questions. The student Meng Deqiang had been kind to Xi when Xi was incarcerated in a dormitory early in the Cultural Revolution. Xi would later remark that while some "leftist rebels" had said hurtful words to prove they were "revolutionary," other Red Guards were "relatively good" and treated him well, even occasionally giving special food delicacies from Xi'an to the old revolutionaries.[60] Another example was Guo Yongtai, a worker who had moved to a high position in the Luoyang refractory-material factory at the expense of the "old comrades." Even though Guo had been a prominent "leftist," he had been kind and polite to Xi after he was reassigned to the factory near the end of the Cultural Revolution. When Jinping applied to Tsinghua University in 1975, it was Guo who wrote that Xi Zhongxun's issue was "a contradiction among the people"—a characterization that paved the way for Jinping to be admitted to the university. Xi Zhongxun said that although Guo had been a "leftist rebel" without a lot of talent, he was not evil: "It is necessary to help this kind of person and to give them a hand."[61]

Xi's support for individuals with problematic records from the Cultural Revolution only went so far, however. He Zai, secretary general of the Organization Department, drafted a report warning that if all Red Guards were to be labeled "leftist rebels," then too many individuals would be punished, and 80 percent of the civilians and cadres would be opposed. Hu Yaobang liked the report, but it was very unpopular among people who thought He Zai was defending dangerous individuals. Zhou Hui, party secretary of Inner Mongolia, called Xi to say that if the report were to be disseminated, it would result in chaos. Xi accepted Zhou's recommendation and ordered that the report be recalled.[62]

Party rectification and the purge of the "three types of people" left behind a mixed record. While Hu Yaobang explicitly claimed that rectification had avoided the mistakes of the Rescue the Fallen Campaign of 1943, in many areas throughout the country, rectification once again led to abuses. At the same time, rectification also failed to eliminate behavior such as corruption and infighting. Yan Huai, who worked in the Young Cadres Bureau of the Organization Department, later wrote in his memoirs that he was "ashamed" of how the three types of people were treated. The real problem facing rectification, Yan thought, was that it focused on punishment, not on establishing more democratic norms within the party. Yet when Hu Yaobang was removed from his position in 1987, one of the charges against him was that he had not been tough enough on the three types of people—and Xi would have shared the blame.[63]

NATIONAL PEOPLE'S CONGRESS AND LEGAL AFFAIRS

Xi was not only involved in clearing out the young and old cadres whom Deng believed had no role in the new order. After the Cultural Revolution had so seriously undermined the National People's Congress and the rule of law, Xi was committed to restoring them. In 1980, he became one of the vice-chairmen of the standing committee of the congress, allowing him to assume the role of head of its Legislative Committee in 1981.

This was not the first time Xi participated in legal affairs—that dated back to his time as a regional leader in the base areas. At the first session of the Second Shaan-Gan-Ning Border Region Assembly in November 1941, he was extraordinarily active. He sponsored more than twenty bills, including one on strengthening legal work and institutions.[64] In Xi's regions of Guanzhong and Suide, the quasi-representative institutions the party established had genuine deliberative elements, unlike in the Communist capital of Yan'an. In November 1944, Xi had pledged to establish a judiciary that would "serve the common people." "It is necessary to wholeheartedly and honestly take our butts and sit them upright on the side of the common people," he said. In the past, "the butts of the old judicial organs did not sit on the side of the common people. They sat in the bosom of a small group of rulers." In these remarks, Xi was demonstrating his own style. According to He Weifang, one of China's leading legal scholars of law, "The language is very unique. It is simple, even a little vulgar. The stuff about butts sitting straight up, this kind of double-meaning expression, has a strong Shaanxi style."[65]

In 1980, the Chinese legislature, even by authoritarian standards, had been politically irrelevant for years—something Xi himself had witnessed before his fall. During the Great Leap Forward, for example, the State Council did not even provide the congress with an economic plan for deliberation, as was technically required. When the head of the congress asked Xi for some discussion documents, Xi went to Zhou Enlai, who said there was no material to be provided or even anyone to give a report.[66] Mao was totally dismissive of the rule of law. No one could recall how many laws were on the books, he complained in 1958. "I participated in the drafting of the constitution, but even I can't remember what is in it," Mao remarked. It was the party that mattered: "Every decision we make is a law. Holding a meeting is a law."[67]

When Xi joined the congress as a vice-chairman in 1980, Ye Jianying was technically chairman, but Ye was largely uninvolved in the body's daily affairs, so Xi worked the most closely with Peng Zhen, secretary general of the congress. It was Peng who, in January 1981, proposed that Xi become head of the Legislative Committee.[68] This was an odd pairing—Peng had played a significant role in the persecution of Xi during the Mao era. Now, they were working together to strengthen China's legal system. Peng even tasked a subordinate with introducing and welcoming Xi to the committee. In October, Peng, who now believed that "ultimately, law serves economic development," told the Legislative Committee, "I believe the Legislative Committee under the leadership of Comrade Zhongxun will quickly overcome deficiencies and legislation will proceed quickly."[69]

China faced a dizzying array of areas that required attention from a legal perspective. One was the laogai, or the "reform-through-labor" system. By the early 1980s, the camps were no longer full of alleged enemies of the people. Now, most of them were younger people with worker, peasant, or cadre backgrounds. The party believed that although these people had hurt others, they themselves had also been victims of the "leftover poison" of the Cultural Revolution. Yet the cadres who ran the camps still often prioritized the use of force, even abuse, over education and protection of the rights of the prisoners. At a major conference held by the Ministry of Public Security from August to September 1981, the party tried to shift to an approach that emphasized "revolutionary humanism." "Reform through labor," the resultant document asserted, should be run like parents treating a sick child or teachers disciplining an unruly student.[70]

Xi, who gave the keynote speech at the conference, did not oppose laogai—he merely thought it should be less cruel. He acknowledged that sometimes the system was too "soft," but he also argued that the bigger problem was "leftism": "After criminals are sentenced and they are laboring at a laogai facility, if you do not treat them as people, if you abuse and humiliate them or even engage in a fascist dictatorship, wouldn't that also be the influence of 'leftism'?" In Xi's mind, most of the problems in society were "contradictions among the people," not manifestations of class struggle. He pointed to the earlier years of the People's Republic as a model: "Before and after the Great Leap Forward, I saw a few prisons. The criminals played basketball. They were as orderly as the military—very clean and very civilized. Life was good."[71]

Xi moved forward cautiously but deliberately. In 1982, members of the Legislative Committee could not decide whether to pass a full civil code or specific laws on particular issues. Xi chose the latter path, concluding that drafting work on a civil code was meaningless until certain basic issues related to reform were solved. According to one individual who participated in the drafting group, "Some civil-code scholars did not understand and felt disappointed by" Xi's decision. However, several legal experts would later say that the step-by-step approach made possible the 1986 General Principles of Civil Law of the Chinese People's Republic.[72] Also in 1982, the Legislative Committee debated whether long-distance transportation by small private businesses should be considered a crime. While some members of the group believed the practice allowed for certain individuals to grow rich unfairly and brought chaos to the economy, others thought it helped supplement deficiencies in the market. When the committee asked for guidance from the party leadership, they were told long-distance transportation should be allowed but better controlled. Xi, acting carefully, temporarily set the matter aside entirely, reasoning that it was still hard to determine what constituted a crime.[73]

Xi also faced the issue of whether to support the reintroduction of the position of state president in the constitution. This was an extraordinarily sensitive question. Liu Shaoqi had been state president from 1959 until his purge during the Cultural Revolution. After Lin Biao's death in 1971, one of the charges against him was that he had wanted China to have a state president so he could assume the role. But between 1975 and 1982, China's constitution had no provisions for a state president. At an enlarged session of the politburo on February 20, 1982, some members of the leadership opposed reestablishing the presidency. Only Deng could take that position, they believed, but Deng's health would not allow it, and it would only force Deng to do more work. Deng, however, said there were other viable candidates. After the meeting, Hu Qiaomu wrote to Hu Yaobang, Wan Li, Yang Shangkun, and Xi to enlist their support for Deng's view. On February 22, Peng Zhen also told them they should support Deng. When the politburo reconvened on February 23, Deng's position carried the day.[74] It was Xi, as executive chairman of the session, who announced, in December 1982, passage of the new constitution, which saw the return of the state presidency but, this time, with term limits and with Li Xiannian assuming the position.[75] Rumors that Xi would become vice president circulated beforehand, but Ulanhu instead assumed the role.[76]

At the subsequent National People's Congress session, Xi was tasked with explaining four comprehensive new laws.[77] His words were a disappointment to the reformers who had spent the previous two years making the case for more serious changes. Proreform thinkers had hoped that candidates for the congress would be allowed to campaign for their positions, as Beijing often knew little about local conditions. An earlier law had indeed allowed for "various kinds" of propaganda during campaign season, but Xi announced a new law that made it illegal for candidates to campaign openly for local legislatures. "It was discovered that, in practice, this regulation was not rigorous enough and left itself open to varying interpretations," Xi said.[78] The new laws did give "deputations," or groups of thirty or more deputies, the right to submit motions. However, Xi explained, it was "subject to the decision of the Presidium on whether they should be included in the National People's Congress sessions' agenda or will first be scrutinized by a special commission."[79]

After the chaos of the Mao era, this was finally a chance to place China on a different course, and Xi was a designated player. Yet, once again, the party acted cautiously. Kevin O'Brien describes the "final scorecard" of the session as "mixed": "The leadership flirted with truly liberal reform (longer, more frequent sessions; professional deputies; meaningful votes), but then pulled away. Several moderate reforms were adopted, but not without accompanying explanations or countermeasures that reduced their effect. . . . Support for radical session and size reform peaked during a wave of reform in late 1980, but faded within a year. Perhaps a change of heart occurred."[80]

Xi left his position as a vice-chairman at the beginning of the next congress in June 1983. Yet he continued to pay attention to legal affairs, including the vexing issue of how to address the massive crime wave that swept the country in the aftermath of the Cultural Revolution. The situation was so bad that many women were afraid to walk alone at night, but some cadres were afraid that a campaign-style crackdown would lead to another explosion in wrongful verdicts. In 1980 and 1981, Deng Xiaoping decisively supported a party policy of "severity" and "rapidity" even though certain party members believed that the formal legal system was enough. Yet crime persisted. In the first five months of 1983, the country saw twenty-five thousand cases of major crimes like murder, arson, rape, and robbery, as well as a plane hijacking. Deng demanded that the party launch a series of so-called Strike Hard Campaigns that prioritized punishment over the rights of people under investigation.[81]

When the second Strike Hard Campaign began in July 1984, it was Xi, along with Song Renqiong and Qiao Shi, who provided guidance to the public-security officials who had convened in Beijing. The meeting concluded that the "unnatural situation" had yet to achieve a fundamental change for the better, which meant the struggle could not be relaxed. The policy of "severe and fast, make a clean sweep" would remain, and it was necessary to integrate "steadfastness, accuracy, and brutality." Along with "striking," the party also identified "prevention" and "transformation" as prominent goals, but those two latter objectives were to be achieved by mobilizing the masses. In part because they were so numerous, repeat offenders who were young and did not violate serious laws could be taken care of by their families, not public security.[82] Xi seemed to support a tough approach. In August, Zheng Tianxiang, president of the Supreme People's Court, wrote a letter to Hu Yaobang in which he noted that after the party center had added the word "accurate" to the slogan "Severe and swift, make a clean sweep," some comrades felt constrained. Consequently, the death penalty became increasingly rare. Zheng was essentially calling for a freer hand. Hu asked Xi to read the letter closely. Xi agreed with Zheng that "accurate" should be removed.[83]

These conflicting tendencies—support for the rule of law but strong worries about security—manifested again in October 1984, when Xi represented the party leadership by giving the address at the opening of the new

Public Security and Police University. He explicitly identified stability as key to China's increasingly ambitious reforms. "Without a political situation of stability and unity and without good public order, smooth execution of socialist modernization will be impossible," he said. Xi then praised the guideline "Severe and swift, make a clean sweep" launched by the party leadership the previous year. He noted that when the campaign had started, it was a little "coarse," but the problems were quickly resolved. Many of Xi's comments reveal the party's continuing conservative instincts:

> It should be seen that because of internal factors and international influence, class struggle will continue to exist to a certain extent. The destructive activities of those who look upon socialism with an enemy mindset still sometimes continue in the areas of economics, politics, ideology, culture, and social life. . . . International criminal organizations, triads, and other counterrevolutionaries also use the opportunity of our opening up to infiltrate. They collude with domestic antiparty and antisocialist so-called dissidents to engage in destruction and subversion. We must not only struggle against the open enemy but also struggle against the hidden enemy.

Nevertheless, Xi did not come off entirely as a reactionary. He spoke of the contradictions between "people's democracy" and "executing dictatorship over the enemy," as well as between maintaining public order and growing the economy. He even recognized the tensions between punishment, on the one hand, and "education, reform, and saving," on the other. He reminded his audience that it was necessary to "completely reject the Cultural Revolution and to reject the theory of 'continuous revolution under the dictatorship of the proletariat.'"[84]

Even as he favored the Strike Hard Campaign, Xi, remarkably, also supported giving more space for China's burgeoning community of lawyers. In February 1985, he attended the inaugural reception of the China Legal Affairs Company at the Great Hall of the People. The company was China's first national legal firm to be run as a business. During the festivities, Xi said, "The work of lawyers is a kind of intellectual work, and the value created by this work must not be underestimated." He emphasized, "We must establish a sound legal system, strengthen legislative work, and act according to established laws." He even wrote an impromptu inscription for the company: "Strictly enforcing the legal system, building a contingent of lawyers who serve the people heart and soul."[85] In June, when hundreds of fishermen surrounded the local party headquarters in a Tianjin suburb to demand urban citizenship and food subsidies, Xi and Hu Qili provided instructions to the relevant grassroots cadres. The standoff was solved through negotiations and the "criticism and education," not imprisonment, of the protesters' leaders. An account of the peaceful resolution along with the instructions given by Xi and Hu were shared with public-security officials throughout the country as a model for such situations.[86]

Just as in the 1950s, Xi continued to emphasize the party's petitioning system, which he still saw as serving as a bulwark against separation from the masses and falling into "bureaucratism." In May 1986, the party held a nationwide petition-work discussion meeting in Beijing, at which Xi delivered the main speech. He stated that party officials often "subconsciously make the mistake" of thinking they are better than other people, and he warned that respecting the petitions is a crucial mechanism for avoiding this problem. Xi joked that it was much more "convenient" to take petitions seriously than for party members to go on investigation trips. "We should treat those who come with petitions as our teachers," he said, arguing that "as a ruling party, it is necessary to take monitoring by the masses seriously." He continued, "Without the rule of law, everything would be in chaos. We are a country with one billion people. I ask our comrades to think for a moment, could we get by without the rule of law? . . . Some of the masses are backward, but, generally speaking, the masses support the country's long-term stability. If you become involved with that Cultural Revolution business again, the masses will not be supportive."[87]

21
PRINCELING POLITICS

Xi Zhongxun had seen how much the party had sacrificed to defeat the Nationalists, even nearly losing his own life on a number of occasions. But could the revolution survive past the first generation? The Cultural Revolution was a cautionary tale. Young people loyal to Mao had rejected the legacy of the old comrades even while these revolutionaries who established the People's Republic were still alive. Ironically, the Cultural Revolution was such a failure that it then created the opposite problem. In 1980, in Shaanxi, Xi's home province and a cradle of the revolution, the Propaganda Department discovered that 30 percent of the population believed Mao's mistakes were greater than his accomplishments, and a majority of those individuals were students.[1]

What would happen when the old guard passed from the scene? Perhaps, some of them thought, they should select their own children to guarantee that the "Red mountains and rivers" would not fall into the history books like so many previous dynasties. After all, the members of the founding generation were the ones who, against all odds, had emerged victorious in the decades-long battle for China—Why shouldn't they be allowed to pass the baton to their own family, they wondered.

But who were the so-called cadre offspring, or "princelings," and how viable were they as a potential group of successors? Although trusted by their parents, they had sullied their reputation during the first months of the Cultural Revolution when, as the first "old Red Guards," many of them beat, sometimes killed, their teachers, and smashed temples and monasteries. As the campaign deepened, these young people felt wronged when they were then persecuted as the sons and daughters of purged leaders. After the Cultural Revolution concluded, they were still disdained but then for another reason—they were seen as beneficiaries of nepotism. They demonstrated a complicated mix of entitlement and insecurity. They were proud, often arrogant, of their status as heirs to the revolution, but they also felt subject to unfair exacting standards. Some of them believed that the suffering they experienced during the Mao era meant they had the right to enjoy themselves by making money or studying overseas.

Xi Jinping, one such cadre offspring, benefited from his father's position. Jinping was climbing the ranks in provinces whose leaderships his father was managing. Zhongxun may have sometimes allowed people around him to support Jinping's career without giving them direct instructions. Yet even individuals who sincerely respected Zhongxun believe that the nepotism he openly displayed toward Jinping was a rare black mark on Zhongxun's storied career. And Zhongxun encouraged other cadre offspring to dedicate themselves to the party too. Shortly before leaving to study overseas, the son of another senior leader visited Xi. Xi said to him, "You should be like my son—stay in China to climb the ladder of success." When the man met Xi a second time years later, Xi said, "Of course I remember you, I told you not to go overseas."[2]

Yet, as in so many other areas of his life, Xi was a man of competing impulses. In a documentary about Xi Zhongxun released in November 2023, Qi Xin claimed that her late husband told his children never to "wag their tails." Xi, she said, hated the sense of superiority of cadre offspring, especially when they compared the ranks of their fathers.[3] Other than Jinping, Xi's other children often complain in reminiscences that Zhongxun actively undercut their careers. While these hagiographic accounts by family members should always be treated skeptically, the diary of Li Rui, who led the Young Cadres Bureau of the Party Organization Department for much of the 1980s, revealed that, privately, Xi Zhongxun was indeed deeply worried about the behavior and reputation of powerful families. For example, he spoke disparagingly about the business interests of Hu Qiaomu's family. Mockingly, he told Li Rui that Hu had had a temper tantrum because he was not forewarned that his son would be arrested for corruption.[4]

Why, then, did Xi Zhongxun make an exception for his own son? It is impossible to say for sure, but apparently none of Zhongxun's children were members of the initial Red Guards who behaved riotously during the early Cultural Revolution. Jinping, who had begun his climb from the grass roots in Hebei Province, was indeed different from those cadre offspring who were little better than wastrels, and he spoke publicly about how he was different from others in his generation. Whatever the reason, Zhongxun was impressed. "Among the children in our household," Jinping's half brother Zhengning said, "Jinping was the most mischievous and the most intelligent, and father liked him the best."[5] Zhongxun even told the daughter of one high-ranking cadre that Jinping "has the makings of a premier!"[6] But even Zhongxun could not guarantee that Jinping's rise would be a smooth one. On one occasion when Zhongxun intervened directly to support his son, the attempt blew up disastrously. Zhongxun often tried but failed to protect his son's patrons in the provincial party leaderships—more early lessons in Jinping's life about the cutthroat nature of party politics.

Even as a student at Tsinghua University, Jinping could not escape from political struggles. In April 1976, he counseled his fellow classmates against participating in the Tiananmen protests that commemorated the death of Zhou Enlai and criticized the extremism of the Cultural Revolution. According to a family friend, when Jinping, who did go to the square to take a look, saw his younger brother, he demanded that Yuanping leave so that no pictures of them could be taken.[7] Jinping's care was well justified—Tsinghua students who had brought wreaths to the square were declared "counter-revolutionary" elements, and as a result, the militia was sent to patrol the campus grounds. More than one hundred individuals were investigated.[8]

After the arrest of the Gang of Four in October 1976, mass rallies continued, though, this time, targeted against the gang. The situation had deteriorated so seriously that, in February 1979, the school leaders made a special decision regarding students who (like Xi) had entered the university in 1975—they would be allowed to graduate even if they failed more than two classes.[9] So-called worker-peasant-soldier students, like Jinping, who had relied upon their family backgrounds or personal recommendations for admission faced suspicion by a younger generation who had gained admission to their respective universities based on test scores.[10]

While in Guangdong, during inspection tours to Huiyang in August 1978 and Hainan Island in January 1979, Zhongxun brought Jinping along.[11] After graduating from Tsinghua in the spring of 1979, Jinping became secretary to Geng Biao, another case of a cadre offspring serving in such a role.[12] Xi

Zhongxun and Geng had known each other since 1936, when they served in the same region of eastern Gansu. Their families were so close that Zhongxun's children, except for Jinping, called Geng "Uncle Geng" and Geng's children called Zhongxun "Uncle Xi." Geng's daughter Yan also worked closely with Zhongxun. As an employee at the New China News Agency in Hong Kong, which, at the time, served as the China's informal embassy, before the handover, Geng Yan often stopped in Guangzhou, where she discussed Hong Kong affairs with Zhongxun.[13]

Ye Jianying probably played a role in Xi Jinping's appointment. Zhongxun, Jinping, and Ye were all in Hainan together in January 1979—shortly before Jinping began working for Geng. Ye and Geng were exceptionally close, and Ye had even tasked Geng with seizing control of the central radio and television stations in October 1976 when the Gang of Four was arrested.[14] One credible account suggests that it was Ye Xuanning, one of Ye Jianying's sons, who recommended that Jinping work for Geng and that Xuanning directly contacted Geng about the matter.[15]

Since Geng was secretary of the Central Military Commission, Jinping was forced to join the military to accept the position of confidential secretary. As Geng's secretary, Jinping had to memorize hundreds of phone numbers, but he occasionally cheated by sneaking into his own office and taking notes. To relax, he listened to the romantic, decidedly nonrevolutionary musician Teresa Teng. According to Geng's chauffeur, Jinping listened to Teresa Teng's "Small Town Story" so often that the recording broke.[16]

In 1982, Jinping left his job with Geng in Beijing for an assignment in Zhengding County of Hebei Province. Zhongxun clearly played a role in the decision. After a man named Cai Wenbin reported on the situation in Sichuan at a meeting in Xi's home, Zhongxun said to Jinping, "Look at how great your big brother Cai is doing. You should go to the grass roots too."[17] According to the memoirs of one well-connected individual working at a central research institute in Beijing, when Xi Zhongxun learned of plans to rapidly promote members of the younger generation, he summoned a family meeting at his home to tell them to take advantage of this situation by finding work at the county level.[18]

An American embassy contact, however, claimed that Jinping had concluded that "staying with Geng Biao would eventually shrink his power base, which would ultimately rest primarily on his father's and Geng's networks and political support."[19] Geng's official biographer provides yet another account: Jinping left because Geng had to cut the number of secretaries who worked for him. One of those secretaries was Geng's wife, and the other two had high ranks, so Jinping took the hint and offered to resign.[20]

Whatever really happened and whatever Jinping really thought, he would often depict his decision to go to the grass roots as an idealistic and unique choice. While working in Beijing, he often met with other cadre offspring who, like him, had also been sent-down youth. In Jinping's mind, many of these people developed a view that the tribulations that they had suffered justified making up for lost time and enjoying themselves. Although Jinping could understand this viewpoint at first, as time passed, he felt increasingly dissatisfied with such a worldview. He wanted to return to the grass roots for work to prevent the occurrence of another Cultural Revolution. After consulting with his father and other elders, he left for Hebei. Jinping felt sorrow, he said, when the other princelings, who only wanted to have fun, could not understand his choice. He claimed to have told them, "We must step forward! In the past, when the old generation came forth, they were enthusiastic and fervent. During the Cultural Revolution, when we were 'sent down,' that was forced upon us. The lack of alternatives forced us to learn and experience many things. Now everything is better. Those 'leftist' things that restricted us in the past have disappeared. Now, it is even more necessary than ever to struggle, to persist, to really do something big!"[21]

Jinping has suggested that Liu Shaoqi's son Liu Yuan was essentially the only other person who gave up the comforts of the capital or a life overseas to accept a low-level post.[22] Liu Yuan's choice was an interesting one. The Xi family had suffered greatly during the Cultural Revolution, but Liu's mother had been incarcerated for twelve years, one brother had committed suicide by laying on railroad tracks, and another brother died shortly after spending eight years in prison. While Xi Jinping wanted to go to Hebei, Liu Yuan decided to go to Henan, where his father—who had been sent there after poor treatment and whose mental stress had already put him in a vegetative state—died.[23]

Yet Liu Yuan did not feel wronged by the party; he felt he had unfinished business. "I enjoy great natural advantages, and that is because I have my father and mother's old comrades in arms. They, too, hope that the younger generation will do a few good things for the people and complete the mission that they did not have time to finish," Liu said. He admitted to undergoing a "period of extraordinarily intense pain" during the Cultural Revolution, when he was "the black son of a capitalist roader." After Mao's death, he was still treated unfairly but now for a different reason—because of his "princeling" status. He decided that he could not force anyone to understand him. "I can only use my own actions to win the trust of the people," so he decided to leave the capital for Henan.[24]

Xi was exaggerating when he said only a small number of people decided to pursue careers at the grass roots. In fact, so many young people went to the countryside to climb the political ranks that author Ke Yunlu wrote a novel about them.[25] At the same time, Xi's choice was not typical. Among his generation, many young people did indeed want to make up for the time they had lost during the Cultural Revolution by having fun, making money, or leaving China. According to one US Embassy contact, while some people "descended into the pursuit of romantic relationships, drink, movies and Western literature as a release from the hardships of the time," Jinping, by contrast, "chose to survive by becoming redder than red."[26]

HEBEI

Hebei had some advantages for Xi Jinping. It was close to Beijing, and his father, as part of his bailiwick on the secretariat, played a role overseeing personnel issues in the province. Yet Hebei was famous, at the time, for its factional politics, resistance to reform, and dissatisfied population. More people from Hebei were going to Beijing to complain about local officials than from any other province.[27] During the Cultural Revolution, 1.02 million people were falsely accused there.[28] In March 1979, Jiang Yizhen became second provincial secretary with the expectation that he would soon become party secretary. Jiang enthusiastically tried to reverse the wrongful verdicts and support reform, but his aggressive nature led to such poor relations with the rest of the Hebei leadership that, in December, Jin Ming took the top position instead. Li Erzhong joined the leadership in January of the next year as governor, forming a troika of Jiang, Jin, and Li.[29]

In May 1981, Jiang was summoned to a Hebei Party Standing Committee meeting, where he was subjected to criticism for more than twenty days. Each side in the debate then wrote letters to the top leadership complaining about the other side. Between July 9 and 15, 1981, the secretariat held a Hebei work meeting to address the continuing factionalism in the province. Several hundred party members from Hebei attended, a scale unseen for any other secretariat meeting that was held to discuss one province, thereby demonstrating the severity of the dysfunction.[30]

Hu Yaobang began the meeting by saying he had been shocked that the new arrivals in Hebei were getting along so poorly. He complained that Jiang Yizhen had too aggressively tried to punish people who had made mistakes during the Cultural Revolution. Xi Zhongxun told the Hebei leadership that "it is necessary to believe that the Central Committee manages affairs justly." He complained that matters had gotten so out of hand that counterrevolutionary posters calling for opposition to the Central Committee had appeared in at least three cities. He then demonstrated his characteristic focus on putting party interests above personal interests: "We are old comrades. If we do not unite, what kind of model is that for the people below us? I will say one thing: it is necessary to trust the Central Committee and stay in line. These are all big matters." He promised fair treatment fundamentally different from what had happened during the Cultural Revolution: "The current Central Committee will not make things up. It will be just. Yaobang spoke correctly, we will not beat each side fifty times. And we won't beat one side seventy times and the other side thirty times. The key is not to beat. What can never happen again is this: if a mistake is made, you can never stand up again." He made one of the greatest understatements of party life: "It is easy to make grudges but not easy to get rid of them." He warned, "Do not push the Central Committee into a corner." He also strongly emphasized the importance of inner-party democracy: "Both correct and incorrect things can be said. What was said in the secretariat yesterday can be overturned. As long as there is truth, do not worry about other people knocking it over.... The previous atmosphere of accusations has changed." Typically, he reminded the participants of the importance of the ability of party members to suffer: "For the good of the party, it is necessary to accept it when you are wronged. Among us comrades, there are a lot of this kind of person. Premier Zhou compromised on behalf of the general interest. He was able to defend a large number of people. You also suffered persecution. You must accept the lessons of the Cultural Revolution."[31] Although Jiang self-criticized for being too aggressive, Jin Ming and Li Erzhong were the main targets of the meeting, and several especially problematic old provincial standing committee members were removed.[32]

In January 1982, two months before Xi Jinping arrived to work in Hebei, party cadres in Feixiang County engineered a campaign to defeat a proreform official. They used drinking bouts, vote soliciting, anonymous big-character posters, and even threats to install a more conservative, factional figure. Feixiang was not the only difficult place to work in Hebei; before starting in Zhengding, Jinping had said he was also willing to work in Pingshan County but was told not to go there because the factions were (literally) throwing explosives at each other. The Feixiang County incident was so serious that it even caught the attention of Deng Xiaoping, who demanded an investigation. Jiang Yizhen used Feixiang to emphasize the importance of selecting new cadres who more closely matched the new direction of the party. Jinping was one of the young, educated individuals whom Jiang assigned to a county-leadership position for precisely this reason. Jinping was indebted. When Jiang died in 1994, Jinping, in a telegram, called him Uncle Jiang and his "old leader."[33]

Yet "Uncle Jiang" was removed almost as soon as Jinping arrived. In May 1982, two months after Jinping appeared in Zhengding, Hu Yaobang visited the province, where he was infuriated by continued infighting. "I did not expect that even now your problems have not been solved!" Hu said.[34] In June of that year, the secretariat decided to send Gao Yang, former minister of State Farms and Land Reclamation, to take charge of the province. The choice was unconventional—Gao was already retired and seventy-three years old, thus violating Central Committee policy of rejuvenating the provincial leaderships. But Gao was a trusted former subordinate of Deng Xiaoping, and the situation in Hebei was dire. On June 9, Xi Zhongxun officially told Gao the news that he would be transferred.[35] At a secretariat meeting on June 16, Hu Yaobang declared that Jin, Jiang, and Li would all leave their posts. When Jiang, furious at being replaced by a much older man, complained to Xi, Xi sympathized, but he could not change the decision.[36]

Despite the setback of losing Jiang, Jinping quickly revealed his usefulness. Zhengding was a poor county even though it exported massive amounts of grain. Along with another vice–party secretary, Jinping traveled to Beijing numerous times to complain about the overly burdensome state grain requisitions. In the early summer, the State Council sent an investigation group to the county, and by the fall, it had lowered Zhengding's yearly grain allocation from seventy-six million *jin* to forty-eight million *jin*—a major victory.[37]

In late 1982, He Zai, who had previously worked for Xi Zhongxun in the Northwest Bureau, traveled to Hebei as a member of an investigation group. He, director of the Cadre Review Bureau of the Organization Department and also the department's secretary, took several trips to Zhengding to get to know Jinping. On December 28, He Zai wrote a letter to Hu Yaobang about why Beijing should support low-ranking cadres to rejuvenate the party and specifically referred to Jinping: "After half a year of work, because of an ability to bear hardship and hard work and to reach the masses, he did a few important things. Not only was he praised by cadres and the masses, but the Organization Department is preparing to investigate his performance and promote him at the appropriate time." Two days later, Hu forwarded the letter to several other leaders and asked for a concrete plan to promote educated young people more systematically. In February 1983, He Zai again referred to Jinping when he wrote a second letter to Hu about rejuvenating the ranks:

> For example, the county party secretary in Zhengding, Xi Jinping, and the vice–party secretary in Beijing's Chaoyang District, Liu Yandong, are both recognized by the party, city, and region as "good sprouts" and "outstanding cadres who can be trusted." Some comrades suggest that they should be fully used. Although they were university students, they have already tumbled at the grass roots for seven or eight years, and they have demonstrated an ability to work with the masses. Although they are cadre offspring, they can work hard, are loyal to the party and are patriotic, study enthusiastically, and are good at uniting cadres.[38]

To make a name for himself, Xi Jinping settled on a project to attract "talent" to Zhengding. In early 1983, he traveled to the provincial capital of Shijiazhuang to find an engineer to help a local enterprise with a technology patent. By the time Jinping arrived, everyone had gone home from work, and Jinping did not know where the engineer lived, so he walked along the street in the middle of a snowstorm shouting the man's name.[39] Wang Jianxun, who grew up with Jinping and had also been sent down in Shaanxi, recalled a similar incident. When Jinping read a newspaper article about a chemist, he decided to seek the man's help to build a factory. When Wang and Xi arrived at the dormitory of the Chinese Medical University in Beijing's Zhongguancun District to find the chemist, they were not sure about his exact place of residence. So Jinping stood on their jeep's running board and repeatedly yelled the chemist's name. Someone shouted back at him, "People are taking naps. What the hell are you shouting about?" Wang Jianxun concluded at the time that Jinping was an individual desperate for quick success.[40]

Jinping understood the value of good publicity. He met with Li Naiyi, a journalist from *Hebei Daily* and said he wanted the provincial newspaper to report on the policy for attracting talent that he was preparing. After Li finished an article based on Xi's ideas, the journalist proposed that Xi first ask a subprovincial paper to publish it. When that local paper refused because some of Xi's proposals were considered sensitive, *Hebei Daily* went ahead with it and the article appeared on March 29, portraying Zhengding's "nine points on attracting talent" as a model.[41]

Jinping successfully brought other famous scholars, such as mathematician Hua Luogeng and economist Yu Guangyuan, to the county.[42] In February 1984, on a trip to Zhengding, Yu met with Jinping and proposed the establishment of what would become the Agricultural Research Institute. Jinping was very interested in the idea and sent his underlings to Beijing to meet with Yu. Progress was swift—less than two months later, the Zhengding County People's Government established a leading group. Three weeks after that, the Agricultural Research Institute was officially established. Yet the plan went nowhere. Yu later wrote, "In the beginning, this work proceeded extremely smoothly, and that was because county party secretary Xi Jinping actively supported it . . . but, unexpectedly, Xi Jinping was soon sent to Fujian to become vice-mayor of Xiamen. After the transfer, Zhengding County never contacted me again, and I no longer heard anything at all about the situation with the Agricultural Research Institute."[43]

In October 1983, Yan Huai—who worked for the Young Cadres Bureau of the Organization Department, an office created to identify and promote trustworthy young cadres—arrived in Shijiazhuang on an inspection trip. After his official assignment was over, he then traveled to Zhengding to make a report on Jinping. As Yan himself admitted, the trip was highly irregular. Li Rui, the head of the Youth Bureau, had personally told Yan to go to Zhengding and had named Jinping specifically—something Li had never done before. Jinping had much less experience than most individuals whom Yan usually reviewed. Yan suspected the reason for the trip was because of Jinping's father. However, he also believed that Li Rui was taking the initiative without a direct order from Zhongxun.[44]

Before and during the trip, Jinping was referred to as "secretary" of Zhengding, but Jinping did not actually assume that post officially until a month later—evidence of the party's cavalier attitude to formal procedures. It would be more than forty years before Yan learned that Jinping was technically not yet secretary.[45] According to a history of the county, Jinping's promotion was the result of a demand by the Hebei Party Committee to make the cadre corps more "revolutionary, young, educated, and professional." The average age of the members of the Zhengding Standing Committee was 41.7—five years younger than that of the previous standing committee—and 45 percent of them had a college education. Xi was only thirty years old.[46]

Yan took his visit very seriously. After meeting with a group of local cadres, he told them that if they had anything more to say about Jinping, they could visit his hotel room to talk off the record with no notes. When Yan met with Jinping individually, Yan provided the feedback he had gotten from Jinping's colleagues. Yan was impressed. Jinping had graduated from a university. He had deliberately asked for a lower position than what most cadres who left Beijing for the grass roots initially enjoyed. Moreover, Jinping did not request work in a nicer region. And Jinping was unusually accessible and open-minded. "Sticking your head in the ground won't make you rich," Jinping told Yan.[47]

Yan reported to Beijing that Jinping's experiences in Shaanxi had taught him to understand the problems with collectivization. Jinping believed that Zhengding should not focus exclusively on agriculture, and he supported the idea of building a mansion, based on the one described in the classic Chinese novel *Dream of a Red Chamber*, for both tourists and television companies. Yan noticed that, although most county leaders took buses when visiting the countryside, Jinping rode a bicycle. He ate in a cafeteria, and people even felt comfortable just walking into his office. He did not have the air of a princeling, and his style was friendly. Yet not everyone spoke highly of him. Since conservative party members still believed that grain should be Zhengding's priority, some people whom Yan interviewed said that Jinping was ignoring his proper duties. One individual complained that even though he was too young to grow facial hair, Jinping still dared to introduce harebrained schemes. Although Yan did not hide these criticisms in his report, he explained them away as the frustrations of older comrades with not much education who did not understand the party's proreform policies.[48]

In certain ways, 1983 was a good time for Jinping and other cadre offspring. Sometime that year, Chen Yun and Deng Xiaoping sent Wang Zhen to Hu Yaobang to stress the need to give special attention to the children of high-ranking officials. Hu, skeptical, suggested that cadre offspring not be allowed to rise to leading positions in a province or central ministry. Wang stressed that such a policy would be unfair to "terrific" candidates. Hu relented but only a little, suggesting that the party only promote the children of those cadres who had already died or retired to such high levels. But Wang was insistent. Finally, Hu fatefully agreed that each family would be allowed one child to rise to a top-ranking position in the provinces or Beijing.[49]

Yet it was that same year that dissatisfaction with cadre offspring as a group became particularly intense. A corruption crackdown revealed just how bad the situation had become. Hu, concerned about the growing anger among the population, proposed in December 1983 that the Central Committee release a special document to manage them. However, the members of the Young Cadres Bureau in the Organization Department could not agree whether this was a good idea.[50]

The cadre offspring were not only worried about their reputation because of corruption and nepotism among their ranks. They also feared that the new rectification campaign would target them for their behavior during the early months of the Cultural Revolution. Fearing punishment, in February 1984, two cadre offspring, including Kong Dan, the son of Kong Yuan (who was responsible for sending the cadres who persecuted Xi to Shaanxi in 1935), wrote a letter to Chen Yun complaining that the "old Red Guards" faced punishment as the three types of people. The speed of Chen's positive response, which came only four days later, raised suspicions that it had all been planned. At the time, Kong Dan was participating in a Philosophy Small Group with Chen Yuan, Chen Yun's son, as well as Chen's secretaries, including Zhu Jiamu (whose father, Zhu Lizhi, led the 1935 Shaanxi purge). Xi Zhongxun believed that the entire incident was "staged" by a "clique." Yan Huai found Chen's decision reprehensible—essentially, it meant that cadre offspring would get a free pass for violence because of their family relations.[51]

Li Rui decided to hold a discussion meeting with prominent children of the revolutionary generation on March 3, 1984. It was a remarkable moment in the party's history, revealing the dramatic extent to which the members of the "second Red generation" felt both pride and vulnerabilities in their position—emotions almost certainly shared by Jinping, although he was not present. Li Rui began by asking the group whether a special document was needed and if so, what it should say. Chen Yuan described the issue as a dilemma. "It is necessary to make the issue clear," he said, "but also not to slander." He asked plaintively when they could "remove the label of 'offspring of cadres.'" He stated, "If a class cannot grasp its own children well, then this class does not deserve to be called a ruling class."[52]

Another participant argued that "disseminating a document on the offspring of cadres is itself a case of preferential treatment." In his mind, "during the Cultural Revolution, we suffered a lot of pressure. At the time, it was an issue of survival. Now we still suffer from invisible pressure." Yu Xiaohong claimed that she had suffered precisely because her father was Yu Guangyuan, and, therefore, she always had to avoid something that could be interpreted as special treatment: "If you were to ask me to make a personal decision," she said, "I actually would not be willing to be the daughter of Yu Guangyuan and to be called a 'cadre offspring.'" Kong Dan complained about how he had commonly heard comments such as "This person's behavior is pretty good; they're not like a cadre offspring." Kong was blunt: "Now, with so many big issues, this document would really only create more chaos."[53]

Li Rui concluded the meeting by acknowledging that they all opposed a special document, and he agreed with them. However, he continued, "Perhaps it is because of blood ties; we care about the cadre offspring, both the good ones and the bad ones. Ultimately, we hope that they will fight to excel. Family influence still exists, especially in China. Of course, in the future, whether that will be true and to what extent is another matter. Family upbringing and family style exist objectively and cannot be denied."[54] In September, during a private conversation, Xi Zhongxun told Li that they held the same worried view on the question of "high cadre offspring," and they discussed two cases of nepotism that they both found distasteful.[55] Ten years later, Li Rui and Yan Huai recalled the March 1984 meeting with the princelings and concluded, "At the time, a document controlling the cadre offspring was truly necessary!"[56]

Yet sometimes a document was not necessary to arrest the ambitions of the cadre offspring. In 1983, Chen Yun strongly hinted to Jiang Zemin, then minister of Machine Building and Electronics Industries, that Chen Yuan should be given a job in Jiang's ministry. Jiang complained to Li Rui, and Li counseled Jiang to pretend he had not understood what Chen wanted.[57] Chen Yuan faced a similar situation in Beijing. After the party introduced a municipal voting system in which there were more candidates than seats, Chen Xitong, the mayor of the city, stated that everyone should vote for Chen Yuan for membership on the Beijing Party Committee since the Organization Department had already named him as vice–party secretary in charge of daily affairs. This act of nepotism was so unpopular that Chen Yuan failed to receive enough votes to join the Beijing Party Committee, either as a full member or even as a candidate member. One individual familiar with the incident wondered whether Chen Xitong had deliberately hurt Chen Yuan's chances by making such a statement.[58]

Despite these growing concerns about cadre offspring, Jinping continued to increase his visibility. In May, two months after the dramatic meeting chaired by Li Rui, he published an article in *China Youth*. It was a patriotic, nationalist screed about his love for Zhengding history from ancient times to the present, and it also included a description of the industrial- and agricultural-production improvements in the country since his arrival.[59] In June 1984, Jinping's name appeared for the first time in *People's Daily*. At that time, the editor of the paper was Qin Chuan, a northwesterner and a close associate of Xi Zhongxun. The article describes the "great changes" that took place in the county under Xi Jinping as it moved away from its status as a typical so-called high-yield, but poor, county. Through "commodity production," the province had achieved rapid growth, and the "roar of machinery" could be heard everywhere.[60]

Just a month later, in July 1984, a glowing portrait of Jinping appeared in *Hebei Youth*.[61] Jinping supported publication of this article, which depicted his devotion to the party and nation as the source of meaning in his life. Jinping saw the article as a response to the societal debates sparked in 1980 by a letter entitled "Why Is Life's Road Becoming Narrower and Narrower?" in *China Youth*. That letter had reflected the ennui that many young Chinese felt in the 1980s. "I am twenty-three this year," the letter's author wrote. "I should say that I am just beginning life, but all of life's mysteries and charms are gone for me already. I feel as if I have reached the end." While the letter described how the disillusionment caused by the trauma of the Cultural Revolution had led people to focus on their personal interests to make up for lost time, Jinping was portraying himself as someone "forged" and rededicated to the people by the experience.[62] In September, He Zai summoned ten county leaders to report to Beijing. Four of them came from Hebei, and one of them was Jinping. He Zai was allegedly impressed by Jinping's ability to think strategically. In his report on the meeting to Hu Yaobang, He Zai praised Jinping in particular as a "mainstay." When Hu Yaobang read the report, he underlined "mainstay" three times.[63]

But trouble was brewing in Beijing. Four individuals, including Deng

Liqun and Li Rui's ex-wife, wrote letters to Chen Yun complaining about Li Rui. When Chen Yun read them, he responded, "Since so many people are unhappy with Li Rui, it seems it would not be appropriate for him to remain in the Organization Department." It was Chen who had originally sent Li to the Organization Department to counter Hu Yaobang. Yet Li gave his loyalties to Hu instead, infuriating Chen, who used the letters as a weapon to remove Li. When Xi Zhongxun heard about what Chen Yun had done, he was upset, but it was too late for him to change Chen's decision. On September 17, Li Rui was told that he had to leave his position. The next day, during a three-hour conversation at Xi's home, Xi explained what had happened and blamed Chen. Li Rui told Xi Zhongxun that it had been Chen Yun who had sent him to the Organization Department in the first place. After their meeting, Xi arranged for Li Rui to officially leave the department, both as the result of Chen's notification *and* Li's own decision, and he commended Li's performance as head of the Youth Cadre Bureau.[64]

Soon after his dismissal, Li left for Shijiazhuang to present a lecture. Four days after Li arrived, on November 23, he visited Jinping in Zhengding together with Chen Zhiping, who, as vice-director of the Organization Department in Hebei, had established a provincial Young Cadres Bureau and was in charge of promoting rising officials. Li made no other such trips to visit a young official while in Hebei. Over lunch at a hotel, Li and Jinping had a long, detailed discussion about why party committees should be smaller and why they should focus more on big issues and not duplicate government functions.[65]

In December, Jinping published his first article in *People's Daily*: "Middle and Young Cadres Must 'Respect the Elderly,'" in which he argues that in feudal times, "respecting the elderly" was an idea manipulated by the "past dynastic feudal ruling class" to hide what was in actuality a history of brutal power struggles. The "laboring people," however, took the idea very seriously. Under socialism, "respecting the elderly" had lost its feudal connotations and had "added new societal content." Decades of revolution had created a generation whose dedication had made China's recent advances possible. Taking care of retired cadres, Jinping argued, should not be seen as a burden. That said, he argued that the new generation should not be bound to its ways, using an old expression meaning "blind ambition": "Of course, when advocating 'respecting the elderly,' that absolutely does not mean that middle and young cadres should only blindly mimic the old cadres, wholesale copy, or even draw a tiger with a cat as their model to adapt to some work forms and methods that are already outdated, daring not to go outside the limits by one step."[66]

By this point, there was clearly a concerted effort in the propaganda apparatus to boost Xi Jinping's image. The very next month, in January 1985, both *China Youth* and *Guangming Daily* published flattering reports about him. Jiang Feng, the author of the *China Youth* article, described Jinping's "rustic style" and praised his ability to manage older cadres who have less education. The most interesting content, however, are the quotes Jiang included that are attributed to Jia Dashan, a local author. "Here, you don't hear everyone shouting, 'Reform,'" Jia said, "but reform is everywhere." Jia described Jinping as a man without sharp elbows whose focus is practicality and results, not reform for reform's sake: "He is a reformer who does not wear Western-style clothes, and he forges ahead without acting aggressively. While persuading people to accept the historical necessity of reform, he can still leisurely have a drink of alcohol. This is a reformer who makes progress with a smile on his face." Xi Jinping was quoted as saying, "Reform is the wish of the Chinese people, and it is the 'great trend' in Chinese society, so individuals need not do anything deliberately shocking." Jinping cautioned that, "In the process of reform, it is necessary to study national characteristics, grasp the thinking of the masses, and avoid any destructive shocks. Otherwise, blind reform is just a romantic lyrical poem. In the worst case, it may even damage any endeavor."[67]

Yet, in the spring of 1985, Jinping's career suddenly hit a serious snag, and it was his father's fault. Zhongxun directly requested that Gao Yang help facilitate Jinping's career, which triggered a political scandal that forced Jinping out of the province. It was a remarkable mistake for Zhongxun—one that was uncharacteristic for him. Zhongxun could have hinted about what he wanted to Gao in partyspeak, which would have allowed him to deny he was actually asking for favoritism. But instead, Zhongxun was too obvious. It was so brazen that Gao complained about Zhongxun at a provincial party standing committee meeting. Zhongxun may have believed Gao would be more willing to help, perhaps because Zhongxun sent Gao to Hebei despite his advanced age. But there is a simpler possible explanation too. When asked how Zhongxun could have made such an error, Yan Huai surmised that Zhongxun "really loved his son a lot."[68] Another credible account suggests that Qi Xin, whose power within the family was formidable, pressured Zhongxun to act more forcefully to support Jinping.[69]

Gao's "bullish temper" surprised even Li Rui.[70] He Zai had to go to Hebei to get permission from Gao to let Jinping leave—a request that further upset Gao. Soon after returning from a trip to Iowa, Jinping went to take leave of Gao, and Gao treated him disdainfully. "You are a cadre managed by the party center," he said. "Don't talk to me."[71] When Jinping left for Fujian, He Zai escorted him to the airport himself and, while waiting for the plane, offered some advice. Jinping thanked him for the trust and support from the Organization Department. He reported for work in the port city of Xiamen on June 15—his thirty-second birthday. When his new secretary noticed that Jinping's face was red, Jinping explained, "Today is my birthday. I drank a bit of alcohol."[72]

FUJIAN

Two prominent cadre offspring already had positions in Xiamen. The previous December, Ye Xiaonan, the daughter of Ye Fei, a former party boss in Fujian, became vice-secretary, and An Li, who not only was the daughter of An Ziwen, former head of the Organization Department, but also was married to one of Hu Yaobang's sons, became a vice-mayor. Very soon after An Li assumed her position, she returned to Beijing because of poor health, although records show her serving as vice-mayor until February 1986.[73] Yan stated that the original plan was for Jinping to become head of Xiamen's Tourism Bureau, a position that had been empty since January 1985, which would have been another "neutral transfer." However, because of the issues with An, Jinping was instead given the position of vice-mayor.[74]

The propaganda apparatus kept Jinping's disgrace well hidden. In November 1985, *China Youth* published a hagiographic article about Jinping's time in Zhengding. It claimed that Jinping could talk about everything: literature, history, modern science, genetic engineering, renewable energy, ancient Zhengding history, and Buddhist art. When he had time, the authors wrote, he would go to Beijing to see Shakespeare and ballet. He was a modern man who was "really good at ballroom dancing" and wore a "well-ironed suit." "He is not the kind of county secretary who wears blue clothes and green canvas shoes in the style of the Eighth Route Army; he is a new model of a county-level leader at the forefront of the trend of the times."[75]

The party boss of Jinping's new province of Fujian, Xiang Nan, was the son of Xiang Yunian, who had a long history in the party's intelligence apparatuses and had spent time doing United Front work in both Guanzhong and Suide under the leadership of Xi Zhongxun. When Xiang Yunian died in 1978, Xi wrote in a memorial that they "were strongly connected by fate" and that Xiang was a "Communist warrior."[76] In 1982, Xiang Nan accompanied Xi Zhongxun on a trip to North Korea, where Xiang gave a report on reform in Fujian. On their return to Beijing, Xi and Xiang had a long chat during which they realized they had similar ideas on China's future. Xi was impressed that Xiang turned the gifts he had been given from the North Koreans over to the state.[77]

In 1983, Xi, along with Qi Xin and Qiaoqiao, visited Fujian for more than ten days on a Lunar New Year's vacation that clearly doubled as a work trip. Xi spoke out against local factionalism in words that echoed his previous comments to the Hebei leadership: "We are all working for the party's business and the people's business! As long as comrades who make mistakes acknowledge those mistakes and change, that is enough. Why is it necessary to have personal grudges? What kind of problems cannot be overcome?" When Xi returned to Beijing, he drafted a report to the central leadership in which he strongly praised Xiang personally and highlighted the economic and political achievements in the province, including a controversial Japanese investment project.[78] Privately, Xi would even say that Xiang did a better job in the special economic zones than Ren Zhongyi, his successor, had done in Guangdong.[79]

According to one account, Jinping had expressed some interest in moving to Guangdong, but when Li Rui casually mentioned Jinping's intentions to Xiang Nan during a meal in Beijing, Xiang said it would be better for Jinping to go to Fujian. Since Zhongxun had worked in Guangdong, Xiang Nan reasoned, that might create unforeseen difficulties for Jinping in case any grudges remained. Furthermore, Guangdong was still dominated by the Ye family, which would make it difficult to maneuver.[80]

Long before Jinping's arrival in Fujian, Xiang Nan's position was already precarious. Deng Xiaoping visited Fujian in February 1984 and strongly affirmed the party's commitment to the special economic zones. Yet only several months later, rumors began to spread that Beijing planned to remove Xiang.[81] Xi Zhongxun did his best to help him. In October of that year, at a celebration marking the 110th anniversary of the birth of Tan Kah Kee, a famous overseas businessman who had contributed to Fujian's development, Xi, who was sitting in the front row, looked around but could not find Xiang.

He waved over an official and asked where Xiang was. Thereafter, the man realized Xiang was in the second row. He brought a chair forward so Xiang could move to the front. When the festivities concluded, Xi was furious with the official. "You worked for so many years in the State Council—don't you know this guy is the *fumu guan* of Fujian?" using an old expression for "powerful leader." This official, who had worked for Xi in the 1950s as well, could not remember any other instance he had been scolded so severely by Xi.[82]

In late April 1985, in preparation for the upcoming Fujian party congress, Xi met with Hu Hong, the province's party secretary for daily affairs, and Ma Xingyuan, the head of its Central Advisory Commission Planning Committee. Ma complained that Xiang had rehabilitated too many former underground party members who had been persecuted prior to the reform era. When Ma refused to admit he had participated in dirty political tricks against Xiang, Xi accused him of encouraging Hu Ping, the governor, to make accusations against Xiang. Xi then severely criticized Ma's role in spreading rumors about Xiang's removal. Xi ended the meeting by affirming Xiang's work, and Xiang was reelected party boss at the subsequent congress.[83]

It was only a temporary victory. The opening salvo in the political attack that did finally cost Xiang his career appeared the day after Jinping arrived to work in Fujian. On June 16, 1985, an article appeared in *People's Daily* under the headline "The Shocking Case of Fujian Jinjiang Fake Medicine." Xiang was truly confused. The incident had not led to a single death. It had already been discovered and addressed. Why did Beijing suddenly make such a huge deal of the matter? On July 13, *People's Daily* published both an editorial and a New China News Agency article on Jinjiang. The next day, media organizations throughout China published an open letter from the Central Commission for Discipline Inspection to the Jinjiang leadership.[84]

Xi Zhongxun strongly opposed punishing Xiang. When a politburo member with a personal grudge against Xiang brought up an old accusation from 1958, when Xiang had worked in the Youth League, to prove that Xiang had always been a "rightist," Xi lost his temper. "Comrade Xiang Nan is from a house full of martyrs; he does not have the slightest selfish attitude toward the party!" In February 1986, Xiang went to Beijing for a meeting with the secretariat. Xi and Wan Li both praised Xiang's record, but the writing was on the wall—Xiang would not be allowed to remain in Fujian. Later that year, Wang Heshou, who worked for the Central Commission for Discipline Inspection, frankly admitted to Xiang that Chen Yun himself had come up with the deeply unfair verdict regarding the Jinjiang fake-medicine incident.[85]

The new party boss of Fujian, Chen Guangyi, was a close associate of Chen and allegedly disliked the young Xi Jinping.[86] Fujian became an even more difficult place to work in early 1987 when Wang Zhaoguo was fired from his job as head of the Party General Office for his allegedly close ties to Hu Yaobang and sent to Fujian to assume the position of governor. Chen Guangyi and Wang Zhaoguo feuded viciously with one another, with each continuously complaining to Beijing.[87]

These were certainly troubling developments, but Jinping was still making new contacts. In October 1985, he was part of a delegation to France, and in February 1988, he traveled to Australia with Huang Ju, vice-mayor of Shanghai, and Wei Fuhai, mayor of Dalian.[88] While in Australia, Wei and Huang did not get along—Wei refused to travel in the same car as Huang, and Huang treated Wei like a "hick." Xi, who was very quiet the entire time, used the experience to "brownnose" Huang, never leaving his side.[89]

In mid-1988, Jinping became the party secretary of Fujian's Ningde region, a particularly poor area. By his own account, the assignment was a frustrating one. Local cadres talked about him as someone who could use his connections as the son of a top-ranking leader to push for rapid development and big projects. "This kind of introduction really makes me afraid," Jinping told a friend. Rumors spread that he only dared to attack corruption so aggressively because of his father's support. When a journalist asked Jinping if he relied on family ties, Jinping responded, "It can't be said that there is absolutely no connection, but it also can't be said that I completely rely on my father to eat. It should be honestly said that currently there is still no complete system for selecting cadres. It is easy for people who are close to leaders, whom leaders know, to be quickly promoted. It is necessary to tell you all, my first position as an 'official' was a secretary in a village; at the time, my father's verdict had still not been reversed."[90]

HOME LIFE IN THE 1980s

National politics and family life mixed in another way as well—one of Xi Zhongxun's bailiwicks on the secretariat was women's issues. He personally approved the construction of a new building for the All-China Women's Federation. According to Zhang Guoying, who held high-ranking positions in the Women's Federation throughout the 1980s, "I always received the love and care of Comrade Zhongxun and Big Sister Qi Xin. When problems came up, they always gave help and support."[91]

On May 17, 1982, Xi gave the keynote at the Fourth Session of the Enlarged Executive Committee of the Fourth Nationwide Women's Congress. He believed a core task for women was the raising of children, and he spoke of a major notification by the secretariat in February of the previous year, *Document No. 19*, which instructed the Women's Federation to improve its role in the upbringing of China's youth. This notification, according to Xi, "greatly strengthens leadership toward children, young adults, and women's work." He explicitly stated that children should be the Women's Federation's top priority. Yet Xi also complained that the number of women in leadership positions was actually declining and that some people were worried the situation was becoming worse. He described the problems faced by China's women and children: "Currently, women and children are abused. The problems of tyrannizing and persecuting are extremely severe; terrible incidents continue to occur. Feudal chauvinism and customs continue to cause problems in people's heads. Husbands and mothers-in-law often discriminate against women, treat each woman coldly, or scold and beat women who give birth to a girl. Baby girls are often drowned." But feudal traditions were not the only problem: "Currently, some young women workers lack great ideals and a correct worldview," he said. "And therefore, in the three areas of love, marriage, and family, many problems are appearing." Xi criticized women who only wanted to marry men from overseas and have big houses or many home appliances: "They pursue money and material enjoyment. They carelessly marry and carelessly divorce."[92]

Little is known about Xi Zhongxun's views on the One-Child Policy, which limited each Chinese family to one child and was highly controversial and opposed by the Women's Federation.[93] He seems to have found the forceful elements of the policy distasteful. On a trip to his home county of Fuping in 1984, he said, "The population must be controlled, but we should be careful about that and not use any coercive measures. Discuss with the masses. The masses understand reason. Two of my daughters have only one child."[94]

Zhongxun's own wife, Qi Xin, assumed a handful of significant positions in Beijing in the early 1980s. In 1981, she became director of the Department of Supervision of the State Personnel Bureau, and by the end of the year, she had assumed the position of vice-head of the Central Commission for Discipline Inspection's Seventh Office, which was responsible for East China. In 1983, she started serving as deputy chief of the Retired Cadre Bureau of the Ministry of Labor and Personnel. In the spring of 1984, she started to work as her husband's secretary, a position she held for the remainder of his life.[95] Throughout the 1980s, her most prominent contribution was to help Xi manage cultural affairs. According to He Jingzhi, who worked in the Department of Propaganda, Qi Xin often worked as a courier.[96] Wu Zuguang, a playwright, wrote in his memoirs that Qi Xin "was a very enthusiastic fan who paid close attention to the art of plays" and often appeared at shows.[97]

Despite Zhongxun's criticism of divorce, Jinping's first marriage ended in failure. His first wife was a fellow "second Red generation": Ke Xiaoming, the daughter of Ke Hua, who had served in the Department of Propaganda of the Northwest Bureau in the 1940s and as director of Public Security Department in Xi'an in 1949.[98] After their marriage, Jinping and Ke Xiaoming lived first with Zhongxun and Qi Xin in the Nanshagou housing compound in Beijing, according to a cable from the American embassy. Despite their revolutionary pedigrees and their fathers' friendship, Jinping and Xiaoming did not make a good match. They constantly fought and eventually drifted apart.[99] The Ke family seemed to be more cosmopolitan. One witness recalled seeing Ke show off her new socks to Jinping and his sisters at the Jingxi Hotel in 1979. Ke finally left for England, where her father was ambassador, and Jinping remained behind to work at the party grass roots.[100]

Close ties with the Xi family did not save Ke Hua from an ignominious end to his career. In late 1982 or in the spring of 1983, shortly after Xi Jinping divorced Ke's daughter, Xi Zhongxun told Ke that after his post as ambassador to the United Kingdom ended, Ke would lead the New China News Agency in Hong Kong. When the politburo discussed Ke's assignment, some noted that there had been letters complaining about him. Although the politburo still approved of Ke's nomination, soon after the meeting, Ke was suddenly told that he was too old for the position. According to new regulations, first secretaries could be no older than sixty-five. Several days later, Xi met with Ke to provide more details about what had happened. Hu Yaobang had been overseas during the politburo meeting, and when he returned, he made three decisions: first, Ke, at sixty-seven years old, was over the age limit; cadres sent to Hong Kong should understand science and culture; and the nominee should be able to work in Hong Kong until 1997. Xi praised Hu for making the right decision. Yet the person sent in Ke's stead, Xu Jiatun, was also sixty-seven, and he had even less formal education than Ke. Ke decided that Xi had lied to him; it had to be the letters of complaint about him that sunk the nomination. Ke instead became an advisor to the Hong Kong and Macau Affairs Office. Xi tried to console him: "As an advisor, you are under one person but above everyone else."[101]

Jinping remarried in September 1987—this time not to a daughter of a compatriot of his father but to a famous folk singer and member of the People's Liberation Army, Peng Liyuan. At first glance, it was an odd pair. When a friend introduced them in early 1986, Peng thought Jinping not only looked like a bumpkin but also gave off the air of an old man. She was surprised when she later learned that he was only thirty-three years old. She wanted to cancel their first date as soon as she saw him, and she only stayed because her friend had strategically promised to meet her an hour later so that Peng would not leave early. She had originally believed she would never, under any circumstances, marry someone involved in politics, as she was completely uninterested in the subject and did not understand it.[102] Additionally, both their parents initially opposed the match but for different reasons. Peng's family believed that all princelings were playboys and feared that Peng would be treated unfairly.[103] Qi Xin, on the other hand, was concerned that Jinping was sacrificing the career for which he had worked so hard for personal, emotional reasons.[104]

Yet powerful similarities between Peng Liyuan and Xi Jinping pulled them together—they both had seen their families suffer horrendously during the Cultural Revolution, and yet they both had decided to pursue the same careers as their parents. Peng was born in 1962 in Shandong, shortly after the Great Leap Forward had devastated the province, to Peng Longkun, the head of a county cultural center and an amateur singer, and Li Xiuying, who was a renowned performer in the county Chinese opera troupe. When the Cultural Revolution started four years later, Peng Longkun was expelled from the party and confined in a cowshed. Li Xiuying's parents had been landlords, and her older brother had fled to Taiwan in 1949. She was subjected to struggle sessions and exiled to the countryside. Since traditional Chinese operas were banned during the Cultural Revolution, she changed her career entirely and became a worker at a food company. According to a short biography of Peng Liyuan published in 1984, "the political persecution and constraints" caused her mother to experience "great devastation" to her emotional state.[105]

Other children refused to play with Peng Liyuan when she was a little girl, even calling her the "fawn of a landlord." With little to no income, the family went hungry. Peng believed, "My current success is connected to the suffering I experienced as a child. Without that suffering, I would never be able to exert myself so fiercely." She was sent to live with her grandmother, a peasant who taught her how to sew. Her grandmother tried to convince her not to pursue a career in music, reminding her what had happened to her mother and father. Years later, when Peng's parents were allowed to return home, they worried that allowing Peng to pursue her dream would be dangerous. Yet their political status made a successful career for Peng at the time unthinkable anyway. On one occasion, when she applied to attend school in the provincial capital, although she had scored well on the admissions tests, when her background was investigated, her name was struck from the list. She tried again later, and after six months of investigation, she was finally admitted in 1978—although her father had not yet been rehabilitated.[106]

As a student, Peng made an unconventional choice. Hong Kong and Taiwan pop songs were sweeping the nation, but she wanted to study patriotic folk music even though she was told that there was no future in the genre. For three years, she studied seven days a week, refusing to stop working even when she was too sick to eat.[107] In 1980, at eighteen years old, she joined the People's Liberation Army and was subject to military discipline. Only several days after she had enlisted, to her great surprise, she was ordered to perform for soldiers on the border with Vietnam.[108]

In a way, her behavior roughly reflected Jinping's own decision to devote his life to his career while other young people were simply trying to live for themselves. According to Peng, "He is very strict with himself. He is dedicated to his work and willing to suffer. Many of his fellow classmates went overseas to make money; it was not that he was unable to go overseas, but he selected a difficult path—the path of serving the people. Therefore, I not only love him, one can say that I worship him."[109] During a television interview in 1999, she would say that she married Jinping because he was someone great enough to "dominate my emotions and thinking."[110]

Peng Liyuan became extraordinarily famous in 1982 during the first televised New Year's Gala with a song that included a lyric about generations of struggle for happiness and glory. Yet Peng did not feel as if her own life of struggle had finally concluded. An article she wrote in 1985 revealed a deeply unhappy individual. "As for me, I am a bit famous. But what came in the wake of fame is only unspeakable difficulties and troubles," she wrote. "People who do not understand my situation always think that I put on airs and that I am conceited, but I truly have challenges that are difficult to describe." Peng tried to suggest that rumors did not affect her: "That's OK; I am a person with a sunny disposition, otherwise I would spend all my days crying." But journalists did bother her. She loathed their "lies" and "empty talk," and she hated how they kept asking her about her life, family, interests, and love life. She concluded the article by asserting a disdain for materialism: "The truth is that wealth does not really have any attraction for me. Wealth can buy material things, but it cannot buy art. I am someone who pursues art."[111]

Family legacy, soaring ambition, patriotism, a fetishization of suffering, discipline, a stated lack of interest in materialism—the collection of shared values between Xi Jinping and Peng Liyuan is striking. A biography of Peng published in 1992 asserted that "from their very first meeting, she could innately understand that they were rooted together in painful hardship." Jinping would later tell Peng that he had decided after only forty minutes that she would be his wife. At the end of their second meeting, he gave her his business card and said, "We have both suffered a great deal. However, we have maintained our original purity and benevolence. We have both escaped our status as ugly ducklings. I hope we can see each other again." She was shocked to see written on his business card that he was vice-mayor of Xiamen—he still had not told her.[112]

First it was necessary to convince their parents. Jinping told Liyuan to tell her mother and father that "my father is the son of a peasant. He is modest and unassuming. All the children in my family matched with the children of regular people. Moreover, family will not be with us forever. I will explain clearly to your parents, and they will accept me."[113] Peng, on the other hand, stressed with her future in-laws that she was no diva. On one occasion, Qi Xin suddenly embraced Liyuan and said emotionally, "Liyuan, I am so sorry; in the past, I wrongly blamed you. I like your simplicity and kindness. Please do not be angry with me."[114] When Zhongxun was asked what he thought of Peng, he replied, "She told Jinping to focus on doing his work well—'for raising the family, there is me'—that is great, really great."[115]

Qi Xin's worries that love would hurt Jinping's future proved unfounded as Jinping and Liyuan would spend very little time together in subsequent years while they each focused on their careers. Jinping even missed the birth of his daughter in 1992.[116]

People who worked for the Xi family later asserted that although Jinping was Xi's favorite son, Qiaoqiao was his favorite daughter.[117] Like Jinping, Qiaoqiao's first marriage was a failed one to a cadre offspring.[118] Also like Jinping, her father's connections would a play key role at important moments in her early career. Qiaoqiao escaped from the horrors of the construction corps in Inner Mongolia when the daughter of Ulanhu arranged a transfer for her. Because Xi Zhongxun's move to Guangdong in 1978 was so rushed, the party leadership decided to send Qiaoqiao along with him as a secretary. While Qiaoqiao was working in Guangdong and she had an opportunity to study overseas, her father convinced her not to go. He reasoned that he had just been rehabilitated and that her leaving the country would create a poor impression.[119]

Ye Jianying arranged for Qiaoqiao to study at the First Military Medicine University, part of the People's Liberation Army, but she was forced to end her studies for health reasons. After recuperating, she began to work in the Liaison Bureau of the Guangzhou Military Region, probably with the help of her father. Her primary responsibility was to carry out "political work" on Vietnamese prisoners of war and convince them to support China. Qiaoqiao later claimed that the prisoners of war were so moved by how they were treated that "they cried and did not want to be released."[120]

After Xi Zhongxun returned to work in the capital, Qiaoqiao transferred to the military's Capital Construction Engineers and studied at China Foreign Affairs University. She then worked as vice-chairwoman in the office of the People's Armed Police Headquarters and as director of its Foreign Affairs Office. He Jiesheng, one of He Long's daughters, also worked with the People's Armed Police and was married to the commissar of the organization. He Jiesheng later wrote that when Qiaoqiao worked with the People's Armed Police, she and her husband had treated Qiaoqiao as one of their own children.[121]

In their writings about their father, Zhongxun's other children often betrayed a sense of frustration that he not only refused to help but actively worked to sabotage their careers. Before his daughter An'an married, he told her, "From now on, you must understand how to respect your husband, you must be filial to your mother-in-law, and you must be a good wife who is industrious in managing the household."[122] Zhengning, Zhongxun's eldest son, worked for thirteen years in a Shaanxi ravine largely because of his father's status as a fallen leader. In 1978, Zhengning was hired by the General Logistics Academy in Beijing, but his father did not allow the transfer. Xi believed that the optics would be bad since he had just returned to work. He made this decision without even discussing it with his son, and Zhengning never had another chance to return to the capital.[123] Even so, Zhengning climbed the government ranks in the family's home province, according to organizational histories. Between 1987 and 1990, he was one of four vice-directors of the provincial Organization Department, after which he became the sole vice-secretary of the provincial Political and Legal Affairs Committee. He also served as director of the Social Security Comprehensive Management Committee, which ran security affairs.[124]

When Qianping was given a job offer by Guangda Company, Xi told her not to take it. Qianping was upset and told her father that she had studied foreign languages and wanted to contribute to China's reform. But Xi was adamant. "You are the daughter of Xi Zhongxun," he lectured her. "You must keep your tail between your legs." Later, during a meal, when Xi learned that Qianping had traveled overseas for her work as a reporter, he demanded that she explain herself. When she said that leaving China was a requirement for her job, he stood up and threw down his chopsticks. "How can it be possible to have so many work demands like that!" he yelled. "You cannot justify any behavior by saying it is for work!" Xi did not calm down until she promised not to leave China again.[125]

22
THE UNITED FRONT RESTORED AND RESTRAINED

In 1985, Xi Zhongxun visited Wu Yifang—one of the great Chinese educators of the twentieth century—on her death bed. A Christian who never joined the party, Wu had served as president of Ginling College and, as a diplomat, was one of only four women to sign the United Nations Charter in San Francisco. One individual present during the visit watched in surprise as Xi, an old United Front hand, continued talking with Wu for half an hour even though she was already in a vegetative state.[1] In early 1986, Xu Deheng, another prominent nonparty official, entered the hospital, where, for the next four years, Xi regularly visited him. When Xu said he felt guilty about so many people taking care of him, Xi said to him, "Old Xu, if you live to a hundred years, that would be the biggest contribution to the party."[2]

As these anecdotes reveal, Xi Zhongxun was someone who took United Front policies very seriously. In part due to his ability to charm but also because of his experiences with United Front work both before and after 1949, in the 1980s, Xi was an unsurprising choice to become the party's highest-ranking liaison to nonparty communities both within the mainland as well as the diaspora. This was a sensitive and difficult task as Mao had essentially destroyed United Front work, even blaming the party's alleged failures on Xi Zhongxun and Li Weihan.

The long and slow reconstruction of the United Front began in 1979 while Xi was still in Guangdong. In March of that year, the Central Committee declared that ministries doing United Front, ethnic, and religious work had not, in fact, executed "surrenderism" or "revisionism" before the Cultural Revolution. In June 1979, Deng Xiaoping gave a speech in which he said the United Front should rally "all positive forces" for modernization, and, in August of that year, the party finally held the Fourteenth National United Front Work Meeting—the first such event since 1963.[3] By the time Xi arrived in Beijing, more than five hundred thousand "rightists" saw verdicts against them reversed. But much work remained to be done. Many party members were still convinced that the United Front was a waste of time. Cadres assigned to United Front work still feared they were vulnerable to charges of being "rightists." Solving these problems was a daunting task—Xi would acknowledge that he spent 70 or 80 percent of his effort and time on the United Front during this period.[4]

Along with Hu Yaobang, Xi was the leading figure at the Fifteenth National United Front Work Conference from December 21, 1981, to January 6, 1982. The participants determined that "leftist" thinking was still the "main tendency." Even "some leading comrades" lacked a "United Front mindset" and saw the department's work as "troublesome" and "unnecessary."[5] In his speech to the work conference on January 5, Hu acknowledged that there were those who felt that the party had gone "too far" to restore the United Front, but he insisted the opposite was true. The policies had not been emphasized enough.[6] In his own remarks, Xi argued that the party's mistakes predated the Cultural Revolution—the problems went back to the antirightist crackdown in 1957. He reminded the audience that this was a personal issue for him. "Premier Zhou assigned me many tasks," he said. "He regularly had me contact friends from outside the party." He also noted that many United Front targets had suffered even worse than the party cadres during the Cultural Revolution: "This counts as having gone through a severe test. This much must be affirmed."[7]

The party had to fully rehabilitate these long-suffering individuals. In a September 1983 letter, Hu Yaobang noted the extraordinary difficulties of the process and assigned Xi to the task. "Grasping this issue requires the greatest practical spirit and the greatest boldness, and you can truly meet this challenge," Hu wrote to Xi.[8] Xi moved swiftly. He sent eight investigation teams to spend a month traveling throughout the country. At a meeting in December 1983, Xi said that the teams were "a vivid reflection of the cooperation between party and nonparty people and the spirit of treating each other with all sincerity."[9] Yet some party officials were not taking the matter seriously, and some cadres even drafted false reports to resist the policy. Xi asked whether it would be a big problem if a leading party cadre had taken someone's wristwatch during the Cultural Revolution. "I think this is absolutely not a small matter," Xi answered himself, continuing, "Some of our party members and party cadres took someone else's watch or other possession, but they are at ease, and they act like nothing happened. If it were me, I would not be able to sleep. I would hurry over and return the watch; if the watch was broken, I would give them a new one." Xi suggested that if party members returned such possessions on their own volition, they would not be punished. Otherwise, they would be treated according to the law.[10]

But the party not only had to resolve the matter of stolen watches. Theoretical questions about United Front work had yet to be resolved as well. Between February 2 and 12, 1985, Xi held an extraordinary meeting with 221 participants, including nonparty individuals, from around the country to discuss the United Front as a concept—the very first such meeting ever held. On the opening day, Xi said United Front work must serve the three missions of economic reform, national reunification, and opposing hegemonism while protecting world peace. He admitted that efforts thus far could boast of significant achievements, but he identified three problems. First, "leftist" thinking still had yet to be eliminated: "Now, many comrades, including comrades in the United Front Work Department, are not willing to consult with nonparty individuals, they do not listen to the opinions and criticisms of nonparty individuals, or they adopt an attitude of going through the motions, they do not have heart-to-heart discussions, and they even act in a domineering fashion, tyrannically abusing their power, and they suppress different opinions."[11]

Second, those engaged in United Front work were not adequately managing personnel issues, like rehabilitation and employment with regard to nonparty officials. Finally, organizationally, the United Front departments at different levels "do not understand United Front policies." He went on, "Their thinking is stagnant. Foolish and ignorant people are still in high-ranking positions, where they do not do what they are assigned, and they have few triumphs and numerous failures." Xi railed against ossified thinking: "We must continuously overcome dogmatism and empiricism, but especially dogmatism. Because comrades with this way of thinking continuously separate theory from practice, they turn theory into something empty and dead. They can only mechanically repeat from memory and simplistically repeat Marxist-Leninist principles and phrases to evaluate practices that have already been developed; they can only 'conform to convention,' and they do not dare go beyond established limits." In his mind, theoretical debate had suffered not only from leftist thinking but also from "some crude methods that violate academic democracy." He said, "It must be seen that for more than thirty years, and especially during the Cultural Revolution, every area was constrained by 'leftist' thinking without us realizing it. Moreover, the thinking and habits left behind by several centuries of feudal society are still having an effect on our brains." To overcome such problems, Xi called for "free discussion with different opinions" under the guidance of Marxism-Leninism and Mao Zedong thought: "Even if someone goes too far and says something wrong, they should not be casually given a 'label' like 'incorrect position,' 'political mistake,' 'not in line with the Central Committee,' 'does not maintain the Four Cardinal Principles,' and so on. With regard to mistakes in thinking or even political mistakes, we must proceed from hopes of unity and use criticism and self-criticism to achieve a new unity."[12] And, indeed, the discussions were frank and broad. They argued about whether "one country, two systems" ever existed in China's past and if the conservative Four Cardinal Principles formulation should be treated as the basis for United Front work. Even economic issues were on the table, and the participants also raised the question of whether the phrase "Religion is the opium of the masses" should still be used.[13]

Xi took seriously the work of listening to opinions from nonparty figures about the party's general direction. On March 22, 1986, he chaired a meeting with nonparty leaders to discuss the upcoming National People's Congress and Chinese People's Political Consultative Conference. Between September 1 and 6, more than two hundred nonparty individuals held a meeting to discuss the draft of a decision on spiritual civilization that was to be passed at the upcoming Sixth Plenum of the Twelfth Party Congress. On the first day of the September session, at the Great Hall of the People, Xi addressed the group: "In the last few years, due to the close cooperation between our party and the democratic parties and dignitaries with different backgrounds, we have formed a habit of every time our party is going to hold an important meeting and make an important decision, a discussion meeting like this one is held beforehand to inform people of the relevant situation and to engage in discussion and consultation on the relevant issues."[14]

Xi led the efforts to hold the largest United Front work meeting since the Cultural Revolution: the Sixteenth National United Front Work Meeting, held between November 27 and December 4, 1986. The participants declared that Reform and Opening had created many new types of people who could participate in the United Front. In the future, the United Front should dare to cross social systems as well as different ideologies and lifestyles. In terms of work style, the correct methods were guidance, convincing, attracting, dialogue, and "warm patience." The United Front was given enormous tasks: national reunification, supporting reform, and "multiparty cooperation" under the party's leadership. For the first time, nonparty officials were allowed to attend such an event.[15]

On December 3, 1986, Xi again returned to the topic of non-Communist parties. He said, "Each of the democratic parties has its own characteristics and represents the interests of a certain social status or social group. They should exist for a long time under the socialist system." He then returned to the idea that lay at the core of Mao's 1957 failed plan to use nonparty officials to prevent the Communists from degrading into a bureaucratic class: "Leaders within the Communist Party should subject themselves to the supervision of the non-communists. They should study carefully their criticisms and suggestions, adopt the correct ones while giving honest answers to others." Xi said this would be an important way to "overcome bureaucracy, set the party's style to right and improve the efficiency of the party and the government."[16]

Xi was a powerful patron to Yan Mingfu, head of the United Front Work Department from 1985 to 1989, who adopted a liberal attitude toward the "democratic parties." Yan had spent most of his career as a translator and, after the Cultural Revolution, helped edit an encyclopedia. He then briefly served as vice-secretary of the National People's Congress Standing Committee. Therefore, his background had little with which he could impress high-ranking leaders. According to Tao Siliang, a United Front cadre and the daughter of a prominent revolutionary, Yan "could not win over many people" because of his weak résumé. "People who disagreed with his way of thinking and methods were even more numerous," she went on. "Some people wrote anonymous letters to complain about him." Xi's support turned out to be essential: "Because of this situation, if not for his direct superior—the good care and protection from the kind and generous Xi Zhongxun—even if Yan Mingfu had much more ability, in such a complicated place as China's officialdom, it would have been difficult to take even an inch forward."[17]

THE UNITED FRONT'S SLOW COLLAPSE

By the end of the decade, the problem was no longer how to keep moving forward inch by inch; it was how to stop the party from moving backward in giant leaps. Hu Yaobang's removal from office in January 1987 raised questions about whether the new United Front approach would be reversed entirely. In March, the United Front Work Department released a document warning that "personnel changes in the Central Committee" had created doubts among "comrades inside and outside the party" that policies would change. To counter that sentiment, the document emphasized that struggle against bourgeois liberalization would be limited to inside the party. United Front workers were informed that Hu's fall "will not change our guidelines and policies but, in fact, will mean the party's guidelines and policies will be executed better." However, the document included new warning signs. The struggle against bourgeois liberalization was "directly related to the future and the fate of the patriotic United Front." Moreover, the document emphasized, the party was the "leading core," and the basis for United Front work in the mainland was still socialism.[18]

Although the more liberal guidelines narrowly survived the removal of Hu Yaobang, the June 4 crackdown in 1989 was a much more serious challenge. Key nonparty leaders tried to reverse the martial law decision.[19] That behavior led to conclusions that United Front work had gone too far in terms of empowering individuals who had questionable loyalties to party leadership. In his memoirs, Hu Zhi'an, a high-ranking figure within the United Front Work Department, wrote, "Some people even said the 'turmoil' was 'united out' by the United Front Work Department. In 1991, several ministries were making a biographical dictionary, and when collecting specific entries, a bureau head at a certain ministry fought with me—that guy stirred up a hornet's nest, his face went dark, and he shouted, 'It was you in United Front, United Front! You "united" to destroy the party's principles, "united" to destroy the party's style, "united" the nation into chaos, "united" out a turbulence!'"[20]

And, indeed, although documents on United Front work after June 4 never explicitly rejected the policies introduced during the 1980s under Xi's leadership, they very clearly pushed the United Front in a new direction. In December 1989, the Central Committee wrote an opinion that laid new emphasis on the party's essential primacy over the nonparty activity it permitted: "Our nation's multiparty cooperation must maintain the leadership of the party, and it must maintain the Four Cardinal Principles. This is the political basis for cooperation between the party and the democratic parties. Party leadership over the democratic parties is political leadership, which includes political principles, political direction, and major guidelines and policies."[21] In June 1990, Jiang Zemin said the party would only "unite" if such a relationship helped "defeat the infiltration, subversion, and peaceful evolution of domestic and foreign enemy forces." He even emphasized the importance of opposing the "accommodationist attitude."[22]

History had repeated itself. In the 1950s, Xi presided over a conducive environment for United Front targets, but then he was blamed when those individuals allegedly grew too aggressive. In the 1980s, Xi led a liberalization of United Front policies and pointed to the 1950s as a golden era—and just as before, the approach ended with a view that co-optation encouraged resistance. The party had once again failed to resolve a fundamental question at the heart of its governance model—how to empower potential allies and include them in governance without giving up control.

THE CHINESE DIASPORA

The United Front did not just target Chinese at home. During the 1980s, it had an international agenda. Like other areas of the United Front, however, it faced an uphill challenge. During the Cultural Revolution, individuals with relatives overseas and returned Chinese were targeted for persecution, and most of their properties were confiscated.[23] Given the number of Chinese with Guangdong ancestry throughout the world, addressing that legacy had been one of Xi's priorities while still leading that province. In March 1979, the Guangdong leadership decided that most members of the diaspora were patriotic and that those who had been punished during the Cultural Revolution were to be rehabilitated—a number that reached 14,271 people.[24] Yet even as late as 1981, Hu Yaobang complained that party members had trouble getting along with visiting foreign Chinese because of their colorful clothes and blue jeans.[25]

In April 1984, Xi laid the foundation for the future direction of Beijing's relationship with overseas Chinese, emphasizing that the most important task was to overcome the party's outdated attitudes. Although many overseas Chinese had supported the civil war against the Nationalists, after 1949, returned Chinese and the families of overseas Chinese suffered because of "political campaigns that came one after another," he said. Despite some progress, "leftism" continued to hamper closer ties: "Many comrades lack a clear understanding of the importance of overseas-Chinese work even today. In their work, the first thing they think of is always something like 'foreign connections,' 'unclear ties,' 'complicated backgrounds,' and other so-called problems." Yet Xi understood the benefits of engaging with overseas Chinese and tried to spell them out: "Not a single country in the whole world has as many nationals and individuals with that country's blood living abroad, and there are not as many returned nationals and relatives of nationals living abroad. This is a special characteristic of our country." Xi went on to appeal to the nation's deep shared history, citing two legendary emperors: "No matter whether they are Chinese nationals or Chinese who have adopted the citizenship of another nation, they are all descendants of Yandi and Huangdi." Overseas Chinese could serve as a crucial source of investment. To convince them of the seriousness of Beijing's position, however, much work remained to be done. "Anything that damages the legal interests of Chinese compatriots and hurts or suppresses the concept or enthusiasm for love of nation and home of the overseas compatriots is incorrect. It violates the guidelines and policies of the national constitution and the party." Xi was sensitive to the difference between Chinese nationals living overseas and Chinese with foreign citizenship:

> It is necessary to avoid two tendencies. The first is to see Chinese with foreign citizenship and overseas Chinese nationals in exactly the same way and to ignore different citizenships, thus causing Chinese with foreign citizenship to feel uncomfortable, creating doubt and concern in the country where they live and giving them difficulties where they have long lived. The second is to see Chinese with foreign citizenship and other foreigners in exactly the same way, thereby not paying attention to the former and not doing the work that can be done. . . . Some things should be done more and said less; some things should be done but not said. It is imperative that we not make mistakes that people can use against us.[26]

TAIWAN

The United Front's most ambitious overseas goal was unification with Taiwan, and Xi led those efforts too. Taiwanese people were not always entirely sure what to make of Xi. When Huang Shun-hsing, a Taiwanese citizen who would join the National People's Congress as a delegate in 1988, met

Xi for the first time at a banquet, Xi seemed to him like "a bumpkin with a cheerful attitude who lacked the airs of an official." Huang was surprised to learn later that Xi had made such major contributions to the revolution, although he was sensitive to the fact that Xi was not a Long Marcher. According to Huang, "Among the old guard in the party, Xi Zhongxun was certainly the individual who had the longest ties to United Front efforts against Taiwan, and he was also the mysterious individual most criticized by Taiwanese who were in the mainland. To a certain extent, people felt a trace of affection toward this local product of Shaanxi with a generous heart who said whatever he wanted. Still, everyone always thought it would have been better if he was moved away from Taiwan affairs."[27]

Huang explained this contradictory attitude toward Xi with a telling anecdote. The first time the two men met for a formal chat, Xi did something remarkable: while talking about his time working in Guangdong, he told Huang that the province grew many bananas. He then made the shape of a banana with his hands and asked Huang if Taiwan had bananas. Huang was stunned by Xi's coarseness and lack of knowledge of the outside world. Huang then complained to the party leadership about having someone with so little understanding of Taiwan run Beijing's policies toward the island. Then Xi surprised Huang again. At a tea session, Xi, in a friendly fashion, said to Huang, "I don't understand Taiwan. I said some unprofessional things. I'm sorry!" Then, at a banquet soon afterward, Xi, in his welcoming remarks, began by saying, "First, I want to express my respect to Mr. Huang. I am simply not modest enough!" This was already six months since the banana incident. Huang started to feel guilty about criticizing Xi. He approached Xi to console him. In his memoirs, Huang expressed how confusing Xi could be: "After that, I thought if Mr. Xi was not a very simple and kind person, then he was the absolute greatest United Front master." But henceforth, they became "partners who worked in perfect harmony."[28]

Xi might not have known much about bananas, but he knew a thing or two about politics. After the United States and China established formal diplomatic relations in 1979, Beijing began introducing a host of new policies toward Taiwan. The People's Republic stopped emphasizing "liberation" as its principal goal, recognized the Nationalist's "governing position," and called for greater links across the Taiwan Strait. The People's Liberation Army ceased its regular artillery attacks on the offshore islands controlled by Taipei, and Beijing promised that, after reunification, Taiwan would remain a "specially administered area" with autonomy and its own military.[29] These changes had begun before Xi moved to Beijing and assumed control over United Front work in 1981, but his expertise as an old United Front hand further refined these policies—and worried Taiwanese leaders.

Xi paid close attention to Taiwanese affairs. He directed the new magazine *Voice of Taiwan*, established in 1982, to be readable for Taiwanese people—it should be a bit "soft," not too political. On one occasion, Xi read aloud an article that demanded that the Taiwanese leadership hand over power to the "people," thus ending their status as "second-class citizens." "This was written very well!" he exclaimed, promptly suggesting the magazine be published every month instead of bimonthly.[30] Xi's remarks were not off the cuff. As declassified intelligence files from Taiwan revealed, the party, at this time, was using prodemocracy, proindependence forces in Taiwan against the regime of President Chiang Ching-kuo, who had succeeded his father, Chiang Kai-shek, as leader.[31]

China's efforts were working enough to frighten Chiang's government. The Nationalists established a special group to counter Beijing's influence operations: the Liu Shaokang Office, under the direction of Wang Sheng, an old master at political warfare. In a self-criticism, the office characterized 1982 as a year of especially intense struggle.[32] The office was extraordinarily powerful, had a global reach, and won several victories in the contest with Beijing. Years later, Wang would tell an interviewer that China had established a special Beat Wang Small Group, which was under the direct leadership of Xi Zhongxun. Wang, however, lost the trust of the Taiwan leadership. To be successful, the Liu Shaokang Office necessarily concentrated a great deal of authority, and Chiang decided Wang had grown too powerful. In April 1983, Chiang summoned Wang Sheng, accused his office of abusing power, and dissolved the organization.[33] Xi, by contrast, had the full support of the party.

Taipei's own human rights problems and the successful Hong Kong–handover negotiations made Taiwan feel vulnerable to Beijing's political warfare. And the party kept improving its strategies. In June 1983, Deng Xiaoping further clarified Taiwan policy in a set of important remarks to Chinese American professor Winston L. Y. Yang. Deng promised that talks with the Nationalists could take place "on an equal footing" and that, after reunification, Taiwan could maintain its own army and judicial system. Furthermore, the mainland would not send troops or administrative personnel to the island.[34] The coastal provinces set up stations to help Taiwanese fishermen, and Beijing lobbied famous members of the Chinese diaspora, even targeting famous musicians such as Teresa Teng (Xi Jinping's favorite singer) and Hou Dejian, whose trip to the mainland in June 1983 caused a sensation in Taiwan. Hou's visit included a public meeting with Xi even though the Beijing government had told Hou there would be no meetings with officials. Hou was impressed with his treatment, later writing in his memoirs that the party, "at this time, really took the United Front policy seriously."[35]

Xi turned to history to win over the old guard in Taiwan. He approved the establishment and organization of the Alumni Association of Huangpu Military Academy, a school which, decades earlier, before Chiang Kai-shek had marched north to unify much of the country in 1926, had included both Nationalists and Communists.[36] In October 1986, Xi watched a private showing of *The Bloody Battle of Taierzhuang*, a movie on a 1938 Nationalist battle against the Japanese. The director, Yang Guangyuan, was afraid that the movie would not be released because of its positive portrayal of the Nationalists. After the private showing, someone from the Department of Propaganda said it would be necessary to make extensive edits. But Xi looked around the room and, in a friendly tone, addressed Cheng Siyuan, vice-chairman of the Chinese People's Political Consultative Conference, who had defected from Taiwan to the mainland in 1965. Xi said that he and others in the room did not understand this history, and he asked Cheng, as someone with direct experience, to express an opinion. Cheng fully approved of the movie. Xi then held the director's hand tightly and thanked him for making such a good film. Its release without edits was an important signal that Beijing was reevaluating the Nationalists' contribution to the war effort.[37]

Two months later, on December 12, Xi gave a speech on the fiftieth anniversary of the Xi'an Incident—the moment in Chinese history when Chiang Kai-shek was captured by two of his generals who believed the Nationalists should focus more on the threat from Japan than on the Communist insurgency. Xi's speech was significant because it was the first time a party leader officially commended Chiang, Soong Mei-ling, and T. V. Soong for the roles they had played in the outcome, which resulted in a promise to cooperate with the Communist Party against Japan. Xi emphasized that "brothers" should unite to fight against those who might wish to humiliate China.[38] Xi's speech marked a major shift in the historiography of the war against the Japanese.

In September 1987, just a few months after *The Bloody Battle of Taierzhuang*'s release and Xi's speech on the Xi'an Incident, Chiang Ching-kuo finally allowed the establishment of some ties with the mainland. He might have been touched by the party's changing views of the Nationalists' historical role, but his policy options were limited. At the end of his life, he may also have hoped for a last breakthrough in cross-strait relations so he could die at home.[39] Riding on these triumphs, Xi began to reach out to Taiwan through a secret back channel.[40] For a time, Beijing's policies seemed to be working, but after generational change and democratization in Taiwan, along with the tragedy of June 4, Xi's approach lost effectiveness. Unification would not be achieved in his lifetime.

THE HONG KONG NEGOTIATIONS

As the former party boss of Guangdong, Xi probably had a better understanding of Hong Kong than others in the leadership. The special economic zones were inspired largely by the achievements of Hong Kong and Macau. The rapid growth in Shenzhen would not have been possible without investments by overseas Chinese, especially by those in Hong Kong. Xi understood very well the motivations of the Hong Kong and Macanese investors. "Now, everyone is saying that when you invest in the motherland, it is patriotism first and making money second," he told a group of investors on one occasion. "That's not right. In actuality, for you, making money is first and patriotism is second. If you do not make money, why would you feel patriotic?"[41]

While still in Guangdong, Xi engaged in diplomacy with the British about the future of the colony. In the spring of 1979, Murray MacLehose, governor of Hong Kong, visited Guangzhou. On April 3, he gave a banquet, attended by Xi, at which he expressed hope for more cooperation between the mainland and Hong Kong.[42] David Wilson, a British diplomat, was particularly struck by Xi's willingness to discuss his difficult past. "I found him an extremely interesting man talking about what life had been like when he was under house arrest," Wilson said, adding "and the books he'd read—he read a huge number of books. He read all sorts of things."[43] In MacLehose's summary report on the trip, he was cautiously optimistic about ways to deepen connections, including the vexatious problem of freshwater supplies that Xi's government promised to resolve. "It was also encouraging that, at every level, there was a recognition of the role that could be played in China's modernization by Hong Kong's capital and expertise," he wrote.[44]

In December, Xi passed through Hong Kong, where he met with acting governor Jack Cater to discuss the colony's future. The British raised the issue of the land leases in the New Territories, which were scheduled by treaty to be returned to China in 1997, so that Xi "would register that this was an unresolved difficulty which could damage the way in which Hong Kong contributes to the economic development of Guangdong." The British explained to Xi that the issue of the New Territories "could not be solved by general assurances." In two or three years, this issue would "become a real problem." The British emphasized that "what mattered was that confidence in Hong Kong should not be allowed to erode. This was a subject both sides needed to keep in mind, but it was one which should be kept to ourselves and treated confidentially. It would be easy for harmful misunderstandings to arise." Xi replied that Deng had given assurances on this question. But Cater pressed, warning that "a problem was building up; it would not go away." Xi was not concerned. The lease, he noted, still had eighteen years before expiration.[45]

Once negotiations finally started in earnest a few years later, Xi influenced the discussions on Hong Kong's Basic Law—the city's constitution. Xu Jiatun, director of the Hong Kong branch of the New China News Agency for much of the 1980s, asserted that, during the negotiations over the law, Hu Yaobang and Xi Zhongxun both supported giving Hong Kong people more rights: "At the time, during internal discussions, I proposed this and that freedom suggested by Hong Kong people should be agreed to, should be written. . . . The reason I proposed this was because Hu Yaobang and Xi Zhongxun both expressed this opinion."[46] Taiwan's Foreign Ministry even believed that Xi was in charge of a secret Hong Kong and Macau Affairs Small Group, directly subordinate to the secretariat. "On the Hong Kong issue," the ministry wrote, "the bandit Xi is the second most powerful decision-maker in the bandit party after Deng Xiaoping."[47]

Xi repeatedly held meetings with officials from the colony during the 1980s. According to Sze-yuen Chung, a politician in Hong Kong, "China began waging a 'United Front' campaign for the hearts and minds of the Hong Kong people" in September 1982, after Margaret Thatcher's visit to China. "The Chinese hoped to win us over with their sincerity and hospitality."[48] That goal was especially important because concern over Hong Kong's future was devastating the colony's economy.

On November 1, 1982, Xi met with a Hong Kong Trade Development Council delegation led by Sir Y. K. Kan. Xi had already met Kan at least two times: once when Kan traveled with MacLehose in 1979 and again in May

1980 when Kan led the first trade mission to Guangdong to discuss greater economic cooperation.[49] Xi began by giving a long talk on the domestic situation in China until Kan's neck started to hurt.[50] Xi struck a diplomatic tone. "The Hong Kong issue and the near future of Hong Kong concerns all of us," he assured them. "We will try to keep the stability and prosperity of Hong Kong after 1997." He praised Hong Kong in strong terms: "Hong Kong is a world financial centre and is a very famous free port. Although limited in area, it is very important, not militarily but in economic and foreign trade terms." He promised that all its "current systems" would remain unchanged, and "the interests of both the Hong Kong people and of foreigners" would be protected.[51] Xi's conversation with Kan apparently achieved its intended goal of stabilizing the mood in Hong Kong. When Kan spoke to reporters about the meeting, the Hang Seng Index rose fifty points.[52]

Yet Xi apparently did not feel that the mainland had a good grasp of politics in Hong Kong. In February 1983, he proposed sending people from the mainland to Hong Kong to better understand the colony, noting that thirty thousand to fifty thousand graduates of Tsinghua, Peking, and Jiaotong Universities were living in Hong Kong, which made it possible to arrange reunions and attract people back to China. He even proposed creating a research institute. "We simply do not understand Hong Kong," he warned.[53]

That same month, the Hong Kong branch of the New China News Agency asked Allen Lee, a member of the Hong Kong Legislative Council, to form a delegation of young professionals to visit Beijing. Allen Lee invited Martin Lee, chairman of the Hong Kong Bar Association and future head of the Democratic Party, to join. For months, the group worked every Sunday on a position paper to submit to Beijing. In their paper, they praised China's new focus on economic modernization and expressed a "fervent hope that China will be strong." Yet Hong Kong people feared, they claimed, that fourteen years in the future, a gap would continue to exist between Hong Kong and the mainland. They warned that if Beijing took administrative control of Hong Kong in 1997, then "public confidence in the territory will immediately nosedive and it will lose its prosperity in a very short time indeed." Only a small number of people were comfortable with the mainland's "self-administration" formula because Hong Kong citizens had "been following repeated political changes to the north of the border with concern and sometimes alarm." "Grave doubts" persisted that Beijing would renege on its promises. People were already leaving the colony. Although "we are all Chinese both by race and heart," they warned, "we do not think that the present capitalist system in Hong Kong can continue after sovereignty reverts back to China." "Furthermore," they asked, "if Hong Kong should experience any social unrest, would the self-administration formula still be workable or be allowed to continue? And if so, who can guarantee this?"[54]

The delegation sent its position paper shortly before leaving for Beijing in May. When the group departed from Hong Kong, its members still did not know whom they would meet. Their handlers on the bus from the Beijing airport to the city told them that they would be meeting Xi, who, they said, was number five on the list of top Chinese leaders. They said he was liberal and open-minded. Years earlier, Allen Lee had met Xi at a Guangzhou restaurant in Guangdong when Lee was part of the delegation that included David Wilson. During that meeting, the weather was so hot that the air conditioning overwhelmed the local electricity grid, and the entire area turned dark, prompting Xi to ask if Hong Kong was a decade ahead of the mainland. Lee replied that it was *several* decades ahead, and they both laughed. Lee had a positive impression of Xi after this meeting, believing him to be very casual and likeable, though he was disappointed that, on this second trip, the group would not be meeting a more senior leader, such as Deng.[55]

The next day, they met Xi in the Great Hall of the People. Martin Lee told Xi that they were delighted to see the fall of the Gang of Four. Lee said he could understand that the Chinese leaders felt as if they were leaving a tunnel after the Cultural Revolution and had a sense of hope for the future. People in Hong Kong, however, believed they were walking *into* a tunnel. Explaining why people were emigrating from Hong Kong, Lee said they were like swimmers suddenly approaching a waterfall and trying to grasp at any rock to save themselves. Xi listened quietly, saying little at first. Lee concluded that Xi's purpose was solely to convince the delegation to bring a return message to the British side: start negotiations about the handover. In other words, Xi had no interest in their position paper or speaking with them about Hong Kong.[56]

In his remarks to the delegation, Xi exuded nationalist sentiments. He complained about the "absolutely unequal treaties" signed after the Opium War. Xi told his audience, "Hong Kong is your home, but it is also a part of China; not just today, but forever. Without a doubt, all of us are Chinese compatriots." Xi demonstrated a classic Marxist interpretation of capitalist markets. He denied that the economic problems in Hong Kong were confidence related; instead, the problems were part of the habit of capitalist economies to rise and fall: "As early as in 1980, when I visited the United States, I had already discovered that the US economy was declining. You may have heard of some problems which cannot in the end be solved by capitalism, but can be solved by socialism. There are ups and downs in a capitalist economy.... The United States and the Soviet Union are engaged in an armaments race and expansionist activities because they want to eliminate the economic crises. We do not have such problems." Xi promised there would not be another Cultural Revolution. He was blunt, however, about China's power: "Hong Kong's prosperity cannot be separated from China's Four Modernizations, but not the other way round; that is, this relationship should be that China does not need Hong Kong in carrying out the Four Modernizations." He also used the occasion to make strong anti-American remarks: "You can have two homes, one in Hong Kong and the other in a foreign county. Go out and see things for yourself and then return. Go! Life is not so good in foreign countries. Go to the United States and see things for yourself. Life in the United States is not all that good. People have told me that if one deposits money in the United States, the interest is so meager that he cannot use it to pay for the bank services." Xi promised that Hong Kong would be allowed to maintain its system after the handover: "Freedom in life will remain unchanged, the system will remain unchanged, and the way of life will remain unchanged." But then he displayed his lingering phobia—fear of chaos: "People in foreign countries have much freedom to enjoy. People in our country also enjoy enough freedom. Of course, it is impossible to have absolute freedom. Absolute freedom will cause all systems to crumble!"[57]

This meeting with Xi did little to change Beijing's position, and, in December 1984, the British promised to return Hong Kong in 1997. Martin Lee came to believe that the meeting with Xi had just been an obfuscation by the party. "I think their tactic was to postpone the arrival of democracy," he said in an interview two decades after the meeting with Xi. "They thought they would be able to win the hearts of Hong Kong people in ten years," he said.[58]

CLEANING HOUSE AT THE HONG KONG BRANCH OF THE NEW CHINA NEWS AGENCY

Xi's bailiwick did not only include meeting with people from Hong Kong but also personnel policy for the Hong Kong branch of the New China News Agency, which served as the party's de facto embassy. In 1983, he invited

Xu Jiatun, the new head of the branch, to his home for a discussion prior to Xu's departure for Hong Kong. In his memoirs, Xu claimed that Xi criticized mainland policy toward Hong Kong as "too leftist and too narrow," and he complained that Liao Chengzhi, the man in charge of Hong Kong and Macau policy in the State Council, was "monopolizing" policy. Xi also had choice words for Wang Kuang, former head of the New China News Agency Hong Kong branch, and He Mingsi, who led its United Front Department, whom he considered "crude." "It is truly absurd that Wang Kuang would let someone of this caliber become the head of the United Front Department in the Hong Kong branch of the New China News Agency or even nominate him to become a member of the Chinese People's Political Consultative Conference!" Xi said.[59]

In a series of articles, He Mingsi later acknowledged that Xi Zhongxun had targeted him. Given Xi's stature, He Mingsi was surprised Xi would even know about low-level individuals like himself. He admitted that the accusations had to do with alleged "leftism." However, he vociferously denied that the charges were accurate, and he portrayed his fall as an issue of pure power politics: "What is 'too leftist and too narrow'? What is its precise content? I am still confused. How can it be explained? Ultimately, if someone in power says that you are a 'rightist,' then you are a 'rightist'; if they say you are a 'leftist,' you are a 'leftist.' This is a two-edged sword; whether it goes to the 'left' or to the 'right,' it still can kill you."[60]

In any case, Xu Jiatun's arrival signified a new approach. In the past, China's most reliable allies in the territory—and the targets of United Front efforts—had been the trade unionists and other leftists. But the United Front policy in Hong Kong after Xu's appointment explicitly identified the "bourgeoisie" as the top targets, not the proletariat. As Cindy Yik-yi Chu shows in her careful research on the topic, "Hong Kong's business leaders constituted the primary target of Beijing's United Front work in the territory." But, after 1989, the scale of cooperation decreased dramatically. China's leaders "were prepared to listen only to close allies in Hong Kong," Chu writes. "Conciliation had given way to struggles, allegations, and news headlines." In other words, after the Tiananmen upheaval, the party had essentially given up on the possibility that it could win over people with different views, such as potentially friendly members of the democratic camp.[61]

23
A NEW ERA IN ETHNIC AND RELIGIOUS AFFAIRS

In the early years of the People's Republic, the Communists mixed cooptation and coercion to gradually assert power in ethnic-minority regions. This was an approach that was especially valuable in Xi's vast Northwest, where the fledgling regime faced uneasy Tibetans, Hui, Uyghurs, and Kazakhs. Yet even before Xi was purged, the party had rejected this approach. As early as 1956, mass violence against Tibetans began in Sichuan. By 1958, the People's Liberation Army was waging war against ethnic minorities throughout the Northwest. In 1962, the party turned against the Panchen Lama, its most prominent non-Han and nonparty ally, and Xi was viciously criticized for his "accommodationist" attitude toward him.

The phrase "The essence of the ethnic problem is class" first appeared as a comment written by the party center on a report regarding the April 1958 Xunhua Incident, when Muslim Salars and Tibetans in Qinghai launched an uprising against party rule to oppose collectivization and the arrest of local leaders. Particularly during the first years of the Cultural Revolution, this idea that any non-Han ethnic or religious characteristics were a manifestation of class struggle reached a new extreme. Although outright warfare had ended, beginning in 1966, the Smash the Four Olds Campaign destroyed mosques, churches, and monasteries, banned ethnic customs, and punished acts of religious faith, with the party attacking even its own minority cadres with brutal ferocity.[1]

Yet Han cadres also suffered at Mao's hands, and, in a certain way, the anguish bound Han and non-Han together. Xi respected people who survived such "forging," and he knew what it was like to be persecuted. When the Panchen Lama apologized to Xi for writing the seventy-thousand-character petition and for implicating him in the incident, Xi told him, "This is not a problem of someone implicating someone. We were all forged and tested, and we all learned something. The party understands you."[2] In an interview, Arjia Rinpoche, the reincarnation of the abbot of Kumbum Monastery, theorized that Xi and the Panchen Lama had "a common ground and a common language" because of similar experiences during the Cultural Revolution.[3]

When Xi reunited with his old allies, the experience was emotional. Apa Alo had trouble controlling himself when he saw Xi at Beijing's Jingxi Hotel in 1978. They hugged each other and wept bitterly. "Comrade Zhongxun again gave me the greatest encouragement and comfort. He made me understand the important significance of unity and of looking ahead," he later wrote.[4] Burhan Shahidi's daughter recalled how her father held Xi and cried when they finally saw each other again in that same year. "When he found out that many of my father's problems had not been resolved, he consoled my father, urging him to trust the central government and assuring him that the party would arrive at a fair and just conclusion to his case."[5] Not all of Xi's old associates survived, however. The prominent Tibetan scholar Sherab Gyatso—who had helped Xi on several occasions during the 1950s and who had often treated Xi to homemade bean porridge—had been persecuted to death in 1968.[6]

In the 1980s, history seemed to repeat itself as the party reintroduced a softer touch that was reminiscent of the nation's founding period. Economic development and the United Front, not class struggle, once again became the top priorities. Yet even Xi did not seem to fully understand that the decades of violence, restrictions on religious activity, and poverty had created problems that could not be easily solved with the co-optation of grievances and economic growth. Xi could be openly dismissive of past injustices; since everyone had suffered during the Cultural Revolution, he did not always believe that the non-Han complaints deserved special attention.

Beijing could not simply turn back the clock to 1952. Although the party's failures, as well as many years away from the center of power, facilitated a zeal among senior cadres to right the ship of the revolution in the twilight of their lives, decades of persecution meant something quite different for many of China's ethnic minorities and religious faithful. While everyone went through tribulations, the ethnic minorities suffered at the hands of the Han. And it was not only the Bolsheviks who could find meaning in the "forge" of adversity. As China exited the long tunnel of the Mao years, party leaders were shocked when religious activity exploded after the Cultural Revolution.

Thinking that the influence of the Dalai Lama had been extinguished, when a group from Dharamsala visited Lhasa, the local authorities asked the crowds not to attack the members of the group or to spit at them. The cadres were then stunned when the prostrating crowds mobbed the Dalai Lama's representative, weeping and shouting anti-Han slogans.[7] In 1979, near the Catholic pilgrimage site of Sheshan, a demon, before it was exorcised, foretold the coming of Mary. In March 1980, about ten thousand Catholics who heard the news of the prophecy traveled to Sheshan. They broke into the church, which was still officially closed, and knelt down in the dust. One elderly man shouted, "Open the gates of Heaven!" A number of those present experienced visions of Mary and Jesus, and one underground priest on a fishing boat listened to three days and three nights of confessions.[8]

Class struggle, therefore, had not ended religion in China, and in fact, it had made many of the religious believers even more dedicated. And since so many Chinese were losing faith in Communism and the country was moving in a more materialistic direction, the spiritual vacuum of the 1980s facilitated a rapid growth in the number of the religious faithful. Even Xi pursued an interest in quasi-religious elements of traditional Chinese culture in the 1980s. He supported a relative in the Xi family ancestral home in Henan who wanted to establish a university for the study of traditional Chinese medicine.[9] When Qi Xin's younger brother, Ruixin, was fighting cancer, Xi sent Fan Ming—his former associate in the Northwest who had studied traditional Chinese medicine after his purge in the 1950s—to treat him. Fan believed that the medicine he gave to Ruixin was magical and capable of "starving" the cancer cells. (Ruixin died three months later.)[10] Xi was also interested in qigong, the breathing exercises, similar to tai chi, that are intended to build up one's qi, or life essence. In November 1989, when the World Medical Qigong Study Association was formally established, Xi Zhongxun became its first honorary chairman.[11] According to a Chinese professor in touch with the American embassy in Beijing, Zhongxun's son Jinping was someone who "displayed a fascination with Buddhist martial arts, qigong, and other mystical powers said to aid health, as well as with Buddhist sacred sites such as Wutaishan." The professor "was extremely surprised by how much Xi knew about the subject and Xi's seeming belief in supernatural forces."[12]

Yet it must be remembered that although Zhongxun and Jinping showed some curiosity about history, superstition, and mystical phenomena, as a Communist, Zhongxun did not subscribe to genuine religious beliefs. He primarily saw religious figures as people who needed to be controlled and rallied to participate in economic development. This was a practical worldview, and during the first half of the 1980s, it seemed to work well, especially given the instability that marked the beginning of the decade. The victory was not easy, as Xi Zhongxun had to defeat numerous forces within the party that doubted the new approach. But by 1985, Xi had reason to feel confident that he had successfully achieved a new political equilibrium with both China's ethnic minorities and Christians.

THE TIBET ISSUE REDUX

Beijing was already paying close attention to Tibet before Xi left Guangdong for the capital to serve as the party's leading figure on ethnic and religious affairs. Hu Yaobang found the challenges in Tibet so pressing that the very first meeting of the secretariat after its reestablishment, held on March 14 and 15, 1980, was devoted entirely to the subject. After listening to reports from the Tibet Autonomous Region leadership, the participants decided it was necessary to do "everything possible" to develop the economy there. The "pernicious influence" of the "radical left line" had to be eliminated. Religious practices were to be "addressed carefully," with the party taking better care of "upper-class" personages. This ambitious agenda included a gradual empowerment of Tibetan cadres, especially those at the lower levels.[13]

After a year of trying to find a suitable candidate, the secretariat selected Yin Fatang as the new leader for the Tibet Autonomous Region. During the war against the Nationalists, Yin had served in Deng Xiaoping's Second Field Army, and he had entered Tibet with Zhang Guohua, although he was forced out of Tibet in the early years of the Cultural Revolution (Zhang Guohua was persecuted to death). At the secretariat meeting in March 1980, Yin asserted that the party's first thirty years in Tibet were "glorious, a victory of

Marxism-Leninism and Mao Zedong thought." Yin would soon prove to be a powerful opponent to Xi's agenda.[14]

In May 1980, Hu Yaobang traveled to Tibet himself. He was struck by the poverty he found there, and he made provocative statements, even asserting that, "to a certain extent," the poor ethnic relations were the result of "some leading Han cadres having a problem in their ideological thinking and work style." He proposed that the "majority" of Han cadres depart from Tibet, "leaving only a minority who are absolutely necessary."[15] In August, the party center approved a proposal to remove twenty-one thousand Han cadres (about two-thirds of those present) and twenty-five thousand Han workers from Tibet.[16]

The party returned to its old allies. Four months after Hu's trip to Tibet, in September 1980, the Panchen Lama (as well as Xi) became vice-chairman of the National People's Congress. This signified a partial rehabilitation, but the Panchen Lama's relationship with Deng Xiaoping remained complicated. On August 16, 1980, Deng told the Panchen Lama that he was "one of the best patriots."[17] However, according to a former high-ranking official who managed ethnic issues, Deng only said this because, at the time, he was engineering the removal of Hua Guofeng, a man beloved by many ethnic minorities because of their affection for Mao.[18] In another conversation with the Panchen Lama, Deng asserted that some parts of the Panchen Lama's 1962 petition had been "wrong," although he allowed that the Tibetan's behavior under persecution was "good."[19] Xi's own relationship with the Panchen Lama deepened, and the friendship extended to their families. One hundred days after the Panchen Lama's daughter was born to the Chinese daughter of a high-ranking military official, Xi went to visit them.[20] The Panchen Lama even let Xi hold the baby.[21]

Yet unity was difficult to achieve given the level of distrust between the party leadership in the Tibet Autonomous Region and the Panchen Lama. In 1980, the New China News Agency published an internal document that described the Dalai Lama, the Panchen Lama, and Phunwang Wangye—founder of the Tibetan Communist Party and a high-ranking Tibetan Communist who had been persecuted throughout much of the Mao era—as challenges to work in Tibet. An assistant editor of the New China News Agency branch in Tibet accidentally saw a version of this document, which was intended only for politburo members, and quickly informed Wangye. Xi

FIGURE 13. Xi Zhongxun holds the tenth Panchen Lama's baby daughter, 1983. *Left to right*: Qi Xin, Xi, Yabshi Pan Rinzinwangmo, the Panchen Lama, and Li Jie (the Panchen Lama's wife). Source: author's personal collection.

began an investigation and met with Yin Fatang to ask for an explanation. When the local Tibetan authorities started pressuring the New China News Agency reporter into making a self-criticism, Xi's intervention prevented the man from suffering any more than a small demotion within the agency.[22]

RECTIFICATION IN XINJIANG

Tibet presented significant challenges to the leadership, but it was in Xinjiang that the party faced the prospect of continuous uprisings at this time. Uyghurs had suffered from decades of failed policies and colonialist exploitation, and Han cadres there had had trouble communicating with them because of language difficulties. Education levels among the cadres were so low that even those at the level of office were unable to take notes.[23] Conservative figures in the Xinjiang leadership were openly skeptical about the 1978 Third Plenum and China's reforms. Those cadres became even more worried about general trends when they heard about Hu Yaobang's new policies toward Tibet, which they felt should not apply to Xinjiang.[24]

The first sign of real trouble was in April 1980, when an employee of the Public Security Bureau in Aksu County put a towel in the mouth of a drunken Uyghur, accidentally killing him. More than three thousand Uyghurs marched and, according to an official Chinese source, shouted political slogans while trying to storm the local party headquarters.[25] In June, a military facility in Artux was attacked by four or five hundred people.[26] On July 10 and 14, the secretariat held two meetings to discuss the situation and passed a *Summary of the Central Secretariat's Discussion on Work in Xinjiang*. The document proposed that Han cadres should act like "advisers" or "assistants" to the minority cadres and that, at the level of commune and below, Han cadres should gradually be replaced by minority cadres. From August 11 to 23, a massive "three-level" meeting was held in Xinjiang, comprising 643 cadres from the city, county, and village levels, to disseminate the secretariat's conclusions and the Xinjiang party leadership's plans to implement them. The three-level meeting was extremely controversial in Xinjiang—minority cadres were delighted, whereas many Han cadres were humiliated.[27]

Dissatisfaction with this new direction among the Han erupted in a spectacular fashion when some of them attacked the headquarters of the South Xinjiang Military Region in Kashgar. The Urumqi Military Region and the Xinjiang Party Committee had decided to execute a Han soldier who killed a Uyghur man, and on September 17, the day after the conclusion of the trial, the military headquarters was besieged by a mob that was primarily made up of People's Liberation Army soldiers. Writing for internal consumption, one New China News Agency journalist concluded that senior civilians, and especially military cadres in Xinjiang, were delighted by the incident, hoping that it would be used to pressure Beijing into rejecting the new approach to ethnic minorities.[28]

Wang Zhen—the man Xi had purged from the Xinjiang leadership in 1952 for "leftism"—suddenly and forcefully reappeared. On September 23, the party decided to send him to Xinjiang, and he arrived there later that month. On November 14, Deng Xiaoping read a report on the situation in southern Xinjiang and wrote, "Comrade Wang Zhen should read this. When necessary, he should go to Xinjiang to help out a bit to manage this kind of problem." At a Xinjiang discussion meeting held between late December and early January, Wang Zhen seemed to be trying to win back the legacy that Xi had stolen from him. Wang affirmed the "democratic reforms, land reform, suppression, and the internal ferreting out" of the early 1950s. But the challenges in the region were becoming worse. Just as high-ranking cadres were discussing Xinjiang in Beijing, the East Xinjiang Military Region was sending forces from two divisions to stop more than ten thousand sent-down youth from Shanghai who were rioting because they wanted to return home. On January 8, 1981, Wang rushed back to Urumqi, where, on January 14, he met with representatives of the sent-down youths. But his arrival in the region could not prevent almost one thousand Uyghurs in southern Xinjiang's Kargilik County from assaulting party and government buildings after a mosque had caught on fire, leading to a declaration of martial law on January 16. Two days later, at a rally of party cadres, Wang affirmed that martial law had been the right choice, saying that it was necessary to "exercise dictatorship" over individuals who were causing trouble. He stated, "As soon as dictatorship is mentioned, some people are afraid of matters going too far, but just how many people are there? Their crimes are so obvious, how can this not be clear?"[29]

Wang's approach seemed to have little effect. On May 27, 1981, weapons were allegedly stolen during an event labeled by the authorities as a "counterrevolutionary armed riot," and 149 people were caught or killed. Twelve were executed.[30] That same month, the Urumqi Party Standing Committee neglected to punish the head of the city's Federation of Literary and Art Circles Preparatory Group for making comments critical of the party. Deng was furious—in July, at a meeting with propaganda workers, he would describe the man's words as "going beyond some antisocialist incorrect opinions from [the Antirightist Campaign] in 1957."[31]

It was in this troubling situation that Xi began to work at the secretariat in June. His return to Beijing coincided with big political changes. He was unable, or unwilling, to save Xinjiang party secretary Wang Feng, his old comrade from the Northwest who was associated with reformist, liberal policies. Wang moved into a hospital in Beijing, which essentially signified the end of his tenure, and Second Secretary Gu Jingsheng started managing daily affairs.[32]

The next month, July, the secretariat, including Xi, held a special session to discuss Xinjiang. It was concluded that, in the past and especially during the Cultural Revolution, the party had made "the serious mistake of taking class struggle too far." Minority rights to autonomy were not being respected and more minority cadres needed to be promoted. Party policy did not mean forcing people to give up their religion; it only meant preventing them from propagating incorrect ideas. Yet the meeting also, for the first time, used the formulation "Two cannot leave," which means that Han cadres and minority cadres should both understand that without each other, nothing is possible. That language signified a departure from the July 1980 secretariat meeting on Xinjiang and indicated that Han cadres would no longer be asked to leave Xinjiang (or Tibet) in the dramatic way that had originally been planned. Moreover, Xinjiang would no longer become "entangled" with historical issues. Instead, the priority was now on the "big picture" and "unity." Altogether, the meeting signified a somewhat more conservative direction.[33]

That agenda was accentuated in August when Deng Xiaoping, on a trip to Xinjiang, told Gu Jingsheng that "the big picture for Xinjiang is stability; without stability, absolutely nothing can be achieved."[34] Yet Deng made it clear that he was not planning to manage Xinjiang affairs directly. "The secretariat is in charge of Xinjiang work," he said. "It is enough for me to know that the situation is complicated."[35] Xi had apparently won back control over Xinjiang from Wang.

Uyghur cadres saw hope in Xi. During a September and October inspection trip to Xinjiang, an employee at the party school discovered that non-Han cadres were furious because Beijing was moving away from Hu Yaobang's earlier positions. Uyghur cadres were especially concerned by Wang Zhen, and one of them asked for Xi to visit: "Long ago, Wang Zhen and Deng Liqun repressed ethnic cadres in Xinjiang. This was remedied by Xi Zhongxun. Xi Zhongxun understands the people in Xinjiang. Only if he were to come here would Xinjiang be managed well." Han cadres, in contrast, claimed that the firing of Wang Zhen and Deng Liqun back in 1952 had been a great mistake that bred dangerous regional tendencies.[36]

In mid-October, Wang Enmao became the new party boss of Xinjiang. Wang Enmao was the man who replaced Wang Zhen in 1952, and when Wang Enmao was persecuted at the beginning of the Cultural Revolution, he was identified as Xi's "representative" in Xinjiang.[37] In 1981, Xi Zhongxun and Wang Enmao quickly proved to be strong partners. On October 30, a Han Chinese killed a Uyghur in Kashgar with a hunting rifle. More than 630 Han were beaten up, fifty-nine severely, and two died. Yet the crisis was resolved primarily by asking Uyghur party cadres to convince the people to calm down. In a speech given shortly after the situation was resolved, Wang Enmao revealed that it had been Xi who had guided this successful and peaceful response:

> Comrade Zhongxun and Comrade [Song] Renqiong together wrote a notification saying that the Kashgar incident should not be treated as a counterrevolutionary incident. If it were to be treated in that way, then more than ten thousand people would have been affected, which is too many. . . . Comrades Zhongxun and Renqiong also issued a joint notification stating that it was necessary to believe that the vast majority of minority cadres and masses were good. . . . Comrades Zhongxun and Renqiong acknowledged there are evil people who are counterrevolutionaries among the ethnic minorities, but they are only a small minority, and their number should not be broadened.

Wang credited the peaceful resolution especially to the "several notifications by telephone from Comrade Zhongxun." Yet Xi's preferred solution was not inevitable. Wang Enmao admitted that some comrades did not believe it was appropriate to treat the incident primarily as a contradiction among the people. Some wanted to use the military, but Wang asserted that "the main priority of the People's Liberation Army is to deal with invasion and protect the security of the motherland."[38]

Still, force also played a role. After the so-called October 30 incident, sixty-seven people were arrested, and the organization supposedly behind the incident was destroyed.[39] Moreover, just two months later, the party decided to reestablish Beijing's most powerful colonialist tool to assert power in Xinjiang: the so-called *bingtuan*, the massive Han-run industrial and agricultural enterprises managed according to military discipline. In 1952, Xi had tried to rein in the expansion of what would officially become the *bingtuan* two years later, but the *bingtuan* had exploded in size during the Great Leap Forward. After the beginning of the Cultural Revolution, the *bingtuan* spent more time on fighting factional struggles than production, and many of the workers returned to eastern China. In 1975, the *bingtuan* were dissolved.[40]

In July 1981, Wang Zhen admitted that some people still did not want to reestablish the *bingtuan*. He threatened to "persecute" them. "The more people oppose reestablishing the *bingtuan*, the more the necessity and importance of reestablishing the *bingtuan* is proven," he said. He finally won the case in December 1981.[41] Xi, however, never seemed to get over his skepticism. In June 1984, he wrote to Wang Enmao with a list of concerns about households that had contracted land from the *bingtuan* to farm. They faced heavy burdens from the state and could not make much money because they mostly produced grain. Households with official urban-type jobs feared that they would be treated like farmers. "Ultimately, it is necessary to proceed from the concrete situation in Xinjiang and come up with an innovative set of policies that can both stabilize morale and stimulate the economy," Xi warned.[42]

CRACKDOWN IN INNER MONGOLIA

Xi was less familiar with Mongolian affairs than he was with those in either Tibet or Xinjiang, as most of what would become Inner Mongolia had fallen outside of his Northwest Bureau. But he had played a significant role guiding party efforts in southwest Mongolia's Yekejuu League. Moreover, after the revolution, he had continued his close friendship with Ulanhu, the party's top Mongol cadre. In the 1950s, the two had been neighbors in Beijing. In 1961, Ulanhu invited Xi and Qi Xin to Hohhot, the capital of Inner Mongolia, to celebrate the Lunar New Year.[43]

The visit was later used against them. During the Cultural Revolution, investigators claimed that after returning to Beijing, Xi did not report on the problems in Inner Mongolia because Ulanhu had prepared a banquet for him. This was only one of the many charges against the two men. The accusations against them were crude: "They were extraordinarily intimate. Xi was extremely attentive to Ulanhu's stinking wife and his children. He often invited Ulanhu's children to eat and play. Their relations were out of the ordinary."[44]

After the founding of the People's Republic, the existence of Ulanhu was only one reason that the party seemed to be better positioned in Inner Mongolia compared to Tibet or Xinjiang. The Han made up a larger proportion of the population, and the Inner Mongolia Autonomous Region, established in 1947, was seen as a prototype for how the party would handle ethnic affairs more broadly after the Communist victory. Furthermore, Mongolian forces had helped defeat the Nationalists.[45] Yet, it was the Mongolians who had suffered the most during the Cultural Revolution. Ulanhu was purged in 1966, and the region was subjected to horrific racial violence during a notorious Root Out and Eradicate Campaign that was targeted overwhelmingly against ethnic Mongolians. Throughout Inner Mongolia, twenty thousand to thirty thousand perished and five hundred thousand were imprisoned. The Yekejuu League was a special target. More than one-fifth of the population was persecuted: 1,260 died, 2,322 were maimed, and 5,016 were injured.[46]

Xi understood the nature of the calamity. He even manipulated the politics of suffering during a conversation with the Dalai Lama's emissaries in 1982 when he said that the Mongolians had suffered more than the Tibetans: "Among the minority nationalities, the biggest loss of life was among the Inner Mongolians." Yet Xi was still impressed with their loyalty: "Even after enduring such a struggle, they petitioned Chairman Mao."[47]

Xi and Ulanhu worked together to run ethnic affairs. Between 1977 and 1983, Ulanhu led the United Front Work Department, and from 1983 to 1988, he served as a vice president. In the 1980s, Xi and Ulanhu again lived right next door to each other, and they often shared delicacies from Shaanxi and Inner Mongolia.[48] In a commemorative article after Ulanhu's death, Xi would write, "After I returned from Guangdong to the Central Committee, he and I managed United Front work and ethnic work together."[49]

But how would Xi and Ulanhu address the legacy of mass violence in Inner Mongolia? Zhou Hui—who had been purged in 1959 along with Peng Dehuai but who would become party leader of Inner Mongolia in 1978—was worried about Hu Yaobang's new policies toward Tibet. When Zhou saw the new secretariat report on Tibet in 1980, he believed that it would be totally impractical to apply its conclusions to Inner Mongolia.[50] Yet, on July 14, 1981, Ulanhu published an article in *People's Daily* that strongly emphasized "ethnicization" and "autonomy" in the minority regions. He also called for "rapidly ending the blind inflow" of Han Chinese into those areas. In July 1981, Hu Yaobang hosted a meeting of the secretariat, attended by Xi, to discuss a report by Zhou Hui. Shortly thereafter, the secretariat released the *Summary of the Secretariat's Discussion of Work in the Inner Mongolian Autonomous Region*, also known as *Document No. 28*.[51]

It was a disaster. Students in Inner Mongolia believed that *Document No. 28* was a move in the wrong direction. Instead of prioritizing Mongol cadres, the summary emphasized both Han and Mongol cadres. Crucially, *Document No. 28* also determined that Han Chinese should not be blocked from relocating to the province. These two decisions were seen as a violation of both what Ulanhu had promised just the previous month and also Hu Yaobang's comments on Tibet. Furthermore, the document did not promise punishment for those Han Chinese leaders who had killed many Mongols during the Cultural Revolution.[52]

When students started protesting in September, Zhou Hui believed that they were not spontaneously expressing real grievances. In his mind, these protests were planned and organized with the help of someone from within the Inner Mongolia party leadership. Regardless of whether this was true, some Mongol members of the Inner Mongolia party leadership did believe that the students' demands were justified, and they hoped to use their protests to promote change. On October 29, after giving the leaders in Inner Mongolia one last chance to respond, a group of student representatives arrived in Beijing to plead their case. The secretariat decided to take a very tough position, and Zhou Hui conveyed Hu Yaobang's hard-line view: "We cannot adopt an unclear and weak position. This is different from the ethnic dispute in Xinjiang. We will not be tricked." In other words, despite the extent of the catastrophe in Inner Mongolia, the secretariat did not see the protests as a natural outgrowth of the mistakes of the Cultural Revolution or of legitimate nationalist sentiments. Three high-ranking cadres in Inner Mongolia were punished for their alleged roles as the "black hands" behind the incident.[53]

A NEW APPROACH TO RELIGIOUS AFFAIRS

Ethnic affairs were intrinsically linked to the party's approach to religion more generally. In January 1982, while addressing religious issues at a nationwide meeting on United Front work, Xi warned that "leftism" was still the main problem. He referred to the Muslim practice of invoking Allah's name while slaughtering chicken and cattle: "This kind of thing cannot be resisted. The more it is restricted, the worse it becomes. The more it is restricted, the more powerful it becomes." Blaming the Cultural Revolution, he warned of a new religious "fever" in the country. "During the Cultural Revolution, people were not allowed to believe in religion. Everything became cow demons and snake spirits," he said.[54]

The 1982 constitution ended the ban on religious activities that had existed during the Cultural Revolution. In that same year, the so-called *Document No. 19: The Basic Viewpoint and Policy on Religious Questions during Our Country's Socialist Period* further clarified the party's position. *Document No. 19* included an extensive self-criticism of the antireligious policies during the Cultural Revolution. However, as Karrie J. Koesel's work on politics and religion demonstrates, liberalization only went so far. *Document No. 19* continued to adhere to the Marxist view that religion would eventually disappear. The purpose of ending the persecution of religious groups was practical—

underground religious practices were more difficult to dominate. "Patriotic" religious organizations were tasked with resisting "the designs of all reactionary religious forces from abroad who desire to once again exert control over religions in our country." The rules on how to return confiscated property suffered from a lack of precision. Only five "normal" religions were given space to operate (Buddhism, Daoism, Catholicism, Islam, and Protestantism). Because the local authorities were the ones who decided whether a practice was legal, consistency in implementation was often problematic.[55]

Furthermore, any religious activity that the party could not control was still unacceptable. Although *Document No. 19* signified a looser approach, in that same year, the Ministry of Public Security issued a report warning about the Christian "Shouters" in Zhejiang Province. When Xi read the report, his notification included extremely tough language: "Foreign Christianity and Catholicism use our country's policy of opening to, by hook or by crook, infiltrate our country and also to instigate a core group of reactionary disciples to attempt to organize counterrevolutionary power, to summon the believing masses to openly oppose the party and the people's government, to occupy churches and meeting points, to besiege police offices, and to disrupt county governments and public-security departments. They are extraordinarily arrogant. They pick on us for being weak. If a serious counterblow is not delivered, then this will spread and expand." In March 1983, Xi stated the "problem" of the Shouters was so severe that it could not be ignored: "It is necessary to take decisive measures to solve the situation practically." After a bit more than a year, the group had essentially been suppressed.[56]

OVERSEEING RELATIONS WITH THE DALAI LAMA AND THE PANCHEN LAMA

Would the Dalai Lama have a home in this rapidly changing China? In 1979, Deng Xiaoping told the Dalai Lama's brother Gyalo Thondup that "except for independence, everything is negotiable."[57] Although Xi did not meet Gyalo Thondup in 1979, he did on Thondup's subsequent trips. Once again, this was a challenging relationship for Xi to get right. Thondup, like many United Front targets, struggled to maintain the trust of his own compatriots. Furthermore, as a back channel between Beijing and the Dalai Lama, he could carry sensitive messages, but since he was an unofficial interlocutor, Thondup also contributed to several important miscommunications.

Like other prominent figures whom the party cultivated, Thondup could display a poor temper. On one such occasion, Thondup's son Khedroob had drinks with United Front officials on the night before they were to meet with Xi. When the Chinese drunkenly told Khedroob that they would only be allowed to visit Qinghai, not the Tibet Autonomous Region, Khedroob woke up his father to relay this news. Because they feared the room was bugged, they went outside to discuss this disappointing revelation. Xi entered the meeting the next day in a friendly mood, but Gyalo Thondup demanded to know where they would be allowed to visit. Xi, who seemed embarrassed, said the party could not guarantee Thondup's security in Tibet because of tensions with India (on one occasion, Xi would tell them not to trust the Indians and that Beijing could "teach the Indians a lesson anytime"). Thondup was furious, accusing the Chinese of an approach of "one step forward, two steps back." Xi "first shook with fury and then turned profusely apologetic." He seemed to be "in a panic." He begged them to go to Qinghai, but Thondup refused and told Xi that the Chinese were not acting with sincerity.[58]

Dharamsala took advantage of the thaw in the early part of the decade and sent several delegations on inspection trips to the Tibetan regions. One of those groups passed through Guangdong and met with Xi. Xi showed the group the watch that the Dalai Lama had given him, and he even expressed the hope that he would see the Dalai Lama once again before dying. When the delegation returned to Dharamsala, the Dalai Lama was moved to hear the part about the watch, but his heart became heavy when he learned about Xi's hope to see him again before his death.[59]

In 1981, Gyalo Thondup again visited Beijing. On this occasion, he met with Hu Yaobang, not Deng Xiaoping. Instead of simply reiterating Deng's earlier claim that everything could be discussed except for independence, Hu now listed five conditions for the Dalai Lama's return. Beijing's terms suggested that the Chinese were now only willing to discuss the Dalai Lama's status, not the Tibet question more broadly. The main sticking point was the fourth one, which stipulated that the Dalai Lama would stay in Beijing and only sometimes go to Tibet. Thondup suggested to the Dalai Lama that Hu's five points should remain secret. If the Tibetans were to know that he would be required to stay in Beijing, they might conclude that the Chinese wanted to hold the Dalai Lama hostage.[60] The Panchen Lama believed that the five points represented a violation of the constitution, and he doubted that the Dalai Lama would ever return under such conditions.[61]

Despite this apparent hardening, China was indeed taking small steps to prepare for the possibility of an agreement with Dharamsala. In April 1982, the party committee in Tibet internally disseminated Hu's so-called Five-Point Proposal and announced that although the 1959 "uprising" was a historical fact that could not be denied, the current policy was to "let bygones be bygones." "It is permissible to no longer become tangled up with that period of history," the members of the committee said. They even stated that the party would "sincerely" welcome the Dalai Lama and his followers to return.[62]

On May 29, 1982, Xi met with representatives of the Dalai Lama in the reception guesthouse of the Great Hall of the People. He found the group still profoundly skeptical of the party and its intentions. Juchen Thupten Namgyal, the head of the delegation, later recalled when he first landed in Beijing, "For a moment, I did not know what to do: if I shake hands with them, it would be a betrayal of the thousand Tibetans as well as my family members. At that moment, I had a flashback of my grandmother and my brothers who died under indescribable circumstances. I thought that if I shook hands, I would betray all those Tibetans who died."[63]

The negotiations immediately hit a snag—the Chinese interlocutors thought the Tibetans had come to discuss the Five-Point Proposal, but the Tibetan delegation did not even know about it. This misunderstanding, according to one participant, Lodi Gyari, rendered the first round of talks "confrontational and unproductive," much to his later regret. Had the delegation known about the five points, it could have brought its own counter-proposal for serious discussions. Moreover, despite their restrictive nature, the five points did not demand that the Dalai Lama declare that Tibet had always been part of China, as Beijing would demand later. "The proposal was actually forward-looking and indicated that we should not focus on past events. But we never had the chance," Gyari later wrote.[64]

At the beginning of the meeting with the emissaries, Xi claimed that the five points did not represent a change in Chinese policy. "You cannot say that Hu Yaobang's proposal has a different meaning." He quoted a statement by Deng that "whether one should negotiate on behalf of the government or on behalf of the Dalai Lama as a person is directly related to the root cause of the problem." Generally, Xi's subsequent remarks were welcoming and positive. He stated that China would "welcome the Dalai Lama if he decides to come back." The return of the Dalai Lama and the return of "Tibetan brothers and sisters in foreign lands" would be seen in China as a "step toward our fulfilment of the socialist state."[65]

Xi carefully addressed the Tibetans' hopes that through negotiation, they could win the same conditions that Beijing was promising Taiwan. Xi said, "Tibet is unlike Taiwan. If we treat Tibet like Taiwan, it is actually reducing the status of Tibet. Tibet is part of the motherland. We conducted peaceful negotiations in 1951. It has been over thirty years since the socialist system was established. Taiwan is a colony of America, and over the years, it has incurred over 110 billion in debt."[66] Xi asserted that unifying all Tibetan regions was impossible, warned about Soviet influence over Dharamsala, and criticized representatives of the Dalai Lama who condemned Beijing. He tried to point to a brighter future for Tibetans living in China as he acknowledged the mistakes of the past: "The aim of the constitution is to avoid Cultural Revolution–like chaos and to promote political stability and economic development. We cannot say there were no leftist mistakes in Tibet."[67]

Lodi Gyari asserted that the Dalai Lama would never submit to the influence of a foreign power. There was no need to worry about connections with the Soviet Union. Phuntsok Tashi Takla, another member of the delegation, added that Tibet was different from Inner Mongolia and Xinjiang because the Tibetans constituted a higher percentage of the population in Tibet. He pointed out that before the People's Republic was established, Inner Mongolia was divided into small regions, which were all united only after liberation. Takla also said he had been a translator during the 1951 Seventeen-Point Agreement discussions, and when the Tibetans mentioned unification of the Tibetan regions, they were told by Zhou Enlai that it was too early to consider such an idea, but they could return to it later. Ulanhu, who was also present, confirmed Takla's claim about Zhou.[68]

Xi Zhongxun wrapped up by saying, "Now you have to trust the Central Committee. Our aim is to avoid repeating past mistakes in the future. Today, our country is extremely famous." He boasted about his travels to Australia and the United States. He continued, "We must look to the present. We must not look into the past but rather into the future. Today's conversation may not have been pleasant. It was sharply worded; this is because free and open conversation is important." The meeting lasted for over two hours and was emotionally tense. However, it ended with a show of friendship, and the two sides agreed to meet again. Takla wrote, "That day, when we expressed ourselves without restraint, Xi Zhongxun was always smiling; however, sometimes, when explaining a point, he used sarcastic, patronizing words, which is reflective of Red China's tradition of a sense of superiority."[69]

In subsequent years, Lodi Gyari would speak positively of Xi. When other leaders were unhappy with Gyari and told him to be quiet, Xi would chastise them, saying that it was necessary to always give young people an opportunity to speak. Gyari believed that, "in a nice way," Xi had a feeling of ownership of Tibet because he had helped incorporate the Tibetan areas into China.[70] Gyari also described how Xi and Ulanhu spoke of their suffering during the Cultural Revolution. "These individuals' own personal sufferings combined with their having witnessed the unprecedented upheaval at the time made them quite sensitive to the Tibetans' plight," Gyari wrote.[71]

The visit by the Dalai Lama's delegation was not the only historic event for Tibet in 1982. In the same year, the Panchen Lama returned to Lhasa and Shigatse for the first time since the Cultural Revolution. Initially, the secretariat had decided that the Panchen Lama could only go to areas outside the Tibet Autonomous Region. However, on March 21, the Panchen Lama wrote a letter to Xi Zhongxun asking for permission to visit. Xi forwarded the letter to Hu Yaobang, and on the following day, Hu approved the Panchen's request.[72] Yin Fatang wanted another year to prepare for the Panchen Lama's return. He was worried that the Panchen Lama would cause a big commotion if he were to visit too soon.[73] Yin was surprised when the United Front Work Department sided with the Panchen Lama, not the Tibet Party Committee.[74]

Although permission was granted, Xi cautioned the Panchen Lama on May 25, at a meeting before the trip. Xi noted that they had already known each other for thirty-one years. "In the past we were friends; after experiencing the Cultural Revolution, we are now both friends and comrades," he said. Xi accentuated the importance of organizational discipline: "I think that not letting you go these past two years was correct. Now, your status is different. Your actions are not a matter of one person. It is necessary to consider our policies toward the Dalai clique, and this is a sensitive political issue." Xi reminded the Panchen Lama of his obligations: "For example, we members of the party do whatever the party tells us. It is impossible to act freely. That is what it means to maintain the party nature and discipline. The only difference between us is that you are not a member of the party. Everything else is the same. We are both engaged in revolution." Xi informed the Panchen Lama that his role as a religious figure was secondary to his role as vice-chairman of the National People's Congress. "It is not that religious activities cannot be carried out," Xi said, "but there should not be too many." Xi included a warning not to speak in too much detail about the Cultural Revolution and not to seek revenge on those who had wronged him.[75] Six days later, Xi met with Yin Fatang to explain the decision to allow the trip. Xi said that there was a fundamental difference between the Panchen Lama and the Dalai Lama, who had "betrayed the nation and now wants to make some kind of Greater Tibet." The Panchen Lama, on the other hand, had always been loyal to the party. Xi referred to Deng's comment in 1980 that the Panchen Lama was a patriot, and he demanded that the party leadership in Tibet treat the Panchen Lama "warmly, sincerely, and politely."[76]

On June 29, the Panchen Lama arrived in Tibet. He tried to do as Xi had instructed by calling on Tibetans to obey the party. He criticized "reactionary views" that supported "a high degree of autonomy" or "independence." Yet the trip did not go smoothly. On July 6, one person was trampled to death and eleven people were injured during a religious ceremony at Jokhang Temple in downtown Lhasa. Nevertheless, Beijing still supported the Panchen Lama. On July 15, the United Front Work Department sent a telegram instructing the region's leaders to try to get along better with him. It was necessary to "win him over and unite with him."[77]

The telegram was ineffective. On July 20, before the Panchen Lama was to continue on to Shigatse, the historic home of the panchen lamas, he met with the party leaders of the Tibet Autonomous Region. Yin Fatang raised some of the problems that had occurred on the trip, and the Panchen Lama promised to discuss them when he returned to Lhasa. Yet the Panchen Lama also said that they should report to the Central Committee when they had different views instead of working them out on their own. When the Panchen Lama met them again on August 18, he criticized them for "restraining and not loosening" party policies on religion—an accusation the regional leadership fiercely disputed. They were also deeply unhappy about the "religious fever" that had manifested during the Panchen Lama's visit.[78] After reading the internal report on the Panchen Lama's trip, Xi made it clear that the party's challenges in Tibet could not be resolved without a clear policy regarding the Dalai Lama and Panchen Lama—two individuals whom he described as "the key to the Tibet issue." "Otherwise, our thinking will be chaotic, and our guidelines will be unclear, which, in turn, will cause contradictions in policy and mistakes in work," he believed.[79]

The party tried to do as Xi had suggested. In February 1983, the General

Office released a notification combining a classic approach that included both "hard" and "soft" elements toward the Dalai Lama: "Our guideline for the Dalai Lama is still to continue to work and to win him over to behave better. If he is willing to return, we welcome that. If he wants to engage in activities opposed to the motherland, he wants to engage in so-called Tibetan independence, and he wants to send people to the Tibetan areas to cause trouble and chaos, we must stubbornly expose this and engage in necessary struggle." In April, the United Front Work Department held a meeting to discuss how exactly to achieve that. When the General Office disseminated the resultant report, it included an introduction emphasizing that the key to the Dalai Lama issue was "to do work within the nation well, especially in Tibet and the other Tibetan areas. We must take another step to overcome the 'leftist' incorrect thinking, to execute all the party's policies, to stubbornly develop production, to make the economy more prosperous, to adamantly develop culture, education, science, and hygiene, and to continuously raise material and cultural standards for Tibetans and other ethnic groups. Only in this way can we more effectively expand the work of winning over the Dalai clique and overseas Tibetans so that they will return to the motherland." Some of the individuals surrounding the Dalai Lama had changed their "counterrevolutionary positions," and the Dalai Lama himself rarely openly discussed Tibetan independence. He recognized the positive changes that had come about in Tibet. However, the report also warned about the continued support of the US and Indian governments to the Dalai Lama: "Over the last few years, the Dalai Lama himself changed his attitude a little and said some nice words to us, but some of what he said he did not believe, and some of what he said were lies. Many facts prove that the Dalai clique is now playing both sides of the situation, and we cannot be tricked by some of his open activities."[80]

XI RETURNS TO THE CATHOLIC CHURCH

The same month that the United Front Work Department was seriously discussing how the party might be able to win over the Dalai Lama, April 1983, Xi attended the annual meeting of Chinese Catholic Bishops to celebrate the twenty-fifth anniversary of the founding of the Catholic Patriotic Association—an act that the Western press, at the time, interpreted as a sign of respect.[81] Despite this apparent "respect," shortly before the proceedings began, the party had released a verdict against underground priests in Shanghai who were arrested in November 1981, shortly after Xi joined the secretariat. The members of the underground church regarded their punishment as a "second September 8"—a reference to the arrest of Cardinal Kung and hundreds of other Catholics in 1955, when Xi had been running Catholic affairs.[82]

Those "above ground" at the official 1983 anniversary celebrations saw a sense of historic continuity too. Xi had been the key party figure at the first two meetings of the Catholic Patriotic Association in 1957 and 1962, and official coverage of the 1983 festivities made the connection explicit: Xi's "speech serves as a link between past and future" and "once again guides the future direction for us down the path of love of nation and love of religion."[83] Vice-Minister Jiang Ping of the United Front Work Department said, "On this twenty-fifth anniversary of the establishment of the Catholic Patriotic Association, I believe it is meaningful to repeat Comrade Xi Zhongxun's speech of July 16, 1957, at the first meeting of this association." Jiang then repeated Xi's earlier comments about how "patriotism is the sacred duty of every Chinese person. Religious people are no exception."[84] Bishop Louis Zhang Jiashu, who had become bishop of Shanghai in 1960, concluded his own submitted remarks by "expressing the deepest gratitude" to Xi Zhongxun for "encouraging us to escape from the Vatican" in 1957.[85]

In his own speech, Xi noted that some of the men present had become bishops prior to 1957, and others, after 1957—that is, without Vatican approval. Yet all of them had made contributions, including "opposing the interference and sabotage of the Vatican." Still, Xi warned that "foreign reactionary forces" would never give up their nefarious plans to "return to the Chinese mainland, control the Chinese Catholic Church, and change our country's socialist system." This struggle would continue into the future. Any Catholic who "willingly accepts domination by a foreign power" or who opposes officially approved Catholic organizations would be punished by the law.[86] The very next month, four elderly priests in Shanghai were sentenced to up to fifteen years in prison for maintaining ties with the Vatican and for sharing information about the Catholics in China with those living overseas.[87]

SMALL VICTORIES IN TIBET AND XINJIANG

Xi believed that overcoming the leftist mistakes in Tibet would help to either win over the Dalai Lama or, if necessary, make him irrelevant. At the same time, he saw the Panchen Lama as a crucial intermediary for party interests and, if necessary, a possible replacement for the Dalai Lama. Yet one of the biggest challenges to this agenda came from a fellow Han Chinese, Tibet party secretary Yin Fatang, together with Yin's allies in the Tibet Autonomous Region leadership. These men believed that Xi's call for reforms went too far, and they were skeptical of the Panchen Lama.[88]

In June 1983, *Tibet Daily* published eight pictures from the meeting of the Sixth National People's Congress, but none of them included a picture of the Panchen Lama, although he was a vice-chairman. Xi told Yin Fatang that this was a serious political incident and demanded an investigation. When Yin looked into the matter, he learned that the pictures had all been supplied by the New China News Agency and that the Panchen Lama happened not to be present when the photographer was taking the pictures. When Yin went to explain the incident to Xi, Xi was unsated. "Regardless, this is a political incident," Xi said. "Why didn't you manage this well at the time, or why is it that even after the incident, you did not address the problem, even if the material was from the New China News Agency?" According to Zhang Xiangming, a high-ranking cadre involved in Tibet policy, "Xi Zhongxun stubbornly believed that this was a political mistake, but Yin Fatang naturally did not accept this criticism."[89]

At one meeting between Xi and Yin, Xi spoke the entire two hours. He claimed that he was incredibly busy and had no time to talk. He hardly gave Yin a moment to speak, so Yin only had time to make two comments: that the Panchen Lama could not replace the Dalai Lama and that it was inappropriate for the Panchen Lama's religious activities to flourish too much because that would make the Dalai Lama religion more powerful too. Yet "Xi Zhongxun was extremely stubborn on these issues," Zhang later wrote.[90]

In November 1983, Yin enraged Xi again. The Tibet Autonomous Region party leadership reacted to the new Eliminate Spiritual Pollution Campaign by declaring that spiritual pollution was "even more prominent" in Tibet than it was in the rest of the country. Xi complained that Tibet and Jilin were the only places where the party leadership had passed a resolution on spiritual pollution. Only a month later, the Central Committee pointedly reminded the Tibet Party Committee that religion and spiritual pollution were two separate issues.[91]

Struggling to resolve these differences, the party held another major forum on the Tibetan question in February and March 1984. Xi wanted to use the forum as an opportunity to remove Yin. Insisting on his position, Yin went directly to Hu Yaobang. Originally, Xi was going to chair that meeting, but when it was about to start, Hu Yaobang showed up and took over. Xi's plan, for the moment, had failed.[92] In his remarks to the forum, Hu Yaobang explained that the meeting was necessary because the secretariat was still hearing "many opinions" about work in Tibet. He recognized that some of those present were furious about the criticisms lodged against them. He tried to calm nerves: "Recently, there have been some rumors that the Central Committee was going to do something or other about Tibet. That is complete fantasy; that is not the case." Xi kept interrupting the proceedings. When Hu Qili said it was necessary to "seek truth from facts" and "develop democracy," Xi said, "That means listening a bit more to the opinions of the Panchen Lama and other living buddhas." With regard to the Dalai Lama, Hu Yaobang stated that China's policy was to welcome his return, but he would have to make a declaration acknowledging his mistakes. Xi's own interjections about the Dalai Lama were tough. If the Dalai Lama were to get what he wants, Xi said, Tibet "will definitely become a colony of the foreign invaders." Xi accused the Dalai Lama of rallying support with "the ethnic issue and the religion issue" and by promising people they would "become feudal lords."[93]

During the forum, regional officials from Tibet criticized Xi by name. At one session, Wan Li remarked that this was the first time in the country's history that local cadres summoned to a meeting in Beijing openly criticized a leader in the party center.[94] During a break, the leadership of the Tibet Autonomous Region was sent to Jiangsu, as well as to Guangdong, Xi's former province, to take a look at those areas that, despite their impoverished beginning, had developed quickly. Although lower-ranking leaders were impressed, the top leadership from Tibet was not, believing that Tibet lacked the conditions for such development.[95]

On March 26, back in Beijing, the secretariat met with the leaders of the Tibet Autonomous Region. When it was Yin's turn to speak, he complained that the draft summary report of the forum was too negative as economic conditions in Tibet truly were harsh, in particular because of an ongoing drought. Although "leftism" was present, it was also true that the Dalai Lama's teachings were still a threat. Some individuals were allegedly using religion to rape women. The Panchen Lama wanted to raise the status of religion, but that meant, in Yin's mind, that "when the water rises, all boats rise," so "the Dalai Lama rises as well." In an act sure to infuriate Xi given his role in the incident, Yin even raised the Panchen Lama's seventy-thousand-character petition. "Was the Panchen Lama always patriotic?" Yin asked.[96]

In his own remarks, Hu Yaobang reflected on Yin's reaction to the criticisms: "The comrades of the Tibet Autonomous Region Party Committee do not agree. That's not all bad; they do not pretend to trick us. If they don't understand now, they will have to stay here a few more days." Hu, worried about instability, affirmed that Yin would continue in his position. Hu Qili then made the stunning announcement to the secretariat that Yin was trying to use Deng Xiaoping, Yin's former leader in the Southwest Bureau, against Xi. Hu Qili claimed that Yin had told Deng that Xi, Li Weihan, and Zhou Enlai's widow, Deng Yingchao, were the ones who supported the Panchen Lama, and Deng responded, "I understand; I understand." In his diary that day, Li Rui wrote that Xi was "absolutely furious" at the meeting.[97]

Two days later, the forum passed the summary, which ordered that the regional leadership focus on three areas: Tibet's special characteristics and improvements to the economy, Tibetan culture, and "highly emphasizing and practically implementing United Front work, ethnic work, and religion work, especially in terms of uniting with high-ranking dignitaries."[98] After the leaders returned to Lhasa, they still heard rumors that Xi was constantly pressuring the Organization Department to fire them.[99] On April 25, Yin Fatang gave a self-criticism at an enlarged session of the region's standing committee. He professed to not having opened his mind enough and "one-sidedly emphasizing national enterprises and the planned economy." In terms of the United Front, he criticized himself for being insufficiently welcoming to prominent nonparty figures. He did not have "enough understanding" of the "mass nature, long-term nature, and complicated nature" of religion. The root of all these problems was "leftism": "the Tibet Autonomous Region Party Committee, and especially me, are responsible."[100] Although Yin remained in his position, Xi had forced him to bend his knee.

Xi also made some progress in Xinjiang in 1984. At a meeting on Xinjiang at his home in January, Xi said that "ethnic unity is the absolute top priority." Yet political infighting persisted among the top leadership in the province, and Wang Enmao had yet to win over his detractors. Xi complained that members of the Xinjiang Party Standing Committee continued to oppose decisions on rehabilitation of Cultural Revolution–era cases. Xi warned that it was necessary for all the factions to be appropriately represented, no matter their size.[101]

In April 1984, Xi spent four days in Xinjiang on his way back from the funeral of Ahmed Sékou Touré in Guinea. On Tomb Sweeping Day, he visited the graves of Communist martyrs, including Mao's brother.[102] He also went to a *bingtuan* near Urumqi. But one of the main purposes of his trip had been to declare his support for Wang Enmao. After listening to a report from the party standing committee, he praised Wang's two years as head of the region: "It is precisely because ethnic-unity work has begun a new stage that economic construction and other work in Xinjiang has finally achieved such big successes."[103]

After returning to Beijing, Xi drafted a glowing report about his trip. Although a full version of this document has yet to be released, a short description claimed that Xi called Xinjiang "a treasure, a good place!" He again praised Wang Enmao's record in Xinjiang during the previous two years. Xi was impressed that Xinjiang, for the first time in fifteen years, had become self-sufficient in food production. In February, the Xinjiang Party Committee had established a target for Xinjiang's gross output of industry and agriculture by the year 2000, but Xi thought the plan was too slow. Under Xi's supervision, the State Council organized a large group of experts from seventeen ministries to inspect the region, and in August, the Xinjiang Party Committee had revised its earlier economic targets, accepting Xi's proposal to grow at a much faster rate.[104]

MEETING REPRESENTATIVES OF THE DALAI LAMA AGAIN

Beijing was growing more confident about its position vis-à-vis Dharamsala. The months after the Second Tibet Work Forum signified a clear toughening in the party's position. Yin Fatang insulted the Dalai Lama, saying that "his greatest mistake is treason." Yin said that China still welcomed the Dalai Lama to return but only "as long as he has patriotic feeling and is willing to admit his mistakes."[105] In October, a new official document was much tougher and less keen on compromise with Dharamsala than before. It began by stating that the Dalai Lama was "unworthy of the nation, unworthy of the Tibetan people, and [he] had destroyed his own reputation." Tibet would not be granted "half independence," be given the same rights as those promised to Taiwan, or be expanded to include all Tibetan areas, so there was nothing to "negotiate."[106]

Shortly after this policy was disseminated, on October 21, another Tibetan exile delegation arrived in Beijing. Lodi Gyari, again among the delegates, noticed that "there was a noticeable hardening of attitude and even a sense of arrogance" across the table, which he attributed to Beijing's successful negotiations with London to reassert political control over Hong Kong.[107] Xi tried to avoid provoking them. On November 19, the secretariat met to discuss the twentieth anniversary of the founding of the Tibet Autonomous Region, and Xi opposed holding any troop inspections or any large-scale parades.[108]

The visit veered toward total failure on November 27 when Yang Jingren, head of the United Front Work Department, publicly revealed, for the very first time, Hu Yaobang's Five-Point Proposal. These actions deeply upset the Tibetans, who had not been warned beforehand.[109] On November 30, Xi hosted a dinner for them to cheer them up and to encourage them to continue relations. While the meal was being prepared, he spoke warmly of the Dalai Lama: "Earlier, we both were colleagues. He was vice-chairman of the Standing Committee of the National People's Congress. We worked together. It has been twenty-five years since he left for abroad. In between, I have very much missed him, especially knowing of his status and livelihood challenges to living abroad. I have always been worried about him." Xi showed the delegation a picture of the Dalai Lama that had been given to him in 1980 and asked about the Dalai Lama's health. Xi then tried to explain why Yang Jingren had publicly referred to the Five-Point Proposal: "The reason we made the announcement about the Five-Point Proposal is not only because some of the earlier Tibetan delegates to China, upon their return, did not accurately report the real situation in China but also because some people around the Dalai Lama had made unfriendly statements." Xi acknowledged Beijing's previous mistakes in Tibet, but he heavily qualified them: "We must not say everything that has happened was because of our Chinese comrades in Tibet. . . . This issue is different from the issue of the Dalai Lama living abroad. We must not make direct connections between the two. During the time of far-left mistakes, the Panchen Lama endured much suffering. I also had to suffer for years. Even Deng was demoted on two occasions." Xi tried to put distance between the Dalai Lama and some of the Dalai Lama's associates, who were, in the party's view, the source of the troubles. Xi suggested that discussions would be smoother if the Dalai Lama himself were to visit Beijing. "In any case," he continued, "if we can have a direct face-to-face conversation with the Dalai Lama after he returns, issues will be more easily resolved." But Xi concluded with a powerful warning about China's growing strength. "We are very confident about succeeding in our endeavors. Given what we have achieved during the last few years, we are confident about our future prospects."[110]

When Xi completed speaking, Juchen, again the head of the delegation, continued to argue with Yang Jingren about the announcement of the five points without prior consultation. Yang claimed that he had warned Juchen, but Juchen said that Yang had only very briefly referred to it during an informal dinner. However, Juchen did acknowledge that Xi's explanation had helped with some of their concerns. He suggested that they issue a collective statement to limit any negative media coverage of the trip. Xi and Yang agreed.[111] Soon thereafter, a New China News Agency report publicly revealed that Xi had showed to the delegation a picture of him together with the Dalai Lama. The announcement even included Xi's kind remarks about the Dalai Lama. The New China News Agency quoted Xi as saying, "I know him well. I think he is an intelligent person and a statesman." The article also included Xi's regards: that he "wished the Dalai Lama good luck."[112] Yet, despite Xi's efforts to smooth out the rough edges, the talks failed. The Tibetan leadership would soon fatefully conclude that diplomacy was going nowhere and that Beijing was simply playing for time.[113]

THE HIGH TIDE OF 1985

Xi had achieved real breakthroughs in 1984, but his record in 1985 was even more remarkable, including with Catholics who continued to present special challenges. The bishop of Shanghai, Louis Zhang Jiashu, was growing old, which made the search for his replacement a pressing task. Catholic leaders often held dim views of one another, and official Catholic doctrine had not changed: the Vatican was still supposed to approve any new bishops, so anyone who violated this stricture risked excommunication. In January 1985, after years of vetting, a new auxiliary bishop of Shanghai was finally consecrated: Aloysius Jin Luxian, a man who had been swept up in the 1955 crackdown (when Xi was managing Catholic affairs) but one who would, nevertheless, tell an American diplomat in 2007 that Xi was "a good person."[114]

As Paul Mariani explains, Bishop Jin faced a difficult moral choice. As an ally of Beijing, he could work to strengthen the party-approved church and live a comfortable life. Defying the party would make it impossible for him to advocate on behalf of Catholic interests from within the system, and it would probably mean his continued persecution. Still, without the Vatican's approval, he knew he would be seen as a traitor among the many Chinese Catholics who still refused to work with the government. Jin had once said, "The government thinks I'm too close to the Vatican, and the Vatican thinks I'm too close to the government. I'm a slippery fish squashed between government control and Vatican demands." In the summer of 1985, on a trip to Hong Kong, Jin told American priest Laurence Murphy that he was "personally committed to union with the Universal Church" and he would "like his own ordination legitimated." Yet he would prove so loyal to party interests that, on one occasion in 1986 or 1987, he told Xi that pursuing a closer relationship with the Vatican would be "harmful."[115]

It was not only with the Catholic Church that Xi won a big victory in 1985. In April, at a discussion meeting on religious policy, Xi complained that 40 percent of the confiscated religious venues and property that should have been returned remained in party hands. The problem was that "'leftist' thinking continues to shackle many of the comrades' brains." Xi made a strikingly practical case: "Looking back on history, countless facts prove that, with regard to dealing with religious issues, the more that our policies are tight and inflexible, the more that religion is suppressed in practical terms, then the more things run counter to one's wishes and the exact opposite result occurs." Because some religious activities "are indeed difficult to distinguish from superstition," it was easy for the party to perpetrate abuses. He called for a lighter touch. "Our cadres can only support and help monks manage their own temples," he said. "They cannot exceed their mandate."[116] Based on Xi's directives, by the end of the year, more than forty-three thousand places for religious worship had been opened.[117]

Xi's weight on Tibetan issues was also especially visible in 1985. Yin Fatang was finally removed on June 1. Yin's move to become vice-commissar of China's nuclear forces was a clear demotion. His memoirs depicted his transfer with bitterness, alleging that some people even "cried out against the injustice."[118] Yin was replaced by Wu Jinghua, who had been born in Yunnan to ethnic Yi parents and had served in both Sichuan (under Deng Xiaoping) and in the State Ethnic Affairs Commission. Yin was gone, but Wu did not find a welcoming environment. A representative of the Organization Department who escorted Wu there to assume his new position concluded that Wu would likely not be able to effectively manage the situation. The other party leaders in the region considered Wu as a "young brother who wants to manage his elder siblings."[119] But for Xi, Wu's ascent to the top was a victory. After the decision was made to send Wu to Tibet, Xi went to the head of the Tibet Advisory Council to pressure him to support the decision.[120]

There were, in 1985, significant developments in Xinjiang as well. Despite longstanding concern that the departure of elderly Wang Enmao would destabilize the region, the top leadership finally felt comfortable promoting younger cadres. On September 17, Xi met with Wang to talk about the leadership team in Xinjiang (and, immediately after, to discuss personnel in Tibet with Wu Jinghua).[121] A few days later, Hu Yaobang announced that Song Hanliang—a regional vice-chairman who was studying at the party school in Beijing at that time—would cut his studies short and return to Xinjiang to replace Wang Enmao as party secretary. Song lacked the experience and authority that Wang enjoyed, and he expressed the wish that Wang continue on at least a little longer, but Beijing refused.[122]

By late 1985, Xi had reasons to look at his record with confidence. The looming succession crisis in the Catholic Church had been solved. Confiscated religious properties were returning to their original owners. Winning over the Dalai Lama seemed less pressing as the party was growing more confident in its new policies, and Xi's foe, Yin Fatang, had finally been removed. Xinjiang appeared stable enough to pursue even more rapid economic growth and to promote younger leaders. It would have been difficult to predict at the time that Xi's entire approach to ethnic and religious affairs would collapse less than four years later.

24
"THINGS WERE GOING SO WELL!"

During the first half of the 1980s, Beijing's new policies helped stabilize the relationship between the party and China's ethnic minorities and religious faithful. The leadership had reason to believe that it was successfully overcoming the legacies of the Cultural Revolution. But everything came crashing down by the end of the decade. When disturbances shook Lhasa in March 1989, Hu Yaobang, by then purged from the leadership, simply could not understand why Tibetans had still not come around to party rule. "Things were going so well! What could have caused this?" he wondered.[1] Martial law was soon declared, and People's Liberation Army soldiers were again used to suppress Tibetans. Further crackdowns, two months later, followed in Xinjiang and Inner Mongolia. Just as in the 1950s, the party had swung dramatically from one direction to another.

What happened? Beginning in late 1985, protests and the continued spread of religious activities started to concern party leaders. They were confused and not quite sure how to react. Were these "growing pains" as the regime moved to a more consultative and open model? Could these problems be solved by better executing the current guidelines? Powerful individuals within the party did not think so. They saw darker forces at work: "splittists" supported by nefarious foreigners. Conservative figures such as Yin Fatang, who had been defeated by Xi, felt vindicated when China's ethnic minorities took to the streets.

Yet Xi too was uncomfortable with these new trends that appeared in the 1980s. He believed that the party needed to act swiftly to get a better handle on the situation. His immediate inclination was to tighten control, not double down on openness and give further space for religious activity. At the same time, he still had faith that economic growth and the co-optation of grievances could play significant roles in reducing ethnic tensions. He may even have believed that adjustments in a conservative direction might protect this broader approach.

This was a difficult balance to get right. And it was not just ethnic and religious minorities who refused to bend to Xi's will. Other issues remained out of his grasp too. One significant problem was mortality—the party heavily relied on unique, irreplaceable figures, such as Ulanhu and the Panchen Lama, whose deaths (December 1988 and January 1989, respectively) stripped the party of powerful intermediaries. But even more important was the longevity and power of Deng Xiaoping. Despite their common fear of chaos, Deng was comparatively less patient than Xi. It was Deng who sent the tanks into Lhasa in March 1989, signifying the collapse of this period of experimentation.

ADJUSTING AND PROTECTING THE NEW APPROACH

Until December 1985, the central and Xinjiang leaderships were confident that affairs in the region had never been better. Yet several issues rankled students there: restrictions on education, signs of increased Han migration, and the replacement of Ismail Amat, the head of government, with Tomur Dawamat, who was viewed as a party puppet (but who had visited Xi on every trip he made to Beijing). In December 1985, students began to march at Xinjiang University. On the fourteenth, seven universities sent representatives to meet the provincial leadership, including Song Hanliang, who listened carefully to their demands and agreed to continue a dialogue. Significantly, the student leaders were not punished for their behavior.[2]

Some members of the Xinjiang Party Committee were not especially alarmed. Amudong Niyazi, head of the People's Congress in Xinjiang, noted that, just as during the Kashgar incident in 1981, the protests were ultimately solved by "persuasion and education work" and by using "democratic personages" to "prevent the situation from becoming bigger." Yet Niyazi could not deduce why the protests, "contrary to expectation, are occurring now when the situation is very good." Since people could use "normal channels" to express their dissatisfaction, he wondered why they chose instead to cause "trouble."³ Wang Enmao, who had recently stepped down as party head of Xinjiang, had an answer, and it was a distressing one. Wang reported directly to Xi that this was a case of "local nationalists behind the scenes scheming, leading, planning, and guiding." Strengthening party leadership and providing more education on the Marxist view of ethnicity were imperative, Wang told Xi. He suggested increasing the size of the People's Armed Police and the *bingtuan*.⁴

Xi was worrying about the explosion of religious activity throughout the country. In April 1985, he had given a major address with an emphasis on righting previous wrongs and giving more space for religious services. But in January 1986, in yet another significant speech, he was clearly moving in a tougher direction. He still said the most important task was to "oppose and defeat 'leftist' thinking." However, he also warned against "catering" to "inappropriate demands" from certain religious figures and ignoring illegal activities. It was necessary to protect freedom of religion, but, at the same time, the party had to "further strengthen ideological-political work" since "witches" and "holy men" were engaged in "superstitious activities." Since 1979, Xi said, too many temples had been built, and mosque renovations were spending too much money. "All religious activities must be executed under the parameters permitted by the constitution and policy. Religion must not interfere in government, law, education, or other national affairs. The feudal privileges and systems that suppress and exploit that have already been eliminated must not be allowed to return," Xi said. He warned about foreigners "using any method or any form to engage in penetration and subversion in our country."⁵ This meeting was a controversial one—religious figures complained directly to Xi about the idea of strengthening party "management" of religious venues.⁶

In February, Xi received a report about "irregular activities" by Christians in Henan. Furious, he scribbled numerous comments in the margins: "Why weren't they prosecuted according to the law?"; "There can be no mercy"; "Any party member who believes in Christianity should be encouraged to stop, and anyone who stubbornly maintains their belief should be expelled from the party."⁷ In May, Xi explicitly said that, henceforth, the priority of the religious departments should shift from rehabilitation to strengthening control.⁸

Meanwhile, Xi's attempts to maintain some kind of dialogue with the Dalai Lama were becoming bogged down. Xi resorted to private channels and personal connections. He decided to use Li Youyi, a prominent Tibetologist then lecturing at UCLA, as an intermediary. Li's children referred to Xi as "uncle," and Qi Xin once asked Li's wife to suggest a professor from Minzu University to tutor her on modern history. Xi told Li that after the Dalai Lama had fled, Beijing had a poor understanding of the Dalai Lama's living situation, and Xi asked Li to visit Dharamsala as a representative of Beijing.[9] In March 1986, Li arrived in India. Juchen recalled that, at the time, there was still some hope that the negotiations would ultimately be successful. At Hotel Tibet, in a meeting with Juchen and Takla, Li praised Tibetan history, literature, and culture as being equal to those of any people. He even spoke of the benefits that the Dalai Lama could bring to China, recognized India's support for the Tibetans in Dharamsala, and criticized Communist ideology. After Li returned to Beijing, he sent a note to Takla about Xi's wishes to continue to remain in contact.[10]

Yet the relationship was hitting serious snags. In that same month, Takla approached the Chinese ambassador to India and asked for permission for Gyalo Thondup to visit Tibet. Takla spoke of a 1984 promise from Xi that the Chinese government would welcome him. However, Takla was told that the Chinese government had decided not to issue an invitation after all. The Chinese embassy also informed the Tibetans that in the future, they would no longer be able to acquire visas in Hong Kong; Tibetans would thereafter be forced to acquire "travel certificates" from the Chinese embassy in Delhi. Dharamsala refused those conditions. In July, Hu Qili and Xi Zhongxun approved a report that suggested the Dalai Lama was making an issue of the visa situation because of his "counterrevolutionary position on 'Tibetan independence.'" The document concluded that the Tibetans were not interested in closing the distance between Dharamsala and Beijing.[11]

After a period of debate on how much religious and ethnic policy should change, the party reached enough of a consensus to hold a major meeting of local cadres from throughout the country in October and November 1986. The message was clear: party policies were correct but did need to be implemented better. Xi affirmed the development-focused policies and declared that "it is difficult for a nationality that keeps itself closed to achieve progress and development." In Xi's mind, although a few of the old ways of thinking still had to be changed, the party now required more concrete action and fewer empty words. Solving these matters was pressing: "Currently, among minorities, fifteen million people have still not solved the problem of having enough to eat and wear, which, nationally, is a small number. But there are only seventy million minority people! So that is nearly one-quarter. This deserves our attention."[12]

Xi betrayed culturally essentialist views, warning that many minority people did not understand how to do business, the importance of contracts, or the meaning of commodity products. "Han comrades should not take advantage of them. They should go help them." He emphasized the role that "mutually dependent economic ties" could play in forging close relations among the nationalities. He said, "In our nation, historically speaking, ever since the Qin and Han dynasties, we, as a nationality, were very open. Our ethnic culture absorbed culture also from the Middle East and South Asia. In terms of ethnic work, it is necessary to actively help each minority ethnicity change its closed status and execute openness." The most significant part of his speech, however, was his affirmation that the party should never again use campaign-style purges to attack people who hold different opinions: "Now, and in the future, it is still the case that each issue should be managed with precision. Do not, as soon as there is a problem, hastily say that this is a case of this-or-that-ism, and also do not say that it is this or that line. In 1957, opposing regional nationalism became a campaign. As soon as there is a campaign, things go bad. No campaigns must ever occur again."[13]

THE FALL OF HU YAOBANG

Shortly after this warning about turning differences of opinion into political struggle, Hu Yaobang lost his position as general secretary of the party in January 1987. That turn of events immediately suggested the possibility of a more fundamental review of ethnic and religious policy. Xi fought hard against that prospect. On January 23, the United Front Work Department and the State Ethnic Affairs Commission together affirmed the results of the meeting on ethnic affairs held the previous fall. Xi directly oversaw the drafting of an official *Report on a Few Important Issues in Ethnic Work*, which continued to prioritize economic development. In that document, party members were again warned not to use "labels." Special attention was to be given to the Law on Autonomous Regions. Specific guidelines were necessary to make sure real autonomy was achieved. The party needed to cultivate minority cadres, the document asserted, and existing minority cadres were to be given freer reign. On March 16, the secretariat held a meeting on Tibet that affirmed that current policies in the region would continue. That same month, in a speech to the Fifth Congress on Islamic Affairs, Xi stated explicitly that the attacks on bourgeois liberalization, an outgrowth of Hu's fall, were limited to inside the party and they would not affect religious policies. Xi's words helped assuage some worries.[14]

But Hu's departure from the leadership was a watershed moment. Many years later, Lodi Gyari expressed regret that the Tibetans had not done more to support Hu while he still held power. "We should have seen the genuineness and seriousness of Hu Yaobang," he remarked. "We did a disservice to him."[15] At this time of acute political sensitivity, over January and February, Takla again visited China. During conversations with both the Panchen Lama and Yan Mingfu, then head of the United Front Work Department, Takla proposed that Xi Zhongxun or Hu Qili meet with the Dalai Lama.[16]

On February 1, Takla met with Xi at the United Front Work Department building. Xi began by saying he was glad Takla had come to Beijing, and he asked whether the Dalai Lama was still healthy. Takla explained that the main reason for his visit was a letter from Li Youyi claiming that Xi still saw a need for continued contacts. After Takla described his meeting with Yan Mingfu, Xi praised the Dalai Lama in extraordinary terms. "The Dalai Lama's wisdom, like his fame, is like an ocean. In general, I have huge respect for him. He not only has great wisdom in religious affairs but also has become very experienced in political affairs. If he were to return to the motherland, his wisdom would not only harmoniously unite the motherland and contribute to the Four Modernizations but also benefit development of the Tibetan people's economy, religion, and culture." Like the last time, Xi tried to distinguish the Dalai Lama from other Tibetan exiles who were more critical of China.[17]

Xi told Takla that a meeting with the Dalai Lama outside of China, even in Hong Kong, would be inappropriate because of the inability to maintain security or secrecy. Xi warned that, as time went by, if the Dalai Lama were to remain overseas, he would become increasingly irrelevant to the international community and become a "playing card":

> As the Dalai Lama reaches age fifty-two, if he stays long in a foreign land, foreigners will eventually treat him patronizingly, and they will take him for granted. This is the nature of the world. Currently, even if the Indian government is treating the Dalai Lama with huge respect, you should know

the purpose is to use all of you. Unless there is peace on the border between the two countries, they will, like a playing card, use you all. The Dalai Lama should know this well. You all must remain suspicious of the Indian government, or you all will later face the consequences.

At this point, Takla interjected to say that the Dalai Lama had never been under anyone's influence, nor would he be so in the future. Xi said, "In that case, this is good." After the meeting, they had dinner together. When they finished, Xi held Takla's hand and said that if the Dalai Lama could briefly come to the motherland and, after meeting with his old friends, could say something about not separating from the motherland, it would be consequential.[18]

Xi had always believed an effective policy toward Dharamsala required China getting its own house in order. But troubles were starting to mount in the Tibet Autonomous Region, where Wu Jinghua—the man Xi had sent to Lhasa to replace Yin Fatang—was struggling to achieve unity with other party leaders. High-ranking officials there believed Wu was "shortsighted and impulsive." Some Tibetan and Han cadres were still afraid that policies would change after the fall of Hu Yaobang, and they worried that if Hu Yaobang had committed rightist mistakes, then that might mean policy on religion was also too liberal. Certain Tibetan cadres were upset that poor peasants and herders had previously been valued by the party, but now only high-ranking dignitaries were taken seriously.[19]

The party was struggling in Inner Mongolia too, where tensions ran so deep that no one wanted to work there. In the middle of July 1987, on the eve of the fortieth anniversary of the Inner Mongolia Autonomous Region, Sun Qi, the vice-secretary of the Liaoning Party Committee, was distressed to learn that Beijing wanted him to become the top party leader in Inner Mongolia. Sun's colleagues told him not to go. They warned him that "interpersonal relations there are very complicated, and the past few previous party secretaries all left unhappily." Representing the Central Committee, Song Ping told Sun that relations between Han and Mongols, as well as among Mongols, were tense because of a competition over high-ranking positions. The current party secretary in Inner Mongolia, Song said, "was in a hurry to resign." Despite weeks of pressure, Sun continued to refuse the position, and, in the middle of August, the party finally decided to send someone else.[20]

In the midst of this turbulence, Xi went to Inner Mongolia to celebrate the anniversary of its founding. Ulanhu led the official delegation, and Xi was his deputy. When they got off the train, they were welcomed by Ulanhu's son Buhe, who was then chairman of the Inner Mongolian government. At the station, nine singing young women in traditional Mongolian clothing presented the delegation with ceremonial scarves and fermented horse milk.[21] Ulanhu worked to build up Xi's prestige by deliberately not appearing at the same events as Xi so that Xi would be the center of attention. But whenever Xi appeared, he would say, "Representing Comrade Ulanhu, I have come to visit everyone!"[22]

On July 30, Xi gave a speech at a rally celebrating the anniversary. He praised the party's "long-term stable policies" in the early years of the People's Republic and condemned the Cultural Revolution. "With regard to handling ethnic contradictions," Xi said, "it is necessary to seek truth from facts, to carefully and reasonably manage issues related to ethnic relations, and to maintain the methods of education and persuasion."[23] On August 4, he accompanied Buhe to visit Genghis Khan's mausoleum in the Yekejuu League region. It was Xi's second trip to the tomb; in December 1951, he had visited it when the tomb was still in Qinghai. The next day, Xi, back in the capital of Hohhot, gave a farewell speech. He was happy with what he had seen, describing Inner Mongolia as a "steed galloping" toward socialist modernization. Leftist radicalism, not rightist liberalism, was still the greater threat: "When engaging in reform, it is necessary to oppose both 'leftism' and rightism, but primarily to overcome the power of habitual 'leftism.' Otherwise, reform will die in the cradle. It will be unfinished."[24]

GROWING CHALLENGES FROM THE TIBETAN AND CHRISTIAN COMMUNITIES

Soon after Xi's speech, events in Tibet led some to conclude that more "leftism" was exactly what the party needed. On September 21, 1987, in a speech to the US Congress, the Dalai Lama introduced a Five-Point Peace Plan, proposing that Tibet become a "zone of peace." He referred to the "holocaust inflicted upon our people during the past decades of occupation." Over three paragraphs, he provided an account of the negotiations that had been overseen on Beijing's side by Xi, accusing China of having "misused the opportunity for a genuine dialogue." It was "against this background" of an impasse that the Dalai Lama openly proposed the departure of the Chinese troops, the abandonment of China's population-transfer policy, respect for Tibetan rights and the environment, and "earnest negotiations" on Tibet's status.[25]

Beijing saw his words as a provocation, especially after demonstrators took to the streets of Lhasa. Between six to twenty Tibetans were killed.[26] Raidi, who at the time was head of the Tibet Autonomous Region's Chinese People's Political Consultative Conference, wrote that "Comrade Zhongxun stated clearly that the riots in Lhasa were a serious political incident caused by the Dalai clique's careful plan to split the motherland and undermine the stability and unity of Tibet."[27]

On November 25, Xi, along with other leaders, including the Panchen Lama, listened to a report on the protests in Tibet.[28] The top leadership, however, still resisted any pressure for a fundamental shift. At a January 24 enlarged Politburo Standing Committee meeting, General Secretary Zhao Ziyang blamed the disturbances on the legacy of radical leftism in the region. The Panchen Lama was put in charge of a new policy of restricting monasteries and exerting greater control.[29]

The Panchen Lama also helped prepare for the Tibetan celebration of Monlam Chenmo. For twenty years, the party had banned the celebration. In February 1986, Xi had personally given the Panchen Lama permission to restore it in order to "expand" the Panchen Lama's "political influence."[30] Monlam Chenmo had gone smoothly on the two previous occasions, but, in March 1988, a violent incident occurred at Jokhang Temple. Tibetans and one member of the People's Armed Police were killed. As a result, even the Panchen Lama condemned what happened. According to him, the monks had assumed "the more violently they riot, the more we [the authorities] will give in."[31] The Panchen Lama realized that Beijing's policies were in an increasingly precarious position. At a meeting of the National People's Congress in March, he expressed the worry that some cadres had concluded that all Tibetans hated the party: "I recently heard that, because of what happened in Tibet, many people have an incorrect opinion about Tibetans. They say that when Tibetans are treated well, they become dishonest. But if they are repressed a bit, then they will become honest, so, according to this thinking, it is necessary to brutally suppress them to make them honest. These words are very wrong."[32]

Cadres in Xinjiang were worried as well. In May, Wang Enmao gave a tough speech in which he said that the greatest threat to Xinjiang was "ethnic separatism from both inside and outside the country, but primarily ethnic separatism from foreign enemies." He warned of external forces that wanted to establish an "independent Turkestan." Tibet clearly rested heavily on his mind: "We saw a real videotape on the March 5 riot in Tibet. It was bloodcurdling, and the riot seemed extremely serious. We in Xinjiang absolutely must treat the Tibet riot as a lesson and prevent similar incidents from taking place." Wang acknowledged that not everyone agreed with his views: "With regard to opposing splittism, everyone's opinion is the same. But about whether to say, 'Oppose bourgeois nationalism,' there are some different opinions. I believe it must be said; it must be used."[33] Wang Enmao probably felt prescient when, on June 15, Uyghur students again marched in Urumqi.[34]

On that same day as the student protests in Xinjiang, the Dalai Lama delivered another address, this time in Strasbourg. For the first time, he explicitly proposed an arrangement whereby Tibet would be allowed to remain "in association with the People's Republic of China" and Beijing could "remain responsible for Tibet's foreign policy." Some figures in the Tibetan leadership felt that the Dalai Lama's speech was a "big disappointment" and a "huge compromise." They believed that, even if the Tibetans were not to pursue independence, Dharamsala should be more vocal in its criticisms of China and avoid a stance that was "too passive" and "too appeasing."[35]

Party leaders in Beijing, however, were increasingly convinced that the recent problems in Tibet were the fault of the Dalai Lama, not any fault or shortcomings in the party's own policies. Also in June, Politburo Standing Committee member Qiao Shi arrived in Tibet for an inspection tour. It was a major turning point in the direction of more conservative policies. Qiao warned that it had been the Dalai Lama who had planned the recent disturbances. Speaking directly to the debates in the party about whether the problem was due to "splittists" or to previously failed policies, he said, "It cannot be said that the riots were simply the result of a long period of 'leftism.'" He added that less time and effort should be spent on rehabilitating and supporting prominent personages because these policies "cannot be limitless, cannot go on forever."[36]

By this point, Wu Jinghua was losing Xi's support. Xi thought that Wu had "made too many enemies." Yin Fatang, however, thought that Xi's analysis was incorrect. "If Wu is the problem, then replacing one person would be enough. But that is not the problem. It is a problem of the Central Committee's guidelines for ruling Tibet," Yin thought.[37] He blamed Xi for what had occurred in Tibet, even alleging that the protests would not have occurred if Xi had not fired him.[38]

Yin's take on the situation was winning adherents. On October 30, another inspection group arrived in Lhasa. This one, led by Yan Mingfu, included a man by the name of Hu Jintao, then party boss of Guizhou. For health reasons, Yan quickly went back to Beijing, so Hu Jintao led the trip. He and his group returned to Beijing on November 20, and four days later, they reported to Xi.[39] On December 1, the Central Committee released a notification that Hu Jintao was to replace Wu Jinghua.[40]

At a meeting of the leadership with the Tibet Autonomous Region Standing Committee held in Beijing later that month, the party tried to give Wu a soft landing. His removal was officially characterized as "a normal personnel change," as his health was "bad, and it would be difficult for him to continue work in Tibet." Wu's tenure was praised for its achievements. But the summary document, *A Few Issues Regarding Current Work in Tibet*, included seven points that signified a leftist turn. The first priority was to "to grasp the struggle against splittism." That struggle was characterized as one "between us and our enemies." Developing the economy was point three. The importance of winning over Tibetans, especially with regard to the Panchen Lama, was relegated to a far lower priority.[41]

THE DEATHS OF ULANHU, THE PANCHEN LAMA, AND THE NEW APPROACH TO ETHNIC MINORITIES

Xi's legacy had suffered a major defeat, and he was about to suffer two serious losses of both a political and personal nature—the deaths of his two closest non-Han friends, Ulanhu and the Panchen Lama. In December 1988, before leaving on a trip for Guangdong, Xi visited Ulanhu, who had just undergone surgery. Xi told him not to leave the hospital until he had entirely recovered. Shortly after Xi departed, Ulanhu passed. One senior Mongol told a historian that Ulanhu "died with regret and shame." His death deeply affected Xi. One year later, when discussing the draft of a commemorative article to be published under Xi's name, the drafter read, "I lost a close comrade in arms," but Xi told him to change it to "I lost my closest comrade in arms." Xi's article describes Ulanhu's death as "a major, irreparable loss for the party and for the nation."[42]

The very next month after Ulanhu's death, the Panchen Lama died during a trip to Tashilhunpo Monastery. Before leaving on the trip, Xi had told him to be careful because there was even less oxygen in Tibet during that season. Xi also warned the Tibetan that he was getting too fat. When the Panchen Lama jokingly said that he was becoming fatter deliberately to better fit the image of an old buddha, Xi warned that the image of an old buddha also needed to meet the demands of a healthy lifestyle. The Panchen Lama explained that the trip was crucial because it would mean achieving his life's greatest desire—to place the remains of his predecessors, which had been desecrated during the Cultural Revolution, in a stupa near a new temple.[43] In response, Xi told him, "The Buddha does not want you to go, and Marx does not want you to go either."[44]

As soon as Beijing learned that the Panchen Lama had collapsed in Shigatse, Wen Jiabao, then a candidate member of the secretariat, left his office directly for the airport with a group that included multiple top doctors. They risked dangerous weather to land in Lhasa. But it was not enough, and they were unable to save the life of the Panchen Lama.[45] In an obituary published in February, Xi, perhaps to make a point about the current situation, recalled that, in 1951, he had told the Panchen Lama to adopt gradualist policies and not to do anything that "leading patriotic individuals and leaders" would not support. The main task was still the united anti-imperialist, patriotic front. Xi then added, "Upon reflection, this spirit of the Central Committee still has meaning even now."[46]

The Panchen Lama's death was a missed opportunity to further a rapprochement between Dharamsala and Beijing. Beijing had issued an invitation through Gyalo Thondup to the Dalai Lama to attend the funeral. According to Gyalo Thondup's son Khedroob, the invitation was extended by Xi himself. But Xi did not extend the offer formally. Instead, a written invitation came from Zhao Puchu, chair of the Chinese Buddhist Association, thus raising suspicions that Beijing's intentions were not really serious. The Dalai Lama's aides asked if he would be able to meet with Deng Xiaoping or visit Kumbum Monastery in Qinghai. But the Chinese refused to agree explicitly, and the visit never took place.[47]

Xi predicted that the process of selecting the next Panchen Lama might end in disaster if Beijing were not to cooperate with the Dalai Lama. At a banquet held by the United Front Work Department, Xi warned that if Tibetan cadre Phunwang Wangye did not quickly visit India to see the Dalai

Lama, "regardless of anything else, as for the matter of the reincarnation of the Panchen Lama, it is possible there will be both a foreign and a Chinese Panchen Lama." One leading figure in the United Front Work Department responded, "We will not delay. It will definitely be done this way." But, for unclear reasons, it was not done in that way. No conversation about the reincarnation ever took place. "Later, developments really did validate Comrade Zhongxun's words," Phunwang Wangye wrote in his memoirs, referring to what would happen in 1995 when the party rejected the Dalai Lama's selection of the eleventh Panchen Lama and arrested the abbot of Tashilhunpo Monastery. The location and circumstances of the Dalai Lama's pick remain unclear to this day.[48]

THE FINAL BREAK OF 1989

During the next few months, the party's failings became clearer, and its policies, more brutal. Bishop Jin had severely damaged his credibility as a Catholic in November 1988 when he savaged the underground church and asserted that Chinese bishops should be completely autonomous from the Vatican. Several weeks later, he consecrated a bishop, an act so provocative that Jin's own priests in training refused to attend the ceremony. The underground church continued to select bishops with the implicit permission of the Vatican, and the party was drawing lessons about the role of the church during the 1988 protests in Poland. Concerned about these developments, in February 1989, the party released the document *Stepping Up Control over the Catholic Church to Meet the New Situation*, which, in the words of Paul Mariani, was "a point-by-point program on how to control and destroy the underground Catholic Church in China." Nevertheless, a deal between the Vatican and the party seemed more possible than ever at about this time—until the June 4 crackdown on Tiananmen Square decisively ended any such hopes for decades.[49]

With the Panchen Lama gone, the party had even fewer options to control the situation in Tibet. This left Beijing poorly prepared when, beginning on March 1, 1989, more protests started in Lhasa.[50] One credible account suggests that Zhao Ziyang appealed to Xi Zhongxun to personally manage the crisis, reasoning that Xi was one of the party's "experts on ethnic policy."[51] At first, Beijing adopted a somewhat restrained position. The head of security in Lhasa later told a *People's Liberation Army Daily* journalist that during the disturbances, even when Han businesses were under attack, he was under orders from above not to do anything. He finally acted only when the police station was in danger. The commander of the garrison in Lhasa also asserted that the People's Liberation Army had been mobilized but was told not to move. It was waiting for the party center because, in actuality, the Tibet Autonomous Region was not autonomous, and Hu Jintao had no authority to make any decisions.[52]

Finally, on March 3, Deng told Zhao Ziyang that "the key is stability." Anything that hurts stability, Deng warned, "must be opposed. . . . There can be no stepping back. There can be no compromise." In Deng's mind, the party could not allow any spontaneous marches. If it were to do so, then they would occur daily.[53] On March 6, Zhao called a Politburo Standing Committee meeting at which, according to "the spirit" of Deng's March 3 warnings, it was decided that martial law would be announced two days later. On March 7, army forces in Tibet were ordered to enter Lhasa. The leadership of the Thirteenth Army Group, which was rushed to the city, was shocked by the suddenness of the command.[54] The decision was not universally embraced. Even local cadres skeptical of Wu Jinghua and the liberal policies toward religion thought it was not only an excessive reaction but also unnecessary, setting back relations between Tibetans and Han.[55]

Hu Yaobang died on April 15, shortly after the crackdown in Lhasa, and students began protesting in Tiananmen Square. Although the world's attention was focused on the capital, there were disturbances in Inner Mongolia and Xinjiang as well. Students in the Inner Mongolian cities of Hohhot, Baotou, and Tongli boycotted class in support of their colleagues in Beijing.[56] On May 15, anger about a book that misconstrued Muslim sexual customs led to an incident in Urumqi. The book was immediately declared illegal and existing copies were destroyed, but that was not enough—people still took to the streets to protest the book. Party and government buildings were attacked, and the People's Armed Police, public-security cadres, and other party members were injured. One thousand public-security officers and 1,200 People's Armed Police were used to quell the disturbance—clearly a different approach than the ones used in 1981 and 1985.[57]

Soon thereafter, the party signified definitively that the old way of handling ethnic relations was over. In November 1989, Jiang Zemin, the new general secretary, chaired a meeting of the Politburo Standing Committee that concluded that the events in Lhasa had been a continuation of the struggle against the imperialist invaders. The riots represented a "severe political struggle" against domestic and foreign forces that wanted to tear up the nation and oppose the Communist Party of China. The party was to rely on "farmers and herdsmen, workers, intellectuals, and other laborers," not the high-ranking religious figures who had been a hallmark of Xi's tenure.[58]

We do not know for sure how Xi felt about these new policies. But when Premier Li Peng visited him in Shenzhen in 1990, Xi showed him the watch given to him by the Dalai Lama. Xi spoke metaphorically to make his point: "Recently this watch stopped working. I sent people to a Swiss watch store in Hong Kong. Soon it was fixed, and now it works very well." According to an assistant who was present, Xi clung to the hope that those in Tibet who had fought Communist Party rule would one day come around—even the Dalai Lama himself.[59]

25
XI AND THE FATE OF GLOBAL COMMUNISM

After moving from Guangdong back to Beijing, Xi Zhongxun was distant from the big decisions about China's grand strategy and relationship with the outside world. But then again, so was everyone else except for Deng Xiaoping. The party had always centralized authority in a "core" leader, yet, even so, foreign policy was a special prerogative dominated first by Mao and then Deng. In 1982, General Secretary Hu Yaobang was warned that he was playing too much of an independent role in foreign policy. "I was a mouse who stepped on the scales to weigh himself," Hu said, using a Chinese expression meaning he did not understand his own place. Chen Yun, the most senior elder after Deng, was subjected to the humiliation of reading a prepared document when meeting with a Soviet representative. Both Hu Yaobang and Chen Yun believed that China's policy toward the Soviet Union was unnecessarily conflictual, but Deng imposed his own strongly anti-Moscow views upon them.[1]

Like Hu and many other leading figures, Xi thought China should use the threat of expanded ties with the Soviet Union to pressure Washington to better heed Beijing's interests. Deng did not agree.[2] Although Xi had seen the partnership with the Soviet Union collapse, he had also witnessed the benefits of cooperating with Moscow in both the Northwest and the State Council. Deng's history with the Soviet Union, however, stands out for its negativity. During the incessant debates about ideology that shaped the Soviet split, it was Deng who served as Mao's most impressive attack dog against "revisionism," meaning the idea that the Soviet Union had betrayed the principles of Marxism-Lenin. It was an ironic task, given that Deng would face accusations of revisionism when he was purged (twice) during the Cultural Revolution.[3]

China's position in the strategic triangle had changed. The inherent political dangers for high-ranking cadres who regularly met foreigners had not. Hu Yaobang's alleged mistakes in foreign policy, characterized as violations of collective leadership, would become one of the main attacks against him at his 1987 forced resignation, which would so upset Xi as unfair. The charges, especially about Hu's relationship with Japan, were fanciful. In 1984, on a trip to Tokyo, Hu invited three thousand young Japanese to visit China. Although such a trifling decision might seem well within the purview of the general secretary of the party, Deng, who was not consulted ahead of time, was furious.[4] Then, at a reception with Japanese prime minister Nakasone Yasuhiro in 1986, Hu proposed to the Japanese leader that another three thousand go to China. A report in the newsletter of the Chinese Foreign Ministry did not clearly characterize Hu's words, and Deng apparently misunderstood what Hu had said—Deng had wrongly concluded that Hu had invited the three thousand young Japanese to attend China's National Day celebrations. It was a misunderstanding, but it illustrated how easy it was to incur Deng's wrath.[5]

Neither Hu nor Xi, therefore, were the primary architects of China's grand strategy. Domestic affairs consumed much of Xi's attention too. When the Romanians invited him to visit their country in 1982, he said he would "very much like to visit," but he explained he was "very busy," and he "underlined that he was personally and directly responsible to the leadership for the streamlining and simplification of the party apparatus."[6]

Nevertheless, Xi was deeply engaged in China's interactions with the outside world in the 1980s. Drawing upon his experience with spy craft during the civil war, he worked hard to help Beijing improve its intelligence capabilities. The Central Investigation Department, China's spy ministry, had been utterly devastated during the Cultural Revolution. Luo Yuan, the son of Minister Luo Qingchang, went so far as to claim that Xi "*managed* the work of the Central Investigation Department." At the very least, Xi helped conduct a rectification of the department. That work included a detailed investigation and separate meetings between Xi and its leaders, including Minister Luo Qingchang, a close Kang Sheng associate who, by this point, was widely distrusted within the elite. In March 1982, the secretariat decided to dissolve the department and establish the new Ministry of State Security.[7]

The next month, Xi held a joint discussion meeting with the top twelve leaders of the department. Succession problems were especially challenging for the Central Investigation Department, Xi said, because "specialization and continuity" were crucial elements for intelligence work. Moreover, during the Cultural Revolution, the department "was beset by disasters and suffered a great deal." He called for compromise and unity: "The situation at the time of the Cultural Revolution was so complicated. When looking at the mistakes of a few comrades, they cannot be separated by the special historical conditions. Do not get entangled with these issues anymore, and do not grab people and refuse to let them go. Some people said a few wrong words or did a few wrong things. Some of them executed orders against their will. Some of them did not think things through or made a few mistakes." He urged younger cadres to learn from the retiring leaders and, when necessary, invite them to continue to attend meetings.[8] The next year, the new Ministry of State Security officially replaced the Central Investigation Department.

Xi also drew upon the Chinese diaspora to learn about the outside world, including the United States. The Chinese People's Association for Friendship with Foreign Countries, a United Front organization led by Shaanxi native Wang Bingnan, twice invited Julia Li Wu to Beijing to meet with Xi. Wu was born in Nanjing and fled to Taiwan at the age of fifteen with the Nationalists. She later moved to America and was nominated by Ronald Reagan to the National Commission on Libraries and Information Science. While in China, she was given extraordinarily courteous treatment, and she was completely charmed by Xi. In her memoirs, she described him in superlative terms: "His boundless hospitality was deeply touching." It was like "having an easy chat with an elder, and everyone was totally at ease." He was very interested in American politics, economics, and society. Although Xi was "quite unfamiliar" with those subjects, "he clearly had an open mind," Wu thought.[9]

Yet Xi and other leaders often still demonstrated a poor grasp of other countries. The prosperity he witnessed in Sweden in 1981 was a shock. "Not an easy thing!" Xi said in a surprised tone when he learned that the elderly in a hospital he visited were not high-ranking officials. The sixty-five-square-meter home and personal possessions of a thirty-three-year-old single worker astounded his delegation. Xi suspected things were too good to be true. He pressed his translator to investigate. "You understand Swedish," he said. "You should learn a bit about whether social benefits in other regions are the same." He wondered whether taxes were "very heavy" and whether the economy could tolerate the burden.[10]

These early interactions with advanced European countries did not always go smoothly. In September 1981, Xi played official host to Their Majesties King Carl XVI Gustaf and Queen Silvia of Sweden. A scheduled-interview opportunity for Swedish journalists with Deng Xiaoping fell through when Deng showed up late to a banquet. In the last days of the trip, the Chinese tried to accommodate the Swedes by arranging a meeting with Xi instead, but, in a telegram, the Swedish ambassador wrote, "Needless to say Xi is not as rewarding as Deng." Xi was "second best."[11] After Beijing, Xi accompanied the king and queen to Xi'an. Xi, the son of a peasant who fought for decades in a Communist revolution, brought these members of the European royalty to visit ancient dynastic sites, such as the terracotta soldiers, the Huaqing Pool, and the Stele Forest. Xi beamed in pictures from the trip.[12] Yet he was often fuming. The next month, Xi wrote a notification complaining, "As soon as you leave the airport, there is dust everywhere. It was like that around the whole city. It's so distressing!" Since most foreign guests who went to China would travel to Xi'an, this impression was "too unbearable; it fails the civilizational dignity of the ancient capital."[13] Still, Xi, as usual, impressed his guests. In a letter, King Gustaf wrote his host, "Your always kind attention made us feel very much at home." The king thanked Xi "for all the informative talks we had on various occasions. Much value was added to our experiences in China, making it unforgettable."[14]

This would prove to be one of Xi's last encounters with major Western figures. His greatest contribution during this era was helping to restore ties with foreign Communist, leftist, and revolutionary parties. It was no easy task. During the Mao era, Beijing's radicalism had destroyed its relationship with most foreign parties. The People's Republic of China had criticized any calls for moderation, refused to interact with any organization that did not attack the Soviet Union, and called upon the rest of the world to study China's revolutionary and governing experiences. As historian Jeremy Friedman argues, China's self-isolation, as well as Moscow's adoption of some of Beijing's revolutionary rhetoric, led to a complete victory by the Soviet Union in the global campaign for influence among the global left.[15] Deng—the individual on the secretariat in charge of relations with foreign parties until 1966—had helped create this disastrous situation before his own purge.

"We've learned our lesson," Deng told the head of the French Communist Party, George Marchais, in 1982.[16]

Xi worked hard to fix the mess created by Mao and Deng. The key breakthrough was the Twelfth Party Congress in September 1982, when Hu Yaobang announced what would henceforth guide Beijing's relationship with other parties: "Marxism and the principles of independence, complete equality, mutual respect and non-interference in each other's internal affairs."[17] In March 1983, in a meeting that signified ties had officially been restored, Xi used precisely the same language with Yuji Soga, the deputy general secretary of the Japan Socialist Party.[18]

Since the People's Republic of China itself was introducing market principles and welcoming foreign investment, rejoining the Communist world could assuage concerns at home and abroad that China was giving up on socialism. As late as November 1978, Deng had tasked a writing group with drafting yet another new book on why the Soviet Union had become revisionist. The project was never completed. Since the party would soon approve household contracting, as well as township and village enterprises, attacking revisionism in another country became impossible. "According to the standards set by the Mao Zedong era, our level of 'revisionism' had already passed the Soviet Union. How could we keep working on such a book?" one member of the writing group asked.[19] Xi had feared outsiders would accuse China of revisionism when he supported the special economic zones, later recalling, "I thought the new and old Trotskyites in Hong Kong would scold us, saying that we were reverting to capitalism. People in the socialist countries would scold us as well, but the capitalist countries would be happy that we were embarking on the road of capitalism."[20] Moreover, Beijing wanted to learn more about how fellow Communist states were approaching reform. China could learn about technology and economics from the West but not politics.[21]

The International Liaison Department, the party's mysterious body for managing relations with foreign parties, launched a charm offensive under Xi's guidance. Xi excelled at his task. In 1982, the party had relations with fourteen Communist parties, three socialist parties, and forty-five nationalist parties. By 1985, China had established or reestablished ties with eighty-four Communist parties, twenty-eight socialist parties, and seventy-eight nationalist parties.[22] Beijing's new approach paid dividends. At a Soviet politburo meeting in August 1983, some of those present suggested that

Moscow terminate its financial support for Hungary. Bankrolling Eastern Europe was a massive drain on Soviet finances. Yet Soviet leader Iurii Andropov rejected the proposal. "Consider what is happening: the Chinese are successfully drawing various communist parties into their orbit, they are deftly and cleverly pursuing their line of isolating the [Communist Party of the Soviet Union]. We should not help them by taking the kind of actions that were proposed here."[23]

THE DEVELOPED WORLD

Xi's trip with Qiao Shi, head of the International Liaison Department, to France at the invitation of the French Communist Party between November 23 and December 3, 1983, revealed the difficulties Beijing faced in rejoining the international community. The French Communist Party had insisted that Xi, as a politburo member, could not be officially hosted by General Secretary Marchais. The Chinese ambassador to France was concerned that the French Communist Party was still too close to the Soviet Union. Government ties complicated party ties: the Chinese had to decide whether Vice-Premier Geng Biao should go as an official guest of the French government before Xi's visit, as President François Mitterrand, the head of the Socialist Party, had extended an invitation for an official government delegation while on a trip to China as early as March 1981. Ultimately, the Chinese prioritized party relations and decided Xi would first visit as a guest of the French Communist Party, which delighted the French Communists.[24]

Politics at home further complicated Xi's trip. In 1959, the Lushan plenum and the Great Leap Forward had raised challenges for Xi's visit to Moscow. Now, just as Xi was leaving for France in 1983, the new Eliminate Spiritual Pollution Campaign was leading many party members as well as outside observers, like the French, to wonder about the possibility of another Cultural Revolution. The day before Xi and Qiao left China, Charles Malo, the French ambassador, invited them to dinner. Delicately, Malo asked whether "some of the political debates, which the press recently reported on, did not risk disrupting production and development efforts." The diplomat noted that the campaign against spiritual pollution brought up "worrying memories." Xi urged Malo not to be concerned and said that the abuses were already being addressed. The French record of the meeting described how Xi emphasized economic development and stressed that China would not once again descend into a persecutorial mania:

> For China, the main task is development of the economy. . . . The issue of spiritual pollution is "a small problem" affecting the country's cultural life. Some unhealthy phenomena have recently been observed. China wishes—like other countries—to harshly condemn those importing or circulating decadent or pornographic material, whose impact is disastrous on youth. Those engaging in those kinds of activities are criminals. There is, however, no need to regard those who, in cultural or intellectual circles, express divergent views, even if they are erroneous, as criminals. People should be able to talk and share ideas. If possible, comrades should acknowledge their mistakes but certainly not be threatened or terrorized. We should above all avoid that "some people attempt to make issues in that field look worse than they actually are in order to harm the atmosphere of stability and unity." That is the reason why the Central Committee had, very recently, given instructions to newspapers to silence that campaign.

Xi impressed Malo, who described him as someone of "uncommon character." He felt that Xi's revolutionary history and the hardships he had faced at the hands of his own party had strengthened him. Xi, Malo wrote in a cable back to Paris, "came across as a man of the land, direct, cheerful, confident, speaking with ease as a leader." The much younger Qiao Shi, on the other hand, "came across like a man from another world."[25]

After his arrival in France, Xi gave a report to the French Communist Party on the domestic political situation in China, and Qiao Shi spoke on foreign policy. Xi proved a powerful advocate for a changing China, arguing that "the first successes accomplished after the disastrous period of the Cultural Revolution were even better than expected." He spoke of hopes to fix the problem of rationing. He praised the latest Chinese People's Political Consultative Conference because only 35 percent of its members were Communists.[26]

Xi then gave an account of the nature of party leadership. He said there was a "first group" consisting of Deng Xiaoping, Li Xiannian, and others who were over seventy years old. Those veterans were providing guidance. A second group, led by Hu Yaobang and Zhao Ziyang, who were over the age of sixty, managed day-to-day activities (Xi had turned seventy the previous month). Xi described a third group, including Qiao Shi, Hu Qili, and Hao Jianxiu, in their forties and fifties, who were "key" and "the future." He also spoke of the difficulties of intergenerational change, but he assured the French that those "comrades who have been promoted are demonstrating a lot of respect toward veterans."[27]

Xi then moved on to talk about the legal reforms he had been leading on the National People's Congress:

> There is no socialism without democracy. There is no socialist modernization without democracy. Chaos and arbitrariness were the rule during the Cultural Revolution. Since the Third Plenum, effective measures have been taken, as is demonstrated by the new statutes of the Party and the Constitution. The statutes specify that, even though the Party plays a leading role, any cult of personality is forbidden, and activists are not above the law. The Constitution widens the role of various mechanisms. The role of mass organizations and spokespersons for the people is also improved. The union between the Party and the democratic parties and personalities without parties is therefore strengthened. So is [the union between] the Han population and the national minorities (without that "Tibet would be an Indian colony" . . .). The Party is not above the law and on the contrary must respect it in an exemplary fashion.

Xi's comments on fighting crime sounded much less liberal:

> Class struggle still exists in socialism, even though it is less acute. Moreover, there is the impact of ten years of trouble, from 1966 to 1976. Delinquency has increased as well as individualism and anarchism. In addition to that, there is the corrosive influence of the bourgeois lifestyle. . . . Severe blows were struck since the September 2, 1982, decision of the Standing Committee of the National People's Congress: it was decided that criminals would be harshly punished. Many arrests were in August and September. . . . The crime rate has lowered but three more years of fighting are needed.[28]

Xi also discussed the rectification campaign. Former "rebels" who had fought as factions during the Cultural Revolution "must be unmasked." Yet he emphasized that this rectification was different from those in the past and that, this time, there would be "no purges." He noted that some people thought that a three-year rectification was too long and that it would harm economic work, but he countered that "it is necessary to reform ideologically. In order to properly do criticism and self-criticism, time is needed." Xi admitted that there was "some pollution of the minds": "Corrupted ideas of the bourgeoisie are spreading. Distrust toward socialism and extreme individualism are both developing. Bourgeois liberalism: consequences can be severe." Yet just as in his earlier conversation with Malo, he stressed that these problems should not be overestimated. Ideological problems were only "contradictions among the people." "It is important to clearly distinguish criminal acts and those that are 'of an antagonistic nature,'" he asserted, emphasizing that no personal attacks were tolerable, only attacks on ideas.[29]

Xi felt there was "a real spark" between the Chinese Communists and the French Communists, according to a French account. "We belong to the same family," he told the French. "We all bear the name of Communists." He expressed a comfortableness with areas where they continued to disagree: "That spark does not mean Chinese and French Communists do not have points of disagreement. They do and they say so." The Chinese and French agreed that "there is no model for the construction of socialism."[30] Xi told reporters that "the differences between our party and the [French Communist Party] on Afghanistan, Vietnam, and Cambodia do not in any way harm the friendship between the two parties."[31]

Beijing also appreciated the long history and political power of the Italian Communist Party, and some members of the Chinese Communist Party elite saw this sensitive relationship with the Italian Communists as an opportunity to hurt competitors in their own country. In 1985, employees of the pro–Hu Yaobang, well-connected International Liaison Department came to believe that Deng Liqun, a man loathed by Xi, was being groomed to replace Hu. Qian Liren, then the head of the department, tasked one individual with reporting on everything that Deng Liqun said and did on a trip to Italy in October 1985. It was immediately clear that Qian was asking the cadre to spy on Deng. Deng would later refer to the incident in bitter terms during a closed speech on party history—right after complaining about Xi's treatment of him on the secretariat.[32]

THE DEVELOPING WORLD

In his speech at the Twelfth Party Congress, Hu Yaobang declared that "Socialist China belongs to the Third World" and stressed the "great strategic significance of South-South cooperation."[33] Xi went to great lengths to expand ties with the Global South. He repeatedly met leftist and Communist parties from the developing world.[34] In 1984, he twice led delegations to Africa: one in March and April for the funeral of Guinea's president Sékou Touré, a major figure in the Non-Aligned Movement, and one in October and November for the thirtieth anniversary of the Algerian revolution.[35]

When Xi arrived in Guinea on the morning of March 30, he found a chaotic situation at the airport and sweltering, humid heat above 104 degrees Fahrenheit. A few hours later, his delegation arrived at the stadium, where they found seventy thousand to eighty thousand Guinean citizens but no protocol officers to guide them. Along with Chinese embassy officials, members of the delegation surrounded Xi to protect him as they moved through the masses of people. When they finally reached the platform, no seats were available, but one African representative saw the elderly Xi in a black Mao suit and gave up his seat. Six to seven hours of intense heat left Xi and the others exhausted and dehydrated.[36]

The next day, Xi met with acting president Louis Lansana Beavogui. The meeting, largely ceremonial, was held in a small room in a building still under construction, with few lights. Xi expressed hope that friendship between the two countries would strengthen and develop, and Beavogui told Xi that he had already been to China three times. Xi returned to China one day later to begin an inspection tour of Xinjiang, where he soon learned that Beavogui had fled to the Chinese embassy seeking asylum because a colonel had executed a coup. The Ministry of Foreign Affairs in Beijing decided that the coup would probably succeed, and they asked Beavogui to leave. Three Chinese diplomats escorted Beavogui out of the embassy, and he was arrested as soon as he left the building. Beavogui, who had diabetes, died shortly thereafter in a hospital.[37] It was another powerful lesson for Xi about the fragility of political order.

While in Algeria later that year, Xi said, "China adopts a policy of opening to the outside world and hopes, in particular, for an all-round cooperation with all other Third World nations in attaining joint development."[38] Xi was unimpressed with China's diplomats during the trip, however, later remarking, "There are many, many problems with cadres involved in foreign affairs. How is their language ability? Everyone in Algeria was a generalist."[39] But trips like the one to Algeria were especially important to Xi for providing evidence that the People's Republic was winning global stature and demonstrating the superiority of its socialist model. He later bragged about the trip to the Dalai Lama's representatives, describing how the Algerian premier, who had recently been to India, allegedly had said that "China, despite having a population over a billion, is able to decisively act upon its people's livelihood because of the socialist system." The Algerian leader, according to Xi, was less impressed by India: "Despite having a similar population, when it comes to making a decision on people's livelihood and national affairs, there is a huge problem. That is because of the capitalist system and also because of a lack of harmony and unity among the people."[40]

THE COMMUNIST BLOC

As China was rejoining its comrades in the global left, the movement was facing serious headwinds across the world. Xi was long aware that the Communist system in other countries was far from perfect. He had visited Hungary just three years after the revolution of 1956. In 1961, he hosted Hermann Matern, a politburo member from East Germany, who warned Xi that because West Germany had a higher standard of living, illegal migration from East Germany was a major problem. The Chinese record of Matern's trip was dismissive: "Whether it was during the evening banquet or in the vehicle, he was always mouthing off that [East] Germany, both in terms of production and the struggle against enemies, faced many difficulties."[41]

Such difficulties were even more obvious in the 1980s. In 1983, the party leadership concluded that, except in a few specific countries, there was no longer a revolutionary trend of proletariats directly seizing power. Global Communism was in a state of "overcoming difficulties, exploring the path forward by summarizing historical experiences, and developing among twists and turns."[42] Over the decade, the International Liaison Department reported on the failures of Arab Communist parties, the rejection of armed struggle in South Asia, the poor electoral performance by Communist parties in Western Europe, persistent weaknesses among Latin American Communists, and the decline of Communist parties in Southeast Asia.[43]

Xi watched carefully as Communist states tried to find a way out of the crises they faced. In Yugoslavia, hope for real change reached a crescendo at the Thirteenth Party Congress of the League of Communists in June 1986, and Xi was present. He would have seen how the Yugoslavian leadership, facing debilitating foreign debt and economic inefficiencies, was pursuing economic decentralization and political reform, including multiple candidates and secret elections. One high-ranking Yugoslavian leader believed the congress signified "a decisive breakthrough to reforms of the economic and political system."[44]

Xi was impressed. He told the president of Yugoslavia's presidium, Vidoje Žarković, that there is "no gap between us." He praised the Yugoslavs, saying that China was "paying extreme attention to Yugoslavia's evolution as the country has a pioneering role in all reforms," and the "experience of Yugoslav communists is of great value" to China's own development. He thanked the Yugoslavs for supporting economic reform in China as "some believe that these reforms lead to restoring capitalism." Xi said, "The League of Communists of Yugoslavia stood for overcoming bureaucratism," a phenomenon that commonly occurs "when one party comes to power, which was not the case during the revolution." He continued, "The Communist Party of China shares the same problem; during the revolution, it was at one with the people. The party was completely merged with the people, and, later on, due to bureaucratism within the party, it separated from the masses." Xi was particularly impressed with how the Yugoslavs prepared for their Thirteenth Party Congress: "The League of Communists of Yugoslavia nurtures a very good method of leadership that the Chinese call mass line. While preparing for the Thirteenth Party Congress, detailed and open discussions were led to collect the invaluable opinions of the members of the League of Communists of Yugoslavia."[45]

Heydar Aliyev—who represented the Soviets at the congress and who would later become the leader of independent Azerbaijan—was more skeptical. He wrote a report back to Moscow warning that the country was coming apart at the seams along ethnic lines.[46] He proved more prescient than Xi. For those who supported reform in Yugoslavia, the congress was an exciting moment full of possibilities, yet the conservative backlash came swiftly, and subsequent years proved that hope for change was ephemeral. Slobodan Milošević, warning about "genocide" in Kosovo and using dirty political tricks, soon led conservatives to victory in Serbia and ultimately Yugoslavia as a whole, thus ending the reformist experiments.[47] Xi was distressed as events there unfolded. In May 1990, he wrote his reaction to a report about Slovenia's new non-Communist government—the first such regime to appear in one of the constituent states of Yugoslavia: "Looking at this, who knows how chaotic Yugoslavia will be in the coming period?!"[48]

Xi also saw Poland as a reference. In 1981, after months of strikes and protests by Solidarity, the Polish government introduced martial law and started a draconian political crackdown. The next major strike occurred on April 25, 1988—the exact same day that Xi met in Beijing with members of Poland's Democratic Party, which ruled in a coalition with the Communists. Xi told them that "the Polish reforms are of a similar kind and that they pay close attention to them." He was self-reflective about history: "In the past we engaged in socialism for decades. But the result was we were not clear about things. We created a poor socialism." He talked about the need for reform in existential terms: "Time does not wait for people. Waiting a year would make the problem very big."[49] But time had run out for Warsaw. It was much less than a year later that the strikes would grow so large that they triggered negotiations between the regime and Solidarity in the form of the Round Table Talks. Slightly less than a year after Xi's words, Solidarity was officially legal. By August 1990, Poland would no longer be a Communist country.[50]

Naturally, change in the Soviet Union also caught Xi's attention. Although he was competing against Soviet influence in the world of global Communism, he had high praise for Mikhail Gorbachev's reforms. In August 1986, Senator Giuseppe Chiarante, a member of the Italian Communist Party, described Xi's favorable views of the Soviet leader in a letter back to headquarters: "Perhaps the most significant aspect of the meeting with Xi Zhongxun was the positive assessment he made regarding the political prospects of Gorbachev concerning economic reform: with the tendency to highlight analogies to China."[51] The Soviet Union could provide negative lessons too, however. In May 1990, an inner-party newsletter published an article translated from Russian into Chinese about the Chernobyl nuclear disaster. Xi penned that the article was "worthy of great learning and special study. We also have a lot of mistakes like this in our work. It's certainly true that 'bureaucratism is much more terrible than radiation'!"[52]

The next month, Xi saw something he liked in Moscow. In 1990, political groupings had started to appear within the Communist Party of the Soviet Union in the months before the Twenty-Eighth Party Congress. Xi was struck by the Marxist Platform, which rejected both social democracy as too capitalist and the Soviet past as a "totalitarian-bureaucratic system" that had ignored "objective laws." Soviet citizens had become "alienated" from the means of production and subjected to spiritual degradation. The Marxist Platform emphasized decentralization, empowered workers, self-management, a strong state economy, and a regulated market. They wanted the Communist Party of the Soviet Union to cease management of the economy, allow for different ideological platforms, cleanse those members of the party who had abused their privileges, and pursue democratization, including secret ballots and ensuring the right of the minority to defend its point of view even after a decision was made. The authors characterized their positions as a return to Marx and Lenin, but they also emphasized that true Marxism assumed a "critical attitude" to "its own predecessors," just like Lenin had done toward Marx.[53]

Although this "platform" was essentially a faction that marked the further deterioration of party discipline in the Soviet Union, Xi was impressed: "This 'platform' should be explored in depth, researched further, and integrated with the situation in China for sincere study. That would benefit us. I support its general themes." Through this notification, Xi was signaling that he believed the Soviet Union, and probably the People's Republic of China as well, might be able to save themselves by rejecting the totalitarian legacy and returning to "classic Marxism."[54]

How did Xi feel during these trials and tribulations in the socialist camp? Xi's confidence seemed unshaken. In the same month that Xi wrote of his hopes for rejuvenation in the Soviet Union by returning to past principles, the Communist Youth League completed a book called *Historical Necessity—Socialism in China*, for which Xi wrote a preface. He wrote, "Scientific socialism represents the inevitable law governing the development of human society, revealed by proletarian revolutionary teachers Marx and Engels through studying the profound contradictions in capitalist society." He tried to distinguish what made the Chinese Communist Party special: "Only the Chinese Communists, who represented the fundamental interests of the proletariat and the broad masses of people, could find the correct road, socialism, for China through combining the universal truth of Marxism-Leninism with China's revolutionary practice." He referred directly to Communism's global setbacks during the last year. At least publicly, he blamed the West: "Recently, an adverse current of negating socialism has appeared in the world. The international hostile forces more intensively pursued the 'peaceful evolution' strategy in an attempt to subvert and sabotage socialism."[55] During his previous tour of duty in Beijing, Xi had witnessed the beginning of the end of China's communion with the Communist bloc. By the end of his second one, he was witnessing the collapse of the bloc itself.

NORTH KOREA

North Korea survived the cataclysm, however, and it was there that Xi played the most significant role in his work with foreign parties. This was an extraordinarily important relationship but one which had suffered during the Cultural Revolution, during which North Korean leader Kim Il-sung was labeled a revisionist by the Chinese, including by diplomats in Pyongyang. On the border, soldiers entered North Korean territory and loudspeakers called for Kim to be overthrown. Kim told the Soviets, "Mao Zedong hates us, the Chinese are embittered, and we can expect anything from them."[56] In the Deng years, the relationship faced new problems. Now, it was Kim who believed that Pyongyang had become the center of global revolution and the last stronghold against revisionism. He was furious as Beijing expanded ties with Seoul and introduced market reforms.[57] In May 1984, Kim Il-sung confided to East German leader Erich Honecker. "What we are most afraid of," he said, "is that China will not stick with socialism."[58]

Like with Japan, it was a relationship that could get Hu Yaobang into trouble. According to Zhao Ziyang, Deng believed that Hu was "too warm" toward Kim Il-sung and "granted North Korea's demands too casually."[59] Yet Beijing's policies toward Pyongyang were clearly far from casual. Before any trip by a senior Chinese leader to Pyongyang during this period, the entire hallway of the International Liaison Department's Asia Bureau would be full of gifts stacked on top of one another. "It's all for Master Kim," the cadres who worked there would jokingly say.[60]

Xi himself visited "Master Kim" twice during the 1980s, both times during moments of exceptional political sensitivity. The first trip was very clearly about the Kim-dynasty succession, something for which Kim Il-sung had spent many years preparing. The Chinese, however, had been skeptical.[61] The breakthrough seems to have finally occurred in September 1982, when Kim visited China for the first time in seven years. Succession was clearly on his mind: on the train from Beijing to Chengdu, Kim asked several questions about Mao's initial successor, Hua Guofeng, and Deng provided Kim with a long, tendentious account of why Hua had been removed from power. Deng also made a case for the Chinese reforms, noting that most of the countryside still could not meet the basic needs of its inhabitants.[62] In Chengdu, Kim emphatically affirmed China's reforms for the first time as a triumph of "socialist construction."[63] And North Korea got what it wanted too: the US State Department Bureau of Intelligence and Research concluded that "the

Chinese probably accepted Kim Il Song's succession arrangements" during this trip.[64]

The next month, Xi went to North Korea. Before departing Beijing, Xi told his delegation that their task was to study the country's urbanization, afforestation, organizational discipline, and moral values.[65] Yet the evidence also strongly suggests that Xi was sent on this delicate mission to express, for the first time, Chinese acceptance of Kim Jong-il as successor. On October 8, Xi gave an address at a banquet held for him by the Standing Committee of the Supreme People's Assembly. Xi attributed "historic significance" to Kim Il-sung's recent trip to China, and he described Kim's "high evaluation" of China's progress as "massive support and encouragement." Crucially, he toasted "the dear leader of the Korean people, Comrade Secretary Kim Jong-il."[66] The following day, Xi went to the Red Flag Mangyongdae Revolutionary School, an educational institution that was originally created for war orphans but later became the premier institution for educating the country's elite (a rough equivalent to the kind of schools his own children had attended).[67] The next day, he paid respects at a statue of his former boss Zhou Enlai in South Hamgyong Province, where he laid a wreath, observed a moment's silence, and walked around the statue.[68]

He continued to spread the word that China had accepted North Korea's succession plans. While in South Hamgyong, Xi again raised a toast to Kim Jong-il.[69] Xi then traveled to Kaesong, on the border with South Korea, where, at a banquet, he discussed Kim Jong-il in strong terms: "People say it takes 10 years to grow a big tree and 100 years to make a man. But, in Korea the great leader Comrade Kim Il-song and the dear leader Comrade Kim [Jong-il] have successfully solved the problem of training cadres."[70]

Finally, on October 14, Xi met Kim Il-sung at the Kumsusan Assembly Hall, the North Korean leader's official residence. The two men met individually for two hours before Kim met the rest of the delegation.[71] Xi noted that he had not seen Kim for twenty-one years, and he cited the Chinese expression "A day's separation seems as long as three years." Kim responded, "Something went wrong for you in 1962." Xi said that was correct, explaining that "because of a problem in a book, I was pushed to the side. It was not until February 1978, after almost sixteen years, that I returned to work." Kim pressed, asking what Xi did during that time. Xi demurred, "That's a long story. It's all in the past; it does not need to be discussed." And indeed,

Xi almost never talked in detail about how he had suffered during those years. However, under pressure from Kim, Xi did agree to talk about his experiences—one of the only times he spoke about what he had endured. Xi took the opportunity to apologize for how the Cultural Revolution had affected relations between China and North Korea: "It not only hurt us, but it also hurt the friendship between the Chinese and Korean peoples."[72]

When Kim met the full delegation, Xiang Nan, party boss of Fujian who was a member of the group, talked about Reform and Opening in his province.[73] While they all ate dinner together afterward, Kim said to Xi, "Your arrival makes me extremely happy. It has been too long since I saw you. You did a lot of work during the war against Japan." Kim said that without the traditional education at the Red Flag Mangyongdae Revolutionary School, young people would not know how hard it had been to achieve socialism. He lectured the Chinese: "China can certainly achieve its planned goal for the next twenty years, but that will only be possible if something like the chaos of the Cultural Revolution never happens again. This is extremely important. Spiritual civilization is very important. The Soviet Union gave up on political work and spiritual civilization. Studying is extremely important. In North Korea, we have a nationwide system for report meetings every Wednesday and studying every Saturday."[74]

At a banquet held by the Chinese embassy the following day, Xi flattered his North Korean hosts. "It felt as if we returned to our own home," he told them. "It was a happy experience." He even went so far as to say that "we deeply feel, for many reasons, that, in many areas, we are inferior to you." China could "especially" learn from North Korea's "socialist spiritual civilization." Xi was clearly impressed by the "firm beliefs and high political consciousness" of the North Koreans, noting that they "are self-disciplined, civilized, and polite and have high energy."[75]

In subsequent years, Xi tried to convince his North Korean counterparts to seriously consider the kind of reforms China was pursuing. In April 1983, Xi, along with a host of International Liaison Department officials, met a friendship delegation of North Korean central and regional leaders. In his speech at the welcoming ceremony, Xi said that thanks to the new agenda introduced at the 1978 Third Plenum, China's political and economic situations were "very good." However, he acknowledged that China still faced "many difficulties and numerous new problems." China's reforms had "only just begun," and "many things are still in a trial phase." He welcomed the North Koreans to criticize what they saw in China and "leave their own valuable experiences."[76] The Chinese leadership was clearly trying to impress upon the North Koreans the need for change. The friendship delegation traveled to Xi's old stomping grounds—Guangzhou and Shenzhen. On its way back to Pyongyang, Xi thanked the members of the delegation for providing a "high evaluation and sincere support" for what they saw. He welcomed the North Koreans to return in the future to "see the results of today's tests."[77]

In June 1983, Kim Jong-il finally met the top leadership in Beijing. Hu Yaobang and Xi Zhongxun greeted him at the train station, and Kim and Xi were filmed sitting next to one another at a concert. In 2018, when Kim Jong-un—the son of Kim Jong-il and, by then, the country's supreme leader—met Xi Jinping in China, the two leaders watched footage of that video. It showed Xi Zhongxun and Kim Jong-il enjoying one performer in particular—Peng Liyuan—who sang "Flower-Selling Girl" in both Mandarin and Korean.[78]

Although relations between Beijing and South Korea had been slowly improving throughout the 1980s, breakthroughs only became possible after Roh Tae-woo became president of the Republic of Korea in 1988. In July of that year, Deng wrote on an internal notification, "The time is ripe for us to develop economic and cultural relations with South Korea. We should move a bit faster and wider." For Deng, "this was an important chess piece for us. We must grasp it closely."[79] That same month, Xi arrived in Pyongyang. He tried to reassure China's allies that nothing had changed. At a banquet held by the Supreme People's Assembly at the Mansudae Assembly Hall, Xi said, "Deepest fraternal friendship has been established between the parties and peoples of China and Korea. We will keep this flower of friendship in full bloom forever."[80] Kim Il-sung invited Xi to a luncheon and Xi gave the North Korean leader a gift.[81]

According to New China News, after Xi returned to China, he submitted a report to the Standing Committee of the National People's Congress that praised the North Koreans in powerful terms: "Through this visit, we also feel that the Korean people's sense of organization and discipline, their strict enforcement of orders and prohibitions, their decorum and courtesy, and their moral accomplishment are worth learning. In addition, Korea attaches great importance to culture, education, education in revolutionary traditions, making the country green, and blazing new trails in planning for urban construction, which left a deep impression on the delegation."[82] Xi's words pointed to an interesting contradiction. On the one hand, he had been trying to convince the North Koreans to pursue economic change. Yet, on the other hand, he admired the political discipline and ideological cohesion he found in North Korea. This tension spoke to the dilemmas he was facing in China as the secretariat struggled to somehow unify the principles of Reform and Opening with the Four Cardinal Principles. Xi tried hard to help Hu Yaobang effectively integrate the two. They would fail.

PART VI **CATASTROPHE AGAIN**

26
"IT IS NECESSARY TO ALSO HAVE A SPIRITUAL CIVILIZATION"

When Xi finally returned to work after years of persecution and exile, it was obvious that something had gone seriously wrong with the revolutionary project—especially in Guangdong, his first assignment. The socialist economic system had proven to be a failure, and the hunt for class traitors within the party had led to mass persecution. The party was now united by the idea that change was imperative. But what would that look like, and how should it be understood? Xi admitted, "In the past, we did not understand socialism enough. We saw it too narrowly." Blindly copying the Soviet Union had proven unworkable. He asked, "Is it better to do socialism with full stomachs or empty stomachs?" His answer: "Only full stomachs can manifest the superiority of the socialist system." This was a lesson, Xi said, "that was learned through decades of struggle." Yet Xi did not have an answer for what the future looked like: "China has already done socialism for thirty-two years. But we are still groping for just exactly what kind of road we will take. The groping might take a long time before a relatively complete socialist system is achieved."[1]

Xi's words suggest fundamental questions about the party's agenda. What did it mean to be a good Communist if no one could say what Communism really was? How could the party continue to win loyal adherents as it acknowledged the severity of past mistakes and moved in a fundamentally new direction? How deep could self-reflection go without losing faith in the cause as a whole? From his position on the secretariat, Xi was at the very center of discussions about how the party should think about—and explain—what it was trying to achieve.

These were debates that could not easily be resolved. Historians of this era typically describe a long struggle between competing factions with mutually incompatible views. Deng Liqun, director of the Propaganda Department, and Hu Qiaomu, who managed ideological affairs for the secretariat, are often referred to as two "leftist kings" who were motivated by inherently conservative tendencies.[2] There is a great deal of truth to this assessment. Throughout the 1980s, Deng Liqun and Hu Qiaomu would often write alarming reports to Deng Xiaoping about alleged political heresies. In contrast, Hu Yaobang never went to Deng Xiaoping with such concerns.[3] Xi came to despise both Hu Qiaomu and Deng Liqun. Yet Xi's life during this period reveals the messy ways that apparently "ideological" differences were shaped by more than the content of ideas. Historical relationships, personalities, political styles, confusion, contingency, fear, weak institutions, party discipline, and, most importantly, Deng Xiaoping's status as final arbiter all deeply complicated the ways that ideas manifested and mattered.

These were people who had known one another for decades. When Xi moved to Beijing from the Northwest in the early 1950s to become director of the Propaganda Department, Hu Qiaomu had served as his deputy. In the 1980s, although Xi had previously been Hu Qiaomu's superior, Xi had to recognize that Hu, who had once served as Mao's secretary, had special experience and status in the ideological realm. Xi's historic relationship with Deng Liqun, in contrast, was more negative. Deng apparently never forgave Xi for what had happened in 1952 when Xi removed him from the Xinjiang leadership.

Old grudges and loyalties shaped political contestation, and no figure fit perfectly into either the "leftist" or "rightist" label. People as diverse as Li Rui, Li Xiannian, and Bo Yibo did not regard Hu Qiaomu as a true conservative. Instead, they thought Hu was, at heart, weak and unprincipled. In Li Rui's mind, Hu did not have strong ideological views; instead, Hu just wanted to take sole credit for both enforcing orthodoxy and introducing innovation. Hu was known for his slavish attitude to both Mao and Deng rather than for promoting his own agenda.[4] Wang Ruoshui, who was deputy editor in charge of theoretical and ideological issues at *People's Daily*, believed that "Hu Qiaomu's own position changed back and forth, but he did not permit others to hold different opinions from his."[5] In fact, Hu often made remarkably "rightist" comments. During the discussions on the second official history resolution that appeared in 1981, he said that Mao had established a "fascist socialist nation that even surpassed Stalin's." In 1985, Deng Xiaoping would conclude that Hu Qiaomu was weak on ideology and subsequently refused to meet with him even though, up until that point, on other occasions, Hu Qiaomu had proven to be "conservative." Shortly before death in 1992, he said Marxism had "done people great harm."[6]

The idea of a "left-right" spectrum is further complicated by the differences between the two most prominent supposed "leftists" of the decade. Deng Liqun was the first to call for the arrest of Hu Qiaomu's son on corruption charges, and Hu did not think Deng was capable of good writing.[7] Li Xiannian once remarked that Hu Qiaomu "had meat but no bones," whereas Deng Liqun "had bones but no meat."[8] In other words, one had no nerve, and the other had no flexibility.

These characteristics could manifest in despicable ways. In 1984, Li Rui told Xi Zhongxun about one especially egregious case. In April 1943, Li had come under suspicion for being a spy and was incarcerated. Deng Liqun led the Rescue the Fallen Campaign at the Central Politics Research Office, where Li's wife was working and was under investigation. Although Deng was married and had two children, he started a sexual relationship with her. After an inquiry into the incident, Yang Shangkun stated that Deng had committed a "political mistake." By having sex with a woman whom he was investigating while her husband was still in detention, Deng had, in Yang's words, shown "wild individualism." Deng behaved in this way because of his arrogance as a longstanding member of the party and his overconfidence in his own skills, but his only real ability was to "show off his dogmatism," Yang said.[9]

Yet Deng Liqun's stubbornness had powerful admirers, and many high-ranking cadres saw him as a potential candidate for general secretary to replace Hu Yaobang. In the words of Chinese historian Xu Qingquan, "Deng Liqun was someone who, when confronted with a problem, dared to buck thunder, and this won a strong reputation for him among the elite."[10] In particular, Deng was supported by individuals like Chen Yun and Wang Zhen—figures who sometimes had strained relations with Xi. However, Deng Liqun also won admirers from members of the reformist camp, like Chen Yizi, who was very close to both Deng and Xi. Chen Yizi wrote in his memoirs, "Many people overseas thought he was a 'leftist king,' and there is some truth there. But this assessment makes the mistake of being too absolute."[11]

The extraordinary complexities of the era are visible especially in the curious case of He Weiling. In 1981, Deng Liqun helped He Weiling establish a research institute called the China Rural Development Research Group. After 1982, the strongly proreform intellectuals who worked at the research group came under attack by conservatives, but Deng Liqun nonetheless continued to support them. Later, He Weiling attracted the attention of the Ministry of Public Security because of a misunderstanding over the content of some letters he had written to his ex-wife in America. He's situation became more serious when his former mother-in-law let it slip that He Weiling had attempted to introduce a young woman to Deng Pufang, the son of Deng Xiaoping—an act seen as violating a serious political taboo. Deng Xiaoping demanded an investigation, which then connected with the "evidence" collected earlier by the Ministry of Public Security. According to He, Xi Zhongxun personally took command of the investigation. Because the evidence was weak, Xi apparently had to be creative: "The old man [Xi], with a wave of his hand (he even used a pencil!), came up with an abstract conviction, an abominable conviction: 'He's character is problematic.'" He Weiling was furious, describing what had occurred as "a stupid case, a group of stupid officials, a stupid notification." Deng Liqun, who was tasked with punishing He, thought the charge of a "problematic character" was ridiculous. However, He Weiling claimed that Xi had an "ultimate weapon"—a document that misleadingly tied He Weiling to Deng's own Political Research Office. So Deng Liqun was forced by Xi to punish a strongly proreform intellectual on trumped-up charges.[12]

Confusion often reigned about who held what views. He Jingzhi, vice-director of the Department of Propaganda, noted with exasperation that anyone with any influence was often incorrectly classified as inherently rightist or leftist.[13] Wishful thinking played a role too. Hu Yaobang's vibrance and open demeanor suggested a liberality not fully deserved. Critics of party policy often hoped that Hu Yaobang would protect them—a hope that caused some in the party to worry about the effect the general secretary was having on stability. Xi was savvy enough to recognize this problem, and he often tried to persuade outspoken cadres not to create trouble for Hu. Yet Xi was unsuccessful. Gradually, Deng Xiaoping came to believe that Hu Yaobang kept a certain distance because he wanted to maintain good relations with young intellectuals, although Hu emphatically denied that this was the case.[14] At the same time, however, there was a limitation to such "factional" thinking, especially at the highest levels. Zhao Ziyang's former secretary Bao Tong recalled, "There is a kind of Communist Party culture. Asking, or even wondering, about the relationship between one leader and another is a major taboo. After I joined the party, I was involved in organizational work. Moreover, I did organization work at the very top. This rule never changed."[15]

When differences did appear, it was often extremely difficult to parse their meaning. Did an argument represent a reasonable concern that could be resolved with discussion, or was it a political attack? In a strikingly high number of cases, political contestation emerged because of simple misunderstandings. Arguments often came down to tone or even to just how many times someone used a particular expression. When this was the case, it was hard to parse what the differences represented. Were they merely part of a simple debate, or was there something more nefarious going on? In his memoirs, Deng Liqun vehemently denied that his behavior toward Hu Yaobang was motivated by political ambitions: "When Hu Yaobang wanted to edit his speeches, he always asked me and Qiaomu to take a look. He usually adopted revisions and additions based on our opinions. Such a relationship continued until he no longer was general secretary. Saying that I wanted to overthrow him is untrue. I never had such an opinion."[16] Xi Zhongxun thought otherwise. Even today, it is challenging to discern which one of them was right.

But Xi had good reason to have such fears. After the horrors of the Mao era, any criticism was terrifying as it might portend a purge. Leading party figures continued to pick "ideological" fights because they felt personally threatened or because they wanted to damage someone else politically. Sometimes a debate had a different meaning for different individuals at the same time—whereas one individual might have been motivated by narrow work-related concerns, another might have been using the debate as a wedge to improve their own position.

Xi was a brawler who did not shrink from using "leftist" methods against people whom he thought were "leftists," as one of the targets of his wrath put it.[17] In a speech for internal consumption, Deng Liqun later complained that during much of the 1980s, "there was a strange phenomenon. Xi Zhongxun apparently helped Hu Yaobang with his work. Hu Qiaomu could no longer manage propaganda and education work. I too could no longer engage in such work, so in actuality it was managed by them." Deng Liqun accused Xi of helping to create a "pestilential atmosphere." Because of this situation, Deng Liqun wanted to resign, but, according to him, "Xi Zhongxun unctuously said, 'Don't talk about things like that.'"[18] Deng Liqun saw Xi as the top protector of the director of *People's Daily*, Hu Jiwei, and editor in chief Qin Chuan. In his memoirs, Deng Liqun wrote, "Hu Jiwei and Qin Chuan were both from the Northwest. They were cadres under Xi Zhongxun. At the time, they often went to visit Xi and gossip about this and that. During rectification, Qin Chuan said, 'It is good that we have Comrade Xi Zhongxun, otherwise, our days would be rough. Only by relying on him were we able to pass through the narrow gate.'"[19]

Despite such clear antipathies, everyone was limited by party discipline. Xi did not engage in open political warfare to push his policy inclinations. Everyone had to at least pretend to respect one another. On repeated occasions, Xi either reined in or failed to protect individuals with whom he agreed and with whom he shared regional or career ties. He knew too much about the party's historic taboo against factions to go too far, and his opponents felt similarly constrained. But when Xi did discipline his supposed protégés, which was often, it is possible, perhaps likely, that he himself decided that the punished had crossed a line. Even if Xi often disagreed with Hu Qiaomu and Deng Liqun, he certainly did not sponsor party critics, let alone dissidents.

Although party discipline kept a lid on political infighting, institutions were too weak to systematically resolve problems. Political contestation instead took the form of spying, the use of compromising material, lying, and plotting. One cadre involved in cultural policy believed that intrigue and character assassination sometimes would reach levels reminiscent of the Cultural Revolution. He blamed Deng Xiaoping, who "did not achieve unity by using methods of collective leadership in the party or the principles of democratic centralism or democratic life in the leadership core. Instead, he used the old special method of past emperors."[20]

Hu Yaobang's inclinations toward party critics were not as aggressive as Deng Xiaoping's. But the crux of the difficulties between the two men was not so much policy differences as the inherent tensions in the party's ideological agenda. Deng wanted rapid economic growth and did not want political campaigns to distract from that goal. But he was also a political conservative. Opponents on any given issue often believed that they understood what Deng really wanted better than the other side. Repeatedly, leading figures attributed certain decisions to others among the elite when it was, in fact, Deng who was driving policy. Hu Qiaomu and Deng Liqun were especially vulnerable to resentment because their official positions required them to act as Deng Xiaoping's enforcers. Deputies sometimes felt as if they were under attack for doing what Deng wanted because no one was willing to criticize Deng directly. Xi Zhongxun, sensitive to the potentially explosive nature of this political model, often encouraged Hu Yaobang to visit Deng as often as possible. But it was to no avail: Hu Yaobang, like Deng Liqun and Hu Qiaomu before him, would fall out of favor.

Deng's model of rule both limited and facilitated agency. Within those confines, Xi's own views resist neat categorization. Xi was no stranger to the ways that ideology could both serve but also endanger party interests. As a young man in the Northwest, he had seen how ideology provided a way to understand a troubled world and to unite a disparate group in a violent and dangerous environment. At the same time, however, ideology often limited policy flexibility and could lead to overly ambitious and counterproductive strategies. Most dangerously, ideology intensified inner-party struggles—as Xi personally experienced on multiple occasions throughout his life.

Relatively speaking, Xi felt more comfortable trusting intellectuals and cultural figures to manage their own affairs, and he knew them better than many other party leaders. As Kang Sheng wrote in a 1963 letter, Xi "is fond of making friends with figures in theatrical circles."[21] Yet Xi did not fully understand them. In his autobiography, Wang Meng recalled a conversation with Xi Zhongxun about whether Wang would take the position of minister of culture—a position Wang did not want. But Xi put heavy pressure on Wang, telling him it was necessary to obey the order. When Xi told Wang not to worry about lacking time to write, Wang believed that Xi simply did not understand that Wang wanted to write novels, not policy-related materials.[22] The endless feuds among Chinese intellectuals could exasperate Xi. He was furious that, after Hu Feng's death, Hu's nemeses continued to oppose rehabilitation. Xi complained plaintively, "The person has already passed on. Why is it that it is still necessary to hold him by a tight grip in terms of literary ideology? It is said that Hu Feng's literary thinking has mistakes, but who can guarantee that their own literary thinking is 100 percent correct?"[23]

In his own remarks on ideology and reform, Xi emphasized the need for balance. He recognized it was hard to tell when critical views were "antiparty." He wanted protection for new ideas; without people breaking the party line, he thought, how could the special economic zones have appeared? Without some openness, reform was impossible, he believed.[24] Although he supported many of the political and economic changes that became possible in this new atmosphere, he went to great lengths to emphasize that faith in socialism was crucial. He believed that only trust in the party's historic mission could provide reform with the stability necessary for success. He was unambiguously not a pro-Western liberal, and he found consumer values distasteful, even asking, "Once people have money, how should they spend it? That is a problem. Material civilization is not enough. It is necessary to also have a spiritual civilization."[25]

PRACTICE IS THE SOLE CRITERION OF TRUTH

In the history of Chinese Communist Party ideology, 1978 is considered a watershed year. Both Chinese and Western accounts describe a momentous showdown between two competing factions over the fate of the nation: the proreform Deng Xiaoping and the neo-Maoist Hua Guofeng. According to this narrative, Deng supported the idea that "practice is the sole criterion of truth," whereas Hua tried to end any discussion of the idea. Yet the latest historiography reveals a very different story. Hua and Deng were not separated by real policy differences. Instead, the debate over "practice" was really about something else—misunderstandings and overreactions.[26]

In May 1978, soon after Xi became the top party leader in Guangdong, an article appeared in *Guangming Daily* asserting that "practice is the sole criterion of truth," or, in other words, if theories failed to achieve their goals, they should be changed in the face of experience. As Frederick Teiwes and Warren Sun note, the *Guangming Daily* article itself was "relatively unremarkable," and none of its authors believed they were making a grand political statement. The writers were therefore shocked when the article incurred the wrath of party vice-chairman Wang Dongxing, who was in charge of ideology. Wang's overreaction would make a mountain out of a molehill, thus turning a narrow theoretical debate into a growing political problem.[27]

On June 2, Deng Xiaoping made a strong case for "seeking truth from facts" at the People's Liberation Army General Political Department Conference. He was probably aware of the *Guangming Daily* article, but his immediate motivation was fury toward the head of propaganda in the department, Li Mancun. For esoteric reasons, Li had criticized two rather formulaic expressions Deng had introduced. It was "another accidental conflict, one that reflected procedural rigidity," in the words of Teiwes and Sun. On June

24, *People's Liberation Army Daily* published a second article on "practice," suggesting the military supported the position. Outside observers quickly linked Deng's speech and the new article as a trend, although Deng was not involved in its publication.[28]

On June 30, Xi approvingly spoke of both articles at an enlarged session of the provincial Guangdong Party Standing Committee. "If you read a lot of Marx and Lenin, but you do not combine it with practice, then what is the use?" he asked. On July 4, at a meeting on education work, he criticized the view that universities should focus primarily on physical labor, not academic learning. "Universities should not be transformed into farms or production brigades," he said. To justify this position, he once again referred to "practice."[29]

At the time, Xi's comments were not openly published. But later that year, regional officials publicly spoke out one by one in favor of "practice." On September 19, Xi was the fourth to do so—one of the earliest.[30] He asserted that "this absolutely is not a simple theoretical issue" but an issue with "major practical significance." Mao himself believed practice was the sole criterion of truth, Xi said. When figures like Lin Biao or the Gang of Four treated Mao's authority as absolute, they did so for their own nefarious political purposes. By grabbing isolated phrases, they could "label you a traitor or an agent. They could arrest people, kill people." Treating Mao's words as "lifeless dogmatism" was a "violation of Mao Zedong thought," he said.[31]

In March of 1979, Xi would brag of his bravery in speaking out so early. "At the time, everyone had a lingering fear. I also had a lingering fear. . . . A comrade from Beijing saw me and said that I expressed my position on the criterion of truth too early."[32] Teiwes and Sun, however, decisively show that the timing of the expressed support for "practice" by the provincial leaders had little or nothing to do with "reformist or conservative tendencies." Instead, these individuals who expressed support thought that "practice" was "commonsense" and that its acknowledgment would facilitate the narrow goal of addressing wrongful Mao-era verdicts. Wan Li, Anhui party leader, was dismissive of such "declarations," thinking they were a distraction from real work.[33]

By the end of the year, however, the party elite understood that "practice" was a political issue. At the work conference prior to the Third Plenum, Wang Dongxing was criticized for quashing the debate. Xi saw a need for resolution before things got out of hand. "With regard to 'Practice is the sole criterion of truth,' I am afraid that it would be bad if a few words about it are not said at this meeting. This issue concerns an ideological line. It has a big implication for practical work, and there has been a lot of outside discussion. If right and wrong are not clear, it is impossible to seek truth from facts. I hope that Chairman Hua will ultimately say a few words," Xi said.[34] And Hua responded positively. He explained that he had been overseas when the "practice" article had first appeared, and at the time, he was too busy to address the issue directly. Ye Jianying had wanted to hold a theory conference to resolve the issue, Hua said, but there had been no time before the work conference.[35]

When that theory conference finally began in January 1979, party leaders, including Hu Yaobang, were increasingly worried about instability, especially because of the Democracy Wall protestors who were posting big-character posters that called for more rapid political reform. This was a challenge, albeit a much larger one, that was similar to what Xi had faced in the Li Yizhe case in Guangzhou. Although proreform intellectuals in the party did not support the Democracy Wall activists, they were doubling down on their greater calls for openness.[36] Concerned about these developments, in March, Deng Xiaoping gave one of the most consequential speeches of his long career. He demanded that party members uphold the Four Cardinal Principles: the socialist path, the people's democratic dictatorship, the leadership of the Chinese Communist Party, and the principle of Mao Zedong thought and Marxism-Leninism. Party members who hoped China would move more quickly in a new liberal direction were distressed by Deng's speech. But Xi, still in Guangdong, was delighted. He told a former secretary that he strongly supported the speech and that it was "very timely and important."[37]

Deng's speech did not permanently resolve the question of how much the party should change. Instead, it created a new problem. Increasingly, party members were seeing a contradiction between the "third" and the "fourth": the "reformist" *Third* Plenum and the "conservative" *Four* Cardinal Principles. Deng had tried to emphasize continuity, even asking, "Is there anything I have said here that is out of keeping with the Third [Plenum]?"[38] But party cadres in Guangdong were not convinced. In fact, they were confused. At a provincial conference, Xi tried to explain that there was no contradiction: "Only with the Cardinal Principles can thought be liberated in a way that is right and not wrong, effective and not formulaic." Xi, like Deng, was still primarily worried about leftist thinking, which was "more likely to seduce people and therefore will be more damaging to us and thus requires that everyone increase their vigilance."[39]

Still problems persisted—especially from the "Left." Xi was worried about three groups of people in his province. Some cadres were opposed to the Third Plenum entirely and feared that "liberating thought" had "liberated all the way to America and Japan." One grassroots cadre in Guangdong, a former "leftist rebel," had even written an open letter that brazenly asserted the party and the nation "have already become a revisionist traitor clique like that of Khrushchev." The "practice" debate was "a big conspiracy," the man claimed. Other people were less worried about the content of the new ideological direction than they were about the signs of a "line struggle." The "practice" debate was threatening the stability that the party had finally achieved, they thought. Finally, a third group thought the discussion was irrelevant and a waste of time, a "matter for the leadership" that a bunch of intellectuals had stirred up. They thought that "power is truth: whoever holds the most power also holds the most truth."[40]

Deng was worried about similar problems throughout the country. Although he had tried to restrict ideological and political reforms in his speech on the Four Cardinal Principles, he would soon signal once again that the *Left* was still the greater danger—one of the many zigzags he would make in subsequent years. In early August, he spoke of the need for a "remedial class" on the "practice" criterion. Xi disseminated Deng's messages at a meeting of regional leaders in Guangzhou held between September 13 and 21, 1979, and he warned that people were using Deng's Four Cardinal Principles inappropriately—by trying to use them as a weapon against the spirit of the Third Plenum.[41]

The following year, 1980, Xi was still clearly worried about the continued use of leftist, radical language from the Mao era—even when it came out of the military, which would repeatedly pressure the top leadership to adopt a more conservative attitude. At a Beijing meeting on political work held by the People's Liberation Army in late April 1980, Hua Guofeng used the leftist slogan "Promote what is proletarian, and liquidate what is bourgeois." At a meeting of the Guangzhou Military Region Standing Committee several weeks later, Xi argued against using such language. "This slogan is not very scientific," he said. "When people use this slogan now, it's hard for people to understand. It is better not to use it. Even when not using this slogan, it is possible to make revolution." Other members of the standing committee disagreed, arguing that in Guangdong, which bordered Macau and Hong Kong, the slogan was especially necessary. Xi asked the Political Department of the Guangzhou Military Region to send a special telegram for clarification.[42]

Like Xi, Deng Liqun criticized Hua's phrase for being too leftist even though Deng Xiaoping had originally approved of the formulation. But instead of defending it, Deng Xiaoping decided to attack the expression, suggesting that Hua's mouthing of the slogan at the political work meeting was inappropriate. For Deng, the problem was not those specific words; it was Hua's use of those words during a meeting with the army—the ultimate arbiter of power in the Chinese political system. Perhaps fearing that Hua was trying to make inroads with the military (an idea that was almost certainly fanciful) or maybe just using it as an excuse, Deng turned it into another wedge issue to hurt Hua. Hua offered his resignation shortly thereafter.[43]

BITTER LOVE

After Mao's death, cultural figures in the party gradually tried to build a more open environment for their work. At a meeting held by three publications in Beijing in October 1978, the earlier attacks on the novel *Liu Zhidan* were portrayed front and center as something that had to be avoided in the future.[44] In December of that year, Xi invited Zhou Yang, chairman of the China Federation of Literary and Art Circles, to Guangzhou, where Zhou gave his first systematic approach to literature since the Cultural Revolution. He addressed the debate about whether the so-called scar literature should be suppressed. Some believed that this form of literature, which describes in detail the tragedy of the Cultural Revolution, was too negative, but Zhou argued that such works played a crucial role in exposing those individuals who had persecuted others. Referring to this meeting, a party intellectual later described the cultural world in Guangdong at this time as "at the forefront" of making breakthroughs.[45]

Zhou Yang often remarked that "culture and the arts are a barometer of class struggle."[46] He was right. In 1962, *Liu Zhidan* had destroyed Xi Zhongxun's career in a way that foreshadowed the Cultural Revolution. Now, at the beginning of the 1980s, just as Xi was returning to the center of power in Beijing to work on the secretariat, it was another cultural product, this time a movie, that threatened to again throw the nation into chaos. First published as a screenplay named *The Sun and the Man* in September 1979, the movie *Bitter Love* was completed at the end of 1980. Created by Bai Hua and Peng Ning, the movie tells the story of a painter who returned to China in 1949 but was later viciously persecuted by the Gang of Four. Famously, his daughter asked him, "You love your motherland, but does your motherland love you?" The ensuing attacks on *Bitter Love* were so aggressive that observers wondered if another Cultural Revolution–style campaign was impending.[47]

Xi was reluctantly dragged into the affair. In some ways, he would have found resonance in the movie. It castigated Mao's personality cult by comparing it to religious superstition. Like *Bitter Love*'s main character, Xi was devoted to the nation, yet the party had betrayed him. After the experience of the *Liu Zhidan* novel, Xi would have had every reason to sympathize with a movie director who had made a mistake. He certainly did not want to let criticism spin out of control and shake the country's newly won stability. But if the cultural sphere was not carefully controlled, Xi, too, understood that confidence in the party's ideals might waver. He could not simply reject attempts by Deng Xiaoping and Hu Qiaomu to reinforce discipline on the intellectuals. Throughout the incident, Xi would variously play the role of enforcer and peacekeeper before finally washing his hands of it entirely.

Bitter Love was not significantly more provocative than other cultural productions that appeared in the years after the Cultural Revolution. It was the medium—a movie—that proved significant, especially the power of the closing scene, when the painter digs the shape of a huge question mark in the snow and then completes it with his freezing body as the dot dying in the wintry wilderness. This was a call to reflect upon the terror of the Mao years—a common goal for authors at the time and one supported by party leaders who wanted to justify the new direction. Still, no one among the top leadership had wanted this particular movie to be filmed in the first place. On May 21, 1980, when members of the secretariat previewed a sample of the movie, they all felt that it should not be made, and after it was filmed, it was almost universally seen as problematic by top-ranking cadres. The ensuing debate within the party was about how far the attacks should go, not whether the movie was good or bad. Leading cultural figures—like Zhou Yang and Zhang Guangnian, another member of Federation of Literary and Art Circles, as well as the director of the Propaganda Department, Wang Renzhong—proceeded cautiously. They encouraged Bai and Peng to "edit" the movie to "save" it. But political workers in the People's Liberation Army, such as Liu Baiyu and Hua Nan, did not think that would be enough. While the movie was undergoing substantial revisions, Deng Xiaoping had a fateful meeting with members of the military leadership on March 27, 1981. Deng said it was necessary to oppose both the "Left" and the "Right," but now it was imperative to place more emphasis on the Four Cardinal Principles and to criticize *Bitter Love*. When an editorial attacking *Bitter Love* appeared in the *People's Liberation Army Daily* on April 20, terror spread among party intellectuals.[48]

On May 17, Hu Yaobang said that *Bitter Love* was "unhealthy" and "harmful," but he also asserted that the article went too far. On July 17, Deng Xiaoping said *People's Liberation Army Daily* had criticized the movie in an inappropriate fashion, but he still affirmed that *Bitter Love* was problematic. In Deng's mind, it was necessary to be careful when addressing deficiencies in cultural products, but the bigger problem was the reluctance to criticize at all. After Deng's remarks, the attacks mellowed, but the controversy prompted the party to address the broader issue of how to approach cultural issues in this new era. The secretariat decided to hold a meeting of three hundred party officials from the party center, regions, and military, beginning on August 3, to discuss Deng's remarks.[49]

On the first day of the meeting, known as the Discussion Meeting on the Ideological Battlefront, Hu Yaobang said that Bai Hua should not be "beaten to death in one strike," but he also denounced the film: "*Bitter Love* does not benefit the people and does not benefit socialism. It should be criticized!" On August 8, Hu Qiaomu gave a long speech in which he stated that cultural figures and party leaders should engage in a self-criticism for their "weakness" in leadership of the cultural sphere. Emphasizing the importance of opposing bourgeois liberalization, he complained about those people who thought they could write whatever they wanted. Hu Qiaomu had conferred with both Hu Yaobang and Xi before giving this speech.[50]

Privately, Xi told Bai Hua that he appreciated the "poised" reaction to *Bitter Love* displayed by one regional military commissar.[51] But Xi could not ignore the attacks on the movie. On August 13, shortly before leaving for Nanjing to rest, Hu Qiaomu wrote a letter to Xi saying that a forthcoming discussion meeting of the Federation of Literary and Art Circles must "be held successfully; it cannot be held poorly." Hu noted that some individuals still had "very strong opinions" about the film, and he suggested that Xi meet with some of them to affirm that they should "keep the big picture in mind" and that they should not "each sing their own tune." The same day that Xi received Hu Qiaomu's letter, Xi decided to have Yang Shangkun speak with Liu Baiyu and Hua Nan, while he, Xi, would speak with their opponents Zhou Yang and Zhang Guangnian. On August 14, Xi showed the two men Hu Qiaomu's letter and said, "It is absolutely necessary to stay in line" with Deng Xiaoping and Hu Yaobang.[52]

On August 15, Xi met with both sides in the debate. According to one account of what Xi said, he tried his best to emphasize the need to criticize a bad work while not going too far: "Comrade Zhongxun said that while holding this meeting, some comrades might be a little nervous, but it is necessary to keep the big picture in mind. It is necessary to engage in criticism and self-criticism and to carry out the spirit of the discussion meeting on the ideological battlefront. . . . The purpose of this discussion meeting is primarily to engage in criticism and self-criticism, to carry out the spirit of Comrade Xiaoping's remarks, to increase unity, and to improve work—not to debate the past." After the meeting, Xi took special care to meet with Hu Qiaomu's secretary to explain what had happened. On August 19, at a preparatory session preceding the full discussion meeting, the first speaker began by relating Xi's guidance.[53] On September 17, Xi wrote a positive affirmation of Hu Qiaomu's conservative August 8 speech: "This speech is a little too long, but it addresses a lot of problems, and it explains matters very clearly. . . . It is a clear elaboration of the situation. I believe it is a very important speech. If disseminated, it will clarify a lot of muddled thinking."[54]

Yet, even as Xi was helping Hu Qiaomu, Xi was betraying frustration with the entire incident. Party intellectuals struggled to get the balance right in an article that would provide a definitive analysis of *Bitter Love*. On September 8, Zhou Yang sent a sixth draft of the article to Xi. Xi thought that the draft was too rough and lacked persuasive power. Next to a line in the draft stating, "If the enormous changes in the social status and historical mission of China's intellectuals since the Third Plenum are not clarified," Xi wrote, "The movie only goes up to the smashing of the Gang of Four; it's impossible to demand that it reflect the changes at the Third Plenum." In the segment that faulted the movie for using a metaphor of religious superstition to criticize the personality cult, Xi wrote, "It is necessary to pay attention to the historical background of the movie. Requiring that the author reflect the historical facts demanded in this document will not persuade people." Next to another line, he simply wrote a question mark. In his general remarks, Xi said that he had not completed reading the draft, but he thought the beginning was "too crude. At the time, the masses really did think in that way." He warned that "it is necessary for Bai Hua and people with similar thinking to easily accept the criticisms that are made." Xi had clearly lost patience with the controversy. "I am busy," he said. "In the future, I will not manage this affair."[55]

STRUGGLES OVER THE DIRECTION OF *PEOPLE'S DAILY* AND "SPIRITUAL POLLUTION"

Xi's position on the secretariat also drew him into struggles over the direction of *People's Daily*, the party's main mouthpiece. This was not the first time Xi found himself involved in the party's media outlets. As head of the Northwest Bureau in the late 1940s and early 1950s, he had managed the top newspaper in the region, *Masses' Daily*. The leader of the paper at the time was Hu Jiwei—the same man who would later become head of *People's Daily* when Xi worked on the secretariat. Hu's memoirs are very nostalgic about his time in the Northwest under Xi. It was, in his words, the "most satisfactory and comfortable period" of his life of newspaper work, "particularly because of the leadership of Comrade Xi Zhongxun." Xi was "modest and unassuming, gentle and affable." Under Xi's leadership, the Northwest Bureau "created a positive atmosphere of treating people equally, a friendly and hospitable atmosphere."[56] In November 1981, Xi announced a new approach for the media, summarized by five goals: truthfulness, brevity, speed, liveliness (meaning avoidance of old, boring formulations that no one would read), and strength to make people feel that what they are reading is meaningful.[57]

Despite these apparently open views on media work as well as Xi's close career ties with Hu Jiwei, in the early 1980s, Xi did not always support Hu. For example, on September 10, 1981, *People's Daily* and other newspapers published a New China News Agency news dispatch on the Federation of Literary and Art Circles meetings that had been closely managed by Xi Zhongxun and Hu Qiaomu after the *Bitter Love* incident. Probably because of the "leftist" nature of the meeting, Hu Jiwei decided to publish the report only on the second page. Xi believed that it was inappropriate to give it such little attention, and he asked Hu Yaobang to confront Hu Jiwei. At the meeting with Hu Yaobang, Hu Jiwei said he had already sent a self-criticism to Xi. He admitted that he heard the meeting was "held poorly." Yet Hu Jiwei did defend himself by noting that Yang Shangkun had approved putting the news of the discussion meeting on the second page. Hu Yaobang admitted that someone had previously asked him as well whether the news should be on the first or second page, and he had said both options were fine, but he described Xi's criticisms as "well intentioned."[58]

That was not the only time Xi supported Hu Qiaomu over Hu Jiwei. In March 1983, Hu Qiaomu wrote a long letter to Hu Jiwei complaining about his statement that party newspapers must have both a "party nature" and a "people's nature." Hu Yaobang, Xi Zhongxun, and Wang Renzhong all read the letter and not only agreed with Hu Qiaomu but decided to publish Hu's letter in an official collection of important documents since the Third Plenum.[59] Although Xi supported Hu Qiaomu on this issue, in his memoirs, Hu Jiwei claimed that his thinking on a newspaper's simultaneous appeal to the "people" and the "party" had been shaped by his time serving under Xi in the Northwest.[60]

After 1981, the country seemed to move past the criticism of *Bitter Love*, and party intellectuals felt emboldened to raise difficult issues. Wang Ruoshui, deputy editor in charge of theoretical and ideological issues at *People's Daily*, argued openly that Marx's idea of "alienation" existed not only in capitalist societies but in China as well. To combat such a trend, the party needed to embrace "humanism," he argued. By the end of 1982, more than four hundred articles had debated these concepts in the spirit of an academic discussion. Deng Liqun himself, shortly after replacing Wang Renzhong as director of the Propaganda Department, approved one such speech on the topic by Zhou Yang in May 1982 for publication in *People's Daily*. But in March 1983, Zhou Yang gave a major address on the occasion of Marx's centennial that rapidly turned these academic debates into a political scandal.[61]

Years earlier, Zhou Yang had developed a reputation for viciously attacking other cultural figures in the party. But at the beginning of the Cultural Revolution, Zhou himself came under attack, in part for supporting publication of *Liu Zhidan*. After years of extreme suffering in prison during the Cultural Revolution, Zhou Yang apologized to those individuals whom he had previously persecuted, and he contemplated what had gone wrong. At the same time, however, Zhou also believed that, after Mao's death, many "unhealthy" cultural products had appeared that did indeed need to be criticized, and he sought to support and legitimate Deng Xiaoping's leadership.[62]

The remarks Zhou made in March 1983 were not the speech of a dissident. He was still a dedicated Marxist. He even allowed that "of course, we still need theories of Marxist class struggle and the dictatorship of the proletariat." But he was clearly wrestling with thinking about the problems left for China to still overcome. He believed that the attacks on "humanism" during the Cultural Revolution had been misguided, although he was careful to distinguish between "bourgeois" and "Marxist" humanism. His most daring claim was to apply Marx's theory of alienation to China, where, in the economy, alienation meant mistakes in economic construction. Problems in democracy and the rule of law meant "the people's servants" sometimes abused their power, and alienation in the ideological sphere manifested as a personality cult. For Zhou, acknowledging the existence of humanism in socialism facilitated combating alienation. He expressed confidence that the party was already well on the path to solving its problems and that alienation was not fundamental to the socialist system. After his speech, Deng Liqun and Wang Zhen approached him to shake hands.[63] An individual present later remarked, "At the time, no one could have ever imagined that this speech would cause such a big uproar."[64]

Zhou Yang's speech was provocative, but it was not so much its content that sparked a major political firestorm as a complicated mix of confusion and big egos. On March 8, Qin Chuan, then editor in chief of *People's Daily*, called Deng Liqun and asked if Zhou's speech could be published. Deng told them to ask Hu Qiaomu. On March 10, Hu Qiaomu went to speak with Zhou Yang. Hu, in a polite tone, said that he supported the idea of humanism. He did not even raise the issue of alienation, which greatly relieved Wang Ruoshui, who was also present. Moreover, Hu did not provide any fundamental critiques other than to assert that Zhou had not paid enough attention to certain issues. But Hu also explicitly said he represented Hu Yaobang, and he told Zhou Yang that there were too many problems with the speech for it to be published without revisions. Zhou asked, "I absolutely cannot publish it?" Hu Qiaomu started to say, "Of course, it is not totally impossible," but then someone walked into the room, and Zhou did not hear the end of the sentence: "You can consider publishing it in the academic journal *Philosophy Research*." This was a pure misunderstanding, but it helped spark one of the most famous incidents in the history of ideology in China.[65]

Wang Ruoshui told Qin Chuan to go ahead and publish Zhou's speech. Wang, who had been present for the conversation between Hu and Zhou on March 10, had concluded that the two men did not hold fundamentally different positions.[66] When Zhou's article appeared in *People's Daily* on March 16, Deng Liqun was livid. He called Qin Chuan, who admitted that he had not asked Hu Qiaomu directly for guidance as Deng Liqun had demanded. Deng said that this was no longer a problem of different opinions: it had become a question of organizational discipline. The leaders of *People's Daily* quickly wrote a self-criticism.[67]

The secretariat met to discuss a report on what had occurred. Xi Zhongxun strongly opposed forcing Zhou Yang to do a self-criticism too. "There's really no reason to force Zhou Yang to express an opinion at some kind of meeting, is there?" he asked.[68] Hu Qiaomu reported to the secretariat again on April 20, but it never met to discuss the incident, probably because a consensus on the matter could not be reached.[69]

Momentarily, it seemed as if Zhou Yang was safe. But at the end of August, Deng Xiaoping suddenly summoned Hu Qiaomu, who was on a break because of heart disease, to return to Beijing to discuss ideological problems at the upcoming Second Plenum. Deng was clearly motivated by the kerfuffle over alienation and concerns about Zhou's behavior. Both Hu Qiaomu and Deng Liqun have claimed that Deng Xiaoping's sudden turn to the left had nothing to do with them and that in fact they themselves had been caught by surprise.[70]

On October 12, Deng Xiaoping gave a speech at the Second Plenum of the Twelfth Party Congress in which he emphatically stated that "on the ideological battlefront there must be no spiritual pollution." "In the theoretical and cultural worlds," Deng warned, "there are many problems, significant chaos still persists, especially manifestations of spiritual pollution."[71] Zhou Yang was forced to carry out a self-criticism at the plenum, but to little effect—most people who did not specialize in ideology simply could not understand the nature of the problem.[72] On October 22, the members of the secretariat, including Xi, approved an official notification, known as *Document No. 36*, that was attached to speeches by Deng Xiaoping and Chen Yun for dissemination to the rest of the party. A notorious new campaign to eliminate "spiritual pollution" had begun. Deng Liqun, who helped draft the notification, would later carry out a self-criticism about how it had been formulated. By giving regional leaders, not the party center, the right to decide when to share the material, it created a rush that contributed to the subsequent leftist excesses.[73]

In the newly charged environment, the top editors at *People's Daily* could no longer survive. On October 28, the secretariat summoned the paper's leaders to Zhongnanhai. At the meeting, Hu Qili, director of the General Office and a member of the secretariat, announced that Hu Jiwei would "resign," and Qin Chuan would become director of the paper, while Wang Ruoshui would be removed from his position as deputy editor in charge of theoretical and ideological issues. Hu Qiaomu then proceeded to list the alleged mistakes committed by Hu Jiwei and Wang Ruoshui and accused them of losing faith in the party. According to Wang, Xi Zhongxun "did not say anything new." Wang sensed that Xi was not very happy but could do nothing to change the outcome. "At the meeting, [Xi] had to demonstrate that he was in line with the Central Committee," Wang wrote.[74]

On October 31, the paper began publishing a series of editorials about the need to eliminate spiritual pollution. Qin Chuan blamed Deng Liqun and Hu Qiaomu for "ordering" the paper to publish such articles: "They wanted to expand and heighten the struggle," Qin has said.[75] However, also on October 31, at a meeting of the secretariat, Deng Liqun and Hu Qiaomu proposed that the elimination of spiritual pollution should not be considered a legal matter or an attack on enemies of the people. Instead, it was to be simply a matter of fixing problematic thinking. On the following day, Deng Liqun warned that the purpose of the campaign was not to "persecute" anyone and that the mistakes of the Cultural Revolution were not to be repeated.[76] Nevertheless, in the subsequent weeks, the so-called Eliminate Spiritual Pollution Campaign moved beyond ideology and culture and began to affect the economy and the lives of ordinary people, even their hairstyles and clothing.

On November 11, Hu Yaobang said to close associates that *Document No. 36* had been wrong to include the word "eliminate" (even though apparently the original notification did not actually include the term). "Some people" had put pressure on regional officials to openly express support for the campaign, which "scared everyone; no one knew what was going on at the party center," Hu continued.[77] Two days later, Hu Qiaomu read a report from Tianjin that proposed more restrictions on what kinds of published material should be attacked as spiritual pollution. He immediately forwarded the document to Deng Liqun, Xi Zhongxun, and Hu Qili and said an editorial should be published to pass on that message so as to "avoid terror in society."[78]

By late November, with Deng Xiaoping's approval, the party started to rein in the excesses of the campaign (how much of a role Xi played in this, however, is unclear as he was in France from November 23 to December 3).

On December 14, Hu Yaobang gave a speech in which he stated that although the campaign should continue, leftism and feudalism should be avoided. Less than one month after it began, the campaign was coming to a close.[79]

Xi believed that the entire incident was farcical. He was surprised when his old partner from Guangdong Yang Shangkun spoke out strongly in support of "eliminating spiritual pollution."[80] One account even suggests that Xi told He Jingzhi, vice-director of the Propaganda Department, "You want to carry out a small Cultural Revolution in the literature and arts world."[81] Deng Liqun alleged that while Zhao Ziyang and Hu Qiaomu were fully on board with opposing spiritual pollution, Hu Yaobang and Wan Li were more skeptical, "as well as Xi Zhongxun," Deng wrote. "Xi Zhongxun wanted to ingratiate himself with Hu Yaobang."[82] Hu Yaobang would later say that he had put an end to a plan to accuse Zhou Yang and Wang Ruoshui of attempting to establish an antiparty clique.[83]

But were the differences really so pronounced at the time? In April 1983, Xi had told a delegation from Tanzania that if the party did not "strengthen discipline and vigilance," then "bourgeois thinking" would "pollute us."[84] At the beginning of the campaign, Deng Liqun had warned about avoiding mass persecution, and, on November 28, he helped spread the word that the secretariat had officially decided that something had gone seriously wrong. At the time, Deng admitted that people feared another antirightist campaign or a cultural revolution, and he criticized people who said, "Spiritual pollution is a basket, and everything should be thrown into it."[85] In subsequent years, Deng Liqun tried to distance himself from the debacle. Privately, he would say that it had been Deng Xiaoping's idea and that "it was nothing more than lukewarm water." "I couldn't help it. The top had me do it, so I had to," he once sighed.[86] In January 1984, Hu Yaobang said privately that he was still not sure what to make of Deng Liqun (although by 1989 he was more critical about the role Hu Qiaomu and Deng Liqun had played in the campaign).[87]

Crucially, although credited with ending the Eliminate Spiritual Pollution Campaign, neither Hu Yaobang nor Xi Zhongxun had opposed *Document No. 36*, and after the attacks on spiritual pollution were restrained, both Hu and Xi were very careful not to entirely reject the concept. In an interview, He Jingzhi later said that the idea that Hu Yaobang would "oppose" the campaign was inconceivable, as Hu was bound by Deng Xiaoping's words and party discipline.[88] On December 18, Xi said that the party was "actively and steadily engaging in work to eliminate spiritual pollution." Although some people had "misunderstandings and doubts," the secretariat had already fixed the problem by clarifying its "scope, methods, and restrictions," he explained. Xi did not say that the campaign had been a mistake.[89]

Xi even supported Hu Qiaomu's decisive conclusion to the affair. On December 30, Hu Qiaomu paid a visit to Xi in Zhongnanhai seeking guidance. The party school had asked him to deliver a speech on humanism and alienation. He had already completed a draft, but he wanted to know whether or not he should give the speech. Xi gave Hu his blessing. In the speech, Hu acknowledged that the party still had to overcome its mistakes, but he argued that lumping those problems together as "alienation" disregarded the specific challenges that each of those issues posed and created doubts about the party's mission. Too much emphasis on "humanism" failed to acknowledge the need for sacrifice and a sense of mission, Hu asserted. When an elderly party intellectual saw a copy of this speech that Xi had given Hu permission to deliver, he concluded that it was "one of the worst" things Hu had ever produced, and it was full of illogical inconsistencies. It still was not clear what the entire debate had been about.[90]

The events of 1983 left behind strong feelings, especially about the treatment of Zhou Yang. Deng Liqun has asserted that he thought that Zhou Yang's self-criticism at the Second Plenum was sufficient. However, Deng Xiaoping wanted Zhou to publicly publish a long self-criticism. When Zhou proved recalcitrant, Hu Qiaomu went to his home. He greeted Zhou with a bow, and then he began to weep as he begged Zhou to relent. Hu had come up with the idea that Zhou would make a self-criticism during an interview with a New China News Agency reporter so he would not have to write up a self-criticism on his own. Zhou wanted to include an addendum to his self-criticism that indicated that he still held to his own views about humanism and alienation, but when the members of the secretariat discussed the matter, even Hu Yaobang said, "Doing both a self-criticism and maintaining one's own views—how can that be a self-criticism?" Zhou was incensed when his self-criticism was broadcast widely on television and printed in newspapers. Moreover, the criticisms against him did not end. Zhou ultimately concluded that Hu Qiaomu had betrayed him.[91]

Zhou, who had survived years of persecution during the Cultural Revolution as well as treatment for cancer, simply could not bear this latest humiliation. He began to show signs of psychological deterioration. One close associate remarked, "Based on my observations of several people whom I knew well, I have reached the following conclusion: if someone does a self-criticism against their wishes and is unhappy about it, it is very easy for senility to set in." Another colleague attributed Zhou's "emotional breakdown" to an inability to resolve the "ceaseless struggle" between "the old habits of servility and the rationality of political awakening." In September 1984, Zhou entered a hospital that he was never to leave. Qi Xin, but not Xi, often visited him there, as Xi's presence would have signified Zhou had been forgiven. In January 1985, Zhou's colleagues tried to find a way to fully rehabilitate him. But it was too difficult to convince anyone in the leadership to visit Zhou in the hospital. Instead, Xi proposed that Zhou's March 1983 speech on alienation be again published openly. But if the speech were to simply be rereleased, that would be too sudden, so Xi cleverly proposed that it be included in a book of Zhou's recent works. The book was published in June 1985, but, by the summer of that year, Zhou was no longer able to speak or recognize anyone, so it is unclear whether he understood the nature of this victory.[92] He died in July 1989.

AN "IDEOLOGICAL" STALEMATE

In the aftermath of the spiritual-pollution fiasco, Hu Yaobang tried to protect Deng Xiaoping's reputation by emphasizing that Deng had never demanded spiritual pollution be "eliminated." Hu sincerely believed he correctly understood that this is what Deng had wanted.[93] The party's official position, expressed by Zhao Ziyang in April 1984, stated that the party would not end its war against spiritual pollution.[94] But, once again, it was easy to get the politics of a course correction wrong—Hu's statement that the term "spiritual pollution" was not precise enough and that it should disappear over time displeased Deng Xiaoping.[95]

The need for a new party decision that decisively settled the ideological debates seemed more pressing than ever—but also more distant. On March 29, 1984, the secretariat met to discuss a draft document on ideology written by Deng Liqun and Hu Qiaomu. Those present pushed back, saying that the document tried too hard to cover everything, that it was too general, and that it did not make any clear points. Xi was especially outspoken. He acknowledged that the problem the document was supposed to solve was "extremely pressing." But he was concerned that conditions were not yet ripe. "I am worried that if another meeting is held, it will cause even more unsteadiness," he warned.[96]

In July 1984, Deng Xiaoping sent the director of the General Office, Hu Qili, to warn Hu Yaobang that he was too weak on the issue of "bourgeois liberalization." But it is unclear whether Hu Yaobang fully understood Deng's position; Deng had sent Hu Qili instead of going himself because otherwise the issue might have seemed too serious.[97] Xi came to believe that Hu was not meeting with Deng enough, and he pressured Hu, telling him this was a mistake. Finally, in August, Hu met with Deng at the summer resort of Beidaihe. The meeting proved to be very significant. Hu and Deng finally seemed to have a heart-to-heart. Deng acknowledged that the Eliminate Spiritual Pollution Campaign had a "bad reputation." Deng, like Xi, saw danger in a big meeting on ideology if it were to be held too soon. Deng told Hu that the party would refrain from any major new decisions on ideology for three years.[98]

Meanwhile, the battle over *People's Daily* persisted. Some of the top leaders in the Organization Department hoped to send Wang Renzhi and three other figures, viewed by Xi and others as too leftist, to work at the paper. In January 1984, at a meeting at Xi's home, Li Rui, who was vice-director of the Organization Department at the time, warned Xi about such plans. All the participants at the meeting emphatically stated that any more changes at the *People's Daily* at this time would cause "further chaos." Li Rui then used Xi's support to block the Organization Department's plans to send Wang Renzhi to the paper. In his memoirs, Deng Liqun claims that Wang Renzhi had been framed.[99]

On July 9, the secretariat again discussed *People's Daily*. According to Li Rui, this meeting turned into "a big struggle." Qin Chuan and Hu Qiaomu each gave speeches that lasted for more than an hour. Qin complained that the Department of Propaganda was directly running the newspaper, and he accused the department of leftist views. Hu Yaobang cut in to say that he did not understand the situation at *People's Daily*, but he questioned whether Hu Jiwei and Wang Ruoshui had been treated appropriately. Xi added, "The situation is so bad that for a year, Yaobang has not dared to approach the newspaper."[100]

It was not only the editors but also the journalists at *People's Daily* who posed a dilemma for the leadership. In 1984, one such journalist, Liu Binyan, made three trips to Shaanxi and was shocked by what he saw, concluding that Shaanxi was extremely backward. In March, he published an article with the headline "Dirt under a Surgical Gown," detailing how intellectuals were still suffering persecution by those who had been promoted during the Cultural Revolution.[101]

In August, *People's Daily* published another article by Liu—"The Rights and Wrongs of Thirty-Eight Years." The article—about a man who had helped the Red Army before 1949 and then was persecuted by the party after it came to power—caused a firestorm, interrupting the work of the secretariat for an entire month. On September 13, a furious Xi held a meeting in Beijing to criticize *People's Daily.* Years later, Ma Wenrui, party leader of Shaanxi, would recall, "If not for Comrade Xi Zhongxun coming forward to hold a meeting and speak just words, it would have been difficult to clarify right and wrong, and *People's Daily* might not have accepted the criticism . . . but in actuality it did not submit, the people who made mistakes were not punished, and, in fact, they were promoted and became even more active."[102]

THE FOURTH CONGRESS OF THE CHINESE WRITERS ASSOCIATION AND ITS CONSEQUENCES

In June 1984, the party began preparing for the Fourth Congress of the Chinese Writers Association. The meeting had been repeatedly delayed because of infighting within the organization about who should assume the new leadership positions. Previously, its membership, like that of other "civilian" bodies, was determined by the relevant body of the Central Committee and then "approved" by the congress. However, Hu Yaobang, Xi Zhongxun, and Wan Li all believed that this process did not accord with the party's purported democratic principles, and they used the occasion of the forthcoming Fourth Congress as an opportunity to take a new approach.[103]

As planning proceeded, Zhang Guangnian, the association's party secretary, feuded with He Jingzhi, deputy director of the Propaganda Department. The reasons for their strained relationship remain somewhat obscure. Certainly, one element was Zhang's fear that He Jingzhi was not sufficiently on board with a more open direction. Yet that seems to have been only one small part of the problem. An expert on this era writes that it was not so much a "struggle" between them as something "rooted in misunderstandings, moods, and personalities. Once you are stuck, then there's a back-and-forth, and things move along in that direction. In other words, there's a lot of contingency. . . . Assuming that everything is an ideological conflict, or even simply assuming people are either 'leftist' or 'rightist,' is to divide them and is not in accordance with fact." It is certainly clear, however, that Zhang was cunning when it came to party politics, and he knew how to fight dirty—along with his chief patron, Xi Zhongxun.[104]

For Zhang, the challenge was how to avoid interference by the Propaganda Department, which officially oversaw the association. On July 10, he met with Xi. He Jingzhi would later complain that this was in fact a violation of party protocol as Zhang was skipping over the Propaganda Department and reaching out directly to the secretariat. When Zhang arrived at Xi's home, Xi's secretary said that his boss had been feeling dizzy and had gone to see a doctor. Zhang had to wait an hour for Xi to return. When Xi finally entered the room, he required assistance walking. Zhang suggested that they cancel the meeting, but Xi insisted. Zhang then said they should speak for only about ten minutes, but it turned into an hour-long chat. When the meeting ended, Xi walked unstably, which made Zhang nervous. Despite worrying signs about Xi's health, the meeting was a victory for Zhang. He spoke little, but Xi spoke a great deal, and Xi supported Zhang's plan to create a "reference list of names" for the members of the new party organization within the association. Xi also said he would inform Hu Yaobang about their conversation, which made it quite clear that the secretariat would directly manage the upcoming congress. In the ensuing weeks, Zhang and his people met with Xi so often that He Jingzhi concluded that it was Xi who was "playing politics."[105]

In September, He Jingzhi organized a meeting at Jingxi Hotel in Beijing to discuss cultural affairs and politics. At that those sessions, Zhao Xun, chairman of the Chinese Theater Association, complained that Hu Yaobang's remarks to a Japanese delegation had included positions that differed from the Central Committee's official policy on spiritual pollution. Zhao Xun questioned how it would be possible to work when the general secretary was not in line with the party. Rumors started to spread that the sessions at Jingxi Hotel were intended to persecute people, strengthen vigilance against spiritual pollution, and criticize Hu Yaobang even though many of the participants at the meeting also attacked "leftist" positions. One participant, Feng Mu, reported on Zhao Xun's remarks to Qi Xin, who immediately told Xi. (Feng would later describe this operation as "just like doing underground work back in the day.") He Jingzhi was summoned to the Party General Office, where Xi Zhongxun, while leafing through the complaint, accused the Jingxi Hotel meeting of attacking Hu Yaobang, and he asserted, falsely, that the meeting had not been approved beforehand. Xi was furious: "At the discussion meeting at Jingxi Hotel, someone shockingly opposed the general secretary and said that the general secretary is not in line with the Central Committee." The Jingxi Hotel sessions were labeled a "black meeting." The atmosphere finally calmed down when Deng Liqun reminded Hu Yaobang that he had in fact told Hu about He Jingzhi's plans. He Jingzhi wanted to clarify matters further, but he decided that speaking to Xi would be useless.[106]

As the date of the Congress of the Chinese Writers Association approached, tensions continued to mount. On December 20, at a high-level meeting to discuss the association's leadership, Hu Yaobang criticized the name list that had been put together by the small group run by the Propaganda and Organization Departments. Hu said it was necessary to avoid the two extremes with regard to civilian organizations. While direct leadership by the party and government was inappropriate, allowing such "civilian" bodies to select whomever they wanted was also wrong. Still, Hu stated that the Propaganda Department and the Organization Department should not directly interfere in the elections for the leadership of the association. "Even if their choices are not ideal," he said, "let them be responsible." Xi then interrupted to agree, asserting that the list prepared by the two departments should not be seen as final: "Some people say the names are determined by the Central Committee. How can it be put that way? Is that merely intended to scare the masses?" The congress was told to select its membership on its own with a secret vote.[107]

This move in the direction of greater openness was accentuated on December 21, when Xi addressed a meeting of members of the non-Communist political parties. He seemed to be more critical of the campaign against spiritual pollution than Zhao Ziyang had been in his official statement earlier that year: "We made a mistake. We conducted the Eliminate Spiritual Pollution Campaign, and moreover, it immediately spread to the society for twenty-seven days. Later, the party center turned things around. At the time, you were worried, we also were worried, and both China and the outside world were worried—there was a fear that the Cultural Revolution had returned."[108] Although this was a major speech, it was not openly published at the time, and it never appeared in any of Xi's later collected works.

On December 29, the day that the congress finally opened, when a congratulatory telegram written by Hu Qiaomu was read, three or four people clapped for a moment, but when no one else responded, those applauding stopped. The atmosphere was incredibly awkward. Next came Deng Liqun's celebratory telegram, and no one made a sound. Hu Yaobang, Xi Zhongxun, and Hu Qili all laughed. When a letter written in Zhou Yang's name was read, everyone applauded, including Hu Yaobang and Xi.[109]

During the free elections for the members of the presidium of the congress, Zhang Guangnian won the most votes, followed by Liu Binyan. He Jingzhi won so few votes that he was not allowed to join the presidium. The congress was one of the most open meetings on Chinese cultural issues since 1949. But He Jingzhi was furious—he believed the outcome was the result of behind the scenes dishonest machinations and manipulation. But the election was not the only issue—speakers such as Liu Binyan and playwright and director Wu Zuguang expressed comments on openness in Chinese society that some participants found explosive.[110]

Zhang Guangnian knew the congress was a disaster. He never could have expected He Jingzhi would do that poorly, and even Zhang did not like the bomb-thrower Liu Binyan. The victors "were all very nervous, worrying: What now? The results of this election will make future work very difficult."[111] The congress was extraordinarily costly for both Hu Yaobang and Xi Zhongxun. Powerful party cadres whispered that they had been "too careless" and "one-sided," while some even accused Hu and Xi of "bourgeois liberalization." The counterattack was so strong that plans to introduce free elections in other civilian organizations, from the non-Communist Party parties to the Association of Industry and Commerce to the Chinese Academy of Sciences, all came to nothing.[112] Xi was upset that, after the congress, Hu Qiaomu complained to marshal Xu Xiangqian, as well as to Deng Yingchao, Zhou Enlai's widow (although they had not been "tricked," Xi believed).[113] Most dangerously, the congress, which Xi had managed so closely, significantly damaged Hu Yaobang's relationship with Deng Xiaoping. Hu was frustrated that Deng had incorrectly concluded that he had been trying to win over supporters of bourgeois liberalization.[114]

Later, the congress would face official accusations of opposing the Four Cardinal Principles, not resisting bourgeois liberalization, and supporting "limitless creative freedom." But just how "liberal" and "proreform" was the congress? In his welcoming remarks, Hu Qili spoke in great detail about the need for "creative freedom," and he warned against political interference and campaign-style criticism in the cultural sphere. However, he also clearly stated that these creative freedoms only applied "within the confines of legality." Although he did not specifically mention the Four Cardinal Principles, Chinese laws, including the constitution, did, which meant that cultural products that did not adhere to the Four Cardinal Principles would be illegal. Hu Qili did not use the term "eliminate spiritual pollution," but Deng Xiaoping himself had already told Hu Yaobang that the campaign had a "bad reputation." Moreover, the word "socialism" appeared fifteen times, and the leadership of the party was accentuated throughout. Unambiguously, the congress did not signify freedom of speech. Hao Huaiming, who helped write Hu Qili's speech, later said the charges were a "fabricated crime" used to criticize Hu Yaobang.[115]

Xi and Hu seemed to worry about what had happened at the Writers' Congress. On January 29, 1985, Xi wrote approvingly on a petition from a party cadre in Hangzhou complaining about a "deluge of spiritual pollution." Xi claimed that such problems had actually appeared all over the country: "Many things are a manifestation of this new bad style of 'putting money first.'"[116] Then, on February 8, 1985, Hu Yaobang gave an extremely conservative speech at a secretariat meeting, attended by Xi, held to discuss party-media work. Deng Liqun, who thought Hu's speech was "very good," saw it as an attempt to rein in "rightism" after the congress. Deng Liqun asserted that Hu Yaobang had been "surprised" by what occurred at the congress, implying that the congress went beyond what Hu had wanted.[117] When Hu Jiwei saw the text of Hu Yaobang's February speech, he did not believe Hu Yaobang was reacting to pressure. "Actually, this was a reappearance of the old views that took decades to form," Hu Jiwei concluded.[118]

Some people had misunderstood the issue of spiritual pollution, Hu Yaobang said. The problem of spiritual pollution had been raised by Deng Xiaoping himself. Hu recited, in full, Zhao Ziyang's May 1984 statement that affirmed the struggle against spiritual pollution was necessary. The party had never given up on the fight, Hu said. Although it was not imperative to constantly use the expression, "that absolutely does not mean that there is anything wrong with the principle of combating spiritual pollution." Hu was strident: "Ultimately, with regard to the problem of opposing spiritual pollution, the Central Committee and the people have already made a final decision. No party member is allowed to act on their own and depart from this conclusion!"[119] Hu Jiwei and other cadres involved in media work then wrote Hu Yaobang a letter in which they complained that these remarks represented a "retreat" from Xi's speech in December 1984 when Xi had said the campaign raised fears of another Cultural Revolution.[120]

Were Hu and Xi doing a bit of political maneuvering? Eight days after Hu Yaobang's speech, Xi held a meeting to criticize Deng Liqun and Deng's Political Research Office. "Turn your face to reform, your face to the world, your face to the future," Xi said. "You must effectively use Marxism to clarify socialist modernization, thereby developing and advancing Marxism." Xi told them to "eliminate every single old viewpoint that does not accord with reality."[121]

THE FINAL BREAK BETWEEN HU YAOBANG AND DENG XIAOPING

Despite his antipathy for leftist campaign-style attacks and hidebound views, Xi clearly understood that critical voices were a political problem—even when they came from his closest associates. Wu Zuguang wrote in his memoirs that after he was persecuted during the Antirightist Campaign in 1957, the only high-ranking figure who maintained ties with him was Xi. Wu had been one of the most outspoken participants at the Congress of the Chinese Writers Association, and this severely damaged his relationship with Hu Qiaomu. Understanding clearly that mending ties between the "rightist" Wu and the "leftist" Hu would contribute to party stability, Xi demanded that Wu meet with Hu, but Wu's son suspected that this was because Xi feared that if Wu were to be punished, it would also reflect badly on him. At first, Wu refused to visit Hu, but Xi insisted. "I already picked a time. You absolutely must go!" When Wu arrived at Hu's residence, it was clear that Xi had already convinced Hu to make amends, and only a few days later, Hu also visited Wu's home. According to Zhongxun's son Yuanping, Zhongxun told Hu that if it proved to be impossible to unite with people like Wu, the party would lose many friends. This was a significant victory for Xi but only a short one. In 1987, after the student protests of late 1986, Hu Qiaomu persuaded Wu to submit his party resignation.[122]

Xi similarly tried to rein in Liu Binyan. In April 1985, Liu Binyan was invited to visit Harvard University as a fellow, but at Xi's insistence, he was not given permission to leave the country. Xi told Liu that he could become a lightning rod for Hu's critics: "It was my idea that you not go to America. The length of time was too long. It would be difficult for you to avoid public talks. If a newspaper misrepresents something you say, those people will make a big deal again. If you people run into any trouble, Hu Yaobang is always blamed. Those people believe Hu Yaobang is an umbrella for the liberalizers."[123]

Xi was right. Hu Yaobang continued to struggle to win Deng Xiaoping's confidence. In the summer of 1985, Deng told Qiao Shi, then secretary of the Political and Legal Affairs Commission, and Hu Qili that they should tell Hu Yaobang that some people were "raising Hu's flag" to criticize party policy.[124] Around the time of Deng's warning, Xi spoke furiously about his colleagues who managed ideological affairs. He complained to Li Rui that Wang Zhen defended both Deng Liqun and Hu Qiaomu. Deng Liqun, Xi said, kept "crying" to Chen Yun, Wang Zhen, and Li Xiannian, complaining that Hu Yaobang was "persecuting people." The situation was not entirely bad, however. Deng Liqun and Hu Qiaomu no longer possessed the power they previously enjoyed—Xi told Li Rui that Deng Xiaoping no longer met with either one of them.[125]

The man who replaced Deng Liqun as minister of propaganda in the summer of 1985, Zhu Houze, had possibly been directly selected by Xi. Although Xi left the secretariat in September 1985, he still tried to support Zhu. In March 1986, Xi complained that Deng Liqun had said at a secretariat meeting that Zhu did not understand theory. In August 1986, *People's Daily* published parts of an official speech that Zhu had given on what would become known as the "three relaxations," which suggested more openness for political debate. Xi's support for the speech was a significant reason that opponents could not attack it. In fact, Xi liked the article so much that on the day it was published, he invited Zhu to his home to eat watermelon. He also had his wife send Deng Xiaoping a copy of that day's newspaper.[126]

Finally, in the summer of 1986, Hu Yaobang and Deng Xiaoping seemed to be on the same page. Two years earlier, the party had abandoned work on a major new document on ideology. But now, Hu Yaobang was making good progress on the project. Vice-Premier Tian Jiyun recalled that while the document was going through multiple drafts, "I could see that Comrade Yaobang was indeed steadfast and faithful to Xiaoping. He took action on everything Deng said."[127] Yet when Hu Yaobang submitted a draft for review by the party leadership, Deng Liqun criticized it. On August 9, at a meeting of the secretariat, Deng Liqun stated that there was not enough continuity with previous party documents. He submitted his proposed revisions widely within the leadership, thus infuriating Hu Yaobang. No one had ever before seen Hu become so angry.[128]

Deng Xiaoping thought Deng Liqun had gone too far, and he unambiguously chose to support Hu Yaobang. When Hu Yaobang reported to Deng Xiaoping in mid-September, Deng complained that Deng Liqun was "trying to pull us to the left" with the revised draft. "Our policies must become more open, not narrower," Deng said. Hu Yaobang told Deng that Lu Dingyi did not want to include the phrase "bourgeois liberalization" in the document. Lu, who decades earlier had been minister of propaganda both before and after Xi and had served as one of Xi's deputies in the ministry, opposed including the words because he feared they would be used as a leftist weapon. Crucially, even though Hu said it was unclear whether the expression was "scientific," Hu did also tell Deng that it was still necessary to include the phrase for now. If it were suddenly to disappear, that would not be conducive for social stability, he said, and Deng agreed. The interference by either leftism or rightism must be opposed, Deng said. Hu Yaobang, who similarly believed that the party had to navigate carefully between both the Left and Right, was thrilled by this conversation.[129]

At what might have been a moment of triumph for Hu Yaobang, disaster struck—and it had nothing to do with policy differences between him and Deng Xiaoping or the machinations of Deng Liqun. On September 28, the Central Committee, including Xi, met to pass the finalized document on ideology. Hu Yaobang, who chaired the meeting, asked whether anyone had any further recommendations. Lu Dingyi rose to criticize inclusion of the phrase "bourgeois liberalization." Beforehand, Hu had specifically reached out to Lu to achieve consensus, but Lu was too stubborn. When Lu finished his remarks, the room filled with applause. Lu had placed Hu in an impossible position. Hu could have cut the debate short, but that would have been disrespectful to Lu, whose credentials as a revolutionary far outweighed Hu's. Also, intervening would have made a mockery of inner-party democracy. So, instead, Hu Yaobang talked about the history of the expression and allowed for discussion without taking a definite position. Wan Li spoke in support of Lu, but then others, such as Yang Shangkun and Bo Yibo, opposed removing the phrase, and they were applauded as well. Deng Xiaoping was livid. "I have spoken the most about opposing bourgeois liberalization, and I was the most insistent," he said. Even though Hu had initially supported including the phrase in the document, the damage was already done. As one party intellectual who was present later wrote in his memoirs, "Deng Xiaoping's speech at the meeting in actuality presaged the final break between him and Hu Yaobang and brought a conclusion to Hu Yaobang's political fate." Hu later plaintively said in private, "Everything was blamed on me."[130]

At the end of the year, student protests erupted in Anhui and Shanghai. During a session of the secretariat, Hu Yaobang betrayed hard-line tendencies. He believed that some of the students wanted China to take a Western, capitalist path. "When you ask them what capitalism is, or about its insurmountable disadvantages, they don't know. They want freedom and democracy, but they don't know what freedom and democracy are. They don't know how to develop freedom and democracy. They think they know, but they don't," he said.[131] Later that month at a meeting with regional leaders, Hu was even tougher. He was shocked by the biggest case of "troublemaking" since the Gang of Four. Tens of thousands of students were not marching with the party despite its triumphs. "Why are they leaving us, hating us?" he wondered. Views that denigrated the party and praised capitalism "are indeed spreading without restraint." "Our own top institutions are not stubbornly propagating the Four Cardinal Principles," he complained, and although most cadres are "good," others "whose heads lack any hope for socialism" should be fired.[132]

On December 25, Xi expressed his own views to a nationwide meeting of provincial secretaries. It was a programmatic statement about what the party was doing right and wrong given at a moment of crisis in state-society relations and elite politics. He frankly admitted that the party was still struggling in numerous areas: prices, salaries, bureaucratism, and cadres abusing privileges. Some of these problems were inevitable and temporary, and, with "appropriate democratic channels," the party could explain itself and win forgiveness and support. However, he continued, some people with "nefarious motives" whose "only fear was peace under heaven" wanted to "overemphasize the dark side." They did everything in their power to tarnish the party, even "inciting" the masses to cause "turmoil" to "pressure the party center" into "comprehensive westernization."[133]

In Xi's mind, the party's main priority should be elimination of the underlying causes for dissatisfaction by improving performance. "Correct opinions and reasonable ideas" should be listened to carefully. Education and "correct democratic channels" were effective for handling such views. He emphasized adherence to the Four Cardinal Principles and opposing "comprehensive westernization," but he was careful to say that "the old methods of refusing to reform, refusing to open up" were not the right way to achieve those goals. "If we use a mistake to correct a mistake, our economy will not improve, and that is exactly what these people will use to fan the flames and oppose us." Stale theories and propaganda were "precisely what would cede to these people the ideological battlefield." With a good economy, the party could "use facts to fundamentally smash their designs."[134]

In the meantime, Xi was still doing his best to stop figures like Liu Binyan and Fang Lizhi, an astrophysicist, from creating more difficulties for Hu Yaobang. Sociologist Fei Xiaotong warned the party leadership that Fang and Liu were planning to hold an academic discussion meeting in March 1987 on the thirtieth anniversary of the Antirightist Campaign. On the same day as his speech to the regional leaders, Xi summoned the heads of the democratic parties to warn them that holding a meeting like the one proposed by Fang and Liu "would divert attention, would drag us back to history, would entangle us in old accounts, would influence unity, and would not benefit reform or the Four Modernizations." Xi's intervention worked: the meeting was canceled several months ahead of time.[135]

Hu Yaobang's tough words about the students and Xi's effective use of the United Front were not enough. On December 30, Deng summoned Hu Yaobang to a fateful meeting. Deng acknowledged that using peaceful means to "guide" the students in the right direction had been correct. He even said the goal was to do everything possible to minimize bloodshed. Yet, at the same time, the party had failed to also punish the students. Furious, Deng blamed the protests on years of failing to take the threat of bourgeois liberalization seriously.[136]

Hu understood that he had lost Deng's confidence. Yet he was still stunned, and he felt deeply wronged. He had never felt there was any distance between him and Deng Xiaoping on the question of ideology. But the problem, of course, was not the reality of the situation. What really mattered was Deng's own subjective views, and those were shaped by one particular problem: the student protests. Nevertheless, Hu swiftly submitted a letter of resignation to Deng. He accepted Deng's charge that he had not taken opposition to bourgeois liberalization seriously enough. But, mournfully, Hu complained about "some bastards who went so far as to treat me as their protective umbrella" to engage in nefarious activities. He described Liu Binyan as a "rightist" who had never changed his position, even though

Liu had never lost faith in socialism. Hu claimed to have told *People's Daily* that Liu should not be allowed to be a journalist. "Of course, it is necessary to state honestly I never deliberately resisted you," Hu wrote to Deng.[137] Hu's request to resign was swiftly accepted—punished for being someone he never truly was. Yet Deng did not give up on Hu simply because, in Deng's mind, the general secretary had failed to impose sufficient discipline in the ideological and cultural spheres. Hu had also struggled in managing another explosive issue as well: the politics of succession and the "two-line" system. And Xi, just as in the 1950s when he was close to Gao Gang and Zhou Enlai, was an integral part of the drama.

27
THE DEEP WATERS OF ZHONGNANHAI

Party rectification. The rule of law and the National People's Congress. Cadre offspring. The United Front. Ethnic and religious affairs. The global left. Ideology. In the wake of the Cultural Revolution, the Chinese Communist Party tried new approaches to the fundamental challenge of how to handle contradictions in society, within the party, and with the outside world. Yet the same dilemmas that appeared in the earliest days of the revolution persisted. What was the right balance between stability and transformation, co-optation and repression, zeal and pragmatism, openness and control? In the second half of the 1980s, these questions became increasingly difficult to answer as challenges mounted. Was a new and tougher approach imperative for the party to survive, or would staying the course finally lead to a new equilibrium? Finding a balance between the party's competing goals was a profound dilemma. As Hu Yaobang stated in a self-criticism he gave after submitting his resignation, "Overall, Reform and Opening should, and can, be unified with the Four Cardinal Principles. But when it comes to many specific problems, I still believe there are contradictions. To unify them effectively is very difficult. It requires a high level of leadership ability and skill."[1] The right approach was not immediately clear to the aging leaders in Beijing, and even Xi Zhongxun—who for much of the decade had been tasked with execution of party policies in these sensitive areas—had shifting and complicated attitudes.

Yet the policy response was not the result of a simple calculation of pros and cons. For, despite the tragedy of the Mao era, the party had still not escaped another enduring predicament: the issue of how to arrange power at the very heart of the leadership compound of Zhongnanhai. And Xi, just as in the 1950s, was once again one of the closest witnesses to the inherent pathologies of succession politics and leader-deputy relations in the Leninist system.

Certainly, in some ways, the Deng years were an improvement over Mao. Deng often had a hands-off approach, and he could be persuaded when policies were not working.[2] In the secretariat, where Xi worked, the atmosphere was very open. Li Rui, who attended secretariat meetings from 1982 to 1984, was impressed by its democratic sensibilities. He compared those meetings to the ones he had experienced in 1958 and 1959, when Mao was present. "I felt that we had truly entered a new era," Li believed. "The system of one person speaking had become a system of many people speaking."[3] Xi agreed. "Now it is possible to speak in the party center. Don't be afraid," Xi told Li in 1985.[4]

Many in the party had learned from Mao a powerful lesson about the danger of strongman rule. Xi told Peng Zhen that it was "necessary to have a system, to have some kind of power that can prevent the kind of pressure of the Cultural Revolution." Xi went on to say that China could not afford another Mao. "The problem is that if, in the future, there is another strongman like Mao Zedong, what is to be done? If he stubbornly acts in that way, what is to be done? I think it will be difficult—difficult!"[5] Xi was afraid that the party, which was full of former peasants, still suffered from too much feudal thinking. The understanding of Communism held by most cadres remained at the level of "beating up the landlords and dividing their land." Most cadres believed that whoever conquered the nation had the right to rule it. The party, Xi worried, lacked democratic traditions.[6]

Yet the Cultural Revolution contained another lesson as well: the danger of the entire system falling apart if there was not a single powerful leader to hold everything together. Deng once stated, "Because Chairman Mao was the core of the leadership at the time, during the Cultural Revolution, the party was not overthrown." In other words, the peril of a powerful leader making colossal mistakes was less serious than the hazard of not having a leader who could demand obedience. Deng believed that "a collective leadership requires a core. Without a core, any leadership is unreliable."[7] These two legacies, fear of dictatorship and fear of collapse, sat together uncomfortably. One cadre who worked for the Central Advisory Commission, a body established for elderly cadres in semiretirement, wrote, "After a life of difficulties and turbulence, especially the catastrophe of the Cultural Revolution, the elders reflected upon and even criticized the personality cult and the superstition of the Mao Zedong era, and they all believed that this was the most painful historical lesson. But a new personality cult and superstition were again quietly appearing around Deng Xiaoping."[8]

Deng, in the words of Li Rui, was actually "half a Mao Zedong." Hu Yaobang had wanted to create a presidium with multiple chairmen, each with one vote, thereby establishing real collective leadership—an idea quashed by Deng.[9] Deng saw real efficiencies in strongman rule. He admired the Soviet Union, which could swiftly and easily make decisions, like the 1979 invasion of Afghanistan. America, on the other hand, had "three governments," with each restraining the other.[10]

With the reestablishment of the secretariat, the "two-line" system that had created so many problems under Mao and that Xi had witnessed so intimately had resurfaced. Hu Yaobang did not immediately see the dangers. In March 1980, he told an associate that Deng "understands me." Hu believed he had Deng's trust for three reasons. First, Hu understood what Deng wanted. Second, he was good at mobilizing the system to achieve Deng's goals. And third, Deng knew that "I [Hu] am an upright person. I do not engage in unjust practices."[11] At heart, Hu believed he was just "doing a few things for Deng Xiaoping and Chen Yun." "I'm not the head," he once said privately. "I'm the bottom of the foot."[12]

Hu believed that his relationship with Deng was strong enough to occasionally allow candor. Hu told Xi, "Of course, it is imperative to protect [Deng's authority]. But necessary words must be spoken."[13] On exceptionally rare occasions, Hu did not accede to Deng's wishes. When Deng wanted Hu to serve as first vice-chairman of the Central Military Commission, Hu refused, reasoning that it would violate the party's organizational principles (probably because Deng was chairman of the Central Military Commission, and thus Hu's assumption of the lower post of general secretary would have raised troubling questions about civil-military relations).[14] After the abuses of the late Mao era, there was a desire to not treat Deng like Mao, and Deng did not want people to think he acted like Mao. Yet this more "democratic" environment could be even harder to maneuver than Mao's leadership, when everyone did nothing but think about making sure they were fully in line with the chairman. In a way, Deng gave Hu enough rope with which to hang himself. Deng complained to individual members of the secretariat that "Yaobang does not have the right to not report to me."[15] After the break between the two was final, Deng said to Hu, "You always thought I was trying to hinder you! You kept trying to establish your own image!"[16]

Mao had often expressed similar sentiments to Zhou Enlai, Xi's former boss. Yet Hu Yaobang, Xi's new superior, was very different from Zhou. Zhou's reputation has suffered in recent years as more evidence revealed how much he facilitated the worst abuses of the Cultural Revolution.[17] At heart, Zhou was a survivor. He once told Geng Biao, "When people attack you, you must not fall; when people push you, you must not run; when people persecute you, you must not die."[18] Hu Yaobang, who led the party's rehabilitation of fallen comrades after the Cultural Revolution, would have known how much Zhou had personally managed the persecution of high-ranking cadres, including Xi. Yet Hu was upset when Wang Dongxing, who had been director of the Central Office during the Cultural Revolution, severely criticized Zhou at a politburo session in 1980. "Everyone understands what the premier's predicament was at the time," Hu had said.[19]

Xi and the rest of the party leadership went to great lengths to protect Zhou's reputation. In August 1983, the secretariat decided to burn some of the most damning documents. The evidence revealed, among other things, that Zhou had proposed an even more severe punishment for Liu Shaoqi than what Jiang Qing, a member of the Gang of Four, had suggested. Zhou even proposed that Liu's wife be executed as a spy. It is hard to guess how Xi felt when he learned about the behavior of his former superior, but, less than a month after the decision to destroy the documents was made, Xi expressed "some negative ideas about Zhou" to Li Rui.[20]

While Zhou was a preternaturally careful politician, Hu was impulsive, incautious, and naïve. In the words of Frederick Teiwes, "Hu's fall is best understood as a product of his own shortcomings as a politician."[21] As early as October 1979, Marshal Xu Xiangqian sent Xi to tell Hu to be more careful when he spoke.[22] When Hu and Xi were both on the secretariat, Xi and others would often criticize Hu for saying whatever came into his head or for making careless remarks. Hu welcomed such input, but he did not significantly change his behavior.[23] Part of the problem was his personality, but Hu also wanted to change the party's style. When confronted about his behavior, he tried to explain: "What I wanted was to create an atmosphere for people to speak in a relaxed manner." In the past, people had not dared to reveal their true thoughts because they were afraid one wrong word would get them into trouble. "When conducting research or discussing problems, it should be OK to speak a bit casually," he said.[24]

Crucially, the politics of a two-line system complicated the politics of succession. To a significant extent, it was Deng's view that the party needed a "core" that made it so difficult to get any leadership transition right. Deng would only feel comfortable handing over the reins of power to someone in whom he had absolute trust. He told Jiang Zemin, who would replace Zhao Ziyang as general secretary in 1989, "When Mao was around, he was the boss. When I am around, I am the boss. Only when you are the boss will I relax."[25] After an extended conversation with Hu in the spring of 1989, Li Rui came away convinced that Hu's mismanagement of the politics of succession was the primary reason for his fall. "The trigger was [Hu] agreeing to [Deng's] resignation," Li wrote in his diary.[26]

The great irony in Deng's behavior was that he should have understood Hu's plight. He had experienced a very similar situation—twice. In 1958, Zhou Enlai had lost control over the economy to Deng's secretariat. Mao gave it back to Zhou in 1965. Then, at the beginning of the Cultural Revolution, Deng was purged entirely from the leadership. The problem was not policy differences between Mao and Deng or that Deng resisted Mao's authority. After the Great Leap Forward, Mao decided to spend more time thinking big thoughts, not about the daily business of government. Since Mao was largely absent and refused to give clear guidance, it was easy for Deng, despite his total loyalty, to accidentally act in ways that enraged the chairman, especially since it seemed like Deng was growing too close to Liu Shaoqi. As historian Chung Yen-lin writes, Deng desperately tried to assuage Mao's concerns, but the chairman's "suspicions were too great," and Deng was cast away in 1966.[27]

Deng was gradually rehabilitated, and by the middle of 1975, he was Mao's preeminent deputy. Yet in October of the very same year, he had lost Mao's trust once again. Deng, overconfident, was fully convinced that his attempts to rebuild the country after years of devastation were exactly what Mao wanted. And Deng was right, until Mao, worried that Deng was not loyal enough to the legacy of the Cultural Revolution, changed his mind. In the words of Frederick Teiwes and Warren Sun, "It was Deng's political skill that let him down even as he worked within Mao's parameters, something striking in a perceptive leader who had worked closely with the Chairman over a long period."[28] In 1987, Hu Yaobang would suffer the same fate as Deng—this time, at Deng's own hands. The enduring nature of the system proved more powerful than the lessons it taught.

Other old problems persisted too, such as the relationship between the secretariat and the State Council. In the 1950s, as Zhou Enlai's deputy in the State Council, Xi saw the complicated mix of cooperation and competition between that body and Deng's secretariat. In the 1980s, Xi, by then a member of the secretariat, had to worry about how it would coexist with Zhao Ziyang's State Council. As Zhao's former secretary Bao Tong noted, the views of Hu Yaobang and Zhao Ziyang were "not often the same." When it came to the economy, Hu and Xi wanted speed and Zhao wanted efficiency. There were also turf wars—Zhao was upset when the secretariat wanted the party committees in the State Council ministries to report their views on reform during the rectification campaign.[29] When Zhao complained to Deng that Hu was interfering too much in the economy, Deng summoned Hu to explain. Hu took a notebook out of his pocket and used it to demonstrate that everything he had done was at Deng's instruction.[30] In a January 1987 self-criticism, Wan Li said that Deng Xiaoping had given him the task of improving relations between Zhao and Hu—a mission that he failed to fulfil.[31]

Deng and the State Council were not the only problem for the secretariat under Hu and Xi, however. As Teiwes notes, now, in addition to having to deal with Deng, they also had to deal with "a number of extremely prestigious party elders who could and did interfere in the affairs of the 'first front.'"[32] In 1984, Xi complained to Li Rui that he had been trying to no avail to meet with Chen Yun for three years. Chen only met Hu Yaobang once a year. When Li Rui asked Hu why the Politburo Standing Committee never met to resolve differences, Hu explained that Deng had said, "Since we can't come to an agreement, it is better that we not have a meeting."[33]

This state of affairs left Hu vulnerable to accusations that the powerful secretariat was operating with no oversight and that Hu was violating the principle of collective leadership. In 1987, a senior party historian privately told sinologist Michel Oksenberg that some high-ranking cadres believed that the politburo, which rarely met, was too weak, and the secretariat, which met about once a week and was tasked with running the country, was too powerful.[34] Even a northwesterner close to Xi, Ma Wenrui, feared that Xi and Hu had grown so close that the two of them, along with Hu Qili, had formed a small clique.[35]

THE CLOSE CALL IN 1983

Despite his popularity within much of the party, Hu Yaobang's position at the top was precarious long before 1987. By 1983, Chen Yun was increasingly dissatisfied with Hu's statements on the economy. Chen was rarely in Beijing, and he only spoke briefly with Hu when they did meet, so when Chen suddenly severely criticized Hu at a joint session of the Politburo Standing Committee and secretariat on March 17, 1983, the participants were stunned. Chen believed that Hu was pursuing economic growth too rapidly, even suggesting, insultingly, that Hu "should study economic affairs a bit." Chen recommended that Zhao Ziyang's Leading Group for Financial and Economic Affairs at the State Council take over management of the economy from the secretariat. Hu believed that many of Chen's words were the result of misunderstandings, and he politely thanked Chen for his comments. Deng accepted Chen's proposal to give control over the economy to Zhao, while warning that this would be "the end of the matter."[36] The incident had powerful similarities to when, in 1958, the State Council—when Chen was a vice-premier and Xi was secretary—lost economic authority to Deng Xiaoping's secretariat.

Deng Xiaoping had said the matter should end then and there, but Deng Liqun described what happened at the meeting between Chen and Hu to New China News Agency leaders from throughout the country and employees at *Red Flag* magazine. They then reported what they had learned to party committees throughout the country. Deng Liqun would later admit that "this was a serious mistake that violated discipline." It seemed that Hu Yaobang was in trouble. Hu Qiaomu even suggested holding a plenum to discuss Chen's remarks, and he told Hu Yaobang, "If you are no longer general secretary, you can do something else. Our friendship is eternal."[37]

A vice-secretary of the Guangdong Party Committee sent a record of Deng Liqun's comments directly to Xi. A number of local officials also called Qin Chuan, who worked at *People's Daily*, to better understand what was going on in Beijing. Qin rushed to see Xi. Xi privately told Qin that there had been no move against Hu, possibly because that is what Xi believed at the time or perhaps because he did not think Qin's rank was high enough to hear such a view. Xi even defended Chen's right to make such criticisms: "Comrade Chen Yun raised some sincere but severe criticisms toward some areas of Comrade Yaobang's work. I believe it is normal for a member of the old generation of leadership to seriously criticize Comrade Yaobang. For us comrades on the first line, this is helpful. It is necessary to accept the lessons of history, right?" However, Xi did comment on Deng Liqun's behavior: "The meeting decided not to disseminate the comments made by Comrade Chen Yun; I don't know why Deng Liqun disseminated them in a few places." Both Xi and Wan Li went to complain to Deng Xiaoping, and Deng expressed support for Hu Yaobang. Deng declared that no party session would be held to air Chen's criticisms.[38] One individual familiar with the situation claimed that Deng felt ambivalent about Hu at this time, and it was only Ye Jianying's forceful intervention that convinced Deng that Hu needed to be protected.[39] Whether Hu's critics really wanted to remove him from power at this time is questionable—Zhao Ziyang, for one, believed that this was not the case.[40]

Xi was clearly upset about what had happened. When Chen Yizi, a pro-reform intellectual from Shaanxi, went to see Xi in the summer of 1983, he found a man deeply distressed about the recent developments. Xi, "with a face marked by life's hardships but a captivating smile," remarked that "managing affairs at the provincial level is not difficult; once you get a handle on the situation, if you set your mind to it, you can do it." Then he continued, confidentially. "Affairs in the party center are difficult to manage," Xi warned. "Our party engaged in leftist activities for twenty years. Plus China's autocratic traditions have a distant source and a long stream! Every step forward is difficult."[41]

In private conversations with Li Rui in subsequent years, Xi would express fury in even more direct terms about the 1983 incident. He thought that Hu Yaobang had been "taught a lesson." Hu Qiaomu was "a conspirator, a careerist," Xi said, who had pressured Hu Yaobang to resign. Xi described Deng Liqun's dissemination of Chen Yun's critical comments as a "problem of discipline." Xi was also nonplussed by Zhao Ziyang's behavior. In Xi's mind, Chen Yun was using Zhao, as well as fellow secretariat member Wan Li, to counter Hu. Xi, who had witnessed so many top deputies lose Mao's trust decades earlier, encouraged Hu Yaobang to see Deng Xiaoping and Chen Yun more often.[42]

THE THORNY SUCCESSION PROBLEM

In May 1985, Hu made one of the biggest mistakes of his career: accepting a wide-ranging interview with the Hong Kong journalist Lu Keng. Hu cavalierly discussed several high-ranking figures, and when Lu Keng bluntly asked about the succession, Hu, in dangerous terms, referred to Deng's position as head of the Central Military Commission: "With Comrade Deng Xiaoping taking charge, it is sufficient for him to say one sentence, but we have to say five sentences." Yet, Hu continued, "to tell the truth, there are not a lot of things to do in the army." Zhao Ziyang later believed that the interview, especially Hu's remarks about the military, fatally soured Deng's views of Hu.[43]

Hu Yaobang and Xi Zhongxun were offending old comrades other than Deng as well. In July and August 1985, during the party's summer retreat in the beach resort of Beidaihe, they questioned numerous old revolutionaries whether they would be willing to retire. In response, they angrily asked which other individuals were retiring and when, even asking to know why they were being forced to go. Some went to complain to Deng directly. They demanded that Hu and Xi be denounced for their behavior. Deng used the occasion of his birthday in August to summon these unhappy cadres and explain that the changes were based on a decision of the standing committee.[44] At the Fifth Plenum in September, Xi, Gu Mu, and Yao Yilin left their positions on the secretariat to make way for five new additions. However, Gu retained his position on the State Council, and Yao remained as vice-premier. Xi was put in the rare position of being a politburo member but not holding any other *formal* titles, although he continued to attend secretariat meetings.

In May 1986, Deng Xiaoping held a fateful meeting with Hu Yaobang to discuss the succession. Deng said that he would fully retire, along with Chen Yun and Li Xiannian. Deng wanted Hu, however, to only "half retire," meaning that he would retire as general secretary but would spend another term as either head of the Central Military Commission or as state president. Hu expressed agreement with Deng's decision to resign but stated that he was already over seventy years old and that he wanted to fully retire at the Thirteenth Party Congress in the coming year too. On his way out, Hu said to his bodyguard that Deng was "as great as George Washington." But rumors soon spread that Hu was power hungry and wanted to push Deng out, and Deng himself seems to have drawn the same conclusion. Deng later asked Wan Li why Hu wanted him to step down. When Wan said it was possible that Hu had misspoken, Deng responded, "No, he wants to replace me." Hu hated these rumors that he had pressured Deng to retire. Hu emphasized that it had been only a private chat. After Hu's fall, when his bodyguard said that Hong Kong and Taiwan media were claiming that Hu's biggest mistake had been not to oppose Deng's stated wish to step down, Hu said nothing but bitterly smiled.[45]

As the party debated how to structure political reform and succession politics, some evidence suggests that over the course of 1986, Xi was increasingly vocal about the need for greater institutionalization. Significantly, one official source states Xi made strong claims about collective leadership "at a party meeting in 1986." His words suggest that the speech was made at a meeting of real significance:

> Rule of law is the best method for modern governments to manage society. It is also the best choice for us to exit difficulties and walk toward tomorrow. Today's meeting is being held precisely to make a choice between today and tomorrow. We are faced with two roads: one is to continue to walk the old road of universal government "rule by man"; the other is to take the road of rule by law. We must not build up the authority of the individual. It is necessary that we build up the authority of the collective and build up the authority of democratic and scientific decisions. Henceforth, we should persist in the transition from rule of man to rule of law, persist in universal equality before the law, and persist in ruling the nation with law.[46]

At least two memoir accounts published outside of mainland censorship suggested Xi was quite explicit that Deng should give up power. For example, Lin Mu, who briefly worked for Hu Yaobang in the 1950s, claimed that, at a politburo meeting sometime around May 1986, both Hu Yaobang and Xi Zhongxun called on Deng Xiaoping to retire at the upcoming Thirteenth Party Congress for age-related reasons. Xi, Lin wrote, said that it was necessary for the country to move away from the rule of man toward the rule of law and that Deng's resignation would leave a good example to posterity. Lin even asserted that Xi criticized Deng with "vicious words." When Deng complained that people must think he was interfering too much in their work, Xi responded that this was not the case. He claimed his concern was primarily about political reform and about Deng's health.[47] Hu Jiwei referred to this meeting as well in his memoirs, although he qualified what he said by using the word "reportedly," and he included far fewer details. Hu Jiwei claimed that Xi was joined by several others, including Marshal Nie Rongzhen, Wan Li, and Ulanhu, in supporting Deng's resignation, but Hu Jiwei put special emphasis on Xi's role in expressing the hope that Deng would go.[48] These accounts have spread widely, contributing to Xi's positive reputation among many proreform Chinese elders and intellectuals. Yet they should be treated skeptically until better documentation becomes available. Lin's narrative in particular has serious problems. He claimed that Liao Chengzhi attended the meeting, but Liao died in June 1983. Lin also asserted that Marshal Nie Rongzhen had said that if Deng resigned, then he (Nie) would resign as well, but Nie had already announced his retirement.[49]

In June 1986, during the summer conference in Beidaihe, Deng told party elders that his biggest mistake over the past few years had been that he had misjudged Hu Yaobang.[50] Although Hu seems to have badly managed his conversation with Deng about the succession, on September 2 and 4, the secretariat, with Xi present, discussed political reform. They used Deng's famous August 1980 speech "On the Reform of the System of Party and State Leadership" as a reference. In those remarks, Deng had called for the establishment of collective leadership and a stable handover to a younger generation. "Patriarchal ways are an antiquated social phenomenon, which has existed from time immemorial and has had a very damaging influence on the party," Deng had said, criticizing the idea of "tenure for life." Yet if Hu and Xi were taking Deng's words seriously, they were making a mistake. As both Deng Liqun and Zhao Ziyang would later note, Deng's 1980 speech was primarily about providing a justification to remove Hua Guofeng. The same month as the secretariat's September 1986 meeting, Deng tasked Zhao Ziyang, not Hu, with devising a plan for political reform—a choice indicating that Deng did not trust the general secretary with the job.[51] Nevertheless, Xi's involvement continued. When Hu Qili criticized the individuals who were researching reform of the political system, even going so far as to assert that the situation was reminiscent of the summer of 1957 (before the Antirightist Campaign), Xi ordered that the Department of Propaganda not disseminate Hu Qili's remarks.[52]

In October 1986, the question of succession became more pressing after three party elders—Han Xianchu, Liu Bocheng, and Ye Jianying—all died within the same month. It was a powerful reminder of the mortality of the revolutionary generation and of the need to pass the baton to the next one. At the end of October, Deng Xiaoping, Chen Yun, and Li Xiannian met privately, with no secretaries in attendance, to discuss the matter of their continued roles. When Deng arrived, he took out two or three pieces of paper and said, "Today we will discuss this matter a bit." The meeting was apparently tense—Deng smoked six cigarettes within an hour and twenty minutes.[53]

On November 4, Deng Xiaoping met with Hu Yaobang, Zhao Ziyang, and Hu Qili. Deng told them that Hu Yaobang would retire and Zhao would become general secretary at the upcoming party congress. However, Zhao would remain in charge of the economy. Deng warned that if he, Chen, and Li did not completely retire, then that would influence many other people, and "our society will not make any progress." Deng said that Zhao Ziyang, Hu Yaobang, Hu Qili, Li Peng, Qiao Shi, Wan Li, and Tian Jiyun would be selected as members of the new Politburo Standing Committee at the forthcoming party congress.[54]

Yet shortly after that crucial November 4 meeting, Hu once again demonstrated his poor ability to manage relations with Deng. On November 9, Hu incautiously discussed succession politics during a conversation in Beijing with Japanese prime minister Nakasone Yasuhiro. Hu, breaking a taboo, spoke of the retirement of the elderly cadres and then he pointed at Hu Qili and Wang Zhaoguo, saying they were among seven or eight young cadres who would be promoted to the central leadership. When Deng met with Nakasone the following day, he apparently tried to correct what Hu had said. "This is not something that can be accomplished within three or five years; it will take about fifteen years," Deng asserted. "Next year's Thirteenth Party Congress will take a step forward, but it very much is not a done deal."[55]

Xi Zhongxun could tell that Hu Yaobang was in trouble. On or shortly after December 10, Xi told Chen Yizi that party elders had long wanted to remove Hu from power, partly because of his liberal positions but even more so because he had expressed support for Deng's retirement. "Little Chen, this thing, power, degrades people," Xi said. "It is easy to say something, but it is much more difficult to do something. Yaobang honestly said he would retire, and he agreed to Xiaoping's retirement, but if things go wrong, it will cause trouble for him." When Chen Yizi expressed worries that Hu was acting too naïvely, Xi responded that he agreed with Hu's views. "There are two roads. We cannot rely on rule by man; it is necessary that we rely on democracy and rule of law!" Xi said.[56]

At about this time, Deng also concluded that Hu Yaobang had failed to fully extinguish the influence of Hua Guofeng within the party. Deng received a mysterious letter from Hua's home province of Shanxi warning about cadres who supported Hua and opposed Deng. In response, Deng demanded that the secretariat investigate the situation, and on the morning of December 16, 1986, the entire Shanxi Party Standing Committee was told to immediately report to Beijing. Xi met with some of the members of the group on the following day. Xi showed them the letter and said, "To protect the person who is complaining, the signature at the end has been removed." The next day, Xi told the visitors from Shanxi that they should work together to write an explanation. Li Ligong, the party boss of Shanxi, was flabbergasted. He thought the charges in the letter were a deliberate attempt to frame him by a fellow member of the Shanxi Party Standing Committee, and he carefully explained why the charges were outrageous. Yet here, once again, Xi was serving as Deng's hatchet man. On December 22, Hu Yaobang castigated the Shanxi leadership for not supporting the party center, behavior which had "cultivated enemy elements, who had created trouble."[57] The incident clearly upset Deng, who thought Hu Yaobang had never been hard enough on Hua Guofeng.[58] After Hu Yaobang fell, Deng Xiaoping would mockingly ask him, "Do you still think about Hua Guofeng in the same way?"[59]

The student protests further worsened Hu's position. On December 27, several old revolutionaries went to Deng's home to complain about Hu. Three days later, Deng summoned Hu to his home and savagely criticized him. Hu Jiwei claimed that on New Year's Eve, Xi Zhongxun and Zhao Ziyang warned Hu Yaobang that he should take the initiative and admit his mistakes to Deng Xiaoping. But under such intense pressure, Hu instead wrote a letter to Deng and requested that he be allowed to resign. Several days later, Deng accepted Hu's resignation. Deng then called for a "party-life" meeting to criticize Hu's mistakes, which was held between January 10 and 15.[60]

The issue of how Xi responded is an essential one. Some claim that he was openly furious with Deng—a version of events that is a core element in Xi's legend as a reformist hero. Both Hu Jiwei, who noted that his account might not be entirely reliable, as well as Lin Mu claimed that Xi banged on a table and complained that a party-life meeting could not discuss the firing of a party general secretary. Xi allegedly even yelled at Deng.[61] Hu Yaobang's own son Hu Dehua later told Li Rui's daughter, "At the party-life meeting, Xi Zhongxun not only said, 'You are staging a coup,' he also said, 'I too am partly responsible for the things for which you are criticizing Hu Yaobang.'"[62] In December 2002, Li Rui reported to Xi Jinping that his father had thrown a "terrible tantrum" at the party-life meeting.[63]

But how credible is the legend that Xi Zhongxun lost his patience and openly bucked the decision to get rid of Hu Yaobang? A showdown between Deng and Xi could not have happened—Deng did not even attend the party-life sessions. More likely to omit than to mislead, Jia Juchuan, the author of the official biography of Xi Zhongxun, said in an interview that with regard to Xi losing his temper about Hu's removal, "I believe that this never occurred, but Xi definitely sympathized" with Hu.[64]

More reliable evidence suggests a measured reaction. Bo Yibo, who chaired the party-life sessions, began the first session on January 10 by saying that the Politburo Standing Committee had assigned him, Zhao Ziyang, Yang Shangkun, Wan Li, and Hu Qili the responsibility of managing the meeting. Yu Qiuli spoke first, and then Hu Yaobang presented a self-criticism about his mistakes with regard to the Four Cardinal Principles, spiritual pollution, personnel decisions, and foreign policy. Bo then affirmed that Hu Yaobang had made mistakes in many areas. Other members of the secretariat had committed errors as well, Bo remarked, and he told them to prepare their own statements. Bo then criticized how the secretariat had run the party rectification. When he finished speaking, the participants at the meeting all fell silent. Xi spoke up: "Such a big affair, and I did not know a thing about it. What's this all about?" He then said that rumors were spreading throughout society and that a cadre from Shaanxi had written him a letter expressing fear that the party center was unstable. Then Xi walked out, bringing the first session to an end.[65]

Hu Yaobang was shocked by what happened next—he thought he would simply be allowed to resign, not tarnished and humiliated. But during the subsequent several days, he was subjected to brutal attacks, including in a particularly vicious speech by Wang Heshou, one of his closest friends—an act that devastated him. At one point, Hu collapsed on a sofa and Xi Zhongxun had to help him up. When Hu said, "I was going to resign at the Thirteenth Party Congress," Xi said loudly, "I heard Hu say this three times!" This was Xi's way of rebutting the charges that Hu was ambitious and wanted to replace Deng. The entire experience was deeply emotional and unfair to Hu. Whenever Hu tried to defend himself, he was told, "Listen to all these criticisms patiently!" As Xi and Hu exited the meeting room together, Hu started to sob uncontrollably. But Hu still accepted the party's decision, later explaining this was "in order to put the big picture first, in order to protect a group of cadres, and in order to protect this home," meaning the party.[66]

But it was not only Hu Yaobang who came under attack—the entire secretariat was held to account. Gao Yang, the man who essentially had expelled Xi Jinping from Hebei, believed that Hu Yaobang's fall was the inevitable outcome of "years of contradictions" during which the secretariat's "arbitrariness" had replaced the Politburo Standing Committee.[67] Chen Yun was especially upset. Years earlier, he had strongly supported the restoration of the secretariat after the Cultural Revolution.[68] But at the politburo enlarged session held to confirm Hu Yaobang's defeat, he savaged the institution. Chen's remarks were deeply unjust. He accused the secretariat of not conducting investigations before making big decisions. Chen complained that Hu never held politburo or Politburo Standing Committee meetings, even though he probably knew it was in fact Deng—not wanting to give Chen an opportunity to speak at such meetings—who prevented them from convening.[69] Chen's criticisms of the inability of the "first line" to properly consult were reminiscent of Mao's complaints about the State Council in 1958 when Chen and Xi both worked there.

Xi in particular was in trouble. At one session of the party-life meetings, Yang Shangkun stated that Xi had "gone even further"—a criticism meant to imply Xi's mistakes were even greater than Hu's.[70] Given these circumstances, Xi could not directly oppose Hu's fall, although both he and Wan Li did note at the session that, along with his mistakes, Hu also had some achievements. Xi and Wan both stated that they, as members of the secretariat, should share responsibility, but they denied that Hu Yaobang had wanted to replace Deng or Chen.[71] Xi himself engaged in a self-criticism: "I am a member of the collective leadership. When the top leader makes a mistake, the collective leadership has a responsibility. I also have responsibility. This demonstrates that our role as assistants was done badly."[72] According to Xi's official biographer, he "supported Deng Xiaoping's speech on the current student troubles and supported the criticism and management of Hu Yaobang's mistakes by Deng Xiaoping as representative of the Politburo Standing Committee."[73]

Yet Xi was clearly upset about what had happened, later remarking that he was "opposed to the kind of attack without rhyme or reason that took place at the party-life sessions."[74] Shortly after Hu's removal, Xi Zhongxun and *People's Daily* editor in chief Qin Chuan went for a stroll in Zhongnanhai, during which time Xi said, "With regard to me at least, during my entire life, I never persecuted anyone. During my entire life, I never made any leftist mistakes."[75] Hu Yaobang's daughter wrote that Xi told visitors around the Lunar New Year the events surrounding Hu's ouster had "no precedent in party history." "How is it possible to hold a party-life meeting to solve the issue of a general secretary? How could a vice-chairman of the Central Advisory Commission [Bo Yibo] be allowed to chair a meeting to solve a problem of a general secretary?!" Xi asked.[76] Bo felt deeply wronged by this view, later saying that he was the only person who could have played such a role because it would have been inappropriate to select either an elderly cadre or one of the deputies on the "front line" to chair the sessions.[77] Once again, the nature of the system was deepening animosities.

AGAIN RALLYING TO DENG

Despite Xi's frustrations about what had occurred, within weeks, he was praising Deng and lambasting Hu. In Shenzhen on February 15, in a speech not included in Xi's official collected works, Xi gave credit to Deng for the astonishing changes in Guangdong: "If not for the support of Comrade Xiaoping, the special economic zones would have found it difficult to be established and develop like this." Then Xi made a series of deeply conservative statements. "With regard to opposing bourgeois liberalization, it is absolutely necessary to be clearcut in our stance and to take a firm stand," he said. He then attacked the recent student protests: "Recently, students have stirred up some trouble, and the students in Shenzhen have also caused a bit of a fuss. They want freedom and democracy, but actually they are not clear about what freedom and democracy are."[78]

Xi said that collective leadership was extremely important, but that Hu Yaobang, not Deng, was the problem: "Comrade Yaobang's mistake was that he violated the party's principle of collective leadership. He made mistakes on major political principles. That was the main problem. Of course, there were other problems as well, such as him not respecting discipline and separating himself from the party organization." Xi said that "the democratic [party-]life meeting was extremely productive." He noted that neither praise nor criticism should be 100 percent—if someone makes a mistake, always "leave space." Yet that was unambiguously not what happened at the party-life meeting, when many leading individuals had savaged Hu with their criticisms. Xi concluded his speech with praise for his old nemesis. "Comrade Chen Yun recently said that cadres must engage in 'five oceans and four seas,'" Xi said, referring to an expression meaning not to engage in factionalism. "This point is very important."[79]

Why would Xi put so much distance between him and his former boss Hu Yaobang? In another speech in Zhuhai on February 19, Xi revealed that party stability was high on his mind: "Without stability and unity, nothing can be accomplished. Stability and unity are a precondition. When we speak of the Four Cardinal Principles, the core is to maintain the leadership of the party." He still believed that conservative guardrails could somehow facilitate reform: "Only by maintaining the Four Cardinal Principles can reform be guaranteed, can openness have a correct direction, can things be done better."[80]

Xi again spoke positively of Deng Xiaoping: "Comrade Xiaoping strongly emphasizes collective leadership, emphasizes democratic centralism." Xi told his listeners that Deng had expressed willingness to change his mind if the minority was correct. Most importantly, Xi said, "Comrade Xiaoping was the first to oppose irregularities in party life. . . . At every level of the party, it is especially necessary to have a regular party life, to perfect democratic centralism." Strikingly, in this speech full of comments that did not reflect Xi's true feelings, he also railed against the habit of lying within the party: "In the late 1950s, no one could speak the truth! If you spoke the truth, that meant trouble, and many people were turned into rightists or rightist opportunists. The result was that it made people lie. Does this situation continue now? Yes! In some matters people do not dare to speak the truth! Those who speak the truth face retribution, whereas people who lie are promoted." Xi even said it was Hu Yaobang, not Deng, who had been responsible for making people lie, because Hu, according to Xi, had told local leaders to pursue goals beyond their means. This speech was heavily edited before publication in an official collection in 2013.[81]

Yet Xi's trip to the South was not only intended to support Deng Xiaoping's decision to remove Hu Yaobang; Xi also used the opportunity to emphasize that reforms would continue. *People's Daily* reported that Xi had commented that Guangdong had "changed even better than expected." "It truly makes people feel all sorts of emotions," Xi said. He met with Hong Kong and Macau industrialists and tried to ensure them that people in Hong Kong should continue to have confidence in the mainland. He told them, "Our Reform and Opening Policy is determined collectively" by the Central Committee, and it "cannot change because of individual personnel changes."[82]

In a report to the Central Committee on his trip, Xi described how he visited the village where, in May 1978, he had first witnessed a mass migration out of the People's Republic into Hong Kong. Now, according to Xi, all those who had left had returned. The special economic zone experience, in Xi's words, was a success, and its role as a "window" could only become more important in the future. However, Xi warned that Hu Yaobang's dismissal had caused many people to worry that the policy of Reform and Opening would end. Those people who had become rich were afraid they would lose everything, whereas the poor thought they would never become wealthy.[83]

To the outside world, it briefly appeared that Xi would benefit from Hu's fall. The *South China Morning Post* twice claimed that Xi was a "strong contender" as Hu's replacement for general secretary, although one of the articles noted that the rumors were "apparently spread deliberately."[84] In September, the newspaper suggested that Xi would probably become head of the Chinese People's Political Consultative Conference.[85] Behind the scenes, however, Xi was frustrated. In September 1987, Feng Wenbin, a high-ranking figure involved in personnel issues, told Li Rui that Xi wanted to completely resign and that he refused to become a vice-chair of the Central Advisory Commission—the body created by Deng in 1982 for elderly, mostly retired revolutionaries. Xi did, however, agree to later replace Chen Pixian as the top-ranking vice-chairman of the National People's Congress at the forthcoming Seventh National People's Congress.[86] After the Thirteenth Party Congress, held in October and November 1987, Xi left the politburo, although he would still often attend its enlarged sessions.

Xi, believing he deserved better, was disappointed. In 1991, he complained that he had never served as general secretary or as head of the National People's Congress. He was especially incensed that Wan Li, who became head of the National People's Congress in 1988, "had been merely a county secretary in his early years"—in other words, Wan's revolutionary credentials fell far short of Xi's own weighty contributions.[87] In 1998, Ren Zhongyi told Li Rui that Xi was also upset that Yang Shangkun, who had been his deputy in Guangdong, had become state president in 1988. Hu Yaobang himself was uncertain about Xi's leadership abilities—Hu even told Ren Zhongyi that neither Xi nor Yang should ever be given a top position.[88]

Xi was in a poor mood. In February or March 1988, while strolling in Shenzhen, Chen Yizi ran into Xi and Qi Xin, and the couple invited Chen to tea. When Chen praised Xi for his role in the special economic zones, Xi responded, "Whenever I go to the grass roots, I am happy. All I see is vitality. As soon as I return to Beijing, it is stuffy, and the only thing you hear is bullshit." Xi took a sip of tea and continued, "At the grass roots, whether you do good or bad depends on what you actually achieve. It is immediately obvious. But in Beijing, people who do real work are rare. There are too many pundits. All they do is engage in lame arguments." When Chen said that everyone was unhappy with how Hu Yaobang had been treated, Xi slammed the table and said, "Ah, Mao Zedong ran a patriarchal system! Deng Xiaoping is the same way—he engages in a patriarchal system too! This is a disaster for the party and for the nation!"[89]

After the Thirteenth Party Congress, Xi held no official positions until the spring session of the Seventh National People's Congress in April 1988 when he became its first vice-chairman and head of its newly established Internal and Judicial Affairs Committee. This session of the National People's Congress was a particularly vibrant one. According to Kevin O'Brien, the meeting is noteworthy for its openness: "Unlike past sessions, barbed comments were not dulled by the National People's Congress Press Bureau or circulated primarily in restricted journals; nor did an ad hoc censorship group select speeches for publication. . . . Personal anecdotes and jokes abounded, and interruptions and rejoinders added an element of real debate."[90]

Congressional regulations had always allowed delegates to make remarks on their own initiative at the end of the session, but no one had ever exercised that right. It fell to Xi, after the work report was presented, to ask whether any delegates wanted to raise an opinion. Four delegates, sensing the new atmosphere, took advantage of the opportunity. The congress appeared to finally be shaking its reputation as a "rubber-stamp" parliament—but this would prove to be the last time people would speak out in such a way.[91] Xi sometimes betrayed the habits of the past, raising the question of how meaningful these changes really were—he declared that one resolution was passed even before the delegates could raise their hands to vote.[92]

Over the next year, Xi concentrated his energies on improving China's legal system. In 1988, twenty-four members of the congress requested that the Internal and Judicial Affairs Committee investigate a four-year-old case in which the head of an industrial research institute in Hangzhou had been accused of speculation and profiteering and held in detention for a period that surpassed the legal limit. In a speech at a committee meeting, Xi demanded an objective, unemotional investigation. He warned that it was a complicated issue, but he told the investigators not to be afraid. "If you face any resistance during your investigation, tell me immediately," he said. In August 1988, a court in Hangzhou declared the man to be innocent.[93]

Xi also intervened to support lawyers who had been persecuted for defending their clients. In May 1984, a court in Anshan, Liaoning Province, tried a rape case. The two lawyers sent by the county legal-advisory office to defend the client argued that the evidence was not persuasive enough for a conviction. In response, the Anshan Procuratorate arrested both lawyers, as well as the head of the legal-advisory office, charging them with covering up the crime. The Internal and Judicial Affairs Committee asked the Supreme People's Procuratorate to investigate. The lawyers, who remained detained for four years, were released.[94]

Xi once stated that he had personally experienced ten to twenty cases in which people were accused of belonging to "antiparty groups" simply because they held different opinions. That history led to his support for a Dissident Opinion Protection Law. "From the perspective of party history, there have been too many disasters caused by differing opinions!" he said during a discussion meeting, arguing that a law was needed to determine "under what circumstances different opinions can be raised even if the opinions are wrong." When one of the attendees reminded Xi that the constitution guaranteed members of the National People's Congress the right to speak and vote, he noted that the number of members of the congress was, relatively speaking, very small and that any citizen should have the right to speak. This was more than a legal problem. "Other than legal punishments, there are also denunciations, detentions, demotions and pay cuts, transfers, removals, and other forms of punishment." Xi wanted protection from any form of punishment. No such law was ever passed.[95]

In March and April 1989, Xi personally shepherded through a law that allowed regular Chinese citizens to sue the government. After it was passed, he often asked whether people at the grass roots dared to sue local officials and whether the problem of the masses having nowhere to complain had been solved.[96] But these incipient steps toward more respect for the rule of law and citizen rights would soon face a severe test—the mass protests centered on Beijing's Tiananmen Square—and Xi would once again find himself near the very center of one of the most consequential moments in modern Chinese history.

28
TIANANMEN SQUARE

In 1988, China's reformist agenda was in decline, as was Xi's physical and political health. This new tide against reform was the result of yet another dramatic turn of events. The previous year, after the purge of Hu Yaobang, Zhao Ziyang—the acting general secretary whose position became permanent at the Thirteenth Party Congress—successfully defeated efforts to use attacks on "bourgeois liberalization" to undermine economic reform. Zhao even did what Hu and Xi had tried to achieve but could not: remove Deng Liqun from the secretariat and dissolve his Political Research Office. At the beginning of 1988, Zhao identified the party's top economic priority as development in the coastal provinces, which included Xi's beloved Guangdong, as well as Fujian, where his son Jinping was working.[1]

Then, disaster struck. In the spring, Deng Xiaoping suddenly decided to liberalize prices, and Zhao supported the idea. When the party announced its plan, inflation skyrocketed and panic buying ensued. Price reform was abandoned, and, in September, Zhao announced a new policy of Rectification and Consolidation—meaning austerity and retrenchment—to stabilize the situation. Politburo Standing Committee members Li Peng and Yao Yilin tried to use the debacle to undermine reform more broadly and steal control over the economy away from Zhao. Malaise set in throughout the country.[2]

Sometime in 1988, Xi slipped while bathing and hurt his femur. The medicine he took put him in a foul mood. According to a friend of the family, the stress of recent developments in Chinese politics was taking a toll too. He had trouble sleeping, and he lost weight. In December 1988, Xi went to

Guangdong on sick leave. In February of the following year, Jinping, worried about his father's health, took time to accompany Zhongxun on a trip to Shaanxi.[3]

Yet Xi was very active on these trips to the two regions closest to his heart. In December, he wrote warnings to the party center about the situation in Guangdong. Suppression of investment into foreign, private, and joint ventures had made it difficult to meet contractual demands, damaged foreign investment, and raised worries about China's policy of opening to the outside world. He described shortages in grain, capital, and raw materials. Xi also urged the Guangdong leadership to somehow integrate Rectification and Consolidation with the strategy of developing coastal regions. In a subsequent report about Shaanxi, he noted that the provincial leadership had recently proposed that stability be addressed as a "strategic problem." Xi stressed the need to strengthen political work now to "eliminate destabilizing factors in a timely fashion before they have time to grow."[4]

Xi was sick and worried about the nation, but Hu Yaobang was faring even worse. A passionate and lonely individual by nature, after his fall, he was regretful, cautious, and frightened. Hu first spent three months meeting no one, instead reading all his previous reports and speeches to find any errors. He finally concluded, "There were no mistakes. I have a clear conscience." He told one visitor, "It looks as if my self-criticism went too far." When some tourists caught sight of him in November 1988 in Hunan, they were delighted and still referred to him as "general secretary." Scared that word of such events might reach Beijing, he henceforth rarely appeared in public. He worried that the persecution had not concluded and that even worse attacks could be forthcoming. Fearful that he was bugged, he never referred to Deng Xiaoping or Chen Yun by name during conversations, instead touching his right ear to refer to the former and his left ear to refer to the latter. He hoped that the verdict against him would be reversed, but, out of dread, he remained silent. He continued to read internal party reports about increased tensions in society. The emotional torment damaged his health, and he suffered a heart attack during a politburo meeting on April 8, 1989. He died on April 15.[5]

The next day, Li Rui went to visit Xi's office at the National People's Congress. Xi told him that he already called General Secretary Zhao Ziyang and President Yang Shangkun to tell them that if the funeral arrangements were not managed well, chaos would occur. Hu Qili—a member of the Politburo

Standing Committee who was also present—started sobbing. Xi interjected brusquely. "This is no time for crying," he said. Xi disdainfully said that when Hu Yaobang was removed from power, Yang Shangkun, Bo Yibo, and Deng Liqun had all wanted to take the position of general secretary.[6]

In the early months of 1989, students had already been planning to march on the anniversary of the 1919 May 4 protests against imperialism. Hu's death moved up those plans, and, on April 17, thousands of students went to Tiananmen Square.[7] On April 18, students from Peking University brought a list of demands to the Great Hall of the People. That evening and the following one, clashes took place at the Xinhua Gate of Zhongnanhai, and several students were beaten, thus seriously escalating the tensions.[8]

Meanwhile, a first draft of the eulogy for Hu Yaobang was shared with the top party elite. Many of the individuals who received the document proposed extensive edits—some of the readers wanted more about Hu's alleged mistakes, while others thought that Hu should receive more praise.[9] On April 19, the media outlets *World Economic Herald* and *New Observer* summoned a group of proreform party elders to discuss Hu's career. Hu Yaobang's son Deping began the event by requesting that the proceedings take place in a "peaceful atmosphere." The subsequent speakers, especially Xi's close associate Qin Chuan, made rather incautious remarks, but it was Dai Qing, the adopted daughter of Ye Jianying, who changed the atmosphere. She said the most pressing task was to achieve inner-party democracy as Hu Yaobang's removal was a clear violation of organizational principles. She even described Hu's self-criticism, written "against his will," as the "most tragic" moment of his career. Members of Zhao Ziyang's circle came to believe that Deng Xiaoping concluded that she was representing a significant group of unhappy senior cadres.[10]

On April 20, two days after the clashes began outside Zhongnanhai, Xi's close associate Qin Chuan told Li Rui that Xi was "extremely agitated."[11] The next day, Zheng Bijian, a speechwriter in the General Office, visited Hu's home to discuss a second draft of the eulogy. During the tense negotiations over the speech, Xi visited the Hu household. The Hu family wanted the eulogy to provide a "just statement" about Hu's purge in 1987, but the top leadership refused. Although the members of the Hu family were not happy with the final version of the memorial speech, they said they would obey the party's decision.[12] Deng refused to give Hu Yaobang the appellation of a "great Marxist" even though many party elders feared such an omission would further enflame the protesters. At an enlarged politburo session that day, a final eulogy was approved. Trying to manage Deng's feelings but also not further incense the students, those present sought language that could meet the concerns of both. Hu was not declared to be a "great Marxist," but he was described as a "great proletarian revolutionary" who, "as a Marxist," had "led a glorious life."[13]

At Hu's funeral on April 22, students seemed satisfied that he had been given a proper send-off. Yet Deng appeared to be furious, leading Zhao's secretary to conclude that Deng was upset that the final eulogy still described Hu in such positive terms. Moreover, the students were angry when they discovered that Hu's body had been removed from the Great Hall of the People from the west side so that no public procession would take place. Kneeling in front of the Great Hall of the People, several students demanded to meet Li Peng. When Li did not appear, the students were outraged.[14] As Xi had feared, the handling of Hu's death was exacerbating the situation. The students were increasingly upset, while Deng seemed to be worried that Zhao was not doing enough about either the old cadres who favored Hu or the protests.

THE NATIONAL PEOPLE'S CONGRESS

When the students started protesting, Zhao believed that only those individuals involved in beating, smashing, looting, burning, or trespassing should be punished. His strategy consisted of three points: persuading the students to return to class, establishing a dialogue to reduce tensions, and avoiding bloodshed no matter what. These three points were accepted by every member of the Politburo Standing Committee on the day of Hu's funeral. On the afternoon of April 23, Zhao, at the train station about to depart for North Korea, told Premier Li Peng that the government should continue to implement those three points. At this time, Zhao still had no sense that any member of the standing committee opposed his position.[15]

Yet on the afternoon or evening of the very next day, April 24, Qin Chuan told Li Rui that Xi had some misgivings about where things were headed. Xi worried specifically about Li Peng, who, Xi feared, wanted "to manage things forcefully." "He has no scruples about suppression," Xi said, according to Qin.[16] For Xi to have made those comments about Li Peng at that particular moment suggests that Xi either had extraordinary insight into Li as an individual or he was extremely well informed. An enlarged Politburo Standing Committee meeting on April 24 had completely disregarded Zhao Ziyang's directives from the day before and had adopted a much tougher stance. This sudden turnaround remains one of the most mysterious moments of the entire crisis. Two of Zhao's former assistants later concluded that Deng might have secretly told Li to take a harder line as early as the evening of April 23. Without instructions from Deng, it is difficult to explain Li's sudden change, given Zhao's seniority and explicit guidance. Li himself suggested in his memoirs that on April 23 Yang Shangkun had proposed that they go to see Deng together, but Li was vague about whether they actually went.[17]

In any case, at the April 24 evening session, the participants drastically departed from Zhao's April 23 instructions. They agreed that the situation was extremely serious—behind the student protests were manipulators, they concluded, and this was an organized, planned political struggle against the leadership of the party. The next day, Deng explicitly labeled the protests "turmoil." A *People's Daily* article that used Deng's language was broadcast on the radio on the night of the twenty-fifth and then published in print the following day. The so-called April 26 editorial became infamous, inflaming the protesting students. Now, if the party wanted to resolve the challenge peacefully, it would have to somehow move away from the editorial's conclusion that characterized the student movement as turmoil.[18]

As the protests escalated, Xi remained publicly active until May 8.[19] He then disappeared from public view until early June. But behind the scenes during those weeks, Xi would face one of the most difficult challenges of his life. Party leaders saw the National People's Congress as a potential escape from two disastrous outcomes: state collapse or brutal crackdown.[20] Xi necessarily would have been at the center of these maneuvers. Although Wan Li was the head of the legislature, Xi was the top-ranked vice-chairman. Moreover, Xi was the second-highest ranking member, after Wan, of the critical Party Leading Group of the Congress, the top party branch within the state legislature.[21]

Apart from Hu Yaobang, Wan and Xi were the two figures who had suffered the most criticism at the January 1987 party-life meeting. Now, together, they led an institution that, at least in name, was the final arbiter of legal authority in the nation. Xi was also in charge of the Internal and Judicial Affairs Committee, which theoretically gave him a special right to speak out on the constitutionality of martial law. And although Xi was only a vice-chairman of the National People's Congress, the title did not fully reflect his revolutionary credentials, which outranked Wan and President Yang Shangkun, let alone Li Peng.

Zhao Ziyang believed that the students might end their protests if the leadership were to acknowledge and address their concerns, and he saw the National People's Congress as a crucial ally in this endeavor. Despite their common reputation as reformers, Zhao and Wan generally had a poor relationship, but on May 3, they reached an understanding on the need for a peaceful solution. Zhao told Wan that many of the older generation with a "class-struggle" worldview believed that any criticism represented a desire to overthrow them. But that mindset made the situation unnecessarily conflictual. Wan agreed.[22]

At a Politburo Standing Committee meeting on May 8, Zhao stated that it would be too difficult to formally change the conclusions of the April 26 editorial. However, the leadership could use democratic and legal reforms, as well as addressing corruption, to win over the students. Those actions, Zhao explained, could only be taken by the National People's Congress Standing Committee. Wan Li—who attended Politburo Standing Committee meetings without voting rights—was the first to express "full support" for Zhao's opinion.[23]

The next day, May 9, Wan informed the congressional vice-chairmen with party membership about the Politburo Standing Committee meeting. The group of vice-chairmen, which should have included Xi, unanimously decided that if the Central Committee or the State Council did not publish Zhao's proposals, then the National People's Congress Standing Committee should do so. When Li Peng heard about this, he called Wan to say that the full politburo had yet to discuss these issues, and, therefore, they should not be publicized. Li also called Zhao to say that these issues should not be included on the agenda of the next National People's Congress Standing Committee.[24]

At a full politburo meeting the following day, May 10, Zhao again made a set of recommendations to assuage the students' demands, and Wan proposed that the congress establish a Clean Government Committee. Li Peng claimed to have told the politburo that Zhao's proposals were "his personal opinions." Later that afternoon, Wan held a meeting with all the congressional vice-chairmen, and Xi was confirmed to have attended this meeting.

The participants decided to hold the Eighth Session of the National People's Congress Standing Committee on June 20 to listen to a report by the State Council on the student protests and to discuss laws on protesting and combatting corruption in enterprises (the meeting might have been scheduled sooner, but Wan had a trip to Canada and the United States planned). Wan told the vice-chairmen that Li Peng had forbidden publication of their support for Zhao's positions. The participants were furious and asked whether they supervised the government or the government supervised the congress. But it was Li Peng who thought it was Wan who was acting inappropriately. According to protocol, the legislature's Leading Party Group should first send any proposals to the Politburo Standing Committee for approval. Li was also angered because the proposed agenda used the words "student movement" instead of the word "turmoil."[25]

On May 12, Zhao went to Wan's home to say that the differences in the party leadership meant it could no longer solve any problems, leaving only the National People's Congress Standing Committee.[26] Suddenly, for the first time in its history, party control over the legislature appeared to be threatened. Wan left for his trip to Canada and the United States later that afternoon—a change making Xi the most senior figure in the National People's Congress who was still in Beijing.

The next day, after repeatedly refusing for unclear reasons, Deng finally agreed to see Zhao. Zhao used the opportunity to press Deng to allow the National People's Congress Standing Committee to discuss with the students their demands for improved transparency. Deng's response was confusing and vague. Yes, it was necessary to oppose corruption, Deng acknowledged, but the party should carefully research what "transparency" really meant so that people would not "use it" for nefarious purposes. Deng also told Zhao, "I am very tired right now, my brain is inadequate, my tinnitus is terrible, and I cannot clearly hear what you are saying." Zhao interpreted Deng's words to mean support, but Li Peng drew the opposite conclusion when he heard a report about the conversation.[27]

Zhao, a skilled political operative, was trying to work within the confines of what he thought Deng approved. Nevertheless, like so many other top deputies who preceded him, Zhao failed to get the politics right. When he met with Soviet leader Mikhail Gorbachev on May 16, Zhao told the Soviet leader that Deng was still officially in charge. It was the truth: at the Central Committee's First Plenum after the Thirteenth Party Congress in 1987, Zhao had announced that Deng would still "continue to take the helm at key junctures," and everyone applauded, signifying acceptance.[28] Zhao's motivations for revealing this fact to Gorbachev at that time are now clear—he thought that this public declaration would assuage widespread criticisms that Deng was trying to rule illegitimately from behind the scenes, and Zhao needed to affirm Deng's role with Gorbachev for protocol reasons (the meeting between Deng and Gorbachev was to officially signal the end of the Sino-Soviet split). Deng, however, believed that Zhao had sold him out. Perhaps even more dangerously, at a Politburo Standing Committee meeting on May 16, Zhao offered to take personal responsibility for the April 26 editorial. Deng probably felt humiliated by Zhao's offer to take responsibility for his own mistake.[29]

On May 17, Deng met with all five Politburo Standing Committee members at his home and, to Zhao's great surprise, suddenly ordered that martial law be imposed. In Deng's mind, the protesters' demands could not be met—they would simply keep asking for more and more until the party collapsed. Zhao refused to execute Deng's command to impose martial law and requested leave. On May 19, Li Peng and Yang Shangkun publicly declared that martial law would begin on May 20. Zhao, who was suffering from cerebral anemia, ceased working entirely from May 19 to May 21.[30]

Zhao was on the ropes, but, on May 19, the same day that martial law was declared, Peng Chong, general secretary of the National People's Congress, chaired an explosive meeting of the congressional Leading Party Group. Those present noted that many standing committee members had written letters urging that a standing committee meeting, or even a full session of the congress, resolve the situation without force. They concluded that "legal guidelines determine that a meeting of the chairmen can summon a standing committee meeting at any time," and, thus, the party group "unanimously believes that it is already completely necessary to summon early a standing committee meeting to discuss the student protests and hunger strikes." The Leading Party Group even requested permission to send a telegram to Wan Li summoning him home early. Li Peng immediately responded, "It is best that foreign matters do not change," and he forwarded the request to Qiao Shi and Yao Yilin—two other members of the Politburo Standing Committee—for their opinions.[31]

On May 20, Peng Chong called Hu Qili to inquire about the status of the request. Hu then called Zhao Ziyang, and Zhao gave oral permission to summon Wan to end his trip early. But the next day, when Hu Qili asked the head of the General Office, Wen Jiabao, to send the telegram, Wen refused. Zhao then told Hu to tell Peng Chong to telegram Wan directly in the name of the Leading Party Group of the congress. When Hu asked if he could say that Zhao had agreed to this, Zhao answered yes. When Wan, then in Canada, received the telegram, he worried that canceling the trip to Washington would hurt Sino-American relations. He was also concerned that the telegram "might have some problems," so he prepared to send an inquiry to the Central Committee for guidance. Before Wan could respond, however, Li Peng learned what had happened. Afraid that if Wan returned early, he would be "used" by supporters of the "turmoil," Li, Qiao Shi, and Yao Yilin wrote a second telegram and, in the name of the Central Committee, told Wan to continue on with his trip. Wan decided, at least for the moment, to obey the second telegram.[32] Xi thus remained the top leader of the congress in Beijing.

On the afternoon of May 22, Peng Chong chaired a meeting of the vice-chairmen of the National People's Congress, which Xi should have attended. An account of the meeting provided by Li Peng does not indicate who said what, but the points made by those present were incendiary: the party had wrongly given up on attempts to channel the students' unhappiness in a positive direction; Zhao's removal might not have adhered to the party's own constitution; the congress was the "most authoritative institution," but so far it had expressed no voice; the congress should summon the presidents of the universities to affirm that the students were patriotic and that the government would not punish them after they returned to their campuses; if the congress and State Council were in conflict, the congress could disband the government; the students had already limited their demands as much as possible, and they would return home if their patriotism was affirmed; the congress could reverse the "incorrect" declaration of martial law; and the standing committee should stop waiting and hold a full session immediately. One participant even demanded that they publicly declare that the students were patriotic, though another said that they had to reach unanimity before taking such a step. When Li Peng saw the report, he was stunned and suspected that "black hands" were using the congress to force him from his position as premier. "At this critical moment, it was necessary to activate the leadership role of the party over the congress," he concluded.[33]

Responding rapidly, Li Peng, Yang Shangkun, Yao Yilin, and Qiao Shi summoned the vice-chairmen in the Leading Party Group that very evening to convince them to support martial law. Li Peng did not list Xi as one of the individuals present. At the conclusion of the three-hour meeting, Vice-Chairmen Chen Muhua and Wang Hanbin acquiesced to Li's demands. Liao Hansheng "complained," but his attitude was "correct" (in Li's words). Peng Chong and Ye Fei, however, remained skeptical.[34]

The situation in the congress had still not stabilized. On May 22, dozens of standing committee members signed a petition written by Hu Jiwei—former chief editor of *People's Daily* and another close associate of Xi Zhongxun—that called for the holding of an emergency session. Hong Kong's *Wen wei po* published an article on the following day that claimed that the petitioners needed only thirty more signatures for their request to take effect. Even more concerning for the party leadership, the article also claimed that some standing committee members understood "why people want Li Peng to resign," thus implying, misleadingly, that this was the explicit goal of the petition.[35] On May 24, the Beijing Stone Group, a private business that had used its resources to help collect the signatures, provided Hu Jiwei with a list of fifty-seven members—more than one-third of the members of the standing committee—who wanted an emergency meeting to be held between May 24 and 26 (some members only agreed by telephone, which created problems for Hu Jiwei when the incident would later be investigated). Hu then submitted both the petition and letters addressed directly to Wan Li, Xi Zhongxun, and Peng Chong.[36]

At 4:00 a.m. Beijing time on May 24, a *People's Daily* reporter stationed in Washington, DC, Cang Lide, called headquarters to say that Wan Li had decided to return to China and that this news should appear in that day's paper. The news item, the journalist said, should state that Wan was returning for health reasons. This had been a collective decision by the entire delegation, Cang clarified. By then, word about the two competing telegrams had gotten out, and the man at headquarters in Beijing who took the call hoped that this meant Wan was returning home early to support Zhao.[37]

As Wan made the decision to return to China, Yang Shangkun—who was not only state president but also a vice-chairman and secretary general of the Central Military Commission—addressed an emergency session of the country's military leadership. He was clearly worried about morale among the troops. Between May 19 and 22, the army had tried to seize the capital, but its forces had been blocked by the citizens of Beijing. The commander of the elite Thirty-Eighth Group Army was fired from his position for expressing doubt and asking the politburo, National People's Congress, or State Council to "investigate" the crisis. Seven retired high-ranking generals had written a joint letter to the leadership pleading for a peaceful resolution. One signatory was Ye Fei, one of Xi's fellow vice-chairmen of the National People's Congress—a man who, on the first day after the crackdown, would weep and say, "Our military is finished; it fired upon the people!" The head of the military's Political Department, Yang Baibing, admitted that the soldiers had been afraid they would "commit a crime" by using force against civilians. According to Li Peng, "Deng Xiaoping worried that morale in the military was not stable."[38]

In his speech on May 24, Yang Shangkun saw a clear link between these difficulties in the military and the party's inability to bring the National People's Congress Standing Committee to heel. He said, "Some students believe that some people in the party center support them. Therefore, they are causing even more and more trouble. They demand an emergency session of the National People's Congress Standing Committee, an emergency session of the National People's Congress. Their goal is to use these organizations to make a decision that rejects the April 26 editorial and acknowledges their view that the student movement is a spontaneous patriotic democracy movement. Right now, they are actively engaged in this; they are still collecting signatures." "Given this situation, what is to be done?" Yang Shangkun asked. Instead of referring to party bodies like the politburo or the Central Committee, he instead spoke about how the elders had come together to support martial law and save the revolution.[39]

Early the next morning, May 25, the outside world learned just how active some members of the National People's Congress Standing Committee had been—Hong Kong's *Wen wei po* reported that Hu Jiwei had finally submitted the petition to the leadership of the National People's Congress.[40] By this time, through one way or another, more than one-third of its standing committee members had expressed support for holding an emergency meeting. Stone Group's Cao Siyuan—who not only had helped Hu collect signatures but also had previously worked on legal affairs for the National People's Congress—later stated in an interview that, legally, "at the time, if Peng Chong wanted to summon an emergency session, the conditions were ready." Cao claimed that they were not so naïve as to believe they would succeed. But the organizers of the petition felt that, by at least trying, they would be leaving an example for the future: "It will bring people's attention to the People's Congress, that the People's Congress is the highest legal authority." "We achieved that," Cao said.[41]

If Cao was indeed pessimistic, he had reason to be. It was on May 25, the same day that Hu Jiwei submitted the petition, that Wan Li was neutralized. At 3:00 a.m., Wan finally arrived back in China and was swiftly isolated. The hard-liners in Beijing were clearly worried about what he might do, so his plane flew to Shanghai, not Beijing—a diversion that came as a shock even to him, according to historian-cum-journalist Yang Jisheng, although, in June, Wan would tell the enlarged politburo session that he had wanted to go to Shanghai for a few days to get a better sense of the situation in the country. Whatever the truth, even before Wan's plane arrived in China, Li Peng had completed a written statement for him to sign. When Wan arrived at the airport, he found four people waiting for him: Ding Guan'gen, who had been sent from Beijing to brief him; Shanghai party secretary Jiang Zemin; Mayor Zhu Rongji; and one of his own sons. Jiang even had a plan to throw off any possible pursuers. As soon as Wan disembarked, he was taken out a side door of the airport and then brought to stay somewhere other than the usual Xijiao Hotel. One car, without Wan, went to the Xijiao Hotel to fool anyone who might have wanted to reach him. A public statement was released that falsely claimed that "Wan was found in need of medical treatment after being examined by doctors here."[42]

That afternoon, when *People's Daily* journalists met to discuss this news, one of them said that almost all the reformist party leaders had either been purged or isolated. "The only ones who are left are Wan Li, Xi Zhongxun, and a few standing committee members of the National People's Congress," the individual said. "Li Peng, at this very moment, is marshaling all of his resources to besiege them, and very quickly the reformist faction will be completely annihilated at the very highest levels and the conservative faction will achieve a total restoration."[43]

The party was indeed taking no chances. Peng Zhen—former chairman of the National People's Congress—was deployed to stop the situation in the capital from spinning out of control. At the beginning of the crisis, Peng had supported Zhao's attempts to reach a peaceful solution, but Peng quickly shifted when Deng made his views clear.[44] Hours after Wan, Xi's official boss, was essentially detained in Shanghai, Peng met with Xi and other congressional leaders at Jade Spring Hill, a residential leadership compound west of Beijing. It is unclear why Xi attended the May 25 meeting but not the one summoned by Li Peng three days earlier. One possibility is that Xi believed that the seniority enjoyed by Peng Zhen demanded such respect. Peng also brought along Xi's old associate and Jinping's former boss Geng Biao, who was a former National People's Congress vice-chairman. No record of Geng's words at the meeting is available, but on the next day, at a meeting of the Central Advisory Commission—the body of revolutionary elders—Geng spoke of the twenty million lives that had been lost in exchange for "all under heaven" (*tianxia*—a dynastic term referring to the nation), and he called on his comrades to "stubbornly struggle" for the sake of the party and its martyrs.[45]

Peng told Xi and the others that "bourgeois liberalization" violated the constitution and that the protests were "turmoil." "The congress represents the entire population of China, not only the small group of people on the streets," Peng said. He also emphasized that martial law was legal and that the congress could intervene only if the government were to declare martial law throughout the entire country, not only Beijing. Peng and Xi had previously spoken of the need for rule of law to prevent the appearance of a new strongman. Now, Peng was telling Xi it was time to rally to Deng and support an unpopular decision.[46]

Peng's words were almost certainly something Xi did not want to hear. On the same day as the meeting with Peng, Xi expressed his views by writing a notification on an article in the New China News Agency newsletter *Final Proofs of Domestic Trends*, a publication restricted to only a small number of the elite. This report described the situation in Zhejiang Province, where Party Secretary Li Zemin had taken a soft line. On May 1, Li met with one hundred students at Zhejiang University in Hangzhou for three hours. He explained that the word "turmoil" was not directed "against the broad masses of students," described student views on democratization as "identical" to the party's, and apologized for "shortcomings and mistakes." He begged the students to take down big-character posters, saying that approach had caused a "great deal" of suffering to their parents and intellectuals during the Cultural Revolution. He concluded by promising to listen to their views regularly. On May 18, Li again received the students and told them, "We have called the central authorities to express our views and the wishes of the teachers and students in Zhejiang." He even promised to contact Beijing again to urge "the principal leaders to hold dialogues with the hunger strikers in Tiananmen Square and hear their reasonable views and requests so that problems can be resolved democratically and lawfully."[47]

The account published in *Final Proofs of Domestic Trends* described the guidelines the Zhejiang party leadership had used to manage the students, which included "channeling," not suppressing, their demands, cleaning up corruption, developing democracy and the rule of law, and "using real steps to win the trust of the people." Xi approved: "Knowing how to work with the masses well to stabilize a situation is a good approach. It is worth promoting."[48] Yet time was slipping away. On May 24, Li Zemin, on a trip to Beijing, had already declared his support for the hard-liners.[49]

Even at this late stage, Xi might not have fully come around to martial law. On the morning of May 26, the day after Xi saw Peng and wrote the notification about Zhejiang, Wang Zhen and Xi had an apparently decisive encounter. During this period, Wang's emotional state seemed unstable. He told a baffled Li Peng that they should summon six or seven thousand cadres to Beijing for a giant meeting to unite thinking and resolve the "turmoil." Later, Wang, with a cane trembling in his hand, told Li that he wanted to march onto Tiananmen Square with his bodyguards to fight a "last-stand" battle with the protesters.[50] Yet Wang was the one who convinced Xi to declare his support for the party line. At 2:00 p.m. on May 26, Xi wrote a letter to Wang and had copies sent to the Central Committee: "At 10:00 a.m. this morning, on an assignment delegated to you by comrades Xiaoping, Xiannian, and Chen Yun, you met me to discuss the current turbulence in the capital. I firmly support Comrade Xiaoping's orders regarding the turbulence. I support the speeches by Comrades Li Peng and Shangkun. I support the policies and measures of the Central Committee and State Council to end this turbulence. This completely meets the fundamental interests of the party and nation, as well as the fundamental interests of all its people."[51] Xi's remark that the three party elders had told Wang to see him is a curious one. On May 23, Chen Yun, Li Xiannian, Wang Zhen, and Peng Zhen had met at Chen's home to plan a campaign to win over doubters, which raises the question of why Xi did not meet Wang until three days later.[52]

In any case, the Leading Party Group of the National People's Congress shifted its position dramatically that very day. It not only ended its search for a negotiated solution but also tried to bring others in line as well. On May 26 and 27, the group pressured other standing committee members who were also party cadres to rally to martial law. On May 29, the group submitted a report to the Central Committee that declared support for Li Peng, again using the word "turmoil." The New China News Agency published this report on the following day. "There should never be the slightest hesitation in this serious political struggle," the report said. "It is necessary to resolutely put down the turmoil stirred up by a very, very few people. Otherwise, there will be no peace in the party and the country." The group claimed that "the demands of the vast numbers of young students to promote democracy and overcome corruption put forward out of ardent patriotism are identical with the wishes of the party and government," and it called for distinguishing between the "ardently patriotic young students and the very, very few people who instigated turmoil." Despite those caveats, the report was clear evidence that the Leading Party Group, which included Xi, had openly supported the imposition of martial law.[53]

Evidence of Xi's role in this remarkable attempt to find a peaceful solution to one of the party's greatest crises in its history is tantalizing but ultimately inconclusive. He might have supported this rearguard action to end martial law, tried to ignore the opportunity, or done something in-between. Given his stature in the congress, especially with Wan overseas, it is difficult to imagine that the leadership of the legislature could have taken so many dramatic steps if Xi had strongly opposed such actions. Afterward, the party leadership certainly would have wondered whether he could have done a better job minding his shop.

In interviews conducted for this book, many interlocutors familiar with Chinese politics assumed Xi opposed the violence because of his reputation as a liberal reformer. Given what we know about Xi, that argument does have some merit. Xi had previously warned about pushing young people in a radical direction. In 1979, an internal party journal on youth affairs featured Xi's treatment of young people, claiming that he "always opposes the simplistic and harsh approach." Xi, according to this article, believed that "the vast majority of young people are reasonable and obey the party. The more critical the moment, the more this view must not waver." If young people were criticized for no good reason, it would just "push them into opposition," Xi thought. "As for those young people with active thinking, Comrade Xi Zhongxun does not try to oppress them but correctly guide them," the article asserted.[54]

It was not the only time Xi was praised for such a view. In 1984, public-security officials complained to Xi about Zhou Weimin, who had participated in the 1978–1979 Democracy Wall protests but had later worked in Guangdong's port at Shekou. At first, Xi sided with public security and demanded that Zhou return to Beijing. But at the urging of a local Guangdong official, Xi decided to investigate the matter more closely. When Hu Yaobang drafted a document in support of Zhou, he used Xi's own words to justify the decision. "Comrade Xi Zhongxun," Hu wrote, "always suggested at all previous meetings, with regard to young people with overly radical thinking, do not push them toward the enemy. Education should be primary."[55]

Xi was savvy enough to see that many young Chinese were losing faith in Communism. He understood the power of dialogue and reform to win over their generation. Yet his other solutions, the study of party history and the spirit of sacrifice, were rooted in the past. In January 1982, he spoke of the "Yan'an Spirit": "We should promote the idea of seeking hardship among young people. Now, we rarely talk about 'suffering first, enjoyment later.'"[56] In April 1985, he addressed a group of young people who were preparing to move to the Northwest to help develop China's poorer regions: "Now, many young people have no ideals or aspirations. They are willing to be flowers in a greenhouse." Xi said that the party should educate young people in "revolutionary idealism" so that they "leave on their own initiative for difficult places to endure trial and hardships."[57] In March 1987, after student protests triggered Hu's downfall, Xi said old comrades should go to campuses to talk about their revolutionary experiences "in a lively way that connects to the real world so that young people understand both history and the present."[58]

These general sensibilities toward young people, however, do not tell us whether Xi acted and, if so, with how much courage in the spring of 1989. Not all party elders with strong "reformist" credentials supported the students. Xi Zhongxun's old associate from the Propaganda Department, Lu Dingyi, for example, held many liberal views, but he did not support the protests. "It is necessary to think about the negative side effects," he said. Moreover, the students were too "arrogant," in his view. In 1990, Lu even said that the turmoil in Eastern Europe demonstrated that if the students had not been suppressed, then they would have engaged in "another Cultural Revolution."[59] While in the United States, Wan Li had given mixed signals. He warned Secretary of State James Baker that avoiding bloodshed might be impossible "given that a tiny handful of people wanted to overthrow Deng Xiaoping and the leadership of the Communist Party." Wan even said that under the Chinese constitution, "the State Council had the right to declare martial law" and that calling for the removal of Li Peng, Deng Xiaoping, or Yang Shangkun would be an act of "subversion." Wan did, however, say that "all kinds of means should be utilized to prevent bloodshed."[60] In his meeting with President George H. W. Bush, Wan asserted that the student demands were legitimate and that "under no circumstances should there be bloodshed." But he also warned about Taiwanese provocateurs and used the word "turmoil" four times. "China cannot accomplish anything without stability and unity," he said, according to an American summary of his remarks.[61] When one party elder later asked Wan Li, "At the time, was there any other option?" Wan replied, "Whenever there is chaos facing a regime, in order to maintain rule, it is always necessary to have some suppression. Suppression is legal."[62]

Zhongxun's own son was skeptical of the students. These young people were marching for reform, yet Jinping saw in their behavior echoes of the Red Guards during the Cultural Revolution. In mid-May, at a meeting on media work, he had admitted that democratization and more respect for rule of law were necessary. However, the extent of such changes, Jinping argued, "must have a certain amount of scientific content." "Otherwise, if democratization is made absolute, if it goes beyond what current conditions can handle, if it lacks a step-by-step approach, then something that should be extremely wise might then become something extremely wrong." He went on to ruminate on the meaning of democracy. His answer was that democracy should be "a certain kind of manifestation of rule of law in the interests of the people." It was not, in Jinping's mind, a way for someone to simply achieve his will. Taking democracy to the extreme is just a way, according to Jinping, of "escaping any constraints or sense of responsibility. That is no good." In village elections, sometimes good people were selected, but in other cases, the winners were so bad that the grass roots fell into a "paralysis." He referred to the chaos of the Cultural Revolution: "Wasn't the 'Cultural Revolution' the manifestation of 'big democracy'? This kind of 'big democracy' is not in accord with science, not in accord with the rule of law but is instead in accord with superstition, in accord with stupidity, and the result is major chaos. Anyone can organize a few people to go and ransack homes; anyone can pull together a struggle unit; today, I knock you down; tomorrow, you knock me down. Can these days be repeated? Without stability and unity, nothing is possible!" The speech was a deeply conservative statement about the dangers of chaos caused by too many freedoms.[63]

Although the behavior of the National People's Congress leadership was remarkably brave, its attempts were ultimately the country's last hope for a peaceful solution, and they failed. With Wan gone, Xi could have done more. He could have called an emergency session of the National People's Congress Standing Committee. He also could have made declarations in the media, which was acting independently at the time. He chose not to.

The counterfactual is meaningless. Sooner or later, Deng would have won. He was the senior revolutionary, and, as Zhao Ziyang himself put it, the National People's Congress would always be a "rubber stamp" while Deng was still alive because "authority is formed under many historical conditions; it is not possible to confer authority and have it suddenly appear."[64] The Central Committee's First Plenum after the Thirteenth Party Congress had voted to consult Deng on major issues. And, crucially, Deng was head of the Central Military Commission. As the party deliberated on how to respond to the protests, without informing the politburo or even Zhao Ziyang, Deng was already mobilizing the People's Liberation Army.[65] Even those most supportive of a peaceful solution understood this reality. Zhao would later say in an interview that once Deng made up his mind to use violence, even a united Politburo Standing Committee could not have stopped him.[66] Wan Li told an associate, "I cannot oppose Deng. When Deng is wrong, I am wrong along with him. When Deng is right, I am right along with him."[67]

Given these circumstances, the question for Xi was how costly the crackdown would be for him and the party if it had to come. In that sense, Xi's behavior is less a case of cowardice than a demonstration of political judgment. Not too long ago he had been criticized, along with Hu Yaobang, at the January 1987 party-life meeting, so he was already in a vulnerable position. Moreover, acting too brazenly might have led to accusations of a Zhao-Xi clique, which would have hurt not only Xi but many others as well. Openly opposing a crackdown might have made the coming violence more costly by leading to false hopes among the protesters of support or instability within the party. He could not have known that martial law would turn out as bloody as it did. But Xi did miss an opportunity to go down in history, like Zhao Ziyang, as a man of principle who refused to go along with the decision for martial law.[68]

Xi reappeared in public on June 1 at a Children's Day activity in Beijing's Longtan Park.[69] He was accompanied by Yan Mingfu, a protégé who, as head of the United Front Work Department, had engaged in desperate talks with the student representatives two weeks earlier. Although Xi had supported

FIGURE 14. Xi Zhongxun visits Beijing's Longtan Park shortly before the 1989 crackdown, June 1, 1989. Source: *Xi Zhongxun huace*, 84.

Yan during earlier difficulties, Yan would soon be fired from his position under suspicion that he had wavered during the crisis. Liao Hansheng, a fellow member of the National People's Congress leadership, was also present, as well as Chen Xitong, the mayor of Beijing. A few years later, Chen would be imprisoned on charges of corruption; after his release, he would bitterly complain that Li Peng's memoirs attempted to use him as a scapegoat, placing him in charge of enforcing martial law.[70]

At 6:30 a.m. on June 3, Radio Beijing broadcast an announcement by the spokesperson of the National People's Congress Standing Committee Office that, under the current "chaotic" circumstances, it would be difficult to hold the standing committee session on June 20 as scheduled.[71] A few hours later, in the early evening, Chinese military units were ordered to move toward Tiananmen Square "at any cost." Students and high-ranking elites alike knew something was coming, but the brazen scale of the violence during the ensuing hours stunned them. Despite widespread skepticism within the party and the People's Liberation Army, Deng had successfully engineered the outcome that he had wanted: to "spill a little blood," as he put it on May 19.[72] Up until the very last moment, protestors were still placing their greatest hopes on the possibility of an emergency meeting of the congress.[73] If they were no longer in the square, they reasoned, "the National People's Congress would be held under bayonets."[74] More than seven hundred of them were killed in the onslaught.[75]

TIANANMEN'S AFTERMATH

Ultimately, whatever Xi Zhongxun might have thought of the crackdown and whatever he did in the immediately preceding weeks, he supported the party after a decision was made, as he had done so many other times earlier in his life. He appeared at a study session led by Premier Li Peng on June 14.[76] The next day, Xi and other vice-chairmen of the National People's Congress publicly "extended cordial regards" to the People's Liberation Army and paid a visit to the wounded soldiers. According to a chronology of Xi's life, he was "assigned" this task by Wan Li.[77] On this occasion, Xi told the soldiers:

> On the morning of June 3, in the capital of our motherland, Beijing, a small minority of rioters instigated some people who did not understand the true situation to create a horrifying counterrevolutionary riot. At this critical moment, under the correct leadership of the Central Committee, State Council, and the Central Military Commission, you resolutely executed the brilliant policy of the Central Committee, took decisive measures, and quickly suppressed this counterrevolutionary riot to defend the socialist system, protect the people's government, protect the security of the lives and property of the people in the capital, and make a monumental contribution. I represent Chairman Wan Li and all the comrades in the National People's Congress's agencies to express to you sincere greetings and also to express the highest respect!

Xi called the crackdown "a glorious page" in the history of the People's Republic of China, and he said the soldiers' "mighty historical contribution will forever be etched into the hearts of all the peoples of the nation." He went on to strike a cautionary note: the forces behind the "counterrevolutionary riot" had not been completely stifled and could yet again rise up.[78] Li Peng described this visit by Xi and the other vice-chairmen as "an important act" that showed they had supported the crackdown "as soon as they understood the real situation."[79]

Xi attended the enlarged politburo sessions held from June 19 to 21 to affirm the decision to use violence and to remove Zhao Ziyang.[80] Xi was featured prominently near the beginning of the news footage on the event. He turned to look at the camera and then folded his hands together in front of his stomach while continuing to stare.[81] The meeting must have been extremely uncomfortable for Xi as the participants focused intensely on the issue of Zhao's attempted "use" of the congress to "oppose" the Central Committee. Wu Xueqian, Peng Chong, Zhao Ziyang, and Hu Qili all tried to blame each other for the May 21 telegram that summoned Wan Li to return to China. The participants were especially shocked when they learned about Hu Qili's role. Although some of them had originally supported his continued membership on the politburo, this news ensured that Hu Qili—who had wept in Xi's office the day after Hu Yaobang's death—would be dismissed from that body as well as from its standing committee. Wan Li was also criticized at the meetings. "Hu, Zhao, and Wan, Hu, Zhao, and Wan, out of the three of them, two and a half fell," Wan said to his family at home after the sessions were over, meaning that he had only narrowly survived and was weakened at that as official head of the congress.[82]

In late June and early July, the National People's Standing Committee finally held a plenary session in Beijing. Many of its members had originally hoped that this session would have been convened on June 20 and that it would have somehow convinced the students to end their protests. Now, hundreds of civilians were dead, and the purpose of the session was to affirm the legitimacy of the violence. During a television broadcast on July 4, Xi was shown first. He occasionally looked up from his notes to glance quickly at his audience. He said that the congress unanimously endorsed a report on the events that concluded that the protests were "an antiparty and antisocialist political upheaval and a counterrevolutionary rebellion created by an extremely small number of people taking advantage of the student unrest." He continued,

> After repeated study and deep thought, I have come to respect wholeheartedly the proletarian revolutionaries of the older generation represented by Comrade Deng Xiaoping for their foresight, decisiveness, and their key pillar role in thwarting the turmoil and suppressing the counterrevolutionary rebellion.
>
> The study has also enabled me to deeply understand that after going through the test of this severe political struggle, our party has been proven to be firm and strong and is worthy of being called the leadership core ca-

pable of leading our case. Our Army has also gone through the test of this severe political struggle, which also proves that it is a qualified Army worthy of the name of the steel great wall of our state and the Army of the people.[83]

The purpose of the standing committee sessions was not only to praise Deng and the army. They were also to mete out punishment. Members of the standing committee demanded an investigation into Hu Jiwei's campaign to collect enough signatures to summon an emergency meeting of the congress. On the same day that Xi's speech was broadcast, Hu was forced to submit a document explaining his behavior. Bravely, he wrote, "Even now, I believe that what I did was completely correct, legal, and necessary at the time." But another standing committee member, Zhang Chengxian, was savage: "One of the struggle tactics of the creators of the turmoil was to force the National People's Congress Standing Committee to convene ahead of schedule and to cancel the martial law decision and even summon a full National People's Congress to dissolve the government," he said. Lamely, Zhang said that collecting signatures for an emergency session was not problematic; Hu's "mistake" had been how he had gone about collecting the signatures, such as enlisting a private enterprise, Stone, to help, which "created severe consequences."[84]

A special group was established to investigate the matter, and a report was completed in October. Later that month, Xi Zhongxun, Wan Li, and Peng Chong had a long discussion with Hu Jiwei. After criticizing him, they officially stated that any member of the congress still had the right to collect signatures to suggest a meeting. Even if Hu had supported removing Li Peng—a charge that Hu denied—that also should be considered legal. Therefore, the standing committee would not punish him. They even stated that their opinion had been conveyed to the party's Central Committee. Hu was thrilled, reasoning that they would never dare to make such a clear statement if it had not already been cleared with the party leadership.[85]

Hu Jiwei probably did not realize how much pressure the leadership of the congress was still under. Also in October, Li Ruihuan, a new addition to the Politburo Standing Committee, gave a speech to the Tianjin City party leadership revealing that Hu would be expelled from the legislature at the next National People's Congress. Even more ominously for Xi, Li also said that "the bourgeois liberalism in the National People's Congress has spread unchecked"—an extraordinarily serious charge. "At heart, this was a struggle over de facto supreme power," Li stated. "They were not willing to exercise supreme power under the leadership of the party committee at the same level."[86]

At a full National People's Congress meeting in March 1990, Xi, as executive chairman of one session, announced that the congress had approved Deng's resignation from chairmanship of the state Central Military Commission (a position his son Jinping would assume twenty-two years later).[87] At a session for the representatives from Shaanxi, Xi said that the forty years of the People's Republic had demonstrated that when the nation was stable and unified, everything could develop smoothly. During times of chaos, however, nothing could move forward. Xi told the delegation that his sixty-plus years as a revolutionary had taught him that the "most important condition" for stability was unity among cadres at every level. "In the past, during the era of guerrilla warfare, unity meant victory," he said. "Lack of unity meant defeat, even complete annihilation."[88]

Despite his continuing public-facing role at the National People's Congress, as well as his constant affirmations of loyalty to the party, Xi was unable to protect Hu Jiwei, who was stunned when his membership on that body was revoked at these sessions.[89] And the party's priority was now clearly reigning in the legislature. Jiang Zemin, who had replaced Zhao Ziyang as general secretary, revealed, at this meeting of the congress, that the Politburo Standing Committee had met the previous August to discuss the work of the legislature. The party leadership had tasked the Leading Party Group of the National People's Congress Standing Committee with investigating how to "improve and perfect" the body. Jiang warned that any attempts to weaken party control over the legislature were wrong. "The Leading Party Group of the National People's Congress Standing Committee must establish and perfect a request for guidance and a reporting system to party committees at the same level to guarantee the party's line, guidelines, and policies are executed in congress work," he ordered.[90]

Xi was touched, once again, by yet another quasi-legal search for enemies within the party. In September 1989, the Organization Department launched a comprehensive rescreening that included even the National People's Congress Standing Committee. To remain within the party, cadres were required to describe their feelings and concrete activities during the "political struggle" and to submit a form to reregister. Anyone whose activities were seen to be too problematic during the protests would be dismissed.[91] On July 22, 1990, Xi himself completed a self-summary to "reregister."[92]

Privately, Xi was still expressing hope for political reform and better relations with the capitalist West. Gao Zimin—who had grown up in Taiwan, studied medicine in the United States, and later became a White House doctor—claimed that Xi treated him to lunch sometime after June 4 in the Great Hall of the People. Gao told Xi, "I was born in Taiwan. I also lived in America for a long time, so my custom is to directly speak my mind. That's not criticism." Xi laughed and said, "Criticism is not a bad thing. Without criticism, how are progress and reform possible? But criticism must come from sincerity and accord with fact." Gao then asked how countries should manage protests without them spiraling out of control. According to Gao's memory of the meeting, Xi responded along the following lines:

> The answer is rule of law. There are no exceptions, no matter whether it is an imperial, socialist, or capitalist political system. Didn't Chinese dynasties collapse because rules and regulations became lax, the role of rule of law was broken?
>
> If the emperor wants people to obey the law, he himself must also obey the law. Now, we are in chaos. There's no need to gloss over that. It is necessary to escape the dilemma and chaotic situation. What's needed is rule of law. Rule by man sooner or later will cause chaos, because never in history has there been a person who is always perfect.[93]

The two men then discussed Sino-American relations. Gao started to tell Xi that the United States would probably end China's most-favored-nation status for three months. Before Gao could finish, Xi interrupted and said, "Stopping for one day is no good, even for one day is no good." Xi described the agreement, which had been reached in July 1979, as beneficial to both countries. The Chinese people had been able to escape poverty through international trade and thereby had achieved self-confidence. If the agreement were to be canceled, exports would be affected: "The common people would lose confidence, and the consequences would be extremely serious." Xi recalled his experience in Guangdong when people were fleeing to Hong Kong. Everyone was a patriot, Xi said, but they left to make a living. Xi pleaded that the Tiananmen crackdown was not a good reason to make ordinary people suffer. When the meeting concluded, Xi provided Gao with a car so he could immediately go to the American Embassy, where he told Ambassador James Lilley about their conversation.[94]

After the June 4 crackdown, more than thirty elderly party members wrote a joint letter to the leadership suggesting that retired cadres should establish a nationwide organization that could facilitate their role in educating younger people in the revolutionary traditions. One year later, in June 1990, Xi Zhongxun and Wang Renzhong were named honorary chairmen of the new Care for the Next Generation Committee. At its first session that same month, Xi described China's generational challenge in apocalyptic terms:

> History and reality teach us that enemy forces at home and abroad have always concentrated their goal of "peaceful evolution" in young people. The fight for young people is a life-and-death struggle without gunpowder. The outcome of this struggle is directly related to the future of the country and the fate of the nation; it is related to whether there will be successors to this socialist nation, for which we in the older generation risked our lives in battles across the country to found; it is related to whether the hopes of achieving the Four Modernizations and the rejuvenation of the Chinese people will be achieved; and it is related to whether the cause of socialism and Communism will never lose its Red color for thousands of years. Therefore, caring for the next generation is a major affair for the entire party and nation, and, even more so, it is an unshirkable responsibility for us old comrades.[95]

It was soaring language, but privately he was under intense stress—a situation that deteriorated further on August 9, 1990, when Liu Jingfan, the brother of Liu Zhidan and one of Xi's closest friends, died. Although the family did not immediately release the news, Xi somehow heard, and he showed up in the middle of the night at the Liu household.[96] Around August 25, Tie Liu—a man who had been declared a rightist in 1957—hosted a ceremony for the Chinese Market Information Compilation Bureau at the Great Hall of the People. Tie spent the evening with Xi, who attended the festivities. When Xi learned that Tie had been labeled a rightist, Xi laughed and said, "Good, then we are even closer than before—you're a rightist, I'm an old rightist; we're the same, we're the same. Ah! What's 'right'! 'Left'! It's all caused by 'class struggle.'"[97]

A few days later, Xi demonstrated extremely odd behavior at a National People's Congress Standing Committee meeting. On August 30, Li Peng presented a draft proposal on consular privileges and immunities at a session chaired by Xi.[98] When Li finished his report, he ran into Xi, who said to him, "I want to denounce you!" which seriously frightened Li. Li Rui wrote in his diary that the incident demonstrated Xi's "mental situation has, at the very least, completely lost control."[99]

On the same day, Chinese foreign minister Qian Qichen gave a speech on Li Peng's proposal.[100] Qian's speech was simple, and it ended in just twenty minutes. Although Xi was not chairing the meeting, when the speech was over, he stood up and said, "Using such a little bit of time to speak so clearly deserves praise; I suggest everyone clap." No one reacted. Then he said, "In the past, the standing committee did not take the discussion of drafts seriously enough. I hope that this meeting can begin a new style. I suggest extending the meeting for another day." No one supported Xi's proposal, and the man chairing the session then said that everyone had already bought their train and plane tickets to depart. "I am the first vice-chairman and not a single member of the standing committee agrees!" Xi said. When Li Rui heard what had happened, he concluded, "This was the result of several years of pent-up resentment."[101]

Later that day, the session broke into four small discussion groups. During a break, Xi walked around the room chatting with various people. "The National People's Congress must represent the people," he said. "It must speak for the people." When they reconvened at 4:30 p.m., according to custom, one more person would speak, and then the meeting would be adjourned. But Xi stood up and said he wanted to speak a bit about history. "I ask that everyone remain one more hour." Then, according to someone who was present, Xi spoke about the early history of the revolution in the Northwest: "Relations among the various base camps were very complicated; many good comrades gave up their lives for nothing. He spoke in a very touching way, and his main idea was not to see those with different opinions as an 'opposition faction' and, even more importantly, not to turn them into a 'counterrevolutionary faction.' It is necessary to protect other opinions, and it is necessary to take seriously and research different opinions." That evening, Xi refused to let a doctor see him, and he spent the night sleeping on the couch. The next day, the participants were informed that Xi was sick, and the "Central Committee had approved that he would rest in the South and no longer participate in this meeting." He never again participated in a National People's Congress session.[102] On September 4, Deng Yingchao, Zhou Enlai's widow, wrote a letter to Xi—who was recuperating in a hospital by then—wishing him better health. The next day, Jiang Zemin not only wrote a letter but also sent Wen Jiabao to visit Xi on his behalf.[103]

Although Liu Jingfan died on August 9, his funeral was not held until September 8. Xi did not attend the service; Qi Xin went in his stead.[104] After the ceremony was over, Xi went by himself to the mourning hall to stand in front of Liu's photo, and he sobbed uncontrollably.[105] In late September, Xi went to Shenzhen, allegedly to treat a tooth ailment. He was accompanied by Yang Dezhong, who was head of the Central Guards Bureau at the time. During this trip, Xi "emotionally" said, "In the future, I will stay in Shenzhen—Shenzhen restored my health, Shenzhen is my home, [and] I want to help develop Shenzhen."[106] On October 11, Li Rui, after chatting with Qin Chuan, wrote in his diary that "Zhongxun is already back to normal. Lots of people are going to visit him." Xi was looking for people to write his biography. His wife was "already active," but she had reached a troubling conclusion: her husband's "political life is now over."[107]

29
THE FINAL YEARS

In the late summer of 1990, Xi's departure from the capital to Guangdong was imminent. Several of his best friends had died in rapid succession, the party was turning away from the political legacies he had helped shape after the disaster of the Cultural Revolution, Communism was collapsing throughout the world, and Deng had just used massive violence against the Chinese people—for whom the revolution had been fought to serve. But despite his failing political, physical, and emotional health, Xi was not quite finished. His last political act was tied inextricably to his first. Desperately hoping to achieve his dream of unification before death, Xi reached out to an individual in Taiwan with whom he had committed his first revolutionary act.

When Xi was a teenager, he had two best friends—Song Wenmei and Cheng Jianwen—and the three were so close that they were known as the "Three Heroes of Guanzhong." In 1928, Cheng led the two other boys in a failed attempt to poison an academic administrator at their school. Cheng later became head of the Organization Department for the party in Shaanxi and worked with Xi after the Liangdang mutiny. However, in 1933, Cheng betrayed the Shaanxi Communist leadership to the Nationalists. He then changed his name to Chen Jianzhong and, having gained Chiang Kai-shek's trust, later worked in Xi'an running operations against the Communists.

After the party seized Xi'an in 1949, Xi had his regional intelligence apparatus repeatedly send Sun Zhigang, a former Nationalist agent, to contact Chen and convince him to defect back. Sun was so good at his work that he won the trust of the Nationalist spymasters, thereby raising Communist suspicions. The Ministry of Public Security in Beijing warned that Sun might in fact be a Nationalist agent. In November 1950, he was placed under investigation, but no problems were immediately discovered. According to Cultural Revolution–era documents, Xi sent him on a second mission to Hong Kong without permission from the central authorities, and Sun continued to supply intelligence from the colony and then from Taiwan until October 1953, when he subsequently disappeared.[1] During the Cultural Revolution, Xi was attacked for his relationship with Chen.[2] Chen fared better than Xi as he was trusted enough by Chiang Kai-shek to be put in charge of the Sixth Bureau—the organization in charge of Communist Party research and psychological warfare. However, when Chen later suggested that the party no longer be referred to as "bandits," he was accused of being a Communist because of his colored past.[3]

In the winter of 1988, a former professor at National Chengchi University in Taiwan, Jing Zhiren, fell ill while in the mainland, and he was hospitalized at Beijing's Xiehe Hospital. Xi happened to be in the hospital at the same time, and he told Jing, "My illness is extremely serious. Please deliver my message. I hope my old friend from the past, Chen Jianzhong, will come to the mainland no matter what." After returning to Taiwan, Jing told Chen that he had seen Xi in the hospital. "His illness seems serious; he desperately hopes to see you as soon as possible," Jing said.[4]

Shortly after the June 4 crackdown, Chen Jianzhong passed through Hong Kong. While in the colony, Xi called Chen on the phone from Xiehe Hospital and said, "Are you Brother Jianzhong? I am Zhongxun." In a trembling voice, Chen responded, "Yes, I am Jianzhong. After decades apart, I still recognize your voice. How is your health?" Xi responded, "My health is very bad. I am now in a hospital. I must ask that you visit Beijing quickly. If there is any delay, I'm afraid there will be no chance to meet!" Xi's voice became softer, leading Chen to believe that Xi was very sad. And yet Chen demurred. "Your intention is very good," Chen said. "A certain individual also delivered a message, but for me personally, because of my status, it is a little inconvenient." After returning to Taiwan, Chen submitted a report to President Lee Teng-hui. Lee approved a visit and said to Chen, "You are most clear about the party's situation. It is best that you go." Lee even gave him some money for the trip.[5]

On October 12, 1990, Chen Jianzhong returned to China.[6] According to Chen's assistant at the time, his main purpose was to visit "an old friend with whom he had survived life-and-death trials and tribulations."[7] In his memoirs, Chen wrote that the trip was more personal than political; his most important motivation was his desire to see Xi.[8] When Chen stepped off the plane in Beijing, he was met by Qi Xin. Qi told Chen that because Xi was ill, he had been unable to go to the airport himself, but he had organized a dinner for Chen that night. Qi also told Chen that a doctor had asked her to relay a message: when Chen met Xi, they should "avoid becoming too excited so as to prevent any accident." When the two old men finally saw each other, they embraced, but they did not speak for a long time. Xi was clearly quite ill and could not walk stably, but he was delighted to see his old comrade in arms. Chen and Xi enjoyed a joint celebration for their eightieth birthdays as Xi was only a few days older than Chen, and Xi took care to invite all their friends and classmates from Shaanxi who were in Beijing at the time. Xi commissioned a famous artist to paint a picture of a bull, their shared Chinese zodiac sign, to present to Chen.[9]

Xi arranged for Chen to live at Diaoyutai, the state guest house. He met top leaders, such as Jiang Zemin and Yang Shangkun. Jiang told Chen that he hoped to restore discussions between the two sides. In response, Chen told Jiang that the purpose of his visit was to see his sick friend, but he promised to relay the message back to Taiwan. Chen did not meet Li Peng, however. Unsurprisingly, Chen came away with the impression that Xi's relations with Li Peng "apparently were not very good." Xi had hoped that his friendship with Chen would not mean that Li would refuse to meet Chen, but Chen decided not to meet with Li anyway.[10]

Xi sent his chief secretary and a number of other cadres to accompany Chen back to Shaanxi. When Chen saw the poor state of the graves of his mother, father, and younger brother, he was so distraught that he fell to his knees and started to howl sobs so strongly that he fainted several times. He began digging with his hands, hoping to see his mother's corpse one last time because, according to his assistant, "someone had said that his father and mother had died under extremely agonizing circumstances."[11]

After Chen returned to Taipei, he suggested that Lee Teng-hui select someone to enter into discussions with Xi, who would represent the Communists. Political heavyweights in Taipei supported Chen's proposal, and

Lee expressed interest, but after two or three days, Lee changed his mind. Lee remained distrustful of those party elders who had been born on the mainland. He decided to use his own trusted confidantes to engage in the secret negotiations that began in December 1990.[12] One individual close to Lee claimed that another worry was that too many different back channels would have made it easy for misunderstandings to occur, which, in a worst-case scenario, could negatively affect democratization in Taiwan or, even worse, could lead to war.[13]

Xi's hopes to see unification in his lifetime never came to pass. His last desperate political attempt before leaving Beijing under difficult circumstances came to nothing. In fact, his entire approach to the United Front in Taiwan was increasingly outdated. The new generation of leaders in Taiwan lacked the emotional and personal attachments to the mainland that had made the classic United Front approaches so powerful. Taiwanese society was changing too. One high-ranking party official admitted to a Taiwanese negotiator that democratization on the island made United Front work much more difficult.[14] And June 4 made China's efforts harder as well. Shortly after the crackdown, Premier Hau Pei-tsun appeared on Taiwanese television to triumphantly say that the party's influence operations on the island would now collapse and that the trend in the direction of more positive affection toward the mainland would end.[15]

THE MOVE SOUTH

On October 26, a few days after Chen returned to Taiwan, Xi left for Guangdong. The exact circumstances remain mysterious. According to a former high-ranking official involved in ethnic issues, when Xi left the capital, Yin Fatang and his allies cheered the news. "Deng Xiaoping drove him away," Yin was reported to have said, "and will never let him return."[16] In an interview with Voice of America, Li Rui said that Xi had been "dispatched to Guangdong" and would not be "allowed to return to Beijing for ten years."[17] In his diary, however, Li characterized Xi's departure as his own choice.[18] A vice-chairman in the office of the Shaanxi Institute of Socialism stated, at a 2016 meeting of princelings and scholars, that Xi's departure for the South was one of the "four great disasters" of Xi's life: "In 1983, Xi Zhongxun and Deng Xiaoping had held different opinions on Reform and Opening, and [Xi] gradually left the center of power. In 1990, seventy-seven-year-old Xi

Zhongxun was still young and in good health, and his political life was in full swing. But he retired too early, he had unfulfilled ambitions, and he was extremely depressed."[19]

Rumors that Deng somehow played a role in Xi's departure at the time spread, but Deng probably did not officially exile him. Xi had not been formally criticized like Zhao Ziyang, which makes the idea that Xi would be confined to house arrest somewhat problematic, although he probably still needed permission to return to the capital.[20] Perhaps Xi was behaving like his old patron Ye Jianying, who had similarly gone south and rarely returned to Beijing after falling out with Deng over the latter's dictatorial style. But it is clear that his political and health problems did not mean Xi was entirely isolated. Even right after he first moved to Guangdong, Xi repeatedly met with top leaders. On August 3, 1991, Xi even met Deng Pufang, Deng Xiaoping's son.[21]

Wild rumors about the exact state of Xi's mental health spread. In November 1990, a *South China Morning Post* article began with "Xi Zhongxun has gone crazy. So say staff in the People's Liberation Army, where the elder military commander once wielded great power." The story, based on unnamed sources, described increasingly erratic behavior. "It did not take much to provoke the breakdown," the article alleged. "At a committee meeting of the National People's Congress, Mr. Xi asked that a pencil be sharpened—twice. Finally, he launched into a tirade that soon became incomprehensible. The ranting did not subside for nearly 48 hours."[22] In December, *Hongkong Standard* offered another version of Xi's deteriorating psychological condition. It quoted a "high-level Chinese source" who claimed that Xi had opposed the June 4 crackdown and that "he boldly criticized the party and the Government." Once his outbursts were reported to party leaders, he was told it would be better if he rested at home. But, "instead of relaxing, Mr. Xi's health began to deteriorate."[23] In August 1991, the *South China Morning Post* interviewed Jinping about his father and asserted, "The elder Mr. Xi, 78, a former party boss of Guangdong, is widely reported by diplomats in Beijing to have suffered a nervous breakdown last year. The diplomats said Mr. Xi was hounded by visions of the Communist Party having fallen victim to 'peaceful evolution.'" Jinping, though, "denied that his father . . . had had mental problems." Jinping said Zhongxun was "very well" and continued to travel the country.[24]

The exact nature of Xi's illness is unclear, but according to Yang Ping, a friend of the Xi family, Xi's health had completely collapsed because of the stress he felt during the June 4 crisis.[25] Du Daozheng, the former head of the liberal party-history journal *Yanhuang chunqiu*, wrote that "friends from the South" said that the stress of June 4 had caused Xi to "go crazy."[26] Qi Xin tried to protect Xi's psychological state by warning visitors not to discuss three people with him—Mao Zedong, Deng Xiaoping, or Hu Yaobang—or three topics—party history in the Northwest, the Cultural Revolution, or June 4.[27] At least occasionally, Xi was known to have suffered from paranoia. He sometimes claimed that "those old people," meaning Deng Xiaoping and Chen Yun, wanted to assassinate him.[28] Xi could become "hotheaded," according to one high-ranking official.[29]

One example of Xi becoming "hotheaded" occurred soon after he left Beijing for the South. Initially, he lived briefly in a villa in Zhuhai. The local party leader, Liang Guangda, knew that Xi had occasionally displayed signs of poor mental health even though Xi acted normally much of the time. Xi thought that nurses were spies, and when local cadres visited him, he would sometimes believe they were Taiwanese agents sent to harm him. When Yang Shangkun and Jiang Zemin planned a visit to the city in late November to celebrate the tenth anniversary of its status as a special economic zone, Liang decided it was a good excuse not only to remove Xi but also to curry favor with a top leader by turning over the villa to Yang Shangkun. However, Xi refused to leave, and he believed that the people who came to remove him were trying to harm him. Xi even demanded that someone bring him a gun. Finally, when the time of Yang's arrival approached, medical personnel gave Xi a shot, and he was brought to Shenzhen sleeping in a car.[30]

Despite instances like this, Xi still had moments when he was exceptionally sharp. One possibility is that the rumors of Xi's "insanity" were partly the result of the machinations of his political enemies, like Deng Xiaoping. Xi's "breakdowns" tended to occur when he was talking to particularly odious people, like Li Peng.[31] On December 29, 1990, Li Rui wrote in his diary that Xi was already "completely normal."[32] Xi continued to express strong opinions about elite politics. "It is possible that Hu Yaobang made a few mistakes," he told a vice-chairman of the Guangdong People's Congress in May 1991, "but one simply cannot make the case that Zhao Ziyang made any mistakes!"[33]

Over the following years, even people who intimately knew the Xi family had different ideas about the nature of Xi Zhongxun's infirmity. One close friend, Hao Zhiping, the widow of military chief of staff Luo Ruiqing, did not believe Xi had any serious afflictions.[34] In 1993, Liu Mila, the niece of Liu Zhidan and the daughter of Li Jiantong, went to Guangdong to visit Zhongxun. In an article commemorating Xi, she wrote,

> Later, I heard that Uncle Xi was sick and was convalescing in Shenzhen. I heard rumors that Uncle Xi's mental condition was bad, and that surprised me. In 1993, while on a work trip to Shenzhen, I went to visit Uncle Xi. When Uncle Xi saw me, with only one glance, he recognized me, grabbed my hand, and said, "Mila, quickly sit down." We talked about this and that in a very friendly atmosphere. I was thinking, Uncle Xi's mental condition is so good, why is it said that he has a mental disorder? What kind of evil motive do these people have?[35]

However, that same year, Kong Shujing, the daughter of a close friend of Xi Zhongxun, felt differently when she visited Xi. At that time, he was in a wheelchair and much thinner than when she had last seen him in Beijing: "He was like a completely different person," she sadly wrote in her memoirs.[36] In March 1994, Qin Chuan told Li Rui that on a recent trip to Shenzhen, it had only been possible to speak to Xi for ten minutes "to avoid upsetting him." But in early May, Jinping told Li Rui that Zhongxun's health was getting back to normal, although he was not planning to return to Beijing.[37]

Xi Jinping's career continued to progress even as his father's was collapsing. They shared the same interests. In October 1989, Jinping published an article on the relationship between the cultural world and politics. He seemed to be striving to find a middle approach between leftism and rightism. "Art and literature cannot be separated from politics, but they are not the same thing either," Jinping wrote. Whether cultural products exposed the bad or praised the good, they must all summon "a sense of historic responsibility." He praised scar literature, but he castigated avant-garde art. "The heart of the matter is not how much culture is managed but the principles and direction of that management," he concluded. It was a balanced view reminiscent of his father.[38]

Also like his father, he did not trust Catholics. In February and March 1990, Jiang Ping—an old Northwest cadre and then an advisor to the United Front Work Department—went on an inspection trip to Ningde. In a report about his trip, Jiang expressed strong admiration for Jinping's tough approach. Sixty percent of Ningde's Catholics fell under the influence of "underground forces." So few Catholics went to official churches that they were running out of money. The situation in Ningde demonstrated that underground Catholics "openly opposed the party and government." The regional party committee, under Jinping's guidance, had developed an effective approach. "Religion-work small groups" appeared at every government level, as well as "church-management small groups" for every place of worship. Yet Ningde required more, including laws that would allow punishment of the underground Catholics and funding for official churches.[39]

In April 1990, Jinping became party secretary of Fuzhou, the provincial capital. A May 1990 *People's Daily* article praised Jinping's attack on cadres who illegally seized land to build private property in Ningde.[40] In September, he published a short article, "The Way of an Official," providing thoughts on how history remembered great figures. Although China had seen many emperors and premiers over the millennia of its history, he wrote, only a handful have been remembered by the common people. But many leaders who were not even officials have been remembered for their contributions. What matters is not someone's position but what they achieve. Those who want to become officials for selfish reasons will face annihilation. In Jinping's mind, one should join the party to help the people, not for personal benefit. "I believe that to be a true official in the Chinese Communist Party is toilsome. I never heard a true leader say that being an official was really comfortable." The basic goal of any official should be at least to leave behind a clean reputation, Jinping asserted.[41]

Jinping continued to demonstrate political ambition. When the Fujian Leadership Science Research Association prepared a special nationwide academic discussion meeting on "cross-century leadership qualities," it asked Jinping to participate. He not only offered financial support but also provided advice on how the meeting should be run, and when the association met, he was selected as the leader of the new Fujian Province Young Leadership Science Subassociation. In remarks published in November 1991, near the final demise of the Soviet Union, Jinping argued that to avoid the collapse of the Chinese Communist Party, his generation must study theoretical matters, act as servants of the people, feel a sense of long-term historic responsibility, and inherit the traditions of the revolutionary generation.[42]

After the Tiananmen crackdown, the party wavered on further economic reforms. But in January 1992, the party boss of Shenzhen, Li Yi, gave Xi Zhongxun some good news. Deng had just visited the province to jumpstart the focus on rapid economic growth—a trip that soon became known as the Southern Tour. At the time, Deng no longer held any formal titles, but his words were a clear threat to Jiang Zemin. While in Shenzhen, Deng flaunted his relationship with the military, even having a picture taken of him with Minister of Defense Liu Huaqing and Vice-Chairman of the Central Military Commission Yang Shangkun. In the spring of 1989, Deng had displayed a blatant disregard for party norms to engineer the crackdown; now, he was doing the same to restart the reforms. Xi told Li Yi to act according to the spirit of Deng's words and raise high the banner of Reform and Opening. Deng's comments, according to Xi, were an "imperial sword" that would allow them to fight for reform without fear.[43]

Yang Shangkun reminded Deng that Xi Zhongxun was living nearby, but Deng declined to see him. Instead, Deng sent his son Pufang to say hello on his behalf.[44] In July, Xi Zhongxun wrote in the foreword to a book on the reforms in Guangdong that the "encouraging power" of Deng's words on the Southern Tour were "difficult to underestimate."[45] Whatever the relationship between Deng and Xi might have been at the time, Xi had reason to be grateful that Deng had helped restart the reform process that Xi cared so much about—especially in his beloved Shenzhen, the physical manifestation of one of his most treasured legacies.

Although the Southern Tour would have been happily received by Xi, the Fourteenth Party Congress held later that year that enshrined Deng's message was not a positive event for the Xi family's ambitions. In July, two Hong Kong media outlets reported that Jinping had scored an impressive vote count in Fujian to be a delegate to the Fourteenth Party Congress and predicted he would soon receive a big promotion to join the Central Committee.[46] But Xi was not even made a candidate member. Rumor spread that Chen Guangyi had ended such a possibility by writing a letter to the leadership arguing that Xi Jinping had demonstrated "a loss of political principle" by asking Xiang Nan to write the introduction to a collection of his speeches.[47] Xiang did indeed write such a foreword, in which he praised Xi Jinping for always making economic growth the absolute top priority and characterized Xi's speeches as "spiritual wealth."[48] Jinping may have also suffered simply because of antipathy against cadre offspring as a group. Bo Xilai and Chen Yuan were also on the ballot to join but not elected, likely because of their unpopular princeling status.[49]

In September 1993, Jinping visited Guanzhong, where his father had served as party leader from 1936 to 1942. He brought a map Zhongxun had drawn of Malanbao, the former site of the local Communist headquarters. He went to the cave where his father had lived at the time, and he spent the night—Zhongxun had wanted Jinping to taste the difficulties he himself had experienced decades earlier.[50] The old days were clearly on Zhongxun's mind. The next month, October, he published an article in *People's Daily* about his old mentor Liu Zhidan on the anniversary of Liu's ninetieth birthday. Xi chose to use the occasion to emphasize the importance of democracy and open-minded leaders. "Why should anyone care about some kind of democracy?" he said some cadres had believed at the time. But Liu, according to Xi, had responded, "Even in primitive societies, everyone knew to select people with ability and talent to be the leaders, let alone people today. First, the villages select the representatives, then the townships select the representatives, and then the members of the government are selected."[51]

On one occasion, Xi Zhongxun exhibited a remarkable sign of respect for Tibetan Buddhism. In the summer of 1994, the Tibetan lama Arjia Rinpoche—who was then head of Qinghai's Kumbum Monastery (he later defected to the West)—and the tenth Panchen Lama's mother visited Xi in Shenzhen. When they arrived at what Arjia Rinpoche described as a "very luxurious" resort, they found Xi to be energetic and strong, even though he did not get out of his wheelchair. When Xi noticed that Arjia Rinpoche was dressed in robes, he became very interested and asked who he was. The rinpoche said that when he was two years old and enthroned as a living buddha, Xi had dispatched a delegation to the ceremony and had even sent a banner with some encouraging words and a clock inscribed with Xi's name. As the group was preparing to leave, Xi put his hands in a prayer position, raised them up to his head, and closed his eyes. "In this life, I am most devoted to only two people: the Dalai Lama and the Panchen Lama," Xi said. Arjia Rinpoche was shocked, interpreting the gesture and these words as a sign of religious faith, done perhaps because Xi understood that his health was deteriorating.[52]

In his later years, Xi met with several figures who had run afoul of Deng. In December 1995, while on a trip to Shenzhen, Hua Guofeng asked to meet with Xi, but Hua's request was denied on the grounds that Xi was ill. Hua persisted, and permission was finally granted.[53] When they met on December 22, Hua asked about Xi's health, but Xi answered dismissively, "How am I sick? It is just that they do not want to let us meet. That is because I keep saying that the special economic zones were suggested by me and approved by Chairman Hua, that they have nothing to do with Xiaoping.... Because I said this openly, they said I was insane." Hua conveyed that he would like to talk with Xi again after a trip to Hainan. But a second conversation never took place—while Hua was in Hainan, a senior official from the National People's Congress was murdered during a botched robbery, and the Central Committee ordered that all top leaders return to Beijing.[54]

Xi also saw Yang Shangkun, whom Deng had unceremoniously dropped from the leadership in 1992. That year, before the Fourteenth Party Congress, both Yang Shangkun and Wan Li had believed that Jiang Zemin would be removed and Yang Shangkun would assume power after Deng's death.[55] But Yang had lost Deng's favor. At the end of a Politburo Standing Committee meeting in September 1992, Yang raised an issue that was not on the agenda. He proposed that his half brother, Yang Baibing—head of the military's General Political Department—join the standing committee at the upcoming party congress. Yang claimed that Deng had said, "When it comes to recommending talented people, you need not deliberately avoid your relatives and friends." Jiang Zemin then asked Wang Ruilin—Deng's secretary who was present for the meeting—whether Deng had actually said this. Wang was silent. Song Ping—who had joined the standing committee after the 1989 crackdown—said he had never heard Deng say such words. Yang pressed, saying the matter could be discussed even if Deng had never said that. Qiao Shi tapped Yang Shangkun on the leg to warn him to stop. Jiang said the matter was not on the agenda and refused to discuss it. As soon as the meeting was over, Jiang and Yang jumped into their cars and raced to see Deng. Jiang won the race, and Yang did not enter Deng's home. Deng, possibly afraid that Yang Shangkun would later say that June 4 had been a mistake, decided to strip Yang—whom he had known since 1932—of all his power.[56] Yang was indeed thoughtful about the crackdown in his later years, even saying, in 1998, that June 4 "was the most serious mistake ever made in the history of the party."[57]

The relationship between Xi Zhongxun and Yang Shangkun was a complicated one. Despite their partnership in Guangdong, Yang had criticized Xi at the January 1987 party-life meeting, and, as secretary general of the Central Military Commission, Yang was implicated in the June 4 incident. Xi was also upset that Yang, not he, had become state president. For a period, Yang did not dare to go see Xi. But later, Yang was firm about wanting a meeting.

When they finally met in February 1996, they hugged three times while their eyes brimmed with tears. After Li Rui heard about the meeting, he wrote in his diary, "Does this mean Yang regrets what he did?"[58]

Xi was less forgiving of Li Peng. In March 1996, Xi met with Li, who was still premier, and a picture of the conversation shows the two men looking generally relaxed.[59] However, a former editor of a Shenzhen newspaper claimed that, once again, Xi had lost his temper. After that, high-ranking officials would sometimes try to avoid spending the night in Shenzhen when they visited—lest they be expected to visit the ailing leader. But despite Xi's reputation for a poor temper, he maintained an earthy humor. In May 1997, that same editor, who had grown up in Shaanxi, visited Xi's home. When the editor departed, Xi pointed with his cane, which he held with a white handkerchief, to the man's posterior and quoted an old Shaanxi aphorism: "When fellow countrymen meet each other, they shoot each other in the butt."[60]

Jinping's status as the son of a prominent revolutionary continued to hurt his prospects. In February 1997, he tried to separate himself from the other princelings:

> First, I want to correct an impression. The cadre offspring are not a single unit or a single model. They all have different experiences, desires, and methods, and they all are affected by different trends. With regard to the cadre offspring, public opinion now can take one of two directions. One is that "a dragon gives birth to a dragon, and a phoenix gives birth to a phoenix." The other is that "they are all dandies and entirely worthless." I think that another old expression says it best: "The dragon birthed nine sons, and each is different." . . . As the son of a high-ranking cadre, I believe that the most important thing is not to rely on my father's credit but instead to rely on my own abilities and not have a sense of superiority over everyone else.[61]

But this attempt at self-defense did not seem to work. The Fifteenth Party Congress in September 1997 was once again a rough one for Jinping, at that time vice–party secretary of Fujian. He did not receive enough votes to enter the Central Committee outright, and instead, he became a candidate member. But even among the candidate members, Jinping's name was the very last on the list, meaning that his share of votes was the smallest. Even worse, Jinping was number 151, suggesting that the top leadership had changed precedent so as to be able to include him because, in previous cases, the number of candidates was always a multiple of ten. Deng Pufang, the son of Deng Xiaoping, came in second to last. This outcome was widely seen to be the result of the unpopularity of the princelings at the time. It was a lesson for Jinping that elections were hard to control and could lead to undesirable outcomes.[62]

Just one month later, the Xi family received another piece of bad news—the death by heart attack of Xi Zhengning, one of Zhongxun's children with Hao Mingzhu. He was only fifty-seven years old. Because the death of Xi Heping during the Cultural Revolution had been so devastating, Qi Xin made the people who worked in the Xi household promise never to tell Zhongxun about his son's death. According to Xi's former secretary Zhang Zhigong, "After a long time during which the old man never saw anything of Zhengning and did not hear any news of him, he gradually had a bad feeling. When he asked about Zhengning's situation, the family and workers used well-intentioned excuses to cover it up. But Secretary Xi was, of course, a revolutionary, and he had experienced all kinds of winds and waves. He then stopped asking about Zhengning."[63]

Xi met Li Rui, apparently for the last time, in March 1998. The formalities were significant—the reception office of Shenzhen City Hall sent a wreath to Xi ahead of the meeting, even without Li making such a request. When Li and his wife arrived, a secretary said Xi was resting and asked that they wait. Qi Xin heard the conversation and rushed downstairs to explain that the secretary was new and did not know who Li was. The two couples spoke for about twenty minutes. Xi was in a good mood, better than the last time they had met, and he seemed happy to tell Li that many people had visited him over the Lunar New Year's holiday. When the topic of recent articles and documentaries came up, Xi complained that "giving Deng Xiaoping credit for everything is bad." They had a picture taken of the two of them, and then Xi walked the Li couple to the door. Xi and Li did not shake hands, however—Li was told Xi's two hands were suffering from an old wound. As Li left, Xi said goodbye very loudly and never stopped waving.[64]

The next month, on their wedding anniversary, Xi called Beijing to speak to Qi Xin. He asked her, "How many years have we been married?" "Fifty-five!" she replied. He responded with flowery words: "I wish you a long life, may your happiness be as deep as the Eastern Sea, and may you live to be as old as Zhongnan Mountain!" Qi emotionally told Xi, "I haven't taken care of you well enough!" Then Xi became upset: "How can you say that? You are loyal to the party and the people, you did much work for the revolution, and you did a lot of work for me, some of which was very important. . . . You must make a record of this conversation and tell the children—make them understand reason." After the phone call, Xi said to Qiaoqiao, "Your mother is an excellent party member."[65]

FIFTY YEARS OF THE PEOPLE'S REPUBLIC

In 1999, two years after the death of Deng Xiaoping, Xi Zhongxun finally returned to the capital for the October 1 National Day celebrations—the People's Republic had reached its fiftieth year. When he arrived in Beijing, Zhengning's son greeted him at the airport. "What about your father?" Xi asked his grandson. A former secretary ran forward to shake his boss's hand and to stop the conversation from continuing.[66] Xi told a group of individuals sent by Jiang Zemin to greet him, "This return to the capital to participate in the fiftieth anniversary celebrations was the result of careful consideration." Xi said he had decided to attend to express support for the "party center with Jiang Zemin as the core." On September 30, on the eve of the holiday, Hu Jintao also paid him a visit. That evening, Jiang toasted Xi at a banquet: "Knowing that Old Xi returned to Beijing and today is participating in this banquet makes us very happy. I already sent Comrade Hu Jintao to see you. I wish you good health!" Xi responded, "Having just returned from overseas, I know that you are busy. I already saw Comrade Jintao. Thank you very much for your attention. I also wish you good health!" When Xi and Jiang clinked their glasses, the people around them applauded.[67]

When Li Zhao, the widow of Hu Yaobang, heard that Xi Zhongxun was present at the banquet, she asked to be taken to him. When Xi saw her, he extended his hands to hold her in a tight embrace, and he began muttering, "Yaobang, Yaobang!" The two spoke little, mostly just looking at each other with tears in their eyes. The scene silenced the room and moved the other old revolutionaries present. "Comrade Zhongxun," Li Zhao said suddenly, "you must take care of yourself!" Xi then raised a glass and toasted her—but they still did not engage in any conversation.[68]

The morning after the dramatic meeting with Li Zhao, Xi Zhongxun watched the annual military parade in Tiananmen Square while sitting on the balcony where Mao had declared the founding of the People's Republic fifty years earlier. One picture from that day shows Xi smiling with Chi

Haotian—the man who had been military chief of staff at the time of the June 4 crackdown.[69] That night, at another banquet, Jiang Zemin again went over to talk with Xi. "I really did not expect that you, as an old man, would have such good health," Jiang told him, holding his hand throughout their conversation. "You participated in all the activities. That's truly remarkable. Tonight is so cold, but you have come here as well, and you are not even wearing a scarf. Look, even I am wearing a scarf." Jiang asked about Qi Xin and promised to send his own wife to visit her. Xi's response was fawning: "You are even more extraordinary; you participated in the events all day and all night. You have the masses in your heart. Look—this grand occasion, this impressive scene—it clearly demonstrates that the people are the nation, and the nation is the people."[70]

Xi invited both Li Zhao and Hao Zhiping, the widow of Luo Ruiqing, to a banquet he was hosting for ordinary people—no officials were invited. After the meal, Hao called her son in America to tell him what Li Zhao had told her: "Do you know why Deng Xiaoping did not allow Xi Zhongxun to return to Beijing? It is precisely because, in 1987, when Yaobang was persecuted, Xi Zhongxun did not agree. He had said that Yaobang was a good person. With one word, he offended Deng Xiaoping, so he was not allowed to live in Beijing. He could only live in Guangzhou and Shenzhen."[71]

After the trip to Beijing, Xi continued to express public support for Jiang. On December 31, 1999, Xi published New Year's greetings in a local Shenzhen newspaper, in which he expressed confidence that the entire party, military, and nation would "closely unite around the Central Committee with Comrade Jiang Zemin as the core."[72] In February 2000, while on a trip to Shenzhen, Jiang visited Xi and told him, "You raised good children."[73]

Although Xi's trip to Beijing at the twilight of his life suggests a rapprochement with the party, Xi never achieved one of his greatest desires—the rehabilitation of Gao Gang. In January 2000, Li Liqun, Gao's widow, called Li Rui and told him that she had seen Xi in Shenzhen to discuss the matter of rehabilitating Gao. "Zhongxun was very agitated," she said, recounting that he had said that even Chen Duxiu, one of the founders of the party, had been rehabilitated even though he had once been labeled a Trotskyite.[74]

As Xi Zhongxun aged, Chinese historians were slowly beginning to reveal secrets about sensitive moments in the party's past. One of the most important venues for these disclosures was *Yanhuang chunqiu*, a monthly journal that celebrated its tenth anniversary in 2001. Du Daozheng, the publisher, decided to ask Xi to write an inscription for the occasion. Before going to see Xi, the leaders of *Yanhuang chunqiu* were unsure what words of commemoration would be most appropriate. When they arrived at Xi's home, he met them at the door and told them that the journal was "pretty good." Then he turned around with his hands behind his back and walked back inside. The visitors decided that Xi's words would be perfect for the inscription.[75] Xi was one of dozens of senior figures who, over the years, had written such inscriptions for the journal, but he was the most prominent among them, and only his inscription was included in an article published in the journal that described the commemorative ceremony.[76]

Xi never wrote a historical account of his life as a party member. According to one of his daughters, the reasons were both that he was a person who "never lifted up his tail," meaning he was too modest, and that he had suffered so much due to the lack of freedom of speech in China.[77] In 2001, when discussing the pending publication of his *Selected Works*, he remarked, "If you want to describe my life, just a few words can summarize it: I did justice for the party, did justice for the people, and did justice for myself; I did not make 'leftist' mistakes, I did not persecute people. My accomplishments have been ordinary. I feel no guilt."[78] He also asked a friend of the family to write down the phrase "Let things be what they may" and treat it as a maxim; Xi himself used a fan with the four characters for this expression etched on it.[79]

In late 2001, cancer was discovered in Xi's body. In January of the following year, scans showed cancer in the left kidney. During the 2002 Lunar New Year's season, Wan Li went to visit Xi in Guangdong. Wan had spent his last years living in fear, remarking, when he retired, that "finally, I have landed peacefully." When Wan arrived at Xi's home, they hugged each other. Wan said that he had come to see an "old partner," but Xi corrected him. "What old partner?" he said. "We are old comrades in arms!" In April, Xi returned to Beijing, where he died on May 24. When Bo Yibo learned of Xi's death, he sent a secretary with a message to Xi's family, recalling the words Mao had used with him in the early 1950s: "I was shocked to learn that the pure-blue flame in the stove unfortunately has died." On May 30, Xi's body was cremated at Baobaoshan Cemetery. In 2005, on the third anniversary of his death, his ashes were buried in Fuping.[80] After his death, Qi Xin revealed a sixteen-character aphorism that Xi had written for himself, which was later carved into his memorial in Fuping:

A life of fighting
A life of happiness
Every day, struggle
Every day, happy.[81]

Less than two months after Xi Zhongxun had died, a journalist from Reuters asked Xi Jinping, then governor of Fujian, whether he was a member of China's new generation who should be watched as a future leader. Jinping's "eyes went wide," the journalist wrote. "He flushed. He nearly spilt his drink. Then he quickly regained his composure." "I nearly spilt water all down my shirt," Xi said. "Are you trying to give me a fright?"[82] Yet by October, Xi was promoted to be acting governor of the economic powerhouse of Zhejiang, and one month after that, he became party secretary of the province. In the following year, he finally joined the Central Committee as a full member. Zhongxun did not live to see his son's career take off.

30
FATHERS AND SONS

In December 2002, less than one month after he became the top party leader in Zhejiang Province, Xi Jinping treated his father's old friend Li Rui to breakfast at an extremely expensive restaurant intended to host ministerial officials. They discussed Zhongxun's behavior when Hu Yaobang was removed from power as well as how Li had left Hu's wake to visit Zhongxun at the Great Hall of the People. "Now your position is different," Li told Xi Jinping at the end of their meeting. "You can raise a few ideas with the higher-ups." Xi responded cautiously. "How can I compare to you?" Xi said. "You know how to walk a fine line. I don't dare." This was to be the last meeting between Li Rui and Xi Jinping. Li would later say, "Of course, at the time, I did not look down on him because he was the son of Zhongxun."[1]

In 2009, Hu Dehua, the youngest of Hu Yaobang's sons, met with Jinping for an hour when Jinping went to visit Hu's widow for the Lunar New Year. Hu Dehua later described his conversation with Xi, who was the heir apparent by then: "I spoke a lot. I said that now the issue is not whether to reform or not. It is that without reform everything will be over. I said that reform does not need to wait until you are in charge. . . . When my father and your father embarked on reform, your father was in Guangdong, and my father was vice president of the party school. The party school had no status at all in the past, and he was only third vice president, but he was still able to cause big waves." Xi said little in response. When pressed, he responded noncommittally, "I am listening to you sing."[2]

That was not the last meeting between a member of the Hu family and Xi.

In 2012, Hu Yaobang's older son Deping, a man whom Xi had once referred to as "big brother," also met with Jinping to encourage a reformist path.[3] Jinping listened patiently, and Hu Deping left the meeting feeling confident that Jinping would steer the party in a better direction.[4] Xi told Hu that the problems China had accumulated were unprecedented, and it was necessary to achieve progress while remaining steady. Although Xi promised to deliver on political reform, he expressed opposition to radical change.[5]

After Xi succeeded Hu Jintao as the country's top leader, proreform party elders and intellectuals were not sure what to make of him at first. In November, Zhao Ziyang's former secretary Bao Tong told the Hong Kong newspaper *Apple Daily* that he expected Jinping could "surpass his father" as a leader. "If he does poorly, he will disappoint and not do justice to his father," Bao said, "but I believe he will do better than his father."[6] On February 6, 2013, the proreform journal *Yanhuang chunqiu* held a meeting during which Feng Jian, a former high-ranking official at the New China News Agency, expressed optimism about Jinping because of who his father was: "He cannot completely give up his father's legacy." But He Fang, a party elder who for decades had worked on foreign policy, interrupted. "Political genes cannot be inherited," he warned.[7]

The proreform elites returned to the question of Xi Jinping on February 27 at a Lunar New Year's celebration, again held by *Yanhuang chunqiu*. Du Daozheng, the director of the journal, pointed out that Jinping had already made a trip to Shenzhen to signify support for the reforms, and, on the anniversary of the 1982 constitution, he had given a major speech praising rule of law. Du was worried, however, by comments Jinping had made for internal consumption that emphasized the loss of control over ideology and the military that had led to the collapse of the Soviet Union. "My meaning is not to be pessimistic," Du said, "but currently one also cannot feel optimistic." Another attendee was Ma Xiaoli, daughter of Ma Wenrui—a northwesterner who, because of his ties to Zhongxun, had also been persecuted during the Mao era. Ma drew upon her understanding of the princelings to warn the participants about what might be coming. She said that "80 or 90 percent of the second Red generation" was leftist. "They all have genes they inherited from their parents, beginning from Old Mao; it is all the same. . . . I say Chairman Mao inherently spoiled us as a group: we're aggressive; what he taught is to be bellicose roosters all the time." Ma believed that the Hu family, given its historic relationship to the Xi family, had a special obligation to push matters in the right direction.[8] In his own speech, Hu Dehua made a cutting remark about Xi Jinping's recent comments that neither the thirty years before or the thirty years after the beginning of Reform and Opening should be rejected. Hu wondered aloud whether such a position also meant that "what Chairman Mao said about General Secretary Xi's father, Zhongxun, 'Using a novel to oppose the party is a great invention,' also cannot be rejected."[9]

Li Rui did not quickly change his mind about Xi Jinping. Despite more and more evidence that Xi would pursue an authoritarian line, Li repeatedly told his daughter that "Xi Jinping is still the son of Xi Zhongxun." In October 2014, Li claimed that nefarious individuals had cut important segments of a speech Xi had given on the constitution the previous year when it was published by the New China News Agency and *People's Daily*: "Some people say this is a serious political incident. I also believe this." When asked explicitly if he was optimistic about Jinping's leadership, Li said he had "big hopes," referring specifically to Jinping's war on corruption, the dismantling of the "reform-by-labor" camps, and the new policies against perks for party members. Li's feelings toward Xi Jinping were based on his attitude toward Xi Zhongxun: "Xi Zhongxun and I were intimate friends. We got along very well. Xi Jinping recently said, 'In the struggle against corruption, the life and reputation of one individual do not matter.' That is enough to see in him his father's courage, strength of character, and sense of responsibility."[10]

In 2016, *Yanhuang chunqiu*, which had been praised by Xi Zhongxun himself, was finally shut down by the authorities under Xi Jinping's watch. Furious because of this turn of events, Li Rui shared a clever play on words with the journal's director, Du Daozheng: "Maobing bugai, ji'e chengxi." The expression can be interpreted both as "If a fault is not corrected, it will become a bad habit" or as "If the disease of Mao is not changed, the evil will accumulate and turn into Xi." Li was asserting that because the legacy of the Maoist era had never truly been overturned, it was now manifesting itself in Xi's behavior.[11] In October 2017, when Xi was reappointed general secretary, Li noted in his diary that the front pages of party newspapers were covered with big headshots of Xi Jinping. "Not even in the Mao era did it ever reach this level," he wrote.[12]

In April 2018, as he lay on his death bed, Li Rui asked his daughter Nanyang how the outside world was reacting to the recent decision to amend the constitution to allow Xi Jinping to stay in power potentially for life. Two days later,

Hu Dehua came to visit him. Li was devastated by the turn Chinese politics had taken: "The appearance of Xi Jinping is your responsibility. You need to figure out who he is. Is it a lack of education? Mao's problem was precisely that he was uneducated; he scored an F in math. Xi's education is also very low. I am very sad. His father was so good. It is so painful that he had such a son."[13]

THE MYSTERY OF XI JINPING

So what, then, were the lessons of Xi Zhongxun's life for his son Jinping? That, of course, raises another question: What are the lessons contained in this biography? The evidence presented here touches upon perhaps the most perennial question of scholarly research into Communist regimes: the question of "possibility-hood."[14] Did the life of Xi Zhongxun, especially his actions during the 1980s, suggest that, under different circumstances, the party might have taken a more "humane," liberal path? Or did the characteristics inherent in the party, as well as Xi's own personal limitations, demonstrate that, as the Russian rock 'n' roll musician Boris Grebenshchikov once put it in a song, "there is no road, and there never was one"?

The question of possibility-hood is inherently dramatic regardless of the answer. Storytelling certainly has its place in history. It can vivify past voices and convey the emotional atmosphere experienced by the participants.[15] Yet, with no disrespect to Li Jiantong's purposes in writing *Liu Zhidan*, "lives are not novels," as Arlette Farge writes.[16] Biographies should not ignore "the disjunctures and anomalies of human experiences, of radically different contexts . . . in service to a literary imperative to give meaning and recognizable shape to the life as a whole," in the words of Ronald Suny.[17] Poetics, partisanship, and presentism are not a free pass to deny the concrete methodological challenges inherent in historical counterfactuals.[18] A serious investigation into historical moments can give us a sense of how politics works and teach us how to structure questions. But the past cannot give us a precise constellation of the variables that deterministically explain an outcome, nor can it help us predict the future.[19]

While books that overemphasize contingency or continuity might make for a good read, Xi's life is a powerful statement about the misleading nature of grand narratives.[20] It shows that power is tricky, slippery, and contingent even for an organizational weapon like the party. Each of the chapters in this book is about a different topic, but they are interconnected in a way that makes counterfactuals about the regime's broader trajectory challenging. All the "characters" in this book, not only Xi but also the people whom he despised, were full of contradictions. They were both victims and perpetrators. While Western historians and official party histories have both long seen the party's past as a constant struggle between "good people" and "bad people," such approaches simply do not do justice to the extraordinary subtleties of personal interactions in an organization like the Chinese Communist Party. Despite organizational discipline, people remained complicated. They could seem "rightist" in one situation and "leftist" in another. They could also change their minds. And even if Hu Yaobang, Zhao Ziyang, or Xi Zhongxun had become the top leader, they too, if they survived, might have changed. Xi himself whispered privately that power corrupted.

Moreover, despite the findings provided in this book, many aspects of Xi's life remain a mystery. This point is not an attempt to shy away from drawing conclusions but a reflection of the peculiarities of party life in China. When Xi met with potential challengers to party rule, he often charmed them. Was he acting sincerely or instrumentally or a bit of both? While this is an academic question for historians, it was an existential puzzle for United Front targets. Even within the party, discipline often made it impossible to discern what Xi, who spent years doing underground work, really thought. He existed in an inherently opaque system in which even people at the top often had a very poor idea of what was transpiring, and he himself often had extremely mixed feelings about events. Because competing versions of the past hold a special charge for party members, writing party history faces special challenges. As Michel-Rolph Trouillot notes, the "play of power in the production of alternative narratives" extends even to the evidence upon which histories are written.[21] In many cases, the vagaries of evidence and intention simply cannot bear the weight of the big questions we would most like to ask.

It is precisely these ambiguities that make the question of what lessons Jinping learned from his father so meaningful. Ironically, guessing what Jinping "really thinks" of his father is difficult in part because he grew up in the Xi household—a place where a person would have learned the need for caution and reticence at a young age. As the Chinese historian Gao Wenqian notes, "Xi Jinping was only nine years old when his father fell [four years before the Cultural Revolution], so the tough environment directly influenced his personality. He is therefore good at forbearance and concealing his intentions, not revealing anything."[22] In a rare moment of candor, Jinping once even said, "My father entrusted me with two things: don't persecute people and tell the truth. The first is possible, while the second is not."[23] Certainly, the Zhongxun-Jinping relationship is a powerful context for understanding the son, yet, at the same time, Jinping, like his father, is the product of a multiplicity of different motives, influences, and contexts.

The possibility of multiple meanings that could be derived from Zhongxun's life is also evidenced by the very different paths taken by his children. Xi Heping committed suicide during the Cultural Revolution. Before his death in 1998, Xi Zhengning, as minister of justice in Hainan Province, fought to strengthen rule of law there—the same task that his father pursued on a national level during his final years in Beijing. In two speeches Zhengning gave on the subject, in 1994 and 1995, the word "party" appeared only once. Instead, he emphasized the importance of learning from Western legal systems. Lawyers should never be punished, he said, for exercising their right to independently practice the law.[24]

Xi Qianping became a journalist at *International Business Daily*, where one journalist who knew both her and her father later wrote that she "dressed simply, was low-key, and had the style of the Xi family. She could not be more different from the show-off style and arrogance of some children of high-ranking officials."[25] In October 2011, she attended an event marking the thirtieth anniversary of the defeat of the Gang of Four that had been organized by *Yanhuang chunqiu*, the history journal.[26] When she attended another *Yanhuang chunqiu* event in March 2014 celebrating the Lunar New Year, those who saw her thought she looked like "a rustic old revolutionary from a base area."[27]

Except for Jinping, Xi Zhongxun's other children, who were born to Qi Xin and grew up after the revolution, have all received extensive attention because of their wealth. In 1990, Xi's daughter Qiaoqiao quit her job in Beijing as vice–division commander in the People's Armed Police to help take care of Xi.[28] As early as 1991, one year after she moved to Shenzhen with her father, she purchased an apartment in Hong Kong that cost $387,000. In 1996, she married the Yunnan businessman Deng Jiagui. Just a few years later, in 1997, she and her husband Deng had an investment of 15.3 million yuan in a company.[29]

In an interview, Qiaoqiao claimed that after her father's death in 2002, Qi Xin wanted to write a letter to the leadership requesting that Qiaoqiao, by then already fifty-four years old, be allowed to return to her old job in

Beijing. Qiaoqiao rejected that option, she claimed, and instead decided to start all over again by entering the world of business. She completed Tsinghua University's executive master's program in business administration in 2006.[30] That same year, in an interview with *Successful Marketing*, Qiaoqiao described her approach to real estate as "looking at things from the perspective of a housewife." She asserted that "the most important thing is that you must be trustworthy! Tricking other people means tricking yourself." Unlike other real estate companies, she would not purchase advertisements. While Mao had described her father as "putting the party's interests first," in this interview, Qiaoqiao stated that it was necessary to "always proceed from the interests of the customer."[31] In 2008, Deng Jiagui spent $71 million to buy a stake in Jiangxi Rare Earth.[32] In 2009, for unclear reasons, Qiaoqiao and Deng were given an early opportunity to buy a $28.6 million stake in Wanda, the giant shopping-center conglomerate owned by oligarch Wang Jianlin, before the company went public.[33]

In 1977, Yuanping entered the Luoyang Foreign Language Academy of the People's Liberation Army. After he graduated, he worked in the military and the government, including in the area of foreign trade, although the details remain unclear.[34] An American embassy contact claimed that, by the 1980s, Yuanping "had become both obese and very wealthy." He sported "expensive jewelry and designer clothing," moving to Hong Kong when it was still under British rule.[35] In October 2000, a man who had previously served as a bodyguard for Ye Jianying, Zhu De, and Hu Yaobang but then later became a businessman told Li Rui that he had run into Yuanping at a hotel and not only paid the 8,000-yuan check but also gave Yuanping all the 10,000-yuan bills he had on hand. This remarkable display of generosity did not impress Qi Xin, who allegedly made a sneering remark: "Get rid of the beggar." He decided to give up on the Xi family.[36]

SELF-REVOLUTION

On Zhongxun's eighty-eighth birthday in October 2001, Jinping, who was too busy to visit, wrote his father a congratulatory letter that listed his father's five characteristics he wanted to emulate. First, Jinping wanted to study how his father treated people: "You once instructed me that, in your entire life, you never persecuted people, and you always maintained the truth while not speaking any falsehoods." Second, Jinping admired how his father "handled affairs." He wrote, "Compared to father, I am too mediocre, and I am blushed with shame." He praised his father for "never claiming credit, never publicizing himself." In Jinping's mind, this was the "style of people who achieved great works." Third, Xi wrote of his father's persevering pursuit of ideals: "No matter whether it was the era of the White Terror [meaning the Nationalists] or the period of extreme leftism, no matter whether you were libeled or you were in a difficult situation, in your heart, you continuously had a bright lantern that always lit the correct path forward. When people yelled at us for being bastards, I always stubbornly believed that my father was a great hero, that he was a father most worthy of feeling proud of." Fourth, Jinping spoke of his wish to emulate his father's innocence and trustfulness: "You are the son of a peasant, you warmly love the Chinese people, warmly love your revolutionary comrades, warmly love the elders in the countryside, and warmly love your mother, wife, and children." The last quality was thriftiness: "Everyone knows about the strictness in our upbringing." Jinping concluded, "With a heart of reverence, from now on in my work, affairs, and life, I will do my utmost to respectfully study father." He signed the letter "Son. Jinping. Kowtow."[37]

These remarks put some of Jinping's behavior in context. First, and perhaps most obviously, is his dedication to the party. While some may wonder why Jinping would remain so devoted to an organization that severely persecuted his own father, perhaps the better question is, How could Jinping betray the party for which his father sacrificed so much? With such a strong belief in the need for unity in the face of adversity, not stepping forward would be treachery. This sensibility is commonly shared by children of revolutionaries. Many of those from the "second Red generation" remained loyal not only to the party but even to the person who had hurt their families the most: Mao Zedong. "Logically speaking, I should not like Mao Zedong," said Bo Xilai, the son of Bo Yibo. "Because of the Cultural Revolution, my father was persecuted for twelve years, and I also spent time imprisoned." However, Bo continued, "after thinking about it a lot, China can only walk the path of Mao Zedong." His mother was persecuted to death during the Cultural Revolution.[38]

For the princelings, this common loyalty to the party often even overrides the grudges and antagonisms of their parents' generation. Some of them subscribe to the view that everyone persecuted everyone else, so it makes little sense to hold a grudge.[39] Zhu Jiamu not only served as Chen

Yun's secretary in the 1980s but also is the son of Zhu Lizhi, the man who helped lead the 1935 persecution of Xi Zhongxun. Yet Zhu would later continuously ply Xi Jinping with "leftist" ideas, and Jinping's famous declaration that neither of the "thirty years"—meaning both the Mao era and the reform era—should be rejected originally had been Zhu's idea.[40] In the 1980s, when Xi Zhongxun and Chen Yun were still in power, but often on different political sides, Jinping regularly visited Chen Yuan, Chen Yun's son.[41] Xi Zhongxun's children often visited the Bo household as well, where Bo Yibo (falsely) told Xi's daughters, who called him Uncle Bo, that he "was always on very good terms with Comrade Zhongxun."[42]

Not explicitly rejecting the party is one thing, but what explains the extraordinary drive and sense of mission Jinping has demonstrated since a very young age? After Zhongxun's fall in 1962, the emotional pressure on a child who was denied participation in the grand adventure of revolution because of family ties must have been intense. As a young man in the late 1980s and early 1990s, Jinping witnessed his father wronged once again. Without drifting too far into psychology, the answer to how someone would react to such a situation might be found in party history. When Xi Zhongxun's great mentor Liu Zhidan found himself under suspicion for being a "rightist," his answer was simple: he would take even greater risks and sacrifice even more to prove his worth—a choice that eventually would cost him his life.

But Liu Zhidan's parents were not revolutionaries. For his entire life, Jinping was loyal to two groups that demanded absolute obedience—the party and the family—and he has often publicly reflected upon the linkages between the two. In his mind, "the family is the basic cell of society; it is the first school of life." For Jinping, "history and reality tell us that the future and the fate of the family are intrinsically tied to the future and the fate of the nation and the people." The family should thus "cultivate and practice socialist core values."[43] The party and the father, often both "unfairly" disciplinarian and strict, might, perhaps counterintuitively, together have inspired a particularly potent form of zeal.

Jinping's sense of destiny and obligation appear to extend through his father to countless generations of Chinese before him. He has regularly referred to the duty he feels as the guarantor of Chinese civilization. "Whoever throws away those things left behind by our ancestors," he once told Taiwanese president Ma Ying-jeou, "is a traitor!"[44] Jinping's nationalism was especially clear when he told Japanese prime minster Shinzo Abe, "If

I were born in the United States, I would not join the Communist Party of the United States. I would join the Democratic Party or Republican Party." Abe understood Jinping's meaning to be that "a party that cannot exercise political influence is meaningless." "It can be seen that he joined the party not for ideological beliefs but for the purpose of seizing political power," Abe concluded. "He's a strong realist."[45]

In an internal speech Jinping delivered to an enlarged session of the Central Military Commission in December 2012, he said, "An old leader once said to me that we comrades who are governing must always remember three things: five thousand years of excellent culture must not be lost, the political system established by the old generation must not be damaged, and the territory left by the ancestors must not shrink." Those three tasks, however, faced a set of interrelated existential crises, Jinping warned. Western countries were using strategic pressure and ideological infiltration to prevent the rise of socialist China—and these attempts would only become more brazen as China grew more powerful. It was necessary to strengthen economic and technological ties with the West to facilitate China's rise, Jinping argued, but Beijing should have no illusions about enemies that want to destroy the nation. "Taiwanese-independence" forces have not given up. The "Dalai Lama clique" is strengthening its "splittist" activities. "East Turkestan ethnic-splittist forces" are plotting terrorist incidents. The "democracy movement" and Falungong want to stage "massive political incidents," and some organizations want to use the Rights Protection movement to cause trouble.[46]

These remarks, made soon after he became China's new leader, reveal a dark vision of the nature of politics and a sense of existential crisis. Years earlier, he had explicitly tied this Hobbesian view of the world to his family's story:

> With regard to my career in politics, many people connect this to my family. To be honest, I can't say there is no connection. But the connection is definitely not what people think. For people who rarely encounter power and who are distant from it, they always see these things as very mysterious and fresh. But what I saw was more than the surface of things. I didn't just see power, flowers, glory, and applause. I also saw the cowsheds [where people were confined during the Cultural Revolution] and the fickleness of the world. I have a deeper understanding of politics.[47]

Chinese scholar Xu Youyu writes that Jinping's generation learned that "in order to receive benefits, it is necessary to have power. The desire for power among this generation, the sensitivity to how power is divided, is definitely beyond that of others."[48]

Could Jinping's concentration of power to combat these threats be an explicit rejection of his father's views on the dangers of autocracy? Perhaps, but Jinping's approach could also be seen as a reaction to the leadership pathologies that Zhongxun understood so vividly. Given Zhongxun's relationships with former leading deputies, such as Gao Gang, Zhou Enlai, and Hu Yaobang, Jinping knows that history intimately. In the Mao and Deng eras, the so-called two-line system created a recipe for misunderstandings and suspicions—a problem further compounded by the fraught politics of succession and course correction. By centralizing both authority and decision-making, as well as temporarily putting a halt to succession, Jinping may be trying to solve some of the problems the associates of his father faced. Jinping's tenure is arguably now more institutionalized than Deng's—Politburo Standing Committee meetings are held regularly, and Jinping has, apparently, put a decisive end to the chaotic "old-person politics" of the Deng era.

Yet the travails of Jinping's own deputies suggest he has not fully resolved the problems at the heart of the Leninist system, and he might have created new ones that remain poorly understood. The old challenges may reappear with new intensity if an aging Jinping is inevitably forced to grant more authority to his deputies. And just like Mao and Deng before him, sooner or later, Jinping will need to think seriously about who will replace him.

In terms of ideology, has Jinping made a deliberate "left turn" away from what his father represented? Certainly, Jinping saw how dangerous it was for his father and other patrons to become associated with a particular ideological tendency. He also witnessed the demise of Zhongxun's reformist agenda of the 1980s. But it is also difficult to guess whether Jinping sees himself as more "left" or more "right" than his father because those terms have always been arbitrary. In the 1980s, when Zhongxun was a prominent leader, the party had concluded that the Cultural Revolution overemphasized "class struggle," but there was no consensus about how far it should move away from this preoccupation with vigilance. Jinping and his associates have similarly concluded that the Cultural Revolution went too far, yet they also believe that, later, the party began to not care about "struggle" enough.[49]

Just how far this course correction will go remains unclear. For any leader of a Leninist regime, getting the level of "struggle" right is like catching lightning in a bottle. Who is a friend, who is an enemy, and who can be won over has always been shifting for Chinese leaders. Within this vague spectrum of "too much" or "not enough" struggle, Jinping may not believe his purge of corrupt party members and persecution of dissidents are entirely antithetical to Zhongxun's own values: a distaste for materialism, skepticism of Western values, an obsession with unity, and a terrible fear of chaos. Jinping may also believe that while earlier campaigns were wrong because they targeted innocent people like his father, he is instead attacking people who deserve it. Many of Jinping's apparently "leftist" statements about ideology and regime security sit comfortably with Zhongxun's earlier pronouncements that Reform and Opening would be impossible without continuing to enforce the conservative Four Cardinal Principles. Guessing about whether Jinping cares more about "ideology/security" or "development" is a distraction from the basic point that the party has always cared about both, even though the pursuit of two such goals simultaneously inevitably creates tensions.

In a way, by trying to avoid the errors of both the Maoist and Dengist periods with a sort of middle path, the contradiction is even more obvious now. Despite claims that he is rejecting the era of Reform and Opening, Jinping has repeatedly used extraordinarily strong language to affirm that the Third Plenum of 1978 was fundamentally correct and to emphasize that China will continue to move in that direction.[50] He has also regularly spoken of his personal distaste for dogmatism and leftism, even claiming that he joined the party to prevent another Cultural Revolution.[51] As leader, Xi has twice visited Deng's statue in Shenzhen—once as early as December 2012 and then again in October 2020.

At the same time, Jinping has accentuated the conservative principles that the party never abandoned. Zhu Jiamu, the theoretician who has apparently helped shape Xi's thinking about history, has stressed "leftist" continuities from Mao to Xi *through* Deng, noting that Deng himself also warned that "bourgeois liberalization" existed both in society and in the party—a very similar motivation, Zhu argues, for why Mao launched the Cultural Revolution.[52] Jinping's legitimation narrative is that he is achieving what previous leaders wanted as well, not that he is rejecting their failed agenda. Hu Jintao—who as Jinping's predecessor had called upon the party to study the Cuban and North Korean approaches to ideology—has emotionally praised

Jinping for doing what he could not.[53] As the economy slows and relations with the West deteriorate, balancing "right" and "left" may become increasingly difficult.

Importantly, Jinping's common musings on the relationship between legacy and innovation suggest that he does not find new approaches to be a rejection of the past. His first article ever published in *People's Daily* argued that older cadres should be respected but that the younger generation should still think creatively.[54] In January 2022, he wrote, "We must seek truth from facts when analyzing change and continuity, keep pace with the times when examining our theories, persist in what must be persisted and adjust what must be adjusted, and innovate what must be innovated. . . . There is no doubt that we must adhere to the basic principles, tenets, and viewpoints of party theory, but, at the same time, the specific theoretical theses during a certain period cannot remain unchanged." He continued, "If for everything it is necessary to look one hundred or one dozen years in the past to see what people said and not go one step farther, then how can there be progress?! That is not true Marxism!"[55] Therefore, instead of seeing his forebears as wrong, he may see party history as a long process of trial, error, and adaptation to suit changing needs.

Whether Jinping really means what he says about party history is an open question, however. He has good reason to stress continuities even if he is breaking with previous practice. One of the most obvious lessons of Zhongxun's life is the explosively dangerous and destabilizing nature of debates on party history. If anyone understands the benefits of caution when it comes to competing versions of the past, it is Xi Jinping. At the same time, for him, history is not just something that should be ignored or avoided. In a very real way, he sees history as a battlefield. One of the reasons the old guard in Beijing was so worried by Jinping's comments in Shenzhen in 2012 was his assertion that the Soviet Union collapsed in part because the Communist Party of the Soviet Union lost control over the narrative of its own past.

The study of history, in Xi's mind, can save the revolution by preventing the party from becoming a bureaucratic, self-interested organization divorced from the people. In February 2021, Jinping launched a new party-history-study campaign, and, in his speech at a rally marking its beginning, he described the party's own history as the "best nutrient." "Revisiting this great history can vividly educate the party's original mission, nature, purpose, ideals, and beliefs," he said, "and we must always bear in mind the glorious history and inherit the Red genes." Study of the past, Xi promised, will inculcate a "revolutionary spirit" in a party full of weak individuals seeking their own personal benefit.[56]

In October 2021, Xi went even further in his use of the past by introducing a new resolution on party history. Eighty years earlier, Mao, too, had wanted a new version of party history to affirm his leadership and permanently tarnish his opponents. That agenda, which tied Mao's experiences in Jiangxi to those of Xi and the other northwesterners, culminated in the first party-history resolution in 1945. The second party-history resolution, passed in 1981, marked the rise of Deng Xiaoping. Xi Jinping's own history resolution, the party's third, is explicitly intended to enhance "our confidence in the path, theory, system, and culture of socialism with Chinese characteristics."[57] But the third resolution served another goal as well: Xi was legitimizing his ambitious political agenda. One year later, at the Twentieth Party Congress in October 2022, Xi began a historic third term as the top Chinese leader.

That congress was a moment of triumph and tribulation. Beijing's partners in Moscow were losing on the battlefield in Ukraine, and relations with the United States had severely deteriorated. Jinping's response to the COVID-19 pandemic that had spread globally from Wuhan—taking extreme measures to ensure virtually zero cases—debilitated the economy and risked social unrest. Young people increasingly spoke of the attraction of *tangping* ("lying flat" in the face of societal pressures) and *runxue* ("run-ology," the art of moving overseas). In the midst of these challenges, Xi Jinping's first trip after the Twentieth Party Congress in 2022 was to Shaanxi—the province of his father's birth and early revolutionary years, the Yan'an base area, and Jinping's place of exile during the Cultural Revolution. Jinping's sense of the grand sweep of history and his family's role in it was palpable. While visiting historic sites in Yan'an, he said,

> I lived and worked in the Yan'an region for seven years, and my parents' generation came out from here too, so I am very familiar with it. When I was a sent-down youth in Northern Shaanxi, every time I passed by Yan'an, I would visit the site of the Seventh Party Congress, Yangjialing, Zaoyuan, Fenghuang Mountain, and other revolutionary sites. After I went to work in the party center, I came to Yan'an three times for investigation and research.

546   CHAPTER 30

This time, I am here with comrades from the Politburo Standing Committee to declare that the new leadership collective will inherit and carry forward the fine revolutionary tradition and style of the party that was formed during the Yan'an period and will carry forward the Yan'an spirit.[58]

Jinping—who, like his father, faced the choice of dedication or desperation in the poor but storied land of Shaanxi as a lonely and frightened teenager—was drawing upon a version of the party and his family's past to tell a country of 1.5 billion people why, in his mind, they should recommit to lives of struggle and sacrifice. No stranger to the extraordinary emotional, organizational, and coercive power of the party, Jinping dreams of no less than permanently breaking the wheel of dynastic succession by integrating traditional Chinese culture with continuous self-revolution.[59] Left out of this narrative is a full account of the terrible costliness in human suffering that has come along with the revolutionary project—a Faustian bargain seen so clearly in the life of the man Xi Zhongxun.

Acknowledgments

As I finished writing the last pages of this book, my thoughts turned to Li Jiantong, the author of *Liu Zhidan*. By writing about the Northwest, she herself was dragged into party history—and faced the consequences. *Liu Zhidan* had a specific political agenda, while *The Party's Interests Come First* is motivated by a belief in the inherent value of shining as much light into the darkness of the past as possible and the need to understand the nature of authoritarian politics. Its purpose is not competition with Xi Jinping's use of history as moral education. Nevertheless, this book will likely not be welcomed in the People's Republic of China at the time of its publication. It is a somewhat ironic outcome. Xi Jinping once said that his devotion to the legacy of the revolution was the result of undergoing a period of doubt when seeing the past at its worst. If the evidence shared in this book helps explain his own choices, why would the party doubt that others would draw different conclusions about his family's "forging"?

Given these circumstances, I have decided not to include specific names in the acknowledgments of this book. Including some individuals but not others would be unfair. I make this decision regretfully. One good definition of research is the asking of friends for help, and my book would have been impossible without such assistance. Six people in particular made this project possible. You know who you are. Thank you.

Any book on history is only the latest draft, and that is especially true for books about the Chinese Communist Party—one of the most difficult research targets in the world. I have done my best to do justice to the lives of the women and men in this book. Inevitably, in many places, I will have failed. I hope that the research presented in this book is not the end of the conversation about the meaning of Xi Zhongxun's life but the beginning, and I look forward to learning what I got wrong from anyone who chooses to engage with me.

I am grateful to the following for their institutional support and other assistance: the Hoover History Lab at Stanford University, the Lieberthal-Rogel Center for Chinese Studies at the University of Michigan, the History and Public Policy Program and the Asia Program at the Woodrow Wilson International Center for Scholars, the China in the World Program at Australian National University, the Council on Foreign Relations, the China and the World Program (Princeton and Harvard), the Harvard Fung Library, the Princeton East Asian Library, and especially the School of International Service at American University. And of course, I thank my mother and father, who always put my interests first.

Abbreviations

Archives and Libraries

AHT	Academia Historica, Taipei
AP RF	Archive of the President of the Russian Federation
AVP RF	Archive of the Foreign Policy of the Russian Federation
CREST	Central Intelligence Agency Records Search Tool
DML	David M. Lampton personal archives
DNSA	Digital National Security Archive
FCFL	Fairbank Collection, Fung Library, Harvard University
FNACP	French National Archives of the Communist Party
HIA	Hoover Institution Archives
ISA	Iowa State Archives
JCL	Jimmy Carter Presidential Library
MHS	Minnesota Historical Society
NAA	National Archives of Australia
NCUSCR	National Committee on US-China Relations
PLUSD	WikiLeaks Public Library of US Diplomacy
PRC FMA	People's Republic of China Foreign Ministry Archive
RAC	Rockefeller Archive Center
RGANI	Russian State Archive of Contemporary History
SAPMO-BA	Foundation Archives of the Political Parties and Mass Organizations of the German Democratic Republic in the Federal Archives
TNA	The National Archives of the UK
TsDAHOU	Central State Archives of Public Organizations and Ukrainica
UWML	University of Wisconsin Milwaukee Libraries
WCDA	Wilson Center Digital Archive
WFM	Walter F. Mondale Papers

Publications

CCTP	*Comprehensive Compilation of Tabloids in the Provinces*, vol. 21 of *NCRGP*
CCTV	China Central Television

ABBREVIATIONS

CND	*China News Digest*
FBIS	Foreign Broadcast Information Service
HCCPM	History of Contemporary Chinese Political Movements, ed. Song Yongyi (Hong Kong: Chinese University Press) (database)
JPRS	Joint Publications Research Service
LD	*Liberation Daily* [*Jiefang ribao*]
LAD	*Liberation Army Daily* [*Jiefangjun bao*]
NCRGP	*New Collection of Red Guard Publications* [*Xinbian hongweibing ziliao*], ed. Song Yongyi, 52 vols. (Oakton, VA: Center for Chinese Research Materials, 2005)
NYRB	*New York Review of Books*
NYT	*New York Times*
PD	*People's Daily* [*Renmin ribao*]
RFA	Radio Free Asia
SCCP	Service Center for Chinese Publications
SCMP	*South China Morning Post*
SMH	*Sydney Morning Herald*
TML	The Maoist Legacy (database)
VoA(C)	Voice of America (China edition)
WP	*Washington Post*

Notes

Chapter 1: The Party's Interests Come First

1. *Chen Jianzhong xiansheng koushu lishi fangwen dagang* (self-pub., n.d.).
2. Li Rui, diary (vol. 22, 1990), p. 67, HIA.
3. Wu Jiang, "Qin Chuan tan Xi Zhongxun er san shi," *Yanhuang chunqiu*, no. 11 (2003): 56–57.
4. Hao Ping, "Yi sheng xinshou 'shemi wuguo, qinjian xingbang,'" in *Xi Zhongxun jinian wenji*, ed. Zhonggong zhongyang dangshi yanjiushi (Beijing: Zhonggong dangshi, 2013), 762.
5. Xi Jinping, "Gei baba bashiba zhousui shengri de hexin," in *Xi Zhongxun jinian wenji*, ed. Zhonggong zhongyang dangshi yanjiushi (Beijing: Zhonggong dangshi, 2013), 806.
6. Gao Wenqian, "Mao de wenge yichan yu Xi Jinping zhiguo moshi," in *Wenge wushinian: Mao Zedong yichan he dangdai Zhongguo*, ed. Song Yongyi, vol. 2 (Deer Park, NY: Mingjing, 2016), 406–24.
7. Ibid., 417.
8. Jiang Xun, "Xi Jinping xiang zuo zhuanshi zuojia dongzuo," *Yazhou zhoukan*, Sept. 22, 2013, 34–35.
9. Hu Ping, "Buxiaozi Xi Jinping," RFA, May 4, 2015.
10. Xi Jinping, "Gei baba," 806–7.
11. Yang Ping, "Mudu ganren de Xi jia fuzi qing," *Yanhuang shijie* 132, no. 2 (2013): 9.
12. Evan Osnos, "Born Red," *New Yorker*, Apr. 6, 2015.
13. Yang Ping, "Xi jia," 11; He Yao, *Xi Zhongxun jiafeng* (n.p.: Hunan renmin, n.d.), 415.
14. Long Fei and Jing Jing, "Zuihou yi ren mishu yanzhong de Xi Zhongxun," *Dang'an chunqiu*, no. 1 (2008): 8.
15. *Zhang Guoying shenqie huainian Xi Zhongxun: Xi Zhongxun danchen yibai zhounian jinian, 1913–2013* (Guangzhou: self-pub., 2013), 250.
16. Andrew Higgins, "For China's Next Leader, the Past Is Sensitive," WP, Feb. 13, 2012.
17. Kevin Rudd, *The PM Years* (Sydney: Macmillan, 2018), 301; Kevin Rudd (former prime minister of Australia), in discussion with the author, Feb. 2020.

18. Iu. V. Tavrovskii, *Si Tszin'pin: Po stupeniam kitaiskoi mechty* (Moscow: Eksmo, 2015), 246; "Vstrecha Predsedatelia KNR Si Tszin'pina s rossiiskimi kitaevedami," *Problemy Dal'nego Vostoka*, no. 4 (2013): 7.

19. Higgins, "For China's Next Leader."

20. Titles in running text are generally given in English for ease of reading. The original language is presented in citations where applicable.

21. Interview with Western historian. All interviews without identifying information were conducted in confidentiality, and the names of interviewees and dates and locations of interviews are withheld by mutual agreement to protect the identity of the interviewees.

22. Joseph Torigian, "Historical Legacies and Leaders' Worldviews: Communist Party History and Xi's Learned (and Unlearned) Lessons," *China Perspectives*, no. 1–2 (2018): 8.

23. Roi Medvedev, *Iurii Andropov: Neizvestnoe ob izvestnom* (Moscow: Vremia, 2004), 29.

Chapter 2: *The Young Wanderer*

1. Yang Ping, "Xi jia," 10.

2. Liu Shaoqi, "Liu Shaoqi dui zhongyang zuzhibu fuzeren de tanhua," Nov. 12, 1962, HCCPM.

3. Mark Selden, *The Yenan Way in Revolutionary China* (Cambridge, MA: Harvard University Press, 1971), 5.

4. *Chen Jianzhong.*

5. Zhonggong Fuping xianwei dangshi yanjiushi, "Fengrong suiyue: Xi Zhongxun de shaonian shidai," in *Xiangyin: Jinian Xi Zhongxun tongzhi danchen jiushiwu zhounian*, ed. Zhonggong Fuping xianwei and Fuping xian renmin zhengfu (Weinan: Zhonggong Fuping xianwei, 2008), 54–59.

6. Hu Peiyuan, "Nanwang de licheng: Xi Zhongxun Yan'an suiyue Huifang," *Zhongguo zuojia* 20 (2013): 5.

7. Zhonggong Fuping xianwei dangshi yanjiushi, "Fengrong suiyue," 56.

8. Xia Meng and Wang Xiaoqiang, *Xi Zhongxun: Father of a Great Nation's Leader* (London: ACA, 2014), 2–3.

9. Zhonggong Yan'an shiwei dangshi yanjiushi, ed., *Xi Zhongxun zai Yan'an* (Beijing: Zhongyang wenxian, 2013), 2.

10. Liang Jian, *Xi Jinping xin zhuan* (Hong Kong: Mingjing, 2012), 301.

11. *Xi Zhongxun zhuan*, 2 vols. (Beijing: Zhongyang wenxian, 2013), 1:13–14.

12. Ding Min, "Xi Zhongxun zai Luonai," *Luoyang wenshi ziliao*, no. 32 (2012): 86.

13. Jia Juchuan, "Xi Zhongxun: Xiongyou guojia, pinzi gaojie," *Xin xiang pinglun*, no. 4 (2018): 16.

14. *Xi Zhongxun zhuan*, 1:313.

15. Jia Juchuan, "Xi Zhongxun nianpu (1913.10–1937.7)," *Weinan shifan xueyuan xuebao* 26, no. 9 (2011): 16 (hereafter cited as Jia Juchuan, "1913.10–1937.7"). See also Xiong Xiaofang, "Qingnian Xi Zhongxun xianwei renzhi de wangshi," *Wen wei po*, Feb. 21, 2008.

16. Zhonggong Yan'an shiwei dangshi yanjiushi, *Xi Zhongxun zai Yan'an*, 3–4; Xiong Xiaofang, "Qingnian Xi Zhongxun."

17. Chen Jianzhong, *Huaipu suibi* (self-pub., n.d.), 45.

18. Jia Juchuan, "1913.10–1937.7," 3.

19. Ibid., 4; Choubei weiyuanhui bangongshi, *Fuping xian Licheng zhongxue jianshi (zhengqiu yijian gao)* (n.p.: n.p., 1985), 3–4.

20. *Xi Zhongxun zhuan*, 1:313–14.

21. *Chen Jianzhong.*

22. Duan Weishao, "Xi Zhongxun yu Yang Hucheng mishu Tian Pingxuan de xiongdi qingyi," *Wenshi tiandi*, no. 2 (2013): 14; Jia Juchuan, "1913.10–1937.7," 4.

23. Wen Xiang, *Gaoceng enyuan yu Xi Zhongxun: Cong Xibei dao Beijing* (Hong Kong: Mingjing, 2008), 9–10; Zanchen Mi, *The Life of General Yang Hucheng* (Hong Kong: C&C, 1981), 23–39; Joseph Esherick, *Accidental Holy Land: The Communist Revolution in Northwest China* (Oakland: University of California Press, 2022), 41–43.

24. Zhonggong Shaanxi shengwei dangshi yanjiushi, ed., "Tudi geming zhanzheng shiqi de Zhonggong Shaanxi shengwei zongshu," in *Shaanxi dangshi ziliao congshu*, vol. 18 (Xi'an: Shaanxi renmin, 1991), 1–2 (hereafter cited as Zhonggong Shaanxi, "Zhonggong Shaanxi shengwei zongshu").

25. Ibid., 4; Esherick, *Accidental Holy Land*, 47–53.

26. Wen Xiang, *Gaoceng enyuan*, 23–24; Zhonggong Shaanxi, "Zhonggong Shaanxi shengwei zongshu," 7–8; *Zhonggong Shaanxi shengwei dangshi yanjiushi, ed.*, "Zhonggong Shaanxi shengwei tonggao (di san shi jiu hao)," in *Shaanxi dangshi ziliao congshu*, vol. 18 (Xi'an: Shaanxi renmin, 1991), 226–31.

27. Zhonggong Shaanxi shengwei dangshi yanjiushi and Gongqingtuan Shaanxi shengwei qingyun shi yanjiushi, eds., "Tudi geming zhanzheng shiqi gongqingtuan Shaanxi shengwei he Shaanxi qingnian yundong zongshu," in *Shaanxi dangshi ziliao congshu*, vol. 20 (Xi'an: Shaanxi renmin, 1992), 7.

28. "Zhonggong Shaanxi shengwei tonggao," 228–29.

29. *Xi Zhongxun nianpu*, 4 vols. (Beijing: Zhongyang wenxian, 2024), 1:5–6.

30. *Xi Zhongxun zhuan*, 1:41–42; Zhonggong Yan'an shiwei dangshi yanjiushi, *Xi Zhongxun zai Yan'an*, 10–11; Tuo Hongwei and Zhang Huamin, "Shixi Shaanxi ji gongchandang ren zai Cha'ha'er kangzhan zhong de zhongyao zuoyong," *Yan'an daxue xuebao* 35, no. 4 (Aug. 2013): 27–31; Zhonggong Shaanxi shengwei dangshi ziliao zhengji yanjiu weiyuanhui and Zhonggong Xianyang shiwei dangshi bangongshi, eds., "Weibei geming genjudi zongshu," in *Shaanxi dangshi ziliao congshu*, vol. 11 (Xi'an: Shaanxi renmin, 1990), 3; Xi Zhonggun, Huang Li, and Tan Jinhang, "Xi Zhongxun: Yi min wei tian de Zhongguo gongchandang ren," *Caijing jie*, no. 7 (2015): 79. Note that Xi, Huang, and Tan have three publications with the same title, and the shortened citations hereafter are thus differentiated by page numbers only.

31. Zhonggong Yan'an shiwei dangshi yanjiushi, *Xi Zhongxun zai Yan'an*, 11.

32. Ibid., 13.

33. Xia Meng and Wang, *Xi Zhongxun: Father*, 11–12.

34. He Zai, *Hongqi manjuan Xibei gaoyuan: Xi Zhongxun zai Xibei* (Beijing: Zhonggong dangshi, 2013), 9–10.

35. *Xi Zhongxun zhuan*, 1:51.

36. Jia Juchuan, "1913.10–1937.7," 5.

37. Xibei gongda "jiefang da Xibei" bingtuan, "Sanfan fenzi Xi Zhongxun de zui'e lishi," ed. Song Yongyi (Xibei gongda), Sept. 12, 1967, 252, *NCRGP*, pt. 3, *CCTP*, pp. 18875–76.

38. Jia Juchuan, "1913.10–1937.7," 5.

39. Xia Meng, "Xibei zhi hun," in *Huainian Xi Zhongxun*, ed. Cao Zhenzhong and Wu Jiang (Beijing: Zhongyang dangshi, 2005), 497–98; Cao Zhenzhong, "Shenqing huainian Xi Zhongxun tongzhi: Jijian wangshi de zhuiyi," *Zongheng*, no. 7 (2011): 13–14.

40. Xia Meng and Wang Xiaoqiang, *Xi Zhongxun huazhuan* (Beijing: Renmin, 2014), 12; Zhonggong Yan'an shiwei dangshi yanjiushi, *Xi Zhongxun zai Yan'an*, 12; Zhang Aisheng, *Cong qunzhong zhong zou chulai de qunzhong lingxiu Xi Zhongxun (Xibei suiyue)* (Beijing: Zhonggong zhongyang dangxiao, 2017), 16; *Xi Zhongxun zhuan*, 1:52, 313; Xi, Huang, and Tan, "Xi Zhongxun," 80; Jia Juchuan, "1913.10–1937.7," 5; Xiong Xiaofang, "Qingnian Xi Zhongxun."

41. Zhonggong Yan'an shiwei dangshi yanjiushi, *Xi Zhongxun zai Yan'an*, 16.
42. Ibid., 12–13.
43. Zhonggong Shaanxi, "Zhonggong Shaanxi shengwei zongshu," 9.
44. Esherick, *Accidental Holy Land*, 72.
45. Zhonggong Shaanxi shengwei dangshi ziliao zhengji yanjiu weiyuanhui and Zhonggong Xianyang shiwei dangshi bangongshi, eds., "Zhonggong Shaanxi shengwei guanyu Weibei youji zhanzheng qingkuang de baogao," in *Shaanxi dangshi ziliao congshu*, vol. 11 (Xi'an: Shaanxi renmin, 1990), 30–42; Jia Juchuan, "1913.10–1937.7," 5.
46. Xia Meng and Wang, *Xi Zhongxun: Father*, 12–14.
47. Jia Juchuan, "1913.10–1937.7," 5.
48. Xiong Xiaofang, "Qingnian Xi Zhongxun."
49. *Xi Zhongxun nianpu*, 4:201.
50. Xia Meng and Wang, *Xi Zhongxun: Father*, 14; Zhonggong Yan'an shiwei dangshi yanjiushi, *Xi Zhongxun zai Yan'an*, 13–14.
51. Zhonggong Yan'an shiwei dangshi yanjiushi, *Xi Zhongxun zai Yan'an*, 13.
52. Tsi-an Hsia, *The Gate of Darkness: Studies on the Leftist Literary Movement* (Hong Kong: Chinese University Press, 2015), 60–70.
53. Jiang Guangci, "Shaonian piaobozhe," in *Jiang Guangci wenji* (Shanghai: Shanghai wenyi, 1982), 74–75.
54. Ibid., 22, 23.
55. Xibei gongda "jiefang da Xibei" bingtuan, "Sanfan fenzi Xi Zhongxun de zui'e lishi," 252.
56. Cao Zhenzhong, "Shenqing," 14.
57. *Xi Zhongxun zhuan*, 1:63.
58. Xi, Huang, and Tan, "Xi Zhongxun," 79.
59. Lu Jianren, "Huiyi Liangdang bingbian," in *Shaanxi wenshi ziliao*, ed. Zhongguo renmin zhengzhi xieshang huiyi, Shaanxi sheng weiyuanhui, and Wenshi ziliao yanjiu weiyuanhui, vol. 11 (Xi'an: Shaanxi renmin, n.d.), 4–11.
60. Zhonggong Yan'an shiwei dangshi yanjiushi, *Xi Zhongxun zai Yan'an*, 16–17.
61. Li Donglang, "Xi Zhongxun yu Liangdang bingbian," *Gansu ribao*, Oct. 15, 2013; Liu Xixian, "Wo yu Xi Zhongxun yijie jinlan," in *Hongse Liangdang*, ed. Liangdang bingbian ji hongjun changzheng zai Liangdang dangshi ziliao bianzuan bangongshi (Lanzhou: Gansu wenhua, 2008), 60.
62. Lu Jianren, *Wode huiyi* (Xi'an: Shaanxi renmin, 1997), 37–39.
63. Ibid., 38–39; Xia Meng and Wang, *Xi Zhongxun: Father*, 15–22; Zhonggong Yan'an shiwei dangshi yanjiushi, *Xi Zhongxun zai Yan'an*, 30; Xi Zhongxun, "1945 nian 7 yue Xi Zhongxun zai Shaan-Gan-Ning bianqu lishi zuotan huishang de fayan (jiexuan)," July 1945, reprint, Huangtu lianyihui, Nov. 6, 2019, https://archive.ph/jSY7Q.
64. Guo Zengyi, "Shenqie mianhuai Liu Linpu lieshi," in *Guanghui de qingchun: Liu Linpu jinian wenji*, ed. Guo Jianmin and Guo Zengyi (Tongchuan: Tongchuan shi xinqu zuojia xiehui, 2010), 172.
65. Esherick, *Accidental Holy Land*, 64; Du Lijun [Du Heng], "Shaanxi daibiao Du Lijun baogao," in *Gansu dangshi ziliao*, ed. Zhonggong Gansu shengwei dangshi ziliao zhengji yanjiu weiyuan hui, vol. 3 (Lanzhou: Gansu renmin, 1986), 77–81.
66. Zhonggong Gansu shengwei dangshi ziliao zhengji yanjiu weiyuan hui, ed., "Longyuan bingbao gaishu," in *Gansu dangshi ziliao*, vol. 3 (Lanzhou: Gansu renmin, 1986), 1–6; Esherick, *Accidental Holy Land*, 64.
67. Jia Juchuan, "1913.10–1937.7," 7; Zhonggong Yan'an shiwei dangshi yanjiushi, *Xi Zhongxun zai Yan'an*, 33.

Chapter 3: Who Saved Whom?

1. Wang Xiaozhong, *Zhongguwei gongzuo jishi 1982–1987* (Hong Kong: Cosmos Books, 2013), 74.
2. Ren Xueling, *Shaan-Gan geming genjudi shi* (Beijing: Renmin, 2013), 105.
3. Ibid., 109.
4. Philip Billingsley and Xu Youwei, "Liu Zhidan and His 'Bro's in the Hood': Bandits and Communists in the Shaanbei Badlands (1)," *Human Sciences Review*, no. 44 (Mar. 2013): 158–67.
5. Esherick, *Accidental Holy Land*, 68–70.
6. Liu Jingfan, "'Sanjiayuan shijian' de zhenxiang," in *Fandang xiaoshuo "Liu Zhidan" an shilu*, ed. Li Jiantong (Hong Kong: Thinker, 2007), 258–72.
7. *Guanyu Xibei hongjun zhanzheng lishi zhong de jige wenti*, *Dangshi tongxun*, no. 8 (1986): 3–4.
8. Ding Min, "Xi Zhongxun zai Luonai," 86–87.
9. Xi Zhengqin, "'Sanyuan Dongxiang' wangshi," in *Sanyuan renwen* (Sanyuan: Sanyuanxian dang'an ju, 2015), 136.
10. Zhonggong Yan'an shiwei dangshi yanjiushi, *Xi Zhongxun zai Yan'an*, 43.
11. Xi Zhongxun, "Qunzhong lingxiu, minzu yingxiong," in *Xi Zhongxun wenji*, vol. 1 (Beijing: Zhonggong dangshi, 2013), 558–74.
12. Xi Zhengqin, "'Sanyuan Dongxiang' wangshi"; Wang Xiaoxin, "Xi Zhongxun yu Sanyuan Dongxiang 'Henan huiguan,'" in *Sanyuan renwen shilüe* (Sanyuan: Sanyuan xia, 2015), 128–34.
13. Esherick, *Accidental Holy Land*, 76.
14. Zhou Baojin, Li Yong, and Ling Shangwen, "Huang Ziwen zhuanlue," in *Huang Ziwen*, ed. Zhou Baojin, Li Yong, and Ling Shangwen (Shaanxi: Zhonggong Sanyuan xianwei zuzhibu, 2004), 12–14.
15. Zhonggong Yan'an shiwei dangshi yanjiushi, *Xi Zhongxun zai Yan'an*, 46–47.
16. Li Donglang, "Xi Zhongxun yu Chenjiapo huiyi," *Dangshi bolan*, no. 10 (2013): 11–16.
17. Ibid.; Xia Meng and Wang, *Xi Zhongxun: Father*, 23–35; Zhonggong Shaanxi shengwei zuzhibu, Zhonggong Shaanxi shengwei dangshi yanjiushi, and Shaanxi sheng dang'anguan, eds., *Zhongguo gongchandang Shaanxi sheng zuzhishi ziliao: 1925.10–1987.10* (Xi'an: Shaanxi renmin, 1994), 148 (hereafter cited as Zhonggong Shaanxi shengwei zuzhibu et al., *1925.10–1987.10*).
18. Xi Zhongxun, "Nanwang de jiaohui: Jinian Liu Zhidan tongzhi jiu shi danchen," *PD*, Oct. 24, 1993.
19. *Xi Zhongxun zhuan*, 1:134–35.
20. Zhonggong Yan'an shiwei dangshi yanjiushi, *Xi Zhongxun zai Yan'an*, 57–58.
21. Li Donglang, "Chenjiapo huiyi."
22. Ibid., 13.
23. Tian Runmin, "Du Heng panbian qianhou," *Yanhuang chunqiu*, no. 3 (2017): 86–92; Esherick, *Accidental Holy Land*, 85.
24. Li Donglang, "Chenjiapo huiyi."
25. Ibid., 15.
26. Zhang Siquan, *Gao Gang* (Beijing: Zhongguo wenshi, 2011), 46; Xia Meng and Wang, *Xi Zhongxun: Father*, 36–41.
27. Wang Qiuying, "Yu Xi lao yi jia qingshen yinong," in *Zai Xibeiju de rizi li*, ed. Shi Jie and Si Zhihao (Xi'an: Shaanxi shifan daxue chubanshe, 2018), 151–56.
28. Gao Wen, *Nanliang shihua* (Lanzhou: Gansu renmin, 1984), 85–87, 95.
29. Xia Meng and Wang, *Xi Zhongxun: Father*, 42–50; Cai Ziwei, "Nanliang genjudi geming douzheng pianduan huiyi," in *Nanliang shuguang*, ed. Li Guo (Lanzhou: Gansu renmin, 1983), 52–66.

30. Wen Xiang, *Gaoceng enyuan*, 46; Esherick, *Accidental Holy Land*, 90.

31. Hongweibing pipan wenzhang, "Tong sanfan fenzi Xi Zhongxun pin cidao dahui jiyao," in *Gao Gang "fandang" zhenxiang*, ed. Wu Ming and Shi Jian (Hong Kong: Xianggang wenhua yishu, 2008), 266–67; Zhang Siquan, *Gao Gang*, 57–63, 684.

32. *Xi Zhongxun zai Shaan-Gan-Ning bianqu* (Beijing: Zhongguo wenshi, 2014), 152–53; Zhonggong Yan'an shiwei dangshi yanjiushi, *Xi Zhongxun zai Yan'an*, 98; Gao Wen, *Nanliang shihua*, 132–33; Ding Min, "Xi Zhongxun zai Luonai," 89.

33. Youwei Xu and Philip Billingsley, "Heroes, Martyrs, and Villains in 1930s Shaanbei: Liu Zhidan and His 'Bandit Policy,'" *Modern China* 44, no. 3 (2018): 243–84.

34. Liu Zhidan and Xi Zhongxun, "Shaan-Gan bian genjudi 'shi da zhengce,'" in *Liu Zhidan wenji* (Beijing: Renmin, 2012), 35–39.

35. Xi Zhongxun, "Guanyu jiaqiang he gaishan budui zhengzhi gongzuo de jidian yijian," in *Xi Zhongxun wenji*, vol. 1 (Beijing: Zhonggong dangshi, 2013), 625–38.

36. Xi Zhongxun, "Nanwang de jiaohui."

37. Billingsley and Xu, "Liu Zhidan."

38. Esherick, *Accidental Holy Land*, 61.

39. Tong Guirong, "Xi Zhongxun cong qunzhong zhong lai," in *Xi Zhongxun zai Xunyi*, ed. Zhonggong Xianyang shiwei, Dangshi yanjiushi, and Zhonggong Xunyi xianwei (Beijing: Zhongyang wenxian, 2012), 217–20.

40. Liang Xingliang and Yao Wenqi, *Zhonggong zhongyang zai Yan'an shisannian shi*, vol. 1. (Beijing: Zhongyang wenxian, 2016), 53–58.

41. Xibei Yan, *Zhenxiang: 1935 nian Shaan-bei cuowu sufan shimo* (Beijing: Huaxia wenhua yishu, 2014), 32–34.

42. Zhang Xiushan, *Wode bashiwunian: Cong Xibei dao Dongbei* (Beijing: Zhonggong dangshi, 2007), 75; Esherick, *Accidental Holy Land*, 99–100.

43. Zhang Siquan, *Gao Gang*, 67.

44. Xi Zhongxun, "1942 nian 11 yue Xi Zhongxun zai Xibeiju gaogan huiyishang guanyu Shaan-Gan bian dangshi wenti de fayan (zhaiyao)," Nov. 1942, reprint, Huangtu lianyihui, Aug. 20, 2024, https://archive.ph/LzR5u.

45. Xibei, *Zhenxiang*, 36–38.

46. Wu Dianyao and Song Lin, *Zhu Lizhi zhuan* (Beijing: Zhonggong dangshi, 2007), 58–65.

47. Xi Zhongxun, "1942 nian."

48. Zhang Huamin, *Xie Zichang zhuan* (Beijing: Zhonggong zhongyang dangxiao, 2015), 283–87; Esherick, *Accidental Holy Land*, 103.

49. Esherick, *Accidental Holy Land*, 110–12.

50. Zhu Lizhi, "Wo dao Shaan-bei hou de cuowu," in *Xibei geming genjudi*, ed. Zhonggong Shaanxi shengwei dangshi yanjiushi (Beiing: Zhonggong dangshi, 1998), 430–33.

51. Xibei, *Zhenxiang*, 71.

52. Xi Zhongxun, "1942 nian."

53. Wen Xiang, *Gaoceng enyuan*, 166.

54. Xi Zhongxun, "1942 nian 11."

55. Li Donglang, "Shaan-bei sufan ji ze shishi zhi kaobian," *Dangshi yanjiu yu jiaoxue*, no. 5 (2010): 78.

56. Tian Runmin, "Shaan-bei 'sufan' yu Zhang Mutao," *Xibu xuekan*, no. 7 (2014): 38–42; Song Jinshou, "Wo liaojie de Xibei geming genjudi sufan," *Yanhuang chunqiu*, no. 10 (2012): 47–55.

57. Xi Zhongxun, "1942 nian."

58. Xibei, *Zhenxiang*, 142; Wen Xiang, *Gaoceng enyuan*, 196.

59. Li Donglang, "Shaan-bei."

60. Xi Zhongxun and Ma Wenrui, "Shanzuo tuanjie gongzuo de mofan: Jinian Liu Zhidan tongzhi danchen 95 zhou nian," *PD*, Oct. 18, 1998.

61. Hao Zaijin, *"Wenge" qianshi: Yan'an "qiangjiu yundong" jishi* (Hong Kong: Liwen, 2006), 49.

62. Wen Xiang, *Gaoceng enyuan*, 214, 221; *Xi Zhongxun zhuan*, 1:204.

63. *Liu Peizhi wencun* (Beijing: Zhonggong dangshi, 2017), 57–58.

64. Xi Zhongxun, "Hongri zhaoliangle Shaan-Gan gaoyuan," in *Xi Zhongxun wenxuan* (Beijing: zhongyang wenxian, 1995), 289.

65. Huang Luobin, "Xi Zhongxun yu Shaan-Gan bian geming genjudi de chuangjian," in *Xi Zhongxun jinian wenji*, ed. Zhonggong zhongyang dangshi yanjiushi (Beijing: Zhonggong dangshi, 2013), 119; Wen Xiang, *Gaoceng enyuan*, 221.

66. Li Donglang, "Shaan-bei," 80–83.

67. Xia Lina, "Zou Yu yi Xi Zhongxun zai quanguo renda de rizi," *Zhongguo renda zazhi*, no. 1 (2014): 47.

68. Marc Opper, "Revolution Defeated: The Collapse of the Chinese Soviet Republic," *Twentieth-Century China* 43, no. 1 (2018): 45–66.

69. Liu Tong, *Bei shang: Dang zhongyang yu Zhang Guotao douzheng shimo* (Beijing: Shenghuo-dushu-xinzhi sanlian shudian, 2016), 180–96.

70. Xi Zhongxun, "1942 nian."

71. Tian Fang, "Xi Zhongxun he Liu Zhidan de rongrong ruru," *Yanhuang chunqiu*, no. 10 (1995): 72.

72. Li Donglang, "Shaan-bei," 83–84; Wei Deping, "'Zhongyang jiu le Shaan-bei': Guanyu 'daoxia liuren' shuo kaobian," *Zhongguo Yan'an ganbu xueyuan xuebao* 11, no. 2 (Mar. 2018): 130.

73. *Wang Shoudao huiyilu* (Beijing: Jiefangjun, 1987), 167.

74. Li Donglang, "'Xibei lishi wenti' de youlai," *Dangshi bolan*, no. 9 (2014): 6–7; Wei, "Zhongyang," 128–29; Li Donglang, "Shaan-bei," 79; Wei Deping, "Zhonggong zhongyang shifang Liu Zhidan juti shijian kao," *Zhongguo Yan'an ganbu xueyuan xuebao* 12, no. 4 (July 2019): 114.

75. Wei Deping, "Zhang Wentian zhuchi jiejue 'Shaan-bei sufan' wenti kao," *Beijing ribao*, Aug. 28, 2014.

76. He Fang, "Liu Ying yi Yan'an suiyue," *Yanhuang chunqiu*, no. 4 (2016): 16.

77. Wu Dianyao and Song, *Zhu Lizhi zhuan*, 429.

78. Song Lin, "Wushi lixing, chizheng buyi," in *Zhu Lizhi bainian dachen jinian wenji*, ed. Zhonggong Nantong shiwei dangshi gongzuo bangongshi (Beijing: Zhonggong dangshi, 2008), 116.

79. He Fang, ed., "Guo Hongtao tong He Fang tan Shaan-bei sufan deng wenti," in *Dangshi biji: Liu Ying yu He Fang tan zhonggong dangshi* (Hong Kong: City University of Hong Kong, 2019), 152–53.

80. Li Donglang, "Xibei," 6.

81. Song Jinshou, "Wo liaojie."

82. Li Rui, diary (vol. 9, Dec. 1942), HIA.

83. Wen Xiang, *Gaoceng enyuan*, 452.

84. Wei Deping, "Li Weihan yu 'Shaan-bei sufan' zhenglun de jiejue," *Dangshi bolan*, no. 3 (2017): 22.

85. Wen Xiang, *Gaoceng enyuan*, 248; Wei Deping, "Liu Zhidan xisheng zhi 'mi' kaobian," *Yan'an daxue xuebao (shehui kexue ban)* 41, no. 2 (Apr. 2019): 62.

86. Wei Deping, "Yan'an zhengfeng dui 'Shaan-bei sufan' de chongxin dingxing," *Dangshi yanjiu yu jiaoxue*, no. 3 (2012): 18–19.

87. Esherick, *Accidental Holy Land*, 171.

88. Xi Zhongxun, "1942 nian."
89. Zhongyang dang'anguan and Shaanxi sheng dang'anguan, eds., "Suqu dang daibiao dahui mishuchu guanyu Shaan-Gan-Ning tequ dangwei xuanju jieguo de tongzhi," in *Zhonggong Shaan-Gan-Ning bianqu dangwei wenjian huiji (1937 nian–1939 nian)*, ser. 35, vol. 8 (n.p.: SCCP, 2016), 3–4.
90. Xibei, *Zhenxiang*, 235.
91. Song Jinshou, "Wo liaojie."

Chapter 4: The Yan'an Era

1. Jia Juchuan, "1913.10–1937.7," 14; Xi Zhongxun, "Guanzhong dangshi jianshu (jiexuan)," in *Longdong geming genjudi de xingcheng* (Qingyang: Zhonggong Qingyang diwei dangshi ziliao zhengji bangongshi, 1990), 262.
2. Zhao Xiaohong, "Dangde liyi zai diyi wei," in *Hongse Nanliang, lianzheng fengbei*, ed. Zhonggong Qingyang shiwei and Zhonggong Gansu sheng jiwei xuanjiao shi (Lanzhou: Lanzhou wanyi yinwu, 2011), 194–98.
3. Zhang Wuji, "Xi Zhongxun zai Huan xian," in *Hongse Nanliang, lianzheng fengbei*, ed. Zhonggong Qingyang shiwei and Zhonggong Gansu sheng jiwei xuanjiao shi (Lanzhou: Lanzhou wanyi yinwu, 2011), 199–212.
4. Yang Kuisong, *Shiqu de jihui? Kangzhan qianhou guogong tanpan shilu* (Beijing: Xinxing, 2010), 7.
5. Jia Juchuan, "1913.10–1937.7," 15.
6. Zhang Zhiying, "Xi Zhongxun tongzhi zai Zhengning xian geming huodong shilüe," *Zhengning wenshi ziliao xuanji* 2 (2002): 81.
7. Li Manxing, "Xi Zhongxun he 'lao guanxi' Tian Pingxuan de yisheng qingyi," *Yanhuang chunqiu*, no. 4 (2017): 27–31; Duan Weishao, "Xi Zhongxun."
8. *Xi Zhongxun zhuan*, 1:269–70.
9. Yang Tianshi, *Jiang Jieshi zhenxiang zhi er: Kangzhan ji zhanhou* (Taipei: Fengyun shidai, 2009), 100–102.
10. Yang Kuisong, *Shiqu de jihui?*, 76, 105, 114.
11. *Xi Zhongxun zhuan*, 1:271–72; Esherick, *Accidental Holy Land*, 177; "Huatong" [pseud.?], "Shaan-Gan-Ning bianqu quanmao," in *Zhonggong bianqu genjudi de lishi wenjian xuanji* (n.p.: n.p., 1985). I thank Joseph Esherick for sharing this document.
12. *Xi Zhongxun zhuan*, 2:268–76; Zhonggong Yan'an shiwei tongzhanbu, ed., "Gao Zili tongzhi zai Shaan-Gan-Ning bianqu zhengfu diyici quzhang lianxi huiyishang de guanyu tongyi zhanxian gongzuo de baogao," in *Yan'an shiqi tongyi zhanxian shiliao xuanbian* (Beijing: Huawen, 2010), 451.
13. Zhonggong Shaanxi shengwei zuzhibu et al., *1925.10–1987.10*, 275.
14. Zhongyang dang'anguan and Shaanxi sheng dang'anguan, eds., "Bianqu dangwei tongzhanbu guanyu tongzhan gongzuo ruogan wenti gei Guanzhong fenwei de zhishi xin," in *Zhonggong Shaan-Gan-Ning bianqu dangwei wenjian huiji (1940 nian–1941 nian)*, ser. 35, vol. 9 (n.p.: SCCP, 2016), 4–7.
15. *Xi Zhongxun zhuan*, 1:277–81.
16. Zhonggong Yan'an shiwei tongzhanbu, ed., "Wang Guanlan tongzhi gei Xi Zhongxun tongzhi de xin: Guanyu tongyi zhanxian wenti," in *Yan'an shiqi tongyi zhanxian shiliao xuanbian* (Beijing: Huawen, 2010), 512–13.
17. Zhongyang dang'anguan and Shaanxi sheng dang'anguan, eds., "Shaanxi shengwei changwei zhi Luo Fu dian," in *Shaanxi geming lishi wenjian huiji: 1940 nian* (Beijing: Zhongyang dang'anguan, 1991), 124–25; Zhongyang dang'anguan and Shaanxi sheng dang'anguan, eds., "Yang Qing zhi Wu Yunfu, Li Hua dian," in *Shaanxi geming lishi wenjian huiji: 1940 nian* (Beijing: Zhongyang dang'anguan, 1991), 120–21; *Xi Zhongxun zhuan*, 1:286.

18. Gao Gang, "Xiao Jingguang, Gao Gang, Gao Zili gei Guanzhong fenqu Xi Zhongxun Zhang Zhongliang dian," in *Gao Gang tongzhi: Shuxin dianwen xuanji*, ed. Xue Junfu and An Mingwen (Beijing: Huaxia wenhua yishu, 2013).

19. Zhongyang dang'anguan and Shaanxi sheng dang'anguan, eds., "Xiao Jingguang, Gao Gang, Gao Zili zhi Xi Zhongxun, Zhang Zhongliang dian," in *Zhonggong Shaan-Gan-Ning bianqu dangwei wenjian huiji (1940 nian–1941 nian)*, ser. 35, vol. 9 (n.p.: SCCP, 2016), 121; Esherick, *Accidental Holy Land*, 177.

20. Zhongyang dang'anguan and Shaanxi sheng dang'anguan, eds., "Bianqu dangwei gei Guanzhong fenwei de zhishi xin," in *Zhonggong Shaan-Gan-Ning bianqu dangwei wenjian huiji (1940 nian–1941 nian)*, ser. 35, vol. 9 (n.p.: SCCP, 2016), 122–26.

21. Tian Runmin, ed., *Xi Zhongxun zai Xunyi de gushi* (Xi'an: Shaanxi renmin, 2013), 6–91, 213–14; Li Manxing, "Xi Zhongxun."

22. Tian Runmin, *Xi Zhongxun*, 189–90.

23. Zhonggong Yan'an diwei tongzhanbu and Zhonggong zhongyang tongzhanbu yanjiusuo, eds., "Zhonggong Shaan-Gan-Ning bianqu weiyuanhui gei Guanzhong fenwei de zhishi," in *KangRi zhanzheng shiqi Shaan-Gan-Ning bianqu tongyi zhanxian he san san zhi* (Xi'an: Shaanxi renmin, 1989), 341–43.

24. Zhonggong Yan'an diwei tongzhanbu and Zhonggong zhongyang tongzhanbu yanjiusuo, eds., "Zhonggong Shaan-Gan-Ning bianqu zhongyang ju gei Guanzhong fenwei de zhishi," in *KangRi zhanzheng shiqi Shaan-Gan-Ning bianqu tongyi zhanxian he san san zhi* (Xi'an: Shaanxi renmin, 1989), 347–50.

25. Zhongyang dang'anguan and Shaanxi sheng dang'anguan, eds., "Ouyang Qin deng ren zhi Mao Zedong deng ren dian," in *Shaanxi geming lishi wenjian huiji: 1941 nian*, vol. 1 (Beijing: Zhongyang dang'anguan, 1991), 50–51.

26. Zhongyang dang'anguan and Shaanxi sheng dang'anguan, eds., "Ouyang Qin, Xi Zhongxun deng zhi Mao Zedong deng ren zhuan bianqu zhongyang ju dian," in *Shaanxi geming lishi wenjian huiji: 1940 nian* (Beijing: Zhongyang dang'anguan, 1991), 86.

27. Zhonggong Shaanxi shengwei zuzhibu et al., *1925.10–1987.10*, 275–77.

28. Zhongyang dang'anguan and Shaanxi sheng dang'anguan, eds., "Zhang Desheng zai xin shengwei diyici huiyishang guanyu Guanzhong bianqu gongzuo wenti de fayan," in *Shaanxi geming lishi wenjian huiji: 1941 nian*, vol. 1 (Beijing: Zhongyang dang'anguan, 1991), 139–48.

29. Qin Ping, "Yi Bu Lu," in *Dute yingxiang: Jinian renmin yingxiong Bu Lu danchen yibaizhounian*, ed. Jia Yanyan (Haikou: Hainan, 2009), 55.

30. Jiang Wei, *Hongse Fuermosi: Bu Lu yu gong'an xitong diyi qi'an* (Shanghai: Xuelin, 2003), 102.

31. Jia Juchuan, "1913.10–1937.7," 16.

32. Zhongyang dang'anguan and Shaanxi sheng dang'anguan, eds., "Xin xingshi xia Shaanxi dangde renwu," in *Shaanxi geming lishi wenjian huiji: 1940 nian* (Beijing: Zhongyang dang'anguan, 1991), 161–78.

33. "Gongfei renwu zhi diyibu: Xi Zhongxun. Minguo siwunian buzheng ziliao," n.d., AHT, Diancang hao 129-100000-1129, Junshi weiyuanhui weiyuan zhang shicong shi, ser. 10, pp. 13–15.

34. Luo Wenzhi, *Zhonggong Shaanxi dixiadang fan dite douzheng jishi* (Xi'an: Shaanxi renmin, 1998), 363–65.

35. Chung Yen-lin, "Peng Zhen zai Zhonggong Yan'an zhengfeng yundong zhong de juese he huodong," *Guoli Zhengzhi daxue lishi xuebao* 49 (May 2018): 39–92; Frederick C. Teiwes and Warren Sun, *The Formation of the Maoist Leadership: From the Return of Wang Ming to the Seventh Party Congress* (London: Contemporary China Institute, School of Oriental and African Studies, University of London, 1994), 11–17; Hua Gao,

How the Red Sun Rose: The Origins and Development of the Yan'an Rectification Movement, 1930–1945 (Hong Kong: University of Hong Kong, 2018), 318–26.

36. Gao, *Red Sun*, 419–23.
37. *Yan'an zhengfeng yundong jishi* (Beijing: Qiushi, 1982), 97–98.
38. Gao, *Red Sun*, 423–38, 453–58.
39. *Yan'an zhengfeng yundong jishi*, 199–200, 253.
40. Huang Daoxuan, "Huang Daoxuan, a Xinling History of the Rectification Campaign," trans. Dayton Lekner, Timothy Cheek, and Nathan Gan, PRC History Group, Dec. 17, 2023, http://prchistory.org/huang-daoxuan-a-xinling-history-of-the-rectification-campaign/.
41. Pauline B. Keating, *Two Revolutions: Village Reconstruction and the Cooperative Movement in Northern Shaanxi, 1934–1945* (Stanford: Stanford University Press, 1997), 17.
42. Harrison Forman, *Report from Red China* (New York: Henry Holt, 1945), 195; Harrison Forman, diary, China (pt. 3, July–Sept. 1944), Travel Diaries and Scrapbooks of Harrison Forman, 1932–1973, UWML.
43. Israel Epstein, "Communist Suiteh Different," *NYT*, Sept. 25, 1944, 9.
44. He Fang, *Dangshi biji: Cong Zunyi huiyi dao Yan'an zhengfeng*, 2 vols. (Hong Kong: Liwen, 2005), 1:318.
45. "Suide shenru zhengfeng xuexi," *LD*, May 4, 1943.
46. Lu Huang, "'Hongse Fuermosi': Bu Lu de zaoyu," *Yanhuang chunqiu*, no. 5 (2014): 78; Wu Jun, "Zhuiyi Xi Zhongxun dui Suide shifan xuexiao de guanhuai," in *Xi Zhongxun jinian wenji*, ed. Zhonggong zhongyang dangshi yanjiushi (Beijing: Zhonggong dangshi, 2013), 557–61; Bai Bingshu, "1942 nian zhengfeng pianduan," in *Zhengrong suiyue* (Xi'an: Shaanxi renmin, 2011), 356–58.
47. Feng Zushun, "Qingxi muxiao," in *Zhengrong suiyue: Huiyilu* (n.p.: Shaanxi sheng Suide shifan xuexiao, 1993), 173.
48. Bai Bingshu, "1942 nian zhengfeng pianduan"; Gao Putang and Zeng Luping, *Yan'an qiangjiu yundong shimo: 200 ge qinlizhe jiyi* (Hong Kong: Shidai guoji, 2008), 264–65.
49. Gao Putang and Zeng, *Yan'an qiangjiu yundong shimo*, 230–32.
50. Ibid., 232–33.
51. Ibid., 233–34.
52. Wen Xiang, *Gaoceng enyuan*, 293.
53. Wei Junyi, *Sitong lu* (Beijing: Beijing shiyue wenyi, 1998), 9–11.
54. Zhuang Qidong, "'Qiangjiu yundong' zhong Xi Zhongxun zai Yan'an," *Shiji*, no. 3 (1994): 23.
55. Feng Zushun, "Qingxi muxiao," 173–74.
56. Wei Junyi, *Sitong lu*, 11–15.
57. Zhuang Qidong, "Qiangjiu yundong," 23–24.
58. Wei Junyi, *Sitong lu*, 17, 90.
59. Shi Zhe, *Wode yi sheng* (Beijing: Renmin, 2001), 170; Lei Jia, *Sishi nianjian: Lei Jia huiyilu* (Shenyang: Chunfeng wenyi, 2020), 101; Shi Zhe, *Feng yu gu: Shi Zhe huiyilu* (Beijing: Hongqi, 1992), 6–8; Li Rui, diary (vol. 30, 1998), p. 47, HIA.
60. Shi Zhe, "Wo suo zhidao de Kang Sheng," *Yanhuang chunqiu*, no. 5 (Mar. 1992): 11.
61. Yuan Renyuan, *Zhengtu jishi* (Changsha: Hunan renmin, 1985), 138.
62. "Suide juxing wanren dahui," *LD*, Aug. 2, 1943.
63. Gao, *Red Sun*, 628.
64. Gao Gang, "Gao Gang, Zhou Xing zhi Xi Zhongxun, Shi Zhe dian," in *Gao Gang tongzhi: Shuxin dianwen xuanji*, ed. Xue Junfu and An Mingwen (Beijing: Huaxia wenhua yishu, [2013]). This document is incorrectly dated 1942.

65. "Suide tewu jiguan yinmou bailu," *LD*, Sept. 15, 1943.
66. "Suide fenqu minzhong daibiao jihui kongsu Guomindang tewu zuixing," *LD*, Oct. 2, 1943.
67. Gao, *Red Sun*, 628–29; *Suide xianzhi* (Xi'an: Sanqin, 2003), 21; "Dangde kuanda zhengce ganzhao xia Suide shizu qingnian fenfen huiguo, kongsu Guomindang tewu jiguan wan'e zuixing," *LD*, Sept. 22, 1943.
68. He Jin, "Dui Yan'an qiangjiu yundong de chubu tantao," *Dangshi yanjiu*, no. 6 (1980): 64–65.
69. Gao, *Red Sun*, 642–47; Wang Jiangong, *Jiushinian jian: Wang Jiangong huiyilu* (Hohhot: Nei Menggu renmin, 2006), 320–21; *Hu Qiaomu huiyi Mao Zedong* (Beijing: Renmin, 2003), 276; He Fang, *Dangshi biji*, 1:353; Cheng Min, ed., *Dangnei dajian* (Beijing: Tuanjie, 1993), 141.
70. "Zhongyang guanyu zai fanjian douzheng zhong ying zhuyi de jige wenti gei gedi de zhishi," in *Zuzhi gongzuo wenjian xuanbian (1935–1945.8)*, ser. 28, vol. 28 (n.p.: SCCP, 2007), 460.
71. Kang Sheng, "Guanyu fanjian douzheng de fazhan qingxing yu dangqian renwu," in *Kangzhan shiqi chubao wenjian (dangnei mimi wenjian)*, vol. 2 (n.p.: Zhonggong zhongyang shehuibu, 1949), 110.
72. "Zhongyang guanyu zai fante douzheng zhong jiuzheng guo zuo ji bi gong xin de zhishi," in *Zuzhi gongzuo wenjian xuanbian (1935–1945.8)*, ser. 28, vol. 28 (n.p.: SCCP, 2007), 462–65.
73. Zhuang Qidong, "Qiangjiu yundong," 24; Bai Bingshu, "1942 nian zhengfeng pianduan," 359.
74. Teiwes and Sun, *Maoist Leadership*, 57–58.
75. Qin Jun, "Xi Zhongxun qingxi zuju di Nanyang," *Dangshi bolan*, no. 10 (2008): 40.
76. Xi Zhongxun, introduction to *Zhonggong Shaanxi dixiadang fan dite douzheng jishi*, by Luo Wenzhi (Xi'an: Shaanxi renmin, 1998), 3.
77. Shi Zhe, *Wode yi sheng*, 175–79; Shi Zhe, *Feng yu gu*, 8.
78. Suide xian laoqu jianshe cujinhui, *Suide xian geming laoqu fazhan shi* (Xi'an: Shaanxi renmin, 2021), 172.
79. Zhonggong Yan'an shiwei tongzhanbu, ed., "Ge fenqu ganbu dui tongzhan gongzuo de yixie sixiang biaoxian: Xibeiju bangongting tongzhan yanjiu cailiao," in *Yan'an shiqi tongyi zhanxian shiliao xuanbian* (Beijing: Huawen, 2010), 367.
80. *Wang Shangrong jiangjun* (Beijing: Dangdai Zhongguo, 2000), 192–94.
81. Sun Zuobin and Lu Jianren, "Huiyi Xi Zhongxun tongzhi de geming shengya," in *Sun Zuobin*, ed. Zhonggong Shanxi shengwei dangshi yanjiu (Xi'an: Shaanxi renmin, 1997), 439.
82. He Jiadong, "Zhengzhi gaige cong zhixuan kaishi: Zhi youren shu," in *He Jiadong wenji*, vol. 1 (Fort Worth: Fellows, 2007), 391; Xi Zhongxun, "Huiyi Huang Ziwen," in *Weibei Huang shi xiongdi* (Sanyuan: Shaanxi sheng Sanyuanxian wenshi ziliao weiyuanhui, 2009), 59–61.
83. Zhuang Qidong, "Qiangjiu yundong," 24.
84. Suide xian laoqu jianshe cujinhui, *Suide xian*, 174.
85. He Fang, *Dangshi biji*, 1:362; Li Donglang, "Shaan-bei," 80; Song Jinshou, "Wo liaojie," 51–52.
86. "Zhonggong zhongyang guanyu shencha ganbu de jueding," in *Kangzhan shiqi chubao wenjian (dangnei mimi wenjian)*, vol. 2 (n.p.: Zhonggong Zhongyang shebuibu, 1949), 16.
87. Wu Yidi, "Yan'an's Iron Bodhisattva: Hunting Spies in the Rectification Campaign," in *1943: China at the Crossroads*, ed. Joseph Esherick and Matthew Combs (Ithaca, NY: Cornell University East Asia Program, 2015), 208–11.

88. Xiong Xianghui, *Wode qingbao yu waijiao shengya* (Beijing: Zhonggong dangshi, 1999), 12–16; Yang Tianshi, *Jiang Jieshi*, 100–102.

89. He Fang, *Dangshi biji*, 1:311–13.

90. Yu Ruxin, *Kang Sheng nianpu (1898–1975): Yige Zhongguo gongchandang ren de yisheng* (Hong Kong: Xin shiji, 2023), 135–39; *Hu Qiaomu*, 278.

91. Chen Yongfa, *Yan'an de yinying* (Taipei: Zhongyang yanjiuyuan jindaishi yanjiusuo, 1990), 229–43.

92. "Zhongyang guanyu shencha ganbu de jueding," in *Zuzhi gongzuo wenjian xuanbian (1935–1945.8)*, ser. 28, vol. 28 (n.p.: SCCP, 2007), 449–55.

93. He Fang, *Dangshi biji*, 1:363.

94. *Xi Zhongxun nianpu*, 1:81.

95. Teiwes and Sun, *Maoist Leadership*, 13–14.

96. David E. Apter and Tony Saich, *Revolutionary Discourse in Mao's Republic* (Cambridge, MA: Harvard University Press, 1994), 50.

97. Dai Maolin and Zhao Xiaoguang, *Gao Gang zhuan* (Xi'an: Shaanxi renmin, 2011), 119–33; Wen Xiang, *Gaoceng enyuan*, 255–86; Teiwes and Sun, *Maoist Leadership*.

98. Raymond F. Wylie, *The Emergence of Maoism: Mao Tse-Tung, Ch'en Po-Ta, and the Search for Chinese Theory, 1935–1945* (Stanford: Stanford University Press, 1980).

99. *Yang Shangkun huiyilu* (Beijing: Zhongyang wenxian, 2001), 152.

100. Mao Zedong, "1942 nian 11 yue Mao Zedong zai Xibei gaogan huiyishang de baogao," Nov. 1942, reprint, Huangtu lianyihui, 2012, https://web.archive.org/web/20130915180509/http://htqly.org/detail.aspx?DocumentId=3195.

101. Xi Zhongxun, "1942 nian."

102. *Xi Zhongxun nianpu*, 1:73–74.

103. Ma Songlin, "Huainian Xi Zhongxun shuji," in *Zai Xibeiju de rizi li*, ed. Shi Jie and Si Zhihao (Xi'an: Shaanxi shifan daxue chubanshe, 2018), 17–38; Zhongguo xinwenshe, "Chicheng," pt. 2, YouTube, Nov. 30, 2023, video, https://www.youtube.com/watch?v=qZfoMNjFY2Q.

104. Gao, *Red Sun*, 263–70.

105. Shi Zhe, *Wode yi sheng*, 155.

106. Mao Zedong, "Zhengdun dangde zuofeng," in *Mao Zedong xuanji*, vol. 3 (Beijing: Renmin, 1953), 845.

107. Zhang Xiushan, *Wode bashiwunian*, 155–60.

108. Gao Gang, "Zai lishi zuotan huishang de jianghua," in *Gao Gang wenji*, ed. Xue Junfu and Bai Haoting (Beijing: Huaxia wenhua yishu, 2013).

109. He Jinnian, "1945 nian 6 yue He Jinnian zai Shaan-Gan-Ning bianqu lishi zuotan huishang de diyici fayan," June 1945, reprint, Huangtu lianyihui, 2012, https://web.archive.org/web/20130915181315/http://htqly.org/detail.aspx?DocumentId=3013.

110. Xi Zhongxun, "1945 nian."

111. He Fang, *Dangshi biji*, 2:529.

112. Li Xin, *Qinli Yan'an suiyue* (Xi'an: Shaanxi renmin, 2015), 331.

113. "Gongfei renwu zhi diyi bu: Xi Zhongxun," n.d., AHT, Diancang hao 129-100000-1129, Junshi weiyuanhui weiyuan zhang shicong shi, ser. 10, p. 11.

114. Wen Xiang, *Gaoceng enyuan*, 295; Wang Enhui, "Canjia 'qi da': Wo nanyi wanghuai de yi duan jingli," *Zongheng*, no. 4 (2002): 17–19.

115. Wen Xiang, *Gaoceng enyuan*, 274.

Chapter 5: Love and Revolution

1. Xi Qianping, "Wayaobu de yi zhi Mudanjiang: Xi Zhongxun qian furen Hao Mingzhu de gushi," *Huaxia jizhe wang*, Sept. 25, 2017, https://web.archive.org/web/20240419191404/https://m.sohu.com/n/8310172089/.

2. Ibid.
3. Zhang Siquan, *Gao Gang*, 725–27; Esherick, *Accidental Holy Land*, 194–95.
4. Liu Maogong, *Menghui chuijiao lianying: Yige lao zhanshi de huiyi* (Beijing: Zhonggong dangshi, 2000), 105–6.
5. Xie Tielun, *Huanghe bian jishi* (Beijing: Zhongyang wenxian, 2014), 73–74.
6. Zhonggong Jiangsu shengwei dangshi gongzuo bangongshi, ed., *Zhang Zhongliang jinian wenji* (Beijing: Zhonggong dangshi, 2008), 29.
7. Xi Qianping, "Wayaobu."
8. Zhongguo renmin zhengzhi xieshang huiyi and Gansu sheng weiyuanhui wenshi ziliao weiyuanhui, eds., *Jinxiandai mingren zai Gansu* (Lanzhou: Gansu renmin, 1994), 32.
9. Zhonggong Shaanxi shengwei zuzhibu et al., *1925.10–1987.10*, 96, 163, 196.
10. Xi Qianping, "Wayaobu."
11. Tian Runmin, *Xi Zhongxun*.
12. Daoxuan Huang, "Disciplined Love: The Chinese Communist Party's Wartime Restrictions on Cadre Love and Marriage," *Journal of Modern Chinese History* 13, no. 1 (2019): 61–75.
13. Xi Qianping, "Wayaobu."
14. *Xi Zhongxun zhuan*, 1:296.
15. Xi Qianping, "Wayaobu."
16. Xiao Jun, *Yan'an riji, 1943–1945*, vol. 2 (Hong Kong: Oxford University Press, 2013), 389.
17. Liu Bingrong, *Zoujin Qi Ruixin* (Beijing: Zhongguo renmin daxue xiaoyouhui, 2014), 8–10.
18. Ibid.; Dai Yugang, *Qi jia kangzhan* (Hefei: Huangshan shushe, 2015), 26–27.
19. *Xi Zhongxun zhuan*, 1:374–75; "Zhongzhen: Xi Zhongxun furen Qi Xin (I)," Tengxun shipin, Feb. 10, 2016, video, https://v.qq.com/x/page/z01844imonn.html; Qi Xin, "Jiqing ranshao de qingchun suiyue: Yi wo zai Taihang kangRi qianxian Kangda de zhandou shenghuo," *Bainianchao*, no. 8 (2015): 25–26; Zhonggong Shanxi shengwei dangshi bangongshi, ed., *Qi Yun zai Taihang* (Beijing: Zhongyang wenxian, 2014), 81.
20. Liu Bingrong, *Zoujin Qi Ruixin*, 14–17.
21. Qi Xin, "Jiqing," 26–27.
22. Ibid., 31; *Xi Zhongxun zhuan*, 1:374–75; "Zhongzhen"; *Qunxing cuican* (Xi'an: Shaanxi renmin, 2011), 707.
23. Qi Xin, "Jiqing," 32–34.
24. *Xi Zhongxun zhuan*, 1:374–75; Qi Xin, "Wo zai Kangda de zhandou shenghuo," *Xinxiang pinglun*, Feb. 2016, 39–41; "Zhongzhen."
25. *Qunxing cuican*, 707; *Yan'an zhengfeng yundong jishi*, 219–20.
26. Nie Chenyong, "Xiangwang yangguang canlan de difang," in *Yanhe ernü: Yan'an qingnian de chengcai zhilu*, ed. Jia Zhi (Beijing: Renmin, 1999), 102.
27. *Li Peng huiyilu (1928–1983)* (Beijing: Zhongyang dianli, 2014), 58, 65.
28. Wang Yunfeng, *Yan'an daxue xiaoshi* (Xi'an: Shaanxi renmin, 1994), 301–3; Han Xueben, "Ji 1949 nian yiqian de Lin Disheng tongzhi," in *Jinian Lin Disheng wenji* (Lanzhou: Lanzhou daxue chubanshe, 2007), 385–87.
29. Tian Fang, "He Xi Zhongxun shenghuo zai yiqi," *Yangcheng wanbao*, May 4, 1996.
30. Qi Xin, "Yi Zhongxun," in *Xi Zhongxun jinian wenji*, ed. Zhonggong zhongyang dangshi yanjiushi (Beijing: Zhonggong dangshi, 2013), 747–60.
31. Xi Qianping, "Wayaobu."
32. Yang Wenyu, "Yan'an shiqi de aiqing," *Dangshi bolan*, no. 5 (1998): 27–31.
33. Qi Xin, "Yi Zhongxun"; *Xi Zhongxun zhuan*, 1:379–80; "Zhongzhen."
34. Shaanxi sheng fulian fuyun shi xiaozu, ed., *Shaan-Gan-Ning bianqu funü yundong*

zhuanti xuanbian (Xi'an: Shaanxi sheng fulian yundong shi xiaozu, 1984), 26–32; Zhonghua quanguo funü lianhehui, *Zhongguo funü yundong shi (Xin minzhu zhuyi shiqi)* (Beijing: Chunqiu, 1989), 544.

35. Xi Qianping, "Wayaobu."
36. Zhonggong Shaanxi shengwei zuzhibu et al., *1925.10–1987.10*, 418, 422.
37. Zhu yuan shengji jiguan zonghe kou gongren and Jiefangjun Mao Zedong sixiang xuanchuan dui yi si liu dui, "Yi Mao zhuxi de zhengce he celüe sixiang wei tongshuai dadan jiefang fan zuowu you le juewu de ganbu," *Shaanxi qingkuang* 11 (Apr. 1969): 17–18.
38. Lu Huang, "Hongse Fuermosi"; Jiang Wei, *Hongse Fuermosi*, 142, 244–45.
39. Qi Xin, "Yi Zhongxun"; *Xi Zhongxun zhuan*, 2:627; "Zhongzhen"; Hu Peiyuan, "Nanwang de licheng," 24; *Qunxing cuican*, 708.
40. *Xi Zhongxun zhuan*, 1:382.
41. Qi Xin, "Wo yu Xi Zhongxun xiangban wushibanian," *Juece yu xinxi*, no. 7 (2012): 44.
42. Liu Bingrong, *Zoujin Qi Ruixin*, 116–18.
43. Jia Juchuan, "1913.10–1937.7," 15.
44. Zhang Zhigong, *Nanwang de ershinian: Zai Xi Zhongxun shenbian gongzuo de rizi li* (Beijing: Jiefangjun, 2013), 214.
45. Xi Qianping, "Wayaobu."
46. *Xi Zhongxun zhuan*, 1:299.
47. Xi Zhengning, "Fuqin dui wode zhunzhun jiaohui," in *Xi Zhongxun jinian wenji*, ed. Zhonggong zhongyang dangshi yanjiushi (Beijing: Zhonggong dangshi, 2013), 767–73.
48. "Xi Yuanping: Mingji lishi, bu wang chuxin," *Xi'an ribao*, May 21, 2019; Hu Peiyuan, "Nanwang de licheng," 25.
49. Qi Xin, "Wo yu Xi Zhongxun fengyu xiangban 55 ge chunqiu," in *Xi Zhongxun geming shengya* (Beijing: Zhongguo wenshi, 2000), 655–56 (hereafter cited as Qi Xin, "Fengyu").
50. Zhang Zhenbang, "Wo wei Xibeiju zhong liangshi," in *Zai Xibeiju de rizi li*, ed. Shi Jie and Si Zhihao (Xi'an: Shaanxi shifan daxue chubanshe, 2018), 58–64; Shao Jiyao, "Xibeiju: Wo yisheng meihao de jiyi," in *Zai Xibeiju de rizi li*, ed. Shi Jie and Si Zhihao (Xi'an: Shaanxi shifan daxue chubanshe, 2018), 71–82; Zhang Zhigong, *Nanwang de ershinian*, 201.

Chapter 6: War on the Nationalists and the Peasants

1. *Yidai zhanjiang: Huiyi Wang Jinshan* (Beijing: Junshi kexue, 1992), 145.
2. Zhonggong Xianyang shiwei dangshi yanjiushi, ed., *Zhengrong suiyue: Xi Zhongxun zai Guanzhong fenqu* (Beijing: Zhongyang wenxian, 2013), 271–80.
3. Xu Ruiyuan and Han Jinqiang, "Cong Mao Zedong jiu feng shuxin qianxi Xi Zhongxun dui jieying zhongyuan tuwei Wang Zhen bu beifan Yan'an de lishi gongxian," *Dang'an*, no. 10 (2016): 19–27.
4. *Peng Dehuai quanzhuan*, 4 vols. (Beijing: Zhongguo da baike quanshu, 2009), 2:586–93; Wang Zhengzhu, *Peng zong zai Xibei jiefang zhanchang* (Xi'an: Shaanxi renmin, 1981), 7–8; Yuan Zhigang, "Jiefangjun gaoji jiangling pingshu Xibei zhanchang (I)," *Dangshi bolan*, no. 2 (2012): 38; Jiefangjun di yi yezhanjun zhanshi bianshen weiyuanhui, ed., "Zhang Zongxun, Xi Zhongxun deng guanyu Xihuachi zhandou wei da jiandi mudi zhi junwei dian," in *Diyiye zhanjun wenxian xuanbian*, vol. 1 (Beijing: Jiefangjun, 2000), 88–89.
5. *Peng Dehuai quanzhuan*, 2:594–98; Meng Deqiang, "Xi Zhongxun de Xi'an yishi," *Zongheng* 280, no. 4 (2013): 21; Tian Runmin, "Xibei jiefang zhanzheng zhong de qingbao zhan," *Yanhuang chunqiu*, no. 2 (2019): 21–27.

6. Yang Zhesheng, *Zai Hu Zongnan shenbian de shiernian* (Shanghai: Shanghai renmin, 2007), 290, 292, 295.
7. *Peng Dehuai quanzhuan*, 2:598–618.
8. Ibid., 618–26.
9. Xi Zhongxun, "Yi dang zhongyang zai zhuanzhan Shaan-bei zhong zhaokai de Xiaohe huiyi," *Zhonggong dangshi ziliao* 52 (1994): 2.
10. "Renmin jiefangjun Peng fu zongsiling yanshuo: Wo junmin tuanjie lida wudi, ding neng quanbu xiaomie Jiang-Hu jun," *PD*, May 23, 1947.
11. Xi Zhongxun, "Yi dang zhongyang," 4.
12. Xia Meng and Wang, *Xi Zhongxun: Father*, 123–24.
13. *Peng Dehuai quanzhuan*, 2:729–38.
14. Wang Yan, "Yongyuan huainian Xi Zhongxun bobo," Zhonghong wang, May 24, 2018, https://archive.ph/5NMZx.
15. Yuan Zhigang, "Jiefangjun gaoji jiangling pingshu Xibei zhanchang (II)," *Dangshi bolan*, no. 3 (2012): 24.
16. Wang Zhengzhu, *Peng zong*, 39–41.
17. Ding Min, "Xi Zhongxun zai Luonai," 97–98.
18. Yuan Zhigang, "Jiefangjun (I)," 37–41.
19. Miao Pingjun, "Zhandou zai diren xinzang de yingxiong men," *Dangshi wenhui*, no. 3 (2017): 41–45.
20. Gao Bulin, "Jiefang zhangzheng houqi zai Guomindang Hu Zongnan zongbu jianli qingbao guanxi de qingkuang," in *Shaan-Gan-Ning bianqu zhengfu bao'anchu nan xian qingbao gongzuo shiliao xuanbian*, ed. Zhonggong Shaanxi shengwei dangshi yanjiushi and Shaanxi sheng gong'anting, ser. 35, vol. 45 (n.p.: SCCP, 2012), 257.
21. Yuan Zhigang, "Jiefangjun (I)," 42; Wang Yan, "Xi Zhongxun bobo."
22. *Zhongguo renmin jiefangjun diyiye zhanjun zhanshi* (Beijing: Jiefangjun, 1995), 373.
23. *Xi Zhongxun nianpu*, 1:194–96.
24. Li Rui, diary (vol. 2–1, 1948, 1949, 1992), p. 11, HIA.
25. Wei Tong, *Hu Xizhong* (Xi'an: Shaanxi renmin jiaoyu, 2003), 25, 78–117, 185–86.
26. Tang Jiayu and Zhang Zhouya, "Xi Zhongxun 'geming shengya zhong zui deyi de yibi,'" *Dangshi bolan*, no. 12 (2017): 14–18.
27. Tang Jiayu, "Xi Zhongxun yu 'Yulin fangshi,'" *Dangshi zonglan*, no. 12 (2017): 4–12.
28. Ibid.
29. Ibid., 5.
30. Ibid., 12.
31. Deng Rong, "Xi Zhongxun zai Guanzhong tequ de tongzhan gongzuo chutan," *Keji xinxi*, Feb. 2013, 78.
32. Yang Kuisong, *Zhonghua renmin gongheguo jianguo shi yanjiu* (Nanchang: Jiangxi renmin, 2015), 29–38; Marc Opper, *People's Wars in China, Malaya, and Vietnam* (Ann Arbor: University of Michigan Press, 2020), 136–38.
33. Yang Kuisong, *Zhonghua renmin gongheguo*, 29–38.
34. Ibid., 38–59; Kyoko Tanaka, "Mao and Liu in the 1947 Land Reform: Allies or Disputants?," *China Quarterly*, no. 75 (Sept. 1978): 566–93.
35. Brian DeMare, *Land Wars: The Story of China's Agrarian Revolution* (Stanford: Stanford University Press, 2019), 15.
36. Zhi Xiaomin, *Liu Shaoqi yu Jin-Sui tugai* (Taipei: Xiuwei zixun keji, 2008), 197.
37. Yang Kuisong, *Zhonghua renmin gongheguo*, 62–63; Zhang Huamin, "Wu Daifeng tongzhi er san shi," *Yan'an wenxue*, no. 1 (2013): 161–64.
38. Yang Kuisong, *Zhonghua renmin gongheguo*, 62–63; Forman, *Report*.
39. Zhi, *Liu Shaoqi*, 213–18.

40. Ibid., 228–29; Jia Juchuan, "Xi Zhongxun nianpu (1937.7–1949.9)," *Weinan shifan xueyuan xuebao* 26, no. 11 (2011): 17.

41. Xi Yuanping, "Fuqin Xi Zhongxun yisheng cong bu fan 'zuo' de cuowu," Xinhua, July 27, 2015; Zhongguo xinwenshe, "Chicheng."

42. Liu Bingrong, "He Long yu Yihe huiyi," *Xiangchao* 10 (Oct. 2007): 20–24.

43. *Xi Zhongxun nianpu*, 1:199.

44. *Lin Boqu zhuan* (Beijing: Hongqi, 1986), 341; *Ren Bishi zhuan (xiuding ben)* (Beijing: Zhongyang wenxian, 2004), 789–94.

45. Xi Zhongxun, "Hongri," 296–97.

46. Yang Kuisong, *Zhonghua renmin gongheguo*, 73–74.

47. Zhongyang dang'anguan, ed., "Xi Zhongxun guanyu Xibei tugai qingkuang de baogao," in *Jiefang zhanzheng shiqi tudi gaige wenjian xuanbian 1945–1949* (Beijing: Zhonggong zhongyang dangxiao, 1981), 128–31; DeMare, *Land Wars*, 113–14; Yang Kuisong, *Zhonghua renmin gongheguo*, 78–79.

48. Yang Kuisong, *Zhonghua renmin gongheguo*, 80–81.

49. Ibid., 81–84.

50. "Xi Zhongxun tongzhi guanyu xinqu gongzuo wenti gei Mao zhuxi de baogao," in *Zhonggong dangshi jiaoxue cankao ziliao*, vol. 18 (Beijing: Zhongguo renmin jiefangjun zhengzhi xueyuan dangshi jiaoyanshi, 1986), 449–50, 452 (hereafter cited as "Xinqu gongzuo wenti").

51. Ibid., 450.

52. Zhongyang dang'anguan, ed., "Xi Zhongxun zai Xibeiju ganbu huiyishang de jielun tigang," in *Jiefang zhanzheng shiqi tudi gaige wenjian xuanbian 1945–1949* (Beijing: Zhonggong zhongyang dangxiao, 1981), 469–73.

53. Ibid., 473.

54. Ibid., 474.

55. "Xinqu gongzuo wenti," 452.

Chapter 7: King of the Northwest

1. Jia Juchuan, "Xi Zhongxun nianpu (1949.10–1962.9)," *Weinan shifan xueyuan xuebao* 27, no. 1 (2012): 5–6 (hereafter cited as Jia Juchuan, "1949.10–1962.9").

2. Xi'an shi dang'anju and Xi'an shi dang'anguan, eds., *Xi'an shi junguan hui jieguan Xi'an gongzuo zongjie (jielu)*, in *Xi'an jiefang dang'an shiliao xuanji* (Xi'an: Shaanxi renmin, 1989), 201–15.

3. Zhonggong Gansu shengwei dangshi yanjiushi, ed., "Xibeiju guanyu Xibei, quxian, quxiang san ji huiyi zhengfeng qingkuang de baogao," in *20 shiji 50 niandai chu Gansu de zhengdang zhengfeng*, ser. 35, vol. 43 (n.p.: SCCP, 2010), 70–71.

4. Xi Zhongxun, "Fandui guanliao zhuyi, mingling zhuyi," *Xibei zhengbao* 1, no. 3 (May 1950): 25–31.

5. Xi Zhongxun, "Xibei qu yijiuwuyi nian de gongzuo renwu," *Xibei zhengbao* 1, no. 10 (Jan. 1951): 1–2.

6. Xi Zhongxun, "Ruhe zuohao yijiuwuyi nian de nongye shengchan gongzuo," *Xibei zhengbao* 1, no. 11 (Feb. 1951): 16–18.

7. Yang Kuisong, *Zhonghua renmin gongheguo*, 147.

8. Ibid., 190.

9. "Shaanxi moxie xianfen dui zhenya fangeming fenzi cunzai youqing pianxiang," *Neibu cankao*, Oct. 16, 1950 (internal circulation).

10. Zhonggong Gansu shengwei, ed., "Xi Zhongxun dui Gansu gongzuo de yijian," in *Xi Zhongxun yu Gansu* (Lanzhou: Gansu renmin, 2013), 414–16.

11. Zhonggong Gansu shengwei, ed., "Xi Zhongxun zai Gansu shengwei weiyuan

huiyishang de jianghua," in *Xi Zhongxun yu Gansu* (Lanzhou: Gansu renmin, 2013), 417–21.

12. Zhonggong Gansu shengwei, ed., "Xi Zhongxun zai Gansu sheng, shi liangji ganbu huiyishang de jianghua," in *Xi Zhongxun yu Gansu* (Lanzhou: Gansu renmin, 2013), 422–26.

13. Xi Zhongxun, "Gonggu chengji, kefu quedian, zhengqu gengde de shengli," *Xinjiang zhengbao* 2, no. 5 (May 1951): 4–6.

14. Zhonggong zhongyang wenxian yanjiushi and Zhongyang dang'anguan, eds., "Zhongyang tongyi Xi Zhongxun guanyu sanyuefen gongzuo zonghe baogao de dianbao," in *Jianguo yilai Liu Shaoqi wengao*, vol. 3 (Beijing: Zhongyang wenxian, 2005), 353–55.

15. "Lanzhou zhenya fangeming fenzi hou de shehui fanying," *Neibu cankao*, Apr. 9, 1951 (internal circulation).

16. "Xibei diqu zhenya fangeming yundong de qingkuang," *Neibu cankao*, Apr. 18, 1951 (internal circulation).

17. Xi Zhongxun, "Dongyuan yiqie liliang wei wancheng quansheng tudi gaige er douzheng," *Gansu zhengbao* 2, no. 5 (Sept. 1951): 1–8.

18. Sun Zuobin and Lu, "Huiyi Xi Zhongxun," 444–46.

19. Tang Fei, "Hu Yaobang zhu Shaan jiu 'zuo,'" *Bainianchao*, no. 10 (Nov. 2005): 4–14.

20. "Zhonggong Shaanxi shengwei guanyu wei Li Qiming tongzhi pingfan de tongzhi," June 10, 1980, HCCPM (hereafter cited as "Li Qiming tongzhi").

21. Xi Zhongxun, "Dongyuan yiqie liliang."

22. Yang Kuisong, *Zhonghua renmin gongheguo*, 271; Zhonggong Gansu shengwei, ed., "Mao Zedong pizhuan Xi Zhongxun guanyu chedi fan tanwu douzheng gei zhongyang de dianbao," in *Xi Zhongxun yu Gansu* (Lanzhou: Gansu renmin, 2013), 438–41.

23. Feng Hui and Pang Xianzhi, eds., *Mao Zedong nianpu 1949–1976*, 6 vols. (Beijing: Zhongyang wenxian, 2013), 1:437.

24. "Xi Zhongxun zhishi bixu yansu zhixing zhengce," Jan. 4, 1952, HCCPM; "Xi'an shi renmin fayuan panchusi shi ming tanwu fan zhong bufen liangxing guozhong: Xi Zhongxun tongzhi yi banling jianqi yi mian yingxiang sanfan yundong de kaizhan," *Neibu cankao*, Jan. 8, 1952 (internal circulation).

25. Xi Zhongxun, "Dazhang qigu di fazhan qunzhong," Jan. 6, 1952, HCCPM.

26. Xi Zhongxun, "Xibei qu ji jiguan yi ri kaishi da laohu de zhandou," Feb. 1, 1952, HCCPM.

27. Ibid.

28. "Mao Zedong guanyu Xibei junqu eryuefen ying shenru sanfan zhaozhong dahu de dianbao," Feb. 1, 1952, HCCPM.

29. "Mao Zedong dui Zhang Zongxun deng guanyu Xibei junqu zhengbian wenti zhishi de piyu," Feb. 10, 1952, HCCPM.

30. "Mao Zedong zhuanfa Xi Zhongxun guanyu Xibeiqu dahu xin yusuan baogao de piyu," Feb. 17, 1952, HCCPM.

31. Zhonggong Gansu shengwei, ed. "Xi Zhongxun guanyu Xibei diqu gongzuo de dierci zonghe baogao," in *Xi Zhongxun yu Gansu* (Lanzhou: Gansu renmin, 2013), 449–56 (hereafter, the title is cited as "Xibei diqu gongzuo").

32. "Sanfanhou Xibeiqu shichang xiaotiao chengxiang neiwu jiaoliu shuaitui: Xibeiqu lingdao jiguan yi juti zhishi gu bumen chouqiao renli jiaqiang yewu gongzuo," *Neibu cankao*, Mar. 3, 1952 (internal circulation).

33. Frank Dikötter, *The Tragedy of Liberation: A History of the Chinese Revolution, 1945–57* (London: Bloomsbury, 2013), 149.

34. Yang Kuisong, *Zhonghua renmin gongheguo*, 300.

Chapter 8: "Political Means, with Military Force as a Supplement"
1. Li Weihan, *Huiyi yu yanjiu*, 2 vols. (Beijing: Zhonggong dangshi ziliao, 1986), 1:467.
2. Zhang Zhiyang, "Xi Zhongxun," 78–79.
3. Zhongyang dang'anguan and Shaanxi sheng dang'anguan, eds., "Bianqu dangwei guanyu Huimin wenti gei Xi Zhongxun de xin," in *Zhonggong Shaan-Gan-Ning bianqu dangwei wenjian huiji* (1940 nian–1941 nian), ser. 35, vol. 9 (n.p.: SCCP, 2016), 140.
4. Yun Shubi, "Cong Tumochuan dao Yan'an: Zhuixun fuqin Wulanfu de zuji," *Shenjian* 4 (2011): 4–24; Xiaoyuan Liu, *Reins of Liberation: An Entangled History of Mongolian Independence, Chinese Territoriality, and Great Power Hegemony* (Stanford: Stanford University Press, 2006), 86, 108; Zhang Zhigong, *Nanwang de ershinian*, 102; Ding Min, "Xi Zhongxun zai Luonai," 99.
5. *Etuoke qi zhi* (Hohhot: Nei Menggu renmin, 1993), 605; Zhonggong zhongyang tongzhanbu, ed., *Zhonggong zhongyang Xibeiju dui Yimeng gongzuo fangzhen de zhishi dian* (Beijing: Zhonggong zhongyang dangxiao, 1991), 982.
6. Tianjin hongdaihui Nankai daxue bayiba huoju zongdui, Nei Menggu Hu sansi yixueyuan dongfanghong gongshe zhuanqiu Gao Gang louwang fenzi lianluozhan, and Nei Menggu Yimeng hongzongsi lianwei "zhanqiu Gao Gang yudang lianluozhan," "Chedi chanchu Gao Gang yudang (I)," in *Mongorujin jenosaido ni kansuru kiso shiryō*, ed. Yang Haiying, vol. 7 (Tokyo: Fukyosha, 2015), 266–68 (hereafter cited as Tianjin hongdaihui Nankai daxue bayiba huoju zongdui et al., "Gao Gang"); Zhou Nansheng, "Qinghai, Xizang, Xinjiang renzhi jishi: Ji Zhonggong zhongyang dui Zhou Renshan de sanci renming," in *Zhou Renshan tongzhi danchen bainian jinian wenji*, ed. Zhonggong Gansu shengwei dangshi yanjiushi (Pingliang: Pingliang Hongqi yinshua, 2014), 17.
7. Mao Zedong, "Jianqu zhengzhi fangshi jiejue xibei diqu," in *Mao Zedong junshi wenji*, vol. 5 (Beijing: Junshi kexue; Beijing: Zhongyang wenxian, 1993), 654.
8. Zhonggong zhongyang tongzhanbu and Zhonggong zhongyang wenxian yanjiushi, eds., "Xibei gongzuo de tedian shi zuohao minzu gongzuo," in *Xi Zhongxun lun tongyi zhanxian* (Beijing: Zhongyang wenxian, 2013), 35.
9. Sun Zuobin and Lu, "Huiyi Xi Zhongxun," 442.
10. Zhonggong zhongyang tongzhanbu and Zhonggong zhongyang wenxian yanjiushi, eds., "Zai xibei tongzhan minzu gongzuo huiyishang de jianghua," in *Xi Zhongxun lun tongyi zhanxian* (Beijing: Zhongyang wenxian, 2013), 61–83.
11. Benno Weiner, "'This Absolutely Is Not a Hui Rebellion!': The Ethnopolitics of Great Nationality Chauvinism in Early Maoist China," *Twentieth-Century China* 48, no. 3 (2023): 211.
12. James Z. Gao, "The Call of the Oases: The 'Peaceful Liberation' of Xinjiang, 1949–1953," in *Dilemmas of Victory: The Early Years of the People's Republic of China*, ed. Jeremy Brown and Paul G. Pickowicz (Cambridge, MA: Harvard University Press, 2007), 184–204.
13. Benno Weiner, *The Chinese Revolution on the Tibetan Frontier* (Ithaca, NY: Cornell University Press, 2020), 55–56.
14. Dikötter, *Tragedy of Liberation*, 205; Yuan Zhigang, *Xibei da jiaofei jishi* (Beijing: Jiefangjun, 2008), 153–61; Weiner, "Hui Rebellion," 220–21.
15. Zhonggong Shaanxi shengwei dangshi yanjiushi, ed., "Guanyu Pingliang feiluan xiang Zhonggong zhongyang Xibeiju de baogao," in *Zhang Desheng* (Xi'an: Shaanxi renmin, 1996), 468–71; Dikötter, *Tragedy of Liberation*, 205.
16. Zhonggong Hebei shengwei tongzhanbu, ed., "Xi Zhongxun tongzhi zai quanguo tongzhan gongzuo huiyishang de jianghua," in *Tongyi zhanxian wenjian xuanbian*, ser. 38, vol. 189, pt. 1 (n.p.: SCCP, 2016), 68.
17. Dikötter, *Tragedy of Liberation*, 205; Yuan Zhigang, *Xibei da jiaofei jishi*, 153–61.

18. Fei Jianxian, "Jianguo chuqi xianwei renzhi de Qinghai pingpan," *Zhongshan fengyu* (Apr. 2014): 7–9.

19. Linda Benson and Ingvar Svanberg, "Osman Batur: The Kazak's Golden Legend," in *The Kazaks of China: Essays on an Ethnic Minority*, ed. Linda Benson and Ingvar Svanberg (Uppsala: Uppsala University, 1988), 141–88; Justin Jacobs, "The Many Deaths of a Kazakh Unaligned: Osman Batur, Chinese Decolonization, and the Nationalization of a Nomad," *American Historical Review* 115, no. 5 (Dec. 2010): 1291–314; Charles Kraus, "To Die on the Steppe: Sino-Soviet American Relations and the Cold War in Chinese Central Asia, 1944–1952," *Cold War History* 14, no. 3 (2014): 293–313.

20. Zizhiqu dangwei jiguan wuchanjieji geming lianluobu "dousi pixiu" zhandoutuan and Honggelian xinda "geming daodi" bingtuan, "Zizhiqu liangtiao luxian douzheng de youlai he fazhan: Jianping Wang Enmao tongzhi de wenti" (Geming daodi), Oct. 16, 1967, *NCRGP*, pt. 3, *CCTP*, pp. 6343–45.

21. *Zhang Zongxun huiyilu* (Beijing: Jiefangjun, 2008), 368; Deng Lifeng, *Jianguo hou junshi xingdong quanlu* (Taiyuan: Shanxi renmin, 1992), 183.

22. Zhonggong Qinghai shengwei dangshi ziliao zhengji weiyuanhui and Zhongguo renmin jiefangjun Qinghai sheng junqu zhengzhiju, eds., "Zhonggong zhongyang zhuanfa Xibeiju guanyu chuli shaoshu minzu diqu panluan baogao de zhishi," in *Jiefang Qinghai shiliao xuanbian* (Xining: Zhonggong Qinghai shengwei dangshi ziliao zhengji weiyuanhui and Zhongguo renmin jiefangjun Qinghai sheng junqu zhengzhiju,1990), 301–2.

23. Zhonggong Gansu shengwei, "Xibei diqu gongzuo," 453.

24. "Xi Zhongxun gei Mao Zedong he zhongyang de baogao (jielu)," Apr. 10, 1951, HCCPM.

25. Zhongguo shehui kexueyuan and Zhongyang dang'anguan, eds., *Zhonghua renmin gongheguo jingji dang'an ziliao xuanbian, 1949–1952: Nongcun jingji tizhi juan* (Beijing: Shehui kexue wenxian, 1992), 229.

26. *Deng Liqun guoshi jiangtanlu*, 7 vols. (Beijing: Zhonghua renmin gongheguo shigao bianweihui, 2000), 5:273.

27. "Xi Zhongxun gei Mao."

28. Zhonggong Gansu shengwei, "Xibei diqu gongzuo," 453.

29. Ibid.; Jiang Ping, "Shenqie huainian wode zhanyou wode shizhang," *Bianianchao*, no. 10 (2013): 15.

30. Zhonggong Gansu shengwei, "Xibei diqu gongzuo," 453–55.

31. Zhonggong zhongyang wenxian yanjiushi and Zhongyang dang'anguan, eds., "Guanyu Xinjiang ruogan gongzuo fangzhen wenti de dianbao," in *Jianguo yilai Liu Shaoqi wengao*, vol. 4 (Beijing: Zhongyang wenxian, 2005), 178–80.

32. Zhonggong zhongyang wenxian yanjiushi and Zhongyang dang'anguan, eds.,"Zhongyang zhuanfa Xi Zhongxun guanyu Xibeiju huiyi qingkuang baogao de tongzhi," in *Jianguo yilai Liu Shaoqi wengao*, vol. 4 (Beijing: Zhongyang wenxian, 2005), 160–62.

33. Zhonggong zhongyang wenxian yanjiushi and Zhongyang dang'anguan, "Guanyu Xinjiang," 175–76.

34. Chen Wuguo and Liu Xianghui, *Xinjiang wangshi* (Beijing: Dangdai Zhongguo, 2006), 26.

35. Fang Xiaochun, *Zhongguo daxingzhengqu: 1949–1954 nian* (Shanghai: Dongfang, 2011), 251–52.

36. *Deng Liqun guoshi jiangtanlu*, 5:267–68; Mao Yinghui, "Dangbao minzu huayu de kuangjia bianqian yanjiu: Xinjiang ribao (hanwen ban) 1949–2009 nian minzu baodao fenxi" (PhD diss., Fudan University, 2010), 74–75.

37. *Xunmi zhenshi de Liu Geping* (Beijing: Zhongguo fazhan, 2016), 213.

38. *Wang Zhen zhuan*, 2 vols. (Beijing: Dangdai Zhongguo, 1999–2001), 1:516–17.
39. Liu Geping zhuanji bianweihui, *Liu Geping*, 214.
40. *Xi Zhongxun zhuan*, 2:194–96; Feng Hui and Pang, *Mao Zedong nianpu*, 1:595–96.
41. Li Kaiquan, "Bingtuan zaoqi gongyehua fangtanlu," *Xinjiang shengchan jianshe bingtuan shiliao xuanji* 16 (2007): 408–12.
42. Deng, "Wode jiantao," *Xinjiang ribao*, July 17, 1952; Xi Zhongxun, "Wu ge yue gongzuo zongjie he dangqian de renwu," *Xinjiang ribao*, July 17, 1952.
43. Xi Zhongxun, "Xibei ju zhuanfa Xi Zhongxun tongzhi gei Mao zhuxi guanyu jiancha Xinjiang gongzuo de jianyao baogao," Aug. 23, 1952, HCCPM; Zhonggong zhongyang wenxian yanjiushi and Zhongyang dang'anguan, "Zhongyang zhuanfa Xi Zhongxun," 481.
44. Feng Shou, *Wang Zhen he women* (Urumqi: Xinjiang renmin, 2008), 202.
45. *Deng Liqun guoshi jiangtanlu*, 5:270.
46. Ibid.
47. Liu Geping zhuanji bianweihui, *Liu Geping*, 217.
48. Li Rui, diary (vol. 30, 1998), p. 119, HIA; Li Rui, diary (vol. 33, 2001), p. 63, HIA; Wu Jiang, "Qin Chuan," 57.
49. Huang Zhengqing, *Huang Zhengqing yu wu shi Jiamuxiang* (Lanzhou: Gansu renmin, 1989), 71–75, 94.
50. Ibid., 82–83.
51. Tang Luo, "Mao Zedong pingzan Xi Zhongxun," *Yanhuang chunqiu*, no. 11 (1999): 20–22.
52. Zhonggong Jiangsu shengwei dangshi gongzuo bangongshi, *Zhang Zhongliang jinian wenji*, 82–89; Tian Runmin, *Xi Zhongxun*, 153; Weiner, *Chinese Revolution*, 56–62.
53. Ding Dong, *Xi Zhongxun yu Xiang Qian*, *Liaowang Zhongguo* 195 (Mar. 2013), http://www.outlookchina.net/html/news/201303/4891.html; Weiner, *Chinese Revolution*, 193.
54. Melvyn C. Goldstein, *A History of Modern Tibet*, 4 vols. (Berkeley: University of California Press, 1989–2019), 2:265–78.
55. Ibid., 2:27–28; Ji Youquan, *Baixue: Jiefang Xizang jishi* (Beijing: Zhongguo wuzi, 1993), 26–28.
56. Che Minghuai, "Xi Zhongxun guanxin Xizang geming he jianshe shiye," *Bainianchao*, no. 8 (2016): 17–25; Xizang zizhiqu dangshi ziliao zhengji weiyuanhui and Xizang junqu dangshi ziliao zhengji lingdao xiaozu, eds., "Zhongyang guanyu Xibeiju fudan Houzang he Ali diqu zhengzhi renwu dian," in *Heping jiefang Xizang* (Chengdu: Xizang renmin, 1995), 104.
57. Wang Xiaobin, *Zhongguo gongchandang Xizang zhengce yanjiu* (Beijing: Renmin, 2013), 374.
58. Goldstein, *History of Modern Tibet*, 2:278–90.
59. "Zhao Fan huiyilu" (unpublished manuscript, 1996), 9.
60. Che, "Xi Zhongxun"; Jiacuo Jiangbian [Jambey Gyatso], *Banchan dashi* (Beijing: Dongfang, 1989), 21–22.
61. Tang Luo, "Song Banchan E'erdeni gui Zang ji," in *Xi Zhongxun geming shengya* (Beijing: Zhongguo wenshi, 2000), 341–42.
62. Ibid., 343–44.
63. Goldstein, *History of Modern Tibet*, 2:387; Fan Ming and Hao Rui, *Xizang neibu zhizheng* (Carle Place: Mingjing, 2009), 185–86.
64. Guo Zhengqing and Guo Xiaomei, *Ya Hanzhang zhuan* (Lanzhou: Gansu renmin, 2016), 152.
65. Fan Ming and Hao, *Xizang neibu zhizheng*, 185–88; Xiaoyuan Liu, *To the End of Revolution: The Chinese Communist Party and Tibet, 1949–1959* (New York: Columbia University Press, 2020), 72.

66. Du Shu'an, "Zongjie jingyan, tigao renshi," *Xizang geming huiyilu* 3 (1984): 259–68; Xiao Sheng, "Xibei jin Zang de houqin gongzuo," *Xizang geming huiyilu* 3 (1984): 269–83; Yang Zhijun, *Wangming xingji* (Beijing: Zhongguo gongren, 2002), 114.

67. Fan Ming, *Ba wuxing hongqi gaogao di chazai Ximalaya shan shang* (Haikou: Nanhai, 2016), 34.

Chapter 9: Ideology and Power Politics in the Beijing of the Early People's Republic

1. Jia Juchuan, "'Luhuo chunqing' Xi Zhongxun," *Dangshi bolan*, no. 3 (2003): 40–42.
2. Yang Kuisong, *Zhonghua renmin gongheguo*, 372–74.
3. Jia Juchuan, "1949.10–1962.9," 15.
4. Ma Songlin, "Huainian Xi Zhongxun shuji," 34–36.
5. Li Rui, diary (vol. 26, 1994), p. 68, HIA.
6. Ding Min, "Xi Zhongxun zai Luonai," 96.
7. Jia Jichuan, "Xi Zhongxun nianpu (1962.10–2002.5)," *Weinan shifan xueyuan xuebao* 27, no. 3 (2012): 8 (hereafter cited as Jia Jichuan, "1962.10–2002.5").
8. Lin Yunhui, *Chongkao Gao Gang, Rao Shushi "fandang" shijian* (Hong Kong: Chinese University Press, 2017), 136.
9. Tian Fang, *Suiyue yinhen: Tian Fang wenji* (Beijing: Jincheng, 1998), 283.
10. Mao Zedong, "Zhongyang zhuanfa Xi Zhongxun guanyu wenwei fen dangzu buzhi fan guanliao zhuyi douzheng de baogao de piyu," in *Jianguo yilai Mao Zedong wengao*, vol. 4 (Beijing: Zhongyang wenxian, 1993), 74–75.
11. *Ye Shengtao ji*, vol. 22 (Nanjing: Jiangsu jiaoyu, 2004), 413, 449.
12. *Qi Benyu huiyilu*, 2 vols. (Hong Kong: Zhongguo wenge lishi, 2016), 2:228.
13. *Zhou Enlai nianpu*, 3 vols. (Beijing: Zhongyang wenxian, 1997), 1:264–65.
14. Xi Zhongxun, "Duiyu dianying gongzuo de yijian," *Dianying juzuo tongxun*, May 10, 1953, 3.
15. Ibid., 5–7.
16. Ibid., 8–11.
17. Wang Lin, *Wenyi shiqi nian: Wang Lin riji* (self-pub., 2013), 69.
18. Zhonggong zhongyang tongzhanbu and Zhonggong zhongyang wenxian yanjiushi, eds., "Ruhe zuohao wenjiao tongyi zhanxian gongzuo," in *Xi Zhongxun lun tongyi zhanxian* (Beijing: Zhongyang wenxian, 2013), 124–52; "Disici quanguo tongzhan gongzuo huiyi gaikuang," in *Lici quanguo tongzhan gongzuo huiyi gaikuang he wenxian* (Beijing: Dang'an, 1988), 122–30.
19. Charles J. Alber, *Embracing the Lie: Ding Ling and the Politics of Literature in the People's Republic of China* (Westport, CT: Praeger, 2004), 65–66; "Hu Feng: Wenyi gongzuo bu ying zhengzhi pipan, jianyan yuanhuo zhong huo pingfan," *Fenghuang weishi*, Jan. 9, 2012; Lu Yuan, *Hu Feng he wo*, ed. Ji Xianlin (Beijing: Beijing shiyue wenyi, 2001), 221; Hu Feng, "Cong shiji chufa," in *Zhiman congcong de huiyi*, ed. Ji Xianlin (Beijing: Beijing shiyue wenyi, 2001), 132.
20. Li Shitao, "Wo jiechuguo de Zhou Yang, Lin Mohan he Hu Qiaomu: Li Zhi xiansheng fangtanlu," *Xin wenxue shiliao*, no. 2 (2011): 76.
21. Lin Mohan, "Hu Feng shijian de qianqian houhou (Lin Mohan wenda lu zhi yi)," *Xin wenxue shiliao*, no. 8 (1989): 17–23; Shi Yun and Li Xin, "Hu Feng cuo'an shimo," *Wenshi yuekan*, no. 6 (2003): 29–30.
22. Xi Zhongxun, "Dangde xuanchuan gongzuo wei guanche dangde zong luxian he dangde qijie sizhong quanhui jueyi er douzheng," May 1954, HCCPM.
23. Han Gang, "Zhonggong lishi yanjiu de ruogan nandian redian wenti zhi 'Gao-Rao shijian' wenti," in *Gao Gang shijian kaobian*, ed. Yang Haofu (Beijing: Dazhong wenyi, 2011), 184–85; Jia Juchuan, "1949.10–1962.9," 15; *Zhou Enlai nianpu*, 1:285.

24. Michael Sheng, "Mao and Chinese Elite Politics in the 1950s: The Gao Gang Affair Revisited," *Twentieth-Century China* 36, no. 1 (2011): 67–96.
25. Lin Yunhui, *Chongkao Gao Gang*, 122.
26. Ibid., 125–28; Chung Yen-lin, "Deng Xiaoping zai 'Gao-Rao shijian' zhong zhi juese yu zuowei," *Renwen ji shehui kexue jikan* 22, no. 12 (2012): 524–27.
27. Yang Kuisong, *Mao Zedong yu Mosike de en'en yuanyuan*, 4th ed. (Nanchang: Jiangxi renmin, 2009), 121.
28. Lin Yunhui, *Chongkao Gao Gang*, 126.
29. Zhao Jialiang and Zhang Xiaoji, *Banjie mubei xia de wangshi: Gao Gang zai Beijing* (Hong Kong: Dafeng, 2008), 151–52.
30. Wen Xiang, *Gaoceng enyuan*, 431–32.
31. Zhang Xiushan, *Wode bashiwunian*, 303–9.
32. *Fan Ming huiyilu*, 3 vols. (Hong Kong: Xin shiji, 2021), 2:638, 2:725–26; "Xi Zhongxun de dier fen 'renzui shu,'" Aug. 9, 1967, HCCPM.
33. Lin Yunhui, *Chongkao Gao Gang*, 133, 310–11.
34. Ibid., 309; Li Rui, diary (vols. 16–17, 1985), p. 42, HIA.
35. Li Liqun, "Nanwang de huiyi," in *Yi Gao Gang tongzhi*, ed. Hengshanxian Gao Gang yu Zhongguo geming yanjiuhui (Beijing: Dazhong wenyi, 2010), 285.
36. Ibid., 264–89; Li Rui, *Lushan huiyi shilu* (Hong Kong: Tiandi tushu, 2009), 375; Zhao Jialiang, "Gao Gang liang ren mishu tan Gao Gang," in *Zhongguo dangdai mingren zhengyao fang shuping ji*, ed. Yang Jisheng (Hong Kong: Tiandi tushu, 2013), 83–100.
37. Chung Yen-lin, "Zhonggong jianzheng hou Zhou Enlai yu Deng Xiaoping guanxi zhi yanjiu (1949–1976)," *Guoli zhengzhi daxue lishi xuebao* 32 (Nov. 2009): 175–76.
38. Zhao Jialiang and Zhang, *Banjie mubei*, 51–53.
39. Li Liqun, "Gao Gang shengming zhong de zuihou wunian," in *Yi Gao Gang tongzhi*, ed. Hengshanxian Gao Gang yu Zhongguo geming yanjiuhui (Beijing: Dazhong wenyi, 2010), 78–79; Li Liqun, "Nanwang de huiyi."
40. Lin Yunhui, *Chongkao Gao Gang*, 311.
41. Shoudu hongdaihui Beijing dianli xueyuan: Jinggangshan gongshe "Peng, Gao, Rao, Xi" zhuan'an xiaozu, *Gao Gang wushinian zui'e shi (1904–1954)*, ser. 6, vol. 6 (n.p.: SCCP, 2007), 32–33 (hereafter cited as Shoudu hongdaihui, *Gao Gang*).
42. Hongweibing pipan wenzhang, "Tong sanfan fenzi," 262–63.
43. "Li Liqun tongzhi dui Lin Biao zuixing de jiefa," May 1972, HCCPM.
44. Hongweibing pipan wenzhang, "Tong sanfan fenzi."
45. Ibid.
46. Zhao Jialiang and Zhang, *Banjie mubei*, 13–14, 29–30, 35; Zhao Jialiang, "Gao Gang diyici zisha jingguo," *Bainianchao*, no. 7 (2003): 25–30; Zhang Siquan, *Gao Gang*, 629–34; Zhao Jialiang and Zhang Xiaoli, "Gao Gang fanxing jiancha," *Wangshi*, no. 72 (Sept. 2008).
47. "Zhou Enlai tongzhi zai guanyu Gao Gang wenti de zuotan huishang de fayan tigang," in *Youguan 1954–1955 nian qijian suowei "Gao-Rao fandang lianmeng" de ruogan zhongyao lishi wenxian*, ser. 6, vol. 1 (n.p.: SCCP, 2000), 59–61.
48. *Fan Ming huiyilu*, 2:726.
49. Li Liqun, "1949 zhi hou: Gao Gang yishuang hanyuan," VoA(C), Dec. 28, 2007; Li Liqun, "Nanwang de huiyi"; Li Su, "1949 zhi hou: Mao dui Gao Gang shiluan zhongqi," VoA(C), Dec. 14, 2007.
50. Two interviews.
51. Zhang Siquan, *Gao Gang*, 645.
52. Ibid., 672.
53. Shoudu hongdaihui, *Gao Gang*, 29.
54. Li Rui, diary (vols. 13–15, 1984), p. 80, HIA.

55. Li Rui, diary (vol. 30, 1998), p. 63, HIA.
56. Shoudu hongdaihui, *Gao Gang*, 32–33.
57. "Zhao Fan huiyilu," 28; X. Liu, *End of Revolution*, 82.
58. Lin Yunhui, *Chongkao Gao Gang*, 130.
59. *Fan Ming huiyilu*, 2:723–27.
60. Hongweibing pipan wenzhang, "Tong sanfan fenzi."
61. Li Liqun, "Nanwang de huiyi."
62. Deng Xiaoping, speech [in Chinese], Mar. 19, 1980. I thank an anonymous scholar for sharing with me Deng's original speech, as the official version of the speech does not include these words.
63. *Zhou Enlai nianpu*, 1:423–24, 1:478.
64. Zhonggong dangshi renwu yanjiuhui, ed., *Zhonggong dangshi renwu zhuan*, vol. 88 (Beijing: Zhonggong dangshi, 2016), 54.
65. Long Liwei and Bai Yuche, "Jiefangjun shouci shixing junxian zhi neimu zhenwen," *Wenshi jinghua*, no. 3 (2006): 4–13.
66. *Fan Ming huiyilu*, 2:723–27.
67. Xibei gongda "jiefang da Xibei" bingtuan, "Sanfan fenzi Xi Zhongxun de zui'e lishi" (Xibei gongda), Sept. 12, 1967, *NCRGP*, pt. 3, *CCTP*, pp. 18875–76; *Zhongguo gongchandang dibajie zhongyang weiyuanhui weiyuan he houbu weiyuan mingdan* (Beijing: Renmin, 1957), 860–61.

Chapter 10: The Perils of Intimacy at Home and Abroad

1. "Suide fenqu zhuanyuan gongxu [1944] qiyuefen gongzuo jianbao," Sept. 2, 1944, 2-1-236, 5, Shaanxi Provincial Archives. I thank Joseph Esherick for sharing this document with me.
2. "Letters from Major W. J. Peterkin, Somewhere in China," Oct. 8, 1944, box 1, Correspondence and Diary/Journal Entries, Wilbur J. Peterkin Papers, HIA; David D. Barrett, *Dixie Mission: The United States Army Observer Group in Yenan, 1944* (Berkeley: Center for Chinese Studies, University of California, 1970), 40.
3. Harrison Forman, diary, China (pt. 3, July–Sept. 1944), Travel Diaries and Scrapbooks of Harrison Forman, 1932–1973, UWML. Though quoting the original wording, I do not mean to endorse the ethnic slur.
4. Charles Kraus, "Creating a Soviet 'Semi-colony'? Sino-Soviet Cooperation and Its Demise in Xinjiang, 1949–1955," *Chinese Historical Review* 17, no. 2 (2010): 129–65; Zhonggong Gansu shengwei, ed., *Guanghui yeji chonggao fengfan: Jinian Xi Zhongxun tongzhi danchen 100 zhounian* (Lanzhou: Gansu renmin, 2013), 194.
5. Jia Juchuan, "1949.10–1962.9," 8, 13.
6. Xia Meng and Wang, *Xi Zhongxun: Father*, 179; Ding Min, "Xi Zhongxun zai Luonai," 95–96.
7. Zhang Peisen, ed., *Zhang Wentian nianpu (1942–1976)* (Beijing: Zhonggong dangshi, 2000), 965.
8. Many of the documents from the archives of the Chinese Foreign Ministry include Xi's name on the list of addressees.
9. Yang Shangkun, "Huiyi Gao-Rao Shijian," *Dang de wenxian*, no. 1 (2001): 14–22; "From the Journal of Ambassador Pavel Yudin: Memorandum of Conversation with Liu Shaoqi and Zhou Enlai," Mar. 9, 1954, WCDA, AVP RF. Obtained by Paul Wingrove.
10. Mao Zedong, "Zai Zhongguo gongchandang dibajie zhongyang weiyuanhui dierci quanti huiyishang de jianghua," in *Mao Zedong xuanji*, vol. 5 (Beijing: Renmin, 1977), 321.
11. Li Yueran, *Waijiao wutaishang de xin Zhongguo lingxiu* (Beijing: Waiyu jiaoxue yu yanjiu, 1994), 170.

574 NOTES TO CHAPTERS 10

12. Ma Yongshun, "Women de hao lingdao: Jinian Xi Zhongxun tongzhi danchen 100 zhounian," *Yaobang yanjiu*, no. 53 (Oct. 2013): 212–14, FCFL.

13. Ibid., 215–17.

14. Shen Zhihua, *Sulian zhuanjia zai Zhongguo (1948–1960)* (Beijing: Zhongguo guoji guangbo, 2003), 268; "Xi Zhongxun zai quanguo waiguo zhuanjia zhaodai gongzuo huiyishang de zhishi," June 28, 1956, ZE1-2-138, pp. 2–5, Liaoning Provincial Archives.

15. Shen Zhihua, *Sulian zhuanjia*; "Xi Zhongxun zai quanguo waiguo zhuanjia."

16. *Xi Zhongxun nianpu*, 2:340.

17. Tao Chen, "Between Economy and Politics: China and the Leipzig Trade Fair (1950–1966)," *European Review of History / Reveue européenne d'histoire* 30, no. 3 (2023): 348–55.

18. "Memorandum on the Chinese Government Delegation," n.d., MNL OL XIX-J-1-k, 1945–1964, China 1/26–6, item no. 26, National Archives of Hungary.

19. *Xi Zhongxun nianpu*, 2:341.

20. "Plan perebuvannia u Kyievi delegatsii Komunistychnoi partii Kytaiu," Mar. 23, 1959, f. 1, op. 31, spr. 1412, ark. 55–56, TsDAHOU; "Perelik suveniriv chlenam delegatsii Komunistychnoi partii Kytaiu," Mar. 23, 1959, f. 1, op. 31, spr. 1412, ark. 57, TsDAHOU.

21. "Ot"ezd iz Moskvy delegatsii KNR," *Izvestiia*, Mar. 28, 1959, 1.

22. Nikita Petrov, *Vremia Andropova* (Moscow: ROSSPEN, 2023), 184–218.

23. Jia Juchuan, "1949.10–1962.9," 20.

24. A. Mikoian, "Zapiska A. Mikoiana v TsK KPSS," Aug. 25, 1959, f. 3, op. 12, d. 565, l. 201, RGANI; "Reshenie TsK KPSS ot 26.VIII.59 g. 'O prieme delegatsii KNR vo glave s Zamestitelem Prem'era Gosudarstvennogo Soveta t. Si Chzhun-siunem,'" Aug. 26, 1959, f. 3, op. 14, d. 317, l. 103, RGANI.

25. "Zapis' besedy s glavoi Pravitel'stvennoi delegatsii KNR–zamestitelem Prem'era Gosudarstvennogo Soveta t. Si Chzhun-siunem na prieme chlenov delegatsii u Zamestitelia Predsedatelia Soveta Ministrov SSSR tovarishchia Zasiad'ko A. F.," Aug. 28, 1959, f. 0100, op. 52, p. 442, d. 5, ll. 36–41, AVP RF.

26. *Peng Dehuai quanzhuan*, 3:1265–77.

27. Wu Lengxi, *Shinian lunzhan: 1956–1966 ZhongSu guanxi huiyilu* (Beijing: Zhongyang wenxian, 1999), 205–8.

28. Mikoian, "Zapiska A. Mikoiana"; "1959 nian 8 yuefen wo tong Sulian zhu Hua dashiguan jiaoshe he qita duiwai huodong jiankuang," Sept. 5, 1959, 109-01338-08_18–20, PRC FMA.

29. "Zapis' besedy."

30. "Prebyvanie v Moskve pravitel'stvennoi delegatsii KNR," *Pravda*, Aug. 29, 1959, 3; "Korotko," *Leninskoe znamia*, Aug. 30, 1959, 1.

31. "Kitaiskie gosti v Moskve," *Pravda*, Aug. 31, 1959, 3.

32. "Vizit pravitel'stvennoi delegatsii KNR Predsedateliu Soveta Ministrov USSR N. T. Kal'chenko," *Pravda Ukrainy*, Sept. 1, 1959, 3.

33. *Xi Zhongxun nianpu*, 2:355–56.

34. Wu Lengxi, *Shinian lunzhan*, 210.

35. "Druzheskie vstrechi: Kitaiskie gosti v Moskve," *Izvestiia*, Sept. 10, 1959, 1.

36. "TASS Statement on China-India Rift," FBIS, Sept. 9, 1959; Zhihua Shen and Yafeng Xia, *Mao and the Sino-Soviet Partnership, 1945–1959: A New History* (Lanham, MD: Lexington Books, 2015), 329–30.

37. "Druz'ia iz Kitaia v Moskve," *Izvestiia*, Sept. 11, 1959, 2.

38. "Zhaxiadike zai wo zhu Su shiguan zhaodai huishang shuo Zhongguo renmin shixian le dayuejin," PD, Sept. 12, 1959.

39. "Dui Sulian Zhong Yin bianjing shijian de shengming de kanfa," Sept. 10, 1959,

105-00946-04_36–37, PRC FMA; "Ot″ezd iz Moskvy zamestitelia prem′era Gosudarstvennogo soveta KNR Si Chzhun-siunia," *Moskovskaia pravda*, Sept. 12, 1959, 1.

40. Joachim Glaubitz, "China im Ostblock," *Osteuropa* 10, no. 4 (Apr. 1960): 257–65.

41. "Discussion between N. S. Khrushchev and Mao Zedong," Oct. 2, 1959, f. 52, op. 1, d. 499, ll. 1–33, WCDA, AP RF, copy in Volkogonov Collection, Manuscript Division, Library of Congress, Washington, DC, trans. Vladislav M. Zubok.

42. V. Zorin and Iu. Andropov, "Perechen′ podarkov rukovodiashchim partiinym i gosudarstvennym rabotnikam Kitaiskoi Narodnoi Respubliki ot Partiino-pravitel′stvennoi delegatsii Sovetskogo Soiuza, vyezzhaiushchei na prazdnovanie 10-letiia KNR," Sept. 17, 1959, f. 3, op. 12, d. 573, l. 55, RGANI.

43. "Qing chunjie yan jiabing: Xi Zhongxun fu zongli zhaodai Sulian zhuanjia fuze ren," *PD*, Jan. 29, 1960.

44. Shen Zhihua, *Sulian zhuanjia*, 386.

45. V. Sanfirov, "Otkliki v KNR na rabotu i resheniia 5-i sessii Verkhovnogo Soveta SSSR," May 11, 1960, f. 5, op. 49, d. 332, ll. 106–10, RGANI.

46. I. Rogachev, "Osveshchenie v kitaiskoi pechati ekonomicheskoi pomoshchi, okazyvaemoi Sovetskim Soiuzom KNR," Sept. 10, 1960, f. 5, op. 49, d. 333, ll. 309–15, RGANI.

47. Zhongyang dang'anguan, ed., "Yinggai zhongshi he jiaqiang dui waiguo zhuanjia de gongzuo," in *Zhonggong zhongyang wenjian xuanji*, vol. 33 (Beijing: Renmin, 2013), 470–79.

48. *Zhu Kezhen riji*, vol. 4 (Beijing: Renmin, 1989), 469–70; Shen Zhihua, *Sulian zhuanjia*, 308–23; Zhonggong Gansu shengwei, ed., "Xi Zhongxun dashiji," in *Xi Zhongxun yu Gansu* (Lanzhou: Gansu renmin, 2013), 578.

49. *Xi Zhongxun nianpu*, 2:372; Wang Qinping, *Xin Zhongguo waijiao 50 nian Zhong* (Beijing: Beijing chubanshe, 1999), 905; Zhang Bing, *Wang Guoquan zhuan* (Kaifeng: Henan daxue chubanshe, 2006), 95; Chen, "Between Economy and Politics," 356.

50 Tao Chen, "East German Pragmatism, China's Policy of Differentiation, and Soviet Miscalculation: Hermann Matern's 1961 Trip to China Revisited," *Cold War History* 19, no. 1 (2019): 92–93, 97–98; "Deguo zhengfu daibiao tuan jiedai jianbao," Jan. 19, 1961, 109-03760-04, PRC FMA; S. Chervonenko, "Zapis′ besedy s poslom GDR v KNR Vandelem," Feb. 3, 1961, f. 0100, op. 54, p. 466, d. 7, ll. 18–23, AVP RF.

51. "Vo imia mira na zemle," *Komsomol′skaia pravda*, July 27, 1962, 3.

52. "Sulian dashiuan linshi daiban juxing jiuhui qingzhu liangsou yuzhou feichuan shengli fanhang, Xi Zhongxun fu zongli deng yingyao chuxi," *PD*, Aug. 19, 1962.

53. *He Fang zishu: Cong Yan'an yi lu zoulai de fansi* (self-pub., 2011), 220.

54. Lin Mu, *Zhu jin meng you xu: Hu Yaobang zhu shou Lin Mu huiyilu* (Hong Kong: Xin shiji, 2008), 194–95.

55. Xibei gongda "jiefang da Xibei" bingtuan, "Sanfan fenzi Xi Zhongxun de zui'e lishi" (Xibei gongda), Sept. 12, 1967, *NCRGP*, pt. 3, *CCTP*, pp. 18875–76.

56. Laixia laiqu zhijian, "Xi Zhongxun," pt. 6, CCTV, YouTube, May 28, 2022, video, https://www.youtube.com/watch?v=OWoFdeYC9KE&t=27s.

57. Zhou Erfu, "Tongyi zhanxian de guanghui: Ji Xi Zhongxun tongzhi er san shi," in *Zhou Erfu sanwen ji*, vol. 2 (Beijing: Huaxia, 1999), 312.

58. Jin Zhijian, "Zhen shi cong xinli ganji zongli," in *Bairen fangtan Zhou Enlai*, ed. Zhou Erjun and Zhou Bingde (Nanjing: Jiangsu wenyi, 1998), 428.

59. Qi Xin, "Zhongxun, wo yong weixiao song ni yuanxing," in *Huainian Xi Zhongxun*, ed. Cao Zhenzhong and Wu Jiang (Beijing: Zhongyang dangshi, 2005), 18–19; Qi Qiaoqiao, "Fuqin yongyuan huo zai wode xinzhong," in *Xi Zhongxun jinian wenji*, ed. Zhonggong zhongyang dangshi yanjiushi (Beijing: Zhonggong dangshi, 2013), 779.

60. Dandan Zhu, *1956: Mao's China and the Hungarian Crisis* (Ithaca, NY: Cornell University East Asia Program, 2013), 12.

61. Shen Zhihua, *Sikao yu xuanze: Cong zhishifenzi huiyi dao fanyoupai yundong 1956–1957* (Hong Kong: Chinese University Press, 2008), 523–36.

62. Ibid., 551–608.

63. "Tingqu jiguan ganbu yijian gaijin shiji gongzuo," PD, May 28, 1957.

64. "Guowuyuan dangwai renshi jixu juxing zuotan," PD, May 30, 1957; "Guowuyuan dangwai renshi jixu zuotan," PD, June 1, 1957; "Guowuyuan dangwai renshi jixu zuotan," PD, June 5, 1957.

65. Qin Chao, "Qin Chao dui shehui zhuyi zhidu de kanfa," May 29, 1957, HCCPM.

66. "Zhonggong zhongyang bangongting 'qingkuang jianbao (zhengfeng zhuanji) huibian' (3)," July 6, 1957, HCCPM.

67. "Guowuyuan dangwai renshi jixu zuotan," PD, June 7, 1957.

68. Hu Xinmin, "Zhou Enlai yu fanyoupai douzheng," *Dangshi bocai*, no. 1 (2015): 22; Hu Shangyuan, "Lu Yuwen niming xin shijian yu fanyoupai douzheng," in *Fengyu licheng* (Beijing: Zhongguo wenshi, 2011), 9–19; Shen Zhihua, *Sikao yu xuanze*, 615–16.

69. "Zai guowuyuan feidang renshi zuotan huishang Li Zhonggong Wang Genzhong fandui yanhu fandong sixiang. Xi Zhongxun mishu zhang ye shoudao niming kongxia xin," PD, June 11, 1957.

70. "Xi Zhongxun zai Guowuyuan dangwai renshi zuotanhui jieshu huishang shuo gongchandang bu huanying de shi fan shehui zhuyi yanlun. Zhiyao shehui zhuyi youli de yanlun, na pa shuo de guofen, women ye huanying," PD, June 20, 1957.

71. Hu Zhi'an, "Zhang Naiqi: Zhengzhi yundong zhong bushi junzi bense," *Yanhuang chunqiu*, no. 11 (2011): 35–36; Zhang Naiqi, "Qishi zishu," *Wenshi ziliao xuanji* 82 (1982): 43–44.

72. Li Rui, diary (vols. 16–17, 1985), p. 41, HIA.

73. Zhou Erfu, "Tongyi zhanxian de guanghui," 316–24; Zhonggong Hebei shengwei tongzhanbu, "Xi Zhongxun," 65–66.

74. *Qunxing cuican*, 708.

75. Du Guang, "Zhongyang gaoji dangxiao fanyoupai neimu," *Yanhuang chunqiu*, no. 9 (2005): 1–8; Chung Yen-lin, *Wenge qian de Deng Xiaoping: Mao Zedong de "fushuai," 1956–1966* (Hong Kong: Chinese University Press, 2013), 109–11, 147.

76. "Dijiuci quanguo tongzhan gongzuo huiyi gaikuang," in *Lici quanguo tongzhan gongzuo huiyi gaikuang he wenxian* (Beijing: Dang'an, 1988), 362–66.

77. "Dishierci quanguo tongzhan gongzuo huiyi gaikuang," in *Lici quanguo tongzhan gongzuo huiyi gaikuang he wenxian* (Beijing: Dang'an, 1988), 389–94.

78. Gerry Groot, *Managing Transitions: The Chinese Communist Party, United Front Work, Corporatism, and Hegemony* (New York: Routledge, 2004), 113–14; "Dishisanci quanguo tongzhan gongzuo huiyi gaikuang," in *Lici quanguo tongzhan gongzuo huiyi gaikuang he wenxian* (Beijing: Dang'an, 1988), 421–24; Zhonggong zhongyang tongzhanbu, ed., *Zhongguo gongchandang tongyi zhanxian shi* (Beijing: Huawen, 2017), 300–326.

79. Wang Guocheng, *Xin Zhongguo tongyi zhanxian 50 nian* (Beijing: Taihai, 1999), 115–16.

80. Li Rui, diary (vols. 16–17, 1985), p. 41, HIA.

81. Zhou Erfu, "Tongyi zhanxian de guanghui," 324–25.

Chapter 11: "Military Suppression Combined with Political Struggle"

1. *Zhou Enlai nianpu*, 1:50.

2. "Zhonggong zhongyang dui zhongyang xuanchuanbu guanyu quanguo zongjiao gongzuo huiyi de baogao ji Lu Dingyi tongzhi zai quanguo zongjiao gongzuo huiyi-

shang de zongjie de pishi," in *Zongjiao gongzuo wenjian xuanbian*, ser. 28, vol. 96 (n.p.: SCCP, 2011), 23–24, 29.

3. Xu Danlu, *Fengxue gaoyuan: Kang-Zang diqu gongzuo jishi* (Beijing: Guojia anquan bu bangong ting qingbao shi yanjiu chu, 1996), 184–85.

4. *Fan Ming huiyilu*, 2:626.

5. Ibid., 2:627.

6. Ibid., 2:649.

7. X. Liu, *End of Revolution*, 82–83.

8. Ibid., 83–84; "Zhao Fan huiyilu," 17–21.

9. *Fan Ming huiyilu*, 2:643.

10. Zhao Shenying, *Zhang Guohua jiangjun zai Xizang* (Beijing: Zhongguo Zangxue, 2001), 94–96.

11. Deng Xiaoping, Xi Zhongxun, and Li Weihan, "Guanyu shenpi Xinjiang minzu quyu zizhi shishi jihua cao'an de liangfen baogao," in *Xinjiang gongzuo wenxian xuanbian 1949–2010*, ed. Zhonggong zhongyang wenxian yanjiushi and Zhonggong Xinjiang Weiwuer zizhiqu weiyuanhui (Beijing: Zhongyang wenxian, 2010), 97–101; Justin Jacobs, *Xinjiang and the Modern Chinese State* (Seattle: University of Washington Press, 2016), 180.

12. Deng Xiaoping, Xi, and Li, "Guanyu shenpi."

13. Ibid.; Jacobs, *Xinjiang*, 179–80; Lu Wenmei, "Yu xin Zhongguo zouguo wushinian," *Minzu tuanjie*, no. 10 (1999): 16–18.

14. Liu Chun, *Guanyu minzu gongzuo de huigu* (n.p.: n.p., 2001), 127; Xi Zhongxun, "Shenqie huainian Zhongguo gongchandang de zhongcheng pengyou Banchan dashi," *PD*, Feb. 20, 1989.

15. Melvyn C. Goldstein, Dawei Sherap, and William R. Siebenschuh, *A Tibetan Revolutionary: The Political Life and Times of Bapa Phuntso Wangye* (Berkeley: University of California Press, 2004), 188.

16. "Zhao Fan huiyilu," 23.

17. Fan Ming and Hao, *Xizang neibu zhizheng*, 275.

18. Dalai Lama, in discussion with the author, May 2023.

19. "Zhao Fan huiyilu," 56–58.

20. Liu Xiaoyuan, "'Beijing shijian': 1950 niandai Zhonggong dui Xizang gaige de dengdai fangzhen," *Ershiyi shiji shuangyue kan*, no. 163 (Oct. 2017): 73–90; X. Liu, *End of Revolution*, 218, 226; Mo Dan, *Tongzhan fengyun (1949–1983)* (Hong Kong: Lanyue, 2019), 92.

21. *Fan Ming huiyilu*, 2:810.

22. X. Liu, *End of Revolution*, 226.

23. Ibid., 226–27; Goldstein, *History of Modern Tibet*, 3:306–34, 3:445–66.

24. X. Liu, *End of Revolution*, 229–31.

25. *Fan Ming huiyilu*, 2:822–23.

26. X. Liu, *End of Revolution*, 231.

27. Zhang Xiangming, "55 nian Xizang gongzuo shilu" (unpublished manuscript, 2006), 70–77; Li Meijie and Zhao Shishu, "'Liu duo' jiangjun Fan Ming," *Yanhuang chunqiu*, no. 3 (2007): 41; Xi'an diqu 926 zhuan'an lianhe diaochatuan, "Peng Dehuai, Xi Zhongxun goujie Fan Ming wangluo niugui sheshen da gao fangeming fubi huodong" (Fan fubi), Oct. 13, 1967, *NCRGP*, vol. 12, p. 4876.

28. *Fan Ming huiyilu*, 2:955, 3:1320.

29. Ibid., 2:974.

30. Ibid., 2:978.

31. Ibid., 3:1005.

32. Xu Mingde, *Wo zhe yi beizi* (n.p.: [PRChina], n.d.), 300.

33. Zhou Nansheng, "Qinghai," 17.

34. Xi'an diqu 926 zhuan'an lianhe diaochatuan, "Xi Zhongxun maizai Xizang de di er ke dingshi zhadan: Zhou Renshan" (Fan fubi), 1968, *NCRGP*, vol. 12, p. 4882; Xi'an diqu 926 zhuan'an lianhe diaochatuan, "Zai ci he sanfan fenzi Xi Zhongxun pin cidao" (Fan fubi), 1968, *NCRGP*, vol. 12, p. 4882.

35. Paul P. Mariani, *Church Militant: Bishop Kung and Catholic Resistance in Communist Shanghai* (Cambridge, MA: Harvard University Press, 2011), 157–62; Amanda C. R. Clark, *China's Last Jesuit: Charles J. McCarthy and the End of the Mission in Catholic Shanghai* (Singapore: Palgrave Macmillan, 2017), 83–84; Feng Hui and Pang, *Mao Zedong nianpu*, 2:118; *Jin Luxian huiyilu*, vol. 1 (Hong Kong: Hong Kong University Press, 2013), 122.

36. "Zhonggong zhongyang guanyu kaizhan Shanghai tianzhujiao gongzuo de zhishi," in *Zongjiao gongzuo wenjian xuanbian*, ser. 28, vol. 171 (n.p.: SCCP, 2016), 13–14.

37. "Xi Zhongxun tongzhi zai di sanci quanguo zongjiao gongzuo huiyishang de zongjie," in *Tongzhan zhengce wenjian huibian*, vol. 4 (n.p.: Zhonggong zhongyang tongyi zhanxian gongzuobu, 1958), 2010–12.

38. Ibid., 2012–13, 2015.

39. Ibid., 2016–17.

40. Mariani, *Church Militant*, 1.

41. Zhongguo tianzhujiao aiguohui and Zhongguo tianzhujiao zhujiaotuan, eds., *Zhongguo tianzhujiao duli zizhu ziban jiaohui jiaoyu jiaocai* (Beijing: Zongjiao wenhua, 2002), 121; Zhang Jiashu, "Wu ling zan song wu zhu," *Zhongguo tianzhujiao*, no. 3 (1987): 17.

42. "Guowuyuan zongjiao shiwuju dangzu guanyu Zhongguo tianzhujiao daibiao huiyi de baogao," Dec. 10, 1957, HCCPM.

43. Zhonggong zhongyang tongzhanbu and Zhonggong zhongyang wenxian yanjiushi, eds., "Zai Zhongguo tianzhujiao you aiguohui quanguo daibiao huiyishang de jianghua," in *Xi Zhongxun lun tongyi zhanxian* (Beijing: Zhongyang wenxian, 2013), 174–94.

44. "Guowuyuan zongjiao shiwuju."

45. "Zhonggong zhongyang guanyu zai shaoshu minzuzhong jinxing zhengfeng he shehuizhuyi jiaoyu de zhishi (caogao)," Oct. 7, 1957, 1–13/1–1957.64, pp. 103–8, Jilin Provincial Archives; "M. Zimianin to the Department of the Central Committee of the CPSU and to Comrade Iu. V. Andropov," trans. David Brophy, Aug. 18, 1958, f. 5, op. 49, d. 130, ll. 164–76, WCDA, RGANI; "Memorandum on a Discussion with Wang Huangzhang, Head of the Foreign Affairs Office of the Prefectural People's Committee," trans. David Brophy, Jan. 22, 1958, f. 5, op. 49, d. 130, ll. 61–64, WCDA, RGANI; "Zhongyang zhuanfa Xinjiang zizhiqu dangwei quanti huiyi (kuoda) de qingkuang baogao," in *Tongzhan zhengce wenjian huibian*, vol. 3 (n.p.: Zhonggong zhongyang tongyi zhanxian gongzuo bu, 1958), 1897.

46. Weiner, *Chinese Revolution*, 166, 169.

47. Liu Chun, *Guanyu minzu gongzuo*, 172–73.

48. Jianglin Li, *When the Iron Bird Flies: China's Secret War in Tibet* (Stanford: Stanford University Press, 2022), 111–12, 150, 160.

49. Ding Dong, "Xi Zhongxun"; Weiner, *Chinese Revolution*, 193.

50. Hao Tingzao, "Zhunzhun zhutuo, yinyin shenqing: Huiyi Xi Zhongxun tongzhi dui wode sanci jiejian," *Gongchandang ren*, no. 9 (2010): 48–51.

51. Cai Liezhou, "Xi Zhongxun yu Xirao Jiacuo dashi," in *Xi Zhongxun jinian wenji*, ed. Zhonggong zhongyang dangshi yanjiuhui (Beijing: Zhonggong dangshi, 2013), 465–66.

52. Jia Juchuan, "1949.10–1962.9," 19.

53. Zhonggong Jiuquan shiwei dangshi yanjiushi, "Xi Zhongxun shicha Akesai Hasake zu zizhi xian," in *Xi Zhongxun yu Gansu*, ed. Zhonggong Gansu shengwei (Lanzhou: Gansu renmin, 2013), 323–29.

54. "Zhongyang pizhuan minwei dangzu guanyu dangqian Yisilanjiao Lamajiao gongzuo wenti de baogao," in *1956–1978 nianjian shiyizhong xijiang ziliao: Zhaibian*, special ser., vol. 119 (n.p.: SCCP, 2016), 23–33; Weiner, *Chinese Revolution*, 176.

55. Goldstein, *History of Modern Tibet*, vol. 4.

56. Xu Mingde, *Wo zhe yi beizi*, 302.

57. Jia Juchuan, "1949.10–1962.9," 20.

58. Xizang zizhiqu gong'anting, *Xizang gong'an dashiji 1950–1995*, vol. 16 (Lhasa: Zhonggong Xizang zhongyao lishi wenxian ziliao huibian, 1999), 103, 108, 110, 112, 117–18.

59. Jiacuo, *Banchan dashi*, 126.

60. Panchen Lama, *A Poisoned Arrow: The Secret Report of the 10th Panchen Lama* (London: Tibet Information Network, 1997).

61. Wang Shusheng, *Wulanfu zhuan* (Beijing: Zhongyang wenxian, 2007), 471–72; Zhang Peitian and Dong Xiaolong, eds., "Guanyu minzu gongzuo huiyi de baogao," in *Xin Zhongguo fazhi yanjiu shiliao tongjian*, vol. 7 (Beijing: Zhongguo zhengfa daxue chubanshe, 2003), 7959–60.

62. Jiacuo Jiangbian [Jambey Gyatso], *1954: Mao Zedong huijian Dalai, Banchan* (Hong Kong: Xin dalu, 2008), 106.

63. Yin Fatang, "Zhou Enlai dui Xizang minzu fazhan de zhuoyue gongxian," in *Zhou Enlai yu Xizang*, ed. Zhonggong Gansu shengwei (Beijing: Zhongguo Zangxue, 1998), 266.

64. Liu Chun, *Guanyu minzu gongzuo*, 200.

65. "Xi Zhongxun, Li Weihan deng tongzhi he Banchan tanhua jiyao," in *Youguan Banchan yinyan huozui de ruogan xijian shiliao (1962 nian 8 yue)*, ser. 31, vol. 10 (n.p.: SCCP, 2010), 1–3.

66. Ibid., 10, 16.

67. Ibid., 20–21.

68. Ibid., 24–28.

69. Liu Chun, *Guanyu minzu gongzuo*, 201.

70. "Zongli jiejian Banchan deng ren de tanhua jiyao," in *Youguan Banchan yinyan huozui de ruogan xijian shiliao (1962 nian 8 yue)*, ser. 31, vol. 10 (n.p.: SCCP, 2010), 1–11.

71. Jiacuo, *Banchan dashi*, 136; Jiacuo Jiangbian [Jambey Gyatso], *Mao Zedong yu Dalai, Banchan* (Hong Kong: Xin dalu, 2008), 262–63; interview.

72. Liu Chun, *Guanyu minzu gongzuo*, 200.

73. Interview.

74. Jiacuo, *Banchan dashi*, 138.

75. "Zhou Enlai jiejian zhongyang minzu xueyuan ganxunban Xizang xuesheng tanhua jilu," Oct. 15, 1966, HCCPM.

Chapter 12: Home Life in the Capital

1. Yuri Slezkine, *The House of Government: A Saga of the Russian Revolution* (Princeton, NJ: Princeton University Press, 2017), 230, 271.

2. Qi Qiaoqiao, "Fangqi chuguo liuxue: Xi Jinping de jiejie Qi Qiaoqiao," *Qinghua jingguan xueyuan guanwang*, Nov. 18, 2016, http://news.creaders.net/china/2016/11/18/1748354.html.

3. Chen Chusan, *Renjian zhong wan qing: Yige suowei "hong er dai" de rensheng guiji* (Deer Park, NY: Mingjing, 2017), 46–47.

4. Xi Qianping, "Baowei xiao bianzi!," in *Zai Yuying, women zouguo tongnian*, ed. Zhongzhi yuying xiaoxue tongxue hui (Beijing: Zhonggong dangshi, 2007), 133–35.

5. Ibid.

6. Liu Huixuan, "Dangshi nianshao ceng qingkuang," in *Dangshi nianshao ceng qingkuang*, ed. Mi Hedu (Hong Kong: Ruitian wenhua, 2015), 1–151; Mi Hedu, "Dayuan wenhua, yingxiong guan, shengli texing ji qita," in *Wenge wushinian: Mao Zedong yichan he dangdai Zhongguo*, ed. Song Yongyi, vol. 2 (Deer Park, NY: Mingjing, 2016), 119–44.

7. Ma Yuping, "Wo zai bayi xuexiao shi wu nian," Difang wenge shi jiaoliu wang, May 12, 2015, https://www.difangwenge.org/forum.php?mod=viewthread&tid=11127.

8. Liu Huixuan, "Dangshi nianshao ceng qingkuang," 15.

9. Mi Hedu, *Xinlu: Toushi gongheguo tongling ren* (Beijing: Zhongyang wenxian, 2011), 63–64.

10. Xi Jinping, "Sizheng ke shi luoshi lide shuren genben renwu de guanjian kecheng," *Qiushi*, Aug. 31, 2020.

11. Zheng Zhonghua, ed., "Geming houdai de yaolan, 'si hua' rencai de ronglu: Beijing bayi xuexiao xiaoshi," in *Bayi ban shiji* (Beijing: Zhongguo gongren, 1997), 19.

12. Liu Ningzhe and Kai Lei, "Shaonian Jinping ceng wuhui fuqin shi 'fu jingli,'" *Wen wei po*, Sept. 10, 2015.

13. Ye Xiaoling, "Wo shi yige nenggou tixing ziji, yueshi ziji de ren," *Lingdao wencui*, no. 5 (2004): 74.

14. Hao Ping, "Yi sheng," 763.

15. Qi Xin, "Zhongxun," 26.

16. Hao Ping, "Yi sheng," 762.

17. Li Weidong and Wang Lihui, "Shenji shi ge hao bangshou: Fang Fujian sheng shengzhang Xi Jinping," *Jingji yuekan*, no. 6 (2001): 17.

18. Ding Min, "Xi Zhongxun zai Luonai," 98.

19. Li Rui, diary (vol. 30, 1998), p. 29, HIA.

20. John Garnaut, "The Creation Myth of Xi Jinping," *Foreign Policy*, Oct. 19, 2012.

21. Interview with journalist for top Western media organization.

22. Kong Dan, *Nande bense ren tianran*, ed. Mi Hedu (Hong Kong: CNHK, 2013), 24–25.

23. Interview with grandchild of former high-ranking official.

24. Yang Ping, "Xi jia," 9.

25. Yang Fajin, "Beijing bayi xuexiao weishenme tuichi huahui difang guanli," *Dangshi bolan*, no. 4 (2019): 30–31.

26. Zheng Zhonghua, "Geming," 17–20.

27. Guo Dexun, "Mao Zedong: Ba 'Hajun gong' jianshe cheng dierge Huangpu junxiao," *Dangshi bolan*, no. 4 (2006): 16–17.

28. Li Min, *Wode fuqin Mao Zedong* (Shenyang: Liaoning renmin, 2000), 317.

29. Yang Ping, "Xi jia," 8.

30. Qi Qiaoqiao, "Fangqi chuguo liuxue."

31. Xi Yuanping, "Wode fubei Xi Zhongxun," *Xinmin wanbao*, Dec. 30, 2009.

32. Gao Fuyou and Gao Ying, *Gonghe guo yuanxun yishi: Guowuyuan jiguan shiwu guanliju yuan changwu fujuzhang Gao Fuyou huiyilu* (Beijing: Zhongyang wenxian, 2013), 304.

33. Ma Ying-jeou and Xiao Xucen, *Banian zhizheng huiyilu* (Taipei: Yuanjian tianxia wenhua, 2019), 367.

34. Qi Qiaoqiao, "Fuqin," 774–75, 776–77.

35. Xi Jinping, "Zai huijian diyijie quanguo wenming jiating daibiao shi de jianghua," Xinhua, Dec. 15, 2016.

36. Qi Xin, "Fengyu," 654–57.

37. Xi Yuanping, "Wode fubei."

Chapter 13: The Great Leap Forward

1. Li Rui, diary (vols. 12–13, 1983), p. 58, HIA.
2. Zhao Wei, *Xihua ting suiyue: Wo zai Zhou Enlai Ding Yingchao shenbian sanshiqinian* (Beijing: Shehui kexue wenxian, 2009), 6.
3. Chang Lifu, "Geming de yi sheng, zhandou de yi sheng," in *Zhang Desheng*, ed. Zhonggong Shaanxi shengxie dangshi yanjiushi (Xi'an: Shaanxi renmin, 1996), 125; *He Fang zishu*, 214; Wen Jize, *Diyige pingfan de "youpai": Wen Jize zishu* (Beijing: Zhongguo qingnian, 1999), 260.
4. Ding Min, "Xi Zhongxun zai Luonai"; Wen Jize, *Diyige*, 261.
5. Jia Juchuan, "Gongpu de kaimo Xi Zhongxun," *Guangdong dangshi*, no. 6 (2003): 24–23.
6. Zhonggong zhongyang bangongting and Guowuyuan bangongting xinfangju, eds., "Xi Zhongxun tongzhi de baogao," in *Quanguo xinfang gongzuo huiyi ziliao huibian*, ser. 28, vol. 101, pt. 1 (n.p.: SCCP, 2011), 22–25.
7. *Xi Zhongxun nianpu*, 2:327.
8. Diao Jiecheng, *Zhou Enlai yu xinfang gongzuo* (Beijing: Renmin, 2014), 209–10.
9. Zhonggong zhongyang bangongting and Guowuyuan bangongting xinfangju, "Xi Zhongxun tongzhi de baogao," 22.
10. "Ji yao you sixiang lingdao, you yao you qunzhong yundong: Xi Zhongxun tan zhongyang guojia jiguan dangqian zhengfeng yundong de qingkuang he wenti," *PD*, Nov. 26, 1957.
11. Yu Zhiheng, "'Ziyou wangguo': Guanzhuang," *PD*, Nov. 30, 1957.
12. "Guowuyuan zhuajin ducu jiancha Guanzhuang de zhenggai," *Neibu cankao*, Dec. 27, 1957, HIA (internal circulation).
13. Lai Jifa, "Guanyu 'ziyou wangguo': Guanzhuang wenti de jiantao," *PD*, Jan. 15, 1958.
14. Mao Zedong, "Dui Zhonggong zhongyang, guowuyuan guanyu qinjian banshe de lianhe zhishi de piyu," in *Jianguo yilai Mao Zedong wengao*, vol. 6 (Beijing: Zhongyang wenxian, 1992), 57–58; Zhou Enlai, "Guowuyuan guanyu chungeng shengchan de zhishi," *PD*, Apr. 1, 1956.
15. Lin Yunhui, *Xiang shehui zhuyi guodu: Zhongguo jingji shehui de zhuanxing* (Hong Kong: Chinese University Press, 2009), 412–20; Frederick C. Teiwes and Warren Sun, *China's Road to Disaster: Mao, Central Politicians, and Provincial Leaders in the Unfolding of the Great Leap Forward* (New York: Routledge, 2015), 21–47.
16. Lin Yunhui, *Wutuobang yundong: Cong dayuejin dao dajihuang* (Hong Kong: Chinese University Press, 2008), 19–27; Bo Yibo, *Ruogan zhongda juece yu shijian de huigu*, 2 vols. (Beijing: Zhonggong zhongyang dangxiao, 1993), 2:651.
17. Interview; Li Rui, diary (vols. 16–17, 1985), p. 41, HIA.
18. Bo, *Ruogan zhongda juece*, 2:639.
19. Zhou Bingde, *Wode bofu Zhou Enlai* (Shenyang: Liaoning renmin, 2000), 222–25.
20. Yen-lin Chung, "The CEO of the Utopian Project: Deng Xiaoping's Roles and Activities in the Great Leap Forward," *China Journal* 69 (Jan. 2013): 155–56; Fan Ruoyu, *Zai Zhou Enlai shenbian de rizi li* (Nanjing: Jiangsu renmin, 1984), 47.
21. Chung Yen-lin, "Zhonggong," 82–87; Y.-L. Chung, "Utopian Project"; Yen-lin Chung, "The Unknown Standard-Bearer of the Three Red Banners: Peng Zhen's Roles in the Great Leap Forward," *China Journal* 74 (July 2015): 129–43.
22. "Zhengfeng yundong dailai shehui zhuyi geming de xin xingshi," *LAD*, Mar. 27, 1958.
23. Wen Jize, *Diyige*, 262–63.
24. "Ba zhengfeng yundong tong jishu geming, wenhua geming yanjie qilai," *LAD*, June 23, 1958.

25. Y.-L. Chung, "Utopian Project," 158; Li Rui, diary (vols. 16–17, 1985), p. 41, HIA; Xibei gongda "jiefang da Xibei" bingtuan, "Sanfan fenzi Xi Zhongxun de zui'e lishi" (Xibei gongda), Sept. 12, 1967, *NCRGP*, vol. 44, pt. 3, *CCTP*, pp. 18875–76.

26. Yue Yufeng, "Huainian lao shouzhang Xi Zhongxun tongzhi," in *Huainian Xi Zhongxun*, ed. Cao Zhenzhong and Wu Jiang (Beijing: Zhongyang dangshi, 2005), 281; Tian Fang, "Xi Zhongxun mingyun zhong jici zhuanzhe," *Yanhuang chunqiu*, no. 8 (2002): 7.

27. "Ba hongqi gaoju daodi: Xi Zhongxun tongzhi tan qingnian yao buduan jinxing sixiang geming," *Anhui jiaoyu*, no. Z1 (Aug.–Sept. 1958): 16–17.

28. "Yong zhengfeng jingyan kaizhan jishu geming he wenhua geming," *LAD*, Aug. 15, 1958.

29. Tian Fang, *Suiyue yinhen*, 293.

30. "Xi Zhongxun tongzhi lai wo sheng tanwang xiafang ganbu shi mianli dajia zuo gongchan zhuyi de quanxin de ren," *Shaanxi ribao*, Sept. 17, 1958.

31. Jisheng Yang, *Tombstone: The Untold Story of Mao's Great Famine* (London: Allen Lane, 2012), 123–25; Tian Fang, *Suiyue yinhen*, 294.

32. "Gansu Dingxi diwei zhuanbao ge xianwei kuoda huiyi dui zhongyang he shengwei fuze tongzhi de yixie yijian," Nov. 25, 1961, HCCPM.

33. Zhonggong Jiuquan shiwei dangshi yanjiushi, "Xi Zhongxun."

34. Zhonggong Gansu shengwei, ed., "Xi Zhongxun zai Dunhuang xian dangtuan huiyishang guanyu gongshehua he shengchan zhong ruogan wenti de jianghua," in *Xi Zhongxun yu Gansu* (Lanzhou: Gansu renmin, 2013), 459–62.

35. Jia Juchuan, "1949.10–1962.9," 19–20.

36. *Xi Zhongxun nianpu*, 2:335–36.

37. Y.-L. Chung, "Standard-Bearer," 137–38.

38. Tian Fang, *Suiyue yinhen*, 298.

39. Y.-L. Chung, "Utopian Project," 163.

40. Jia Juchuan, "1949.10–1962.9," 20; Tian Fang, *Suiyue yinhen*.

41. Li Rui, diary (vols. 16–17, 1985), p. 41, HIA.

42. Jia Juchuan, "'Luhuo chunqing' Xi Zhongxun," 40.

43. Diao, *Zhou Enlai*, 220; *Xi Zhongxun nianpu*, 2:342–43.

44. Mao Zedong, "Guanyu jiejue chunhuang queliang wenti de piyu," in *Jianguo yilai Mao Zedong wengao*, vol. 8 (Beijing: Zhongyang wenxian, 1993), 209.

45. Ma Yongshun, *Zhou Enlai zujian yu guanli zhengfu shilu* (Beijing: Zhongyang wenxian, 1995), 322; Xia Meng and Wang, *Xi Zhongxun: Father*, 209–10.

46. "Niederschriften über Besuche in Werken der chinesischen Feinmechanik/Optik-Industrie," May 1959, BACZ 23852, ZEISS Archives.

47. Bo, *Ruogan zhongda juece*, 2:835–36.

48. Cao Xin, "Xi Zhongxun: Ta yi beizi meiyou zhengguo ren," *Baokan huicui*, no. 6 (2009): 80; Tian Fang, "Wo he Peng Dehuai jiaowang shiernian," *Yanhuang chunqiu*, no. 9 (1994): 7; Lin Yunhui, *Wutuobang yundong*, 451–55; Zhonggong Gansu shengwei, ed., "Xi Zhongxun guanyu guowuyuan renmin jiedai shi 'guanyu Gansu sheng bufen diqu queliang wenti de jianbao' de pishi," in *Xi Zhongxun yu Gansu* (Lanzhou: Gansu renmin, 2013), 463–64.

49. Tian Fang, "Wo," 7; *Peng Dehuai quanzhuan*, 4:1309–10.

50. Tian Fang, "Wo," 8.

51. Li Rui, *Lushan huiyi shilu*; Lin Yunhui, *Wutuobang yundong*, 463–64.

52. *Peng Dehuai quanzhuan*, 4:394.

53. An Zhiwen, "An Zhiwen tan Zhao Ziyang he Zhongguo gaige," in *Zhongguo dangdai mingren zhengyao fang shuping ji*, ed. Yang Jisheng (Hong Kong: Tiandi tushu, 2013), 49–50.

54. Wu Wenjun, "Longshang dajihuang ji qi jiaoxun," in *Gansu liushi niandai dajihuang kaozheng*, special ser., vol. 74 (n.p.: SCCP, 2007), 23; "Gansu shengji danwei shijiuji yishang dangyuan ganbu xuexi taolun kuoda de zhongyang gongzuo huiyi wenjian zhong dui zhongyang, zhongyang youguan fuze tongzhi he zhongyang youguan bumen tichu de yijian," 1962, HCCPM; Zhang Tianheng, "Zai yu Huo laogong huannan de rizi li," in *Huo Weide*, ed. Xiong Meijie (Beijing: Nanhai, 1994), 175–76.
55. Tian Fang, "Wo," 9.
56. Interview.
57. Li Rui, *Lushan huiyi shilu*, 375.
58. Li Rui, "Li Rui 1959 nian Lushan huiyi youguan ziliao," Oct. 30, 1980, pp. 13–14, HIA.
59. Chung Yen-lin, "Peng Zhen zai 1959 nian Zhonggong 'fan youqing' yundong zhong de juese he zuowei," *Zhongguo dalu yanjiu* 57, no. 1 (Mar. 2014): 97–125.
60. J. Yang, *Tombstone*, 57–58; Zhang Shufan, "Xinyang shijian: Yige chentong de lishi jiaoxun," *Bainianchao*, no. 6 (1998): 42–43; Qian Zhengwang, "Xinyang shijian yu Zhongnanju diyici huiyim," *Yanhuang chunqiu*, no. 2 (2016): 14–17.
61. Wang Yongqin, *Monan zhong de Zhou Enlai* (Beijing: Hongqi, 2009), 184.
62. Lin Yunhui, *Wutuobang yundong*, 627–32.
63. *Zhonghua renmin gongheguo minzhengbu dashiji* (Beijing: Zhongguo shehui, 2003), 113–14.
64. Zhongyang dang'anguan, ed., "Zhonggong zhongyang guanyu zhongyang zhengfa jiguan jingjian jigou he gaibian guanli tizhi de pifu," in *Zhonggong zhongyang wenjian xuanji*, vol. 35 (Beijing: Renmin, 2013), 388–89.
65. Diao, *Zhou Enlai*, 157–59.
66. Ibid., 159–60.
67. Bo, *Ruogan zhongda juece* 2:906–7; Lin Yunhui, *Wutuobang yundong*, 667–70.
68. Kong Xianrui, "Huiyi Xi Zhongxun zai Changge," *Xuchang wenshi ziliao* 8 (1995): 140–42.
69. Xi Zhongxun, "Guowuyuan fuzongli Xi Zhongxun tongzhi zai Zhonggong Changge xianwei (kuoda) huiyishang de jianghua," in *Changge xianzhi* (Beijing: Shenghuo-dushu-xinzhi sanlian shudian, 1992), 2–9.
70. Wu Zhongxian, *Xi Zhongxun zai Changge* (Zhengzhou: Henan renmin, 2014); Xi Zhongxun, "Guowuyuan fuzongli Xi Zhongxun guantian Changge xian nongcun de liangci diaocha bao," May 23, 1961, HCCPM.
71. Y.-L. Chung, "Utopian Project," 166; Tian Fang, *Suiyue yinhen*, 304.
72. "Xi Zhongxun tongzhi shicha Shenzhen, Zhuhai shi de jianghua," in *Zhongyang dui Guangdong gongzuo zhishi huibian (1986 nian–1987 nian)*, ser. 28, vol. 41, pt. 1 (n.p.: SCCP, 2007), 270.
73. Lin Yunhui, *Wutuobang yundong*, 684–786.
74. "Xi Zhongxun, Tan Zhenlin dui Shandong Cao Shuli zhi Mao Zedong xin de pishi ji Zhou Enlai gei Tan Qilong de xin," Oct. 26, 1961, HCCPM.
75. *Zhonghua renmin gongheguo*, 123.
76. Zhonggong Fuping xianwei dangshi yanjiushi, "Nanshe sangzi qing," in *Xiangyin: Jinian Xi Zhongxun tongzhi danchen jiushiwu zhounian*, ed. Zhonggong Fuping xianwei and Fuping xian renmin zhengfu ([Weinan]: [Zhonggong Fuping xianwei], 2008), 84–85.
77. Lin Mu, *Zhu jin meng*, 185–86.
78. Huang Zhengqing, "Zangbao xinmu zhong de qinren," in *Xi Zhongxun geming shengya* (Beijing: Zhongguo wenshi, 2000), 313.
79. Zheng Zhongzhong, "Bayi xuexiao shi zheyang de," in *Wo xinzhong de bayi*, ed. Li Heshun (Beijing: Tuanjie, 2007), 97–98.

80. Zhang Suhua, *Bianju: Qiqian ren dahui shimo* (Beijing: Zhongguo qingnian, 2012); Lu Di, "Lishi zhuanzhe zhong de Xi Zhongxun," *Bainianchao*, no. 4 (2018): 50.
81. *Zeng Shan zhuan* (Nanchang: Jiangxi renmin, 2019), 478.
82. *Zhou Enlai nianpu*, 2:467.
83. *Xi Zhongxun zhuan*, 2:326.
84. Li Rui, diary (vols. 16–17, 1985), p. 41, HIA.
85. Shen Zhihua, *Sikao yu xuanze*, 669–70.
86. Lin Yunhui, *Wutuobang yundong*, 232, 624.

Chapter 14: *Liu Zhidan*

1. Qi Xin, "Fengyu," 659.
2. Xi Zhongxun, "Yongyuan nanwang de huainian," in *Xi Zhongxun wenxuan* (Beijing: Zhongyang wenxian, 1995), 315.
3. Ding Min, "Xi Zhongxun zai Luonai," 94.
4. Chung Yen-lin, "1962 nian Xi Zhongxun wenti ji qi xiangguan zhengzhi yingxiang" (unpublished manuscript, n.d.).
5. Jia Juchuan, "Xi Zhongxun yuan'an shimo," *Yanhuang chunqiu*, no. 1 (2011): 6.
6. Xi Zhongxun, "Yongyuan nanwang de huainian," 28.
7. He Jiadong, "Fengyu '*Liu Zhidan*,'" in *Siren yi shi jingshen yongcun: He Jiadong jinian wenji*, ed. Chen Ziming and Bi Yimin (self-pub., Shidai wenxian, 2012), 307; *Xi Zhongxun zhuan*, 2:276–81; Tian Fang, "Xi Zhongxun he Liu Zhidan."
8. *Guo Hongtao huiyilu* (Beijing: Zhongyang dangshi, 2004), 84–88; Wu Dianyao and Song, *Zhu Lizhi zhuan*, 435.
9. He Jiadong, "Cong Wu Yunduo dao '*Liu Zhidan*,'" in *Wangshi huisheng: Zhongguo zhuming zhishi fenzi fangtanlu*, ed. Xing Xiaoqun (Hong Kong: Shidai guoji, 2004), 74.
10. Wu Wenxiao, "'*Liu Zhidan*' beihou de xuanran dabo," *Fujian dangshi yuekan*, no. 6 (2010): 44–46.
11. *Xi Zhongxun zhuan*, 2:281.
12. Li Yuan, "Yan Hongyan he xiaoshuo '*Liu Zhidan*,'" *Bainianchao*, no. 3 (2003): 17–22; Dong Cunfa, "'*Liu Zhidan*' yinqi de zhengzhi fengbo," in *Dangnei dajian*, ed. Cheng Min (Beijing: Tuanjie, 1993), 235–37.
13. *Liu Peizhi wencun*, 58.
14. Wu Wenxiao, "*Liu Zhidan*."
15. Dong Cunfa, "*Liu Zhidan*," 237; Jia Juchuan, "1949.10–1962.9," 22; Bo, *Ruogan zhongda juece*, 2:1096.
16. Frederick C. Teiwes and Warren Sun, *The End of the Maoist Era: Chinese Politics during the Twilight of the Cultural Revolution, 1972–1976* (Armonk, NY: M. E. Sharpe, 2007), 366.
17. Ding Min, "Xi Zhongxun zai Luonai," 92.
18. Xiao Donglian, *Wenge qian shinian shi 1956–1966*, vol. 2 (Hong Kong: Heping tushu, 2013), 727–36; Qian Xiangli, *Lishi de bianju: Cong wanjiu weiji dao fanxiu fangxiu, 1962–1965* (Hong Kong: Chinese University Press, 2008), 272–74.
19. Qian Xiangli, *Lishi de bianju*, 277–78.
20. Xiao Donglian, *Wenge*, 739.
21. Yan Changgui, "Kang Sheng de mishu tan Kang Sheng," *Yanhuang chunqiu*, no. 2 (2013): 45–47; Yan Mingfu, "Cong wo qinli de ji jian shi kan Kang Sheng," *Yanhuang chunqiu*, no. 5 (2005): 40–45.
22. Interview.
23. Chung Yen-lin, "1962"; Chung Yen-lin, *Wenge*, 425–29.
24. Dong Cunfa, "*Liu Zhidan*," 235–36.

25. Li Jiantong, *Fandang xiaoshuo "Liu Zhidan" an shilu* (Hong Kong: Thinker, 2007), 53–57.
26. Li Jiantong, "Zhou Yang he xiaoshuo 'Liu Zhidan,'" in *Yi Zhou Yang*, ed. Wang Meng and Yuan Ying (Hohhot: Nei Menggu renmin, 1998), 374–75.
27. Jia Juchuan, "Xi Zhongxun yuan'an shimo," 5.
28. Zhang Zhigong, *Nanwang de ershinian*, 11–12; Bo, *Ruogan zhongda juece*, 2:1096.
29. *Xi Zhongxun nianpu*, 2:423–24.
30. Li Zhi, *Wentan fengyun lu* (Beijing: Renmin wenxue, 2015), 281; Jia Juchuan, "Xi Zhongxun yuan'an shimo," 8.
31. Mo, *Tongzhan fengyun*, 211.
32. Si Tao, *Liu Lantao shengping jishi* (Beijing: Zhongguo wenshi, 2010), 121.
33. Zhonggong dangshi renwu yanjiuhui, *Zhonggong*, 54.
34. *Deng Xiaoping nianpu (1904–1974)*, 3 vols. (Beijing: Zhongyang wenxian, 2009), 2:1725.
35. Mao Zedong, "Zai bajie shizhong quanhui de jianghua," Sept. 24, 1962, HCCPM.
36. Si, *Liu Lantao*, 121–22.
37. Li Zhi, *Wentan fengyun lu*, 284.
38. Wei Xinsheng, "Xiaoshuo 'Liu Zhidan' an shuping," in *Huainian Xi Zhongxun* (Beijing: Zhonggong dangshi, 2005), 450–52.
39. *Xi Zhongxun zhuan*, 2:283.
40. "Chedi qingsuan Xi, Jia, Liu fandang jituan: Paozhi da ducao—xiaoshuo 'Liu Zhidan' de taotian zuixing" (Dongfang hong bao), June 2, 1967, NCRGP, vol. 9, pt. 2, A Special Compilation of Newspapers in Beijing Area, p. 3330.
41. Xi'an diqu wenyijie geming zaofan zongsilingbu doupigai bangongshi, *Chedi qingsuan Peng, Gao, Xi fandang jituan liyong wenxue yishu fandang de taotian zuixing*, ser. 6, vol. 6, pt. 4 (n.p.: SCCP, 2007), 28.
42. "Zui'e shengya wushinian: Fandang yexinjia Xi Zhongxun choushi" (unpublished manuscript, n.d.). Held by this author.
43. "Liu Shaoqi dui zhongyang zuzhibu fuze ren de tanhua," Nov. 12, 1962, HCCPM.
44. "Deng Xiaoping zai zuzhi gongzuo huiyi quanguo jiancha gongzuo huiyishang de baogao," Nov. 29, 1962, HCCPM.
45. Qian Liqun, *Huashuo Zhou shi xiongdi: Beida yanjiang lu* (Ji'nan: Shandong huabao, 1999), 271; He Jiadong, "Fengyu 'Liu Zhidan,'" 311.
46. Zhang Zhigong, *Nanwang de ershinian*, 29.
47. Lin Mu, *Zhu jin meng*, 194–95.
48. Qi Xin, "Fengyu," 658.
49. Interview.
50. Zhang Zhigong, *Nanwang de ershinian*, 16.
51. Xi Zhongxun, "Yongyuan nanwang de huainian," 315–16; *Xi Zhongxun zhuan*, 2:284–85.
52. "Vice Premier Hsi Chung-Hsun Reportedly Removed from Office: United States Consulate General; Hong Kong; Secret," Apr. 7, 1964, DNSA; *Qu Wu wenxuan* (Beijing: Tuanjie, 1988); "Chinese Deputy Premier Is Reported to Be Purged," NYT, Apr. 7, 1964; "Purge of Hsi Chung-Hsun," n.d., ref. no. A0076081, Leading Personal of the Chinese Communist Regime Biographic Data (1956–1969), Archive of Christian Study Centre on Chinese Religion and Culture, https://repository.lib.cuhk.edu.hk/tc/item/cuhk-2994867; interview.
53. Chen Feng, *Dao tianhuo de shiren: Ke Zhongping pingzhuan* (Xi'an: Shaanxi renmin, 1992), 228–42.
54. Wang Chaobei, *Mengyuan jishi* (self-pub., Beijing shidai nongchao wenhua

fazhan, 2013), 58, 139, 159, 181–82; Hao Ting and Zhang Zhong'e, *Wenhua dageming zhong de zhongyang diaochabu* (n.p.: 2013), 89; Luo Qingchang, "Mianhuai jing'ai de Li Kenong buzhang," in *Jinian Li Kenong wenji* (Beijing: n.p., 1989), 68.

55. Wang Chaobei, *Mengyuan jishi*, 203–15; Shi Wan, "Daozhi 'Hongqi piaopiao' tingkan de yi pian wenzhang," *Renmin zhengxie bao*, Jan. 24, 2008; Fu Canglong, "Liu-Deng hei silingbu baopi xia baobi xia de Xi Zhongxun fandang jituan cehua de youyi fangeming shijian," in *Xiang wenyi heixian menglie kaihuo* (Tianjin: Nankai daxue weidong hongweibing weidong bianjibu, 1968), 241–42.

56. Wang Chaobei and Shi Ning, *Laizi mimi zhanxian de baogao* (Tianjin: Baihua wenyi, 1997), 101.

57. "Zhonggong zhongyang zuzhi bu guanyu zhongyang jiguan yuan fubuzhang he sheng, shi, zizhi qu yuan fu shengzhang yishang ganbu de shencha qingkuang (liushiyi ren) caogao," Feb. 1976, HCCPM; "Li Qiming tongzhi."

58. Hao Ting and Zhang, *Wenhua dageming*, 90–91.

59. Han Gang, "Xiaoshuo 'Liu Zhidan' anjian yu Zhongguo zhengzhi de zouxiang," in *Jinian Liu Jingfan tongzhi danchen 100 zhounian zuotanhui ziliao huibian*, ed. Liu Mila (self-pub., Beijing shidai nongchao wenhua fazhan, 2011), 55–57.

60. Kang Sheng, "Guanyu liangtiao luxian douzheng ji qita," in *Kang Sheng yanlun xuanbian*, vol. 3 (Beijing: Zhonggong Beijing shiwei dangxiao ziliao shi, 1979), 25.

Chapter 15: The Cultural Revolution

1. *Xi Zhongxun nianpu*, 2:426.

2. *Xi Zhongxun zhuan*, 2:290–91; Hu Shihou, "Mianhuai Xi lao: Jinian Xi Zhongxun tongzhi danchen 100 zhounian," *Dangshi bolan*, no. 5 (2013): 17.

3. Jia Juchuan, "1962.10–2002.5," 6.

4. Qi Qiaoqiao, "Fuqin," 788.

5. Xia Meng and Wang, *Xi Zhongxun: Father*, 233–35.

6. Jia Juchuan, "1962.10–2002.5," 5.

7. "Liu-Deng hei silingbu paozhi he bihu fandang xiaoshuo 'Liu Zhidan' zuize nantao," *Weidong*; *Jinggangshan*; *Dongfanghong bao*, July 8, 1967, *NCRGP*, vol. 9, pt. 2, A Special Compilation of Newspapers in the Beijing Area, p. 3377; "Zhonggong zhongyang zuzhibu guanyu wei xiaoshuo 'Liu Zhidan' pingfan de baogao," in *"Wuchan jieji wenhua dageming": You tuichao er fanxing*, ser. 26, vol. 5 (n.p.: SCCP, 2004), 7.

8. *Peng Dehuai quanzhuan*, 4:1587.

9. Jia Juchuan, "1962.10–2002.5," 6.

10. *Peng Dehuai quanzhuan*, 4:1589.

11. A. L. Verchenko, "Vklad SSSR v sozdanie krupnykh industrial′nykh tsentrov v Kitae," in *Uchastie SSSR v rekonstruktsii i stroitel′stve "156 proizvodstvennykh ob″ektov" v KNR v 1950-e gody. Novye fakty i obstoiatel′stva sovetsko-kitaiskogo sotrudnichestva*, ed. N. L. Mamaeva (Moscow: Ves′ mir, 2018), 521–53.

12. *Xi Zhongxun moji* (Beijing: Zhongyang wenxian, 2013); *Xi Zhongxun zhuan*, 2:295; Qi Qiaoqiao, "Fuqin"; Sun Bin, "Shuiru jiaorong: Xi Zhongxun zai Luoyang de rizi," *Dahe bao*, Oct. 18, 2013; Liu Xingshi, "Xi Zhongxun tongzhi zai kuangshan jiqi chang gongzuo de pianduan," *Luoyang wenshi ziliao* 17 (1996): 54–58; Luo Zixing, "Xi Zhongxun teshu de gongchang suiyue," *Jingji daokan*, no. 8 (2018): 91.

13. *Xi Zhongxun zhuan*, 2:303–4.

14. Xia Meng and Wang, *Xi Zhongxun: Father*, 238.

15. Liu Xingshi, "Xi Zhongxun," 57–58.

16. Shinichi Tanigawa, "The Policy of the Military 'Supporting the Left' and the Spread of Factional Warfare in China's Countryside: Shaanxi, 1967–1968," *Modern*

China 44, no. 1 (2018): 35–67; Bai Lei, "Xi'an zaofanpai de qingqi yu fenhua," in *Zhonghua xueren wenge lunwenji*, ed. Qi Zhi, vol. 3 (Austin, TX: Meiguo huayi, 2019), 301–18.

17. *Xi Zhongxun zhuan*, 2:309; Meng Deqiang, "He Xi Zhongxun zai yiqi de 72 tian," *Zongheng* 277, no. 1 (2013): 4–5.
18. Meng Deqiang, "He Xi Zhongxun," 4–5.
19. Ibid., 6–7, 9–10.
20. Han Sanzhou, "Xi Zhongxun xie gei Mao Zedong de liangfeng xin," *Xiangsheng bao*, Jan. 7, 2013.
21. Meng Deqiang, "Xi Zhongxun 'wenge' mengnan xiangqing," *Changjiang ribao*, Mar. 15, 2013; *Xi Zhongxun zhuan*, 2:313–15.
22. Liu Yunyue, *Liu Bangxian* (Xi'an: Shaanxi renmin, 2008), 115.
23. Meng Deqiang, "Xi Zhongxun de Xi'an yishi," 20.
24. Zhang Zhigong, *Nanwang de ershinian*, 37.
25. *Xi Zhongxun zhuan*, 2:315.
26. Zhang Zhigong, *Nanwang de ershinian*, 38.
27. Meng Deqiang, "He Xi Zhongxun," 10–11.
28. Ibid., 11; *Xi Zhongxun zhuan*, 2:315–27; Bai Lei, "Xi'an 'qishisan hao' jishi," *Yanhuang chunqiu*, no. 7 (2015): 69.
29. Bai Lei, "Xi'an 'qishisan hao' jishi," 70–71.
30. Wang Lin, *Wode geming licheng* (Beijing: Dangdai Zhongguo, 2001), 199.
31. Bai Lei, "Xi'an 'qishisan hao' jishi," 69.
32. *Xi Zhongxun zhuan*, 2:315–17.
33. Hongweibing pipan wenzhang, "Tong sanfan fenzi," 261–70.
34. Jia Juchuan, "1962.10–2002.5," 8.
35. "Ba fangeming xiuzhengzhuyi fenzi Xi Zhongxun pidao douchou," *Renmin jiaoda*, no. 70 (Aug. 1967).
36. Xi'an diqu 926 zhuan'an lianhe diaochatuan, "Zai ci he sanfan fenzi Xi Zhongxun pin cidao" (Fan fubi), 1968, *NCRGP*, vol. 12, p. 4882.
37. Xia Meng and Wang, *Xi Zhongxun: Father*, 239.
38. *Xi Zhongxun zhuan*, 2:315–27.
39. Xi Yuanping, "Fuqin wangshi," in *Xi Zhongxun jinian wenji*, ed. Zhonggong zhongyang dangshi yanjiushi (Beijing: Zhonggong dangshi, 2013), 810.
40. Ding Min, "Xi Zhongxun zai Luonai," 94.
41. Yang Ping, "Xi jia," 11.
42. "Zhonggong zhongyang wenge shouzhang jiejian Shaanxi sheng fu Jing daibiaotuan de zhishi jilu" (Shanghai shiyuan), May 16, 1968, 16564, *NCRGP*, pt. 3, *CCTP*, pp. 16563–65.
43. Zhou Enlai, "Zai 'Yan'an diqu chadui qingnian gongzuo zuotanhui' shang de jianghua," in *1970–1973 nian Zhou Enlai zhuchi zhongyang richang gongzuo qijian 33 pian wei gongkai kanyin zhi wengao shibian*, ser. 5, vol. 601, pt. 1 (n.p.: SCCP, 2022), 1–11.
44. Fan Ziju, *Sun Dingguo zhuan* (Beijing: Zhongguo wenlian, 1999), 170–71; Xiao Yiping, "Kongsu Kang Sheng, Cao Yiou zai zhongyang dangxiao de zuixing," in *Xiao Yiping wengao juan yi* (Hong Kong: Zhongguo wenhua chuanmei, 2008), 322.
45. *Zhongguo gongchandang Beijing shi Haidian qu zuzhishi ziliao (1949–1987)* (n.p.: Zhonggong Beijing shi Haidian quwei zuzhibu, 1990), 16, 38; Qi Xin, "Fengyu," 659.
46. Wang Haiguang, "Liu Shaoqi yu siqing yundong," *Dang de wenxian*, no. 5 (1999): 54–60; Liao Wanqing, "Wode 'siqing' jingli," *Xiaoyou wengao ziliao xuanbian* 24 (n.d.): 110–15; Zhao Youfu, "Peng Zhen yu jingjiao nongcun shejiao yundong," *Beijing dangshi*, no. 2 (2004): 10–13; Guo Dehong and Lin Xiaobo, *Siqing yundong shilu* (Hangzhou: Zhejiang renmin, 2005), 62.

47. Qi Xin, "Fengyu," 659.
48. Zhonggong Beijing shiwei dangshi yanjiushi, *Neiluan de shinian: Beijing qu xian "wenhua dageming" shiqi jilue* (Beijing: Zhonggong Beijing shiwei dangshi yanjiushi, 2002), 197–206.
49. Hu Shihou, "Hu Yaobang ting wo shensu," *Dangshi bolan*, no. 8 (2010): 37; Sun Chunshan, *Wuhui rensheng: Yang Xianzhen* (Ji'nan: Shandong huabao, 2001), 152; Yu Ruxin, *Kang Sheng nianpu*, 409, 426–27; "Kang Sheng zai zhonggong zhongyang gaoji dangxiao gongzuo renyuan dahuishang de jianghua," Apr. 23, 1967, HCCPM.
50. Liu Bingrong, *Zoujin Qi Ruixin*, 223.
51. Xi Yuanping, "Zhuiyi Xi Zhongxun de shaolin jingshen," *Shenzhen tequ bao*, Oct. 15, 2014.
52. Qi Qiaoqiao, "Fangqi chuguo liuxue."
53. Xi Yuanping, "Zhuiyi Xi Zhongxun."
54. Ibid.
55. "Zhongzhen"; Xi Yuanping, "Wode fubei Xi Zhongxun," *Xinmin wanbao*, Dec. 30, 2009; Wan Bo'ao, "Lao Lei zongheng di huangsha," *Meizhong shibao*, Sept. 28, 2021.
56. "Zhongguo fazhi xin meiti changwu fu zhuren: Ma Baoshan jianjie, qi furen Xi Qianping," *Zhongguo fazhi*, Nov. 14, 2015; Dai Yannian and Chen Rinong, *Zhongguo waiwenju wushinian dashiji* (Beijing: Xinxing, 1999), 214–65; interview with individual familiar with situation.
57. Qi Qiaoqiao, "Fangqi chuguo liuxue."
58. Bi Ruxie, "Cong 1968 nian Beijing jianghu jiaodu kan Xi Jinping," *Beijing zhi chun*, Aug. 2023, http://beijingspring.com/bj2/2010/140/81202375445.htm; Bi Ruxie, "Songren Xi Jinping," *CND kanwu he luntan*, Dec. 29, 2022, http://hx.cnd.org/2022/12/29/%E6%AF%95%E6%B1%9D%E8%B0%90%E6%80%82%E4%BA%A%E4%B9%A0%E8%BF%91%E5%B9%B3/; Bi Ruxie (former student at the Beijing Foreign Studies University School), in discussion with the author, Oct. 2023; Xia Meng and Wang, *Xi Zhongxun: Father*, 240.
59. Liu Huixuan, "Dangshi nianshao ceng qingkuang," 23.
60. Garnaut, "Creation Myth."
61. Chen Qiuying, "Shizhang ningju taoliqing," in *Wo xinzhong de Bayi*, ed. Li Heshun (Beijing: Tuanjie, 2007), 232.
62. "Xi Jinping zhongxue shixi du Du Fu ai tiqiu," *Beijing qingnian bao*, Mar. 2, 2015.
63. Wang Youqin, "Wumai xia de wenge lishi," *Huaxia wenzhai zengkan*, no. 99 (Dec. 2014).
64. Interview.
65. Two interviews.
66. Bu Weihua, *"Zalan jiu shijie": Wenhua dageming de dongluan yu haojie* (Hong Kong: Chinese University Press, 2009), 209–17.
67. Mi Hedu, *Xinlu*, 233–49; Sun Yancheng, "Xuetong lun he Daxing 'ba san yi' shijian," *Yanhuang chunqiu*, no. 2 (2012): 32–37.
68. Mu Guodong, "Yige liudu quanguo de zhengzhi dapianju de youlai," in *Wo xinzhong de Bayi*, ed. Li Heshun (Beijing: Tuanjie, 2007), 330–34; Zheng Zhonghua, "Geming," 22.
69. "Qianglie de fanying, fennü de qianze: Guangda gongnongbing canguan Bayi xuexiao liandong zuixing zhanlanhou," *Chunlei*, Mar. 12, 1967.
70. Nie Weiping and Wang Duanyang, *Nie Weiping: Weiqi rensheng* (Beijing: Wenhua yishu, 2011), 109.
71. Yang Xiaohuai, "Xi Jinping: Wo shi ruhe kuaru zhengjie de," *Zhonghua ernü*, no. 7 (2000): 43; Yang Ping, "13 sui dacheng fangeming, Xi Zhongxun bu ku zhi, Xi Jinping wenge xuelei shi," *Xianggang chengbao*, July 6, 2012.

72. Yang Ping, "13 sui dacheng fangeming."
73. Lu Ying and Zhou Weisi, "Er li zhi nian," *Hebei qingnian*, no. 7 (1984): 8.
74. Meng Xiangfeng, "Zuo you zhiqi you zuowei de yidai," *Jiazhang*, no. 2 (1997): 4.
75. "Xi Jinping he mama," *PD*, Feb. 3, 2022.
76. Yuhao wang, "Wo shi Yan'an ren," YouTube, Oct. 20, 2019, video, https://www.youtube.com/watch?v=a_hx9ZXT2BU.
77. Jin Guangyao and Jin Dalu, *Zhongguo xin fangzhi: Zhishi qingnian shangshan xiaxiang shiliao jilu*, vol. 3 (Shanghai: Shanghai shudian, 2014), 1456.
78. Li Zizhuang, "Suiyue de fansi," in *Qingxi huang tudi*, ed. Sun Lizhe (Beijing: Zhongguo guoji guangbo, 1996), 71.
79. Li Huasong, "Yige weiren de qidai," in *Qingxi huang tudi*, ed. Sun Lizhe (Beijing: Zhongguo guoji guangbo, 1996), 4–5, 7.
80. Ma Ying-jeou and Xiao, *Banian zhizheng huiyilu*, 367.
81. Yuhao wang, "Wo shi Yan'an ren."
82. *Liangjiahe* (Xi'an: Shaanxi renmin, 2018), 54–55.
83. Lu Jianfeng, "Qi Yun zai Yangcheng," *Wenshi yuekan*, no. 9 (2014): 4; "Geming yisheng, fendou yisheng, guangrong yisheng: Jinian yeye shishi 40 zhounian" (unpublished manuscript, 2020).
84. Interview.
85. Yang Xiaohuai, "Xi Jinping," 42.
86. Jin Guangyao and Jin, *Zhongguo xin fangzhi*, 1375, 1386.
87. Lei Rongsheng and Lei Pingsheng, "Jinping ba ziji kanzuo huang tudi de yi bufen," in *Xi Jinping de qinian zhiqing suiyue*, ed. Zhongyang dangxiao caifang shilu bianjishi (Beijing: Zhonggong zhongyang dangxiao, 2017), 15.
88. *Liangjiahe*, 54.
89. Ibid., 87; Lena H. Sun, "Post for a 'Princeling,'" *WP*, June 8, 1992.
90. Yang Xiaohuai, "Xi Jinping," 43.
91. Liang Yuming, "Jinping gan shuo gan zuo gan dandang," in *Xi Jinping de qinian zhiqing suiyue*, ed. Zhongyang dangxiao caifang shilu bianjishi (Beijing: Zhonggong zhongyang dangxiao, 2017), 170–71; Yang Shizhong, "Jinping dang cun zhishu jiu shi yinwei dajia dou yonghu ta," in *Xi Jinping de qinian zhiqing suiyue*, ed. Zhongyang dangxiao caifang shilu bianjishi (Beijing: Zhonggong zhongyang dangxiao, 2017), 367.
92. Lei Rongsheng and Lei, "Jinping," 18.
93. Xi Yuanping, "Zhuiyi Xi Zhongxun"; Yang Ping, "Xi jia," 9.
94. Xi Yuanping, "Zhuiyi Xi Zhongxun."
95. Yaita Akio and Huang Yiyun, *Xi Jinping: Gongchan Zhongguo zui tuoshi de lingxiu* (Taipei: Tianxia zazhi, 2012), 128.
96. Lu Ying and Zhou, "Er li zhi nian," 9.
97. "Xi Jinping mantan wangxi 30 nian," *Dangshi wenyuan*, no. 3 (2004): 53.
98. Lu Ying and Zhou, "Er li zhi nian," 8.
99. Ye Xiaoling, "Wo," 76.
100. Evgenii Bazhanov, "Si Tszin′pin i Chernyshevskii," *Nezavisimaia gazeta*, Apr. 1, 2013; Sun Peidong, "Wenge shiqi Jing-Hu zhiqing jiecenghua de geren yuedu," *Ershiyi shiji shuangyue kan*, no. 8 (2016): 80, 90.
101. *Xi Zhongxun nianpu*, 4:234–35.
102. Bian Tiejian, "Jundui waiyu, jishu rencai de yaolan," in *Yuanxiao: Huiyi shiliao* (Beijing: Jiefangjun, 1995), 727–35; Lu Xukang, "Ji 793 buhui san xi er ban," *BlackHair-WhiteHair*, Nov. 19, 2009, https://blackhairwhitehair.blogspot.com/2009/11/793-19641968.html.
103. Garnaut, "Creation Myth"; interview.
104. Yuhao wang, "Wo shi Yan'an ren."

105. Zhang Zhigong, *Nanwang de ershinian*, 216.
106. "Diandi," 163–67.

Chapter 16: The Xi Family Slowly Rebuilds

1. Xi Yuanping, "Fuqin wangshi," 809.
2. *Qunxing cuican*, 709.
3. Qi Xin, "Yi Zhongxun," 755.
4. Xi Zhongxun, "Yongyuan nanwang de huainian," 318.
5. *Xi Zhongxun zhuan*, 2:332–33; Qi Qiaoqiao, "Fuqin," 791; Meng Deqiang, "Xi Zhongxun de Xi'an yishi," 22; Meng Xiangfeng, "Zuo you."
6. *Xi Zhongxun nianpu*, 2:442–43.
7. Zhonggong Henan shengwei dangshi yanjiushi, "Xi Zhongxun zai Henan," *Bainianchao*, no. 11 (2013): 28.
8. *Peng Zhen nianpu 1979–1997*, 5 vols. (Beijing: Zhongyang wenxian, 2002), 4:510.
9. Interview.
10. *Luoyang naihuo cailiao changzhi (1956–1984)* (Xi'an: n.p., 1986), 7–8, 325, 339, 351.
11. Ding Min, "Xi Zhongxun zai Luonai," 85–86.
12. Yang Ping, "Xi jia," 7; Luo Zixing, "Xi Zhongxun," 92.
13. Sun Bin, "Shuiru jiaorong."
14. Xi Zhonggun, Huang Li, and Tan Jinhang, "Xi Zhongxun: Yi min wei tian de Zhongguo gongchandang ren," *Caijing jie*, no. 3 (2015): 95; Ding Min, "Xi Zhongxun zai Luonai," 96.
15. Yang Ping, "Xi jia," 10.
16. Cao Zhenzhong, "Shenqing," 16.
17. Zhonggong Henan shengwei dangshi yanjiushi, "Xi Zhongxun zai Henan," 29.
18. Xi Zhonggun, Huang Li, and Tan Jinhang, "Xi Zhongxun: Yi min wei tian de Zhongguo gongchandang ren," *Caijing jie*, no. 2 (2015): 74.
19. *Xi Zhongxun zhuan*, 2:339–41.
20. Xi Yuanping, "Fuqin wangshi," 815; Xi Zhonggun, Huang, and Tan, "Xi Zhongxun," 71.
21. Xi Yuanping, "Fuqin wangshi," 816; Sun Bin, "Shuiru jiaorong."
22. Xu Renjun, "20 shiji 70 niandai mo de zhiqing fancheng langchao," *Dangshi bolan*, no. 2 (2004): 9.
23. Qi Xin, "Fengyu," 660.
24. Li Nanyang, "Mieshi mingyun bian neng chaoyue," *"Li Nanyang gaozhuang haiguan an" genjin baodao*, no. 100 (Nov. 2022), FCFL; Torigian, "Historical Legacies," 8; Li Nanyang (daughter of Li Rui), in discussion with the author, Feb. 2020; interview.
25. *Liangjiahe*, 115; *Fujian boshi fengcai* (Fuzhou: Haichao sheying yishu, 2003), 3.
26. Liu Bing, *Fengyu suiyue: 1964–1976 nian de Qinghua* (Beijing: Dangdai Zhongguo, 2010), 178–219.
27. Yang Ping, "Xi jia," 8.
28. Ibid., 9.
29. Laixia laiqu zhijian, "Xi Zhongxun," pt. 3, CCTV, YouTube, May 28, 2022, video, https://www.youtube.com/watch?v=OWoFdeYC9KE&t=27s&ab_channel=%E6%9D%A5%E5%A4%B9%E6%9D%A5%E5%8E%BB%E4%B9%8B%E9%97%B4.
30. Luo Zixing, "Xi Zhongxun," 94.
31. Ding Min, "Xi Zhongxun zai Luonai," 97.
32. Xi, Huang, and Tan, "Xi Zhongxun," 75–77.
33. Yang Ping, "Xi Zhongxun, Hao Ran, he wo," *Hongse wenhua wang*, May 15, 2017, https://www.kunlunce.com/llyj/fl11111111111/2017-05-16/115935.html.
34. Gao Xin, "Xi zhuxi shuo: 'meiyou Mao zhuxi, nalai jintian de wo,'" RFA, Dec. 12,

2013; Mao Yushi and Xia Youxin, "Dang he guojia lingdao ren canguan Shaoshan ganyan jiyu," *Zhonghua hun*, no. 12 (2003): 17–19.

35. Kong Shujing, *Suiyue jiyi: Yiwei jiangjun nü'er de suantian kule* (Beijing: Huayi, 2011), 156–57.

36. Interview.

37. Lishi, "Xi Zhongxun chang 'Dongfang hong,'" YouTube, June 22, 2017, video, https://www.youtube.com/watch?v=IxgNY-qFWjk&ab_channel=lishi.

38. Xue Qingchao, *Lishi de jianzheng: "Wenge" de zhongjie* (Beijing: Jiuzhou, 2011), 362.

39. *Xi Zhongxun zhuan*, 2:348.

40. Frederick C. Teiwes and Warren Sun, *Hua Guofeng, Deng Xiaoping, and the Dismantling of Maoism: From Restoration toward Reform, 1976–1981* (New York: Routledge, forthcoming).

41. Wu Wenxiao, "Liu Zhidan," 46.

42. Hu Shihou, "Mianhuai Xi lao," 19.

43. Ibid., 19–20; *Xi Zhongxun nianpu*, 3:1.

44. Zhang Zhigong, *Nanwang de ershinian*, 107; Jia Juchuan, "1962.10–2002.5," 10.

45. *Xi Zhongxun nianpu*, 2:447–48.

46. Ding Min, "Xi Zhongxun zai Luonai," 101; Warren Sun (historian of modern China), in discussion with the author, July 2022.

47. Laixia laiqu zhijian, "Xi Zhongxun," pt. 3.

48. *Wang Zhen zhuan*, 1:520–21.

49. Sun, discussion.

50. Ding Min, "Xi Zhongxun zai Luonai," 101.

51. *Xi Zhongxun nianpu*, 2:449.

52. Li Shengyu, *Pingfan suiyue* (self-pub., Beijing shidai nongchao wenhua fazhan, 2012), 105.

53. Wang Hui, "Yi yu Xi Lao de yici huanju," in *Xi Zhongxun jinian wenji*, ed. Zhonggong zhongyang dangshi yanjiushi (Beijing: Zhonggong dangshi, 2013), 242–43.

54. Yang Lin and Bu Changjiong, "'Renzhe' Xi Zhongxun," *Boke tianxia* 158 (Apr. 2014).

55. Li Rui, diary (vols. 19–20, 1987), p. 81, HIA.

Chapter 17: Facing the Consequences of the Cultural Revolution

1. Yang Li, *Gu Dacun chenyuan lu* (Hong Kong: Tiandi tushu, 2000), 342; Huang Ziyun, "Gaige kaifang chuqi de Ye Jianying yu Xi Zhongxun," *Dangzhi zonglan*, no. 10 (2018): 90–96.

2. Zhonggong Guangdong shengwei dangshi yanjiushi, ed., *Xi Zhongxun zhuzheng Guangdong fengcai lu* (Guangzhou: Guangdong renmin, 2013), 9–11.

3. Hu Shihou, "Mianhuai Xi lao," 20.

4. Zeng Dingshi, "Huiyi sheng zhengfu de hao banzhang Tianfu tongzhi," in *Huiyi Liu Tianfu* (Hong Kong: Xianggang rongyu, 2003), 153.

5. *Qunxing cuican*, 709.

6. *Liu Peizhi wencun*, 59.

7. Mo, *Tongzhan fengyun*, 435.

8. "Zhonggong zhongyang pizhuan zhonggong zhongyang zuzhibu guanyu wei xiaoshuo 'Liu Zhidan' pingfan de baogao," Aug. 4, 1979, TML; "Zhongyang zuzhibu zhuanfa Zhonggong Shaanxi shengwei 'guanyu wei suowei 'Peng, Gao, Xi fandang jituan' wenti chedi pingfan de qingshi baogao' de tongzhi," Jan. 11, 1980, TML; "Zhonggong zhongyang guanyu wei suowei 'Xi Zhongxun fandang jituan' pingfan de tongzhi," Feb. 25, 1980, TML.

9. Yan Hongwei and Qiu Ran, eds., *Xi Zhongxun yu qunzhong luxian*, vol. 1 (Beijing: Zhonggong zhongyang dangxiao, 2015), 172.

10. Yang Lin and Bu, "'Renzhe' Xi Zhongxun."

11. Cheng Guanjun, "Xi Zhongxun weihe zai 1978 nian zhongyang gongzuo huiyishang bei zanyang," *Tongzhou gongjin*, no. 6 (2016): 29–31; "Bu yao pa ting ci'er de hua: Guli ganbu qunzhong jianghua; Guangdong Huiyang diqu Mai Zican tongzhi xie xin piping shengwei di'er shuji Xi Zhongxun, Xi Zhongxun tongzhi fuxin, chengken jieshou yijian, bing xie gei gedi, yaoqiu jiuzheng quedian, gaijin zuofeng," *PD*, Nov. 8, 1978.

12. "Ye Jianying zai zhongyang gongzuo huiyi bimu huishang de jianghua" (unpublished manuscript, Dec. 13, 1978). Held by Warren Sun.

13. Lu Di, "Lishi."

14. Cheng Guanjun, "Xi Zhongxun."

15. Yu Guangyuan, *Wo yanzhong de tamen* (Hong Kong: Shidai guoji, 2005), 7–8.

16. Xi Zhongxun, "Zai quansheng jijian ganbu xuexiban jieye huishang de jianghua," in *Guangdong jijian jiancha ji: 1950–1995 nian*, ed. Zhonggong Guangdong sheng jilü jiancha weiyuanhui and Guangdong sheng jianchating (Guangzhou: Guangzhou renmin, 1998), 886–87.

17. Wu Nansheng, "Wu Nansheng: Wo suo qinli de jingji tequ de juece guocheng," in *Zhongguo dangdai mingren zhengyao fang shuping ji*, ed. Yang Jisheng (Hong Kong: Tiandi tushu, 2013), 141, 143.

18. Song Chundan, "Xi Zhongxun zai 1978," *Zhongguo xinwen zhoukan*, Dec. 17, 2018.

19. Cheng Kai, "He Pin zhuanfang Cheng Kai," in *Xi Jinping jiazu yu Chuanpu maoyizhan*, ed. Ho Pin (Deer Park, NY: Mingjing, 2018), 13–94.

20. Ju Liming, "Yi zhizheng zhaoxi de geming jingshen zhua Guangdong gongzuo," in *Xi Zhongxun zhuzheng Guangdong yishu lu*, ed. Zhonggong Guangdong shengwei dangshi yanjiushi (Beijing: Zhonggong dangshi, 2013), 253.

21. Interview.

22. He Yao, *Xi Zhongxun jiafeng*, 199.

23. Lian Zhengbao, "Zhongguo shengzhang daibiaotuan shouci fangmei: Wan Li zhiding Xi Zhongxun dang tuanzhang," *Ta Kung Pao*, Sept. 26, 2013; Si, *Liu Lantao*, 272.

24. *Xi Zhongxun zhuan*, 2:630.

25. Cheng Kai (former Chinese journalist), in discussion with the author, Feb. 2020.

26. Li Rui, diary (vol. 22, 1990), p. 47, HIA.

27. Lu Di, "Ji Xi Zhongxun canjia shiyijie sanzhong quanhui," in *Zhongguo mingyun da juice: Shiyijie sanzhong quanhui qinli*, ed. Zheng Hui (Shenzhen: Shenzhen baoye jituan, 2008), 314.

28. Zhonggong Guangdong sheng jilü jiancha weiyuanhui and Guangdong sheng jianchating, eds., *Guangdong jijian jiancha ji: 1950–1995 nian* (Guangzhou: Guangzhou renmin, 1998), 32.

29. Wu Nansheng, "Wu Nansheng," 141.

30. *Liu Tianfu huiyilu* (Beijing: Zhonggong dangshi, 1995), 428–29; Zhu Senlin, "Chuanhao gaige kaifang jieli bang: Zhu Senlin fangtanlu," in *Guangdong gaige kaifang juecezhe fangtanlu*, ed. Zhonggong Guangdong shengwei dangshi yanjiushi (Guangzhou: Guangdong renmin, 2008), 478; Zhu Senlin, "Gaodu zhihui kaiqi Guangdong gaige kaifang," in *Xi Zhongxun zhuzheng Guangdong yishu lu*, ed. Zhonggong Guangdong shengwei dangshi yanjiushi (Beijing: Zhonggong dangshi, 2013), 9–10.

31. Wu Nansheng, "Wu Nansheng," 141–43.

32. David Shambaugh, *The Making of a Premier: Zhao Ziyang's Provincial Career* (New York: Routledge, 2019); Yang Li, *Gu Dacun chenyuan lu*, 342–43; Nian Ren, "Hu Yaobang, Xi Zhongxun zhongshi 'Feng Gu difang zhuyi fandang lianmeng' de pingfan," in

Guangdong lishi wenti yanjiu: Guangdong difang zhuyi: Pingfan yanjiu ziliao, ed. Zhang Jiangming, special ser., vol. 81 (n.p.: SCCP, 2000), 379–80.

33. Zhang Zhigong, "Lingdao ganbu he qunzhong shi pingdeng de," in *Caifang shilu: Xi Zhongxun zai Guangdong de gushi*, ed. Yan Hongwei and Qiu Ran (Hong Kong: Xianggang zhonghe, 2016), 209–10.
34. Yang Li, *Gu Dacun chenyuan lu*, 343–53; Nian, "Hu Yaobang," 381–82.
35. Yang Li, *Gu Dacun chenyuan lu*, 360–69.
36. Fernando Galbiati, *P'eng P'ai and the Hai-Lu-Feng Soviet* (Stanford: Stanford University Press, 1985), 368–69.
37. Lu Di, "Ji Xi Zhongxun," 314.
38. Li Shenping, "Xi Zhongxun zai Guangdong zhuchi pingfan yuanjia cuo'an," *Yanhuang chunqiu*, no. 6 (2012): 58.
39. Zhang Zhigong, "Lingdao ganbu," 208–9.
40. Yang Lin and Bu, "'Renzhe' Xi Zhongxun."
41. Xi Zhongxun, "Tongdao jingai de Ye shuai," *PD*, Oct. 31, 1986; Zhang Hanqing, "Yinling Guangdong gaige kaifang xian zou yi bu," in *Xi Zhongxun zhuzheng Guangdong yishu lu*, ed. Zhonggong Guangdong shengwei dangshi yanjiushi (Beijing: Zhonggong dangshi, 2013), 151–52.
42. Su Weimin, "Gaige kaifang zhi chu Yang Shangkun zai Guangdong," *Bainianchao*, no. 2 (2008): 21.
43. Zhang Hanqing, "Ta yong ziji yi sheng de shijian lai shuxie 'qunzhong luxian' zhe sige dazi," in *Caifang shilu: Xi Zhongxun zai Guangdong de gushi*, ed. Yan Hongwei and Qiu Ran (Hong Kong: Xianggang zhonghe, 2016), 177–80.
44. Su Weimin, "Gaige kaifang," 20.
45. Zhonggong Guangdong shengwei dangshi yanjiushi, ed., *Guangdong gaige kaifang fazhan shi: 1978–2018* (Guangzhou: Guangdong renmin, 2019), 13.
46. Li Rui, *Li Rui koushu wangshi* (Hong Kong: Dashan wenhua, 2013), 418; Lu Di, "Ji Xi Zhongxun," 311.
47. Lu Di, "Lishi."
48. Li Liqun, "Nanwang de huiyi," 284–85.
49. Li Liqun, "1949 zhi hou."
50. Hu Jiwei, *Hu Zhao xinzheng qishilu: Bingdui "xin minzhu zhuyi" jinxing poxi* (Hong Kong: Xin shiji, 2012), 87.
51. Gao Yu, "He Jiadong yu qijin wei liao de xiaoshuo 'Liu Zhidan' yuan'an," in *Siren yi shi jingshen yongcun: He Jiadong jinian wenji*, ed. Chen Ziming and Bi Yimin (self-pub., Shidai wenxian, 2012), 88; He Jiadong, "Zhengzhi gaige," 391; Li Jiantong, *Fandang xiaoshuo "Liu Zhidan,"* 238–39.
52. Guo Hongtao, "Shaan-bei fenghuo," *Geming shi ziliao*, no. 5 (1981): 40–69; Guo Hongtao, "Dierci guonei geming zhanzheng shiqi Shaan-bei geming douzheng shishi huiyi," *Shaanxi wenshi ziliao* 12 (1981): 1–26.
53. Liu Jingfan et al., "Guanyu Shaan-bei 'sufan' yu luxian douzheng de zhenxiang," n.d., reprint, Huangtu lianyihui, 2012, https://web.archive.org/web/20171112011408/http://www.htqly.org/Detail.aspx?Id=271.
54. Wang Xiaozhong, *Zhongguwei gongzuo jishi*, 68–72; Zhang Xiushan, *Wode bashiwunian*, 355–59; Ren Xueling, *Shaan-Gan*, 260–62.
55. Wang Xiaozhong, *Zhongguwei gongzuo jishi*, 81–82.
56. Ibid., 83–84.
57. Ibid., 85.
58. Ibid., 86–89.
59. Zhang Xiangming, "55 nian," 354; *Fan Ming huiyilu*, 3:1587–93, 1:1.

60. Wang Chaobei, *Mengyuan jishi*, 275–76.
61. Anita Chan, Stanley Rosen, and Jonathan Unger, eds., introduction to *On Socialist Democracy and the Chinese Legal System: The Li Yizhe Debates*, ed. Chan, Rosen, and Unger (Armonk, NY: M. E. Sharpe, 1985), 1–16.
62. Yang Lin and Bu, "'Renzhe' Xi Zhongxun."
63. Zhonggong Guangdong shengwei dangshi yanjiushi, *Xi Zhongxun*, 201–3.
64. *Wang Xizhe zizhuan: Zouxiang hei'an* (Hong Kong: Minzhu daxue chubanshe, 1996), 188–89.
65. Li Zhengtian, "Xi Zhongxun xiuzheng wode 'wu zhengfu zhuyi,'" *Nanfang dushi bao*, Feb. 6, 2008.
66. *Wang Xizhe zizhuan*, 194–95.
67. Ibid., 197–98.
68. Ibid., 205–6; Chan, Rosen, and Unger, introduction, 24.
69. Li Haidong, "Guanxin qingnian, qiadang chuli 'Li Yizhe' anjian," in *Xi Zhongxun zhuzheng Guangdong yishu lu*, ed. Zhonggong Guangdong shengwei dangshi yanjiushi (Beijing: Zhonggong dangshi, 2013), 211–12.
70. Zhonggong Guangdong shengwei dangshi yanjiushi, *Xi Zhongxun*, 210–12.
71. *Wang Xizhe zizhuan*, 206–9.
72. Zhonggong Guangdong shengwei dangshi yanjiushi, *Xi Zhongxun*, 212–13.
73. *Wang Xizhe zizhuan*, 209.
74. Ibid., 219.
75. Wang Xizhe, "An Interview with Wang Xizhe by the Guangzhou *People's Voice*," *Chinese Law and Government* 14, no. 2 (Summer 1991): 77–83.
76. Stanley Rosen, "Guangzhou's Democracy Movement in Cultural Revolution Perspective," *China Quarterly*, no. 101 (1985): 1–31.
77. Ding Dong and Xing Xiaoqun, *Bashi niandai Zhongguo zhenggai yaozhe neimu* (Hong Kong: Dashan wenhua, 2015), 83–84.
78. Rosen, "Guangzhou's Democracy Movement," 22.
79. Chan, Rosen, and Unger, introduction, 24–26.

Chapter 18: Blazing a Bloody Trail

1. Yang Jisheng, *Zhongguo gaige niandai de zhengzhi douzheng* (Hong Kong: Excellent Culture, 2004), 206–7.
2. Lu Di, "Xi Zhongxun yu Guangdong fan 'toudu waitao,'" *Bainianchao*, no. 10 (2007): 21.
3. Fang Bao, "Gaige kaifang yi jiefang sixiang wei xiandao: Fang Bao fangtanlu," in *Guangdong gaige kaifang juecezhe fangtanlu*, ed. Zhonggong Guangdong shengwei dangshi yanjiushi (Guangzhou: Guangdong renmin, 2008), 443.
4. "1978 nian 9 yue 5 ri Guangdong sheng gong'anting guanyu dangqian wo sheng toudu waitao yanzhong de qingkuang baogao," *Guangdong wenshi ziliao* 85 (2002): 505.
5. Lu Di, "Xi Zhongxun," 22.
6. Huang Ziyun, "Gaige kaifang."
7. Yang Lin and Bu, "'Renzhe' Xi Zhongxun"; Fang Bao, "Wei qunzhong banshi, bu yao pa cuo, you xie shiqing zuocuole, yao ganyu chengdan zeren le," in *Caifang shilu: Xi Zhongxun zai Guangdong de gushi*, ed. Yan Hongwei and Qiu Ran (Hong Kong: Xianggang zhonghe, 2016), 94–95; Liu Lizhen, "Shenqie mianhuai wode shufu Liu Jingfan," in *Jinian Liu Jingfan tongzhi danchen 100 zhounian zuotanhui ziliao huibian*, ed. Liu Mila (self-pub., Beijing shidai nongchao wenhua fazhan, 2011), 3–4; Lu Di, "Xi Zhongxun," 23; Liu Jingfan, "Guanyu Shenzhen shi shourong zhan guanya, nuedai shouren renyuan qingkuang de baogao," in *Liu Jingfan jinian wenji*, ed. Liu Mila and Liu Dudu (Beijing: Zhongyang wenxian, 2015), 858–60.

8. Lu Di, "Xi Zhongxun," 24.
9. Ibid., 25.
10. Fang Bao, "Wei qunzhong banshi," 96–99.
11. Chen Bing'an, *Da tao gang* (Guangdong: Guangdong renmin, 2010), 334.
12. Ibid., 335–36.
13. Ibid., 337–38.
14. Ibid., 338; Fang Bao, "Wei qunzhong banshi," 105.
15. Fang Bao, "Wei qunzhong banshi," 106–7.
16. "Guangdong Province: Relations with New South Wales," Dec. 14, 1979, A7327, BJ830/1/1 pt. 1, Peking China—Australia and China General—Sister State and Province Relationships NSW—Guangdong, NAA; "Record of Meeting at Government House," Nov. 22, 1979, FCO 21/1739, TNA; "Visit by Chairman of the Guangdong Provincial Revolutionary Committee," Dec. 1, 1979, FCO 21/1739, TNA; Lu Di, "Xi Zhongxun," 26–27; "Guangdong Province Chief Visits Hong Kong," Dec. 14, 1979, PLUSD.
17. *Deng Xiaoping nianpu (1975–1997)*, 3 vols. (Beijing: Zhongyang wenxian, 2004), 1:646.
18. Xi Zhongxun, "Zai quansheng jijian ganbu," 886–87.
19. Li Shengyu, *Pingfan suiyue*, 76–77.
20. Duan Yun, "Gang'Ao jingji suo jian," in *Duan Yun xuanji* (Taiyuan: Shanxi renmin, 1987), 349–62; Li Haiwen, "Bilu lanlu, yiqi shanlin," *Jingji daokan* 237 (Dec. 2018): 86–96.
21. Li Haiwen, "Xi Zhongxun lizheng zhongyang rang Guangdong xian xing yi bu," *Shiji* 3 (2018): 5–10.
22. Lin Yajie, ed., "Wu Nansheng tongzhi gei shengwei de baogao (1979 nian 2 yue 21 ri)," in *Tequ de youlai* (Guangzhou: Guangdong renmin, 2010), 32–34.
23. Lin Yajie, ed., "Shengwei changwei huiyi jilu (jiexuan) (1979 nian 4 yue 2 ri xiawu)," in *Tequ de youlai* (Guangzhou: Guangdong renmin, 2010), 35–37; Wu Nansheng, "Wu Nansheng."
24. Li Haiwen, "Xi Zhongxun"; Wang Quanguo, "Jiefang sixiang, ganyu chuangxin, ganyu gaige," in *Xi Zhongxun zhuzheng Guangdong yishu lu*, ed. Zhonggong Guangdong shengwei dangshi yanjiushi (Beijing: Zhonggong dangshi, 2013), 63.
25. Li Haiwen, "Xi Zhongxun"; Xi Zhongxun, "Zai shengwei sijie sanci changwei kuoda huiyishang de jianghua," in *Jingji tequ de youlai* (Guangzhou: Guangdong renmin, 2002), 194–97.
26. Ezra F. Vogel, *Deng Xiaoping and the Transformation of China* (Cambridge, MA: Belknap Press of Harvard University Press, 2011), 398–99.
27. Teiwes and Sun, *Dismantling of Maoism*.
28. Xia Meng, "Xibei zhi hun," 491–92.
29. Wu Nansheng, "Zhenshi de lishi: 'Ganchuang' de jilu," in *Jingji tequ de youlai*, ed. Lin Yajie (Guangzhou: Guangdong renmin, 2010), 142–52.
30. Lin Yajie, ed., "Shengwei changwei huiyi jilu (jiexuan) (1979 nian 5 yue 3 ri xiawu)," in *Tequ de youlai* (Guangzhou: Guangdong renmin, 2010), 40–42.
31. Wu Nansheng, "Wu Nansheng," 132.
32. *Liu Tianfu huiyilu*, 407.
33. *Deng Liqun zishu: Shierge chunqiu (1975–1987)* (Hong Kong: Dafeng, 2006), 145.
34. Xi Zhongxun, "Zai shengwei," 197.
35. Li Lanqing, *Tuwei: Guomen chukai de suiyue* (Beijing: Zhongyang wenxian, 2008), 89–92; Lawrence C. Reardon, *A Third Way: The Origins of China's Current Economic Development Strategy* (Cambridge, MA: Harvard University Asia Center, 2020), 60–61.
36. Gu Mu, "Guanyu zhixing 'Zhonggong zhongyang, guowuyuan pizhuan Guangdong shengwei, Fujian shengwei guanyu duiwai jingji huodong shixing teshu zhengce

he linghuo cuoshi de liangge baogao' de ruogan wenti," in *Zhongyang dui Guangdong gongzuo zhishi huibian (1979 nian–1982 nian)*, ser. 28, vol. 40 (n.p.: SCCP, 2007), 41–49.

37. Xiao Donglian, *Lishi de zhuanzhe—cong boluan fanzheng dao gaige kaifang* (Hong Kong: Quanqiu faxing zhongwen daxue, 2008), 552–53.

38. Ibid., 552–53; Warren Sun, "Chronology of Hua Guofeng (1971–1981)," China Studies Centre, University of Sydney (website), forthcoming.

39. "Zhonggong zhongyang guanyu 'Guangdong, Fujian liangsheng huiyi jiyao' de pishi," in *Zhongyang dui Guangdong gongzuo zhishi huibian (1979 nian–1982 nian)*, ser. 28, vol. 40 (n.p.: SCCP, 2007), 62.

40. *Xi Zhongxun nianpu*, 3:109.

41. Liu Tianfu, "Jiefang sixiang, jinxing jingji tizhi gaige de shiyan," in *Liu Tianfu wenxuan* (Guangzhou: Guangdong renmin, 1995), 357–72.

42. Wu Nansheng, "Zai Shenzhen ganbu dahuishang de jianghua," in *Jingji tequ de youlai* (Guangzhou: Guangdong renmin, 2002), 243–47.

43. "Zhongyang shujichu tongzhi tingqu Guangdong gongzuo huibao de tanhua jiyao," in *Zhongyang dui Guangdong gongzuo zhishi huibian (1979 nian–1982 nian)*, ser. 28, vol. 40 (n.p.: SCCP, 2007), 94–108.

44. Liu Tianfu, "Yong dang gaige kaifang de paitou bing: Liu Tianfu caifang lu," in *Guangdong gaige kaifang juecezhe fangtanlu*, ed. Zhonggong Guangdong shengwei dangshi yanjiushi (Guangzhou: Guangdong renmin, 2008), 122–25, 127.

45. Zhu Senlin, "Chuanhao gaige kaifang," 479; Wu Nansheng, "Wu Nansheng," 141; Bi Ping, *Liang Xiang: Zhuazhu laoshu bu shi hao mao* (Hong Kong: Gonghe, 2007), 96–100.

46. Han Gang, "Jiannan de zhuanxing: Yijiuqiba nian zhongyang gongzuo huiyi de nongye yiti," *Zhonggong dangshi yanjiu*, no. 9 (2011): 25, 27.

47. Frederick C. Teiwes and Warren Sun, *Paradoxes of Post-Mao Rural Reform: Initial Steps toward a New Chinese Countryside, 1976–1981* (New York: Routledge, 2016), 182–83.

48. Du Ruizhi, "Guangdong nongcun gaige de jianxing lu: Du Ruizhi fangtanlu," in *Guangdong gaige kaifang juecezhe fangtanlu*, ed. Zhonggong Guangdong shengwei dangshi yanjiushi (Guangzhou: Guangdong renmin, 2008), 290.

49. Ibid.; Lin Ruo, "Zai kaituo chuangxin zhong yingde xin fazhan: Lin Ruo caifang lu," in *Guangdong gaige kaifang juecezhe fangtanlu*, ed. Zhonggong Guangdong shengwei dangshi yanjiushi (Guangzhou: Guangdong renmin, 2008), 57–58.

50. Cheng Kai, "He Pin," 21–23; Cheng Kai, discussion.

51. Ezra F. Vogel, *One Step Ahead in China: Guangdong under Reform* (Cambridge, MA: Harvard University Press, 1989), 88.

52. Interview.

53. Li Rui, diary (vols. 19–20, 1987), p. 62, HIA.

54. Zhang Gensheng, "Ting Hua Guofeng tan jijian dashi," *Yanhuang chunqiu*, no. 10 (2008): 9–10.

55. Xiao Donglian, *Tanlu zhi yi: 1978–1992 nian de Zhongguo jingji gaige* (Beijing: Shehui kexue wenxian, 2019), 86.

56. Ibid., 89–90.

57. *Xi Zhongxun nianpu*, 3:176.

58. "Hu Yaobang tongzhi zai Guangdong, Fujian liangsheng zuotan huishang de fayan," in *Zhongyang dui Guangdong gongzuo zhishi huibian (1979 nian–1982 nian)*, ser. 28, vol. 40 (n.p.: SCCP, 2007), 272.

59. "Peng Chong tongzhi zai Guangdong, Fujian liangsheng zuotan huishang de fayan," in *Zhongyang dui Guangdong gongzuo zhishi huibian (1979 nian–1982 nian)*, ser. 28, vol. 40 (n.p.: SCCP, 2007), 289–91.

60. Wu Nansheng, "Wu Nansheng," 138.
61. Guan Shan, "Ren Zhongyi tan Deng Xiaoping yu Guangdong de gaige kaifang," *Yanhuang chunqiu*, no. 8 (2008): 13.
62. Xiao Donglian, *Tanlu zhi yi*, 91–92.
63. "1983-11-22 Malo, Entretien avec M Xi Zhongxun," Nov. 22, 1983, Ministère des Affaires Etrangères, 2882 TOPO 2917, Direction Asie and Océanie, 1980–1986, série CH sous-série 1 dossier 4.
64. Zhou Ke and Gu Xunzhong, *Fengyu qishinian: Shidai dachao zhong de wo he wode yijia* (Shanghai: Wenhui, 2006), 333.

Chapter 19: Opening to the West

1. Quan Yanchi, "Xu Shiyou hejiu xuanjiang," *Yanhuang chunqiu*, no. 1 (Jan. 1992): 49.
2. Li Yu, "Daonian Li Shenzhi xiansheng," in *Huainian Li Shenzhi*, ed. Ding Dong (Hong Kong: Shidai chaoliu, 2003), 297.
3. "From Neville Wran to J. M. Fraser," Oct. 8, 1979, A1838, 3107/38/8/14 pt. 1, China—Relations with Australia—Cultural NSW Special Relations with Guangdong, NAA.
4. "Xi Zhongxun," Dec. 1979, A1838, 3107/38/8/14 pt. 1, China—Relations with Australia—Cultural NSW Special Relations with Guangdong, NAA.
5. "Welcome in Australia," FBIS, Nov. 26, 1979.
6. "Record of Conversation between the Minister, Mr. Xi Zhongxun, Chairman of Revolutionary Committee, Guangdong Province, China, and Six Members of the Guangdong Delegation," Dec. 14, 1979, A7327, BJ830/1/1 pt. 1, Peking China—Australia and China General—Sister State and Province Relationships NSW—Guangdong, NAA.
7. "Guangdong Province: Relations with New South Wales," Dec. 14, 1979, A7327, BJ830/1/1 pt. 1, Peking China—Australia and China General—Sister State and Province Relationships NSW—Guangdong, NAA.
8. *Xi Zhongxun nianpu*, 3:103.
9. Andrew Watson, "No Oil, but a Red Carpet," *SMH*, Apr. 11, 1980.
10. "Visit of Premier of NSW: Call on Premier Hua Guofeng," Apr. 17, 1980, A7327, BJ830/1/1 pt. 1, Peking China—Australia and China General—Sister State and Province Relationships NSW—Guangdong, NAA.
11. "Australia/China Relations—Visit of the Premier of New South Wales," Apr. 16, 1980, A7327, BJ830/1/1 pt. 1, Peking China—Australia and China General—Sister State and Province Relationships NSW—Guangdong, NAA.
12. Andrew Watson, "As PM, Neville Has a Long Hua to Go," *SMH*, Apr. 13, 1980.
13. "Future of Hong Kong: Relevance of the Status of Macao," Oct. 5, 1982, PREM 19/790, TNA.
14. "Guangdong Chief in Macau," *SCMP*, June 5, 1980; He Yueming, "Xi Zhongxun fangwen Aomen yugao 'tequ' anpai," *Shiji*, Jan. 2019.
15. "Guangdong Chief in Macau."
16. Yong Yi, "Huiyi Xi Zhongxun yu Aomen miqie xianggang de jijian shi," *Xinhua Aobao*, May 25, 2017; Shiu Hing Lo, *Political Development in Macau* (Hong Kong: Chinese University Press, 1995), 31–33.
17. He Yueming, "Xi Zhongxun"; Bertil Lintner, *Blood Brothers: The Criminal Underworld of Asia* (New York: Palgrave Macmillan, 2003), 101–23.
18. He Yueming, "Xi Zhongxun."
19. Ibid.; "Guangdong Governor Speaks on Macao, Hong Kong Status," FBIS, June 16, 1980; Yong Yi, "Huiyi Xi Zhongxun."
20. "Vice President Walter F. Mondale's Visit to Canton, the People's Republic of China, Aug. 30–31, Sept. 1, 1979," n.d., box 21, 154-I-16–10F, Vice President: Trip Files, WFM, MHS.

21. "Office of the Vice President's Press Secretary," Aug. 31, 1979, box 11, 154-I-2-11B, Press Releases and Related Materials, WFM, MHS.

22. "Remarks of Vice President Walter F. Mondale: Guangzhou Consulate Opening," Aug. 31, 1979, Speeches Given on Vice President's Trip to China, Aug. 1979, pt. 3., WFM, MHS.

23. "Suggested Guidelines for Activities Related to the Visit of the Provincial Governors Delegation of the People's Republic of China," Oct. 1, 1980, ser. 4, box 36, folder 348, RG 4, Accession 4 (FA1186), RAC, NCUSCR; Jan Berris, *Report on the Visit of the Chinese Provincial Governors Delegation to the United States, Oct. 20–Nov. 6, 1980*, Nov. 10, 1980, ser. 4, box 36, folder 350, RG 4, Accession 4 (FA1186), RAC, NCUSCR.

24. Lian, "Zhongguo."

25. "Guangdong Governor Xi Zhongxun Hails Bilateral Ties," FBIS, Oct. 23, 1980; "Itinerary: Delegation of Provincial Leaders of the People's Republic of China, 20 Oct.–6 Nov. 1980," Nov. 6, 1980, ser. 4, box 36, folder 348, RG 4, Accession 4 (FA1186), RAC, NCUSCR.

26. "Subject: Appointment for PRC Provincial Governors Delegation," Oct. 9, 1980, Records of the Office of the National Security Advisor—Zbigniew Brzezinski Material—Country File (NSA 6), China (PRC), 10/80–1/81, JCL.

27. "Subject: Your Meeting with Chinese Provincial Governors Delegation," Oct. 17, 1980, Records of the Office of the National Security Advisor—Zbigniew Brzezinski Material—Country File (NSA 6), China (PRC), 10/80–1/81, JCL.

28. "Subject: Your Meeting with Xi Zhongxun, Governor of Guangdong Province and Members of His Party on Thursday, Oct. 23 at 4:30 p.m.," Oct. 22, 1980, White House Central File, Subject File, Container CO-17, File unit: Co 34-2, Confidential, 4/1/80–1/20/81, JCL.

29. "Translator to Arthur Rosen and Jan Berris," Nov. 10, 1980, ser. 4, box 36, folder 350, RG 4, Accession 4 (FA1186), RAC, NCUSCR; "Itinerary."

30. Kenneth Quinn (former deputy assistant secretary of state), in discussion with the author, June 2021.

31. Evan Roth, "Chinese Eye Purchase of Farm Gear," *Des Moines Tribune*, Oct. 27, 1980.

32. Interview with American participant of the delegation.

33. Quinn, discussion.

34. Lian, "Zhongguo"; "Schedule for Governor's Delegation from China to Iowa," Oct. 24, 1980, RG 43 Governor, Gov. Robert D. Ray, Departmental and Subject Files—Kenneth Quinn, ISA.

35. Kenneth M. Quinn, "The Journey in Retrospect," in *Old Friends: The Xi Jinping-Iowa Story*, ed. Sarah D. Lande and Albert Lin (Muscatine: Sarah D. Lande US-China Friendship Education, 2017); Quinn, discussion.

36. Wang Huning, *Meiguo fandui Meiguo* (Shanghai: Shanghai wenyi, 1991), 20–24; Diane L. Barthel, *Amana: From Pietist Sect to American Community* (Lincoln: University of Nebraska Press, 1984).

37. Berris, *Report*.

38. Ibid.

39. Susan Levine (translator during trip), in discussion with the author, June 2024.

40. Ibid.

41. Ibid.

42. Ibid.; Lian, "Zhongguo"; "Tom Bradley to Yang Shangkun," Oct. 17, 1980, ser. 4, box 36, folder 352, RG 4, Accession 4 (FA1186), RAC, NCUSCR.

43. Erwin Baker, "Prospects for Sister-City Tie to Canton Improve," *Los Angeles Times*, Nov. 7, 1980; "Translator to Arthur Rosen"; Berris, *Report*.

44. Levine, discussion.
45. "Itinerary."
46. Lian, "Zhongguo."
47. "Translator to Arthus Rosen."
48. Ibid.; Jeremy Page, "Like Father Like Son: Xi Jinping Not First in Family to Visit Iowa," *Wall Street Journal*, Feb. 6, 2012.
49. Lian, "Zhongguo."
50. Berris, *Report*.
51. Levine, discussion.
52. "Translator to Arthur Rosen."
53. Osnos, "Born Red"; "Miscellaneous Notes of Conversations in Henan (Luoyang, Zhengzhou, and Shaolin Monastery) about Ji Dengkui and Xu Shiyou," n.d., Zhengzhou Foreign Affairs Bureau, Shaolin Temple/Monastery, Luoyang Mining Machinery Factory, Zhengzhou Communes, and Guangzhou Commune, Nov. 22–Dec. 1, 1980, DML.
54. "Arthur Rosen to Xi Zhongxun," July 31, 1981, box 40, folder 374, Rosen Chron Files, RG 9, (FA1191), RAC, NCUSCR.
55. Xi Zhongxun, "Xuexiao yao jiaqiang sixiang zhengzhi jiaoyu gongzuo," in *Xi Zhongxun wenxuan* (Beijing: Zhongyang wenxian, 1995), 363.
56. "Xi Zhongxun Meets, Fetes US Delegation," FBIS, Nov. 12, 1982; "Brief Sit-Down with Xi Zhongxun, Vice Chairman Standing Committee, NPC, Secretary CCP, Politburo Member, Beijing, November 12, 1982, 6:30 p.m.," Nov. 12, 1982, DML.

Chapter 20: A New Order at the Secretariat and the National People's Congress

1. Zhang Shujun, *Da zhuanzhe: Zhonggong shiyijie sanzhong quanhui shilu* (Hangzhou: Zhejiang renmin, 1998), 270.
2. Lu Di, "Lishi," 51.
3. Ye Jianying, "Zai dangde shiyijie wuzhong quanhui diyici huiyishang de jianghua," in *Sanzhong quanhui yilai zhongyao wenxian huibian*, vol. 1 (Beijing: Renmin, 1982), 388–92.
4. Jia Juchuan, "1962.10–2002.5," 12–13.
5. Zhong Peizhang, "Changliu yize zai renjian," *Yaobang yanljiu* 85 (June 2022): 212, FCFL.
6. Li Rui, diary (vol. 26, 1994), p. 7, HIA.
7. Li Rui, diary (vol. 23, 1991), p. 88, HIA.
8. "Telegram from Sundfelt," Sept. 9, 1981, dossier C 50 G/7 del 3, Regeringskansliet, Centralarkivet Utrikesdepartementet.
9. "The Chinese Communist Party's Sixth Plenum: Deng Firms His Grip," Nov. 1, 1981, CIA-RDP03T02547R000100100001-0, CREST.
10. Bryan Johnson, "Haymaker from Deng Likely to End a Backroom Brawl," *Globe and Mail*, July 25, 1981; David Chen, "Country Has a Far Better Track Record than Many Others," *SCMP*, July 4, 1981.
11. Li Rui, diary (vols. 11–12, 1981–1982), p. 39, HIA.
12. *Deng Xiaoping nianpu (1975–1997)*, 2:845; *Xi Zhongxun zhuan*, 2:504–5.
13. Re Di [Raidi], "Zhongxun tongzhi yu Xizang gongzuo," in *Xi Zhongxun jinian wenji*, ed. Zhonggong zhongyang dangshi yanjiushi (Beijing: Zhonggong dangshi, 2013), 28–37; Li Xiangchao et al., "Xi Zhongxun yu 'mishu gongzuo' chuangkan," *Mishu gongzuo*, no. 7 (2015): 4–7.
14. Joseph Torigian, *Prestige, Manipulation, and Coercion: Elite Power Struggles in the Soviet Union and China after Stalin and Mao* (New Haven, CT: Yale University Press, 2022), 192.
15. *Deng Liqun guoshi jiangtanlu*, 3:410.

16. Chung Yen-lin, "Peng Zhen he Zhonggong Dongbeiju zhenglun," *Zhongyang yanjiusuo jindaishi yanjiusuo jikan*, no. 3 (2016): 99–151.

17. Li Rui, diary (vols. 12–13, 1983), p. 58, HIA.

18. Huang Da, Zhu Yu, and Gao Jingzeng, "Shuobujin de Li Xiannian," in *Zhongguo gongchandang koushu shiliao congshu*, vol. 6, pt. 1 (Beijing: Zhonggong dangshi, 2013), 449–61.

19. Wang Xiaozhong, *Zhongguwei gongzuo jishi*, 161–67.

20. Ye Bing, "Bao Tong yi wenge: Xi Zhongxun shi Mao Zedong 'dada de shouhaizhe,'" VoA(C), May 6, 2021.

21. Wu Jiang, "Qin Chuan," 56–57.

22. Gao Kai, "Ta ceng shexiang zhiding baohu butong yijian zhidu," *21 shiji jingji baodao*, Oct. 15, 2013.

23. Li Rui, diary (vols. 13–15, 1984), p. 26, HIA.

24. Du Daozheng, *Yi ke pingchang xin* (Hong Kong: Yanhuang wenhua chanye, 2009), 201–2.

25. Sun Yuting, "Nanwang de enqing," in *Huainian Zhongxun*, ed. Cao Zhenzhong and Wu Jiang (Beijing: Zhongyang dangshi, 2005), 273–74.

26. Interview with individual who witnessed described events.

27. Teiwes and Sun, *Dismantling of Maoism*; Sun, discussion; Han Gang, "Guanyu Hua Guofeng de ruogan shishi," *Yanhuang chunqiu*, no. 2 (2011): 16.

28. Zhonggong zhongyang shujichu yanjiushi, ed., *Dangde shiyijie sanzhong quanhui yilai dashiji: 1978–1985* (Beijing: Hongqi, 1987), 118.

29. *Li Erzhong biji zhaichao*, vol. 2 (self-pub., Zhongguo zhanwang, 2014), 562–68.

30. Torigian, *Prestige*, 139–41.

31. *Ye Jianying nianpu (1897–1986)*, vol. 2 (Beijing: Zhongyang wenxian, 2007), 1228–29.

32. Teiwes and Sun, *Maoist Era*, 223–26; Luo Yinsheng, *Qiao Guanhua quanzhuan* (Shanghai: Dongfang chuban zhongxin, 2006), 427–30.

33. Xi Wei and Liang Ping, "Huiyi bofu Xi Zhongxun," in *Jinian Xi Zhongxun danchen 100 zhounian wenji*, ed. Zhonggong Shaanxi shengwei dangshi yanjiushi (Xi'an: Shaanxi renmin, 2015), 113–14; He Pin [Ho Pin] and Gao Xin, *Zhonggong taizidang* (Taipei: Shibao wenhua, 1992).

34. Zhang Liqun et al., *Hu Yaobang zhuan*, 3 vols. (n.p.: Zhengqiu yijian gao, 2008), 3:69.

35. Jia Juchuan, "1962.10–2002.5," 14.

36. Zhonggong Gansu shengwei, ed., "Xi Zhongxun guanyu Gansu sheng lingdao banzi tiaozheng de jianghua," in *Xi Zhongxun yu Gansu* (Lanzhou: Gansu renmin, 2013), 469–71; Li Rui, diary (vols. 12–13, 1983), p. 23, HIA; Li Ziqi, "Gansu shengwei yuan shuji Li Ziqi: Shenqie huainian Xi Zhongxun tongzhi," *Guangming ribao*, Oct. 22, 2013.

37. Li Rui, diary (vols. 12–13, 1983), pp. 63–64, HIA.

38. Li Rui, diary (vols. 13–15, 1984), p. 1, HIA; Hu Yaobang, "Guanyu zhengdang de ruogan wenti," in *Hu Yaobang wenxuan 1975–1986*, vol. 3 (n.p.: Zhengqiu yijian gao, n.d.), 203–4.

39. Li Rui, diary (vols. 16–17, 1985), p. 41, HIA; Li Rui, diary (vol. 24, 1992), p. 101, HIA; *Xi Zhongxun zhuan*, 2:520.

40. Xiao Jin, *Zhengdang dashiji* (Harbin: Heilongjiang renmin, 1985), 151–53.

41. Mingjing huopai, "Tongzhi jieji yishi: Yan Huai de 'Jinchu zhongzubu' jiedu zhi er," YouTube, Oct. 2, 2017, video, https://www.youtube.com/watch?v=UicDF3Vgwdw; Hong Yung Lee, *From Revolutionary Cadres to Party Technocrats in Socialist China* (Berkeley: University of California Press, 1991), 245–46.

42. Deng Xiaoping, "Gaoji ganbu yao daitou fayang dangde youliang chuantong," in *Deng Xiaoping wenxuan*, vol. 2 (Beijing: Renmin, 1994), 222, 225.

43. Mingjing huopai, "Tongzhi jieji yishi"; H. Lee, *From Revolutionary Cadres*, 248–50; Yan Huai, *Jinchu zhongzubu: Yige hongerdai lixiangzhuyizhe de linglei rensheng* (Deer Park, NY: Mingjing, 2017), 201–2.
44. Li Rui, diary (vols. 11–12, 1981–1982), p. 23, HIA.
45. Zhang Zhigong, *Nanwang de ershinian*, 165–66.
46. Hu Sisheng, *Gaoceng fangtanlu* (Hong Kong: Xianggang xin dalu, 2012), 52–53.
47. "Xi Zhongxun Views Treatment of Younger Generation," FBIS, June 26, 1984.
48. Zhou Ke and Gu, *Fengyu qishinian*, 334.
49. Zhu Jintian, "Beijing shida er fuzhong zhong wenge jishi," *Huaxia wenzhai zengkan* 1145 (Oct. 2018).
50. Shan Shi and Fu Bo, "Li Wenfang jianjie," in *Jiqing yongyuan ranshao: Li Wenfang jinian wenji*, ed. Shan Shi (Beijing: Zuojia, 2007), 34.
51. Jia Yanyan, "Zhiqing suiyue," in *Jiqing Molidawa: Huiyi women zai Xingnong chadui de qingchun suiyue*, ed. Fang Fenglei (Beijing: Renmin wenxue, 2015), 376.
52. Zhonggong Beijing shiwei zuzhibu, *Zhongguo gongchandang Beijing shi zuzhishi ziliao* (Beijing: Renmin, 1992), 349, 399; Shan Shi and Fu, "Li Wenfang jianjie," 34–35.
53. Jia Yanyan, "Wangshi lili: Xi Zhongxun bu buxiu," in *Huainian Xi Zhongxun*, ed. Cao Zhenzhong and Wu Jiang (Beijing: Zhongyang dangshi, 2005), 266.
54. Xiao Ming, *Guangxi wenge tongshi gouchen* (Hong Kong: Xin shiji, 2013).
55. *Xi Zhongxun nianpu*, 3:251.
56. "Zhongyang lingdao dui Guangxi gongzuo de zhishi yaodian," July 1, 1983, TML.
57. "Huang Yun tongzhi chuanda zhongyang lingdao tongzhi zai taolun Guangxi liangge chuyi wenjian shi de jianghua jingshen," Sept. 12, 1983, TML; Li Rui, diary (vols. 12–13, 1983), p. 54, HIA.
58. "Hu Yaobang, Xi Zhongxun, Li Rui deng jiejian Guangxi zhongyang gongzuo zu he shengwei lingdao shi de jianghua," Jan. 14, 1984, HCCPM.
59. Xiao Ming, *Guangxi wenge tongshi gouchen*, 203.
60. Ding Min, "Xi Zhongxun zai Luonai," 92.
61. Hu Shihou, "Mianhuai Xi lao," 21.
62. He Zai, "Huainian Yaobang tongzhi," *Hong tudi*, no. 11 (2005).
63. Zhang Liqun et al., *Hu Yaobang zhuan*, 3:81–83; Yan Huai, *Jinchu zhongzubu*, 201–2.
64. "Shaan-Gan-Ning bianqu dierjie canyihui diyici dahui ti'an huilu," in *Shaan-Gan-Ning bianqu canyihui* (Beijing: Zhonggong zhongyang dangxiao keyan bangongshi, 1985), 306–50.
65. He Weifang, "Tongguo sifa shixian shehui zhengyi: Dui Zhongguo faguan xianzhuang de yige toushi," in *Zouxiang quanli de shidai*, ed. Xia Yong (Beijing: Zhongguo zhengfa daxue chubanshe, 1999), 230–31; Xi Zhongxun, "Guanche sifa gongzuo de zhengque fangxiang," LD, Nov. 5, 1944; He Weifang (Chinese legal scholar), in discussion with the author, Mar. 2020.
66. A Ji, "Lishi de xuanze: Renda 50 nian (xupian yi) (I)," *Zhengfu fazhi* 9 (2004): 15.
67. Yin Shusheng, "Gong'an gongzuo 'da yuejin,'" *Yanhuang chunqiu*, no. 1 (2010): 22.
68. *Xi Zhongxun nianpu*, 3:144.
69. *Peng Zhen nianpu*, 5:111, 5:117–18.
70. Zhonggong zhongyang tongzhanbu and Zhonggong zhongyang wenxian yanjiushi, eds., "Zhonggong zhongyang bangongting, Guowuyuan bangongting zhuanfa gong'anbu di baqi quanguo laogai gongzuo huiyi jiyao de tongzhi," in *Zhonghua renmin gongheguo xianxing fagui huibian (1949–1985)*, vol. 6 (Beijing: Renmin, 1987), 185–93.
71. "Xi Zhongxun tongzhi zai di baci quanguo laogai gongzuo huiyishang de jianghua (jielu)," Sept. 7, 1981, Laogai Research Foundation (database). Originally compiled by the PRC Ministry of Justice, Selected Reference Documents concerning Reform-

through-Labor Laws (vol. 2, Sept. 1987). I thank Lucy Hornby for sharing this document with me.

72. Zhang Chunsheng and Lü Wan, "Zai zuo 30 nian, women ye bu neng hezhe yanjing lifa: Zhang Chunsheng fangtanlu," *Difang lifa yanjiu* 4, no. 6 (Nov. 2019): 115–16; Zhang Chunsheng, "1979–1986: Liang du nanchan de Zhongguo minfa dian shi ruhe kaishi tupo de," *Zhongguo xinwen zhoukan*, Oct. 16, 2018.

73. Zhang Chunsheng, "Xin shiqi de fazhi jianshe cong zheli qibu," *Fazhi ribao*, Dec. 18, 2018.

74. *Hu Qiaomu zhuan*, vol. 2 (Beijing: Dangdai Zhongguo, 2015), 666.

75. "Zhonghu renmin gongheguo di sibu xianfa zhuangyan dansheng," *PD*, Dec. 5, 1982.

76. Siegmund Ginzberg, "Deng Xiaoping è stato eletto capo delle forze armate è Li Xiannian il nuovo presidente," *L'Unita*, June 19, 1983.

77. "Further Coverage of Fifth Session of Fifth NPC: Xi Zhongxun's Speech," FBIS, Dec. 16, 1982.

78. "Law to Rule Out Election Propaganda," *SCMP*, Dec. 17, 1982; Kevin J. O'Brien, *Reform without Liberalization: China's National People's Congress and the Politics of Institutional Change* (New York: Cambridge University Press, 1990), 127–31.

79. "Further Coverage."

80. O'Brien, *Reform*, 147.

81. *Liu Fuzhi huiyilu* (Beijing: Zhongyang wenxian, 2010), 311–12, 349–56.

82. *Jianguo yilai gong'an gongzuo dashi yaolan* (Beijing: Qunzhong, 2002), 565–66; Ye Fang, *Shehui zhi'an zonghe zhili shiwu quanshu* (Beijing: Zhongguo renmin gong'an daxue chubanshe, 1997), 208–10.

83. Zheng Tianxiang, *Xingcheng jilüe* (Beijing: Beijing chubanshe, 1994), 411–16.

84. "Xi Zhongxun tongzhi jianghua," *Gong'an daxue xuebao*, no. 1 (1985): 2–4.

85. "Xi Zhongxun Inaugurates Legal Affairs Company," FBIS, Feb. 13, 1985.

86. *Jianguo*, 596.

87. Zhonggong zhongyang bangongting and Guowuyuan bangongting xinfangju, eds., "Xi Zhongxun tongzhi de jianghua," in *Quanguo xinfang gongzuo huiyi ziliao huibian*, ser. 28, vol. 101, pt. 2 (n.p.: SCCP, 2011), 576–78.

Chapter 21: Princeling Politics

1. Jiang Huajie, "Zhidu jingxiang: Bolan tuanjie gonghui shijian yu Zhongguo gaige kaifang de bianzou," *Ershiyi shiji shuangyue kan* 6, no. 185 (June 2021): 102.

2. Sun, discussion.

3. Zhongguo xinwenshe, "Chicheng."

4. Li Rui, diary (vols. 17–18, 1986), p. 21, HIA.

5. Yan Huai, *Jinchu zhongzubu*, 219; Chun Han Wong, *Party of One: The Rise of Xi Jinping and China's Superpower Future* (New York: Avid Reader, 2023), 20.

6. Yan Huai (former cadre in Organization Department), in discussion with the author, Feb. 2024.

7. Torigian, "Historical Legacies," 11.

8. Liu Bing, *Fengyu suiyue*, 229; He Chongling, ed., *Qinghua daxue jiushinian* (Beijing: Qinghua daxue chubanshe, 2001), 290.

9. He Chongling, *Qinghua daxue jiushinian*, 288–99.

10. Xu Youyu, "1977: Gaibian mingyun de kaiduan," in *Kaifang Zhongguo: Gaige de 30 nian jiyi*, ed. Jingji guancha bao (Beijing: Zhongxin, 2008), 9.

11. Zhonggong Guangdong shengwei dangshi yanjiushi, *Xi Zhongxun*, 42–47.

12. Kong Dan, *Nande bense ren tianran*, 173.

13. "Daoshi yu jiyao mishu," *Boke tianxia* 34 (2013).

14. Zhonggong Guangdong shengwei dangshi yanjiushi, *Xi Zhongxun*, 47; Kong Xiangxiu, *Geng Biao zhuan*, vol. 2 (Beijing: Jiefangjun, 2009), 277–78, 530–31.
15. Sun, discussion.
16. "Daoshi yu jiyao mishu."
17. Yan, discussion.
18. He Weiling, *Chuanshuo zhong de He Weiling shougao* (Hong Kong: Dafeng, 2015), 388. However, the author of these memoirs despised Xi Zhongxun, so this story should be treated with caution.
19. "Portrait of Vice President Xi Jinping: 'Ambitious Survivor' of the Cultural Revolution," Nov. 16, 2009, PLUSD.
20. "Daoshi yu jiyao mishu."
21. Zhou Weisi, "Jinping ba zhanlüe yanguang he wushi jingshen jiehe qilai, hen liaobuqi," in *Xi Jinping zai Zhengding*, ed. Zhongyang dangxiao caifang shilu bianjishi (Beijing: Zhonggong zhongyang dangxiao, 2019), 142–44; Yang Xiaohuai, "Xi Jinping," 42.
22. Yang Xiaohuai, "Xi Jinping," 42.
23. Li Chao, "Liu Shaoqi shi bei pohai zhisi de," *Yanhuang chunqiu*, no. 1 (2010): 80–81.
24. Bei Ling and Yu Caiqian, *Hongse guizu* (Beijing: Hongqi, 1993), 233.
25. Ke Yunlu, "Liberating China's Past: An Interview with Ke Yunlu," interview by Ian Johnson, *NYRB*, Mar. 29, 2017.
26. "Portrait."
27. Du Lirong, "Guxi zhi nian tiao zhongdan: Hebei sheng zhengxie yuanfuzhuxi Han Licheng tan Gao Yang," *Lingdao zhi you*, no. 7 (2013): 48.
28. Zhonggong Hebei shengwei zuzhibu, Zhonggong Hebei shengwei dangshi ziliao zhengji bianshen weiyuanhui, and Hebei sheng dang'anju, eds., *Zhongguo gongchandang Hebei sheng zuzhishi ziliao (1922–1987)* (Shijiazhuang: Hebei renmin, 1990), 744.
29. Zhong Zhaoyun and Wang Shengze, *Chizi zhi xin: Jiang Yizhen zhuan*, vol. 2 (Hong Kong: Tiandi tushu, 2008), 684–761.
30. Ibid., 811–13.
31. *Li Erzhong biji zhaichao*, 539–64.
32. Zhong Zhaoyun and Wang, *Chizi zhi xin*, 813–14.
33. Ibid., 834–35, 974; Yong Huaqi, "Xi Jinping hui Zhengding (I)," *Lingdao wencui*, no. 11 (2009): 66.
34. Zhong Zhaoyun and Wang, *Chizi zhi xin*, 835–36.
35. Du Lirong, "Gao Yang yu Hebei 'fengping langjing' zhengzhi jumian de xingcheng," *Dangshi bocai*, no. 12 (2018): 10–13.
36. Zhong Zhaoyun and Wang, *Chizi zhi xin*, 836–37; *Li Erzhong biji zhaichao*, 586–88.
37. Li Chunlei, *Pengyou: Xi Jinping yu Jia Dashan jiaowang wangshi* (Beijing: Zhongguo yanshi, 2014), 12–13.
38. He Zai, "Xi Jinping tongzhi dang xianwei shuji shi jiu bei renwei shi dongliang zhi cai," in *Xi Jinping zai Zhengding*, ed. Zhongyang dangxiao caifang shilu bianjishi (Beijing: Zhonggong zhongyang dangxiao, 2019), 112–14; He Zai, "Guanyu pai daxuesheng xiaqu danren dangzheng lingdao de jianyi xin," in *Wode bashinian: Nanwang suiyue* (Beijing: Zhonggong dangshi, 2016), 49; He Zai, "Guanyu luoshi zhengce deng wenti de jianyi," in *Wode bashinian: Nanwang suiyue* (Beijing: Zhonggong dangshi, 2016), 56.
39. Rui Feng and Geng Fu, "Xi Jinping 'chushan,'" *Dangdai qingnian*, no. 11 (1985): 8.
40. Li Nanyang, "Yi Wang Jianxun: 'Genjin' shengao ren," *Dongxiang* 371 (July 2016).
41. Li Naiyi, "Zhengding xianwei youzhi zhi shi changkai damen," *Hebei ribao*, Mar. 29, 1983; Li Naiyi, "Xi shuji zhiding 'rencai jiu tiao' de guocheng, ye shi Zhengding jiefang sixiang, cujin gaige de guocheng," in *Xi Jinping zai Zhengding*, ed. Zhongyang dangxiao caifang shilu bianjishi (Beijing: Zhonggong zhongyang dangxiao, 2019), 167–79.

42. Li Naiyi, "Xi shuji," 174.

43. Yu Guangyuan, *Wode jiaoyu sixiang* (Suzhou: Suzhou daxue chubanshe, 2000), 260.

44. Yan Huai, *Jinchu zhongzubu*, 216; Mingjing zhuanfang, "Kaocha Xi Jinping de ren," pt. 2, YouTube, Oct. 13, 2016, video, https://www.youtube.com/watch?v=-gcrogGSwzY; Yan, discussion.

45. Yan, discussion. Yan explained to the author that this kind of procedure was quite common if the decision for a promotion had already been made.

46. Zhonggong Zhengding xianwei zuzhibu, Zhonggong Zhengding xianwei dangshi ziliao zhengji bianshen bangongshi, and Zhengding xian dang'anju, eds., *Zhongguo gongchandang Hebei sheng Zhengding xian zuzhishi ziliao (1924–1987)* (Shijiazhuang: Hebei renmin, 1991), 127.

47. Yan, discussion.

48. Yan Huai, *Jinchu zhongzubu*, 217–18; Wong, *Party of One*, 33.

49. Yan, discussion.

50. Yan Huai, *Jinchu zhongzubu*, 205; Cui Wunian, *Wode 83ge yue* (Hong Kong: Gaowen, 2003), 17–18.

51. Yan Huai, *Jinchu zhongzubu*, 202–6; Kong Dan, *Nande bense ren tianran*, 167–74; Li Rui, diary (vols. 13–15, 1984), p. 75, HIA; Chen Chusan, *Renjian zhong wan qing*, 381–84.

52. Cui, *Wode 83ge yue*, 18.

53. Ibid., 18–20.

54. Ibid., 21.

55. Li Rui, diary (vols. 13–15, 1984), p. 75, HIA.

56. Yan Huai, *Jinchu zhongzubu*, 205.

57. Li Rui, *Li Rui koushu wangshi*, 452–53.

58. Wan Runnan, *Shanghai yunfan: Sitong gushi* (Hong Kong: Tianyu, 2013), 382; Wan Runnan (formerly of Stone Company), in discussion with the author, May 2023.

59. Xi Jinping, "Zhi zhi zhen, ai zhi qie," *Zhongguo qingnian*, no. 5 (1984): 20–21.

60. Zhao Derun and Gao Peiqi, "Zhengding fanshen ji," *PD*, June 17, 1984.

61. Lu Ying and Zhou, "Er li zhi nian," 4–9.

62. Zhou Weisi, "Jinping," 161; Luo Xu, *Searching for Life's Meaning: Changes and Tensions in the Worldviews of Chinese Youth in the 1980s* (Ann Arbor: University of Michigan Press, 2002), 49–71.

63. He Zai, "Xi Jinping," 114–15.

64. Yan Huai, *Jinchu zhongzubu*, 245–46; Li Rui, diary (vols. 13–15, 1984), pp. 75–77, HIA; Li Rui, diary (vols. 16–17, 1985), p. 12, HIA; Li Nanyang, *Wo you zheyang de yige muqin* (Keller, TX: Fellows Press of America, 2020), 35–36.

65. Li Rui, diary (vols. 13–15, 1984), pp. 92–94, HIA.

66. Xi Jinping, "Zhongqingnian ganbu yao 'zun lao,'" *PD*, Dec. 7, 1984.

67. Jiang Feng, "Ta gengyun zai Zhengding de yuanye shang," *Zhongguo qingnian*, no. 1 (1985): 27–31.

68. Yan, discussion.

69. Interview.

70. Li Nanyang, "Liangge banben," "*Li Nanyang gaozhuang haiguan an*" *genjin baodao*, no. 112 (Nov. 2023), FCFL.

71. Li Rui, diary (vols. 19–20, 1987), p. 29, HIA; Du Lirong, "Gao Yang," 13; Wu Wen, "Gao Yang yu Xi Jinping de 'enyuan,'" *Dongxiang zazhi*, May 2009.

72. Wang Taixing, "Jinping tongzhi dui wo zuoren zuoshi yingxiang zhishen," in *Xi Jinping zai Xiamen*, ed. Zhongyang dangxiao caifang shilu bianjishi (Beijing: Zhongyang dangxiao, 2020), 76.

73. Yan Huai, *Jinchu zhongzubu*, 218; Zhonggong Xiamen shiwei zuzhibu, Zhonggong

Xiamen shiwei dangshi bangongshi, and Xiamen shi dang'anguan, eds., *Zhongguo gongchandang Fujian sheng Xiamen shi zuzhishi ziliao* (Fuzhou: Fujian renmin, 1989), 248.

74. Yan Huai, *Jinchu zhongzubu*, 218.
75. Rui and Geng, "Xi Jinping 'chushan,'" 9.
76. Wang Shu'en, "Xiang Yunian de chuanqi rensheng," *Yanhuang zongheng*, Dec. 5, 2013; Hu Shao'an, *Jingwei renmin: Xiang Nan zhuan*, vol. 1 (Hong Kong: Tiandi tushu, 2004), 91–92, 200.
77. Hu Shao'an, *Jingwei renmin*, 396; Zhong Zhaoyun, "Xiang Nan yu Xi Zhongxun de jiaowang," *Dangshi bolan*, no. 3 (2021): 14.
78. Zhong, "Xiang Nan," 14–18.
79. Gao Xin, "Daji gaigei pai zhong chen Chen Yun buze shouduan," RFA, May 12, 2017.
80. Interview with former associate of Li Rui.
81. Zhong, "Xiang Nan," 19.
82. Ma Yongshun, "Women de hao lingdao," 221.
83. Hu Shao'an, *Jingwei renmin*, 558–62.
84. Ibid., 594–600.
85. Ibid., 611–13, 639, 671, 673–74, 684.
86. Gao Xin, "You ci yi shuo: Xi Jinping yin Xiang Nan shisida wei jin houbu zhongwei," RFA, May 17, 2017.
87. Cai Wenbin, ed., "Zhao Ziyang zai Beijing shinian (1980–1989): Bao Tong fangtanlu" (unpublished manuscript, n.d.).
88. Zheng Jinmu, "Zhiding fazhan zhanlüe shi Jinping tongzhi dui Xiamen de yige quanju xing gongxian," in *Xi Jinping zai Xiamen*, ed. Zhongyang dangxiao caifang shilu bianjishi (Beijing: Zhongyang dangxiao, 2020), 68–69.
89. Interview with individual familiar with the trip.
90. Shan Lan, "Liuxing de pianjian yongyuan bushi zhenli: Xi Zhongxun de erzi Xi Jinping," in *Hongqiangnei de zinümen*, vol. 2 (Yanbian: Yanbian renmin, 1998), 471; Wu Zhifei, "Xi Jinping: Cong huangtu gaopo dao Shanghai tan," *Dangshi zongheng*, no. 5 (2007): 16–21.
91. Lin Zhiwen and Luo Min, "Xi Zhongxun tongzhi zhongshi zhichi fulian ban yiqie hao shi shishi," *Zhongguo funü bao*, Oct. 18, 2013.
92. Xi Zhongxun, "Zai quanguo funü di sijie zhixing weiyuanhui disici kuoda huiyishang de jianghua," in *"Si da" yilai funü yundong wenxuan* (Beijing: Zhongguo funü, 1983), 54–59.
93. Hu Yaobang, "Jihua shengyu zhengce yao jianli zai guangda qunzhong nenggou jieshou de jichu shang," in *Hu Yaobang wenxuan 1975–1986*, vol. 2 (n.p.: Zhengqiu yijian gao, n.d.), 189–91.
94. Zhonggong Yan'an shiwei dangshi yanjiushi, *Xi Zhongxun zai Yan'an*, 326–27.
95. *Qunxing cuican*, 709.
96. Chen Weiren, *Tang Dacheng: Wentan fengyu wushinian* (Carle Place: Mingjing, 2007), 245.
97. Wu Zuguang, *Yi beizi: Wu Zuguang huiyilu* (Beijing: Zhongguo wenlian, 2004), 379.
98. Ke Hua, *Xin Zhongguo waijiao qisu Ke Hua 95 sui shuhuai* (Beijing: Wenhua yishu, 2013), 77.
99. "Portrait."
100. Interview with individual present.
101. Xu Huangang and Li Zhaoxiang, *Ke Hua dashi de waijiao shengya* (Beijing: Zhongguo qingnian, 2001), 185–87.
102. Li Musheng, "Ta cong 'xiwang de tianye shang' zoulai," *Mingren zhuanji* 11 (1992): 73.

103. "Peng Liyuan tan xingfu jiating shenghuo," *Zhanjiang wanbao*, Oct. 5, 2007 (hereafter cited as "Xingfu jiating shenghuo").
104. Li Musheng, "Ta," 94.
105. Ibid., 67, 70; Fu Xipeng, "Aoxiang ba, zhankai ni gesheng de chibang," *Hai'ou* 12 (1984): 43–44.
106. Fu Xipeng, "Aoxiang ba," 44–46; Li Musheng, "Ta," 70.
107. Fu Xipeng, "Aoxiang ba," 46–47; Wang Yinxuan, "Wo he Peng Liyuan," in *Shandong wentan jishi*, ed. Shandong sheng wenlian (Ji'nan: Shandong wenyi, 1989), 233–36.
108. "Peng Liyuan jiangshu ziji de junlü qinghuai," *Xinlang*, June 30, 2004.
109. Chen Huiying, "Tingting yuhe yi fangxin," *Jiating*, no. 6 (1989): 5–6.
110. Xin Zhongguo pindao, "Peng Liyuan 1999 fangtan," YouTube, Oct. 13, 2013, video, https://youtu.be/TWT00gv1m3Y?si=0ebOVZagyLMagZQr.
111. Peng Liyuan, "Chengming yu kunao: Peng Liyuan yi xi tan," *Yinyue shijie* (May 1985): 41–42.
112. Li Musheng, "Ta," 73–74.
113. "Xingfu jiating shenghuo."
114. Li Musheng, "Ta," 74.
115. Yang Ping, "Xi jia," 11.
116. "Xingfu jiating shenghuo."
117. Interview by Louisa Lim, notes.
118. Interview. Qiaoqiao was married to the son of Zhang Zhiyi, a high-ranking United Front Work Department official.
119. Qi Qiaoqiao, "Fuqin"; Qi Qiaoqiao, "Fangqi chuguo liuxue."
120. Qi Qiaoqiao, "Fangqi chuguo liuxue."
121. Liu Bingrong, *Zoujin Qi Ruixin*, 11–13.
122. Xi An'an, "Baba, cong mei likaiguo women," in *Xi Zhongxun jinian wenji*, ed. Zhonggong zhongyang dangshi yanjiushi (Beijing: Zhonggong dangshi, 2013), 796–805.
123. Xi Zhengning, "Fuqin," 767–73.
124. Zhonggong Shaanxi shengwei zuzhibu, Zhonggong Shaanxi shengwei dangshi yanjiushi, and Shaanxi sheng dang'anguan, eds., *Zhongguo gongchandang Shaanxi sheng zuzhishi ziliao: 1987.11–1993.5* (Xi'an: Shaanxi renmin, 1994), 20, 29, 35–36.
125. Zhang Zhigong, *Nanwang de ershinian*, 230; *Xi Zhongxun zhuan*, 2:638.

Chapter 22: The United Front Restored and Restrained
1. Interview.
2. Meng Hong, "Zhonggong lingdaoren yu Xu Deheng," *Wenshi yuekan*, no. 9 (2017): 17.
3. Groot, *Managing Transitions*, 125–36; "Dishisici quanguo tongzhan gongzuo huiyi gaikuang," in *Lici quanguo tongzhan gongzuo huiyi gaikuang he wenxian* (Beijing: Dang'an, 1988), 436–40.
4. Alex Joske, "The Central United Front Work Leading Small Group: Institutionalising United Front Work," Sinopsis: China in Context and Perspective, July 23, 2019, https://sinopsis.cz/en/joske-united-front-work-lsg/.
5. "Dishiwuci quanguo tongzhan gongzuo huiyi gaikuang," in *Lici quanguo tongzhan gongzuo huiyi gaikuang he wenxian* (Beijing: Dang'an, 1988), 465–70.
6. Hu Yaobang, "Zai quanguo tongzhan gongzuo huiyishang de jianghua," in *Lici quanguo tongzhan gongzuo huiyi gaikuang he wenxian* (Beijing: Dang'an, 1988), 470–83.
7. Zhonggong Hebei shengwei tongzhanbu, "Xi Zhongxun," 64, 67.
8. Hu Yaobang, "Guanyu luoshi tongzhan zhengce gei Xi Zhongxun dengde yizu xinhan," in *Hu Yaobang wenxuan 1975–1986*, vol. 3 (n.p.: Zhengqiu yijian gao, n.d.), 160–63.

9. "Xi Zhongxun Addresses CPPCC, United Front," FBIS, Dec. 28, 1983.
10. Xi Zhongxun, "Zai luoshi zhengce zuotan huishang de jianghua," in *Minzu zhengce wenxuan* (Urumqi: Xinjiang renmin, 1985), 274–86.
11. Xi Zhongxun, "Tongyi zhanxian rengran shi yi da fabao," in *Lici quanguo tongzhan gongzuo huiyi gaikuang he wenxian* (Beijing: Dang'an, 1988), 568–69.
12. Xi Zhongxun, "Tongyi zhanxian," 569–72.
13. "Quanguo tongyi zhanxian lilun gongzuo huiyi gaikuang," in *Lici quanguo tongzhan gongzuo huiyi gaikuang he wenxian* (Beijing: Dang'an, 1988), 529–44.
14. "Xin Zhongguo tongyi zhanxian liushinian dashiji" bianji zu, ed., *Xin Zhongguo tongyi zhanxian liushinian dashiji* (Beijing: Huawen, 2000), 237, 241–42.
15. "Dishisiliu quanguo tongzhan gongzuo huiyi gaikuang," in *Lici quanguo tongzhan gongzuo huiyi gaikuang he wenxian* (Beijing: Dang'an, 1988), 495–502.
16. "Xi Zhongxun on Importance of Democratic Parties," FBIS, Dec. 3, 1986.
17. Tao Siliang, "Wo zuo zhishi fenzi gongzuo de wangshi," *Yanhuang chunqiu*, no. 6 (2015): 9–15.
18. "Guanyu quanguo tongzhan buzhang zuotanhui qingkuang de baogao," in *Lici quanguo tongzhan gongzuo huiyi gaikuang he wenxian* (Beijing: Dang'an, 1988), 520–28.
19. Groot, *Managing Transitions*, 171–77.
20. Hu Zhi'an, *Tongzhan mixin: Wo suo renshi de minzhu renshi* (Hong Kong: Tiandi tushu, 2010), 374–75.
21. Zhonggong zhongyang tongzhanbu and Zhonggong zhongyang wenxian yanjiushi, eds., "Zhonggong zhongyang guanyu jianchi he wanshan Zhongguo gongchandang lingdao de duodang hezuo he zhengzhi xieshang zhidu de yijian," in *Xin shiqi tongyi zhanxian wenxian xuanbian (xubian)* (Beijing: Zhonggong zhongyang dangxiao, 1997), 146.
22. Jiang Zemin, "Nuli fazhan zui guangfan de aiguo tongyi zhanxian," in *Tongyi zhanxian gongzuo ganbu jiben duwu*, ed. Zhonggong zhongyang tongyi zhanxian gongzuobu (Beijing: Beijing Yanshan, 1992), 348–59.
23. Mao Qixiong and Lin Xiaodong, *Zhongguo qiaowu zhengce gaishu* (Beijing: Zhongguo huaqiao, 1993), 122–23.
24. Zhonggong Guangdong shengwei dangshi yanjiushi, *Guangdong*, 18–19.
25. "Zhonggong zhongyang bangongting zhuanfa 'Zhongyang lingdao tongzhi zai guonei qiaowu gongzuo zuotan huishang de jianghua yaodian,'" in *Qiaowu fagui wenjian huibian* (n.p.: Guowuyuan, Qiaowu bangongshi, Zhengce yanjiushi, 1989), 20.
26. "Xi Zhongxun tongzhi zai sheng, zizhiqu, zhixiashi qiaoban zhuren huiyishang de jianghua," in *Qiaowu fagui wenjian huibian* (n.p.: Guowuyuan, Qiaowu bangongshi, Zhengce yanjiushi, 1989), 38–50.
27. Huang Shun-hsing, *Beijing jianwen* (Taipei: self-pub., 1993), 90, 92–93.
28. Ibid., 93–94.
29. Lin Hsiao-ting, *Jiang Jingguo de Taiwan shidai: Zhonghua minguo yu lengzhan xia de Taiwan* (Xinbei: Yuanzu wenhua, 2021), 435–37.
30. "Biaoda xinsheng: 'Taisheng' zazhi de dansheng," *Taibao zhi jia wang*, Nov. 23, 2021, http://www.tailian.org.cn/ztzz/tlss/tlclsss/202111/t20211123_12392313.htm.
31. Lin Hsiao-ting, *Jiang Jingguo*, 156.
32. "Outline on Enhancing Struggle against Enemies, Liu Shaokang Office Self-Criticism, 1982–1983," n.d., box 5, folder 5, Wang Sheng Papers, HIA.
33. Lin Hsiao-ting, *Jiang Jingguo*, 148–54; Wu Jianguo, *Poju: Jiemi! Jiang Jingguo wannian quanli buju gaibian de neimu* (Taipei: Shibao wenhua, 2017), 161–62; Zhong Shunan, "Wang Sheng Jiang Yanshi de zaoyu," *Zhongguo baodao* 1143 (May 1986): 10.
34. Deng Xiaoping, "Zhongguo dalu he Taiwan heping tongyi de shexiang," in *Deng Xiaoping wenxuan*, vol. 3 (Beijing: Renmin, 1994), 30–31.

35. Lin Hsiao-ting, *Jiang Jingguo*, 450–51; Linda Jaivin, *The Monkey and the Dragon: A True Story about Friendship, Music, Politics, and Life on the Edge* (Melbourne: Text, 2001), 100, 113; Hou Dejian, *Huotouzi zheng zhuan* (Taipei: Lianjing, 1990), 36.

36. *Xu Xiangqian nianpu*, vol. 2 (Beijing: Jiefangjun, 2016), 587, 591–92.

37. Meng Weijun, "'*Xuezhan Taierzhuang*' dansheng ji," *Dangshi zongheng* 2 (2009): 49–50; Sun Jingyan, "Zheng hai mishi," *Shi jie*, no. 1 (1994): 192.

38. Ma Jianli et al., *Haixia liang'an guanxi sishinian* (Wuhan: Hubei jiaoyu, 1995), 236–37.

39. Lin Hsiao-ting, *Jiang Jingguo*, 450–51, 456.

40. See chapter 29.

41. Wu Yongjia, "Guangdong gaige kaifang de dianji ren," *Shenzhen tequ bao*, Oct. 12, 2013.

42. "The Governor's Visit to Guangzhou," Apr. 6, 1979, FCO 40/1050, TNA.

43. Stuart Lau, "David Wilson Reflects on His Time as Former Governor of Hong Kong: 'It Was the Most Worthwhile Job in the World,'" *SCMP*, June 25, 2017.

44. "C. M. MacLehose to David Owen," Apr. 11, 1979, FCO 40/1050, TNA.

45. "Extract from Meeting in Government House on 7 December with Delegation from Guangdong," Dec. 12, 1979, FCO 40/1061, TNA; David Wilson, "New Territories Leases," Dec. 13, 1979, FCO 40/1061, TNA.

46. Xu Jiatun, *Xu Jiatun liuxia de mimi* (Hong Kong: Mingjing, 2016), 172.

47. "Tongzhan huodong," n.d., AHT, Diancang hao 020-010399-0014, Waijiao bu, Yadong Taiping yang si, Xianggang Aomen, p. 42.

48. Sze-yuen Chung, *Hong Kong's Journey to Reunification: Memoirs of Sze-Yuen Chung* (Hong Kong: Chinese University Press, 2001), 63.

49. "Sir YK Optimistic over Closer Guangdong Ties," *SCMP*, May 30, 1980.

50. Mark Roberti, *The Fall of Hong Kong: China's Triumph and Britain's Betrayal* (New York: John Wiley, 1994), 56.

51. "Future of Hong Kong," Nov. 1, 1982, Margaret Thatcher Foundation, PREM 19/791 f12.

52. Roberti, *Fall of Hong Kong*, 56–57.

53. Xi Zhongxun, "Yong gaige jingshen kaichuang zhengxie gongzuo xin jumian," in *Lao yidai gemingjia lun renmin zhengxie* (Beijing: Zhongyang wenxian, 1997), 362–64.

54. Gary Cheung, "Thirty Years On, a Young Turk Recalls Historic Trip," *SCMP*, May 20, 2013; Martin Lee (Hong Kong democracy activist), in discussion with the author, May 2019; Allen Lee (Hong Kong political figure), in discussion with the author, May 2019; Martin Lee, "Zhong-Ying tanpan de 'chuxin' (er)," *Taizhou kan*, June 8, 2016; Joseph Y. S. Cheng, "Position Paper of the Young Professional Group Submitted to Xi Zhongxun, a Member of the Secretariat of the Central Committee of the Chinese Communist Party, during Their Visit to Beijing in May 1983 (the Group Was Led by Three Legislative Councillors and Consisted of Twelve Leading Professionals) (in Chinese)," in *Hong Kong: In Search of a Future*, ed. Yushuo Zheng (Hong Kong: Oxford University Press, 1984), 197–203.

55. A. Lee, discussion; M. Lee, discussion.

56. M. Lee, discussion; A. Lee, discussion; M. Lee, "Zhong-Ying tanpan de 'chuxin' (er)."

57. Hsin Pao Tsai Ching Yue Kan, *Xi Zhongxun Discusses Future of Hong Kong*, China Report: Political, Sociological and Military Affairs, no. 439, JPRS 83966 (July 1983): 65–69, https://apps.dtic.mil/sti/tr/pdf/ADA346017.pdf; "Xi Zhongxun xiang gejie qingniantuan tanhua shilu," *Xinbao caijing yuekan* 7, no. 4 (July 1983): 35–36.

58. Stuart Lau and Jun Mai, "Like Father, Like Son: Xi Jinping's Occupy Challenge in Hong Kong Similar to Father's Experience 30 Years Before," *SCMP*, June 30, 2017.

59. Xu Jiatun, *Xu Jiatun Xianggang huiyilu*, vol. 1 (Hong Kong: Xianggang lianhebao, 1993), 77; Xu Jiatun, *Xu Jiatun huiyi yu suixiang lu* (Carle Place: Mingjing, 1998), 87.
60. He Mingsi, "Wo yinggai you shenbian de quanli," *Xinbao*, June 28, 1993.
61. Cindy Yik-yi Chu, *Chinese Communists and Hong Kong Capitalists: 1937–1997* (New York: Palgrave Macmillan, 2011), 69–101.

Chapter 23: A New Era in Ethnic and Religious Affairs

1. *Dangdai Zhongguo de minzu gongzuo*, 2 vols. (Beijing: Dangdai Zhongguo, 1993), 1:114–19.
2. Xi Zhongxun, "Shenqie huainian Zhongguo gongchandang."
3. Arjia Rinpoche (Buddhist lama), in discussion with the author, Jan. 2019.
4. Huang Zhengqing, *Huang Zhengqing*, 94.
5. Xia Meng and Wang, *Xi Zhongxun: Father*, 246.
6. Jiacuo, *Mao Zedong*, 273.
7. Melvyn C. Goldstein, *The Snow Lion and the Dragon: China, Tibet and the Dalai Lama* (Berkeley: University of California Press, 1999), 62–63.
8. Paul P. Mariani, *China's Church Divided* (Cambridge, MA: Harvard University Press, forthcoming).
9. Qin Jun, "Xi Zhongxun," 41.
10. Liu Bingrong, *Zoujin Qi Ruixin*, 729–31.
11. Feng Junjun, "Shijie yixue qigong xuehui zai Jing chengli," *PD*, Nov. 18, 1989, overseas edition.
12. Ian Johnson, *The Souls of China: The Return of Religion after Mao* (New York: Pantheon Books, 2017), 224.
13. "Zhonggong zhongyang guanyu zhuanfa 'Xizang gongzuo zuotanhui jiao' de tongzhi," in *Sanzhong quanhui yilai zhongyao wenxian xuanbian*, vol. 1 (Guangdong: Renmin, 1982), 478–93.
14. Yin Fatang, *Cong Taishan dao Zhufeng* (Beijing: Zhongguo Zangxue, 2021), 204, 250–59, 286–87; Li Rui, huiyi jilu / gongzuo biji (vol. 14, Aug. 1983), p. 23, HIA.
15. Zhang Liqun et al., *Hu Yaobang zhuan*, 3:57–58.
16. "Zhonggong zhongyang, guowuyuan pizhuan Xizang zizhiqu dangwei he renmin zhengfu 'guanyu dapi diaochu jin Zang ganbu, gongren de qingshi baogao' de tongzhi," in *"Wuchan jieji wenhua dageming": You tuichao er fanxing*, ser. 26, vol. 6 (n.p.: SCCP, 2006), 1–7.
17. Deng Xiaoping, "Tong Banchan E'erdeni de tanhua," in *Xizang gongzuo wenxian xuanbian 1949-2005 nian*, ed. Zhonggong zhongyang wenxian yanjiushi and Zhonggong Xizang zizhiqu weiyuanhui (Beijing: Zhongyang wenxian, 2005), 318–19.
18. Interview with former high-ranking official.
19. Xin Guangwu, *Banchan chuanqi* (Hong Kong: Dafeng, 2008), 371.
20. Yaoxi Ban Renji Wangmu (Yabshi Pan Rinzinwangmo), "Shishi Banchen nü'er jiangshu: Wo bala weishenme quqi shengnu," *Kunlun ce*, Mar. 19, 2019, https://www.kunlunce.com/e/wap/show.php?bclassid=15&classid=140&id=132018.
21. Untitled, photograph, 1983, author's personal collection.
22. Wangjie Pingcuo [Phunwang Wangye], *Pingdeng tuanjie lu man man, Pingdeng tuanjie lu man man: Dui woguo minzu guanxi de fansi* (Hong Kong: Xin shiji, 2014), 96–97; Zhang Xiangming, "55 nian," 178–79; Goldstein, Sherap, and Siebenschuh, *Tibetan Revolutionary*, 291–93.
23. Liu Yuanhang, "Simayi Aimaiti, zhege xinwen lianbo li zai ye tingbudao de mingzi, ta daodi shi shei," *Zhongguo xinwen zhoukan*, Nov. 2018.
24. Zhu Peimin, *20 shiji Xinjiang shi yanjiu* (Urumqi: Xinjiang renmin, 2000), 332–33.
25. *Wang Feng zhuan* (Beijing: Zhonggong dangshi, 2011), 608–9.

26. Xinjiang Weiwuer zizhiqu difangzhi bianzuan weiyuanhui, *Xinjiang dashiji* (Urumqi: Xinjiang renmin, 2016), 513.

27. Zhu Peimin, Chen Hong, and Yang Hong, *Zhongguo gongchandang yu Xinjiang minzu wenti*, 184–86.

28. Lan Sisi, *Zhongguo X dang'an: Zhonggong yangai de "neibu lishi"* (Deer Park, NY: Mingjing, 2014), 167–89.

29. *Wang Zhen zhuan*, 2:216, 2:219–20; *Deng Xiaoping nianpu (1975–1997)*, 1:691; Xinjiang Weiwuer zizhiqu difangzhi bianzuan weiyuanhui, *Xinjiang dashiji*, 518–19.

30. Ma Dazheng, *Guojia liyi gaoyu yiqie: Xinjiang wending wenti de guancha yu sikao* (Urumqi: Xinjiang renmin, 2002), 46–47.

31. Deng Xiaoping, "Guanyu sixiang zhanxianshang de wenti de tanhua," in *Deng Xiaoping wenxuan*, vol. 2 (Beijing: Renmin, 1994), 389–90.

32. Zhu Peimin, Chen, and Yang, *Zhongguo*, 206.

33. "Zhongyang shujichu taolun Xinjiang gongzuo wenti de jiyao," in *Minzu zhengce wenxuan* (Urumqi: Xinjiang renmin, 1985), 19–22; Chen Wuguo, *Wang Enmao zhuan* (Beijing: Zhongguo wenshi, 2014), 542; Zhu Peimin, *20 shiji Xinjiang*, 356–57; Guojia minzu shiwu weiyuanhui and Zhonggong zhongyang wenxian yanjiushi, eds., "Gaohao minzu guanxi, jiaqiang minzu tuanjie: Zhaizi Zhonggong zhongyang zhuanfa de 'zhongyang shujichu taolun Xinjiang gongzuo wenti de jiyao,'" in *Xin shiqi minzu gongzuo wenxian xuanbian* (Beijing: Zhongyang wenxian, 1990), 147–49; Yin Fatang, *Cong Taishan dao Zhufeng*, 313.

34. *Deng Xiaoping nianpu (1975–1997)*, 2:762.

35. *Wang Zhen zhuan*, 2:221.

36. Ruan Ming, "Shiqu de lishi jihui: Yi shinian qian Xinjiang zhi xing," *Minzhu Zhongguo* 8 (Feb. 1992): 18.

37. Qu dangwei zongtuan "Fenglei," "Jiekai 'Xi Zhongxun zhuan'an xiaozu' zhi mi," in *Xinjiang wenti zhiyi: Hongqi pinglun*, ser. 16, vol. 32 (n.p.: SCCP, 1999), 54–56.

38. Wang Enmao, "Zai zizhuqu dangwei changwei kuoda huiyishang guanyu Kashi wenti de jianghua (jiexuan)," in *Guanche minzu zhengce wenjian xuanbian* (Urumqi: Xinjiang renmin, 1985), 123–42.

39. Xinjiang Weiwuer zizhiqu difangzhi bianzuan weiyuanhui, *Xinjiang dashiji*, 524.

40. James A. Millward, *Eurasian Crossroads: A History of Xinjiang* (New York: Columbia University Press, 2007), 264–65.

41. "Wang Zhen guanyu huifu bingtuan wenti dui youguan lingdao de tanhua (jielu)," *Xinjiang shengchan jianshe bingtuan shiliao xuanji* 19 (Nov. 2009): 11–13.

42. *Xi Zhongxun nianpu*, 3:296.

43. Song Chundan, "'Hongse zhizi' Wulanfu," *Zhongguo xinwen zhoukan*, Mar. 2018; Zhang Zhigong, *Nanwang de ershinian*, 100–101.

44. Tianjin hongdaihui Nankai daxue bayiba huoju zongdui et al., "Gao Gang," 268; Nei Menggu zizhiqu Yikezhaomeng lianwei, Neimeng Yimeng Yijin Huoluo qi lianzong "doupi Wulanfu lianluozhan," and Hu sansi Nei Menggu daxue Jinggangshan "doupi Wulanfu lianluozhan," "Wulanfu zai Yimeng de zuixing: 'Chedi chanchu Gao Gang yudang' (II)," in *Mongorujin jenosaido ni kansuru kiso shiryō*, ed. Yang Haiying, vol. 7 (Tokyo: Fukyosha, 2015), 382–83.

45. X. Liu, *Reins of Liberation*, 151–94.

46. Qi Zhi, *Neimeng wenge shilu: "Minzu fenlie" yu "wasu" yundong* (Hong Kong: Tianxing jian, 2010); Jisheng Yang, *The World Turned Upside Down: A History of the Chinese Cultural Revolution* (New York: Farrar, Straus and Giroux, 2021), 322–33; Tiejun Cheng, Uradyn Bulag, and Mark Selden, *A Chinese Rebel beyond the Great Wall: The Cultural Revolution and Ethnic Pogrom in Inner Mongolia* (Chicago: University of Chicago Press, 2023), 241–42.

47. Thupten Namgyal Juchen, *'Ju chen thub bstan gyi sku tshe'i lo rgyus*, 21 vols. (Chauntra: Juchentsang, 2014), 10:103.
48. Song Chundan, "'Hongse zhizi' Wulanfu."
49. Xi Zhongxun, "Wulanfu tongzhi yongyuan huo zai gezu renmin xinzhong," *PD*, Dec. 7, 1989.
50. Tian Congming, *Mama de xin* (Beijing: Xinhua, 2014), 134.
51. Qi Zhi, *Neimeng wenge shilu*, 533–38.
52. Ibid., 534–35.
53. Ibid., 535–66.
54. Zhonggong Hebei shengwei tongzhanbu, "Xi Zhongxun," 68.
55. Karrie J. Koesel, *Religion and Authoritarianism: Cooperation, Conflict, and the Consequences* (New York: Cambridge University Press, 2014), 42–49.
56. Jiang Ping, "Shenqie," 16.
57. Gyalo Thondup and Anne F. Thurston, *The Noodle Maker of Kalimpong: The Dalai Lama's Brother and His Struggle for Tibet* (New York: PublicAffairs, 2015), 258.
58. Ibid., 289–90; Khedroob Thondup, "Meeting Xi's Father," *The Week*, Oct. 30, 2022; Khedroob Thondup (son of Gyalo Thondup), in discussion with the author, Dec. 2022.
59. Dalai Lama, interview by Ho Pin, 2017, unpublished video.
60. Thondup and Thurston, *Noodle Maker*, 269–70.
61. Interview with former high-ranking official involved in ethnic politics.
62. Xizang zizhiqu gong'anting, *Xizang*, 249–51.
63. Claude Arpi, *Dharamsala and Beijing: The Negotiations That Never Were* (New Delhi: Lancer, 2009), 77–78.
64. Lodi Gyaltsen Gyari, *The Dalai Lama's Special Envoy: Memoirs of a Lifetime in Pursuit of a Reunited Tibet* (New York: Columbia University Press, 2022), 270–71, 273.
65. Juchen, *'Ju chen*, 10:96.
66. Ibid.
67. Ibid., 10:98.
68. Ibid., 10:107.
69. Ibid., 10:95–109; Phuntsok Tashi Takla, *Mi tshe'i byung ba brjod pa*, vol. 3 (Dharamsala: Bod kyi dpe mdzod khang, 1995), 244–48; Zhonggong zhongyang tongzhanbu and Zhonggong zhongyang wenxian yanjiushi, eds.,"Jiejian Dalai Lama daibiao tanhua yaodian," in *Xi Zhongxun lun tongyi zhanxian* (Beijing: Zhongyang wenxian, 2013), 238–41.
70. Lee Kuan Yew School of Public Policy, "Lodi Gyaltsen Gyari on Resolving Tibet: Crucial for China's Stability," YouTube, Aug. 12, 2014, video, https://www.youtube.com/watch?v=kalpvzGcWqU.
71. Gyari, *Dalai Lama's Special Envoy*, 244–45.
72. Che, "Xi Zhongxun."
73. *Zhonggong Xizang dangshi dashiji 1949–1994* (Lhasa: Xizang renmin, 1995), 258.
74. Zhang Xiangming, "55 nian," 181.
75. Che, "Xi Zhongxun."
76. Zheng Ying, "Yi Xi Zhongxun yu Xizang tongyi zhanxian gongzuo," in *Zangzu bainian shilu*, vol. 2 (Beijing: Shehui kexue wenxian, 2018), 655.
77. *Zhonggong Xizang*, 264–65.
78. Ibid., 264.
79. Fan Minxin, "Yi Xi Zhongxun yu di shishi Banchan de youyi," *Xizang ribao*, Sept. 25, 2015.
80. Zhonggong Hebei shengwei tongzhanbu, ed., "Zhongyang bangongting zhuanfa zhongyang tongzhanbu 'guanyu zhengqu Dalai jituan he guowai Zangbao gongzuo

zuotanhui ruogan wenti de baogao,'" in *Tongyi zhanxian wenjian xuanbian*, ser. 38, vol. 189, pt. 2 (n.p.: SCCP, 2016), 1145–51.

81. William Sexton, "From Peking Hierarchy, a Gesture to Chinese Catholics," *Philadelphia Inquirer*, Apr. 26, 1983.

82. Mariani, *China's Church Divided*.

83. "Zhongguo tianzhujiao aiguohui, Zhongguo tianzhujiao jiaowu weiyuanhui zhaokai weiyuan (kuoda) huiyi," *Zhongguo tianzhujiao*, no. 7 (1983): 4.

84. Jiang Ping, "Zhongyang tongzhanbu fubuzhang Jiang Ping tongzhi zai Zhongguo tianzhujiao lianghui weiyuan (kuoda) huiyishang de jianghua," *Zhongguo tianzhujiao*, no. 7 (1983): 22–25.

85. "Zhang Jiashu zhujiao de fayan (Shen Baozhi shenfu xuandu)," *Zhongguo tianzhujiao*, no. 7 (1983): 46.

86. Xi Zhongxun, "Quanguo renda changwei wei fuweiyuanzhang Xi Zhongxun tongzhi zai tianzhujiao qingzhu aiguohui chengli he zixuan zisheng zhujiao ershiwu zhounian dahuishang de jianghua yaodian," *Zhongguo tianzhujiao*, no. 7 (1983): 43–45.

87. Christopher Wren, "Peking Sends Priests Back to Jail," *NYT*, May 3, 1983; "China Imprisons Four 'Subversive' Jesuits," *SCMP*, May 3, 1983.

88. Zhang Xiangming, "55 nian," 199.

89. Ibid., 198–201; *Zhonggong Xizang*, 279.

90. Zhang Xiangming, "55 nian," 200.

91. *Zhonggong Xizang*, 278–80; Wang Xiaobin, *Zhongguo gongchandang Xizang zhengce de lishi kaocha* (Beijing: Zhonggong zhongyang dangxiao Zhonggong dangshi jiaoyanbu, 2003); Li Rui, diary (vol. 21, 1989), p. 60, HIA.

92. Zhang Xiangming, "55 nian," 204–13.

93. Zhang Liqun et al., *Hu Yaobang zhuan*, 3:64; "Hu Yaobang tongzhi zai Xizang gongzuo zuotan huishang de jianghua (jielu)," in *Xizang zizhiqu guanche yijiubasi nian Zhonggong zhongyang shujichu zhaokai de Xizang gongzuo zuotanhui jingshen wenjian xuanbian*, ser. 28, vol. 69, pt. 1 (n.p.: SCCP, 2009), 28–46.

94. Interview.

95. Li Rui, diary (vols. 13–15, 1984), p. 23, HIA; Li Rui, Huiyi jilu / gongzuo biji (vol. 14), p. 21, HIA.

96. Li Rui, Huiyi jilu / gongzuo biji (vol. 14), p. 22, HIA.

97. Ibid., p. 23; Li Rui, diary (vols. 13–15, 1984), p. 23, HIA.

98. "Xizang gongzuo zuotanhui jiyao," in *Xizang zizhiqu guanche yijiubasi nian Zhonggong zhongyang shujichu zhaokai de Xizang gongzuo zuotanhui jingshen wenjian xuanbian*, ser. 28, vol. 69, pt. 1 (n.p.: SCCP, 2009), 1–25; Warren W. Smith Jr., *Tibetan Nation: A History of Tibetan Nationalism and Sino-Tibetan Relations* (Boulder, CO: Westview, 1996), 586–91.

99. Zhang Xiangming, "55 nian," 204–13.

100. "Yin Fatang tongzhi zai Zhonggong Xizang zizhiqu sanjie erci quanwei kuoda huiyishang de jianghua," in *Xizang zizhiqu guanche yijiubasi nian Zhonggong zhongyang shujichu zhaokai de Xizang gongzuo zuotanhui jingshen wenjian xuanbian*, ser. 28, vol. 69, pt. 1 (n.p.: SCCP, 2009), 74–100.

101. Li Rui, Huiyi jilu / gongzuo biji (vol. 14), p. 1, HIA.

102. "Xi Zhongxun jisao geming lieshi lingyuan," *Xinjiang ribao*, Apr. 5, 1984.

103. "Xi Zhongxun li Wulumuqi huidao Beijing," *Xinjiang ribao*, Apr. 7, 1984.

104. Chen Tongwei and Qin Zhi, *Qingxi Tianshan: Dang he guojia lingdaoren zai Xinjiang* (Beijing: Zhonggong dangshi, 1995), 146–51.

105. "Xizang's Yin Fatang Urges Dalai Lama to Return," FBIS, May 13, 1984; Tsering Shakya, *The Dragon in the Land of Snows: A History of Modern Tibet since 1947* (New York: Columbia University Press, 1999), 394–400.

NOTES TO CHAPTERS 23 AND 24

106. Xizang zizhiqu gong'anting, *Xizang*, 266–77.
107. Gyari, *Dalai Lama's Special Envoy*, 264.
108. Jia Juchuan, "1962.10–2002.5," 19.
109. *Late Report: Yang Jingren Meets Dalai Lama Representatives*, FBIS, Nov. 27, 1984; "China Senior Official Reaffirms Five-Point Policy toward Dalai Lama," FBIS, Nov. 27, 1984; "Yang Jingren Says Dalai Lama Welcome to Return," FBIS, Nov. 27, 1984.
110. Juchen, *'Ju chen*, 11:192–99.
111. Ibid., 201–3.
112. "Xi Zhongxun Receives Dalai Lama's Representatives," FBIS, Nov. 30, 1984.
113. Gyari, *Dalai Lama's Special Envoy*, 274–75.
114. "Shanghai Bishop Jin on China-Vatican Ties," Apr. 16, 2007, PLUSD; Mariani, *China's Church Divided*.
115. Mariani, *China's Church Divided*; *Report of a Trip to Hong Kong Part I, Chinese Delegation's Visit—Fr. Laurence Murphy*, 1985, Mission Research and Planning Department Records, 1985, Maryknoll Fathers and Brothers Archives, Maryknoll Mission Archives, Maryknoll, New York; Jin Luxian, *The Memoirs of Jin Luxian* (Hong Kong: Hong Kong University Press, 2012), xvi.
116. Xi Zhongxun, "Yiding yao zhuajin luoshi dang de zongjiao zhengce," Apr. 3, 1985, TML.
117. Ren Wuzhi, "Huainian Xi Zhongxun tongzhi," *Zhongguo zongjiao*, no. 35 (2002): 15.
118. Yin Fatang, *Cong Taishan dao Zhufeng*, 388–89.
119. Interview.
120. Zhang Xiangming, "55 nian," 210–13.
121. *Xi Zhongxun nianpu*, 3:387.
122. Dong Zhaohe, "Rensheng de biaogan," in *Gongpu fengfan: Jinian Song Hanliang tongzhi wenji*, ed. Zhonggong Xinjiang Weiwuer zizhiqu weiyuanhui dangshi yanjiushi (Beijing: Zhongyang wenxian, 2014), 106.

Chapter 24: "Things Were Going So Well!"

1. Sun Hongquan, "Zuihou de jiaotan," in *Huainian Yaobang*, ed. Zhang Liqun and Zhang Ding, vol. 1 (Hong Kong: Lingtian, 1999), 293.
2. Brian Spivey, "The December 12th Student Movement: Uyghur Student Protest in Reform-Era China," *Journal of Asian Studies* 71, no. 4 (2022): 733–37; Dawamaiti Tiemu'er, *Shengming zhi yuan jicui* (Beijing: Minzu, 2009), 358.
3. Niyazi Amudong, "Jiaqiang dang de lingdao, zuohao sixiang zhengzhi gongzuo, buduan gonggu he fazhan zizhi qu anding tuanjie de dahao xingshi," in *Guanche minzu zhengce wenjian xubian* (Urumqi: Xinjiang renmin, 1990), 369–87.
4. Wang Enmao, "Xiang zhongyang shujichu huibao guanyu Xinjiang fasheng de bufen shaoshu minzu xuesheng shangjie youxing shijian de qingkuang he zhongyang shujichu taolun Xinjiang wenti huiyi jingshen de chuanda tigang," in *Guanche minzu zhengce wenjian xubian* (Urumqi: Xinjiang renmin, 1990), 40–47; Xinjiang Weiwuer zizhiqu difangzhi bianzuan weiyuanhui, *Xinjiang dashiji*, 560.
5. "Xi Zhongxun tongzhi zai quanguo zongjiao ju (chu) zhang huiyishang de jianghua," in *Zongjiao zhengce wenjian huibian*, ser. 32, vol. 75 (n.p.: SCCP, 2016).
6. Ren, "Huainian Xi Zhongxun tongzhi," 16.
7. *Xi Zhongxun nianpu*, 4:13.
8. Yan Mingfu, "Yi Xi lao," in *Xi Zhongxun jinian wenji*, ed. Zhonggong zhongyang dangshi yanjiushi (Beijing: Zhonggong dangshi, 2013), 89.
9. Two interviews.
10. Juchen, *'Ju chen*, 12:436–37; Takla, *Mi tshe'i*, 296; "Cable, Amconsul Hong Kong to

Secstate 6875, Subject: 'Chinese Communication with the Dalai Lama,'" Apr. 18, 1986, Tibet Documentation Project, DNSA.

11. Yeshi Dhondup, "Chronology of Sino-Tibetan Contacts from 1978 to 2012," *Tibet Journal* 38, no. 3–4 (2013): 127; "Guanyu Dalai jinnian bupairen huiguo ji women de chuli yijian" (unpublished manuscript, July 3, 1986). Held by this author.

12. Xi Zhongxun, "Shao shuo konghua, duo ban shishi, ba shaoshu minzu diqu de jingji wenhua jianshe gaoshangqu," in *Xin shiqi tongyi zhanxian wenxian xuanbian (xubian)*, ed. Zhonggong zhongyang tongzhanbu and Zhonggong zhongyang wenxian yanjiushi (Beijing: Zhonggong zhongyang dangxiao, 1997), 44–46.

13. "Xi Zhongxun Urges 'Open Policy' for Minorities," FBIS, Nov. 1, 1986; Xi Zhongxun, "Shao shuo konghua," 51–56.

14. Liu Yuanhang, "Simayi Aimaiti"; *Zhongguo gongchandang lishi dacidian: Shehuizhuyi shiqi* (Beijing: Zhonggong zhongyang dangxiao, 1991), 536; Zhonggong zhongyang tongzhanbu and Zhonggong zhongyang wenxian yanjiushi, eds., "Zhonggong zhongyang tongzhanbu, guojia minzu shiwu weiyuanhui guanyu minzu gongzuo ji ge zhongyao wenti de baogao," in *Xin shiqi tongyi zhanxian wenxian xuanbian (xubian)* (Beijing: Zhonggong zhongyang dangxiao, 1997), 78–93; "Dishisiliu," 495–502; Ren, "Huainian Xi Zhongxun tongzhi," 16.

15. Lee Kuan Yew School of Public Policy, "Lodi Gyaltsen Gyari."

16. Takla, *Mi tshe'i*, 293.

17. Ibid., 296.

18. Ibid., 300–302.

19. Cui, *Wode 83ge yue*, 324–35.

20. Sun Qi, "Kenqing buren Nei Menggu zizhiqu dangwei shuji," in *Qinli sanshinian: "Ye Fanghuai" zhengwenji*, ed. Xu Qingquan and Wang Wenyun (Beijing: Zhongguo wenshi, 2009), 64–66.

21. Yang Yankui and Guo Dongsheng, "Wulanfu shuai zhongyang daibiaotuan dida Huhehaote," *Nei Menggu ribao*, July 30, 1987.

22. Song Chundan, "'Hongse zhizi' Wulanfu."

23. Wulanfu [Ulanhu], "Zai qingzhu Nei Menggu zizhiqu chengli sishi zhounian ganbu dahuishang de jianghua," *Nei Menggu ribao*, Aug. 1, 1987.

24. "Zhongyang daibiaotuan yu zizhiqu lingdao qinqie huabie," *Nei Menggu ribao*, Aug. 6, 1987.

25. Dalai Lama, "Five Point Peace Plan," public statement, Sept. 21, 1987.

26. Goldstein, *Snow Lion*, 79; Smith, *Tibetan Nation*, 602–3.

27. Re, "Zhongxun tongzhi," 33.

28. Jia Juchuan, "1962.10–2002.5," 22–23.

29. *Zhonggong Xizang*, 333.

30. *Xi Zhongxun nianpu*, 4:11.

31. Smith, *Tibetan Nation*, 508.

32. Lu Xiaofei, Su Ning, and Xu Jianzhong, "Lasa saoluan zhijie shouhaizhe shi Zangzu renmin, Dalai fangqi fenlie lichang jiu huanying ta huiguo," *PD*, Apr. 5, 1988.

33. Chen Wuguo, *Wang Enmao zhuan*, 598–600; Wang Enmao, "Zai zizhiqu dangwei dishiqici changwei huishang de fayan," in *Guanche minzu zhengce wenjian xubian* (Urumqi: Xinjiang renmin, 1990), 96–106.

34. Spivey, "Student Movement," 741–42.

35. Interview with former high-ranking official involved in ethnic politics.

36. *Zhonggong Xizang*, 337–38; Xu Mingxu, *Xueshan xia de chouxing: Xizang baoluan de lailong qumai* (Chengdu: Sichuan jiaoyu, 2010), 215; Luobu Jiangcun [Gyaincain Norbu], "Xizang zou shang le kuaisu fazhan de guidao," in *Jianzheng Xizang: Xizang*

zizhiqu zhengfu liren xianren zhuxi zishu, ed. Ma Lihua and Feng Liang (Beijing: Zhongguo Zangxue, 2005), 170–71.

37. Zhang Xiangming, "55 nian," 238.

38. Interview with former high-ranking official involved in ethnic politics.

39. Jia Juchuan, "1962.10–2002.5," 24; "Jiemi: Hu Jintao zai Xizang gongzuo de 4 nian ruhe wending dangdi jushi," *Xilu wang*, Mar. 25, 2016, http://lishi.xilu.com/20160325/1000010000936942_4.html.

40. *Zhonggong Xizang*, 341.

41. Xizang zizhiqu dangwei bangongting, "Qu dangwei yinfa Zhonggong zhongyang guanyu 'Dangqian Xizang gongzuo de jige wenti de tongzhi,'" in *Xizang zizhiqu zhongyao wenjian xuanbian 1985–1990 xia ce, Zhonggong Xizang zhongyao lishi wenxian ziliao huibian*, vol. 27 (n.p.: SCCP, 2011), 1–4.

42. Song Chundan, "'Hongse zhizi' Wulanfu"; Uradyn E. Bulag, *The Mongols at China's Edge: History and the Politics of National Unity* (Lanham, MD: Rowman and Littlefield, 2002), 244.

43. Arjia Rinpoche, *Surviving the Dragon: A Recent History of Tibet through the Looking Glass of a Tibetan Lama* (New York: Rodale, 2010), 160; He Yao, *Xi Zhongxun jiafeng*, 390.

44. Xi Zhongxun, "Shenqie huainian Zhongguo gongchandang."

45. Xin, *Banchan chuanqi*, 436.

46. Xi Zhongxun, "Shenqie huainian Zhongguo gongchandang."

47. Gyari, *Dalai Lama's Special Envoy*, 310–14; Khedroob Thondup, discussion.

48. Wangjie, *Pingdeng*, 61–62.

49. Mariani, *China's Church Divided*.

50. "1989 nian '3.5' Lasa saoluan jie hou muji ji," in *Xizang wenti beiwanglu*, ser. 31, vol. 6 (n.p.: SCCP, 2009), 55–59.

51. Interview with former high-ranking official involved in ethnic politics.

52. "1989 nian 3 yue: Lasa 'jieyan,'" n.d., Jiang Lin Papers, HIA.

53. Deng Xiaoping, "Zhongguo buyunxu luan," in *Deng Xiaoping wenxuan*, vol. 3 (Beijing: Renmin, 1994), 286–87; Wu Wei, *Zhongguo 80 niandai zhengzhi gaige de taiqian muhou* (Hong Kong: Xin shiji, 2013), 429.

54. Wang Xuedong, *Fu Quanyou zhuan*, vol. 1 (Beijing: Jiefangjun, 2015), 505–7.

55. "1989 nian 3 yue: Lasa 'jieyan,'" n.d., Jiang Lin Papers, HIA.

56. "Inner Mongolia's Bu He Speaks on Student Unrest," FBIS, May 19, 1989; "Unrest in Inner Mongolia," FBIS, May 18, 1989.

57. Ma Dazheng, *Guojia liyi gaoyu yiqie*, 54–56; Song Hanliang, "Renzhen xuexi guanche dangde shisanjie sizhong quanhui jingshen, nuli zuohao wo qude gexiang gongzuo," in *Guanche minzu zhengce wenjian xubian* (Urumqi: Xinjiang renmin, 1990), 240–60.

58. Wang Xiaobin, *Lishi kaocha*, 107–8.

59. Yang Lin and Bu, "'Renzhe' Xi Zhongxun"; Zhang Guoying, "Buyi yuli, zhichi Shenzhen gaige kaifang shiye," in *Xi Zhongxun zhuzheng Guangdong yishu lu*, ed. Zhonggong Guangdong shengwei dangshi yanjiushi (Beijing: Zhonggong dangshi, 2013), 433; *Zhang Guoying*, 242–43. Zhang Guoying is inconsistent about whether the watch was given to Xi by the Dalai Lama or the Panchen Lama, but it was almost certainly the one from the Dalai Lama.

Chapter 25: Xi and the Fate of Global Communism

1. Joseph Torigian, "Elite Politics and Foreign Policy in China from Mao to Xi," Brookings Institution, Jan. 22, 2019, https://www.brookings.edu/articles/elite-politics-and-foreign-policy-in-china-from-mao-to-xi/.

2. Interview.
3. Chung Yen-lin, *Wenge*, 407.
4. Ziyang Zhao, *Prisoner of the State: The Secret Journal of Zhao Ziyang*, trans. Pu Bao, Renee Chiang, and Adi Ignatius (New York: Simon and Schuster, 2010), 167.
5. Zhang Liqun et al., *Hu Yaobang zhuan*, 3:94, 3:105.
6. "Telegram to Ministry of Foreign Affairs," Mar. 25, 1982, Problem 220/C, 1982_460, Relations on Party and Mass Organizations Line with the People's Republic of China, p. 19, Romanian Ministry of Foreign Affairs Archives.
7. Jiang Shan et al., "Xi Zhongxun yu dangde qunzhong luxian zhuanti yantaohui zai Jing zhaokai," Zhongguo baoxie wang, May 26, 2016, http://zgbx.people.com.cn/n1/2016/0526/c347565-28382766.html; Wang Jun, *Zhengcheng fengyun lu* (Hong Kong: Boxue, 2012), 171.
8. *Xi Zhongxun nianpu*, 3:188.
9. Wu Li Yaohua [Julia Li Wu], *Zuobuwan de Meiguo meng* (Beijing: Dongfang, 2011), 248–50, 257. The Chinese asked Wu to serve as a secret emissary between the mainland and Taiwan, but she refused.
10. Gao Feng, "Ruidian shemindang de ziwo gaige zhi lu," *Tongzhou gongjin*, no. 3 (2011): 32–33.
11. "Telegram from Sundfelt," Oct. 19, 1981, dossier C 50 G/7 del 3, Regeringskansliet, Centralarkivet Utrikesdepartementet.
12. Zhonggong Fuping xianwei and Fuping xian renmin zhengfu, eds., *Xiangyin: Jinian Xi Zhongxun tongzhi danchen jiushiwu zhounian* ([Weinan]: [Zhonggong Fuping xianwei], 2008).
13. *Xi Zhongxun nianpu*, 3:159.
14. "Telegram from Sundfelt," Sept. 30, 1981, dossier C 50 G/7 del 3, Regeringskansliet, Centralarkivet Utrikesdepartementet.
15. Jeremy Friedman, *Shadow Cold War: The Sino-Soviet Competition for the Third World* (Chapel Hill: University of North Carolina Press, 2015).
16. *Deng Xiaoping nianpu (1975–1997)*, 2:864.
17. "Text of Hu Yaobang's Report to 12th CPC Congress," FBIS, Sept. 7, 1982.
18. Soga Yūri, *Tajō busshin: Waga Nihon Shakaitō kōbōshi* (Tokyo: Shakai Hyōronsha, 2014), 342.
19. Li Shenzhi, "Tantan Zhonghua renmin gongheguo de waijiao," in *Li Shenzhi wenji* (n.p., 2004), 334.
20. Zhonggong zhongyang tongzhanbu and Zhonggong zhongyang wenxian yanjiushi, eds., "Huijian Bolan minzhu dang fanghua daibiaotuan tanhua yaodian," in *Xi Zhongxun lun tongyi zhanxian* (Beijing: Zhongyang wenxian, 2013), 525–27.
21. Jiang Huajie, "Zhidu jingxiang," 94.
22. Qian Liren, *Bange shiji de canghai sangtian: Qian Liren huiyilu* (Beijing: Waijiao bu, 2013), 146.
23. "The Diary of Anatoly S. Chernyaev," 1983, p. 23, DNSA.
24. "Memo to the Secretariat of the Central Committee," Dec. 7, 1983, AD-093NI_0000002431–2438, FNACP; Jiang Huanghua, *Fangwen waiguo zhengdang jishi* (Beijing: Shijie zhishi, 1997), 151–65.
25. "1983-11-22 Malo, Entretien avec M Xi Zhongxun," Nov. 22, 1983, Ministère des Affaires Etrangères, 2882 TOPO 2917, Direction Asie and Océanie, 1980–1986, série CH sous-série 1 dossier 4.
26. "Memo to the Secretariat"; "Meeting PCF-CCP. 11.24.1983 Session," Dec. 4, 1983, AD093NI_0000002455–2458, FNACP.
27. Ibid.

28. Ibid.
29. Ibid.
30. Unnamed, Dec. 2, 1983, AD093NI_0000002455–2458, FNACP.
31. Ibid.; "Xi Zhongxun's Declaration to FR3 on November 28, 83, Monday," Nov. 28, 1983, AD093NI_00000024440, FNACP; "PRC CP Delegation Meets Marghais [sic], Ends Visit," FBIS, Dec. 2, 1983.
32. *Deng Liqun guoshi jiangtanlu*, 5:273; interview with former cadre in the International Liaison Department.
33. "Hu Yaobang's Report."
34. *Zhongguo gongchandang duiwai gongzuo dashiji*, vol. 2 (Beijing: Dangdai shijie, 2001).
35. "Thousands Mourn Sekou Toure," United Press International, Mar. 31, 1984; Gu Jiaji, "Aile shengzhong de zhengbian nao," in *Hongzhao yizong*, ed. Luo Guibo, Han Nianlong, and Gong Dafei (Nanjing: Jiangsu renmin, 1995), 164.
36. Gu Jiaji, "Aile shengzhong," 165–66.
37. Ibid., 167–71.
38. "Xi Zhongxun, Party Leave Conakry for Home," FBIS, Apr. 1, 1984; "Meet Algerian President 3 Nov," FBIS, Nov. 4, 1984.
39. Li Rui, diary (vol. 14, Aug. 1983), p. 30, HIA.
40. Juchen, '*Ju chen*, 11:199.
41. "Deguo zhengfu daibiao tuan jiedai jianbao," Jan. 19, 1961, 109-03760-04, PRC FMA.
42. Qian Liren, *Bage shiji*, 141.
43. Shen Zhihua, "Tongmeng wajie: Deng Xiaoping shidai de Zhong-Chao guanxi, 1977–1992 (I)," *Ershiyi shiji shuangyue kan* 8, no. 166 (Apr. 2018): 116.
44. V. P. Gagnon, *The Myth of Ethnic War: Serbia and Croatia in the 1990s* (Ithaca, NY: Cornell University Press, 2006), 60–61, 65.
45. "Note on the Conversation between Comrade Vidoje Žarković, the President of the Presidium of the Central Committee of the League of Communists of Yugoslavia, with Xi Zhongxun, Member of the Politburo of the Central Committee of the Communist Party of China and the Chief of the Chinese Delegation on the 13th Congress of the LCY, June 24, 1986," June 24, 1986, AJ, CK SKJ, IX 60/I-223, Archives of Yugoslavia, Commission for International Relations and Contacts, People's Republic of China.
46. Elmira Akhundova, *Geidar Aliev: Lichnost´ i epokha*, vol. 2 (Moscow: Kanon+, 2017), 303–4.
47. Gagnon, *Myth of Ethnic War*, 65–69.
48. *Xi Zhongxun nianpu*, 4:183.
49. "Warsaw Reports End to Strike," FBIS, Apr. 25, 1988; "Huijian Bolan"; "Cryptogram No. 1323/II," Apr. 26, 1988, "Meeting with Representatives of Polish Democratic Party," Department II, 24/92, w. 6, Archive of the Polish Ministry of Foreign Affairs. I thank Marek Hańderek for sharing this document with me.
50. Grzegorz Ekiert and Jan Kubik, *Rebellious Civil Society: Popular Protest and Democratic Consolidation in Poland, 1989–1993* (Ann Arbor: University of Michigan Press, 2001), 43–44.
51. "Giuseppe Chiarante to Italian Communist Party Directorate," Aug. 30, 1986, Fondazione Gramsci, APC, Partito 1986, Estero: Cina, mf. 587 / pp. 135–39.
52. *Xi Zhongxun nianpu*, 4:184.
53. A. V. Buzgalin, *Belaia vorona: Poslednii god zhizni TsK KPSS* (Moscow: n.p., 1993), 38–49.
54. *Xi Zhongxun nianpu*, 4:185.

55. "Historical Necessity of Socialism Stressed," FBIS, June 30, 1990.

56. Joseph Torigian, "Prestige, Manipulation, and Coercion: Elite Power Struggles and the Fate of Three Revolutions" (PhD diss., MIT, 2016), 621–23.

57. Shen Zhihua, "Tongmeng wajie: Deng Xiaoping shidai de Zhong-Chao guanxi, 1977–1992 (II)," *Ershiyi shiji shuangyue kan* 8, no. 168 (Aug. 2018): 117–18.

58. "Memorandum of Conversation between Erich Honecker and Kim Il Sung," trans. Grace Leonard, May 31, 1984, DY 30, 2460, WCDA, SAPMO-BA.

59. Z. Zhao, *Prisoner*, 167.

60. Interview with former cadre in the International Liaison Department.

61. John Delury, "Feudal Contradictions between Communist Allies: Deng Xiaoping, Kim Il-Sung, and the Problem of Succession, 1976–1984," *Journal of Cold War Studies* 24, no. 2 (2022): 4–28.

62. Shi Binhai, *Lishi zhuanzhe zhong de Hua Guofeng (1973–1981)* (Beijing: Beijing chuanshi jiashu wenhua fazhan, 2020), 332–38.

63. Kim Il-sung, "Jin Richeng tongzhi zai Chengdu shi qunzhong huanying dahuishang de jianghua," in *Zhong-Chao liangdang, liangguo lingdaoren jianghua he heyan dian huibian* (n.p.: Zhonggong zhongyang duiwai lianluobu erju, 1983), 106–13.

64. "INR's East Asia and Pacific Weekly Highlights, December 5–11, 1982, Report No. 46, Supplement 1," Dec. 10, 1982, DNSA.

65. Dawamaiti, *Shengming zhi yuan jicui*, 40.

66. Xi Zhongxun, "Xi Zhongxun fuweiyuanzhang zai huanying yanhuishang de jianghua," in *Zhong-Chao liangdang, liangguo lingdaoren jianghua he heyan dian huibian* (n.p.: Zhonggong zhongyang duiwai lianluobu erju, 1983), 127–29; Delury, "Feudal Contradictions," 21–22.

67. "Visits Pyongyang," FBIS, Oct. 9, 1982.

68. "Visit to Zhou Enlai Statue," FBIS, Oct. 10, 1982.

69. "NPC's Xi Zhongxun Addresses Hamhung Banquet," FBIS, Oct. 10, 1982.

70. "Kaesong Banquet Speeches," FBIS, Oct. 13, 1982.

71. Dawamaiti, *Shengming zhi yuan jicui*, 42.

72. Jia Juchuan, "'Luhuo chunqing' Xi Zhongxun," 42; Delury, "Feudal Contradictions," 21–22.

73. Zhong, "Xiang Nan," 14.

74. Dawamaiti, *Shengming zhi yuan jicui*, 42–43.

75. "Xi Zhongxun fuweiyuanzhang zai gaobie yanhuishang de jianghua," in *Zhong-Chao liangdang, liangguo lingdaoren jianghua he heyan dian huibian* (n.p.: Zhonggong zhongyang duiwai lianluobu erju, 1983), 130–33.

76. Xi Zhongxun, "Xi Zhongxun tongzhi zai huanying yanhuishang de jianghua," in *Zhong-Chao liangdang, liangguo lingdaoren jianghua he heyan dian huibian* (n.p.: Zhonggong zhongyang duiwai lianluobu erju, 1983), 137–39.

77. Xi Zhongxun, "Xi Zhongxun tongzhi zai gaobie yanhuishang de jianghua," in *Zhong-Chao liangdang, liangguo lingdaoren jianghua he heyan dian huibian* (n.p.: Zhonggong zhongyang duiwai lianluobu erju, 1983), 146–47.

78. Kieran Corcoran, "Vintage Video of Kim Jong Un and Xi Jinping's Dads on a Diplomatic Trip in 1983 Shows Their Deep Family Bond," *Business Insider*, May 10, 2018; Delury, "Feudal Contradictions," 22–23.

79. Shen, "Tongmeng wajie," pt. 2, 115–16.

80. "Banquet Held for Delegation," FBIS, July 9, 1988.

81. "Received by Kim Il-song," FBIS, July 13, 1988.

82. "Xi Zhongxun Reports on DPRK Visit," FBIS, Aug. 30, 1988.

Chapter 26: "It Is Necessary to Also Have a Spiritual Civilization"

1. *Xi Zhongxun nianpu*, 3:157, 3:199.
2. Frank Dikötter, *China after Mao: Rise of a Superpower* (New York: Bloomsbury, 2022), 56–57; Julian Gewirtz, *Never Turn Back: China and the Forbidden History of the 1980s* (Cambridge, MA: Belknap Press of Harvard University Press, 2022), 44–45.
3. Z. Zhao, *Prisoner*, 162.
4. Li Rui, diary (vol. 26, 1994), p. 8, HIA; Li Rui, *Li Rui koushu wangshi*, 426–29; Lu Zhichao, "Haibian yiwang: Weirao Zhongnanhai de huiyi yu sikao" (unpublished manuscript, 2008), 261.
5. Wang Ruoshui, "Zhou Yang dui Makesizhuyi de zuihou tansuo," in *Yi Zhou Yang*, ed. Wang Meng and Yuan Ying, (Hohhot: Nei Menggu renmin, 1998), 435.
6. *Deng Liqun guoshi jiangtanlu*, 7:99, 7:101; interview.
7. Li Rui, "Yaobang qushi qian de tanhua," in *Huainian Yaobang*, ed. Zhang Liqun et al., vol. 4 (Hong Kong: Yatai guoji, 2001), 285; interview.
8. Lu Zhichao, "Haibian yiwang," 261.
9. Li Rui, "Li Rui baocun de lishi jiazhi xinjian 9.1: Li Rui zhi Zhao Ziyang bing Deng Xiaoping fandui Deng Liqun ren Zhonggong zong shuji de xin," n.d., HIA; Li Nanyang, *Fumu zuori shu*, vol. 1 (Hong Kong: Shidai guoji, 2005); Li Rui, diary (vols. 13–15, 1984), p. 75, HIA.
10. Xu Qingquan, "Xuanxiao guohou zai shuo Deng Liqun," *Aisixiang*, Nov. 2, 2015, https://www.aisixiang.com/data/93397.html.
11. *Chen Yizi huiyilu* (Hong Kong: Xin shiji, 2013), 324–25.
12. He Weiling, *Chuanshuo*, 40, 84, 88, 130, 267–84.
13. He Jingzhi, "Zai zhongxuanbu gongzuo de qian qinian (I)," in *He Jingzhi wenji*, vol. 6 (Beijing: Zuojia, 2004), 387.
14. Li Rui, diary (vol. 27, 1995), p. 88, HIA.
15. Cai, "Zhao Ziyang."
16. *Deng Liqun zishu*, 192–93.
17. Jia Man, *Shiren He Jingzhi* (Beijing: Dazhong wenyi, 2000), 308–9.
18. *Deng Liqun guoshi jiangtanlu*, 3:461, 3:465, 3:468, 3:470.
19. *Deng Liqun zishu*, 304.
20. Lu Zhichao, "Haibian yiwang," 159.
21. Liu Xicheng, *Zai wentan bianyuan*, vol. 1 (Kaifeng: Henan daxue chubanshe, 2003), 160.
22. *Wang Meng zizhuan*, vol. 2 (Guangzhou: Huacheng, 2007), 254.
23. Li Xin, "Du 'Ding Ling yu Hu Feng' yi wen suo xiangqi de," *Xin wenxue shiliao*, no. 2 (2008): 117.
24. Gao Kai, "Xi Zhongxun jianyi zhiding 'butong yijian baohufa,'" *Yanhuang chunqiu*, no. 12 (2013): 21.
25. Zheng Rong, *Wo yu Beijingren yi* (Beijing: Dongfang, 2000), 210.
26. Torigian, *Prestige*, 151–55, 172–78; Frederick C. Teiwes and Warren Sun, "CCP Ideology, 1976–1980: From the 'Two Whatevers,' to the 'Criterion of Truth,' to the 'Four Cardinal Principles,' and Beyond" (China Studies Working Paper, China Studies Centre, University of Sydney, 2023), 104–24.
27. Teiwes and Sun, "CCP Ideology," 72–85.
28. Ibid., 87–91.
29. Li Yi, "Ta qizhi xianming di tichu gei Guangdong fangquan," in *Xi Zhongxun zhuzheng Guangdong yishu lu*, ed. Zhonggong Guangdong shengwei dangshi yanjiushi (Beijing: Zhonggong dangshi, 2013), 27–29.
30. Shen Baoxiang, *Zhenli biaozhun wenti taolun shimo* (Beijing: Zhongguo qingnian, 1997), 229.

31. "Shishi qiushi, jiefang sixiang, jiakuai qianjin bufa," *PD*, Sept. 20, 1978.
32. *Xi Zhongxun zhuzheng Guangdong* (Beijing: Zhonggong dangshi, 2008), 36.
33. Teiwes and Sun, "CCP Ideology," 112–16.
34. Lu Di, "Lishi," 50.
35. Torigian, *Prestige*, 154–55.
36. Teiwes and Sun, "CCP Ideology," 179–242.
37. Tian Fang, *Suiyue yinhen*, 308–14.
38. Teiwes and Sun, "CCP Ideology," 216.
39. "Jianding bu yi jixu guanche sanzhong quanhui jingshen," *PD*, June 11, 1979.
40. *Xi Zhongxun zhuzheng Guangdong*, 42–43.
41. Ibid., 43–46; "Guangdong's Xi Zhongxun Stresses Truth Criterion," FBIS, Sept. 15, 1979.
42. Jia Juchuan, "Xi Zhongxun zhiyi 'xingwu miezi,'" *Bainianchao*, no. 11 (2001): 78.
43. Torigian, *Prestige*, 182–83.
44. Liu Xicheng, *Zai wentan bianyuan*, 154.
45. Ibid., 152; Liu Xicheng, "'Xin shiqi wenyi' de tichu yu wenyi zhengce de queli: Yi Zhongguo wenlian sanci huiyi weili," *Zhongguo dangwei wenxue yanjiu*, no. 2 (2020): 30–31.
46. Xu Qingquan, ed., "Yu Zhou Weizhi tan Zhou Yang," in *Zhiqingzhe shuo Zhou Yang* (Beijing: Jingji ribao, 2003), 49.
47. Merle Goldman, *Sowing the Seeds of Democracy in China: Political Reform in the Deng Xiaoping Era* (Cambridge, MA: Harvard University Press, 1994), 88–112; Richard Baum, *Burying Mao: Chinese Politics in the Age of Deng Xiaoping* (Princeton, NJ: Princeton University Press, 1994), 126–30.
48. Xu Qingquan, *Fengyu song chungui: Xin shiqi wentan sixiang jiefang yundong jishi* (Kaifeng: Henan daxue chubanshe, 2005), 321–64; Li Jiefei, "Fengyu wanlai fangding," in *Huiyi Zhang Guangnian* (Beijing: Zuojia, 2013), 450–51.
49. Xu Qingquan, *Fengyu song chungui*, 386–95.
50. Ibid., 395–97; *Hu Qiaomu zhuan*, 690–94.
51. "Bai Hua: 'Kulian' de wengu er zhixin," *Nanyang ribao*, Dec. 2, 2008.
52. Xu Qingquan, *Fengyu song chungui*, 398–99; Zhang Guangnian, *Wentan huichun jishi*, vol. 1 (Shenzhen: Haitian, 1998), 267–76.
53. Xu Qingquan, *Fengyu song chungui*, 399.
54. *Hu Qiaomu zhuan*, 690–95.
55. Xu Qingquan, *Fengyu song chungui*, 417; Tang Yin and Tang Dacheng, "Lun 'Kulian' de cuowu qingxiang," *PD*, Oct. 7, 1981; Zhang Guangnian, *Wentan huichun jishi*, 276–77; Li Jiefei, "Fengyu wanlai fangding," 455.
56. *Hu Jiwei zishu*, 4 vols. (Hong Kong: Zhuoyue wenhua, 2006), 1:391.
57. Xi Zhongxun, "Zai Xinhuashe jianshe wushi zhounian jinian huishang de jianghua," in *Xi Zhongxun wenji*, vol. 2 (Beijing: Zhonggong dangshi, 2013), 694–95.
58. Xu Qingquan, *Fengyu song chungui*, 412; Hu Jiwei, "Jiehou cheng zhongren, yindui zhuyi cheng: Wei Yaobang shishi shi zhounian er zuo," *Shuwu*, no. 4 (2000): 18, 21.
59. Wang Ruoshui, *Hu Yaobang xiatai de beijing* (Hong Kong: Mingjing, 1997), 121–22, 170; *Hu Qiaomu zhuan*, 696–99.
60. *Hu Jiwei zishu*, 1:400.
61. Goldman, *Seeds of Democracy*, 116–19; Hao Huaiming, *Gaige kaifang zai Zhongnanhai*, vol. 1 (Hong Kong: Xianggang xinhua, 2018), 150–51.
62. Xu Qingquan, "Yu Zhou Weizhi," 50; Xu Qingquan, ed., "Yu Qin Chuan tan Zhou Yang," in *Zhiqingzhe shuo Zhou Yang* (Beijing: Jingji ribao, 2003), 58–60, 74; Yao Wenyuan, "Ping fangeming liangmian pai Zhou Yang," *PD*, Jan. 3, 1967; Li Jiantong, "Zhou Yang," 373–74.

63. *Deng Liqun guoshi jiangtanlu*, 7:361; Hao Huaiming, *Gaige kaifang*, 150–51.
64. Yu Guangyuan, "Zhou Yang he wo," in *Yi Zhou Yang*, ed. Wang Meng and Yuan Ying (Hohhot: Nei Menggu renmin, 1998), 195.
65. *Deng Liqun guoshi jiangtanlu*, 7:361–62; Wang Ruoshui, "Zhou Yang," 420, 422–23.
66. Hao Huaiming, *Gaige kaifang*, 155; Xu Qingquan, "Yu Qin Chuan," 60–61.
67. *Deng Liqun guoshi jiangtanlu*, 7:363.
68. Gu Xiang, "Zhou Yang yu qingchu jingshen wuran," *Yanhuang chunqiu*, no. 10 (2013): 34; *Deng Liqun zishu*, 267.
69. *Deng Liqun guoshi jiangtanlu*, 7:364–65.
70. Ibid., 7:367–70; Lu Zhichao, "Haibian yiwang," 124, 129; *Hu Qiaomu zhuan*, 714–16.
71. Yang Jisheng, *Zhongguo gaige*, 249–51.
72. Yu Guangyuan, "Zhou Yang he wo," 200.
73. *Deng Liqun guoshi jiangtanlu*, 7:371; *Deng Liqun zishu*, 418.
74. Wang Ruoshui, *Hu Yaobang*, 174.
75. Xu Qingquan, "Yu Qin Chuan," 73.
76. Deng Liqun, "Deng Liqun chuanda dangde shierjie erzhong quanhui jingshen," in *Deng Liqun wenji*, vol. 2 (Beijing: Dangdai Zhongguo, 1998), 302–40.
77. Gao Yong, "Conglai lishi fei qinding, ziyou shi jian yan weizhen," *Hu Yaobang shiliao xinxi wang*, Mar. 25, 2009, https://web.archive.org/web/20201103090526; Lu Zhichao, "Haibian yiwang," 132.
78. *Hu Qiaomu zhuan*, 727.
79. Yen-lin Chung, "The Ousting of General Secretary Hu Yaobang," *China Review* 19, no. 1 (Feb. 2019): 101–2; Yang Jisheng, *Zhongguo gaige*, 252–53; *Deng Liqun guoshi jiangtanlu*, 7:429, 7:433.
80. Li Rui, diary (vols. 17–18, 1986), p. 21, HIA.
81. Lin Mu, "Xi Zhongxun wannian de jijian dashi," *Beijing zhichun*, no. 89 (Oct. 2000): 24.
82. *Deng Liqun guoshi jiangtanlu*, 3:461.
83. Hao Huaiming, *Gaige kaifang*, 316.
84. *Xi Zhongxun nianpu*, 3:241–42.
85. Deng Liqun, "Guanyu qingchu jingshen wuran de ruogan zhengce jiexian," in *Deng Liqun wenji*, vol. 2 (Beijing: Dangdai Zhongguo, 1998), 348–73.
86. *Chen Yizi huiyilu*, 285.
87. Li Rui, "Yaobang," 284–85, 297.
88. He Jingzhi, "Zai zhongxuanbu gongzuo de qian qinian (II)," in *He Jingzhi wenji*, vol. 6 (Beijing: Zuojia, 2004), 420–21.
89. Xi Zhongxun, "Zai luoshi zhengce," 286.
90. *Hu Qiaomu zhuan*, 731, 741; Hu Qiaomu, "Guanyu rendao zhuyi he yihua wenti," *PD*, Jan. 27, 1984; Yu Guangyuan, "Zhou Yang he wo," 202–3.
91. *Deng Liqun guoshi jiangtanlu*, 3:454–55; "Zhou Yang Criticized, Makes Self-Criticism in Interview," FBIS, Nov. 5, 1983; Yu Guangyuan, "Zhou Yang he wo," 200–201.
92. Gu Xiang, *Wannian Zhou Yang* (Beijing: Wenhui, 2003), 102–3, 106, 113–15, 123, 127–28; *Zhou Yang jinzuo* (Beijing: Zuojia, 1985); Yu Guangyuan, "Zhou Yang he wo," 207; Li Ziyun, *Wo qinli de naxie ren he shi* (Shanghai: Wenhui, 2005), 134.
93. Li Rui, diary (vol. 27, 1995), p. 88, HIA.
94. *Deng Liqun guoshi jiangtanlu*, 3:460–61.
95. Y.-L. Chung, "Ousting," 101–2.
96. Hao Huaiming, *Gaige kaifang*, 210.
97. Li Rui, diary (vol. 27, 1995), p. 88, HIA.

98. Li Rui, diary (vols. 13–15, 1984), pp. 56–57, HIA; *Deng Liqun zishu*, 317–18.
99. Li Rui, "Yaobang," 282–83; Li Rui, diary (vols. 13–15, 1984), pp. 56–57, HIA; *Deng Liqun zishu*, 335.
100. Li Rui, diary (vols. 13–15, 1984), p. 56, HIA.
101. Binyan Liu, *A Higher Kind of Loyalty: A Memoir by China's Foremost Journalist* (New York: Pantheon Books, 1990), 176–82.
102. Ibid., 187–88; *Ma Wenrui zhuan* (Beijing: Dangdai Zhongguo, 2005), 602; Hu Peiyuan, *Haohai: Ma Wenrui yu gaige kaifang* (Beijing: Zhongyang wenxian, 2014), 266.
103. Zhang Liqun et al., *Hu Yaobang zhuan*, 3:175.
104. Li Jiefei, "Fengyu wanlai fangding," 464, 471.
105. Ibid., 473–74; Chen Weiren, *Tang Dacheng*, 235–46.
106. Jia Man, *Shiren He Jingzhi*, 300–305; He Jingzhi, "Zai zhongxuanbu," pt. 2, 452–60; *Deng Liqun zishu*, 319–20; *Deng Liqun guoshi jiangtanlu*, 3:463; Li Jiefei, "Fengyu wanlai fangding," 475.
107. Zhang Liqun et al., *Hu Yaobang zhuan*, 3:175.
108. Lu Chaoqi, *Liu si neibu riji* (Hong Kong: Zhuoyue wenhua, 2006), 280–81.
109. Chen Weiren, *Tang Dacheng*, 250.
110. Ibid., 252–55.
111. Li Jiefei, "Fengyu wanlai fangding," 477.
112. Zhang Liqun et al., *Hu Yaobang zhuan*, 3:176.
113. Li Rui, diary (vols. 17–18, 1986), p. 21, HIA.
114. Li Rui, diary (vol. 27, 1995), p. 89, HIA.
115. Hao Huaiming, *Gaige kaifang*, 220–22.
116. *Xi Zhongxun nianpu*, 3:332.
117. *Deng Liqun guoshi jiangtanlu*, 7:99, 7:389.
118. Hu Jiwei, *Cong Hua Guofeng xiatai dao Hu Yaobang xiatai* (Brampton, ON: Mingjing, 1997), 352.
119. Zheng Zhongbing, ed., *Hu Yaobang nianpu ziliao changbian*, vol. 2 (Hong Kong: Shidai guoji, 2005), 989–90.
120. Hu Jiwei, *Cong Hua Guofeng*, 360.
121. *Xi Zhongxun nianpu*, 3:338.
122. Wu Zuguang, *Yi beizi*, 378–83; Wang Fan, "Wu Zuguang he tade jiwei lao pengyou," *Tongzhou gongjin*, no. 2 (2015): 34; Wu Huan, "Xi Zhongxun xiansheng de jijian wangshi," *Gonghui xinxi* 23 (2014): 28–30.
123. Hu Jiwei, "Hu Yaobang yu Liu Binyan," *China Digital Times*, Feb. 2, 2012, https://chinadigitaltimes.net/chinese/208002.html.
124. Li Rui, diary (vol. 27, 1995), p. 88, HIA.
125. Li Rui, diary (vols. 16–17, 1985), pp. 40–41, HIA.
126. Li Rui, diary (vols. 17–18, 1986), p. 21, HIA; Wu Xiang, "Zhu Houze he tade 'san kuan,'" *Yanhuang chunqiu*, no. 11 (2010): 20; Zheng Zhongbing, "Shei jujian de Zhu Houze," *Yanhuang chunqiu*, no. 1 (2016): 30–34.
127. Tian Jiyun, "Jin juli ganshou Hu Yaobang," *Yanhuang chunqiu*, no. 10 (2004): 4.
128. *Deng Liqun zishu*, 578–606; Hao Huaiming, *Gaige kaifang*, 272.
129. Tian Jiyun, "Jin juli," 4–5; Hao Huaiming, *Gaige kaifang*, 273–75.
130. Jia Juchuan, "1962.10–2002.5," 21; Hao Huaiming, *Gaige kaifang*, 282–86; Li Rui, "Yaobang," 279.
131. Sheng Ping and Wang Zaixing, eds., *Hu Yaobang sixiang nianpu*, special ser., vol. 70 (n.p.: SCCP, 2007), 1297.
132. Hao Huaiming, *Gaige kaifang*, 327–28.
133. *Xi Zhongxun nianpu*, 4:62–63.
134. *Xi Zhongxun nianpu*, 3:63.

135. Hu Zhi'an, *Tongzhan mixin*, 545–46; Zhao Ziyang, "San fang Zhao Ziyang," in *Zhongguo dangdai mingren zhengyao fang shuping ji*, ed. Yang Jisheng (Hong Kong: Tiandi tushu, 2013), 16–17.

136. Deng Xiaoping, "Take a Clear-Cut Stand against Bourgeois Liberalization," in *Selected Works of Deng Xiaoping (1982–1992)*, vol. 2 (Beijing: Foreign Languages, 1994), 194, 195.

137. Hu Yaobang to Deng Xiaoping, letter (unpublished), Jan. 1, 1987. I thank Warren Sun for sharing this document.

Chapter 27: The Deep Waters of Zhongnanhai

1. [Hu Yaobang], Hu Yaobang's self-criticism [in Chinese], Jan. 10, 1987. I thank Warren Sun for sharing this document.

2. Barry Naughton, "Deng Xiaoping: The Economist," *China Quarterly*, no. 135 (Sept. 1993): 500.

3. Zhang Liqun et al., *Hu Yaobang zhuan*, 3:173.

4. Li Rui, diary (vols. 16–17, 1985), p. 41, HIA.

5. Gao Kai, "Xi Zhongxun," 19.

6. *Chen Yizi huiyilu*, 494.

7. Deng Xiaoping, "Disandai lingdao jiti de dangwu zhi ji," in *Deng Xiaoping wenxuan*, vol. 3 (Beijing: Renmin, 1994), 310.

8. Wang Xiaozhong, *Zhongguwei gongzuo jishi*, 237.

9. Torigian, *Prestige*, 166.

10. Torigian, "Elite Politics."

11. Wang Zhongfang, *Jiu shi youyu* (Beijing: self-pub., 2015), 36.

12. Wang Yuanyuan and Yan Bin, "Richang shenghuo zhong de Yaobang shushu," in *Wangshi huisheng: Zhongguo zhuming zhishifenzi fangtanlu*, ed. Xing Xiaoqun (Hong Kong: Shidai guoji, 2005), 13.

13. Li Rui, diary (vols. 19–20, 1987), p. 13, HIA.

14. "Zuotan Zhonggong dangshi" (unpublished manuscript, June 30, 2010). Held by Frederick Teiwes.

15. Zhang Liqun et al., *Hu Yaobang zhuan*, 2:160.

16. Liu Chongwen, "Hu Yaobang shishi qian bannian de xintai," *Yanhuang chunqiu*, no. 9 (2009): 4.

17. Sima Qingyang and Ouyang Longmen, *Xin faxian de Zhou Enlai* (Carle Place: Mingjing, 2009).

18. Kong Xiangxiu, *Geng Biao zhuan*, 253.

19. Wang Zhongfang, *Jiu shi youyu*, 35.

20. Li Rui, diary (vols. 12–13, 1983), pp. 50, 58, HIA; Yan, discussion; Shan Shaojie, "Mao Zedong: Zhengren yu pa shi—Mao Zedong shishi sanshi zhounian ji (I)," *Huaxia wenzhai zengkan* 559 (Mar. 2007).

21. Frederick C. Teiwes, "The Politics of Succession: Previous Patterns and a New Process," in *China's Post-Jiang Leadership Succession: Problems and Perspectives*, ed. John Wong and Yongnian Zheng (Singapore: Singapore University Press, 2002), 39.

22. *Xu Xiangqian nianpu*, 380.

23. Zhang Liqun et al., *Hu Yaobang zhuan*, 2:149, 3:194.

24. Xing Xiaoqun, "Richang shenghuo zhong de Yaobang shushu," *Lao zhaopian* 42 (Aug. 2005): 26.

25. Li Rui, *Li Rui koushu wangshi*, 191.

26. Li Rui, diary (vol. 21, 1989), p. 36, HIA.

27. Chung Yen-lin, *Wenge*, 429–45.

28. Teiwes and Sun, *Maoist Era*, 380.

29. Bao Tong, "Wo kan Hu Zhao guanxi," in *Bao Tong wenji* (Hong Kong: Xin shiji, 2012), 407–27.
30. Wang Yuanyuan and Yan, "Richang shenghuo," 10.
31. Wu Jiaxiang, *Zhongnanhai riji* (Carle Place: Mingjing, 2002), 264; Li Rui, diary (vols. 20–21, 1988), p. 61, HIA.
32. Teiwes, "Politics of Succession," 39.
33. Li Rui, "Yaobang," 290; Li Rui, diary (vols. 13–15, 1984), p. 75, HIA.
34. Hu Hua, interview by Michel Oksenberg, notes, file 1987, box 19, Michel Oksenberg Papers, Bentley Historical Library, University of Michigan.
35. Li Rui, diary (vol. 28, 1996), p. 69, HIA.
36. Zhang Liqun et al., *Hu Yaobang zhuan*, 3:110–11; Sheng Ping and Wang, *Hu Yaobang sixiang nianpu*, 854–56.
37. Zhang Liqun et al., *Hu Yaobang zhuan*, 3:111; *Deng Liqun zishu*, 417.
38. Qin Chuan, "Yijiubasannian 'qing wu' yundong zhuiyi," *Jingbao yuekan*, no. 12 (1996): 48–55; Wang Ruoshui, *Hu Yaobang*, 39; *Hu Jiwei zishu*, 4:292; Zhang Liqun et al., *Hu Yaobang zhuan*, 3:111.
39. Interview.
40. Zhao Ziyang, "San fang Zhao Ziyang," 18.
41. *Chen Yizi huiyilu*, 337.
42. Li Rui, diary (vols. 13–15, 1984), p. 75, HIA; Li Rui, diary (vols. 17–18, 1986), p. 21, HIA.
43. Li Rui, diary (vol. 27, 1995), p. 90, HIA; Frank Dikötter, *The Age of Openness: China before Mao* (Berkeley: University of California Press, 2008), 85.
44. Zhang Liqun et al., *Hu Yaobang zhuan*, 2:168.
45. Li Rui, "Yaobang," 278, 291, 305; Y.-L. Chung, "Ousting," 109; Gao Yong, "Conglai lishi fei qinding."
46. Yan Qiying, *Xi Zhongxun huazhuan* (Beijing: Xuexi, 2013), 412–13.
47. Lin Mu, "Xi Zhongxun," 26–27.
48. *Hu Jiwei zishu*, 4:299.
49. I thank Warren Sun for these insights.
50. Li Rui, diary (vol. 27, 1995), p. 89, HIA.
51. Wu Wei, *Zhongguo*, 75; *Xi Zhongxun nianpu*, 4:44; Torigian, *Prestige*, 161–62.
52. Wu Jiaxiang, *Zhongnanhai riji*, 152–53.
53. Zhao Tianyuan, *Zai Chen Yun shenbian de shinian* (Beijing: Zhongyang wenxian, 2005), 357–59.
54. Interview.
55. Yamaguchi Shinji, "New Evidence on Hu Yaobang's Fall and Japan-China Relations in the 1980s: Prime Minister Nasakone Yasuhiro's Visit to China, 1986," Wilson Center, Feb. 16, 2021, https://www.wilsoncenter.org/blog-post/new-evidence-hu-yaobangs-fall-and-japan-china-relations-1980s-prime-minister-nakasone.
56. *Chen Yizi huiyilu*, 423.
57. Li Ligong, *Wangshi huigu* (Beijing: Zhonggong dangshi, 2008), 448–50.
58. Torigian, *Prestige*, 166.
59. Zhang Liqun et al., *Hu Yaobang zhuan*, 3:199.
60. Y.-L. Chung, "Ousting," 110–12; Yamaguchi, "New Evidence"; *Hu Jiwei zishu*, 4:304.
61. *Hu Jiwei zishu*, 4:306; Lin Mu, "Xi Zhongxun," 28.
62. Li Nanyang, "Li Rui juechang," in *Jingji Li Rui*, ed. Li Nanyang (Hong Kong: Chuban gongfang, 2019), 464.
63. Li Rui, dairy (vols. 34–35, 2002), p. 121, HIA.

64. Song Jiangjun, "Xi Zhongxun de jinian xushi," *21 shiji jingji baodao*, Oct. 14, 2013.
65. Li Rui, diary (vols. 19–20, 1987), p. 10, HIA; Sheng Ping and Wang, *Hu Yaobang sixiang nianpu*, 1302–3; Zhang Liqun et al., *Hu Yaobang zhuan*, 3:188; two interviews.
66. Li Rui, diary (vols. 20–21, 1988), p. 61, HIA; Zhang Liqun et al., *Hu Yaobang zhuan*, 3:190–91; Hao Huaiming, *Gaige kaifang*, 331; interviews.
67. Li Rui, diary (vols. 19–20, 1987), p. 2, HIA.
68. Zheng Hewei, "Chen Yun weihe changdao huifu zhongyang shujichu," *Dangshi wenhui*, no. 2 (2021): 46–48.
69. Chen Yun, "Diaocha yanjiu he dangnei minzhu shenghuo zhidu wenti," in *Chen Yun wenxuan*, vol. 3 (Beijing: Renmin, 1995), 358–59.
70. Li Rui, diary (vol. 22, 1990), p. 17, HIA.
71. Sheng Ping and Wang, *Hu Yaobang sixiang nianpu*, 1303; Zhang Liqun et al., *Hu Yaobang zhuan*, 3:189.
72. Jia Juchuan, "'Luhuo chunqing' Xi Zhongxun," 41.
73. Jia Juchuan, "1962.10–2002.5," 21.
74. Li Rui, diary (vol. 32, 2000), p. 44, HIA.
75. Wu Jiang, "Qin Chuan," 56–57.
76. Man Mei, *Huiyi fuqin Hu Yaobang*, vol. 2 (Hong Kong: Tiandi tushu, 2016), 766–67, 769.
77. Interview.
78. "Xi Zhongxun tongzhi shicha Shenzhen," 264–65.
79. Ibid., 265–66.
80. Ibid., 268–69.
81. Ibid., 269–71; Xi Zhongxun, "Tingqu Zhuhai jingji tequ fuze ren gongzuo huibao hou de jianghua," in *Xi Zhongxun wenji*, vol. 2 (Beijing: Zhonggong dangshi, 2013), 1144–53.
82. "Xi Zhongxun kuobie liunian chongkan Guangdong zantan bujue," *PD*, Mar. 14, 1987.
83. Xi Zhongxun, "Guanyu Guangdong zhi xing de baogao," in *Xi Zhongxun wenxuan* (Beijing: Zhongyang wenxian, 1995), 447–56.
84. Terry Cheng and David Chen, "Zhao's Political Future Remains Up in the Air," *SCMP*, Mar. 31, 1987; Terry Cheng and David Chen, "Congress Clues to Power Struggle," *SCMP*, Feb. 25, 1987.
85. David Chen, "Contest for Top Consultative Job Is Far from Over," *SCMP*, Sept. 18, 1987; He Pin and Gao, *Zhonggong taizidang*, 196.
86. Li Rui, diary (vols. 19–20, 1987), p. 62, HIA.
87. Li Rui, diary (vol. 23, 1991), p. 88, HIA.
88. Li Rui, diary (vol. 30, 1998), p. 29, HIA.
89. *Chen Yizi huiyilu*, 495.
90. O'Brien, *Reform*, 117–18.
91. Wang Hongliang, "Wang Gong: Di yi wei lüshi de kanke," *Sanlian shenghuo zhoukan*, no. 37 (Sept. 2009).
92. Daniel Southerland, "China's People's Congress Gets Whiff of Democracy: Limited Public Debate, Open Voting Tested," *WP*, Apr. 13, 1988.
93. Xia Lina, "Zou Yu," 48.
94. Ibid.
95. Gao Kai, "Xi Zhongxun," 20; Gao Kai, "Ta."
96. Xia Lina, "Zou Yu," 48.

Chapter 28: Tiananmen Square

1. Wu Wei, *Zhongguo*, 118–46, 364.
2. Ibid., 366–99.
3. Lu Ruihua, "Wennuan qinqie de guli," in *Xi Zhongxun zhuzheng Guangdong yishu lu*, ed. Zhonggong Guangdong shengwei dangshi yanjiushi (Beijing: Zhonggong dangshi, 2013), 23–24; Yang Ping, "Xi jia"; *Xi Zhongxun nianpu*, 4:130–31.
4. *Xi Zhongxun nianpu*, 4:130–33, 4:141.
5. Li Chang, "Wo yu Yaobang gongshi," *Yanhuang chunqiu*, no. 1 (2006): 23; Gao Yong, "Conglai lishi fei qinding"; Liu Chongwen, "Hu Yaobang"; Teiwes and Sun, "CCP Ideology," 236.
6. Li Rui, diary (vol. 21, 1989), pp. 38–39, HIA; Li Rui, "Yaobang," 274; Cai, "Zhao Ziyang."
7. Jeremy Brown, *June Fourth: The Tiananmen Protests and Beijing Massacre of 1989* (New York: Cambridge University Press, 2021), 43–46.
8. Ibid., 43–48.
9. Zhang Liqun et al., *Hu Yaobang zhuan*, 4:242.
10. Li Rui, "Fu: 'Yaobang tongzhi huo zai women xin zhong' zuotanhui fayan ji," in *Li Rui wenji*, vol. 10 (Shenzhen: Zhongguo shehui jiaoyu, 2009), 118–39; Dai Qing, "Wode 1989," *Xin shiji* 27 (2015); Zhang Ganghua, *Li Peng riji zhenxiang* (Hong Kong: Aoya, 2010), 87; Cai, "Zhao Ziyang."
11. Li Rui, diary (vol. 21, 1989), p. 40, HIA.
12. Zhang Lifan, "Hu Yaobang zhisang shouji," *Yanhuang chunqiu*, no. 6 (2012): 4; Wu Wei, *Zhongguo*, 444.
13. Zhang Liqun et al., *Hu Yaobang zhuan*, 3:242–43.
14. Brown, *June Fourth*; "Zhao Ziyang Speech at Meeting," FBIS, Apr. 22, 1989; Cai, "Zhao Ziyang."
15. Zhao Ziyang, *Gaige licheng* (Hong Kong: Xin shiji, 2009), 25–26.
16. Li Rui, diary (vol. 21, 1989), p. 41, HIA.
17. Wu Wei, *Zhongguo*, 452; Wu Guoguang, "Zhengzhi quanli, xianzhang zhidu yu lishi beiju 'Li Peng [Liu si] riji' chudu," *CND kanwu he luntan*, June 18, 2010, http://hx.cnd.org/2010/06/18/%E5%90%B4%E5%9B%BD%E5%85%89%EF%BC%9A%E6%94%BF%E6%B2%BB%E6%9D%83%E5%8A%9B%E3%80%81%E5%AE%AA%E7%AB%A0%E5%88%B6%E5%BA%A6%E4%B8%8E%E5%8E%86%E5%8F%B2%E6%82%B2%E5%89%A7%E2%80%95%E2%80%95%E3%80%8A%E6%9D%8E/; Zhang Ganghua, *Li Peng riji zhenxiang*, 79. However, Deng's instructions were usually transmitted immediately, so this version of events remains only a possibility.
18. Torigian, "Prestige," 464–65.
19. "Qiao Shi deng huijian Xizang ganbu canguan tuan," *PD*, May 1, 1989; "Huanjing wuran zai manyan shengtai zhuangkuang ehua. Zhengfu jiang yi geng youxiao cuoshi jianjue zhili," *PD*, May 2, 1989; "Shoudu qingnian jihui jinian wu si," *PD*, May 4, 1989; "Zhonghua zhijiao she zhili yucai chengji feiran," *PD*, May 7, 1989; "Duiwai youxie juban youhao ri lianhuan," *PD*, May 7, 1989; "Hu Qili deng huijian wenwu gongzuozhe," *PD*, May 8, 1989; "Li Jingquan yiti gaobie yishi zai Jing juxing," *PD*, May 9, 1989.
20. Chung Yen-lin, "Peng Zhen zai 1989 nian Zhonggong 'Tiananmen shijian' zhong de juese he huodong," *Zhongguo dalu yanjiu* 62, no. 1 (Mar. 2019): 1–20.
21. Zhonggong zhongyang zuzhibu, Zhonggong zhongyang dangshi yanjiushi, and Zhongyang dang'anguan, eds., *Zhongguo gongchandang zuzhishi ziliao*, vol. 7, pt. 1 (Beijing: Zhonggong dangshi, 2000), 274.
22. Wu Jiaxiang, *Zhongnanhai riji*, 152; Ma Ya, *Dafeng qixi: Ma Hong zhuan* (Hong Kong: Mingjing, 2014), 250; Wu Wei, *Zhongguo*, 465; Zhao Ziyang, "San fang Zhao Ziyang," 24.

23. Zhang Wanshu, *Lishi de da baozha: "Liu si" shijian quanjing shilu* (Hong Kong: Tiandi, 2009), 138; Wu Wei, *Zhongguo*, 483–84; Zhang Ganghua, *Li Peng riji zhenxiang*, 134–36; Cai, "Zhao Ziyang."
24. *Chen Yizi huiyilu*, 588; Wu Wei, *Zhongguo*, 484.
25. Zhang Ganghua, *Li Peng riji zhenxiang*, 140; Cai, "Zhao Ziyang"; *Chen Yizi huiyilu*, 588; "Qijie renda changweihui baci huiyi jiangyu liuyue ershiri zuoyou juxing," *Jiefangjun bao*, May 12, 1989.
26. Zhang Ganghua, *Li Peng riji zhenxiang*, 350.
27. Ibid., 150–51; Z. Zhao, *Prisoner*, 21; Zhang Wanshu, *Lishi de da baozha*, 162.
28. Zhao Ziyang, "Zai dangde shisanjie yizhong quanhui jieshu shi de jianghua," in *Zhao Ziyang wenji (1980–1989)*, vol. 4 (Hong Kong: Chinese University Press, 2016), 255–56.
29. Wu Wei, *Zhongguo*, 494–507; interview.
30. Brown, *June Fourth*, 76–81; Zhang Ganghua, *Li Peng riji zhenxiang*, 171–73; Cai, "Zhao Ziyang."
31. Chung Yen-lin, "Peng Zhen zai 1989 nian," 14; Zhang Ganghua, *Li Peng riji zhenxiang*, 213.
32. Zhang Ganghua, *Li Peng riji zhenxiang*, 240–41, 350; Z. Zhao, *Prisoner*, 33; Cai Yongmei, ed., "Wan Li tongzhi zai Zhonggong zhongyang zhengzhiju kuoda huiyishang de fayan," in *Zuihou de mimi: Zhonggong shisanjie sizhong quanhui "liu si" jielun wendang* (Hong Kong: Xin shiji, 2019), 244–45.
33. Zhang Ganghua, *Li Peng riji zhenxiang*, 204–8, 251.
34. Ibid., 208–13; Chung Yen-lin, "Peng Zhen zai 1989 nian," 15.
35. "NPC Meeting Called For," FBIS, May 23, 1989.
36. "Sitong Clarifies 'Refutation of Rumor,'" FBIS, May 31, 1989; Wan, *Shanghai yunfan*, 627–29.
37. Lu Chaoqi, *Liu si neibu riji*, 112.
38. Ibid., 97–99; Timothy Brook, *Quelling the People: The Military Suppression of the Beijing Democracy Movement* (New York: Oxford University Press, 1992), 48–77; Jiefangjun Beijing junqu zhengzhiju bangongshi, "Yang Baibing tongzhi zai jieyan budui zhenggong huishang de jianghua," in *Beijing junqu budui zhixing jieyan renwu zhong de zhengzhi gongzuo*, ser. 27, vol. 37 (n.p.: SCCP, 2009), 30; Zhang Ganghua, *Li Peng riji zhenxiang*, 205; Dai Qing, "Ye Jianying yangnu Dai Qing," *NYT*, June 4, 2014, China edition; Jiang Lin, "Wei Zhang Aiping shangjiang xie zhuanji de rizi," n.d., Jiang Lin Papers, HIA.
39. Jiefangjun Beijing junqu zhengzhiju bangongshi, "Yang Shangkun tongzhi zai zhongyang junwei jinji kuoda huiyishang de jianghua yaodian," in *Beijing junqu budui zhixing jieyan renwu zhong de zhengzhi gongzuo*, ser. 27, vol. 37 (n.p.: SCCP, 2009), 14–19.
40. "57 NPC Members Urge Meeting," FBIS, May 25, 1989.
41. Dai Qing, "Kaihui bi kaiqiang hao: Caifang Cao Siyuan" (unpublished manuscript, n.d.). Held by Dai Qing.
42. Zhang Ganghua, *Li Peng riji zhenxiang*, 240–42; Yang Jisheng, *Zhongguo gaige*, 412; "Wan Li to Undergo Treatment," FBIS, May 25, 1989; Cai Yongmei, "Wan Li," 245–46. In his memoirs, Li Peng incorrectly dated Wan's return to May 26, not May 25.
43. Zhang Wanshu, *Lishi de da baozha*, 288.
44. Chung Yen-lin, "Peng Zhen zai 1989 nian."
45. Zhang Ganghua, *Li Peng riji zhenxiang*, 235.
46. Chung Yen-lin, "Peng Zhen zai 1989 nian," 16–17; *Peng Zhen nianpu*, 5:448; *Liao Hansheng huiyilu* (Beijing: Jiefangjun, 2012), 665–66.
47. "Zhejiang Leaders Meet with Teachers, Students," FBIS, May 19, 1989; "Li Zemin Conducts Dialogue with Zhejiang Students," FBIS, May 3, 1989; Keith Forster, "The

Popular Protest in Hangzhou," in *The Pro-democracy Protests in China: Reports from the Provinces*, ed. Jonathan Unger (Armonk, NY: M. E. Sharpe, 1991), 166–85.

48. *Xi Zhongxun nianpu*, 4:148.
49. Zhang Ganghua, *Li Peng riji zhenxiang*, 227.
50. Ibid., 145, 265–66.
51. *Xi Zhongxun nianpu*, 4:148.
52. *Peng Zhen nianpu*, 5:447.
53. "NPC Party Group Voices Support," FBIS, May 30, 1989; "Wan Li Returns to Beijing," FBIS, May 31, 1989.
54. Li Musheng, "Ta," 66–74.
55. "Luoshi zhengce, pingfan yuanjia cuo'an de yi zu piyu," in *Hu Yaobang wenxuan 1975–1986*, vol. 1 (n.p.: Zhengqiu yijian gao, n.d.), 115; Zhu Jianguo, "Hu Yaobang qi bao 'Shekou zhenggai,'" in *Renmin xin zhong de Hu Yaobang*, ed. Su Shaozhi, Chen Yizi, and Gao Wenqian (Carle Place: Mingjing, 2006), 219–20.
56. *Xi Zhongxun nianpu*, 3:175.
57. Xi Zhongxun, "Nimen shi you lixiang you zhiqi de hao er'nü," *Liaowang*, no. 19 (Apr. 1985): 9–10.
58. *Xi Zhongxun nianpu*, 4:75.
59. Li Rui, diary (vol. 21, 1989), p. 52, HIA; Li Rui, diary (vol. 22, 1990), pp. 32–33, HIA.
60. Secretary of state to American Embassy in Beijing, cable, "Re: Secretary's Meeting with Wan Li," May 26, 1989, ID# CF01722-007, Bush Presidential Records, National Security Council, White House Situation Room Files, Tiananmen Square Crisis Files, China pt. 2 of 5 Tiananmen Square Crisis (1989) (2), George Bush Presidential Library.
61. Memorandum of conversation, "Meeting with Wan Li, Chairman of the Standing Committee of the National People's Congress and Member of the Politburo, People's Republic of China," Bush Memcon, George Bush Presidential Library.
62. Yao Jianfu, "Du Runsheng: Zaodian fangxia 'liu si' zhe ge baofu," *Xin shiji* 8 (June 2012): 84.
63. Xu Yiming, "Bawo hao xinwen gongzuo de jidian," *Zhongguo jizhe* (July 1989): 13.
64. Du Daozheng, *Zhao Ziyang hai shuoguo shenme? Du Daozheng riji* (Hong Kong: Tiandi, 2010), 77.
65. Torigian, "Prestige," 554–52, 559–61.
66. Zhao Ziyang, "San fang Zhao Ziyang," 13.
67. Interview; Cai, "Zhao Ziyang."
68. Cai, "Zhao Ziyang." For these points, I draw upon Bao Tong's comments about Wan Li's behavior.
69. Li Xiangqian, *Xi Zhongxun: Cong "luojiaodian" dao "kaifangquan"* (Beijing: Zhongyang wenxian, 2014), 62; "Shoudu juxing dahui jinian 'liu yi' jie," PD, June 2, 1989.
70. Yao Jianfu, *Chen Xitong qinshu* (Hong Kong: Xin shiji, 2012), 1–8, 28–29, 62.
71. Gongqingtuan Beijing shiwei, *70 tian dashiji: Hu Yaobang bingshi dao Zhao Ziyang jiezhi* (Beijing: Beijing chubanshe, 1990), 77.
72. Torigian, "Prestige," 570–78.
73. Zhou Fengsuo (former Tiananmen Square leader), in discussion with the author, Nov. 2023.
74. Ling Chai, *A Heart for Freedom* (Carol Stream, NY: Tyndale House, 2011), 166; Lu Li, *Moving the Mountain: My Life in China from the Cultural Revolution to Tiananmen Square* (London: Macmillan, 1990), 180.
75. Zhang Wanshu, *Lishi de da baozha*, 461.
76. "Li Peng Chairs Study Meeting," FBIS, June 14, 1989.

77. Jia Juchuan, "1962.10–2002.5," 24.
78. "15 wei fuweiyuanzhang weiwen zhixing jieyan renwu guanbing," *PD*, June 16, 1989.
79. Zhang Ganghua, *Li Peng riji zhenxiang*, 340–41.
80. "Xi Zhongxun, Others Speak," FBIS, July 4, 1989.
81. Lailailai qu zhijian, "1989 nian 6 yue 23 ri–24 ri, dangde shisanjie di sizhong quanhui zhaokai," YouTube, June 24, 2022, video, https://www.youtube.com/watch?v=qlJHTNPyaSM&ab_channel=%E6%9D%A5%E5%A4%B9%E6%9D%A5%E5%8E%BB%E4%B9%8B%E9%97%B4.
82. Zhang Ganghua, *Li Peng riji zhenxiang*, 349–51; Yang Jisheng, *Zhongguo gaige*, 447–48.
83. "Xi Zhongxun, Others Speak."
84. "Renda changwei tan qianming shijian yaoqiu chengli diaochazu chedi qingcha," *PD*, July 5, 1989.
85. *Hu Jiwei zishu*, 4:218–19, 4:236.
86. Lu Chaoqi, *Liu si neibu riji*, 224.
87. "Deng Resigns from Post," FBIS, Mar. 21, 1990.
88. Xi Zhongxun, "Wending shi guojia de zuigao liyi," in *Xi Zhongxun wenxuan* (Beijing: Zhongyang wenxian, 1995), 476.
89. *Hu Jiwei zishu*, 4:212.
90. Jiang Zemin, "Zai qijie quanguo renda sanci huiyi he quanguo zhengxie ji jie sanci huiyi dangnei fuzeren huishang de jianghua (jielu)," in *Renda gongzuo wenxian ziliao huibian*, ser. 38, vol. 182 (n.p.: SCCP, 2005), 56.
91. Zhongjiwei bangongting, ed., "Zhonggong zhongyang zhuanfa 'zhongyang zuzhibu guanyu zai bufen danwei jinxing dangyuan chongxin dengji gongzuo de yijian' de tongzhi," in *"Liu si" bennian jijian shiliao*, ser. 28, vol. 188 (n.p.: SCCP, 2009), 37–42.
92. Jia Juchuan, "1962.10–2002.5," 25.
93. Gao Ximin, "Zai zui weiji shike shuochu zui zhongken de hua: Zhuihuai he Xi Zhongxun xiansheng de yi xi tan (I)," *Zhongguo shibao*, Mar. 9, 2020.
94. Gao Ximin, "Zuihui guo daiyu yi tian dou buneng ting (II)," *Zhongguo shibao*, Mar. 10, 2020.
95. *Xi Zhongxun nianpu*, 4:188; "Fahui lao tongzhi zuoyong, cujin qingshaonian chengzhang, guanxin xia yidai weiyuanhui zai Jing chengli," *PD*, May 18, 1990.
96. Liu Mila, "Huainian Xi Zhongxun shushu," Zhonghong wang, Sept. 9, 2013, https://archive.ph/lGA4l.
97. Tie Liu, "Xi Jinping fuqin wenge bei pidou neimu," Kan niuyue, Mar. 22, 2019, https://www.kannewyork.com/culture/2019/03/22/60868.html.
98. Zhang Sutang and Sun Benyao, "Renda changweihui shiwuci huiyi juxing quanhui," *Guangming ribao*, Aug. 31, 1990.
99. Li Rui, diary (vol. 22, 1990), p. 67, HIA.
100. "Qian Qichen on Consular Privileges Draft," FBIS, Aug. 30, 1990.
101. Gao Kai, "Xi Zhongxun," 21–22; Li Rui, diary (vol. 22, 1990), p. 67, HIA.
102. Gao Kai, "Xi Zhongxun," 22; Yang Lin and Bu, "'Renzhe' Xi Zhongxun"; Li Rui, diary (vol. 22, 1990), p. 67, HIA.
103. Jia Juchuan, "1962.10–2002.5," 25.
104. "Leaders Pay Last Respects to Liu Jingfan," FBIS, Sept. 8, 1990.
105. Interview.
106. Yan Hongwei and Qiu, *Xi Zhongxun*, 28; Yang Lin and Bu, "'Renzhe' Xi Zhongxun"; *Zhang Guoying*, 238.
107. Li Rui, diary (vol. 22, 1990), p. 78, HIA.

Chapter 29: The Final Years

1. "Zhonggong zhongyang zuzhibu guanyu zhongyang jiguan yuan fubuzhang he sheng, shi, zizhi qu yuan fushengzhang yishang ganbu de shencha qingkuang (liushiyi ren) caogao," Feb. 1976, HCCPM; "Li Qiming tongzhi."
2. Ding Min, "Xi Zhongxun zai Luonai," 93.
3. Chen Sanjing, *Bashi wencun: Da shidai zhong de shijia yu shixue* (Taipei: Xiuwei zixun keji, 2017), 180; Chen Sanjing, *Tiaotiao mishi lu: Chuansuo liang'an mishi qunxiang* (Taipei: Duli zuojia, 2016), 146; *Chen Jianzhong*.
4. *Chen Jianzhong*; Li Yi, "Ta"; Chen Sanjing, *Tiaotiao mishi lu*, 146–47.
5. Chen Sanjing, *Tiaotiao mishi lu*, 146–47; *Chen Jianzhong*; Chen Jianzhong, *Huaipu suibi*, 49.
6. Chen Jianzhong, *Huaipu suibi*, 51.
7. Fang Shuwen, "Wo zhuisui Chen Jianzhong xiansheng de dalu zhi xing," in *Caihui rensheng bashinian: Chen Jianzhong xiansheng baqiu huadan wenji*, ed. Guo Zhe (self-pub., n.d.), 536.
8. Ma Jianli et al., *Haixia liang'an guanxi sishinian*, 429; Chen Sanjing, *Tiaotiao mishi lu*, 146–48; *Xi Zhongxun zhuan*, 2:557.
9. Fang Shuwen, "Wo," 538; *Chen Jianzhong*; Chen Jianzhong, *Huaipu suibi*, 53.
10. *Chen Jianzhong*.
11. Ibid.; Fang Shuwen, "Wo," 541.
12. *Chen Jianzhong*; Su Chi [Su Qi], *Liang'an botao ershinian jishi* (Taipei: Yuanjian tianxia wenhua, 2014), 20–30; Wei Chengsi, "Li Denghui shidai, liang'an jiu du mitan shilu," *Shangye zhoukan* 661 (July 24, 2000): 60–82; Lee Teng-hui, *Li Denghui zhizheng gaobai shilu* (Taipei: Yinshua, 2001), 180–81; interview.
13. Zhang Rongfeng, *Wu Yanxiao de zhanchang: Cong weiquan dao minzhu zhuanzhe de guo'an shouji* (Taipei: Dongmei, 2022), 246–47.
14. Ibid., 220.
15. Hau Pei-tsun, *Banian canmou zongzhang riji*, 2 vols. (Taipei: Commonwealth, 2000), 2:1476.
16. Interview with former high-ranking official involved in ethnic politics.
17. Li Rui, "Li Rui ping Xi: Mei xiangdao wenhua chengdu zheme di," VoA(C), Apr. 18, 2018.
18. Li Rui, diary (vols. 34–35, 2002), p. 47, HIA.
19. Jiang Shan et al., "Xi Zhongxun."
20. Interview.
21. *Zhang Guoying*, 27, 32, 39, 40, 43, 45, 80, 89, 96.
22. Seth Faison, "Power Balance Shifting with Casualty List," *SCMP*, Nov. 4, 1990.
23. "NPC's Xi Zhongxun Said Recovering from Stress," FBIS, Dec. 21, 1990.
24. Chris Yeung, "Rumours of Offsprings' Promotion Denied," *SCMP*, Aug. 9, 1991.
25. Yang Ping, "Xi jia."
26. Du Daozheng, *Yi ke pingchang xin*, 201.
27. Dai Qing (journalist and activist), in discussion with the author, Sept. 2023.
28. Interview with assistant of former official.
29. Interview with offspring of former high-ranking official.
30. "Liang Guangda pai Yang Shangkun mapi, shouyi ganzou Xi Zhongxun," *Waican* 8 (Aug. 2012); Mingjing huopai, "Xi Jinping fuzi Zhuhai Shenzhen enyuan, Gang-Zhu-Ao daqiao xian qiangguo qiang gongcheng," YouTube, Oct. 23, 2018, video, https://www.youtube.com/watch?v=bFhIeTeRk1s; "Jiang Attends Celebration Meeting," FBIS, Nov. 28, 1990; Li Rui, diary (vol. 30, 1998), p. 29, HIA. In an interview, the journalist Ho Pin emphasized that he learned this information from someone present during the incident, and he stated that the *Waican* article was written by this individ-

ual. Ren Zhongyi referred to the incident later during a conversation with Li Rui. Ho Pin, in discussion with the author, Oct. 2022.

31. Interview.
32. Li Rui, diary (vol. 22, 1990), p. 99, HIA.
33. Du Daozheng, *Zhao Ziyang*, 303.
34. Luo Yu (son of Luo Ruiqing), in discussion with the author, Feb. 2020.
35. Liu Mila, "Huainian Xi Zhongxun."
36. Kong Shujing, *Suiyue jiyi*, 159.
37. Li Rui, diary (vol. 26, 1994), p. 32, HIA.
38. Xi Jinping, "Lun wenyi yu zhengzhi de guanxi," *Caibei* 30 (Oct. 1989): 3–5.
39. Jiang Ping, "Guanyu Fujian sheng zongjiao gongzuo wenti de diaocha baogao," in *Minzu zongjiao wenti lunwenji* (Beijing: Zhonggong dangshi, 1995), 396–99.
40. Zhang Mingqing, "Ban hao yi jian shi, yingde wanren xin: Fujian Ningde diqu chacha ganbu weiji jian sifang jishi," *PD*, May 21, 1990.
41. Xi Jinping, "Wei guan zhi dao," *Lingdao kexue*, no. 9 (1990): 32.
42. Xi Jinping, "Kua shiji lingdao ganbu de lishi zhongren ji bibei suzhi," *Lilun xuexi yuekan*, no. 11 (1991): 32–36.
43. *Zhang Guoying*, 55, 257; Wu Songying, *Qinlizhe jishu: 1992 nian Deng Xiaoping nanxun neiqing* (Hong Kong: Mingbao, 2012), 185–94.
44. Sun, discussion.
45. Xi Zhongxun, introduction to *Gaige kaifang zai Guangdong: Xian zou yibu de shijian yu sikao*, ed. Lin Ruo (Guangzhou: Guangdong gaodeng jiaoyu, 1992), 4.
46. Willy Wo-lap Lam, "Fujian Cadres Face Dismissal for Reform Failures," *SCMP*, July 17, 1992; Li Feng, "Fujian Reformists Said Elected Congress Deputies," FBIS, July 16, 1992.
47. Gao Xin, "You ci yi shuo: Xi Jinping yin Xiangnan shi sida wei jin houbu zhongwei," RFA, May 17, 2017.
48. Xiang Nan, introduction to *Baituo pinkun*, by and ed. Xi Jinping (Fuzhou: Fujian renmin, 1992), 1–3.
49. Cheng Li, *Chinese Politics in the Xi Jinping Era: Reassessing Collective Leadership* (Washington, DC: Brookings Institution Press, 2016), 267–68.
50. Zhongguo xinwenshe, "Chicheng."
51. Xi Zhongxun, "Nanwang de jiaohui."
52. Arjia Rinpoche, discussion.
53. *Zhang Guoying*, 24.
54. Sun, discussion.
55. Du Daozheng, *Zhao Ziyang*, 319.
56. Interview.
57. Jiang Yanyong, "Yaoqiu wei liu si zhengming de shangshu," in *Zhao Ziyang yu Zhongguo gaige: Jinian Zhao Ziyang*, ed. Chen Yizi (Carle Place: Mingjing, 2005), 364.
58. Li Rui, diary (vol. 27, 1995), p. 10, HIA; Li Rui, diary (vol. 30, 1998), p. 29, HIA; *Zhang Guoying*, 27.
59. *Zhang Guoying*, 26.
60. Interview with former editor of Shenzhen newspaper.
61. Meng Xiangfeng, "Zuo you."
62. Minemura Kenji, *Zhanshang shisanyi ren de dingduan: Xi jinping zhangquan zhi lu* (Taipei: Lianjing, 2018), 218–19; Zong Hairen, *Di sidai* (Carle Place: Mingjing, 2005), 397; Cary Huang, "Princelings Shunned in Party Vote," *Hong Kong iMail*, Sept. 19, 1997.
63. Zhang Zhigong, *Nanwang de ershinian*, 216–17.
64. Li Rui, diary (vol. 30, 1998), p. 27, HIA; Li, discussion.
65. Qi Xin, "Yi Zhongxun," 758.

632   NOTES TO CHAPTERS 29 AND 30

66. Zhang Zhigong, *Nanwang de ershinian*, 217.
67. *Xi Zhongxun zhuan*, 2:654–55.
68. Jiang Wei, "Wo gei Li Zhao he Xi Zhongxun paile yizhang zhengui zhaopian," *Zhonghua ernü*, no. 4 (2008): 56–57.
69. *Zhang Guoying*, 25.
70. *Xi Zhongxun zhuan*, 2:658.
71. Luo Yu, *Gaobie zongcanmou bu* (Hong Kong: Open Books, 2015), 354; Luo, discussion.
72. Xi Zhongxun, "Xi Zhongxun tongzhi de yuandan zhuci," *Shenzhen shangbao*, Dec. 31, 1991.
73. *Xi Zhongxun zhuan*, 2:654.
74. Li Rui, diary (vol. 32, 2000), p. 2, HIA.
75. Interview with former *Yanhuang chunqiu* employee.
76. "Yanhuang chunqiu zazhishe jihui qingzhu chuangkan shizhounian," *Yanhuang chunqiu*, no. 8 (2001): 17.
77. Zhang Zhigong, *Nanwang de ershinian*, 254.
78. Ibid., 253.
79. *Zhang Guoying*, 270.
80. Jia Juchuan, "1962.10–2002.5," 40; Jia Juchuan, "'Luhuo chunqing' Xi Zhongxun," 40; "Wan Li zhi zi tan fuqin: Kanwang bingzhong Xi Zhongxun yu qi jidong yongbao," *PD*, Nov. 9, 2012; interview.
81. Qi xin, "Yi Zhongxun," 760.
82. Edwin Chan, "China's Fujian Governor Flushes over Rosy Future," Reuters, July 3, 2002.

Chapter 30: Fathers and Sons

1. Li Rui, "Li Rui ping Xi"; Li Rui, *Li Rui koushu wangshi*, 459; Li Rui, diary (vols. 34–35, 2002), p. 121, HIA.
2. Wang Jian, "Xi Jinping xiang he chu qu," *Yangguang shiwu zhoukan* 30 (Nov. 2012); Li Rui, diary (vol. 46, 2013), p. 28, HIA.
3. Li Rui, diary (vol. 45, 2012), pp. 4, 19, HIA.
4. Interview.
5. Chris Buckley, "China President-in-Waiting Signals Quicker Reform," Reuters, Sept. 7, 2012.
6. "Fu Xi Zhongxun shi Zhao Ziyang qinmi zhanyou," *Pingguo ribao*, Nov. 16, 2012.
7. Li Rui, diary (vol. 46, 2013), p. 8, HIA.
8. Lu Yue, "Renu gaoceng de 'Yanhuang chunqiu' xinchun lianyihui fayan," *Qianshao*, June 2013, 30–34.
9. Li Rui, diary (vol. 46, 2013), p. 16, HIA; Hu Dehua, "Hu Dehua zai 'Yanhuang chunqiu' juhui shi de fayan," NewCenturyNet, June 16, 2013, https://2newcenturynet.blogspot.com/2013/06/blog-post_16.html.
10. Li Rui, "Li Rui fangtanlu: Guanyu 'wode fuqin Li Rui' yi shu," interview, Oct. 2–3, 2014. Held by Li Nanyang.
11. Lu Yue, "Xi Jinping yu Li Rui," in *Jingji Li Rui*, ed. Li Nanyang (Hong Kong: Chuban gongfang, 2019), 357–59. The first character in the Chinese word for "deficiency" (*maobing*) is the same as that for Chairman Mao's surname. Alone, the second character in the word means "disease." The character for "habit" is the same as Xi's surname.
12. Li Rui, diary (vol. 50, 2017), p. 49, HIA.
13. Li Nanyang, "Li Rui juechang," 459, 464.
14. George W. Breslauer, "Counterfactual Reasoning in Western Studies of Soviet

Politics and Foreign Relations," in *Counterfactual Thought Experiments in World Politics: Logical, Methodological, and Psychological Perspectives*, ed. Philip E. Tetlock and Aaron Belkin (Princeton, NJ: Princeton University Press, 1996), 71–94; Howard W. French, "China's Foreclosed Possibilities," *NYRB*, Nov. 2, 2023.

15. Maya Jasanoff, "The Power of a Well-Told History," in *History and Human Flourishing*, ed. Darrin M. McMahon (New York: Oxford University Press, 2023), 73.

16. Arlette Farge, *The Allure of the Archives* (New Haven, CT: Yale University Press, 2013), 76.

17. Ronald Suny, *Red Flag Wounded* (Brooklyn, NY: Verso, 2020), 23.

18. Richard Ned Lebow and Janice Gross Stein, "Back to the Past: Counterfactuals and the Cuban Missile Crisis," in *Counterfactual Thought Experiments in World Politics: Logical, Methodological, and Psychological Perspectives*, ed. Philip E. Tetlock and Aaron Belkin (Princeton, NJ: Princeton University Press, 1996), 119–48.

19. Joseph Torigian, "A New Case for the Study of Individual Events in Political Science," *Global Studies Quarterly* 1, no. 4 (Dec. 2021): 1–11.

20. Hayden White, *Metahistory: The Historical Imagination in Nineteenth-Century Europe* (Baltimore: Johns Hopkins University Press, 2014).

21. Michel-Rolph Trouillot, *Silencing the Past: Power and the Production of History* (New York: Penguin Random House, 2015), 29.

22. Gao Wenqian, "Mao de wenge yichan," 414.

23. Li Rui, diary (vol. 37, 2004), p. 105, HIA.

24. Xi Zhengning, "Wanshan Hainan jingji tequ falü fuwu shichang de yanjiu," in *Hainan sheng lilun yantaohui lunwen ji*, ed. Ruan Chongwu (Haikou: Hainan, 1994), 514–24; Xi Zhengning, "Hainan fazhi xuanchuan jiaoyu gongzuo tantao," *Hainan sheng lilun yantaohui lunwen ji*, ed. Ruan Chongwu (Haikou: Hainan, 1994), 273–80.

25. "Zhongguo fazhi xin meiti changwu fuzhuren: Ma Baoshan jianjie, qi furen Xi Qianping," *Zhongguo fazhi*, Nov. 14, 2015; Hu Sisheng, *Gaoceng fangtanlu*, 53.

26. Cheng Min and Jian Jun, "Jinian fensui 'Sirenbang' 35 zhounian zuotan zongshu," *Yanhuang chunqiu*, no. 11 (2011): 1.

27. Jiang Xun, "Xi Jinping jiejie liting gaige pai," *Yazhou zhoukan*, Mar. 23, 2014, 30.

28. Qi Qiaoqiao, "Fangqi chuguo liuxue."

29. "Xi Jinping Millionaire Relations Reveal Elite Chinese Fortunes," Bloomberg, June 29, 2012; Cheng Ming [Gao Yu], "Chengqing Xi Jinping jiazu de caifu chuanwen," *Mingjing (waican)*, July 13, 2012.

30. Qi Qiaoqiao, "Fangqi chuguo liuxue."

31. "Guanyuan fangchan: Didiao de linglei yingxiao," *Chenggong yingxiao*, Oct. 18, 2006, http://news.ppzw.com/Article_Print_73317.html.

32. Forsythe et al., "Xi Jinping."

33. Michael Forsythe, "Billionaire at the Intersection of China's Business and Power," *NYT*, Apr. 29, 2015; Michael Forsythe, "Chinese Tycoon Defends Xi's Relatives, and Himself, on Business Deal," *NYT*, Oct. 31, 2015.

34. Xi Yuanping, "Wode fubei."

35. "Portrait."

36. Li Rui, diary (vol. 32, 2000), p. 87, HIA.

37. Xi Jinping, "Gei baba."

38. Zhou Zhixing, "Bo Xilai xiao congming zhizao de da wenti," *Financial Times*, Aug. 30, 2013, China edition, http://www.ftchinese.com/story/001052270?full=y.

39. Tao Siliang, "Xiangfeng yi xiao zai Meizhou," *Aisixiang*, July 27, 2021, http://www.aisixiang.com/data/127740.html.

40. Gao Yu, *Nan'er Xi Jinping: Dui Zhongguo quangui de dongchali* (Deer Park, NY: Mingjing, 2015), 148; Li Rui, diary (vol. 46, 2013), p. 18, HIA.

41. Gao Xin, "Xu Yongyue huiyi zhong de Deng Chen gongdou mixin," RFA, Feb. 26, 2021; Xu Yongyue, "Yuan Chen Yun mishu Xu Yongyue: Wannian Chen Yun yu Deng Xiaoping," *Bainianchao*, no. 3 (2006): 17.

42. Tang Luo, "Mao Zedong," 21; Xi Qianping, "Bo Yibo tan 'luhuo chunqing' yu '*Liu Zhidan* xiaoshuo yuan'an' neimu," in *Huainian Xi Zhongxun*, ed. Cao Zhenzhong and Wu Jiang (Beijing: Zhongyang dangshi, 2005), 433–41.

43. Zhao Yinping, "Shibada yilai, Xi Jinping zheyang tan 'jiafeng,'" Xinhua, Mar. 29, 2017; "Xi Jinping tan jiafeng jianshe," *PD*, July 22, 2020, overseas edition.

44. Ma Ying-jeou and Xiao, *Banian zhizheng huiyilu*, 371.

45. Abe Shinzo and Kitamura Shigeru, *Abe Shinzo kaikoroku* (Tokyo: Chuo Koron Shinsha, 2023), 187.

46. Xi Jinping, "Zengqiang youhuan yishi, weiji yishi, shiming yishi," in *Xi Jinping guanyu guofang he jundui jianshe zhongyao lunshu xuanbian* (Beijing: Jiefangjun, 2014), 50–52.

47. Chen Peng, "Qinfen, zhencheng, tanran, jinze: Xi Jinping tan zuoguan yu zuoren," *Shidai chao*, no. 8 (2000): 34.

48. Xu Youyu, *Xingxing sese de zaofan: Hongweibing jingshen suzhi de xingcheng ji yanbian* (Hong Kong: Zhongwen daxue chubanshe, 1999), 236.

49. Zhu Jiamu, "Shenke renshi dangde di sange lishi jueyi de shidai tese," *Makesi zhuyi yanjiu*, no. 1 (2022): 29–30.

50. "Highlights of Xi's Speech at a Conference Celebrating 40 Years of Reform, Opening-Up," *China Daily*, Dec. 18, 2018.

51. Joseph Torigian, "Xi Jinping and Ideology," *Wilson China Fellowship Essays on China and US Policy*, no. 22 (2021): 308–38.

52. Zhu Jiamu, "Zai tan guoshi fenqi wenti," *Dangdai Zhongguoshi yanjiu* 28, no. 2 (Mar. 2021): 9.

53. Interview.

54. Xi Jinping, "Zhong qingnian ganbu yao 'zun lao,'" *PD*, Dec. 7, 1984.

55. Xi Jinping, "Geng hao bawo he yunyong dangde bainian fendou lishi jingyan," *Qiushi*, June 30, 2022.

56. Xi Jinping, "Zai dangshi xuexi jiaoyu dongyuan dahuishang de jianghua," *Qiushi*, Mar. 31, 2021.

57. "Full Text: Resolution of the CPC Central Committee on the Major Achievements and Historical Experience of the Party over the Past Century," Xinhua, Nov. 16, 2021.

58. Xi Jinping, "Jicheng he fayang dangde youliang geming chuantong he zuofeng," *Qiushi*, Dec. 16, 2022.

59. Xi Jinping, "Jianchi he fazhan Zhongguo tese shehui zhuyi yao yi yi guan zhi," *Qiushi*, Sept. 15, 2022.

Bibliography

Chinese Sources

A Ji. "Lishi de xuanze: Renda 50 nian (xupian yi) (I)." *Zhengfu fazhi* 9 (2004): 14–21, 31.
An Zhiwen. "An Zhiwen tan Zhao Ziyang he Zhongguo gaige." In *Zhongguo dangdai mingren zhengyao fang shuping ji*, edited by Yang Jisheng, 36–52. Hong Kong: Tiandi tushu, 2013.
"Ba fangeming xiuzhengzhuyi fenzi Xi Zhongxun pidao douchou." *Renmin jiaoda*, no. 70 (Aug. 1967).
"Ba hongqi gaoju daodi: Xi Zhongxun tongzhi tan qingnian yao buduan jinxing sixiang geming." *Anhui jiaoyu*, no. Z1 (Aug.–Sept. 1958): 16–17.
Bai Bingshu. "1942 nian zhengfeng pianduan." In *Zhengrong suiyue*, 350–70. Xi'an: Shaanxi renmin, 2011.
Bai Lei. "Xi'an 'qishisan hao' jishi." *Yanhuang chunqiu*, no. 7 (2015): 69–73.
Bai Lei. "Xi'an zaofanpai de qingqi yu fenhua." In *Zhonghua xueren wenge lunwenji*, edited by Qi Zhi, 301–18. Vol. 3. Austin, TX: Meiguo huayi, 2019.
Bao Tong. "Wo kan Hu Zhao guanxi." In *Bao Tong wenji*, 407–27. Hong Kong: Xin shiji, 2012.
Bei Ling and Yu Caiqian. *Hongse guizu*. Beijing: Hongqi, 1993.
Bi Ping. *Liang Xiang: Zhuazhu laoshu bu shi hao mao*. Hong Kong: Gonghe, 2007.
Bi Ruxie. "Songren Xi Jinping." *CND kanwu he luntan*, Dec. 29, 2022. http://hx.cnd.org/2022/12/29/%E6%AF%95%E6%B1%9D%E8%B0%90%E6%80%82%E4%BA%BA%E4%B9%A0%E8%BF%91%E5%B9%B3/.
Bian Tiejian. "Jundui waiyu, jishu rencai de yaolan." In *Yuanxiao: Huiyi shiliao*, 727–35. Beijing: Jiefangjun, 1995.
Bo Yibo. *Ruogan zhongda juece yu shijian de huigu*. 2 vols. Beijing: Zhonggong zhongyang dangxiao, 1993.
Bu Weihua. *"Zalan jiu shijie": Wenhua dageming de dongluan yu haojie*. Hong Kong: Chinese University Press, 2009.
Cai Liezhou. "Xi Zhongxun yu Xirao Jiacuo dashi." In *Xi Zhongxun jinian wenji*, edited by Zhonggong zhongyang dangshi yanjiuhui, 464–66. Beijing: Zhonggong dangshi, 2013.

635

Cai Wenbin, ed. "Zhao Ziyang zai Beijing shinian (1980–1989): Bao Tong fangtanlu." Unpublished manuscript, n.d.
Cai Yongmei, ed. "Wan Li tongzhi zai Zhonggong zhongyang zhengzhiju kuoda huiyishang de fayan." In *Zuihou de mimi: Zhonggong shisanjie sizhong quanhui "liu si" jielun wendang*, 243–49. Hong Kong: Xin shiji, 2019.
Cai Ziwei. "Nanliang genjudi geming douzheng pianduan huiyi." In *Nanliang shuguang*, edited by Li Guo, 52–66. Lanzhou: Gansu renmin, 1983.
Cao Xin. "Xi Zhongxun: Ta yi beizi meiyou zhengguo ren." *Baokan huicui*, no. 6 (2009): 80–81.
Cao Zhenzhong. "Shenqing huainian Xi Zhongxun tongzhi: Jijian wangshi de zhuiyi." *Zongheng*, no. 7 (2011): 13–16.
Chang Lifu. "Geming de yi sheng, zhandou de yi sheng." In *Zhang Desheng*, edited by Zhonggong Shaanxi shengxie dangshi yanjiushi, 94–135. Xi'an: Shaanxi renmin, 1996.
Che Minghuai. "Xi Zhongxun guanxin Xizang geming he jianshe shiye." *Bainianchao*, no. 8 (2016): 17–25.
Chen Bing'an. *Da tao gang*. Guangdong: Guangdong renmin, 2010.
Chen Chusan. *Renjian zhong wan qing: Yige suowei "hong er dai" de rensheng guiji*. Deer Park, NY: Mingjing, 2017.
Chen Feng. *Dao tianhuo de shiren: Ke Zhongping pingzhuan*. Xi'an: Shaanxi renmin, 1992.
Chen Huiying. "Tingting yuhe yi fangxin." *Jiating*, no. 6 (1989): 4–6.
Chen Jianzhong. *Huaipu suibi*. Self-published, n.d.
Chen Jianzhong xiansheng koushu lishi fangwen dagang. Self-published, n.d.
Chen Peng. "Qinfen, zhencheng, tanran, jinze: Xi Jinping tan zuoguan yu zuoren." *Shidai chao*, no. 8 (2000): 34–35.
Chen Qiuying. "Shizhang ningju taoliqing." In *Wo xinzhong de Bayi*, edited by Li Heshun, 231–33. Beijing: Tuanjie, 2007.
Chen Sanjing. *Bashi wencun: Da shidai zhong de shijia yu shixue*. Taipei: Xiuwei zixun keji, 2017.
Chen Sanjing. *Tiaotiao mishi lu: Chuansuo liang'an mishi qunxiang*. Taipei: Duli zuojia, 2016.
Chen Tongwei and Qin Zhi. *Qingxi Tianshan: Dang he guojia lingdaoren zai Xinjiang*. Beijing: Zhonggong dangshi, 1995.
Chen Weiren. *Tang Dacheng: Wentan fengyu wushinian*. Carle Place: Mingjing, 2007.
Chen Wuguo. *Wang Enmao zhuan*. Beijing: Zhongguo wenshi, 2014.
Chen Wuguo and Liu Xianghui. *Xinjiang wangshi*. Beijing: Dangdai Zhongguo, 2006.
Chen Yizi huiyilu. Hong Kong: Xin shiji, 2013.
Chen Yongfa. *Yan'an de yinying*. Taipei: Zhongyang yanjiuyuan jindaishi yanjiusuo, 1990.
Chen Yun. "Diaocha yanjiu he dangnei minzhu shenghuo zhidu wenti." In *Chen Yun wenxuan*, 358–59. Vol. 3. Beijing: Renmin, 1995.
Cheng Guanjun. "Xi Zhongxun weihe zai 1978 nian zhongyang gongzuo huiyishang bei zanyang." *Tongzhou gongjin*, no. 6 (2016): 29–31.
Cheng Kai. "He Pin zhuanfang Cheng Kai." In *Xi Jinping jiazu yu Chuanpu maoyizhan*, edited by Ho Pin, 13–94. Deer Park, NY: Mingjing, 2018.
Cheng Min, ed. *Dangnei dajian*. Beijing: Tuanjie, 1993.
Cheng Min and Jian Jun. "Jinian fensui 'Sirenbang' 35 zhounian zuotan zongshu." *Yanhuang chunqiu*, no. 11 (2011): 1–7.
Cheng Ming [Gao Yu]. "Chengqing Xi Jinping jiazu de caifu chuanwen." *Mingjing (waican)*, July 13, 2012.
Choubei weiyuanhui bangongshi. *Fuping xian Licheng zhongxue jianshi (zhengqiu yijian gao)*. N.p.: n.p., 1985.

Chung Yen-lin. "Deng Xiaoping zai 'Gao-Rao shijian' zhong zhi juese yu zuowei." *Renwen ji shehui kexue jikan* 22, no. 12 (2012): 521–62.
Chung Yen-lin. "1962 nian Xi Zhongxun wenti ji qi xiangguan zhengzhi yingxiang." Unpublished manuscript, n.d.
Chung Yen-lin. "Peng Zhen he Zhonggong Dongbeiju zhenglun." *Zhongyang yanjiusuo jindaishi yanjiusuo jikan*, no. 3 (2016): 99–151.
Chung Yen-lin. "Peng Zhen zai 1989 nian Zhonggong 'Tiananmen shijian' zhong de juese he huodong." *Zhongguo dalu yanjiu* 62, no. 1 (Mar. 2019): 1–20.
Chung Yen-lin. "Peng Zhen zai 1959 nian Zhonggong 'fan youqing' yundong zhong de juese he zuowei." *Zhongguo dalu yanjiu* 57, no. 1 (Mar. 2014): 97–125.
Chung Yen-lin. "Peng Zhen zai Zhonggong Yan'an zhengfeng yundong zhong de juese he huodong." *Guoli Zhengzhi daxue lishi xuebao* 49 (May 2018): 39–92.
Chung Yen-lin. *Wenge qian de Deng Xiaoping: Mao Zedong de "fushuai," 1956–1966*. Hong Kong: Chinese University Press, 2013.
Chung Yen-lin. "Zhonggong jianzheng hou Zhou Enlai yu Deng Xiaoping guanxi zhi yanjiu (1949–1976)." *Guoli zhengzhi daxue lishi xuebao* 32 (Nov. 2009): 169–220.
Cui Wunian. *Wode 83ge yue*. Hong Kong: Gaowen, 2003.
Dai Maolin and Zhao Xiaoguang. *Gao Gang zhuan*. Xi'an: Shaanxi renmin, 2011.
Dai Qing. "Kaihui bi kaiqiang hao: Caifang Cao Siyuan." Unpublished manuscript, n.d. Held by Dai Qing.
Dai Qing. "Wode 1989." *Xin shiji* 27 (2015).
Dai Yannian and Chen Rinong. *Zhongguo waiwenju wushinian dashiji*. Beijing: Xinxing, 1999.
Dai Yugang. *Qi jia kangzhan*. Hefei: Huangshan shushe, 2015.
Dangdai Zhongguo de minzu gongzuo. 2 vols. Beijing: Dangdai Zhongguo, 1993.
"Daoshi yu jiyao mishu." *Boke tianxia* 34 (2013).
Dawamaiti Tiemu'er. *Shengming zhi yuan jicui*. Beijing: Minzu, 2009.
Deng Lifeng. *Jianguo hou junshi xingdong quanlu*. Taiyuan: Shanxi renmin, 1992.
Deng Liqun. "Deng Liqun chuanda dangde shierjie erzhong quanhui jingshen." In *Deng Liqun wenji*, 302–40. Vol. 2. Beijing: Dangdai Zhongguo, 1998.
Deng Liqun. *Deng Liqun guoshi jiangtanlu*. 7 vols. Beijing: Zhonghua renmin gongheguo shigao bianweihui, 2000 (internal circulation).
Deng Liqun. *Deng Liqun zishu: Shierge chunqiu (1975–1987)*. Hong Kong: Dafeng, 2006.
Deng Liqun. "Guanyu qingchu jingshen wuran de ruogan zhengce jiexian." In *Deng Liqun wenji*, 348–73. Vol. 2. Beijing: Dangdai Zhongguo, 1998.
Deng Rong. "Xi Zhongxun zai Guanzhong tequ de tongzhan gongzuo chutan." *Keji xinxi*, Feb. 2013, 78.
Deng Xiaoping. "Disandai lingdao jiti de dangwu zhi ji." In *Deng Xiaoping wenxuan*, 309–14. Vol. 3. Beijing: Renmin, 1994.
Deng Xiaoping. "Gaoji ganbu yao daitou fayang dangde youliang chuantong." In *Deng Xiaoping wenxuan*, 215–30. Vol. 2. Beijing: Renmin, 1994.
Deng Xiaoping. "Guanyu sixiang zhanxianshang de wenti de tanhua." In *Deng Xiaoping wenxuan*, 389–90. Vol. 2. Beijing: Renmin, 1994.
Deng Xiaoping. Speech. [In Chinese.] Mar. 19, 1980.
Deng Xiaoping. "Tong Banchan E'erdeni de tanhua." In *Xizang gongzuo wenxian xuanbian 1949–2005 nian*, edited by Zhonggong zhongyang wenxian yanjiushi and Zhonggong Xizang zizhiqu weiyuanhui, 318–19. Beijing: Zhongyang wenxian, 2005.
Deng Xiaoping. "Zhongguo buyunxu luan." In *Deng Xiaoping wenxuan*, 286–87. Vol. 3. Beijing: Renmin, 1994.
Deng Xiaoping. "Zhongguo dalu he Taiwan heping tongyi de shexiang." In *Deng Xiaoping wenxuan*, 30–31. Vol. 3. Beijing: Renmin, 1994.

Deng Xiaoping nianpu (1904–1974). 3 vols. Beijing: Zhongyang wenxian, 2009.
Deng Xiaoping nianpu (1975–1997). 3 vols. Beijing: Zhongyang wenxian, 2004.
Deng Xiaoping, Xi Zhongxun, and Li Weihan. "Guanyu shenpi Xinjiang minzu quyu zizhi shishi jihua cao'an de liangfen baogao." In *Xinjiang gongzuo wenxian xuanbian 1949–2010*, edited by Zhonggong zhongyang wenxian yanjiushi and Zhonggong Xinjiang Weiwuer zizhiqu weiyuanhui, 97–101. Beijing: Zhongyang wenxian, 2010.
Diao Jiecheng. *Zhou Enlai yu xinfang gongzuo*. Beijing: Renmin, 2014.
"Dijiuci quanguo tongzhan gongzuo huiyi gaikuang." In *Lici quanguo tongzhan gongzuo huiyi gaikuang he wenxian*, 362–66. Beijing: Dang'an, 1988 (internal circulation).
Ding Dong and Xing Xiaoqun. *Bashi niandai Zhongguo zhenggai yaozhe neimu*. Hong Kong: Dashan wenhua, 2015.
Ding Min. "Xi Zhongxun zai Luonai." *Luoyang wenshi ziliao*, no. 32 (2012): 85–106 (internal circulation).
"Dishierci quanguo tongzhan gongzuo huiyi gaikuang." In *Lici quanguo tongzhan gongzuo huiyi gaikuang he wenxian*, 389–94. Beijing: Dang'an, 1988 (internal circulation).
"Dishisanci quanguo tongzhan gongzuo huiyi gaikuang." In *Lici quanguo tongzhan gongzuo huiyi gaikuang he wenxian*, 421–24. Beijing: Dang'an, 1988 (internal circulation).
"Dishisici quanguo tongzhan gongzuo huiyi gaikuang." In *Lici quanguo tongzhan gongzuo huiyi gaikuang he wenxian*, 436–40. Beijing: Dang'an, 1988 (internal circulation).
"Dishisiliu quanguo tongzhan gongzuo huiyi gaikuang." In *Lici quanguo tongzhan gongzuo huiyi gaikuang he wenxian*, 495–502. Beijing: Dang'an, 1988 (internal circulation).
"Dishiwuci quanguo tongzhan gongzuo huiyi gaikuang." In *Lici quanguo tongzhan gongzuo huiyi gaikuang he wenxian*, 465–70. Beijing: Dang'an, 1988 (internal circulation).
"Disici quanguo tongzhan gongzuo huiyi gaikuang." In *Lici quanguo tongzhan gongzuo huiyi gaikuang he wenxian*, 122–30. Beijing: Dang'an, 1988 (internal circulation).
Dong Cunfa. "'Liu Zhidan' yinqi de zhengzhi fengbo." In *Dangnei dajian*, edited by Cheng Min, 233–37. Beijing: Tuanjie, 1993.
Dong Zhaohe. "Rensheng de biaogan." In *Gongpu fengfan: Jinian Song Hanliang tongzhi wenji*, edited by Zhonggong Xinjiang Weiwuer zizhiqu weiyuanhui dangshi yanjiushi, 105–18. Beijing: Zhongyang wenxian, 2014.
Du Daozheng. *Yi ke pingchang xin*. Hong Kong: Yanhuang wenhua chanye, 2009.
Du Daozheng. *Zhao Ziyang hai shuoguo shenme? Du Daozheng riji*. Hong Kong: Tiandi, 2010.
Du Guang. "Zhongyang gaoji dangxiao fanyoupai neimu." *Yanhuang chunqiu*, no. 9 (2005): 1–8.
Du Lijun [Du Heng]. "Shaanxi daibiao Du Lijun baogao." In *Gansu dangshi ziliao*, edited by Zhonggong Gansu shengwei dangshi ziliao zhengji yanjiu weiyuan hui, 77–81. Vol. 3. Lanzhou: Gansu renmin, 1986.
Du Lirong. "Gao Yang yu Hebei 'fengping langjing' zhengzhi jumian de xingcheng." *Dangshi bocai*, no. 12 (2018): 10–13.
Du Lirong. "Guxi zhi nian tiao zhongdan: Hebei sheng zhengxie yuanfuzhuxi Han Licheng tan Gao Yang." *Lingdao zhi you*, no. 7 (2013): 48–51.
Du Ruizhi. "Guangdong nongcun gaige de jianxing lu: Du Ruizhi fangtanlu." In *Guangdong gaige kaifang juecezhe fangtanlu*, edited by Zhonggong Guangdong shengwei dangshi yanjiushi, 270–90. Guangzhou: Guangdong renmin, 2008.
Du Shu'an. "Zongjie jingyan, tigao renshi." *Xizang geming huiyilu* 3 (1984): 259–68.
Duan Weishao. "Xi Zhongxun yu Yang Hucheng mishu Tian Pingxuan de xiongdi qingyi." *Wenshi tiandi*, no. 2 (2013): 13–17.
Duan Yun. "Gang'Ao jingji suo jian." In *Duan Yun xuanji*. Taiyuan: Shanxi renmin, 1987, 349–62.

Etuoke qi zhi. Hohhot: Nei Menggu renmin, 1993.
Fan Ming. *Ba wuxing hongqi gaogao di chazai Ximalaya shan shang: Husong shi shi Banchan dashi fan Zang jishi*. Haikou: Nanhai, 2016.
Fan Ming and Hao Rui. *Xizang neibu zhizheng*. Carle Place: Mingjing, 2009.
Fan Ming huiyilu. 3 vols. Hong Kong: Xin shiji, 2021.
Fan Ruoyu. *Zai Zhou Enlai shenbian de rizi li*. Nanjing: Jiangsu renmin, 1984.
Fan Ziju. *Sun Dingguo zhuan*. Beijing: Zhongguo wenlian, 1999.
Fang Bao. "Gaige kaifang yi jiefang sixiang wei xiandao: Fang Bao fangtanlu." In *Guangdong gaige kaifang juecezhe fangtanlu*, edited by Zhonggong Guangdong shengwei dangshi yanjiushi, 434–73. Guangzhou: Guangdong renmin, 2008.
Fang Bao. "Wei qunzhong banshi, bu yao pa cuo, you xie shiqing zuocuole, yao ganyu chengdan zeren le." In *Caifang shilu: Xi Zhongxun zai Guangdong de gushi*, edited by Yan Hongwei and Qiu Ran, 79–116. Hong Kong: Xianggang zhonghe, 2016.
Fang Shuwen. "Wo zhuisui Chen Jianzhong xiansheng de dalu zhi xing." In *Caihui rensheng bashinian: Chen Jianzhong xiansheng baqiu huadan wenji*, edited by Guo Zhe, 536–41. Self-published, n.d.
Fang Xiaochun. *Zhongguo daxingzhengqu: 1949–1954 nian*. Shanghai: Dongfang, 2011.
Fei Jianxian. "Jianguo chuqi xianwei renzhi de Qinghai pingpan." *Zhongshan fengyu* (Apr. 2014): 7–9.
Feng Hui and Pang Xianzhi, eds. *Mao Zedong nianpu 1949–1976*. 6 vols. Beijing: Zhongyang wenxian, 2013.
Feng Shou. *Wang Zhen he women*. Urumqi: Xinjiang renmin, 2008.
Feng Zushun. "Qingxi muxiao." In *Zhengrong suiyue: Huiyilu*, 163–75. N.p.: Shaanxi sheng Suide shifan xuexiao, 1993.
Fu Canglong. "Liu-Deng hei silingbu baopi xia baobi xia de Xi Zhongxun fandang jituan cehua de youyi fangeming shijian." In *Xiang wenyi heixian menglie kaihuo*, 234–46. Tianjin: Nankai daxue weidong hongweibing weidong bianjibu, 1968.
Fu Xipeng. "Aoxiang ba, zhankai ni gesheng de chibang." *Hai'ou* 12 (1984): 43–48.
Fujian boshi fengcai. Fuzhou: Haichao sheying yishu, 2003.
Gao Bulin. "Jiefang zhangzheng houqi zai Guomindang Hu Zongnan zongbu jianli qingbao guanxi de qingkuang." In *Shaan-Gan-Ning bianqu zhengfu bao'anchu nan xian qingbao gongzuo shiliao xuanbian*, edited by Zhonggong Shaanxi shengwei dangshi yanjiushi and Shaanxi sheng gong'anting, 253–57. Ser. 35, vol. 45. N.p.: SCCP, 2012.
Gao Feng. "Ruidian shemindang de ziwo gaige zhi lu." *Tongzhou gongjin*, no. 3 (2011): 32–34.
Gao Fuyou and Gao Ying. *Gonghe guo yuanxun yishi: guowuyuan jiguan shiwu guanliju yuan changwu fuzhang Gao Fuyou huiyilu*. Beijing: Zhongyang wenxian, 2013.
Gao Gang. "Gao Gang, Zhou Xing zhi Xi Zhongxun, Shi Zhe dian." In *Gao Gang tongzhi: Shuxin dianwen xuanji*, edited by Xue Junfu and An Mingwen. Beijing: Huaxia wenhua yishu, [2013].
Gao Gang. "Xiao Jingguang, Gao Gang, Gao Zili gei Guanzhong fenqu Xi Zhongxun Zhang Zhongliang dian." In *Gao Gang tongzhi: Shuxin dianwen xuanji*, edited by Xue Junfu and An Mingwen. Beijing: Huaxia wenhua yishu, 2013.
Gao Gang. "Zai lishi zuotan huishang de jianghua." In *Gao Gang wenji*, edited by Xue Junfu and Bai Haoting. Beijing: Huaxia wenhua yishu, 2013.
Gao Kai. "Xi Zhongxun jianyi zhiding 'butong yijian baohufa.'" *Yanhuang chunqiu*, no. 12 (2013): 18–22.
Gao Putang and Zeng Luping. *Yan'an qiangjiu yundong shimo: 200 ge qinlizhe jiyi*. Hong Kong: Shidai guoji, 2008.
Gao Wen. *Nanliang shihua*. Lanzhou: Gansu renmin, 1984.
Gao Wenqian. "Mao de wenge yichan yu Xi Jinping zhiguo moshi." In *Wenge wushinian*:

Mao Zedong yichan he dangdai Zhongguo, edited by Song Yongyi, 406–24. Vol. 2. Deer Park, NY: Mingjing, 2016.

Gao Yong. "Conglai lishi fei qinding, ziyou shi jian yan weizhen." *Hu Yaobang shiliao xinxi wang*, Mar. 25, 2009. https://web.archive.org/web/20201103090526.

Gao Yu. "He Jiadong yu qijin wei liao de xiaoshuo '*Liu Zhidan*' yuan'an." In *Siren yi shi jingshen yongcun: He Jiadong jinian wenji*, edited by Chen Ziming and Bi Yimin, 82–91. Self-published, Shidai wenxian, 2012.

Gao Yu. *Nan'er Xi Jinping: Dui Zhongguo quangui de dongchali*. Deer Park, NY: Mingjing, 2015.

"Geming yisheng, fendou yisheng, guangrong yisheng: Jinian yeye shishi 40 zhounian." Unpublished manuscript, 2020.

Gongqingtuan Beijing shiwei. *70 tian dashiji: Hu Yaobang bingshi dao Zhao Ziyang jiezhi*. Beijing: Beijing chubanshe, 1990.

Gu Jiaji. "Aile shengzhong de zhengbian nao." In *Hongzhao yizong*, edited by Luo Guibo, Han Nianlong, and Gong Dafei, 162–75. Nanjing: Jiangsu renmin, 1995.

Gu Mu. "Guanyu zhixing 'Zhonggong zhongyang, guowuyuan pizhuan Guangdong shengwei, Fujian shengwei guanyu duiwai jingji huodong shixing teshu zhengce he linghuo cuoshi de liangge baogao' de ruogan wenti." In *Zhongyang dui Guangdong gongzuo zhishi huibian (1979 nian–1982 nian)*, 41–49. Ser. 28, vol. 40. N.p.: SCCP, 2007.

Gu Xiang. *Wannian Zhou Yang*. Beijing: Wenhui, 2003.

Gu Xiang. "Zhou Yang yu qingchu jingshen wuran." *Yanhuang chunqiu*, no. 10 (2013): 33–37.

Guan Shan. "Ren Zhongyi tan Deng Xiaoping yu Guangdong de gaige kaifang." *Yanhuang chunqiu*, no. 8 (2008): 8–17.

"Guanyu Dalai jinnian bupairen huiguo ji women de chuli yijian." Unpublished manuscript, July 3, 1986. Held by this author.

"Guanyu quanguo tongzhan buzhang zuotanhui qingkuang de baogao." In *Lici quanguo tongzhan gongzuo huiyi gaikuang he wenxian*, 520–28. Beijing: Dang'an, 1988 (internal circulation).

Guanyu Xibei hongjun zhanzheng lishi zhong de jige wenti. Dangshi tongxun, no. 8 (1986): 3–4.

Guo Dehong and Lin Xiaobo. *Siqing yundong shilu*. Hangzhou: Zhejiang renmin, 2005.

Guo Dexun. "Mao Zedong: Ba 'Hajun gong' jianshe cheng dierge Huangpu junxiao." *Dangshi bolan*, no. 4 (2006): 14–17.

Guo Hongtao. "Dierci guonei geming zhanzheng shiqi Shaan-bei geming douzheng shishi huiyi." *Shaanxi wenshi ziliao* 12 (1981): 1–26.

Guo Hongtao. "Shaan-bei fenghuo." *Geming shi ziliao*, no. 5 (1981): 40–69.

Guo Hongtao huiyilu. Beijing: Zhongyang dangshi, 2004.

Guo Zengyi. "Shenqie mianhuai Liu Linpu lieshi." In *Guanghui de qingchun: Liu Linpu jinian wenji*, edited by Guo Jianmin and Guo Zengyi, 167–76. Tongchuan: Tongchuan shi xinqu zuojia xiehui, 2010.

Guo Zhengqing and Guo Xiaomei. *Ya Hanzhang zhuan*. Lanzhou: Gansu renmin, 2016.

Guojia minzu shiwu weiyuanhui and Zhonggong zhongyang wenxian yanjiushi, eds. "Gaohao minzu guanxi, jiaqiang minzu tuanjie: Zhaizi Zhonggong zhongyang zhuanfa de 'zhongyang shujichu taolun Xinjiang gongzuo wenti de jiyao.'" In *Xin shiqi minzu gongzuo wenxian xuanbian*, 147–49. Beijing: Zhongyang wenxian, 1990.

Han Gang. "Guanyu Hua Guofeng de ruogan shishi." *Yanhuang chunqiu*, no. 2 (2011): 9–18.

Han Gang. "Jiannan de zhuanxing: Yijiuqiba nian zhongyang gongzuo huiyi de nongye yiti." *Zhonggong dangshi yanjiu*, no. 9 (2011): 21–28.

Han Gang. "Xiaoshuo 'Liu Zhidan' anjian yu Zhongguo zhengzhi de zouxiang." In *Jinian Liu Jingfan tongzhi danchen 100 zhounian zuotanhui ziliao huibian*, edited by Liu Mila, 55–57. Self-published, Beijing shidai nongchao wenhua fazhan, 2011.

Han Gang. "Zhonggong lishi yanjiu de ruogan nandian redian wenti zhi 'Gao-Rao shijian' wenti." In *Gao Gang shijian kaobian*, edited by Yang Haofu, 183–86. Beijing: Dazhong wenyi, 2011.

Han Xueben. "Ji 1949 nian yiqian de Lin Disheng tongzhi." In *Jinian Lin Disheng wenji*, 360–89. Lanzhou: Lanzhou daxue chubanshe, 2007.

Hao Huaiming. *Gaige kaifang zai Zhongnanhai*. Vol. 1. Hong Kong: Xianggang xinhua, 2018.

Hao Ping. "Yi sheng xinshou 'shemi wuguo, qinjian xingbang.'" In *Xi Zhongxun jinian wenji*, edited by Zhonggong zhongyang dangshi yanjiushi, 761–66. Beijing: Zhonggong dangshi, 2013.

Hao Ting and Zhang Zhong'e. *Wenhua dageming zhong de zhongyang diaochabu*. N.p.: 2013 (internal circulation).

Hao Tingzao. "Zhunzhun zhutuo, yinyin shenqing: Huiyi Xi Zhongxun tongzhi dui wode sanci jiejian." *Gongchandang ren*, no. 9 (2010): 48–51.

Hao Zaijin. *"Wenge" qianshi: Yan'an "qiangjiu yundong" jishi*. Hong Kong: Liwen, 2006.

Hau Pei-tsun. *Banian canmou zongzhang riji*. 2 vols. Taipei: Commonwealth, 2000.

He Chongling, ed. *Qinghua daxue jiushinian*. Beijing: Qinghua daxue chubanshe, 2001.

He Fang. *Dangshi biji: Cong Zunyi huiyi dao Yan'an zhengfeng*. 2 vols. Hong Kong: Liwen, 2005.

He Fang, ed. "Guo Hongtao tong He Fang tan Shaan-bei sufan deng wenti." In *Dangshi biji: Liu Ying yu He Fang tan zhonggong dangshi*, 151–59. Hong Kong: City University of Hong Kong, 2019.

He Fang. "Liu Ying yi Yan'an suiyue." *Yanhuang chunqiu*, no. 4 (2016): 15–23.

He Fang zishu: Cong Yan'an yi lu zoulai de fansi. Self-published, 2011.

He Jiadong. "Cong Wu Yunduo dao 'Liu Zhidan.'" In *Wangshi huisheng: Zhongguo zhuming zhishi fenzi fangtanlu*, edited by Xing Xiaoqun, 66–85. Hong Kong: Shidai guoji, 2004.

He Jiadong. "Fengyu 'Liu Zhidan.'" In *Siren yi shi jingshen yongcun: He Jiadong jinian wenji*, edited by Chen Ziming and Bi Yimin, 303–12. Self-published, Shidai wenxian, 2012.

He Jiadong. "Zhengzhi gaige cong zhixuan kaishi: Zhi youren shu." In *He Jiadong wenji*, 371–400. Vol. 1. Fort Worth: Fellows, 2007.

He Jin. "Dui Yan'an qiangjiu yundong de chubu tantao." *Dangshi yanjiu*, no. 6 (1980): 63–67.

He Jingzhi. "Zai zhongxuanbu gongzuo de qian qinian (I)." In *He Jingzhi wenji*, 373–414. Vol. 6. Beijing: Zuojia, 2004.

He Jingzhi. "Zai zhongxuanbu gongzuo de qian qinian (II)." In *He Jingzhi wenji*, 414–68. Vol. 6. Beijing: Zuojia, 2004.

He Jinnian. "1945 nian 6 yue He Jinnian zai Shaan-Gan-Ning bianqu lishi zuotan huishang de diyici fayan." June 1945. Reprint, Huangtu lianyihui, 2012. https://web.archive.org/web/20130915181315/http://htqly.org/detail.aspx?DocumentId=3013.

He Pin [Ho Pin] and Gao Xin. *Zhonggong taizidang*. Taipei: Shibao wenhua, 1992.

He Weifang. "Tongguo sifa shixian shehui zhengyi: Dui Zhongguo faguan xianzhuang de yige toushi." In *Zouxiang quanli de shidai*, edited by Xia Yong, 179–250. Beijing: Zhongguo zhengfa daxue chubanshe, 1999.

He Weiling. *Chuanshuo zhong de He Weiling shougao*. Hong Kong: Dafeng, 2015.

He Yao. *Xi Zhongxun jiafeng*. N.p.: Hunan renmin, n.d.

He Yueming. "Xi Zhongxun fangwen Aomen yugao 'tequ' anpai." *Shiji*, Jan. 2019.

He Zai. "Guanyu luoshi zhengce deng wenti de jianyi." In *Wode bashinian: Nanwang suiyue*, 52–56. Beijing: Zhonggong dangshi, 2016.
He Zai. "Guanyu pai daxuesheng xiaqu danren dangzheng lingdao de jianyi xin." In *Wode bashinian: Nanwang suiyue*, 48–50. Beijing: Zhonggong dangshi, 2016.
He Zai. *Hongqi manjuan Xibei gaoyuan: Xi Zhongxun zai Xibei*. Beijing: Zhonggong dangshi, 2013.
He Zai. "Huainian Yaobang tongzhi." *Hong tudi*, no. 11 (2005).
He Zai. "Xi Jinping tongzhi dang xianwei shuji shi jiu bei renwei shi dongliang zhi cai." In *Xi Jinping zai Zhengding*, edited by Zhongyang dangxiao caifang shilu bianjishi, 105–20. Beijing: Zhonggong zhongyang dangxiao, 2019.
Hongweibing pipan wenzhang. "Tong sanfan fenzi Xi Zhongxun pin cidao dahui jiyao." In *Gao Gang "fandang" zhenxiang*, edited by Wu Ming and Shi Jian, 261–70. Hong Kong: Xianggang wenhua yishu, 2008.
Hou Dejian. *Huotouzi zheng zhuan*. Taipei: Lianjing, 1990.
Hu Feng. "Cong shiji chufa." In *Zhiman congcong de huiyi*, edited by Ji Xianlin, 79–156. Beijing: Beijing shiyue wenyi, 2001.
Hu Jiwei. *Cong Hua Guofeng xiatai dao Hu Yaobang xiatai*. Brampton, ON: Mingjing, 1997.
Hu Jiwei. *Hu Zhao xinzheng qishilu: Bingdui "xin minzhu zhuyi" jinxing poxi*. Hong Kong: Xin shiji, 2012.
Hu Jiwei. "Jiehou cheng zhongren, yindui zhuyi cheng: Wei Yaobang shishi shi zhounian er zuo." *Shuwu*, no. 4 (2000): 4–30.
Hu Jiwei zishu. 4 vols. Hong Kong: Zhuoyue wenhua, 2006.
Hu Peiyuan. *Haohai: Ma Wenrui yu gaige kaifang*. Beijing: Zhongyang wenxian, 2014.
Hu Peiyuan. "Nanwang de licheng: Xi Zhongxun Yan'an suiyue huifang." *Zhongguo zuojia* 20 (2013): 4–83.
Hu Qiaomu huiyi Mao Zedong. Beijing: Renmin, 2003.
Hu Qiaomu zhuan. Vol. 2. Beijing: Dangdai Zhongguo, 2015.
Hu Shangyuan. "Lu Yuwen niming xin shijian yu fanyoupai douzheng." In *Fengyu licheng*, 9–19. Beijing: Zhongguo wenshi, 2011.
Hu Shao'an. *Jingwei renmin: Xiang Nan zhuan*. Vol. 1. Hong Kong: Tiandi tushu, 2004.
Hu Shihou. "Hu Yaobang ting wo shensu." *Dangshi bolan*, no. 8 (2010): 36–37.
Hu Shihou. "Mianhuai Xi lao: Jinian Xi Zhongxun tongzhi danchen 100 zhounian." *Dangshi bolan*, no. 5 (2013): 17–21.
Hu Sisheng. *Gaoceng fangtanlu*. Hong Kong: Xianggang xin dalu, 2012.
Hu Xinmin. "Zhou Enlai yu fanyoupai douzheng." *Dangshi bocai*, no. 1 (2015): 19–24.
Hu Yaobang. "Guanyu luoshi tongzhan zhengce gei Xi Zhongxun dengde yizu xinhan." In *Hu Yaobang wenxuan 1975–1986*, 160–63. Vol. 3. N.p.: Zhengqiu yijian gao, n.d.
Hu Yaobang. "Guanyu zhengdang de ruogan wenti." In *Hu Yaobang wenxuan 1975–1986*, 200–207. Vol. 3. N.p.: Zhengqiu yijian gao, n.d.
[Hu Yaobang]. Hu Yaobang's self-criticism. [In Chinese.] Jan. 10, 1987. Held by Warren Sun.
Hu Yaobang. "Jihua shengyu zhengce yao jianli zai guangda qunzhong nenggou jieshou de jichu shang." In *Hu Yaobang wenxuan 1975–1986*, 189–91. Vol. 2. N.p.: Zhengqiu yijian gao, n.d.
Hu Yaobang. "Zai quanguo tongzhan gongzuo huiyishang de jianghua." In *Lici quanguo tongzhan gongzuo huiyi gaikuang he wenxian*, 470–83. Beijing: Dang'an, 1988 (internal circulation).
"Hu Yaobang tongzhi zai Guangdong, Fujian liangsheng zuotan huishang de fayan." In *Zhongyang dui Guangdong gongzuo zhishi huibian (1979 nian–1982 nian)*, 261–78. Ser. 28, vol. 40. N.p.: SCCP, 2007.

"Hu Yaobang tongzhi zai Xizang gongzuo zuotan huishang de jianghua (jielu)." In *Xizang zizhiqu guanche yijiubasi nian Zhonggong zhongyang shujichu zhaokai de Xizang gongzuo zuotanhui jingshen wenjian xuanbian*, 28–46. Ser. 28, vol. 69, pt. 1. N.p.: SCCP, 2009.

Hu Zhi'an. *Tongzhan mixin: Wo suo renshi de minzhu renshi*. Hong Kong: Tiandi tushu, 2010.

Hu Zhi'an. "Zhang Naiqi: Zhengzhi yundong zhong bushi junzi bense." *Yanhuang chunqiu*, no. 11 (2011): 32–42.

Huang Da, Zhu Yu, and Gao Jingzeng. "Shuobujin de Li Xiannian." In *Zhongguo gongchandang koushu shiliao congshu*, 449–61. Vol. 6, pt. 1. Beijing: Zhonggong dangshi, 2013.

Huang Luobin. "Xi Zhongxun yu Shaan-Gan bian geming genjudi de chuangjian." In *Xi Zhongxun jinian wenji*, edited by Zhonggong zhongyang dangshi yanjiushi, 114–20. Beijing: Zhonggong dangshi, 2013.

Huang Shun-hsing. *Beijing jianwen*. Taipei: self-published, 1993.

Huang Zhengqing. *Huang Zhengqing yu wu shi Jiamuxiang*. Lanzhou: Gansu renmin, 1989.

Huang Zhengqing. "Zangbao xinmu zhong de qinren." In *Xi Zhongxun geming shengya*, 298–316. Beijing: Zhongguo wenshi, 2000.

Huang Ziyun. "Gaige kaifang chuqi de Ye Jianying yu Xi Zhongxun." *Dangzhi zonglan*, no. 10 (2018): 90–96.

"Huatong" [pseud.?]. "Shaan-Gan-Ning bianqu quanmao." In *Zhonggong bianqu genjudi de lishi wenjian xuanji*. N.p.: n.p.,1985.

Ji Youquan. *Baixue: Jiefang Xizang jishi*. Beijing: Zhongguo wuzi, 1993.

Jia Juchuan. "Gongpu de kaimo Xi Zhongxun." *Guangdong dangshi*, no. 6 (2003): 23–26.

Jia Juchuan. "'Luhuo chunqing' Xi Zhongxun." *Dangshi bolan*, no. 3 (2003): 40–42.

Jia Juchuan. "Xi Zhongxun nianpu (1949.10–1962.9)." *Weinan shifan xueyuan xuebao* 27, no. 1 (2012): 5–22, 32.

Jia Juchuan. "Xi Zhongxun nianpu (1962.10–2002.5)." *Weinan shifan xueyuan xuebao* 27, no. 3 (2012): 5–25, 40.

Jia Juchuan. "Xi Zhongxun nianpu (1913.10–1937.7)." *Weinan shifan xueyuan xuebao* 26, no. 9 (2011): 3–16.

Jia Juchuan. "Xi Zhongxun nianpu (1937.7–1949.9)." *Weinan shifan xueyuan xuebao* 26, no. 11 (2011): 3–19.

Jia Juchuan. "Xi Zhongxun: Xiongyou guojia, pinzi gaojie." *Xin xiang pinglun*, no. 4 (2018): 16–17.

Jia Juchuan. "Xi Zhongxun yuan'an shimo." *Yanhuang chunqiu*, no. 1 (2011): 4–10.

Jia Juchuan. "Xi Zhongxun zhiyi 'xingwu miezi.'" *Bainianchao*, no. 11 (2001): 78.

Jia Man. *Shiren He Jingzhi*. Beijing: Dazhong wenyi, 2000.

Jia Yanyan. "Wangshi lili: Xi Zhongxun bu buxiu." In *Huainian Xi Zhongxun*, edited by Cao Zhenzhong and Wu Jiang, 265–72. Beijing: Zhongyang dangshi, 2005.

Jia Yanyan. "Zhiqing suiyue." In *Jiqing Molidawa: Huiyi women zai Xingnong chadui de qingchun suiyue*, edited by Fang Fenglei, 365–87. Beijing: Renmin wenxue, 2015.

Jiacuo Jiangbian [Jambey Gyatso]. *Banchan dashi*. Beijing: Dongfang, 1989.

Jiacuo Jiangbian [Jambey Gyatso]. *Mao Zedong yu Dalai, Banchan*. Hong Kong: Xin dalu, 2008.

Jiacuo Jiangbian [Jambey Gyatso]. *1954: Mao Zedong huijian Dalai, Banchan*. Hong Kong: Xin dalu, 2008.

Jiang Feng. "Ta gengyun zai Zhengding de yuanye shang." *Zhongguo qingnian*, no. 1 (1985): 27–31.

Jiang Guangci. "Shaonian piaobozhe." In *Jiang Guangci wenji*, 1–82. Shanghai: Shanghai wenyi, 1982.

Jiang Huajie. "Zhidu jingxiang: Bolan tuanjie gonghui shijian yu Zhongguo gaige kaifang de bianzou." *Ershiyi shiji shuangyue kan* 6, no. 185 (June 2021): 91–110.
Jiang Huanghua. *Fangwen waiguo zhengdang jishi*. Beijing: Shijie zhishi, 1997.
Jiang Ping. "Guanyu Fujian sheng zongjiao gongzuo wenti de diaocha baogao." In *Minzu zongjiao wenti lunwenji*, 396–404. Beijing: Zhonggong dangshi, 1995.
Jiang Ping. "Shenqie huainian wode zhanyou wode shizhang." *Bainianchao*, no. 10 (2013): 12–16.
Jiang Ping. "Zhongyang tongzhanbu fubuzhang Jiang Ping tongzhi zai Zhongguo tianzhujiao lianghui weiyuan (kuoda) huiyishang de jianghua." *Zhongguo tianzhujiao*, no. 7 (1983): 22–25.
Jiang Shan et al. "Xi Zhongxun yu dangde qunzhong luxian zhuanti yantaohui zai Jing zhaokai." Zhongguo baoxie wang, May 26, 2016. http://zgbx.people.com.cn/n1/2016/0526/c347565-28382766.html.
Jiang Wei. *Hongse Fuermosi: Bu Lu yu gong'an xitong diyi qi'an*. Shanghai: Xuelin, 2003.
Jiang Wei. "Wo gei Li Zhao he Xi Zhongxun paile yizhang zhengui zhaopian." *Zhonghua ernü*, no. 4 (2008): 56–57.
Jiang Xun. "Xi Jinping jiejie liting gaige pai." *Yazhou zhoukan*, Mar. 23, 2014, 30.
Jiang Xun. "Xi Jinping xiang zuo zhuanshi zuojia dongzuo." *Yazhou zhoukan*, Sept. 22, 2013, 34–36.
Jiang Yanyong. "Yaoqiu wei liu si zhengming de shangshu." In *Zhao Ziyang yu Zhongguo gaige: Jinian Zhao Ziyang*, edited by Chen Yizi, 357–66. Carle Place: Mingjing, 2005.
Jiang Zemin. "Nuli fazhan zui guangfan de aiguo tongyi zhanxian." In *Tongyi zhanxian gongzuo ganbu jiben duwu*, edited by Zhonggong zhongyang tongyi zhanxian gongzuobu, 348–59. Beijing: Beijing Yanshan, 1992 (internal circulation).
Jiang Zemin. "Zai qijie quanguo renda sanci huiyi he quanguo zhengxie ji jie sanci huiyi dangnei fuzeren huishang de jianghua (jielu)." In *Renda gongzuo wenxian ziliao huibian*, 54–59. Ser. 38, vol. 182. N.p.: SCCP, 2005.
Jianguo yilai gong'an gongzuo dashi yaolan. Beijing: Qunzhong, 2002 (internal circulation).
Jiefangjun Beijing junqu zhengzhiju bangongshi. "Yang Baibing tongzhi zai jieyan budui zhenggong huishang de jianghua." In *Beijing junqu budui zhixing jieyan renwu zhong de zhengzhi gongzuo*, 27–36. Ser. 27, vol. 37. N.p.: SCCP, 2009.
Jiefangjun Beijing junqu zhengzhiju bangongshi. "Yang Shangkun tongzhi zai zhongyang junwei jinji kuoda huiyishang de jianghua yaodian." In *Beijing junqu budui zhixing jieyan renwu zhong de zhengzhi gongzuo*, 14–19. Ser. 27, vol. 37. N.p.: SCCP, 2009.
Jiefangjun di yi yezhanjun zhanshi bianshen weiyuanhui, ed. "Zhang Zongxun, Xi Zhongxun deng guanyu Xihuachi zhandou wei da jiandi mudi zhi junwei dian." In *Diyiye zhanjun wenxian xuanbian*, 88–89. Vol. 1. Beijing: Jiefangjun, 2000.
Jin Guangyao and Jin Dalu. *Zhongguo xin fangzhi: Zhishi qingnian shangshan xiaxiang shiliao jilu*. Vol. 3. Shanghai: Shanghai shudian, 2014.
Jin Luxian huiyilu. Vol. 1. Hong Kong: Hong Kong University Press, 2013.
Jin Zhijian. "Zhen shi cong xinli ganji zongli." In *Bairen fangtan Zhou Enlai*, edited by Zhou Erjun and Zhou Bingde, 423–30. Nanjing: Jiangsu wenyi, 1998.
Ju Liming. "Yi zhizheng zhaoxi de geming jingshen zhua Guangdong gongzuo." In *Xi Zhongxun zhuzheng Guangdong yishu lu*, edited by Zhonggong Guangdong shengwei dangshi yanjiushi, 240–57. Beijing: Zhonggong dangshi, 2013.
Kang Sheng. "Guanyu fanjian douzheng de fazhan qingxing yu dangqian renwu." In *Kangzhan shiqi chubao wenjian (dangnei mimi wenjian)*, 103–38. Vol. 2. N.p.: Zhonggong zhongyang shehuibu, 1949.
Kang Sheng. "Guanyu liangtiao luxian douzheng ji qita." In *Kang Sheng yanlun xuanbian*, 23–28. Vol. 3. Beijing: Zhonggong Beijing shiwei dangxiao ziliao shi, 1979.

Ke Hua. *Xin Zhongguo waijiao qisu Ke Hua 95 sui shuhuai*. Beijing: Wenhua yishu, 2013.
Kim Il-sung. "Jin Richeng tongzhi zai Chengdu shi qunzhong huanying dahuishang de jianghua." In *Zhong-Chao liangdang, liangguo lingdaoren jianghua he heyan dian huibian*, 106–13. N.p.: Zhonggong zhongyang duiwai lianluobu erju, 1983 (internal circulation).
Kong Dan. *Nande bense ren tianran*. Edited by Mi Hedu. Hong Kong: CNHK, 2013.
Kong Shujing. *Suiyue jiyi: Yiwei jiangjun nü'er de suantian kule*. Beijing: Huayi, 2011.
Kong Xiangxiu. *Geng Biao zhuan*. Vol. 2. Beijing: Jiefangjun, 2009.
Kong Xianrui. "Huiyi Xi Zhongxun zai Changge." *Xuchang wenshi ziliao* 8 (1995): 140–42 (internal circulation).
Lailailai qu zhijian. "1989 nian 6 yue 23 ri–24 ri, dangde shisanjie di sizhong quanhui zhaokai." YouTube, June 24, 2022. Video. https://www.youtube.com/watch?v=qlJHTNPyaSM&ab_channel=%E6%9D%A5%E5%A4%B9%E6%9D%A5%E5%8E%BB%E4%B9%8B%E9%97%B4.
Laixia laiqu zhijian. "Xi Zhongxun." Pt. 3. CCTV, YouTube, May 28, 2022. Video. https://www.youtube.com/watch?v=a17QeFBgirM&ab_channel=%E6%9D%A5%E5%A4%B9%E6%9D%A5%E5%8E%BB%E4%B9%8B%E9%97%B4.
Laixia laiqu zhijian. "Xi Zhongxun." Pt. 6. CCTV, YouTube, May 28, 2022. Video. https://www.youtube.com/watch?v=OWoFdeYC9KE&t=27s.
Lan Sisi. *Zhongguo X dang'an: Zhonggong yangai de "neibu lishi."* Deer Park, NY: Mingjing, 2014.
Lee Kuan Yew School of Public Policy. "Lodi Gyaltsen Gyari on Resolving Tibet: Crucial for China's Stability." YouTube, Aug. 12, 2014. Video. https://www.youtube.com/watch?v=kalpvzGcWqU.
Lee Teng-hui. *Li Denghui zhizheng gaobai shilu*. Taipei: Yinshua, 2001.
Lei Jia. *Sishi nianjian: Lei Jia huiyilu*. Shenyang: Chunfeng wenyi, 2020.
Lei Rongsheng and Lei Pingsheng. "Jinping ba ziji kanzuo huang tudi de yi bufen." In *Xi Jinping de qinian zhiqing suiyue*, edited by Zhongyang dangxiao caifang shilu bianjishi, 3–58. Beijing: Zhonggong zhongyang dangxiao, 2017.
Li Chang. "Wo yu Yaobang gongshi." *Yanhuang chunqiu*, no. 1 (2006): 18–23.
Li Chao. "Liu Shaoqi shi bei pohai zhisi de." *Yanhuang chunqiu*, no. 1 (2010): 80–81.
Li Chunlei. *Pengyou: Xi Jinping yu Jia Dashan jiaowang wangshi*. Beijing: Zhongguo yanshi, 2014.
Li Donglang. "Shaan-bei sufan ji ze shishi zhi kaobian." *Dangshi yanjiu yu jiaoxue*, no. 5 (2010): 78–86.
Li Donglang. "'Xibei lishi wenti' de youlai." *Dangshi bolan*, no. 9 (2014): 4–11.
Li Donglang. "Xi Zhongxun yu Chenjiapo huiyi." *Dangshi bolan*, no. 10 (2013): 11–16.
Li Erzhong biji zhaichao. Vol. 2. Self-published, Zhongguo zhanwang, 2014.
Li Haidong. "Guanxin qingnian, qiadang chuli 'Li Yizhe' anjian." In *Xi Zhongxun zhuzheng Guangdong yishu lu*, edited by Zhonggong Guangdong shengwei dangshi yanjiushi, 204–17. Beijing: Zhonggong dangshi, 2013.
Li Haiwen. "Bilu lanlu, yiqi shanlin." *Jingji daokan* 237 (Dec. 2018): 86–96.
Li Haiwen. "Xi Zhongxun lizheng zhongyang rang Guangdong xian xing yi bu." *Shiji* 3 (2018): 5–10.
Li Huasong. "Yige weiren de qidai." In *Qingxi huang tudi*, edited by Sun Lizhe, 2–9. Beijing: Zhongguo guoji guangbo, 1996.
Li Jiantong. *Fandang xiaoshuo "Liu Zhidan" an shilu*. Hong Kong: Thinker, 2007.
Li Jiantong. "Zhou Yang he xiaoshuo 'Liu Zhidan.'" In *Yi Zhou Yang*, edited by Wang Meng and Yuan Ying, 372–78. Hohhot: Nei Menggu renmin, 1998.
Li Jiefei. "Fengyu wanlai fangding." In *Huiyi Zhang Guangnian*, 430–79. Beijing: Zuojia, 2013.

Li Kaiquan. "Bingtuan zaoqi gongyehua fangtanlu." *Xinjiang shengchan jianshe bingtuan shiliao xuanji* 16 (2007): 405–35 (internal circulation).
Li Lanqing. *Tuwei: Guomen chukai de suiyue*. Beijing: Zhongyang wenxian, 2008.
Li Ligong. *Wangshi huigu*. Beijing: Zhonggong dangshi, 2008.
Li Liqun. "Gao Gang shengming zhong de zuihou wunian." In *Yi Gao Gang tongzhi*, edited by Hengshanxian Gao Gang yu Zhongguo geming yanjiuhui, 41–92. Beijing: Dazhong wenyi, 2010.
Li Liqun. "Nanwang de huiyi." In *Yi Gao Gang tongzhi*, edited by Hengshanxian Gao Gang yu Zhongguo geming yanjiuhui, 264–89. Beijing: Dazhong wenyi, 2010.
Li Manxing. "Xi Zhongxun he 'lao guanxi' Tian Pingxuan de yisheng qingyi." *Yanhuang chunqiu*, no. 4 (2017): 27–31.
Li Meijie and Zhao Shishu. "'Liu duo' jiangjun Fan Ming." *Yanhuang chunqiu*, no. 3 (2007): 37–42, 51.
Li Min. *Wode fuqin Mao Zedong*. Shenyang: Liaoning renmin, 2000.
Li Musheng. "Ta cong 'xiwang de tianye shang' zoulai." *Mingren zhuanji* 11 (1992): 66–74.
Li Naiyi. "Xi shuji zhiding 'rencai jiu tiao' de guocheng, ye shi Zhengding jiefang sixiang, cujin gaige de guocheng." In *Xi Jinping zai Zhengding*, edited by Zhongyang dangxiao caifang shilu bianjishi, 167–79. Beijing: Zhonggong zhongyang dangxiao, 2019.
Li Nanyang. *Fumu zuori shu*. Vol. 1. Hong Kong: Shidai guoji, 2005.
Li Nanyang. "Li Rui juechang." In *Jingji Li Rui*, edited by Li Nanyang, 456–89. Hong Kong: Chuban gongfang, 2019.
Li Nanyang. *Wo you zheyang de yige muqin*. Keller, TX: Fellows Press of America, 2020.
Li Nanyang. "Yi Wang Jianxun: 'Genjin' shengao ren." *Dongxiang* 371 (July 2016).
Li Peng huiyilu (1928–1983). Beijing: Zhongyang dianli, 2014.
Li Rui. "Fu: 'Yaobang tongzhi huo zai women xin zhong' zuotanhui fayan ji." In *Li Rui wenji*, 118–39. Vol. 10. Shenzhen: Zhongguo shehui jiaoyu, 2009.
Li Rui. *Li Rui koushu wangshi*. Hong Kong: Dashan wenhua, 2013.
Li Rui. *Lushan huiyi shilu*. Hong Kong: Tiandi tushu, 2009.
Li Rui. "Yaobang qushi qian de tanhua." In *Huainian Yaobang*, edited by Zhang Liqun, Zhang Ding, Yan Ruping, and Li Gongtian, 274–305. Vol. 4. Hong Kong: Yatai guoji, 2001.
Li Shengping. "Xi Zhongxun zai Guangdong zhuchi pingfan yuanjia cuo'an." *Yanhuang chunqiu*, no. 6 (2012): 57–60.
Li Shengyu. *Pingfan suiyue*. Self-published, Beijing shidai nongchao wenhua fazhan, 2012.
Li Shenzhi. "Tantan Zhonghua renmin gongheguo de waijiao." In *Li Shenzhi wenji*, 325–37. N.p.: n.p., 2004.
Li Shitao. "Wo jiechuguo de Zhou Yang, Lin Mohan he Hu Qiaomu: Li Zhi xiansheng fangtanlu." *Xin wenxue shiliao*, no. 2 (2011): 70–98.
Li Weidong and Wang Lihui. "Shenji shi ge hao bangshou: Fang Fujian sheng shengzhang Xi Jinping." *Jingji yuekan*, no. 6 (2001): 16–17.
Li Weihan. *Huiyi yu yanjiu*. 2 vols. Beijing: Zhonggong dangshi ziliao, 1986.
Li Xiangchao, Ni Shang, Li Hengjian, Wang Zeyang, and Yan Yuhan. "Xi Zhongxun yu 'mishu gongzuo' chuangkan." *Mishu gongzuo*, no. 7 (2015): 4–7.
Li Xiangqian. *Xi Zhongxun: Cong "luojiaodian" dao "kaifangquan."* Beijing: Zhongyang wenxian, 2014.
Li Xin. "Du 'Ding Ling yu Hu Feng' yi wen suo xiangqi de." *Xin wenxue shiliao*, no. 2 (2008): 115–19.
Li Xin. *Qinli Yan'an suiyue*. Xi'an: Shaanxi renmin, 2015.

Li Yi. "Ta qizhi xianming di tichu gei Guangdong fangquan." In *Xi Zhongxun zhuzheng Guangdong yishu lu*, edited by Zhonggong Guangdong shengwei dangshi yanjiushi, 26–39. Beijing: Zhonggong dangshi, 2013.
Li Yu. "Daonian Li Shenzhi xiansheng." In *Huainian Li Shenzhi*, edited by Ding Dong, 295–99. Hong Kong: Shidai chaoliu, 2003.
Li Yuan. "Yan Hongyan he xiaoshuo 'Liu Zhidan.'" *Bainianchao*, no. 3 (2003): 17–22.
Li Yueran. *Waijiao wutaishang de xin Zhongguo lingxiu*. Beijing: Waiyu jiaoxue yu yanjiu, 1994.
Li Zhi. *Wentan fengyun lu*. Beijing: Renmin wenxue, 2015.
Li Ziyun. *Wo qinli de naxie ren he shi*. Shanghai: Wenhui, 2005.
Li Zizhuang. "Suiyue de fansi." In *Qingxi huang tudi*, edited by Sun Lizhe, 68–74. Beijing: Zhongguo guoji guangbo, 1996.
"Liang Guangda pai Yang Shangkun mapi, shouyi ganzou Xi Zhongxun." *Waican* 8 (Aug. 2012).
Liang Jian. *Xi Jinping xin zhuan*. Hong Kong: Mingjing, 2012.
Liang Xingliang and Yao Wenqi. *Zhonggong zhongyang zai Yan'an shisannian shi*. Vol. 1. Beijing: Zhongyang wenxian, 2016.
Liang Yuming. "Jinping gan shuo gan zuo gan dandang." In *Xi Jinping de qinian zhiqing suiyue*, edited by Zhongyang dangxiao caifang shilu bianjishi, 161–81. Beijing: Zhonggong zhongyang dangxiao, 2017.
Liangjiahe. Xi'an: Shaanxi renmin, 2018.
Liao Hansheng huiyilu. Beijing: Jiefangjun, 2012.
Liao Wanqing. "Wode 'siqing' jingli." *Xiaoyou wengao ziliao xuanbian* 24 (n.d.): 110–15.
Lin Boqu zhuan. Beijing: Hongqi, 1986.
Lin Hsiao-ting. *Jiang Jingguo de Taiwan shidai: Zhonghua minguo yu lengzhan xia de Taiwan*. Xinbei: Yuanzu wenhua, 2021.
Lin Mohan. "Hu Feng shijian de qianqian houhou (Lin Mohan wenda lu zhi yi)." *Xin wenxue shiliao*, no. 8 (1989): 4–28.
Lin Mu. "Xi Zhongxun wannian de jijian dashi." *Beijing zhichun*, no. 89 (Oct. 2000): 22–28.
Lin Mu. *Zhu jin meng you xu: Hu Yaobang zhu shou Lin Mu huiyilu*. Hong Kong: Xin shiji, 2008.
Lin Ruo. "Zai kaituo chuangxin zhong yingde xin fazhan: Lin Ruo caifang lu." In *Guangdong gaige kaifang juecezhe fangtanlu*, edited by Zhonggong Guangdong shengwei dangshi yanjiushi, 50–87. Guangzhou: Guangdong renmin, 2008.
Lin Yajie, ed. "Shengwei changwei huiyi jilu (jiexuan) (1979 nian 5 yue 3 ri xiawu)." In *Tequ de youlai*, 40–42. Guangzhou: Guangdong renmin, 2010.
Lin Yajie, ed. "Shengwei changwei huiyi jilu (jiexuan) (1979 nian 4 yue 2 ri xiawu)." In *Tequ de youlai*, 35–37. Guangzhou: Guangdong renmin, 2010.
Lin Yajie, ed. "Wu Nansheng tongzhi gei shengwei de baogao (1979 nian 2 yue 21 ri)." In *Tequ de youlai*, 32–34. Guangzhou: Guangdong renmin, 2010.
Lin Yunhui. *Chongkao Gao Gang, Rao Shushi "fandang" shijian*. Hong Kong: Chinese University Press, 2017.
Lin Yunhui. *Wutuobang yundong: Cong dayuejin dao dajihuang*. Hong Kong: Chinese University Press, 2008.
Lin Yunhui. *Xiang shehui zhuyi guodu: Zhongguo jingji shehui de zhuanxing*. Hong Kong: Chinese University Press, 2009.
Lishi. "Xi Zhongxun chang 'Dongfang hong.'" YouTube, June 22, 2017. Video. https://www.youtube.com/watch?v=IxgNY-qFWjk&ab_channel=lishi.
Liu Bing. *Fengyu suiyue: 1964–1976 nian de Qinghua*. Beijing: Dangdai Zhongguo, 2010.
Liu Bingrong. "He Long yu Yihe huiyi." *Xiangchao* 10 (Oct. 2007): 20–24.

Liu Bingrong. *Zoujin Qi Ruixin*. Beijing: Zhongguo renmin daxue xiaoyouhui, 2014 (internal circulation).

Liu Chongwen. "Hu Yaobang shishi qian bannian de xintai." *Yanhuang chunqiu*, no. 9 (2009): 1–5.

Liu Chun. *Guanyu minzu gongzuo de huigu*. N.p.: n.p., 2001 (internal circulation).

Liu Fuzhi huiyilu. Beijing: Zhongyang wenxian, 2010.

Liu Huixuan. "Dangshi nianshao ceng qingkuang." In *Dangshi nianshao ceng qingkuang*, edited by Mi Hedu, 1–151. Hong Kong: Ruitian wenhua, 2015.

Liu Jingfan. "Guanyu Shenzhen shi shourong zhan guanya, nuedai shouren renyuan qingkuang de baogao." In *Liu Jingfan jinian wenji*, edited by Liu Mila and Liu Dudu, 858–60. Beijing: Zhongyang wenxian, 2015.

Liu Jingfan. "'Sanjiayuan shijian' de zhenxiang." In *Fandang xiaoshuo "Liu Zhidan" an shilu*, edited by Li Jiantong, 258–72. Hong Kong: Thinker, 2007.

Liu Jingfan et al. "Guanyu Shaan-bei 'sufan' yu luxian douzheng de zhenxiang." N.d. Reprint, Huangtu lianyihui, 2012. https://web.archive.org/web/20171112011408/http://www.htqly.org/Detail.aspx?Id=271.

Liu Lizhen. "Shenqie mianhuai wode shufu Liu Jingfan." In *Jinian Liu Jingfan tongzhi danchen 100 zhounian zuotanhui ziliao huibian*, edited by Liu Mila, 3–4. Self-published, Beijing shidai nongchao wenhua fazhan, 2011.

Liu Maogong. *Menghui chuijiao lianying: Yige lao zhanshi de huiyi*. Beijing: Zhonggong dangshi, 2000.

Liu Mila. "Huainian Xi Zhongxun shushu." Zhonghong wang, Sept. 9, 2013. https://archive.ph/lGA4l.

Liu Peizhi wencun. Beijing: Zhonggong dangshi, 2017.

Liu Tianfu. "Jiefang sixiang, jinxing jingji tizhi gaige de shiyan." In *Liu Tianfu wenxuan*, 357–72. Guangzhou: Guangdong renmin, 1995.

Liu Tianfu. "Yong dang gaige kaifang de paitou bing: Liu Tianfu caifang lu." In *Guangdong gaige kaifang juecezhe fangtanlu*, edited by Zhonggong Guangdong shengwei dangshi yanjiushi, 88–143. Guangzhou: Guangdong renmin, 2008.

Liu Tianfu huiyilu. Beijing: Zhonggong dangshi, 1995.

Liu Tong. *Bei shang: Dang zhongyang yu Zhang Guotao douzheng shimo*. Beijing: Shenghuo-dushu-xinzhi sanlian shudian, 2016.

Liu Xiaoyuan. "'Beijing shijian': 1950 niandai Zhonggong dui Xizang gaige de dengdai fangzhen." *Ershiyi shiji shuangyue kan*, no. 163 (Oct. 2017): 73–90.

Liu Xicheng. "'Xin shiqi wenyi' de tichu yu wenyi zhengce de queli: Yi Zhongguo wenlian sanci huiyi weili." *Zhongguo dangwei wenxue yanjiu*, no. 2 (2020): 29–34.

Liu Xicheng. *Zai wentan bianyuan*. Vol. 1. Kaifeng: Henan daxue chubanshe, 2003.

Liu Xingshi. "Xi Zhongxun tongzhi zai kuangshan jiqi chang gongzuo de pianduan." *Luoyang wenshi ziliao* 17 (1996): 54–58 (internal circulation).

Liu Xixian. "Wo yu Xi Zhongxun yijie jinlan." In *Hongse Liangdang*, edited by Liangdang bingbian ji hongjun changzheng zai Liangdang dangshi ziliao bianzuan bangongshi, 60. Lanzhou: Gansu wenhua, 2008.

Liu Yuanhang. "Simayi Aimaiti, zhege xinwen lianbo li zai ye tingbudao de mingzi, ta daodi shi shei." *Zhongguo xinwen zhoukan*, Nov. 30, 2018.

Liu Yunyue. *Liu Bangxian*. Xi'an: Shaanxi renmin, 2008.

Liu Zhidan and Xi Zhongxun. "Shaan-Gan bian genjudi 'shi da zhengce.'" In *Liu Zhidan wenji*, 35–39. Beijing: Renmin, 2012.

Long Fei and Jing Jing. "Zuihou yi ren mishu yanzhong de Xi Zhongxun." *Dang'an chunqiu*, no. 1 (2008): 4–8.

Long Liwei and Bai Yuche. "Jiefangjun shouci shixing junxian zhi neimu zhenwen." *Wenshi jinghua*, no. 3 (2006): 4–13.

Lu Chaoqi. *Liu si neibu riji*. Hong Kong: Zhuoyue wenhua, 2006.
Lu Di. "Ji Xi Zhongxun canjia shiyijie sanzhong quanhui." In *Zhongguo mingyun da juice: Shiyijie sanzhong quanhui qinli*, edited by Zheng Hui, 309–19. Shenzhen: Shenzhen baoye jituan, 2008.
Lu Di. "Lishi zhuanzhe zhong de Xi Zhongxun." *Bainianchao*, no. 4 (2018): 45–56.
Lu Di. "Xi Zhongxun yu Guangdong fan 'toudu waitao.'" *Bainianchao*, no. 10 (2007): 20–27.
Lu Huang. "'Hongse Fuermosi': Bu Lu de zaoyu." *Yanhuang chunqiu*, no. 5 (2014): 76–80.
Lu Jianfeng. "Qi Yun zai Yangcheng." *Wenshi yuekan*, no. 9 (2014): 4–8.
Lu Jianren. "Huiyi Liangdang bingbian." In *Shaanxi wenshi ziliao*, edited by Zhongguo renmin zhengzhi xieshang huiyi, Shaanxi sheng weiyuanhui, and Wenshi ziliao yanjiu weiyuanhui, 4–11. Vol. 11. Xi'an: Shaanxi renmin, n.d.
Lu Jianren. *Wode huiyi*. Xi'an: Shaanxi renmin, 1997.
Lu Ruihua. "Wennuan qinqie de guli." In *Xi Zhongxun zhuzheng Guangdong yishu lu*, edited by Zhonggong Guangdong shengwei dangshi yanjiushi, 12–25. Beijing: Zhonggong dangshi, 2013.
Lu Wenmei. "Yu xin Zhongguo zouguo wushinian." *Minzu tuanjie*, no. 10 (1999): 16–18.
Lu Ying and Zhou Weisi. "Er li zhi nian." *Hebei qingnian*, no. 7 (1984): 4–9.
Lu Yuan. *Hu Feng he wo*, edited by Ji Xianlin. Beijing: Beijing shiyue wenyi, 2001.
Lu Yue. "Renu gaoceng de 'Yanhuang chunqiu' xinchun lianyihui fayan." *Qianshao*, June 2013, 30–34.
Lu Yue. "Xi Jinping yu Li Rui." In *Jingji Li Rui*, edited by Li Nanyang, 357–59. Hong Kong: Chuban gongfang, 2019.
Lu Zhichao. "Haibian yiwang: Weirao Zhongnanhai de huiyi yu sikao." Unpublished manuscript, 2008.
Luo Qingchang. "Mianhuai jing'ai de Li Kenong buzhang." In *Jinian Li Kenong wenji*, 62–78. Beijing: n.p., 1989.
Luo Wenzhi. *Zhonggong Shaanxi dixiadang fan dite douzheng jishi*. Xi'an: Shaanxi renmin, 1998.
Luo Yinsheng. *Qiao Guanhua quanzhuan*. Shanghai: Dongfang chuban zhongxin, 2006.
Luo Yu. *Gaobie zongcanmou bu*. Hong Kong: Open Books, 2015.
Luo Zixing. "Xi Zhongxun teshu de gongchang suiyue." *Jingji daokan*, no. 8 (2018): 90–96.
Luobu Jiangcun [Gyaincain Norbu]. "Xizang zou shang le kuaisu fazhan de guidao." In *Jianzheng Xizang: Xizang zizhiqu zhengfu liren xianren zhuxi zishu*, edited by Ma Lihua and Feng Liang, 167–206. Beijing: Zhongguo Zangxue, 2005.
"Luoshi zhengce, pingfan yuanjia cuo'an de yi zu piyu." In *Hu Yaobang wenxuan 1975–1986*, 98–117. Vol. 1. N.p.: Zhengqiu yijian gao, n.d.
Luoyang naihuo cailiao changzhi (1956–1984). Xi'an: n.p., 1986 (internal circulation).
Ma Dazheng. *Guojia liyi gaoyu yiqie: Xinjiang wending wenti de guancha yu sikao*. Urumqi: Xinjiang renmin, 2002 (internal circulation).
Ma Jianli, Tan Kesheng, Xiao Decai, and He Zhengzhou. *Haixia liang'an guanxi sishinian*. Wuhan: Hubei jiaoyu, 1995.
Ma Songlin. "Huainian Xi Zhongxun shuji." In *Zai Xibeiju de rizi li*, edited by Shi Jie and Si Zhihao, 17–38. Xi'an: Shaanxi shifan daxue chubanshe, 2018.
Ma Wenrui zhuan. Beijing: Dangdai Zhongguo, 2005.
Ma Ya. *Dafeng qixi: Ma Hong zhuan*. Hong Kong: Mingjing, 2014.
Ma Ying-jeou and Xiao Xucen. *Banian zhizheng huiyilu*. Taipei: Yuanjian tianxia wenhua, 2019.
Ma Yongshun. *Zhou Enlai zujian yu guanli zhengfu shilu*. Beijing: Zhongyang wenxian, 1995.

Ma Yuping. "Wo zai bayi xuexiao shi wu nian." *Difang wenge shi jiaoliu wang*, May 12, 2015. https://www.difangwenge.org/forum.php?mod=viewthread&tid=11127.

Man Mei. *Huiyi fuqin Hu Yaobang*. Vol. 2. Hong Kong: Tiandi tushu, 2016.

Mao Qixiong and Lin Xiaodong. *Zhongguo qiaowu zhengce gaishu*. Beijing: Zhongguo huaqiao, 1993 (internal circulation).

Mao Yinghui. "Dangbao minzu huayu de kuangjia bianqian yanjiu: Xinjiang ribao (hanwen ban) 1949–2009 nian minzu baodao fenxi." PhD diss., Fudan University, 2010.

Mao Yushi and Xia Youxin. "Dang he guojia lingdao ren canguan Shaoshan ganyan jiyu." *Zhonghua hun*, no. 12 (2003): 17–19.

Mao Zedong. "Dui Zhonggong zhongyang, guowuyuan guanyu qinjian banshe de lianhe zhishi de piyu." In *Jianguo yilai Mao Zedong wengao*, 57–58. Vol. 6. Beijing: Zhongyang wenxian, 1992 (internal circulation).

Mao Zedong. "Guanyu jiejue chunhuang queliang wenti de piyu." In *Jianguo yilai Mao Zedong wengao*, 209. Vol. 8. Beijing: Zhongyang wenxian, 1993 (internal circulation).

Mao Zedong. "Jianqu zhengzhi fangshi jiejue Xibei diqu." In *Mao Zedong junshi wenji*, 654–57. Vol. 5. Beijing: Junshi kexue; Beijing: Zhongyang wenxian, 1993.

Mao Zedong. "1942 nian 11 yue Mao Zedong zai Xibei gaogan huiyishang de baogao." Nov. 1942. Reprint, Huangtu lianyihui, 2012. https://web.archive.org/web/20130915180509/http://htqly.org/detail.aspx?DocumentId=3195.

Mao Zedong. "Zai Zhongguo gongchandang dibajie zhongyang weiyuanhui dierci quanti huiyishang de jianghua." In *Mao Zedong xuanji*, 313–29. Vol. 5. Beijing: Renmin, 1977.

Mao Zedong. "Zhengdun dangde zuofeng." In *Mao Zedong xuanji*, 833–50. Vol. 3. Beijing: Renmin, 1953.

Mao Zedong. "Zhongyang zhuanfa Xi Zhongxun guanyu wenwei fen dangzu buzhi fan guanliao zhuyi douzheng de baogao de piyu." In *Jianguo yilai Mao Zedong wengao*, 74–75. Vol. 4. Beijing: Zhongyang wenxian, 1993 (internal circulation).

Meng Deqiang. "He Xi Zhongxun zai yiqi de 72 tian." *Zongheng* 277, no. 1 (2013): 4–11.

Meng Deqiang. "Xi Zhongxun de Xi'an yishi." *Zongheng* 280, no. 4 (2013): 19–22.

Meng Hong. "Zhonggong lingdaoren yu Xu Deheng." *Wenshi yuekan*, no. 9 (2017): 4–17.

Meng Weijun. "'*Xuezhan Taierzhuang*' dansheng ji." *Dangshi zongheng* 2 (2009): 49–50.

Meng Xiangfeng. "Zuo you zhiqi you zuowei de yidai." *Jiazhang*, no. 2 (1997): 4.

Mi Hedu. "Dayuan wenhua, yingxiong guan, shengli texing ji qita." In *Wenge wushinian: Mao Zedong yichan he dangdai Zhongguo*, edited by Song Yongyi, 119–44. Vol. 2. Deer Park, NY: Mingjing, 2016.

Mi Hedu. *Xinlu: Toushi gongheguo tongling ren*. Beijing: Zhongyang wenxian, 2011.

Miao Pingjun. "Zhandou zai diren xinzang de yingxiong men." *Dangshi wenhui*, no. 3 (2017): 41–45.

Minemura Kenji. *Zhanshang shisanyi ren de dingduan: Xi jinping zhangquan zhi lu*. Taipei: Lianjing, 2018.

Mingjing huopai. "Tongzhi jieji yishi: Yan Huai de 'Jinchu zhongzubu' jiedu zhi er." YouTube, Oct. 2, 2017. Video. https://www.youtube.com/watch?v=UicDF3Vgwdw.

Mingjing huopai. "Xi Jinping fuzi Zhuhai Shenzhen enyuan, Gang-Zhu-Ao daqiao xian qiangguo qiang gongcheng." YouTube, Oct. 23, 2018. Video. https://www.youtube.com/watch?v=bFhIeTeRk1s.

Mingjing zhuanfang. "Kaocha Xi Jinping de ren." Pt. 2. YouTube, Oct. 13, 2016. Video. https://www.youtube.com/watch?v=-gcrogGSwzY.

Mo Dan. *Tongzhan fengyun (1949–1983)*. Hong Kong: Lanyue, 2019.

Mu Guodong. "Yige liudu quanguo de zhengzhi dapianju de youlai." In *Wo xinzhong de Bayi*, edited by Li Heshun, 330–34. Beijing: Tuanjie, 2007.

Nei Menggu zizhiqu Yikezhaomeng lianwei, Neimeng Yimeng Yijin Huoluo qi lianzong "doupi Wulanfu lianluozhan," and Hu sansi Nei Menggu daxue Jinggangshan "doupi Wulanfu lianluozhan." "Wulanfu zai Yimeng de zuixing: 'Chedi chanchu Gao Gang yudang' (II)." In *Mongorujin jenosaido ni kansuru kiso shiryō*, edited by Yang Haiying, 374–85. Vol. 7. Tokyo: Fukyosha, 2015.

Nian Ren. "Hu Yaobang, Xi Zhongxun zhongshi 'Feng Gu difang zhuyi fandang lianmeng' de pingfan." In *Guangdong lishi wenti yanjiu: Guangdong difang zhuyi: Pingfan yanjiu ziliao*, edited by Zhang Jiangming, 379–85. Special ser., vol. 81. N.p.: SCCP, 2000.

Nie Chengyong. "Xiangwang yangguang canlan de difang." In *Yanhe ernü: Yan'an qingnian de chengcai zhilu*, edited by Jia Zhi, 96–105. Beijing: Renmin, 1999.

Nie Weiping and Wang Duanyang. *Nie Weiping: Weiqi rensheng*. Beijing: Wenhua yishu, 2011.

"1989 nian '3.5' Lasa saoluan jie hou muji ji." In *Xizang wenti beiwanglu*, 55–59. Ser. 31, vol. 6. N.p.: SCCP, 2009.

"1978 nian 9 yue 5 ri Guangdong sheng gong'anting guanyu dangqian wo sheng toudu waitao yanzhong de qingkuang baogao." *Guangdong wenshi ziliao* 85 (2002): 505.

Niyazi Amudong. "Jiaqiang dang de lingdao, zuohao sixiang zhengzhi gongzuo, buduan gonggu he fazhan zizhi qu anding tuanjie de dahao xingshi." In *Guanche minzu zhengce wenjian xubian*, 369–87. Urumqi: Xinjiang renmin, 1990 (internal circulation).

"Peng Chong tongzhi zai Guangdong, Fujian liangsheng zuotan huishang de fayan." In *Zhongyang dui Guangdong gongzuo zhishi huibian (1979 nian–1982 nian)*, 289–91. Ser. 28, vol. 40. N.p.: SCCP, 2007.

Peng Dehuai quanzhuan. 4 vols. Beijing: Zhongguo da baike quanshu, 2009.

Peng Liyuan. "Chengming yu kunao: Peng Liyuan yi xi tan." *Yinyue shijie* (May 1985): 41–42.

Peng Zhen nianpu 1979–1997. 5 vols. Beijing: Zhongyang wenxian, 2002.

Qi Benyu huiyilu. 2 vols. Hong Kong: Zhongguo wenge lishi, 2016.

Qi Qiaoqiao. "Fuqin yongyuan huo zai wode xinzhong." In *Xi Zhongxun jinian wenji*, edited by Zhonggong zhongyang dangshi yanjiushi, 774–95. Beijing: Zhonggong dangshi, 2013.

Qi Xin. "Jiqing ranshao de qingchun suiyue: Yi wo zai Taihang kangRi qianxian Kangda de zhandou shenghuo." *Bainianchao*, no. 8 (2015): 25–34.

Qi Xin. "Wo yu Xi Zhongxun fengyu xiangban 55 ge chunqiu." In *Xi Zhongxun geming shengya*, 649–65. Beijing: Zhongguo wenshi, 2000.

Qi Xin. "Wo yu Xi Zhongxun xiangban wushibanian." *Juece yu xinxi*, no. 7 (2012): 43–48.

Qi Xin. "Wo zai Kangda de zhandou shenghuo." *Xinxiang pinglun*, Feb. 2016, 39–41.

Qi Xin. "Yi Zhongxun." In *Xi Zhongxun jinian wenji*, edited by Zhonggong zhongyang dangshi yanjiushi, 747–60. Beijing: Zhonggong dangshi, 2013.

Qi Xin. "Zhongxun, wo yong weixiao song ni yuanxing." In *Huainian Xi Zhongxun*, edited by Cao Zhenzhong and Wu Jiang, 12–33. Beijing: Zhongyang dangshi, 2005.

Qi Zhi. *Neimeng wenge shilu: "Minzu fenlie" yu "wasu" yundong*. Hong Kong: Tianxing jian, 2010.

Qian Liqun. *Huashuo Zhou shi xiongdi: Beida yanjiang lu*. Ji'nan: Shandong huabao, 1999.

Qian Liren. *Bange shiji de canghai sangtian: Qian Liren huiyilu*. Beijing: Waijiao bu, 2013.

Qian Xiangli. *Lishi de bianju: Cong wanjiu weiji dao fanxiu fangxiu, 1962–1965*. Hong Kong: Chinese University Press, 2008.

Qian Zhengwang. "Xinyang shijian yu Zhongnanju diyici huiyi." *Yanhuang chunqiu*, no. 2 (2016): 14–17.

Qin Chuan. "Yijiubasannian 'qing wu' yundong zhuiyi." *Jingbao yuekan*, no. 12 (1996): 48–55.
Qin Jun. "Xi Zhongxun qingxi zuju di Nanyang." *Dangshi bolan*, no. 10 (2008): 39–41.
Qin Ping. "Yi Bu Lu." In *Dute yingxiang: jinian renmin yingxiong Bu Lu danchen yibaizhounian*, edited by Jia Yanyan, 55–57. Haikou: Hainan, 2009.
Qu dangwei zongtuan "Fenglei." "Jiekai 'Xi Zhongxun zhuan'an xiaozu' zhi mi." In *Xinjiang wenti zhiyi: Hongqi pinglun*, 54–56. Ser. 16, vol. 32. N.p.: SCCP, 1999.
Qu Wu wenxuan. Beijing: Tuanjie, 1988.
Quan Yanchi. "Xu Shiyou hejiu xuanjiang." *Yanhuang chunqiu*, no. 1 (Jan. 1992): 48–49.
"Quanguo tongyi zhanxian lilun gongzuo huiyi gaikuang." In *Lici quanguo tongzhan gongzuo huiyi gaikuang he wenxian*, 529–44. Beijing: Dang'an, 1988 (internal circulation).
Qunxing cuican. Xi'an: Shaanxi renmin, 2011.
Re Di [Raidi]. "Zhongxun tongzhi yu Xizang gongzuo." In *Xi Zhongxun jinian wenji*, edited by Zhonggong zhongyang dangshi yanjiushi, 28–37. Beijing: Zhonggong dangshi, 2013.
Ren Bishi zhuan (xiuding ben). Beijing: Zhongyang wenxian, 2004.
Ren Wuzhi. "Huainian Xi Zhongxun tongzhi." *Zhongguo zongjiao*, no. 35 (2002): 14–16.
Ren Xueling. *Shaan-Gan geming genjudi shi*. Beijing: Renmin, 2013.
Ruan Ming. "Shiqu de lishi jihui: Yi shinian qian Xinjiang zhi xing." *Minzhu Zhongguo* 8 (Feb. 1992): 17–18.
Rui Feng and Geng Fu. "Xi Jinping 'chushan.'" *Dangdai qingnian*, no. 11 (1985): 8–9.
"Shaan-Gan-Ning bianqu dierjie canyihui diyici dahui ti'an huilu." In *Shaan-Gan-Ning bianqu canyihui*, 306–50. Beijing: Zhonggong zhongyang dangxiao keyan bangongshi, 1985 (internal circulation).
Shaanxi sheng fulian fuyun shi xiaozu, ed. *Shaan-Gan-Ning bianqu funü yundong zhuanti xuanbian*. Xi'an: Shaanxi sheng fulian yundong shi xiaozu, 1984.
Shan Lan. "Liuxing de pianjian yongyuan bushi zhenli: Xi Zhongxun de erzi Xi Jinping." In *Hongqiangnei de zinümen*, 467–76. Vol. 2. Yanbian: Yanbian renmin, 1998.
Shan Shaojie. "Mao Zedong: Zhengren yu pa shi—Mao Zedong shishi sanshi zhounian ji (I)." *Huaxia wenzhai zengkan* 559 (Mar. 5, 2007).
Shan Shi and Fu Bo. "Li Wenfang jianjie." In *Jiqing yongyuan ranshao: Li Wenfang jinian wenji*, edited by Shan Shi, 11–51. Beijing: Zuojia, 2007.
Shao Jiyao. "Xibeiju: Wo yisheng meihao de jiyi." In *Zai Xibeiju de rizi li*, edited by Shi Jie and Si Zhihao, 71–82. Xi'an: Shaanxi shifan daxue chubanshe, 2018.
Shen Baoxiang. *Zhenli biaozhun wenti taolun shimo*. Beijing: Zhongguo qingnian, 1997.
Shen Zhihua. *Sikao yu xuanze: Cong zhishifenzi huiyi dao fanyoupai yundong 1956–1957*. Hong Kong: Chinese University Press, 2008.
Shen Zhihua. *Sulian zhuanjia zai Zhongguo (1948–1960)*. Beijing: Zhongguo guoji guangbo, 2003.
Shen Zhihua. "Tongmeng wajie: Deng Xiaoping shidai de Zhong-Chao guanxi, 1977–1992 (I)." *Ershiyi shiji shuangyue kan* 8, no. 166 (Apr. 2018): 111–21.
Shen Zhihua. "Tongmeng wajie: Deng Xiaoping shidai de Zhong-Chao guanxi, 1977–1992 (II)." *Ershiyi shiji shuangyue kan* 8, no. 168 (Aug. 2018): 109–21.
Sheng Ping and Wang Zaixing, eds. *Hu Yaobang sixiang nianpu*. Special ser., vol. 70. N.p.: SCCP, 2007.
Shi Binhai. *Lishi zhuanzhe zhong de Hua Guofeng (1973–1981)*. Beijing: Beijing chuanshi jiashu wenhua fazhan, 2020.
Shi Yun and Li Xin. "Hu Feng cuo'an shimo." *Wenshi yuekan*, no. 6 (2003): 26–34.
Shi Zhe. *Feng yu gu: Shi Zhe huiyilu*. Beijing: Hongqi, 1992.
Shi Zhe. *Wode yi sheng*. Beijing: Renmin, 2001.

Shi Zhe. "Wo suo zhidao de Kang Sheng." *Yanhuang chunqiu*, no. 5 (Mar. 1992): 10–17, 30.
Shoudu hongdaihui Beijing dianli xueyuan: Jinggangshan gongshe "Peng, Gao, Rao, Xi" zhuan'an xiaozu. *Gao Gang wushinian zui'e shi (1904–1954)*. Ser. 6, vol. 6. N.p.: SCCP, 2007.
Si Tao. *Liu Lantao shengping jishi*. Beijing: Zhongguo wenshi, 2010.
Sima Qingyang and Ouyang Longmen. *Xin faxian de Zhou Enlai*. Carle Place: Mingjing, 2009.
Song Chundan. "'Hongse zhizi' Wulanfu." *Zhongguo xinwen zhoukan*, Mar. 2018.
Song Chundan. "Xi Zhongxun zai 1978." *Zhongguo xinwen zhoukan*, Dec. 17, 2018.
Song Hanliang. "Renzhen xuexi guanche dangde shisanjie sizhong quanhui jingshen, nuli zuohao wo qude gexiang gongzuo." In *Guanche minzu zhengce wenjian xubian*, 240–60. Urumqi: Xinjiang renmin, 1990 (internal circulation).
Song Jinshou. "Wo liaojie de Xibei geming genjudi sufan." *Yanhuang chunqiu*, no. 10 (2012): 47–55.
Song Lin. "Wushi lixing, chizheng buyi." In *Zhu Lizhi bainian dachen jinian wenji*, edited by Zhonggong Nantong shiwei dangshi gongzuo bangongshi, 107–18. Beijing: Zhonggong dangshi, 2008.
Su Chi [Su Qi]. *Liang'an botao ershinian jishi*. Taipei: Yuanjian tianxia wenhua, 2014.
Su Weimin. "Gaige kaifang zhi chu Yang Shangkun zai Guangdong." *Bainianchao*, no. 2 (2008): 18–24.
Suide xian laoqu jianshe cujinhui. *Suide xian geming laoqu fazhan shi*. Xi'an: Shaanxi renmin, 2021.
Suide xianzhi. Xi'an: Sanqin, 2003.
Sun Chunshan. *Wuhui rensheng: Yang Xianzhen*. Ji'nan: Shandong huabao, 2001.
Sun Hongquan. "Zuihou de jiaotan." In *Huainian Yaobang*, edited by Zhang Liqun and Zhang Ding, 285–95. Vol. 1. Hong Kong: Lingtian, 1999.
Sun Jingyan. "Zheng hai mishi." *Shi jie*, no. 1 (1994): 178–94.
Sun Peidong. "Wenge shiqi Jing-Hu zhiqing jiecenghua de geren yuedu." *Ershiyi shiji shuangyue kan*, no. 8 (2016): 78–98.
Sun Qi. "Kenqing buren Nei Menggu zizhiqu dangwei shuji." In *Qinli sanshinian: "Ye Fanghuai" zhengwenji*, edited by Xu Qingquan and Wang Wenyun, 64–66. Beijing: Zhongguo wenshi, 2009.
Sun Yancheng. "Xuetong lun he Daxing 'ba san yi' shijian." *Yanhuang chunqiu*, no. 2 (2012): 32–37.
Sun Yuting. "Nanwang de enqing." In *Huainian Zhongxun*, edited by Cao Zhenzhong and Wu Jiang, 273–74. Beijing: Zhongyang dangshi, 2005.
Sun Zuobin and Lu Jianren. "Huiyi Xi Zhongxun tongzhi de geming shengya." In *Sun Zuobin*, edited by Zhonggong Shanxi shengwei dangshi yanjiu, 436–46. Xi'an: Shaanxi renmin, 1997.
Tang Fei. "Hu Yaobang zhu Shaan jiu 'zuo.'" *Bainianchao*, no. 10 (Nov. 2005): 4–14.
Tang Jiayu. "Xi Zhongxun yu 'Yulin fangshi.'" *Dangshi zonglan*, no. 12 (2017): 4–12.
Tang Jiayu and Zhang Zhuoya. "Xi Zhongxun 'geming shengya zhong zui deyi de yibi.'" *Dangshi bolan*, no. 12 (2017): 14–18.
Tang Luo. "Mao Zedong pingzan Xi Zhongxun." *Yanhuang chunqiu*, no. 11 (1999): 20–22.
Tang Luo. "Song Banchan E'erdeni gui Zang ji." In *Xi Zhongxun geming shengya*, 338–49. Beijing: Zhongguo wenshi, 2000.
Tao Siliang. "Wo zuo zhishi fenzi gongzuo de wangshi." *Yanhuang chunqiu*, no. 6 (2015): 9–15.
Tian Congming. *Mama de xin*. Beijing: Xinhua, 2014.

BIBLIOGRAPHY

Tian Fang. *Suiyue yinhen: Tian Fang wenji*. Beijing: Jincheng, 1998.
Tian Fang. "Wo he Peng Dehuai jiaowang shiernian." *Yanhuang chunqiu*, no. 9 (1994): 4–9.
Tian Fang. "Xi Zhongxun he Liu Zhidan de rongrong ruru." *Yanhuang chunqiu*, no. 10 (1995): 69–73.
Tian Fang. "Xi Zhongxun mingyun zhong jici zhuanzhe." *Yanhuang chunqiu*, no. 8 (2002): 6–7.
Tian Jiyun. "Jin juli ganshou Hu Yaobang." *Yanhuang chunqiu*, no. 10 (2004): 1–5.
Tian Runmin. "Du Heng panbian qianhou." *Yanhuang chunqiu*, no. 3 (2017): 86–92.
Tian Runmin. "Shaan-bei 'sufan' yu Zhang Mutao." *Xibu xuekan*, no. 7 (2014): 38–42.
Tian Runmin, ed. *Xi Zhongxun zai Xunyi de gushi*. Xi'an: Shaanxi renmin, 2013.
Tian Runmin. "Xibei jiefang zhanzheng zhong de qingbao zhan." *Yanhuang chunqiu*, no. 2 (2019): 21–27.
Tianjin hongdaihui Nankai daxue bayiba huoju zongdui, Nei Menggu Hu sansi yi-xueyuan dongfanghong gongshe zhuanqiu Gao Gang louwang fenzi lianluozhan, and Nei Menggu Yimeng hongzongsi lianwei "zhanqiu Gao Gang yudang lianlu-ozhan." "Chedi chanchu Gao Gang yudang (I)." In *Mongorujin jenosaido ni kansuru kiso shiryō*, edited by Yang Haiying, 263–301. Vol. 7. Tokyo: Fukyosha, 2015.
Tong Guirong. "Xi Zhongxun cong qunzhong zhong lai." In *Xi Zhongxun zai Xunyi*, edited by Zhonggong Xianyang shiwei, Dangshi yanjiushi, and Zhonggong Xunyi xianwei, 217–20. Beijing: Zhongyang wenxian, 2012.
Tuo Hongwei and Zhang Huamin. "Shixi Shaanxi ji gongchandang ren zai Cha'ha'er kangzhan zhong de zhongyao zuoyong." *Yan'an daxue xuebao* 35, no. 4 (Aug. 2013): 27–31.
Wan Runnan. *Shanghai yunfan: Sitong gushi*. Hong Kong: Tianyu, 2013.
Wang Chaobei. *Mengyuan jishi*. Self-published, Beijing shidai nongchao wenhua fazhan, 2013.
Wang Chaobei and Shi Ning. *Laizi mimi zhanxian de baogao*. Tianjin: Baihua wenyi, 1997.
Wang Enhui. "Canjia 'qi da': Wo nanyi wanghuai de yi duan jingli." *Zongheng*, no. 4 (2002): 17–19.
Wang Enmao. "Xiang zhongyang shujichu huibao guanyu Xinjiang fasheng de bufen shaoshu minzu xuesheng shangjie youxing shijian de qingkuang he zhongyang shu-jichu taolun Xinjiang wenti huiyi jingshen de chuanda tigang." In *Guanche minzu zhengce wenjian xubian*, 40–47. Urumqi: Xinjiang renmin, 1990 (internal circula-tion).
Wang Enmao. "Zai zizhiqu dangwei dishiqici changwei huishang de fayan." In *Guanche minzu zhengce wenjian xubian*, 96–106. Urumqi: Xinjiang renmin, 1990 (internal cir-culation).
Wang Enmao. "Zai zizhuqu dangwei changwei kuoda huiyishang guanyu Kashi wenti de jianghua (jiexuan)." In *Guanche minzu zhengce wenjian xuanbian*, 123–42. Urumqi: Xinjiang renmin, 1985 (internal circulation).
Wang Fan. "Wu Zuguang he tade jiwei lao pengyou." *Tongzhou gongjin*, no. 2 (2015): 33–36.
Wang Feng zhuan. Beijing: Zhonggong dangshi, 2011.
Wang Guocheng. *Xin Zhongguo tongyi zhanxian 50 nian*. Beijing: Taihai, 1999.
Wang Haiguang. "Liu Shaoqi yu siqing yundong." *Dang de wenxian*, no. 5 (1999): 54–60.
Wang Hongliang. "Wang Gong: Di yi wei lüshi de kanke." *Sanlian shenghuo zhoukan*, no. 37 (Sept. 2009).
Wang Hui. "Yi yu Xi lao de yici huanju." In *Xi Zhongxun jinian wenji*, edited by Zhong-gong zhongyang dangshi yanjiushi, 241–44. Beijing: Zhonggong dangshi, 2013.

Wang Huning. *Meiguo fandui Meiguo*. Shanghai: Shanghai wenyi, 1991.
Wang Jian. "Xi Jinping xiang he chu qu." *Yangguang shiwu zhoukan* 30 (Nov. 2012).
Wang Jiangong. *Jiushinian jian: Wang Jiangong huiyilu*. Hohhot: Nei Menggu renmin, 2006.
Wang Jun. *Zhengcheng fengyun lu*. Hong Kong: Boxue, 2012.
Wang Lin. *Wenyi shiqi nian: Wang Lin riji*. Self-published, 2013.
Wang Lin. *Wode geming licheng*. Beijing: Dangdai Zhongguo, 2001.
Wang Meng zizhuan. Vol. 2. Guangzhou: Huacheng, 2007.
Wang Qinping. *Xin Zhongguo waijiao 50 nian zhong*. Beijing: Beijing chubanshe, 1999.
Wang Qiuying. "Yu Xi lao yi jia qingshen yinong." In *Zai Xibeiju de rizi li*, edited by Shi Jie and Si Zhihao, 151–56. Xi'an: Shaanxi shifan daxue chubanshe, 2018.
Wang Quanguo. "Jiefang sixiang, ganyu chuangxin, ganyu gaige." In *Xi Zhongxun zhuzheng Guangdong yishu lu*, edited by Zhonggong Guangdong shengwei dangshi yanjiushi, 52–71. Beijing: Zhonggong dangshi, 2013.
Wang Ruoshui. *Hu Yaobang xiatai de beijing*. Hong Kong: Mingjing, 1997.
Wang Ruoshui. "Zhou Yang dui Makesizhuyi de zuihou tansuo." In *Yi Zhou Yang*, edited by Wang Meng and Yuan Ying, 414–39. Hohhot: Nei Menggu renmin, 1998.
Wang Shangrong jiangjun. Beijing: Dangdai Zhongguo, 2000.
Wang Shoudao huiyilu. Beijing: Jiefangjun, 1987.
Wang Shusheng. *Wulanfu zhuan*. Beijing: Zhongyang wenxian, 2007.
Wang Taixing. "Jinping tongzhi dui wo zuoren zuoshi yingxiang zhishen." In *Xi Jinping zai Xiamen*, edited by Zhongyang dangxiao caifang shilu bianjishi, 75–86. Beijing: Zhongyang dangxiao, 2020.
Wang Xiaobin. *Zhongguo gongchandang Xizang zhengce de lishi kaocha*. Beijing: Zhonggong zhongyang dangxiao Zhonggong dangshi jiaoyanbu, 2003 (internal circulation).
Wang Xiaobin. *Zhongguo gongchandang Xizang zhengce yanjiu*. Beijing: Renmin, 2013.
Wang Xiaoxin. "Xi Zhongxun yu Sanyuan Dongxiang 'Henan huiguan.'" In *Sanyuan renwen shilüe*, 128–34. Sanyuan: Sanyuan xia, 2015 (internal circulation).
Wang Xiaozhong. *Zhongguwei gongzuo jishi 1982–1987*. Hong Kong: Cosmos Books, 2013.
Wang Xizhe zizhuan: Zouxiang hei'an. Hong Kong: Minzhu daxue chubanshe, 1996.
Wang Xuedong. *Fu Quanyou zhuan*. Vol. 1. Beijing: Jiefangjun, 2015.
Wang Yan. "Yongyuan huainian Xi Zhongxun bobo." *Zhonghong wang*, May 24, 2018. https://archive.ph/5NMZx.
Wang Yinxuan. "Wo he Peng Liyuan." In *Shandong wentan jishi*, edited by Shandong sheng wenlian, 233–36. Ji'nan: Shandong wenyi, 1989.
Wang Yongqin. *Monan zhong de Zhou Enlai*. Beijing: Hongqi, 2009.
Wang Youqin. "Wumai xia de wenge lishi." *Huaxia wenzhai zengkan*, no. 99 (Dec. 2014).
Wang Yuanyuan and Yan Bin. "Richang shenghuo zhong de Yaobang shushu." In *Wangshi huisheng: Zhongguo zhuming zhishifenzi fangtanlu*, edited by Xing Xiaoqun, 1–28. Hong Kong: Shidai guoji, 2005.
Wang Yunfeng. *Yan'an daxue xiaoshi*. Xi'an: Shaanxi renmin, 1994.
"Wang Zhen guanyu huifu bingtuan wenti dui youguan lingdao de tanhua (jielu)." *Xinjiang shengchan jianshe bingtuan shiliao xuanji* 19 (Nov. 2009): 11–13.
Wang Zhen zhuan. 2 vols. Beijing: Dangdai Zhongguo, 1999–2001.
Wang Zhengzhu. *Peng zong zai Xibei jiefang zhanchang*. Xi'an: Shaanxi renmin, 1981.
Wang Zhongfang. *Jiu shi youyu*. Beijing: Self-published, 2015.
Wangjie Pingcuo [Phunwang Wangye]. *Pingdeng tuanjie lu man man: Dui woguo minzu guanxi de fansi*. Hong Kong: Xin shiji, 2014.
Wei Chengsi. "Li Denghui shidai, liang'an jiu du mitan shilu." *Shangye zhoukan* 661 (July 2000): 60–82.

Wei Deping. "Liu Zhidan xisheng zhi 'mi' kaobian." *Yan'an daxue xuebao (shehui kexue ban)* 41, no. 2 (Apr. 2019): 56–65.
Wei Deping. "Li Weihan yu 'Shaan-bei sufan' zhenglun de jiejue." *Dangshi bolan*, no. 3 (2017): 19–25.
Wei Deping. "Yan'an zhengfeng dui 'Shaan-bei sufan' de chongxin dingxing." *Dangshi yanjiu yu jiaoxue*, no. 3 (2012): 16–29.
Wei Deping. "Zhonggong zhongyang shifang Liu Zhidan juti shijian kao." *Zhongguo Yan'an ganbu xueyuan xuebao* 12, no. 4 (July 2019): 110–18.
Wei Deping. "'Zhongyang jiu le Shaan-bei': Guanyu 'daoxia liuren' shuo kaobian." *Zhongguo Yan'an ganbu xueyuan xuebao* 11, no. 2 (Mar. 2018): 125–30.
Wei Junyi. *Sitong lu*. Beijing: Beijing shiyue wenyi, 1998.
Wei Tong. *Hu Xizhong*. Xi'an: Shaanxi renmin jiaoyu, 2003.
Wei Xinsheng. "Xiaoshuo '*Liu Zhidan*' an shuping." In *Huainian Xi Zhongxun*, 442–55. Beijing: Zhonggong dangshi, 2005.
Wen Jize. *Diyige pingfan de "youpai": Wen Jize zishu*. Beijing: Zhongguo qingnian, 1999.
Wen Xiang. *Gaoceng enyuan yu Xi Zhongxun: Cong Xibei dao Beijing*. Hong Kong: Mingjing, 2008.
Wu Dianyao and Song Lin. *Zhu Lizhi zhuan*. Beijing: Zhonggong dangshi, 2007.
Wu Guoguang. "Zhengzhi quanli, xianzhang zhidu yu lishi beiju 'Li Peng [Liu si] riji' chudu." *CND kanwu he luntan*, June 18, 2010. http://hx.cnd.org/2010/06/18/%E5%90%B4%E5%9B%BD%E5%85%89%EF%BC%9A%E6%94%BF%E6%B2%BB%E6%9D%83%E5%8A%9B%E3%80%81%E5%AE%AA%E7%AB%A0%E5%88%B6%E5%BA%A6%E4%B8%8E%E5%8E%86%E5%8F%B2%E6%82%B2%E5%89%A7%E2%80%95%E2%80%95%E3%80%8A%E6%9D%8E/.
Wu Huan. "Xi Zhongxun xiansheng de jijian wangshi." *Gonghui xinxi* 23 (2014): 28–30.
Wu Jiang. "Qin Chuan tan Xi Zhongxun er san shi." *Yanhuang chunqiu*, no. 11 (2003): 56–57.
Wu Jianguo. *Poju: Jiemi! Jiang Jingguo wannian quanli buju gaibian de neimu*. Taipei: Shibao wenhua, 2017.
Wu Jiaxiang. *Zhongnanhai riji*. Carle Place: Mingjing, 2002.
Wu Jun. "Zhuiyi Xi Zhongxun dui Suide shifan xuexiao de guanhuai." In *Xi Zhongxun jinian wenji*, edited by Zhonggong zhongyang dangshi yanjiushi, 557–61. Beijing: Zhonggong dangshi, 2013.
Wu Lengxi. *Shinian lunzhan: 1956–1966 ZhongSu guanxi huiyilu*. Beijing: Zhongyang wenxian, 1999.
Wu Li Yaohua [Julia Li Wu]. *Zuobuwan de Meiguo meng*. Beijing: Dongfang, 2011.
Wu Nansheng. "Wu Nansheng: Wo suo qinli de jingji tequ de juece guocheng." In *Zhongguo dangdai mingren zhengyao fang shuping ji*, edited by Yang Jisheng, 129–52. Hong Kong: Tiandi tushu, 2013.
Wu Nansheng. "Zai Shenzhen ganbu dahuishang de jianghua." In *Jingji tequ de youlai*, 243–47. Guangzhou: Guangdong renmin, 2002.
Wu Nansheng. "Zhenshi de lishi: 'Ganchuang' de jilu." In *Jingji tequ de youlai*, edited by Lin Yajie, 142–52. Guangzhou: Guangdong renmin, 2010.
Wu Songying. *Qinlizhe jishu: 1992 nian Deng Xiaoping nanxun neiqing*. Hong Kong: Mingbao, 2012.
Wu Wei. *Zhongguo 80 niandai zhengzhi gaige de taiqian muhou*. Hong Kong: Xin shiji, 2013.
Wu Wenjun. "Longshang dajihuang ji qi jiaoxun." In *Gansu liushi niandai dajihuang kaozheng*, 1–39. Special ser., vol. 74. N.p.: SCCP, 2007.
Wu Wenxiao. "'*Liu Zhidan*' beihou de xuanran dabo." *Fujian dangshi yuekan*, no. 6 (2010): 44–46.

Wu Xiang. "Zhu Houze he tade 'san kuan.'" *Yanhuang chunqiu*, no. 11 (2010): 19–24.
Wu Zhifei. "Xi Jinping: Cong huangtu gaopo dao Shanghai tan." *Dangshi zongheng*, no. 5 (2007): 16–21.
Wu Zhongxian. *Xi Zhongxun zai Changge*. Zhengzhou: Henan renmin, 2014.
Wu Zuguang. *Yi beizi: Wu Zuguang huiyilu*. Beijing: Zhongguo wenlian, 2004.
Xi An'an. "Baba, cong mei likaiguo women." In *Xi Zhongxun jinian wenji*, edited by Zhonggong zhongyang dangshi yanjiushi, 796–805. Beijing: Zhonggong dangshi, 2013.
Xi Jinping. "Gei baba bashiba zhousui shengri de hexin." In *Xi Zhongxun jinian wenji*, edited by Zhonggong zhongyang dangshi yanjiushi, 806–7. Beijing: Zhonggong dangshi, 2013.
Xi Jinping. "Geng hao bawo he yunyong dangde bainian fendou lishi jingyan." *Qiushi*, June 30, 2022.
Xi Jinping. "Jianchi he fazhan Zhongguo tese shehui zhuyi yao yi yi guan zhi." *Qiushi*, Sept. 15, 2022.
Xi Jinping. "Jicheng he fayang dangde youliang geming chuantong he zuofeng, hongyang Yan'an jingsheng." *Qiushi*, Dec. 16, 2022.
Xi Jinping. "Kua shiji lingdao ganbu de lishi zhongren ji bibei suzhi." *Lilun xuexi yuekan*, no. 11 (1991): 32–36.
Xi Jinping. "Lun wenyi yu zhengzhi de guanxi." *Caibei* 30 (Oct. 1989): 3–5.
Xi Jinping. "Sizheng ke shi luoshi lide shuren genben renwu de guanjian kecheng." *Qiushi*, Aug. 31, 2020.
Xi Jinping. "Wei guan zhi dao." *Lingdao kexue*, no. 9 (1990): 32.
Xi Jinping. "Zai dangshi xuexi jiaoyu dongyuan dahuishang de jianghua." *Qiushi*, Mar. 31, 2021.
Xi Jinping. "Zengqiang youhuan yishi, weiji yishi, shiming yishi." In *Xi Jinping guanyu guofang he jundui jianshe zhongyao lunshu xuanbian*, 47–53. Beijing: Jiefangjun, 2014 (internal circulation).
Xi Jinping. "Zhi zhi zhen, ai zhi qie." *Zhongguo qingnian*, no. 5 (1984): 20–21.
"Xi Jinping mantan wangxi 30 nian." *Dangshi wenyuan*, no. 3 (2004): 52–53.
Xi Qianping. "Baowei xiao bianzi!" In *Zai Yuying, women zouguo tongnian*, edited by Zhongzhi yuying xiaoxue tongxue hui, 133–35. Beijing: Zhonggong dangshi, 2007.
Xi Qianping. "Bo Yibo tan 'luhuo chunqing' yu '*Liu Zhidan* xiaoshuo yuan'an' neimu." In *Huainian Xi Zhongxun*, edited by Cao Zhenzhong and Wu Jiang, 433–41. Beijing: Zhongyang dangshi, 2005.
Xi Wei and Liang Ping. "Huiyi bofu Xi Zhongxun." In *Jinian Xi Zhongxun danchen 100 zhounian wenji*, edited by Zhonggong Shaanxi shengwei dangshi yanjiushi, 113–15. Xi'an: Shaanxi renmin, 2015.
Xi Yuanping. "Fuqin wangshi." In *Xi Zhongxun jinian wenji*, edited by Zhonggong zhongyang dangshi yanjiushi, 808–19. Beijing: Zhonggong dangshi, 2013.
Xi Zhengning. "Fuqin dui wode zhunzhun jiaohui." In *Xi Zhongxun jinian wenji*, edited by Zhonggong zhongyang dangshi yanjiushi, 767–73. Beijing: Zhonggong dangshi, 2013.
Xi Zhengning. "Hainan fazhi xuanchuan jiaoyu gongzuo tantao." *Hainan sheng lilun yantaohui lunwen ji*, edited by Ruan Chongwu, 273–80. Haikou: Hainan, 1994.
Xi Zhengning. "Wanshan Hainan jingji tequ falü fuwu shichang de yanjiu." In *Hainan sheng lilun yantaohui lunwen ji*, edited by Ruan Chongwu, 514–24. Haikou: Hainan, 1994.
Xi Zhengqin. "'Sanyuan Dongxiang' wangshi." In *Sanyuan renwen*, 135–40. Sanyuan: Sanyuanxian dang'an ju, 2015 (internal circulation).
Xi Zhonggun, Huang Li, and Tan Jinhang. "Xi Zhongxun: Yi min wei tian de Zhongguo gongchandang ren." *Caijing jie*, no. 2 (2015): 68–77.

Xi Zhonggun, Huang Li, and Tan Jinhang. "Xi Zhongxun: Yi min wei tian de Zhongguo gongchandang ren." *Caijing jie*, no. 3 (2015): 86–95.
Xi Zhonggun, Huang Li, and Tan Jinhang. "Xi Zhongxun: Yi min wei tian de Zhongguo gongchandang ren." *Caijing jie*, no. 7 (2015): 75–85.
Xi Zhongxun. "Dongyuan yiqie liliang wei wancheng quansheng tudi gaige er douzheng." *Gansu zhengbao* 2, no. 5 (Sept. 1951): 1–8.
Xi Zhongxun. "Duiyu dianying gongzuo de yijian." *Dianying juzuo tongxun*, May 10, 1953, 3–12 (internal circulation).
Xi Zhongxun. "Fandui guanliao zhuyi, mingling zhuyi." *Xibei zhengbao* 1, no. 3 (May 1950): 25–31.
Xi Zhongxun. "Gonggu chengji, kefu quedian, zhengqu gengde de shengli." *Xinjiang zhengbao* 2, no. 5 (May 1951): 4–6.
Xi Zhongxun. "Guanyu Guangdong zhi xing de baogao." In *Xi Zhongxun wenxuan*, 447–56. Beijing: Zhongyang wenxian, 1995.
Xi Zhongxun. "Guanyu jiaqiang he gaishan budui zhengzhi gongzuo de jidian yijian." In *Xi Zhongxun wenji*, 625–38. Vol. 1. Beijing: Zhonggong dangshi, 2013.
Xi Zhongxun. "Guanzhong dangshi jianshu (jiexuan)." In *Longdong geming genjudi de xingcheng*, 261–65. Qingyang: Zhonggong Qingyang diwei dangshi ziliao zhengji bangongshi, 1990.
Xi Zhongxun. "Guowuyuan fuzongli Xi Zhongxun tongzhi zai Zhonggong Changge xianwei (kuoda) huiyishang de jianghua." In *Changge xianzhi*, 2–9. Beijing: Shenghuo-dushu-xinzhi sanlian shudian, 1992.
Xi Zhongxun. "Hongri zhaoliangle Shaan-Gan gaoyuan." In *Xi Zhongxun wenxuan*, 286–300. Beijing: zhongyang wenxian, 1995.
Xi Zhongxun. "Huiyi Huang Ziwen." In *Weibei Huang shi xiongdi*, 59–61. Sanyuan: Shaanxi sheng Sanyuanxian wenshi ziliao weiyuanhui, 2009 (internal circulation).
Xi Zhongxun. Introduction to *Gaige kaifang zai Guangdong: Xian zou yibu de shijian yu sikao*, edited by Lin Ruo, 1–5. Guangzhou: Guangdong gaodeng jiaoyu, 1992.
Xi Zhongxun. Introduction to *Zhonggong Shaanxi dixiadang fan dite douzheng jishi*, by Luo Wenzhi, 1–5. Xi'an: Shaanxi renmin, 1998.
Xi Zhongxun. "Nimen shi you lixiang you zhiqi de hao er'nü." *Liaowang*, no. 19 (Apr. 1985): 9–10.
Xi Zhongxun. "1945 nian 7 yue Xi Zhongxun zai Shaan-Gan-Ning bianqu lishi zuotan huishang de fayan (jiexuan)." July 1945. Reprint, Huangtu lianyihui, Nov. 6, 2019. https://archive.ph/wip/jSY7Q.
Xi Zhongxun. "1942 nian 11 yue Xi Zhongxun zai Xibeiju gaogan huiyishang guanyu Shaan-Gan bian dangshi wenti de fayan (zhaiyao)." Nov. 1942. Reprint, Huangtu lianyihui, Aug. 20, 2024. https://archive.ph/wip/LzR5u.
Xi Zhongxun. "Quanguo renda changwei wei fuweiyuanzhang Xi Zhongxun tongzhi zai tianzhujiao qingzhu aiguohui chengli he zixuan zisheng zhujiao ershiwu zhounian dahuishang de jianghua yaodian." *Zhongguo tianzhujiao*, no. 7 (1983): 43–45.
Xi Zhongxun. "Qunzhong lingxiu, minzu yingxiong." In *Xi Zhongxun wenji*, 558–74. Vol. 1. Beijing: Zhonggong dangshi, 2013.
Xi Zhongxun. "Ruhe zuohao yijiuwuyi nian de nongye shengchan gongzuo." *Xibei zhengbao* 1, no. 11 (Feb. 1951): 16–18.
Xi Zhongxun. "Shao shuo konghua, duo ban shishi, ba shaoshu minzu diqu de jingji wenhua jianshe gaoshangqu." In *Xin shiqi tongyi zhanxian wenxian xuanbian (xubian)*, edited by Zhonggong zhongyang tongzhanbu and Zhonggong zhongyang wenxian yanjiushi, 44–56. Beijing: Zhonggong zhongyang dangxiao, 1997.
Xi Zhongxun. "Tingqu Zhuhai jingji tequ fuze ren gongzuo huibao hou de jianghua." In *Xi Zhongxun wenji*, 1144–53. Vol. 2. Beijing: Zhonggong dangshi, 2013.

Xi Zhongxun. "Tongyi zhanxian rengran shi yi da fabao." In *Lici quanguo tongzhan gongzuo huiyi gaikuang he wenxian*, 567–72. Beijing: Dang'an, 1988 (internal circulation).
Xi Zhongxun. "Wending shi guojia de zuigao liyi." In *Xi Zhongxun wenxuan*, 476–79. Beijing: Zhongyang wenxian, 1995.
Xi Zhongxun. "Xibei qu yijiuwuyi nian de gongzuo renwu." *Xibei zhengbao* 1, no. 10 (Jan. 1951): 1–2.
Xi Zhongxun. "Xi Zhongxun fuweiyuanzhang zai huanying yanhuishang de jianghua." In *Zhong-Chao liangdang, liangguo lingdaoren jianghua he heyan dian huibian*, 127–29. N.p.: Zhonggong zhongyang duiwai lianluobu erju, 1983 (internal circulation).
Xi Zhongxun. "Xi Zhongxun tongzhi zai gaobie yanhuishang de jianghua." In *Zhong-Chao liangdang, liangguo lingdaoren jianghua he heyan dian huibian*, 146–7. N.p.: Zhonggong zhongyang duiwai lianluobu erju, 1983 (internal circulation).
Xi Zhongxun. "Xi Zhongxun tongzhi zai huanying yanhuishang de jianghua." In *Zhong-Chao liangdang, liangguo lingdaoren jianghua he heyan dian huibian*, 137–39. N.p.: Zhonggong zhongyang duiwai lianluobu erju, 1983 (internal circulation).
Xi Zhongxun. "Xuexiao yao jiaqiang sixiang zhengzhi jiaoyu gongzuo." In *Xi Zhongxun wenxuan*, 363–65. Beijing: Zhongyang wenxian, 1995.
Xi Zhongxun. "Yi dang zhongyang zai zhuanzhan Shaan-bei zhong zhaokai de Xiaohe huiyi." *Zhonggong dangshi ziliao* 52 (1994): 1–12.
Xi Zhongxun. "Yong gaige jingshen kaichuang zhengxie gongzuo xin jumian." In *Lao yidai gemingjia lun renmin zhengxie*, 362–64. Beijing: Zhongyang wenxian, 1997.
Xi Zhongxun. "Yongyuan nanwang de huainian." In *Xi Zhongxun wenxuan*, 301–19. Beijing: Zhongyang wenxian, 1995.
Xi Zhongxun. "Zai luoshi zhengce zuotan huishang de jianghua." In *Minzu zhengce wenxuan*, 274–86. Urumqi: Xinjiang renmin, 1985 (internal circulation).
Xi Zhongxun. "Zai quanguo funü di sijie zhixing weiyuanhui disici kuoda huiyishang de jianghua." In *"Si da" yilai funü yundong wenxuan*, 54–59. Beijing: Zhongguo funü, 1983.
Xi Zhongxun. "Zai quansheng jijian ganbu xuexiban jieye huishang de jianghua." In *Guangdong jijian jiancha ji: 1950–1995 nian*, edited by Zhonggong Guangdong sheng jilü jiancha weiyuanhui and Guangdong sheng jianchating, 886–87. Guangzhou: Guangzhou renmin, 1998.
Xi Zhongxun. "Zai shengwei sijie sanci changwei kuoda huiyishang de jianghua." In *Jingji tequ de youlai*, 194–97. Guangzhou: Guangdong renmin, 2002.
Xi Zhongxun. "Zai Xinhuashe jianshe wushi zhounian jinian huishang de jianghua." In *Xi Zhongxun wenji*, 694–95. Vol. 2. Beijing: Zhonggong dangshi, 2013.
"Xi Zhongxun fuweiyuanzhang zai gaobie yanhuishang de jianghua." In *Zhong-Chao liangdang, liangguo lingdaoren jianghua he heyan dian huibian*, 130–33. N.p.: Zhonggong zhongyang duiwai lianluobu erju, 1983 (internal circulation).
Xi Zhongxun huace. Shenzhen: Haitian, 2006.
"Xi Zhongxun, Li Weihan deng tongzhi he Banchan tanhua jiyao." In *Youguan Banchan yinyan huozui de ruogan xijian shiliao (1962 nian 8 yue)*, 1–43. Ser. 31, vol. 10. N.p.: SCCP, 2010.
Xi Zhongxun moji. Beijing: Zhongyang wenxian, 2013.
Xi Zhongxun nianpu. 4 vols. Beijing: Zhongyang wenxian, 2024.
"Xi Zhongxun tongzhi guanyu xinqu gongzuo wenti gei Mao zhuxi de baogao." In *Zhonggong dangshi jiaoxue cankao ziliao*, 449–52. Vol. 18. Beijing: Zhongguo renmin jiefangjun zhengzhi xueyuan dangshi jiaoyanshi, 1986.
"Xi Zhongxun tongzhi jianghua." *Gong'an daxue xuebao*, no. 1 (1985): 2–4.
"Xi Zhongxun tongzhi shicha Shenzhen, Zhuhai shi de jianghua." In *Zhongyang dui*

Guangdong gongzuo zhishi huibian (1986 nian–1987 nian), 262–77. Ser. 28, vol. 41, pt. 1. N.p.: SCCP, 2007.
"Xi Zhongxun tongzhi zai di sanci quanguo zongjiao gongzuo huiyishang de zongjie." In *Tongzhan zhengce wenjian huibian*, 2010–21. Vol. 4. N.p.: Zhonggong zhongyang tongyi zhanxian gongzuobu, 1958 (internal circulation).
"Xi Zhongxun tongzhi zai quanguo zongjiao ju (chu) zhang huiyishang de jianghua." In *Zongjiao zhengce wenjian huibian*. Ser. 32, vol. 75. N.p.: SCCP, 2016.
"Xi Zhongxun tongzhi zai sheng, zizhiqu, zhixiashi qiaoban zhuren huiyishang de jianghua." In *Qiaowu fagui wenjian huibian*, 38–50. N.p.: Guowuyuan, Qiaowu bangongshi, Zhengce yanjiushi, 1989.
"Xi Zhongxun xiang gejie qingniantuan tanhua shilu." *Xinbao caijing yuekan* 7, no. 4 (July 1983): 35–36.
Xi Zhongxun zai Shaan-Gan-Ning bianqu. Beijing: Zhongguo wenshi, 2014.
Xi Zhongxun zhuan. 2 vols. Beijing: Zhongyang wenxian, 2013.
Xi Zhongxun zhuzheng Guangdong. Beijing: Zhonggong dangshi, 2008.
Xia Lina. "Zou Yu yi Xi Zhongxun zai quanguo renda de rizi." *Zhongguo renda zazhi*, no. 1 (2014): 47–48.
Xia Meng. "Xibei zhi hun." In *Huainian Xi Zhongxun*, edited by Cao Zhenzhong and Wu Jiang, 489–522. Beijing: Zhongyang dangshi, 2005.
Xia Meng and Wang Xiaoqiang. *Xi Zhongxun huazhuan*. Beijing: Renmin, 2014.
Xi'an diqu wenyijie geming zaofan zongsilingbu doupigai bangongshi. *Chedi qingsuan Peng, Gao, Xi fandang jituan liyong wenxue yishu fandang de taotian zuixing*. Ser. 6, vol. 6, pt. 4. N.p.: SCCP, 2007.
Xi'an shi dang'anju and Xi'an shi dang'anguan, eds. *Xi'an shi junguan hui jieguan Xi'an gongzuo zongjie (jielu)*. In *Xi'an jiefang dang'an shiliao xuanji*, 201–15. Xi'an: Shaanxi renmin, 1989.
Xiang Nan. Introduction to *Baituo pinkun*, by and edited by Xi Jinping, 1–3. Fuzhou: Fujian renmin, 1992.
Xiao Donglian. *Lishi de zhuanzhe—cong boluan fanzheng dao gaige kaifang*. Hong Kong: Quanqiu faxing zhongwen daxue, 2008.
Xiao Donglian. *Tanlu zhi yi: 1978–1992 nian de Zhongguo jingji gaige*. Beijing: Shehui kexue wenxian, 2019.
Xiao Donglian. *Wenge qian shinian shi 1956–1966*. Vol. 2. Hong Kong: Heping tushu, 2013.
Xiao Jin. *Zhengdang dashiji*. Harbin: Heilongjiang renmin, 1985.
Xiao Jun. *Yan'an riji, 1943–1945*. Vol. 2. Hong Kong: Oxford University Press, 2013.
Xiao Ming. *Guangxi wenge tongshi gouchen*. Hong Kong: Xin shiji, 2013.
Xiao Sheng. "Xibei jin Zang de houqin gongzuo." *Xizang geming huiyilu* 3 (1984): 269–83.
Xiao Yiping. "Kongsu Kang Sheng, Cao Yiou zai zhongyang dangxiao de zuixing." In *Xiao Yiping wengao juan yi*, 319–24. Hong Kong: Zhongguo wenhua chuanmei, 2008.
Xibei Yan. *Zhenxiang: 1935 nian Shaan-bei cuowu sufan shimo*. Beijing: Huaxia wenhua yishu, 2014.
Xie Tielun. *Huanghe bian jishi*. Beijing: Zhongyang wenxian, 2014.
Xin Guangwu. *Banchan chuanqi*. Hong Kong: Dafeng, 2008.
Xin Zhongguo pindao. "Peng Liyuan 1999 fangtan." YouTube, Oct. 13, 2013. Video. https://youtu.be/TWToogv1m3Y?si=0ebOVZagyLMagZQr.
"Xin Zhongguo tongyi zhanxian liushinian dashiji" bianji zu, ed. *Xin Zhongguo tongyi zhanxian liushinian dashiji*. Beijing: Huawen, 2000.
Xing Xiaoqun. "Richang shenghuo zhong de Yaobang shushu." *Lao zhaopian* 42 (Aug. 2005): 1–28.
Xinjiang Weiwuer zizhiqu difangzhi bianzuan weiyuanhui. *Xinjiang dashiji*. Urumqi: Xinjiang renmin, 2016.

Xiong Xianghui. *Wode qingbao yu waijiao shengya*. Beijing: Zhonggong dangshi, 1999.
"Xizang gongzuo zuotanhui jiyao." In *Xizang zizhiqu guanche yijiubasi nian Zhonggong zhongyang shujichu zhaokai de Xizang gongzuo zuotanhui jingshen wenjian xuanbian*, 1–25. Ser. 28, vol. 69, pt. 1. N.p.: SCCP, 2009.
Xizang zizhiqu dangshi ziliao zhengji weiyuanhui and Xizang junqu dangshi ziliao zhengji lingdao xiaozu, eds. "Zhongyang guanyu Xibeiju fudan Houzang he Ali diqu zhengzhi renwu dian." In *Heping jiefang Xizang*, 104. Chengdu: Xizang renmin, 1995 (internal circulation).
Xizang zizhiqu dangwei bangongting. "Qu dangwei yinfa Zhonggong zhongyang guanyu 'Dangqian Xizang gongzuo de jige wenti de tongzhi.'" In *Xizang zizhiqu zhongyao wenjian xuanbian 1985–1990 xia ce, Zhonggong Xizang zhongyao lishi wenxian ziliao huibian*, 1–4. Vol. 27. N.p.: SCCP, 2011.
Xizang zizhiqu gong'anting. *Xizang gong'an dashiji 1950–1995*. Vol. 16. Lhasa: Zhonggong Xizang zhongyao lishi wenxian ziliao huibian, 1999.
Xu Danlu. *Fengxue gaoyuan: Kang-Zang diqu gongzuo jishi*. Beijing: Guojia anquan bu bangong ting qingbao shi yanjiu chu, 1996 (internal circulation).
Xu Huangang and Li Zhaoxiang. *Ke Hua dashi de waijiao shengya*. Beijing: Zhongguo qingnian, 2001.
Xu Jiatun. *Xu Jiatun huiyi yu suixiang lu*. Carle Place: Mingjing, 1998.
Xu Jiatun. *Xu Jiatun liuxia de mimi*. Hong Kong: Mingjing, 2016.
Xu Jiatun. *Xu Jiatun Xianggang huiyilu*. Vol. 1. Hong Kong: Xianggang lianhebao, 1993.
Xu Mingde. *Wo zhe yi beizi*. N.p.: [PRChina], n.d.
Xu Mingxu. *Xueshan xia de chouxing: Xizang baoluan de lailong qumai*. Chengdu: Sichuan jiaoyu, 2010.
Xu Qingquan. *Fengyu song chungui: Xin shiqi wentan sixiang jiefang yundong jishi*. Kaifeng: Henan daxue chubanshe, 2005.
Xu Qingquan, ed. "Yu Qin Chuan tan Zhou Yang." In *Zhiqingzhe shuo Zhou Yang*, 53–76. Beijing: Jingji ribao, 2003.
Xu Qingquan, ed. "Yu Zhou Weizhi tan Zhou Yang." In *Zhiqingzhe shuo Zhou Yang*, 3–52. Beijing: Jingji ribao, 2003.
Xu Renjun. "20 shiji 70 niandai mo de zhiqing fancheng langchao." *Dangshi bolan*, no. 2 (2004): 9–15.
Xu Ruiyuan and Han Jinqiang. "Cong Mao Zedong jiu feng shuxin qianxi Xi Zhongxun dui jieying zhongyuan tuwei Wang Zhen bu beifan Yan'an de lishi gongxian." *Dang'an*, no. 10 (2016): 19–27.
Xu Xiangqian nianpu. Vol. 2. Beijing: Jiefangjun, 2016.
Xu Yiming. "Bawo hao xinwen gongzuo de jidian." *Zhongguo jizhe* (July 1989): 13–14.
Xu Yongyue. "Yuan Chen Yun mishu Xu Yongyue: Wannian Chen Yun yu Deng Xiaoping." *Bainianchao*, no. 3 (2006): 13–17.
Xu Youyu. "1977: Gaibian mingyun de kaiduan." In *Kaifang Zhongguo: Gaige de 30 nian jiyi*, edited by Jingji guancha bao, 3–10. Beijing: Zhongxin, 2008.
Xu Youyu. *Xingxing sese de zaofan: Hongweibing jingshen suzhi de xingcheng ji yanbian*. Hong Kong: Zhongwen daxue chubanshe, 1999.
Xue Qingchao. *Lishi de jianzheng: "Wenge" de zhongjie*. Beijing: Jiuzhou, 2011.
Xunmi zhenshi de Liu Geping. Beijing: Zhongguo fazhan, 2016.
Yaita Akio and Huang Yiyun. *Xi Jinping: Gongchan Zhongguo zui tuoshi de lingxiu*. Taipei: Tianxia zazhi, 2012.
Yan Changgui. "Kang Sheng de mishu tan Kang Sheng." *Yanhuang chunqiu*, no. 2 (2013): 45–47.
Yan Hongwei and Qiu Ran, eds. *Xi Zhongxun yu qunzhong luxian*. Vol. 1. Beijing: Zhonggong zhongyang dangxiao, 2015.

Yan Huai. *Jinchu zhongzubu: Yige hongerdai lixiangzhuyizhe de linglei rensheng.* Deer Park, NY: Mingjing, 2017.
Yan Mingfu. "Cong wo qinli de ji jian shi kan Kang Sheng." *Yanhuang chunqiu*, no. 5 (2005): 40–45.
Yan Mingfu. "Yi Xi lao." In *Xi Zhongxun jinian wenji*, edited by Zhonggong zhongyang dangshi yanjiushi, 72–89. Beijing: Zhonggong dangshi, 2013.
Yan Qiying. *Xi Zhongxun huazhuan.* Beijing: Xuexi, 2013.
Yan'an zhengfeng yundong jishi. Beijing: Qiushi, 1982.
Yang Fajin. "Beijing bayi xuexiao weishenme tuichi huahui difang guanli." *Dangshi bolan*, no. 4 (2019): 29–31.
Yang Jisheng, ed. *Zhongguo dangdai mingren zhengyao fang shuping ji.* Hong Kong: Tiandi tushu, 2013.
Yang Jisheng. *Zhongguo gaige niandai de zhengzhi douzheng.* Hong Kong: Excellent Culture, 2004.
Yang Kuisong. *Mao Zedong yu Mosike de en'en yuanyuan.* 4th ed. Nanchang: Jiangxi renmin, 2009.
Yang Kuisong. *Shiqu de jihui? Kangzhan qianhou guogong tanpan shilu.* Beijing: Xinxing, 2010.
Yang Kuisong. *Zhonghua renmin gongheguo jianguo shi yanjiu.* Nanchang: Jiangxi renmin, 2015.
Yang Li. *Gu Dacun chenyuan lu.* Hong Kong: Tiandi tushu, 2000.
Yang Lin and Bu Changjiong. "'Renzhe' Xi Zhongxun." *Boke tianxia* 158 (Apr. 2014).
Yang Ping. "Mudu ganren de Xi jia fuzi qing." *Yanhuang shijie* 132, no. 2 (2013): 6–11.
Yang Shangkun. "Huiyi Gao-Rao Shijian." *Dang de wenxian*, no. 1 (2001): 14–22.
Yang Shangkun huiyilu. Beijing: Zhongyang wenxian, 2001.
Yang Shizhong. "Jinping dang cun zhishu jiu shi yinwei dajia dou yonghu ta." In *Xi Jinping de qinian zhiqing suiyue*, edited by Zhongyang dangxiao caifang shilu bianjishi, 363–72. Beijing: Zhonggong zhongyang dangxiao, 2017.
Yang Tianshi. *Jiang Jieshi zhenxiang zhi er: Kangzhan ji zhanhou.* Taipei: Fengyun shidai, 2009.
Yang Wenyu. "Yan'an shiqi de aiqing." *Dangshi bolan*, no. 5 (1998): 27–31.
Yang Xiaohuai. "Xi Jinping: Wo shi ruhe kuaru zhengjie de." *Zhonghua ernü*, no. 7 (2000): 39–44.
Yang Zhesheng. *Zai Hu Zongnan shenbian de shiernian.* Shanghai: Shanghai renmin, 2007.
Yang Zhijun. *Wangming xingji.* Beijing: Zhongguo gongren, 2002.
"Yanhuang chunqiu zazhishe jihui qingzhu chuangkan shizhounian." *Yanhuang chunqiu*, no. 8 (2001): 17.
Yao Jianfu. *Chen Xitong qinshu.* Hong Kong: Xin shiji, 2012.
Yao Jianfu. "Du Runsheng: Zaodian fangxia 'liu si' zhe ge baofu." *Xin shiji* 8 (June 2012): 80–84.
Ye Fang. *Shehui zhi'an zonghe zhili shiwu quanshu.* Beijing: Zhongguo renmin gong'an daxue chubanshe, 1997.
Ye Jianying. "Zai dangde shiyijie wuzhong quanhui diyici huiyishang de jianghua." In *Sanzhong quanhui yilai zhongyao wenxian huibian*, 388–92. Vol. 1. Beijing: Renmin, 1982.
Ye Jianying nianpu (1897–1986). Vol. 2. Beijing: Zhongyang wenxian, 2007.
"Ye Jianying zai zhongyang gongzuo huiyi bimu huishang de jianghua." Unpublished manuscript, Dec. 13, 1978. Held by Warren Sun.
Ye Shengtao ji. Vol. 22. Nanjing: Jiangsu jiaoyu, 2004.
Ye Xiaoling. "Wo shi yige nenggou tixing ziji, yueshi ziji de ren." *Lingdao wencui*, no. 5 (2004): 71–76.

Yidai zhanjiang: Huiyi Wang Jinshan. Beijing: Junshi kexue, 1992.
Yin Fatang. *Cong Taishan dao Zhufeng*. Beijing: Zhongguo Zangxue, 2021.
Yin Fatang. "Zhou Enlai dui Xizang minzu fazhan de zhuoyue gongxian." In *Zhou Enlai yu Xizang*, edited by Zhonggong Gansu shengwei, 249–88. Beijing: Zhongguo Zangxue, 1998.
"Yin Fatang tongzhi zai Zhonggong Xizang zizhiqu sanjie erci quanwei kuoda huiyishang de jianghua." In *Xizang zizhiqu guanche yijiubasi nian Zhonggong zhongyang shujichu zhaokai de Xizang gongzuo zuotanhui jingshen wenjian xuanbian*, 74–100. Ser. 28, vol. 69, pt. 1. N.p.: SCCP, 2009.
Yin Shusheng. "Gong'an gongzuo 'da yuejin.'" *Yanhuang chunqiu*, no. 1 (2010): 17–23.
Yong Huaqi. "Xi Jinping hui Zhengding (I)." *Lingdao wencui*, no. 11 (2009): 63–68.
Yu Guangyuan. *Wo yanzhong de tamen*. Hong Kong: Shidai guoji, 2005.
Yu Guangyuan. *Wode jiaoyu sixiang*. Suzhou: Suzhou daxue chubanshe, 2000.
Yu Guangyuan. "Zhou Yang he wo." In *Yi Zhou Yang*, edited by Wang Meng and Yuan Ying, 154–208. Hohhot: Nei Menggu renmin, 1998.
Yu Ruxin. *Kang Sheng nianpu (1898–1975): Yige Zhongguo gongchandang ren de yisheng*. Hong Kong: Xin shiji, 2023.
Yuan Renyuan. *Zhengtu jishi*. Changsha: Hunan renmin, 1985.
Yuan Zhigang. "Jiefangjun gaoji jiangling pingshu Xibei zhanchang (I)." *Dangshi bolan*, no. 2 (2012): 36–42.
Yuan Zhigang. "Jiefangjun gaoji jiangling pingshu Xibei zhanchang (II)." *Dangshi bolan*, no. 3 (2012): 21–24.
Yuan Zhigang. *Xibei da jiaofei jishi*. Beijing: Jiefangjun, 2008.
Yue Yufeng. "Huainian lao shouzhang Xi Zhongxun tongzhi." In *Huainian Xi Zhongxun*, edited by Cao Zhenzhong and Wu Jiang, 275–84. Beijing: Zhongyang dangshi, 2005.
Yuhao wang. "Wo shi Yan'an ren." YouTube, Oct. 20, 2019. Video. https://www.youtube.com/watch?v=a_hx9ZXT2BU.
Yun Shubi. "Cong Tumochuan dao Yan'an: Zhuixun fuqin Wulanfu de zuji." *Shenjian* 4 (2011): 4–24.
Zeng Dingshi. "Huiyi sheng zhengfu de hao banzhang Tianfu tongzhi." In *Huiyi Liu Tianfu*, 153–62. Hong Kong: Xianggang rongyu, 2003.
Zeng Shan zhuan. Nanchang: Jiangxi renmin, 2019.
Zhang Aisheng. *Cong qunzhong zhong zou chulai de qunzhong lingxiu Xi Zhongxun (Xibei suiyue)*. Beijing: Zhonggong zhongyang dangxiao, 2017.
Zhang Bing. *Wang Guoquan zhuan*. Kaifeng: Henan daxue chubanshe, 2006.
Zhang Chunsheng. "1979–1986: Liang du nanchan de Zhongguo minfa dian shi ruhe kaishi tupo de." *Zhongguo xinwen zhoukan*, Oct. 16, 2018.
Zhang Chunsheng and Lü Wan. "Zai zuo 30 nian, women ye bu neng hezhe yanjing lifa: Zhang Chunsheng fangtanlu." *Difang lifa yanjiu* 4, no. 6 (Nov. 2019): 112–25.
Zhang Ganghua. *Li Peng riji zhenxiang*. Hong Kong: Aoya, 2010.
Zhang Gensheng. "Ting Hua Guofeng tan jijian dashi." *Yanhuang chunqiu*, no. 10 (2008): 9–10.
Zhang Guangnian. *Wentan huichun jishi*. Vol. 1. Shenzhen: Haitian, 1998.
Zhang Guoying. "Buyi yuli, zhichi Shenzhen gaige kaifang shiye." In *Xi Zhongxun zhuzheng Guangdong yishu lu*, edited by Zhonggong Guangdong shengwei dangshi yanjiushi, 424–35. Beijing: Zhonggong dangshi, 2013.
Zhang Guoying shenqie huainian Xi Zhongxun: Xi Zhongxun danchen yibai zhounian jinian, 1913–2013. Guangzhou: Self-published, 2013.
Zhang Hanqing. "Ta yong ziji yi sheng de shijian lai shuxie 'qunzhong luxian' zhe sige dazi." In *Caifang shilu: Xi Zhongxun zai Guangdong de gushi*, edited by Yan Hongwei and Qiu Ran, 157–85. Hong Kong: Xianggang zhonghe, 2016.

Zhang Hanqing. "Yinling Guangdong gaige kaifang xian zou yi bu." In *Xi Zhongxun zhuzheng Guangdong yishu lu*, edited by Zhonggong Guangdong shengwei dangshi yanjiushi, 146–63. Beijing: Zhonggong dangshi, 2013.

Zhang Huamin. "Wu Daifeng tongzhi er san shi." *Yan'an wenxue*, no. 1 (2013): 161–64.

Zhang Huamin. *Xie Zichang zhuan*. Beijing: Zhonggong zhongyang dangxiao, 2015.

Zhang Jiashu. "Wu ling zan song wu zhu." *Zhongguo tianzhujiao*, no. 3 (1987): 16–19.

"Zhang Jiashu zhujiao de fayan (Shen Baozhi shenfu xuandu)." *Zhongguo tianzhujiao*, no. 7 (1983): 45–46.

Zhang Lifan. "Hu Yaobang zhisang shouji." *Yanhuang chunqiu*, no. 6 (2012): 1–8.

Zhang Liqun, Yan Ruping, Tang Fei, and Li Gongtian. *Hu Yaobang zhuan*. 3 vols. N.p.: Zhengqiu yijian gao, 2008.

Zhang Naiqi. "Qishi zishu." *Wenshi ziliao xuanji* 82 (1982): 36–59.

Zhang Peisen, ed. *Zhang Wentian nianpu (1942–1976)*. Beijing: Zhonggong dangshi, 2000.

Zhang Peitian and Dong Xiaolong, eds. "Guanyu minzu gongzuo huiyi de baogao." In *Xin Zhongguo fazhi yanjiu shiliao tongjian*, 7959–60. Vol. 7. Beijing: Zhongguo zhengfa daxue chubanshe, 2003.

Zhang Rongfeng. *Wu Yanxiao de zhanchang: Cong weiquan dao minzhu zhuanzhe de guo'an shouji*. Taipei: Dongmei, 2022.

Zhang Shufan. "Xinyang shijian: Yige chentong de lishi jiaoxun." *Bainianchao*, no. 6 (1998): 39–44.

Zhang Shujun. *Da zhuanzhe: Zhonggong shiyijie sanzhong quanhui shilu*. Hangzhou: Zhejiang renmin, 1998.

Zhang Siquan. *Gao Gang*. Beijing: Zhongguo wenshi, 2011.

Zhang Suhua. *Bianju: Qiqian ren dahui shimo*. Beijing: Zhongguo qingnian, 2012.

Zhang Tianheng. "Zai yu Huo laogong huannan de rizi li." In *Huo Weide*, edited by Xiong Meijie, 171–77. Beijing: Nanhai, 1994.

Zhang Wanshu. *Lishi de da baozha: "Liu si" shijian quanjing shilu*. Hong Kong: Tiandi, 2009.

Zhang Wuji. "Xi Zhongxun zai Huan xian." In *Hongse Nanliang, lianzheng fengbei*, edited by Zhonggong Qingyang shiwei and Zhonggong Gansu sheng jiwei xuanjiao shi, 199–212. Lanzhou: Lanzhou wanyi yinwu, 2011 (internal circulation).

Zhang Xiangming. "55 nian Xizang gongzuo shilu." Unpublished manuscript, 2006.

Zhang Xiushan. *Wode bashiwunian: Cong Xibei dao Dongbei*. Beijing: Zhonggong dangshi, 2007.

Zhang Zhenbang. "Wo wei Xibeiju zhong liangshi." In *Zai Xibeiju de rizi li*, edited by Shi Jie and Si Zhihao, 58–64. Xi'an: Shaanxi shifan daxue chubanshe, 2018.

Zhang Zhigong. "Lingdao ganbu he qunzhong shi pingdeng de." In *Caifang shilu: Xi Zhongxun zai Guangdong de gushi*, edited by Yan Hongwei and Qiu Ran, 201–24. Hong Kong: Xianggang zhonghe, 2016.

Zhang Zhigong. *Nanwang de ershinian: Zai Xi Zhongxun shenbian gongzuo de rizi li*. Beijing: Jiefangjun, 2013.

Zhang Zhiying. "Xi Zhongxun tongzhi zai Zhengning xian geming huodong shilüe." *Zhengning wenshi ziliao xuanji* 2 (2002): 75–81 (internal circulation).

Zhang Zongxun huiyilu. Beijing: Jiefangjun, 2008.

"Zhao Fan huiyilu." Unpublished manuscript, 1996.

Zhao Jialiang. "Gao Gang diyici zisha Jingguo." *Bainianchao*, no. 7 (2003): 25–30.

Zhao Jialiang. "Gao Gang liang ren mishu tan Gao Gang." In *Zhongguo dangdai mingren zhengyao fang shuping ji*, edited by Yang Jisheng, 83–100. Hong Kong: Tiandi tushu, 2013.

Zhao Jialiang and Zhang Xiaoji. *Banjie mubei xia de wangshi: Gao Gang zai Beijing*. Hong Kong: Dafeng, 2008.

Zhao Jialiang and Zhang Xiaoli. "Gao Gang fanxing jiancha." *Wangshi*, no. 72 (Sept. 2008).
Zhao Shenying. *Zhang Guohua jiangjun zai Xizang*. Beijing: Zhongguo Zangxue, 2001.
Zhao Tianyuan. *Zai Chen Yun shenbian de shinian*. Beijing: Zhongyang wenxian, 2005.
Zhao Wei. *Xihua ting suiyue: Wo zai Zhou Enlai Ding Yingchao shenbian sanshiqinian*. Beijing: Shehui kexue wenxian, 2009.
Zhao Xiaohong. "Dangde liyi zai diyi wei." In *Hongse Nanliang, lianzheng fengbei*, edited by Zhonggong Qingyang shiwei and Zhonggong Gansu sheng jiwei xuanjiao shi, 194–98. Lanzhou: Lanzhou wanyi yinwu, 2011 (internal circulation).
Zhao Youfu. "Peng Zhen yu jingjiao nongcun shejiao yundong." *Beijing dangshi*, no. 2 (2004): 10–13.
Zhao Ziyang. *Gaige licheng*. Hong Kong: Xin shiji, 2009.
Zhao Ziyang. "San fang Zhao Ziyang." In *Zhongguo dangdai mingren zhengyao fang shuping ji*, edited by Yang Jisheng, 6–35. Hong Kong: Tiandi tushu, 2013.
Zhao Ziyang. "Zai dangde shisanjie yizhong quanhui jieshu shi de jianghua." In *Zhao Ziyang wenji (1980–1989)*, 255–56. Vol. 4. Hong Kong: Chinese University Press, 2016.
Zheng Hewei. "Chen Yun weihe changdao huifu zhongyang shujichu." *Dangshi wenhui*, no. 2 (2021): 46–48.
Zheng Jinmu. "Zhiding fazhan zhanlüe shi Jinping tongzhi dui Xiamen de yige quanju xing gongxian." In *Xi Jinping zai Xiamen*, edited by Zhongyang dangxiao caifang shilu bianjishi, 49–74. Beijing: Zhongyang dangxiao, 2020.
Zheng Rong. *Wo yu Beijingren yi*. Beijing: Dongfang, 2000.
Zheng Tianxiang. *Xingcheng jilüe*. Beijing: Beijing chubanshe, 1994.
Zheng Ying. "Yi Xi Zhongxun yu Xizang tongyi zhanxian gongzuo." In *Zangzu bainian shilu*, 653–58. Vol. 2. Beijing: Shehui kexue wenxian, 2018.
Zheng Zhongbing, ed. *Hu Yaobang nianpu ziliao changbian*. Vol. 2. Hong Kong: Shidai guoji, 2005.
Zheng Zhongbing. "Shei jujian de Zhu Houze." *Yanhuang chunqiu*, no. 1 (2016): 30–34.
Zheng Zhonghua, ed. "Geming houdai de yaolan, 'si hua' rencai de ronglu: Beijing bayi xuexiao xiaoshi." In *Bayi ban shiji*, 1–35. Beijing: Zhongguo gongren, 1997.
Zheng Zhongzhong. "Bayi xuexiao shi zheyang de." In *Wo xinzhong de bayi*, edited by Li Heshun, 97–98. Beijing: Tuanjie, 2007.
Zhi Xiaomin. *Liu Shaoqi yu Jin-Sui tugai*. Taipei: Xiuwei zixun keji, 2008.
Zhong Shunan. "Wang Sheng Jiang Yanshi de zaoyu." *Zhongguo baodao* 1143 (May 1986): 6–10.
Zhong Zhaoyun. "Xiang Nan yu Xi Zhongxun de jiaowang." *Dangshi bolan*, no. 3 (2021): 14–20.
Zhong Zhaoyun and Wang Shengze. *Chizi zhi xin: Jiang Yizhen zhuan*. Vol. 2. Hong Kong: Tiandi tushu, 2008.
Zhonggong Beijing shiwei dangshi yanjiushi. *Neiluan de shinian: Beijing qu xian "wenhua dageming" shiqi jilue*. Beijing: Zhonggong Beijing shiwei dangshi yanjiushi, 2002.
Zhonggong Beijing shiwei zuzhibu. *Zhongguo gongchandang Beijing shi zuzhishi ziliao*. Beijing: Renmin, 1992 (internal circulation).
Zhonggong dangshi renwu yanjiuhui, ed. *Zhonggong dangshi renwu zhuan*. Vol. 88. Beijing: Zhonggong dangshi, 2016.
Zhonggong Fuping xianwei and Fuping xian renmin zhengfu, eds. *Xiangyin: Jinian Xi Zhongxun tongzhi danchen jiushiwu zhounian*. [Weinan]: [Zhonggong Fuping xianwei], 2008 (internal circulation).
Zhonggong Fuping xianwei dangshi yanjiushi. "Fengrong suiyue: Xi Zhongxun de shaonian shidai." In *Xiangyin: Jinian Xi Zhongxun tongzhi danchen jiushiwu zhounian*, edited by Zhonggong Fuping xianwei and Fuping xian renmin zhengfu, 53–78. Weinan: Zhonggong Fuping xianwei, 2008 (internal circulation).

Zhonggong Fuping xianwei dangshi yanjiushi. "Nanshe sangzi qing." In *Xiangyin: Jinian Xi Zhongxun tongzhi danchen jiushiwu zhounian*, edited by Zhonggong Fuping xianwei and Fuping xian renmin zhengfu, 84–85. [Weinan]: [Zhonggong Fuping xianwei], 2008 (internal circulation).

Zhonggong Gansu shengwei, ed. *Guanghui yeji chonggao fengfan: Jinian Xi Zhongxun tongzhi danchen 100 zhounian*. Lanzhou: Gansu renmin, 2013.

Zhonggong Gansu shengwei, ed. "Mao Zedong pizhuan Xi Zhongxun guanyu chedi fan tanwu douzheng gei zhongyang de dianbao." In *Xi Zhongxun yu Gansu*, 438–41. Lanzhou: Gansu renmin, 2013.

Zhonggong Gansu shengwei, ed. "Xi Zhongxun dashiji." In *Xi Zhongxun yu Gansu*, 515–88. Lanzhou: Gansu renmin, 2013.

Zhonggong Gansu shengwei, ed. "Xi Zhongxun dui Gansu gongzuo de yijian." In *Xi Zhongxun yu Gansu*, 414–16. Lanzhou: Gansu renmin, 2013.

Zhonggong Gansu shengwei, ed. "Xi Zhongxun guanyu Gansu sheng lingdao banzi tiaozheng de jianghua." In *Xi Zhongxun yu Gansu*, 469–71. Lanzhou: Gansu renmin, 2013.

Zhonggong Gansu shengwei, ed. "Xi Zhongxun guanyu guowuyuan renmin jiedai shi 'guanyu Gansu sheng bufen diqu queliang wenti de jianbao' de pishi." In *Xi Zhongxun yu Gansu*, 463–64. Lanzhou: Gansu renmin, 2013.

Zhonggong Gansu shengwei, ed. "Xi Zhongxun guanyu Xibei diqu gongzuo de dierci zonghe baogao." In *Xi Zhongxun yu Gansu*, 449–56. Lanzhou: Gansu renmin, 2013.

Zhonggong Gansu shengwei, ed. "Xi Zhongxun zai Dunhuang xian dangtuan huiyishang guanyu gongshehua he shengchan zhong ruogan wenti de jianghua." In *Xi Zhongxun yu Gansu*, 459–62. Lanzhou: Gansu renmin, 2013.

Zhonggong Gansu shengwei, ed. "Xi Zhongxun zai Gansu sheng, shi liangji ganbu huiyishang de jianghua." In *Xi Zhongxun yu Gansu*, 422–26. Lanzhou: Gansu renmin, 2013.

Zhonggong Gansu shengwei, ed. "Xi Zhongxun zai Gansu shengwei weiyuan huiyishang de jianghua." In *Xi Zhongxun yu Gansu*, 417–21. Lanzhou: Gansu renmin, 2013.

Zhonggong Gansu shengwei dangshi yanjiushi, ed. "Xibeiju guanyu Xibei, quxian, quxiang san ji huiyi zhengfeng qingkuang de baogao." In *20 shiji 50 niandai chu Gansu de zhengdang zhengfeng*, 69–75. Ser. 35, vol. 43. N.p.: SCCP, 2010.

Zhonggong Gansu shengwei dangshi ziliao zhengji yanjiu weiyuan hui, ed. "Longyuan bingbao gaishu." In *Gansu dangshi ziliao*, 1–8. Vol. 3. Lanzhou: Gansu renmin, 1986.

Zhonggong Guangdong sheng jilü jiancha weiyuanhui and Guangdong sheng jianchating, eds. *Guangdong jijian jiancha ji: 1950–1995 nian*. Guangzhou: Guangzhou renmin, 1998.

Zhonggong Guangdong shengwei dangshi yanjiushi, ed. *Guangdong gaige kaifang fazhan shi: 1978–2018*. Guangzhou: Guangdong renmin, 2019.

Zhonggong Guangdong shengwei dangshi yanjiushi, ed. *Xi Zhongxun zhuzheng Guangdong fengcai lu*. Guangzhou: Guangdong renmin, 2013.

Zhonggong Hebei shengwei tongzhanbu, ed. "Xi Zhongxun tongzhi zai quanguo tongzhan gongzuo huiyishang de jianghua." In *Tongyi zhanxian wenjian xuanbian*, 61–71. Ser. 38, vol. 189, pt. 1. N.p.: SCCP, 2016.

Zhonggong Hebei shengwei tongzhanbu, ed. "Zhongyang bangongting zhuanfa zhongyang tongzhanbu 'guanyu zhengqu Dalai jituan he guowai Zangbao gongzuo zuotanhui ruogan wenti de baogao.'" In *Tongyi zhanxian wenjian xuanbian*, 1145–51. Ser. 38, vol. 189, pt. 2. N.p.: SCCP, 2016.

Zhonggong Hebei shengwei zuzhibu, Zhonggong Hebei shengwei dangshi ziliao zhengji bianshen weiyuanhui, and Hebei sheng dang'anju, eds. *Zhongguo gongchandang Hebei sheng zuzhishi ziliao (1922–1987)*. Shijiazhuang: Hebei renmin, 1990 (internal circulation).

Zhonggong Henan shengwei dangshi yanjiushi. "Xi Zhongxun zai Henan." *Bainianchao*, no. 11 (2013): 22–31.
Zhonggong Jiangsu shengwei dangshi gongzuo bangongshi, ed. *Zhang Zhongliang jinian wenji*. Beijing: Zhonggong dangshi, 2008.
Zhonggong Jiuquan shiwei dangshi yanjiushi. "Xi Zhongxun shicha Akesai Hasake zu zizhi xian." In *Xi Zhongxun yu Gansu*, edited by Zhonggong Gansu shengwei, 323–29. Lanzhou: Gansu renmin, 2013.
Zhonggong Qinghai shengwei dangshi ziliao zhengji weiyuanhui and Zhongguo renmin jiefangjun Qinghai sheng junqu zhengzhiju, eds. "Zhonggong zhongyang zhuanfa Xibeiju guanyu chuli shaoshu minzu diqu panluan baogao de zhishi." In *Jiefang Qinghai shiliao xuanbian*, 299–310. Xining: Zhonggong Qinghai shengwei dangshi ziliao zhengji weiyuanhui and Zhongguo renmin jiefangjun Qinghai sheng junqu zhengzhiju, 1990.
Zhonggong Shanxi shengwei dangshi bangongshi, ed. *Qi Yun zai Taihang*. Beijing: Zhongyang wenxian, 2014.
Zhonggong Shaanxi shengwei dangshi yanjiushi, ed. "Guanyu Pingliang feiluan xiang Zhonggong zhongyang Xibeiju de baogao." In *Zhang Desheng*, 468–71. Xi'an: Shaanxi renmin, 1996.
Zhonggong Shaanxi shengwei dangshi yanjiushi, ed. "Tudi geming zhanzheng shiqi de Zhonggong Shaanxi shengwei zongshu." In *Shaanxi dangshi ziliao congshu*, 1–24. Vol. 18. Xi'an: Shaanxi renmin, 1991.
Zhonggong Shaanxi shengwei dangshi yanjiushi, ed. "Zhonggong Shaanxi shengwei tonggao (di san shi jiu hao)." In *Shaanxi dangshi ziliao congshu*, 226–31. Vol. 18. Xi'an: Shaanxi renmin, 1991.
Zhonggong Shaanxi shengwei dangshi yanjiushi and Gongqingtuan Shaanxi shengwei qingyun shi yanjiushi, eds. "Tudi geming zhanzheng shiqi gongqingtuan Shaanxi shengwei he Shaanxi qingnian yundong zongshu." In *Shaanxi dangshi ziliao congshu*, 1–27. Vol. 20. Xi'an: Shaanxi renmin, 1992.
Zhonggong Shaanxi shengwei dangshi ziliao zhengji yanjiu weiyuanhui and Zhonggong Xianyang shiwei dangshi bangongshi, eds. "Weibei geming genjudi zongshu." In *Shaanxi dangshi ziliao congshu*, 1–23. Vol. 11. Xi'an: Shaanxi renmin, 1990.
Zhonggong Shaanxi shengwei dangshi ziliao zhengji yanjiu weiyuanhui and Zhonggong Xianyang shiwei dangshi bangongshi, eds. "Zhonggong Shaanxi shengwei guanyu Weibei youji zhanzheng qingkuang de baogao." In *Shaanxi dangshi ziliao congshu*, 30–42. Vol. 11. Xi'an: Shaanxi renmin, 1990.
Zhonggong Shaanxi shengwei zuzhibu, Zhonggong Shaanxi shengwei dangshi yanjiushi, and Shaanxi sheng dang'anguan, eds. *Zhongguo gongchandang Shaanxi sheng zuzhishi ziliao: 1987.11–1993.5*. Xi'an: Shaanxi renmin, 1994.
Zhonggong Shaanxi shengwei zuzhibu, Zhonggong Shaanxi shengwei dangshi yanjiushi, and Shaanxi sheng dang'anguan, eds. *Zhongguo gongchandang Shaanxi sheng zuzhishi ziliao: 1925.10–1987.10*. Xi'an: Shaanxi renmin, 1994.
Zhonggong Xiamen shiwei zuzhibu, Zhonggong Xiamen shiwei dangshi bangongshi, and Xiamen shi dang'anguan, eds. *Zhongguo gongchandang Fujian sheng Xiamen shi zuzhishi ziliao*. Fuzhou: Fujian renmin, 1989.
Zhonggong Xianyang shiwei dangshi yanjiushi, ed. *Zhengrong suiyue: Xi Zhongxun zai Guanzhong fenqu*. Beijing: Zhongyang wenxian, 2013.
Zhonggong Xizang dangshi dashiji 1949–1994. Lhasa: Xizang renmin, 1995.
Zhonggong Yan'an diwei tongzhanbu and Zhonggong zhongyang tongzhanbu yanjiusuo, eds. "Zhonggong Shaan-Gan-Ning bianqu weiyuanhui gei Guanzhong fenwei de zhishi." In *KangRi zhanzheng shiqi Shaan-Gan-Ning bianqu tongyi zhanxian he san san zhi*, 341–43. Xi'an: Shaanxi renmin, 1989.

Zhonggong Yan'an diwei tongzhanbu and Zhonggong zhongyang tongzhanbu yanjiusuo, eds. "Zhonggong Shaan-Gan-Ning bianqu zhongyang ju gei Guanzhong fenwei de zhishi." In *KangRi zhanzheng shiqi Shaan-Gan-Ning bianqu tongyi zhanxian he san san zhi*, 347–50. Xi'an: Shaanxi renmin, 1989.

Zhonggong Yan'an shiwei dangshi yanjiushi, ed. *Xi Zhongxun zai Yan'an*. Beijing: Zhongyang wenxian, 2013.

Zhonggong Yan'an shiwei tongzhanbu, ed. "Gao Zili tongzhi zai Shaan-Gan-Ning bianqu zhengfu diyici quzhang lianxi huiyishang de guanyu tongyi zhanxian gongzuo de baogao." In *Yan'an shiqi tongyi zhanxian shiliao xuanbian*, 442–63. Beijing: Huawen, 2010.

Zhonggong Yan'an shiwei tongzhanbu, ed. "Ge fenqu ganbu dui tongzhan gongzuo de yixie sixiang biaoxian: Xibeiju bangongting tongzhan yanjiu cailiao." In *Yan'an shiqi tongyi zhanxian shiliao xuanbian*, 367–69. Beijing: Huawen, 2010.

Zhonggong Yan'an shiwei tongzhanbu, ed. "Wang Guanlan tongzhi gei Xi Zhongxun tongzhi de xin: Guanyu tongyi zhanxian wenti." In *Yan'an shiqi tongyi zhanxian shiliao xuanbian*, 512–13. Beijing: Huawen, 2010.

Zhonggong Zhengding xianwei zuzhibu, Zhonggong Zhengding xianwei dangshi ziliao zhengji bianshen bangongshi, and Zhengding xian dang'anju, eds. *Zhongguo gongchandang Hebei sheng Zhengding xian zuzhishi ziliao (1924–1987)*. Shijiazhuang: Hebei renmin, 1991.

Zhonggong zhongyang bangongting and Guowuyuan bangongting xinfangju, eds. "Xi Zhongxun tongzhi de baogao." In *Quanguo xinfang gongzuo huiyi ziliao huibian*, 21–27. Ser. 28, vol. 101, pt. 1. N.p.: SCCP, 2011.

Zhonggong zhongyang bangongting and Guowuyuan bangongting xinfangju, eds. "Xi Zhongxun tongzhi de jianghua." In *Quanguo xinfang gongzuo huiyi ziliao huibian*, 576–82. Ser. 28, vol. 101, pt. 2. N.p.: SCCP, 2011.

"Zhonggong zhongyang bangongting zhuanfa 'Zhongyang lingdao tongzhi zai guonei qiaowu gongzuo zuotan huishang de jianghua yaodian.'" In *Qiaowu fagui wenjian huibian*, 19–25. N.p.: Guowuyuan, Qiaowu bangongshi, Zhengce yanjiushi, 1989.

Zhonggong zhongyang dangshi yanjiushi, ed. *Xi Zhongxun huace*. Beijing: Zhonggong dangshi, 2013.

"Zhonggong zhongyang dui zhongyang xuanchuanbu guanyu quanguo zongjiao gongzuo huiyi de baogao ji Lu Dingyi tongzhi zai quanguo zongjiao gongzuo huiyishang de zongjie de pishi." In *Zongjiao gongzuo wenjian xuanbian*, 21–33. Ser. 28, vol. 96. N.p.: SCCP, 2011.

"Zhonggong zhongyang guanyu 'Guangdong, Fujian liangsheng huiyi jiyao' de pishi." In *Zhongyang dui Guangdong gongzuo zhishi huibian (1979 nian–1982 nian)*, 60–71. Ser. 28, vol. 40. N.p.: SCCP, 2007.

"Zhonggong zhongyang guanyu kaizhan Shanghai tianzhujiao gongzuo de zhishi." In *Zongjiao gongzuo wenjian xuanbian*, 13–14. Ser. 28, vol. 171. N.p.: SCCP, 2016.

"Zhonggong Zhongyang guanyu shencha ganbu de jueding." In *Kangzhan shiqi chubao wenjian (dangnei mimi wenjian)*, 15–25. Vol. 2. N.p.: Zhonggong Zhongyang shebuibu, 1949.

"Zhonggong zhongyang guanyu zhuanfa 'Xizang gongzuo zuotanhui jiao' de tongzhi." In *Sanzhong quanhui yilai zhongyao wenxian xuanbian*, 478–93. Vol. 1. Guangdong: Renmin, 1982 (internal circulation).

"Zhonggong zhongyang, guowuyuan pizhuan Xizang zizhiqu dangwei he renmin zhengfu 'guanyu dapi diaochu jin Zang ganbu, gongren de qingshi baogao' de tongzhi." In "*Wuchan jieji wenhua dageming*": *You tuichao er fanxing*, 1–7. Ser. 26, vol. 6. N.p.: SCCP, 2006.

Zhonggong zhongyang shujichu yanjiushi, ed. *Dangde shiyijie sanzhong quanhui yilai dashiji: 1978–1985*. Beijing: Hongqi, 1987.
Zhonggong zhongyang tongzhanbu, ed. *Zhongguo gongchandang tongyi zhanxian shi*. Beijing: Huawen, 2017.
Zhonggong zhongyang tongzhanbu, ed. *Zhonggong zhongyang Xibeiju dui Yimeng gongzuo fangzhen de zhishi dian*. Beijing: Zhonggong zhongyang dangxiao, 1991.
Zhonggong zhongyang tongzhanbu and Zhonggong zhongyang wenxian yanjiushi, eds. "Huijian Bolan minzhu dang fanghua daibiaotuan tanhua yaodian." In *Xi Zhongxun lun tongyi zhanxian*, 525–27. Beijing: Zhongyang wenxian, 2013.
Zhonggong zhongyang tongzhanbu and Zhonggong zhongyang wenxian yanjiushi, eds. "Jiejian Dalai Lama daibiao tanhua yaodian." In *Xi Zhongxun lun tongyi zhanxian*, 238–41. Beijing: Zhongyang wenxian, 2013.
Zhonggong zhongyang tongzhanbu and Zhonggong zhongyang wenxian yanjiushi, eds. "Ruhe zuohao wenjiao tongyi zhanxian gongzuo." In *Xi Zhongxun lun tongyi zhanxian*, 124–52. Beijing: Zhongyang wenxian, 2013.
Zhonggong zhongyang tongzhanbu and Zhonggong zhongyang wenxian yanjiushi, eds. "Xibei gongzuo de tedian shi zuohao minzu gongzuo." In *Xi Zhongxun lun tongyi zhanxian*, 35–39. Beijing: Zhongyang wenxian, 2013.
Zhonggong zhongyang tongzhanbu and Zhonggong zhongyang wenxian yanjiushi, eds. "Zai Xibei tongzhan minzu gongzuo huiyishang de jianghua." In *Xi Zhongxun lun tongyi zhanxian*, 61–83. Beijing: Zhongyang wenxian, 2013.
Zhonggong zhongyang tongzhanbu and Zhonggong zhongyang wenxian yanjiushi, eds. "Zai Zhongguo tianzhujiao you aiguohui quanguo daibiao huiyishang de jianghua." In *Xi Zhongxun lun tongyi zhanxian*, 174–94. Beijing: Zhongyang wenxian, 2013.
Zhonggong zhongyang tongzhanbu and Zhonggong zhongyang wenxian yanjiushi, eds. "Zhonggong zhongyang bangongting, Guowuyuan bangongting zhuanfa gong'anbu di baqi quanguo laogai gongzuo huiyi jiyao de tongzhi." In *Zhonghua renmin gongheguo xianxing fagui huibian (1949–1985)*, 185–93. Vol. 6. Beijing: Renmin, 1987.
Zhonggong zhongyang tongzhanbu and Zhonggong zhongyang wenxian yanjiushi, eds. "Zhonggong zhongyang guanyu jianchi he wanshan Zhongguo gongchandang lingdao de duodang hezuo he zhengzhi xieshang zhidu de yijian." In *Xin shiqi tongyi zhanxian wenxian xuanbian (xubian)*, 145–55. Beijing: Zhonggong zhongyang dangxiao, 1997.
Zhonggong zhongyang tongzhanbu and Zhonggong zhongyang wenxian yanjiushi, eds. "Zhonggong zhongyang tongzhanbu, guojia minzu shiwu weiyuanhui guanyu minzu gongzuo ji ge zhongyao wenti de baogao." In *Xin shiqi tongyi zhanxian wenxian xuanbian (xubian)*, 78–93. Beijing: Zhonggong zhongyang dangxiao, 1997.
Zhonggong zhongyang wenxian yanjiushi and Zhongyang dang'anguan, eds. "Guanyu Xinjiang ruogan gongzuo fangzhen wenti de dianbao." In *Jianguo yilai Liu Shaoqi wengao*, 175–80. Vol. 4. Beijing: Zhongyang wenxian, 2005.
Zhonggong zhongyang wenxian yanjiushi and Zhongyang dang'anguan, eds. "Zhongyang tongyi Xi Zhongxun guanyu sanyuefen gongzuo zonghe baogao de dianbao." In *Jianguo yilai Liu Shaoqi wengao*, 353–55. Vol. 3. Beijing: Zhongyang wenxian, 2005.
Zhonggong zhongyang wenxian yanjiushi and Zhongyang dang'anguan, eds. "Zhongyang zhuanfa Xi Zhongxun guanyu Xibeiju huiyi qingkuang baogao de tongzhi." In *Jianguo yilai Liu Shaoqi wengao*, 160–62. Vol. 4. Beijing: Zhongyang wenxian, 2005.
"Zhonggong zhongyang zuzhibu guanyu wei xiaoshuo 'Liu Zhidan' pingfan de baogao." In *"Wuchan jieji wenhua dageming": You tuichao er fanxing*, 1–24. Ser. 26, vol. 5. N.p.: SCCP, 2004.
Zhonggong zhongyang zuzhibu, Zhonggong zhongyang dangshi yanjiushi, and Zhong-

yang dang'anguan, eds. *Zhongguo gongchandang zuzhishi ziliao*. Vol. 7, pt. 1. Beijing: Zhonggong dangshi, 2000.

Zhongguo gongchandang Beijing shi Haidian qu zuzhishi ziliao (1949–1987). N.p.: Zhonggong Beijing shi Haidian quwei zuzhibu, 1990.

Zhongguo gongchandang dibajie zhongyang weiyuanhui weiyuan he houbu weiyuan mingdan. Beijing: Renmin, 1957.

Zhongguo gongchandang duiwai gongzuo dashiji. Vol. 2. Beijing: Dangdai shijie, 2001 (internal circulation).

Zhongguo gongchandang lishi dacidian: Shehuizhuyi shiqi. Beijing: Zhonggong zhongyang dangxiao, 1991.

Zhongguo renmin jiefangjun diyiye zhanjun zhanshi. Beijing: Jiefangjun, 1995.

Zhongguo renmin zhengzhi xieshang huiyi and Gansu sheng weiyuanhui wenshi ziliao weiyuanhui, eds. *Jinxiandai mingren zai Gansu*. Lanzhou: Gansu renmin, 1994.

Zhongguo shehui kexueyuan and Zhongyang dang'anguan, eds. *Zhonghua renmin gongheguo jingji dang'an ziliao xuanbian, 1949–1952: Nongcun jingji tizhi juan*. Beijing: Shehui kexue wenxian, 1992.

Zhongguo tianzhujiao aiguohui and Zhongguo tianzhujiao zhujiaotuan, eds. *Zhongguo tianzhujiao duli zizhu ziban jiaohui jiaoyu jiaocai*. Beijing: Zongjiao wenhua, 2002.

"Zhongguo tianzhujiao aiguohui, Zhongguo tianzhujiao jiaowu weiyuanhui zhaokai weiyuan (kuoda) huiyi." *Zhongguo tianzhujiao*, no. 7 (1983): 3–4.

Zhongguo xinwenshe. "Chicheng." Pt. 2. YouTube, Nov. 30, 2023. Video. https://www.youtube.com/watch?v=qZf0MNjFY2Q.

Zhonghua quanguo funü lianhehui. *Zhongguo funü yundong shi (Xin minzhu zhuyi shiqi)*. Beijing: Chunqiu, 1989.

Zhonghua renmin gongheguo minzhengbu dashiji. Beijing: Zhongguo shehui, 2003.

Zhongjiwei bangongting, ed. "Zhonggong zhongyang zhuanfa 'zhongyang zuzhibu guanyu zai bufen danwei jinxing dangyuan chongxin dengji gongzuo de yijian' de tongzhi." In *"Liu si" bennian jijian shiliao*, 37–42. Ser. 28, vol. 188. N.p.: SCCP, 2009.

Zhongyang dang'anguan, ed. "Xi Zhongxun guanyu Xibei tugai qingkuang de baogao." In *Jiefang zhanzheng shiqi tudi gaige wenjian xuanbian 1945–1949*, 128–31. Beijing: Zhonggong zhongyang dangxiao, 1981 (internal circulation).

Zhongyang dang'anguan, ed. "Xi Zhongxun zai Xibeiju ganbu huiyishang de jielun tigang." In *Jiefang zhanzheng shiqi tudi gaige wenjian xuanbian 1945–1949*, 468–97. Beijing: Zhonggong zhongyang dangxiao, 1981 (internal circulation).

Zhongyang dang'anguan, ed. "Yinggai zhongshi he jiaqiang dui waiguo zhuanjia de gongzuo." In *Zhonggong zhongyang wenjian xuanji*, 470–79. Vol. 33. Beijing: Renmin, 2013.

Zhongyang dang'anguan, ed. "Zhonggong zhongyang guanyu zhongyang zhengfa jiguan jingjian jigou he gaibian guanli tizhi de pifu." In *Zhonggong zhongyang wenjian xuanji*, 388–89. Vol. 35. Beijing: Renmin, 2013.

Zhongyang dang'anguan and Shaanxi sheng dang'anguan, eds. "Bianqu dangwei gei Guanzhong fenwei de zhishi xin." In *Zhonggong Shaan-Gan-Ning bianqu dangwei wenjian huiji (1940 nian–1941 nian)*, 122–26. Ser. 35, vol. 9. N.p.: SCCP, 2016.

Zhongyang dang'anguan and Shaanxi sheng dang'anguan, eds. "Bianqu dangwei guanyu Huimin wenti gei Xi Zhongxun de xin." In *Zhonggong Shaan-Gan-Ning bianqu dangwei wenjian huiji (1940 nian–1941 nian)*, 140. Ser. 35, vol. 9. N.p.: SCCP, 2016.

Zhongyang dang'anguan and Shaanxi sheng dang'anguan, eds. "Bianqu dangwei tongzhanbu guanyu tongzhan gongzuo ruogan wenti gei Guanzhong fenwei de zhishi xin." In *Zhonggong Shaan-Gan-Ning bianqu dangwei wenjian huiji (1940 nian–1941 nian)*, 4–7. Ser. 35, vol. 9. N.p.: SCCP, 2016.

Zhongyang dang'anguan and Shaanxi sheng dang'anguan, eds. "Ouyang Qin deng ren zhi Mao Zedong deng ren dian." In *Shaanxi geming lishi wenjian huiji: 1941 nian*, 50–51. Vol. 1. Beijing: Zhongyang dang'anguan, 1991.

Zhongyang dang'anguan and Shaanxi sheng dang'anguan, eds. "Ouyang Qin, Xi Zhongxun deng zhi Mao Zedong deng ren zhuan bianqu zhongyang ju dian." In *Shaanxi geming lishi wenjian huiji: 1940 nian*, 86. Beijing: Zhongyang dang'anguan, 1991.

Zhongyang dang'anguan and Shaanxi sheng dang'anguan, eds. "Shaanxi shengwei changwei zhi Luo Fu dian." In *Shaanxi geming lishi wenjian huiji: 1940 nian*, 124–25. Beijing: Zhongyang dang'anguan, 1991.

Zhongyang dang'anguan and Shaanxi sheng dang'anguan, eds. "Suqu dang daibiao dahui mishuchu guanyu Shaan-Gan-Ning tequ dangwei xuanju jieguo de tongzhi." In *Zhonggong Shaan-Gan-Ning bianqu dangwei wenjian huiji (1937 nian–1939 nian)*, 3–4. Ser. 35, vol. 8. N.p.: SCCP, 2016.

Zhongyang dang'anguan and Shaanxi sheng dang'anguan, eds. "Xiao Jingguang, Gao Gang, Gao Zili zhi Xi Zhongxun, Zhang Zhongliang dian." In *Zhonggong Shaan-Gan-Ning bianqu dangwei wenjian huiji (1940 nian–1941 nian)*, 121. Ser. 35, vol. 9. N.p.: SCCP, 2016.

Zhongyang dang'anguan and Shaanxi sheng dang'anguan, eds. "Xin xingshi xia Shaanxi dangde renwu." In *Shaanxi geming lishi wenjian huiji: 1940 nian*, 161–78. Beijing: Zhongyang dang'anguan, 1991.

Zhongyang dang'anguan and Shaanxi sheng dang'anguan, eds. "Yang Qing zhi Wu Yunfu, Li Hua dian." In *Shaanxi geming lishi wenjian huiji: 1940 nian*, 120–21. Beijing: Zhongyang dang'anguan, 1991.

Zhongyang dang'anguan and Shaanxi sheng dang'anguan, eds. "Zhang Desheng zai xin shengwei diyici huiyishang guanyu Guanzhong bianqu gongzuo wenti de fayan." In *Shaanxi geming lishi wenjian huiji: 1941 nian*, 139–48. Vol. 1. Beijing: Zhongyang dang'anguan, 1991.

"Zhongyang guanyu shencha ganbu de jueding." In *Zuzhi gongzuo wenjian xuanbian (1935–1945.8)*, 449–55. Ser. 28, vol. 28. N.p.: SCCP, 2007.

"Zhongyang guanyu zai fanjian douzheng zhong ying zhuyi de jige wenti gei gedi de zhishi." In *Zuzhi gongzuo wenjian xuanbian (1935–1945.8)*, 458–61. Ser. 28, vol. 28. N.p.: SCCP, 2007.

"Zhongyang guanyu zai fante douzheng zhong jiuzheng guo zuo ji bi gong xin de zhishi." In *Zuzhi gongzuo wenjian xuanbian (1935–1945.8)*, 462–65. Ser. 28, vol. 28. N.p.: SCCP, 2007.

"Zhongyang pizhuan minwei dangzu guanyu dangqian Yisilanjiao Lamajiao gongzuo wenti de baogao." In *1956–1978 nianjian shiyizhong xijiang ziliao: Zhaibian*, 23–33. Special ser., vol. 119. N.p.: SCCP, 2016.

"Zhongyang shujichu taolun Xinjiang gongzuo wenti de jiyao." In *Minzu zhengce wenxuan*, 19–22. Urumqi: Xinjiang renmin, 1985 (internal circulation).

"Zhongyang shujichu tongzhi tingqu Guangdong gongzuo huibao de tanhua jiyao." In *Zhongyang dui Guangdong gongzuo zhishi huibian (1979 nian–1982 nian)*, 94–108. Ser. 28, vol. 40. N.p.: SCCP, 2007.

"Zhongyang zhuanfa Xinjiang zizhiqu dangwei quanti huiyi (kuoda) de qingkuang baogao." In *Tongzhan zhengce wenjian huibian*, 1894–902. Vol. 3. N.p.: Zhonggong zhongyang tongyi zhanxian gongzuo bu, 1958 (internal circulation).

"Zhongzhen: Xi Zhongxun furen Qi Xin (I)." Tengxun shipin, Feb. 10, 2016. Video. https://v.qq.com/x/page/z01844imonn.html.

Zhou Baojin, Li Yong, and Ling Shangwen. "Huang Ziwen zhuanlue." In *Huang Ziwen*, edited by Zhou Baojin, Li Yong, and Ling Shangwen, 1–73. Shaanxi: Zhonggong Sanyuan xianwei zuzhibu, 2004.

Zhou Bingde. *Wode bofu Zhou Enlai*. Shenyang: Liaoning renmin, 2000.

Zhou Enlai. "Zai 'Yan'an diqu chadui qingnian gongzuo zuotanhui' shang de jianghua." In *1970–1973 nian Zhou Enlai zhuchi zhongyang richang gongzuo qijian 33 pian wei gongkai kanyin zhi wengao shibian*, 1–11. Ser. 5, vol. 601, pt. 1. N.p.: SCCP, 2022.

Zhou Enlai nianpu. 3 vols. Beijing: Zhongyang wenxian, 1997.

"Zhou Enlai tongzhi zai guanyu Gao Gang wenti de zuotan huishang de fayan tigang." In *Youguan 1954–1955 nian qijian suowei "Gao-Rao fandang lianmeng" de ruogan zhongyao lishi wenxian*, 59–61. Ser. 6, vol. 1. N.p.: SCCP, 2000.

Zhou Erfu. "Tongyi zhanxian de guanghui: Ji Xi Zhongxun tongzhi er san shi." In *Zhou Erfu sanwen ji*, 303–28. Vol. 2. Beijing: Huaxia, 1999.

Zhou Ke and Gu Xunzhong. *Fengyu qishinian: Shidai dachao zhong de wo he wode yijia*. Shanghai: Wenhui, 2006.

Zhou Nansheng. "Qinghai, Xizang, Xinjiang renzhi jishi: Ji Zhonggong zhongyang dui Zhou Renshan de sanci renming." In *Zhou Renshan tongzhi danchen bainian jinian wenji*, edited by Zhonggong Gansu shengwei dangshi yanjiushi, 11–28. Pingliang: Pingliang Hongqi yinshua, 2014.

Zhou Weisi. "Jinping ba zhanlüe yanguang he wushi jingshen jiehe qilai, hen liaobuqi." In *Xi Jinping zai Zhengding*, edited by Zhongyang dangxiao caifang shilu bianjishi, 139–66. Beijing: Zhonggong zhongyang dangxiao, 2019.

Zhou Yang jinzuo. Beijing: Zuojia, 1985.

Zhu Jiamu. "Shenke renshi dangde di sange lishi jueyi de shidai tese." *Makesi zhuyi yanjiu*, no. 1 (2022): 23–35.

Zhu Jiamu. "Zai tan guoshi fenqi wenti." *Dangdai Zhongguoshi yanjiu* 28, no. 2 (Mar. 2021): 4–16.

Zhu Jianguo. "Hu Yaobang qi bao 'Shekou zhenggai.'" In *Renmin xin zhong de Hu Yaobang*, edited by Su Shaozhi, Chen Yizi, and Gao Wenqian, 211–23. Carle Place: Mingjing, 2006.

Zhu Jintian. "Beijing shida er fuzhong zhong wenge jishi." *Huaxia wenzhai zengkan* 1145 (Oct. 2018).

Zhu Kezhen riji. Vol. 4. Beijing: Renmin, 1989.

Zhu Lizhi. "Wo dao Shaan-bei hou de cuowu." In *Xibei geming genjudi*, edited by Zhonggong Shaanxi shengwei dangshi yanjiushi, 430–33. Beiing: Zhonggong dangshi, 1998.

Zhu Peimin. *20 shiji Xinjiang shi yanjiu*. Urumqi: Xinjiang renmin, 2000.

Zhu Peimin, Chen Hong, and Yang Hong. *Zhongguo gongchandang yu Xinjiang minzu wenti*. Urumqi: Xinjiang renmin, 2004.

Zhu Senlin. "Chuanhao gaige kaifang jieli bang: Zhu Senlin fangtanlu." In *Guangdong gaige kaifang juecezhe fangtanlu*, edited by Zhonggong Guangdong shengwei dangshi yanjiushi, 474–513. Guangzhou: Guangdong renmin, 2008.

Zhu Senlin. "Gaodu zhihui kaiqi Guangdong gaige kaifang." In *Xi Zhongxun zhuzheng Guangdong yishu lu*, edited by Zhonggong Guangdong shengwei dangshi yanjiushi, 2–11. Beijing: Zhonggong dangshi, 2013.

Zhu yuan shengji jiguan zonghe kou gongren and Jiefangjun Mao Zedong sixiang xuanchuan dui yi si liu dui. "Yi Mao zhuxi de zhengce he celüe sixiang wei tongshuai dadan jiefang fan zuowu you le juewu de ganbu." *Shaanxi qingkuang* 11 (Apr. 1969): 15–21 (internal circulation).

Zhuang Qidong. "'Qiangjiu yundong' zhong Xi Zhongxun zai Yan'an." *Shiji*, no. 3 (1994): 22–24.

Zong Hairen. *Di sidai*. Carle Place: Mingjing, 2005.

"Zongli jiejian Banchan deng ren de tanhua jiyao." In *Youguan Banchan yinyan huozui de ruogan xijian shiliao (1962 nian 8 yue)*, 1–11. Ser. 31, vol. 10. N.p.: SCCP, 2010.

"Zui'e shengya wushinian: Fandang yexinjia Xi Zhongxun choushi." Unpublished manuscript, n.d. Held by this author.

"Zuotan Zhonggong dangshi." Unpublished manuscript, June 30, 2010. Held by Frederick Teiwes.

English Sources

Alber, Charles J. *Embracing the Lie: Ding Ling and the Politics of Literature in the People's Republic of China*. Westport, CT: Praeger, 2004.

Apter, David E., and Tony Saich. *Revolutionary Discourse in Mao's Republic*. Cambridge, MA: Harvard University Press, 1994.

Arpi, Claude. *Dharamsala and Beijing: The Negotiations That Never Were*. New Delhi: Lancer, 2009.

Barrett, David D. *Dixie Mission: The United States Army Observer Group in Yenan, 1944*. Berkeley: Center for Chinese Studies, University of California, 1970.

Barthel, Diane L. *Amana: From Pietist Sect to American Community*. Lincoln: University of Nebraska Press, 1984.

Baum, Richard. *Burying Mao: Chinese Politics in the Age of Deng Xiaoping*. Princeton, NJ: Princeton University Press, 1994.

Benson, Linda, and Ingvar Svanberg. "Osman Batur: The Kazak's Golden Legend." In *The Kazaks of China: Essays on an Ethnic Minority*, edited by Linda Benson and Ingvar Svanberg, 141–88. Uppsala: Uppsala University, 1988.

Billingsley, Philip, and Xu Youwei. "Liu Zhidan and His 'Bro's in the Hood': Bandits and Communists in the Shaanbei Badlands (1)." *Human Sciences Review*, no. 44 (Mar. 2013): 147–92.

Breslauer, George W. "Counterfactual Reasoning in Western Studies of Soviet Politics and Foreign Relations." In *Counterfactual Thought Experiments in World Politics: Logical, Methodological, and Psychological Perspectives*, edited by Philip E. Tetlock and Aaron Belkin, 71–94. Princeton, NJ: Princeton University Press, 1996.

Brook, Timothy. *Quelling the People: The Military Suppression of the Beijing Democracy Movement*. New York: Oxford University Press, 1992.

Brown, Jeremy. *June Fourth: The Tiananmen Protests and Beijing Massacre of 1989*. New York: Cambridge University Press, 2021.

Bulag, Uradyn E. *The Mongols at China's Edge: History and the Politics of National Unity*. Lanham, MD: Rowman and Littlefield, 2002.

Chai, Ling. *A Heart for Freedom*. Carol Stream, NY: Tyndale House, 2011.

Chan, Anita, Stanley Rosen, and Jonathan Unger. Introduction to *On Socialist Democracy and the Chinese Legal System: The Li Yizhe Debates*, edited by Chan, Rosen, and Unger, 1–28. Armonk, NY: M. E. Sharpe, 1985.

Chen, Tao. "Between Economy and Politics: China and the Leipzig Trade Fair (1950–1966)." *European Review of History / Reveue européenne d'histoire* 30, no. 3 (2023): 348–55.

Chen, Tao. "East German Pragmatism, China's Policy of Differentiation, and Soviet Miscalculation: Hermann Matern's 1961 Trip to China Revisited." *Cold War History* 19, no. 1 (2019): 85–99.

Cheng, Joseph Y. S. "Position Paper of the Young Professional Group Submitted to Xi Zhongxun, a Member of the Secretariat of the Central Committee of the Chinese Communist Party, during Their Visit to Beijing in May 1983 (the Group Was Led by Three Legislative Councillors and Consisted of Twelve Leading Professionals) (in

Chinese)." In *Hong Kong: In Search of a Future*, edited by Yushuo Zheng, 197–203. Hong Kong: Oxford University Press, 1984.

Cheng, Tiejun, Uradyn Bulag, and Mark Selden. *A Chinese Rebel beyond the Great Wall: The Cultural Revolution and Ethnic Pogrom in Inner Mongolia*. Chicago: University of Chicago Press, 2023.

Chu, Cindy Yik-yi. *Chinese Communists and Hong Kong Capitalists: 1937–1997*. New York: Palgrave Macmillan, 2011.

Chung, Sze-yuen. *Hong Kong's Journey to Reunification: Memoirs of Sze-Yuen Chung*. Hong Kong: Chinese University Press, 2001.

Chung, Yen-lin. "The CEO of the Utopian Project: Deng Xiaoping's Roles and Activities in the Great Leap Forward." *China Journal* 69 (Jan. 2013): 154–73.

Chung, Yen-lin. "The Ousting of General Secretary Hu Yaobang." *China Review* 19, no. 1 (Feb. 2019): 89–122.

Chung, Yen-lin. "The Unknown Standard-Bearer of the Three Red Banners: Peng Zhen's Roles in the Great Leap Forward." *China Journal* 74 (July 2015): 129–43.

Clark, Amanda C. R. *China's Last Jesuit: Charles J. McCarthy and the End of the Mission in Catholic Shanghai*. Singapore: Palgrave Macmillan, 2017.

Corcoran, Kieran. "Vintage Video of Kim Jong Un and Xi Jinping's Dads on a Diplomatic Trip in 1983 Shows Their Deep Family Bond." *Business Insider*, May 10, 2018.

Dalai Lama. "Five Point Peace Plan." Public statement, Sept. 21, 1987.

Delury, John. "Feudal Contradictions between Communist Allies: Deng Xiaoping, Kim Il-Sung, and the Problem of Succession, 1976–1984." *Journal of Cold War Studies* 24, no. 2 (2022): 4–28.

DeMare, Brian. *Land Wars: The Story of China's Agrarian Revolution*. Stanford: Stanford University Press, 2019.

Deng Xiaoping. "Take a Clear-Cut Stand against Bourgeois Liberalization." In *Selected Works of Deng Xiaoping (1982–1992)*, 194–97. Vol. 2. Beijing: Foreign Languages, 1994.

Dhondup, Yeshi. "Chronology of Sino-Tibetan Contacts from 1978 to 2012." *Tibet Journal* 38, no. 3–4 (2013): 121–60.

Dikötter, Frank. *The Age of Openness: China before Mao*. Berkeley: University of California Press, 2008.

Dikötter, Frank. *China after Mao: Rise of a Superpower*. New York: Bloomsbury, 2022.

Dikötter, Frank. *The Tragedy of Liberation: A History of the Chinese Revolution, 1945–57*. London: Bloomsbury, 2013.

Ekiert, Grzegorz, and Jan Kubik. *Rebellious Civil Society: Popular Protest and Democratic Consolidation in Poland, 1989–1993*. Ann Arbor: University of Michigan Press, 2001.

Esherick, Joseph. *Accidental Holy Land: The Communist Revolution in Northwest China*. Oakland: University of California Press, 2022.

Farge, Arlette. *The Allure of the Archives*. New Haven, CT: Yale University Press, 2013.

Forman, Harrison. *Report from Red China*. New York: Henry Holt, 1945.

Forster, Keith. "The Popular Protest in Hangzhou." In *The Pro-democracy Protests in China: Reports from the Provinces*, edited by Jonathan Unger, 166–85. Armonk, NY: M. E. Sharpe, 1991.

French, Howard W. "China's Foreclosed Possibilities." *NYRB*, Nov. 2, 2023.

Friedman, Jeremy. *Shadow Cold War: The Sino-Soviet Competition for the Third World*. Chapel Hill: University of North Carolina Press, 2015.

Gagnon, V. P. *The Myth of Ethnic War: Serbia and Croatia in the 1990s*. Ithaca, NY: Cornell University Press, 2006.

Galbiati, Fernando. *P'eng P'ai and the Hai-Lu-Feng Soviet*. Stanford: Stanford University Press, 1985.

Gao, Hua. *How the Red Sun Rose: The Origins and Development of the Yan'an Rectification Movement, 1930–1945*. Hong Kong: University of Hong Kong, 2018.
Gao, James Z. "The Call of the Oases: The 'Peaceful Liberation' of Xinjiang, 1949–1953." In *Dilemmas of Victory: The Early Years of the People's Republic of China*, edited by Jeremy Brown and Paul G. Pickowicz, 184–204. Cambridge, MA: Harvard University Press, 2007.
Garnaut, John. "The Creation Myth of Xi Jinping." *Foreign Policy*, Oct. 19, 2012.
Gewirtz, Julian. *Never Turn Back: China and the Forbidden History of the 1980s*. Cambridge, MA: Belknap Press of Harvard University Press, 2022.
Goldman, Merle. *Sowing the Seeds of Democracy in China: Political Reform in the Deng Xiaoping Era*. Cambridge, MA: Harvard University Press, 1994.
Goldstein, Melvyn C. *A History of Modern Tibet*. 4 vols. Berkeley: University of California Press, 1989–2019.
Goldstein, Melvyn C. *The Snow Lion and the Dragon: China, Tibet and the Dalai Lama*. Berkeley: University of California Press, 1999.
Goldstein, Melvyn C., Dawei Sherap, and William R. Siebenschuh. *A Tibetan Revolutionary: The Political Life and Times of Bapa Phuntso Wangye*. Berkeley: University of California Press, 2004.
Groot, Gerry. *Managing Transitions: The Chinese Communist Party, United Front Work, Corporatism, and Hegemony*. New York: Routledge, 2004.
Gyari, Lodi Gyaltsen. *The Dalai Lama's Special Envoy: Memoirs of a Lifetime in Pursuit of a Reunited Tibet*. New York: Columbia University Press, 2022.
Hsia, Tsi-an. *The Gate of Darkness: Studies on the Leftist Literary Movement*. Hong Kong: Chinese University Press, 2015.
Hsin Pao Tsai Ching Yue Kan. *Xi Zhongxun Discusses Future of Hong Kong*. China Report: Political, Sociological and Military Affairs, no. 439, JPRS 83966 (July 1983): 65–69. https://apps.dtic.mil/sti/tr/pdf/ADA346017.pdf
Huang, Daoxuan. "Disciplined Love: The Chinese Communist Party's Wartime Restrictions on Cadre Love and Marriage." *Journal of Modern Chinese History* 13, no. 1 (2019): 61–75.
Huang, Daoxuan. "Huang Daoxuan, a Xinling History of the Rectification Campaign." Translated by Dayton Lekner, Timothy Cheek, and Nathan Gan. PRC History Group, Dec. 17, 2023. http://prchistory.org/huang-daoxuan-a-xinling-history-of-the-rectification-campaign/.
Jacobs, Justin. "The Many Deaths of a Kazakh Unaligned: Osman Batur, Chinese Decolonization, and the Nationalization of a Nomad." *American Historical Review* 115, no. 5 (Dec. 2010): 1291–314.
Jacobs, Justin. *Xinjiang and the Modern Chinese State*. Seattle: University of Washington Press, 2016.
Jaivin, Linda. *The Monkey and the Dragon: A True Story about Friendship, Music, Politics, and Life on the Edge*. Melbourne: Text, 2001.
Jasanoff, Maya. "The Power of a Well-Told History." In *History and Human Flourishing*, edited by Darrin M. McMahon, 70–84. New York: Oxford University Press, 2023.
Jin Luxian. *The Memoirs of Jin Luxian*. Hong Kong: Hong Kong University Press, 2012.
Johnson, Ian. *The Souls of China: The Return of Religion after Mao*. New York: Pantheon Books, 2017.
Joske, Alex. "The Central United Front Work Leading Small Group: Institutionalising United Front Work." Sinopsis: China in Context and Perspective, July 23, 2019. https://sinopsis.cz/en/joske-united-front-work-lsg/.

Keating, Pauline B. *Two Revolutions: Village Reconstruction and the Cooperative Movement in Northern Shaanxi, 1934–1945*. Stanford: Stanford University Press, 1997.
Koesel, Karrie J. *Religion and Authoritarianism: Cooperation, Conflict, and the Consequences*. New York: Cambridge University Press, 2014.
Kraus, Charles. "Creating a Soviet 'Semi-Colony'? Sino-Soviet Cooperation and Its Demise in Xinjiang, 1949–1955." *Chinese Historical Review* 17, no. 2 (2010): 129–65.
Kraus, Charles. "To Die on the Steppe: Sino-Soviet American Relations and the Cold War in Chinese Central Asia, 1944–1952." *Cold War History* 14, no. 3 (2014): 293–313.
Lebow, Richard Ned, and Janice Gross Stein. "Back to the Past: Counterfactuals and the Cuban Missile Crisis." In *Counterfactual Thought Experiments in World Politics: Logical, Methodological, and Psychological Perspectives*, edited by Philip E. Tetlock and Aaron Belkin, 119–48. Princeton, NJ: Princeton University Press, 1996.
Lee, Hong Yung. *From Revolutionary Cadres to Party Technocrats in Socialist China*. Berkeley: University of California Press, 1991.
Li, Cheng. *Chinese Politics in the Xi Jinping Era: Reassessing Collective Leadership*. Washington, DC: Brookings Institution Press, 2016.
Li, Jianglin. *When the Iron Bird Flies: China's Secret War in Tibet*. Stanford: Stanford University Press, 2022.
Li, Lu. *Moving the Mountain: My Life in China from the Cultural Revolution to Tiananmen Square*. London: Macmillan, 1990.
Lintner, Bertil. *Blood Brothers: The Criminal Underworld of Asia*. New York: Palgrave Macmillan, 2003.
Liu, Binyan. *A Higher Kind of Loyalty: A Memoir by China's Foremost Journalist*. New York: Pantheon Books, 1990.
Liu, Xiaoyuan. *Reins of Liberation: An Entangled History of Mongolian Independence, Chinese Territoriality, and Great Power Hegemony*. Stanford: Stanford University Press, 2006.
Liu, Xiaoyuan. *To the End of Revolution: The Chinese Communist Party and Tibet, 1949–1959*. New York: Columbia University Press, 2020.
Lo, Shiu Hing. *Political Development in Macau*. Hong Kong: Chinese University Press, 1995.
Mariani, Paul P. *China's Church Divided*. Cambridge, MA: Harvard University Press, forthcoming.
Mariani, Paul P. *Church Militant: Bishop Kung and Catholic Resistance in Communist Shanghai*. Cambridge, MA: Harvard University Press, 2011.
Mi, Zanchen. *The Life of General Yang Hucheng*. Hong Kong: C&C, 1981.
Millward, James A. *Eurasian Crossroads: A History of Xinjiang*. New York: Columbia University Press, 2007.
Naughton, Barry. "Deng Xiaoping: The Economist." *China Quarterly*, no. 135 (Sept. 1993): 491–514.
O'Brien, Kevin J. *Reform without Liberalization: China's National People's Congress and the Politics of Institutional Change*. New York: Cambridge University Press, 1990.
Opper, Marc. *People's Wars in China, Malaya, and Vietnam*. Ann Arbor: University of Michigan Press, 2020.
Opper, Marc. "Revolution Defeated: The Collapse of the Chinese Soviet Republic." *Twentieth-Century China* 43, no. 1 (2018): 45–66.
Osnos, Evan. "Born Red." *New Yorker*, Apr. 6, 2015.
Panchen Lama. *A Poisoned Arrow: The Secret Report of the 10th Panchen Lama*. London: Tibet Information Network, 1997.
Quinn, Kenneth M. "The Journey in Retrospect." In *Old Friends: The Xi Jinping–Iowa*

Story, edited by Sarah D. Lande and Albert Lin. Muscatine: Sarah D. Lande US-China Friendship Education, 2017.

Reardon, Lawrence C. *A Third Way: The Origins of China's Current Economic Development Strategy*. Cambridge, MA: Harvard University Asia Center, 2020.

Rinpoche, Arjia. *Surviving the Dragon: A Recent History of Tibet through the Looking Glass of a Tibetan Lama*. New York: Rodale, 2010.

Roberti, Mark. *The Fall of Hong Kong: China's Triumph and Britain's Betrayal*. New York: John Wiley, 1994.

Rosen, Stanley. "Guangzhou's Democracy Movement in Cultural Revolution Perspective." *China Quarterly*, no. 101 (1985): 1–31.

Rudd, Kevin. *The PM Years*. Sydney: Macmillan, 2018.

Selden, Mark. *The Yenan Way in Revolutionary China*. Cambridge, MA: Harvard University Press, 1971.

Shakya, Tsering. *The Dragon in the Land of Snows: A History of Modern Tibet since 1947*. New York: Columbia University Press, 1999.

Shambaugh, David. *The Making of a Premier: Zhao Ziyang's Provincial Career*. New York: Routledge, 2019.

Shen, Zhihua, and Yafeng Xia. *Mao and the Sino-Soviet Partnership, 1945–1959: A New History*. Lanham, MD: Lexington Books, 2015.

Sheng, Michael. "Mao and Chinese Elite Politics in the 1950s: The Gao Gang Affair Revisited." *Twentieth-Century China* 36, no. 1 (2011): 67–96.

Slezkine, Yuri. *The House of Government: A Saga of the Russian Revolution*. Princeton, NJ: Princeton University Press, 2017.

Smith, Warren W., Jr. *Tibetan Nation: A History of Tibetan Nationalism and Sino-Tibetan Relations*. Boulder, CO: Westview, 1996.

Spivey, Brian. "The December 12th Student Movement: Uyghur Student Protest in Reform-Era China." *Journal of Asian Studies* 71, no. 4 (2022): 727–46.

Sun, Warren. "Chronology of Hua Guofeng (1971–1981)." China Studies Centre, University of Sydney (website), forthcoming.

Suny, Ronald. *Red Flag Wounded*. Brooklyn, NY: Verso, 2020.

Tanaka, Kyoko. "Mao and Liu in the 1947 Land Reform: Allies or Disputants?" *China Quarterly*, no. 75 (Sept. 1978): 566–93.

Tanigawa, Shinichi. "The Policy of the Military 'Supporting the Left' and the Spread of Factional Warfare in China's Countryside: Shaanxi, 1967–1968." *Modern China* 44, no. 1 (2018): 35–67.

Teiwes, Frederick C. "The Politics of Succession: Previous Patterns and a New Process." In *China's Post-Jiang Leadership Succession: Problems and Perspectives*, edited by John Wong and Yongnian Zheng, 21–58. Singapore: Singapore University Press, 2002.

Teiwes, Frederick C., and Warren Sun. "CCP Ideology, 1976–1980: From the 'Two Whatevers,' to the 'Criterion of Truth,' to the 'Four Cardinal Principles,' and Beyond." China Studies Working Paper, China Studies Centre, University of Sydney, 2023.

Teiwes, Frederick C., and Warren Sun. *China's Road to Disaster: Mao, Central Politicians, and Provincial Leaders in the Unfolding of the Great Leap Forward*. New York: Routledge, 2015.

Teiwes, Frederick C., and Warren Sun. *The End of the Maoist Era: Chinese Politics during the Twilight of the Cultural Revolution, 1972–1976*. Armonk, NY: M. E. Sharpe, 2007.

Teiwes, Frederick C., and Warren Sun. *The Formation of the Maoist Leadership: From the Return of Wang Ming to the Seventh Party Congress*. London: Contemporary China Institute, School of Oriental and African Studies, University of London, 1994.

Teiwes, Frederick C., and Warren Sun. *Hua Guofeng, Deng Xiaoping, and the Dismantling of Maoism: From Restoration toward Reform, 1976–1981*. New York: Routledge, forthcoming.
Teiwes, Frederick C., and Warren Sun. *Paradoxes of Post-Mao Rural Reform: Initial Steps toward a New Chinese Countryside, 1976–1981*. New York: Routledge, 2016.
Thondup, Gyalo, and Anne F. Thurston. *The Noodle Maker of Kalimpong: The Dalai Lama's Brother and His Struggle for Tibet*. New York: PublicAffairs, 2015.
Torigian, Joseph. "Elite Politics and Foreign Policy in China from Mao to Xi." Brookings Institution, Jan. 22, 2019. https://www.brookings.edu/articles/elite-politics-and-foreign-policy-in-china-from-mao-to-xi/.
Torigian, Joseph. "Historical Legacies and Leaders' Worldviews: Communist Party History and Xi's Learned (and Unlearned) Lessons." *China Perspectives*, no. 1–2 (2018): 7–15.
Torigian, Joseph. "A New Case for the Study of Individual Events in Political Science." *Global Studies Quarterly* 1, no. 4 (Dec. 2021): 1–11.
Torigian, Joseph. "Prestige, Manipulation, and Coercion: Elite Power Struggles and the Fate of Three Revolutions." PhD diss., MIT, 2016.
Torigian, Joseph. *Prestige, Manipulation, and Coercion: Elite Power Struggles in the Soviet Union and China after Stalin and Mao*. New Haven, CT: Yale University Press, 2022.
Torigian, Joseph. "Xi Jinping and Ideology." *Wilson China Fellowship Essays on China and US Policy*, no. 22 (2021): 308–38.
Trouillot, Michel-Rolph. *Silencing the Past: Power and the Production of History*. New York: Penguin Random House, 2015.
Vogel, Ezra F. *Deng Xiaoping and the Transformation of China*. Cambridge, MA: Belknap Press of Harvard University Press, 2011.
Vogel, Ezra F. *One Step Ahead in China: Guangdong under Reform*. Cambridge, MA: Harvard University Press, 1989.
Wang Xizhe. "An Interview with Wang Xizhe by the Guangzhou *People's Voice*." *Chinese Law and Government* 14, no. 2 (Summer 1991): 77–83.
Weiner, Benno. *The Chinese Revolution on the Tibetan Frontier*. Ithaca, NY: Cornell University Press, 2020.
Weiner, Benno. "'This Absolutely Is Not a Hui Rebellion!': The Ethnopolitics of Great Nationality Chauvinism in Early Maoist China." *Twentieth-Century China* 48, no. 3 (2023): 208–29.
White, Hayden. *Metahistory: The Historical Imagination in Nineteenth-Century Europe*. Baltimore: Johns Hopkins University Press, 2014.
Wong, Chun Han. *Party of One: The Rise of Xi Jinping and China's Superpower Future*. New York: Avid Reader, 2023.
Wu, Yidi. "Yan'an's Iron Bodhisattva: Hunting Spies in the Rectification Campaign." In *1943: China at the Crossroads*, edited by Joseph Esherick and Matthew Combs, 203–41. Ithaca, NY: Cornell University East Asia Program, 2015.
Wylie, Raymond F. *The Emergence of Maoism: Mao Tse-Tung, Ch'en Po-Ta, and the Search for Chinese Theory, 1935–1945*. Stanford: Stanford University Press, 1980.
Xia Meng and Wang Xiaoqiang. *Xi Zhongxun: Father of a Great Nation's Leader*. London: ACA, 2014.
Xu, Luo. *Searching for Life's Meaning: Changes and Tensions in the Worldviews of Chinese Youth in the 1980s*. Ann Arbor: University of Michigan Press, 2002.
Xu, Youwei, and Philip Billingsley. "Heroes, Martyrs, and Villains in 1930s Shaanbei: Liu Zhidan and His 'Bandit Policy.'" *Modern China* 44, no. 3 (2018): 243–84.
Yamaguchi Shinji. "New Evidence on Hu Yaobang's Fall and Japan-China Relations in the 1980s: Prime Minister Nasakone Yasuhiro's Visit to China, 1986." Wilson Center,

Feb. 16, 2021. https://www.wilsoncenter.org/blog-post/new-evidence-hu-yaobangs-fall-and-japan-china-relations-1980s-prime-minister-nakasone.

Yang, Jisheng. *Tombstone: The Untold Story of Mao's Great Famine*. London: Allen Lane, 2012.

Yang, Jisheng. *The World Turned Upside Down: A History of the Chinese Cultural Revolution*. New York: Farrar, Straus and Giroux, 2021.

Yunlu, Ke. "Liberating China's Past: An Interview with Ke Yunlu." Interview by Ian Johnson. *NYRB*, Mar. 29, 2017.

Zhao, Ziyang. *Prisoner of the State: The Secret Journal of Zhao Ziyang*. Translated by Pu Bao, Renee Chiang, and Adi Ignatius. New York: Simon and Schuster, 2010.

Zhu, Dandan. *1956: Mao's China and the Hungarian Crisis*. Ithaca, NY: Cornell University East Asia Program, 2013.

German Sources

Glaubitz, Joachim. "China im Ostblock." *Osteuropa* 10, no. 4 (Apr. 1960): 257–65.

Japanese Sources

Abe Shinzo and Kitamura Shigeru. *Abe Shinzo kaikoroku*. Tokyo: Chuo Koron Shinsha, 2023.

Soga Yūri. *Tajō busshin: Waga Nihon Shakaitō kōbōshi*. Tokyo: Shakai Hyōronsha, 2014.

Russian Sources

Akhundova, Elmira. *Geidar Aliev: Lichnost´ i epokha*. Vol. 2. Moscow: Kanon+, 2017.

Buzgalin, A. V. *Belaia vorona: Poslednii god zhizni TsK KPSS*. Moscow: n.p., 1993.

Medvedev, Roi. *Iurii Andropov: Neizvestnoe ob izvestnom*. Moscow: Vremia, 2004.

Petrov, Nikita. *Vremia Andropova*. Moscow: ROSSPEN, 2023.

Tavrovskii, Iu. V. *Si Tszin´pin: Po stupeniam kitaiskoi mechty*. Moscow: Eksmo, 2015.

Verchenko, A. L. "Vklad SSSR v sozdanie krupnykh industrial´nykh tsentrov v Kitae." In *Uchastie SSSR v rekonstruktsii i stroitel´stve "156 proizvodstvennykh ob"ektov" v KNR v 1950-e gody: Novye fakty i obstoiatel´stva sovetsko-kitaiskogo sotrudnichestva*, edited by N. L. Mamaeva, 521–53. Moscow: Ves´ mir, 2018.

"Vstrecha Predsedatelia KNR Si Tszin´pina s rossiiskimi kitaevedami." *Problemy Dal´nego Vostoka*, no. 4 (2013): 3–7.

Tibetan Sources

Juchen, Thupten Namgyal. *'Ju chen thub bstan gyi sku tshe'i lo rgyus*. 21 vols. Chauntra: Juchentsang, 2014.

Takla, Phuntsok Tashi. *Mi tshe'i byung ba brjod pa*. Vol. 3. Dharamsala: Bod kyi dpe mdzod khang, 1995.

Index

Locators in *italic* refer to figures.

Abe Shinzo, 540–41
Afghanistan, 292, 419, 470
Amudong, Niyazi, 397
An Li, 339
An Ziwen: An Li (wife of Hu Yaobang's son) identified as his daughter, 339; as vice-minister of the Organization Department, 124, 129, 161, 220
Antirightist Campaign (1957), 169, 374, 466, 478; cancelling of an academic discussion meeting on (Mar. 1987), 466; criticism of the Vatican during, 165–66; decline in the number of petitions received by central agencies during, 203; Deng Xiaoping's toughness during, 190; the party's approach to ethnic and religious affairs shaped by, 155, 165–66, 169; Wu Zuguang's persecution during, 462; Xi Zhongxun's party crackdown against United Front targets, 137, 148, 150–52
Arjia Rinpoche (Lobsang Tubten Jigme Gyatso), 368, 524
Australia: Xi Jinping's meeting with Kevin Rudd, 5; Xi Jinping's visit with Huang Ju and Wei Fuhai (1988), 342; Xi Zhongxun's visit to (1979), 288–89
Azizi, Saifuddin, 157–58, 180

Bao Tong: on Communist Party culture, 437; Hu Yaobang and Zhao Ziyang's views contrasted by, 473; Xi Jinping compared with Xi Zhongxun, 533; Xi Zhongxun described by, 306
Barrett, David D., 137
Berris, Jan, 295, 298
bingtuan (Han-run industrial and agricultural enterprises), 397; dissolution of (1975), 376; Wang Zhen associated with, 115–16, 376; Xi Zhongxun's reservations about (1952), 116, 376–77; Xi Zhongxun's visit to a *bingtuan* near Urumqi, 391
biographical writing: complexity of, 535–36. *See also* Li Jiantong—*Liu Zhidan*, novel
Bo Gu, 58
Bo Xilai, 523, 539
Bo Yibo: Bo Xilai identified as his son, 539; on Hu Yaobang at the Jan. 1987 party-life meeting, 481; resolution of the debate over *Liu Zhidan* demanded by, 266; as a White-area cadre, 128; Xi Zhongxun described to him by Mao as "a pure blue flame in the stove," 123, 530

682 INDEX

Bo Yibo—as vice-premier: selection of, 306; self-criticism after Lushan, 201; weaknesses of, 306
Brzezinski, Zbigniew, 291–92
Bu Lu, 52, 58, 78

cadre offspring: An Li as vice-mayor of Fuzhou, 339; fear of being targeted for their behavior during the Cultural Revolution in the new rectification campaign (1984), 334; Ke Xiaoming as the daughter of Ke Hua, 344; Liu Yuan (Liu Shaoqi's son), 327–28; Mao Zedong's negative view of, 179; proposal to write a special document to manage them (Dec. 1983), 334–35; the second Red generation asserted as 80 or 90 percent leftist, 533–34; the second Red generation asserted as loyal to the party and to Mao Zedong, 539; selection as secretaries for cadres, 313–14; Tao Siliang, 354; Ye Xuanning, identified as a son of Ye Jianying, 251, 326. *See also* Chen Yuan; Qi Qiaoqiao; Qi An'an; Xi Jinping; Xi Qianping; Xi Zhengning; Xiang Nan
Cai Ziwei, 40, 44
Central Advisory Commission: Bo Yibo's management of the affairs of, 266, 483; discussion of its makeup at the Twelfth Party Congress (1982), 304; establishment for elderly cadres in semiretirement, 469–70, 485; Geng Biao's speech during the Tiananmen Square protest, 500; Xi Zhongxun's refusal to become vice-chair of, 485
Central Investigation Department: replacement by the Ministry of State Security, 413; Wang Chaobei's article on Hu Zongnan blocked by, 217; Xi Zhongxun's efforts to rectify it, 412–13
Central Military Commission: Deng Xiaoping as chairman of, 470, 476, 505, 510; Editing and Compilation Committee on the Fighting History of the First Field Army, 86; Geng Biao as secretary of, 326; Hua Guofeng's consideration of Xi Zhongxun as vice-chairman of, 308; Hu Yaobang's refusal to be vice-chairman of, 471; Peng Dehuai as vice-chairman of, 85; Xi Jinping as chairman of, 510; Xi Jinping's speech on three tasks of governing (Dec. 2012), 541; Xi Zhongxun on its role in addressing the Tiananmen Square protests, 507; Xi Zhongxun's report on illiteracy forwarded to, 125; Yang Shangkun as vice-chairman and secretary general of, 497, 525, 529
Chen, Tao, 140
Cheng Kai, 258, 284
Chen Jianzhong (formerly Cheng Jianwen): betrayal of the party, 1, 18–19, 33, 515; meeting with Xi Zhongxun (1990), 1–3, 515–17; and Lee Teng-hui, 516–18
Chen Xitong, 335–36, 506
Chen Yi, 134, 138, 143–44, 171, 185, 198, 214
Chen Yuan: failed effort to join the Beijing Party Committee, 335–36; identified as Chen Yun's son, 334, 540; on the label "offspring of cadres," 334–35
Chen Yun, 134, 185, 187, 191, 280–81, 333; criticism of special economic zones, 285; and Gao Gang, 130–32; infrequent meetings with Politburo Standing Committee, 473; as leader of the Organization Department, 70; leftist rebels (three types of people) disliked by, 312, 334; Li Rui removed from the Organization Department, 337; Mao's criticism of him, 190, 211, 263–64; as a member of the politburo, 303, 306; prepared document read at a meeting with a Soviet representative (1982), 411
Chiang Kai-shek: attack on Communist forces in Hunan, 82–83; Chen Jianzhong as his spymaster, 1; White Terror purges launched against Communists (1927), 4, 17–18, 539; Xi'an Incident, 360
Chiarante, Giuseppe, 423
China Youth: hagiographic article about Xi Jinping's time in Zhengding (Nov. 1985), 339; Jiang Feng's flattering report on Xi Jinping quoting Jia Dashan (Jan. 1985), 338; Xi Jinping's article on Zhengding history published in (June 1984), 336; Xi Jinping's

letter on his devotion to the party and nation published in (July 1984), 336; Xi Zhongxun's discussion of class warfare with writers of, 193–94

Chinese People's Political Consultative Conference: Cheng Siyuan as vice-chairman of, 360; praised by Xi Zhongxun because only 35 percent of its members were Communists, 417; Raidi [Re Di] as head of the Tibet Autonomous Region, 404; the tenth Panchen Lama as vice-chairman of, 159; Xi Zhongxun invited to attend the fifth session of (Feb. 1978), 252; Xi Zhongxun proposed to be head of (1987), 485; Xi Zhongxun's discussion with Catholic leaders at (Feb. 1956), 165; Xi Zhongxun's liaison work with, 305, 353

Chinese Writers Association. *See* Fourth Congress of the Chinese Writers Association

Christianity and Christians: Xi Zhongxun on the problem of "Shouters," 380; Xi Zhongxun's concerns about "irregular activities" by Christians in Henan (1986), 398; Xi Zhongxun's temporary political victory over Christians, 370

Christianity and Christians—Catholics: Bishop Jin (Aloysius Jin Luxian), 393–94, 408; prophesies near the pilgrimage site of Shesan, 369; Protestantism and Catholicism labeled "political" religions by Zhou Enlai, 154; underground Catholics, 386–87, 408, 522; Xi Zhongxun's management of Catholic affairs, 163–66, 387, 393–95

Chu, Cindy Yik-yi, 366

Chung, Sze-yuen, 362

Chung Yen-lin, 130, 208, 212, 472

Cultural Revolution (May 1966–Oct. 1976): failure of, 323; false accusations and aggressive punishments in Hebei during, 328–29; identified by Jinping as a manifestation of "big democracy," 504; legacy of strong personal animosities and distrust within provincial party committees, 310; Peng Liyuan on political persecution and constraints during, 345–46; purging and rehabilitation of Gu Dacun and Feng Baiju, 260–62; purging and rehabilitation of Peng Pai and his family, 262; sent-down youth's experience of, 234–35; sent-down youth subsequent to, 328; the United Front Work Department denounced as a "revisionist headquarters," 151; violence in Guangxi Province during, 314–15; Xi Heping's death during, 239–40, 527, 537; Xi Jinping on his experiences during, 234–38; Xi Jinping's conclusions about, 542–43; Xi Zhongxun on his experiences during, 233–34; Xi Zhongxun's conclusions in the 1980s that it overemphasized "class struggle," 542; Xi Zhongxun's support for individuals with problematic records from, 309–10, 314–15. *See also* Xi Zhongxun—factory work during the Cultural Revolution

cultural space and cultural policy: Qi Xin's helping Xi Zhongxun manage cultural affairs, 344; targeting of Wang Chaobei, 217–18, 266; Xi Zhongxun's trust of intellectuals and cultural figures to manage their own affairs, 126–27, 439. *See also* Li Jiantong—*Liu Zhidan*, novel

Dai Qing, 490

Dalai Lama: thirteenth Dalai Lama's dispute with the ninth Panchen Lama, 119; the party's interest in winning him over, 119, 153–54, 157, 160; the Southwest Bureau's oversight of, 119, 154

Dalai Lama—fourteenth Dalai Lama: Beijing's interest in persuading him not to flee China, 119; delight over the news of Fan Ming's downfall, 162; Five-Point Peace Plan introduced by (1987), 403; flight to India by (1959), 170, 212; selection of the eleventh Panchen Lama by, 408; as vice-chairman of the National People's Congress, 159; viewed as a "centrist," 157; Xi Zhongxun admired by, 160; Xi Zhongxun's meeting representatives of (1982), 382–83; Zhou Enlai's opinion of, 173

684 INDEX

Deng Liqun: the China Rural Development Research Group established with He Weiling (1981), 436; criticism of, 435; as director of the Propaganda Department, 434; Hu Qiaomu's son's arrest on corruption charges called for by, 435; monitoring of his trip to Italy (1985), 419; outrage over the publication of Zhou Yang's article on Marx (Mar. 1983), 451; punishment for his actions in Xinjiang (1952), 112, 114–17, 434; report of Chen Yun's criticism of Hu Yaobang sent by (1983), 474–75; support for him among high-ranking cadres, 435; Xi Zhongxun criticized by, 279, 437

Deng Xiaoping: admiration of the strongman rule of the Soviet Union, 470; criticism of his model of rule, 438–39; declared the main decision maker in the party by Hu Yaobang (1981), 305; Deng Pufang as his son, 436, 519, 526–27; described by Xi Zhongxun as a veteran providing guidance, 417; and Gao Gang, 130, 134, 138; Mao's purging of, 243; participation in the Ming Tombs Reservoir Project, 192; reservations about the wording of Hu Yaobang's eulogy, 490–91; second party-history resolution passed by (1981), 545; speech addressing spiritual pollution at the Second Plenum of the Twelfth Party Congress (Oct. 1983), 451; tanks sent to quell protests in Lhasa (1989), 397; Tiananmen protests labeled by him as "turmoil," 492; vote to consult him on major issues at the First Plenum after the Thirteenth Party Congress (1987), 494–95, 505; Xi Zhongxun's departure for Guangdong blamed on, 518–19; Xi Zhongxun's remaining on the secretariat supported by (1982), 305; Yang Shangkun dropped from leadership by (1992), 525. *See also* field armies—Second Field Army

Deng Xiaoping—retirement of: Hu Yaobang's discussion of succession, 475–79; Xi Zhongxun's supposed call for Deng to give up power, 477–78

Deng Yingchao, 303, 390, 460, 513–14

Document No. 28, published as the *Summary of the Secretariat's Discussion of Work in the Inner Mongolian Autonomous Region* (July 1981), 378

Document No. 28 (report of the Central Advisory Commision), *Liu Zhidan* accused of violating it (1986), 265–66

Du Daozheng: on Xi Zhongxun's habit of wordiness, 307; on Xi Zhongxun's psychological state, 520

Du Heng [Du Lijun], 25, 27, 32–33, 37

East Germany. *See* German Democratic Republic (East Germany)

Eighth Party Congress (1956): Xi Zhongxun at, 135, 135; Zhou Enlai's presentation of Xi's report on institutional reform, 139

Eighth Party Congress—Tenth Plenum of (1962). *See* Tenth Plenum of the Eighth Party Congress (1962)

Eliminate Spiritual Pollution Campaign (1983): concerns that it would lead to another Cultural Revolution, 416; Deng Xiaoping's views of, 456; *Document No. 36*, 451–53; reactions to its enactment in Tibet, 388; Xi Zhongxun's position on it, 452–53, 456, 459

emperors: legendary emperor Yandi, 357; Qin Shi Huang (259–210 BCE), 13, 357; Qing Empress Dowager Cixi and Emperor Guangxu, 14; Qing Emperor Puyi, 147–48; Xi Jinping on how few are remembered by the common people, 522

emperors—political model of: Deng Xiaoping model of rule compared with, 438–39; Xi Zhongxun criticized as a "local emperor," 226–27

Engels, Friedrich, influence of his thought on Xi Zhongxun, 35, 115, 424

Epstein, Israel, 55

Esherick, Joseph, 17, 30, 38

Ethnic Affairs Commission: Liu Chun as head of, 167, 172; *Report on a Few Important Issues in Ethnic Work* (1987), 400; Wu Jinghua's service to, 394; Xi Zhongxun in charge of, 158–59, 167, 169–70, 203; Zhao Fan's management of Tibet on behalf of, 157

Fang Lizhi, 466
Fan Ming: as head of the Northwest Bureau Liaison Office, 119; launching of a rectification campaign in Tibet by, 162; *New Journey to the West* (novelized version of the party's history in Tibet) by, 162, 218; report by him on preparations to establish Back Tibet, 119; as Xi Zhongxun's former subordinate, 129
Fan Ming—downfall of: the fourteenth Dalai Lama's delight over the news of, 162; as a setback for northwesterners, 162–63; the Tibet Work Conference ("Panmunjom" meeting, 1953), 156–57, 160; Zhou Renshan selected as his replacement, 163
Farge, Arlette, 535
Feng Yuxiang, 17, 19, 150
field armies—First Field Army: creation of (Nov. 11, 1948), 86; Soviet support of its power in Xinjiang, 137; Xi Zhongxun's position and contributions to, 86
field armies—Second Field Army: as the main force entering Tibet, 119; territory seized in Shandong, 85; Yan Hongyan's service under Deng Xiaoping in, 212; Yin Fatang's service under Deng Xiaoping in, 370
First Plenum after the Thirteenth Party Congress (1987), vote to consult Deng Xiaoping on major issues, 494–95, 505
Forman, Harrison, 55, 137
Four Modernizations, 280, 365, 401, 466, 512
Fourth Congress of the Chinese Writers Association: Hu Yaobang's criticism of elections for the leadership of, 459; official criticism of, 460–61; planning for, 457–58; Wu Zuguang's comments on openness in Chinese society at, 460, 462
Friedman, Jeremy, 414
Fu Zuoyi, 79, 180
Fujian Province: An Li as vice-mayor of Fuzhou, 339; Deng Xiaoping's visit to (Feb. 1984), 340; Ningde Catholics, 521–22; Xiang Nan as the party boss of, 339. *See also* Xi Jinping—rise of—in Fujian Province

Fuping County. *See* Shaanxi Province—Fuping County

Gang of Four: arrest of (Oct. 1976), 247–48, 325; Guangdong Province faulted by, for failing to attack the legacy of (1978), 260; its defeat organized by *Yanhuang chunqiu*, 537; Mao's authority used for their own political purposes, 441; Qiao Guanhua's punishment for his supposed ties to, 309; Wang Dongxing's role in the move against them, 251. *See also* Jiang Qing
Gansu Province: the anti-Communist forces led by Ma Liang in (1953), 111, 117; famine during the Great Leap Forward in, 196, 199; Hui led by Ma Guo'ai under the Nationalist flag in (1952), 111; Kang Sheng's report on landlords in eastern Gansu, 90; Liangdang mutiny (1932), 24–27, 26, 30, 515; Linxia area, 110, 111; mass uprisings in (1958), 167–68; Pingliang incident (1950), 110, 113; Xi Zhongxun's discussions with Zhang Zhongliang (provincial party leader of), 195, 200; Xi Zhongxun's support of party secretary Feng Jixin (1983), 310; Xi Zhongxun's visit during the Great Leap Forward (1958), 194–97; Xi Zhongxun's visit to Aksay Kazakh Autonomous County (1958), 168–69; Yintao Dam construction, 195–96
Gao Gang: claim that *Liu Zhidan* was meant to reverse the verdict against him, 211–13; death of (1954), 134; marriage to Li Liqun, 70; role in criticism of Guo Hongtao, Zhu Lizhi, and Yan Hongyan (1942 and 1945), 210; support for the Rescue Campaign, 64
Gao Gang—fall of: the Gao Gang incident, 128, 156, 185, 193, 198; labelling as a "rightist," 43; the party's approach to ethnic and religious affairs shaped by, 155–56; suicide attempt by (1954), 43, 132; Xi Zhongxun's criticism of his treatment by the party (1967), 226, 248
Gao Wenqian, 537
Gao Yang, 338–39, 482
Gao Zimin, 511–12

Garnaut, John, 178–79, 230–31

General Office: Hu Qili as director of, 452, 456; Xi Zhongxun offered the post of vice-premier by a representative of (1959), 197; Yang Shangkun as director of, 186, 210, 255

Geng Biao, 471; closeness of his family with Xi Zhongxun's family, 326; speech for the Central Advisory Commission during the Tiananmen Square protests, 500; Xi Jinping as his secretary, 326–27

German Democratic Republic (East Germany): Leipzig Trade Fair, 139–40, 145–46; Hermann Matern's visit to China (1961), 146, 421; Xi Zhongxun's meeting with a delegation visiting Chinese factories (1959), 199; Xi Zhongxun's trip to (1960), 145–47, 296

Germany—West Germany: Beijing's ties with, in the 1950s, 139–40; brick press sent to Xi Zhongxun's factory in Luoyang, 243

Gorbachev, Mikhail, 423, 494–95

Great Leap Forward (1958–1962): August Beidaihe meeting signifying the beginning of, 193; criticism of it at the Lushan plenum (1959), 201; famine caused by, 146, 199, 202–6; Mao Zedong's dismissal of the rule of law during, 317; Oppose Rash Advance, 189–90; Peng Dehuai's criticism of, 141, 201; quantity rather than quality at Chinese factories (1959), 199; showcasing at the Leipzig Trade Fair, 140, 145–46; significance for Xi Zhongxun, 207; Xi Zhongxun's purging in the wake of, attributed to Kang Sheng, 207–8; Xi Zhongxun tasked with implementing the State Council's directive on spring plowing, 189

Gu Jingsheng, 374–75

Gu Mu, 273, 279–82, 467

Guangdong Province: Gu Mu's visit to discuss implementing *Document No. 50*, 280–82; Huang Yongsheng as party boss of, 259; Jiao Linyi as the secretary for daily affairs of the Guandong Party Standing Committee, 259–60, 262, 267; Liu Tianfu (vice-governor) on structural reforms and policies in, 281–82; Ren Zhongyi as Xi Zhongxun's successor as party boss, 177, 284, 485; Whampoa Military Academy located in, 21, 23

Guangdong Province—Guangdong Party Committee: Deng Liqun's record of Chen Yun's criticism of Hu Yaobang sent to Xi by a vice-secretary of (1983), 474–75; the province faulted by, for failing to attack the legacy of the Gang of Four (1978), 260; Wu Nansheng's proposal to use foreign capital to expand trade, 277

Guangdong Province—Guangzhou: American consulate established in Guangzhou (1979), 291; early economic reforms in, interpreted by Xi Zhongxun as a political challenge, 282–83; Liang Xiang, second party secretary of, 259–60, 282–83; Xi Zhongxun as party leader (1936–1942), 524; Yang Shangkun as party boss of, 260, 277–78, 284, 296

Guangdong Province—Shenzhen: described as chaotic by Wu Nansheng, 281; described as reactionary and capitalist (White) by Hu Qiaomu, 284–85; incarceration of migrants in, 272; investment by overseas Chinese in, 361; Li Yi as the party boss of (1992), 522–23; tenth anniversary of the establishment of the Shenzhen Special Economic Zone (1990), 276–77; Xi Jinping's trip to Shenzhen to signify support for reform, 533; Xi Zhongxun's help arranging work for Mao's son-in-law Kong Linghua in, 249; Xi Zhongxun visited by the tenth Panchen Lama's mother in, 524

Guangdong Province—Xi Zhongxun's reforms in: legacy of, 284–86; Xi Zhongxun's reflections on, 433

Guangming Daily: article on "practice is the sole criterion of truth" (May 1978), 440; flattering report on Xi Jinping published in (Jan. 1985), 338

Guangxi Province: violence during the Cultural Revolution in, 314

Guanzhong—Xunyi County: Nationalist annihilation of the Communist operations in, 51; Nationalist siege to a hospital for Red Army soldiers, 47; Tian Pingxuan, as a Nationalist leader in, 46–47

Guo Hongtao: criticism by the party in (1942 and 1945), 94, 210; criticism of, 41–44, 65; criticism of his articles on the Northwest (1981), 264–65; Gao Gang opposed by, 66, 131; as head of the Shaan-bei Organization Department (1934), 37; his son identified as a class prankster, 175; on Liu Zhidan's rightist deviation, 38

Gyari, Lodi Gyaltsen, 382–84, 391–92, 401

Han Gang, 218

Han Xianchu, 478

Hao Mingzhu: birth and life before her marriage to Xi Zhongxun, 69; career working on women's issues, 77; introduction to Xi by Guo Liben, 69–70

Hao Mingzhu—children and family life with Xi Zhongxun: contradictions between her married life and her devotion to the revolution, 71–72; divorce of, 77; Guo Liben's introduction of Hao to Xi Zhongxun, 69–70; Hao's ties with Xi Zhongxun investigated during the Cultural Revolution, 77–78. *See also* Xi Heping; Xi Qianping; Xi Zhengning

Hao Zhiping (widow of Luo Ruiqing), 521, 529

Hau Pei-tsun, 518

He Jingzhi: at the Fourth Congress of the Chinese Writers Association, 457–58, 460; on Hu Yaobang's position on ending the Eliminate Spiritual Pollution Campaign, 453; on Qi Xin's work in cultural affairs, 344; as vice-director of the Propaganda Department, 436, 453, 457

He Jinnian, 67, 265–66

He Long, 171; affirmation by him of the need for land reform in the northwest, 91; as commander of the Shaanxi-Gansu-Ningxia-Shanxi Suide Joint Defense Army, 85; He Jiesheng identified as his daughter, 348; Mao's instruction to combine military force with "political means" in the Northwest Region (1949), 109; recognition for his triumphs in the Northwest, 86; relationship with Xi Zhongxun, 8

He Pin [Ho Pin], 630–31n30

He Weiling, 436

He Zai, 315–16

Hebei Province: factional politics in, 328; Feixiang County incident (1982), 329–30; Gao Yang placed in charge of, 330; *People's Daily* article on Guanzhuang (1958), 188

Hebei Province–Zhengding County—Xi Jinping's assignment as county party secretary: Agricultural Research Institute established in (1984), 332; hagiographic article about Xi Jinping's time in Zhengding (Nov. 1985), 339; Li Rui's visit to, 337; project to attract "talent" to, 331–32; reduction of yearly grain allocations, 330; violence by factions, 330; Xi Jinping's article on Zhengding history (June 1984), 336; Xi Jinping's choice of Zhengding (1982), 326; Xi Jinping's promotion to "secretary" of Zhengding, 332–33; Xi Jinping's views on agriculture in, 333

Hebei Youth, portrait of Xi Jinping published in (July 1984), 336

Henan Province: drought in (1928), 22; Japanese military operations in (1940s), 61; Qi Xin and Yuanping exiled to the May 7 Cadre School in, 230; report sent to Xi Zhongxun on "irregular activities" by Christians in, 398; the Xi ancestral home in Dengzhou, 13; Xi Zhongxun's inspection of steel production, during the Leap, 199, 205; Xi Zhongxun's support of a relative pursuing traditional Chinese medicine in, 369; Xi Zhongzhi's guild in Shaanxi for people from Henan, 19, 30. *See also* Xi Zhongxun—factory work in Luoyang during the Cultural Revolution

Henan Province—Changge County: famine during the Great Leap Forward in, 199, 202–4; self-criticism of party officials prompted by Xi Zhongxun's criticisms of, 205; Xi Zhongxun's remarks on famine, 203–5

688 INDEX

Hong Kong: economic achievement in, as an inspiration for special economic zones, 361; Xi Zhongxun's criticism of mainland policy toward Hong Kong, 366; Xi Zhongxun's meeting with Jack Cater, 275, 362; Xi Zhongxun's meeting with the Hong Kong Trade Development Council delegation (1982), 362–63

Hu Feng: *Report on the Real Situation in Literature and Art since Liberation*, 126–27, 165; Xi Zhongxun's support for, 126–27, 439

Hu Jintao: as the leader of the Tibet Autonomous Region, 406, 409; the party's study of Cuban and North Korean approaches to ideology called on by, 543; visit to Xi Zhongxun during the National Day celebrations (1999), 528; as Xi Jinping's predecessor, 533

Hu Jiwei: campaign to summon an emergency session of the National People's Congress, 497–99, 509; as director of the *People's Daily*, 438, 448; resignation as director of the *People's Daily*, 452; revoking of his membership in the National People's Congress, 510

Hu Ping (Chinese intellectual living in the United States), 4

Hu Ping (Governor of Fujian), 341

Hu Qiaomu: diverse views of his ideological stance, 434–35; ideological affairs of the secretariat managed by, 434; ideological problems discussed with Deng Xiaoping (Aug. 1983), 453; Shenzhen described as reactionary and capitalist (White) by, 284–85; support for Deng Xiaoping as state president enlisted by, 319; as vice-minister of propaganda, 124; Xi Zhongxun's criticism of, 324; Xi Zhongxun's remaining on the secretariat supported by (1982), 305

Hu Qili, 481, 489–90, 495–96; criticism of individuals researching the reform of the political system, 478; described by Xi Zhongxun as key to the future of the party, 418; as director of the General Office, 452, 456; dismissal from the politburo and its standing committee, 508; as secretary in charge of daily affairs of the secretariat (1982), 305

Hu Yaobang: An Li as his daughter-in-law, 339; criticism of elections for the leadership of the Chinese Writers Association, 459; death and eulogy for, 2, 409, 489–91; described by Xi Zhongxun as managing day-to-day activities of the party leadership, 417; on the Eliminate Spiritual Pollution Campaign, 452–53; as general secretary of the party, 304; Lodi Gyari's positive views of, 401; as Hua Guofeng's replacement, 308; on the implementation of special economic zones in Guangdong, 282–85; meeting in 1984 on violence in Guangxi during the Cultural Revolution, 315; meeting with Gyalo Thondup (1981), 381; as a member of the Central Committee (1956), 135; as a member of the politburo, 303; persecution for attempting to end mass arrests and expulsions of party members in the Northwest (1964), 103; persecution of party members by, 64; Tibet and its challenges for the party as his focus, 370–71; Xi Zhongxun as his close associate, 8, 471

Hu Yaobang—fall of: analysis of, 471–72; Chen Yun's critical comments about Hu disseminated by Deng Liqun (1983), 474–75; criticism of him at the party-life meeting (Jan. 1987), 480–83, 491, 505; departure as general secretary of the party (Jan. 1987), 2, 3, 400–401; impact on the United Front Work Department, 355

Hu Yaobang—Five-Point Proposal: Xi Zhongxun's discussion with Tibetans (May 1982), 382–84; Xi Zhongxun's discussion with Tibetans (Oct. 1982), 391–93

Hu Zhi'an, 355

Hu Zongnan (Nationalist general): attack on Yan'an (1946), 83–84; Baoji (in Shaanxi Province) seized by (1948), 85; and Guanzhong, 49, 82; the Northwest Bureau's penetration of his headquarters (1948–1949), 86; Wang Chaobei's article "Fighting against

Hu's Cavalry in an Ancient City," 217–18
Hua Guofeng, 256, 308; Deng Xiaoping's opposition to, 371, 440, 443, 478–80; his request to meet with Xi Zhongxun denied (1995), 524–25; honored by Ye Jianying as a model at the work conference prior to the Third Plenum (1978), 257; Hunan as province he previously led, 310–11; as Mao's named successor at the time of the chairman's death, 251, 425; meeting with Neville Wran, governor of New South Wales, 289; removal of (1980), 308; support for special economic zones, 277–78, 308, 525; visit to the United Kingdom, 273; Ye Jianying's praise of, 257
Huang, Daoxuan, 54–55
Huang Shun-hsing, 357–58
Huang Yongsheng, as party boss of Guangdong, 259
Huang Ziwen, 30, 35, 40, 44, 62–63
Hunan Province: as province where Hua Guofeng previously worked, 310–11; Mao's visit during the Great Leap Forward, 199; rescue mission to save Wang Zhen's retreating forces from (1946), 82–83
Hungary: Iurii Andropov as the Soviet ambassador to (1956), 140–41; Xi Zhongxun's visit to (1959), 140, 421

Inner Mongolia. *See* Mongolia—Inner Mongolia Autonomous Region
Italy and the Italian Communist Party: Deng Liqun's trip to (1985), 419; Xi Zhongxun's views of Gorbachev described by Giuseppe Chiarante, 423

Ji Dengkui, 252, 309–10
Jia Juchuan: on challenges faced by biographers, 6; on Xi Zhongxun's sympathizing with Hu Yaobang, 481
Jia Yanyan, 313–14
Jiang Guangci, *The Young Wanderer*, 7, 22–23, 238
Jiang Qing: Guangdong visited by, 259–60; as a member of the Gang of Four, 259, 314, 471
Jiangxi Province: Xi Zhongxun's visit to, during the Great Leap Forward, 199–201
Jiang Yizhen, 328–30
Jiang Zemin, 499, 514, 517, 520, 523, 525; on the crackdown in Tibet, 409–10; meeting with Xi Zhongxun (1999), 528–29; as minister of Machine Building and Electronics Industries, 335; opposition to accommodationist attitudes, 356; Zhao Ziyang replaced as general secretary by (1989), 472, 510
Jin Ming, 328–29
Juchen, Thupten Namgyal, 382, 394, 399

Kan, Y. K., 362–63
Kang Sheng: activities at the party school where Qi Xin worked supported by, 229; as an advisor to the Central Cultural Revolution Small Group, 222; claim that *Liu Zhidan* was meant to reverse the verdict on Gao Gang, 211–15; distrust of him, within the elite, 412–13; involvement with the Rescue the Fallen Campaign, 59–60, 62, 64; Peng Dehuai and Xi Zhongxun's transfer discussed at the Peng-Xi Special Case Committee (Sept. 1965), 220; promotion to the secretariat (1962), 214; report on famine in Shaan-Gan-Ning, 91; report on landlords in eastern Gansu, 90; Xi Jinping persecuted by his wife, Cao Yi'ou, 233; Xi Zhongxun's fall attributed to, 207–8, 213–14, 218, 270; on Xi Zhongxun's friendship with figures in theatrical circles, 439
Kazakhs: Osman Batur, 110–11; suicide of the deputy chairman of the Ili-Kazakh Autonomous Prefecture, 167; Xi Zhongxun's visit to the Aksay Kazakh Autonomous County in Gansu, 168
Ke Hua, 344–45
Ke Yunlu, 328
Ke Zhongping, epic poem about Liu Zhidan, 217–18
Khrushchev, Nikita: Gao Gang discussed with Deng Xiaoping (1960), 138; Peng Dehuai's criticism of the Great Leap Forward associated with, 141; Stalin denounced at the Soviet Twentieth Party Congress (1956), 138
Koesel, Karrie J., 379–80

690 INDEX

Kong Dan, 334–35
Kong Shujing, on Xi Zhongxun's condition (in 1993), 521
Kong Yuan, 38, 334
Korea: the party's study of Cuban and North Korean approaches to ideology called on by Hu Jintao, 543; relations between Beijing and South Korea, 428
Korea—Korean War (1950–1953): charged atmosphere in China created by, 101; peace talks compared to the Tibet Work Conference (1953), 156; Peng Dehuai and Gao Gang's relationship during, 200
Korea—North Korea: Kim Il-sung's meeting with Erich Honecker (1984), 245; Kim Il-sung's meeting with top leadership in Beijing (1983), 428; Xi Zhongxun's meetings with Kim Il-sung (1980 and 1982), 245, 340, 425–28; Xi Zhongxun's meetings with Kim Il-sung (1988), 428–29

land reform: in Hui regions, 111–12; meeting on land reform arranged in Yihe (Nov. 1947), 90; and Poor Peasants Association, 90–93; Xi Zhongxun's speech on land reform in minority areas at their May 4 meeting, 112–13. *See also* Xi Zhongxun—self-criticism and behavior during land reform
Lee, Allen, 363–64
Lee, Martin, 363–65
Lee Teng-hui, 516–18
Lenin, V. I.: mausoleum of Lenin and Stalin visited by Xi Zhongxun's delegation (1959), 142. *See also* Marxist-Leninist principles
Li Erzhong, 308, 328–29
Li Jiantong: Liu Mila identified as her daughter, 521
Li Jiantong—*Liu Zhidan*, novel: banning of, 6; claim that it was meant to reverse the verdict on Gao Gang, 211–15; Peng Dehuai's pleas for rehabilitation associated with Xi Zhongxun's support for it, 208–9, 211–15, 218, 250, 256; persecution of individuals subsequent to its publication, 215–16; revolutionaries interviewed by, 209; Xi Zhongxun's reservations about it, 209–10, 250; Yan Hongyan's concerns about it, 210–11, 213
Li Liqun, 130; efforts to rehabilitate Gao Gang, 264, 529; Gao Gang's death blamed on Xi Zhongxun, 131, 133; marriage to Gao Gang, 70; writing about Peng Dehuai, during the Cultural Revolution, 131, 214
Li Min, 179
Li Peng: calls for the removal of, 497, 504, 509; Chen Xitong's criticism of, 506; concerns about Wan Li's return to China following the Tiananmen crackdown (1989), 495–96, 499, 627n42; criticism for his handling of Hu Yaobang's funeral (1989), 491; execution of his father by the Nationalists (1931), 75; on the imposition of martial law, 492, 495, 497–98; as a Politburo Standing Committee member, 479, 488; proposal on consular privileges and immunities, 512–13; Xi Zhongxun's denouncing of him at the National People's Congress Standing Committee (1990), 3, 512–13; Xi Zhongxun's visit to soldiers praised by, 507; Xi Zhongxun visited in Shenzhen (1990), 410; Zhao Ziyang's proposal regarding student protests opposed by, 493–94
Li Rui, 193, 390, 473; criticism of his activities (at the Lushan plenum), 201; Deng Liqun criticized by, 435; on how Xi Zhongxun raised his sons, 177; on Hu Qiaomu, 434; removal from the Organization Department, 337; Xi Jinping visited in Zhengding, 337; on Xi Zhongxun's departure for Guangdong (1990), 518; on Xi Zhongxun's mental health, 3, 513, 520
Li Ruihuan, 509–10
Li Weihan, 72, 157; apology to Xi Zhongxun for his unfair treatment, 43; investigation of mass uprising in Gansu (1958), 167; nationwide ethnic work conference led by (May 1962), 171; the Panchen Lama's petition discussed with Xi Zhongxun, 172; United Front work, 152, 155–56; Xi Zhongxun praised for his work in Guanzhong, 52, 107

Li Xiannian: criticism of Deng Liqun and Hu Qiaomu, 434–35; described by Xi Zhongxun as a veteran providing guidance, 417; designation as a full Central Committee member (1945), 306; state presidency with term limits, 319
Li Xiannian—as vice-premier: Cao Shuli's letter to Mao on deaths in Shandong forwarded to, 206; dissatisfaction with Xi Zhongxun's handling migrants fleeing to Hong Kong, 273; selection of (1954), 306; self-criticism after Lushan, 201; speech on the economy, 277–78; Xi Zhongxun's criticism of him for concentrating economic decision-making authority in the capital (Apr. 1979), 280
Li Zhao (widow of Hu Yaobang), 528–29
Li Youyi, 399, 401
Liangdang mutiny, Gansu Province (1932), 24–27, 26, 30, 515
Lian Zhengbao, 291, 296
Liao Chengzhi, 366, 478
Liao Hansheng, 497, 506
Lin Biao, 131, 259–60, 269, 314, 318, 441
Lin Mu, 477, 480
Liu Binyan: his *People's Daily* article on the persecution of intellectuals in Shaanxi, 456; his *People's Daily* article "The Rights and Wrongs of Thirty-Eight Years," 457; on openness in Chinese society at the Fourth Congress of the Chinese Writers Association (1984), 460; Xi Zhongxun's attempt to block his criticism of Hu Yaobang, 462–64, 466
Liu Bocheng, 84, 119, 478
Liu Chun, 167, 172–73
Liu Jingfan: advice to Xi Zhongxun to hide, 40; death of, 2, 512, 514; Li Jiantong identified as his wife, 209; Liu Zhidan identified as his older brother, 209, 272; Mao's releasing him from prison, 242–43; the Special Case Committee's accusations of, 250; Xi Zhongxun's advice to him regarding *Liu Zhidan*, 209, 213
Liu Linpu, 24–25
Liu Maogong, 70
Liu Mila, on Xi Zhongxun's mental condition (in 1993), 521

Liu Shaoqi: Liu Yuan identified as his son, 327–28; notification on Xi Zhongxun's speech at the May 4 meeting of the Northwest Bureau, 113; participation in the Ming Tombs Reservoir Project, 192; as state president, 318; support for the Rescue Campaign, 64; as a White-area cadre, 128; on Xi Zhongxun's interest in his ancestors, 13
Liu Zhidan: investigation of, 39–40; as a key leader in the Northwest, 18, 28–29, 66, 67; Ke Zhongping's epic poem about, 217–18; Liu Jingfan identified as his younger brother, 2, 40, 209; the Shaan-Gan Border Region built up by, 37–38. *See also* Li Jiantong—*Liu Zhidan*, novel
Long March, 6, 41, 74, 130, 288
Lu Dingyi, 464, 503
Luo Qingchang, 412
Lushan plenum (1959): challenges for Xi Zhongxun's visit to Moscow created by, 141–42, 416; criticism of Bo Yibo at, 201; criticism of Li Rui at, 201; criticism of Peng Dehuai at, 141, 199–201, 209; Xi Zhongxun's chat with Peng Dehuai on the way to, 199–200

Ma Wenrui, 457, 473
Ma Xiaoli, the second Red generation asserted as 80 or 90 percent leftist by, 533–34
Ma Zhenwu, 111, 168
Macau: economic achievements in, 361; Ke Hua as advisor to the Hong Kong and Macau Affairs Office, 345; Xi Zhongxun's visit to (1979), 289–91
MacLehose, Murray, 361–63
Mao Zedong: cadre offspring viewed as problematic, 179; death of (Sept. 1976), 247; demands for more violence against supposed counterrevolutionaries, 101; first party-history resolution (1945), 545; individuals under investigation released by (1975), 242–43; reaction to Peng Dehuai's criticism of the Leap (1959), 141, 201; the rule of law dismissed by (1958), 189–90, 317; Zhou Enlai criticized at the Nanning Conference (1958), 189–90

Mao Zedong—and Xi Zhongxun: role in saving Xi Zhongxun's life during the 1935 purge in Shaanxi, 41–42; Xi Jinping's recitation of Mao's speeches from memory encouraged by Xi Zhongxun, 247; Xi Zhongxun characterized with the words "The party's interests come first," 2–3; Xi Zhongxun's comment that Mao made no mistakes until 1953, 248; Xi Zhongxun's help extended to Mao's son-in-law Kong Linghua, 249; Xi Zhongxun's support of, 249; Xi Zhongxun's work on his rescue mission to save Wang Zhen's retreating forces (1946), 82–83

Mariani, Paul P., 393–94, 408

Marxist-Leninist principles: the Communist Youth League's *Historical Necessity—Socialism in China*, 424; influence of Engels's thought on Xi Zhongxun, 35, 115, 424; the Marxist Platform, 423–24; Marxist view that religion would eventually disappear, 379; revisionism in the Soviet Union that betrayed the principles of, 412; succession politics and leader-deputy relations in the Leninist system, 10, 469, 543; Xi Zhongxun's criticism of simplistic understanding of, 352–53. *See also* Xi Zhongxun—socialist values of

Medvedev, Roi, 10

Meng Deqiang, 222–23, 225

Ming Tombs Reservoir Project, 191, *192*

Mondale, Walter, American consulate established in Guangzhou, 291

Mongolia and Mongols: Mongols killed by Han Chinese during the Cultural Revolution, 377–78; role of Mongolian forces in defeating the Nationalists, 377. *See also* Ulanhu (Wulanfu)

Mongolia—Inner Mongolia Autonomous Region, 230; *Document No. 28*, published as the *Summary of the Secretariat's Discussion of Work in the Inner Mongolian Autonomous Region* (July 1981), 378; Jia Yanyan as a sent-down youth in (1970), 313; protests in support of Tiananmen Square protestors (1989), 396, 409; as a prototype for the party's handling of ethnic affairs (1947), 377; Qi Qiaoqiao's work on a construction corps in, 231, 348; Sun Qi warned not to accept a position in (July 1987), 402; Tibet contrasted with, 383; Xi Zhongxun's trip to (1987), 402–3; Zhou Hui as party secretary of, 315–16, 378–79

Mongolia—Mongolian Yekejuu League: Xi Zhongxun as manager of party work in, 108, 163, 377–78; Xi Zhongxun's visit to Genghis Khan's mausoleum in, 403

Nakasone Yasuhiro, 412, 479

Nanfanag Daily, Mai Zican's critical exchange with Xi Zhongxun published in (1978), 257

Nationalist Party and the Nationalists: ambushing of Xi (May 1933), 31–32; Hui led by Ma Guo'ai under the Nationalist flag in Gansu, 111; its apparatus in Shaanxi built by the Communists, 17, 46; Liu Shaokang Office established to counter Beijing's influence, 359; military intelligence file on Xi, 53; Tian Pingxuan (Nationalist leader in Xunyi), 46–47; Yang Zongyao identified as a Nationalist agent (1940), 50. *See also* Chiang Kai-shek; Hu Zongnan (Nationalist general)

Nationalist Party and the Nationalists—battle in the Northwest: defeat of Nationalist forces at Qinghuabian, Yangmahe, and Panlong, 84; meetings on the history of the Northwest battlefield, 85, 86; numbers of soldiers fighting in the Northwest, 86

National People's Congress: the Dalai Lama as vice-chairman of (1954), 159; the State Council and Ethnic Affairs Commission established at its first session (1954), 158–59; Xi Zhongxun's liaison work with, 305, 353; Xi Zhongxun's outburst at a meeting of the Standing Committee of (Aug.1990), 3; Zhu De as the head of, 140

New China News Agency (Xinhua): Bo Gu as head of, 58; document published about issues in the Tibet Autonomous

Region (1980), 371–72; internal report on the murder of a Uyghur (Apr. 1980), 373; Ke Hua nominated to lead it, 344–45; pictures of the Sixth National People's Congress supplied to *Tibet Daily* (June 1983), 388; Xu Jiatun appointed to lead it, 345, 366
Nie Rongzhen, 477–78
Ningxia Hui Autonomous Region, 194, 269; agricultural production reported by Xi (1958), 196; Xi Qianping's participation in the Socialist Education Campaign in (1966), 231. *See also* Shaan-Gan-Ning (Shaanxi-Gansu-Ningxia) Border Region
Northwest Bureau: Back Tibet, the Ali region, and the Panchen Lama as its focus, 119; dire conditions in (late 1954), 186; Fan Ming's downfall as a setback for northwesterners, 162–63; Kang Sheng's report to, on landlords in eastern Gansu, 90; meeting on land reform arranged in Yihe (Nov. 1947), 90; penetration of Hu Zongnan's headquarters (1948–1949), 86; Qi Xin's work for the Northwest Bureau in Yan'an, 80–81; role in convincing the tenth Panchen Lama to remain in China, 119; violence in, during land reform, 90; Xi Zhongxun as dean of the Northwest Bureau Party School, 54. *See also* Fan Ming
Northwest Bureau—Xi Zhongxun as head of: party work in the Mongolian Yekejuu League, 108, 163, 377–78; Xi Zhongxun's speech on land reform in minority areas at May 1952 meeting of, 112–13, 114, 116

O'Brien, Kevin J., 319–20, 486
Oksenberg, Michel, 473
Organization Department: An Ziwen as head of, 124, 129, 161, 220; Bo Gu as head of, 58; Cheng Jianwen as head of the Shaanxi Party Organization Department, 515; Chen Yun as leader of, 70; comprehensive rescreening launched by (Sept. 1989), 510–11; Hu Yaobang as head of (Dec. 1977), 251–52; of the Northwest Women's Federation headed by Hao Mingzhu, 77; Qi Xin as vice-director of the Guangzhou Party Organization Department, 255; Xi Zhongxun given responsibility for, 305, 310; Yan Huai's work for the Young Cadres Bureau of, 316, 332

Panchen Lama: the fourteenth Dalai Lama's selection of the eleventh Panchen Lama (1995), 408; the ninth Panchen Lama's dispute with the thirteenth Dalai Lama, 119; the Northwest Bureau's oversight of, 119; the party's interest in winning him over, 153–54
Panchen Lama—tenth Panchen Lama (Choekyi Gyaltsen): criticized at the Tenth Plenum, 173; death of, 407; enthronement of, 119; pictures published of the Sixth National People's Congress that did not include him (June 1983), 388; role of the Northwest Bureau in his remaining in China, 119; seventy-thousand-character petition, 171–73, 368, 390; as vice-chairman of the Chinese People's Political Consultative Conference, 159; as vice-chairman of the National People's Congress, 371, 384, 388, 404; viewed as a "leftist," 157; visit to Tibet by (1982), 384–85; wife and daughter of, 371, 372; Xi Zhongxun's efforts to upgrade his living quarters, 159; Xi Zhongxun's meetings with, 120, 120–22
party congresses—Seventh Party Congress, Xi Jinping's visit to the site of, 545
party congresses—Twentieth Party Congress (2022), Xi Jinping's presence at, 545
Peng Dehuai: and Fan Ming's book *New Journey to the West*, 162; opposition to paying Tibetan aristocrats, 156; pleas for rehabilitation associated with Xi Zhongxun's support for *Liu Zhidan*, 208–9, 211–15, 218, 250, 256; purging of, 141, 189, 199–201, 209, 214; regional command accepted to address attacks in Yan'an (1946), 83; support for the northwesterners, 155; as vice chairman of the Central Military Commission, 83; Xi Zhongxun as his close associate, 8

694 INDEX

Peng Liyuan: fame as a folk singer, 346–47, 428; marriage to Xi Jinping, 345–48; on the suffering of her family during the Cultural Revolution, 345–46

Peng Zhen: actions during the Tiananmen crackdown, 499–501; as a member of the politburo (1945), 306; support for the Rescue Campaign, 64; unpopularity of, 242, 306; Xi Zhongxun accused of being the Panchen Lama's "backstage supporter," 173; Xi Zhongxun proposed as head of the Legislative Committee, 317

People's Daily: article on Guanzhuang (1958), 188; criticism of (1984), 456–57; Deng Xiaoping's labeling of the Tiananmen protests as a "turmoil" published by, 492; discussion of purges during the Tiananmen protests, 499; Liu Binyan's controversial articles published by (1984), 456–57; Mai Zican's critical exchange with Xi Zhongxun published in (1978), 257; editorial on Oppose Rash Advance, 189; Ulanhu's article on ethnicization and autonomy in the minority regions (July 1981), 378; Xi Jinping's article "Middle and Young Cadres Must 'Respect the Elderly'" (Dec. 1984), 337–38, 544; Xi Jinping's name printed for the first time in (June 1984), 336; Xi's involvement in struggles over the direction of, 448; Zhou Yang's speech on Marx applying his theory of alienation to China published by (Mar. 1983), 449, 451. *See also* Qin Chuan—as editor and chief of the *People's Daily*; Wang Ruoshui

Peterkin, Wilbur, 137

Poland: end of Communism in (1990), 423; martial law introduced in, 422–23; protests in (1988), 408, 423

Qi An'an: her father's view of her career, 348–49; struggles at Beijing Foreign Studies University, 231

Qi Houzhi, 73–74, 79

Qi Qiaoqiao: birth and early years of, 80–81; Deng Jiagui (her husband), 537–38; incarceration in a Mao Zedong-Thought Study Group (1969), 231; wealth of, 537–38; work in a construction corps in Inner Mongolia, 231, 348; as Xi Zhongxun's favorite daughter, 348

Qi Ruixin, 73, 229, 369

Qi Xin: interest in a tutor on modern history, 399; positions in Beijing in the early 1980s, 342–43; restoration of her status as a party member (1972), 241; sixteen-character aphorism carved into Xi Zhongxun's memorial revealed by, 530–31; as a student at the party school in Yan'an, 75; as vice-director of the Guangzhou Party Organization Department, 255–56; views of how she dressed, 181; work for the Northwest Bureau in Yan'an, 80–81; on Xi Zhongxun's complaints about the impact of the imperial tombs in Dancun, 13–14

Qi Xin—children and family life with Xi Zhongxun: challenges faced due to her marriage to Xi Zhongxun, 230; courtship and marriage, 76–78; only her sons allowed to carry Xi Zhongxun's surname, 174; reunion in 1972, 241–42; stories about setting up the Shaan-Gan Border Region told by Xi Zhongxun to his children, 180–81; Xi Qianping raised by, 79–80; Xi Zhongxun as a ferocious disciplinarian, 177–79. *See also* Qi Qiaoqiao; Qi An'an; Xi Jinping; Xi Yuanping

Qi Yun: birth of (1919), 73; Jinping's visit to her and her husband Wei Zhenwu, 235–36; meeting with Qi Houzi (her father) after his defection to the Communists, 79; youth during the Sino-Japanese War, 73–75

Qian Liren, 419

Qian Qichen, 512

Qiao Shi, 320, 405, 416–18, 463, 479, 495–97, 525

Qin Chuan—as editor and chief of the *People's Daily*, 336, 456; appointment of, 452; information about Hu Yaobang's fall requested from Xi Zhongxun by, 474; publication of Zhou Yang's speech by, 450–51; on Xi Zhongxun, 306–7, 438

Qing dynasty, 219; Empress Dowager Cixi and Emperor Guangxu, 14; its collapse attributed to the Manchus' spoiling of their children, 179; Puyi, 147–48; Xinjiang ("new territories") used during, 158

Qinghai Province, 194, 381; Arjia Rinpoche as head of Kumbum Monastery, 368, 524; Xunhua Incident (Apr. 1958), 367; insurgents in Xunhua (Dec. 1949), 109; Nangra Tibetans in, 118; the tenth Panchen Lama enthroned at Kumbum Monastery in, 119; uprisings by Tibetans and Muslims there during the Leap, 167–69; violent uprisings in (1951), 110

Qinghai Province—Xining: the Panchen Lama's meeting at party headquarters in, 120; struggle against Muslims during the Leap in, 168–69

Qu Wu, 180, 216

Quinn, Kenneth M., 293–94

rectification campaigns: Fan Ming's launching of a rectification campaign in Tibet, 162; fear among cadre offspring that they would be targeted in (1984), 334; politics emphasized over practical knowledge (Mar. 1958), 191; Rectification and Socialist Education Campaign (Oct. 1957), 167; Strike Hard Campaign (1984), 320–21. *See also* Rescue the Fallen Campaign in Suide

rectification campaigns—Yan'an (1942–1944): coercive and voluntary elements of, 54–55; drive to achieve transformation through education, 53–54; investigation into its progress among teachers at the Northwest Bureau Party School, 54–55; Mao's launching of (1942), 53, 75; persecution of Lin Disheng, the head of middle school at Yan'an University, 75–76; the secretariat's request for party committees in the State Council ministries to report on their views during, 473; Xi Zhongxun's discussion of it during his visit to France (1983), 418–19

Ren Bishi, 62, 91

Ren Zhongyi, 630–31n30

Rescue the Fallen Campaign in Suide: death of Xi Zhongxun's relative, Zhao Tianxian, 61; Deng Liqun as head of the Central Politics Research Office, 435; Kang Sheng's involvement with, 59–60, 62, 64; launching as a confession movement directed at spies, 55–56; as a lesson on the negative effects of radicalism within the party, 62; Liu Shaoqi, Peng Zhen, and Gao Gang as supporters of, 64; "Mass Rally of All Types of People Denouncing the Nationalist Spies," 60; persecutorial mania of, 56–60; Yuan Renyuan's meeting with Mao regarding, 59

Rudd, Kevin, 5

Russia and the Soviet Union: Iurii Andropov, 140–41, 416; celebration of the October Revolution, 30, 34; Nikolai Chernyshevskii's novel *What Is to Be Done?*, 238; China's adoption of the Soviet model, 138–39; Deng Xiaoping's admiration for the strongman rule of, 470; Gao Gang's closeness to Soviet advisers in Manchuria, 138; Aleksei Kosygin, 140, 145; the Northwest Chinese-Soviet Friendship Association, 187; possible threat of expanding ties with to improve relations with United States, 411–12; Russia's invasion of Ukraine, 140, 545; Sino-Soviet alliance, 146, 220; Sino-Soviet split, 287, 495; Soviet statement on the border clash between China and India (1959), 142–43; Xi Zhongxun on the Chernobyl nuclear disaster, 423; Xi Zhongxun's relationship with, 136–37, 152; Xi Zhongxun's warning about its "southward drive strategy," 292; Xi Zhongxun trips to (1959), 140–43; Aleksandr Zasiad'ko, 141–43. *See also* Khrushchev, Nikita; Marxist-Leninist principles

Second Plenum of the Twelfth Party Congress (1983): Deng Xiaoping's speech on manifestations of "spiritual pollution," 451; Hunan leaders criticized by Xi at, 311; Zhou Yang's self-criticism at, 451, 454

696   INDEX

Shaan-Gan-Ning (Shaanxi-Gansu-Ningxia) Border Region: under the control of Shaanxi Province (1941), 51; its portrayal in *Liu Zhidan* as a revolutionary base, 215; land reform in, 89–90, 93; Shaanxi-Gansu-Ningxia-Shanxi Suide Joint Defense Army, 85; stories about setting it up told by Xi to his children, 180–81; Xi Zhongxun's warning to the leaders of (1940), 48; Xi Zhongxun's work in Guanzhong under the control of the headquarters of, 48, 50–51

Shaan-Gan-Ning (Shaanxi-Gansu-Ningxia) Border Region Assembly: bills sponsored by Xi at (1941), 316; dissatisfaction with Guo Hongtao expressed during elections for (1937), 44; Hao Mingzhu's service on, 77

Shaan-Gan (Shaanxi-Gansu) Border Region: Liu Zhidan's activities in, 39–40; Xi Zichang's visit to Xi Zhongxun's base area in, 37–38

Shaan-Gan (Shaanxi-Gansu) Border Region Congress of Workers, Peasants, and Soldiers, election held in Nanliang to elect a soviet government (1934), 34

Shaan-Gan (Shaanxi-Gansu) Border Region Revolutionary Committee, 31, 236

Shaanxi Province: Baoji seized by Hu Zongnan (1948), 85; drought in (1928), 22; extreme punishments in Weinan during the Suppression of Counterrevolutionaries Campaign, 100–101; flight of its provincial leadership to Guanzhong (1939), 48; Gao Gang's activities in the Red area of Northern Shaanxi, 128; Liu Binyan's article in *People's Daily* on the persecution of intellectuals in, 456; purge in (1935), 6, 38, 42–43, 223–24, 334; Xi Zhongxun's visit there during the Great Leap Forward (1958), 194–97. *See also* Suide; Weibei

Shaanxi Province—Fuping County: Dancun as the Xi ancestral village in, 13–14, 21, 29; during the Great Leap Forward, 206, 227, 238; Xi Zhongxun's memorial in, 530–31; Xi Zhongxun's student days in, 16–20, 87

Shaanxi Province—Shaanxi Party Committee: arrest of most of the leadership of (Feb. 1929), 21; existing structures of local power as its base, 18; Hu Yaobang as the first acting secretary of (1964), 103; infighting within the party there during the revolution, 28; Ma Wenrui as party leader of Shaanxi, 457; Zhang Desheng's critical remarks to, about Xi Zhongxun's area of Guanzhong (1941), 51–52

Shaanxi Province—Suide: alleged Nationalist spy group known as the Renaissance Society, 59–61; described by Dixie Mission officers, 137; location of, 55; Xi Zhongxun appointed the top party leader in (1943), 55; Xi Zhongxun praised by Gao Gang for his work in, 59; Xi Zhongxun's report to the Northwest Bureau on land reform in (1947), 92; Yan'an compared with, 55. *See also* Rescue the Fallen Campaign in Suide; Yihe Township in Suide Province

Shahidi, Burhan, 157–58, 180, 368

Shi Zhe, 58–59, 62, 131

Sichuan Province, 326, 394; mass violence against Tibetans in (1956), 168–69, 367; social reforms enacted in Tibetan regions of, 160–61

Sixth Plenum (June 1981), Deng Xiaoping declared the main decision maker in the Party by Hu Yaobang, 305

Sixth Plenum of the 12th Party Congress (1986), Xi's address to, 353

Sixth Plenum of the Central Committee (Nov.–Dec. 1958), 197

Solts, Aaron, 174

Song Ping, 298, 402, 525

Song Wenmei: attempt to enroll students from Xi Zhongxun's village at Whampoa Military Academy, 21; as one of the "Three Heroes of Guanzhong," 18–19, 515; as Xi Zhongxun's sponsor into the Communist Youth League, 17

South China Morning Post: articles on Xi Zhongxun's health in, 519; speculation that Xi Zhongxun would become general secretary, 304, 485

Southwest Bureau: Front Tibet, the Dalai Lama, and the area around Lhasa

as its focus, 119, 154. *See also* Zhang Guohua
Soviet Union. *See* Russia and the Soviet Union
special case committees: Mao Zedong's releasing of individuals under investigation by the central special case committees (1975), 242–43; meeting of the Peng-Xi Special Case Committee (Sept. 1965), 220; Xi Zhongxun's role in establishing them, 9
special economic zones: criticized by Chen Yun, 285; Deng Xiaoping's contribution to, 285, 483; economic achievements in Hong Kong and Macau as inspiration for, 361; household responsibility system as a, 9, 285–86; Hua Guofeng's contribution identified by Xi Zhongxun, 308, 525; mass protests of 1989 associated with, 2; naming based on "special zones" in Shaan-Gan-Ning, 278; Shenzhen compared to colonial "concession areas" in the nineteenth century, 284; Xi Zhongxun on the purpose of, 281; Xi Zhongxun's role in establishing them, 282, 284, 415. *See also* Guangdong Province—Shenzhen
Strike Hard Campaign (1984), 320–21
Sun Qi, 402
Sun, Warren, 440–41, 472
Sun Zhigang, 515–16
Suny, Ronald, 535
Suppression of Counterrevolutionaries Campaign: extreme punishments in Shaanxi during the Suppression of Counterrevolutionaries Campaign, 100–101; Mao's demands for more violence against counterrevolutionaries, 101; verdict that it had been incomplete reversed (in 1980), 103; Xi Zhongxun criticized for his activities during, 103, 227; Xi Zhongxun's alleged tempering of its reach, 3, 168

Taiwan: Chiang Ching-kuo, 359–61; Guangdong's economic potential compared with, 277; human rights problems in, 359–60; its potential as a "special economic zone" proposed by Xi, 291; Jinping's concerns about Taiwanese-independence forces (2012), 541; Ma Ying-jeou, 180, 235, 540; military intelligence file on Xi Zhongxun in, 53; Oct. 10 declared as the Day of the Republic of China in Los Angeles, 296; Tibet contrasted with, 383; unification with Taiwan as goal of the United Front, 1, 357–61, 515, 518; Wu Li Yaohua's [Julia Li Wu] refusal to serve as a secret emissary between the mainland and, 616n9; Xi Zhongxun's meeting with Chen Jianzhong (1990), 1–3, 515–17
Takla, Phuntsok Tashi: and Li Youyi, 339, 401; told by Zhou Enlai that unification was too early for the Tibetan regions, 383; Xi Zhongxun's discussions with him about the Dalai Lama, 401–2; on Xi Zhongxun's discussions with Tibetans about the Five Point Agreement, 383–84
Tan Zhenlin, 202, 206
Tao Zhu, 261
TASS (Telegrafnoe agentstvo Sovetskogo Soiuza), statement on the border clash between China and India (1959), 143
Teiwes, Frederick C., 440–41, 471–73
Tenth Plenum of the Eighth Party Congress (Sept. 24–27, 1962): *Liu Zhidan* attacked at, 214–15; Mao's call for "class struggle" at the work meeting prior to, 173; the party's approach to ethnic and religious affairs shaped by, 155; Xi Zhongxun criticized at, 151–52, 214–17, 228
Thatcher, Margaret, visit to China (1982), 362
Third Plenum of the Central Committee (1978), 310; promotions of party elders at, 303; skepticism of China's reforms expressed by Xinjiang leadership at, 373; Xi Jinping's affirmation of, 543; Xi Zhongxun on the new agenda introduced at, 428; Ye Jianying's speech absent from the collection of documents of (1982), 257
Third Plenum of the Central Committee (1978)—work conference prior to: Peng Dehuai's contributions lauded by Xi at, 263–64; Wang Dongxing criticized for quashing debate at, 441;

698 INDEX

Third Plenum of the Central Committee (1978) (cont.)
   Xi Zhongxun and Hua Guofeng honored at, by Ye Jianying, 257
Thondup, Gyalo: meeting with Hu Yaobang (1981), 381; request to visit Tibet, 381, 399; as a United Front target, 380; and Xi Zhongxun, 380–81, 407
Thondup, Khedroob, 381, 407
Three Antis Campaign, 104–6, 285
three types of people, 312, 315–16, 334
Tiananmen Square—June 4 crackdown (1989), 529; impact on party relations with the Vatican, 408; impact on the party's cooperation with people with different views, 366; impact on Xi Zhongxun's United Front work, 355–56, 361; violence of, 506–7; Xi Zhongxun's role in finding a peaceful solution to, 502–3; Xi Zhongxun's visit to Longtan Park shortly before, 505, 506
Tian Fang, 76, 152, 194, 200
Tibet: Deng Xiaoping's concerns about his legacy in, 141; Fan Ming's launching of a rectification campaign in, 162; Front and Back Tibet proposed by Beijing, 119–20, 156; Thupten Namgyal Juchen's meetings with Xi Zhongxun as a representative of the Dalai Lama, 382, 393; Lhasa crackdown (1989), 396, 408–10; McMahon Line, 141; pictures of the Sixth National People's Congress without the Panchen Lama published by the *Tibet Daily* (June 1983), 388; rioting at Jokhang Temple (Mar. 1988), 404–6; Tibet Work Conference ("Panmunjom" meeting, 1953), 156–57, 160. *See also* Dalai Lama; Panchen Lama; Takla, Phuntsok Tashi; Thondup, Gyalo
Tibet—Xi Zhongxun's relations with Tibetan leaders: Apa Alo (Huang Zhengqing), 117–18, 206, 368; the Dalai Lama's gifting of a watch to Xi, 159, 381, 410, 615n59; the Five-Point Proposal discussed with Tibetans, 382–84, 391–93; Gyalo Thondup (the Dalai Lama's brother), 380–81, 399, 407; model of ethnic relations championed by Xi Zhongxun, 2; the Panchen Lama's visit to the Tibetan Autonomous Region discussed with Yin Fatang (1982), 384–85; Raidi's [Re Di] criticism of Xi Zhongxun, 404; Wangchen Dondrup, 118, 168; Xi Zhongxun's confession of his "crimes" on Tibet policy, 227
Tibet Autonomous Region: document published by the New China News Agency about issues in, 371–72; Hu Jintao as the leader of, 406, 409; reactions to the enactment of the Eliminate Spiritual Pollution Campaign, 388; reforms begun in (1956), 160; Wu Jinghua as the leader of, 394–95, 406; Xi Zhongxun's challenges in, 154–55, 371; Yin Fatang selected as the leader of (Mar. 1980), 370–71
Trouillot, Michel-Rolph, 536
Tsinghua University: graduates of, living in Hong Kong, 363; Qi Qiaoqiao's studies at (2006), 538; rally criticizing Liu Bing at (1975), 246; students declared "counterrevolutionary elements" at (1976), 325; Xi Jinping's time at, 246, 315, 325
Twelfth Party Congress (Sept. 1982), Xi Zhongxun elected to the politburo and the secretariat of, 304–5

Ukraine, 140, 545
Ulanhu (Wulanfu): article on ethnicization and autonomy in the minority regions (July 1981), 378; Buhe identified as his son, 403; death of (1988), 406; purging during the Cultural Revolution (1966), 377; Qi Qiaoqiao's transfer from Inner Mongolia arranged by his daughter, 348; Qi Xin's friendship with his daughter Yun Shubi, 107–8; selection as vice president (1982), 319; the United Front Work Department led by (1983–1988), 378; Xi Zhongxun's cordial relationship with, 108, 377–78
United Front Work Department, 9; He Mingsi selected by Wang Kuang to head the Hong Kong branch of, 366; impact of Hu Yaobang's removal on, 355; Li Weihan's management of policies for Guanzhong, 52; Sixteenth National United Front Work Meeting (1986), 354; as a top priority in the 1980s, 368;

Ulanhu as the leader of (1983–1988), 378; Xi Zhongxun's role in United Front work attacked at the Tenth Plenum, 151; Yang Jingren as head of, 392
United States: China's expanding ties with the Soviet Union used as a threat toward, 411–12; meeting between Khrushchev and Eisenhower, 143; Nixon's 1972 trip to China, 291; Xi Jinping's meeting with then Vice President Joe Biden (2011), 5. *See also* Xi Zhongxun—delegation of Chinese governors visiting the United States led by (1980)

Vogel, Ezra F., 284

Wan Li: concern about Xi Zhongxun's declining health (1986), 307; declaration of martial law discussed in his meeting with George H. W. Bush, 503–4; on the first delegation of Chinese governors to visit the United States (1980), 291–92; return to China during the Tiananmen protests (1989), 496–97, 499, 508; Zhao Ziyang's proposal regarding student protests supported by, 493–94
Wang Chaobei, 217–18, 266
Wang Dongxing: criticism of him at the work conference prior to the Third Plenum, 441; criticism of the *Guangming Daily* article (May 1978), 440; criticism of Zhou Enlai during a politburo session (1980), 471; support for Xi Zhongxun's rehabilitation, 251
Wang Enmao, 86, 390; on the Kashgar incident, 376; partnering with Xi Zhongxun, 375–76, 391; as party boss of Xinjiang (1981), 375; retirement as party boss of Xinjiang (1985), 375
Wang Meng, 439
Wang Renzhong, 445, 449, 512
Wang Ruoshui: on Hu Qiaomu's ideological position, 434; Hu Yaobang's protection of, 453; on Marx's idea of "alienation," 449; removed as deputy editor in charge of theoretical and ideological issues of the *People's Daily*, 452, 456; Zhou Yang's speech approved for publication in the *People's Daily*, 450–51

Wang Sheng, 359
Wang Xiaozhong, 28
Wang Zhen, 333; and *bingtuan*, 115–16, 376–77; Mao urged to flee Yan'an (1946), 83; as a member of the politburo, 303; punishment for his actions in Xinjiang, 112, 114–17; reappearance in Xinjiang (1952), 373–74; rescue mission to save his retreating forces (1946), 82–83; support for Xi Zhongxun's rehabilitation, 251
Wangye, Phunwang [Wangjie Pingcuo], 371, 407–8
Weibei: severe drought in (1930), 21; Weibei Soviet base area, 30–31
Wei Junyi, 58
Weiner, Benno, 109–10, 167
Wen Jize, 191
West Germany. *See* Germany—West Germany
Wilson, David, 361, 364
Women's Federation: the Northwest Women's Federation, 77; opposition to the One-Child Policy, 343; Xi Zhongxun given responsibility for, 305; Xi Zhongxun's view that children should be a top priority of, 343
Wran, Neville, 288–89
Wu Jinghua: as the leader of the Tibet Autonomous Region (1985), 394–95; removal as the leader of the Tibet Autonomous Region (1988), 406
Wu Li Yaohua [Julia Li Wu], 413, 616n9
Wu Nansheng, 260, 272, 277, 279, 282
Wu Tingjun, 18–19
Wu Yifang, 350
Wu Zuguang: comments on openness in Chinese society at the Fourth Congress of the Chinese Writers Association (1984), 460, 462; persecution during the Antirightist Campaign (1957), 462; on Qi Xin's enthusiasm for theater, 344

Xi Heping: death during the Cultural Revolution, 239–40, 240, 527, 537; her name as the Chinese word for "peace," 46; identified as Hao Mingzhu's daughter with Xi Zhongxun, 79, 174; work at a military academy in Hebei, 238

700   INDEX

Xi Jinping: Bao Tong's assessment of his leadership, 533; He Zai's support of, 331, 336, 339; in Liangjiahe during the Cultural Revolution, 236–37, 239, 245; marriage to Ke Xiaoming, 344; marriage to Peng Liyuan, 345–48; memories of his past, during his visit to Shaanxi (2022), 545–46; persecution by Kang Sheng's wife, Cao Yi'ou, 233; speech for the Central Military Commission on the three tasks of governing (Dec. 2012), 541; Teresa Teng as his favorite singer, 326, 360; on Xi Zhongxun's devotion to the revolution and the party, 4, 539; Yan Huai's assessment of, 332–33

Xi Jinping—early years: attempts to join the party (1973), 237; benefits enjoyed as a cadre offspring, 176–77, 324–25; middle school experience, 175–77; persecution due to being a cadre offspring, 231–33, 236–37; as a student at Tsinghua University, 246, 315, 325; Xi Zhongxun's fall from power when he was nine years old, 536

Xi Jinping—rise of: article, "The Way of an Official" (Sept. 1990), 522; article on the cultural world and politics (1989), 521; the Cultural Revolution identified as a manifestation of "big democracy" by, 504; departure from Hebei, 338–39, 482; as Geng Biao's secretary, 326–27; increased visibility in publications (1984), 336–38. *See also* Hebei Province—Zhengding County—Xi Jinping's assignment as county party secretary

Xi Jinping—rise of—in Fujian Province: as governor of Fujian, 531; as party secretary of Fujian's Ningde region (mid-1988), 342; as party secretary of Fuzhou (Apr. 1990), 522; as vice-party secretary of Fujian (Sept. 1997), 526

Xi Jinping—as the president of China: party-history study campaign launched by (Feb. 2021), 544–45; response to the COVID-19 pandemic, 545; third party-history resolution introduced by (Oct. 2021), 545; trip to Shenzhen to signify his support for the reforms, 533; at the Twentieth Party Congress (2022), 545

Xi Qianping: birth and early years of, 79–80; experience as a schoolgirl, 175, 239; on Hao Mingzhu's miscarriages, 72; identified as Hao Mingzhu's daughter with Xi Zhongxun, 72, 174; Xi Zhongxun's obstruction of her career, 349; as a journalist and supporter of *Yanhuang Chunqiu*, 537

Xi Yuanping: birth and early schooling of, 174–76, 178, 230; exiling to the May 7 Cadre School in Henan, 230; wealth of, 538; on Xi Zhongxun's report to Mao on the Northwest Bureau's meeting at Yangjiagou (1947), 91

Xi Zhengning: birth as Fuping and early life with a foster family, 80; cadre offspring classmates of, 175; identified as Zhongxun's son with Hao Mingzhu, 80, 174, 527; as minister of justice in Hainan Province, 537; Xi Zhongxun's fatherly advice to him, 80; his early death, 527

Xi Zhonggun, 248

Xi Zhongkai (Xi Zhongxun's brother), 225

Xi Zhongxun's biography: lessons of his life for his son Jinping, 533, 535–37, 544; as party history, 5–7, 10; weaponization of his life by his son's detractors and boosters, 6

Xi Zhongxun—basic biography—ancestors and relatives: Dancun as the Xi ancestral village in Fuping County, Shaanxi Province, 13–14, 21, 29; Xi Yongsheng (Xi Zhongxun's grandfather), 13, 24, 61; Zhao Tianxian (Xi Zhongxun's cousin), 61

Xi Zhongxun—basic biography—birth and early years of: ambushing of him by the Nationalists (May 1933), 31–32; childhood name, Xiangjin, 14; the Communist Youth League joined by, 16–17, 250; his father (Xi Zongde) and mother, 7, 14–15, 20, 22; his formative years reflected in Jiang Guangci, *The Young Wanderer*, 7, 22–23, 238; impact of stories from *Romance of the Three Kingdoms* and *The Water Margin* on, 16; meaning of his birth name Zhongxun, 14; participation in the Liangdang mutiny (1932), 24–27, 26, 30, 515; revolutionary activities during his formative years, 21–23

Xi Zhongxun—basic biography—infirmity and death of: death from cancer (2002), 530; declining health in the 1980s, 307, 488–89; Hua Guofeng's request to meet him denied (1995), 524–25; Kong Shujing, on Xi Zhongxun's condition (in 1993), 521; Li Rui, on Xi Zhongxun's mental health, 3, 521; Liu Mila, on Xi Zhongxun's mental condition (in 1993), 521; rumors about his mental health (1990), 519–20; sixteen-character aphorism carved into his memorial in Fuping, 530–31

Xi Zhongxun—character of: Australian diplomats' descriptions of him, 288; described as an individual who got along well with everyone, 306–7; described by Mao to Bo Yibo as "a pure blue flame in the stove," 123, 530; game playing and dancing habits of, 81; his behavior during interrogations in Suide, 56–57; intellectuals and cultural figures trusted to manage their own affairs, 126–27, 439; Lou Shide held up as a model for, 245; Charles Malo's impression of, 417; Mao's positive impression of his organizational discipline, 66; Qin Chuan on his support and consensual style, 306–7, 438; short temper of, 277, 341, 358, 481, 520

Xi Zhongxun—children with Hao Mingzhu. See also Hao Mingzhu—children and family life with Xi Zhongxun; Xi Heping; Xi Qianping; Xi Zhengning

Xi Zhongxun—children with Qi Xin. See also Qi Qiaoqiao; Qi Xin—children and family life with Xi Zhongxun; Qi An'an; Xi Jinping

Xi Zhongxun—ethnic relations: as manager of the Ethnic Affairs Commission, 158–59, 167, 169–70, 203; model of ethnic relations championed by, 2, 111–12, 115; speech to the Fifth Congress on Islamic Affairs (1987), 401; tolerance for the Muslim practice of invoking Allah's name, 379. See also Tibet—Xi Zhongxun's relations with Tibetan leaders

Xi Zhongxun—exile, persecution, and incarceration, 7; departure for Guangdong (1990), 518–19; his advice to Jinping about the value of being a sent-down youth, 242; his return to work after experiences of, 433; impact of his incarceration as a youth on his revolutionary path (1928), 19; imprisonment at the Beijing Garrison (1968), 227; imprisonment in "Number 73" (1967), 225–26; investigation of him following the Tenth Plenum (1962), 151–52, 214–17; persecution during the 1935 purge in Shaanxi, 6, 42–43, 223–24; rumors about him heard by his family, 241; struggle session in Xi'an People's Stadium (Jan. 1967), 222–25. See also Xi Zhongxun—factory work during the Cultural Revolution

Xi Zhongxun—factory work during the Cultural Revolution, impact on Xi Zhongxun's support for individuals with problematic records, 221–22, 315–16

Xi Zhongxun—factory work in Luoyang during the Cultural Revolution: refractory-material factory in Luoyang (1975), 243, 244, 315; as vice-manager of a mining-tool factory in Luoyang (1965), 220–22

Xi Zhongxun—international travel: to Australia (1979), 288–89; China's delegation to the Leipzig Trade Fair led by, 139–40, 145–46; to Hungary (1959), 140, 421; to Macau (1979), 289–91; to Sweden (1981), 414–15; trips to the Soviet Union (1959), 140–43; trip to East Germany (1960), 145–46, 296

Xi Zhongxun—international travel—France: account of the nature of party leadership, 417–18; arrangements for his trip with Qiao Shi (1983), 416; discussion of legal reforms at the National People's Conference, 418; discussion of the rectification campaign, 418–19; report to the French Communist Party on China's domestic political situation, 417, 419

Xi Zhongxun—international travel—United States visit of a delegation of Chinese governors (1980): New York City speech warning about the Soviet Union's "southward drive strategy," 292; Wan Li's appointment of, 291–92

Xi Zhongxun—matchmaking and views of marriage and women: case of an arranged marriage, 71; criticism of divorce, 343–44; Liu Maogong matched with Yu Qun, 70–71; on One-Child Policy, 343; Zhang Fengying introduced to Yao Chungui, 71–72

Xi Zhongxun—as a party member: as chairman of the Central Military Commission's Editing and Compilation Committee on the Fighting History of the First Field Army, 86; criticism of the Ministry of Finance at a conference for regional and central leaders (Mar. 1979), 434; criticism of Wang Kuang for his selection of He Mingsi, 366; as dean of the Northwest Bureau Party School, 54; Gao Yang sent to Hebei, 330, 338; honored by Ye Jianying as a model at the work conference prior to the Third Plenum (1978), 257; as a leader in Guanzhong, 47, 52–53; opposition to forcing Zhou Yang to do self-criticism, 451; outburst at a meeting of the National People's Congress Standing Committee of (Aug. 1990), 3; participation in the Ming Tombs Reservoir Project, 191, 192; persecution of Yang Shu and Wei Junyi, 58; as a politburo and secretariat member (1982), 305; politburo resignation (Nov. 1987), 485; position on the Eliminate Spiritual Pollution Campaign (1983), 452–53, 456, 459; promotion to vice-premier, 197–98; relationship with Yang Shangkun, 65, 525–26; reports on deaths in Xinyang sent to Tan Zhenlin and Zhou Enlai (1960), 202; report to Mao on the Northwest Bureau's meeting at Yangjiagou (1947), 91–92, 96; as secretary of the Military Affairs Committee and the youth organization in Shaanxi, 31; speech on using the countryside to envelope cities (1934), 34; support for his rehabilitation, 251; as the top party leader in Suide (1943), 55; visit to Changge County, 203–5; as Zhou Enlai's deputy in the State Council, 185–86, 198–99, 473

Xi Zhongxun—religion and mystical phenomena: address suggesting more space for religious services (1985), 398; concerns about religious activities (1986), 398–99; his management of Catholic affairs, 393–94; as honorary chairman of the Qigong Study Association, 369; political equilibrium sought with Christians, 370; relations with the fourteenth Dalai Lama, 160, 398–99; response to the Panchen Lama's criticism of persecution of Tibetans, 172

Xi Zhongxun—self-criticism and behavior during land reform: confession of his "crimes" on Tibet policy, 227; the deficiencies of the Yihe meeting accounted for, 94–95; report to Northwest Bureau on land reform in Suide (1947), 92; self-criticism at a high-ranking cadre meeting (Nov. 1–23, 1947), 90–91; speech on land reform in minority areas at the May 4 meeting of the Northwest Bureau, 112–14, 116

Xi Zhongxun—socialist values of: preface written for the Communist Youth League's *Historical Necessity—Socialism in China*, 424; on putting Marx and Lenin's ideas into practice, 441; Xi Zhongxun's criticism of simplistic understanding of Marxist-Leninist principles, 352–53

Xi Zhongzhi, 19, 24, 30

Xiang Nan: as party boss of Fujian, 339–40; trip to North Korea with Xi Zhongxun, 340

Xiang Yunian, 339–40

Xie Zichang: criticism of fellow Shaanxi Communists, 38; death of, 38; as a key leader in the Northwest, 28–29, 66; mutiny in Qingjian (1927), 18; return to Shaan-bei after being expelled from, 37

Xinjiang: concerns about Hu Yaobang's new policies toward Tibet, 372; cooperation with the Soviets in, 137–38;

Deng Liqun punished for his actions in (1952), 112, 114–17, 434; Kashgar incident (1981), 375–76, 397; model of ethnic relations championed by Xi Zhongxun in, 2, 111–12, 115; naming as Xinjiang Uyghur Autonomous Region, 157–58; Rectification and Socialist Education Campaign (Oct. 1957), 167; secretariat meeting discussing party policy prioritizing the "big picture" and "unity" in (1981), 374–75; student protests in Urumqi (June 1988), 405; Three Antis abuses in, 106; Wang Enmao as the party boss of, 375; Wang Zhen's punishment for his actions in Xinjiang (1952), 112, 114–17, 135, 153, 251, 373, 375; Wang Zhen's reappearance in, 373–74; Xi Zhongxun's directive on land reform to the Xinjiang Subbureau, 113. *See also* Wang Enmao

Xinjiang Daily: Deng Liqun's self-criticism published in (July 1952), 116; Xi Zhongxun's May 4, 1952 speech on land reform in minority areas published in, 114

Xinjiang Party Committee: economic targets revised to accept Xi Zhongxun's proposal to grow faster (1984), 391; enlarged session criticizing nationalist sentiment (1958), 167

Xu Jiatun: appointment as the director of New China News Agency, 362, 366; on negotiations on Hong Kong's Basic Law, 362; on Xi Zhongxun's criticism of mainland policy toward Hong Kong, 366

Xu Qingquan, 435

Xu Youyu, 542

Yan Hongyan: concerns about *Liu Zhidan*, 210–13; and Deng Xiaoping, 212; as a key leader in the Northwest, 28–29; opposition to Gao Gang's rise, 66–67; Qingjian mutiny (1927), 18

Yan Huai, 332–34

Yan Mingfu: as head of the United Front Work Department, 354, 401; meeting with Phuntsok Tashi Takla, 401; Xi Zhongxun as his supporter, 354

Yang Jingren: Hu Yaobang's Five-Point Proposal publicly revealed by, 392–93;
Xi Zhongxun accused of targeting Gao Gang, 133

Yang Ping, 246–49, 519–20

Yang Shangkun, 319, 447–48, 464, 492–93; Deng Liqun criticized by, 435; Deng Xiaoping's dropping him from leadership (1992), 525; as director of the General Office, 186, 210, 255; at the Jan. 1987 party-life meeting, 481–82; martial law declaration (1989), 495–98; as party boss of Guangzhou, 260, 277–78, 284, 296; report on famine in Shaan-Gan-Ning, 91; schooling of his children, 175; support of "eliminating spiritual pollution," 453; as vice-chairman and secretary general of the Central Military Commission, 497, 525, 529; and Xi Zhongxun, 65, 259, 278, 284, 485, 489–90, 525–26

Yang Shu, 58

Yanhuang chunqiu: discussion of the Gang of Four's defeat organized by, 537; Xi Zhongxun asked to write an inscription for its tenth anniversary (2001), 529–30; Xi Jinping's ideology discussed at meetings of (2013), 533

Yao Chungui, 49–50, 72

Yao Yilin, 280, 282, 476, 488, 496

Ye Fei, 339, 497–98

Ye Jianying: Dai Qing identified as his adopted daughter, 490; death of, 478; diminishing of his real authority, 309, 519; on the roles of the politburo, Politburo Standing Committee, and the secretariat, 304; Qi Qiaoqiao's studies at the First Military Medicine University arranged by, 348; Xi Zhongxun selected to run affairs in Guangdong, 255; as Xi Zhongxun's supporter, 257, 262

Ye Xuanning, identified as a son of Ye Jianying, 251, 326

Yihe Township in Suide Province: meeting on land reform arranged by the Northwest Bureau (Nov. 1947), 90; Qi Xin as vice-secretary of, 79; Xi Zhongxun on the deficiencies of the Yihe meeting, 94–95

Yin Fatang, 518; criticism of Xi Zhongxun's call for reforms in the Tibet Autonomous Region, 388; the Panchen

Yin Fatang (cont.)
　Lama's visit to the Tibet Autonomous Region discussed with Xi (1982), 384–85; removal as the leader of the Tibet Autonomous Region (1985), 394–95; selection as the leader of the Tibet Autonomous Region (Mar. 1980), 370–71; Xi blamed for protests in Tibet, 397, 405–506
Yugoslavia, 421–22

Zhang Chengxian, 509
Zhang Desheng, 51–52, 110, 206
Zhang Guangnian: He Jingzhi targeted at the Fourth Congress of the Chinese Writers Association, 457–58, 460
Zhang Guohua: as a cadre from the Southwest Bureau, 154–55; discussion of the Panchen Lama's petition (1962), 172; persecution to death of, 371; self-criticism and acceptance of responsibility for tensions with Fan, 157; Xu Danlu's criticism of, 155; as Zhang Jingwu's first deputy secretary, 155
Zhang Guotao, 288, 306
Zhang Jingwu: discussion of the Panchen Lama's petition (1962), 172–73; as first party secretary of the Tibet Work Committee (Mar. 1952), 155, 162; Xu Danlu's criticism of, 155–56; Zhang Guohua identified as his first deputy secretary, 155
Zhang Xiushan: confession under duress (1935), 63; labelled as a "rightist," 43; opium production rationalized by, 35; Xi Zhongxun's criticism of, 35, 129, 131
Zhang Zhongliang, 50, 195, 200
Zhao Fan, 157, 160
Zhao Jialiang, 130, 132
Zhao Ziyang: Bao Tong identified as his former secretary, 533; criticism of, 508–9; on Deng Xiaoping's authority, 505; described by Xi Zhongxun as managing day-to-day activities of the leadership, 417; Hu Yaobang's views contrasted with, 473; proposal regarding student protests, 493–94; replacement by Jiang Zemin as general secretary (1989), 472, 510
Zhejiang Province: Li Zemin's meeting with students at Zhejiang University, 500–501; warning about Christian "Shouters" in, 380; Xi Jinping as party leader of, 532
Zheng Tianxiang, 320
Zhou Enlai: Cao Shuli's letter to Mao on deaths in Shandong sent to, 206; investigations of deaths in Xinyang demanded by (1960), 202; participation in the Ming Tombs Reservoir Project, 191, 192; protection of his reputation by party leadership, 471; Xi Zhongxun as his close associate, 8; Xi Zhongxun as his deputy in the State Council, 185–86, 198–99, 473; Xi Zhongxun criticized by, 225–28
Zhou Enlai—criticism of: Deng Xiaoping's attempts to protect him, 190–91; by Mao at the Nanning Conference (1958), 189–90; Mao's removal of his economic decision making (1958), 190
Zhou Enlai—death of (Jan. 1976): impact on Xi Zhongxun, 244; Tiananmen protests commemorating it, 325
Zhou Hui, 315–16, 378–79
Zhou Renshan, 163, 170
Zhou Weimin, 502–3
Zhou Yang: reputation for attacking cultural figures in the party, 449; self-criticism at the Second Plenum (Oct. 1983), 451, 454; speech on Marx applying his theory of alienation to China (Mar. 1983), 449–51
Zhu De, 129, 140, 166–67
Zhu Jiamu, 334, 539–40, 543
Zhu Lizhi: criticism by the party in (1942 and 1945), 94, 210; purge in Shaanxi Province led by (1935), 38; Zhu Jiamu identified as his son, 540

STANFORD-HOOVER SERIES ON **AUTHORITARIANISM**

Edited by Paul R. Gregory and Norman Naimark

The Stanford–Hoover Series on Authoritarianism is dedicated to publishing peer-reviewed books for scholars and general readers that explore the history and development of authoritarian states across the globe. The series includes authors whose research draws on the rich holdings of the Hoover Library and Archives at Stanford University. Books in the Stanford–Hoover Series reflect a broad range of methodologies and approaches, examining social and political movements alongside the conditions that lead to the rise of authoritarian regimes, and is open to work focusing on regions around the world, including but not limited to Russia and the Soviet Union, Central and Eastern Europe, China, the Middle East, and Latin America. The Stanford–Hoover Series on Authoritarianism seeks to expand the historical framework through which scholars interpret the rise of authoritarianism throughout the twentieth century.

Silvio Pons, *The Rise and Fall of the Italian Communist Party: A Transnational History*
2024

Mark Harrison, *Secret Leviathan: Secrecy and State Capacity under Soviet Communism*
2023

David Brandenberger, *Stalin's Usable Past: A Critical Edition of the 1937 Short History of the USSR*
2024